Foundations of Business

5e

William M. Pride
Texas A&M University

Robert J. Hughes
Dallas County Community Colleges

Jack R. Kapoor
College of DuPage

CENGAGE
Learning·

Australia • Brazil • Mexico • Singapore • United Kingdom • United States

Foundations of Business, Fifth Edition
William M. Pride, Robert J. Hughes, and
Jack R. Kapoor

Vice President, General Manager, Social Science &
Qualitative Business: Erin Joyner

Product Director: Jason Fremder

Product Manager: Heather Mooney

Associate Content Developer: Megan Fischer

Product Assistant: Jamie Mack

Marketing Manager: Jeffrey Tousignant

Content Project Manager: Megan Guiliani

Manufacturing Planner: Ron Montgomery

Production Service: Cenveo Publisher Services

Sr. Art Director: Linda May

Internal Designer: Red Hangar Design

Cover Designer: Tippy McIntosh

Cover Image: IR Stone/Shutterstock.com

Intellectual Property

   Analyst: Diane Garrity

   Project Manager: Sarah Shainwald

Inside Business: © Yuganov Konstantin

Entrepreneurial Success icon: © Stasique

Career Success icon: © Thanapun

Personal App icon: © dolphfyn

Ethical Success of Failure icon: © Davydenko Yuliia

Library of Congress Control Number: 2015947518

Student Edition ISBN: 978-1-305-51106-4

Cengage Learning
20 Channel Center Street
Boston, MA 02210
USA

Cengage Learning is a leading provider of customized learning solutions with employees residing in nearly 40 different countries and sales in more than 125 countries around the world. Find your local representative at **www.cengage.com**.

Cengage Learning products are represented in Canada by Nelson Education, Ltd.

To learn more about Cengage Learning Solutions, visit **www.cengage.com**

Purchase any of our products at your local college store or at our preferred online store **www.cengagebrain.com**

Printed in the United States of America
Print Number: 01   Print Year: 2015

To Nancy, Allen, Carmen, Mike, Ashley, Charlie, J.R., and Gracie Pride

To the memory of my wife Peggy and to my mother Barbara Hughes

*To my wife Theresa; my children Karen, Kathryn, and Dave;
and in memory of my parents Ram and Sheela Kapoor*

Brief Contents

PART 1 The Environment of Business   2

Chapter 1   Exploring the World of Business and Economics   2
Chapter 2   Being Ethical and Socially Responsible   37
Chapter 3   Exploring Global Business   68

PART 2 Business Ownership and Entrepreneurship   104

Chapter 4   Choosing a Form of Business Ownership   104
Chapter 5   Small Business, Entrepreneurship, and Franchises   132

PART 3 Management and Organization   164

Chapter 6   Understanding the Management Process   164
Chapter 7   Creating a Flexible Organization   188
Chapter 8   Producing Quality Goods and Services   210

PART 4 Human Resources   244

Chapter 9   Attracting and Retaining the Best Employees   244
Chapter 10   Motivating and Satisfying Employees and Teams   272

PART 5 Marketing   304

Chapter 11   Building Customer Relationships Through Effective Marketing   304
Chapter 12   Creating and Pricing Products That Satisfy Customers   329
Chapter 13   Distributing and Promoting Products   362

PART 6 Information, Accounting, and Finance   400

Chapter 14   Exploring Social Media and e-Business   400
Chapter 15   Using Management and Accounting Information   433
Chapter 16   Mastering Financial Management   466

Glossary   G-1
Name Index   NI-1
Subject Index   SI-1

The following appendixes appear on the companion site www.cengage.brain.com
Appendix A: Understanding Personal Finances and Investments   A-1
Appendix B: Careers in Business   B-1
Appendix C: Enhancing Union–Management Relations   C-1
Appendix D: Risk Management and Insurance   D-1
Appendix E: Business Law, Regulation, and Taxation   E-1

Contents

About the Author   xii
Acknowledgments   xiii

PART 1   The Environment of Business   2

Chapter 1: Exploring the World of Business and Economics   2

→ *Inside Business:* Visa's Vast Global Payments Empire 3

Your Future in the Changing World of Business 4
Why Study Business? 5 • Special Note to Business Students 8

Personal App: Be the employee you'd like to hire! 7

Business: A Definition 10
*The Organized Effort of Individuals 10 • Satisfying
Needs 11 • Business Profit 12*

Types of Economic Systems 12
*Capitalism 14 • Capitalism in the United States 15 •
Command Economies 17*

Measuring Economic Performance 18
*The Importance of Productivity in the Global Marketplace 18 •
The Nation's Gross Domestic Product 19 • Important Economic
Indicators That Measure a Nation's Economy 20*

The Business Cycle 21

Career Success: Career Moves and the Business Cycle 22

Types of Competition 23
*Perfect Competition 23 • Monopolistic Competition 25 •
Oligopoly 26 • Monopoly 26*

Entrepreneurial Success: Meet the Teenaged Founder of
Fish Flops 26

American Business Today 27
*Early Business Development 27 • Business Development in
the 1900s 28 • A New Century: 2000 and Beyond 29 • The
Current Business Environment 29 • The Challenges Ahead 31*

Social Media: Government Agencies Go Social 30

Summary 32

Key Terms 34

Discussion Questions 34

Video Case: KlipTech Turns Recycled Paper into Products
and Profits 34

Building Skills for Career Success 35

Endnotes 36

Chapter 2: Being Ethical and Socially Responsible 37

→ *Inside Business:* Tesla Motors 38

Business Ethics Defined 39

Ethical Issues 39
*Fairness and Honesty 39 • Organizational Relationships 40 •
Conflict of Interest 40 • Communications 41*

Factors Affecting Ethical Behavior 41
*Individual Factors Affecting Ethics 42 • Social Factors
Affecting Ethics 42 • Opportunity as a Factor Affecting
Ethics 43*

Encouraging Ethical Behavior 43
*Government's Role in Encouraging Ethics 43 • Trade
Associations' Role in Encouraging Ethics 44 • Individual
Companies' Role in Encouraging Ethics 44 • Social
Responsibility 46*

The Evolution of Social Responsibility in Business 47
*Historical Evolution of Business Social Responsibility 47 •
Two Views of Social Responsibility 49 • The Pros and Cons
of Social Responsibility 49*

Ethical Success or Failure Businesses Feel Pressure Over
Conditions in Suppliers' Factories 50

Public Responsibilities of Business 51
Consumerism 51 • Public Health 53

Personal App: Do you always know what you're buying? 52

Social Media: The FTC Blogs and Tweets Too 53

Employment Practices 55
*Affirmative Action Programs 56 • Training Programs for the
Hard-Core Unemployed 57 • Programs to Reduce Sexual
Harassment and Abusive Behavior 57*

Environmental Concerns 58
*Pollution 59 • Effects of Environmental Legislation 59 •
Business Response to Environmental Concerns 60*

Career Success: Aiming to Be a Chief Sustainability
Officer? 59

Implementing a Program of Social Responsibility 62
*Commitment of Top Executives 62 • Planning 62 •
Appointment of a Director 62 • The Social Audit 62*

Summary 63

Key Terms 64

Discussion Questions 64

Video Case: PortionPac Chemical Is People-Friendly,
Planet-Friendly 65

Building Skills for Career Success 65

Endnotes 66

Chapter 3: Exploring Global Business 68

→ *Inside Business:* Walmart's Global Business Strategy 69

The Basis for International Business 70
Absolute and Comparative Advantage 70 • Exporting and Importing 71

Methods of Entering International Business 73
Licensing 73 • Exporting 74 • Joint Ventures 76 • Totally Owned Facilities 77 • Strategic Alliances 77 • Trading Companies 77 • Countertrade 77 • Multinational Firms 78

Entrepreneurial Success: Advice from Global Entrepreneurs 75

Personal App 76

Restrictions to International Business 78
Types of Trade Restrictions 79 • Reasons for Trade Restrictions 81 • Reasons Against Trade Restrictions 82

The Extent of International Business 83
The Economic Outlook for Trade 83

International Trade Agreements 86
The General Agreement on Tariffs and Trade and the World Trade Organization 86 • International Economic Organizations Working to Foster Trade 88

Career Success: Aiming for an Overseas Job? 87

Sources of Export Assistance 90

Financing International Business 91
The Export-Import Bank of the United States 91 • Multilateral Development Banks 91 • The International Monetary Fund 93 • The Challenges Ahead 93

Social Media: The IMF Goes Social Around the World 93

Summary 94

Key Terms 95

Discussion Questions 95

Video Case: Keeping Brazil's Economy Hot 95
Building Skills for Career Success 96
Running a Business: Part 1: Let's Go Get a Graeter's! 98
Building a Business Plan: Part 1 100

Endnotes 102

© ANDY DEAN PHOTOGRAPHY/SHUTTERSTOCK.COM

PART 2 Business Ownership and Entrepreneurship 104

Chapter 4: Choosing a Form of Business Ownership 104

→ *Inside Business:* GoPro's Global Growth Began by Bootstrapping 105

Sole Proprietorships 106
Advantages of Sole Proprietorships 107 • Disadvantages of Sole Proprietorships 108 • Beyond the Sole Proprietorship 109

Social Media: Small Business Resources 109

Partnerships 109
Types of Partners 110 • The Partnership Agreement 111

Advantages and Disadvantages of Partnerships 112
Advantages of Partnerships 112 • Disadvantages of Partnerships 113 • Beyond the Partnership 114

Corporations 114
Corporate Ownership 115 • Forming a Corporation 115 • Corporate Structure 118

Entrepreneurial Success: Should Your Company Be a Benefit Corporation? 116

Personal App: Are you a stockholder? 117

Advantages and Disadvantages of Corporations 119
Advantages of Corporations 119 • Disadvantages of Corporations 120

Special Types of Business Ownership 121
S Corporations 121 • Limited-Liability Companies 122 • Not-for-Profit Corporations 123

Joint Ventures and Syndicates 123
Joint Ventures 124 • Syndicates 124

Ethical Success or Failure Tough Decisions for Entrepreneurs in Tough Situations 124

Corporate Growth 125
Growth from Within 125 • Growth Through Mergers and Acquisitions 125 • Merger and Acquisition Trends for the Future 127

Summary 128

Key Terms 129

Discussion Questions 129

Video Case: Project Repat Gives Old T-Shirts New Life 130
Building Skills for Career Success 130

Endnotes 131

Chapter 5: Small Business, Entrepreneurship, and Franchises 132

→ *Inside Business:* Bark & Co. Provides for Pampered Pooches 133

Small Business: A Profile 133
The Small-Business Sector 134 • Industries That Attract Small Businesses 135

Social Media: Small Business Saturday 135

Personal App: Have you worked for a small business? 136

The People in Small Businesses: The Entrepreneurs 136
Characteristics of Entrepreneurs 137 • Other Personal Factors 137 • Motivation 138 • Women as Small-Business Owners 138 • Teenagers as Small-Business Owners 139 • Why Some Entrepreneurs and Small Businesses Fail 139

Career Success: Plan Now for an Entrepreneurial Venture Later 138

The Importance of Small Businesses in Our Economy 140
Providing Technical Innovation 141 • Providing Employment 142 • Providing Competition 142 • Filling Needs of Society and Other Businesses 142

The Pros and Cons of Smallness 143
Advantages of Small Business 143 • Disadvantages of Small Business 144 • The Importance of a Business Plan 144 • Components of a Business Plan 145

The Small Business Administration 146
SBA Management Assistance 146 • Help for Minority-Owned Small Businesses 148 • SBA Financial Assistance 149

Franchising 150
What Is Franchising? 150 • Types of Franchising 150

Entrepreneurial Success: Is a Franchise in Your Future? 152

The Growth of Franchising 152
Are Franchises Successful? 153 • Advantages of Franchising 153 • Disadvantages of Franchising 154 • Global Perspectives in Small Business 155

Summary 156

Key Terms 157

Discussion Questions 157

Video Case: From Two Men and a Truck to 220 Franchises and 1,400 Trucks 158

> **Building Skills for Career Success 158**

> **Running a Business: Part 2: Graeter's: A Fourth-Generation Family Business 160**

> **Building a Business Plan: Part 2 162**

Endnotes 162

PART 3 Management and Organization 164

Chapter 6: Understanding the Management Process 164

→ **Inside Business:** Managing Walt Disney for a Second Century of Creativity and Success 165

What is Management? 165

Personal App: Are you already a manager? 166

Basic Management Functions 167
Planning 167 • Organizing the Enterprise 171 • Leading and Motivating 171 • Controlling Ongoing Activities 172

Kinds of Managers 173
Levels of Management 173 • Areas of Management Specialization 174

Key Skills of Successful Managers 175
Conceptual Skills 176 • Analytic Skills 176 • Interpersonal Skills 177 • Technical Skills 177 • Communication Skills 177

Career Success: Collaborate Your Way to Success 176

Leadership 177
Formal and Informal Leadership 177 • Styles of Leadership 178 • Which Leadership Style Is the Best? 179

Entrepreneurial Success: Elon Musk's Far-Out Ideas Are Crazy like a Fox 178

Managerial Decision Making 179
Identifying the Problem or Opportunity 180 • Generating Alternatives 180 • Selecting an Alternative 180 • Implementing and Evaluating the Solution 181

Ethical Success or Failure: CVS Backs Words with Actions 181

Managing Total Quality 181

Summary 183

Key Terms 184

Discussion Questions 184

Video Case: Meet Heidi Ganahl, Top Dog at Camp Bow Wow 185

> **Building Skills for Career Success 185**

Endnotes 186

Chapter 7: Creating a Flexible Organization 188

→ **Inside Business:** Can Structural Changes Re-Ignite McDonald's Growth? 189

What is an Organization? 189
Developing Organization Charts 190 • Major Considerations for Organizing a Business 192

Job Design 192
Job Specialization 192 • The Rationale for Specialization 192 • Alternatives to Job Specialization 192

Career Success: Flexible Work Space: Are You Ready to Sit Next to the CEO? 193

Departmentalization 193
By Function 193 • By Product 194 • By Location 194 • By Customer 194 • Combinations of Bases 194

Delegation, Decentralization, and Centralization 195
Delegation of Authority 195 • Decentralization of Authority 196

The Span of Management 197
Wide and Narrow Spans of Management 197 • Organizational Height 198

Forms of Organizational Structure 198
The Line Structure 198 • The Line-and-Staff Structure 199 • The Matrix Structure 201 • The Network Structure 202

Personal App: Do you have a mentor? 199

Ethical Success or Failure: If We Get Ethics Right, Will Compliance Follow? 200

Entrepreneurial Success: Entrepreneurs Set the Tone of Corporate Culture 202

Corporate Culture 203

Committees and Task Forces 204

The Informal Organization and the Grapevine 205

Summary 206

Key Terms 207

© ANDY DEAN PHOTOGRAPHY/SHUTTERSTOCK.COM

Discussion Questions 207

Video Case: Zappos Wants to Make Customers (and Employees) Happy 207

Building Skills for Career Success 208

Endnotes 209

Chapter 8: Producing Quality Goods and Services 210

→ *Inside Business:* How Detroit Bikes Makes Bikes in Detroit 211

What is Production? 212
How American Manufacturers Compete in the Global Marketplace 212 • Careers in Operations Management 214

Social Media: Inside Boeing's Factories 213

The Conversion Process 215
Manufacturing Using a Conversion Process 215

The Increasing Importance of Services 216
Planning Quality Services 216 • Evaluating the Quality of a Firm's Services 217

Where do New Products and Services Come From? 218
Research and Development 218 • Product Extension and Refinement 218

Entrepreneurial Success: Have a New Product Idea? Think Quirky 219

How do Managers Plan Production? 220
Design Planning 220 • Site Selection and Facilities Planning 222 • Operational Planning 224

Career Success: How Would You Plan for Peak Holiday Deliveries? 225

Operations Control 226
Purchasing 226 • Inventory Control 227 • Scheduling 228 • Quality Control 228 • Production Planning: A Summary 231

Personal App: Nobody likes complaints! 229

Improving Productivity with Technology 232
Productivity Trends 232 • Improving Productivity Growth 233 • The Impact of Automation, Robotics, and Computers on Productivity 233 • Sustainability and Technological Displacement 235

Summary 236

Key Terms 237

Discussion Questions 237

Video Case: Chobani Gives the World a Taste for Greek Yogurt 238

Building Skills for Career Success 239

Running a Business: Part 3: Graeter's Grows Through Good Management, Organization, and Quality 240

Building a Business Plan: Part 3 242

Endnotes 242

PART 4 Human Resources 244

Chapter 9: Attracting and Retaining the Best Employees 244

→ *Inside Business:* Netflix Stands Ready to Change 245

Human Resources Management: An Overview 245
HRM Activities 246 • Responsibility for HRM 247

Personal App: How many skills do you have? 246

Human Resources Planning 247
Forecasting Human Resources Demand 247 • Forecasting Human Resources Supply 248 • Matching Supply with Demand 249

Entrepreneurial Success: Hiring Your First Employee: Key Questions to Consider 248

Cultural Diversity in Human Resources 250

Job Analysis 251

Recruiting, Selection, and Orientation 252
Recruiting 252 • Selection 254 • Orientation 256

Social Media: Recruiting Via Social Media 253

Compensation and Benefits 256
Compensation Decisions 256 • Comparable Worth 257 • Types of Compensation 258 • Employee Benefits 259

Career Success: What Are the Job Perks at Apple? 260

Training and Development 260
Analysis of Training Needs 261 • Training and Development Methods 261 • Evaluation of Training and Development 262

Performance Appraisal 262
Common Evaluation Techniques 262 • Performance Feedback 264

The Legal Environment of HRM 265
National Labor Relations Act and Labor–Management Relations Act 265 • Fair Labor Standards Act 265 • Equal Pay Act 266 • Civil Rights Acts 266 • Age Discrimination in Employment Act 266 • Occupational Safety and Health Act 266 • Employee Retirement Income Security Act 267 • Affirmative Action 267 • Americans with Disabilities Act 267

Summary 268

Key Terms 269

Discussion Questions 269

Video Case: The Container Store Hires Great Employees to Sell Empty Boxes 269

Building Skills for Career Success 270

Endnotes 271

Chapter 10: Motivating and Satisfying Employees and Teams 272

→ *Inside Business:* What Makes a "Best Company to Work For"? 273

What is Motivation? 273

Historical Perspectives on Motivation 274
Scientific Management 274 • The Hawthorne Studies 275 • Maslow's Hierarchy of Needs 276 • Herzberg's Motivation–Hygiene Theory 277 • Theory X and Theory Y 279 • Theory Z 280 • Reinforcement Theory 281

Contemporary Views on Motivation 281
Equity Theory 281 • Expectancy Theory 282 • Goal-Setting Theory 283

Key Motivation Techniques 284
Management by Objectives 284 • Job Enrichment 285 • Behavior Modification 286 • Flextime 286 • Part-Time Work and Job Sharing 287 • Telecommuting 288 • Employee Empowerment 289 • Employee Ownership 289

Career Success: Is Flextime for You? 287

Personal App: Can you work from home? 288

Entrepreneurial Success: A Time to Micromanage 290

Teams and Teamwork 290
What Is a Team? 291 • Types of Teams 291 • Developing and Using Effective Teams 292 • Roles Within a Team 293 •

Team Cohesiveness 293 • Team Conflict and How to Resolve It 294 • Benefits and Limitations of Teams 294

Ethical Success or Failure: When Teamwork Doesn't Work 293

Summary 295

Key Terms 296

Discussion Questions 296

Video Case: Putting the Focus on People at the Fruit Guys 297

Building Skills for Career Success 297

Running a Business: Part 4: At Graeter's, Tenure Is "a Proud Number" 299

Building a Business Plan: Part 4 301

Endnotes 301

PART 5 Marketing 304

© ANDY DEAN PHOTOGRAPHY/SHUTTERSTOCK.COM

Chapter 11: Building Customer Relationships Through Effective Marketing 304

→ **Inside Business:** Starbucks: What's Not to Love 305

Managing Customer Relationships 305

Utility: The Value Added by Marketing 307

The Marketing Concept 308
Evolution of the Marketing Concept 308 • Implementing the Marketing Concept 309

Markets and their Classification 310

Developing Marketing Strategies 310
Target Market Selection and Evaluation 310 • Creating a Marketing Mix 313

Entrepreneurial Success: Small Businesses Create Big Buzz 315

Marketing Strategy and the Marketing Environment 316

Social Media: Warby Parker: Social Media Star 316

Developing a Marketing Plan 317

Personal App: Do you have a personal marketing plan? 318

Market Measurement and Sales Forecasting 318

Marketing Information 318
Marketing Information Systems 318 • Marketing Research 319 • Using Technology to Gather and Analyze Marketing Information 319

Types of Buying Behavior 321
Consumer Buying Behavior 321 • Business Buying Behavior 323

Ethical Success or Failure: Should E-Cigarettes Be Marketed to Young People? 322

Summary 324

Key Terms 325

Discussion Questions 325

Video Case: Raleigh Wheels Out Steel Bicycle Marketing 326

Building Skills for Career Success 327

Endnotes 327

Chapter 12: Creating and Pricing Products That Satisfy Customers 329

→ **Inside Business:** GoldieBlox Gets the Gold for Capitalizing on Free Marketing Opportunities 330

Classification of Products 331
Consumer Product Classifications 331 • Business Product Classifications 332

The Product Life-Cycle 332
Stages of the Product Life-Cycle 333 • Using the Product Life-Cycle 335

Personal App: Do you have one of these? 334

Product Line and Product Mix 335

Managing the Product Mix 336
Managing Existing Products 336 • Deleting Products 337 • Developing New Products 338 • Why Do Products Fail? 340

Entrepreneurial Success: BucketFeet: A Gift of Hand-Decorated Sneakers Creates a $1 Million Business 339

Branding, Packaging, and Labeling 340
What Is a Brand? 341 • Types of Brands 341 • Benefits of Branding 341 • Choosing and Protecting a Brand 343 • Branding Strategies 344 • Brand Extensions 344 • Packaging 344 • Labeling 346

Social Media: Going Boldly Where No Cookie Has Gone Before 342

Pricing Products 346
The Meaning and Use of Price 346 • Price and Non-Price Competition 347 • Buyers' Perceptions of Price 347

Ethical Success or Failure: What is the Real Price...? 348

Pricing Objectives 348
Survival 348 • Profit Maximization 348 • Target Return on Investment 349 • Market-Share Goals 349 • Status-Quo Pricing 349

Pricing Methods 349
Cost-Based Pricing 349 • Demand-Based Pricing 351 • Competition-Based Pricing 351

Pricing Strategies 351
   New-Product Pricing 352 • Differential Pricing 352 •
   Psychological Pricing 353 • Product-Line Pricing 354 •
   Promotional Pricing 355

Pricing Business Products 355
   Geographic Pricing 355 • Transfer Pricing 356 •
   Discounting 356

Summary 357

Key Terms 358

Discussion Questions 359

Video Case: Mi Ola Strives for a Marketing Splash 359

   Building Skills for Career Success 360

Endnotes 361

Chapter 13: Distributing and Promoting Products 362

→ **Inside Business:** Under Armour Gaining in the Race against Nike 363

Distribution Channels and Market Coverage 364
   Commonly Used Distribution Channels 364 • Level of Market Coverage 365

Partnering Through Supply-Chain Management 366

Marketing Intermediaries: Wholesalers 367
   Wholesalers Provide Services to Retailers and Manufacturers 367 • Types of Wholesalers 367

Marketing Intermediaries: Retailers 368
   Types of Retail Stores 369 • Types of Nonstore Selling 371 • Types of Shopping Centers 373

Entrepreneurial Success: Mobile Goes Retro: Food Trucks and More 370

Physical Distribution 374

Inventory Management 374 • Order Processing 375 • Warehousing 375 • Materials Handling 376 • Transportation 376

What is Integrated Marketing Communications? 377

The Promotion Mix: An Overview 378

Advertising 379
   Types of Advertising by Purpose 379 • Major Steps in Developing an Advertising Campaign 380 • Advertising Agencies 382 • Social and Legal Considerations in Advertising 382

Personal Selling 383
   Kinds of Salespersons 383 • The Personal-Selling Process 384 • Major Sales Management Tasks 385

Sales Promotion 385
   Sales Promotion Objectives 385 • Sales Promotion Methods 386 • Selection of Sales Promotion Methods 386

Personal App: Do sales promotion tools affect your buying decision? 386

Ethical Success or Failure: On-Campus Branding: What's Your Experience? 388

Public Relations 389
   Types of Public-Relations Tools 389 • Uses of Public Relations 390

Social Media: UPS and FedEx Are Social Media Savvy 389

Summary 391

Key Terms 392

Discussion Questions 393

Video Case: Honest Tea Plus Coca-Cola Equals National Distribution 393

   Building Skills for Career Success 394

   Running a Business: Part 5: Graeter's is "Synonymous with Ice Cream" 396

   Building a Business Plan: Part 5

Endnotes 398

PART 6 Information, Accounting, and Finance 400

© ANDY DEAN PHOTOGRAPHY/SHUTTERSTOCK.COM

Chapter 14: Exploring Social Media and e-Business 400

→ **Inside Business:** Taco Bell's Recipe for Social Media Success 401

Why is Social Media Important? 402
   What Is Social Media and How Popular Is It? 402 • Why Businesses Use Social Media 402

Ethical Success or Failure: Should Social Media Disclose Experiments to Users? 404

Social Media Tools for Business Use 405
   Business Use of Blogs 405 • Photos, Videos, and Podcasts 406 • Social Media Ratings 406 • Social Games 407

Achieving Business Objectives Through Social Media 407
   Social Media Communities 408 • Crisis and Reputation Management 409 • Listening to Stakeholders 409 • Targeting Customers 410 • Social Media Marketing 410 • Generating New Product Ideas 412 • Recruiting Employees 413

Career Success: Do You Have a Future in Social Media? 409

Personal App: Make a Good Impression Using Social Media 413

Developing a Social Media Plan 413
   Steps to Build a Social Media Plan 413 • Measuring and Adapting a Social Media Plan 416 • The Cost of Maintaining a Social Media Plan 417

Defining e-Business 418
   Organizing e-Business Resources 418 • Satisfying Needs Online 419 • Creating e-Business Profit 420

Entrepreneurial Success: Advice from Teenage App Entrepreneurs 419

Fundamental Models of e-Business 421
   Business-to-Business (B2B) Model 421 • Business-to-Consumer (B2C) Model 422

The Future of the Internet, Social Media, and e-Business 423
   Internet Growth Potential 423 • Ethical and Legal Concerns 424 • Future Challenges for Computer Technology, Social Media, and e-Business 425

Summary 427

Key Terms 428

Discussion Questions 429

Video Case: Luke's Lobster: Entrepreneurs Use Social Networking to Claw Their Way Up the Food Chain 429

Building Skills for Career Success 430

Endnotes 431

Chapter 15: Using Management and Accounting Information 433

→ *Inside Business:* Amazon Web Services Delivers in the Cloud 434

How Can Information Reduce Risk When Making a Decision? 435

Information and Risk 435 • Information Rules 436 • The Difference Between Data and Information 436 • Knowledge Management 437

Social Media: The Small Business Administration Is Big on Social Media 437

What is a Management Information System? 438

A Firm's Information Requirements 438 • Costs and Limits of the System 440

How Do Employees Use a Management Information System? 440

Step 1: Collecting Data 441 • Step 2: Storing Data 442 • Step 3: Updating Data 442 • Step 4: Processing Data 442 • Step 5: Presenting Information 443

Personal App: Better Knowledge = Better Decisions 442

Why Accounting Information Is Important 445

Entrepreneurial Success: Avoid These Top Three Accounting Mistakes 445

Why Audited Financial Statements Are Important? 446 • Accounting Fraud, Ethical Behavior, and Reform 446 • Different Types of Accounting 447 • Careers in Accounting 448

The Accounting Equation and the Balance Sheet 449

The Accounting Equation 449 • The Balance Sheet 450 • Assets 451 • Liabilities and Owners' Equity 452

The Income Statement 453

Revenues 454 • Cost of Goods Sold 454 • Operating Expenses 455 • Net Income 456

Ethical Success or Failure: Timing Counts in Tesco's Accounting Scandal 456

The Statement of Cash Flows 456

Evaluating Financial Statements 458

Comparing Financial Data 458 • Financial Ratios 460

Summary 461

Key Terms 463

Discussion Questions 463

Video Case: Making the Numbers or Faking the Numbers? 463

Building Skills for Career Success 464

Endnotes 465

Chapter 16: Mastering Financial Management 466

→ *Inside Business:* Alibaba and the $25 Billion IPO 467

Why Financial Management? 468

The Need for Financial Management 468 • Financial Reform After the Economic Crisis 469 • Careers in Finance 469

The Need for Financing 470

Short-Term Financing 470 • Long-Term Financing 471 • The Risk–Return Ratio 472

Planning—The Basis of Sound Financial Management 472

Developing the Financial Plan 472 • Monitoring and Evaluating Financial Performance 475

Entrepreneurial Success: Celebrity Investors Bring Cash and Star Power 474

Personal App: Do You Have a Financial Plan? 475

Financial Services Provided by Banks and Other Financial Institutions 476

Traditional Banking Services for Business Clients 476 • Credit and Debit Card Transactions 477 • Electronic Banking Services 478 • International Banking Services 478

Sources of Short-Term Debt Financing 479

Sources of Unsecured Short-Term Financing 479 • Sources of Secured Short-Term Financing 481 • Factoring Accounts Receivable 482 • Cost Comparisons 482

Sources of Equity Financing 483

Selling Stock 483 • Retained Earnings 485 • Venture Capital, Angel Investors, and Private Placements 486

Social Media: Tweet to Chuck 485

Ethical Success or Failure: Should Fans Be Able to Buy Securities Linked to Athletes? 487

Sources of Long-Term Debt Financing 487

Long-Term Loans 488 • Corporate Bonds 489 • Cost Comparisons 490

Summary 491

Key Terms 492

Discussion Questions 493

Video Case: Moonworks Partners with Bank Rhode Island to Finance Growth 493

Building Skills for Career Success 494

Running a Business: Part 6: Graeter's Recipe for Growth: New Systems, Social Media, and Financing 495

Building a Business Plan: Part 6 497

Endnotes 498

Glossary G-1

Name Index NI-1

Subject Index SI-1

The following appendixes appear on the companion site **www.cengage.brain.com**

Appendix A: Understanding Personal Finances and Investments A-1

Appendix B: Careers in Business B-1

Appendix C: Enhancing Union–Management Relations C-1

Appendix D: Risk Management and Insurance D-1

Appendix E: Business Law, Regulation, and Taxation E-1

About the Authors

William M. Pride Texas A&M University

William M. Pride is professor of marketing, Mays Business School at Texas A&M University. He received his PhD from Louisiana State University. He is the author of Cengage Learning's *Marketing*, 15th edition, a market leader. Dr. Pride's research interests are in advertising, promotion, and distribution channels. Dr. Pride's research articles have appeared in major journals in the fields of advertising and marketing, such as *Journal of Marketing*, *Journal of Marketing Research*, *Journal of the Academy of Marketing Science*, and the *Journal of Advertising*. Dr. Pride is a member of the American Marketing Association, Academy of Marketing Science, Association of Collegiate Marketing Educators, Society for Marketing Advances, and the Marketing Management Association. Dr. Pride has taught principles of marketing and other marketing courses for more than 30 years at both the undergraduate and graduate levels.

Robert J. Hughes Richland College, Dallas County Community Colleges

Robert J. Hughes (PhD, University of North Texas) specializes in business administration and college instruction. He has taught Introduction to Business for more than 35 years both on campus and online for Richland College— one of seven campuses that are part of the Dallas County Community College District. In addition to *Business* and *Foundations of Business*, published by Cengage Learning, he has authored college textbooks in personal finance and business mathematics; served as a content consultant for two popular national television series, *It's Strictly Business* and *Dollars & Sense: Personal Finance for the 21st Century*; and is the lead author for a business math project utilizing computer-assisted instruction funded by the ALEKS Corporation. He is also active in many academic and professional organizations and has served as a consultant and investment advisor to individuals, businesses, and charitable organizations. Dr. Hughes is the recipient of three different Teaching in Excellence Awards at Richland College. According to Dr. Hughes, after 35 years of teaching Introduction to Business, the course is still exciting: "There's nothing quite like the thrill of seeing students succeed, especially in a course like Introduction to Business, which provides the foundation for not only academic courses, but also life in the real world."

Jack R. Kapoor College of DuPage

Jack R. Kapoor (EdD, Northern Illinois University) has been a professor of business and economics in the Business and Technology Division at the College of DuPage, where he taught Introduction to Business, Marketing, Management, Economics, and Personal Finance for more than 44 years. Professor Kapoor is a recipient of the Business and Services Division's Outstanding Professor Award. He previously taught at Illinois Institute of Technology's Stuart School of Management, San Francisco State University's School of World Business, and other colleges. He has also served as an Assistant National Bank Examiner for the U.S. Treasury Department and as an international trade consultant to Bolting Manufacturing Co., Ltd., Mumbai, India.

Dr. Kapoor is known internationally as a coauthor of several textbooks in Business and Personal Finance including *Foundations of Business*, 5th edition (Cengage Learning); has served as a content consultant for two popular national television series "*The Business File: An Introduction to Business*," and "*Dollars & Sense: Personal Finance for the 21st Century*"; and developed two full-length audio courses in business and personal finance. He has been quoted in many national newspapers and magazines, including *USA Today*, *U.S. News & World Report*, the *Chicago Sun-Times*, *Crain's Small Business*, the *Chicago Tribune*, and other publications.

Dr. Kapoor has traveled around the world and has studied business practices in capitalist, socialist, and communist countries.

Acknowledgments

The quality of this book and its supplements program has been helped immensely by the insightful and rich comments of a special set of instructors. Their thoughtful and helpful comments had real impact in shaping the final product. In particular, we wish to thank:

John Adams,
  San Diego Mesa College
Ken Anglin,
  Minnesota State University, Mankato
Ellen A. Benowitz,
  Mercer County Community College
Michael Bento,
  Owens Community College
Patricia Bernson,
  County College of Morris
Laura Bulas,
  Central Community College, NE
Brennan Carr,
  Long Beach City College
Paul Coakley,
  The Community College of Baltimore County
Jean Condon,
  Mid-Plains Community College
Mary Cooke,
  Surry Community College
Dean Danielson,
  San Joaquin Delta College
John Donnellan,
  Holyoke Community College
Gary Donnelly,
  Casper College
Karen Edwards,
  Chemeketa Community College
Donna K. Fisher,
  Georgia Southern University
Charles R. Foley,
  Columbus State Community College
Mark Fox,
  Indiana University South Bend
Connie Golden,
  Lakeland Community College
Karen Gore,
  Ivy Tech Community College - Evansville

Carol Gottuso,
  Metropolitan Community College
John Guess,
  Delgado Community College
Frank Harber,
  Indian River State College
Linda Hefferin,
  Elgin Community College
Tom Hendricks,
  Oakland Community College
Eileen Kearney,
  Montgomery Community College
Anita Kelley,
  Harold Washington College
Mary Beth Klinger,
  College of Southern Maryland
Natasha Lindsey,
  University of North Alabama
Robert Lupton,
  Central Washington University
John Mago,
  Anoka Ramsey Community College
Rebecca J. Mahr,
  Western Illinois University
Pamela G. McElligott,
  St. Louis Community College Meramec
Myke McMullen,
  Long Beach City College
Carol Miller,
  Community College of Denver
Jadeip Motwani,
  Grand Valley State
Mark Nagel,
  Normandale Community College
Dyan Pease,
  Sacramento City College
Jeffrey D. Penley,
  Catawba Valley Community College

Angela J. Rabatin,
  Prince George's Community College
Anthony Racka,
  Oakland Community College— Auburn Hills Campus
Dwight Riley,
  Richland College
Kim Rocha,
  Barton College
Carol Rowey,
  Community College of Rhode Island
Christy Shell,
  Houston Community College
Cindy Simerly,
  Lakeland Community College
Yolanda I. Smith,
  Northern Virginia Community College
Gail South,
  Montgomery College
Rieann Spence-Gale,
  Northern Virginia Comm. College—Alexandria Campus
Kurt Stanberry,
  University of Houston, Downtown
John Striebich,
  Monroe Community College
Keith Taylor,
  Lansing Community College
Tricia Troyer,
  Waubonsee Community College
Leo Trudel,
  University of Maine - Fort Kent
Randy Waterman,
  Richland College
Leslie Wiletzky,
  Pierce College - Ft. Steilacoom
Anne Williams,
  Gateway Community College

We also wish to acknowledge Colette Wolfson and Linda Hoffman of Ivy Tech Community College for their contributions to the *Instructor's Resource Manual*. We thank the Dallas Center for Distance Learning Solutions for their Telecourse partnership and for providing the related student and instructor materials. Finally, we thank the following people for their professional and technical assistance: Marian Wood, Elisa Reyna, Carolyn Phillips, MacKenzie Staples, Gwyn Walters, Laurie Marshall, Clarissa Means, Theresa Kapoor, David Pierce, Kathryn Thumme, Karen Tucker, and Dave Kapoor.

Many talented professionals at Cengage Learning have contributed to the development of *Foundations of Business, 5e*. We are especially grateful to Erin Joyner, Jason Fremder, Heather Mooney, Kristen Hurd, Megan Fischer, Jamie Mack, Linda May, Megan Guiliani, and Jeff Tousignant. Their inspiration, patience, support, and friendship are invaluable.

W. M. P.

R. J. H.

J. R. K.

MindTap™

Tap into **engagement**

MindTap empowers you to produce your best work—consistently.

MindTap is designed to help you master the material. Interactive videos, animations, and activities create a learning path designed by your instructor to guide you through the course and focus on what's important.

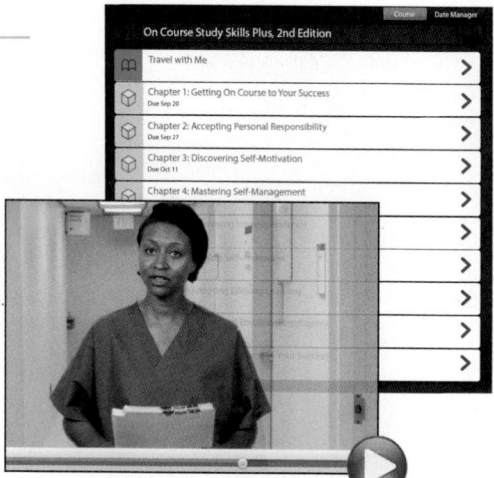

MindTap delivers real-world activities and assignments

that will help you in your academic life as well as your career.

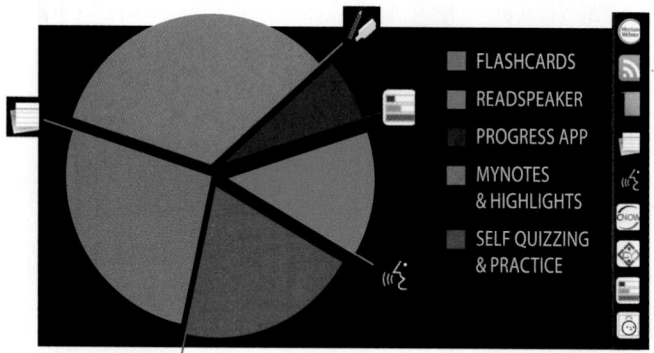

- FLASHCARDS
- READSPEAKER
- PROGRESS APP
- MYNOTES & HIGHLIGHTS
- SELF QUIZZING & PRACTICE

MindTap helps you stay organized and efficient

by giving you the study tools to master the material.

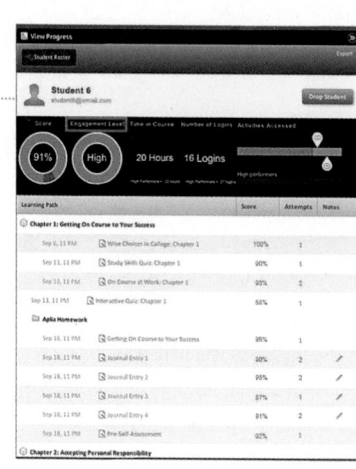

MindTap empowers and motivates

with information that shows where you stand at all times—both individually and compared to the highest performers in class.

"MindTap was very useful – it was easy to follow and everything was right there."
— Student, San Jose State University

"I'm definitely more engaged because of MindTap."
— Student, University of Central Florida

"MindTap puts practice questions in a format that works well for me."
— Student, Franciscan University of Steubenville

Tap into more info at: **www.cengage.com/mindtap**

Source Code: 14M-AA0105

INGA IVANOVA/DREAMSTIME.COM

CHAPTER 1

Exploring the World of Business and Economics

Why Should You Care?

Studying business will help you to choose a career, become a successful employee or manager, start your own business, and become a more informed consumer and better investor.

Learning Objectives

What you will be able to do once you complete this chapter:

1-1 Discuss what you must do to be successful in the world of business.

1-2 Define *business* and identify potential risks and rewards.

1-3 Define *economics* and describe the two types of economic systems: capitalism and command economy.

1-4 Identify the ways to measure economic performance.

1-5 Examine the different phases in the typical business cycle.

1-6 Outline the four types of competition.

1-7 Summarize the factors that affect the business environment and the challenges that American businesses will encounter in the future.

Visa's Vast Global Payments Empire

Handling the burgeoning volume of payments made via credit cards, debit cards, and mobile devices is the backbone of Visa's vast payments empire. Although cash remains popular in many parts of the world, the California-based company processes 96 billion transactions every year for consumers and businesses in 200 countries.

Visa's roots go back to 1958, when it was founded as BankAmericard, the credit card division of Bank of America. During the 1970s, the division became independent and was renamed Visa and became an umbrella for a series of payment-processing networks owned by banks in different regions. In 2007, these far-flung networks were united under the Visa name to form a single business that today is a publicly-traded corporation serving more than 14,000 banks and 2.3 billion cardholders worldwide. Its competition includes MasterCard—the second-largest payment network on the planet—and non-credit payment alternatives such as PayPal and Bitcoin.

During peak purchasing periods—such as the yearend holiday shopping season—Visa can process as many as 56,000 transactions per *second*. Most of these in-store and online payments are made by customers using plastic. However, in today's fast-moving economy, a growing number of payments are digital-only, made by customers using smart phones or tablet computers. Visa has been innovating to serve these customers by offering services such as Visa Checkout, a digital wallet that powers payments made by mobile devices, and is part of the network that enables Apple Pay transactions via iPhones.

Looking ahead, Visa sees a lot of opportunity to expand within countries where cash has traditionally been king. By partnering with mobile-network firms throughout Asia, the company is setting the stage for a huge increase in digital payments made by customers on the go. Visa is also distributing tiny devices that turn a small business owner's smart phone into a mobile checkout terminal. So whether the small business is in Hanoi or Hartford, Visa makes it easy to authorize and complete the purchase within seconds.[1]

Did You Know?

Visa earns $12 billion in revenue every year and has its brand name on 2.3 billion credit and debit cards issued worldwide.

Wow! What a challenging world we live in. Just for a moment, think about how you would answer the question below.

In the future, which of the following is the most serious problem facing Americans?

a. Government spending and the national debt.
b. The high unemployment rate.
c. A volatile stock market.
d. Social unrest.
e. An unstable economy and global business environment.

Unfortunately there is no one best answer because all of the above options are serious problems facing you, American businesses, and the nation. Ask almost anyone, and they will tell you that they are worried about at least one or more of the above problems. At the time of the publication of your text, there are signs of economic improvement. The unemployment rate has dropped, consumers are spending more money, gasoline and the price of crude oil have decreased, and the stock market has reached all-time highs. The fact is that people are more optimistic about their future and the future of our nation. And yet, remember that back in 2008 the nation was beginning one of the worst recession periods since the Great Depression in 1929. Simply put, the economic picture is brighter, but individuals, business leaders, and politicians, still worry about their future and the future of the nation.

Regardless of the current state of the economy, keep in mind that our economy continues to adapt and change to meet the challenges of an ever-changing world and to provide opportunities for those who want to achieve success. Our economic system also provides an amazing amount of freedom that allows businesses like Visa—the company profiled in the Inside Business opening case for this chapter—to adapt to changing business environments. To meet increased demand for its payment services—credit cards, debit cards, and mobile payment systems—Visa and its employees were able to introduce new products and services, earn a profit, and sell stock to the general public.

Within certain limits, imposed mainly to ensure public safety, the owners of a business can produce any legal good or service they choose and attempt to sell it at the price they set. This system of business, in which individuals decide what to produce, how to produce it, and at what price to sell it, is called **free enterprise**. Our free-enterprise system ensures, for example, that Amazon.com can sell everything from televisions, toys, and tools to computers, cameras, and clothing. Our system gives Amazon's owners and stockholders the right to make a profit from the company's success. It gives Amazon's management the right to compete with bookstore rival Barnes & Noble and electronics giant Sony. It also gives you—the consumer—the right to choose.

In this chapter, we look briefly at what business is and how it became that way. First, we discuss what you must do to be successful in the world of business and explore some important reasons for studying business. Next, we define *business*, noting how business organizations satisfy their customers' needs and earn profits. Then we examine how capitalism and command economies answer four basic economic questions. Next, our focus shifts to how the nations of the world measure economic performance, the phases in a typical business cycle, and the four types of competitive situations. Then we look at the events that helped shape today's business system, the current business environment, and the challenges that businesses face.

1-1 YOUR FUTURE IN THE CHANGING WORLD OF BUSINESS

Learning Objective

1-1 Discuss what you must do to be successful in the world of business.

The key word in this heading is *changing*. When faced with both economic problems and increasing competition not only from firms in the United States but also from international firms located in other parts of the world, employees and managers began to ask the question: What do we do now? Although this is a fair question, it is difficult to answer. Certainly, for a college student taking business courses or an employee just starting a career, the question is even more difficult to answer. Yet there are still opportunities out there for people who are willing to work hard, continue to learn, and possess the ability to adapt to change. Let's begin this course with three basic concepts.

- What do you want?
- Why do you want it?
- Write it down!

During a segment on a national television talk show, Joe Dudley, one of the world's most respected black business owners, gave the preceding advice to anyone who wanted to succeed in business. His advice can help you achieve success. What is so amazing about Dudley's success is that he started a manufacturing business in his own kitchen, with his wife and children serving as the new firm's only employees. He went on to develop his own line of hair-care and cosmetic products sold directly to cosmetologists, barbers, beauty schools, and consumers in the United States and 18 foreign countries. Today, Mr. Dudley has a multimillion-dollar empire—one of the most successful minority-owned companies in the nation. He is not only a successful business owner but also a winner of the Horatio Alger Award—an award given to outstanding individuals who have succeeded in the face of adversity.[2]

free enterprise the system of business in which individuals are free to decide what to produce, how to produce it, and at what price to sell it

Although many people would say that Joe Dudley was just lucky or happened to be in the right place at the right time, the truth is that he became a success because he had a dream and worked hard to turn his dream into a reality. He would be the first to tell you that you have the same opportunities that he had. According to Mr. Dudley, "Success is a journey, not just a destination."[3]

Whether you want to obtain part-time employment to pay college and living expenses, begin your career as a full-time employee, or start a business, you must *bring* something to the table that makes you different from the next person. Employers and our economic system are more demanding than ever before. Ask yourself: What can I do that will make employers want to pay me a salary? What skills do I have that employers need? With these two questions in mind, we begin the next section with another basic question: Why study business?

1-1a Why Study Business?

The potential benefits of higher education are enormous. To begin with, there are economic benefits. Over their lifetimes, college graduates on average earn much more than high school graduates. Although lifetime earnings are substantially higher for college graduates, so are annual income amounts (see Figure 1-1). In addition to higher income, you will find at least five compelling reasons for studying business.

FOR HELP IN CHOOSING A CAREER What do you want to do with the rest of your life? Like many people, you may find it a difficult question to answer. This business course will introduce you to a wide array of employment opportunities. In private enterprise, these range from small, local businesses owned by one individual to large companies such as American Express and Marriott International that are owned by thousands of stockholders. There are also employment opportunities with federal, state, county, and local governments and with charitable organizations such as the Red Cross and Save the Children. For help in deciding which career might be right for you, read Appendix B: Careers in Business, which appears on the text website.

In addition to career information in Appendix B, a number of additional websites provide information about career development. For more information, visit the following sites:

- Career Builder at www.careerbuilder.com
- Career One Stop at www.careeronestop.org
- Monster at www.monster.com

To click your career into high gear, you can also use online networking to advance your career. Websites like Facebook, Twitter, LinkedIn, and other social media sites can help you locate job openings and help prospective employers to

FIGURE 1-1 Who Makes The Most Money?

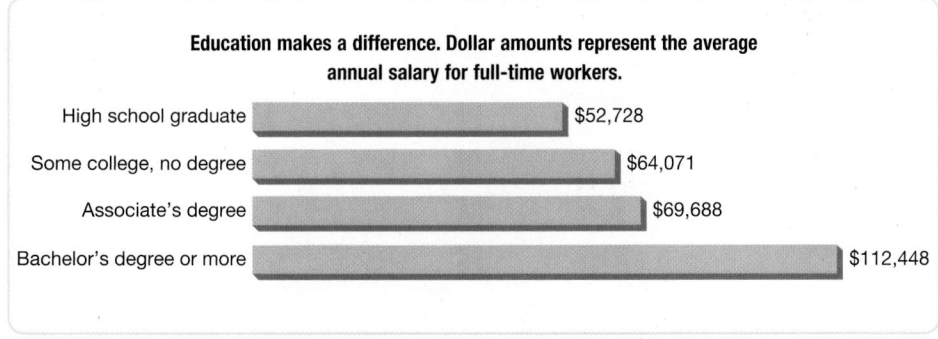

Education makes a difference. Dollar amounts represent the average annual salary for full-time workers.

High school graduate	$52,728
Some college, no degree	$64,071
Associate's degree	$69,688
Bachelor's degree or more	$112,448

Source: "Educational Attainment of Householder—Households with Householder 25 Years Old and Over by Median and Mean Income," The U.S. Census Bureau at www.census.gov (accessed January 12, 2015).

find you. To make the most of online networking, begin by identifying and joining sites where you can connect with potential employers, former classmates, and others who may have or may hear of job openings. Next, be sure your online profiles, photographs, and posts communicate your abilities and interests. Finally, be ready to respond quickly when you spot a job opening.

One thing to remember as you think about what your ideal career might be is that a person's choice of a career ultimately is just a reflection of what he or she values and holds most important. What will give one individual personal satisfaction may not satisfy another. For example, one person may dream of a career as a corporate executive and becoming a millionaire before the age of 30. Another may choose a career that has more modest monetary rewards but that provides the opportunity to help others. What you choose to do with your life will be based on what you feel is most important. And *you* are a very important part of that decision.

TO BE A SUCCESSFUL EMPLOYEE Deciding on the type of career you want is only the first step. To get a job in your chosen field and to be successful at it, you will have to develop a plan, or a road map, that ensures that you have the skills and knowledge the job requires. You will also be expected to have the ability to work well with many types of people in a culturally diverse workforce. **Cultural (or workplace) diversity** refers to the differences among people in a workforce owing to race, ethnicity, and gender.

This course, your instructor, and all of the resources available at your college or university can help you to acquire the skills and knowledge you will need for a successful career. But do not underestimate your part in making your dream a reality. In addition to the job-related skills and knowledge you'll need to be successful in a specific career, employers will also look for the following characteristics when hiring a new employee or promoting an existing employee:

- Honesty and integrity
- Willingness to work hard
- Dependability
- Time management skills

Cultural (or workplace) diversity differences among people in a workforce owing to race, ethnicity, and gender

What do you want to do with the rest of your life? While some people know exactly what they want to do in life, many people have trouble choosing a career. Often it helps to begin a career search by asking "What do I value?" or "What's really important to me?" Ultimately, what you choose to do with your life is based on what you feel is most important. And you may be the most important part of the decision.

SOLARSEVEN/DREAMSTIME.COM

- Self-confidence
- Motivation
- Willingness to learn
- Communication skills
- Professionalism

Employers will also be interested in any work experience you may have had in cooperative work/school programs, during summer vacations, or in part-time jobs during the school year. In addition to job skills and knowledge, experience—even part-time work experience—can make a difference when it is time to apply for the job you really want.

TO IMPROVE YOUR MANAGEMENT SKILLS Many employees want to become managers because managers often receive higher salaries and can earn promotions within an organization. Although management obviously can be a rewarding career, what is not so obvious is the amount of time and hard work needed to achieve the higher salaries and promotions. For starters, employers expect more from managers and supervisors than ever before. Typically, the heavy workload requires that managers work long hours, and most do not get paid overtime. They also face increased problems created by an unstable economy, increased global competition, the quest for improved quality, and the need for efficient use of the firm's resources.

Personal App

Be the employee you'd like to hire!

VALENTIN ARMIANU/DREAMSTIME.COM

Think about what you'd look for if you were making hiring decisions, and strive to become that kind of employee. What characteristics, skills, and knowledge would make you an outstanding employee? Whether you expect to work for a big corporation, small business, government agency, or nonprofit group, understanding the basics of business will add to your attractiveness as an employee.

To be an effective manager, managers must be able to perform four basic management functions: planning, organizing, leading and motivating, and controlling. All four topics are discussed in Chapter 6, Understanding the Management Process. To successfully perform these management functions, managers must also possess four very important skills.

- *Interpersonal skills*—The ability to deal effectively with individual employees, other managers within the firm, and people outside the firm.
- *Analytic skills*—The ability to identify problems correctly, generate reasonable alternatives, and select the "best" alternatives to solve problems.
- *Technical skills*—The skill required to accomplish a specific kind of work being done in an organization. Although managers may not actually perform the technical tasks, they should be able to train employees and answer technical questions.
- *Conceptual skills*—The ability to think in abstract terms in order to see the "big picture." Conceptual skills help managers understand how the various parts of an organization or an idea can fit together.

In addition to the four skills just described, a successful manager will need many of the same characteristics that an employee needs to be successful.

TO START YOUR OWN BUSINESS Some people prefer to work for themselves, and they open their own businesses. To be successful, business owners must possess many of the same characteristics that successful employees and managers have, and they must be willing to work hard and put in long hours.

It also helps if your small business can provide a product or service that customers want. For example, Nick D'Aloisio, who lives in England, created his first app when he was 12. A few apps later he hit upon a new idea that propelled him into the major leagues of the app business world. This new app was based on a simple need: A way to summarize the information contained on a web page without having to read the entire page. To solve this problem and meet the needs of potential customers, D'Aloisio developed an algorithm that summarizes the key points in a few words. The app was called Summly and was sold on Apple's App website. Eventually, Yahoo! became interested in Summly *and* Nick D'Aloisio. The search engine purchased the app and asked D'Aloisio to develop a related product called Yahoo! News Digest which debuted in 2014. Was he just lucky? No, the secret of his success was that he met the needs of customers who were willing to buy the app.[4]

Unfortunately, many business firms fail: Approximately 70 percent of small businesses fail within the first ten years. Typical reasons for business failures include undercapitalization (not enough money), poor business location, poor customer service, unqualified or untrained employees, fraud, lack of a proper business plan, and failure to seek outside professional help. The material in Chapter 5, Small Business, Entrepreneurship, and Franchises, and selected topics and examples throughout this text will help you to decide whether you want to open your own business. The material in this course will also help you to overcome many of these problems.

TO BECOME A BETTER INFORMED CONSUMER AND INVESTOR The world of business surrounds us. You cannot buy a home, a new Ford Fusion Hybrid from the local Ford dealer, a pair of jeans at Gap Inc., or a hot dog from a street vendor without entering into a business transaction. Because you no doubt will engage in business transactions almost every day of your life, one very good reason for studying business is to become a more fully informed consumer.

Many people also rely on a basic understanding of business to help them to invest for the future. According to Julie Stav, Hispanic stockbroker-turned-author/ radio personality, "Take $25, add to it drive plus determination and then watch it multiply into an empire."[5] The author of *Get Your Share* and other personal finance help books believes that it is important to learn the basics about the economy and business, stocks, mutual funds, and other alternatives before investing your money. She also believes that it is never too early to start investing. Although this is an obvious conclusion, just dreaming of being rich does not make it happen. In fact, like many facets of life, it takes planning and determination to establish the type of investment program that will help you to accomplish your financial goals.

1-1b Special Note to Business Students

It is important to begin reading this text with one thing in mind: *This business course does not have to be difficult.* We have done everything possible to eliminate the problems that you encounter in a typical class. All of the features in each chapter have been evaluated and recommended by instructors with years of teaching experience. In addition, business students—just like you—were asked to critique each chapter component. Based on this feedback, the text includes the following features:

- *Learning objectives* appear at the beginning of each chapter.
- *Inside Business* is a chapter-opening case that highlights how successful, real-world companies do business on a day-to-day basis.
- *Margin notes* are used throughout a chapter to reinforce both learning objectives and key terms.
- *Boxed features* in each chapter highlight how both employees and entrepreneurs can be ethical and successful. Topics discussed in the boxed features include career success, entrepreneurial success, ethics, and social media.

- A *Personal App* in each chapter provides special student-centered examples and explanations that help you immediately grasp and retain the material.
- *Concept Checks* at the end of each major section within a chapter help you test your understanding of the major issues just discussed.
- *End-of-chapter materials* provide a chapter summary, a list of key terms, discussion questions, and a video case about a successful, real-world company.
- The last section of every chapter is entitled *Building Skills for Career Success* and includes exercises devoted to enhancing your social media skills, building team skills, and researching different careers.
- *End-of-part materials* provide a continuing video case about Graeter's Ice Cream, a company that operates a chain of retail outlets in the Cincinnati, Ohio, area and sells to Kroger Stores and other retailers throughout the country. Also, at the end of each major part is an exercise designed to help you to develop the components that are included in a typical business plan.

In addition to the text, a number of student supplements will help you to explore the world of business. We are especially proud of the website that accompanies this edition. There, you will find online study aids, such as interactive Test Yourself quizzes, key terms and definitions, student PowerPoint slides, crossword puzzles, and links to the videos for each chapter. If you want to take a look at the Internet support materials available for this edition of *Foundations of Business,*

1. Go to www.cengagebrain.com.
2. At the CengageBrain.com home page, enter the ISBN for your book (located on the back cover of your book) in the search box at the top of the page. This will take you to the textbook website where companion resources can be found.

As authors, we want you to be successful. We know that your time is valuable and that your schedule is crowded with many different activities. We also appreciate the fact that textbooks are expensive. Therefore, we want you to use this text and get the most out of your investment. To help you get off to a good start, a number of suggestions for developing effective study skills and using this text are provided in Table 1-1.

TABLE 1-1 Seven Ways to Use This Text and Its Resources

1. Prepare before you go to class	Early preparation is the key to success in many of life's activities. Certainly, early preparation for this course can help you to participate in class, ask questions, and improve your performance on examinations.
2. Read the chapter	Although it may seem like an obvious suggestion, many students never take the time to really read the material. Find a quiet space where there are no distractions, and invest enough time to become a "content expert."
3. Underline or highlight important concepts	Make this text yours. Do not be afraid to write on the pages of your text or highlight important material. When it is time to review for exams, it is much easier to review material if you have identified important concepts.
4. Take notes	While reading, take the time to jot down important points and summarize concepts in your own words. Also, take notes in class.
5. Apply the concepts	Learning is always easier if you can apply the content to your real-life situation. Think about how you could use the material either now or in the future.
6. Practice critical thinking	Test the material in the text. Do the concepts make sense? To build critical-thinking skills, answer the discussion questions and the questions that accompany the cases at the end of each chapter. Also, many of the exercises in the Building Skills for Career Success feature at the end of each chapter require critical thinking.
7. Prepare for the examinations	Allow enough time to review the material before the examinations. Check out the concept check questions at the end of each major section in the chapter and the summary at the end of the chapter. Then use the resources on the text website.

✓ What reasons would you give if you were advising someone to study business?

✓ What factors affect a person's choice of careers?

✓ Once you have a job, what steps can you take to be successful?

Learning Objective

1-2 Define *business* and identify potential risks and rewards.

business the organized effort of individuals to produce and sell, for a profit, the goods and services that satisfy society's needs

Because a text should always be evaluated by the students and professors who use it, we would welcome and sincerely appreciate your comments and suggestions. Please feel free to contact us by using one of the following e-mail addresses:

Bill Pride: w-pride@tamu.edu

Bob Hughes: bhughes@dcccd.edu

Jack Kapoor: kapoorj@att.net

1-2 BUSINESS: A DEFINITION

Business is the organized effort of individuals to produce and sell, for a profit, the goods and services that satisfy society's needs. The general term *business* refers to all such efforts within a society (as in "American business"). However, *a business* is a particular organization, such as Kraft Foods, Inc., or Cracker Barrel Old Country Stores. To be successful, a business must perform three activities. It must be organized, it must satisfy needs, and it must earn a profit.

1-2a The Organized Effort of Individuals

For a business to be organized, it must combine four kinds of resources: material, human, financial, and informational. *Material* resources include the raw materials used in manufacturing processes as well as buildings and machinery. For example, Mrs. Fields Cookies needs flour, sugar, butter, eggs, and other raw materials to produce the food products it sells worldwide. In addition, this Colorado-based company needs human, financial, and informational resources. *Human* resources are the people who furnish their labor to the business in return for wages. The *financial* resource is the money required to pay employees, purchase materials, and generally keep the business operating. *Information* is the resource that tells the managers of the business how effectively the other three resources are being combined and used (see Figure 1-2).

Today, businesses are usually organized as one of three specific types. *Service businesses* produce services, such as haircuts, legal advice, or tax preparation. H&R Block provides tax preparation, retail banking, and software and digital products to both businesses and consumers in the United States, Canada, and Australia. *Manufacturing businesses* process various materials into tangible goods, such as delivery trucks, towels, or computers. Intel, for example, produces computer chips that, in turn, are sold to companies that manufacture computers. Finally, some firms called *marketing intermediaries* buy products from manufacturers and then resell them. Sony Corporation is a manufacturer that produces stereo equipment, televisions, and other electronic products. These products may be sold to a marketing intermediary—often referred to as a retailer—such as Best Buy or Walmart, which then resells the manufactured goods to consumers in their retail stores.

FIGURE 1-2 Combining Resources

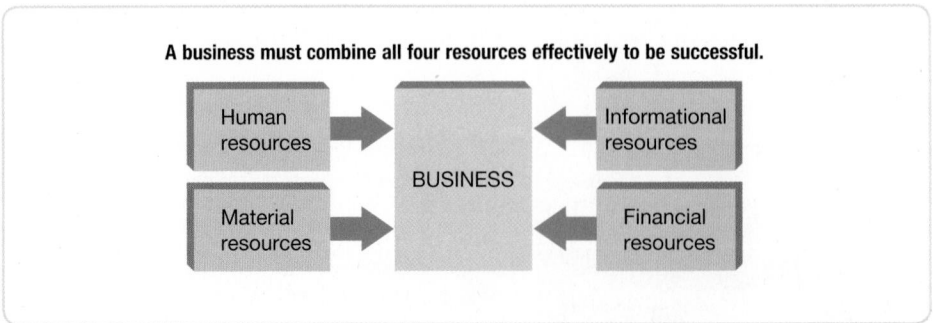

A business must combine all four resources effectively to be successful.

Human resources → BUSINESS ← Informational resources

Material resources → BUSINESS ← Financial resources

While most people think of retailers as the "store around the corner," today many consumers prefer to shop online. To take advantage of the opportunities to sell goods and services online, there are retailers that exist only on the Internet and more traditional business firms that sell goods and services in both their brick-and-mortar stores *and* online. For example, Zappos, a highly successful Internet retailer, only sells merchandise online. Macy's, on the other hand, sells merchandise in both its stores and online. According to market research, the number of people shopping online and using e-business to shop for goods and services continues to grow each year. For our purposes, **e-business** can be defined as the organized effort of individuals to produce and sell for a profit, the goods and services that satisfy society's needs *through the facilities available on the Internet*. e-Business—a topic we will continue to explore throughout this text—has become an accepted method of conducting business and a way for businesses to increase sales and profits and reduce expenses.

1-2b Satisfying Needs

The ultimate objective of every firm must be to satisfy the needs of its customers. People generally do not buy goods and services simply to own them; they buy goods and services to satisfy particular needs. Some of us may feel that the need for transportation is best satisfied by an air-conditioned BMW with navigation system, stereo system, heated and cooled seats, automatic transmission, power windows, and remote-control side mirrors. Others may believe that a Chevrolet Sonic with a stick shift will do just fine. Both products are available to those who want them, along with a wide variety of other products that satisfy the need for transportation.

When firms lose sight of their customers' needs, they are likely to find the going rough. However, when businesses understand their customers' needs and work to satisfy those needs, they are usually successful. Back in 1962, Sam Walton opened his first discount store in Rogers, Arkansas. Although the original store was quite different from the Walmart Superstores you see today, the basic ideas of providing customer service and offering goods that satisfied needs at low prices are part of the reason why this firm has grown to become the largest retailer in the world.

e-business the organized effort of individuals to produce and sell for a profit, the goods and services that satisfy society's needs *through the facilities available on the Internet.*

Some companies just do it right! Starbucks, a company that was started in 1971, has established a history of meeting the needs of its customers. Over the years, the company has grown to be the largest coffeehouse in the world with 20,000 stores in 65 countries. Perhaps the reason for its success is its mission to inspire and nurture the human spirit—one person, one cup, and one neighborhood at a time.

FIGURE 1-3 The Relationship Between Sales Revenue and Profit

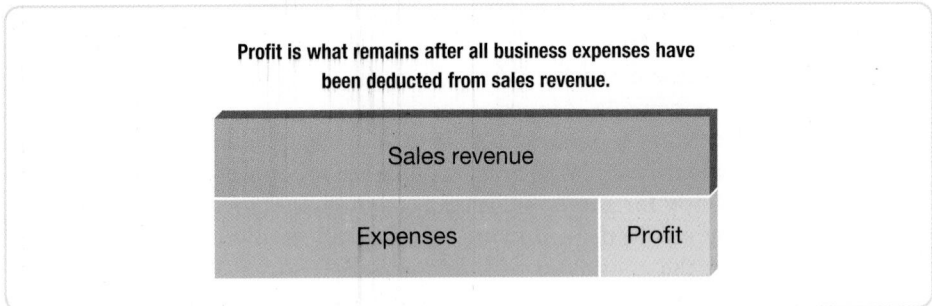

Profit is what remains after all business expenses have been deducted from sales revenue.

Sales revenue	
Expenses	Profit

1-2c Business Profit

A business receives money (sales revenue) from its customers in exchange for goods or services. It must also pay out money to cover the expenses involved in doing business. If the firm's sales revenues are greater than its expenses, it has earned a profit. More specifically, as shown in Figure 1-3, **profit** is what remains after all business expenses have been deducted from sales revenue.

A negative profit, which results when a firm's expenses are greater than its sales revenue, is called a *loss*. A business cannot continue to operate at a loss for an indefinite period of time. Management and employees must find some way to increase sales revenues and reduce expenses to return to profitability. If some specific actions are not taken to eliminate losses, a firm may be forced to close its doors or file for bankruptcy protection. Although many people—especially stockholders and business owners—believe that profit is literally the bottom line or most important goal for a business, many stakeholders may be just as concerned about a firm's social responsibility record. The term **stakeholders** is used to describe all the different people or groups of people who are affected by an organization's policies, decisions, and activities. Many corporations, for example, are careful to point out their efforts to sustain the planet, participate in the green ecological movement, and help people to live better lives in an annual social responsibility report. In its latest social responsibility report, General Mills describes how it contributes $153 million each year to a wide variety of causes, including support for programs that feed the hungry and nonprofit organizations, schools, and communities in the United States and around the globe.[6]

The profit earned by a business becomes the property of its owners. Thus, in one sense, profit is the reward business owners receive for producing goods and services that customers want. Profit is also the payment that business owners receive for assuming the considerable risks of business ownership. One of these is the risk of not being paid. Everyone else—employees, suppliers, and lenders—must be paid before the owners.

A second risk that owners undertake is the risk of losing whatever they have invested into the business. A business that cannot earn a profit is very likely to fail, in which case the owners lose whatever money, effort, and time they have invested.

To satisfy society's needs and make a profit, a business must operate within the parameters of a nation's economic system. In the next section, we define economics and describe two different types of economic systems.

1-3 TYPES OF ECONOMIC SYSTEMS

Economics is the study of how wealth is created and distributed. By *wealth*, we mean "anything of value," including the goods and services produced and sold by business. *How wealth is distributed* simply means "who gets what." Experts often use economics to explain the choices we make and how these choices change as we cope with

---

profit what remains after all business expenses have been deducted from sales revenue

stakeholders all the different people or groups of people who are affected by an organization's policies, decisions, and activities

economics the study of how wealth is created and distributed

Concept Check

✓ Describe the four resources that must be combined to organize and operate a business.

✓ What is the difference between a manufacturing business, a service business, and a marketing intermediary?

✓ Explain the relationship among profit, business risk, and the satisfaction of customers' needs.

Learning Objective

1-3 Define *economics* and describe the two types of economic systems: capitalism and command economy.

the demands of everyday life. In simple terms, individuals, businesses, governments, and society must make decisions that reflect what is important to each group at a particular time. For example, suppose you want to take a weekend trip to some exotic vacation spot, and you also want to begin an investment program. Because of your financial resources, though, you cannot do both, so you must decide what is most important. Business firms, governments, and to some extent society face the same types of decisions. Each group must deal with scarcity when making important decisions. In this case, *scarcity* means "lack of resources"—money, time, natural resources, and so on—that are needed to satisfy a want or need.

Today, experts often study economic problems from two different perspectives: microeconomics and macroeconomics. **Microeconomics** is the study of the decisions made by individuals and businesses. Microeconomics, for example, examines how the prices of homes affect the number of homes individuals will buy. On the other hand, **macroeconomics** is the study of the national economy and the global economy. Macroeconomics examines the economic effect of national income, unemployment, inflation, taxes, government spending, interest rates, and similar factors on a nation and society.

The decisions that individuals, business firms, government, and society make, and the way in which people deal with the creation and distribution of wealth determine the kind of economic system, or **economy**, that a nation has.

Over the years, the economic systems of the world have differed in essentially two ways: (1) the ownership of the factors of production and (2) how they answer four basic economic questions that direct a nation's economic activity.

Factors of production are the resources used to produce goods and services. There are four such factors:

- *Land and natural resources*—elements that can be used in the production process to make appliances, automobiles, and other products. Typical examples include crude oil, forests, minerals, land, water, and even air.
- *Labor*—the time and effort that we use to produce goods and services. It includes human resources such as managers and employees.
- *Capital*—the money, facilities, equipment, and machines used in the operation of organizations. Although most people think of capital as just money, it can also be the manufacturing equipment in a Pepperidge Farm production facility or a computer used in the corporate offices of McDonald's.
- *Entrepreneurship*—the activity that organizes land and natural resources, labor, and capital. It is the willingness to take risks and the knowledge and ability to use the other factors of production efficiently. An **entrepreneur** is a person who risks his or her time, effort, and money to start and operate a business.

A nation's economic system significantly affects all the economic activities of individuals, businesses, government, and society within a country. This far-reaching impact becomes more apparent when we consider that a country's economic system determines how the factors of production are used to meet the needs of society. Today, two different economic systems exist: capitalism and command economies. The way

What does it take to be a successful entrepreneur? Although some people think the life of an entrepreneur is easy, think again. To be successful, entrepreneurs—often referred to as risk takers—must work hard and put in long hours. And they must have an idea for a product or service that has the potential to be successful. Then they must be able to create a plan to turn the idea into a successful product or service.

microeconomics the study of the decisions made by individuals and businesses

macroeconomics the study of the national economy and the global economy

economy the way in which people deal with the creation and distribution of wealth

factors of production resources used to produce goods and services

entrepreneur a person who risks time, effort, and money to start and operate a business

New energy from an old source: The wind. To protect the environment and our natural resources as well as to reduce our dependence on oil, many utility companies are developing alternative energy sources such as wind power. Although the price of oil and gasoline has dropped and the production of oil and gas has increased, once developed, wind-energy may actually be cheaper than using oil in the future.

NIVEK NESLO/PHOTODISC/GETTY IMAGES

each system answers the four basic economic questions listed here determines a nation's economy.

1. *What* goods and services—and how much of each—will be produced?
2. *How* will these goods and services be produced?
3. *For whom* will these goods and services be produced?
4. *Who* owns and who controls the major factors of production?

1-3a Capitalism

Capitalism is an economic system in which individuals own and operate the majority of businesses that provide goods and services. Capitalism stems from the theories of the Scottish economist Adam Smith. In his book *Wealth of Nations*, published in 1776, Smith argued that a society's interests are best served when the individuals within that society are allowed to pursue their own self-interest. According to Smith, when individuals act to improve their own fortunes, they indirectly promote the good of their community and the people in that community. Smith went on to call this concept the "invisible hand." The **invisible hand** is a term created by Adam Smith to describe how an individual's own personal gain benefits others and a nation's economy. For example, the only way a small-business owner who produces shoes can increase personal wealth is to sell shoes to customers. To become even more prosperous, the small-business owner must hire workers to produce even more shoes. According to the invisible hand, people in the small-business owner's community not only would have shoes but also would have jobs working for the shoemaker. Thus, the success of people in the community and, to some extent, the nation's economy are tied indirectly to the success of the small-business owner.

Adam Smith's capitalism is based on the following fundamental issues—also see Figure 1-4.

1. The creation of wealth is the concern of private individuals, not the government.
2. Individuals must own private property and the resources used to create wealth.
3. Economic freedom ensures the existence of competitive markets that allow both sellers and buyers to enter and leave the market as they choose.

capitalism an economic system in which individuals own and operate the majority of businesses that provide goods and services

invisible hand a term created by Adam Smith to describe how an individual's personal gain benefits others and a nation's economy

FIGURE 1-4 Basic Assumptions of Adam Smith's Laissez-Faire Capitalism

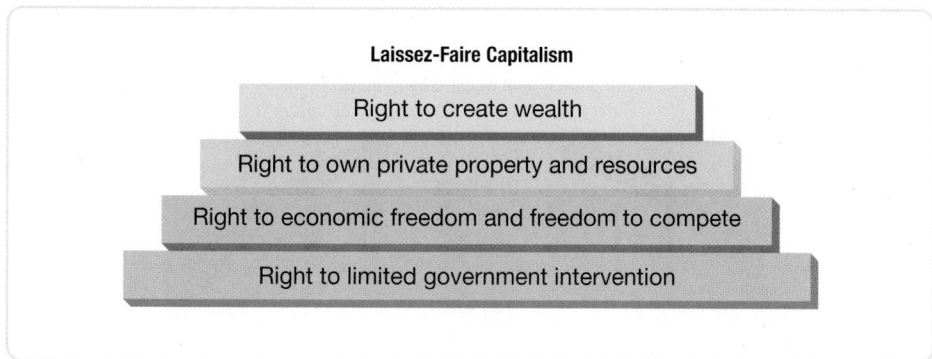

Laissez-Faire Capitalism

Right to create wealth

Right to own private property and resources

Right to economic freedom and freedom to compete

Right to limited government intervention

4. The role of government should be limited to providing defense against foreign enemies, ensuring internal order, and furnishing public works and education.

One factor that Smith felt was extremely important was the role of government. He believed that government should act only as rule maker and umpire. The French term *laissez-faire* describes Smith's capitalistic system and implies that there should be no government interference in the economy. Loosely translated, this term means "let them do" (as they see fit).

Adam Smith's laissez-faire capitalism is also based on the concept of a market economy. A **market economy** (sometimes referred to as a *free-market economy*) is an economic system in which businesses and individuals decide what to produce and buy, and the market determines prices and quantities sold. In today's competitive world, a business like Ford Motor Company must decide *what* type of automobiles it will sell, *how* the automobiles will be produced, and *for whom* the automobiles will be produced. *You,* the consumer, must decide if you will buy a Ford product or an automobile manufactured by another company. Prices are determined by the interaction of consumers and businesses in the marketplace.

1-3b Capitalism in the United States

Our economic system is rooted in the laissez-faire capitalism of Adam Smith. However, our real-world economy is not as laissez-faire as Smith would have liked because government participates as more than umpire and rule maker. Our economy is, in fact, a **mixed economy**, one that exhibits elements of both capitalism and socialism.

market economy an economic system in which businesses and individuals decide what to produce and buy, and the market determines quantities sold and prices

mixed economy an economy that exhibits elements of both capitalism and socialism

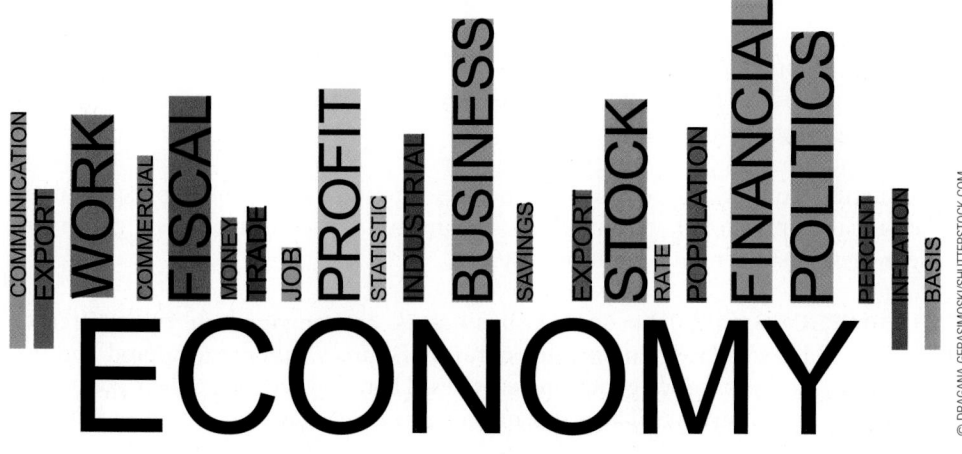

FIGURE 1-5 The Circular Flow in Our Mixed Economy

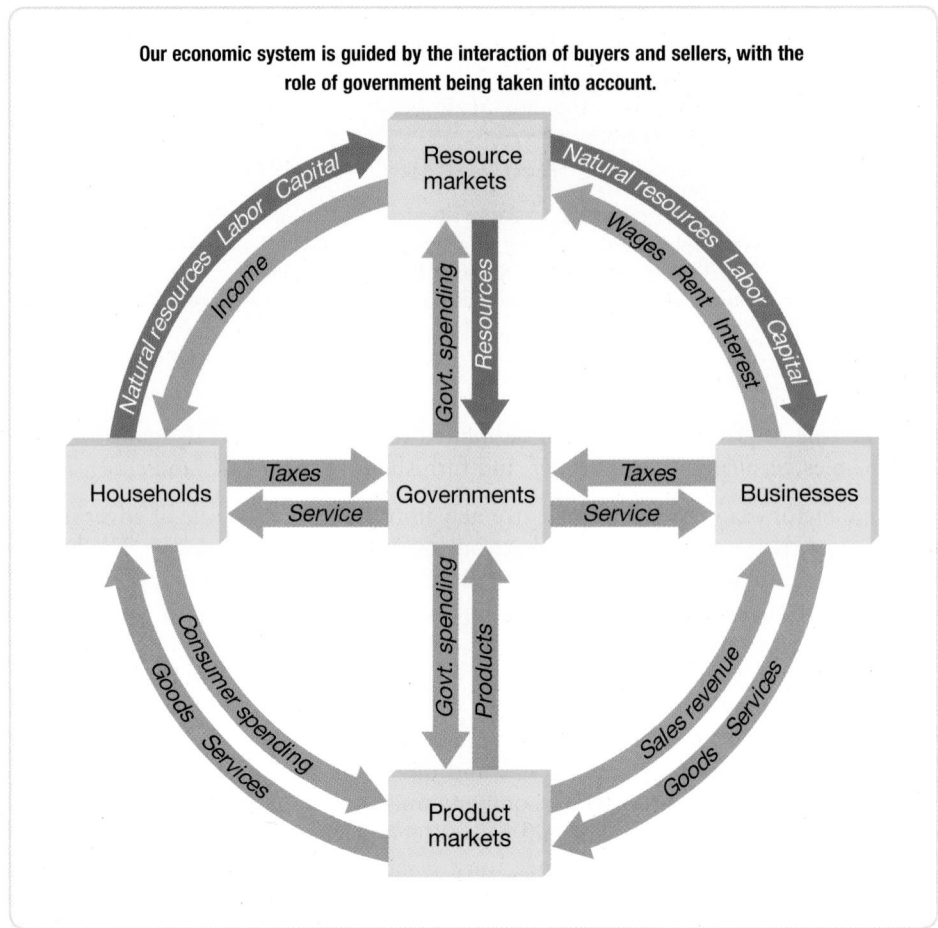

Our economic system is guided by the interaction of buyers and sellers, with the role of government being taken into account.

In a mixed economy, the four basic economic questions discussed at the beginning of this section (*what, how, for whom,* and *who*) are answered through the interaction of households, businesses, and governments. The interactions among these three groups are shown in Figure 1-5.

HOUSEHOLDS Households, made up of individuals, are the consumers of goods and services as well as owners of some of the factors of production. As *resource owners*, people should be free to determine how their resources are used and also to enjoy the income, profits, and other benefits derived from ownership of their resources. For example, members of households provide businesses with labor, capital, and other resources. In return, businesses pay wages, rent, and dividends and interest, which households receive as income.

As *consumers*, household members use their income to purchase the goods and services produced by business. Today, almost 70 percent of our nation's total production consists of **consumer products**—goods and services purchased by individuals for personal consumption.[7] This means that consumers, as a group, are the biggest customers of American business.

BUSINESSES Like households, businesses are engaged in two different exchanges. They exchange money for natural resources, labor, and capital and use these resources to produce goods and services. Then they exchange their goods and services for sales revenue. This sales revenue, in turn, is exchanged for additional resources, which are used to produce and sell more goods and services.

consumer products goods and services purchased by individuals for personal consumption

Along the way, of course, business owners would like to remove something from the circular flow in the form of profits. When business profits are distributed to business owners, these profits become household income. (Business owners are, after all, members of households.) Household members try to retain some income as savings. But are profits and savings really removed from the flow? Usually not! When the economy is running smoothly, households are willing to invest their savings in businesses. They can do so directly by buying stocks issued by businesses, by purchasing shares in mutual funds that purchase stocks in businesses, or by lending money to businesses. They can also invest indirectly by placing their savings in bank accounts. Banks and other financial institutions then invest these savings as part of their normal business operations. Thus, business profits, too, are retained in the business system, and the circular flow in Figure 1-5 is complete. How, then, does government fit in?

© SERGEY YECHIKOV/SHUTTERSTOCK.COM

Can a small business compete with Walmart? That's a tough question to answer. Today, Walmart is recognized as the largest retailer in the world *and* a tough competitor—especially for small businesses in small towns. The mega retailer's policy of low prices has enabled it to build an empire of nearly 11,000 stores in 28 countries that serve more than 245 million household members each week.

GOVERNMENTS The numerous government services are important but they (1) would either not be produced by private business firms or (2) would be produced only for those who could afford them. Typical services include national defense, police, fire protection, education, and construction of roads and highways. To pay for all these services, governments collect a variety of taxes from households (such as personal income taxes and sales taxes) and from businesses (corporate income taxes).

Figure 1-5 shows this exchange of taxes for government services. It also shows government spending of tax dollars for resources and products required to provide these services.

Actually, with government included, our circular flow looks more like a combination of several flows. In reality, it is. The important point is that together the various flows make up a single unit—a complete economic system that effectively provides answers to the basic economic questions. Simply put, the system works.

1-3c Command Economies

A **command economy** is an economic system in which the government decides *what* goods and services will be produced, *how* they will be produced, *for whom* available goods and services will be produced, and *who* owns and controls the major factors of production. Today, two types of economic systems—*socialism* and *communism*—serve as examples of command economies.

SOCIALISM In a socialist economy, the key industries are owned and controlled by the government. Such industries usually include transportation, utilities, communications, banking, and industries producing important materials such as steel. Land, buildings, and raw materials may also be the property of the state in a socialist economy. Depending on the country, private ownership of smaller businesses is permitted to varying degrees. Usually, people may choose their own occupations, although many work in state-owned industries.

What to produce and how to produce it are determined in accordance with national goals, which are based on projected needs and the availability of resources. The distribution of goods and services—who gets what—is also controlled by the state to the extent that it controls taxes, rents, and wages. Among the professed aims of socialist countries are the equitable distribution of income, the elimination of poverty, and the distribution of social services (such as medical care) to all who

command economy an economic system in which the government decides *what* goods and services will be produced, *how* they will be produced, *for whom* available goods and services will be produced, and *who* owns and controls the major factors of production

need them. The disadvantages of socialism include increased taxation and loss of incentive and motivation for both individuals and business owners.

Today, many of the nations that have been labeled as socialist nations traditionally, including France, Sweden, and India, are transitioning to a free-market economy. Currently, many countries that were once thought of as communist countries are now often referred to as socialist countries. Examples of former communist countries often referred to as socialists (or even capitalists) include most of the nations that were formerly part of the Union of Soviet Socialist Republics, China, and Vietnam.

COMMUNISM If Adam Smith was the father of capitalism, Karl Marx was the father of communism. In his writings during the mid-1800s, Marx advocated a classless society whose citizens together owned all economic resources. All workers would then contribute to this *communist* society according to their ability and would receive benefits according to their need.

Since the breakup of the Soviet Union and economic reforms in China and most of the Eastern European countries, the best remaining examples of communism are North Korea and Cuba. Today, these so-called communist economies seem to practice a strictly controlled kind of socialism. The basic four economic questions are answered through centralized government plans. Emphasis is placed on the production of goods and services the government needs rather than on the needs of consumers, so there are frequent shortages of consumer goods.

1-4 MEASURING ECONOMIC PERFORMANCE

Consider for just a moment the following questions:

- Is the gross domestic product for the United States increasing or decreasing?
- Why is the unemployment rate important?
- Are U.S. workers as productive as workers in other countries?

The information needed to answer these questions is easily obtainable from many sources. More important, the answers to these and other questions can be used to gauge the economic health of the nation.

1-4a The Importance of Productivity in the Global Marketplace

One way to measure a nation's economic performance is to assess its productivity. While there are other definitions of productivity, for our purposes, **productivity** is the average level of output per worker per hour. An increase in productivity results in economic growth because a larger number of goods and services are produced by a given labor force. To see how productivity affects you and the economy, consider the following three questions:

Question: *How does productivity growth affect the economy?*

Answer: Because of increased productivity, it now takes fewer workers to produce more goods and services. As a result, employers have reduced costs, earned more profits, and sold their products or services for less. Finally, productivity growth helps American business to compete more effectively with other nations in a global, competitive world.

Question: *How does a nation improve productivity?*

Answer: Reducing costs and enabling employees to work more efficiently are at the core of all attempts to improve productivity. Methods that can be used to increase productivity are discussed in detail in Chapter 8, Producing Quality Goods and Services.

productivity the average level of output per worker per hour

It takes employee communication and teamwork to improve a company's productivity. One of the best and fastest ways to improve a company's productivity is to encourage employees to talk to each other and work in teams. While other methods can be used, the advantage of employees talking and working together is that it is an inexpensive way to improve quality, reduce costs, increase profits, *and* improve productivity.

Question: *Is productivity growth always good?*

Answer: Fewer workers producing more goods and services can lead to lower salary expenses for employers and higher unemployment rates for workers. In this case, increased productivity is good for employers but not good for unemployed workers seeking jobs in a very competitive work environment.

1-4b The Nation's Gross Domestic Product

In addition to productivity, a measure called *gross domestic product* can be used to measure the economic well-being of a nation. **Gross domestic product (GDP)** is the total dollar value of all goods and services produced by all people within the boundaries of a country during a one-year period. For example, the values of automobiles produced by employees in an American-owned General Motors plant and a Japanese-owned Toyota plant in the United States are both included in the GDP for the United States. The U.S. GDP was $17.6 trillion in 2014.[8] (*Note:* At the time of publication, 2014 was the last year for which statistics were available.)

The GDP figure facilitates comparisons between the United States and other countries because it is the standard used in international guidelines for economic accounting. It is also possible to compare the GDP for one nation over several different time periods. This comparison allows observers to determine the extent to which a nation is experiencing economic growth. For example, government economic experts project the U.S. GDP will grow to $24.1 trillion by the year 2022.[9]

To make accurate comparisons of the GDP for different years, we must adjust the dollar amounts for inflation. **Inflation** is a general rise in the level of prices. (The opposite of inflation is deflation.) **Deflation** is a general decrease in the level of prices. By using inflation-adjusted figures, we are able to measure the *real* GDP for a nation. In effect, it is now possible to compare the goods and services produced by a nation in constant dollars—dollars that will purchase the same amount of goods and services. Figure 1-6 depicts the GDP of the United States in current dollars

gross domestic product (GDP) the total dollar value of all goods and services produced by all people within the boundaries of a country during a one-year period

inflation a general rise in the level of prices

deflation a general decrease in the level of prices

FIGURE 1-6 GDP in Current Dollars and in Inflation-Adjusted Dollars

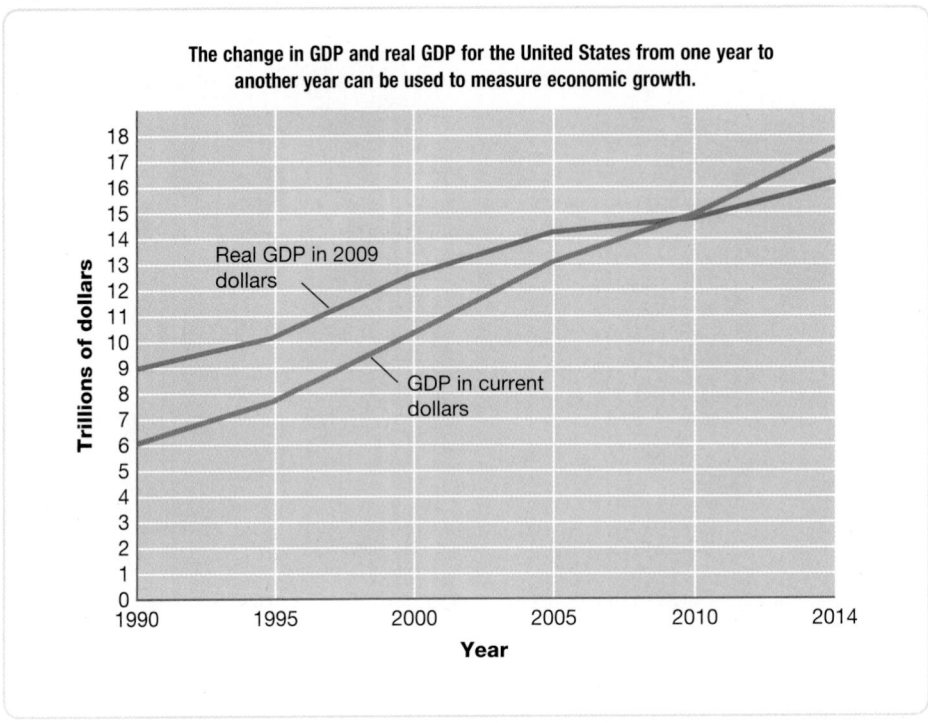

The change in GDP and real GDP for the United States from one year to another year can be used to measure economic growth.

Source: U.S. Bureau of Economic Analysis website at www.bea.gov (accessed December 16, 2014).

and the real GDP in inflation-adjusted dollars. Note that between 1990 and 2014, America's real GDP grew from almost $9 trillion to $16.2 trillion.[10]

1-4c Important Economic Indicators That Measure a Nation's Economy

In addition to productivity, GDP, and real GDP, other economic measures exist that can be used to evaluate a nation's economy. One very important statistic is the unemployment rate. The **unemployment rate** is the percentage of a nation's labor force unemployed at any time. Although the unemployment rate for the United States is typically about 4 to 6 percent, it peaked during the recent economic crisis. At the time of publication, the unemployment rate is just under 6 percent. This is an especially important statistic—especially if you are unemployed.

The **consumer price index (CPI)** is a monthly index that measures the changes in prices of a fixed basket of goods purchased by a typical consumer in an urban area. Goods listed in the CPI include food and beverages, transportation, housing, clothing, medical care, recreation, education, communication, and other goods and services. Economists often use the CPI to determine the effect of inflation on not only the nation's economy but also individual consumers. Another index is the producer price index. The **producer price index (PPI)** measures prices that producers receive for their finished goods. Because changes in the PPI reflect price increases or decreases at the wholesale level, the PPI is an accurate predictor of both changes in the CPI and prices that consumers will pay for many everyday necessities in the future.

Some additional economic measures are described in Table 1-2. Like the measures for GDP, real GDP, unemployment rate, and price indexes, these measures can be used to compare one economic statistic over different periods of time.

unemployment rate the percentage of a nation's labor force unemployed at any time

consumer price index (CPI) a monthly index that measures the changes in prices of a fixed basket of goods purchased by a typical consumer in an urban area

producer price index (PPI) an index that measures prices that producers receive for their finished goods

Concept Check

✓ How does an increase in productivity affect business?

✓ Define gross domestic product. Why is this economic measure significant?

✓ How does inflation affect the prices you pay for goods and services?

✓ How is the producer price index related to the consumer price index?

TABLE 1-2 Common Measures Used to Evaluate a Nation's Economic Health

Economic Measure	Description
1. Balance of trade	The total value of a nation's exports minus the total value of its imports over a specific period of time.
2. Consumer confidence index	A measure of how optimistic or pessimistic consumers are about the nation's economy. This measure is usually reported on a monthly basis.
3. Corporate profits	The total amount of profits made by corporations over selected time periods.
4. Inflation rate	An economic statistic that tracks the increase in prices of goods and services over a period of time. This measure is usually reported monthly and calculated on an annual basis.
5. National income	The total income earned by various segments of the population, including employees, self-employed individuals, corporations, and other types of income.
6. New housing starts	The total number of new homes started during a specific time period.
7. Prime interest rate	The lowest interest rate that banks charge their most credit-worthy customers.

1-5 THE BUSINESS CYCLE

All industrialized nations of the world seek economic growth, full employment, and price stability. However, a nation's economy fluctuates rather than grows at a steady pace every year. In fact, if you were to graph the economic growth rate for a country like the United States, it would resemble a roller-coaster ride with peaks (high points) and troughs (low points). These fluctuations are generally referred to as the **business cycle**, that is, the recurrence of periods of growth and recession in a nation's economic activity.

At the time of publication, many experts believed that the U.S. economy was showing signs of improvement. Key economic indicators including the gross domestic product, the stock market, and consumer spending have improved, and the cost of energy and the unemployment rate have decreased. And yet, the nation's unemployment rate is still high and there are concerns about the size of the national debt—a topic described later in this section. There are also concerns about the long-term stability of the U.S. economy and economies of foreign nations around the globe and the political and social unrest throughout the world.

The changes that result from either economic growth or economic downturn affect the amount of products and services that consumers are willing to purchase and, as a result, the amount of products and services produced by business firms. Generally, the business cycle consists of four phases: the peak (sometimes called prosperity), recession, the trough, and recovery (sometimes called expansion).

During the *peak period* (prosperity), the economy is at its highest point and unemployment is low. Total income is relatively high. As long as the economic outlook remains prosperous, consumers are willing to buy products and services. In fact, businesses often expand and offer new products and services during the peak period to take advantage of consumers' increased buying power.

Generally, economists define a **recession** as two or more consecutive three-month periods of decline in a country's GDP. Because unemployment rises during a recession, total buying power declines. The pessimism that accompanies a recession often stifles both consumer and business spending. As buying power decreases, consumers tend to become more value conscious and reluctant to purchase frivolous or nonessential items. And companies and government at all levels often postpone or go slow on major projects during a recession. In response to a recession, many businesses focus on producing the products and services that provide the most value to their customers.

Economists define a **depression** as a severe recession that lasts longer than a typical recession and has a larger decline in business activity when compared to a

Learning Objective

1-5 Examine the different phases in the typical business cycle.

business cycle the recurrence of periods of growth and recession in a nation's economic activity

recession two or more consecutive three-month periods of decline in a country's GDP

depression a severe recession that lasts longer than a typical recession and has a larger decline in business activity when compared to a recession

Chapter 1 Exploring the World of Business and Economics

21

Career Moves and the Business Cycle

Whether you're at the start of your career or you have entry-level experience and are looking ahead to your next position, keep the business cycle in mind as you plan future career moves. Jobs are more plentiful during the prosperity phase of the business cycle because businesses are booming and they need more employees to keep up with higher demand for goods and services. When employers must compete for talented employees at the peak of the business cycle, they offer higher salaries and more generous benefit packages.

During a recession, however, employers postpone hiring new employees to reduce salary costs in order to cope with stagnant or lower consumer and business spending. Job searches generally take longer, and job applicants face more competition from new graduates, unemployed people, and mid-career employees. Salaries tend to rise slowly during a

recession because employers aren't competing against each other to hire the best employees.

If your job search takes place during a period of prosperity, you'll have more choices of industry and employer—and if your skills and experience closely fit an employer's needs, you'll be in a stronger position to negotiate compensation. During a recession, experts advise thinking about a lateral move (either with your current employer or at the same level with a new employer) to build your skills, increase your knowledge, and add to your experience. The point is to prepare yourself for a higher-level, higher-paying job by the time the recession is over.

Sources: Based on information in Dionissi Aliprantis, Anne Chen, and Chris Vecchio, "Job Search Before and After the Great Recession," *Federal Reserve Bank of Cleveland*, August 12, 2014, www.clevelandfed.org; Anna Zernone, "Is a Lateral Career Move Right for You?" *Times-Union (Albany, NY)*, February 21, 2014, www.timesunion.com; Nick Inglis, "How to Map Your Career Path," *U.S. News and World Report*, January 23, 2014, http://money.usnews.com.

recession. A depression is characterized by extremely high unemployment rates, low wages, reduced purchasing power, lack of confidence in the economy, lower stock values, and a general decrease in business activity.

The third phase of the business cycle is the *trough*. The trough of a recession or depression is the turning point when a nation's production and employment bottom out and reach their lowest levels. To offset the effects of recession and depression, the federal government uses both monetary and fiscal policies. **Monetary policies** are the Federal Reserve's decisions that determine the size of the supply of money in the nation and the level of interest rates. Through **fiscal policy**, the government can influence the amount of savings and expenditures by altering the tax structure and changing the levels of government spending. For example, during the economic crisis that began in 2008, both the Federal Reserve's monetary policies (lower interest rates) and the government's fiscal policies (increased spending) were used to stimulate the economy.

One of the concerns about the government's recent stimulus programs is the national debt. Although the federal government collects approximately $3 trillion in annual revenues, the government usually spends more than it receives, resulting in a **federal deficit**. For example, the government had a federal deficit for each year between 2002 and 2014. The total of all federal deficits is called the **national debt**. Today, the U.S. national debt is $18 trillion or approximately $56,000 for every man, woman, and child in the United States.[11]

Since World War II, the average business cycle has lasted 69 months, or a little less than six years, from one peak period to the next peak period. During the same time period, the average length of recovery (often referred to as expansion) has been 58 months while the average recession has been 11 months.[12] *Recovery* (or *expansion*) is the movement of the economy from the trough, when a nation's production and employment bottom out and reach their lowest levels, to the next peak in a business cycle. Some experts believe that effective use of monetary

monetary policies Federal Reserve's decisions that determine the size of the supply of money in the nation and the level of interest rates

fiscal policy government influence on the amount of savings and expenditures; accomplished by altering the tax structure and by changing the levels of government spending

federal deficit a shortfall created when the federal government spends more in a fiscal year than it receives

national debt the total of all federal deficits

and fiscal policies can speed up recovery and reduce the amount of time the economy is in recession. During the recovery stage of a business cycle, high unemployment rates decline, income increases, and both the ability and the willingness to buy rise.

1-6 TYPES OF COMPETITION

Our capitalist system ensures that individuals and businesses make the decisions about what to produce, how to produce it, and what price to charge for the product. Mattel, Inc., for example, can introduce new versions of its famous Barbie doll, license the Barbie name, change the doll's price and method of distribution, and attempt to produce and market Barbie in other countries or over the Internet at www.mattel.com. Our system also allows customers the right to choose between Mattel's products and those produced by competitors.

As a consumer, you get to choose which products or services you want to buy. Competition like that between Mattel and other toy manufacturers is a necessary and extremely important by-product of capitalism. Business **competition** is essentially a rivalry among businesses for sales to potential customers. In a capitalistic economy, competition also ensures that a firm will survive only if it serves its customers well by providing products and services that meet needs. Economists recognize four different degrees of competition ranging from ideal, complete competition to no competition at all. These are perfect competition, monopolistic competition, oligopoly, and monopoly. For a quick overview of the different types of competition, including numbers of firms and examples for each type, look at Table 1-3.

1-6a Perfect Competition

Perfect (or pure) competition is the market situation in which there are many buyers and sellers of a product, and no single buyer or seller is powerful enough to affect the price of that product. As pointed out in Table 1-3, real-world examples of perfect competition are corn, wheat, peanuts, and many agricultural products. For perfect competition to exist, there are five very important concepts.

- We are discussing the market for a single product, such as bushels of wheat.
- There are no restrictions on firms entering the industry.
- All sellers offer essentially the same product for sale.
- All buyers and sellers know everything there is to know about the market (including, in our example, the prices that all sellers are asking for their wheat).
- The overall market is not affected by the actions of any one buyer or seller.

TABLE 1-3 Four Different Types of Competition

The number of firms determines the degree of competition within an industry.

Type of Competition	Number of Business Firms or Suppliers	Real-World Examples
1. Perfect	Many	Corn, wheat, peanuts, many agricultural products
2. Monopolistic	Many	Clothing, shoes
3. Oligopoly	Few	Automobiles, cereals
4. Monopoly	One	Software protected by copyright, many local public utilities

Concept Check

✓ What are the four phases in the typical business cycle?

✓ At the time you are studying the material in this chapter, which phase of the business cycle do you think the U.S. economy is in? Justify your answer.

✓ How can the government use monetary policy and fiscal policy to reduce the effects of an economic crisis?

Learning Objective

1-6 Outline the four types of competition.

competition rivalry among businesses for sales to potential customers

perfect (or pure) competition the market situation in which there are many buyers and sellers of a product, and no single buyer or seller is powerful enough to affect the price of that product

What company uses the slogan "More Saving, More Doing?" For a clue look at the orange store fixtures in this photo. That's right—the answer is Home Depot. Although it has competition from Lowes, a smaller home improvement store, and local lumber yards and hardware stores, Home Depot is the largest home improvement store in the world with stores in all 50 states, the District of Columbia, Puerto Rico, U.S. Virgin Islands, 10 Canadian provinces, and Mexico.

When perfect competition exists, every seller should ask the same price that every other seller is asking. Why? Because if one seller wanted 50 cents more for his products than all the others, that seller would not be able to sell a single product. Buyers could—and would—do better by purchasing the same products from the competition. On the other hand, a firm willing to sell below the going price would sell all its products quickly. However, that seller would lose sales revenue (and profit) because buyers are actually willing to pay more.

In perfect competition, then, sellers—and buyers as well—must accept the going price. The price of each product is determined by the actions of all buyers and all sellers together through the forces of supply and demand.

THE BASICS OF SUPPLY AND DEMAND The **supply** of a particular product is the quantity of the product that producers are willing to sell at each of various prices. Producers are rational people, so we would expect them to offer more of a product for sale at higher prices and to offer less of the product at lower prices, as illustrated by the supply curve in Figure 1-7.

The **demand** for a particular product is the quantity that buyers are willing to purchase at each of various prices. Buyers, too, are usually rational, so we would expect them—as a group—to buy more of a product when its price is low and to buy less of the product when its price is high, as depicted by the demand curve in Figure 1-7.

supply the quantity of a product that producers are willing to sell at each of various prices

demand the quantity of a product that buyers are willing to purchase at each of various prices

market price the price at which the quantity demanded is exactly equal to the quantity supplied

THE EQUILIBRIUM, OR MARKET, PRICE There is always one certain price at which the demand for a product is exactly equal to the quantity of that product produced. Suppose that producers are willing to *supply* two million bushels of wheat at a price of $8 per bushel and that buyers are willing to *purchase* two million bushels at a price of $8 per bushel. In other words, supply and demand are in balance, or in equilibrium, at the price of $8. Economists call this price the *market price*. The **market price** of any product is the price at which the quantity demanded is exactly equal to the quantity supplied.

FIGURE 1-7 Supply Curve and Demand Curve

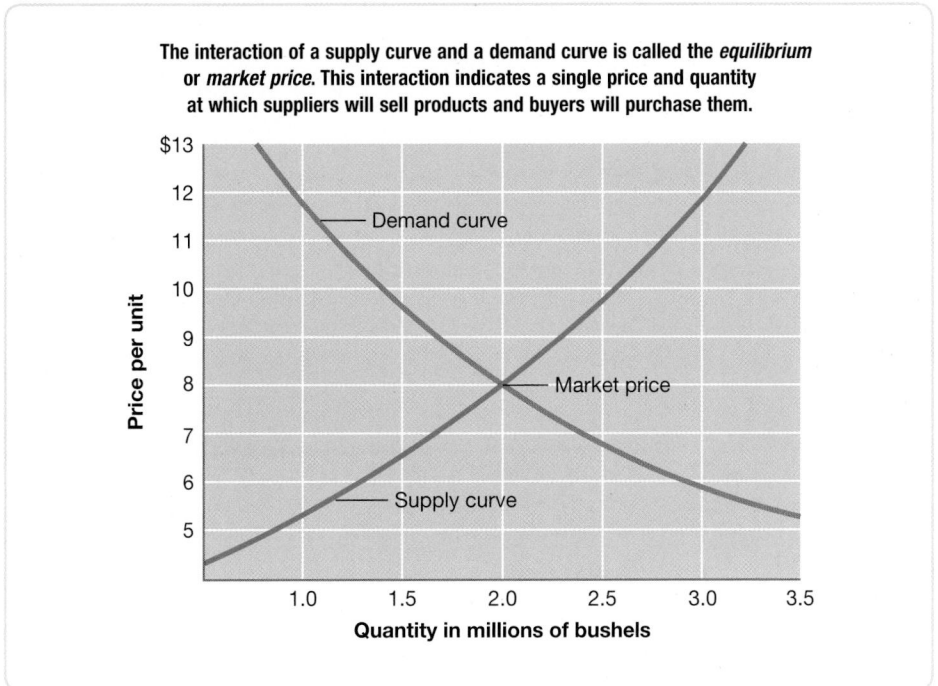

The interaction of a supply curve and a demand curve is called the *equilibrium* or *market price*. This interaction indicates a single price and quantity at which suppliers will sell products and buyers will purchase them.

In theory and in the real world, market prices are affected by anything that affects supply and demand. The *demand* for wheat, for example, might change if researchers suddenly discovered that it offered a previously unknown health benefit. Then buyers would demand more wheat at every price. Or the *supply* of wheat might change if new technology permitted the production of greater quantities of wheat from the same amount of acreage. Other changes that can affect competitive prices are shifts in buyer tastes, the development of new products, fluctuations in income owing to inflation or recession, or even changes in the weather that affect the production of wheat.

Perfect competition is quite rare in today's world. Many real markets, however, are examples of monopolistic competition.

1-6b **Monopolistic Competition**

Monopolistic competition is a market situation in which there are many buyers along with a relatively large number of sellers. Real-world examples of products sold in a monopolistically competitive market include clothing, shoes, soaps, furniture, and many consumer items. The various products available in this type of competitive market are very similar in nature, and they are all intended to satisfy the same need. However, each seller attempts to make its product different from the others by providing unique product features, an attention-getting brand name, unique packaging, or services such as free delivery or a lifetime warranty.

Product differentiation is the process of developing and promoting differences between one's products and all competitive products. It is a fact of life for the producers of many consumer goods, from soaps to clothing to furniture to shoes. A furniture manufacturer such as Thomasville sees what looks like a mob of competitors, all trying to chip away at its share of the market. By differentiating each of its products from all similar products produced by competitors, Thomasville obtains some limited control over the market price of its product.

monopolistic competition a market situation in which there are many buyers along with a relatively large number of sellers who differentiate their products from the products of competitors

product differentiation the process of developing and promoting differences between one's products and all competitive products

© ZHU DIFENG/SHUTTERSTOCK.COM

Entrepreneurial Success

Meet the Teenaged Founder of Fish Flops

When Madison Robinson was 8 years old, she drew colorful fish, starfish, and whales over outlines of flip-flops and called them "Fish Flops." Her father, Dan Robinson, liked the product idea, so he reserved the FishFlops.com domain name. That initial $10 investment in a website address put the Houston-based Robinson family on the road to a fast-growing fashion business that now rings up more than $1.2 million in yearly retail sales.

At first, Robinson was too busy with his T-shirt business to look into manufacturing possibilities. His daughter kept drawing more sea creatures and refining her idea of fun flip-flops for children that would light up with each step. A few years later, Robinson commissioned product samples, took them to a trade show in Florida, and came home with dozens of orders. Fish Flops was officially in business.

Since the beginning, the teenaged founder has been in charge of product design. She also researches potential retail buyers, attends industry shows, and makes media appearances on behalf of Fish Flops. Early on, she wrote the shoe buyer for Nordstrom—and as a result of that contact, she was asked to develop three new flip-flop designs to be sold exclusively in the Nordstrom chain. Fish Flops has sold more than 100,000 pairs of flip-flops in three years. With future growth in mind, the company is currently expanding into a line of casual clothing under the Madison Nicole brand name—the founder's first and middle names.

Sources: Based on information in Joy Sewing, "Teen Grows Fashion Business from FishFlops to Fifth Avenue," *Houston Chronicle*, June 18, 2014, www.houstonchronicle.com; Silvana Ordonez, Andy Rothman, and Tyler Mathisen, "Bright Ideas: Fish Flops," *Nightly Business News*, CNBC, September 9, 2013, http://nbr.com; Adrienne Burke, "How a 15-Year-Old Entrepreneur Got Her Product into Nordstrom," *Yahoo News: Profit Minded*, May 30, 2013, http://news.yahoo.com; http://fishflops.com.

1-6c Oligopoly

An **oligopoly** is a market (or industry) situation in which there are few sellers. Generally, these sellers are quite large, and sizable investments are required to enter into their market. Examples of oligopolies are the automobile, airline, car rental, cereal, and farm implement industries.

Because there are few sellers in an oligopoly, the market actions of each seller can have a strong effect on competitors' sales and prices. If General Motors, for example, reduces its automobile prices, Ford, Honda, Toyota, and Nissan usually do the same to retain their market shares. For instance, when Ford and General Motors began offering cash incentives to encourage consumers to purchase a new automobile at the end of 2015, Chrysler, Honda, Nissan, and Toyota began offering similar incentives and for the same reason—to attract new-car buyers. In the absence of much price competition, product differentiation becomes the major competitive weapon; this is very evident in the advertising of the major automobile manufacturers.

1-6d Monopoly

A **monopoly** is a market (or industry) with only one seller, and there are barriers to keep other firms from entering the industry. In a monopoly, there is no close substitute for the product or service. Because only one firm is the supplier of a product, it would seem that it has complete control over price. However, no firm can set its price at some astronomical figure just because there is no competition; the firm would soon find that it has no customers or sales revenue either. Instead, the firm in a monopoly position must consider the demand for its product and set the price at the most profitable level.

oligopoly a market (or industry) in which there are few sellers

monopoly a market (or industry) with only one seller, and there are barriers to keep other firms from entering the industry

Classic examples of monopolies in the United States are public utilities, including companies that provide local gas, water, or electricity. Each utility firm operates in a *natural monopoly*, an industry that requires a huge investment in capital and within which any duplication of facilities would be wasteful. Natural monopolies are permitted to exist because the public interest is best served by their existence, but they operate under the scrutiny and control of various state and federal agencies. Although many public utilities are still classified as natural monopolies, there is increased competition in many areas of the country. For example, there have been increased demands for consumer choice when selecting a company that provides electrical service to both homes and businesses.

A legal monopoly—sometimes referred to as a *limited monopoly*—is created when a government entity issues a franchise, license, copyright, patent, or trademark. For example, a copyright exists for a specific period of time and can be used to protect the owners of written materials from unauthorized use by competitors that have not shared in the time, effort, and expense required for their development. Because Microsoft owns the copyright on its popular Windows software, it enjoys a legal-monopoly position. Except for natural monopolies and legal monopolies, federal antitrust laws prohibit both monopolies and attempts to form monopolies in order to ensure that competitive markets exist and customers have a choice for products they need or want to purchase.

Concept Check

✓ Is competition good for business? Is it good for consumers?

✓ Compare the four forms of competition.

✓ What is the relationship between supply and demand?

✓ Explain how the equilibrium, or market, price of a product is determined.

1-7 AMERICAN BUSINESS TODAY

Although our economic system is far from perfect, it provides Americans with a high standard of living compared with people in other countries throughout the world. **Standard of living** is a loose, subjective measure of how well off an individual or a society is, mainly in terms of want satisfaction through goods and services. Also, our economic system offers solutions to many of the problems that plague society and provides opportunities for people who are willing to work and to continue learning.

To understand the current business environment and the challenges ahead, it helps to understand how business developed.

1-7a Early Business Development

Our American business system has its roots in the knowledge, skills, and values that the earliest settlers brought to this country. The first settlers in the United States were concerned mainly with providing themselves with basic necessities—food, clothing, and shelter. Almost all families lived on farms, and the entire family worked at the business of surviving. They used their surplus for trading, mainly by barter, among themselves and with the English trading ships that called at the colonies. **Barter** is a system of exchange in which goods or services are traded directly for other goods or services without using money. As this trade increased, small businesses began to appear. Some settlers were able to use their skills and their excess time to work under the domestic system of production. The **domestic system** was a method of manufacturing in which an entrepreneur distributed raw materials to various homes, where families would process them into finished goods. The entrepreneur then offered the goods for sale.

Then, in 1793, a young English apprentice mechanic named Samuel Slater opened a textile factory in Pawtucket, Rhode Island, to spin raw cotton into thread. Slater's ingenuity resulted in America's first use of the **factory system** of manufacturing, in which all the materials, machinery, and workers required to manufacture a product are assembled in one place. The Industrial Revolution in America was born.

Learning Objective

1-7 Summarize the factors that affect the business environment and the challenges that American businesses will encounter in the future.

standard of living a loose, subjective measure of how well off an individual or a society is, mainly in terms of want satisfaction through goods and services

barter a system of exchange in which goods or services are traded directly for other goods or services without using money

domestic system a method of manufacturing in which an entrepreneur distributes raw materials to various homes, where families process them into finished goods to be offered for sale by the merchant entrepreneur

factory system a system of manufacturing in which all the materials, machinery, and workers required to manufacture a product are assembled in one place

A manufacturing technique called *specialization* was used to improve productivity. **Specialization** is the separation of a manufacturing process into distinct tasks and the assignment of the different tasks to different individuals.

The years from 1820 to 1900 were the golden age of invention and innovation in machinery. At the same time, new means of transportation greatly expanded the domestic markets for American products. Certainly, many basic characteristics of our modern business system took form during this time period.

1-7b **Business Development in the 1900s**

Industrial growth and prosperity continued well into the 20th century. Henry Ford's moving automotive assembly line, which brought the work to the worker, refined the concept of specialization and helped spur on the mass production of consumer goods. Fundamental changes occurred in business ownership and management as well. No longer were the largest businesses owned by one individual; instead, ownership was in the hands of thousands of corporate shareholders who were willing to invest in—but not to operate—a business.

The Roaring Twenties ended with the sudden crash of the stock market in 1929 and the near collapse of the economy. The Great Depression that followed in the 1930s was a time of misery and human suffering. People lost their faith in business and its ability to satisfy the needs of society without government involvement. After Franklin D. Roosevelt became president in 1933, the federal government devised a number of programs to get the economy moving again. In implementing these programs, the government got deeply involved in business.

To understand the major events that shaped the United States during the remainder of the 20th century, it helps to remember that the economy was compared to a roller-coaster ride earlier in this chapter—periods of economic growth followed by periods of economic slowdown. The following are major events that shaped the nation's economy during the period from 1940 to 2000:

specialization the separation of a manufacturing process into distinct tasks and the assignment of the different tasks to different individuals

Do you recognize this machine? While quite different than today's technology, this type of computer was the only game in town in the late 1950s. Ironically, even though it is huge by today's standards, it couldn't compute as much information as a laptop computer can today. Looking at this picture, gives you an historical perspective on how far technology, computers, laptops, and tablets have come.

© EVERETT COLLECTION/SHUTTERSTOCK.COM

- World War II, the Korean War, and the Vietnam War
- Rapid economic growth and higher standard of living during the 1950s and 1960s
- The social responsibility movement during the 1960s
- A shortage of crude oil and higher prices for most goods in the mid-1970s
- High inflation, high interest rates, and reduced business profits during the last part of the 1970s and early 1980s
- Sustained economic growth in the 1990s

Unfortunately, by the last part of the 1990s, a larger number of business failures and declining stock values were initial signs that larger economic problems were on the way.

1-7c A New Century: 2000 and Beyond

According to many economic experts, the first part of the 21st century might be characterized as the best of times and the worst of times rolled into one package. On the plus side, technology became available at an affordable price. Both individuals and businesses could now access information with the click of a button. They also could buy and sell merchandise online.

In addition to information technology, the growth of service businesses also changed the way American firms do business in the 21st century. Because service businesses employ approximately 85 percent of the nation's workforce, we now have a service economy.[13] A **service economy** is an economy in which more effort is devoted to the production of services than to the production of goods. Typical service businesses include restaurants, laundries and dry cleaners, real estate, movie theaters, repair companies, and other services that we often take for granted. More information about how service businesses affect the economy is provided in Chapter 8, Producing Quality Goods and Services.

On the negative side, it is hard to watch television, surf the Web, listen to the radio, or read the newspaper without hearing some news about the economy. Because many of the economic indicators described in Table 1-2 on page 21 still indicate troubling economic problems, there is still a certain amount of pessimism surrounding the nation's economy and the global economy. In addition to concerns about the economy, there are other concerns including social unrest and political uncertainty on the national, state, and local levels.

1-7d The Current Business Environment

Before reading on, answer the following question:

In today's competitive business world, which of the following environments affects business?

a. The competitive environment
b. The global environment
c. The technological environment
d. The economic environment
e. All of the above

Correct Answer: e. All the environments listed in the above question affect business today.

THE COMPETITIVE ENVIRONMENT As noted earlier in this chapter, competition is a basic component of capitalism. Every day, business owners must

service economy an economy in which more effort is devoted to the production of services than to the production of goods

Social Media:
Government Agencies Go Social

Do you know what to do in case of a Zombie Apocalypse—or more common disasters, such as hurricanes and tornadoes? If you click to follow the U.S. Centers for Disease Control (CDC) on Twitter (https://twitter.com/CDCgov) or like its Facebook page (https://www.facebook.com/CDC), you'll have the tips you need to cope with emergency situations.

The CDC is only one of many government agencies using social media to increase transparency and facilitate communication with individuals and organizations on the federal, state, and local level. Not only is social media a great way for the government to disseminate information, it also allows agency personnel to answer questions and gauge public reaction to policies and actions. Another plus: social media is a cost-effective way to communicate with geographically-dispersed audiences. The CDC spent less than $100 to launch its "zombie" social media campaign, which attracted national attention and increased awareness of the need for emergency preparedness.

The U.S. Small Business Administration (SBA) is also active in social media, using YouTube, Facebook, Twitter, Google+, and blogs to connect with entrepreneurs and small business owners. In support of Small Business Saturday every November, the SBA posts Facebook messages (on www.facebook.com/SBAgov) and tweets (on http://twitter.com/sbagov) to encourage businesses to prepare and consumers to patronize local shops and restaurants. To verify whether a particular social media account is really connected with the federal government, go to http://www.usa.gov/Agencies.shtml.

Sources: Based on information in M.J. Clark, "Small Business Saturday Set for Nov. 29," *Wyoming Business Report*, November 21, 2014, www.wyomingbusinessreport.com; Melanie Haiken, "Is the CDC Planning for a Walking Dead Zombie Apocalypse?" *Forbes*, March 18, 2014, www.forbes.com; Missy Graham and Elizabeth Johnson Avery, "Government Public Relations and Social Media: An Analysis of the Perceptions and Trends of Social Media Use at the Local Government Level," *Public Relations Journal*, Vol. 7, No. 4 (2013), www.prsa.org.

figure out what makes their businesses successful and how the goods and services they provide are different from the competition. Often, the answer is contained in the basic definition of business provided on page 10. Just for a moment, review the definition:

> *Business is the organized effort of individuals to produce and sell, for a profit, the goods and services that satisfy society's needs.*

In the definition of business, note the phrase *satisfy society's needs*. These three words say a lot about how well a successful firm competes with competitors. If you meet customer needs, then you have a better chance at success.

THE GLOBAL ENVIRONMENT Related to the competitive environment is the global environment. Not only do American businesses have to compete with other American businesses, but they also must compete with businesses from all over the globe. Firms in other countries including China, Japan, India, Germany, and most of the remaining European and Asian countries around the world also compete with U.S. firms. There was once a time when the label "Made in the United States" gave U.S. businesses an inside edge both at home and in the global marketplace. Today, because business firms in other countries manufacture and sell goods, the global marketplace has never been more competitive.

While many foreign firms are attempting to sell goods and services to U.S. customers, U.S. firms are also increasing both sales and profits by selling goods and services to customers in other countries. In fact there are many "potential" customers in developing nations that will buy goods and services manufactured by U.S. firms. For example, Procter & Gamble sells laundry detergent, soap, health and grooming products, and baby products in Asia, Europe, India, the Middle East, Africa, Latin America, and North America.[14] And Procter & Gamble is not alone. Unilever, DuPont, Johnson & Johnson, General Motors, and many more U.S. companies are also selling goods and services to customers in countries all over the globe.

THE TECHNOLOGY ENVIRONMENT The technology environment for U.S. businesses has never been more challenging. Changes in manufacturing equipment, distribution of products, and communication with customers are all examples of how technology has changed everyday business practices. For example, many businesses are now using social media to provide customers with information about products and services. If you ask different people, you will often find different definitions for social media, but for our purposes **social media** is defined as online interaction that allows people and businesses to communicate and share ideas, personal information, and information about products or services. To illustrate how

social media the online interaction that allows people and businesses to communicate and share ideas, personal information, and information about products or services

popular social media is, consider that Facebook with over 1.3 billion monthly active users was launched in 2004.[15] Because of rapid developments in social media and the increased importance of technology and information, businesses will need to spend additional money to keep abreast of an ever-changing technology environment and even more money to train employees to use the new technology.

THE ECONOMIC ENVIRONMENT The economic environment must always be considered when making business decisions. This fact is especially important when the nation's economy takes a nosedive or an individual firm's sales revenue and profits are declining. For example, both small and large business firms reduce both spending and hiring new employees when the economy is in a recession. On the other hand, businesses increase spending and hiring new employees when the economy is recovering and sales and profits are increasing. As pointed out earlier in this chapter, businesses often introduce new products and services during the peak period of the business cycle to take advantage of consumers' increased buying power.

For some businesses, green may be a new way of doing business! When a business wants to help sustain the planet or develop a green initiative, it must create a product or service that enables humans and nature to exist in productive harmony. At the same time, businesses must still generate sales revenues and profits in order to stay in business.

In addition to economic pressures, today's socially responsible managers and business owners must be concerned about the concept of sustainability. According to the U.S. Environmental Protection Agency, **sustainability** creates and maintains the conditions under which humans and nature can exist in productive harmony, that permit fulfilling the social, economic, and other requirements of present and future generations.[16] Although the word *green* used to mean a color in a box of crayons, today green means a new way of doing business. As a result, a combination of forces, including economic factors, growth in population, increased energy use, and concerns for the environment, is changing the way individuals live and businesses operate.

When you look back at the original question we asked at the beginning of this section, clearly, each different type of environment—competitive, global, technological, and economic—affects the way a business does *business*. As a result, there are always opportunities for improvement and challenges that must be considered.

1-7e The Challenges Ahead

There it is—the American business system in brief.

When it works well, it provides jobs for those who are willing to work, a standard of living that few countries can match, and many opportunities for personal advancement for those willing to work hard and continue to learn. However, like every other system devised by humans, it is not perfect. Our business system may give us prosperity, but it also gave us the Great Depression of the 1930s, the economic problems of the 1970s and the early 1980s, and the recent economic crisis.

Obviously, the system can be improved. Certainly, there are plenty of people who are willing to tell us exactly what they think the American economy needs. However, these people often provide us only with conflicting opinions. Who is right and who is wrong? Even the experts cannot agree.

The experts do agree, however, that several key issues will challenge our economic system (and our nation) over the next decade. Some of the questions to be resolved include:

- How can we create a more stable economy and create new jobs for the unemployed?

sustainability creates and maintains the conditions under which humans and nature can exist in productive harmony, that permit fulfilling the social, economic, and other requirements of present and future generations

- How do we reduce the national debt and still stimulate business growth?
- How do we restore investor confidence in the financial and banking system?
- How can we use technology to make American workers more productive and American firms more competitive in the global marketplace?
- How can we preserve the benefits of competition and small business in our American economic system?
- How can we conserve natural resources and sustain our environment?
- How can we resolve social unrest, discrimination, and inequality in society?
- How can we meet the needs of two-income families, single parents, older Americans, and the less fortunate who need health care and social programs to exist?
- How can we combat terrorism and resolve conflict with Iran, North Korea, and other countries throughout the world?

The answers to these questions are anything but simple. In the past, Americans have always been able to solve their economic problems through ingenuity and creativity. Now, as we continue the journey through the 21st century, we need that same ingenuity and creativity not only to solve our current problems but also to compete in the global marketplace and build a nation and economy for future generations.

The American business system is not perfect by any means, but it does work reasonably well. We discuss some of its problems in Chapter 2 as we examine the topics of social responsibility and business ethics.

Summary

1-1 Discuss what you must do to be successful in the world of business.

For many years, people in business—both employees and managers—assumed that prosperity would continue. When faced with both economic problems and increased competition, a large number of these people began to ask the question: What do we do now? Although this is a fair question, it is difficult to answer. Certainly, for a college student taking business courses or an employee just starting a career, the question is even more difficult to answer. And yet there are still opportunities out there for people who are willing to work hard, continue to learn, and possess the ability to adapt to change. By studying business, you can become a better employee or manager or you may decide to start your own business. You can also become a better consumer and investor.

1-2 Define *business* and identify potential risks and rewards.

Business is the organized effort of individuals to produce and sell, for a profit, the goods and services that satisfy society's needs. Four kinds of resources—material, human, financial, and informational—must be combined to start and operate a business. The

three general types of businesses are service businesses, manufacturers, and marketing intermediaries. Today, marketing intermediaries sell goods and services in brick-and-mortar stores, online, or both. Profit is what remains after all business expenses are deducted from sales revenue. It is the payment that owners receive for assuming the risks of business—primarily the risks of not receiving payment and of losing whatever has been invested in the firm. Although many people believe that profit is literally the bottom line or most important goal for a business, the ultimate objective of a successful business is to satisfy the needs of its customers. In addition to profit, many corporations are careful to point out their efforts to sustain the planet, participate in the green ecological movement, and help people to live better lives.

1-3 Define *economics* and describe the two types of economic systems: capitalism and command economy.

Economics is the study of how wealth is created and distributed. An economic system must answer four questions: *What* goods and services will be produced? *How* will they be produced? *For whom* will they be produced? And *Who* owns and who controls the major factors of production? The factors of production are land and natural resources, labor, capital, and entrepreneurship. Capitalism (on which our economic system is based) is an economic system in which individuals own and operate the majority of businesses that provide goods and services. Capitalism stems from the theories of Adam Smith. Smith's pure laissez-faire capitalism is an economic system based on the assumptions described in Figure 1-4.

Our economic system today is a mixed economy and exhibits elements of both capitalism and socialism. In the circular flow that characterizes our business system (see Figure 1-5), households and businesses exchange resources for goods and services, using money as the medium of exchange. In a similar manner, the government collects taxes from businesses and households and purchases products and resources with which to provide services.

In a command economy, government, rather than individuals, owns many of the factors of production and provides the answers to the three other economic questions. Socialist and communist economies are—at least in theory—command economies.

1-4 Identify the ways to measure economic performance.

One way to evaluate the performance of an economic system is to assess changes in productivity, which is the average level of output per worker per hour. Gross domestic product (GDP) can also be used to measure a nation's economic health and is the total dollar value of all goods and services produced by all people within the boundaries of a country during a one-year period. It is also possible to adjust GDP for inflation and thus to measure real GDP. Other economic indicators include a nation's balance of trade, consumer confidence index, consumer price index (CPI), corporate profits, inflation rate, national income, new housing starts, prime interest rate, producer price index (PPI), and unemployment rate.

1-5 Examine the different phases in the typical business cycle.

A nation's economy fluctuates rather than grows at a steady pace every year. These fluctuations are generally referred to as the business cycle. Generally, the business cycle consists of four states: the peak (sometimes called prosperity), recession, the trough, and recovery (sometimes called expansion). Some experts believe that effective use of monetary policy (the Federal Reserve's decisions that determine the size of the supply of money and the level of interest rates) and fiscal policy (the government's influence on the amount of savings and expenditures) can speed up recovery.

A federal deficit occurs when the government spends more than it receives in taxes and other revenues. At the time of publication, the national debt is over $18 trillion or approximately $56,000 for every man, woman, and child in the United States.

1-6 Outline the four types of competition.

Competition is essentially a rivalry among businesses for sales to potential customers. In a capitalist economy, competition works to ensure the efficient and effective operation of business. Competition also ensures that a firm will survive only if it serves its customers well by providing goods and services that meet their needs. Economists recognize four degrees of competition. Ranging from most to least competitive, the four degrees are perfect competition, monopolistic competition, oligopoly, and monopoly. The factors of supply and demand generally influence the price that customers pay producers for goods and services.

1-7 Summarize the factors that affect the business environment and the challenges that American businesses will encounter in the future.

From the beginning of the Industrial Revolution to the phenomenal expansion of American industry in the 1800s and early 1900s, our government maintained an essentially laissez-faire or hands off attitude toward business. However, during the Great Depression of the 1930s, the federal government began to provide a number of social services to its citizens and government got deeply involved in business.

To understand the major events that shaped the United States during the remainder of the 20th and 21st century, it helps to remember that the economy was compared to a roller-coaster ride earlier in this chapter—periods of economic growth followed by periods of economic slowdown. Events and a changing business environment including wars, rapid economic growth, the social responsibility movement, a shortage of crude oil, high inflation, high interest rates, reduced business profits, increased use of technology, and social media all have shaped business and the economy.

Now more than ever before, the way a business operates is affected by the competitive environment, global environment, technological environment, and economic environment. As a result, business has a number of opportunities for improvement and challenges for the future.

Key Terms

You should now be able to define and give an example relevant to each of the following terms:

free enterprise (4)
cultural (or workplace)
   diversity (6)
business (10)
e-business (11)
profit (12)
stakeholders (12)
economics (12)
microeconomics (13)
macroeconomics (13)
economy (13)
factors of production (13)
entrepreneur (13)
capitalism (14)

invisible hand (14)
market economy (15)
mixed economy (15)
consumer products (16)
command economy (17)
productivity (18)
gross domestic product
   (GDP) (19)
inflation (19)
deflation (19)
unemployment rate (20)
consumer price index
   (CPI) (20)
producer price index (PPI) (20)

business cycle (21)
recession (21)
depression (21)
monetary policies (22)
fiscal policy (22)
federal deficit (22)
national debt (22)
competition (23)
perfect (or pure)
   competition (23)
supply (24)
demand (24)
market price (24)

monopolistic
   competition (25)
product differentiation (25)
oligopoly (26)
monopoly (26)
standard of living (27)
barter (27)
domestic system (27)
factory system (27)
specialization (28)
service economy (29)
social media (30)
sustainability (31)

Discussion Questions

1. What factors caused American business to develop into a mixed economic system rather than some other type of economic system?
2. Does an individual consumer really have a voice in answering the basic four economic questions described on pages 14–15?
3. Is gross domestic product a reliable indicator of a nation's economic health? What might be a better indicator?
4. Discuss this statement: "Business competition encourages improved product quality and increased customer satisfaction."
5. Is government participation in our business system good or bad? What factors can be used to explain your position.
6. Choose one of the challenges listed on pages 31–32 and describe possible ways in which business and society could help to solve or eliminate the problem in the future.

Video Case
KlipTech Turns Recycled Paper into Products and Profits

Joel Klippert became an entrepreneur at the urging of his wife, LeeAnn Klippert, who believed in his unusual idea of turning recycled paper into a superstrong surface for skateboard ramps. For months he had tried, without success, to find a manufacturer willing to work with him in developing a durable composite ramp surface made from recycled and eco-friendly materials. Even his closest friends were skeptical. However, because Klippert and his wife were convinced that there was a viable market for this kind of sustainable product, they moved ahead to form KlipTech in 2000.

For the next two years, Klippert wrote and fine-tuned a business plan as he had manufacturing experts test various materials and production processes for transforming his invention from an idea to a reality. Despite unenthusiastic responses from most of the bankers he approached for possible financing, Klippert introduced his new skateboard ramp surface product in 2002. Later that same year, he

pioneered yet another green product by introducing kitchen and bathroom countertops made from a composite of recycled materials.

Despite ever-higher sales of these products, Klippert still faced the challenge of enhancing the aesthetic appearance of his paper-based composite countertops for home use. At the time, such composite products were produced only in dark colors because of the resins used in the manufacturing process. Klippert recognized that a broader range of colors would make the countertops more appealing to more consumers. Working with a partner, he created an innovative countertop composite made with both recycled paper and bamboo and capable of being dyed in either light or dark colors. This new type of countertop attracted the attention of mainstream buyers, not just green-minded buyers, and gave KlipTech the edge it needed to compete more effectively with some of the biggest names in the industry.

KlipTech continues to build revenues and profits by introducing new products made from recycled paper. More recently, it launched EcoClad, a line of composites used for exterior siding on commercial buildings and residences. Not only is EcoClad attractive and durable, it also helps buildings qualify as green under the U.S. Green Building Council's standards, confirming its environmentally-sound qualities.

Today, KlipTech is a profitable business with multiple product lines, a global customer base, two manufacturing plants in the United States, and a reputation for dedication to sustainability. The company also has plans to expand production in foreign countries and introduce its products in Asia, the Middle East, and the United Kingdom.

What lessons has Joel Klippert learned in the years since becoming a successful entrepreneur? First, he found out first hand that an entrepreneur must have the confidence, patience, and perseverance to take the practical steps necessary to turn a good idea into an actual product that can meet customers' needs. It took many months of experimentation to perfect the skateboard ramp surface that gave KlipTech its start in the business world, but Klippert never gave up.

Second, the product must be unique so the company can, in effect, make its own market rather than go head-to-head with major competitors in an established market. When Klippert introduced his first skateboard ramp surface, no one else was making such products from recycled paper. The same was true for KlipTech's first kitchen counter surface, as well as its later products. KlipTech's innovations resulted in unique products that really fit the needs of its customers.

Third, Klippert learned that a nimble startup has an important advantage over large competitors. "The great part about being a small business is you're like a speed boat on the water," he explains. This means KlipTech can respond very quickly, "on the fly," to emerging trends in the business environment. "Innovation is the key to the future and we will be working day after day to bring this to our current and future customers." says Klippert. In contrast, big rivals need more time to make and implement decisions about adapting to the same changes in the business environment.

Klippert also advises entrepreneurs to do their homework early on legal issues and financing possibilities, so they have experts and resources in place before problems arise. From experience, he knows that small business owners must understand finance and plan to pay vendors and employees before paying themselves. He's always thinking about how to improve one of his products or listening to customers talk about a new product they'd like to see. Succeeding in the global economy is far from easy, but Klippert remains enthusiastic about the opportunities he faces every day as the co-founder and co-owner of a successful business.[17]

Questions

1. Joel Klippert says he pays himself last, after he pays his vendors and employees. Explain this decision in terms of the principle of business profit. Do you agree with his payment priorities?
2. When compared to larger manufacturing firms in the building products industry, what advantages have helped KlipTech become successful?
3. How have the competitive, global, technological, and economic environments helped KlipTech to become a successful business? Which of the above environments might pose the most challenges in the next few years, and why?

Building Skills for Career Success

1. Social Media Exercise

Today, many companies have a social media presence on Facebook, Twitter, Flickr, and other sites beyond their corporate website. Think of three of your favorite car companies and conduct a quick search using a search engine like Google or Yahoo! Then answer the following:
1. Name the social networks for each company.
2. Compare each of their Facebook pages. How many "likes" does each company have? Are there multiple pages for the company? How much interaction (or engagement) is on each Facebook page?
3. What business goals do you think each company is trying to reach through their Facebook presence?

2. Building Team Skills

Over the past few years, employees have been expected to function as productive team members instead of working alone. People often believe that they can work effectively in teams, but many people find working with a group of people to be a challenge.

College classes that function as teams are more interesting and more fun to attend, and students generally learn more about the topics in the course. One way to begin creating a team is to learn something about each student in the class. This helps team members to feel comfortable with each other and fosters a sense of trust.

Assignment

1. Find a partner, preferably someone you do not know.
2. Each partner has two to three minutes to answer the following questions:
   a. What is your name, and where do you work?
   b. What interesting or unusual thing have you done in your life? (Do not talk about work or college; rather, focus on such things as hobbies, travel, family, and sports.)

c. Why are you taking this course, and what do you expect to learn? (Satisfying a degree requirement is not an acceptable answer.)

3. Introduce your partner to the class. Use one to two minutes, depending on the size of the class.

3. Researching Different Careers

In this chapter, *entrepreneurship* is defined as the willingness to take risks and the knowledge and ability to use the other factors of production efficiently. An *entrepreneur* is a person who risks time, effort, and money to start and operate a business. Often, people believe that these terms apply only to small business. However, employees with entrepreneurial attitudes have recently advanced more rapidly in large companies as well.

Assignment

1. Go to the local library or use the Internet to research how large firms, especially corporations, are rewarding employees who have entrepreneurial skills.

2. Find answers to the following questions:
   a. Why is an entrepreneurial attitude important in large corporations today?
   b. What makes an entrepreneurial employee different from other employees?
   c. How are these employees being rewarded, and are the rewards worth the effort?

3. Write a two-page report that summarizes your findings.

Endnotes

1 Based on information in Tanya Agrawal, "Visa Sees Mobile Payment as Big Growth Driver," *Reuters*, October 29, 2014, www.reuters.com; Daniel Roberts, "Visa's Open-Armed Leader," *Fortune*, September 22, 2014, p. 22; Gaurav Raghuvanshi, "Visa Aims to Boost Electronic Payments," *Wall Street Journal*, August 10, 2014, www.wsj.com; www.visa.com.

2 The Horatio Alger website at www.horatioalger.org (accessed December 12, 2014).

3 Ibid.

4 "Nick D'Aloisio, Creator of Summly, on the Latest Changes to Yahoo News Digest," The What Mobile website at www.whatmobile.net (accessed December 12, 2014).

5 Idy Fernandez, "Julie Stav," *Hispanic*, June–July 2005, 204.

6 The General Mills website at www.generalmills.com (accessed December 15, 2014).

7 The Bureau of Economic Analysis website at www.bea.gov (accessed December 15, 2014).

8 The Bureau of Economic Analysis website at www.bea.gov (accessed December 15, 2013).

9 The Bureau of Labor Statistics website at www.bls.gov (accessed December 15, 2014).

10 The Bureau of Economic Analysis website at www.bea.gov (accessed December 16, 2014).

11 The U.S. Debt Clock website at www.usdebtclock.org (accessed December 16, 2014).

12 The Investopedia website at www.investopedia.com (accessed December 16, 2014).

13 The Bureau of Labor Statistics website at www.bls.gov (accessed December 16, 2014).

14 The Procter & Gamble website at www.pg.com (accessed December 17, 2014).

15 The Digital Marketing Ramblings website at www.expandedramblings.com (accessed December 17, 2014).

16 The Environmental Protection Agency website at www.epa.gov (accessed December 18, 2014).

17 Sources: Based on information from the KlipTech website at www.kliptech.com (accessed December 18, 2014); "Editor's Choice: The Hot 50 Products 2012," *Green Builder*, February 2012, www.greenbuildermag.com/hot502012; Wanda Lau, "KlipTech EcoClad XP," *Architect*, January 2012, www.architectmagazine.com; and the Cengage video, "The Entrepreneurial Life: KlipTech."

Being Ethical and Socially Responsible

Learning Objectives

Once you complete this chapter, you will be able to:

2-1 Understand what is meant by *business ethics.*

2-2 Identify the types of ethical concerns that arise in the business world.

2-3 Discuss the factors that affect the level of ethical behavior in organizations.

2-4 Explain how ethical decision making can be encouraged.

2-5 Describe how our current views on the social responsibility of business have evolved.

2-6 Discuss the factors that led to the consumer movement and list some of its results.

2-7 Analyze how present employment practices are being used to counteract past abuses.

2-8 Describe the major types of pollution, their causes, and their cures.

2-9 Identify the steps a business must take to implement a program of social responsibility.

Why Should You Care?

Business ethics and social responsibility issues have become extremely relevant in today's business world. Business schools teach business ethics to prepare managers to be more responsible. Corporations are developing ethics and social responsibility programs to help meet these needs in the work place.

Tesla Motors

Tesla Motors, headed by tech-savvy entrepreneur Elon Musk, says its goal is to "accelerate the world's transition to electric mobility with a full range of increasingly affordable electric cars. We're catalyzing change in the industry." The current product line, available in 37 countries, includes cars and SUVs priced about $70,000, with lower priced models soon to be introduced. One model is outfitted with self-driving features, which only adds to the growing interest in Tesla's earth-friendly vehicles and technology.

Tesla's upscale electric vehicles are stylish and much greener than those with gasoline engines or hybrid gas-electric motors. Design is a major strength, as is manufacturing know-how. When Tesla can't find vehicle components that meet its exacting environmental and quality standards, internal experts develop, patent, and produce their own. Tesla invites other automakers to use its patents, and it says a few firms have already taken the company up on this unusual offer.

Now Tesla is spending $5 billion to build a Gigafactory, the world's largest and most sophisticated lithium-ion battery factory, in Nevada. For environmental reasons, it is pioneering a supply chain to use only raw materials from North America at the new factory. The long-term plan is to reduce the cost of batteries and lower the price tag for Tesla's vehicles, giving the firm an even more compelling competitive advantage in the global market for green vehicles.

Knowing that car buyers care about convenience, as well as keeping the planet safe, Tesla is building a multinational network of supercharger stations for its electric vehicles. These publicly-available charging stations will top up one of its batteries to 50 percent of capacity in 20 minutes, and charge to 100 percent of capacity in 75 minutes. The supercharger stations will also be supplied with batteries made in the Nevada Gigafactory, enabling Tesla to use its cutting-edge technology for vital support services, as well as in each of its vehicles.[1]

Did You Know?

Tesla is building a $5 billion Gigafactory in Nevada to make lithium-ion batteries for its electric vehicles.

Obviously, organizations like Tesla Motors want to be recognized as responsible corporate citizens. These companies recognize the need to harmonize their operations with environmental demands and other social concerns. Not all firms, however, have taken steps to include social responsibility and ethics in their decisions and day-to-day activities. Some managers still regard such business programs as a poor investment, in which the cost is not worth the return. Other managers—indeed, most managers—view the cost of these programs as a necessary business expense, similar to wages or rent.

Most managers today are finding ways to balance an agenda of socially responsible activities with the drive to generate profits. This also happens to be a good way for organizations to demonstrate their values and to attract like-minded employees, customers, and shareholders. In a highly competitive global business environment, an increasing number of companies are seeking to set themselves apart by developing a reputation for ethical and socially responsible behavior.

We begin this chapter by defining *business ethics* and examining ethical issues. Next, we look at the standards of behavior in organizations and how ethical behavior can be encouraged. We then turn to the topic of social responsibility. We explore the evolution of the idea of social responsibility, compare and contrast two present-day models of social responsibility, and present arguments for and against increasing the social responsibility of business. We then explore business responsibilities toward the public. We discuss how social responsibility in business has affected employment practices and environmental concerns. Finally, we consider the commitment and planning that go into a firm's program of social responsibility.

2-1 BUSINESS ETHICS DEFINED

Ethics is the study of right and wrong and of the morality of the choices individuals make. An ethical decision or action is one that is "right" according to some standard of behavior. When there is strong consensus regarding a particular unethical action, society may demand laws to outlaw it. **Business ethics** is the application of moral standards to business situations. Recent court cases involving unethical behavior have helped to make business ethics a matter of public concern. In one such case, the former president of Houston's Riverside Hospital, along with several others, was convicted of fraud for submitting false and fraudulent mental health care claims to Medicare. The Department of Justice claimed that Earnest Gibson III, the former president of Riverside, had the hospital bill Medicare for $158 million in psychiatric services that patients did not qualify for or never received.[2] Regardless of their legality, all business decisions can be judged as right or wrong.

Learning Objective

2-1 Understand what is meant by *business ethics*.

2-2 ETHICAL ISSUES

Ethical issues often arise out of a business's relationship with investors, customers, employees, creditors, suppliers, or competitors. Each of these stakeholder groups has specific concerns and usually exerts pressure on the organization's managers. For example, investors want management to make sensible financial decisions that will boost sales, profits, and returns on their investments. Customers expect a firm's products to be safe, reliable, and reasonably priced. Employees demand to be treated fairly in hiring, promotion, and compensation decisions. Creditors require accounts to be paid on time and the accounting information furnished by the firm to be accurate. Competitors expect the firm's competitive practices to be fair and honest. Canadian-based Coffee Club sued Keurig Green Mountain, Inc., which markets Keurig coffee makers and single-serving K-Cups for use in its coffee makers, arguing that Keurig's newest coffee makers include "lock-out technology" that prevent the use of single-serving beverage products made by other firms, such as the environmentally friendly ones marketed by Coffee Club. Coffee Club's suit contends that Keurig's new system effectively excludes competitors from the market and that Keurig's marketers have spread lies about competing products in order to confuse consumers and obtain exclusive agreements with third parties. A court will have to resolve the dispute.[3]

Businesspeople face ethical issues every day, and some of these issues can be difficult to assess. Although some types of issues arise infrequently, others occur regularly. Let's take a closer look at several ethical issues.

Learning Objective

2-2 Identify the types of ethical concerns that arise in the business world.

ethics the study of right and wrong and of the morality of the choices individuals make

business ethics the application of moral standards to business situations

2-2a Fairness and Honesty

Fairness and honesty in business are two important ethical concerns. Besides obeying all laws and regulations, businesspeople are expected to refrain from knowingly deceiving, misrepresenting, or intimidating others. The consequences of failing to do so can be expensive. Recently, for example, Juan Alejandro Rodriguez Cuya faces decades in prison after being convicted of deceiving and intimidating Spanish-speaking customers of a call center into fraudulent settlements. In court, prosecutors explained that Cuya extorted victims into believing that they had to pay for deliveries of nonexistent products or else be subject to huge fines and lawsuits and even deportation.[4] Gerber came under fire for promoting that its Good Start Gentle baby formula can prevent or reduce allergies in children. The Federal Trade Commission ruled that Gerber's claim lacked

PICTURENET/BLEND IMAGES/THINKSTOCK

Ethics Violations Ethics violations can be more than humiliating. Ethics violators sometimes go to prison, pay large fines, lose their jobs, lose their families, and pay expensive legal fees.

scientific evidence and asked the company to remove the statement from its advertising and product labels.[5]

If consumers feel they have been deceived or that companies have been unfair, they will take their business elsewhere and may even ask regulators to intervene. The Federal Trade Commission filed suit against AT&T for "throttling" or reducing Internet speeds for heavy smartphone users who signed up for unlimited plans. Some consumers saw their speeds reduced by as much as 90 percent. The head of the FTC contends that AT&T's actions are unfair to consumers who paid for "unlimited" plans with the expectation of limitless usage and speed.[6]

2-2b Organizational Relationships

A businessperson may be tempted to place his or her personal welfare above the welfare of others or the welfare of the organization. For example, Joyce Ziehli was convicted of misappropriating more than $800,000 of funds belonging to the New Glarus Home, a Wisconsin nursing home where she worked as the bookkeeper.[7] Aside from the legality of such actions, they may threaten the livelihood of employees and the business itself and harm relations with customers, suppliers, and others.

Relationships among co-workers often create ethical problems. Unethical behavior in these areas includes taking credit for others' ideas or work, not meeting one's commitments in a mutual agreement, and pressuring others to behave unethically. One issue related to fairness and honesty is **plagiarism**—knowingly taking someone else's words, ideas, or other original material without acknowledging the source. When exposed, the consequences of plagiarism can be grave. For example, the U.S. Army War College rescinded the master's degree that it had awarded U.S. Senator John Walsh after an academic review by the college determined that Walsh had copied significant parts of his final paper from other sources. Walsh withdrew from his re-election campaign soon after the scandal.[8]

When misconduct occurs in business, investors also suffer. Investors and owners must be able to trust that companies are acting in their best interests and reporting their activities truthfully. They have the right to expect that all actions by a firm contribute toward a return on their investment. Two issues that raise flags for investors are executive compensation packages that are out of line with performance and the conflict of interest that may occur when a chief executive officer also sits on the board of directors—the group that oversees the CEO. Investors have increasingly protested high executive compensation, particularly when those executives do not generate strong profits for the owners. Shareholders have voted against executive compensation packages at a number of companies, including Staples, Abercrombie & Fitch, Chipotle, and more.[9] Activist investors have also protested companies whose CEOs also sit on the board of directors, which can result in a conflict of interest when the CEOs performance is under review.

2-2c Conflict of Interest

Conflict of interest results when a businessperson takes advantage of a situation for his or her own personal interest rather than for the employer's interest. Examples of situations involving conflicts of interest generally involve an employee who has divided loyalties, such as a manager who is dating a subordinate, an employee with a close relative who works for a competitor, a purchasing manager who chooses to do business with another firm in which he is an investor, or a firm

plagiarism knowingly taking someone else's words, ideas, or other original material without acknowledging the source

that advises clients without informing them that it has a relationship with some of the products it recommends. Even the appearance of a conflict of interest can jeopardize a businessperson's credibility. For example, the Securities and Exchange Commission charged a Houston investment advisory firm of fraud because the Robare Group, Ltd. failed to notify clients of mutual funds that it recommended, that it was receiving compensation from the broker offering the mutual funds.[10] In such cases, consumers have the right to know that their investment advisor may be recommending certain funds over others in order to receive the extra compensation received regardless of whether those funds are most suitable.

Conflicts of interest may occur when payments and gifts make their way into business deals. Although bribes—gifts, favors, or payments offered with the intent of influencing an outcome—are often part of business negotiations overseas, it is illegal for American businesspersons to use bribes in the U.S. or abroad. Defending against bribery charges can be costly and affect future business negotiations. Walmart, for example, reported to U.S. regulators that it had uncovered evidence that employees and subcontractors of its Mexican division had paid $24 million in bribes in order to open new stores in Mexico more quickly than if they had gone through conventional channels. Moreover, the firm found evidence that the employees of its Mexican division had attempted to cover up the bribes, which are illegal under the U.S. Foreign Corrupt Practices Act. Although Walmart reported the bribery to U.S. authorities, it spent $439 million investigating the wrongdoing and expects to pay millions more in fines. The company also faces shareholder lawsuits as a result of the crime.[11] A wise rule to remember is that anything given to a person that might unfairly influence that person's business decision is a bribe, and all bribes are unethical.

At Procter & Gamble Company (P&G), all employees are obligated to act at all times solely in the best interests of the company. P&G defines a conflict of interest as when an employee has a personal relationship or financial or other interest that could interfere with this obligation, or when an employee uses his or her position with the company for personal gain. P&G requires employees to disclose all potential conflicts of interest and to take prompt actions to eliminate a conflict when the company asks them to do so. Generally, P&G prohibits employees from receiving gifts, entertainment, or other gratuities from people with whom the company does business because doing so could imply an obligation on the part of the company and potentially pose a conflict of interest.[12]

2-2d Communications

Business communications, especially advertising, can present ethical questions. False and misleading advertising is illegal and unethical, and it can infuriate customers. For example, the makers of Red Bull energy drink agreed to pay $13 million to settle a class-action lawsuit from customers who felt that the company's advertising contained false claims that lacked scientific support, including its longtime slogan, "Red Bull gives you wings."[13] Sponsors of advertisements aimed at children must be especially careful to avoid misleading messages. Advertisers of health-related products also must take precautions to guard against deception when using such descriptive terms as *low fat*, *fat free*, and *light*. In fact, the Federal Trade Commission has issued guidelines on the use of these labels.

2-3 FACTORS AFFECTING ETHICAL BEHAVIOR

Is it possible for an individual with strong moral values to make ethically questionable decisions in a business setting? What factors affect a person's inclination to make either ethical or unethical decisions in a business organization? Although the answers

Concept Check

✓ What is meant by business ethics?

✓ What are the different types of ethical concerns that may arise in the business world?

✓ Explain and give an example of how advertising can present ethical questions.

Learning Objective

2-3 Discuss the factors that affect the level of ethical behavior in organizations

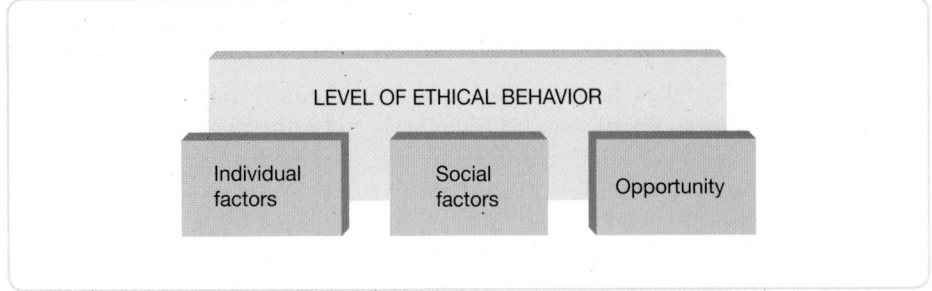

FIGURE 2-1 Factors That Affect the Level of Ethical Behavior in an Organization

LEVEL OF ETHICAL BEHAVIOR

| Individual factors | Social factors | Opportunity |

Source: Based on O. C. Ferrell and Larry Gresham, "A Contingency Framework for Understanding Ethical Decision Making in Marketing," *Journal of Marketing* (Summer 1985), 89.

to these questions are not entirely clear, three general sets of factors do appear to influence the standards of behavior in an organization[14] As shown in Figure 2-1, the sets consist of individual factors, social factors, and opportunities.

2-3a Individual Factors Affecting Ethics

Several individual factors influence the level of ethical behavior in an organization, including personal knowledge, values, and goals. How much an individual knows about an issue is one factor. A decision maker with a greater amount of knowledge regarding a situation may take steps to avoid ethical problems, whereas a less-informed person may take action unknowingly that could lead to ethical problems. An individual's moral values and central, value-related attitudes also clearly influence his or her business behavior and choices. Most organizations do not try to change an employee's personal ethics but instead strive to hire people with good character and values that complement their own. The actions of specific individuals in scandal-plagued companies, such as Adelphia, Arthur Anderson, Enron, Halliburton, Qwest, and WorldCom, often raise questions about individuals' personal character and integrity. Finally, most people join organizations to accomplish personal goals. The types of personal goals an individual aspires to and the manner in which these goals are pursued have a significant impact on that individual's behavior in an organization.

2-3b Social Factors Affecting Ethics

Many social factors can affect ethical behavior within a firm, including cultural norms, actions and decisions of co-workers, values and attitudes of "significant others," and the use of the Internet. A person's behavior in the workplace, to some degree, is determined by cultural norms, and these social factors vary from one culture to another. For example, in some countries it is acceptable and ethical for customs agents to receive gratuities for performing ordinary, legal tasks that are a part of their jobs, whereas in other countries these practices would be viewed as unethical and perhaps illegal. The actions and decisions of co-workers may also shape a person's sense of business ethics. For example, if your co-workers peruse YouTube and Instagram on company time and at company expense, you might view that behavior as acceptable and ethical because everyone does it. The moral values and attitudes of "significant others"—spouses, friends, and relatives, for instance— also can affect an employee's perception of what is ethical and unethical behavior in the workplace.

© ALPHASPIRIT/SHUTTERSTOCK.COM

Even the Internet presents new challenges for firms whose employees enjoy easy access through convenient high-speed connections at work. An employee's behavior online can be viewed as offensive to co-workers and possibly lead to lawsuits against the firm if employees engage in unethical behavior on controversial websites not related to their job. Moreover, if an employee posts controversial content using their employer's email, Instagram, or Twitter account, that content may run counter to the company's core values and reflect negatively on the company. Interestingly, one recent survey of employees found that most workers assume that their use of technology at work will be monitored. A large majority of employees approved of most monitoring methods such as monitoring faxes and e-mail, tracking Web use, and even recording telephone calls.

2-3c Opportunity as a Factor Affecting Ethics

Several opportunity factors affect ethics in an organization. *Opportunity* refers to the amount of freedom an organization affords an employee to behave unethically if he or she makes that choice. If the employee is rewarded in some way for an unethical choice—praise or a bonus, for example—or fails to suffer any kind of consequence, he or she is more likely to make that same choice in the future. In some organizations, certain company policies and procedures reduce the opportunity to be unethical. For example, at some fast-food restaurants, one employee takes your order and receives your payment, and another fills the order. This procedure reduces the opportunity to be unethical because the person handling the money is not dispensing the product, and the person giving out the product is not handling the money.

The existence of codes of ethics and other policies on ethics, as well as the importance management places on these policies are other elements of opportunity (codes of ethics are discussed in more detail in the next section). The degree of enforcement of company policies, procedures, and ethical codes is a major force affecting opportunity. When violations are dealt with consistently and firmly, the opportunity to be unethical is reduced.

Now that we have considered some of the factors believed to influence the level of ethical behavior in the workplace, let us explore what can be done to encourage ethical behavior and to discourage unethical behavior.

Concept Check

✓ Describe several individual factors that influence the level of ethical behavior in an organization.

✓ Explain several social factors that affect ethics in an organization.

✓ How does opportunity influence the level of ethical behavior in the workplace?

2-4 ENCOURAGING ETHICAL BEHAVIOR

Most authorities agree that there is room for improvement in business ethics. A more problematic question is: Can business be made more ethical in the real world? The majority opinion on this issue suggests that government, trade associations, and individual firms indeed can promote acceptable levels of ethical behavior.

Learning Objective

2-4 Explain how ethical decision making can be encouraged.

2-4a Government's Role in Encouraging Ethics

The government can encourage ethical behavior in business by enacting more stringent regulations. For example, the landmark **Sarbanes–Oxley Act of 2002** provides sweeping new legal protection for those who report corporate misconduct. Among other things, the law deals with corporate responsibility, conflicts of interest, and corporate accountability. However, rules require enforcement, and the unethical businessperson frequently seems to "slip something by" without getting caught. Increased regulation may help, but it cannot solve the entire ethics problem.

Sarbanes-Oxley Act of 2002 provides sweeping new legal protection for employees who report corporate misconduct

Sarbanes-Oxley Act The Sarbanes-Oxley Act of 2002 includes tough provisions to deter and punish corporate and accounting fraud and corruption. The legislation passed with unanimous support.

ELLENMCK/FOTOLIA

2-4b Trade Associations' Role in Encouraging Ethics

Trade associations can and often do provide ethical guidelines for their members. These organizations, which operate within particular industries, are in an excellent position to exert pressure on members to stop engaging in questionable business practices that may harm all firms in the industry. For example, a pharmaceutical trade group adopted a new set of guidelines intended to end the extravagant dinners and expensive gifts sales representatives often give to physicians to persuade them to prescribe a particular medicine. However, enforcement and authority vary from association to association. Because trade associations exist for the benefit of their members, harsh measures may be self-defeating. Trade associations must also ensure that their codes do not contain provisions that may run afoul of antitrust laws.

2-4c Individual Companies' Role in Encouraging Ethics

Codes of ethics are perhaps the most effective way to encourage ethical behavior. A **code of ethics** is a written guide to acceptable and ethical behavior as defined by an organization; it outlines uniform policies, standards, and punishments for violations. Because a code of ethics informs employees what is expected of them and what will happen if they violate the rules, it can go a long way toward encouraging ethical behavior. However, codes cannot possibly cover every situation. Companies also must create an environment in which employees recognize the importance of complying with the written code. Managers must provide direction by fostering communication, actively modeling and encouraging ethical decision making, and training employees to make ethical decisions. Figure 2-2 offers snippets of some of the guiding principles behind well-known companies' codes of ethics.

Beginning in the 1980s, an increasing number of organizations created and implemented ethics codes. Today, about 95 percent of *Fortune* 1000 firms have a formal code of ethics or conduct. For example, the ethics code of Starbucks defines the firm's mission and values and includes provisions relating to policies and procedures; laws and regulations; relationships with customers, suppliers, competitors, and the community; conflicts of interest; handling of proprietary information; and more. Starbucks' code also details how employees can express concerns or find guidance in ambiguous situations and even provides a graphical decision-making framework that employees can apply to difficult decisions.[15]

In the wake of a number of corporate scandals and the Sarbanes-Oxley Act, many large companies now have created a new executive position, the chief ethics (or compliance) officer. Assigning an ethics officer who guides ethical conduct provides employees someone to consult if they are not sure of the right thing to do. An ethics officer meets with employees and top management to provide ethical advice, establishes and maintains an anonymous confidential service to answer questions about ethical issues, and takes action on ethics code violations.

Sometimes even employees who want to act ethically may find it difficult to do so. Unethical practices can become ingrained in an organization. Employees with high personal ethics may then take a controversial step called *whistle-blowing*. **Whistle-blowing** is informing the press or government officials about unethical practices within an organization. Consider Josh Harmon, who brought a lawsuit against Trinity Industries under the False Claims Act, which permits whistle-blowers to sue companies they believe have defrauded the government. Harmon, who installed roadway guardrails that are supposed to cushion vehicles in the event of an accident,

code of ethics a guide to acceptable and ethical behavior as defined by the organization

whistle-blowing informing the press or government officials about unethical practices within one's organization

FIGURE 2-2 Defining Acceptable Behavior at Starbucks, Nike, and Apple

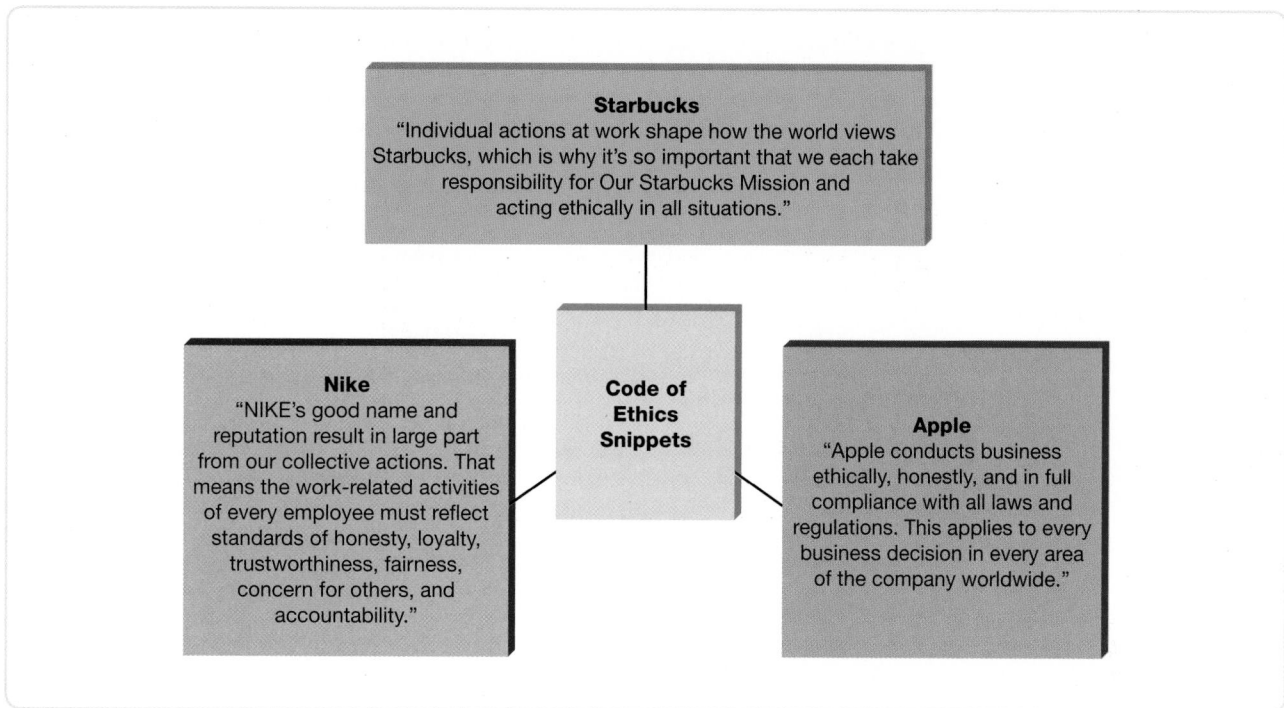

Source: Starbucks, "Business Ethics and Compliance: Standards of Business Conduct," p. 6, http://globalassets.starbucks.com/assets/eecd184d6d2141d58966319744393d1f.pdf (accessed October 30, 2014); Nike, "Inside the Lines: The NIKE Code of Ethics," p. 4, http://nike.q4web.com/files/2011%20Inside%20the%20Lines%20online%20booklet%20FINAL%2011-10-26.pdf (accessed October 30, 2014); Apple, "Business Conduct: The Way We Do Business Worldwide," p. 2, http://files.shareholder.com/downloads/AAPL/3565008853x0x443008/5f38b1e6-2f9c-4518-b691-13a29ac90501/business_conduct_policy.pdf (accessed October 30, 2014).

believed that Trinity failed to notify regulators and others that it had redesigned its guardrail end caps in such a way that they became unsafe and caused injuries and fatalities during vehicle accidents instead of reducing them. A federal jury ultimately decided that Trinity had indeed made false claims to regulators about the product's redesign and owed $175 million in damages.[16]

Whistle-blowing, however, can have serious repercussions for employees: Those who "blow whistles" may face retaliation and sometimes even lose their jobs. The Sarbanes–Oxley Act of 2002 protects whistle-blowers who report corporate misconduct. Any executive who retaliates against a whistle-blower can be held criminally liable and imprisoned for up to ten years. Federal employees who report misconduct are likewise protected by the Whistleblower Protection Act of 1989.

When companies set up anonymous hotlines to handle ethically questionable situations, employees actually may be more likely to engage in whistle-blowing. When firms instead create an environment that educates employees and nurtures ethical behavior, fewer ethical problems arise. Ultimately, the need for whistle-blowing is greatly reduced.

It is difficult for an organization to develop ethics codes, programs, and procedures to deal with all relationships and every situation. Michael Josephson, an expert on workplace ethics, says, "The objective of such programs is to establish a business culture in which it's easier to do the right thing than the wrong thing, and where concerned co-workers and vigilant supervisors repress illegal or improper conduct that can potentially endanger or embarrass the company."[17] When no company policies or procedures exist or apply, a quick test to determine if a behavior is ethical is to see if others—co-workers, customers, and suppliers—approve of it. Ethical decisions will always withstand scrutiny. Openness and communication about choices will often build trust and strengthen business relationships. Table 2-1 provides some general guidelines for making ethical decisions.

TABLE 2-1 Guidelines for Making Ethical Decisions

1. Listen and learn	Recognize the problem or decision-making opportunity that confronts your company, team, or unit. Don't argue, criticize, or defend yourself—keep listening and reviewing until you are sure that you understand others.
2. Identify the ethical issues	Examine how co-workers and consumers are affected by the situation or decision at hand. Examine how you feel about the situation, and attempt to understand the viewpoint of those involved in the decision or in the consequences of the decision.
3. Create and analyze options	Try to put aside strong feelings such as anger or a desire for power and prestige and come up with as many alternatives as possible before developing an analysis. Ask everyone involved for ideas about which options offer the best long-term results for you and the company. Then decide which option will increase your self-respect even if, in the long run, things don't work out the way you hope they will.
4. Identify the best option from your point of view	Consider it and test it against some established criteria, such as respect, understanding, caring, fairness, honesty, and openness.
5. Explain your decision and resolve any differences that arise	This may require neutral arbitration from a trusted manager or taking "time out" to reconsider, consult, or exchange written proposals before a decision is reached.

Source: Based on information in Tom Rusk with D. Patrick Miller, "Doing the Right Thing," *Sky* (Delta Airlines), August 1993, 18–22.

2-4d Social Responsibility

Social responsibility is the recognition that business activities have an impact on society and the consideration of that impact in business decision making. Target, for example, has donated $418 million to public schools through its Take Charge of Education program that rewards more than 84,000 schools designated by Target REDcard holders. The company also offers access to fresh food to families in need through their schools as well as grants for educational programs.[18] Obviously, social responsibility costs money. It is perhaps not so obvious—except in isolated cases—that social responsibility is also good business. Many companies contribute resources, knowledge, and products as well as money to help neighbors and others during times of crisis. For example, Procter & Gamble's orange Loads of Hope trucks are a welcome sight during disaster relief efforts. Residents in disaster areas can drop off loads of dirty laundry at the mobile laundromats, and volunteers use Tide products and high-efficiency machines to wash, dry, and even fold their clothes. Thus far, the program has

social responsibility the recognition that business activities have an impact on society and the consideration of that impact in business decision making

Social responsibility is good business Natural disasters create opportunities for companies to engage in socially responsible behavior. Procter & Gamble's Loads of Hope program takes in disaster victims' dirty laundry and returns it to them clean and folded, allowing them to deal with more important problems.

WORDPRESS.COM

TABLE 2-2 *Corporate Responsibility* Magazine's 10 Best Corporate Citizens

1. Bristol-Myers Squibb Co.
2. Johnson & Johnson
3. Gap, Inc.
4. Microsoft Corporation
5. Mattel, Inc.
6. Weyerhaeuser, Inc.
7. Ecolab, Inc.
8. Intel Corp.
9. Coco-Cola Co.
10. Walt Disney Co.

Source: "CR's 100 Best Corporate Citizens 2014," *CR*, http://www.thecro.com/files/100BestList.pdf (accessed October 24, 2014).

done more than 55,000 loads of laundry and brought a sense of normalcy and hope back to victims so that they can focus on more pressing matters.[19] Efforts like these bring positive associations for brands that can help them stand out in a competitive market. Customers eventually find out which firms act responsibly and which do not. Just as easily as they can purchase a product made by a company that is socially responsible, they can choose against buying from the firm that is not.

Even small businesses can develop social responsibility programs. For example, P. Terry's, which operates nine fast-food hamburger stands in Austin, Texas, donates 100 percent of its profits from one day each quarter to a local charity. The company lets customers know about upcoming charity days through its social media accounts.[20] In general, people are more likely to want to work for and buy from such organizations.

Increasingly, companies large and small are striving to be good corporate citizens. **Corporate citizenship** is adopting a strategic approach to fulfilling economic, ethical, environmental, and social responsibilities. This requires balancing the needs, desires, and demands of a diverse group of stakeholders including investors, employees, customers, regulators, competitors, neighborhoods and communities, and social activists. Hilton Hotels, for example, offers military veterans points from its Hilton HHonors rewards program for free nights in Hilton-owned hotel rooms while they are searching for jobs or undergoing training.[21] Table 2-2 lists the best corporate citizens.

2-5 THE EVOLUTION OF SOCIAL RESPONSIBILITY IN BUSINESS

Business is far from perfect in many respects, but its record of social responsibility today is much better than that in past decades. In fact, present demands for social responsibility have their roots in outraged reactions to the abusive business practices of the early 1900s.

2-5a Historical Evolution of Business Social Responsibility

During the first quarter of the 20th century, businesses were free to operate pretty much as they chose. Government protection of workers and consumers was minimal. As a result, people either accepted what business had to offer or they did without. Working conditions often were deplorable by today's standards.

Concept Check

✓ How can the government encourage the ethical behavior of organizations?

✓ What is trade associations' role in encouraging ethics?

✓ What is whistle-blowing? Who protects the whistle-blowers?

✓ What is social responsibility? How can business be socially responsible?

Learning Objective

2-5 Describe how our current views on the social responsibility of business have evolved.

corporate citizenship adopting a strategic approach to fulfilling economic, ethical, environmental, and social responsibilities

The average workweek in most industries exceeded 60 hours, no minimum-wage law existed, and employee benefits were almost nonexistent. Work places were crowded and unsafe, and industrial accidents were the rule rather than the exception. To improve working conditions, employees organized and joined labor unions. During the early 1900s, however, businesses—with the help of government—were able to use court orders, brute force, and even the few existing antitrust laws to defeat union attempts to improve working conditions.

During this period, consumers generally were subject to the doctrine of **caveat emptor**, a Latin phrase meaning "let the buyer beware." In other words, "what you see is what you get," and if it is not what you expected, too bad. Although victims of unscrupulous business practices could take legal action, going to court was very expensive, and consumers rarely won their cases. Moreover, no consumer groups or government agencies existed to publicize their consumers' grievances or to hold sellers accountable for their actions.

Before the 1930s, most people believed that competition and the action of the marketplace would, in time, correct abuses. Government, therefore, became involved in day-to-day business activities only in cases of obvious abuse of the free-market system. Six of the most important business-related federal laws passed between 1887 and 1914 are described in Table 2-3. As you can see, these laws were aimed more at encouraging competition than at correcting abuses, although two of them did deal with the purity of food and drug products.

The collapse of the stock market on October 29, 1929, triggered the Great Depression. Factory production fell by almost half, and up to 25 percent of the nation's workforce was unemployed. Public pressure soon mounted for the government to "do something" about the economy and about worsening social conditions. Soon after Franklin D. Roosevelt became president in 1933, he instituted programs to restore the economy and improve social conditions. The government passed laws to correct what many viewed as the monopolistic abuses of big business, and provided various social services for individuals. These massive federal programs became the foundation for increased government involvement in the dealings between business and society.

As government involvement has increased, so has everyone's awareness of the social responsibility of business. Today's business owners are concerned about the return on their investment, but at the same time most of them demand ethical behavior from employees. In addition, employees demand better working conditions, and consumers want safe, reliable products. Various advocacy groups echo these concerns and also call for careful consideration of Earth's delicate ecological balance. Therefore, managers must operate in a complex business environment—one in which they are just

TABLE 2-3 Early Government Regulations That Affected American Business

Government Regulation	Major Provisions
Interstate Commerce Act (1887)	First federal act to regulate business practices; provided regulation of railroads and shipping rates
Sherman Antitrust Act (1890)	Prevented monopolies or mergers where competition was endangered
Pure Food and Drug Act (1906)	Established limited supervision of interstate sales of food and drugs
Meat Inspection Act (1906)	Provided for limited supervision of interstate sales of meat and meat products
Federal Trade Commission Act (1914)	Created the Federal Trade Commission to investigate illegal trade practices
Clayton Antitrust Act (1914)	Eliminated many forms of price discrimination that gave large businesses a competitive advantage over smaller firms

caveat emptor a Latin phrase meaning "let the buyer beware"

as responsible for their managerial actions as for their actions as individual citizens. Interestingly, today's high-tech and Internet-based firms fare relatively well when it comes to environmental issues, worker conditions, the representation of minorities and women in upper management, animal testing, and charitable donations.

2-5b Two Views of Social Responsibility

Government regulation and public awareness are *external* forces that have increased the social responsibility of business. However, business decisions are made within the firm—there, social responsibility begins with the attitude of management. Two contrasting philosophies, or models, define the range of management attitudes toward social responsibility.

According to the traditional concept of business, a firm exists to produce quality goods and services, earn a reasonable profit, and provide jobs. In line with this concept, the **economic model of social responsibility** holds that society will benefit most when business is left alone to produce and market profitable products that society needs. The economic model has its origins in the 18th century, when businesses were owned primarily by entrepreneurs or owner-managers. Competition was vigorous among small firms, and short-run profits and survival were the primary concerns. To the manager who adopts this traditional attitude, social responsibility is someone else's job. After all, stockholders invest in a corporation to earn a return on their investment, not because the firm is socially responsible, and the firm is legally obligated to act in the economic interest of its stockholders. Moreover, profitable firms pay federal, state, and local taxes that are used to meet the needs of society. Thus, managers who concentrate on profit believe that they fulfill their social responsibility indirectly through the taxes paid by their firms. As a result, social responsibility becomes the problem of the government, various environmental groups, charitable foundations, and similar organizations.

In contrast, some managers believe that they have a responsibility not only to stockholders but also to customers, employees, suppliers, and the general public. This broader view is referred to as the **socioeconomic model of social responsibility**, which places emphasis not only on profits but also on the impact of business decisions on society.

Recently, increasing numbers of managers and firms have adopted the socioeconomic model, and they have done so for at least three reasons. First, business is dominated by the corporate form of ownership, and the corporation is a creation of society. If a corporation does not perform as a good citizen, society can and will demand changes. Second, many firms have begun to take pride in their social responsibility records, among them Starbucks, Hewlett-Packard, Colgate-Palmolive, and Coca-Cola. Of course, many other corporations are much more socially responsible today than they were ten years ago. Third, many businesspeople believe that it is in their best interest to take the initiative in this area. The alternative may be legal action brought against the firm by some special-interest group; in such a situation, the firm may lose control of its activities.

2-5c The Pros and Cons of Social Responsibility

Business owners, managers, customers, and government officials have debated the pros and cons of the economic and socioeconomic models for years. Each side seems to have four major arguments to reinforce its viewpoint.

Proponents of the socioeconomic model maintain that a business must do more than simply seek profits. To support their position, they offer the following arguments:

1. Because business is a part of our society, it cannot ignore social issues.
2. Business has the technical, financial, and managerial resources needed to tackle today's complex social issues.

economic model of social responsibility the view that society will benefit most when business is left alone to produce and market profitable products that society needs

socioeconomic model of social responsibility the concept that business should emphasize not only profits but also the impact of its decisions on society.

3. By helping resolve social issues, business can create a more stable environment for long-term profitability.

4. Socially responsible decision making by firms can prevent increased government intervention, which would force businesses to do what they fail to do voluntarily.

These arguments are based on the assumption that a business has a responsibility not only to its stockholders but also to its customers, employees, suppliers, and the general public.

Opponents of the socioeconomic model argue that business should do what it does best: earn a profit by manufacturing and marketing products that people want. Those who support this position argue as follows:

1. Business managers are responsible primarily to stockholders, so management must be concerned with providing a return on owners' investments.

2. Corporate time, money, and talent should be used to maximize profits, not to solve society's problems.

3. Social problems affect society in general, so individual businesses should not be expected to solve these problems.

4. Social issues are the responsibility of government officials who are elected for that purpose and who are accountable to the voters for their decisions.

These arguments obviously are based on the assumption that the primary objective of business is to earn profits and that government and social institutions should deal with social problems.

Concept Check

✓ Outline the historical evolution of business social responsibility.

✓ What are the six important business-related federal laws passed between 1887 and 1914?

✓ Explain two views on the social responsibility of business.

✓ What are the arguments for increased social responsibility?

✓ What are the arguments against increased social responsibility?

Ethical Success or Failure

Businesses Feel Pressure Over Conditions in Suppliers' Factories

Should businesses be blamed for problems that occur in suppliers' factories? Even when a supplier is located half a world away, many stakeholders expect manufacturers and retailers to help improve the lives of workers who make the products these businesses sell.

Nike, for example, has worked for years to curb problems like child labor and hazardous conditions in suppliers' facilities. After its brand was tarnished in the 1990s by accusations of unsafe factories and underage workers, Nike established a supplier code of conduct, instituted site visits to check on compliance, and changed production details to improve safety. Company executives will drop suppliers that fail to comply, even if that means higher costs and lower profit margins.

Apple has also felt pressure to deal with reported problems at Chinese factories where phones and computers are assembled for sale in stores worldwide. Like Nike, Apple requires suppliers to meet standards for on-the-job safety and employee living conditions. The company sends inspectors to audit suppliers and also relies on site visits conducted by independent groups like the Fair Labor Association.

The world's largest retailer, Walmart, is well known for low prices—made possible, in part, by buying from low-cost suppliers in China, among other areas. Over the years, Walmart has been criticized for abuses at suppliers' factories, and has set up specific workplace standards for their suppliers. It conducts surprise inspections, maintains a hotline for tips about potential problems, and has a "zero tolerance" policy for suppliers that don't meet its standards.

Should Walmart, Apple, Nike, and other businesses be blamed for the actions of their suppliers?

Sources: Based on information in Christina Farr, "Apple Address Labor Violations at Quanta Chinese Factories After 2013 Audit," *Reuters*, August 15, 2014, www.reuters.com; Shelly Banjo, "Inside Nike's Struggle to Balance Cost and Worker Safety in Bangladesh," *Wall Street Journal*, April 21, 2014, www.wsj.com; Paul Mozur, Chao Deng, and Eva Dou, "Worker Group Alleges Abuses at Apple Supplier in China," *Wall Street Journal*, July 29, 2013, www.wsj.com; Stephanie Clifford and Steven Greenhouse, "Fast and Flawed Inspections of Factories Abroad," *New York Times*, September 1, 2013, www.nytimes.com.

Today, few firms are either purely economic or purely socioeconomic in outlook; most have chosen some middle ground between the two extremes. However, our society generally seems to want—and even to expect—some degree of social responsibility from business. Thus, within this middle ground, businesses are leaning toward the socioeconomic view. In the next several sections, we look at some results of this movement in four specific areas: the public, employment practices, the environment, and implementation of social responsibility programs.

2-6 PUBLIC RESPONSIBILITIES OF BUSINESS

Business responsibilities to the public can be classified with regard to consumers and public health.

2-6a Consumerism

Consumerism consists of all activities undertaken to protect the rights of consumers. The fundamental issues pursued by the consumer movement fall into three categories: environmental protection, product performance and safety, and information disclosure. Although consumerism has been with us to some extent since the early 19th century, the consumer movement became stronger in the 1960s. It was then that President John F. Kennedy declared that the consumer was entitled to a new "Bill of Rights."

THE BASIC RIGHTS OF CONSUMERS President Kennedy's Consumer Bill of Rights asserted that consumers have a right to safety, to be informed, to choose, and to be heard. Two additional rights added since 1975 are the right to consumer education and the right to courteous service. These six rights are the basis of much of the consumer-oriented legislation passed during the last 45 years. These rights also provide an effective outline of the objectives and accomplishments of the consumer movement.

The Right To Safety. The consumers' right to safety means that the products they purchase must be safe for their intended use, must include thorough and explicit directions for proper use, and must be tested by the manufacturer to ensure product quality and reliability. Federal agencies, such as the Food and Drug Administration and the Consumer Product Safety Commission, have the power to force businesses that make or sell defective products to take corrective actions such as offering refunds, recalling defective products, issuing public warnings, and reimbursing consumers—all of which can be expensive. Moreover, consumers and the government have been winning an increasing number of product-liability lawsuits against sellers of defective products. The amount of the awards in these suits has been increasing steadily. For example, a Florida woman won $23.6 billion in a wrongful death lawsuit against R.J. Reynolds Tobacco Company after her husband, a long-time smoker, died of lung cancer.[22] Yet another major reason for improving product safety is consumers' demand for safe products. People simply will stop buying a product they believe is unsafe or unreliable.

The Right To Be Informed. The right to be informed means that consumers must have access to complete information about a product before they buy it. Detailed information about ingredients and nutrition must be provided on food containers, information about fabrics and

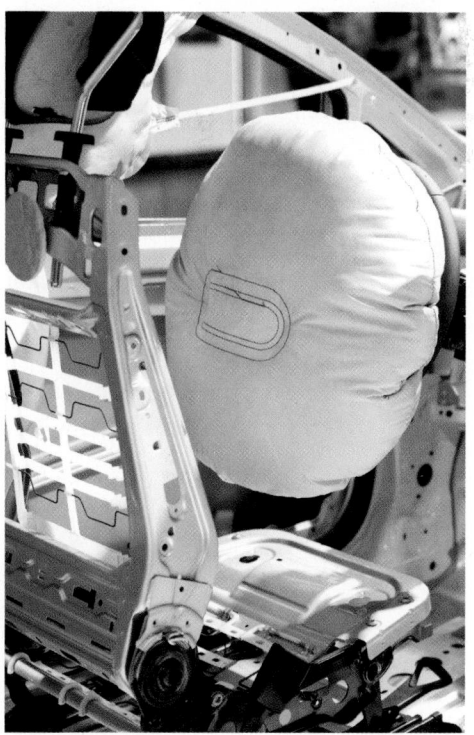

ISTOCKPHOTO.COM/HXDBZXY

Learning Objective

2-6 Discuss the factors that led to the consumer movement and list some of its results.

consumerism all activities undertaken to protect the rights of consumers

The right to safety The Consumer Bill of Rights asserts buyers' basic rights. The right to safety means that products must be safe for their intended use and tested by the producer to ensure product quality and safety.

Personal Apps

Do you always know what you're buying?

Keep these consumer rights in mind when you shop around for goods or services, buy something, or have a problem with a purchase. You're entitled to be informed, to have choices, to be heard, to buy safe products, to have responsive service, and to know your rights.

laundering methods must be attached to clothing, and lenders must disclose the true cost of borrowing the money they make available to customers who purchase merchandise on credit. In addition, manufacturers must inform consumers about the potential dangers of using their products. Manufacturers that fail to provide such information can be held responsible for personal injuries suffered because of their products. For example, Maytag provides customers with a lengthy booklet that describes how they should use a washing machine. Sometimes such warnings seem excessive, but they are necessary if user injuries (and resulting lawsuits) are to be avoided.

The Right To Choose. The right to choose means that consumers must have a choice of products, offered by different manufacturers and sellers, to satisfy a particular need. The government has done its part by encouraging competition through antitrust legislation. The greater the competition, the greater is the choice available to consumers. Competition and the resulting freedom of choice provide additional benefits for customers by reducing prices. For example, when personal computers were introduced, they cost more than $5,000. Thanks to intense competition and technological advancements, personal computers today can be purchased for less than $500.

The Right To Be Heard. The right to be heard means that someone will listen and take appropriate action when customers complain. Actually, management began to listen to consumers after World War II, when competition between businesses that manufactured and sold consumer goods increased. One way that firms gained a competitive edge was to listen to consumers and provide the products they said they wanted and needed. Today, businesses are listening even more attentively, and many larger firms have consumer relations departments that can be contacted easily via toll-free telephone numbers. Other groups listen, too. Most large cities and some states have consumer affairs offices to act on citizens' complaints.

Additional Consumer Rights. In 1975, President Gerald Ford added to the Consumer Bill of Rights the right to consumer education, which entitles people to be fully informed about their rights as consumers. In 1994, President Bill Clinton added a sixth right, the right to service, which entitles consumers to convenience, courtesy, and responsiveness from manufacturers and sellers of consumer products.

MAJOR CONSUMERISM FORCES The major forces in consumerism are individual consumer advocates and organizations, consumer education programs, and consumer laws. Consumer advocates, such as Ralph Nader, take it on themselves to protect the rights of consumers. They band together into consumer organizations, either independently or under government sponsorship. Some consumer advocates and organizations encourage consumers to boycott products and businesses to which they have objections.

Educating consumers to make wiser purchasing decisions is perhaps one of the most far-reaching aspects of consumerism. Increasingly, consumer education is becoming a part of high school and college curricula and adult-education programs. These programs cover many topics—for instance, what major factors should be considered when buying specific products, such as insurance, real estate, automobiles, appliances and furniture, clothes, and food; the provisions of certain consumer-protection laws; and the sources of information that can help individuals become knowledgeable consumers.

Major advances in consumerism have come through federal legislation. Some laws enacted in the last 50 years to protect your rights as a consumer are listed and described in Table 2-4.

Most businesspeople now realize that they ignore consumer issues only at their own peril. Managers know that improper handling of consumer complaints can result in lost sales, bad publicity, and lawsuits.

2-6b Public Health

Many people believe that businesses have a basic responsibility to contribute to the general wellbeing of the public, starting with ensuring that their products do not harm anyone. Beyond this basic responsibility, however, there is contention with regard to how far businesses' responsibility to public health extends, especially about issues such as obesity, smoking, heart disease, alcohol use, and even smartphone use while driving. These issues are not black and white, but exploring them can help us find balance among the desires and demands of various stakeholders.

Obesity has become a major public health topic in recent years, with more than one-third of adult Americans being categorized as obese. Other countries are experiencing similar trends. People who are obese or significantly overweight

Social Media:
The FTC Blogs and Tweets Too

The U.S. lawmakers who wrote the original Federal Trade Commission Act in 1914 never envisioned that a century later, FTC staff members would be responsible for monitoring business activity on Facebook, Twitter, YouTube, Tumblr, and Pinterest—and for using social media to help keep consumers informed about their rights.

When the FTC takes action against a business for an unfair trade practice, staff members tweet about it on the agency's Twitter account (http://twitter.com/ftc). They also tweet consumer tips for saving money, safeguarding credit, avoiding scams, and protecting children's privacy, reaching tens of thousands of followers with each message. Knowing that many U.S. consumers are Facebook users, the FTC also has a very active account there (www.facebook.com/federaltradecommission).

The FTC's blog (at www.consumer.ftc.gov/blog, available in English and Spanish) carries longer messages to alert consumers to recent agency enforcement activities, smart shopping techniques, shady financial practices, and other developments. Businesses can learn more about FTC guidelines through the blog, as well. Videos posted on the FTC YouTube channel (www.youtube.com/user/FTCvideos) educate consumers (in English and Spanish) about how to get a mortgage, how to avoid identity fraud, and how to file a complaint with the agency. More than a million people have viewed FTC videos on YouTube.

In its regulatory role, the FTC is taking steps to prevent consumers from being misled via social media. For instance, companies must disclose when a message, image, or video is posted for advertising purposes. Otherwise, an advertiser or ad agency will get a warning letter or be charged with a violation. And the FTC will blog or tweet about it, too.

Sources: Based on information in "FTC's Charges Against Deutsch LA Seen as a Twitter Wake-Up Call for Industry," *Wall Street Journal*, November 28, 2014, www.wsj.com; Jeremy Quittner, "How to Avoid the FTC's Ire When Advertising on Social Media," *Inc.*, October 22, 2014, www.inc.com; Katy Bachman, "FTC Dings Cole Haan for Wandering Sole Promo on Pinterest," *Adweek*, April 3, 2014, www.adweek.com; www.ftc.gov.

face higher rates of diabetes, strokes, heart disease, and some types of cancer, and the swelling numbers of these illnesses place a great burden on the healthcare system, the costs of which are borne by society. Public health advocates have called for companies—particularly those that market sugary drinks and fast food—to modify their products or at least their advertising in an effort to reduce the consumption of these products, which have been shown to contribute to rising rates of obesity. Perhaps as a result, some producers of these products have suffered losses and are responding with new ideas and products. Coca-Cola, for example, is testing a lower-calorie soft drink called Coca-Cola Life, which has 89 calories and is sweetened by Stevia, compared to regular Coca-Cola, which has 140 calories sweetened by high-fructose corn syrup. Life represents Coke's efforts to find a middle ground between

TABLE 2-4 Major Federal Legislation Protecting Consumers Since 1960

Legislation	Major Provisions
Federal Hazardous Substances Labeling Act (1960)	Required warning labels on household chemicals if they were highly toxic
Kefauver–Harris Drug Amendments (1962)	Established testing practices for drugs and required manufacturers to label drugs with generic names in addition to trade names
Cigarette Labeling Act (1965)	Required manufacturers to place standard warning labels on all cigarette packages and advertising
Fair Packaging and Labeling Act (1966)	Called for all products sold across state lines to be labeled with net weight, ingredients, and manufacturer's name and address
Motor Vehicle Safety Act (1966)	Established standards for safer cars
Truth in Lending Act (1968)	Required lenders and credit merchants to disclose the full cost of finance charges in both dollars and annual percentage rates
Credit Card Liability Act (1970)	Limited credit-card holder's liability to $50 per card and stopped credit-card companies from issuing unsolicited cards
Fair Credit Reporting Act (1971)	Required credit bureaus to provide credit reports to consumers regarding their own credit files; also provided for correction of incorrect information
Consumer Product Safety Commission Act (1972)	Established an abbreviated procedure for registering certain generic drugs
Fair Credit Billing Act (1974)	Amended the Truth in Lending Act to enable consumers to challenge billing errors
Equal Credit Opportunity Act (1974)	Provided equal credit opportunities for males and females and for married and single individuals
Magnuson–Moss Warranty–Federal Trade Commission Act (1975)	Provided for minimum disclosure standards for written consumer-product warranties for products that cost more than $15
Amendments to the Equal Credit Opportunity Act (1976, 1994)	Prevented discrimination based on race, creed, color, religion, age, and income when granting credit
Fair Debt Collection Practices Act (1977)	Outlawed abusive collection practices by third parties
Nutrition Labeling and Education Act (1990)	Required the Food and Drug Administration to review current food labeling and packaging focusing on nutrition label content, label format, ingredient labeling, food descriptors and standards, and health messages
Telephone Consumer Protection Act (1991)	Prohibited the use of automated dialing and prerecorded-voice calling equipment to make calls or deliver messages
Consumer Credit Reporting Reform Act (1997)	Placed more responsibility for accurate credit data on credit issuers; required creditors to verify that disputed data are accurate and to notify a consumer before reinstating the data
Children's Online Privacy Protection Act (2000)	Placed parents in control over what information is collected online from their children younger than 13 years; required commercial website operators to maintain the confidentiality, security, and integrity of personal information collected from children
Do Not Call Implementation Act (2003)	Directed the FCC and the FTC to coordinate so that their rules are consistent regarding telemarketing call practices including the Do Not Call Registry and other lists, as well as call abandonment
Credit Card Accountability, Responsibility, and Disclosure Act (2009)	Provided the most sweeping changes in credit card protections since the Truth in Lending Act of 1968
Dodd–Frank Wall Street Reform and Consumer Protection Act of 2010	Promoted the financial stability of the United States by improving accountability and responsibility in the financial system; established a new Consumer Financial Protection Agency to regulate home mortgages, car loans, and credit cards; became Public Law on July 21, 2010

those decrying sugary soft drinks and those who adamantly oppose artificial sweeteners that may have their own health issues.[23] Other companies, including Panera and Starbucks, are posting the calories in their offerings right on their menus to help people make better choices. Many companies have removed unhealthy trans fats from their product formulas. In the meantime, First Lady Michelle Obama has brought industry representatives and public health advocates together to search for a middle ground that allows firms to continue producing and marketing their products as long as they are within the law, yet dials back marketing toward those most impressionable. Obama recently called for companies to stop marketing junk food at children during the school day.[24]

Another major public health topic facing business relates to smoking and tobacco products. The relationship between smoking—even second-hand smoke—and cancer has been well documented, but some consumers still demand to buy cigarettes and smoking products. While most people agree that businesses should not knowingly sell products that harm customers, what should they do when consumers continue to demand those products? CVS Caremark earned much publicity when it announced that it would no longer sell cigarettes in its stores, even though it would lose $2 billion in revenue from doing so.[25] In recent years, the rise of e-cigarettes, which are battery-powered smoking devices that deliver nicotine as a vapor rather than smoke, has further compounded the issue. Marketers of e-cigarettes insist that their products are safer than cigarettes and even tout them as a method to stop smoking. Health advocates, however, say they are still harmful, and worry that the vapors—which come in flavors such as bubblegum and piña colada—may be especially attractive to minors. Some cities have banned e-cigarettes along with conventional ones, and federal regulators are studying the devices to determine whether further regulation is needed.

There are other issues businesses face with regard to public health, including labeling products that contain genetically modified organisms (GMOs), making questionable claims of the health benefits of supplements and ingredients, where and how to provide affordable housing for the homeless, and many others. One growing concern is the use of smartphones and smartphone apps while driving. Should cell phone service providers take steps to prevent customers from texting and using apps that distract from driving or merely advise them to refrain from these activities? AT&T launched its "It Can Wait" promotion campaign to ask customers to avoid texting while driving, and more than 5 million users pledged not to. The cell phone service provider asked customers to use the hashtag #X to alert their friends and followers that they are about to be unreachable on social media because they are driving.[26]

Concept Check

✓ Describe the six basic rights of consumers.

✓ What are the major forces in consumerism today?

✓ What are some of the federal laws enacted in the last 50 years to protect your rights as a consumer?

✓ What are some of the issues businesses must consider with regard to public health?

2-7 EMPLOYMENT PRACTICES

Everyone should have the opportunity to land a job for which he or she is qualified and to be rewarded on the basis of ability and performance. This is a fundamental issue for Americans, and it also makes good business sense. Yet, over the years, this opportunity has been denied to members of various minority groups. A **minority** is a racial, religious, political, national, or other group regarded as different from the larger group of which it is a part and that is often singled out for unfavorable treatment.

The federal government responded to the outcry of minority groups during the 1960s and 1970s by passing a number of laws forbidding discrimination in the workplace. (These laws are discussed in Chapter 9 in the context of human resources management.) Yet, more than 50 years after passage of the Civil Rights Act of 1964, abuses still exist. An example is the disparity in income levels for whites, blacks, Hispanics, and Asians, as illustrated in Figure 2-3. Lower incomes and higher unemployment rates also characterize Native Americans, handicapped persons, and women. Responsible managers have instituted a number of programs to counteract the results of discrimination.

Learning Objective

2-7 Analyze how present employment practices are being used to counteract past abuses.

minority a racial, religious, political, national, or other group regarded as different from the larger group of which it is a part and that is often singled out for unfavorable treatment

FIGURE 2-3 Comparative Income Levels

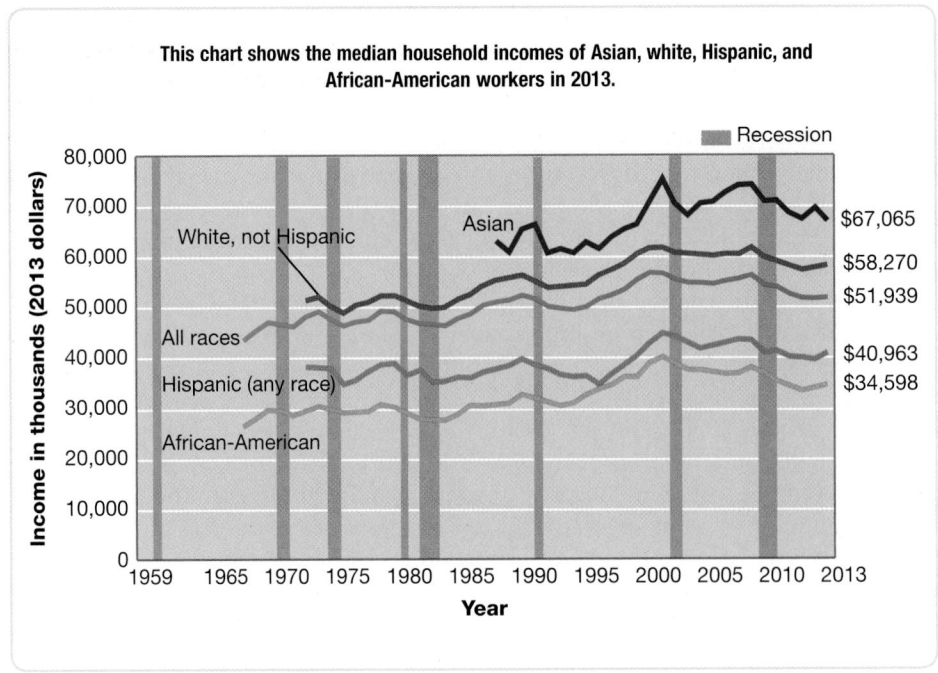

This chart shows the median household incomes of Asian, white, Hispanic, and African-American workers in 2013.

- Recession

Income in thousands (2013 dollars)

White, not Hispanic
Asian
$67,065
$58,270
$51,939
All races
Hispanic (any race)
$40,963
$34,598
African-American

Year
1959 1965 1970 1975 1980 1985 1990 1995 2000 2005 2010 2013

Source: Carmen DeNavas-Walt and Bernadette D. Proctor, Income and Poverty in the United States: 2013, U.S. Census Bureau, September 2014, p. 5, http://www.census.gov/content/dam/Census/library/publications/2014/demo/p60-249.pdf.

2-7a Affirmative Action Programs

affirmative action program a plan designed to increase the number of minority employees at all levels within an organization

Equal Employment Opportunity Commission (EEOC) a government agency with the power to investigate complaints of employment discrimination and the power to sue firms that practice it

An **affirmative action program** is a plan designed to increase the number of minority employees at all levels within an organization. Employers with federal contracts of more than $50,000 per year must have written affirmative action plans. The objective of such programs is to ensure that minorities are represented within the organization in approximately the same proportion as in the surrounding community. If 25 percent of the electricians in a geographic area in which a company is located are African Americans, then approximately 25 percent of the electricians it employs also should be African Americans. Affirmative action plans encompass all areas of human resources management: recruiting, hiring, training, promotion, and pay.

Unfortunately, affirmative action programs have been plagued by two problems. The first involves quotas. In the beginning, many firms pledged to recruit and hire a certain number of minority members by a specific date. To achieve this goal, they were forced to consider only minority applicants for job openings; if they hired nonminority workers, they would be defeating their own purpose. However, the courts have ruled that such quotas are unconstitutional even though their purpose is commendable. They are, in fact, a form of discrimination called *reverse discrimination*.

The second problem is that although most such programs have been reasonably successful, not all businesspeople are in favor of affirmative action programs. Managers not committed to these programs can "play the game" and still discriminate against workers. To help solve this problem, Congress created (and later strengthened) the **Equal Employment Opportunity Commission (EEOC)**, a government agency with the power to investigate complaints of employment discrimination and sue firms that practice it.

INGRAM PUBLISHING/THINKSTOCK

Cultural diversity A company with a culturally diverse workforce benefits in a number of ways.

FIGURE 2-4 Relative Earnings of Male and Female Workers

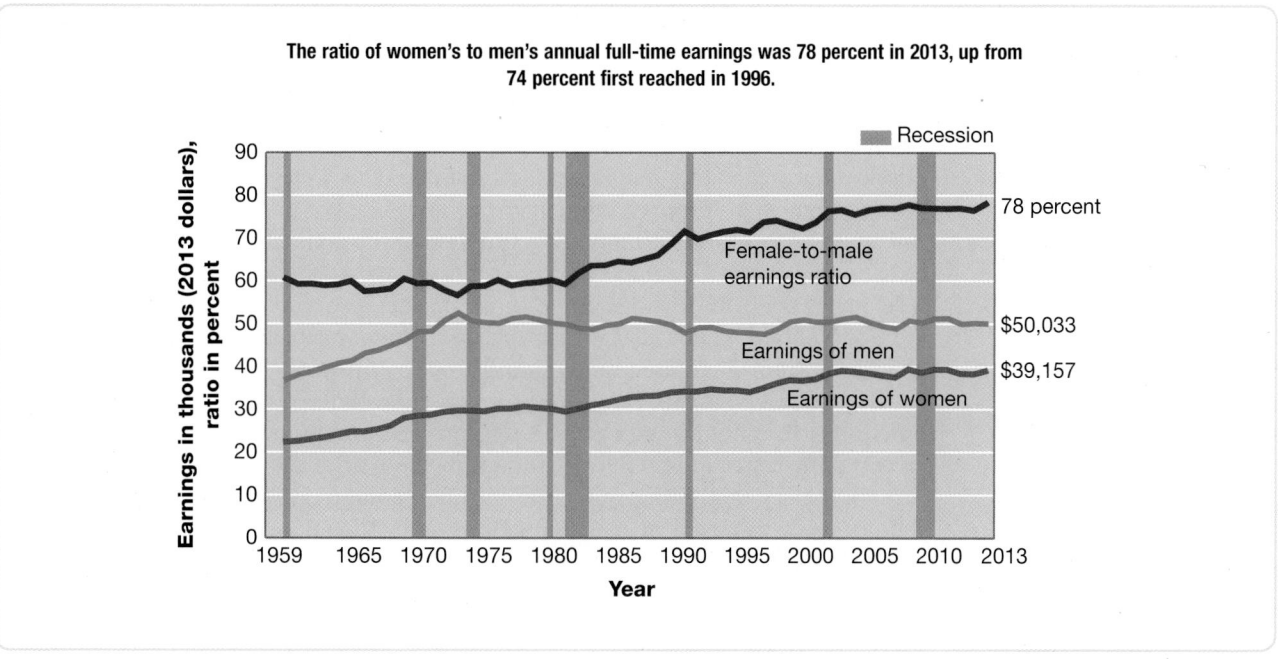

The ratio of women's to men's annual full-time earnings was 78 percent in 2013, up from 74 percent first reached in 1996.

Source: Carmen DeNavas-Walt and Bernadette D. Proctor, Income and Poverty in the United States: 2013, U.S. Census Bureau, September 2014, p. 9, http://www.census.gov/content/dam/Census/library/publications/2014/demo/p60-249.pdf.

The threat of legal action has persuaded some corporations to amend their hiring and promotional policies, but the discrepancy between men's and women's salaries still exists, as illustrated in Figure 2-4. For more than 50 years, women have consistently earned only about 77 cents for each dollar earned by men.

2-7b Training Programs for the Hard-Core Unemployed

For some firms, social responsibility extends far beyond placing a help-wanted advertisement in the local newspaper. These firms have assumed the task of helping the **hard-core unemployed**, workers with little education or vocational training and a long history of unemployment. For example, the Hard Rock Hotel & Casino teamed up with the College of Menominee Nation and Gateway Technical College in Kenosha, Wisconsin, to create a Jobs Training Institute to recruit and train Native Americans for casino and related jobs in the Kenosha area.[27] In the past, such workers often were turned down routinely by personnel managers, even for the most menial jobs.

2-7c Programs to Reduce Sexual Harassment and Abusive Behavior

Another hot button issue in the workplace is addressing sexual harassment and other abusive behaviors. The Workplace Bullying Institute (WBI) defines bullying in the workplace as repeated work sabotage; verbal abuse; and/or abusive conduct that is threatening, humiliating, or intimidating. The stress of bullying can result in physical and mental health issues that can ultimately cost employers many hours of lost worker productivity as well as lower morale and higher turnover. The WBI has found that 27 percent of respondents to a survey have suffered abusive conduct at work; 21 percent say they have witnessed it in the workplace.[28] Other researchers have found much higher rates of bullying. Moreover, research by the WBI suggests that half of victims do not report their bullying out of fear of further harassment because their bully is in a position of power.[29] Even football players can be subject

hard-core unemployed workers with little education or vocational training and a long history of unemployment

to bullying in the workplace: Former Miami Dolphins tackle Jonathan Martin left the team because he felt he could not continue to do his job in the face of repeated bullying from other teammates.[30]

When bullying takes on sexual overtones, it becomes sexual harassment, which the U. S. Equal Employment Opportunity Commission defines as unwelcome sexual advances, requests for sexual favors, and other verbal or physical harassment of a physical nature. Unlike bullying, sexual harassment is illegal.[31] It can also result in poor morale, high turnover, and expensive lawsuits. For example, four women filed suit against Ford Motor Company, claiming that the sexual harassment they endured at a Ford plant in Chicago created a "hostile work environment" for all women working at the plant. In addition to those charges, the women claimed the company did not respond when they complained to its harassment hotline, and that at least one of the women endured retaliation for her complaints.[32]

To create a workplace environment that stifles bullying, sexual harassment, and other abusive conduct, managers need to provide programs, much like the ones that are used, to foster more ethical conduct in the workplace. In addition to creating formal policies that define and prohibit unacceptable abusive conduct, companies should strive to create an anti-bullying organizational culture by modeling good behavior and sending a strong message that improper conduct will be punished. Companies may even want to go a step further and offer training and additional services through employee assistance programs such as counseling to ensure that all employees feel supported.[33]

2-8 ENVIRONMENTAL CONCERNS

Learning Objective

2-8 Describe the major types of pollution, their causes, and their cures.

A growing social consciousness by the public and some business managers, fostered by government legislation, has led to major efforts to reduce environmental pollution, conserve natural resources, and reverse some of the worst damage caused by past negligence in this area.

A significant environmental issue is the amount of waste produced by businesses and society. For example, by some estimates, the United States throws out one-third of all the food produced, and grocery stores are responsible for as much as 10 percent of that. One reason for the large amount of grocery waste is consumer expectations: Consumers bypass fruits and vegetables that do not appear to be perfect, so supermarkets discard any produce that doesn't meet that expectation, even when that produce is otherwise safe and healthy.[34] The disposal problem has been deteriorating over the past few years because modern technology has continued to produce increasing amounts of chemical and radioactive waste. U.S. manufacturers produce an estimated 40 to 60 million tons of contaminated oil, solvents, acids, and sludge each year. Service businesses, utility companies, hospitals, and other industries also dump vast amounts of wastes into the environment. While companies today strive to reduce waste from operations as much as possible, much still winds up in landfills. A shortage of landfills, owing to stricter regulations, makes garbage disposal a serious problem in some areas. Incinerators help to solve the landfill-shortage problem, but they bring with them their own problems. They reduce the amount of garbage but also leave tons of ash to be buried—ash that often has a higher concentration of toxicity than the original garbage.

Another major environmental issue is **pollution**, the contamination of water, air, or land through the actions of people in an industrialized society. Pollution harms water and air quality, threatens human and animal health, degrades habitats, and contributes to climate change. Among the serious threats to people posed by pollutants are respiratory irritation, cancer, kidney and liver damage, anemia, and heart failure. Businesspeople harm the environment when they unwittingly— or knowingly—dump hazardous chemicals and waste in unapproved ways. For example, Leading Edge Aviation Services, Inc., was fined $1 million for improper

Concept Check

✓ What is an affirmative action program? What is its purpose?

✓ Why did Congress create (and later strengthen) the Equal Employment Opportunity Commission?

✓ How can businesses reduce sexual harassment and abusive behavior at the workplace?

pollution the contamination of water, air, or land through the actions of people in an industrialized society

Career Success

Aiming to Be a Chief Sustainability Officer?

Would you like to be a CSO? Nike, Dow Chemical, IKEA, DuPont, and a growing number of other major companies have established the position of chief sustainability officer (CSO) to champion green business practices throughout the organization. The CSO assesses the company's environmental impact, monitors whether the firm is in compliance with laws and regulations, and determines how the company's operations affect natural resources (such as scarce raw materials and energy sources). The next step is to identify opportunities and implement strategies for achieving sustainability goals that complement or enhance financial goals (such as energy-conservation measures that also save money). Some CSOs go further, using innovation to put sustainability at the heart of new operations, new products, and new markets.

At Nike, for instance, CSO Hannah Jones is involved in bringing together an international group of product designers, scientists, and other outside experts working on innovations in sustainable materials and production processes. By forging ties with specialists worldwide, Jones promotes the development of earth-friendly materials and manufacturing approaches—which, in turn, benefits Nike and its customers. Jones's responsibilities are wider ranging: She also looks at environmental and social responsibility issues affecting Nike's suppliers and works for positive change throughout the supply chain.

To be effective at this senior management level, a CSO needs an in-depth understanding of the business and its practices, familiarity with the regulatory process, and a flair for communication. Most important, a CSO should have the conceptual ability to envision far-reaching changes that will protect the planet while supporting the company's mission.

Sources: Based on information in Christopher P. Skroupa, "Building Innovation into Sustainability," *Forbes*, November 3, 2014, www.forbes.com; Dina Gerdeman, "What Do Chief Sustainability Officers Do?" *Forbes*, October 8, 2014, www.forbes.com; "Nike's Launch Project Expands Search for Sustainable Materials Innovations," *The Guardian (UK)*, March 14, 2014, www.theguardian.com.

handling and storage of paint stripping chemicals at a Mississippi airport; the company will also have to pay to clean up the site.[35] For decades, environmentalists have been warning us about the dangers of industrial pollution. Unfortunately, business and government leaders either ignored the problem or were not concerned about it until pollution became a threat to life and health in America.

2-8a Pollution

Oil spills can have long-lasting effects on our wildlife and other natural resources. As our population and businesses expand, the need to reduce pollution at its source becomes more important.

2-8b Effects of Environmental Legislation

As in other areas of concern to our society, legislation and regulations play a crucial role in pollution control. The laws outlined in Table 2-5 reflect the scope of current environmental legislation: laws to promote clean air, clean water, and even quiet work and living environments. Of major importance was the creation of the Environmental Protection Agency (EPA), the federal agency charged with enforcing laws designed to protect the environment.

When they are aware of a pollution problem, many firms respond to it rather than wait to be cited by the EPA. Other owners and managers, however, take the position that environmental standards are too strict.

PREDRAG1/ISTOCK/THINKSTOCK

TABLE 2-5 Summary of Major Environmental Laws

Legislation	Major Provisions
National Environmental Policy Act (1970)	Established the Environmental Protection Agency (EPA) to enforce federal laws that involve the environment
Clean Air Amendment (1970)	Provided stringent automotive, aircraft, and factory emission standards
Water Quality Improvement Act (1970)	Strengthened existing water pollution regulations and provided for large monetary fines against violators
Resource Recovery Act (1970)	Enlarged the solid-waste disposal program and provided for enforcement by the EPA
Water Pollution Control Act Amendment (1972)	Established standards for cleaning navigable streams and lakes and eliminating all harmful waste disposal by 1985
Noise Control Act (1972)	Established standards for major sources of noise and required the EPA to advise the Federal Aviation Administration on standards for airplanes
Clean Air Act Amendment (1977)	Established new deadlines for cleaning up polluted areas; also required review of existing air-quality standards
Resource Conservation and Recovery Act (1984)	Amended the original 1976 act and required federal regulation of potentially dangerous solid-waste disposal
Clean Air Act Amendment (1987)	Established a national air-quality standard for ozone
Oil Pollution Act (1990)	Expanded the nation's oil-spill prevention and response activities; also established the Oil Spill Liability Trust Fund
Clean Air Act Amendments (1990)	Required that motor vehicles be equipped with onboard systems to control about 90 percent of refueling vapors
Food Quality Protection Act (1996)	Amended the Federal Insecticide, Fungicide and Rodenticide Act and the Federal Food Drug and Cosmetic Act; the requirements included a new safety standard—reasonable certainty of no harm—that must be applied to all pesticides used on foods
American Recovery and Reinvestment Act (2009)	Provided $7.22 billion to the EPA to protect and promote "green" jobs and a healthier environment

(Loosely translated, this means that compliance with present standards is too expensive.) Consequently, it often has been necessary for the EPA to take legal action to force firms to install antipollution equipment and to clean up waste storage areas. Oregon-based Jerome Cheese, for example, had to pay $88,000 to settle charges that it failed to follow EPA regulations regarding the uncontrolled or accidental release of toxic anhydrous ammonia.[36]

Experience has shown that the combination of environmental legislation, voluntary compliance, and EPA action can succeed in cleaning up the environment and keeping it clean. However, much still remains to be done.

2-8c Business Response to Environmental Concerns

One of the most effective ways that companies can reduce their impact on the environment is to reduce waste from operations and other activities. Identifying and eliminating inefficiencies in production and operations is where most firms begin that process. Finding alternative uses for waste is another. For example, leftover food from supermarkets and restaurants is often donated to local food banks or sold to farmers who feed it to livestock. Most companies strive to recycle as much as possible. **Recycling** involves converting used materials into new products or components for new products in order to prevent their unnecessary disposal. Companies can recycle waste paper, plastic packaging, glass, rubber, metals, and other chemicals so

Recycling converting used materials into new products or components for new products in order to prevent their unnecessary disposal

that they or their components can be reprocessed into new products and kept out of landfills. The Coca-Cola Bottling Company of Northern New England, for example, donates waste plastic and paper to other manufacturing firms in the area, which turn those leftover materials into synthetic fibers and composite decking material that become components of new products.[37]

Another way businesses strive to be more environmentally conscious is through the use of "greener" forms of power to counter their use of huge quantities of energy during operations and other activities. Companies can audit their operations to identify places where more efficient and environmentally friendly products can be used to save energy, such as using CFL or LED light bulbs—which reduce heat as well as power use—and even natural sunlight to light workplaces. Many companies are turning to alternative forms of power generation, including solar and wind power which do not rely on diminishing sources of fossil fuels. New Belgium Brewing in Fort Collins, Colorado, became the first company to be 100 percent powered by the wind, but many other companies have followed suit. A number of the world's largest businesses, including IKEA, Mars, Nestle, and H&M, have pledged to convert to 100 percent renewable energy sources such as wind and solar by 2020.[38]

Reducing dependence on fossil fuels Today's businesses (and consumers) are more open to alternative sources of energy because they are concerned about the negative impact of conventional energy sources.

Recognizing public demand for greater environmental responsibility, more and more firms are adopting environmentally friendly practices and products that are less harmful to the environment. **Green marketing** is the process of creating, making, delivering, and promoting products that are environmentally safe. It may include making modifications to products, manufacturing processes, packaging, and/or promotion activities to make or deliver products that are better for the environment. Chipotle Mexican Grill, for example, built its reputation as a green marketer by strictly adhering to its "Food with Integrity" manifesto, which describes the company's "commitment to finding the very best ingredients with respect for the animals, the environment, and the farmers." To live by that manifesto, the company's products include only natural animal products (treated humanely and fed a vegetarian diet that does not include growth hormones or antibiotics). It also became the first food chain to label genetically modified ingredients. It is significant that Chipotle has not yet achieved all its sustainability goals, but its manifesto guides the firm in all decision making and activities.[39]

Green marketers must ensure that their claims are backed by evidence that shows a significant environmental benefit and does not mislead consumers or they may run afoul of the Federal Trade Commission.[40] Companies that take their green marketing efforts too far, without relevance or substantiating their environmental claims risk being labeled guilty of green washing.

Who will pay for the environmental cleanup? Many business leaders offer one answer–tax money should be used to clean up the environment and to keep it clean. They reason that business is not the only source of pollution, so business should not be forced to absorb the entire cost of the cleanup. Environmentalists disagree. They believe that the cost of proper treatment and disposal of industrial wastes is an expense of doing business. In either case, consumers probably will pay a large part of the cost—either as taxes or in the form of higher prices for goods and services.

> ## Concept Check
>
> ✓ What are the major environmental issues facing society today?
>
> ✓ Summarize major provisions of federal environmental laws enacted since 1970?
>
> ✓ What is businesses' response to environmental concerns?

green marketing the process of creating, making, delivering, and promoting products that are environmentally safe

2-9 IMPLEMENTING A PROGRAM OF SOCIAL RESPONSIBILITY

Learning Objective

2-9 Identify the steps a business must take to implement a program of social responsibility.

A firm's decision to be socially responsible is a step in the right direction—but only the first step. The firm then must develop and implement a program to reach this goal. The program will be affected by the firm's size, financial resources, past record in the area of social responsibility, and competition. Above all, however, the program must have the firm's total commitment or it will fail.

An effective program for social responsibility takes time, money, and organization. In most cases, developing and implementing such a program will require four steps: securing the commitment of top executives, planning, appointing a director, and preparing a social audit.

2-9a Commitment of Top Executives

Without the support of top executives, any program will soon falter and become ineffective. For example, the Boeing Company's Ethics and Business Conduct Committee is responsible for the ethics program. The committee is appointed by the Boeing board of directors, and its members include the company chairman and CEO, the president and chief operating officer, the presidents of the operating groups, and senior vice presidents. As evidence of their commitment to social responsibility, top managers should develop a policy statement that outlines key areas of concern. This statement sets a tone of positive support and later will serve as a guide for other employees as they become involved in the program.

2-9b Planning

Next, a committee of managers should be appointed to plan the program. Whatever form their plan takes, it should deal with each of the issues described in the top managers' policy statement. If necessary, outside consultants can be hired to help develop the plan.

2-9c Appointment of a Director

After the social responsibility plan is established, a top-level executive should be appointed to implement the organization's plan. This individual should be charged with recommending specific policies and helping individual departments to understand and live up to the social responsibilities the firm has assumed. Depending on the size of the firm, the director may require a staff to handle the program on a day-to-day basis. For example, at the Boeing Company, the director of ethics and business conduct administers the ethics and business conduct program.

2-9d The Social Audit

At specified intervals, the program director should prepare a social audit for the firm. A **social audit** is a comprehensive report of what an organization has done and is doing with regard to social issues that affect it. This document provides the information the firm needs to evaluate and revise its social responsibility program. Typical subject areas include human resources, community involvement, the quality and safety of products, business practices, and efforts to reduce pollution and improve the environment. The information included in a social audit should be as accurate and as quantitative as possible, and the audit should reveal both positive and negative aspects of the program. Caesars Entertainment, which operates casinos, evaluates its corporate citizenship efforts annually and then issues a report describing

social audit a comprehensive report of what an organization has done and is doing with regard to social issues that affect it its performance for a variety of stakeholders including employees, investors, and the media. Caesars' Corporate Citizenship Report details its performance in meeting goals in the areas of responsible gaming, employee development, environmental stewardship, and community investment.[41]

Today, many companies listen to concerned individuals within and outside the company. For example, the Boeing Ethics Line listens to and acts on concerns expressed by employees and others about possible violations of company policies, laws, or regulations, such as improper or unethical business practices, as well as health, safety, and environmental issues. Employees are encouraged to communicate their concerns, as well as ask questions about ethical issues. The Ethics Line is available to all Boeing employees, including Boeing subsidiaries. It is also available to concerned individuals outside the company.

Concept Check

✓ What steps must a business take to implement a program of social responsibility?

✓ What is the social audit? Who should prepare a social audit for the firm?

Summary

2-1 Understand what is meant by business ethics.

Ethics is the study of right and wrong and of the morality of choices. Business ethics is the application of moral standards to business situations.

2-2 Identify the types of ethical concerns that arise in the business world.

Ethical issues arise often in business situations out of relationships with investors, customers, employees, creditors, or competitors. Businesspeople should make every effort to be fair, to consider the welfare of customers and others within the firm, to avoid conflicts of interest, and to communicate honestly.

2-3 Discuss the factors that affect the level of ethical behavior in organizations.

Individual, social, and opportunity factors all affect the level of ethical behavior in an organization. Individual factors include knowledge level, moral values and attitudes, and personal goals. Social factors include cultural norms and the actions and values of co-workers and significant others. Opportunity factors refer to the amount of leeway that exists in an organization for employees to behave unethically if they choose to do so.

2-4 Explain how ethical decision making can be encouraged.

Governments, trade associations, and individual firms can establish guidelines for defining ethical behavior. Governments can pass stricter regulations. Trade associations provide ethical guidelines for their members. Companies provide codes of ethics—written

guides to acceptable and ethical behavior as defined by an organization—and create an atmosphere in which ethical behavior is encouraged. An ethical employee working in an unethical environment may resort to whistle-blowing to bring a questionable practice to light.

2-5 Describe how our current views on the social responsibility of business have evolved.

In a socially responsible business, management realizes that its activities have an impact on society and considers that impact in the decision-making process. Before the 1930s, workers, consumers, and government had very little influence on business activities; as a result, business leaders gave little thought to social responsibility. All this changed with the Great Depression. Government regulations, employee demands, and consumer awareness combined to create a demand that businesses act in socially responsible ways.

The basic premise of the economic model of social responsibility is that society benefits most when business is left alone to produce profitable goods and services. According to the socioeconomic model, business has as much responsibility to society as it has to its owners. Most managers adopt a viewpoint somewhere between these two extremes.

2-6 Discuss the factors that led to the consumer movement and list some of its results.

Consumerism consists of all activities undertaken to protect the rights of consumers. The consumer movement generally has demanded—and received—attention from business in the areas of product safety, product information, product choices through competition, and the resolution of complaints about products and business practices. Although concerns over consumer rights have been around to some extent since the early 19th century, the movement became more powerful in the 1960s when President John F. Kennedy initiated the Consumer Bill of Rights. The six basic rights of consumers include the right to safety, the right to be informed, the right to choose, the right to be heard, and the rights to consumer education and courteous service. Today, many people believe that businesses have a basic responsibility to contribute to the general wellbeing of the public. Other issues businesses face relate to public health, including labeling products that contain genetically modified organisms.

2-7 Analyze how present employment practices are being used to counteract past abuses.

Legislation and public demand have prompted some businesses to correct past abuses in employment practices—mainly with regard to minority groups. Affirmative action and training of the hard-core unemployed are two types of programs that have been used successfully. Another issue in the workplace is addressing sexual harassment and other abusive behaviors, such as bullying and verbal abuse.

2-8 Describe the major types of pollution, their causes, and their cures.

Pollution is the contamination of water, air, or land through the actions of people in an industrialized society. Pollution harms water and air quality, threatens human and animal health, degrades habitats, and contributes to climate change. Current environmental laws, enforced by the Environmental Protection Agency, promote clean air, clean water, and even quiet work and living environments. However, much still remains to be done. Many companies are turning to alternative forms of power generation, including solar and wind power which do not rely on diminishing sources of fossil fuels. More and more firms are adopting environmentally friendly practices and products that are less harmful to the environment.

2-9 Identify the steps a business must take to implement a program of social responsibility.

A program to implement social responsibility in a business begins with total commitment by top management. The program should be planned carefully, and a capable director should be appointed to implement it. Social audits should be prepared periodically as a means of evaluating and revising the program.

Key Terms

You should now be able to define and give an example relevant to each of the following terms:

ethics (39)
business ethics (39)
plagiarism (40)
Sarbanes–Oxley Act
    of 2002 (43)
code of ethics (44)
whistle-blowing (44)

social responsibility (46)
corporate citizenship (47)
caveat emptor (48)
economic model of social
    responsibility (49)
socioeconomic model of
    social responsibility (49)

consumerism (51)
minority (55)
affirmative action
    program (56)
Equal Employment
    Opportunity Commission
    (EEOC) (56)

hard-core unemployed (57)
pollution (58)
recycling (60)
green marketing (61)
social audit (62)

Discussion Questions

1. When a company acts in an ethically questionable manner, what types of problems are caused for the organization and its customers?
2. How can an employee take an ethical stand regarding a business decision when his or her superior already has taken a different position?
3. Overall, would it be more profitable for a business to follow the economic model or the socioeconomic model of social responsibility?

4. Why should business take on the task of training the hard-core unemployed?
5. To what extent should the blame for vehicular air pollution be shared by manufacturers, consumers, and government?
6. Why is there so much government regulation involving social responsibility issues? Should there be less?

Video Case
PortionPac Chemical Is People-Friendly, Planet-Friendly

When Marvin Klein and Syd Weisberg founded PortionPac Chemical Corporation (www.portionpaccorp.com) in 1964, they were thinking "green" long before the word came to describe an international environmental movement. The partners shared the belief that cleaning solutions didn't have to be toxic or caustic to be effective. They also realized that both water and packaging went to waste when manufacturers poured premixed cleaning liquids into spray bottles that customers would throw away when empty. One more thing the cofounders agreed on: They wanted to do business with integrity, dealing with employees, suppliers, and customers in an ethical way.

With commercial customers in mind, Weisberg tested and developed concentrated cleaning formulas that did away with grease and dirt in offices, kitchens, and bathrooms without endangering people or the planet. He and Klein prepared small packages of concentrate to be mixed with water for full-strength cleaning in elementary schools, companies, factories, and correctional facilities. To be sure the cleaning solution wasn't too strong or too weak, the entrepreneurs gave custodians, janitors, and other cleaning staff careful instructions about exactly how to dilute the concentrate. And to avoid mountains of empty bottles piling up in local landfills, they had customers use refillable spray bottles.

Chicago-based PortionPac's core principles of safety and sustainability were way ahead of their time. Now that environmental issues are in the public eye, the company is thriving, with $20 million in annual sales, 84 employees, and an ever-expanding customer base. Unlike most businesses, however, PortionPac rewards its salespeople for selling only the amount of cleaning products that customers need. This policy reflects its respect for the environment as well as its emphasis on ethical business practices. If customers buy too much, they may use too much and put their staff or the environment at risk, not to mention spending more than they should. PortionPac also provides customers with on-site and online training about the proper use of cleaning products and timesaving ways to get the job done. No wonder so many of PortionPac's customers remain loyal buyers year after year.

PortionPac pays just as much attention to the needs of its employees as it does to the needs of its customers and the planet. Machines in the company's Chicago factory have been designed to operate with minimal noise, so that employees can talk or listen to music as they work. Sunshine streams through large skylights, potted plants brighten the factory floor, and thoughtful sculptures follow the themes of plumbing and cleaning. Rather than operate three shifts around the clock, PortionPac arranges family-friendly work schedules that allow managers and employees to balance their personal and professional obligations.

Once every year, on Front to Back Day, top executives and all non production managers and employees go into the factory to work side by side with frontline employees. This experience gives them a better understanding of everyday challenges and conditions on the factory floor, which, in turn, helps senior managers make more informed decisions about production. At the end of the day, the entire workforce joins in a barbecue that reinforces the company's close-knit family feeling. It's not surprising that turnover is exceptionally low. More than half the workforce has been with PortionPac for more than a decade. On the few occasions when positions do open up, employees encourage their brothers, sisters, or adult children to apply. Recognizing the company's commitment to its employees, *Inc.* magazine has named PortionPac to its list of Winning Workplaces.

Marvin Klein, who now serves as chairman, stresses that PortionPac's dedication to business ethics and integrity is actually a matter of common sense. It's also a two-way street: He wants to do business with suppliers and customers that do the right thing. As PortionPac celebrates its 50th anniversary, Klein and the entire management team are planning for a people-friendly, planet-friendly future.[42]

Questions

1. PortionPac is family-owned. How does this private ownership affect the company's ability to follow the socioeconomic model of social responsibility?
2. If you were appointed to conduct a social audit of PortionPac, what type of information would you collect? What questions would you ask? Explain your answer.
3. Do you agree with Marvin Klein's assessment of business ethics as a matter of common sense? Why or why not?

Building Skills for Career Success

1. Social Media Exercise

In 2010, Pepsi decided to develop a new social media–based project, called Pepsi Refresh Project, aimed at Millennials and allowing consumers to post ideas for improving their communities. This replaced the $20 million they spent on Superbowl advertising. The project received more than 57 million votes.

1. Do you think this was an effective strategy for Pepsi? Do you think this resonated with the Millennial generation?
2. Do you think this is a good example of corporate social responsibility (CSR)? Why or why not?
3. How does this CSR example for Pepsi compare with that of its main rival Coca-Cola (see http://www.thecoca-colacompany.com/citizenship/index.html)?

2. Building Team Skills

A firm's code of ethics outlines the kinds of behaviors expected within the organization and serves as a guideline for encouraging ethical behavior in the workplace. It reflects the rights of the firm's workers, shareholders, and consumers.

Assignment

1. Working in a team of four, find a code of ethics for a business firm. Start the search by asking firms in your community for a copy of their codes, by visiting the library, or by searching and downloading information from the Internet.
2. Analyze the code of ethics you have chosen, and answer the following questions:
   a. What does the company's code of ethics say about the rights of its workers, shareholders, consumers, and suppliers? How does the code reflect the company's attitude toward competitors?
   b. How does this code of ethics resemble the information discussed in this chapter? How does it differ?
   c. As an employee of this company, how would you personally interpret the code of ethics? How might the code influence your behavior within the workplace? Give several examples.

3. Researching Different Careers

Business ethics has been at the heart of many discussions over the years and continues to trouble employees and shareholders. Stories about dishonesty and wrongful behavior in the workplace appear on a regular basis in newspapers and on the national news.

Assignment

Prepare a written report on the following:
1. Why can it be so difficult for people to do what is right?
2. What is your personal code of ethics? Prepare a code outlining what you believe is morally right. The document should include guidelines for your personal behavior.
3. How will your code of ethics affect your decisions about:
   a. The types of questions you should ask in a job interview?
   b. Selecting a company in which to work?

Endnotes

1 Sources: Based on information in "Tesla's Electric Man," *The Economist Technology Quarterly*, December 6, 2014, pp. 19-20; Chris Woodyard, "Elon Musk Says Rivals Are Now Using Tesla Patents," *USA Today*, October 15, 2014, www.usatoday.com; Joseph B. White, "Tesla Aims to Leapfrog Rivals," *Wall Street Journal*, October 10, 2014, www.wsj.com; Vivek Wadhwa, "Tesla's Success Is a Victory for Anyone Who Loves the Environment," *Washington Post*, March 4, 2014, www.washingtonpost.com; "Tesla, Citing Environment, to Use North American Materials for Battery Plant," *Bloomberg*, March 29, 2014, www.bloomberg.com; www.teslamotors.com.
2 Press Release, U.S. Department of Justice, October 20, 2014, http://www.justice.gov/opa/pr/president-houston-hospital-and-three-others-convicted-158-million-medicare-fraud-scheme; Dane Schiller, "Riverside Hospital's ex-CEO, 3 Others, Convicted in Medicare Fraud Case," *The Houston Chronicle*, October 20, 2014, http://www.chron.com/news/houston-texas/houston/article/Riverside-Hospital-CEO-3-others-convicted-in-5835279.php.
3 Ashante Infantry, "Canadian Coffee Firm Sues Keurig, Alleges Unfair Competition," *The (Toronto) Star*, October 1, 2014, U.S. Department of Justice website at http://www.thestar.com/business/2014/10/01/canadian_coffee_firm_sues_keurig_alleges_unfair_competition.html.
4 "Jury Convicts Peruvian Man of Defrauding and Extorting Spanish-Speaking Customers through Fraudulent Call Centers," Press Release, U.S. Department of Justice, October 17, 2014, http://www.justice.gov/opa/pr/jury-convicts-peruvian-man-defrauding-and-extorting-spanish-speaking-customers-through.
5 "Gerber Accused of False Claims on Baby Formula," *NBC News*, October 30, 2014, http://www.nbcnews.com/health/kids-health/gerber-accused-false-claims-baby-formula-n237781.
6 "Feds Sue AT&T for Unfair Slowing of Mobile Customer Data," *NBC News*, October 28, 2014, http://nbcnews.com/business/consumer/feds-sue-t-unfair-slowing-mobile-customer-data-n235716.
7 Rob Schulz, "Joyce Ziehli Convicted of Five Counts of Embezzlement from New Glarus Home," *Wisconsin State Journal*, October 8, 2014, http://host.madison.com/news/local/crime_and_courts/joyce-ziehli-convicted-of-five-counts-in-embezzlement-from-new/article_345488e0-00a0-56d1-be3e-63e934b5b19e.html.
8 Jonathan Martin, "Plagiarism Costs Degree for Senator John Walsh," *The New York Times*, October 10, 2014, http://www.nytimes.com/2014/10/11/us/politics/plagiarism-costs-degree-for-senator-john-walsh.html?_r=0
9 Nick Turner, "Staples Shareholders Vote against Executive-Compensation Plan," *Bloomberg News*, June 2, 2014, http://www.bloomberg.com/news/2014-06-03/staples-shareholders-vote-against-executive-compensation-plan.html.
10 U.S. Securities & Exchange Commission, "Houston-Based Advisory Firm and Co-Owners Charged with Failing to Disclose Conflict of Interest," Press Release, September 2, 2014, http://www.sec.gov/News/PressRelease/Detail/PressRelease/1370542808249#.VE6ASfnF8oM.
11 Mark Friedman, "Wal-Mart Spends $230 Million on Mexican Bribery Investigation," *Arkansas Business*, June 10, 2013, http://www.arkansasbusiness.com/article/92905/wal-mart-spends-230-million-on-mexican-bribery-investigation?page=all; David Voreacos and Renee Dudley, "Wal-Mart Says Bribe Probe Cost $439 Million in Two Years," *Bloomberg News*, March 26, 2014, http://www.bloomberg.com/news/2014-03-26/wal-mart-says-bribery-probe-cost-439-million-in-past-two-years.html.
12 Procter & Gamble Company, *Our Worldwide Business Conduct Manual*, p. 23, http://www.pg.com/en_US/downloads/company/governance/Policy_Worldwide_Business_Conduct_Manual.pdf.
13 Lara O'Reilly, "Red Bull Will Pay $10 to Customers Disappointed the Drink Didn't Actually Give Them 'Wings'," *Business Insider*, October 8, 2014, http://www.businessinsider.com/red-bull-settles-false-advertising-lawsuit-for-13-million-2014-10.
14 O. C. Ferrell and Larry Gresham, "A Contingency Framework for Understanding Ethical Decision Making in Marketing," *Journal of Marketing* (Summer 1985), 89.

15 Starbucks, "Business Ethics and Compliance: Standards of Business Conduct," p. 6, http://globalassets.starbucks.com/assets/eecd184d6d2141d58966319744393d1f.pdf (accessed October 30, 2014).

16 Katy Stech, "Trinity Industries Whistleblower Awarded $175 Million in Guardrail Suit," *The Wall Street Journal*, October 20, 2014, http://online.wsj.com/articles/jury-awards-trinity-whistleblower-175-million-in-guardrail-suit-1413838696.

17 Michael Josephson, "Can Corporate Ethics Programs Do Any Good," *Josephson Institute blog*, December 27, 2013, http://josephsoninstitute.org/business/blog/2013/12/can-corporate-ethics-programs-do-any-good/.

18 Target, "Schools," https://corporate.target.com/corporate-responsibility/education/schools (accessed October 31, 2014).

19 Procter & Gamble, Tide's Loads of Hope, http://www.tide.com/en-US/loads-of-hope/index.jspx (accessed November 10, 2014).

20 Lyndsey Taylor, "P. Terry's Burger Stand," *Community Impact (Austin Metro edition)*, September 24, 2014, impactnews.com/austin-metro/northwest-austin/p-terrys-burger-stand/.

21 Barbara Miller, "Hilton Hotels Offer Veterans Hotel 'Points' for Use During Job Searches," The Patriot-News, October 29, 2014, http://www.pennlive.com/midstate/index.ssf/2014/10/hilton_hotels_offer_free_point.html.

22 Jacob Passy, "Florida Jury Awards $23.6B Verdict in Big Tobacco Lawsuit," NBC News, July 19, 2014, http://www.nbcnews.com/news/us-news/florida-jury-awards-23-6b-verdict-big-tobacco-lawsuit-n160241.

23 Claire Suddath, "Coke's New Low-Cal, Low-Sugar Soda is Designed to Quiet Critics," *BusinessWeek*, June 17, 2014, http://www.businessweek.com/articles/2014-06-17/cokes-new-low-cal-low-sugar-soda-is-designed-to-quiet-critics.

24 Alexandra Sifferlin, "Why Michele Obama Went After Junk Food Ads," *Time*, February 25, 2014, http://healthland.time.com/2014/02/25/what-food-marketing-changes-means-for-health/.

25 Sarah Hedgecock, "Lots of Smoke as CVS Withdraws Cigarettes," *Forbes*, September 5, 2014, http://www.forbes.com/sites/sarahhedgecock/2014/09/05/lots-of-smoke-as-cvs-withdraws-cigarettes/.

26 Caitlyn Bohannon, "AT&T's It Can Wait Texting Campaign Adds Hashtag, Sends Unclear Message," *Mobile Marketer*, July 30, 2014, http://www.mobilemarketer.com/cms/news/messaging/18338.html.

27 Brittany Baumann, "Menominee Tribe, Hard Rock Team Up with Colleges for Job Training Program," WDJT, October 31, 2014, http://www.cbs58.com/story/27179838/menominee-tribe-hard-rock-team-up-with-colleges-for-job-training-program.

28 "The 2014 WBI U.S. Workplace Bullying Survey," Workplace Bullying Institute, February 2014, http://workplacebullying.org/multi/pdf/WBI-2014-US-Survey.pdf (accessed October 24, 2014).

29 Lisa Evans, "Why the Office Bully Is Getting Promoted," *Fast Company*, October 23,2014, http://www.fastcompany.com/3037427/why-the-office-bully-is-getting-promoted.

30 Robin Abcarian, "Just as We Thought: Richie Incognito Bullied Jonathan Martin," *Los Angeles Times*, February 14, 2014, http://articles.latimes.com/2014/feb/14/local/la-me-ra-report-miami-dolphins-jonathan-martin-bullied-by-richie-incognito–20140214.

31 "Sexual Harassment," U.S. Equal Employment Opportunity Commission, http://www.eeoc.gov/laws/types/sexual_harassment.cfm (accessed November 4, 2014).

32 Alejandra Cancino, "Years After Sexual Harassment Settlement, Ford Plant Sued Again," *Chicago Tribune*, November 4, 2014, http://www.chicagotribune.com/business/ct-ford-lawsuit-1104-biz-20141103-1-story.html.

33 Evans, "Why the Office Bully Is Getting Promoted."

34 Harrison Jacobs, "Why Grocery Stores Like Trader Joe's Throw Out so Much Perfectly Good Food," Business Insider, October 15, 2014, http://www.businessinsider.com/why-grocery-stores-throw-out-so-much-food-2014-10.

35 "Company Fined $1M on Waste," *Star-Telegram*, November 6, 2014, http://www.star-telegram.com/2014/11/06/6265529/company-fined-1m-on-waste.html.

36 Alison Gene Smith, "Jerome Cheese to Pay $88K Fine to EPA," (Twin Falls) *Times-News*, October 16, 2014, http://magicvalley.com/news/local/jerome-cheese-to-pay-k-fine-to-epa/article_619f9c69-075d-5d46-9dc0-ab50f013ad71.html.

37 "Coca-Cola New England Teaches a Lesson in Recycling," *New Hampshire Business Review*, October 17, 2014, http://www.nhbr.com/October-17-2014/Coca-Cola-New-England-teaches-a-lesson-in-recycling/.

38 Heather Clancy, "IKEA, Swiss Re, Mars, H&M Go All-In on Renewable Energy," *GreenBiz*, September 22, 2014, http://www.greenbiz.com/blog/2014/09/22/ikea-swiss-re-mars-hm-make-100-renewable-energy-pledges.

39 Andrew J. Czaplewski, Erik M. Olson, and Peggy McNulty, Going Green Puts Chipotle in the Black," *Marketing News*, March 2014, https://www.ama.org/publications/MarketingNews/Pages/Going-Green–Puts-Chipotle-in-the-Black.aspx.

40 Missy Baxter, "FTC Clarifies Green Marketing Guidelines," *Credit Union Times*, May 7, 2014, http://www.cutimes.com/2014/05/07/ftc-clarifies-green-marketing-guidelines.

41 "Caesar's Entertainment Exceeds Corporate Citizenship Goals by Taking a Serious Approach to Play," *Entertainment & Travel*, October 11, 2014, p. 76.

42 Based on information in "NIST Visit to Chicago Spotlights Manufacturing Success," *Department of Commerce*, July 20, 2012, http://www.commerce.gov; Hosea Sanders, "Less Is More for Green Business," ABC WLS-TV, January 21, 2011, http://abclocal.go.com; Leigh Buchanan, "A Look Inside the Un-Factory," *Inc.*, June 8, 2010, http://www.inc.com; "Top Workplaces: PortionPac Chemical," *Inc.*, June 1, 2010, http://www.inc.com; Nicole J. Bowman, "PortionPac Chemical Corp.," *ISSA*, March 23, 2010, http://current.issa.com; http://www.portionpaccorp.com (accessed November 9, 2014).

CHAPTER 3

Exploring Global Business

Why Should You Care?

Free trade—are you for or against it? Most economists support free-trade policies, but public support can be lukewarm, and certain groups are adamantly opposed, alleging that "trade harms large segments of U.S. workers," "degrades the environment," and "exploits the poor."

Learning Objectives

Once you complete this chapter, you will be able to:

3-1 Explain the economic basis for international business.

3-2 Explore the methods by which a firm can organize for and enter into international markets.

3-3 Discuss the restrictions nations place on international trade, the objectives of these restrictions, and their results.

3-4 Outline the extent of international business and the economic outlook for trade.

3-5 Discuss international trade agreements and international economic organizations working to foster trade.

3-6 Describe the various sources of export assistance.

3-7 Identify the institutions that help firms and nations finance international business.

Walmart's Global Business Strategy

Walmart has expanded from a single Arkansas store in 1962 to 11,000 outlets worldwide today, plus online stores in 10 countries. The world's largest retailer rings up sales of $485.7 billion in 27 countries. Whether the name over the door or on the web site is Walmart, Bodega Aurrera, Asda, Yihaodian, Seiyu, or Superama, Walmart's global business strategy is to offer merchandise that local customers need at low prices they can afford.

Although Walmart has enjoyed considerable success worldwide, it has also suffered setbacks. The company entered and then left both Germany and South Korea after failing to achieve its financial goals in either market. It became a minority investor in the Japanese supermarket chain Seiyu in 2002 and acquired it as a wholly-owned subsidiary in 2008. Coping with Japan's struggling economy, however, has led Walmart to close as many as 30 Seiyu stores in recent years.

In 1996, Walmart opened its first stores in China, eyeing the ever-higher buying power of local consumers. Since then, the retailer has experienced both ups and downs in China. It recently announced the closing of 29 underperforming stores there, even as it opens dozens of new, smaller stores in more promising urban areas. The retailer is also spending heavily to expand e-commerce operations in China, targeting the growing number of customers who shop by smart phone, tablet, or computer.

To enter India, another market where household incomes have been rising, Walmart formed a joint venture with a local corporation and opened cash-and-carry wholesale outlets starting in 2009. At the time, India protected its small merchants by strictly limiting foreign ownership of wholesale and retail businesses. After some of those restrictions were eased in 2012, the joint venture was dissolved, allowing the local partner to concentrate on its own retail expansion. For its part, Walmart plans to keep adding new cash-and-carry wholesale outlets until India simplifies the rules for foreign direct investment in retailing.[1]

Did You Know?

Founded in 1962, Walmart now rings up $485.7 billion in annual sales and employs 2.2 million people worldwide.

Walmart is just one of a growing number of companies, large and small, that are doing business with firms in other countries. Some companies, such as General Electric, sell to firms in other countries; others, such as Pier 1 Imports, buy goods around the world to import into the United States. Combustion Associates of Corona, California, is a small business founded by husband and wife immigrants of Bangladesh. The company makes and exports large power generators to more than forty developing countries. Whether they buy or sell products across national borders, these companies are all contributing to the volume of international trade that is fueling the global economy.

Theoretically, international trade is every bit as logical and worthwhile as interstate trade between, say, California and Washington. Yet, nations tend to restrict the import of certain goods for a variety of reasons. For example, in the early 2000s, the United States restricted the import of Mexican fresh tomatoes because they were undercutting price levels of domestic fresh tomatoes.

Despite such restrictions, international trade has increased almost steadily since World War II. Many of the industrialized nations have signed trade agreements intended to eliminate problems in international business and to help less-developed nations participate in world trade. Individual firms around the world have seized the opportunity to compete in foreign markets by exporting products and increasing foreign production, as well as by other means.

Signing the Trade Act of 2002, President George W. Bush remarked, "Trade is an important source of good jobs for our workers and a source of higher growth for our economy. Free trade is also a proven strategy for building global prosperity and adding to the momentum of political freedom. Trade is an engine of economic growth. In our lifetime, trade has helped lift millions of people and whole nations out of poverty and put them on the path of prosperity."[2] In his national best seller, *The World Is Flat*, Thomas L. Friedman states, "The flattening of the world has presented us with new opportunities, new challenges, new partners but, also, alas new dangers, particularly as Americans it is imperative that we be the best global citizens that we can be—because in a flat world, if you don't visit a bad neighborhood, it might visit you."

We describe international trade in this chapter in terms of modern specialization, whereby each country trades the surplus goods and services it produces most efficiently for products in short supply. We explore several methods of entering international markets and explain the restrictions nations place on products and services from other countries and present some of the possible advantages and disadvantages of these restrictions. We describe the extent of international trade and identify the organizations working to foster it. We then outline the various sources of export assistance available from the federal government. Finally, we identify some of the institutions that provide the complex financing necessary for modern international trade.

3-1 THE BASIS FOR INTERNATIONAL BUSINESS

Learning Objective

3-1 Explain the economic basis for international business.

International business encompasses all business activities that involve exchanges across national boundaries. Thus, a firm is engaged in international business when it buys some portion of its input from, or sells some portion of its output to, an organization located in a foreign country. (A small retail store may sell goods produced in some other country. However, because it purchases these goods from American distributors, it is not engaged in international trade.)

3-1a Absolute and Comparative Advantage

Some countries are better equipped than others to produce particular goods or services. The reason may be a country's natural resources, its labor supply, or even

International business all business activities that involve exchanges across national boundaries

A U.S. Absolute Advantage. The United States has long specialized in the production of wheat. Because of its natural resource, the United States and some other countries enjoy an absolute advantage—their ability to produce wheat more efficiently than countries in other parts of the world.

LIVESLOW/ISTOCK/THINKSTOCK

customs or a historical accident. Such a country would be best off if it could specialize in the production of such products so that it can produce them most efficiently. The country could use what it needed of these products and then trade the surplus for products it could not produce efficiently on its own.

Saudi Arabia thus has specialized in the production of crude oil and petroleum products; South Africa, in diamonds; and Australia, in wool. Each of these countries is said to have an absolute advantage with regard to a particular product. An **absolute advantage** is the ability to produce a specific product more efficiently than any other nation.

One country may have an absolute advantage with regard to several products, whereas another country may have no absolute advantage at all. Yet it is still worthwhile for these two countries to specialize and trade with each other. To see why this is so, imagine that you are the president of a successful manufacturing firm and that you can accurately type 90 words per minute. Your assistant can type 80 words per minute but would run the business poorly. Thus, you have an absolute advantage over your assistant in both typing and managing. However, you cannot afford to type your own letters because your time is better spent in managing the business. That is, you have a **comparative advantage** in managing. A comparative advantage is the ability to produce a specific product more efficiently than any other product.

Your assistant, on the other hand, has a comparative advantage in typing because he or she can do that better than managing the business. Thus, you spend your time managing, and you leave the typing to your assistant. Overall, the business is run as efficiently as possible because you are each working in accordance with your own comparative advantage.

The same is true for nations. Goods and services are produced more efficiently when each country specializes in the products for which it has a comparative advantage. Moreover, by definition, every country has a comparative advantage in some product. The United States has many comparative advantages—in research and development, high-technology industries, and identifying new markets, for instance.

3-1b Exporting and Importing

Suppose that the United States specializes in producing corn. It then will produce a surplus of corn, but perhaps it will have a shortage of wine. France, on the other hand, specializes in producing wine but experiences a shortage of corn. To satisfy both needs—for corn and for wine—the two countries should trade with each other. The United States should export corn and import wine. France should export wine and import corn.

Exporting is selling and shipping raw materials or products to other nations. The Boeing Company, for example, exports its airplanes to a number of countries for use by their airlines. Figure 3-1 shows the top ten merchandise-exporting states in the United States.

Importing is purchasing raw materials or products in other nations and bringing them into one's own country. Thus, buyers for Macy's department stores may purchase rugs in India or raincoats in England and have them shipped back to the United States for resale.

Importing and exporting are the principal activities in international trade. They give rise to an important concept called the *balance of trade*. A nation's **balance of trade** is the total value of its exports minus the total value of its imports over some period of time. If a country imports more than it exports, its balance of trade is negative and is said to be *unfavorable*. (A negative balance of trade is unfavorable because the country must export money to pay for its excess imports.)

absolute advantage the ability to produce a specific product more efficiently than any other nation

comparative advantage the ability to produce a specific product more efficiently than any other product

exporting selling and shipping raw materials or products to other nations

importing purchasing raw materials or products in other nations and bringing them into one's own country

balance of trade the total value of a nation's exports minus the total value of its imports over some period of time

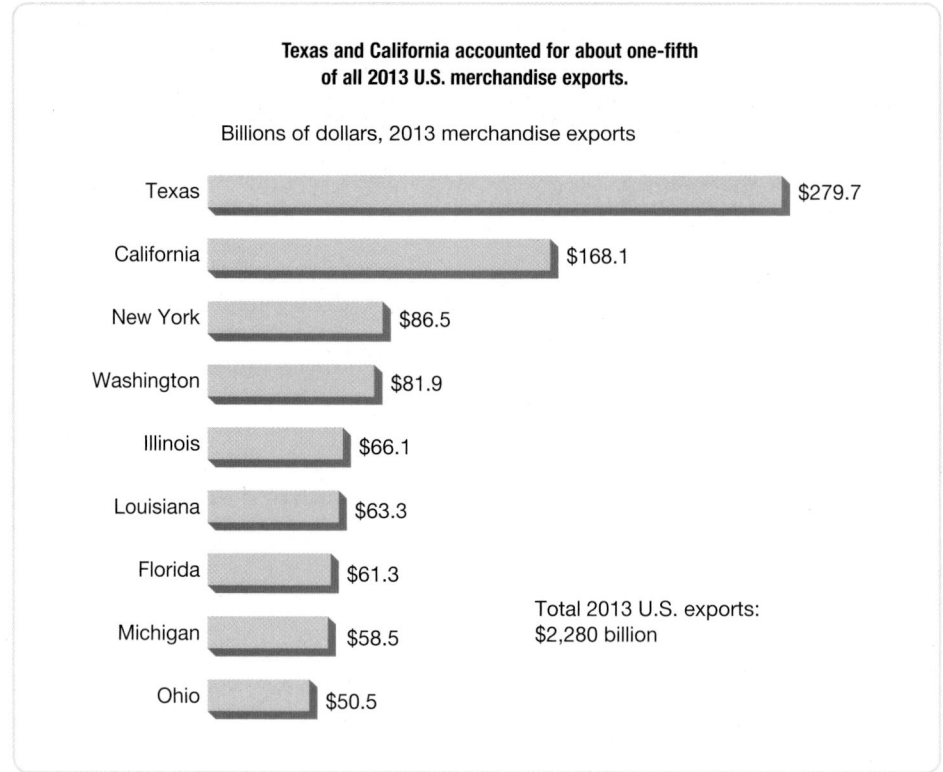

FIGURE 3-1 The Top Ten Merchandise-Exporting States

Texas and California accounted for about one-fifth
of all 2013 U.S. merchandise exports.

Billions of dollars, 2013 merchandise exports

Texas	$279.7
California	$168.1
New York	$86.5
Washington	$81.9
Illinois	$66.1
Louisiana	$63.3
Florida	$61.3
Michigan	$58.5
Ohio	$50.5

Total 2013 U.S. exports:
$2,280 billion

Source: International Trade Administration, www.trade.gov/mas/ian/statereports/ (accessed January 1, 2015).

In 2013, the United States imported $2,757 billion worth of goods and services and exported $2,280 billion worth. It thus had a trade deficit of $477 billion. A **trade deficit** is a negative balance of trade (see Figure 3-2). However, the United States has consistently enjoyed a large and rapidly growing surplus in services. For example, in 2013, the United States imported $462.1 billion worth of services and exported $687.4 billion worth, thus creating a favorable balance of $225.3 billion.[3]

Question: *Are trade deficits bad?*

Answer: In testimony before the Senate Finance Committee, Daniel T. Griswold, associate director of the Center for Trade Policy at the Cato Institute, remarked, "The trade deficit is not a sign of economic distress, but of rising domestic demand and investment. Imposing new trade barriers will only make Americans worse off while leaving the trade deficit virtually unchanged."

On the other hand, when a country exports more than it imports, it is said to have a favorable balance of trade. This has consistently been the case for Japan over the last two decades or so.

A nation's **balance of payments** is the total flow of money into a country minus the total flow of money out of that country over some period of time. Balance of payments, therefore, is a much broader concept than balance of trade. It includes imports and exports, of course. However, it also includes investments, money spent by foreign tourists, payments by foreign governments, aid to foreign governments, and all other receipts and payments.

A continual deficit in a nation's balance of payments (a negative balance) can cause other nations to lose confidence in that nation's economy. Alternatively, a continual surplus may indicate that the country encourages exports but limits imports by imposing trade restrictions.

trade deficit a negative balance of trade

balance of payments the total flow of money into a country minus the total flow of money out of that country over some period of time

Concept Check

✓ Why do firms engage in international trade?

✓ What is the difference between an absolute advantage and a comparative advantage?

✓ What is the difference between balance of trade and balance of payments?

FIGURE 3-2 U.S. International Trade in Goods and Services

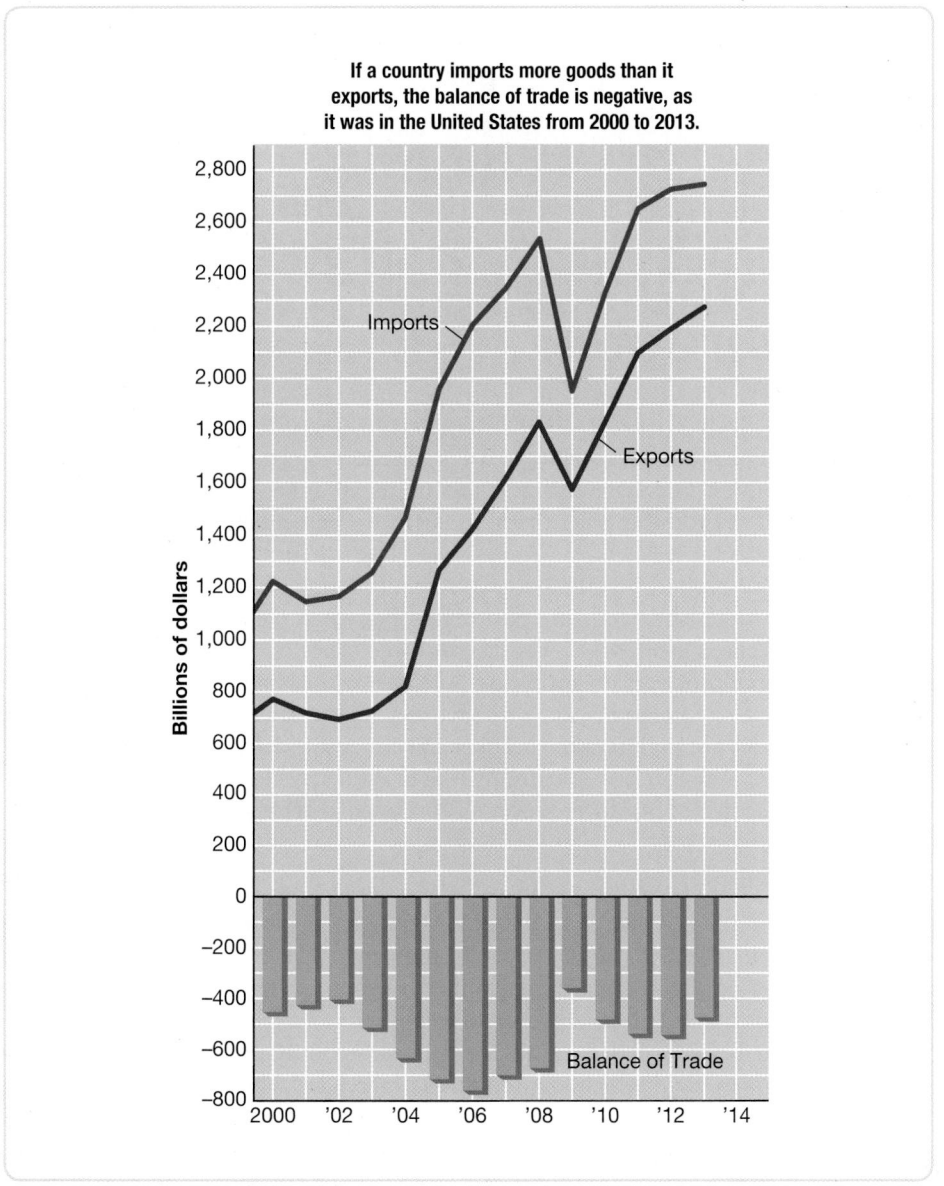

If a country imports more goods than it exports, the balance of trade is negative, as it was in the United States from 2000 to 2013.

Source: U.S. Department of Commerce, International Trade Administration, www.trade.gov/mas/ian/build/groups/public/tg_ian/documents (accessed January 2, 2015).

3-2 METHODS OF ENTERING INTERNATIONAL BUSINESS

A firm that has decided to enter international markets can do so in several ways. We will discuss several different methods. These different approaches require varying degrees of involvement in international business. Typically, a firm begins its international operations at the simplest level. Then, depending on its goals, it may progress to higher levels of involvement.

3-2a Licensing

Licensing is a contractual agreement in which one firm permits another to produce and market its product and use its brand name in return for a royalty or other

Learning Objective

3-2 Explore the methods by which a firm can organize for and enter into international markets.

licensing a contractual agreement in which one firm permits another to produce and market its product and use its brand name in return for a royalty or other compensation

KHENG GUAN TOH/FOTOLIA

compensation. For example, Yoplait yogurt is a French yogurt licensed for production in the United States. The Yoplait brand maintains an appealing French image, and in return, the U.S. producer pays the French firm a percentage of its income from sales of the product.

Licensing is especially advantageous for small manufacturers wanting to launch a well-known domestic brand internationally. For example, all Spalding sporting products are licensed worldwide. The licensor, the Questor Corporation, owns the Spalding name but produces no goods itself. Licensing thus provides a simple method for expanding into a foreign market with virtually no investment. On the other hand, if the licensee does not maintain the licensor's product standards, the product's image may be damaged. Another possible disadvantage is that a licensing arrangement may not provide the original producer with any foreign marketing experience.

3-2b Exporting

A firm also may manufacture its products in its home country and export them for sale in foreign markets. As with licensing, exporting can be a relatively low-risk method of entering foreign markets. Unlike licensing, however, it is not a simple method; it opens up several levels of involvement to the exporting firm.

At the most basic level, the exporting firm may sell its products outright to an *export–import merchant*, which is essentially a merchant wholesaler. The merchant assumes all the risks of product ownership, distribution, and sale. It may even purchase the goods in the producer's home country and assume responsibility for exporting the goods. An important and practical issue for domestic firms dealing with foreign customers is securing payment. This is a two-sided issue that reflects the mutual concern rightly felt by both parties to the trade deal: The exporter would like to be paid before shipping the merchandise, whereas the importer obviously would prefer to know that it has received the shipment before releasing any funds. Neither side wants to take the risk of fulfilling its part of the deal only to discover later that the other side has not. The result would lead to legal costs and complex, lengthy dealings that would waste everyone's resources. This mutual level of mistrust, in fact, makes good business sense and has been around since the beginning of trade centuries ago. The solution then was the same as it still is today—for both parties to use a mutually trusted go-between who can ensure that the payment is held until the merchandise is in fact delivered according to the terms of the trade contract. The go-between representatives employed by the importer and exporter are still, as they were in the past, the local domestic banks involved in international business.

EXPORTING TO INTERNATIONAL MARKETS American companies may manufacture their products in the United States and export them for sale in foreign markets. Exporting can be a relatively low-risk method of entering foreign markets.

Here is a simplified version of how it works. After signing contracts detailing the merchandise sold and terms for its delivery, an importer will ask its local bank to issue a **letter of credit** for the amount of money needed to pay for the merchandise. The letter of credit is issued "in favor of the exporter," meaning that the funds are tied specifically to the trade contract involved. The importer's bank forwards the letter of credit to the exporter's bank, which also normally deals in international transactions. The exporter's bank then notifies the exporter that a letter of credit has been received in its name, and the exporter can go ahead with the shipment. The carrier transporting the merchandise provides the exporter with evidence of the shipment in a document called a **bill of lading**. The exporter signs over title to the merchandise (now in transit) to its bank by delivering signed copies of the bill of lading and the letter of credit.

In exchange, the exporter issues a **draft** from the bank, which orders the importer's bank to pay for the merchandise. The draft, bill of lading, and letter of credit are sent from the exporter's bank to the importer's bank. Acceptance by the importer's bank leads to return of the draft and its sale by the exporter to its bank, meaning that the exporter receives cash and the bank assumes the risk of collecting the funds from the foreign bank. The importer is obliged to pay its bank on delivery of the merchandise, and the deal is complete.

In most cases, the letter of credit is part of a lending arrangement between the importer and its bank. Of course, both banks earn fees for issuing letters of credit and drafts and for handling the import–export services for their clients. Furthermore, the process incorporates the fact that both importer and exporter will have different local currencies and might even negotiate their trade in a third currency. The banks look after all the necessary exchanges. For example, the vast majority of international business is negotiated in U.S. dollars, even though the

letter of credit issued by a bank on request of an importer stating that the bank will pay an amount of money to a stated beneficiary

bill of lading document issued by a transport carrier to an exporter to prove that merchandise has been shipped

draft issued by the exporter's bank, ordering the importer's bank to pay for the merchandise, thus guaranteeing payment once accepted by the importer's bank

Entrepreneurial Success

Advice from Global Entrepreneurs

Entrepreneurial businesses are increasingly looking for growth by expanding into global markets. Here's what seasoned entrepreneurs have learned from their experiences with international business:

- *Get local help.* Asking for suggestions and ideas from consultants, suppliers, or even potential customers in the local area is a good way to avoid potential pitfalls that could hurt a global business. A Boston-based entrepreneur expanding abroad says that talking with customers "allowed us to get a grasp of the local customs" in that area.

- *Innovate, innovate, innovate.* Global markets are ripe with opportunities for entrepreneurs who can provide innovative goods and services to meet the needs of local consumers or businesses. A small business expert sums up international business opportunities this way: "The options are practically limitless."

- *Remember time differences.* As basic as this sounds, it means that entrepreneurs must be available to their local employees or distributors during working hours in the market(s) where they do business. One entrepreneur recalls the challenge of working during the U.S. business day, and then putting in even more hours at night to deal with overseas business issues.

- *Be prepared for the unexpected.* "Nothing ever works out as smoothly as you think, and timelines always get stretched out further," observes a technology entrepreneur. Global entrepreneurs need more than patience and a positive attitude—they should be ready to search for creative, out-of-the-ordinary solutions when problems pop up without warning.

Sources: Based on information in "How to Expand Overseas (and Not Get Overwhelmed), *Inc.*, March 28, 2014, www.inc.com; Tanya Edwards, "Steal This Start-Up Advice from Entrepreneurs Making a Difference," *Glamour*, March 24, 2014, www.glamour.com; Dan Schawbel, "Why You Should Think Globally as an Entrepreneur," *Forbes.com*, October 29, 2013, www.forbes.com.

Personal App

The cars you and your friends drive or admire may have parts made in far-flung parts of the world, one clue to the multinational scale of companies like Ford, Toyota, Volkswagen, and Hyundai. Often multinational automakers open assembly plants close to the markets where they sell—which means a car bearing an international brand may actually be made in North America, not in Japan, Germany or South Korea. Because of their multinational perspective, these automakers can apply what they learn in each region to improve their business operations all over the world.

trade may be between countries other than the United States. Thus, although the importer may end up paying for the merchandise in its local currency and the exporter may receive payment in another local currency, the banks involved will exchange all necessary foreign funds in order to allow the deal to take place.

Alternatively, the exporting firm may ship its products to an *export–import agent*, which arranges the sale of the products to foreign intermediaries for a commission or fee. The agent is an independent firm—like other agents—that sells and may perform other marketing functions for the exporter. The exporter, however, retains title to the products during shipment and until they are sold.

An exporting firm also may establish its own *sales offices*, or *branches*, in foreign countries. These installations are international extensions of the firm's distribution system. They represent a deeper involvement in international business than the other exporting techniques we have discussed—and thus they carry a greater risk. The exporting firm maintains control over sales, and it gains both experience in and knowledge of foreign markets. Eventually, the firm also may develop its own sales force to operate in conjunction with foreign sales offices.

3-2c Joint Ventures

A *joint venture* is a partnership formed to achieve a specific goal or to operate for a specific period of time. A joint venture with an established firm in a foreign country provides immediate market knowledge and access, reduced risk, and control over product attributes. However, joint-venture agreements established across national borders can become extremely complex. As a result, joint-venture agreements generally require a very high level of commitment from all the parties involved.

A joint venture may be used to produce and market an existing product in a foreign nation or to develop an entirely new product. Recently, for example, Archer Daniels Midland Company (ADM), one of the world's leading food processors, entered into a joint venture with Gruma SA, Mexico's largest corn flour and tortilla company. Besides a 22 percent stake in Gruma, ADM also received stakes in other joint ventures operated by Gruma. One of them will combine both companies' U.S. corn flour operations, which account for about 25 percent of the U.S. market. ADM also has a 40 percent stake in a Mexican wheat flour mill. ADM's joint venture increased its participation in the growing Mexican economy, where ADM already produces corn syrup, fructose, starch, and wheat flour.

Joint Venture. Large pipelines can involve multiple countries. They can be organized based on the use of joint ventures.

3-2d Totally Owned Facilities

At a still deeper level of involvement in international business, a firm may develop *totally owned facilities*, that is, its own production and marketing facilities in one or more foreign nations. This *direct investment* provides complete control over operations, but it carries a greater risk than the joint venture. The firm is really establishing a subsidiary in a foreign country. Most firms do so only after they have acquired some knowledge of the host country's markets.

Direct investment may take either of two forms. In the first, the firm builds or purchases manufacturing and other facilities in the foreign country. It uses these facilities to produce its own established products and to market them in that country and perhaps in neighboring countries. Firms such as General Motors, Union Carbide, and Colgate-Palmolive are multinational companies with worldwide manufacturing facilities. Colgate-Palmolive factories are becoming *Eurofactories*, supplying neighboring countries as well as their own local markets.

A second form of direct investment in international business is the purchase of an existing firm in a foreign country under an arrangement that allows it to operate independently of the parent company. When Sony Corporation (a Japanese firm) decided to enter the motion picture business in the United States, it chose to purchase Columbia Pictures Entertainment, Inc., rather than start a new motion picture studio from scratch.

3-2e Strategic Alliances

A **strategic alliance**, the newest form of international business structure, is a partnership formed to create competitive advantage on a worldwide basis. Strategic alliances are very similar to joint ventures. The number of strategic alliances is growing at an estimated rate of about 20 percent per year. In fact, in the automobile and computer industries, strategic alliances are becoming the predominant means of competing. International competition is so fierce and the costs of competing on a global basis are so high that few firms have all the resources needed to do it alone. Thus, individual firms that lack the internal resources essential for international success may seek to collaborate with other companies.

An example of such an alliance is the New United Motor Manufacturing, Inc. (NUMMI), formed by Toyota and General Motors to make automobiles of both firms. This enterprise united the quality engineering of Japanese cars with the marketing expertise and market access of General Motors.

3-2f Trading Companies

A **trading company** provides a link between buyers and sellers in different countries. A trading company, as its name implies, is not involved in manufacturing or owning assets related to manufacturing. It buys products in one country at the lowest price consistent with quality and sells to buyers in another country. An important function of trading companies is taking title to products and performing all the activities necessary to move the products from the domestic country to a foreign country. For example, large grain-trading companies operating out of home offices both in the United States and overseas control a major portion of the world's trade in basic food commodities. These trading companies sell homogeneous agricultural commodities that can be stored and moved rapidly in response to market conditions.

> **strategic alliance** a partnership formed to create competitive advantage on a worldwide basis

> **trading company** provides a link between buyers and sellers in different countries

3-2g Countertrade

In the early 1990s, many developing nations had major restrictions on converting domestic currency into foreign currency. Therefore, exporters had to resort to barter

TABLE 3-1 The Ten Largest Foreign and U.S. Multinational Corporations

2014 Rank	Company	Business	Country	Revenue ($ millions)
1	Walmart Stores	General Merchandise	United States	476,294
2	Royal Dutch Shell	Energy	Netherlands	459,599
3	Sinopec	Energy	China	457,201
4	China National Petroleum	Energy	China	432,007
5	ExxonMobil	Energy	United States	407,666
6	BP	Energy	United Kingdom	396,217
7	State Grid	Power Grids	China	333,386
8	Volkswagen	Automobiles	Germany	261,539
9	Toyota	Automobiles	Japan	256,454
10	Glencore	Commodities	Switzerland	232,694

Source: http://fortune.com/global500/ (accessed January 1, 2015).

countertrade an international barter transaction

multinational enterprise a firm that operates on a worldwide scale without ties to any specific nation or region

Concept Check

✓ Two methods of engaging in international business may be categorized as either direct or indirect. How would you classify each of the methods described in this chapter? Why?

✓ What is a letter of credit? A bill of lading? A draft?

✓ In what ways is a multinational enterprise different from a large corporation that does business in several countries?

✓ What are the steps in entering international markets?

agreements with importers. **Countertrade** is essentially an international barter transaction in which goods and services are exchanged for different goods and services. Examples include Saudi Arabia's purchase of ten 747 jets from Boeing with payment in crude oil and Philip Morris's sale of cigarettes to Russia in return for chemicals used to make fertilizers.

3-2h Multinational Firms

A **multinational enterprise** is a firm that operates on a worldwide scale without ties to any specific nation or region. The multinational firm represents the highest level of involvement in international business. It is equally "at home" in most countries of the world. In fact, as far as the operations of the multinational enterprise are concerned, national boundaries exist only on maps. It is, however, organized under the laws of its home country.

Table 3-1 shows the ten largest foreign and U.S. public multinational companies; the ranking is based on a composite score reflecting each company's best three out of four rankings for sales, profits, assets, and market value. Table 3-2 describes steps in entering international markets.

According to the former chairman of the board of Dow Chemical Company, a multinational firm of U.S. origin, "The emergence of a world economy and of the multinational corporation has been accomplished hand in hand." He sees multinational enterprises moving toward what he calls the "anational company," a firm that has no nationality but belongs to all countries. In recognition of this movement, there already have been international conferences devoted to the question of how such enterprises would be controlled.

3-3 RESTRICTIONS TO INTERNATIONAL BUSINESS

Learning Objective

3-3 Discuss the restrictions nations place on international trade, the objectives of these restrictions, and their results.

Specialization and international trade can result in the efficient production of want-satisfying goods and services on a worldwide basis. As we have noted, international business generally is increasing. Yet the nations of the world continue to erect barriers to free trade. They do so for reasons ranging from internal political and economic pressures to simple mistrust of other nations. We examine first the types of restrictions that are applied and then the arguments for and against trade restrictions.

TABLE 3-2 Steps in Entering International Markets

Step	Activity	Marketing Tasks
1	Identify exportable products.	Identify key selling features. Identify needs that they satisfy. Identify the selling constraints that are imposed.
2	Identify key foreign markets for the products.	Determine who the customers are. Pinpoint what and when they will buy. Do market research. Establish priority, or "target," countries.
3	Analyze how to sell in each priority market (methods will be affected by product characteristics and unique features of country/market).	Locate available government and private-sector resources. Determine service and backup sales requirements.
4	Set export prices and payment terms, methods, and techniques.	Establish methods of export pricing. Establish sales terms, quotations, invoices, and conditions of sale. Determine methods of international payments, secured and unsecured.
5	Estimate resource requirements and returns.	Estimate financial requirements. Estimate human resources requirements (full- or part-time export department or operation). Estimate plant production capacity. Determine necessary product adaptations.
6	Establish overseas distribution network.	Determine distribution agreement and other key marketing decisions (price, repair policies, returns, territory, performance, and termination). Know your customer (use U.S. Department of Commerce international marketing services).
7	Determine shipping, traffic, and documentation procedures and requirements.	Determine methods of shipment (air or ocean freight, truck, rail). Finalize containerization. Obtain validated export license. Follow export-administration documentation procedures.
8	Promote, sell, and be paid.	Use international media, communications, advertising, trade shows, and exhibitions. Determine the need for overseas travel (when, where, and how often?). Initiate customer follow-up procedures.
9	Continuously analyze current marketing, economic, and political situations.	Recognize changing factors influencing marketing strategies. Constantly re-evaluate.

Source: U.S. Department of Commerce, International Trade Administration, Washington, DC.

3-3a Types of Trade Restrictions

Nations generally are eager to export their products. They want to provide markets for their industries and to develop a favorable balance of trade. Hence, most trade restrictions are applied to imports from other nations.

TARIFFS Perhaps the most commonly applied trade restriction is the customs (or import) duty. An **import duty** (also called a **tariff**) is a tax levied on a particular foreign product entering a country. For example, the United States imposes a 2.2 percent import duty on fresh Chilean tomatoes, an 8.7 percent duty if tomatoes are dried and packaged, and nearly 12 percent if tomatoes are made into ketchup or salsa. The two types of tariffs are revenue tariffs and protective tariffs; both have the effect of raising the price of the product in the importing nations, but for different reasons. *Revenue tariffs* are imposed solely to generate income for the government. For example, the United States imposes a duty on Scotch whiskey solely for revenue purposes. *Protective tariffs*, on the other hand, are imposed to protect a domestic industry from competition by keeping the price of competing imports level with or higher than the price of

import duty (tariff) a tax levied on a particular foreign product entering a country

similar domestic products. Because fewer units of the product will be sold at the increased price, fewer units will be imported. The French and Japanese agricultural sectors would both shrink drastically if their nations abolished the protective tariffs that keep the price of imported farm products high. Today, U.S. tariffs are the lowest in history, with average tariff rates on all imports under 3 percent.

Some countries rationalize their protectionist policies as a way of offsetting an international trade practice called *dumping*. **Dumping** is the exportation of large quantities of a product at a price lower than that of the same product in the home market.

Thus, dumping drives down the price of the domestic item. Recently, for example, the Pencil Makers Association, which represents eight U.S. pencil manufacturers, charged that low-priced pencils from Thailand and the People's Republic of China were being sold in the United States at less than fair value prices. Unable to compete with these inexpensive imports, several domestic manufacturers had to shut down. To protect themselves, domestic manufacturers can obtain an antidumping duty through the government to offset the advantage of the foreign product. Recently, for example, the U.S. Department of Commerce imposed antidumping duties of up to 99 percent on a variety of steel products imported from China, following allegations by U.S. Steel Corp. and other producers that the products were being dumped at unfair prices.

NONTARIFF BARRIERS A **nontariff barrier** is a nontax measure imposed by a government to favor domestic over foreign suppliers. Nontariff barriers create obstacles to the marketing of foreign goods in a country and increase costs for exporters. The following are a few examples of government-imposed nontariff barriers:

- An **import quota** is a limit on the amount of a particular good that may be imported into a country during a given period of time. The limit may be set in terms of either quantity (so many pounds of beef) or value (so many dollars' worth of shoes). Quotas also may be set on individual products imported from specific countries. Once an import quota has been reached, imports are halted until the specified time has elapsed.

- An **embargo** is a complete halt to trading with a particular nation or of a particular product. The embargo is used most often as a political weapon. At present, the United States has import embargoes against Iran and North Korea—both as a result of extremely poor political relations.

- A **foreign-exchange control** is a restriction on the amount of a particular foreign currency that can be purchased or sold. By limiting the amount of foreign currency importers can obtain, a government limits the amount of goods importers can purchase with that currency. This has the effect of limiting imports from the country whose foreign exchange is being controlled.

- A nation can increase or decrease the value of its money relative to the currency of other nations. **Currency devaluation** is the reduction of the value of a nation's currency relative to the currencies of other countries.

Devaluation increases the cost of foreign goods, whereas it decreases the cost of domestic goods to foreign firms. For example, suppose that the British pound is worth $2. In this case, an American-made $2,000 computer can be purchased for £1,000. However, if the United Kingdom devalues the pound so that it is worth only $1, that same computer will cost £2,000. The increased cost, in pounds, will reduce the import of American computers—and all foreign goods—into England.

On the other hand, before devaluation, a £500 set of English bone china will cost an American $1,000. After the devaluation, the set of china will cost only $500. The decreased cost will make the china—and all English goods—much more

dumping exportation of large quantities of a product at a price lower than that of the same product in the home market

nontariff barrier a nontax measure imposed by a government to favor domestic over foreign suppliers

import quota a limit on the amount of a particular good that may be imported into a country during a given period of time

embargo a complete halt to trading with a particular nation or in a particular product

foreign-exchange control a restriction on the amount of a particular foreign currency that can be purchased or sold

currency devaluation the reduction of the value of a nation's currency relative to the currencies of other countries

Restricting trade through tariffs. Due to the recent increase in inexpensive solar products from China and Taiwan, many American manufactures were forced out of business. To help fix this issue, the United States placed a tariff on Chinese and Taiwanese produced solar panels. Some industry experts believe that the increased prices caused by the tariffs could curb the adoption of solar energy in the United States.

JEFF_HU/ISTOCK/THINKSTOCK

attractive to U.S. purchasers. Bureaucratic red tape is more subtle than the other forms of nontariff barriers. Yet it can be the most frustrating trade barrier of all. A few examples are the unnecessarily restrictive application of standards and complex requirements related to product testing, labeling, and certification.

CULTURAL BARRIERS Another type of nontariff barrier is related to cultural attitudes. Cultural barriers can impede acceptance of products in foreign countries. For example, illustrations of feet are regarded as despicable in Thailand. Even so simple a thing as the color of a product or its package can present a problem. In Japan, black and white are the colors of mourning, so they should not be used in packaging. In Brazil, purple is the color of death. And in Egypt, green is never used on a package because it is the national color. When customers are unfamiliar with particular products from another country, their general perceptions of the country itself affect their attitude toward the product and help to determine whether they will buy it. Because Mexican cars have not been viewed by the world as being quality products, Volkswagen, for example, may not want to advertise that some of its models sold in the United States are made in Mexico. Many retailers on the Internet have yet to come to grips with the task of designing an online shopping site that is attractive and functional for all global customers.

Gifts to authorities—sometimes quite large ones—may be standard business procedure in some countries. In others, including the United States, they are called bribes or payoffs and are strictly illegal.

3-3b Reasons for Trade Restrictions

Various reasons are given for trade restrictions either on the import of specific products or on trade with particular countries. We have noted that political considerations usually are involved in trade embargoes. Other frequently cited reasons for restricting trade include the following:

- *To equalize a nation's balance of payments.* This may be considered necessary to restore confidence in the country's monetary system and in its ability to repay its debts.

- *To protect new or weak industries.* A new, or infant, industry may not be strong enough to withstand foreign competition. Temporary trade restrictions may be used to give it a chance to grow and become self-sufficient. The problem is that once an industry is protected from foreign competition, it may refuse to grow, and "temporary" trade restrictions will become permanent. For example, a recent report by the Government Accountability Office (GAO), the congressional investigative agency, has accused the federal government of routinely imposing quotas on foreign textiles without "demonstrating the threat of serious damage" to U.S. industry. The GAO said that the Committee for the Implementation of Textile Agreements sometimes applies quotas even though it cannot prove the textile industry's claims that American companies have been hurt or jobs have been eliminated.

- *To protect national security.* Restrictions in this category generally apply to technological products that must be kept out of the hands of potential enemies. For example, strategic and defense-related goods cannot be exported to unfriendly nations.

- *To protect the health of citizens.* Products may be embargoed because they are dangerous or unhealthy (e.g., farm products contaminated with insecticides).

- *To retaliate for another nation's trade restrictions.* A country whose exports are taxed by another country may respond by imposing tariffs on imports from that country.

- *To protect domestic jobs.* By restricting imports, a nation can protect jobs in domestic industries. However, protecting these jobs can be expensive. For example, protecting 9,000 jobs in the U.S. carbon-steel industry costs $6.8 billion, or $750,000 per job. In addition, Gary Hufbauer and Ben Goodrich, economists at the Institute for International Economics, estimate that the tariffs could temporarily save 3,500 jobs in the steel industry, but at an annual cost to steel users of $2 billion, or $584,000 per job saved. Yet recently the United States imposed tariffs of up to 616 percent on steel pipes imported from China, South Korea, and Mexico. Similarly, it is estimated that we spent more than $100,000 for every job saved in the apparel manufacturing industry—jobs that seldom paid more than $35,000 a year.

3-3c Reasons Against Trade Restrictions

Trade restrictions have immediate and long-term economic consequences—both within the restricting nation and in world trade patterns. These include the following:

- *Higher prices for consumers.* Higher prices may result from the imposition of tariffs or the elimination of foreign competition, as described earlier. For example, imposing quota restrictions and import protections adds $25 billion annually to U.S. consumers' apparel costs by directly increasing costs for imported apparel.

- *Restriction of consumers' choices.* Again, this is a direct result of the elimination of some foreign products from the marketplace and of the artificially high prices that importers must charge for products that are still imported.

- *Misallocation of international resources.* The protection of weak industries results in the inefficient use of limited resources. The economies of both the restricting nation and other nations eventually suffer because of this waste.

- *Loss of jobs.* The restriction of imports by one nation must lead to cutbacks— and the loss of jobs—in the export-oriented industries of other nations. Furthermore, trade protection has a significant effect on the composition of employment. U.S. trade restrictions—whether on textiles, apparel, steel, or automobiles—benefit only a few industries while harming many others. The gains in employment accrue to the protected industries and their primary suppliers, and the losses are spread across all other industries. A few states gain employment, but many other states lose employment.

Concept Check

✓ List and briefly describe the principal restrictions that may be applied to a nation's imports.

✓ What reasons are generally given for imposing trade restrictions?

✓ What are the general effects of import restrictions on trade?

3-4 THE EXTENT OF INTERNATIONAL BUSINESS

Restrictions or not, international business is growing. Although the worldwide recessions of 1991 and 2001–2002 slowed the rate of growth, and the 2008–2009 global economic crisis caused the sharpest decline in more than 75 years, globalization is a reality of our time. In the United States, international trade now accounts for over one-fourth of Gross Domestic Product (GDP). As trade barriers decrease, new competitors enter the global marketplace, creating more choices for consumers and new opportunities for job seekers. International business will grow along with the expansion of commercial use of the Internet.

Learning Objective

3-4 Outline the extent of international business and the economic outlook for trade.

3-4a The Economic Outlook for Trade

Although the global economy continued to grow robustly until 2007, economic performance was not equal: growth in the advanced economies slowed and then stopped in 2009, whereas emerging and developing economies continued to grow. Looking ahead, the International Monetary Fund (IMF), an international bank with 188 member nations, expected a gradual global growth to continue in 2014 and 2015 in both advanced and emerging developing economies. The IMF expected the world economic growth to be 3.3 per cent and 3.8 per cent in 2014 and 2015, respectively.[4]

CANADA AND WESTERN EUROPE The U.S.-Canada economic relationship is the most efficient, most integrated, and most dynamic in the world. Together, the two nations generated $736 billion in bilateral trade in 2013—more than $2 billion a day, or $23,000 every second. More than 96,000 American companies currently export to Canada, and 70 percent of Canada's exports come to the United States.[5] In the euro area, expected growth is only about 1 percent. While growth in Spain has resumed, Italy has suffered its third consecutive year of negative growth, and France and Germany showed weak growth. Regardless, the U.S. trade with EU is one of the largest and most complex in the world; generating an estimated goods and trade flow of over $2.7 billion a day, and representing an estimated

International expansion. Netflix continues its globalization efforts by expanding into France, Germany, Austria, Switzerland, Belgium, and Luxembourg. Other regions in which Netflix operates include North America (except Cuba), South America, and the U.K.

WELLESENTERPRISES/DREAMSTIME.COM

30 percent of global trade.[6] In most other advanced economies, including Norway, Sweden, Switzerland, and the United Kingdom, growth is expected to be robust.

MEXICO AND LATIN AMERICA According to the International Monetary Fund (IMF), Latin American exports are growing by a steady 3 to 4 percent annually. This region is home to 11 Free Trade Area countries. In addition to Mexico, these countries include Chile, Colombia, Peru, and the six countries of the Dominican Republic-Central America FTA or "CAFTA-DR" (Costa Rica, The Dominican Republic, El Salvador, Guatemala, Honduras, and Nicaragua)[7].

JAPAN Japan is the world's third largest economy and the United States' fourth largest trading partner. After nearly two decades of deflation and low growth, Japan's economy is showing signs of recovery.

OTHER ASIAN COUNTRIES The economic growth in Asia remained relatively strong in 2013 and 2014 despite the global recession. China's emergence as a global economic power has been among the most dramatic economic developments of recent decades. Indeed, China has grown to be the world's second largest economy, and the United States shares half-trillion dollars in annual bilateral trade—our third-largest trading relationship. Also, as the emerging middle class in India, the world's largest democracy, buys U.S. products, it means jobs and income for U.S. middle class. With a market of 1.2 billion of the world's consumers and per capita incomes expected to grow at a rate of 8 percent over the next several years, India's vast market promises U.S. companies' continued strong demand for goods and services. In short, the key emerging economies in Asia are leading the global recovery.

AFRICA Sub-Saharan Africa is home to seven of the top ten fastest growing economies in the world—with estimated future growth of 5 to 6 percent for each of the next two years. U.S. trade to and from Africa has tripled over the past decade, and U.S. exports to this region exceed $21 billion. The growth in the African continent is projected to be positive, but uncertain.[8]

U.S. Exports. U.S. aircraft and spacecraft products represent the 5th largest U.S. exports.

EXPORTS AND THE U.S. ECONOMY In 2013, U.S. exports supported more than 11.3 million full- and part-time jobs during a historic time, when exports as a percentage of GDP reached the highest levels since 1916. The new record, 13.5 percent of GDP in 2013, shows that U.S. businesses have great opportunities in the global marketplace. Even though the global economic crisis caused the number of jobs supported by exports to decline sharply to 8.5 million in 2009, globalization represents a huge opportunity for all countries—rich or poor. Indeed, in 2013, for the first time, the U.S. exports exceeded $2.3 trillion and supported 11.3 million jobs, an increase of 1.6 million jobs since 2009.[9] The 15-fold increase in trade volume over the past 65 years has been one of the most important factors in the rise of living standards around the world. During this time, exports have become increasingly important to the U.S. economy. Exports as a percentage of U.S. GDP have increased steadily since 1985, except in the 2001 and 2008 recessions. Our exports to developing and newly industrialized countries are on the rise. Table 3-3 shows U.S. exports and imports for selected world areas in 2013, and Table 3-4 shows the value of U.S. merchandise

TABLE 3-3 U.S. Exports and Imports for Selected World Areas in 2013 In billions of dollars

Selected World Area*	Exports	Imports
North America	$433	$611
Europe	$290	$452
Euro Area	$175	$297
European Union	$232	$382
Pacific Rim	$351	$767
South/Central America	$165	$152
Africa	$34	$50
OPEC	$78	$141
Re-Exports	$207	—

*Countries may be included in more than one area grouping.
Source: U.S. Department of Commerce, Census Bureau, www.census.gov/foreign-trade/Press-Release/2013pr/aip/related_party/rp13-exh1.pdf (accessed January 2, 2015).

TABLE 3-4 Value of U.S. Merchandise Exports and Imports, 2014

Rank/Trading Partner	Exports ($ billions)	Rank/Trading Partner	Imports ($ billions)
1) Canada	312.0	1) China	466.7
2) Mexico	240.3	2) Canada	346.1
3) China	124.0	3) Mexico	294.2
4) Japan	67.0	4) Japan	133.9
5) United Kingdom	53.9	5) Germany	123.2
6) Germany	49.4	6) South Korea	69.6
7) South Korea	44.5	7) United Kingdom	54.0
8) Netherlands	43.7	8) Saudi Arabia	47.0
9) Brazil	42.4	9) France	47.0
10) Belgium	34.8	10) India	45.2

Source: U.S. Department of Commerce, Census Bureau, Top Trading Partners http://www.census.gov/foreign-trade/statistics/highlights/top/index.html (accessed May 4, 2015).

FIGURE 3-3 U.S. Goods Export and Import Shares in 2013

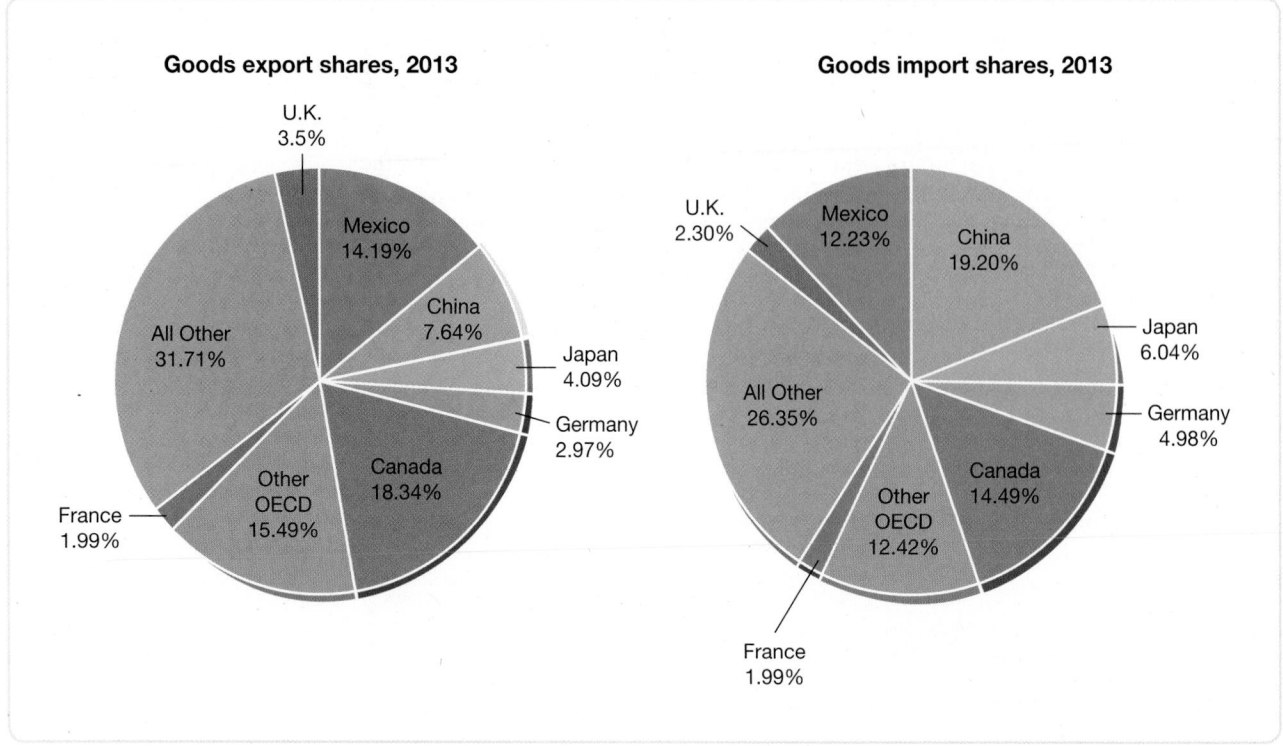

Source: Federal Reserve Bank of St. Louis, *National Economic Trends*, December 2014, p. 18.

Concept Check

✓ According to the IMF, what are the economic growth projections for 2014 and 2015?

✓ What is the importance of exports to the U.S. economy?

✓ Which nations are the principal trading partners of the United States? What are the major U.S. imports and exports?

Learning Objective

3-5 Discuss international trade agreements and international economic organizations working to foster trade.

General Agreement on Tariffs and Trade (GATT) an international organization of 160 nations dedicated to reducing or eliminating tariffs and other barriers to world trade.

exports to, and imports from, each of the nation's ten major trading partners. Note that Canada and Mexico are our best partners for our exports; China and Canada, for imports.

Figure 3-3 shows the U.S. goods export and import shares in 2013. Major U.S. exports and imports are manufactured goods, agricultural products, and mineral fuels.

3-5 INTERNATIONAL TRADE AGREEMENTS

3-5a The General Agreement on Tariffs and Trade and the World Trade Organization

At the end of World War II, the United States and 22 other nations organized the body that came to be known as GATT. The **General Agreement on Tariffs and Trade (GATT)** is an international organization of 160 nations dedicated to reducing or eliminating tariffs and other barriers to world trade. These 160 nations accounted for more than 97 percent of the world's merchandise trade. GATT, headquartered in Geneva, Switzerland, provided a forum for tariff negotiations and a means for settling international trade disputes and problems. Most-favored-nation status (MFN) was the famous principle of GATT. It meant that each GATT member nation was to be treated equally by all contracting nations. Therefore, MFN ensured that any tariff reductions or other trade concessions were extended automatically to all GATT members. From 1947 to 1994, the body sponsored eight rounds of negotiations to reduce trade restrictions. Three of the most fruitful were the Kennedy Round, the Tokyo Round, and the Uruguay Round.

Career Success

Aiming for an Overseas Job?

Are you interested in working abroad? Want the benefits of traveling and living in another country while you gain on-the-job experience? With the global economic climate beginning to improve, businesses are once again planning to create new positions abroad or send U.S. employees on overseas assignments. Many are looking for candidates with specific skills, knowledge, and attitudes, not necessarily familiarity with the local language. Multinational employers in particular understand the value of helping employees and managers develop a global perspective by working in other nations.

Whether you're aiming for a brief overseas stint or want to spend much of your career in another country, start now to prepare for a successful experience. You'll need to think global—so learn more about international events, political trends, and economic issues. Also research social influences and business customs in the region where you expect to work.

Before you apply, determine what employers with international openings are looking for in a job candidate, such as the ability to work independently, good relationship-building skills, solid communication skills, and respect for cultural differences. Ask for advice and suggestions from the professionals in your school's career office and from classmates and alumni who have worked overseas. Most importantly, maintain an open mind and be ready to adapt to situations and decisions that are novel or unexpected—which you will certainly encounter if you work abroad.

Sources: Based on information in Valerie Sweeten, "Who Makes a Good Candidate for Job in Another Country?" *Houston Chronicle*, December 12, 2014, www.chron.com; Francesca Donner, "Want to Work Overseas? Now's Your Chance," *Wall Street Journal*, December 1, 2014, www.wsj.com; Kenny Buck, "Grads Find Work Overseas," *The Advocate (Minnesota State University-Moorhead)*, November 24, 2014, http://msumadvocate.com.

THE KENNEDY ROUND (1964–1967) In 1962, the United States Congress passed the Trade Expansion Act. This law gave President John F. Kennedy the authority to negotiate reciprocal trade agreements that could reduce U.S. tariffs by as much as 50 percent. Armed with this authority, which was granted for a period of five years, President Kennedy called for a round of negotiations through GATT.

These negotiations, which began in 1964, have since become known as the Kennedy Round. They were aimed at reducing tariffs and other barriers to trade in both industrial and agricultural products. The participants succeeded in reducing tariffs on these products by an average of more than 35 percent. However, they were less successful in removing other types of trade barriers.

THE TOKYO ROUND (1973–1979) In 1973, representatives of approximately 100 nations gathered in Tokyo for another round of GATT negotiations. The *Tokyo Round* was completed in 1979. The participants negotiated tariff cuts of 30 to 35 percent, which were to be implemented over an eight-year period. In addition, they were able to remove or ease such nontariff barriers as import quotas, unrealistic quality standards for imports, and unnecessary red tape in customs procedures.

THE URUGUAY ROUND (1986–1993) In 1986, the *Uruguay Round* was launched to extend trade liberalization and widen the GATT treaty to include textiles, agricultural products, business services, and intellectual-property rights. This most ambitious and comprehensive global commercial agreement in history concluded overall negotiations on December 15, 1993, with delegations on hand from 109 nations. The agreement included provisions to lower tariffs by greater than one-third, to reform trade in agricultural goods, to write new rules of trade for intellectual property and services, and to strengthen the dispute-settlement process. These reforms were expected to expand the world economy by an estimated $200 billion annually.

The Uruguay Round also created the **World Trade Organization (WTO)** on January 1, 1995. The WTO was established by GATT to oversee the provisions of the Uruguay Round and resolve any resulting trade disputes. Membership in the WTO obliges 160 member nations to observe GATT rules.

World Trade Organization (WTO) powerful successor to GATT that incorporates trade in goods, services, and ideas

3-5b International Economic Organizations Working to Foster Trade

The primary objective of the WTO is to remove barriers to trade on a worldwide basis. On a smaller scale, an **economic community** is an organization of nations formed to promote the free movement of resources and products among its members and to create common economic policies. A number of economic communities now exist.

THE EUROPEAN UNION Operating as a single market with 28 countries, the European Union (EU), also known as the European Economic Community and the Common Market, was formed in 1957 by six countries—France, the Federal Republic of Germany, Italy, Belgium, the Netherlands, and Luxembourg. Its objective was freely conducted commerce among these nations and others that might later join. As shown in Figure 3-4, many more nations have joined the EU since then. The EU, with a population of over 507 million is now an economic force with a collective economy larger than much of the United States or Japan.

Since January 2002, 19 member nations of the EU have been participating in the new common currency, the euro. The euro, used by over 339 million Europeans, is the single currency of the European Monetary Union nations. However, three EU members, Denmark, the United Kingdom, and Sweden, still maintain their own currencies.

THE NORTH AMERICAN FREE TRADE AGREEMENT The North American Free Trade Agreement (NAFTA) joined the United States with its first- and second-largest export trading partners, Canada and Mexico. Implementation of NAFTA on January 1, 1994, created a market of more than 475 million people. This

economic community an organization of nations formed to promote the free movement of resources and products among its members and to create common economic policies

FIGURE 3-4 The Evolving European Union

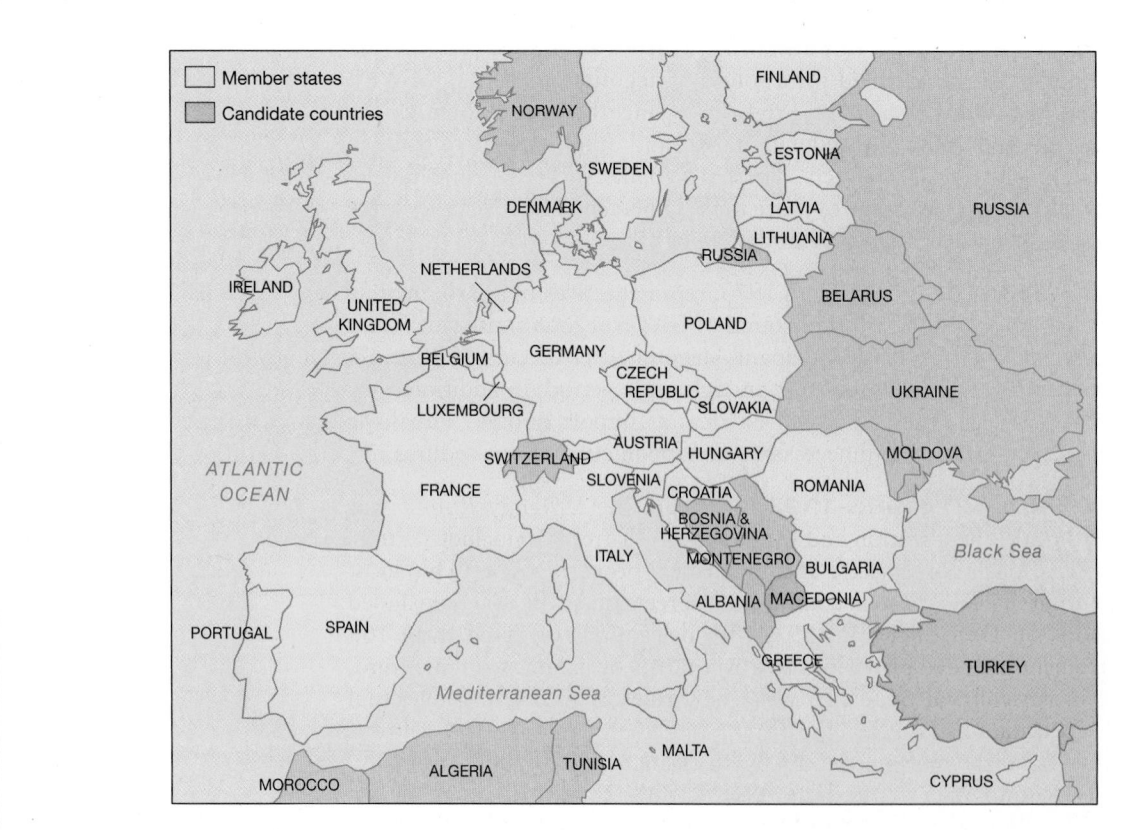

market consists of Canada (population 35 million), the United States (320 million), and Mexico (120 million). According to the Office of the U.S. Trade Representative, after 21 years, NAFTA has achieved its core goals of expanding trade and investment between the United States, Canada, and Mexico. For example, from 1993 to 2013, trade among the NAFTA nations increased nearly five-fold, from $297 billion to $1,400 billion.

NAFTA is built on the Canadian Free Trade Agreement, signed by the United States and Canada in 1989, and on the substantial trade and investment reforms undertaken by Mexico since the mid-1980s. Initiated by the Mexican government, formal negotiations on NAFTA began in June 1991 among the three governments. The support of NAFTA by President Bill Clinton, former Presidents Ronald Reagan and Jimmy Carter, and Nobel Prize–winning economists provided the impetus for U.S. congressional ratification of NAFTA in November 1993. By 2008, NAFTA had gradually eliminated all tariffs and quotas on goods produced and traded among Canada, Mexico, and the United States to provide for a totally free-trade area.

NAFTA. The North American Free Trade Agreement is over 21 years old. NAFTA is the world's largest free trade area, linking 475 million people producing $17 trillion worth of goods and services. NAFTA partners exchange nearly $2.6 billion in products each day.

However, NAFTA is not without its critics. Critics maintain that NAFTA

- has not achieved its goals
- has resulted in job losses
- hurts workers by eroding labor standards and lowering wages
- undermines national sovereignty and independence
- does nothing to help the environment, and
- hurts the agricultural sector

The proponents of NAFTA call the agreement a remarkable economic success story for all three partners. They maintain that NAFTA

- has contributed to significant increases in trade and investment
- has benefited companies in all three countries
- has resulted in increased sales, new partnerships, and new opportunities
- has created high-paying export-related jobs, and
- better prices and selection in consumer goods

THE CENTRAL AMERICAN FREE TRADE AGREEMENT The Central American Free Trade Agreement (CAFTA) was created in 2003 by the United States and four Central American countries—El Salvador, Guatemala, Honduras, and Nicaragua. The CAFTA became CAFTA-DR when the Dominican Republic joined the group in 2007. On January 1, 2009, Costa Rica joined CAFTA-DR as the sixth member. CAFTA-DR creates the third-largest U.S. export market in Latin America, behind only Mexico and Brazil.

THE ASSOCIATION OF SOUTHEAST ASIAN NATIONS The Association of Southeast Asian Nations, with headquarters in Jakarta, Indonesia, was established in 1967 to promote political, economic, and social cooperation among its seven member countries: Indonesia, Malaysia, the Philippines, Singapore, Thailand, Brunei, and Vietnam. With the three new members, Cambodia, Laos, and Myanmar, this region of more than 620 million people, and GDP of $2.2 trillion, is already our fifth-largest trading partner.

THE COMMONWEALTH OF INDEPENDENT STATES The Commonwealth of Independent States was established in December 1991 by the newly independent states as an association of 11 republics of the former Soviet Union.

TRANS-PACIFIC PARTNERSHIP (TPP) On November 12, 2011, the leaders of the nine countries—Australia, Brunei Darussalam, Chile, Malaysia, New Zealand, Peru, Singapore, Vietnam, and the United States—formed the Trans-Pacific Partnership. This partnership will boost economies of the member countries, lower barriers to trade and investment, increase exports, and create more jobs. Together, these eight economies would be America's fifth-largest trading partner.

THE COMMON MARKET OF THE SOUTHERN CONE (MERCOSUR) Headquartered in Montevideo, Uruguay, the Common Market of the Southern Cone (MERCOSUR) was established in 1991 under the Treaty of Asuncion to unite Argentina, Brazil, Paraguay, and Uruguay as a free-trade alliance; Colombia, Ecuador, Peru, Bolivia, and Chile joined later as associates.

THE ORGANIZATION OF PETROLEUM EXPORTING COUNTRIES The Organization of Petroleum Exporting Countries was founded in 1960 in response to reductions in the prices that oil companies were willing to pay for crude oil. The organization was conceived as a collective bargaining unit to provide oil-producing nations with some control over oil prices.

Concept Check

✓ Define and describe the major objectives of the World Trade Organization (WTO) and the international economic communities.

✓ What is the North American Free Trade Agreement (NAFTA)? What is its importance for the United States, Canada, and Mexico?

3-6 SOURCES OF EXPORT ASSISTANCE

Learning Objective

3-6 Describe the various sources of export assistance.

In August 2010, President Obama announced the *National Export Initiative* (NEI) to revitalize U.S. exports. Under the NEI, many federal agencies assist U.S. firms in developing export-promotion programs. The export services and programs of these agencies can help American firms to compete in foreign markets and create new jobs in the United States. For example, recently the International Trade Administration coordinated 77 trade missions to 38 countries. More than 1,120 companies secured over $1.25 billion in export sales during these missions. Table 3-5 provides an overview of selected export assistance programs.

TABLE 3-5 U.S. Government Export Assistance Programs

1	U.S. Export Assistance Centers, www.sba.gov/oit/export/useac.html	Provides assistance in export marketing and trade finance
2	International Trade Administration, www.ita.doc.gov/	Offers assistance and information to exporters through its domestic and overseas commercial officers
3	U.S. and Foreign Commercial Services, www.export.gov/	Helps U.S. firms compete more effectively in the global marketplace and provides information on foreign markets
4	Advocacy Center, www.ita.doc.gov/advocacy	Facilitates advocacy to assist U.S. firms competing for major projects and procurements worldwide
5	Trade Information Center, http://export.gov/exportbasics/eg_main_017458.asp	Provides U.S. companies information on federal programs and activities that support U.S. exports
6	STAT-USA/Internet, www.stat-usa.gov/	Offers a comprehensive collection of business, economic, and trade information on the Web
7	Small Business Administration, www.sba.gov/oit/	Publishes many helpful guides to assist small- and medium-sized companies
8	National Trade Data Bank, www.stat-usa.gov/tradtest.nsf	Provides international economic and export-promotion information supplied by more than 20 U.S. agencies

These and other sources of export information enhance the business opportunities of U.S. firms seeking to enter expanding foreign markets. Another vital energy factor is financing.

3-7 FINANCING INTERNATIONAL BUSINESS

International trade compounds the concerns of financial managers. Currency exchange rates, tariffs and foreign exchange controls, and the tax structures of host nations all affect international operations and the flow of cash. In addition, financial managers must be concerned both with the financing of their international operations and with the means available to their customers to finance purchases.

Fortunately, along with business in general, a number of large banks have become international in scope. Many have established branches in major cities around the world. Thus, like firms in other industries, they are able to provide their services where and when they are needed. In addition, financial assistance is available from U.S. government and international sources.

The U.S. Small Business Administration provides up to $5 million in short-term loans to U.S. small business exporters. The agency also provides small businesses that have exporting potential, but need funds to cover the initial costs of entering an export market with up to $500,000 in export development financing to buy, produce goods, or provide services for exports. Several of today's international financial organizations were founded many years ago to facilitate free trade and the exchange of currencies among nations. Some, such as the Inter-American Development Bank, are supported internationally and focus on developing countries. Others, such as the Export-Import Bank, are operated by one country but provide international financing.

3-7a The Export-Import Bank of the United States

The **Export-Import Bank of the United States**, created in 1934, is an independent agency of the U.S. government whose function is to assist in financing the exports of American firms. *Ex-Im Bank*, as it is commonly called, extends and guarantees credit to overseas buyers of American goods and services and guarantees short-term financing for exports. It also cooperates with commercial banks in helping American exporters to offer credit to their overseas customers. In 2014, the Ex-Im Bank approved $20.5 billion in total guarantees, supporting $27.5 billion in U.S. exports and 164,000 American jobs.

According to Fred P. Hochberg, chairman and president of Ex-Im Bank, "Working with private lenders we are helping U.S. exporters put Americans to work producing the high quality goods and services that foreign buyers prefer. As part of President Obama's National Export Initiative, Ex-Im Bank's export financing is contributing to the goal of doubling of U.S. exports within the next five years."

3-7b Multilateral Development Banks

A **multilateral development bank (MDB)** is an internationally supported bank that provides loans to developing countries to help them grow. The most familiar is the World Bank, a cooperative of 188 member countries, which operates worldwide. Established in 1944 and headquartered in Washington, DC, the bank provides

Concept Check

✓ List some key sources of export assistance. How can these sources be useful to small business firms?

Learning Objective

3-7 Identify the institutions that help firms and nations finance international business.

Export-Import Bank of the United States an independent agency of the U.S. government whose function is to assist in financing the exports of American firms

multilateral development bank (MDB) an internationally supported bank that provides loans to developing countries to help them grow

Mission possible. The Export-Import Bank of the United States (Ex-Im Bank) is the official export credit agency of the United States. Ex-Im Bank's mission is to assist in financing the U.S. goods and services to international markets with more than 79 years of experience, Ex-Im Bank has supported more than $450 billion of the U.S. exports, primarily to developing markets worldwide.

B CHRISTOPHER/ALAMY

low-interest loans, interest-free credits, and grants to developing countries. The loans and grants help these countries to:

- supply safe drinking water
- build schools and train teachers
- increase agricultural productivity
- expand citizens' access to markets, jobs, and housing
- improve health care and access to water and sanitation
- manage forests and other natural resources
- build and maintain roads, railways, and ports, and
- reduce air pollution and protect the environment.[10]

Four other MDBs operate primarily in Central and South America, Asia, Africa, and Eastern and Central Europe. All five are supported by the industrialized nations, including the United States.

THE INTER-AMERICAN DEVELOPMENT BANK The Inter-American Development Bank (IDB), the oldest and largest regional bank, was created in 1959 by 19 Latin American countries and the United States. The bank, which is headquartered in Washington, DC, makes loans and provides technical advice and assistance to countries. Today, the IDB is owned by 48 member states.

THE ASIAN DEVELOPMENT BANK With 67 member nations, the Asian Development Bank (ADB), created in 1966 and headquartered in the Philippines, promotes economic and social progress in Asian and Pacific regions. The U.S. government is the second-largest contributor to the ADB's capital, after Japan.

THE AFRICAN DEVELOPMENT BANK The African Development Bank (AFDB), also known as *Banque Africaines de Development*, was established in 1964 with headquarters in Abidjan, Ivory Coast. Its members include 53 African and 24 non-African countries from the Americas, Europe, and Asia. The AFDB's goal is to foster the economic and social development of its African members. The bank pursues this goal through loans, research, technical assistance, and the development of trade programs.

EUROPEAN BANK FOR RECON-STRUCTION AND DEVELOPMENT

Established in 1991 to encourage reconstruction and development in the Eastern and Central European countries, the London-based *European Bank for Reconstruction and Development* is owned by 64 countries and 2 intergovernmental institutions. Its loans are geared toward developing market-oriented economies and promoting private enterprise.

3-7c The International Monetary Fund

The **International Monetary Fund (IMF)** is an international bank with 188 member nations that makes short-term loans to developing countries experiencing balance-of-payment deficits. This financing is contributed by member nations, and it must be repaid with interest. Loans are provided primarily to fund international trade. Created in 1945 and headquartered in Washington, DC, the bank's main goals are to:

- promote international monetary cooperation
- facilitate the expansion and balanced growth of international trade
- promote exchange rate stability
- assist in establishing a multilateral system of payments, and
- make resources available to members experiencing balance-of-payment difficulties.

3-7d The Challenges Ahead

The challenge of the 21st century is to build on common bonds and shared values to help fully integrate the United States, Europe, and other established economies with a new group of rapidly emerging economies—such as China, India, Brazil, Russia, and others. There are over 302,000 exporters in the United States and more than 58 percent sell to only one foreign country, usually Canada or Mexico. This group of U.S. exporters together represent less than 5 percent of overall U.S. exports. Free Trade Agreements have helped to open markets such as Australia, Canada, Central America, Chile, Israel, Jordan, Korea, Mexico, and Singapore. The challenge, for large and small businesses, is to reach these markets.

In a recent speech at Oxford University, Pascal Lamy, former Director-General of the World Trade Organization stated, "We live in a world of ever-growing

Social Media:
The IMF Goes Social Around the World

No matter where businesses and public policy-makers are located, they can use social media to stay in touch with news and views from the International Monetary Fund. The IMF maintains a Social Media Hub (www.imf.org/external/social.htm) with links to the many social-media networks where it posts messages, files, photos, and videos. The organization uses Twitter (http://twitter.com/IMFNews) for alerts and breaking news about world finance. A separate Twitter account (http://twitter.com/IMFLive) posts announcements made at IMF meetings. For Chinese audiences, the IMF posts messages in Chinese on the Weibo microblog site (www.weibo.com).

Since the IMF joined YouTube in 2009, it has uploaded dozens of videos about economic conditions around the world and in specific regions. It has also posted videos teaching the basics of international finance, the business cycle, and other key concepts. The IMF's *Finance and Development Magazine* has a Facebook page (www.facebook.com/FinanceandDevelopment) with links to articles (in six languages) about the global economic situation, monetary policy, and other timely topics.

To provide more in-depth information and commentary, the IMF has several blogs, including the IMF Direct Forum (http://blog-imfdirect.imf.org/) and the Spanish-language Diálogo a Fondo (http://blog-dialogoafondo.imf.org/). Visitors to the organization's Flickr site (www.flickr.com/photos/imfphoto) can browse thousands of photos taken at IMF events over the years. Finally, the IMF uses LinkedIn (www.linkedin.com/company/international-monetary-fund) to introduce itself to potential job candidates and post open positions.

Concept Check

✓ What is the Export-Import Bank of the United States? How does it assist U.S. exporters?

✓ What is a multilateral development bank (MDB)? Who supports these banks?

✓ What is the International Monetary Fund? What types of loans does the IMF provide?

International Monetary Fund (IMF) an international bank with 188 member nations that makes short-term loans to developing countries experiencing balance-of-payment deficits

independence and interconnectedness. Our interdependence has grown beyond anyone's imagination. The world of today is virtually unrecognizable from the world in which we lived one generation ago." The most striking example of globalization is Apple. Apple's iPod is designed in the United States, manufactured with components from Japan, Korea, and several other Asian countries, and assembled in China by a company from Chinese Taipei. Nowadays, most products are not "Made in the UK" or "Made in France"; they are in fact "Made in the World."[11]

Summary

3-1 Explain the economic basis for international business.

International business encompasses all business activities that involve exchanges across national boundaries. International trade is based on specialization, whereby each country produces the goods and services that it can produce more efficiently than any other goods and services. A nation is said to have a comparative advantage relative to these goods. International trade develops when each nation trades its surplus products for those in short supply.

A nation's balance of trade is the difference between the value of its exports and the value of its imports. Its balance of payments is the difference between the flow of money into and out of the nation. Generally, a negative balance of trade is considered unfavorable.

3-2 Explore the methods by which a firm can organize for and enter into international markets.

A firm can enter international markets in several ways. It may license a foreign firm to produce and market its products. It may export its products and sell them through foreign intermediaries or its own sales organization abroad, or it may sell its exports outright to an export–import merchant. It may enter into a joint venture with a foreign firm. It may establish its own foreign subsidiaries, or it may develop into a multinational enterprise.

Generally, each of these methods represents an increasingly deeper level of involvement in international business, with licensing being the simplest and the development of a multinational corporation the most involved.

3-3 Discuss the restrictions nations place on international trade, the objectives of these restrictions, and their results.

Despite the benefits of world trade, nations tend to use tariffs and nontariff barriers (import quotas, embargoes, and other restrictions) to limit trade. These restrictions typically are justified as being needed to protect a nation's economy, industries, citizens, or security. They can result in the loss of jobs, higher prices, fewer choices in the marketplace, and the misallocation of resources.

3-4 Outline the extent of international business and the economic outlook for trade.

World trade is generally increasing. Trade between the United States and other nations is increasing in dollar value but decreasing in terms of our share of the world market. Exports as a percentage of U.S. GDP have increased steadily since 1985, except in the 2001 and 2008 recessions.

3-5 Discuss international trade agreements and international economic organizations working to foster trade.

The General Agreement on Tariffs and Trade (GATT) was formed to dismantle trade barriers and provide an environment in which international business can grow. Today, the World Trade Organization (WTO) and various economic communities carry on this mission. These world economic communities include the European Union, the NAFTA, the CAFTA, the Association of Southeast Asian Nations, the Pacific Rim, the Commonwealth of Independent States, the Caribbean Basin Initiative, the Common Market of the Southern Cone, the Organization of Petroleum Exporting Countries, and the Organization for Economic Cooperation and Development.

3-6 Describe the various sources of export assistance.

Many government and international agencies provide export assistance to U.S. and foreign firms. Sources of export assistance include U.S. Export Assistance Centers, the International Trade Administration, U.S. and Foreign Commercial Services, Export Legal Assistance Network, Advocacy Center, National Trade Data Bank, and other government and international agencies.

3-7 Identify the institutions that help firms and nations finance international business.

The financing of international trade is more complex than that of domestic trade. Institutions such as the Ex-Im Bank and the International Monetary Fund have been established to provide financing and ultimately to increase world trade for American and international firms.

Key Terms

You should now be able to define and give an example relevant to each of the following terms:

international business (70)
absolute advantage (71)
comparative advantage (71)
exporting (71)
importing (71)
balance of trade (71)
trade deficit (72)
balance of payments (72)
licensing (73)

letter of credit (75)
bill of lading (75)
draft (75)
strategic alliance (77)
trading company (77)
countertrade (78)
multinational enterprise (78)
import duty (tariff) (79)
dumping (80)

nontariff barrier (80)
import quota (80)
embargo (80)
foreign-exchange control (80)
currency devaluation (80)
General Agreement on Tariffs and Trade (GATT) (86)
World Trade Organization (WTO) (87)

economic community (88)
Export-Import Bank of the United States (91)
multilateral development bank (MDB) (91)
International Monetary Fund (IMF) (93)

Discussion Questions

1. The United States restricts imports but, at the same time, supports the WTO and international banks whose objective is to enhance world trade. As a member of Congress, how would you justify this contradiction to your constituents?

2. What effects might the devaluation of a nation's currency have on its business firms, its consumers, and the debts it owes to other nations?

3. Should imports to the United States be curtailed by, say, 20 percent to eliminate our trade deficit? What might happen if this were done?

4. When should a firm consider expanding from strictly domestic trade to international trade? When should it consider becoming further involved in international trade? What factors might affect the firm's decisions in each case?

5. How can a firm obtain the expertise needed to produce and market its products in, for example, the EU?

Video Case
Keeping Brazil's Economy Hot

It's been hot in Brazil. No, we're not talking about the country's temperature: We're talking about its economy, which has been growing at a heated pace. In 2010, the country's GDP grew by 7.5 percent. That's a growth rate developed countries such as the United States haven't experienced for years, if not decades. Although Brazil's growth rate slowed considerably in 2011 and 2012 due to the global economic crisis, it has fared better than many other nations. Recently it surpassed the United Kingdom as the sixth-largest economy in the world.

Why has Brazil done so well economically? Increased world trade is one reason why. The country has an abundant amount of natural resources firms in other countries around the world are eager to buy—especially companies in the fast-growing nation of China. Greater exports have also helped 40 million Brazilians rise up out of poverty and into the middle class. Their massive spending power is creating new markets for multinational companies ranging from McDonald's and Whirlpool to Nestlé, Avon, and Volkswagen. Brazil has become Avon's largest market. Volkswagen now sells more cars in Brazil than it does Germany, where the company is headquartered. "China may have over a billion inhabitants, but Brazil has 200,000 consumers," explains Ivan Zurita, the president of Nestle's Brazil division.

Clouds on the horizon threaten to cool off Brazil's growth, however. To begin with, the country is concerned that its trade with China is out of balance. Although China purchases more natural resources from Brazil than any other nation, it doesn't purchase near as many manufactured goods from Brazil as it exports to it.

A bigger issue is the appreciation of Brazil's currency, the real. Massive amounts of money have been flowing into Brazil to take advantage of the nation's high interest rates and growth opportunities. This has increased the demand for the real, causing its value to rise by nearly 50 percent relative to other currencies. The good news is that the stronger real has made imported products cheaper for Brazilians to buy. The bad news is that products made in Brazil have become more expensive for the rest of the world to purchase, slowing the country's exports and growth.

Businesses in Brazil have lobbied the government to weaken the real so their products are better able to compete against imports. Their efforts appear to have paid off. Recently, Guido Mantega, Brazil's minister of finance, said the country will take steps "as needed" to weaken the real. The government has also imposed tariffs on a number of imported products, including cars, shoes, chemicals, and textiles, and signed a trade deal with Mexico that put a quota on the number of automobiles imported from that country.

Imports and the value of the real are not the only clouds threatening Brazil, though. Businesses in the country face a great deal of bureaucratic red tape, heavy regulations, and tax rates that are some of the highest in the world. To deal with these problems, Brazilian President Dilma Rousseff has announced that her administration will eliminate payroll taxes for employers in industries hardest hit by imports. To further ease the nation's growing pains, Brazil's development bank, BDM, will subsidize business loans to boost the production of many products, including tablets and off-shore oil rigs. The goal is to stimulate technological innovations that will enable manufacturers to produce higher-value products so Brazil doesn't have to rely on natural resources to fuel its growth. "Look, a government isn't made on the second or third day," Rousseff has said about her administration's incremental efforts to keep Brazil's emerging economy moving forward. "It's made over time. Things mature."[12]

Questions

1. Do you think the efforts of Brazil's government to keep the economy growing will be successful? Why or why not?
2. What downsides might Brazil experience by implementing quotas, tariffs, and measures to devalue its currency?

Building Skills for Career Success

1. Social Media Exercise

Although Nike was founded in the Pacific Northwest and still has its corporate headquarters near Beaverton, Oregon, the company has become a multinational enterprise. The firm employs more than 35,000 people across six continents and is now a global marketer of footwear, apparel, and athletic equipment.

Because it operates in 160 countries around the globe and manufactures products in over 900 factories in 47 different countries, sustainability is a big initiative for Nike. Today, Nike uses the YouTube social media site to share its sustainability message with consumers, employees, investors, politicians, and other interested stakeholders. To learn about the company's efforts to sustain the planet, follow these steps:

- Make an Internet connection and go to the YouTube website (www.youtube.com).
- Enter the words "Nike" and "Sustainability" in the search window and click the search button.
1. View at least three different YouTube videos about Nike's sustainability efforts.

2. Based on the information in the videos you watched, do you believe that Nike is a good corporate citizen because of its efforts to sustain the planet? Why or why not?
3. Prepare a one to two page report that describes how Nike is taking steps to reduce waste, improve the environment, and reduce its carbon footprint while manufacturing products around the globe.

2. Building Team Skills

The North American Free Trade Agreement among the United States, Mexico, and Canada went into effect on January 1, 1994. It has made a difference in trade among the countries and has affected the lives of many people.

Assignment

1. Working in teams and using the resources of your library, investigate NAFTA. Answer the following questions:
   a. What are NAFTA's objectives?
   b. What are its benefits?
   c. What impact has NAFTA had on trade, jobs, and travel?

d. Some Americans were opposed to the implementation of NAFTA. What were their objections? Have any of these objections been justified?

e. Has NAFTA influenced your life? How?

2. Summarize your answers in a written report. Your team also should be prepared to give a class presentation.

3. Researching Different Careers

Today, firms around the world need employees with special skills. In some countries, such employees are not always available, and firms then must search abroad for qualified applicants. One way they can do this is through global workforce databases. As business and trade operations continue to grow globally, you may one day find yourself working in a foreign country, perhaps for an American company doing business there or for a foreign company. In what foreign country would you like to work? What problems might you face?

Assignment

1. Choose a country in which you might like to work.

2. Research the country. The National Trade Data Bank is a good place to start. Find answers to the following questions:

   a. What language is spoken in this country? Are you proficient in it? What would you need to do if you are not proficient?

   b. What are the economic, social, and legal systems like in this nation?

   c. What is its history?

   d. What are its culture and social traditions like? How might they affect your work or your living arrangements?

3. Describe what you have found out about this country in a written report. Include an assessment of whether you would want to work there and the problems you might face if you did.

Running a Business
Part 1

Let's Go Get a Graeter's!

Only a tiny fraction of family-owned businesses are still growing four generations after their founding, but happily for lovers of premium-quality ice cream, Graeter's is one of them.

Now a $30 million firm with national distribution, Graeter's was founded in Cincinnati in 1870 by Louis Charles Graeter and his wife, Regina Graeter. The young couple made ice cream and chocolate candies in the back room of their shop, sold them in the front room, and lived upstairs. Ice cream was a special treat in this era before refrigeration, and the Graeters started from scratch every day to make theirs from the freshest, finest ingredients. Even after freezers were invented, the Graeters continued to make ice cream in small batches to preserve the quality, texture, and rich flavor.

After her husband's death, Regina's entrepreneurial leadership became the driving force behind Graeter's expansion from 1920 until well into the 1950s. At a time when few women owned or operated a business, Regina opened 20 new Graeter's stores in the Cincinnati area and added manufacturing capacity to support this ambitious—and successful— growth strategy. Her sons and grandchildren followed her into the business and continued to open ice-cream shops all around Ohio and beyond. Today, three of Regina's great-grandsons run Graeter's with the same attention to quality that made the firm famous. In her honor, the street in front of the company's ultramodern Cincinnati factory is named Regina Graeter Way.

The Scoop on Graeter's Success

Graeter's fourth-generation owners are Richard Graeter II (CEO), Robert (Bob) Graeter (vice president of operations), and Chip Graeter (vice president of retail operations). They grew up in the business, learning through hands-on experience how to do everything from packing a pint of ice cream to locking up the store at night. They also absorbed the family's dedication to product quality, a key reason for the company's enduring success. "Our family has always been contented to make a little less profit in order to ensure our long-term survival," explains the CEO.

Throughout its history, Graeter's has used a unique, time-consuming manufacturing process to produce its signature ice creams in small batches. "Our competition is making thousands and thousands of gallons a day,"

© ISTOCKPHOTO.COM/LUVO

says Chip Graeter. "We are making hundreds of gallons a day at the most. All of our ice cream is packed by hand, so it's a very laborious process." Graeter's "French pot" manufacturing method ensures that very little air gets into the product. As a result, the company's ice cream is dense and creamy, not light and fluffy—so dense, in fact, that each pint weighs nearly a pound.

Another success factor is the use of simple, fresh ingredients like high-grade chocolate, choice seasonal fruits, and farm-fresh cream. Graeter's imports some ingredients, such as vanilla from Madagascar, and buys other ingredients from U.S. producers known for their quality. "We use a really great grade of chocolate," says Bob Graeter. "We don't cut corners on that … Specially selected great black raspberries, strawberries, blueberries, and cherries go into our ice cream because we feel that we want to provide flavor not from artificial or unnatural ingredients but from really quality, ripe, rich fruits." Instead of tiny chocolate chips, Graeter's products contain giant chunks formed when liquid chocolate is poured into the ice-cream base just before the mixture is frozen and packed into pints.

Maintaining the Core of Success

Graeter's "fanatical devotion to product quality" and its time-tested recipes have not changed over the years. The current generation of owners is maintaining this core of the company's success while mixing in a generous dash of innovation. "If you just preserve the core," Bob Graeter says, "ultimately you stagnate. And if you are constantly stimulating progress and looking for new ideas, well, then you risk losing what was important…. Part of your secret to long-term success is knowing what your core is and holding to that. Once you know what you're really all about and what is most important to you, you can change everything else."

One of those "important" things is giving back to the community and its families via local charities and other initiatives. "Community involvement is just part of being a good corporate citizen," observes Richard Graeter. When Graeter's celebrated a recent new store opening, for example, it made a cash donation to the neighborhood public library. It is also a major sponsor of The Cure Starts Now Foundation, a research foundation seeking a cure for pediatric brain cancer. In line with its focus on natural goodness, Graeter's has been doing its part to preserve the environment by recycling and by boosting production efficiency to conserve water, energy, and other resources.

Graeter's Looks to the Future

Even though Graeter's recipes reflect its 19th century heritage, the company is clearly a 21st century operation. It has 170,544 Facebook "likes," connects with brand fans on Twitter, and invites customers to subscribe to its e-mail newsletter. The company sells its products online and ships orders via United Parcel Service to ice-cream lovers across the continental United States. Its newly-opened production facility uses state-of-the-art refrigeration, storage, and sanitation—yet the ice cream is still mixed by hand rather than by automated equipment. With an eye toward future growth, Graeter's is refining its information system to provide managers with all the details they need to make timely decisions in today's fast-paced business environment.

Graeter's competition ranges from small, local businesses to international giants such as Unilever, which owns Ben & Jerry's, and Nestle, which owns Haagen-Dazs.

Throughout the economic ups and downs of recent years, Graeter's has continued to expand, and its ice creams are now distributed through 6,200 stores in 46 states. Oprah Winfrey and other celebrities have praised its products in public. But the owners are just as proud of their home-town success. "Graeter's in Cincinnati is synonymous with ice cream," says Bob Graeter. "People will say, 'Let's go get a Graeter's.'"[13]

Questions

1. How have Graeter's owners used the four factors of production to build the business over time?
2. Which of Graeter's stakeholders are most affected by the family's decision to take a long-term view of the business rather than aiming for short-term profit? Explain your answer.
3. Knowing that Graeter's competes with multinational corporations as well as small businesses, would you recommend that Graeter's expand by licensing its brand to a company in another country? Why or why not?

Building a Business Plan: Part 1

A *business plan* is a carefully constructed guide for a person starting a business. The purpose of a well-prepared business plan is to show how practical and attainable the entrepreneur's goals are. It also serves as a concise document that potential investors can examine to see if they would like to invest or assist in financing a new venture. A business plan should include the following 12 components:

- Introduction
- Executive summary
- Benefits to the community
- Company and industry
- Management team
- Manufacturing and operations plan
- Labor force
- Marketing plan
- Financial plan
- Exit strategy
- Critical risks and assumptions
- Appendix

A brief description of each of these sections is provided in Chapter 5. This is the first of seven exercises that appear at the ends of each of the seven major parts in this textbook. The goal of these exercises is to help you work through the preceding components to create your own business plan. For example, in the exercise for this part, you will make decisions and complete the research that will help you to develop the introduction for your business plan and the benefits to the community that your business will provide. In the exercises for Parts 2 through 6, you will add more components to your plan and eventually build a plan that actually could be used to start a business. The flowchart shown in Figure 3-5 gives an overview of the steps you will be taking to prepare your business plan.

The First Step: Choosing Your Business

One of the first steps for starting your own business is to decide what type of business you want to start. Take some time to think about this decision. Before proceeding, answer the following questions:

- Why did you choose this type of business?
- Why do you think this business will be successful?
- Would you enjoy owning and operating this type of business?

Warning: Do not rush this step. This step often requires much thought, but it is well worth the time and effort. As an added bonus, you are more likely to develop a quality business plan if you really want to open this type of business.

Now that you have decided on a specific type of business, it is time to begin the planning process. The goal for this part is to complete the introduction and benefits-to-the-community components of your business plan.

Before you begin, it is important to note that the business plan is not a document that is written and then set aside. It is a living document that an entrepreneur should refer to continuously in order to ensure that plans are being carried through appropriately. As the entrepreneur begins to execute the plan, he or she should monitor the business environment continuously and make changes to the plan to address any challenges or opportunities that were not foreseen originally.

Throughout this course, you will, of course, be building your knowledge about business. Therefore, it will be appropriate for you to continually revisit parts of the plan that you have already written in order to refine them based on your more comprehensive knowledge. You will find that writing your plan is not a simple matter of starting at the beginning and moving chronologically through to the end. Instead, you probably will find yourself jumping around the various components, making refinements as you go. In fact, the second component—the executive summary—should be written last, but because of its comprehensive nature and its importance to potential investors, it appears after the introduction in the final business plan. By the end of this course, you should be able to put the finishing touches on your plan, making sure that all the parts create a comprehensive and sound whole so that you can present it for evaluation.

The Introduction Component

1.1. Start with the cover page. Provide the business name, street address, telephone number, Web address (if any), name(s) of owner(s) of the business, and the date the plan is issued.

1.2. Next, provide background information on the company and include the general nature of the business: retailing, manufacturing, or service; what your product or service is; what is unique about it; and why you believe that your business will be successful.

1.3. Then include a summary statement of the business's financial needs, if any. You probably will need to revise

FIGURE 3-5 Business Plan

Steps in creating a business plan

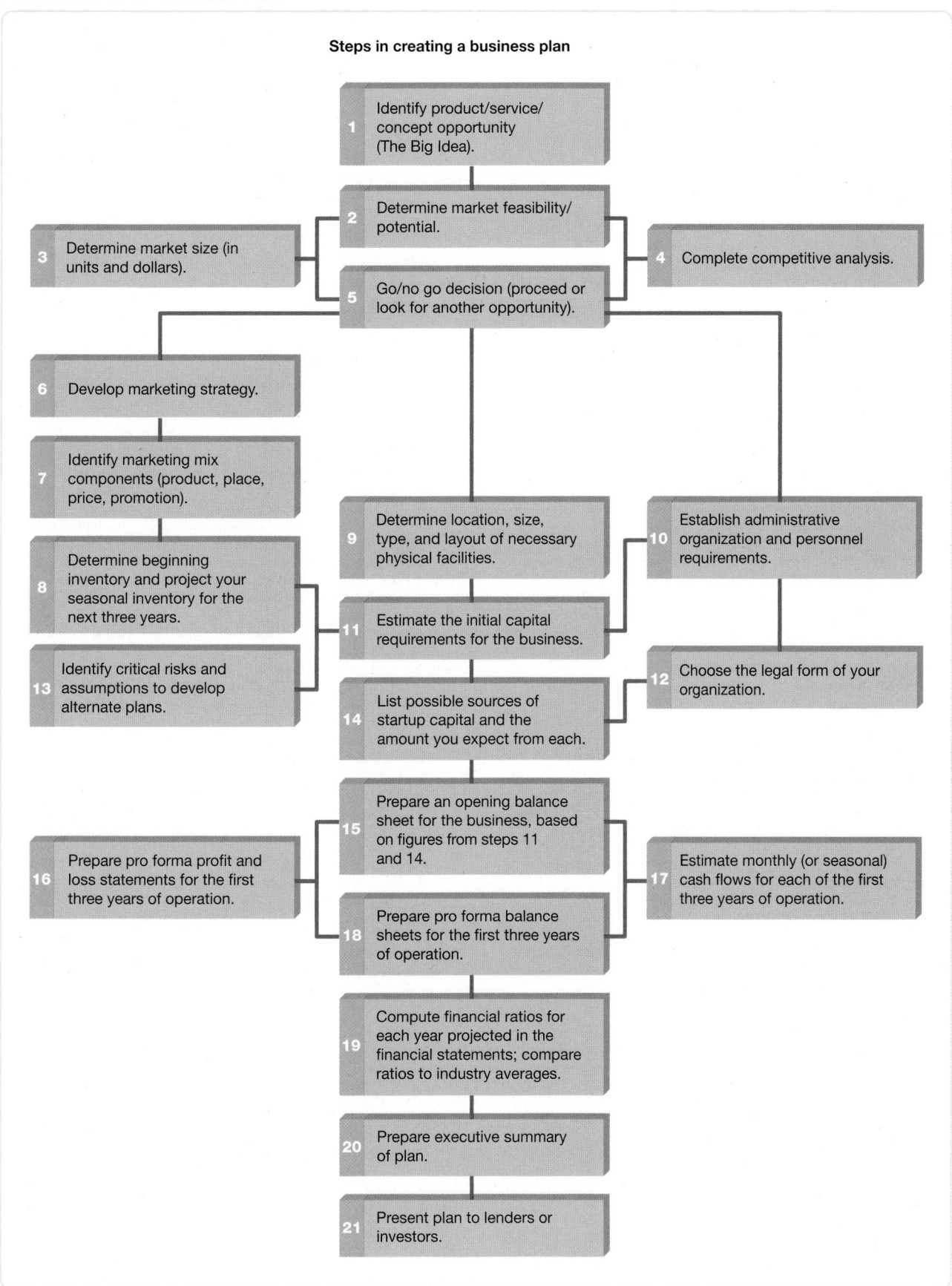

1. Identify product/service/concept opportunity (The Big Idea).
2. Determine market feasibility/potential.
3. Determine market size (in units and dollars).
4. Complete competitive analysis.
5. Go/no go decision (proceed or look for another opportunity).
6. Develop marketing strategy.
7. Identify marketing mix components (product, place, price, promotion).
8. Determine beginning inventory and project your seasonal inventory for the next three years.
9. Determine location, size, type, and layout of necessary physical facilities.
10. Establish administrative organization and personnel requirements.
11. Estimate the initial capital requirements for the business.
12. Choose the legal form of your organization.
13. Identify critical risks and assumptions to develop alternate plans.
14. List possible sources of startup capital and the amount you expect from each.
15. Prepare an opening balance sheet for the business, based on figures from steps 11 and 14.
16. Prepare pro forma profit and loss statements for the first three years of operation.
17. Estimate monthly (or seasonal) cash flows for each of the first three years of operation.
18. Prepare pro forma balance sheets for the first three years of operation.
19. Compute financial ratios for each year projected in the financial statements; compare ratios to industry averages.
20. Prepare executive summary of plan.
21. Present plan to lenders or investors.

Source: Hatten, Timothy, *Small Business Management*, Fifth Edition. Copyright 2012 Cengage Learning.

your financial needs summary after you complete a detailed financial plan later in Part 6.

1.4. Finally, include a statement of confidentiality to keep important information away from potential competitors.

The Benefits-to-the-Community Component

In this section, describe the potential benefits to the community that your business could provide. Chapter 2 in your textbook, "Being Ethical and Socially Responsible," can help you in answering some of these questions. At the very least, address the following issues:

1.5. Describe the number of skilled and nonskilled jobs the business will create, and indicate how purchases of supplies and other materials can help local businesses.

1.6. Next, describe how providing needed goods or services will improve the community and its standard of living.

1.7. Finally, state how your business can develop new technical, management, or leadership skills; offer attractive wages; and provide other types of individual growth.

Review of Business Plan Activities

Read over the information that you have gathered. Because the Building a Business Plan exercises at the end of Parts 2 through 7 are built on the work you do in Part 1, make sure that any weaknesses or problem areas are resolved before continuing. Finally, write a brief statement that summarizes all the information for this part of the business plan.

Endnotes

1   Sources: Based on information in "Not Reversing Multi-Brand Law Gives Walmart Hope for Retail," *Times of India*, December 4, 2014, http://timesofindia.com; Hiroko Tabuchi and Rachel Abrams, "After a Bump in Sales, Walmart Braces for a Competitive Holiday Season," *New York Times*, November 13, 2014, www.nytimes.com; Rhitu Chatterjee, "Indian Shopkeepers Greet Wal-Mart's Expansion Plans with Protests," *National Public Radio*, November 20, 2014, www.npr.org; "Walmart to Incur Higher Charges on India Joint Venture Split," *Economic Times (India)*, February 20, 2014, http://articles.economictimes.indiatimes.com; Bruce Einhorn, "Wal-Mart Tries Again in India," *Bloomberg Businessweek*, October 23, 2014, www.businessweek.com; Nandita Bose and Adam Rose, "Wal-Mart's China Syndrome a Symptom of International Woes," *Reuters*, February 21, 2014, www.reuters.com; www.walmart.com.

2   The White House, Office of the Press Secretary, Press Release, August 6, 2002.

3   U.S. Census Bureau, Foreign Trade Division, www.census.gov/foreign-trade/statistics/historical/exhibit_history (accessed December 27, 2014).

4   International Monetary Fund website at http://www.imf.org/external/ns/cs/aspx?id=29 (accessed January 5, 2015).

5   U.S. Department of Commerce website at http://www.commerce.gov/print/news/secretary-speeches/2014/10/30/us-secretary-commerce-penny-pritzker-discusses-us-canada-trade-and-commercial-relationship-in-ottawa (accessed January 2, 2015).

6   U.S. Department of State website at http://www.state.gov/r/pa/pl/2013/211144.htm (accessed January 1, 2015).

7   U.S. Census Bureau website at http://www.census.gov/foreign-trade/aes/tradesource_july2013.pdf (accessed January 3, 2015).

8   U.S. Census Bureau website at http://www.census.gov/foreign-trade/aes/tradesource_jan2014.pdf (accessed January 3, 2015).

9   U.S. Department of Commerce, Economics and Statistics Administration, International Trade Administration, "The Role of Exports in the U.S. Economy," May 13, 2014, www.trade.gov/neinext/role-of-exports-in-us-economy.pdf (accessed January 4, 2015).

10 The World Trade Organization website at www.wto.org/english/news_e/sppl_e/spp1220_htm (accessed February 6, 2013).

11 Ibid.

12 Sources: Andre Soliani, "Surge," *Bloomberg BusinessWeek*, April 3, 2012, www.businessweek.com; "Invigorated Roussef Shifts Focus to 'Brazil Cost,'" *Reuters*, April 2, 2012, www.reuters.com; Komal Sri-Kumar, "Brazil Should Embrace a Freer Market," *Financial Times*, March 6, 2012, www.ft.com; "Multinationals Choose Brazilian Investment," *Obelisk Investment News*, May 4, 2011, www.obeliskinternational.com.

13 Sources: Based on information from Kimberly L. Jackson, "Graeter's Premium Chocolate Chip Ice Cream Lands at Stop & Shop," *Newark Star-Ledger (NJ)*, April 4, 2012, www.nj.com; "Graeter's Ice Cream Debuts in Bay Area," *Tampa Bay Times (St. Petersburg, FL)*, January 10, 2012, p. 4B; Jim Carper, "Graeter's Runs a Hands-on Ice Cream Plant," *Dairy Foods*, August 2011, pp. 36+; Jim Carper, "The Greater Good," *Dairy Foods*, August 2011, pp. 95+; "Graeter's Unveils New 'Mystery Flavor,'" *Dayton Daily News*, March 29, 2012, www.daytondailynews.com; Bob Driehaus, "A Cincinnati Ice Cream Maker Aims Big," *New York Times*, September 11, 2010, www.nytimes.com; Lucy May, "Graeter's Northern Kentucky Franchisee Puts Stores on the Block," *Business Courier*, August 6, 2010, http://cincinnati.bizjournals.com; www.graeters.com; interviews with company staff and Cengage videos about Graeter's.

©EDBOOKSTOCK/SHUTTERSTOCK.COM

CHAPTER

4

Choosing a Form of Business Ownership

Why Should You Care?

There's a good chance that during your lifetime you will work for a business or start a business. With this fact in mind, the material in this chapter can help you to understand how and why businesses are organized.

Learning Objectives

Once you complete this chapter, you will be able to:

4-1 Describe the advantages and disadvantages of sole proprietorships.

4-2 Explain the different types of partners and the importance of partnership agreements.

4-3 Describe the advantages and disadvantages of partnerships.

4-4 Summarize how a corporation is formed.

4-5 Describe the advantages and disadvantages of a corporation.

4-6 Examine special types of businesses, including S corporations, limited-liability companies, and not-for-profit corporations.

4-7 Discuss the purpose of a joint venture and syndicate.

4-8 Explain how growth from within and growth through mergers can enable a business to expand.

GoPro's Global Growth Began by Bootstrapping

When surfer Nick Woodman graduated from University of California, San Diego in 1997, his goal was to become a successful entrepreneur by the age of 30. However, his first startup was a failure. His second, a contest site named FunBug.com, raised several million dollars in venture capital—but it wasn't successful, either. Even though FunBug was a corporation, which limited his personal liability, Woodman felt terrible about losing other people's money.

After FunBug, Woodman took time off to surf the world while he thought about trying another startup or looking for a job. He rigged a waterproof disposable camera to a wrist strap so he could photograph his surfing adventures. By the time he returned home, five months and many in-water tests later, Woodman was ready to build a new business around his idea of wearable cameras for use while surfing and in other outdoor activities.

He incorporated the new venture as Woodman Labs in 2002 and, remembering how it felt to lose outside investors' money, he initially sought funding only from his family. His mother invested $35,000 and his father invested $200,000, to which the founder added his own $30,000, intending to bootstrap growth as he generated sales revenue. When Woodman launched his first GoPro wearable camera in 2004, demand was so strong that the company quickly became profitable. Before Woodman celebrated his 30th birthday, his company (soon renamed GoPro) was earning millions of dollars.

In 2011 and again in 2012, the firm received tens of millions of dollars in outside investment and welcomed seasoned industry experts to its board of directors, preparing for more aggressive expansion as GoPro products flew off the shelves in Best Buy, REI, and many other stores. In 2014, with worldwide yearly sales approaching $1 billion, GoPro began selling stock to the public. Looking ahead, the founder sees a bright financial future in helping GoPro users find new ways to digitally share their adventures with friends and fans.[1]

Did You Know?

GoPro rings up $1 billion in annual sales of wearable cameras, selling through 25,000 retail outlets in 100 countries.

If at first you don't succeed, try and try again. While many would-be entrepreneurs would just give up after two failures, Nick Woodman still remembered his goal of becoming a successful entrepreneur. To accomplish that goal, he turned an idea for a wearable camera into a very successful business. Along the way, Woodman had to make decisions that would eventually shape his new venture and at the same time find start-up funding to turn his dream into a reality. Remembering how it felt to lose other people's money, initial funding for GoPro came from his mother and father and his own savings. He also made the decision to incorporate his business. Although he could have chosen the sole proprietorship or partnership or other specialized forms of business ownership, he chose the corporation because of the advantages that this type of ownership provides. Within a few months, demand for wearable cameras was so strong that the company enjoyed early profits. Based on continued success, a few years later Woodman was able to obtain millions from outside investors that could be used to grow the business. As the company continued to grow, Woodman made another decision to obtain seasoned experts to help the young company grow—a step that many entrepreneurs don't take because they don't want to give up control of their business. In 2014, GoPro sold stock to the public to obtain even more financing. Today, GoPro is a success because it provides quality products. It also has a management team that makes smart decisions and has developed a business plan that evolved over time to meet the ever-changing needs of a growing company. At a time when many would-be entrepreneurs hear stories about how hard it is start a successful business and the number of business failures, entrepreneurs can still achieve their dreams. If you doubt this statement, remember Nick Woodman and how he turned his dream into a multi-million dollar company.

We begin this chapter by describing the three common forms of business ownership: sole proprietorships, partnerships, and corporations. We discuss how these types of businesses are formed and note the advantages and disadvantages of each. Next, we consider several types of business ownership usually chosen for special purposes, including S corporations, limited-liability companies (LLCs), not-for-profit corporations, joint ventures, and syndicates. We conclude the chapter with a discussion of how businesses can grow through internal expansion or through mergers with other companies.

4-1 SOLE PROPRIETORSHIPS

Learning Objective

4-1 Describe the advantages and disadvantages of sole proprietorships.

A **sole proprietorship** is a business that is owned (and usually operated) by one person. Although a few sole proprietorships are large and have many employees, most are small. In most instances, the owner (the *sole* proprietor) simply decides that he or she is in business and begins operations. Some of today's largest corporations, including Walmart, JCPenney, and Procter & Gamble Company, started out as tiny—and in many cases, struggling—sole proprietorships.

Often entrepreneurs with a promising idea choose the sole proprietorship form of ownership. Annie Withey, for example, created a cheddar cheese–flavored popcorn snack food. Annie's popcorn, called Smartfood, became one of the fastest-selling snack foods in U.S. history. After a few years, Frito-Lay bought the brand for about $15 million. Ms. Withey went on to develop an all-natural white-cheddar macaroni and cheese product. Although her firm, Annie's Homegrown, has grown and become a major player in a very competitive industry, Annie always remained the entrepreneurial heart of the company and still thinks like a sole proprietor. It's still possible for a sole proprietor to develop an idea that meets customer needs, to start a business, and to enjoy the financial rewards of a successful business. If you doubt the above statement, consider this: General Mills paid $820 million for Annie's Homegrown in 2014.[2] And while the money did not all go to Ms. Withey, it does illustrate that a good idea and a successful business can be worth a lot of money.

As you can see in Figure 4-1, there are approximately 31 million sole proprietorships in the United States. They account for 73 percent of the country's

FIGURE 4-1 Relative Percentages of Sole Proprietorships, Partnerships, and Corporations in the United States

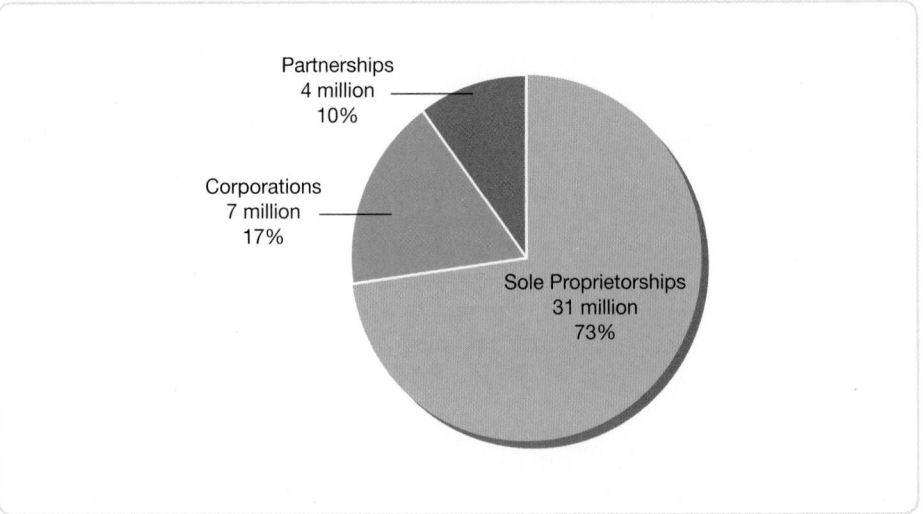

Partnerships
4 million
10%

Corporations
7 million
17%

Sole Proprietorships
31 million
73%

sole proprietorship a business that is owned (and usually operated) by one person

Source: "Statistics of Income," The Internal Revenue Service website at www.irs.gov (accessed January 5, 2014).

FIGURE 4-2 Total Sales Receipts of Sole Proprietorships, Partnerships, and Corporations in the United States

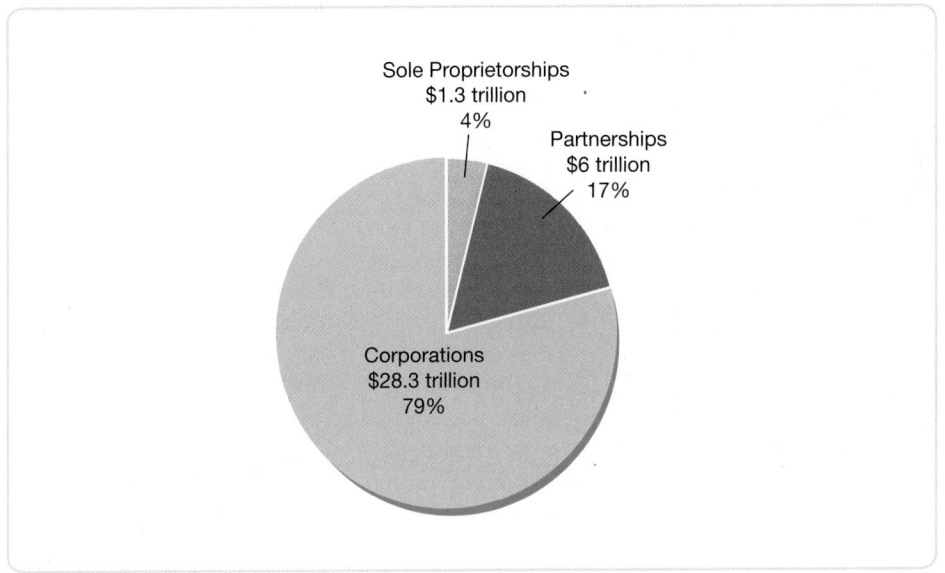

Source: "Statistics of Income," The Internal Revenue Service website at www.irs.gov (accessed January 5, 2014).

business firms. Although the most popular form of ownership when compared with partnerships and corporations, they rank last in total sales revenues. As shown in Figure 4-2, sole proprietorships account for about $1.3 trillion, or about 4 percent of total annual sales.

Sole proprietorships are most common in retailing, service, and agriculture. Thus, the clothing boutique, corner grocery, appliance-repair shop down the street, and small, independent farmers are likely to be sole proprietorships.

4-1a **Advantages of Sole Proprietorships**

Most of the advantages of sole proprietorships arise from the two main characteristics of this form of ownership: simplicity and individual control.

EASE OF START-UP AND CLOSURE Sole proprietorship is the simplest way to start a business. A sole proprietorship can be, and most often is, established without the services of an attorney. The legal requirements often are limited to registering the name of the business and obtaining any necessary licenses or permits.

If the enterprise does not succeed, the firm can be closed as easily as it was opened. Creditors must be paid, of course, but generally, the owner does not have to go through any legal procedure before hanging up an "Out of Business" sign.

PRIDE OF OWNERSHIP A successful sole proprietor is often very proud of her or his accomplishments—and rightfully so. In almost every case, the owner deserves a great deal of credit for solving the day-to-day problems associated with operating a sole proprietorship. Unfortunately, the reverse is also true. When the business fails, it is often the sole proprietor who is to blame.

RETENTION OF ALL PROFITS Because all profits become the personal earnings of the owner, the owner has a strong incentive to succeed. This direct financial reward attracts many entrepreneurs to the sole proprietorship form of business and, if the business succeeds, is a source of great satisfaction.

NO SPECIAL TAXES Profits earned by a sole proprietorship are taxed as the personal income of the owner. As a result, a sole proprietor must report business profit or loss and certain other financial information for a business on the Internal Revenue Service's Schedule C which becomes part of their personal income tax return. They must also make estimated quarterly tax payments to the federal government.

FLEXIBILITY OF BEING YOUR OWN BOSS A sole proprietor is completely free to make decisions about the firm's operations. Without asking or waiting for anyone's approval, a sole proprietor can move a shop's location, open a new store, or close an old one. And, he or she can make an immediate change in business hours. The manager of a store in a large corporate chain such as Best Buy Company may have to seek the approval of numerous managers and company officials before making such changes.

Owning your own business can be frustrating! While there are many advantages to sole proprietorships, there are disadvantages. For many sole proprietors there aren't enough hours in the day to get everything done. For others, the pressure of making decisions on a daily basis can be overwhelming. And yet, even with the disadvantages, sole proprietorships are still the most popular form of business ownership when compared to partnerships and corporations.

4-1b Disadvantages of Sole Proprietorships

The disadvantages of a sole proprietorship stem from the fact that these businesses are owned by one person. Some capable sole proprietors experience no problems. Individuals who start out with few management skills and little money are most at risk for failure.

UNLIMITED LIABILITY Unlimited liability is a legal concept that holds a business owner personally responsible for all the debts of the business. There is legally no difference between the debts of the business and the debts of the proprietor. If the business fails, or if the business is involved in a lawsuit and loses, the owner's personal property—including savings and other assets—can be seized (and sold if necessary) to pay creditors.

Unlimited liability is perhaps the major factor that tends to discourage would-be entrepreneurs with substantial personal wealth from using the sole proprietor form of business organization. Unlimited liability is also a reason why many sole proprietors switch to the corporate form of ownership or some other type of business organization once their businesses become successful.

LACK OF CONTINUITY Legally, the sole proprietor *is* the business. If the owner retires, dies, or is declared legally incompetent, the business essentially ceases to exist. In many cases, however—especially when the business is a profitable enterprise—the owner may sell the business or the owner's heirs may take it over and either sell it or continue to operate it. The business also can suffer if the sole proprietor becomes ill and cannot work for an extended period of time. If the owner, for example, has a heart attack, there is often no one who can step in and manage the business. An illness can be devastating if the sole proprietor's personal skills are what determine if the business is a success or a failure.

unlimited liability a legal concept that holds a business owner personally responsible for all the debts of the business

LACK OF MONEY Banks, suppliers, and other lenders usually are often unwilling to lend large sums of money to sole proprietorships. Only one person—the sole proprietor—can be held responsible for repaying such loans, and the assets of most sole proprietors usually are limited. Moreover, these assets may have been used already as security or collateral for personal borrowing (a home mortgage or car loan) or for short-term credit from suppliers. Lenders also worry about the lack of continuity of sole proprietorships: Who will repay a loan if the sole proprietor dies? Finally, many lenders are concerned about the large number of sole proprietorships that fail—a topic discussed in Chapter 5.

The limited ability to borrow money can prevent a sole proprietorship from growing. It is the main reason that many business owners, when in need of relatively large amounts of capital, change from a sole proprietorship to a partnership or corporate form of ownership.

LIMITED MANAGEMENT SKILLS The sole proprietor is often the sole manager—in addition to being the only salesperson, buyer, accountant, and, on occasion, janitor. Even the most experienced business owner is unlikely to have expertise in all these areas. Unless he or she obtains the necessary expertise by hiring employees, assistants, or consultants, the business can suffer in the areas in which the owner is less knowledgeable. For the many sole proprietors who cannot afford to hire the help they need, there just are not enough hours in the day to do everything that needs to be done.

DIFFICULTY IN HIRING EMPLOYEES The sole proprietor may find it hard to attract and keep competent help. Potential employees may feel that there is no room for advancement in a firm whose owner assumes all managerial responsibilities. And when those who *are* hired are ready to take on added responsibility, they may find that the only way to do so is to quit the sole proprietorship and go to work for a larger firm or start up their own businesses. The lure of higher salaries and increased benefits also may cause existing employees to change jobs.

4-1c Beyond the Sole Proprietorship

Like many others, you may decide that the major disadvantage of a sole proprietorship is the limited amount that one person can do in a workday. One way to reduce the effect of this disadvantage (and retain many of the advantages) is to form a partnership and have more than one owner.

4-2 PARTNERSHIPS

A person who would not think of starting and running a sole proprietorship business alone may enthusiastically seize the opportunity to form a business partnership. The U.S. Uniform Partnership Act defines a **partnership** as a voluntary association of two or more persons to act as co-owners of a business for profit. For example, in 1990, two young African-American entrepreneurs named Janet Smith and Gary Smith started IVY Planning Group—a company that provides full-service

Social Media:
Small Business Resources

Whether you're thinking about starting a sole proprietorship, partnership, or corporation or want to take your business to the next level, check out the many resources available on social-media sites. For example, *Inc.* magazine's popular Facebook page (www.facebook.com/Inc) has informative posts, links, and videos with "everything you need to know to start and grow your business now." More than 600,000 Facebook users have clicked to like the *Inc.* page and follow what the editors' post. The *Inc.* Twitter account (http://twitter.com/inc) has more than 63,000 tweets and well over 1 million followers.

Entrepreneur magazine has attracted nearly 2 million Facebook likes (www.facebook.com/EntMagazine) because of the many resources available on its page. The magazine also keeps entrepreneurs informed through the links, photos, and videos on its Twitter account (http://twitter.com/entrepreneur), inspiring photos on its Pinterest page (www.pinterest.com/entmagazine), and discussions on its LinkedIn page (www.linkedin.com/company/entrepreneur-media).

Every month, American Express uploads a variety of small-business videos to its OPEN YouTube channel (www.youtube.com/user/americanexpressOPEN). The videos cover tips for startups, small business success stories, customer relations, employee relations, marketing ideas, new technology, government contracts, and other topics of interest for entrepreneurs of all ages and in all industries.

Concept Check

✓ What is a sole proprietorship?

✓ What are the advantages of a sole proprietorship?

✓ What are the disadvantages of a sole proprietorship?

Learning Objective

4-2 Explain the different types of partners and the importance of partnership agreements.

partnership a voluntary association of two or more persons to act as co-owners of a business for profit

management consulting for clients. Today, over 25 years later, the company has evolved into a multimillion-dollar company that has hired a diverse staff of employees and provides cultural diversity training for *Fortune* 1000 firms, large not-for-profit organizations, and government agencies including PepsiCo, MetLife, Verizon, Target, and the U.S. Social Security Administration. In recognition of its efforts, IVY Planning Group has been recognized by www.DiversityBusiness.com as one of the top 50 minority-owned companies. And both Janet Smith and Gary Smith have been named "1 of 50 Influential Minorities in Business" by Minority Business and Professionals Network.[3]

As shown in Figures 4-1 and 4-2, there are approximately 4 million partnerships in the United States, and this type of ownership accounts for about $6 trillion in sales receipts each year. Note, however, that this form of ownership is much less common than the sole proprietorship or the corporation. In fact, as Figure 4-1 shows, partnerships represent only about 10 percent of all American businesses. Although there is no legal maximum on the number of partners a partnership may have, most have only two. Regardless of the number of people involved, a partnership often represents a pooling of special managerial skills and talents; at other times, it is the result of a sole proprietor taking on a partner for the purpose of obtaining more capital.

4-2a Types of Partners

All partners are not necessarily equal. Some may be active in running the business, whereas others may have a limited role.

GENERAL PARTNERS A **general partner** is a person who assumes full or shared responsibility for operating a business. General partners are active in day-to-day business operations, and each partner can enter into contracts on behalf of the other partners. He or she also assumes unlimited liability for all debts, including debts incurred by any other general partner without his or her knowledge or consent. To avoid future liability, a general partner who withdraws from the partnership must give notice to creditors, customers, and suppliers.

LIMITED PARTNERS A **limited partner** is a person who invests money in a business but who has no management responsibility or liability for losses beyond his or her investment in the partnership. Typically, the general partner or partners collect management fees and receive a percentage of profits. Limited partners receive a portion of profits and tax benefits. Limited partnerships, for example, may be formed to finance real estate, oil and gas, motion picture, and other business ventures.

Because of potential liability problems, special rules apply to limited partnerships. These rules are intended to protect customers and creditors who deal with limited partnerships. For example, prospective partners in a limited partnership must file a formal declaration, usually with the secretary of state, that describes the essential details of the partnership and the liability status of each partner involved in the business. At least one general partner must be responsible for the debts of the limited partnership. Also, some states prohibit the use of the limited partner's name in the partnership's name.

Partnership Pride. Don't ask these two entrepreneurs about their business unless you want to hear their story. Like most small business owners, talking about their businesses is easy and is a source of pride—especially when the partnership is profitable and the owners pool their management skills to build a successful business.

general partner a person who assumes full or shared responsibility for operating a business

limited partner a person who invests money in a business but has no management responsibility or liability for losses beyond the amount he or she invested in the partnership

VESNAANDJIC/ISTOCK/GETTY IMAGES

4-2b The Partnership Agreement

Articles of partnership refers to an agreement listing and explaining the terms of the partnership. Although both oral and written partnership agreements are legal and can be enforced in the courts, a written agreement has an obvious advantage. It is not subject to lapses of memory.

Figure 4-3 shows a typical partnership agreement. The partnership agreement should state

- Who will make the final decisions
- What each partner's duties will be
- The investment each partner will make
- How much profit or loss each partner receives or is responsible for
- What happens if a partner wants to dissolve the partnership or dies

Concept Check

✓ How does a sole proprietorship differ from a partnership?

✓ Explain the difference between a general partner and a limited partner.

✓ Describe the issues that should be included in a partnership agreement.

FIGURE 4-3 Articles of Partnership

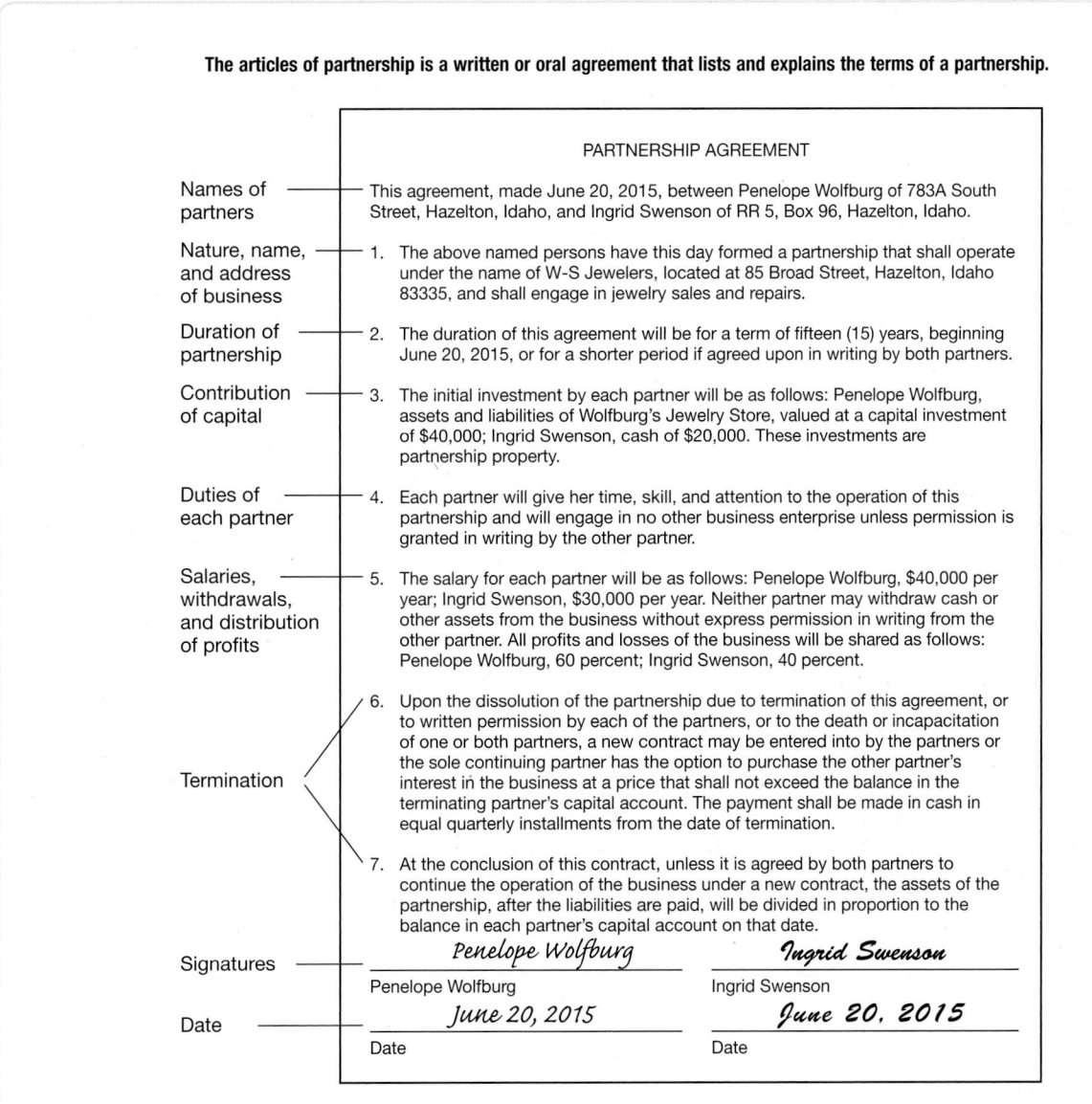

The articles of partnership is a written or oral agreement that lists and explains the terms of a partnership.

PARTNERSHIP AGREEMENT

Names of partners

This agreement, made June 20, 2015, between Penelope Wolfburg of 783A South Street, Hazelton, Idaho, and Ingrid Swenson of RR 5, Box 96, Hazelton, Idaho.

Nature, name, and address of business

1. The above named persons have this day formed a partnership that shall operate under the name of W-S Jewelers, located at 85 Broad Street, Hazelton, Idaho 83335, and shall engage in jewelry sales and repairs.

Duration of partnership

2. The duration of this agreement will be for a term of fifteen (15) years, beginning June 20, 2015, or for a shorter period if agreed upon in writing by both partners.

Contribution of capital

3. The initial investment by each partner will be as follows: Penelope Wolfburg, assets and liabilities of Wolfburg's Jewelry Store, valued at a capital investment of $40,000; Ingrid Swenson, cash of $20,000. These investments are partnership property.

Duties of each partner

4. Each partner will give her time, skill, and attention to the operation of this partnership and will engage in no other business enterprise unless permission is granted in writing by the other partner.

Salaries, withdrawals, and distribution of profits

5. The salary for each partner will be as follows: Penelope Wolfburg, $40,000 per year; Ingrid Swenson, $30,000 per year. Neither partner may withdraw cash or other assets from the business without express permission in writing from the other partner. All profits and losses of the business will be shared as follows: Penelope Wolfburg, 60 percent; Ingrid Swenson, 40 percent.

Termination

6. Upon the dissolution of the partnership due to termination of this agreement, or to written permission by each of the partners, or to the death or incapacitation of one or both partners, a new contract may be entered into by the partners or the sole continuing partner has the option to purchase the other partner's interest in the business at a price that shall not exceed the balance in the terminating partner's capital account. The payment shall be made in cash in equal quarterly installments from the date of termination.

7. At the conclusion of this contract, unless it is agreed by both partners to continue the operation of the business under a new contract, the assets of the partnership, after the liabilities are paid, will be divided in proportion to the balance in each partner's capital account on that date.

Signatures

Penelope Wolfburg   *Ingrid Swenson*

Penelope Wolfburg   Ingrid Swenson

Date

June 20, 2015   *June 20, 2015*

Date   Date

Source: Adapted from Goldman and Sigismond, *Cengage Advantage Books: Business Law 9E.*

Although the people involved in a partnership can draft their own agreement, most experts recommend consulting an attorney.

When entering into a partnership agreement, partners would be wise to let a neutral third party—a consultant, an accountant, a lawyer, or a mutual friend—assist with any disputes that might arise.

4-3 ADVANTAGES AND DISADVANTAGES OF PARTNERSHIPS

Learning Objective

4-3 Describe the advantages and disadvantages of partnerships.

When compared to sole proprietorships and corporations, partnerships are the least popular form of business ownership. Still there are situations when forming a partnership makes perfect sense. Before you make a decision to form a partnership, all the people involved should consider both the advantages and disadvantages of a partnership.

4-3a Advantages of Partnerships

Partnerships have many advantages. The most important are described as follows.

EASE OF START-UP Partnerships are relatively easy to form. As with a sole proprietorship, the legal requirements often are limited to registering the name of the business and obtaining any necessary licenses or permits. It may not even be necessary to prepare written articles of partnership, although doing so is generally a good idea.

AVAILABILITY OF CAPITAL AND CREDIT Because partners can pool their funds, a partnership usually has more capital available than a sole proprietorship does. This additional capital, coupled with the general partners' unlimited liability and combined management skills, may encourage banks and suppliers to extend more credit or approve larger loans to a partnership than to a sole proprietor. This does not mean that partnerships can borrow all the money they need. Many partnerships have found it hard to get long-term financing simply because lenders worry about the possibility of management disagreements and lack of continuity.

PERSONAL INTEREST General partners are very concerned with the operation of the firm—perhaps even more so than sole proprietors. After all, they are responsible for the actions of all other general partners, as well as for their own. The pride of ownership from solving the day-to-day problems of operating a business—with the help of another person(s)—is a strong motivating force and often makes all the people involved in the partnership work harder to become more successful.

COMBINED BUSINESS SKILLS AND KNOWLEDGE Partners often have complementary skills. The weakness of one partner—in manufacturing, for example—may be offset by another partner's strength in that area. Moreover, the ability to discuss important decisions with another concerned individual often relieves some pressure and leads to more effective decision making.

RETENTION OF PROFITS As in a sole proprietorship, all profits belong to the owners of the partnership. The partners share directly in the financial rewards and therefore are highly motivated to do their best to make the firm succeed. As noted, the partnership agreement should state how much profit or loss each partner receives or is responsible for.

NO SPECIAL TAXES Although a partnership pays no income tax, the Internal Revenue Service requires partnerships to file an annual information return that states the names and addresses of all partners involved in the business. Then each partner is required to report his or her share of profit (or loss) from the partnership on his or her individual tax return. Ultimately each partner's share of the partnership profit is taxed in the same way a sole proprietor is taxed.

4-3b Disadvantages of Partnerships

Although partnerships have many advantages when compared with sole proprietorships and corporations, they also have some disadvantages, which anyone thinking of forming a partnership should consider.

UNLIMITED LIABILITY As we have noted, each *general* partner has unlimited liability for all debts of the business. Each partner is legally and personally responsible for the debts, taxes, and actions of any other partner conducting partnership business, even if that partner did not incur those debts or do anything wrong. General partners thus run the risk of having to use their personal assets to pay creditors. *Limited* partners, however, risk only their original investment.

Today, many states allow partners to form a *limited-liability partnership* (LLP), in which a partner may have limited-liability protection from legal action resulting from the malpractice or negligence of the other partners. Many states that allow LLPs restrict this type of ownership to certain types of professionals such as accountants, architects, attorneys, and similar professionals. (Note the difference between a limited partnership and an LLP. A limited partnership must have at least one general partner that has unlimited liability. On the other hand, all partners in an LLP may have limited liability *for the malpractice and negligence of the other partners.*)

MANAGEMENT DISAGREEMENTS What happens to a partnership if one of the partners brings a spouse or a relative into the business? What happens if a partner wants to withdraw more money from the business? Notice that each of these situations—and for that matter, most of the other problems that can develop in a partnership—involves one partner doing something that disturbs the other partner(s). This human factor is especially important because business partners—with egos, ambitions, and money on the line—are especially susceptible to friction. When partners begin to disagree about decisions, policies, or ethics, distrust may build and get worse as time passes—often to the point where it is impossible to operate the business successfully.

LACK OF CONTINUITY Partnerships are terminated if any one of the general partners dies, withdraws, or is declared legally incompetent. However, the remaining partners can purchase that partner's ownership share. For example, the partnership agreement may permit surviving partners to continue the business after buying a deceased partner's interest from his or her estate. However, if the partnership loses an owner whose specific management or technical skills cannot be replaced, it is not likely to survive.

FROZEN INVESTMENT It is easy to invest money in a partnership, but it is sometimes quite difficult to get it out. This is the case, for example, when remaining partners are unwilling to buy the share of the business that belongs to a partner who retires. To avoid such difficulties, the partnership agreement should include some procedure for buying out a partner.

In some cases, a partner must find someone outside the firm to buy his or her share. How easy or difficult it is to find an outsider depends on how successful the business is and how willing existing partners are to accept a new partner.

Concept Check

✓ What are the advantages of a partnership?

✓ What are the disadvantages of a partnership?

4-3c Beyond the Partnership

The main advantages of a partnership over a sole proprietorship are increased availability of capital and credit and the combined business skills and knowledge of the partners. However, some of the basic disadvantages of the sole proprietorship also plague the general partnership. A third form of business ownership, the corporation, overcomes many of these disadvantages.

4-4 CORPORATIONS

Learning Objective

4-4 Summarize how a corporation is formed.

Back in 1837, William Procter and James Gamble—two sole proprietors—formed a partnership called Procter & Gamble (P&G) and set out to compete with 14 other soap and candle makers in Cincinnati, Ohio. Then, in 1890, Procter & Gamble incorporated to raise additional capital for expansion that eventually allowed the company to become a global giant. P&G brands serve over 5 billion of the 7 billion people in the world today because the corporation operates in 180 countries around the globe.[4] Like many large corporations, P&G's market capitalization is greater than the gross domestic product of many countries. Although this corporation is a corporate giant, the firm's executives and employees believe it also has a responsibility to be an ethical corporate citizen. For example, P&G's purpose statement (or mission) is

> We will provide branded products and services of superior quality and value that improve the lives of the world's consumers, now and for generations to come. As a result, consumers will reward us with leadership sales, profit and value creation, allowing our people, our shareholders and the communities in which we live and work to prosper.[5]

While not all sole proprietorships and partnerships become corporations, there are reasons why business owners choose the corporate form of ownership. Let's begin with a definition of a corporation. Perhaps the best definition of a corporation was given by Chief Justice John Marshall in a famous Supreme Court decision in 1819. A corporation, he said, "is an artificial person, invisible, intangible, and existing only in contemplation of the law." In other words, a **corporation** (sometimes referred to as a *regular* or *C-corporation*) is an artificial person created by law, with most of the legal rights of a real person. These include

- The right to start and operate a business
- The right to buy or sell property
- The right to borrow money
- The right to sue or be sued
- The right to enter into binding contracts

Unlike a real person, however, a corporation exists only on paper. There are approximately 7 million corporations in the United States. They comprise about 17 percent of all businesses, but they account for 79 percent of sales revenues (see Figures 4-1 and 4-2).

corporation an artificial person created by law with most of the legal rights of a real person, including the rights to start and operate a business, to buy or sell property, to borrow money, to sue or be sued, and to enter into binding contracts

4-4a Corporate Ownership

The shares of ownership of a corporation are called **stock**. The people who own a corporation's stock—and thus own part of the corporation—are called **stockholders**. Once a corporation has been formed, it may sell its stock to individuals or other companies that want to invest in the corporation. It also may issue stock as a reward to key employees or as a return to investors in place of cash payments.

A **closed corporation** is a corporation whose stock is owned by relatively few people and is not sold to the general public. As an example, Mars—the company famous for M&Ms, Snickers, Dove, Milky Way, Twix, and other chocolate candy—is a privately held, family-owned, closed corporation. Although many people think that a closed corporation is a small company, there are exceptions. Mars, for example, has annual sales of more than $33 billion, employs more than 75,000 associates worldwide, and operates in over 70 different countries.[6]

What a success story. Back in 1955, a man named Ray Kroc founded the McDonald's Corporation. A mere five years later McDonalds had sold 100 million hamburgers. Over the years, the McDonald's Corporation continued to grow and change its menu options to reflect consumer tastes for healthier food. Today, McDonalds is one of the world's leading food service retailers serving nearly 70 million people every day in 36,000 restaurants around the globe.

An **open corporation** is one whose stock can be bought and sold by any individual. Examples of open corporations include General Electric, Microsoft, Apple, and Sony.

4-4b Forming a Corporation

Although you may think that incorporating a business guarantees success, it does not. There is no special magic about placing the word *Incorporated* or the abbreviation *Inc.* after the name of a business. Unfortunately, like sole proprietorships or partnerships, corporations can go broke. The decision to incorporate a business, therefore, should be made only after carefully considering whether the corporate form of ownership suits your needs better than the sole proprietorship or partnership forms.

If you decide that the corporate form is the best form of organization for you, most experts recommend that you begin the incorporation process by consulting a lawyer to be sure that all legal requirements are met. While it may be possible to incorporate a business without legal help, it is well to keep in mind the old saying, "A man who acts as his own attorney has a fool for a client." Table 4-1 lists some aspects of starting and running a business that may require legal help.

WHERE TO INCORPORATE A business is allowed to incorporate in any state that it chooses. Most small- and medium-sized businesses are incorporated in the state where they do the most business. The founders of larger corporations or of those that will do business nationwide often compare the benefits that various states provide to corporations. The decision on where to incorporate usually is based on two factors: (1) the cost of incorporating in one state compared with the cost in another state and (2) the advantages and disadvantages of each state's corporate laws and tax structure. Some states are more hospitable than others, and some offer fewer restrictions, lower taxes, and other benefits to attract new firms. Delaware, Nevada, and Wyoming are often chosen by corporations that do business in more than one state because of their corporation-friendly laws and pro-business climate.[7]

stock the shares of ownership of a corporation

stockholder a person who owns a corporation's stock

closed corporation a corporation whose stock is owned by relatively few people and is not sold to the general public

open corporation a corporation whose stock can be bought and sold by any individual

Should Your Company Be a Benefit Corporation?

Entrepreneurs who put social responsibility high on their list of priorities should investigate the pros and cons of the "benefit corporation." This form of business ownership, currently available in more than two dozen states, gives a for-profit corporation the legal authority to operate for the benefit of societal stakeholders, not just for stockholders. As a result, a benefit corporation's board of directors can't be sued for pursuing non-financial goals such as protecting the environment or giving back to the community.

Becoming a benefit corporation is a way to demonstrate a commitment to social responsibility and attract customers, investors, and employees who share those values. It can also serve as a way to differentiate your company in a competitive marketplace. However, because the benefit corporation is a fairly new form of business ownership, states are still working out the regulatory details. For example, what happens if the benefit corporation does *not* achieve its non-financial goals? Should benefit corporations be subject to special government oversight to ensure that they are actually involved in socially-responsible initiatives?

B Lab, a nonprofit organization, takes the idea of a benefit corporation one step further with its "B Corp" certification. To qualify, a business must follow the legal rules for incorporating as a benefit corporation *and* be certified by B Lab that it meets specific standards of social and environmental performance, community involvement, fair and equitable treatment of employees, accountability, and transparency. Patagonia, Ben & Jerry's, and Etsy are among the hundreds of successful businesses that proudly proclaim their status as certified B Corps. In fact, B Corp certification has become a badge of honor!

Sources: Based on information in Jeffrey Stinson, "Rules Recognizing Benefit Corporations," *Albuquerque Business Journal*, December 28, 2014, www.abqjournal.com; Doug Bend and Alex King, "Why Consider a Benefit Corporation?" *Forbes*, May 30, 2014, www.forbes.com; David R. Sands, "Benefit Corporations Raise Legal, Regulatory Questions," *Washington Times*, December 7, 2014, www.washingtontimes.com; Steve Parrish, "Three Companies Doing Well by Doing Good," *Forbes*, December 15, 2014, www.forbes.com; www.bcorporation.net.

An incorporated business is called a **domestic corporation** in the state in which it is incorporated. In all other states where it does business, it is called a **foreign corporation**. Sears Holdings Corporation, the parent company of Sears and Kmart, is incorporated in Delaware, where it is a domestic corporation. In the remaining 49 states, Sears is a foreign corporation. Sears must register in all states where it does business and also pay taxes and annual fees to each state. A corporation chartered by a foreign government and conducting business in the United States is an **alien corporation**. Volkswagen AG and Sony Corporation are examples of alien corporations.

domestic corporation a corporation in the state in which it is incorporated

foreign corporation a corporation in any state in which it does business except the one in which it is incorporated

alien corporation a corporation chartered by a foreign government and conducting business in the United States

TABLE 4-1 Ten Aspects of Business That May Require Legal Help

1. Choosing either the sole proprietorship, partnership, corporate, or some special form of ownership
2. Constructing a partnership agreement
3. Incorporating a business
4. Registering a corporation's stock
5. Obtaining a trademark, patent, or copyright
6. Filing for licenses or permits at the local, state, and federal levels
7. Purchasing an existing business or real estate
8. Creating valid contracts
9. Hiring employees and independent contractors
10. Extending credit and collecting debts

THE CORPORATE CHARTER Once a home state has been chosen, the incorporator(s) submits *articles of incorporation* to the secretary of state. When the articles of incorporation are approved, they become a contract, often called the corporate charter, between a corporation and the state in which the state recognizes the formation of the artificial person that is the corporation. Usually, the articles of incorporation include the following information:

- The firm's name and address
- The incorporators' names and addresses
- The purpose of the corporation
- The maximum amount of stock and types of stock to be issued
- The rights and privileges of stockholders
- The length of time the corporation is to exist

To help you to decide if the corporate form of organization is the right choice, you may want to visit the library. You can also use an Internet search engine and enter the term "business incorporation" for useful websites. In addition, before making a decision to organize your business as a corporation, you may want to consider two additional areas: stockholders' rights and the importance of the organizational meeting.

Personal App

Are you a stockholder?

© STEPHEN COBURN/SHUTTERSTOCK.COM

Even if you own a single share of common stock, you're legally a part owner of the corporation. You're entitled to receive any dividends paid to stockholders and you can vote on important matters such as electing the board of directors. Your vote is counted—and it counts.

STOCKHOLDERS' RIGHTS There are two basic types of stock. Owners of **common stock** may vote on corporate matters. Generally, an owner of common stock has one vote for each share owned. However, any claims of common-stock owners on profits, dividends, and assets of the corporation are paid after the claims of others. The owners of **preferred stock** usually have no voting rights, but their claims on dividends are paid before those of common-stock owners. Although some large corporations may issue both common and preferred stock, generally smaller corporations issue only common stock.

Perhaps the most important right of owners of both common and preferred stock is to share in the profit earned by the corporation through the payment of dividends. A **dividend** is a distribution of earnings to the stockholders of a corporation. Other rights include receiving information about the corporation, voting on changes to the corporate charter, and attending the corporation's annual stockholders' meeting, where they may exercise their right to vote.

Because common stockholders usually live all over the nation, very few actually may attend a corporation's annual meeting. Instead, they vote by proxy. A **proxy** is a legal form listing issues to be decided at a stockholders' meeting and enabling stockholders to transfer their voting rights to some other individual or individuals. The stockholder can register a vote and transfer voting rights simply by signing and returning the form. Today, most corporations also allow stockholders to exercise their right to vote by proxy by accessing the Internet or using a toll-free phone number.

ORGANIZATIONAL MEETING As the last step in forming a corporation, the incorporators and original stockholders meet to adopt corporate bylaws and elect

common stock stock owned by individuals or firms who may vote on corporate matters but whose claims on profits and assets are subordinate to the claims of others

preferred stock stock owned by individuals or firms who usually do not have voting rights but whose claims on dividends are paid before those of common-stock owners

dividend a distribution of earnings to the stockholders of a corporation

proxy a legal form listing issues to be decided at a stockholders' meeting and enabling stockholders to transfer their voting rights to some other individual or individuals

You will be
missed Steve
-Austin, USA

© PHOTOCRITICAL/SHUTTERSTOCK.COM

What's it take to lead a major corporation? Simple answer: Leadership. Apple co-founder, Steve Jobs, was always known for his leadership style that helped to create technology-based products that enabled Apple to become a leader in the very competitive technology industry. The people at Apple will miss his leadership skills, but the world will miss his creative genius.

Concept Check

✓ Explain the difference between an open corporation and a closed corporation.

✓ How is a domestic corporation different from a foreign corporation and an alien corporation?

✓ Outline the incorporation process, and describe the basic corporate structure.

✓ What rights do stockholders have?

board of directors the top governing body of a corporation, the members of which are elected by the stockholders

corporate officers the chairman of the board, president, executive vice presidents, corporate secretary, treasurer, and any other top executive appointed by the board of directors

their first board of directors. (Later, directors will be elected or reelected at the corporation's annual meetings by the firm's stockholders.) The board members are directly responsible to the stockholders for the way they operate the firm.

4-4c Corporate Structure

The organizational structure of most corporations is more complicated than that of a sole proprietorship or partnership. In a corporation, both the board of directors and the corporate officers are involved in management.

BOARD OF DIRECTORS As an artificial person, a corporation can act only through its directors, who represent the corporation's stockholders. The **board of directors** is the top governing body of a corporation and is elected by the stockholders. In theory, then, the stockholders are able to control the activities of the entire corporation through its directors because they are the group that elects the board of directors (see Figure 4-4).

Board members can be chosen from within the corporation or from outside it. *Note:* For a small corporation, only one director is required in many states although you can choose to have more. Directors who are elected from within the corporation are usually its top managers—the president and executive vice presidents, for example. Those elected from outside the corporation generally are experienced managers or entrepreneurs with proven leadership ability and/or specific talents the organization seems to need. In smaller corporations, majority stockholders usually serve as board members.

The major responsibilities of the board of directors are to set company goals and develop general plans (or strategies) for meeting those goals. The board also is responsible for the firm's overall operation and appointing corporate officers.

CORPORATE OFFICERS Corporate officers are appointed by the board of directors. Although a small corporation may not have all of the following officers, the chairman of the board, president, executive vice presidents, corporate secretary, and treasurer are all corporate officers. They help the board to make plans, carry out strategies established by the board, hire employees, and manage day-to-day business activities. Periodically (usually each month), they report to the board of directors. And at the annual meeting, the directors report to the stockholders.

FIGURE 4-4 Hierarchy of Corporate Structure

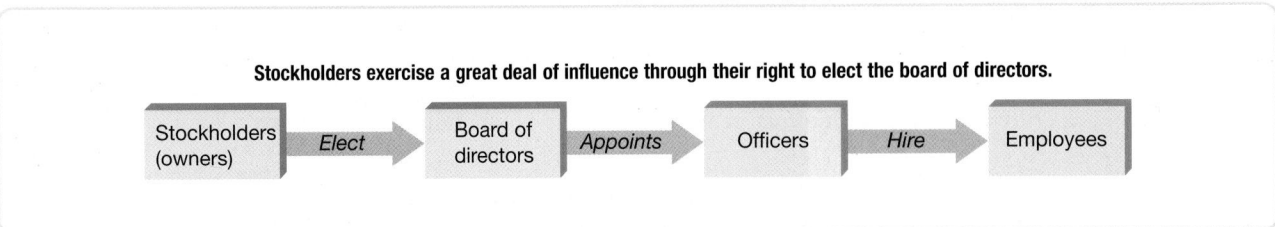

Stockholders exercise a great deal of influence through their right to elect the board of directors.

Stockholders (owners) → *Elect* → Board of directors → *Appoints* → Officers → *Hire* → Employees

4-5 ADVANTAGES AND DISADVANTAGES OF CORPORATIONS

When Warren Buffett started his first partnership more than 50 years ago, he never dreamed he would wind up putting together a wildly diverse collection of businesses under one corporate umbrella. It all started when Buffett set up a series of partnerships with family and friends to pool cash for buying big blocks of stock in companies he had researched. Not all of the companies Buffett chose paid off, but many were so successful that Buffett quickly earned a worldwide reputation for his ability to pick just the "right" company. Today, Berkshire Hathaway now owns more than 50 different corporations, brings in almost $200 billion in annual revenue, and employees 300,000 people.

Although Warren Buffett started with partnerships, he eventually chose the corporate form of ownership because it provided a number of advantages when compared to a partnership or the other forms of business ownership. Typical advantages of the corporate form of ownership include limited liability, ease of raising capital, ease of transfer of ownership, perpetual life, and specialized management.

4-5a Advantages of Corporations

LIMITED LIABILITY One of the most attractive features of corporate ownership is **limited liability**. With few exceptions, each owner's financial liability is limited to the amount of money he or she has paid for the corporation's stock. This feature arises from the fact that the corporation is itself a legal person, separate from its owners. If a corporation fails or is involved in a lawsuit and loses, creditors have a claim only on the corporation's assets. Because it overcomes the problem of unlimited liability connected with sole proprietorships and general partnerships, limited liability is one of the chief reasons why entrepreneurs often choose the corporate form of organization. For example, Manny Ruiz, with the help of a team of media specialists, founded a corporation called Hispanic PR Wire back in 2000. They chose the corporate form of ownership because of limited liability *and* the other advantages this type of ownership provided that other forms of business ownership did not offer. After the firm's initial success, Hispanic PR Wire was sold to PR Newswire—a larger company—but the original company continues to provide important news and entertainment coverage for the Hispanic market.[8]

EASE OF RAISING CAPITAL The corporation is one of the most effective forms of business ownership for raising capital. Like sole proprietorships and partnerships, corporations can borrow from lending institutions. However, they also can raise additional sums of money by selling stock. In fact, the amount of capital that can be raised by selling stock can be staggering. Alibaba, the Chinese e-commerce company, raised $25

Learning Objective

4-5 Describe the advantages and disadvantages of a corporation.

limited liability a feature of corporate ownership that limits each owner's financial liability to the amount of money that he or she has paid for the corporation's stock

CPENLER/DREAMSTIME.COM

How much money can a corporation raise by selling stock? Good question. While the amount of money a corporation can raise by selling stock depends on many factors, Alibaba—the Chinese e-commerce company—raised $25 billion by selling stock. The money can be used to fund expansion, to repay debt, or for any valid business reasons.

billion by selling stock in late 2014. This was the largest global initial public stock offering—often referred to as an IPO—in history.[9] Money from an IPO can be used by a corporation for expansion, to repay debt, or for any valid reason. While not all IPOs are as large as Alibaba's, individuals are more willing to invest in corporations than in other forms of business because of limited liability, and they can generally sell their stock easily—hopefully for a profit.

EASE OF TRANSFER OF OWNERSHIP Accessing a brokerage firm website or a telephone call to a stockbroker is all that is required to put most stock up for sale. Willing buyers are available for most stocks at the current market price. Ownership is transferred when the sale is made, and practically no restrictions apply to the sale and purchase of stock issued by an open corporation.

PERPETUAL LIFE Since it is essentially a legal "person," a corporation exists independently of its owners and survives them. The withdrawal, death, or incompetence of a key executive or owner does not cause the corporation to be terminated. Sears, Roebuck and Co. was originally founded in 1893 and is one of the nation's largest retailing corporations, even though its original founders, Richard Sears and Alvah Roebuck, have been dead for decades.

SPECIALIZED MANAGEMENT Typically, corporations are able to recruit more skilled, knowledgeable, and talented managers than proprietorships and partnerships. This is so because they pay bigger salaries, offer excellent employee benefits, and are large enough to offer considerable opportunity for advancement. Within the corporate structure, administration, human resources, finance, marketing, operations, and manufacturing are placed in the charge of experts in these fields.

4-5b Disadvantages of Corporations

Like its advantages, many of a corporation's disadvantages stem from its legal definition as an artificial person or legal entity. The most serious disadvantages are described in the following text. Also see Table 4-2 for a comparison of some of the advantages and disadvantages of a sole proprietorship, general partnership, and corporation.

DIFFICULTY AND EXPENSE OF FORMATION Forming a corporation can be a relatively complex and costly process. The use of an attorney is usually necessary to complete the legal forms that are submitted to the secretary of state. Application fees, attorney's fees, registration costs associated with selling stock, and other organizational costs can amount to thousands of dollars for even a medium-sized

TABLE 4-2 Some Advantages and Disadvantages of a Sole Proprietorship, Partnership, and Corporation

	Sole Proprietorship	General Partnership	Regular C-Corporation
Protecting against liability for debts	Difficult	Difficult	Easy
Raising money	Difficult	Difficult	Easy
Ownership transfer	Difficult	Difficult	Easy
Preserving continuity	Difficult	Difficult	Easy
Government regulations	Few	Few	Many
Formation	Easy	Easy	Difficult
Income taxation	Once	Once	Twice

corporation. The costs of incorporating, in terms of both time and money, discourage many owners of smaller businesses from forming corporations. Before deciding to incorporate a small business, you may want to review the material in the section "Forming a Corporation" discussed earlier in this chapter.

GOVERNMENT REGULATION AND INCREASED PAPERWORK A corporation must register and meet various government standards before it can sell its stock to the public. Then it must file many reports on its business operations and finances with local, state, and federal governments. In addition, the corporation must make periodic reports to its stockholders. To prepare all the necessary reports, even small corporations often need the help of an attorney, certified public accountant, and other professionals on a regular basis. In addition, a corporation's activities are restricted by law to those spelled out in its corporate charter.

CONFLICT WITHIN THE CORPORATION Because a large corporation may employ thousands of employees, some conflict is inevitable. For example, the pressure to increase sales revenue, reduce expenses, and increase profits often leads to increased stress and tension for both managers and employees. This is especially true when a corporation operates in a competitive industry, attempts to develop and market new products, or must downsize the workforce to reduce employee salary expense. For example, both Coca Cola and McDonalds—two of America's strongest corporations—announced plans to lay off workers in the first part of 2015 in order to reduce expenses. According to Ann Moore, a Coca-Cola spokeswoman, "We do not take decisions about job impacts lightly."[10]

DOUBLE TAXATION Corporations must pay a tax on their profits. In addition, stockholders must pay a personal income tax on profits received as dividends. Corporate profits thus are taxed twice—once as corporate income and a second time as the personal income of stockholders. *Note:* Both the S corporation and the limited-liability company (LLC) discussed in the next section eliminate the disadvantage of double taxation and are a primary reason why business owners choose these special types of business ownership.

LACK OF SECRECY Because open corporations are required to submit detailed reports to government agencies and to stockholders, they cannot keep all of their operations confidential. Competitors can study these corporate reports and then use the information to compete more effectively. In effect, every public corporation has to share some of its secrets about its management, finances, and other business activities with its competitors.

Concept Check

✓ What are the advantages of a corporation?

✓ What are the disadvantages of a corporation?

4-6 SPECIAL TYPES OF BUSINESS OWNERSHIP

In addition to the sole proprietorship, partnership, and the regular corporate form of organization, some entrepreneurs choose other forms of organization that meet their special needs. Additional organizational options include S corporations, LLCs, and not-for-profit corporations.

4-6a S Corporations

If a corporation meets certain requirements, its directors may apply to the Internal Revenue Service for status as an S corporation. An **S corporation** is a corporation that is taxed as though it were a partnership. In other words, the corporation's income is taxed only as the personal income of its stockholders. Corporate profits

Learning Objective

4-6 Examine special types of businesses, including S corporations, limited-liability companies, and not-for-profit corporations.

S corporation a corporation that is taxed as though it were a partnership

or losses "pass through" the business and are reported on the owners' personal income tax returns.

To qualify for the special status of an S corporation, the first step is to file the necessary paperwork to become a corporation. A number of issues described in the section "Forming a Corporation" must be decided and paperwork must be filed with the secretary of state. Once the corporation is established, the corporation must complete Form 2553 and submit it to the IRS. In addition to completing the form, a firm must meet the following criteria:[11]

1. No more than 100 stockholders are allowed.
2. Stockholders must be individuals, estates, or certain trusts.
3. There can be only one class of outstanding stock.
4. The firm must be a domestic corporation eligible to file for S corporation status.
5. All stockholders must agree to the decision to form an S corporation.

Becoming an S corporation can be an effective way to avoid double taxation while retaining the corporation's legal benefit of limited liability.

4-6b Limited-Liability Companies

A **limited-liability company (LLC)** is a form of business ownership that combines the benefits of a corporation and a partnership while avoiding some of the restrictions and disadvantages of those forms of ownership. Chief advantages of an LLC are as follows:

1. Like a sole proprietorship or partnership, an LLC enjoys pass-through taxation. This means that owners—which are called members in an LLC—report their share of profits or losses in the company on their individual tax returns and avoid the double taxation imposed on most corporations. LLCs with at least two members are taxed like a partnership. LLCs with just one member are taxed like a sole proprietorship. LLCs can even elect to be taxed as a corporation or S corporation if there are benefits to offset the corporate double taxation and other restrictions.

2. Like a corporation, it provides limited-liability protection for acts and debts of the LLC. An LLC thus extends the concept of personal-asset protection to small business owners.

3. The LLC type of organization provides more management flexibility and fewer restrictions when compared with corporations. A corporation, for example, is required to hold annual meetings and record meeting minutes; an LLC is not.

Although many experts believe that the LLC is nothing more than a variation of the S corporation, there is a difference. An LLC is not restricted to 100 stockholders—a common drawback of the S corporation. Although the laws for forming an LLC are slightly different in each state, the owners of an LLC may file the required articles of organization in any state. Most choose to file in their home state—the state where they do most of their business.

limited-liability company (LLC) a form of business ownership that combines the benefits of a corporation and a partnership while avoiding some of the restrictions and disadvantages of those forms of ownership

BMW of North America: A Limited Liability Company. A limited liability company doesn't have to be small. BMW sells luxury automobiles all over the world including Europe, Asia, Africa, South America—and of course North America. BMW of North America chose the limited-liability company form of ownership to avoid some of the restrictions and disadvantages of other forms of business ownership.

BISERKO/DREAMSTIME.COM

TABLE 4-3 Some Advantages and Disadvantages of a Regular Corporation, S Corporation, and Limited-Liability Company

	Regular C-Corporation	S Corporation	Limited-Liability Company
Double taxation	Yes	No	No
Limited liability and personal asset protection	Yes	Yes	Yes
Management flexibility	No	No	Yes
Restrictions on the number of owners/stockholders	No	Yes	No
Internal Revenue Service tax regulations	Many	Many	Fewer

Even though most LLCs are small- to medium-sized businesses, an LLC doesn't have to be small. BMW of North America—an LLC that sells luxury automobiles and motorcycles—chose the LLC type of business ownership because it provided limited liability for investors and avoided some of the restrictions and disadvantages of other forms of business ownership.

For help in understanding the differences between a regular corporation, S corporation, and an LLC, see Table 4-3.

4-6c Not-for-Profit Corporations

A **not-for-profit corporation** (sometimes referred to as *non-profit*) is a corporation organized to provide a social, educational, religious, or other service rather than to earn a profit. Various charities, museums, private schools, colleges, and charitable organizations are organized in this way, primarily to ensure limited liability.

While the process used to organize a not-for-profit corporation is similar to the process used to create a regular corporation, each state does have different laws. Once approved by state authorities, not-for-profit corporations must meet specific Internal Revenue Service guidelines in order to obtain tax-exempt status.

Today, there is a renewed interest in not-for-profits because these organizations are often formed to improve communities and change lives. For example, Habitat for Humanity is a not-for-profit corporation and was formed to provide homes for qualified lower income people who cannot afford housing. Even though this corporation may receive more money than it spends, any surplus funds are "reinvested" in building activities to provide low-cost housing to qualified individuals.

Many not-for-profit corporations operate in much the same way as for-profit businesses. Employees of not-for-profit businesses are responsible for making sure the organization achieves its goals and objectives, ensuring accountability for finances and donations, and monitoring activities to improve the performance of both paid employees and volunteers. If you are interested in a business career, don't rule out the non-profit sector. You might consider volunteering in a local not-for-profit organization to see if you enjoy this type of challenge.

not-for-profit corporation a corporation organized to provide a social, educational, religious, or other service rather than to earn a profit

Concept Check

✓ Explain the difference between an S corporation and a limited-liability company.

✓ How does a regular (C) corporation differ from a not-for-profit corporation?

4-7 JOINT VENTURES AND SYNDICATES

Today, two additional types of business organizations—joint ventures and syndicates—are used for special purposes. Each of these forms of organization is unique when compared with more traditional forms of business ownership.

Learning Objective

4-7 Discuss the purpose of a joint venture and syndicate.

Ethical Success or Failure

Tough Decisions for Entrepreneurs in Tough Situations

As an entrepreneur launching a small business, you'll face lots of tough decisions. What do you think is the right thing to do in the following situations?

1. A potential customer wants to visit your place of business. Should you introduce friends as "employees" so your firm looks bigger and busier?
2. Suppliers have sent you free samples so you can examine products before placing an order. Once you buy, is it ethical to sell the samples while you wait for your delivery?
3. A supplier offers to cut its price and not collect sales tax if you pay cash and don't require a receipt. Money is tight—should you do this?

Experts say it's important for entrepreneurs to set a tone of honesty and integrity and earn the trust of their employees, bankers, suppliers, customers, distributors, and investors.

A fledgling business known for ethical dealings will have a smoother path to success than a business that's suspected of shady dealings.

So in situation #1, the ethical course of action is to invite your suppliers and introduce them as your network of experts that are on hand to answer a customer's questions and offer advice. In situation #2, give the freebies away to customers who order other products—a good way to gain goodwill and let *them* sample new products without risk. As for situation #3, do you want to do business with a tax cheat or have this supplier tell others that you participated in a scheme to avoid paying taxes?

Sources: Based on information in Gael O'Brien, "The Ethics Coach's Top 3 Strategies for Creating an Ethical Workplace," *Entrepreneur*, June 2014; Gael O'Brien, "The Ethics Coach on Cash Deals, Transparency, and More," *Entrepreneur*, January 2014; Gael O'Brien, "The Ethics Coach on Misrepresentation," *Entrepreneur*, April 2013.

4-7a Joint Ventures

A **joint venture** is an agreement between two or more groups to form a business entity in order to achieve a specific goal or to operate for a specific period of time. Both the scope of the joint venture and the liabilities of the people or businesses involved usually are limited to one project. Once the goal is reached, the period of time elapses, or the project is completed, the joint venture is dissolved.

Corporations, as well as individuals, may enter into joint ventures. Major oil producers often have formed a number of joint ventures to share the extremely high cost of exploring for offshore petroleum deposits. And many U.S. companies are forming joint ventures with foreign firms in order to enter new markets around the globe. Back in 1991, General Mills and Nestle formed the joint venture Cereal Partners Worldwide to market breakfast cereals in 130 countries around the globe. Today, more than 25 years later, the joint venture accounts for over $1 billion in sales each year. This joint venture has been a great success because it marries the production and marketing expertise of General Mills and the worldwide presence of Nestle, which also has local market knowledge and distribution strength. The General Mills and Nestle joint venture also continues to expand its operations by opening a new factory in western Turkey to produce breakfast cereals for the Turkish market as well as other countries in the Middle East and North Africa.[12]

joint venture an agreement between two or more groups to form a business entity in order to achieve a specific goal or to operate for a specific period of time

syndicate a temporary association of individuals or firms organized to perform a specific task that requires a large amount of capital

JOINT VENTURE

© PICHETW/SHUTTERSTOCK.COM

4-7b Syndicates

A **syndicate** is a temporary association of individuals or firms organized to perform a specific task that requires a large amount of capital. The syndicate is formed because no one person or firm is willing to put up the entire amount required for the undertaking. Like a joint venture, a syndicate is dissolved as soon as its purpose has been accomplished.

Syndicates are used most commonly to underwrite large insurance policies, loans, and investments. To share the risk of default, banks have formed syndicates to provide loans to developing countries. Stock brokerage firms usually join together in the same way to market a new issue of stock. In early 2015, Box, Inc., a company that provides cloud-based data management services to over 32 million people and 275,000 companies, sold stock to investors. With the help of a syndicate of Wall Street firms, including Morgan Stanley, Credit Suisse, and J.P. Morgan, Box raised approximately $150 million through its initial public offering, often referred to as an IPO. (An *initial public offering* is the term used to describe the first time a corporation sells stock to the general public.) Once the stock was sold, Box used the money to improve its cash balance and fund growth and expansion.[13]

4-8 CORPORATE GROWTH

Growth seems to be a basic characteristic of business. One reason for seeking growth has to do with profit: A larger firm generally has greater sales revenue and thus greater profit. Another reason is that in a growing economy, a business that does not grow is actually shrinking relative to the economy. A third reason is that business growth is a means by which some executives boost their power, prestige, and reputation.

Growth poses new problems and requires additional resources that first must be available and then must be used effectively. The main ingredient in growth is capital—and as we have noted, capital is most readily available to corporations.

4-8a Growth from Within

Most corporations grow by expanding their present operations. Some introduce and sell new but related products. Others expand the sale of present products to new geographic markets or to new groups of consumers in geographic markets already served. Although Walmart was started by Sam Walton in 1962 with one discount store, today Walmart has nearly 11,000 stores in the United States and 27 other countries, serves 245 million customers each week, and has long-range plans for expanding into additional international markets.[14]

Growth from within, especially when carefully planned and controlled, can have relatively little adverse effect on a firm. For the most part, the firm continues to do what it has been doing, but on a larger scale. For instance, Larry Ellison, co-founder and CEO of Oracle Corporation of Redwood Shores, California, built the firm's annual revenues up from a mere $282 million in 1988 to approximately $38 billion today.[15] Much of this growth has taken place over the last 25 years as Oracle capitalized on its global leadership in information management software.

4-8b Growth Through Mergers and Acquisitions

Another way a firm can grow is by purchasing another company. The combining of two corporations or other business entities to form one business is called a **merger**. An *acquisition* is essentially the same thing as a merger, but the term usually is used in reference to a large corporation's purchases of other corporations. Although most mergers and acquisitions are often friendly, hostile takeovers also occur. A **hostile takeover** is a situation in which the management and board of directors of a firm targeted for acquisition disapprove of the merger.

merger the combining of two corporations or other business entities to form one business

hostile takeover a situation in which the management and board of directors of a firm targeted for acquisition disapprove of the merger

Facebook continues to grow. Just about everyone knows that Facebook is the world's largest social networking site, but did you know that part of the reason for its success is that management is always on a lookout for companies that the company can acquire. In fact, Facebook has a history of business acquisitions—especially successful companies that have talented people with a vision of the future.

When a merger or acquisition becomes hostile, a corporate raider—another company or a wealthy investor—may make a tender offer or start a proxy fight to gain control of the target company. A **tender offer** is an offer to purchase the stock of a firm targeted for acquisition at a price just high enough to tempt stockholders to sell their shares. Corporate raiders also may initiate a proxy fight. A **proxy fight** is a technique used to gather enough stockholder votes to control a targeted company.

If the corporate raider is successful and takes over the targeted company, existing management usually is replaced. Faced with this probability, existing management may take specific actions, sometimes referred to as "poison pills," "shark repellents," or "porcupine provisions," to maintain control of the firm and avoid the hostile takeover. Whether mergers are friendly or hostile, they are generally classified as *horizontal, vertical*, or *conglomerate* (see Figure 4-5).

HORIZONTAL MERGERS A *horizontal merger* is a merger between firms that make and sell similar products or services in similar markets. The merger between American Airlines and US Airways is an example of a horizontal merger because both firms provide customers with air travel to destinations in the United States and around the globe. This type of merger tends to reduce the number of firms in an industry—and thus may reduce competition. While this merger was challenged by the U.S. Department of Justice on the basis the merger would reduce competition in the airline industry, it was eventually approved when the airlines agreed to divest some takeoff and landing rights at major U.S. airports.

VERTICAL MERGERS A *vertical merger* is a merger between firms that operate at different but related levels in the production and marketing of a product. Generally, one of the merging firms is either a supplier or a customer of the other. A vertical merger occurred when computer software and hardware giant Oracle acquired BlueKai. At the time of the merger, BlueKai, based in Cupertino, California, was a much smaller company that had developed a data management platform used by more than 300 customers to personalize their marketing efforts. Rather than develop its own software and data management program for its marketing products, Oracle simply purchased the BlueKai company.[16]

CONGLOMERATE MERGERS A *conglomerate* merger takes place between firms in completely different industries. A conglomerate merger occurred when financial conglomerate Berkshire Hathaway acquired Duracell. While both companies were recognized as successful companies that have a history of increasing sales revenues and profits, they operate in different industries. Berkshire Hathaway, led by its CEO Warren Buffett, has a long history of acquiring firms that have great financial potential. According to Mr. Buffett, "Duracell is a leading global brand with top quality products and it will fit well within Berkshire Hathaway."[17]

tender offer an offer to purchase the stock of a firm targeted for acquisition at a price just high enough to tempt stockholders to sell their shares

proxy fight a technique used to gather enough stockholder votes to control a targeted company

FIGURE 4-5 Three Types of Growth by Merger

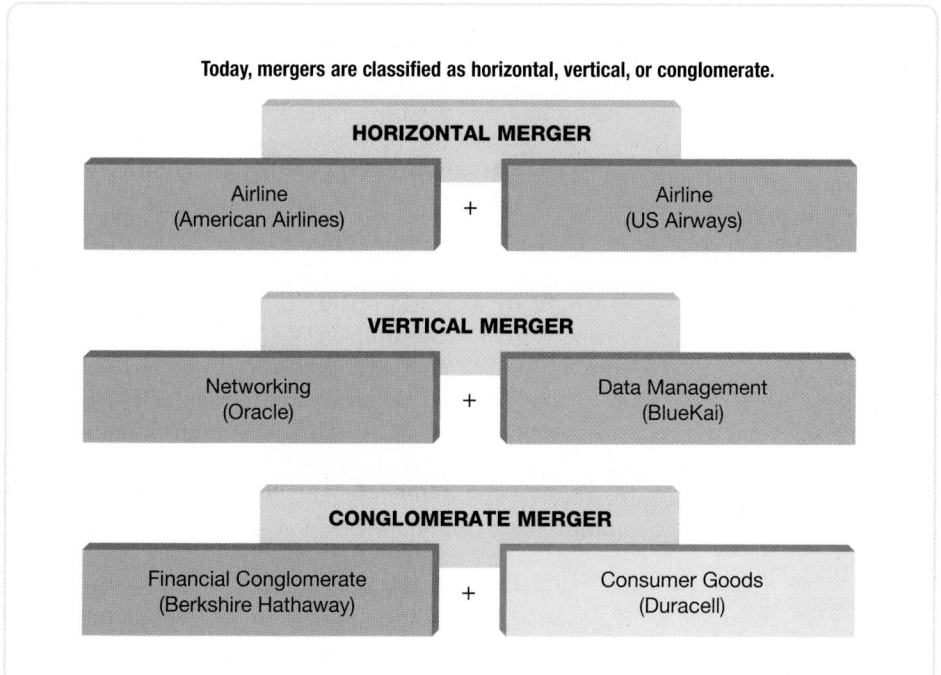

Today, mergers are classified as horizontal, vertical, or conglomerate.

HORIZONTAL MERGER

| Airline (American Airlines) | + | Airline (US Airways) |

VERTICAL MERGER

| Networking (Oracle) | + | Data Management (BlueKai) |

CONGLOMERATE MERGER

| Financial Conglomerate (Berkshire Hathaway) | + | Consumer Goods (Duracell) |

4-8c Merger and Acquisition Trends for the Future

Economists, financial analysts, corporate managers, and stockholders still hotly debate whether mergers and acquisitions are good for the economy—or for individual companies—in the long run. Takeover advocates argue that for companies that have been taken over, the purchasers have been able to make the company more profitable and productive by installing a new top-management team, by reducing expenses, and by forcing the company to concentrate on one main business.

Takeover opponents argue that takeovers do nothing to enhance corporate profitability or productivity. These critics argue that the only people who benefit from takeovers are investment bankers, brokerage firms, and takeover "artists," who receive financial rewards by manipulating corporations rather than by producing tangible products or services.

While there have always been mergers and acquisitions, the current economy has changed the dynamics of how and why firms merge. Most experts now predict that mergers and acquisitions after the 2008 economic crisis will be the result of cash-rich companies looking to acquire businesses that will enhance their position in the marketplace or an industry. Analysts also anticipate more mergers that involve companies or investors from other countries. Regardless of the companies involved or where the companies are from, future mergers and acquisitions will be driven by solid business logic and the desire to compete in the international marketplace.

Whether they are sole proprietorships, partnerships, corporations, or some other form of business ownership, most U.S. businesses are small. In the next chapter, we focus on these small businesses. We examine, among other things, the meaning of the word *small* as it applies to business and the place of small business in the American economy.

Concept Check

✓ What happens when a firm makes a decision to grow from within?

✓ What is a hostile takeover? How is it related to a tender offer and a proxy fight?

✓ Explain the three types of mergers.

✓ Describe the current merger trends and how they affect the businesses involved and their stockholders.

Summary

4-1 Describe the advantages and disadvantages of sole proprietorships.

In a sole proprietorship, all business profits become the property of the owner, but the owner is also personally responsible for all business debts. A successful sole proprietorship can be a great source of pride for the owner. When comparing different types of business ownership, the sole proprietorship is the simplest form of business to enter, control, and leave. It also pays no special taxes. Perhaps for these reasons, 73 percent of all American business firms are sole proprietorships. Sole proprietorships nevertheless have disadvantages, such as unlimited liability and limits on one person's ability to borrow or to be an expert in all fields. As a result, this form of ownership accounts for only 4 percent of total revenues when compared with partnerships and corporations.

4-2 Explain the different types of partners and the importance of partnership agreements.

Like sole proprietors, general partners are responsible for running the business and for all business debts. Limited partners receive a share of the profit in return for investing in the business. However, they are not responsible for business debts beyond the amount they have invested. Regardless of the type of partnership, it is always a good idea to have a written agreement (or articles of partnership) setting forth the terms of a partnership.

4-3 Describe the advantages and disadvantages of partnerships.

Although partnership eliminates some of the disadvantages of sole proprietorship, it is the least popular of the major forms of business ownership. The major advantages of a partnership include ease of start-up, availability of capital and credit, personal interest, combined skills and knowledge, retention of profits, and possible tax advantages. The effects of management disagreements are one of the major disadvantages of a partnership. Other disadvantages include unlimited liability (in a general partnership), lack of continuity, and frozen investment. By forming a limited partnership, the disadvantage of unlimited liability may be eliminated for the limited partner(s). This same disadvantage may be eliminated for partners that form a limited liability partnership (LLP). Of course, special requirements must be met if partners form either the limited partnership or the LLP.

4-4 Summarize how a corporation is formed.

A corporation is an artificial person created by law, with most of the legal rights of a real person, including the right to start and operate a business, to buy or sell property, to borrow money, to be sued or sue, and to enter into contracts. With the corporate form of ownership, stock can be sold to individuals to raise capital. The people who own a corporation's common or preferred stock are called stockholders. Stockholders are entitled to receive any dividends paid by the corporation, and common stockholders can vote either in person or by proxy.

Most experts believe that the services of a lawyer are necessary when making decisions about where to incorporate and about obtaining a corporate charter, issuing stock, holding an organizational meeting, and all other legal details involved in incorporation. In theory, stockholders are able to control the activities of the corporation because they elect the board of directors who appoint the corporate officers.

4-5 Describe the advantages and disadvantages of a corporation.

Perhaps the major advantage of the corporate form is limited liability—stockholders are not liable for the corporation's debts beyond the amount they paid for its stock. Other important advantages include ease of raising capital, ease of transfer of ownership, perpetual life, and specialized management. A major disadvantage of a large corporation is double taxation: All profits are taxed once as corporate income and again as personal income because stockholders must pay a personal income tax on their dividend income. Other disadvantages include difficulty and expense of formation, government regulation, conflict within the corporation, and lack of secrecy.

4-6 Examine special types of businesses, including S corporations, limited-liability companies, and not-for-profit corporations.

S corporations are corporations that are taxed as though they were partnerships but that enjoy the benefit of limited liability. To qualify as an S corporation, a number of criteria must be met. An LLC is a form of business ownership that provides limited liability and has fewer restrictions when compared to a regular corporation or an S corporation. LLCs also avoid the double taxation imposed on most corporations. When compared with a regular corporation or an S corporation, an LLC is more flexible. Not-for-profit corporations are formed to provide social services and to improve communities and change lives rather than to earn profits.

4-7 Discuss the purpose of a joint venture and syndicate.

Two additional forms of business ownership—the joint venture and a syndicate—are used by their owners to meet special needs. A joint venture is formed when two or more groups form a business entity in order to achieve a specific goal or to operate for a specific period of time. Once the goal is reached, the period of time elapses, or the project is completed, the joint venture is dissolved. A syndicate is a temporary association of individuals or firms organized to perform a specific task that requires large amounts of capital. Like a joint venture, a syndicate is dissolved as soon as its purpose has been accomplished.

4-8 Explain how growth from within and growth through mergers can enable a business to expand.

A corporation may grow by expanding its present operations or through a merger or an acquisition. Although most mergers are friendly, hostile takeovers also occur. A hostile takeover is a situation in which the management and board of directors of a firm targeted for acquisition disapprove of the merger. Mergers generally are classified as horizontal, vertical, or conglomerate.

While economists, financial analysts, corporate managers, and stockholders debate the merits of mergers, some trends should be noted. First, experts predict that future mergers will be the result of cash-rich companies looking to acquire businesses that will enhance their position in the marketplace or an industry. Second, more mergers are likely to involve foreign companies or investors. Third, mergers will be driven by business logic and the desire to compete in the international marketplace.

Key Terms

You should now be able to define and give an example relevant to each of the following terms:

sole proprietorship (106)	closed corporation (115)	proxy (117)	joint venture (124)
unlimited liability (108)	open corporation (115)	board of directors (118)	syndicate (124)
partnership (109)	domestic corporation (116)	corporate officers (118)	merger (125)
general partner (110)	foreign corporation (116)	limited liability (119)	hostile takeover (125)
limited partner (110)	alien corporation (116)	S corporation (121)	tender offer (126)
corporation (114)	common stock (117)	limited-liability company	proxy fight (126)
stock (115)	preferred stock (117)	(LLC) (122)	
stockholder (115)	dividend (117)	not-for-profit corporation (123)	

Discussion Questions

1. If you were to start a business, which ownership form would you choose? What factors might affect your choice?
2. Why might an investor choose to become a partner in a limited partnership instead of purchasing the stock of an open corporation?
3. Discuss the following statement: "Corporations are not really run by their owners."
4. What kinds of services do not-for-profit corporations provide? Would a career in a not-for-profit corporation appeal to you?
5. Is growth a good thing for all firms? How does management know when a firm is ready to grow?

Video Case

Project Repat Gives Old T-Shirts New Life

Ross Lohr and Nathan Rothstein have built a thriving small business from the idea of giving old T-shirts new life by having them cut into squares and sewn into comfortable fleece-backed quilts. The Boston-based company is named Project Repat because it is dedicated to repatriating textile-industry jobs and helping U.S. workers earn a living wage by sewing T-shirt quilts made to order.

To start, customers visit the Project Repat website (www.projectrepat.com) and select the size of their quilt, based on the number of T-shirts they want sewn together. Then they choose the color of fleece for the backing, enter their payment information, and place the order. Project Repat responds with detailed instructions for preparing the T-shirts and shipping them to one of its two contract manufacturing centers, the one in Fall River, Massachusetts or the one in Morganton, North Carolina. Once the T-shirts arrive, the company confirms the receipt of the T-shirts by sending an e-mail to the customer. Within a month, the new quilt made of old T-shirts is on its way back to the customer, ready to be enjoyed for the warmth and the memories.

The original business plan was to make good use of T-shirts that had been discarded by U.S. consumers and wound up in Kenya. The cofounders raised money via crowdsourcing to pay for designing fashion accessories made from old T-shirts. Once designs were completed, local Kenyan artisans were then employed to turn the designs into finished products that were then shipped to America for sale. However, feedback from U.S. customers quickly led the company to refocus on creating something new from customers' own T-shirts that had nostalgic value. So Project Repat switched from production of fashion accessories in Kenya to production of T-shirt quilts in America through contract manufacturers that paid and treated their workers well.

Project Repat was set up as a traditional corporation because it had the help of a business accelerator and it was seeking funding from venture capitalists and angel investors. One of the original cofounders and a designer received some shares in the corporation. However, the current management team of CEO Ross Lohr and President Nathan Rothstein—who together are the primary shareholders—would have preferred to establish Project Repat as an S corporation or an LLC, in part because the tax bill would be a little lower. Lohr and Rothstein have also taken Project Repat through the process of qualifying as a B corporation, which signals their commitment to pursuing social responsibility goals as well as financial goals.

Now Project Repat is reaching out to potential customers via social media sites like Facebook, Twitter, YouTube, Pinterest, and Instagram. It sews as many as 1,000 T-shirt quilts every week, enabling customers to hold onto beloved T-shirts in a new form and relive happy memories every time they use the quilt. With over $2 million in annual revenue, the company has been responsible for recycling one million T-shirts that might otherwise have been relegated to landfills. Just as important, Project Repat's rapid growth has resulted in the creation of dozens of jobs for U.S. workers, an economic benefit to the local communities where they live and work.[18]

Questions

1. Considering the tax benefits, why would investors not want Project Repat to be an S corporation?
2. One of the cofounders of Project Repat is no longer with the company, although he retains a small owner-ship stake. What complications might this change have caused if Project Repat was set up as a partnership rather than a corporation?
3. Imagine you're an angel investor looking to invest in young companies. What questions would you ask the management team at Project Repat before making a final decision about investing in it?

Building Skills for Career Success

1. Social Media Exercise

Not-for-profit organizations have used social media to redefine how they can get funding for their missions. There are even a few that exist totally online. Check out www.donorschoose.org and www.kiva.org. Both of these depend on crowds (called crowdfunding) to either fund educational projects (Donors Choose) or lend money to support projects all over the world (Kiva) using the microfinancing model.

a. Take a minute to explore both sites and view some of the projects up for funding. Do you think social media is an effective method of raising money for worthwhile projects? Why or why not?

b. Both Donors Choose and Kiva are not-for-profits; do you think crowdfunding could be useful for "for-profit" businesses? Why or why not?

2. Building Team Skills

Suppose that you have decided to quit your job as an insurance adjuster and open a bakery. Your business is now growing, and you have decided to add a full line of catering services. This means more work and responsibility. You will need someone to help you, but you are undecided about what to do. Should you hire an employee or find a partner? If you add a partner, what type of decisions should be made to create a partnership agreement?

Assignment

1. In a group, discuss the following questions:
   a. What are the advantages and disadvantages of adding a partner versus hiring an employee?
   b. Assume that you have decided to form a partnership. What articles should be included in a partnership agreement?
   c. How would you go about finding a partner?
2. As a group, prepare an articles-of-partnership agreement. Be prepared to discuss the pros and cons of your group's agreement with other groups from your class, as well as to examine their agreements.
3. Summarize your group's answers to these questions, and present them to your class.

3. Researching Different Careers

Many people spend their entire lives working in jobs that they do not enjoy. Why? Often, it is because they have taken the first job they were offered without giving it much thought.

How can you avoid having this happen to you? First, you should determine your "personal profile" by identifying and analyzing your own strengths, weaknesses, things you enjoy, and things you dislike. Second, you should identify the types of jobs that fit your profile. Third, you should identify and research the companies that offer those jobs.

Assignment

a. Take two sheets of paper and draw a line down the middle of each sheet, forming two columns on each page. Label column 1 "Things I Enjoy or Like to Do," column 2 "Things I Do Not Like Doing," column 3 "My Strengths," and column 4 "My Weaknesses."
b. Record data in each column over a period of at least one week. You may find it helpful to have a relative or friend give you input.
c. Summarize the data, and write a profile of yourself.
d. Take your profile to a career counselor at your college or to the public library and ask for help in identifying jobs that fit your profile. Your college may also offer testing to assess your skills and personality. The Internet is another resource.
e. Research the companies that offer the types of jobs that fit your profile.
f. Write a report on your findings.

Endnotes

1 Sources: Based on information in Charlie Rose, "Charlie Rose Talks to GoPro's Nick Woodman," *Bloomberg Businessweek*, October 2, 2014, www.businessweek.com; Serena Renner, "The Best Ride of Our Lives," *Triton (UC San Diego)*, Summer 2013, http://alumni.ucsd.edu; Ryan Mac, "GoPro Plans to Go Public, Files Confidential IPO Docs," *Forbes.com*, February 7, 2014; Lizette Chapman, "How Family Ties Helped Nick Woodman Make GoPro Click," *Wall Street Journal*, June 20, 2013, www.wsj.com.
2 Melvin Backman, "General Mills Buys Annie's for $820 Million," the Money/CNN website at www.money.cnn.com (accessed September 8, 2014).
3 The IVY Planning Group website at www.ivygroupllc.com (accessed January 5, 2015).
4 The Procter & Gamble website at www.pg.com (accessed January 7, 2015).
5 Ibid.
6 The Mars Corporate website at www.mars.com (accessed January 5, 2015).
7 The My New Company website at www.mynewcompany.com (accessed January 6, 2015).
8 The Hispanic PR Wire website at www.hispanicprwire.com (accessed January 6, 2015).
9 Liyan Chen, "Alibaba Claims Title for Largest Global IPO Ever With Extra Share Sales," the Forbes website at www.forbes.com (accessed September 22, 2014).
10 Bruce Horowitz, "Layoffs Hit Icons Coke and McDonalds," the USA Today website at www.usatoday.com (accessed January 8, 2015).
11 The Internal Revenue Service website at www.irs.gov (accessed January 8, 2015).
12 The General Mills Corporate website at www.generalmills.com (accessed January 10, 2015).
13 The Renaissance Capital website at www.renaissancecapital.com (accessed January 9, 2015).
14 The Walmart Corporate website at www.walmartstores.com (accessed January 10, 2015).
15 The Oracle website at www.oracle.com (accessed January 10, 2015).
16 Larry Dignan, "Oracle Acquires BlueKai, Rounds Out Its Marketing Cloud," The ZDNet website at www.zdnet.com (accessed February 14, 2014).
17 "Berkshire Hathaway Acquires Duracell," The Intelligent Insurer website at www.intelligentinsurer.com (accessed November 14, 2014).
18 Sources: Based on information in Autumn Spanne, "Want People to Buy a Product That Lasts? Sell Them an Emotional Connection," *The Guardian (UK)*, January 17, 2015, www.theguardian.com; Mike Ross, "Couch-Based Entrepreneurs," *Boston Globe*, December 15, 2014, www.boston.com; Sara Castellanos, "Project Repat Turns Old T-Shirts into Quilts, Targets $2M in Revenue This Year," *Boston Business Journal*, July 28, 2014, www.bizjournals.com/boston; www.projectrepat.com; Cengage Learning, *Project Repat* video.

MONKEY BUSINESS IMAGES/SHUTTERSTOCK.COM

Small Business, Entrepreneurship, and Franchises

Why Should You Care?

America's small businesses drive the U.S. economy. Small businesses represent 99.7 percent of all employer firms, and there is a good probability that you will work for a small business or perhaps even start your own business. This chapter can help you to become a good employee or a successful entrepreneur.

Learning Objectives

Once you complete this chapter, you will be able to:

5-1 Define what a small business is and recognize the fields in which small businesses are concentrated.

5-2 Identify the people who start small businesses and the reasons why some succeed and many fail.

5-3 Assess the contributions of small businesses to our economy.

5-4 Describe the advantages and disadvantages of operating a small business.

5-5 Explain how the Small Business Administration helps small businesses.

5-6 Explain the concept and types of franchising.

5-7 Analyze the growth of franchising and its advantages and disadvantages.

Bark & Co. Provides for Pampered Pooches

Co-founded in 2011 by Henrik Werdelin, Carly Strife, and Matt Meeker, New York-based Bark & Co. is a fast-growing small business dedicated to helping U.S. and Canadian pet-lovers pamper their pooches. Its first service was BarkBox, offering subscribers a monthly delivery of doggie treats, toys, and accessories, customized for the dog's size and weight (tiny, small and cute, just right, or big and bold).

BarkBox has attracted a highly loyal customer base of 200,000, with more than 90 percent of subscribers choosing to receive deliveries month after month after month. Subscribers also have the option to pay a few more dollars for an extra dog toy every month. One out of five customers chooses this upgrade, boosting the firm's revenues even further. And because BarkBox contributes 10 percent of its profits to dog-related charities, higher sales means higher donations.

Ringing up annual revenues of $30 million, Bark & Co. has raised money through a combination of venture capital and debt to continue its aggressive expansion. The company now offers BarkCare, an on-demand service that arranges for veterinarians to give vaccinations or checkups to dogs at home. In addition, it operates BarkPost.com, a content site loaded with dog-related photos, videos, and information. BarkBuddy is the company's mobile app for matching would-be dog owners with pups in their area. Yet another app, BarkCam, allows dog owners to take better smartphone photos of their pets and embellish with captions and other goodies, then share with friends. Recently-launched BarkShop is an e-commerce site featuring a variety of dog merchandise, from beds and blankets to collars and chews.

Bark & Co. is highly social, staying in touch with dog lovers through Facebook, Twitter, Instagram, and Pinterest. Watch for new tech-fueled services as this entrepreneurial business continues to grow by catering to the needs and interests of pet owners.[1]

Did You Know?

Bark & Co. is a fast-growing small business competing for customers in the $58 billion market for pet products.

Most businesses start small and those that survive usually stay small. However, they provide a solid foundation for our economy—as employers, as suppliers and purchasers of goods and services, and as taxpayers.

In this chapter, we do not take small businesses for granted. Instead, we look closely at this important business sector—beginning with a definition of small business, a description of industries that often attract small businesses, and a profile of some of the people who start small businesses. Next, we consider the importance of small businesses in our economy. We also present the advantages and disadvantages of smallness in business. We then describe services provided by the Small Business Administration, a government agency formed to assist owners and managers of small businesses. We conclude the chapter with a discussion of the pros and cons of franchising, an approach to small-business ownership that has become very popular in the last 55 years.

small business one that is independently owned and operated for profit and is not dominant in its field

5-1 SMALL BUSINESS: A PROFILE

The Small Business Administration (SBA) defines a **small business** as "one which is independently owned and operated for profit and is not dominant in its field." How small must a firm be not to dominate its field? That depends on the particular industry it is in. The SBA has developed the following specific "smallness" guidelines for the various industries, as shown in Table 5-1.[2] The SBA periodically revises and simplifies its small-business size regulations.

Learning Objective

5-1 Define what a small business is and recognize the fields in which small businesses are concentrated.

TABLE 5-1 Industry Group–Size Standards

Small-business size standards are usually stated in number of employees or average annual sales. In the United States, 99.7 percent of all businesses are considered small.

Industry Group	Size Standard
Manufacturing, mining industries	500 employees
Wholesale trade	100 employees
Agriculture	$750,000
Retail trade, barber shops, beauty salons	$7.5 million
General and heavy construction (except dredging)	$36.5 million
Dredging	$27.5 million
Special trade contractors	$15 million
Travel agencies, tour operators	$20.5 million
Department stores	$32.5 million
Discount department stores	$29.5 million
Furniture stores	$20.5 million

Source: www.sba.gov/content/small-business-size-standards (accessed January 13, 2015).

Annual sales in millions of dollars may not seem very small. However, for many firms, profit is only a small percentage of total sales. Thus, a firm may earn only $50,000 or $60,000 on yearly sales of $1 million—and that is small in comparison with the profits earned by most medium-sized and large firms. Moreover, most small firms have annual sales well below the maximum limits in the SBA guidelines.

Small businesses are very important to the U.S. economy. For example, small businesses

- represent 99.7 percent of all employer firms;
- employ about half of all private sector employees;
- pay 42 percent of total U.S. private payroll;
- have generated 63 percent of net new jobs over the past 20 years;
- create more than half of the nonfarm private GDP;
- hire 37 percent of high-tech workers (scientists, engineers, computer programmers, and others);
- are 52 percent home-based and 2 percent franchises;
- made up 97.5 percent of all identified exporters and produced 33 percent of export value; and
- produced 16.5 times more patents per employee than large patenting firms.[3]

5-1a The Small-Business Sector

In the United States, it typically takes less than a week and $600 to establish a business as a legal entity. The steps include registering the name of the business, applying for tax IDs, and setting up unemployment and workers' compensation insurance. In Japan, however, a typical entrepreneur spends more than $3,500 and 11 days to follow 8 different procedures.

A surprising number of Americans take advantage of their freedom to start a business. There are, in fact, about 28.2 million businesses in this country. Only just 17,700 of these employ more than 500 workers—enough to be considered large.

Interest in owning or starting a small business has never been greater than it is today. During the last decade, the number of small businesses in the United States has increased 49 percent. For the last few years, new-business formation in the United States has broken successive records, except during the 2001–2002 and 2008 recessions. In 2013, 1,233,000 new businesses were started. Furthermore, part-time entrepreneurs have increased fivefold in recent years; they now account for one-third of all small businesses.[4]

According to a recent study, 69 percent of new businesses survive at least two years, about 50 percent survive at least five years, and 31 percent survive at least ten years.[5] The primary reason for these failures is mismanagement resulting from a lack of business know-how. The makeup of the small-business sector thus is constantly changing. Despite the high failure rate, many small businesses succeed modestly. Some, like Apple Computer, Inc., are extremely successful—to the point where they can no longer be considered small. Taken together, small businesses are also responsible for providing a high percentage of the jobs in the United States. According to some estimates, the figure is well over 50 percent.

5-1b Industries That Attract Small Businesses

Some industries, such as auto manufacturing, require huge investments in machinery and equipment. Businesses in such industries are big from the day they are started—if an entrepreneur or group of entrepreneurs can gather the capital required to start one.

By contrast, a number of other industries require only a low initial investment and some special skills or knowledge. It is these industries that tend to attract new businesses. Growing industries, such as outpatient-care facilities, are attractive because of their profit potential. However, knowledgeable entrepreneurs choose areas with which they are familiar, and these are most often the more established industries.

Small enterprise spans the gamut from corner newspaper vending to the development of optical fibers. The owners of small businesses sell gasoline, flowers, and coffee to go. They publish magazines, haul freight, teach languages, and program computers. They make wines, movies, and high-fashion clothes. They build new homes and restore old ones. They fix appliances, recycle metals, and sell used cars. They drive cabs and fly planes. They make us well when we are ill, and they sell us the products of corporate giants. In fact, 74 percent of real estate, rental, and leasing industries; 61 percent of the businesses in the leisure and hospitality services; and 86 percent of the construction industries are dominated by small businesses. The various kinds of businesses generally fall into three broad categories of industry: distribution, service, and production.

Social Media:
Small Business Saturday

Started by American Express in 2010, Small Business Saturday has now become a tradition on the Saturday after Thanksgiving. The idea is to support local stores, restaurants, and other small businesses during the busy holiday shopping season. Only four years after the launch of Small Business Saturday, its Facebook page (www.facebook.com/SmallBusinessSaturday) had already attracted 3.5 million likes, 44,000 Twitter followers (http://twitter.com/shopsmall), and more than 6,000 Instagram followers (http://instagram.com/shopsmall). This late-November day even has its own hashtag, #ShopSmall, used on Twitter more than 125,000 times during a recent Small Business Saturday—with a growing number of tweets year after year as more businesses and customers participate.

Individual businesses and regional retail and restaurant trade groups have jumped on the social media bandwagon to promote Small Business Saturday in communities across the country. For example, the Greater Dallas Restaurant Association and the Texas Restaurant Association post #DineSmall and #ShowUsYourMenu messages on social media sites like LinkedIn, Facebook, and Twitter to encourage dining at entrepreneur-owned restaurants.

In Boston, the Olives & Grace gift store begins posting on Facebook, Instagram, and Twitter four weeks ahead of Small Business Saturday, using #ShopSmall and its own #olivesandgrace hashtag. Owner Sophie Madison is delighted by the positive response—especially on Instagram, where it has over 7,000 followers—and plans a new social-media campaign for every year's Small Business Saturday.

Sources: Based on information in Julissa Trevino, "Small Business Saturday Draws Business, Crowds," *Dallas Morning News*, November 29, 2014, www.dallasnews.com; Nicole Leinbach-Reyhle, "Small Business Saturday 2014 Stood Strong among Communities and Small Businesses," *Forbes*, December 2, 2014, www.forbes.com; Amy Gesenhues, "Small Business Saturday Reminds Consumers to Shop Local After Black Friday Deals," *Marketing Land*, November 28, 2014, http://marketingland.com.

Personal App

Have you worked for a small business?

MONKEYBUSINESSIMAGES/ISTOCK/THINKSTOCK.

Sometime in your career, you're likely to have a job in a small business. You might work in a store, in a service business, or in production. If you're thinking of starting your own business, be sure to watch how these entrepreneurs manage their companies. Consider what you'd do differently if you were the owner—and make mental notes, so you can apply your knowledge and experience to any business you may start in the future.

Concept Check

✓ What information would you need to determine whether a particular business is small according to SBA guidelines?

✓ Which two areas of business generally attract the most small business? Why are these areas attractive to small business?

✓ Distinguish among service industries, distribution industries, and production industries.

Learning Objective

5-2 Identify the people who start small businesses and the reasons why some succeed and many fail.

DISTRIBUTION INDUSTRIES This category includes retailing, wholesaling, transportation, and communications—industries concerned with the movement of goods from producers to consumers. Distribution industries account for approximately 33 percent of all small businesses. Of these, almost three-quarters are involved in retailing, that is, the sale of goods directly to consumers. Clothing and jewelry stores, pet shops, bookstores, and grocery stores, for example, are all retailing firms. Slightly less than one-quarter of the small distribution firms are wholesalers. Wholesalers purchase products in quantity from manufacturers and then resell them to retailers.

SERVICE INDUSTRIES This category accounts for more than 48 percent of all small businesses. Of these, about three-quarters provide such nonfinancial services as medical and dental care; watch, shoe, and TV repairs; haircutting and styling; restaurant meals; and dry cleaning. About 8 percent of the small service firms offer financial services, such as accounting, insurance, real estate, and investment counseling. An increasing number of self-employed Americans are running service businesses from home.

PRODUCTION INDUSTRIES This last category includes the construction, mining, and manufacturing industries. Only about 19 percent of all small businesses are in this group, mainly because these industries require relatively large initial investments. Small firms that do venture into production generally make parts and subassemblies for larger manufacturing firms or supply special skills to larger construction firms.

5-2 THE PEOPLE IN SMALL BUSINESSES: THE ENTREPRENEURS

The entrepreneurial spirit is alive and well in the United States. One study revealed that the U.S. population is quite entrepreneurial when compared with those of other countries. More than 70 percent of Americans would prefer being an entrepreneur to working for someone else. This compares with 46 percent of adults in Western Europe and 58 percent of adults in Canada. Another study on entrepreneurial activity found that of 36 countries studied, the United States was in the top third in entrepreneurial activity and was the leader when compared with Japan, Canada, and Western Europe.[6]

Small businesses typically are managed by the people who started and own them. Most of these people have held jobs with other firms and still could be so employed if they wanted. Yet owners of small businesses would rather take the risk of starting and operating their own firms, even if the money they make is less than the salaries they otherwise might earn.

Researchers have suggested a variety of personal factors as reasons why people go into business for themselves. These are discussed next.

5-2a Characteristics of Entrepreneurs

Entrepreneurial spirit is the desire to create a new business. For example, Nikki Olyai always knew that she wanted to create and develop her own business. Her father, a successful businessman in Iran, was her role model. She came to the United States at the age of 17 and lived with a host family in Salem, Oregon, attending high school there. Undergraduate and graduate degrees in computer science led her to start Innovision Technologies while she held two other jobs to keep the business going and took care of her four-year-old son. Recently, Nikki Olyai's business was honored by the Women's Business Enterprise National Council's "Salute to Women's Business Enterprises" as one of 11 top successful firms. For three consecutive years, her firm was selected as a "Future 50 of Greater Detroit Company."

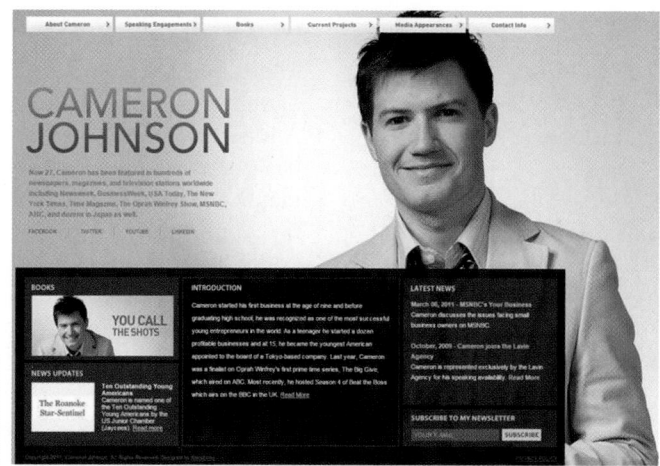

Meet Cameron Johnson, a young entrepreneur. At a young age, Cameron started his own company selling holiday cards. Since then he has successfully created several other companies. Recently, he has been involved in television projects on Animal Planet, BBC, and ABC.

5-2b Other Personal Factors

Other personal factors in small-business success include

- independence;
- a desire to determine one's own destiny;
- a willingness to find and accept a challenge;
- family background (in particular, researchers think that people whose families have been in business, successfully or not, are most apt to start and run their own businesses); and
- age (those who start their own businesses also tend to cluster around certain ages—more than 70 percent are between 24 and 44 years of age; see Figure 5-1).

FIGURE 5-1 How Old is the Average Entrepreneur?

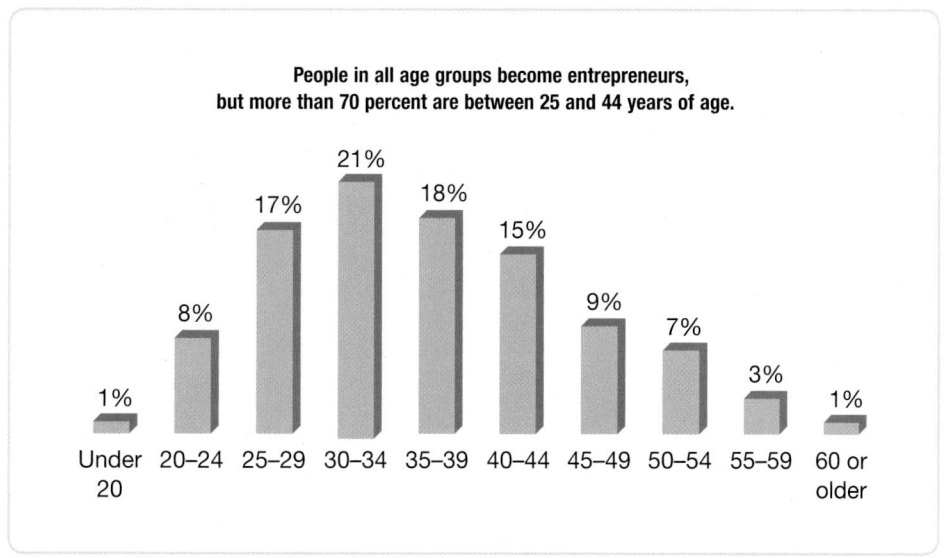

People in all age groups become entrepreneurs, but more than 70 percent are between 25 and 44 years of age.

Under 20: 1%
20–24: 8%
25–29: 17%
30–34: 21%
35–39: 18%
40–44: 15%
45–49: 9%
50–54: 7%
55–59: 3%
60 or older: 1%

Source: Data developed and provided by the National Federation of Independent Business Foundation and sponsored by the American Express Travel Related Services Company, Inc.

5-2c Motivation

There must be some motivation to start a business. A person may decide that he or she simply has "had enough" of working and earning a profit for someone else. Another may lose his or her job for some reason and decide to start the business he or she has always wanted rather than to seek another job. Still another person may have an idea for a new product or a new way to sell an existing product. Or the opportunity to go into business may arise suddenly, perhaps as a result of a hobby. For example, Cheryl Strand started baking and decorating cakes from her home while working full time as a word processor at Clemson University. Her cakes became so popular that she soon found herself working through her lunch breaks and late into the night to meet customer demand.

5-2d Women as Small-Business Owners

According to the latest 2015 data available from the SBA

- Women are 51 percent of the U.S. population, and according to the SBA, they owned at least 36 percent of all small businesses.
- Women already own 66 percent of the home-based businesses in this country, and the number of men in home-based businesses is growing rapidly.
- About 7.8 million women-owned businesses in the United States provide almost 7.6 million jobs and generate $1.2 trillion in sales.
- Women-owned businesses in the United States have proven that they are more successful; more than 40 percent have been in business for 12 years or more.
- Women-owned businesses are financially sound and credit-worthy, and their risk of failure is lower than average.
- Compared to other working women, self-employed women are older, better educated, and have more managerial experience.

Career Success

Plan Now for an Entrepreneurial Venture Later

Every job you hold, part-time or full-time, can help you prepare for the eventual launch of an entrepreneurial venture. What can you learn while working for others that will help you build your own business later?

Training and consulting entrepreneur Susan Steinbrecher says to avoid burning any bridges. Whether you're leaving a job or having a disagreement with a business associate, you don't want to look back in regret at the way you acted toward someone who might become a customer, employee, partner, or supplier when you go out on your own. She also emphasizes the importance of learning to delegate as you move up the career ladder. No entrepreneur can do everything—and delegating allows others to gain experience and demonstrate competence.

John Berkowitz of Yodle, an online marketing firm, points to the need to be prepared for change at any moment. Planning is a vital part of every job and every business

venture. Yet even the most brilliant plan will have to be tweaked if and when a problem pops up. So be realistic and ready to change, which will serve you well in any company and as an entrepreneur.

The advice of Priscilla Claman, cofounder of a career-coaching company, is to locate an experienced mentor, especially when you anticipate making a career change. Look for someone at a higher level who has broad knowledge of multiple companies and industries, and pay close attention to your mentor's ideas and recommendations. Stay in touch as your career develops, be considerate of your mentor's time, and show appreciation for your mentor's support.

Sources: Based on information in Scott Gerber, "The Advice 13 Entrepreneurs Would Give Their Younger Selves," *Mashable.com*, December 9, 2014; Susan Steinbrecher, "5 Golden Pieces of Leadership Advice for Young Entrepreneurs," *Entrepreneur.com*, September 29, 2014; Gwen Moran, "How to Learn to Delegate Without Giving Up All Your Control," *Fast Company*, June 10, 2014, www.fastcompany.com.

- Just over one-half of small businesses are home based, and 91 percent have no employees. About 60 percent of home-based businesses are in service industries, 16 percent in construction, 14 percent in retail trade, and the rest in manufacturing, finance, transportation, communications, wholesaling, and other industries.

Women's Business Centers (WBCs), are the national network of nearly 100 educational centers throughout the United States. WBCs assist women in starting and growing small businesses and seek to "level the playing field" for women entrepreneurs, who still face unique obstacles in the business world. SBA's Office of Women's Business Ownership oversees the WBC Network, which provides entrepreneurs, especially women who are economically or socially disadvantaged, comprehensive training and counseling on business topics in several languages.[7]

Kool Kidz Sno Konez started by young entrepreneurs. At the ages of 11 and 12 years old, siblings Amaya Selmon and Jaden Wheeler started a snow cone business in their front yard. Now, they use a food truck to sell over 20 flavors of snow cones and even a few food items to customers all over Memphis. Jaden said "our goal with the food truck is to franchise it, so I don't have to work when I grow up. What I mean is that I want to work smart instead of working hard."

5-2e Teenagers as Small-Business Owners

High-tech teen entrepreneurship is definitely exploding. "There's not a period in history where we've seen such a plethora of young entrepreneurs," comments Nancy F. Koehn, associate professor of business administration at Harvard Business School. Still, teen entrepreneurs face unique pressures in juggling their schoolwork, their social life, and their high-tech workload. Some ultimately quit school, whereas others quit or cut back on their business activities. Consider Brian Hendricks at Winston Churchill High School in Potomac, Maryland. He is the founder of StartUpPc and VB Solutions, Inc. StartUpPc, founded in 2001, sells custom-built computers and computer services for home users, home offices, small businesses, and students. Brian's services include design, installation of systems, training, networking, and on-site technical support. A year later, Brian founded VB Solutions, Inc., which develops and customizes websites and message boards. The firm sets up advertising contracts and counsels website owners on site improvements. The company has designed corporate ID kits, logos, and websites for clients from all over the world. Brian learned at a very young age that working for yourself is one of the best jobs available. According to Brian, a young entrepreneur must possess "the five P's of entrepreneurship"—planning, persistence, patience, people, and profit. Brian knows what it takes to be a successful entrepreneur. His accolades include Junior Achievement's "National Youth Entrepreneur of the Year" and SBA's "Young Entrepreneur of the Year" awards. The SBA offers a wide range of resources and programs to help young entrepreneurs start, manage, and grow their business.[8]

In some people, the motivation to start a business develops slowly as they gain the knowledge and ability required for success as a business owner. Knowledge and ability—especially, management ability—are probably the most important factors involved. A new firm is very much built around the entrepreneur. The owner must be able to manage the firm's finances, its personnel (if there are any employees), and its day-to-day operations. He or she must handle sales, advertising, purchasing, pricing, and a variety of other business functions. The knowledge and ability to do so are acquired most often through experience working for other firms in the same area of business.

5-2f Why Some Entrepreneurs and Small Businesses Fail

Small businesses are prone to failure. Capital, management, and planning are the key ingredients in the survival of a small business, as well as the most common

TABLE 5-2 U.S. Business Start-ups, Closures, and Bankruptcies

	New (In Thousands)	Closures (In Thousands)	Bankruptcies
2013	1,233	NA	33,212
2012	800	732	40,075
2011	782	752	47,806
2010	741	755	56,282
2009	702	877	60,837
2005	867	737	39,201
2000	826	759	35,472

NA = Not available.

Source: U.S. Small Business Administration, Office of Advocacy, *Small Business Quarterly Bulletin, 2ⁿᵈ Quarter 2014*, released September 9, 2014, https://www.sba.gov/advocacy/small-business-quarterly-bulletins (accessed January 12, 2015).

reasons for failure. Businesses can experience a number of money-related problems. It may take several years before a business begins to show a profit. Entrepreneurs need to have not only the capital to open a business but also the money to operate it in its possibly lengthy start-up phase. One cash flow obstacle often leads to others. Moreover, a series of cash flow predicaments usually ends in a business failure. This scenario is played out all too often by small and not-so-small start-up Internet firms that fail to meet their financial backers' expectations and so are denied a second wave of investment dollars to continue their drive to establish a profitable online firm. According to Maureen Borzacchiello, co-owner of Creative Display Solutions, a trade show products company, "Big businesses such as Bear Stearns, Fannie Mae and Freddie Mac, and AIG can get bailouts, but small-business owners are on their own when times are tough and credit is tight."

Many entrepreneurs lack the management skills required to run a business. Money, time, personnel, and inventory all need to be managed effectively if a small business is to succeed. Starting a small business requires much more than optimism and a good idea.

Success and expansion sometimes lead to problems. Frequently, entrepreneurs with successful small businesses make the mistake of overexpansion. Fast growth often results in dramatic changes in a business. Thus, the entrepreneur must plan carefully and adjust competently to new and potentially disruptive situations.

Every day, and in every part of the country, people open new businesses. For example, in 2012, 800,000 new businesses opened their doors. At the same time, however, 732,000 businesses closed their business and 40,075 businesses declared bankruptcy (see Table 5-2).[9] Although many fail, others represent well-conceived ideas developed by entrepreneurs who have the expertise, resources, and determination to make their businesses succeed. As these well-prepared entrepreneurs pursue their individual goals, our society benefits in many ways from their work and creativity. Billion-dollar companies such as Apple Computer, McDonald's Corporation, and Procter & Gamble are all examples of small businesses that expanded into industry giants.

Concept Check

✓ What kinds of factors encourage certain people to start new businesses?

✓ What are the major causes of small-business failure? Do these causes also apply to larger businesses?

5-3 THE IMPORTANCE OF SMALL BUSINESSES IN OUR ECONOMY

Learning Objective

5-3 Assess the contributions of small businesses to our economy.

This country's economic history abounds with stories of ambitious men and women who turned their ideas into business dynasties. The Ford Motor Company started as a one-man operation with an innovative method for industrial production.

L.L. Bean, Inc., can trace its beginnings to a basement shop in Freeport, Maine. Both Xerox and Polaroid began as small firms with a better way to do a job. Indeed, every year since 1963, the president of the United States has proclaimed National Small Business Week to recognize the contributions of small businesses to the economic well-being of America.

5-3a Providing Technical Innovation

Invention and innovation are part of the foundations of our economy. The increases in productivity that have characterized the past 200 years of our history are all rooted in one principal source: new ways to do a job with less effort for less money. Studies show that the incidence of innovation among small-business workers is significantly higher than among workers in large businesses. Small firms produce two-and-a-half times as many innovations as large firms relative to the number of persons employed. In fact, small firms employ 43 percent of all high-tech workers such as scientists, engineers, and computer specialists. No wonder small firms produce 16 to 17 times more patents per employee than large patenting firms.

Consider Waymon Armstrong, the owner of a small business that uses computer simulations to help government and other clients prepare for and respond to natural disasters, medical emergencies, and combat. In presenting the 2010 National Small Business Person of the Year award, Karen Mills, former Administrator of the U.S. Small Business Administration, said, "Waymon Armstrong is a perfect example of the innovation, inspiration, and determination that exemplify America's most successful entrepreneurs. He believed in his brainchild to the point where he deferred his own salary for three years to keep it afloat. When layoffs loomed for his staff after 9/11, their loyalty and belief in the company was so great that they were willing to work without pay for four months."

"Waymon's commitment to his employees and to his business—Engineering & Computer Simulations, Inc.—demonstrates the qualities that make small businesses such a powerful force for job creation in the American economy and in their local communities," said Mills. "It's the same qualities that will lead us to economic recovery. We are especially proud that his company benefited from two grants under SBA's Small Business Innovation and Research Program." Waymon Armstrong was honored by President Barak Obama in Washington, D.C. during the National Small Business Week where the SBA recognizes small businesses that drive America's economy.[10]

According to the U.S. Office of Management and Budget, more than half the major technological advances of the 20th century originated with individual inventors and small companies. Even just a sampling of those innovations is remarkable:

- Air-conditioning
- Airplane
- Automatic transmission
- FM radio
- Heart valve
- Helicopter
- Instant camera
- Insulin

Using Technical Innovation. AMP Americas makes compressed natural gas from cow manure. One dairy farm is using AMP's technological innovation to power its 42 tractor-trailers to transport milk to neighboring states.

- Jet engine
- Penicillin
- Personal computer
- Power steering

Perhaps even more remarkable—and important—is that many of these inventions sparked major new U.S. industries or contributed to an established industry by adding some valuable service.

5-3b Providing Employment

Small firms traditionally have added more than their proportional share of new jobs to the economy. Seven out of the ten industries that added the most new jobs were small-business-dominated industries. Small businesses creating the most new jobs recently included business services, leisure and hospitality services, and special trade contractors. Small firms hire a larger proportion of employees who are younger workers, older workers, women, or workers who prefer to work part time.

Furthermore, small businesses provide 67 percent of workers with their first jobs and initial on-the-job training in basic skills. According to the SBA, small businesses represent 99.7 percent of all employers, employ more than 50 percent of the private workforce, and provide about two-thirds of the net new jobs added to our economy.

In a 2015 news release, the SBA Administrator Maria Contreras-Sweet, stated, "Once again it was not large corporations, but entrepreneurs and small businesses powering us out of the greatest economic crisis since the Great Depression. Small businesses created nearly 2 million of the roughly 3 million private-sector jobs generated in 2014. More than 7 million of the 11 million jobs created during our recovery have been generated by startups and small enterprises".[11] Small businesses thus contribute significantly to solving unemployment problems.

5-3c Providing Competition

Small businesses challenge larger, established firms in many ways, causing them to become more efficient and more responsive to consumer needs. A small business cannot, of course, compete with a large firm in all respects. However, a number of small firms, each competing in its own particular area and its own particular way, together have the desired competitive effect. Thus, several small janitorial companies together add up to reasonable competition for the no-longer-small ServiceMaster.

5-3d Filling Needs of Society and Other Businesses

Small firms also provide a variety of goods and services to each other and to much larger firms. Sears, Roebuck & Co. purchases merchandise from approximately 12,000 suppliers—and most of them are small businesses. General Motors relies on more than 32,000 companies for parts and supplies and depends on more than 11,000 independent dealers to sell its automobiles and trucks. Large firms generally buy parts and assemblies from smaller firms for one very good reason: It is less expensive than manufacturing the parts in their own factories. This lower cost eventually is reflected in the price that consumers pay for their products.

It is clear that small businesses are a vital part of our economy and that, as consumers and as members of the labor force, we all benefit enormously from their existence. Now let us look at the situation from the viewpoint of the owners of small businesses.

Concept Check

✓ Briefly describe four contributions of small business to the American economy.

✓ Give examples of how small businesses fill needs of society and other businesses.

5-4 THE PROS AND CONS OF SMALLNESS

Do most owners of small businesses dream that their firms will grow into giant corporations—managed by professionals—while they serve only on the board of directors? Or would they rather stay small, in a firm where they have the opportunity (and the responsibility) to do everything that needs to be done? The answers depend on the personal characteristics and motivations of the individual owners. For many, the advantages of remaining small far outweigh the disadvantages.

Learning Objective

5-4 Describe the advantages and disadvantages of operating a small business.

5-4a Advantages of Small Business

Small-business owners with limited resources often must struggle to enter competitive new markets. They also have to deal with increasing international competition. However, they enjoy several unique advantages.

PERSONAL RELATIONSHIPS WITH CUSTOMERS AND EMPLOYEES
For those who like dealing with people, small business is the place to be. The owners of retail shops get to know many of their customers by name and deal with them on a personal basis. Through such relationships, small-business owners often become involved in the social, cultural, and political life of the community.

Relationships between owner-managers and employees also tend to be closer in smaller businesses. In many cases, the owner is a friend and counselor as well as the boss.

These personal relationships provide an important business advantage. The personal service small businesses offer to customers is a major competitive weapon—one that larger firms try to match but often cannot. In addition, close relationships with employees often help the small-business owner to keep effective workers who might earn more with a larger firm.

ABILITY TO ADAPT TO CHANGE Being his or her own boss, the owner-manager of a small business does not need anyone's permission to adapt to change. An owner may add or discontinue merchandise or services, change store hours, and experiment with various price strategies in response to changes in market conditions. And through personal relationships with customers, the owners of small businesses quickly become aware of changes in people's needs and interests, as well as in the activities of competing firms.

SIMPLIFIED RECORD KEEPING
Many small firms need only a simple set of records. Record keeping might consist of a checkbook, a cash-receipts journal in which to record all sales, and a cash-disbursements journal in which to record all amounts paid out. Obviously, enough records must be kept to allow for producing and filing accurate tax returns.

INDEPENDENCE Small-business owners do not have to punch in and out,

FUSE/THINKSTOCK

Getting personal. For those who like dealing with people, small business is the place to be. Here a business owner provides personalized service to a happy customer.

bid for vacation times, take orders from superiors, or worry about being fired or laid off. They are the masters of their own destinies—at least with regard to employment. For many people, this is the prime advantage of owning a small business.

OTHER ADVANTAGES According to the SBA, the most profitable companies in the United States are small firms that have been in business for more than ten years and employ fewer than 20 people. Small-business owners also enjoy all the advantages of sole proprietorships, which were discussed in Chapter 4. These include being able to keep all profits, the ease and low cost of going into business and (if necessary) going out of business, and being able to keep business information secret.

5-4b Disadvantages of Small Business

Personal contacts with customers, closer relationships with employees, being one's own boss, less cumbersome record-keeping chores, and independence are the bright side of small business. In contrast, the dark side reflects problems unique to these firms.

RISK OF FAILURE As we have noted, small businesses (especially new ones) run a heavy risk of going out of business—about 50 percent survive at least five years. Older, well-established small firms can be hit hard by a business recession mainly because they do not have the financial resources to weather an extended difficult period.

LIMITED POTENTIAL Small businesses that survive do so with varying degrees of success. Many are simply the means of making a living for the owner and his or her family. The owner may have some technical skill—as a hair stylist or electrician, for example—and may have started a business to put this skill to work. Such a business is unlikely to grow into big business. In addition, employees' potential for advancement is limited.

LIMITED ABILITY TO RAISE CAPITAL Small businesses typically have a limited ability to obtain capital. Figure 5-2 shows that most small-business financing comes out of the owner's pocket. Personal loans from lending institutions provide only about one-fourth of the capital required by small businesses. About 50 percent of all new firms begin with less than $30,000 in total capital, according to Census Bureau and Federal Reserve surveys. In fact, almost 36 percent of new firms begin with less than $20,000, usually provided by the owner or family members and friends.[12] According to the SBA, average capital for starting a new business is $80,000.

Although every person who considers starting a small business should be aware of the hazards and pitfalls we have noted, a well-conceived business plan may help to avoid the risk of failure. The U.S. government is also dedicated to helping small businesses make it. It expresses this aim most actively through the SBA.

5-4c The Importance of a Business Plan

Lack of planning can be as deadly as lack of money to a new small business. Planning is important to any business, large or small, and never should be overlooked or taken lightly. A **business plan** is a carefully constructed guide for the person starting a business. Consider it as a tool with three basic purposes: communication, management, and planning. As a communication tool, a business plan serves as a concise document that potential investors can examine to see if they would like to invest or assist in financing a new venture. It shows whether a business has the potential to make a profit. As a management tool, the business plan helps to track, monitor, and evaluate the progress. The business plan is a living document;

business plan a carefully constructed guide for the person starting a business

FIGURE 5-2 Sources of Capital for Entrepreneurs

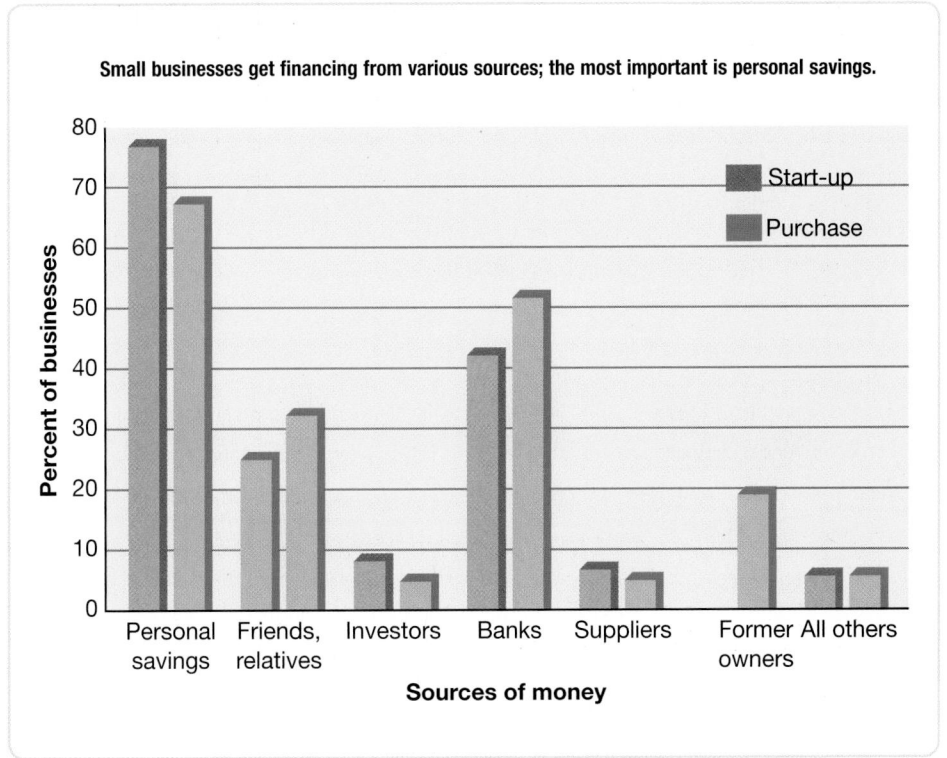

Small businesses get financing from various sources; the most important is personal savings.

Source: Data developed and provided by the National Federation of Independent Business Foundation and sponsored by the American Express Travel Related Services Company, Inc.

it is modified as the entrepreneur gains knowledge and experience. It also serves to establish time lines and milestones and allows comparison of growth projections against actual accomplishments. Finally, as a planning tool, the business plan guides a businessperson through the various phases of business. For example, the plan helps to identify obstacles to avoid and to establish alternatives. According to Robert Krummer, Jr., chairman of First Business Bank in Los Angeles, "The business plan is a necessity. If the person who wants to start a small business can't put a business plan together, he or she is in trouble."

5-4d Components of a Business Plan

Table 5-3 shows the 12 sections that a business plan should include. Each section is further explained at the end of each of the six major parts in the text. The goal of each end-of-the-part exercise is to help a businessperson create his or her own business plan. When constructing a business plan, the businessperson should strive to keep it easy to read, uncluttered, and complete. Like other busy executives, officials of financial institutions do not have the time to wade through pages of extraneous data. The business plan should answer the four questions banking officials and investors are most interested in: (1) What exactly is the nature and mission of the new venture? (2) Why is this new enterprise a good idea? (3) What are the businessperson's goals? (4) How much will the new venture cost?

TABLE 5-3 Components of a Business Plan

1. *Introduction.* Basic information such as the name, address, and phone number of the business; the date the plan was issued; and a statement of confidentiality to keep important information away from potential competitors.

2. *Executive Summary.* A one- to two-page overview of the entire business plan, including a justification why the business will succeed.

3. *Benefits to the Community.* Information on how the business will have an impact on economic development, community development, and human development.

4. *Company and Industry.* The background of the company, choice of the legal business form, information on the products or services to be offered, and examination of the potential customers, current competitors, and the business's future.

5. *Management Team.* Discussion of skills, talents, and job descriptions of management team, managerial compensation, management training needs, and professional assistance requirements.

6. *Manufacturing and Operations Plan.* Discussion of facilities needed, space requirements, capital equipment, labor force, inventory control, and purchasing requirement.

7. *Labor Force.* Discussion of the quality of skilled workers available and the training, compensation, and motivation of workers.

8. *Marketing Plan.* Discussion of markets, market trends, competition, market share, pricing, promotion, distribution, and service policy.

9. *Financial Plan.* Summary of the investment needed, sales and cash flow forecasts, breakeven analysis, and sources of funding.

10. *Exit Strategy.* Discussion of a succession plan or going public. Who will take over the business?

11. *Critical Risks and Assumptions.* Evaluation of the weaknesses of the business and how the company plans to deal with these and other business problems.

12. *Appendix.* Supplementary information crucial to the plan, such as résumés of owners and principal managers, advertising samples, organization chart, and any related information.

Source: From HATTEN, *Small Business Management*, 5E.

Concept Check

✓ What are the major advantages and disadvantages of smallness in business?

✓ What are the major components of a business plan? Why should an individual develop a business plan?

The great amount of time and consideration that should go into creating a business plan probably will end up saving time later. For example, Sharon Burch, who was running a computer software business while earning a degree in business administration, had to write a business plan as part of one of her courses. Burch has said, "I wish I'd taken the class before I started my business. I see a lot of things I could have done differently. But it has helped me since because I've been using the business plan as a guide for my business." Accuracy and realistic expectations are crucial to an effective business plan. It is unethical to deceive loan officers, and it is unwise to deceive yourself.

5-5 THE SMALL BUSINESS ADMINISTRATION

Learning Objective

5-5 Explain how the Small Business Administration helps small businesses.

The **Small Business Administration (SBA)**, created by Congress in 1953, is a governmental agency that assists, counsels, and protects the interests of small businesses in the United States. It helps people get into business and stay in business. The agency provides assistance to owners and managers of prospective, new, and established small businesses. Through more than 1,000 offices and resource centers throughout the nation, the SBA provides both financial assistance and management counseling. Recently, the SBA provided training, technical assistance, and education to more than 3.5 million small businesses. It helps small firms to bid for and obtain government contracts, and it helps them to prepare to enter foreign markets.

5-5a SBA Management Assistance

Small Business Administration (SBA) a governmental agency that assists, counsels, and protects the interests of small businesses in the United States

Statistics show that most failures in small business are related to poor management. For this reason, the SBA places special emphasis on improving the management ability of the owners and managers of small businesses. The SBA's Management Assistance Program is extensive and diversified. It includes free individual counseling, courses, conferences, workshops, and a wide range of publications. Recently, the SBA provided management and technical assistance to nearly 1 million small businesses through its 900 Small Business Development Centers and 11,000 volunteers from the Service Corps of Retired Executives.

The SBA launched its 2015 Emerging Leaders Program in 48 U.S. cities. Since 2008, the program has trained more than 2,400 small business owners in underserved communities. According to SBA Administrator Maria Contreras-Sweet, "The Emerging Leaders Program is a resource that can open lucrative doors for America's small businesses. The addition of over 20 new cities in 2015 will help serve even more entrepreneurs. Graduates of the Leadership Program have measurably increased their revenue, helped create jobs, and drive economic growth in their local communities."[13]

MANAGEMENT COURSES AND WORKSHOPS The management courses offered by the SBA cover all the functions, duties, and roles of managers. Instructors may be teachers from local colleges and universities or other professionals, such as management consultants, bankers, lawyers, and accountants. Fees for these courses are quite low. The most popular such course is a general survey of eight to ten different areas of business management. In follow-up studies, businesspeople may concentrate in depth on one or more of these areas depending on their particular strengths and weaknesses. The SBA occasionally offers one-day conferences. These conferences are aimed at keeping owner-managers up-to-date on new management developments, tax laws, and the like. The SBA Learning Center is an online training network consisting of 23 SBA-run courses, workshops, and resources. Some of the most requested courses include Entrepreneurship, Starting and Managing Your Own Business, Developing a Business Plan, Managing the Digital Enterprise, Identify Your Target Market, and Analyze Profitability. Find out more at www.sba.gov/training. Recently, more than 260,000 small-business owners benefited from SBA's free online business courses.

SCORE The **Service Corps of Retired Executives (SCORE)**, Counselors to America's Small Business, created in 1964, is a group of more than 11,000 retired and active businesspeople, including more than 2,000 women who volunteer their services to small businesses through the SBA. The collective experience of SCORE volunteers spans the full range of American enterprise. These volunteers have worked for such notable companies as Eastman Kodak, General Electric, IBM, and Procter & Gamble. Experts in areas of accounting, finance, marketing, engineering, and retailing provide counseling and mentoring to entrepreneurs. In 2014, SCORE celebrated its 50th Anniversary and the volunteers donated more than 1.1 million hours to assist small businesses.

A small-business owner who has a particular problem can request free counseling from SCORE. An assigned counselor visits the owner in his or her establishment and, through careful observation, analyzes the business situation and the problem. If the problem is complex, the counselor may call on other volunteer experts to assist. Finally, the counselor offers a plan for solving the problem and helping the owner through the critical period.

Consider the plight of Elizabeth Halvorsen, a mystery writer from Minneapolis. Her husband had built up the family advertising and graphic arts firm for 17 years when he was called in 1991 to serve in the Persian Gulf War. The only one left behind to run the business was Mrs. Halvorsen, who admittedly had no business experience. Enter SCORE. With a SCORE management expert at her side, she kept the business on track. Recently, SCORE volunteers served more than 350,000 small-business people like Mrs. Halvorsen through its more than 320 offices. Since its inception, SCORE has assisted more than 10 million small-business people with online and face-to-face small business counseling. Recently, SCORE volunteers

Service Corps of Retired Executives (SCORE) a group of businesspeople who volunteer their services to small businesses through the SBA

Minority-owned businesses. Are you ready to start your business, but don't know where to start or what opportunities are available to minority groups? The SBA provides information on federal government programs and services that help people start their own businesses.

helped start 38,630 businesses, created 67,320 jobs, and mentored 124,600 small business owners and entrepreneurs.[14]

5-5b Help for Minority-Owned Small Businesses

Americans who are members of minority groups have had difficulty entering the nation's economic mainstream. Raising money is a nagging problem for minority business owners, who also may lack adequate training. Members of minority groups are, of course, eligible for all SBA programs, but the SBA makes a special effort to assist those minority groups who want to start small businesses or expand existing ones. For example, the Minority Business Development Agency awards grants to develop and increase business opportunities for members of racial and ethnic minorities.

Helping women become entrepreneurs is also a special goal of the SBA. Emily Harrington, one of nine children, was born in Manila, the Philippines. She arrived in the United States in 1972 as a foreign-exchange student. Convinced that there was a market for hard-working, dedicated minorities and women, she launched Qualified Resources, Inc., a professional staffing services firm. *Inc.* magazine selected her firm as one of "America's Fastest Growing Private Companies" just six years later. Harrington credits the SBA with giving her the technical support that made her first loan possible. Finding a SCORE counselor to work directly with her, she refined her business plan until she got a bank loan. Before contacting the SBA, Harrington was turned down for business loans "by all the banks I approached," even though she worked as a manager of loan credit and collection for a bank. Later, Emily Harrington was SBA's winner of the local, regional, and national Small Business Entrepreneurial Success Award for Rhode Island, the New England region, and the nation! For several years in a row, Qualified Resources, Inc., was named one of the fastest growing private companies in Rhode Island. Now with more than 100 Women's Business Centers, entrepreneurs like Harrington can receive training and technical assistance, access to credit and capital, federal contracts, and international markets. The SBA's Online Women's Business Center (https://www.sba.gov/tools/local-assistance/wbc) is a state-of-the-art Internet site to help women expand their businesses. This free, interactive website offers women information about business principles and practices, management techniques, networking, industry news, market research and technology training, online counseling, and hundreds of links to other sites, as well as information about the many SBA services and resources available to them. In 2014, the SBA approved $6.5 billion in loans for 15,620 minority-owned businesses.

SMALL-BUSINESS INSTITUTES Small-business institutes (SBIs), created in 1972, are groups of senior and graduate students in business administration who provide management counseling to small businesses. SBIs have been set up on more than 520 college campuses as another way to help business owners. The students work in small groups guided by faculty advisers and SBA management-assistance experts. Like SCORE volunteers, they analyze and help solve the problems of small-business owners at their business establishments.

SMALL-BUSINESS DEVELOPMENT CENTERS Small-business development centers (SBDCs) are university-based groups that provide individual

small-business institutes (SBIs) groups of senior and graduate students in business administration who provide management counseling to small businesses

small-business development centers (SBDCs) university-based groups that provide individual counseling and practical training to owners of small businesses

counseling and practical training to owners of small businesses. SBDCs draw from the resources of local, state, and federal governments, private businesses, and universities. These groups can provide managerial and technical help, data from research studies, and other types of specialized assistance of value to small businesses. In 2014, there were more than 900 SBDC locations, primarily at colleges and universities, assisting people such as Kathleen DuBois. After scribbling a list of her abilities and the names of potential clients on a napkin in a local restaurant, Kathleen DuBois decided to start her own marketing firm. Beth Thornton launched her engineering firm after a discussion with a colleague in the ladies room of the Marriott. When Richard Shell was laid off after 20 years of service with Nisource (Columbia Gas), he searched the Internet tirelessly before finding the right franchise option. Introduced by mutual friends, Jim Bostic and Denver McMillion quickly connected, built a high level of trust, and combined their diverse professional backgrounds to form a manufacturing company. Although these entrepreneurs took different routes in starting their new businesses in West Virginia, all of them turned to the West Virginia Small Business Development Center for the technical assistance to make their dreams become a reality.

The SBA provides a variety of services.
When disaster strikes, the SBA makes available relief for stricken businesses. For example, the SBA provided disaster relief to small businesses affected by Hurricane Sandy.

SBA PUBLICATIONS The SBA issues management, marketing, and technical publications dealing with hundreds of topics of interest to present and prospective managers of small firms. Most of these publications are available from the SBA free of charge. Others can be obtained for a small fee from the U.S. Government Printing Office.

5-5c **SBA Financial Assistance**

Small businesses seem to be constantly in need of money. An owner may have enough capital to start and operate the business. But then he or she may require more money to finance increased operations during peak selling seasons, to pay for required pollution control equipment, to finance an expansion, or to mop up after a natural disaster such as a flood or a terrorist attack. In early 2013, 90 days after Hurricane Sandy hit the Northeast, the SBA guaranteed over $1 billion in loans to more than 16,800 businesses, homeowners, and renters. In the year following the storm, the SBA had approved $2.4 billion in low-interest disaster loans.[15] Earlier, the SBA offered economic injury loans to fishing and fishing-dependent small businesses as a result of the Deepwater BP spill that shut down commercial and recreational fishing waters. According to the SBA Administrator, "SBA remains committed to taking every step to help small businesses deal with the financial challenges they are facing as a result of the Deepwater BP oil spill."[16] The SBA offers special financial-assistance programs that cover all these situations. However, its primary financial function is to guarantee loans to eligible businesses.

REGULAR BUSINESS LOANS Most of the SBA's business loans are actually made by private lenders such as banks, but repayment is partially guaranteed by the agency. That is, the SBA may guarantee that it will repay the lender up to 90 percent of the loan if the borrowing firm cannot repay it. Guaranteed loans approved may be as large as $5.0 million (this loan limit may be increased in the future). The average size of an SBA-guaranteed business loan is about $300,000, and its average duration is about eight years.

SMALL-BUSINESS INVESTMENT COMPANIES Venture capital is money that is invested in small (and sometimes struggling) firms that have the potential to become very successful. In many cases, only a lack of capital keeps these firms from rapid and solid growth. The people who invest in such firms expect that their

venture capital money that is invested in small (and sometimes struggling) firms that have the potential to become very successful investments will grow with the firms and become quite profitable. Consider this: 36 years ago, a young computer programmer working out of his parents' garage needed capital to create the world's most user-friendly personal computer. He met a financier, John Hines, who managed an Illinois-based venture capital firm, licensed and supported by the U.S. Small Business Administration. Hines saw the potential and invested half a million dollars in the promising startup. Two years later, the young programmer took his company public, and the venture capital firm sold its stake for $44 million. Who was this programmer? His name is Steve Jobs.

The popularity of these investments has increased over the past 40 years, but most small firms still have difficulty obtaining venture capital. To help such businesses, the SBA licenses, regulates, and provides financial assistance to **small-business investment companies (SBICs)**.

An SBIC is a privately owned firm that provides venture capital to small enterprises that meet its investment standards. Firms such as America Online, Apple Computer, Costco, Jenny Craig, Federal Express, Compaq Computer, Intel Corporation, Outback Steakhouse, and Staples, Inc., all were financed through SBICs during their initial growth period. More than 292 SBICs are intended to be profit-making organizations. The aid that SBA offers allows them to invest in small businesses that otherwise would not attract venture capital. Since Congress created the program in 1958, SBICs have financed more than 120,000 small businesses for a total of about $70 billion. In 2013, SBICs benefited 1,068 small businesses, and 30 percent of these firms were owned by women or other minorities.[17]

We have discussed the importance of the small-business segment of our economy. We have weighed the advantages and drawbacks of operating a small business as compared with a large one. But is there a way to achieve the best of both worlds? Can one preserve one's independence as a business owner and still enjoy some of the benefits of "bigness"? Let's take a close look at franchising.

Concept Check

✓ Identify five ways in which the SBA provides management assistance to small businesses.

✓ Identify two ways in which the SBA provides financial assistance to small businesses.

✓ Why does the SBA concentrate on providing management and financial assistance to small business?

✓ What is venture capital? How does the SBA help small businesses to obtain it?

5-6 FRANCHISING

Learning Objective

5-6 Explain the concept and types of franchising.

A **franchise** is a license to operate an individually owned business as if it were part of a chain of outlets or stores. Often, the business itself is also called a *franchise*. Among the most familiar franchises are McDonald's, H&R Block, AAMCO Transmissions, GNC (General Nutrition Centers), and Dairy Queen. Many other franchises carry familiar names; this method of doing business has become very popular in the last 60 years or so. It is an attractive means of starting and operating a small business.

5-6a What Is Franchising?

Franchising is the actual granting of a franchise. A **franchisor** is an individual or organization granting a franchise. A **franchisee** is a person or organization purchasing a franchise. The franchisor supplies a known and advertised business name, management skills, the required training and materials, and a method of doing business. The franchisee supplies labor and capital, operates the franchised business, and agrees to abide by the provisions of the franchise agreement. Table 5-4 lists the basic franchisee rights and obligations that would be covered in a typical franchise agreement.

5-6b Types of Franchising

Franchising arrangements fall into three general categories. In the first approach, a manufacturer authorizes a number of retail stores to sell a certain brand-name item. This type of franchising arrangement, one of the oldest, is prevalent in sales of passenger cars and trucks, farm equipment, shoes, paint, earth-moving equipment, and petroleum. About 90 percent of all gasoline is sold through franchised,

small-business investment companies (SBICs) privately owned firms that provide venture capital to small enterprises that meet their investment standards

franchise a license to operate an individually owned business as though it were part of a chain of outlets or stores

franchising the actual granting of a franchise

franchisor an individual or organization granting a franchise

franchisee a person or organization purchasing a franchise

TABLE 5-4 Basic Rights and Obligations Delineated in a Franchise Agreement

Franchisee rights include:
1. use of trademarks, trade names, and patents of the franchisor;
2. use of the brand image and the design and decor of the premises developed by the franchisor;
3. use of the franchisor's secret methods;
4. use of the franchisor's copyrighted materials;
5. use of recipes, formulae, specifications, processes, and methods of manufacture developed by the franchisor;
6. conducting the franchised business upon or from the agreed premises strictly in accordance with the franchisor's methods and subject to the franchisor's directions;
7. guidelines established by the franchisor regarding exclusive territorial rights; and
8. rights to obtain supplies from nominated suppliers at special prices.

Franchisee obligations include:
1. to carry on the business franchised and no other business upon the approved and nominated premises;
2. to observe certain minimum operating hours;
3. to pay a franchise fee;
4. to follow the accounting system laid down by the franchisor;
5. not to advertise without prior approval of the advertisements by the franchisor;
6. to use and display such point-of-sale advertising materials as the franchisor stipulates;
7. to maintain the premises in good, clean, and sanitary condition and to redecorate when required to do so by the franchisor;
8. to maintain the widest possible insurance coverage;
9. to permit the franchisor's staff to enter the premises to inspect and see if the franchisor's standards are being maintained;
10. to purchase goods or products from the franchisor or his designated suppliers;
11. to train the staff in the franchisor's methods to ensure that they are neatly and appropriately clothed; and
12. not to assign the franchise contract without the franchisor's consent.

Source: Office of Entrepreneurship Education Resources, http://www.sba.gov/offices/headquarters/oee/resources/3641#Selecting a Franchise (accessed January 12, 2015).

independent retail service stations, and franchised dealers handle virtually all sales of new cars and trucks. In the second type of franchising arrangement, a producer licenses distributors to sell a given product to retailers. This arrangement is common in the soft drink industry. Most national manufacturers of soft drink syrups—The Coca-Cola Company, Dr. Pepper/Seven-Up Companies, PepsiCo, Royal Crown Companies, Inc.—franchise independent bottlers who then serve retailers. In a third form of franchising, a franchisor supplies brand names, techniques, or other services instead of a complete product. Although the franchisor may provide certain production and distribution services, its primary role is the careful development and control of marketing strategies. This approach to franchising, which is the most typical today, is used by Avis, Hampton Hotels, 7-Eleven Inc., Anytime Fitness, Denny's Inc., Pizza Hut Inc., McDonald's, and SUBWAY, to name but a few.

Concept Check

✓ Explain the relationships among a franchise, the franchisor, and the franchisee.

✓ Describe the three general categories of franchising arrangements.

Entrepreneurial Success

Is a Franchise in Your Future?

A small but growing number of franchisees in their 20s see franchising as a path toward entrepreneurial success. Becoming a franchisee requires a sizeable financial investment—but so do many small businesses started from scratch. What attracts young franchisees is the opportunity to build on a recognized brand and proven operational processes. Adding their own creativity and enthusiasm, they can leverage the franchise model to fuel business growth.

Hailey Nault is happy with her decision to own a Pita Pit franchise in Ontario, Canada. Partnering with an existing Pita Pit owner to buy a franchise, Nault and her employees make healthy pita-bread sandwiches to order. Although she works long hours, Nault brings high energy and ambition to her franchise business. "If it succeeds, it's because I did it," she explains. "That's more exciting than anything."

Mit Patel is another franchisee under 30 who enjoys being part of a successful franchise, Forever Yogurt. Patel is the son of an entrepreneur, so he understands the ups and downs of running a business—and he has a mentor in the family. His frozen yogurt shop is located close in a popular Baltimore neighborhood of restaurants and shops. Patel advises young franchisees to "ask a million questions" and take time choosing a location.

After Ivan Kenneth Taw graduated college in the Philippines, he worked in marketing and then shifted gears to consider franchising. His careful research led him to buy a 7-Eleven convenience store, with family financing. "The reliable support system allows me to work on my own, without being entirely on my own," he says.

Sources: Based on information in Tracy Hanes, "Young Entrepreneurs See Big Opportunities in Franchising," *Globe and Mail (Canada)*, November 3, 2014, www.theglobeandmail.com; "Young Franchisee Gives Fresh Business Insights for New Graduates," *Philippine Star*, April 7, 2014, www.philstar.com; Kate Taylor, "Franchise Players: A Young Franchisee Brings Family's Lessons to Forever Yogurt," *Entrepreneur.com*, March 12, 2014.

5-7 THE GROWTH OF FRANCHISING

Learning Objective

5-7 Analyze the growth of franchising and its advantages and disadvantages.

Franchising, which began in the United States around the time of the Civil War, was used originally by large firms, such as the Singer Sewing Company, to distribute their products. Franchising has been increasing steadily in popularity since the early 1900s, primarily for filling stations and car dealerships; however, this retailing strategy has experienced enormous growth since the mid-1970s. The franchise proliferation generally has paralleled the expansion of the fast-food industry.

Of course, franchising is not limited to fast foods. Hair salons, tanning parlors, and dentists and lawyers are expected to participate in franchising arrangements in growing numbers. Franchised health clubs, pest exterminators, and campgrounds are already widespread, as are franchised tax preparers and travel agencies. The real estate industry also has experienced a rapid increase in franchising.

Also, franchising is attracting more women and minority business owners in the United States than ever before. One reason is that special outreach programs designed to encourage franchisee diversity have developed. Consider Angela Trammel, a young mother of two. She had been laid off from her job at the Marriott after 9/11. Since she was a member of a Curves Fitness Center and liked the concept of empowering women to become physically fit, she began researching the cost of purchasing a Curves franchise and ways to finance the business. "I was online looking for financing, and I linked to Enterprise Development Group in Washington, DC. I knew that they had diverse clients." The cost for the franchise was $19,500, but it took $60,000 to open the doors to her fitness center. "Applying for a loan to start the business was much harder than buying a house," said Trammel. Just three years later, Angela and her husband, Ernest, own three Curves Fitness Centers with 12 employees. Recently, since giving birth to her third child, she has found the financial freedom and flexibility needed to care for her busy family. In fact, within a three-year period, the Trammels grew their annual household income from $80,000 to $250,000.[18] Franchisors such as Wendy's, McDonald's, Burger King, and Church's Chicken all have special corporate programs to attract minority and women franchisees. Just as important, successful women and minority franchisees are willing to get involved by offering advice and guidance to new franchisees.

Herman Petty, the first African-American McDonald's franchisee, remembers that the company provided a great deal of help while he worked to establish his first units. In turn, Petty traveled to help other black franchisees, and he invited new franchisees to gain hands-on experience in his Chicago restaurants before starting their own establishments. In 1972, Petty also organized a support group, the National Black McDonald's Operators Association, to help black franchisees in other areas. Today, members of this association own over 1,300 McDonald's restaurants throughout the United States, South Africa, and the Caribbean with annual sales of more than $2.7 billion. "By staying together, we will realize the dream that our forefathers envisioned: an organization of successful African-American entrepreneurs who did not forget their humble beginnings," says Roland G. Parrish, the McDonald's franchisee who leads the group.

Dual-branded franchises, in which two franchisors offer their products together, are a new small-business trend. For example, in 1993, pleased with the success of its first co-branded restaurant with Texaco in Beebe, Arkansas, McDonald's now has more than 400 co-branded restaurants in the United States. Also, an agreement between franchisors Doctor's Associates, Inc., and TCBY Enterprises, Inc., now allows franchisees to sell SUBWAY sandwiches and TCBY yogurt in the same establishment.

5-7a Are Franchises Successful?

Franchising is designed to provide a tested formula for success, along with ongoing advice and training. The success rate for businesses owned and operated by franchisees is significantly higher than the success rate for other independently owned small businesses. In a recent nationwide Gallup poll of 944 franchise owners, 94 percent of franchisees indicated that they were very or somewhat successful, only 5 percent believed that they were very unsuccessful or somewhat unsuccessful, and 1 percent did not know. Despite these impressive statistics, franchising is not a guarantee of success for either franchisees or franchisors. Too rapid expansion, inadequate capital or management skills, and a host of other problems can cause failure for both franchisee and franchisor. Thus, for example, the Dizzy Dean's Beef and Burger franchise is no longer in business. Timothy Bates, a Wayne State University economist, warns, "Despite the hype that franchising is the safest way to go when starting a new business, the research just doesn't bear that out." Just consider Boston Chicken, which once had more than 1,200 restaurants before declaring bankruptcy in 1998.

5-7b Advantages of Franchising

Franchising plays a vital role in our economy and soon may become the dominant form of retailing. Why? Because franchising offers advantages to both the franchisor and the franchisee.

TO THE FRANCHISOR The franchisor gains fast and well-controlled distribution of its products without incurring the high cost of constructing and operating its own outlets. The franchisor thus has more capital available to expand production and to use for

We Do Lines. When three landscape business owners needed their parking lot striped, they discovered a new business opportunity which quickly became their only business. Their Connecticut based We Do Lines grew quickly along the East Coast. They now have franchisees in Arizona, Ohio, New York, New Jersey, and Florida.

The growth of franchising. Franchising is designed to provide a tested formula for success, along with ongoing advice and training. The franchisor, such as McDonald's, Chipotle, or Panda Express, supplies a known and advertised business name, management skills, the required training and materials, and a method of doing business. Franchising, however, is not a guarantee of success for either franchisees or franchisors.

advertising. At the same time, it can ensure, through the franchise agreement, that outlets are maintained and operated according to its own standards.

The franchisor also benefits from the fact that the franchisee—a sole proprietor in most cases—is likely to be very highly motivated to succeed. The success of the franchise means more sales, which translate into higher royalties for the franchisor.

TO THE FRANCHISEE The franchisee gets the opportunity to start a business with limited capital and to make use of the business experience of others. Moreover, an outlet with a nationally advertised name, such as RadioShack, McDonald's, or Century 21, has guaranteed customers as soon as it opens.

If business problems arise, the franchisor gives the franchisee guidance and advice. This counseling is primarily responsible for the very high degree of success enjoyed by franchises. In most cases, the franchisee does not pay for such help.

The franchisee also receives materials to use in local advertising and can take part in national promotional campaigns sponsored by the franchisor. McDonald's and its franchisees, for example, constitute one of the nation's top 20 purchasers of advertising. Finally, the franchisee may be able to minimize the cost of advertising, supplies, and various business necessities by purchasing them in cooperation with other franchisees.

5-7c Disadvantages of Franchising

The main disadvantage of franchising affects the franchisee, and it arises because the franchisor retains a great deal of control. The franchisor's contract can dictate every aspect of the business: decor, design of employee uniforms, types of signs, and all the details of business operations. All Burger King French fries taste the same because all Burger King franchisees have to make them the same way.

Contract disputes are the cause of many lawsuits. For example, Rekha Gabhawala, a Dunkin' Donuts franchisee in Milwaukee, alleged that the franchisor was forcing her out of business so that the company could profit by reselling the downtown franchise to someone else; the company, on the other hand, alleged that Gabhawala breached the contract by not running the business according to company standards. In another case, Dunkin' Donuts sued Chris Romanias, its franchisee in Pennsylvania, alleging that Romanias intentionally underreported gross sales to the company. Romanias, on the other hand, alleged that Dunkin' Donuts, Inc., breached the contract because it failed to provide assistance in operating the franchise. Other franchisees claim that contracts are unfairly tilted toward the franchisors. Yet others have charged that they lost their franchise and investment because their franchisor would not approve the sale of the business when they found a buyer.

To arbitrate disputes between franchisors and franchisees, the National Franchise Mediation Program was established in 1993 by 30 member firms, including Burger King Corporation, McDonald's Corporation, and Wendy's International, Inc. Negotiators have since resolved numerous cases through mediation. Recently, Carl's

CHRIS LAWRENCE/ALAMY

Jr. brought in one of its largest franchisees to help set its system straight, making most franchisees happy for the first time in years. The program also helped PepsiCo settle a long-term contract dispute and renegotiate its franchise agreements.

Because disagreements between franchisors and franchisees have increased in recent years, many franchisees have been demanding government regulation of franchising. In 1997, to avoid government regulation, some of the largest franchisors proposed a new self-policing plan to the Federal Trade Commission.

Franchise holders pay for their security, usually with a one-time franchise fee and continuing royalty and advertising fees, collected as a percentage of sales. For example, a SUBWAY franchisee pays an initial franchise fee of $15,000 and a weekly fee of 12.5 percent of gross sales (8 percent royalty and 4.5 percent advertising fees) In some fields, franchise agreements are not uniform. One franchisee may pay more than another for the same services.

Even success can cause problems. Sometimes a franchise is so successful that the franchisor opens its own outlet nearby, in direct competition—although franchisees may fight back. For example, a court recently ruled that Burger King could not enter into direct competition with the franchisee because the contract was not specific on the issue. A spokesperson for one franchisor contends that the company "gives no geographical protection" to its franchise holders and thus is free to move in on them. Franchise operators work hard. They often put in 10- and 12-hour days, six days a week. The International Franchise Association advises prospective franchise purchasers to investigate before investing and to approach buying a franchise cautiously. Franchises vary widely in approach as well as in products. Some, such as Dunkin' Donuts and Baskin-Robbins, demand long hours. Others, such as Great Clips and SportClips hair salons, are more appropriate for those who do not want to spend many hours at their stores.

5-7d Global Perspectives in Small Business

The world economy has entered a new phase since the ups and downs of the global financial crisis of 2009. For small American businesses, the world is becoming smaller. National and international economies are growing more and more interdependent as political leadership and national economic directions change and trade barriers diminish or disappear. Globalization and instant worldwide communications are rapidly shrinking distances at the same time that they are expanding business opportunities. According to a recent study, the Internet is increasingly important to small-business strategic thinking, with more than 50 percent of those surveyed indicating that the Internet represented their most favored strategy for growth. This was more than double the next-favored choice, strategic alliances reflecting the opportunity to reach both global and domestic customers. The Internet and online payment systems enable even very small businesses to serve international customers. In fact, technology now gives small businesses the leverage and power to reach markets that were once limited solely to large corporations. According to the U.S. Commercial Service, "More than 70 percent of the world's purchasing power is outside of the United States and over the next five years, 85 percent of the world's economic growth will be overseas."[19]

The SBA offers help to the nation's small-business owners who want to enter the world markets. U.S. Export Assistance Centers, staffed by experts from the SBA, Department of Commerce, Export-Import Bank, and other public and private organizations are located in major U.S. metropolitan areas. The SBA's efforts include counseling small firms on how and where to market overseas, matching U.S.

small-business executives with potential overseas customers, and helping exporters to secure financing. The agency brings small U.S. firms into direct contact with potential overseas buyers and partners. The SBA International Trade Loan program provides guarantees of up to $5 million in loans to small-business owners. These loans help small firms in expanding or developing new export markets. The U.S. Commercial Service, a Commerce Department division, aids small- and medium-sized businesses in selling overseas. The division's global network includes more than 100 offices in the United States and 151 others in more than 70 countries around the world.[20]

Consider Daniel J. Nanigian, president of Nanmac Corporation in Framingham, Massachusetts. This company manufactures temperature sensors used in a wide range of industrial applications. With an export strategy aimed at growing revenues in diverse foreign markets including China, the Nanmac Corporation experienced explosive growth in 2009. The company nearly doubled its sales from $2.7 million in 2008 to $5.1 million in 2009. The company's international sales, at $300,000 in 2004, reached $700,000 in 2009, and $1.7 million in 2010. Its administrative, sales, and manufacturing employees have increased by 80 percent.

The company has a strong presence in China and is expanding in other markets, as well, including Latin America, Singapore, and Russia. Under Nanigian's guidance, the company has developed creative solutions and partnerships to help maximize its presence internationally. As part of its China strategy, Nanmac partners with distributors, recruits European and in-country sales representatives, uses a localized Chinese website, and relies for advice on the export assistance programs of the Massachusetts Small Business Development Center Network's Massachusetts Export Center. The strategy, along with travel to China to conduct technical training seminars and attend trade shows and technical conferences, has helped to grow Nanmac's Chinese client list from 1 in 2003 to more than 30 accounts today. Mr. Nanigian received SBA's Small Business Exporter of the Year Award.[21]

International trade will become more important to small-business owners as they face unique challenges in the new century. Small businesses, which are expected to remain the dominant form of organization in this country, must be prepared to adapt to significant demographic and economic changes in the world marketplace.

This chapter ends our discussion of American business today. From here on, we shall be looking closely at various aspects of business operations. We begin, in the next chapter, with a discussion of management—what management is, what managers do, and how they work to coordinate the basic economic resources within a business organization.

Concept Check

✓ What does the franchisor receive in a franchising agreement? What does the franchisee receive? What does each provide?

✓ Cite one major benefit of franchising for the franchisor. Cite one major benefit of franchising for the franchisee.

✓ How does the SBA help small business-owners who want to enter the world markets?

✓ What are the global perspectives in small business?

Summary

5-1 Define what a small business is and recognize the fields in which small businesses are concentrated.

A small business is one that is independently owned and operated for profit and is not dominant in its field. There are about 28.2 million businesses in this country, and 99.7 percent of them are small businesses. Small businesses employ more than half the nation's workforce. About 69 percent of small businesses survive at least two years and about 50 percent survive at least five years. More than half of all small businesses are in retailing and services.

5-2 Identify the people who start small businesses and the reasons why some succeed and many fail.

Such personal characteristics as independence, desire to create a new enterprise, and willingness to accept a challenge may encourage individuals to start small businesses. Various external circumstances, such as special expertise or even the loss of a job, also can supply the motivation to strike out on one's own. Poor planning and lack of capital and management experience are the major causes of small-business failures.

5-3 Assess the contributions of small businesses to our economy.

Small businesses have been responsible for a wide variety of inventions and innovations, some of which have given rise to new industries. Historically, small businesses have created the bulk of the nation's new jobs. Further, they have mounted effective competition to larger firms. They provide things that society needs, act as suppliers to larger firms, and serve as customers of other businesses, both large and small.

5-4 Describe the advantages and disadvantages of operating a small business.

The advantages of smallness in business include the opportunity to establish personal relationships with customers and employees, the ability to adapt to changes quickly, independence, and simplified record keeping. The major disadvantages are the high risk of failure, the limited potential for growth, and the limited ability to raise capital.

5-5 Explain how the Small Business Administration helps small businesses.

The Small Business Administration (SBA) was created in 1953 to assist and counsel the nation's millions of small-business owners. The SBA offers management courses and workshops; managerial help, including one-to-one counseling through SCORE; various publications; and financial assistance through guaranteed loans and SBICs. It places special emphasis on aid to minority-owned businesses, including those owned by women.

5-6 Explain the concept and types of franchising.

A franchise is a license to operate an individually owned business as though it were part of a chain. The franchisor provides a known business name, management skills, a method of doing business, and the training and required materials. The franchisee contributes labor and capital, operates the franchised business, and agrees to abide by the provisions of the franchise agreement. There are three major categories of franchise agreements.

5-7 Analyze the growth of franchising and its advantages and disadvantages.

Franchising has grown tremendously since the mid-1970s. The franchisor's major advantage in franchising is fast and well-controlled distribution of products with minimal capital outlay. In return, the franchisee has the opportunity to open a business with limited capital, to make use of the business experience of others, and to sell to an existing clientele. For this, the franchisee usually must pay both an initial franchise fee and a continuing royalty based on sales. He or she also must follow the dictates of the franchise with regard to operation of the business.

Worldwide business opportunities are expanding for small businesses. The SBA assists small-business owners in penetrating foreign markets. The next century will present unique challenges and opportunities for small-business owners.

Key Terms

You should now be able to define and give an example relevant to each of the following terms:

small business (133)	Service Corps of Retired Executives (SCORE) (147)	small-business development centers (SBDCs) (148)	franchise (150)
business plan (144)		venture capital (149)	franchising (150)
Small Business Administration (SBA) (146)	small-business institutes (SBIs) (148)	small-business investment companies (SBICs) (150)	franchisor (150)
			franchisee (150)

Discussion Questions

1. Most people who start small businesses are aware of the high failure rate and the reasons for it. Why, then, do some take no steps to protect their firms from failure? What steps should they take?
2. Are the so-called advantages of small business really advantages? Wouldn't every small-business owner like his or her business to grow into a large firm?
3. Do average citizens benefit from the activities of the SBA, or is the SBA just another way to spend our tax money?
4. Would you rather own your own business independently or become a franchisee? Why?

Video Case

From Two Men and a Truck to 220 Franchises and 1,400 Trucks

Two Men and a Truck (www.twomenandatruck.com) began in the 1980s as a way for brothers Brig and Jon Sorber to make money while in high school. They started with one old pickup truck, placed a newspaper ad promoting their moving services in and around Lansing, Michigan, and charged $25 per hour to transport household goods. Their mother Mary Ellen Sheets created the hand-drawn logo of stick-figure men inside a truck, which has been part of the company's business identity since the beginning.

When the brothers left for college, their mother took over to keep the moving business on the move. Demand was so strong, in fact, that Sheets decided to buy a larger used truck for $350, hire two more men, and undertake even larger moving jobs. During school breaks, the brothers came home and earned extra spending money by climbing into one of the trucks and helping homeowners move.

Two Men and a Truck continued to attract so many customers that Sheets finally quit her job to operate the business as a full-time entrepreneur. In 1985, she hired more people, purchased a new truck, and set a tone of superior customer service embodied by the "Grandma Rule"—treat every customer with the same care and respect you would show your own grandmother. Within two years, Two Men and a Truck had earned its first profit, which Sheets donated to community charities. This was only the first of many efforts driven by the entrepreneur's core value of taking care of people—the community as well as the customers.

One day, Sheets was part of a panel about entrepreneurship and met a woman who had successfully franchised her business. With this woman's encouragement, Sheets looked into the idea of franchising Two Men and a Truck. She asked her daughter Melanie Bergeron to join the family business as head of the franchising division. Thanks to a grant, Bergeron was able to learn about franchising through weekly consultations with experts at the accounting firm of Deloitte & Touche. Two Men and a Truck started to offer franchises and as its aggressive growth continued, Bergeron's brothers returned to work in the family business a few years later.

Over time, each family member has found ways to apply his or her own strengths to the challenges and opportunities faced by the company, and to function effectively as business partners when they're all in the office dealing with a problem. Today, Brig Sorber is the CEO, Jon Sorber is the executive vice president, and Melanie Bergeron serves as chair of Two Men and a Truck. Looking ahead, the company has a structured succession plan in place for an orderly transition if the next generation chooses to become part of the business. Alicia Sorber, Brig's daughter, is already involved, working for a franchisee and learning from her father's experiences and ideas.

Two Men and a Truck now has 220 franchisees and 1,400 trucks across the United States and is expanding into Europe. The company's annual revenue is $275 million and it handles more than 400,000 moves every year. Franchisees have adopted the company's credo of caring, using their trucks and employees for the benefit of local causes. For example, some have moved boxes of donated food from collection points to food banks for distribution to needy families. Others have delivered cleaning supplies, food, and personal care items to areas hit hard by natural disasters. No matter what cause they support, local franchisees show how Two Men and a Truck cares for its communities as well as its customers.[22]

Questions

1. Which advantages of small business helped Mary Ellen Sheets establish and grow Two Men and a Truck?
2. Which disadvantages of small business did Two Men and a Truck have to overcome? If you had been part of the business at the start, what suggestions would you have offered for overcoming these issues?
3. Do you think it's a good idea for Two Men and a Truck to offer franchises outside of North America? Why or why not? What kinds of questions would international franchisees be likely to ask the company?

Building Skills for Career Success

1. Social Media Exercise

American Express's "Open Forum" is a website that is designed for small-business owners (www.openforum.com). Do a search using a search engine like Google or Bing and you will also find its presence on Tumblr and Pinterest. Take a look at the Open Forum website and answer the following questions.

1. What questions can Open Forum answer for business owners?
2. Develop a list of five issues or topics that you feel illustrates how American Express does an effective job of presenting information on this website.

2. Building Team Skills

A business plan is a written statement that documents the nature of a business and how that business intends to achieve its goals. Although entrepreneurs should prepare a business plan *before* starting a business, the plan also serves as an effective guide later on. The plan should concisely describe the business's mission, the amount of capital it requires, its target market, competition, resources, production plan, marketing plan, organizational plan, assessment of risk, and financial plan.

Assignment

1. Working in a team of four students, identify a company in your community that would benefit from using a business plan, or create a scenario in which a hypothetical entrepreneur wants to start a business.
2. Using the resources of the library or the Internet and/or interviews with business owners, write a business plan incorporating the information in Table 5-3.
3. Present your business plan to the class.

3. Researching Different Careers

Many people dream of opening and operating their own businesses. Are you one of them? To be successful, entrepreneurs must have certain characteristics; their profiles generally differ from those of people who work for someone else. Do you know which personal characteristics make some entrepreneurs succeed and others fail? Do you fit the successful entrepreneur's profile? What is your potential for opening and operating a successful small business?

Assignment

1. Use the resources of the library or the Internet to establish what a successful entrepreneur's profile is and to determine whether your personal characteristics fit that profile. Internet addresses that can help you are www.smartbiz.com/sbs/arts/ieb1.html and www.sba. gov (see "Start your Business" and "FAQ"). These sites have quizzes online that can help you to assess your personal characteristics. The SBA also has helpful brochures.
2. Interview several small-business owners. Ask them to describe the characteristics they think are necessary for being a successful entrepreneur.
3. Using your findings, write a report that includes the following:
   a. A profile of a successful small-business owner
   b. A comparison of your personal characteristics with the profile of the successful entrepreneur
   c. A discussion of your potential as a successful small-business owner

Running a Business
Part 2

Graeter's: A Fourth-Generation Family Business

Independent and family-owned for more than 140 years, Graeter's has successfully made the transition from a 19th century mom-and-pop ice cream business to a 21st century corporation with three manufacturing facilities, dozens of ice cream shops, and hundreds of employees. Much of the company's success over the years has been due to the family's strong and enduring entrepreneurial spirit.

Small Business, Big Ambitions

The road to small-business success started with co-founder Louis Charles Graeter, who developed the startup's first flavors, insisted on only the finest ingredients, and made all his ice cream by hand in small batches to ensure freshness and quality. After his death, his wife and co-founder Regina maintained the same high level of quality as she led the company through three decades of aggressive growth. Her great-grandson, CEO Richard Graeter II, says that "without her strength, fortitude, and foresight, there would be no Graeter's ice cream today."

Richard, Bob, and Chip, great-grandsons of the founders, are the fourth generation to own and operate Graeter's. They grew up in the business, and now they share responsibility for the firm's day-to-day management and for determining its future direction. Bob worked his way up to vice president of operations, starting with a management position in one of the Graeter's ice-cream shops. Chip, currently vice president of retail operations, handled all kinds of jobs in Graeter's stores as a teenager. He uses this first-hand knowledge of customer relations to fine-tune every store function.

Richard Graeter became the company's CEO in 2007. "Even though I have the title of CEO, in a family business titles don't mean a whole lot," he comments. "The functions that I am doing now as CEO, I was doing as executive vice president for years … It really was and remains a partnership with my two cousins … Our fathers brought us into the business at an early age … I think most important is we saw our fathers and their dedication and the fact that, you know, they came home later, they came home tired, they got up early and went to work before we ever got up to go to school in the morning, and you see that dedication and appreciate that—that is what keeps your business going."

© ISTOCKPHOTO.COM/VVO

Graeter continues, "It can be challenging to work with your family. My father and I didn't always see things the same way. But on the other hand, there is a lot of strength in the family relationship … we certainly had struggles, and family businesses do struggle, especially with transition … but we found people to help us, including lawyers, accountants, and a family-business psychologist."

Growing Beyond Cincinnati

To expand beyond Cincinnati without diverting resources from the existing stores and factory, the third generation of Graeter's family owners decided to license a handful of franchise operators. One franchise operation was so successful that it even opened its own factory. A few years ago, however, the fourth generation switched gears on growth and repurchased all the stores of its last remaining franchisee. "When you think about Graeter's," says the CEO, "the core of Graeter's is the quality of the product. You can't franchise your core. So by franchising our manufacturing, that created substantial risk for the organization, because the customer doesn't know that it is a franchise…. They know it is Graeter's…. You really have to rely on the intention and goodwill of the individual franchisees to make the product the way you would make it, and that is not an easy thing to guarantee."

After working with consultants to carefully analyze the situation and evaluate alternative paths to future growth, the founder's great-grandsons decided against further franchising. Instead, they pursued nationwide distribution through a large network of grocery stores and supermarket chains. They also built a new facility to increase production capacity and hired experienced executives to help manage the expanded business.

As a private company, Graeter's can take actions like these without worrying about the reaction of the stock market. Specifically, Graeter's is an S corporation, which allows it limited-liability protection coupled with the benefit of not being taxed as a corporation. Instead, the three owners—who are the stockholders—pay only personal income taxes on the corporation's profits. In the event of significant legal or tax code changes, Graeter's owners do have the option of choosing a different form of corporate organization.[23]

Questions

1. Graeter's current management team bought the business from their parents, who did not have a formal succession plan in place to indicate who would do what. Do you think the current team should have such a plan specifying who is to step into the business, when, and with what responsibilities? Why or why not?

2. Graeter's hired management consultants to help improve its training procedures and expand distribution. "I think my cousins and I all have come to realize we can't do it alone," says the CEO. Why do you think the management team made this decision? Does the involvement of outside consultants move Graeter's further from its roots as a family business?

3. Do you agree with Graeter's decision to stop franchising? Explain your answer.

Building a Business Plan: Part 2

After reading Part 2, "Business Ownership and Entrepreneurship," you should be ready to tackle the company and industry component of your business plan. In this section, you will provide information about the background of the company, choice of the legal business form, information on the product or services to be offered, and descriptions of potential customers, current competitors, and the business's future. This chapter and the previous chapter (Chapter 4) in your textbook, "Choosing a Form of Business Ownership," and Chapter 5, "Small Business, Entrepreneurship, and Franchises," can help you to answer some of the questions in this part of the business plan.

The Company and Industry Component

The company and industry analysis should include the answers to at least the following questions:

2.1. What is the legal form of your business? Is your business a sole proprietorship, a partnership, or a corporation?

2.2. What licenses or permits will you need, if any?

2.3. Is your business a new independent business, a takeover, an expansion, or a franchise?

2.4. If you are dealing with an existing business, how did your company get to the point where it is today?

2.5. What does your business do, and how does it satisfy customers' needs?

2.6. How did you choose and develop the products or services to be sold, and how are they different from those currently on the market?

2.7. What industry do you operate in, and what are the industry-wide trends?

2.8. Who are the major competitors in your industry?

2.9. Have any businesses recently entered or exited? Why did they leave?

2.10. Why will your business be profitable, and what are your growth opportunities?

2.11. Does any part of your business involve e-business?

Review of Business Plan Activities

Make sure to check the information you have collected, make any changes, and correct any weaknesses before beginning Part 3. *Reminder:* Review the answers to questions in the preceding part to make sure that all your answers are consistent throughout the business plan. Finally, write a summary statement that incorporates all the information for this part of the business plan.

Endnotes

1 Sources: Based on information in Kieron Monks, "Fluffy Millions: Start-Ups Booming in the Pet Business," *CNN*, December 9, 2014, www.cnn.com; Darrell Etherington, "BarkCam, BarkBox's Instagram for Dogs, Is Now Available," *Tech Crunch*, July 15, 2014, http://techcrunch.com; Sarah Perez, "Doggie-Focused Bark & Co. (BarkBox) Raises $15 Million Series B," *Tech Crunch*, July 11, 2014, http://techcrunch.com; Thornton McEnery, "BarkBox Creators Feast on $15 M in New Capital," *Crain's New York Business*, July 14, 2014, www.crainsnewyork.com.

2 U.S. Small Business Administration, Office of Advocacy, *Frequently Asked Questions*, updated March 2014, www.sba.gov/content/small-business-size-standards (accessed January 14, 2015).

3 Ibid.

4 U.S. Small Business Administration, Office of Advocacy, *Small Business Quarterly Bulletin*, Second Quarter 2014, released September 9, 2014, Table 1, https://www.sba.gov/advocacy/small-business-quarterly-bulletins (accessed January 15, 2015).

5 SBA Office of Advocacy, *Small Business Facts*, June 2012, https://www.sba.gov/sites/default/files/Business-Survival.pdf (accessed January 14, 2015).

6 Thomas A. Garrett, "Entrepreneurs Thrive in America," *Bridges*, Federal Reserve Bank of St. Louis, Spring 2005, 2.

7 U.S. Small Business Administration website at https://www.sba.gov/tools/local-assistance/wbc (accessed January 14, 2015), and SBA

Office of Advocacy website at http://www.sba.gov/sites/default/files/FAQ_March_2014_0.pdf (accessed January 14, 2015).

8 U.S. Small Business Administration, *News Release*, Number 05–53, September 13, 2005, www.sba.gov/teens/brian_hendricks.html (accessed February 8, 2013), and the SBA website at https://www.sba.gov/offices/district/dc/washington/success-stories?page=10 (accessed January 15, 2015).

9 U.S. Small Business Administration, Office of Advocacy, *Small Business Quarterly Bulletin*, 2nd Quarter 2014, released September 9, 2014, accessed at https://www.sba.gov/advocacy/small-business-quarterly-bulletins (accessed January 12, 2015).

10 SBA Press Release, "Computer Simulation Company from Florida Is National Small Business of the Year," May 25, 2010, www.sba.gov/news (accessed March 15, 2012), and Orlando Chamber of Commerce website at http://www.orlando.org/index.php?src=news&refno=1887&category=Headlines (accessed January 15, 2015).

11 U.S. Small Business Administration, Office of Advocacy website at http://www. sba.gov/sites/default/files/FAQ_March_2014_0.pdf (accessed January 14, 2015 and January 15, 2015), and the SBA Blog at https://www.sba.gov/blogs/smallbusinesses-create-2-million-jobs (accessed January 18, 2015).

12 Timothy S. Hatten, *Small Business Management: Entrepreneurship and Beyond*, 5th ed., Copyright © 2012 by Cengage Learning. Reprinted with permission.

13 BusinessUSA website at http://www/business.usa.gov/external-site? (accessed January 5, 2015).

14 The SCORE Foundation website at http://scorefoundation.org/about-us/our-impact/ (accessed January 4, 2015).

15 The SBA Blog website at https://www.sba.gov/blogs/hurricane-sandy-and-small-business (accessed January 15, 2015), and the SBA website at www.sba.gov (accessed February 8. 2013).

16 U.S. Small Business Administration, *News Release*, Release Number 10–33, May 26, 2010, www.sba.gov/news (accessed March 18, 2012).

17 The SBA website at http://www.sba.gov/content/sbic-program-overview (accessed January 12, 2015).

18 Cindy Elmore, "Putting the Power into the Hands of Small Business Owners," *Marketwise*, Federal Reserve Bank of Richmond, Issue II, 2005, 13.

19 U.S. Commercial Service, U.S. Department of Commerce 2011 Annual Report, accessed at http://www.trade.gov/cs/cs_annualreport12.pdf (accessed January 15, 2015).

20 U.S. Department of Commerce, International Trade Administration website at http://www.trade.gov/cs/ (accessed January 15, 2015), and at http://www.trade.gov/cs/factsheet.asp (accessed January 15, 2015).

21 SBA Press Release, "SBA 2010 Small Business Exporter of the Year," www.sba.gov/news (accessed March 20, 2012); NANMAC Corporation website at http://nanmac.com/press-sba.html (accessed February 9, 2013); and U.S. Small Business Administration website at http://www.sba.gov/offices/district/dc/washington/success-stories?page=8 (accessed January 16, 2015).

22 Sources: Based on information in Joe Boomgaard, "Mother Knows Best: Mary Ellen Sheets Helps Foster Culture for Two Men and a Truck Moving Company," *MiBiz (Grand Rapids, Michigan)*, May 13, 2012, www.mibiz.com; "Janelle Dowley Distinction: President and Franchisee of Two Men and a Truck," *Palm Beach Post (Florida)*, February 20, 2012, p. 2D; "In the Classroom: ABC Academy, Two Men and a Truck Join Forces in Thanksgiving Food Collection," *Michigan Live*, November 19, 2012, www.mlive.com; J. Patrick Pepper, "Woodhaven: From Downriver to Sandy's Downtrodden, a Special Delivery," *News Herald (Downriver, Michigan)*, November 16, 2012, www.thenewsherald.com; www.twomenandatruck.com.

23 Sources: Based on information from Kimberly L. Jackson, "Graeter's Premium Chocolate Chip Ice Cream Lands at Stop & Shop," *Newark Star-Ledger (NJ)*, April 4, 2012, www.nj.com; "Graeter's Ice Cream Debuts in Bay Area," *Tampa Bay Times (St. Petersburg, FL)*, January 10, 2012, p. 4B; Jim Carper, "Graeter's Runs a Hands-on Ice Cream Plant," *Dairy Foods*, August 2011, pp. 36+; Jim Carper, "The Greater Good," *Dairy Foods*, August 2011, pp. 95+; "Graeter's Unveils New 'Mystery Flavor,'" *Dayton Daily News*, March 29, 2012, www.daytondailynews.com; Bob Driehaus, "A Cincinnati Ice Cream Maker Aims Big," *New York Times*, September 11, 2010, www.nytimes.com; Lucy May, "Graeter's Northern Kentucky Franchisee Puts Stores on the Block," *Business Courier*, August 6, 2010, http://cincinnati.bizjournals.com; www.graeters.com; interviews with company staff and Cengage videos about Graeter's.

JACOB WACKERHAUSEN/THINKSTOCK

CHAPTER

6

Understanding the Management Process

Why Should You Care?

Most of the people who read this chapter will advance upward and become managers. Thus an overview of the field of management is essential.

Learning Objectives

Once you complete this chapter, you will be able to:

6-1 Define what management is.

6-2 Describe the four basic management functions: planning, organizing, leading and motivating, and controlling.

6-3 Distinguish among the various kinds of managers in terms of both level and area of management.

6-4 Identify the key management skills of successful managers.

6-5 Explain the different types of leadership.

6-6 Discuss the steps in the managerial decision-making process.

6-7 Describe how organizations benefit from total quality management.

Managing Walt Disney for a Second Century of Creativity and Success

Walt Disney was famous for his attention to quality and detail—two elements that have helped the Walt Disney Company expand into a $49 billion entertainment empire by continuing the creative, yet careful management of its legendary founder. Through more than nine decades of operation, the company has become a business behemoth with brands known on every continent. Beyond characters like Buzz Lightyear and Ariel and blockbuster movies like *Frozen* and *The Avengers*, Walt Disney owns cable television giants ESPN and the Disney Channel as well as ABC Television, Disney World and Disneyland theme parks, and the Penguin Club children's website.

Managing such a diverse group of businesses can be a challenge. Under the leadership of CEO Bob Iger, the managers of each individual business unit handle their own strategic planning and make their own decisions to keep the creativity flowing, yet meet high corporate standards for service and success. This minimizes decision-making bottlenecks and allows each unit to set its own agenda within the framework of Disney's overall strategy and goals. Iger is responsible for corporate-level decisions about acquisitions to enhance Disney's strengths (such as bringing Lucasfilm under the Disney umbrella to add *Star Wars* as a movie brand).

Iger aggressively promotes a global viewpoint and invests in advanced technology as a competitive advantage across businesses as customers' buying and consuming patterns evolve. He also empowers managers in individual units to make decisions and take actions that will improve the customer experience and boost Disney's long-term growth prospects. If actual results are not proceeding according to plan, Disney managers understand the need for early intervention to get performance back on track. On the other hand, Iger allows businesses to delay projects for reasons of creative execution, the way the Pixar unit did when it postponed the animated feature *The Good Dinosaur* to allow more time for development.[1]

Did You Know?

The Walt Disney Company employs 175,000 people and rings up $49 billion in annual revenue worldwide.

The leadership demonstrated at the Walt Disney Company, which fosters the company's unique culture, illustrates that management can be one of the most exciting and rewarding professions available today. Depending on its size, a firm may employ a number of specialized managers who are responsible for particular areas of management, such as marketing, finance, and operations. That same organization also includes managers at several levels within the firm.

In this chapter, we define *management* and describe the four basic management functions of planning, organizing, leading and motivating, and controlling. Then we focus on the types of managers with respect to levels of responsibility and areas of expertise. Next, we focus on the skills of effective managers and the different roles managers must play. We examine several styles of leadership and explore the process by which managers make decisions. We also describe how total quality management can improve customer satisfaction.

6-1 WHAT IS MANAGEMENT?

Management is the process of coordinating people and other resources to achieve the goals of an organization. As we saw in Chapter 1, most organizations make use of four kinds of resources: material, human, financial, and informational (see Figure 6-1).

Material resources are the tangible, physical resources an organization uses. For example, General Motors uses steel, glass, and fiberglass to produce cars and trucks on complex machine-driven assembly lines. A college or university uses books,

Learning Objective

6-1 Define what management is.

management the process of coordinating people and other resources to achieve the goals of an organization

FIGURE 6-1 The Four Main Resources of Management

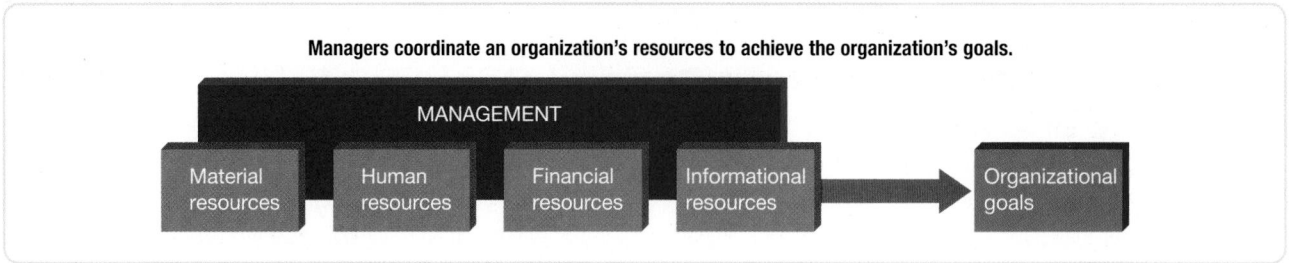

Managers coordinate an organization's resources to achieve the organization's goals.

MANAGEMENT

Material resources → Human resources → Financial resources → Informational resources → Organizational goals

Personal App

Are you already a manager?

Maybe you've never thought of yourself as a manager. But if you've ever headed a committee or organized a new school club, you've actually been involved in management. Understanding more about the way management works can make you more successful in the daily business of *your* life.

Concept Check

✓ What is management?

✓ What are the four kinds of resources?

classroom buildings, desks, and computers to educate students. And the Mayo Clinic uses operating room equipment, diagnostic machines, and laboratory tests to provide health care.

Perhaps the most important resources of any organization are its *human resources*—people. In fact, some firms live by the philosophy that employees are their most important assets. Some managers believe that the way employees are developed and managed has more impact on an organization than other vital components such as marketing, financial decisions, production, or technology. Research supports this belief. It shows that prioritizing human resources and working to ensure that employees are happy can greatly affect productivity and customer relationships.

Financial resources are the funds an organization uses to meet its obligations to investors and creditors. A 7-Eleven convenience store obtains money from customers at the checkout counter and uses a portion to pay its suppliers. Your college obtains money in the form of tuition, income from endowments, and state and federal grants. It uses the money to pay bills, insurance premiums, and salaries.

Increasingly, organizations are finding that they cannot afford to ignore *information*. External environmental conditions—the economy, consumer markets, technology, politics, and cultural forces—are all changing so rapidly that a business must adapt to survive. To adapt to change, the business must gather information about competitors and changes to the industry in order to learn from the failures and successes of others.

It is important to realize that the four types of resources described earlier are only general categories. Within each category are hundreds or thousands of more specific resources. It is this complex mix of specific resources—which varies between companies and industries—that managers must coordinate to produce goods and services.

Another way to look at management is in terms of the different functions managers perform, which are planning, organizing, leading and motivating employees, and controlling. We look at each of these management functions in the next section.

FIGURE 6-2 The Management Process

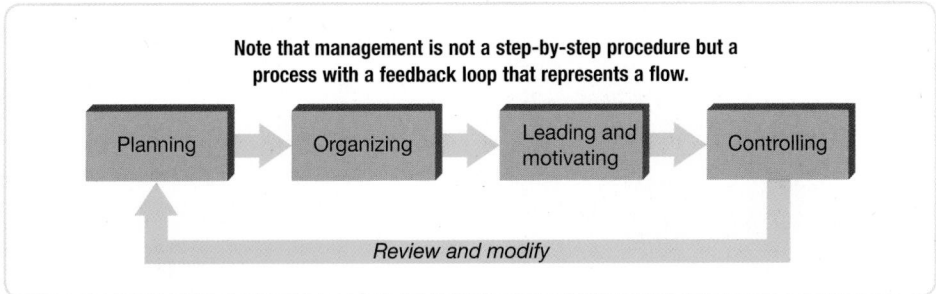

Note that management is not a step-by-step procedure but a process with a feedback loop that represents a flow.

Planning → Organizing → Leading and motivating → Controlling

Review and modify

6-2 BASIC MANAGEMENT FUNCTIONS

After years of declining profits, Hewlett-Packard's new CEO Meg Whitman analyzed its situation and developed a five-year plan to turn the company around. Her plan required revamping the firm's core printer and personal computer business, laying off 45,000 employees, and ultimately, splitting the company into two separate corporations—one for hardware and one for business software.[2]

Management functions do not occur according to some rigid, preset timetable. Managers do not plan in January, organize in February, lead and motivate in March, and control in April. At any given time, managers may engage in a number of functions simultaneously. However, each function tends to lead naturally to others. Figure 6-2 provides a visual framework for a more detailed discussion of the four basic management functions. How well managers perform these key functions determines whether a business is successful.

6-2a Planning

Planning, in its simplest form, is establishing organizational goals and deciding how to accomplish them. It is often referred to as the "first" management function because all other management functions depend on planning. Organizations such as Starbucks, Amazon, and Twitter base the planning process on a mission statement.

An organization's **mission** is a statement of the basic purpose that makes that organization different from others. Starbucks's mission statement, for example, is "to inspire and nurture the human spirit—one person, one cup, and one neighborhood at a time." Amazon.com's mission is "to be earth's most customer-centric company, where people can come to find and discover anything they might want to buy online." Twitter's mission statement is "to give everyone the power to create and share ideas and information instantly, without barriers."[3] Once a mission has been stated, the next step is to engage in strategic planning.

STRATEGIC PLANNING PROCESS The **strategic planning process** involves establishing an organization's major goals and objectives and allocating resources to achieve them. Top management is responsible for strategic planning, although customers, products, competitors, and company resources all factor into the process.

In today's rapidly changing business environment, constant internal or external changes may necessitate changes in a company's goals, mission, or strategy. The timeline for strategic plans is generally one to two years, but can be much longer. Strategic plans should be flexible and include action items, such as outlining how plans will be implemented.

ESTABLISHING GOALS AND OBJECTIVES A **goal** is an end result that an organization is expected to achieve over a one- to ten-year period. An **objective** is

Learning Objective

6-2 Describe the four basic management functions: planning, organizing, leading and motivating, and controlling.

planning establishing organizational goals and deciding how to accomplish them

mission a statement of the basic purpose that makes an organization different from others

strategic planning process the establishment of an organization's major goals and objectives and the allocation of resources to achieve them

goal an end result that an organization is expected to achieve over a one- to ten-year period

objective a specific statement detailing what an organization intends to accomplish over a shorter period of time

Human Resources. Superior human resources management can set a firm apart. Do you have a great business plan or product? A competitor can easily copy both. Great employees, however, are much harder to duplicate. That's why being able to attract, train, and retain talented workers can give a firm a competitive advantage over its rivals.

© RACORN/SHUTTERSTOCK.COM

a specific statement detailing what the organization intends to accomplish over a shorter period of time.

Goals and objectives can involve a variety of factors, such as sales, company growth, costs, customer satisfaction, and employee morale. Whereas a small manufacturer may focus primarily on sales objectives for the next six months, a large firm may be more interested in goals that will drive the firm for several years. While many retailers have scaled back in recent years, Swedish fashion retailer H&M has set ambitious growth targets through opening new stores and online markets that complement its stores. The company aims to open 375 new stores worldwide, especially in the United States and China, as well as eight to ten new online markets around the world.[4] Finally, goals are set at every level of an organization. Every member of an organization—the president of the company, the head of a department, and an operating employee at the lowest level—has a set of goals that he or she hopes to achieve.

It is likely that some conflicts will arise among levels within the organization, but goals must be made consistent across an organization. A production department, for example, may have a goal of minimizing costs. One way to do this is to produce only one type of product and limited customer service. Marketing may have a goal of maximizing sales, which might be achieved by offering a wide range of products and options. As part of goal-setting, the manager responsible for *both* departments must strike a balance between conflicting goals. This balancing process is called *optimization*.

The optimization of conflicting goals requires insight and ability. Faced with the marketing-versus-production conflict just described, most managers would find a middle ground through offering a moderately diverse product line featuring only the most popular products. Such a compromise would be best for the whole organization.

General Motors Mission Statement

"G.M. is a multinational corporation engaged in socially responsible operations, worldwide. It is dedicated to provide products and services of such quality that our customers will receive superior value while our employees and business partners will share in our success and our stock-holders will receive a sustained superior return on their investment."

General Motors

© KURHAN/SHUTTERSTOCK.COM

What is your organization's purpose? How is it different than other organizations? Those are the questions a firm's mission statement like the one shown here should answer. Mission statements are meant for multiple audiences, including a company's customers, investors, the general public, and employees. Most firms familiarize their personnel with their mission statements so they know what's expected of them and what they should strive for.

SWOT ANALYSIS **SWOT analysis** is the identification and evaluation of a firm's strengths, weaknesses, opportunities, and threats. Strengths and weaknesses are internal factors that affect a company's capabilities. Strengths refer to a firm's favorable characteristics and core competencies. **Core competencies** are approaches and processes that a company performs well that may give it an advantage over its competitors. These core competencies may help the firm attract financial and human resources that increase the firm's capacity to produce products that satisfy customers. Weaknesses refer to internal limitations a company faces in developing or implementing plans. At times, managers have difficulty identifying and understanding the negative effects of weaknesses in their organizations.

External opportunities and threats exist independently of the firm. Opportunities refer to favorable conditions in the environment that could benefit the organization if properly exploited. Threats, on the other hand, are conditions or barriers that may prevent the firm from reaching its objectives. Opportunities and threats can stem from many sources within the business environment. Because environmental factors vary between firms and industries, threats for some firms may be opportunities for others. Examples of strengths, weaknesses, opportunities, and threats are shown in Figure 6-3.

TYPES OF PLANS Once goals and objectives have been set for the organization, managers must develop plans for achieving them. A **plan** is an outline of the actions by which an organization intends to accomplish its goals and objectives. The organization develops several types of plans, as shown in Figure 6-4.

An organization's **strategic plan** is its broadest plan, developed as a guide during the strategic planning process for major policy setting and decision making. Strategic plans are set by the board of directors and top management and are generally designed to achieve the organization's long-term goals. Thus, a firm's strategic plan defines what business the company is in or wants to be in and the kind of company

FIGURE 6-3 Elements and Examples of SWOT Analysis

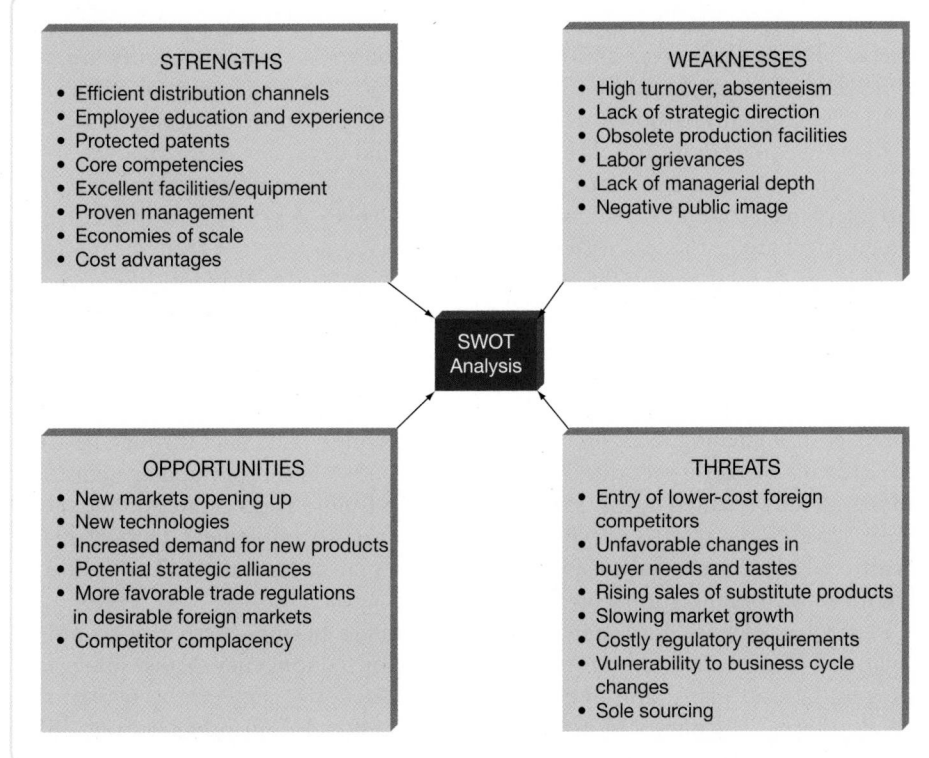

STRENGTHS
- Efficient distribution channels
- Employee education and experience
- Protected patents
- Core competencies
- Excellent facilities/equipment
- Proven management
- Economies of scale
- Cost advantages

WEAKNESSES
- High turnover, absenteeism
- Lack of strategic direction
- Obsolete production facilities
- Labor grievances
- Lack of managerial depth
- Negative public image

SWOT Analysis

OPPORTUNITIES
- New markets opening up
- New technologies
- Increased demand for new products
- Potential strategic alliances
- More favorable trade regulations in desirable foreign markets
- Competitor complacency

THREATS
- Entry of lower-cost foreign competitors
- Unfavorable changes in buyer needs and tastes
- Rising sales of substitute products
- Slowing market growth
- Costly regulatory requirements
- Vulnerability to business cycle changes
- Sole sourcing

SWOT analysis the identification and evaluation of a firm's strengths, weaknesses, opportunities, and threats

core competencies approaches and processes that a company performs well that may give it an advantage over its competitors

plan an outline of the actions by which an organization intends to accomplish its goals and objectives

strategic plan an organization's broadest plan, developed as a guide for major policy setting and decision making

FIGURE 6-4 Types of Plans

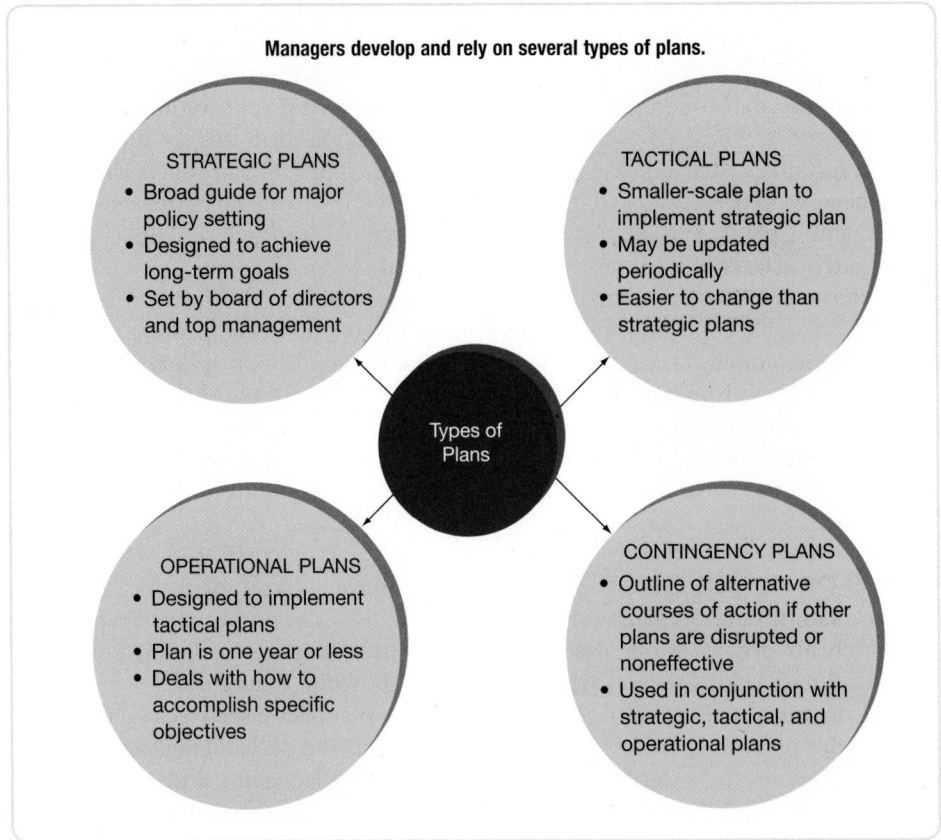

Managers develop and rely on several types of plans.

STRATEGIC PLANS
- Broad guide for major policy setting
- Designed to achieve long-term goals
- Set by board of directors and top management

TACTICAL PLANS
- Smaller-scale plan to implement strategic plan
- May be updated periodically
- Easier to change than strategic plans

Types of Plans

OPERATIONAL PLANS
- Designed to implement tactical plans
- Plan is one year or less
- Deals with how to accomplish specific objectives

CONTINGENCY PLANS
- Outline of alternative courses of action if other plans are disrupted or noneffective
- Used in conjunction with strategic, tactical, and operational plans

it is or wants to be. Although it was an early leader in handheld e-mail devices, in recent years BlackBerry suffered in the face of stiff competition from Apple and Android smartphones. Sharply sagging sales prompted the company to revise its strategic plan to slash costs and focus more on business customers, software, and mobile data services. In addition to its BlackBerry Messenger instant messaging service, the company is developing devices and applications for network security and Internet connectivity for all sorts of commercial devices.[5]

In addition to strategic plans, most organizations also employ several narrower kinds of plans. A **tactical plan** is a smaller scale plan developed to implement a strategy. Most tactical plans cover a one- to three-year period. If a strategic plan will take five years to complete, the firm may develop five tactical plans, one covering each year. Tactical plans may be updated periodically as dictated by conditions and experience. Their more limited scope permits them to be changed more easily than strategies. As part of its tactical plan to improve revenue, Best Buy's CEO is fighting slumping sales with a reinvention effort called "Renew Blue." This plan involves slashing costs, matching Amazon.com's prices, boosting online sales through bestbuy.com, and improving distribution so that stores do not run out of popular items. The plan has already resulted in cost savings of nearly $1 billion and greater online sales.[6]

An **operational plan** is a type of plan designed to implement tactical plans. Operational plans are usually established for one year or less and deal with how to accomplish the organization's specific objectives.

Regardless of how hard managers try, sometimes business activities do not go as planned. Today, most corporations also develop contingency plans along with strategies, tactical plans, and operational plans. A **contingency plan** is a plan that outlines alternative courses of action that may be taken if an organization's other plans are disrupted or become ineffective. Contingency plans may address disruptions

tactical plan a smaller scale plan developed to implement a strategy

operational plan a type of plan designed to implement tactical plans

contingency plan a plan that outlines alternative courses of action that may be taken if an organization's other plans are disrupted or become ineffective caused by natural disasters, criminal or ethical misconduct, political instability, or other unexpected activities. For example, the potential threat of power disruptions caused by lava flows from the Kilauea volcano has led Hawaii Electric Light to draft contingency plans to keep power on throughout the Hawaiian island. The plans include monitoring eruptions and lava flows from the volcano and coordinating with state agencies. The company's plans also include the development of prototype power poles that can better withstand conditions stemming from lava flows across the island of Hawaii, as well as strategically locating generators to fill in transmission gaps as needed.[7]

© GAJUS/SHUTTERSTOCK.COM

Encouraging employees is part of motivating them. Organizations employ numerous motivational messages. There are considerable differences among people regarding the factors and messages that motivate them.

6-2b Organizing the Enterprise

After goal-setting and planning, the manager's second major function is organization. **Organizing** is the grouping of resources and activities to accomplish some end result in an efficient and effective manner. Consider the case of an inventor who creates a new product and goes into business to sell it. At first, the inventor will do everything on his or her own—purchase raw materials, make the product, advertise it, sell it, and keep business records. Eventually, as business grows, the inventor will need help. To begin with, he or she might hire a professional sales representative and a part-time bookkeeper. Later, it also might be necessary to hire sales staff, people to assist with production, and an accountant. As the inventor hires new personnel, he or she must decide what each person will do, to whom each person will report, and how each person can best take part in the organization's activities. We discuss these and other facets of the organizing function in much more detail in Chapter 7.

6-2c Leading and Motivating

The leading and motivating function is concerned with an organization's human resources. Specifically, **leading** is the process of influencing people to work toward a common goal. **Motivating** is the process of providing reasons for people to work in the best interests of an organization. Together, leading and motivating are often referred to as **directing**.

Leading and motivating are critical activities because of the importance of an organization's human resources. Obviously, different people do things for different reasons—that is, they have different *motivations*. Some are interested primarily in earning as much money as they can. Others may be spurred on by opportunities to get promoted. Part of a manager's job, then, is to determine what factors motivate workers and to try to provide those incentives to encourage effective performance. Many people choose to work at the Container Store because of its reputation for treating its employees well (it has been on *Fortune*'s Best Companies to Work For list for 15 years), and they want to be part of a major specialty retailer with strong growth potential. Kip Tindell, CEO and one of the founders of the Container Store, is a top CEO in America and has guided the Container Store to success through his model leadership. The Container Store pays its employees nearly twice the industry average and provides extensive training and development to ensure

organizing the grouping of resources and activities to accomplish some end result in an efficient and effective manner

leading the process of influencing people to work toward a common goal

motivating the process of providing reasons for people to work in the best interests of an organization

directing the combined processes of leading and motivating

If your dreams don't scare you they're not big enough.

they can find the right storage products for each customer. The Container Store also provides generous benefits and strives to create fun workspaces.[8] A lot of research has been done on both motivation and leadership. As you will see in Chapter 10, research on motivation has yielded very useful information. However, research on leadership has been less successful. Despite decades of study, no one has discovered a general set of personal traits or characteristics that makes a good leader. Later in this chapter, we discuss leadership in more detail.

6-2d Controlling Ongoing Activities

Controlling is the process of evaluating and regulating ongoing activities to ensure that goals are achieved. The control function includes three steps (see Figure 6-5). The first is *setting standards* against which performance can be compared. The second is *measuring actual performance* and comparing it with the standard. The third is *taking corrective action* as necessary. Notice that the control function is circular in nature. The steps in the control function must be repeated periodically until the goal is achieved. For example, suppose that Southwest Airlines establishes a goal of increasing profits by 12 percent. Southwest's management will monitor its profit on a monthly basis to ensure success. After three months, if profit has increased by 3 percent, management may assume that plans are effective. In this case, no action will likely be taken. However, if profit has increased only 1 percent, some corrective action will be needed to get the firm on track. The action that is required depends on the reason for the less-than-expected increase.

Concept Check

✓ Why is planning sometimes referred to as the "first" management function?

✓ What is a plan? Differentiate between the major types of plans.

✓ What kind of motivations do different employees have?

✓ What are the three steps of controlling?

FIGURE 6-5 The Control Function

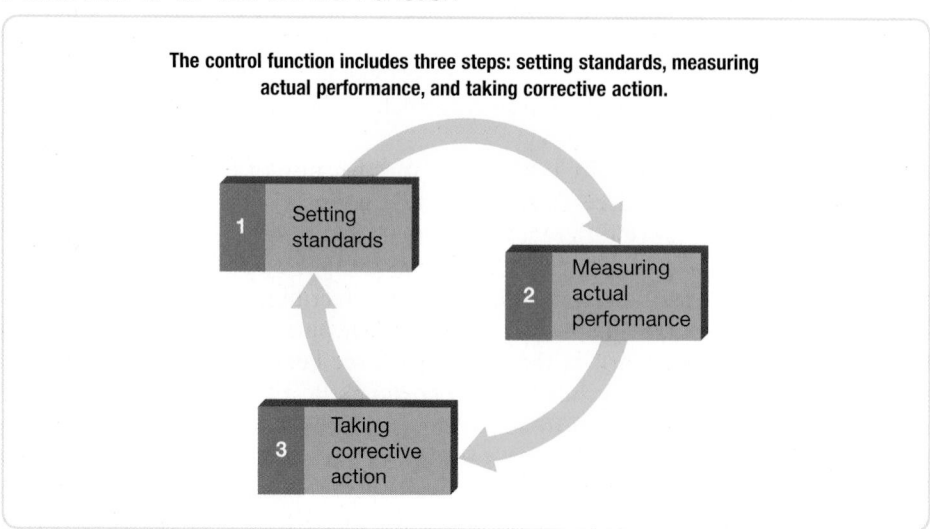

The control function includes three steps: setting standards, measuring actual performance, and taking corrective action.

1. Setting standards
2. Measuring actual performance
3. Taking corrective action

controlling the process of evaluating and regulating ongoing activities to ensure that goals are achieved

6-3 KINDS OF MANAGERS

Managers can be classified in two ways: according to their level within an organization and according to their area of management. In this section, we use both perspectives to explore the various types of managers.

6-3a Levels of Management

For the moment, think of an organization as a three-story structure (as illustrated in Figure 6-6). Each story corresponds to one of the three general levels of management: top managers, middle managers, and first-line managers.

TOP MANAGERS A **top manager** is an upper-level executive who guides and controls an organization's overall fortunes. Top managers represent the smallest of the three groups. In terms of planning, they are generally responsible for developing the organization's mission. They also determine the firm's strategy. It takes years of hard work, long hours, and perseverance, talent, and no small share of good luck to reach the ranks of top management in large companies. Common job titles associated with top managers are president, vice president, chief executive officer (CEO), and chief operating officer (COO).

MIDDLE MANAGERS Middle managers make up the largest group of managers in most organizations. A **middle manager** is a manager who implements the strategy and major policies developed by top management. Middle managers develop tactical and operational plans, and they coordinate and supervise the activities of first-line managers. Titles at the middle-management level include division manager, department head, plant manager, and operations manager.

Learning Objective

6-3 Distinguish among the various kinds of managers in terms of both level and area of management.

© AP IMAGES/MARK LENNIHAN

A top manager's out-of-this-world business strategy. At the age of 16, Richard Branson, the CEO and founder of the Virgin Group, started his first business venture: a magazine called *The Student*. Today, the Virgin Group consists of over 400 companies, including Virgin Telecommunications, Virgin Radio, Virgin Cola, Virgin Wine, Virgin Spa, Virgin Airlines—and the list goes on. In the near future, Virgin Galactic, one of Branson's newest companies, aims to launch paying customers into space.

FIGURE 6-6 Management Levels Found in Most Companies

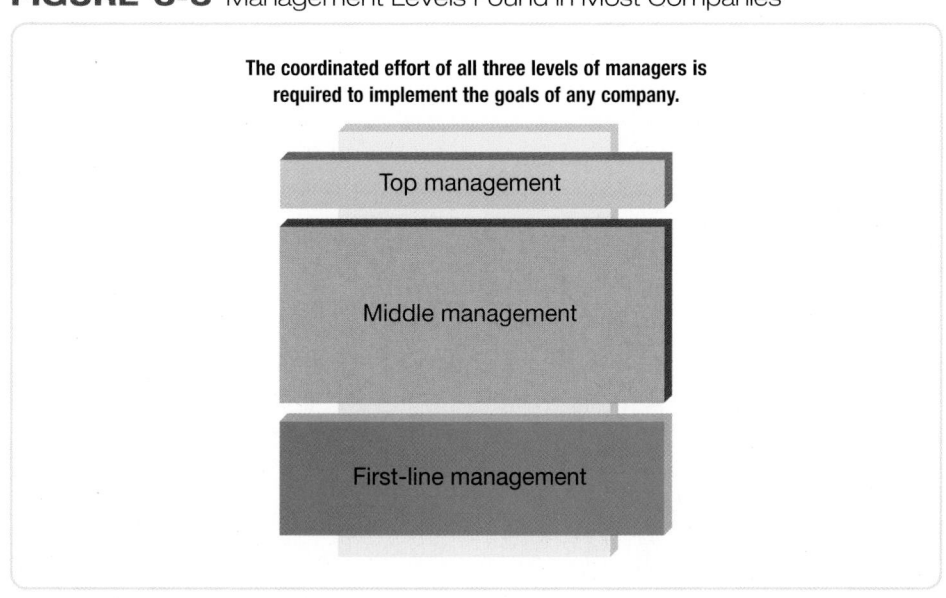

The coordinated effort of all three levels of managers is required to implement the goals of any company.

Top management

Middle management

First-line management

top manager an upper-level executive who guides and controls the overall fortunes of an organization

middle manager a manager who implements the strategy and major policies developed by top management

FIGURE 6-7 Areas of Management Specialization

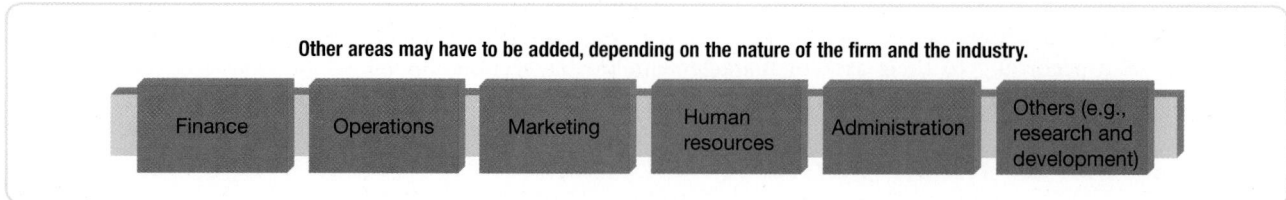

Other areas may have to be added, depending on the nature of the firm and the industry.

Finance | Operations | Marketing | Human resources | Administration | Others (e.g., research and development)

FIRST-LINE MANAGERS A **first-line manager** is a manager who coordinates and supervises the activities of operating employees. First-line managers spend most of their time working with and motivating their employees, answering questions, and solving day-to-day problems. Most first-line managers are former operating employees who were promoted into management. Many of today's middle and top managers began their careers on this first management level. Common titles for first-line managers include office manager, supervisor, and foreman.

6-3b Areas of Management Specialization

Organizational structure can also be divided into areas of management specialization (see Figure 6-7). The most common areas are finance, operations, marketing, human resources, and administration. Depending on its mission, goals, and objectives, an organization may include other areas as well—research and development (R&D), for example.

FINANCIAL MANAGERS A **financial manager** is primarily responsible for an organization's financial resources. Accounting and investment are specialized areas within financial management. Because financing affects the operation of the entire firm, many CEOs and presidents of large companies are people who were first trained as financial managers.

OPERATIONS MANAGERS An **operations manager** manages the systems that convert resources into goods and services. Traditionally, operations management has been equated with manufacturing—the production of goods. However, in recent years, many of the techniques and procedures of operations management have been applied to the production of services and to a variety of nonbusiness activities. As with financial management, operations management has produced a large percentage of today's company CEOs and presidents.

first-line manager a manager who coordinates and supervises the activities of operating employees

financial manager a manager who is primarily responsible for an organization's financial resources

operations manager a manager who manages the systems that convert resources into goods and services

Harnessing the cooperation of an organization's specialized managers. Imagine the managers of different departments as a team of horses. If they—and their employees—don't all work together and pull in the same direction, the organization won't get to the destination it's trying to reach.

© EDHAR/SHUTTERSTOCK.COM

MARKETING MANAGERS A **marketing manager** is responsible for facilitating the exchange of products between an organization and its customers or clients. Specific areas within marketing are marketing research, product management, advertising, promotion, sales, and distribution. A sizable number of today's company presidents have risen from marketing management.

HUMAN RESOURCES MANAGERS A **human resources manager** is charged with managing an organization's human resources programs. He or she engages in human resources planning, designs systems for hiring, training, and evaluating the performance of employees, and ensures that the organization follows government regulations concerning employment practices. There are many technological tools to help human resources managers. For example, Workday, Inc. produces a suite of software and tools for human resources departments, including a program to streamline the recruiting and hiring process and tools that help HR managers collect and process information.

ADMINISTRATIVE MANAGERS An **administrative manager** (also called a *general manager*) is not associated with any specific functional area, but provides overall administrative guidance and leadership. A hospital administrator is an example of an administrative manager. He or she does not specialize in operations, finance, marketing, or human resources management but instead coordinates the activities of specialized managers in all these areas. In many respects, most top managers are really administrative managers.

Whatever their level and specialization in the organization, successful managers generally exhibit certain key skills and are able to play a variety of managerial roles. However, as we shall see, some skills are likely to be more critical at one level of management than at another.

6-4 KEY SKILLS OF SUCCESSFUL MANAGERS

As shown in Figure 6-8, managers need a variety of skills, including conceptual, analytic, interpersonal, technical, and communication skills.

FIGURE 6-8 Key Skills of Successful Managers

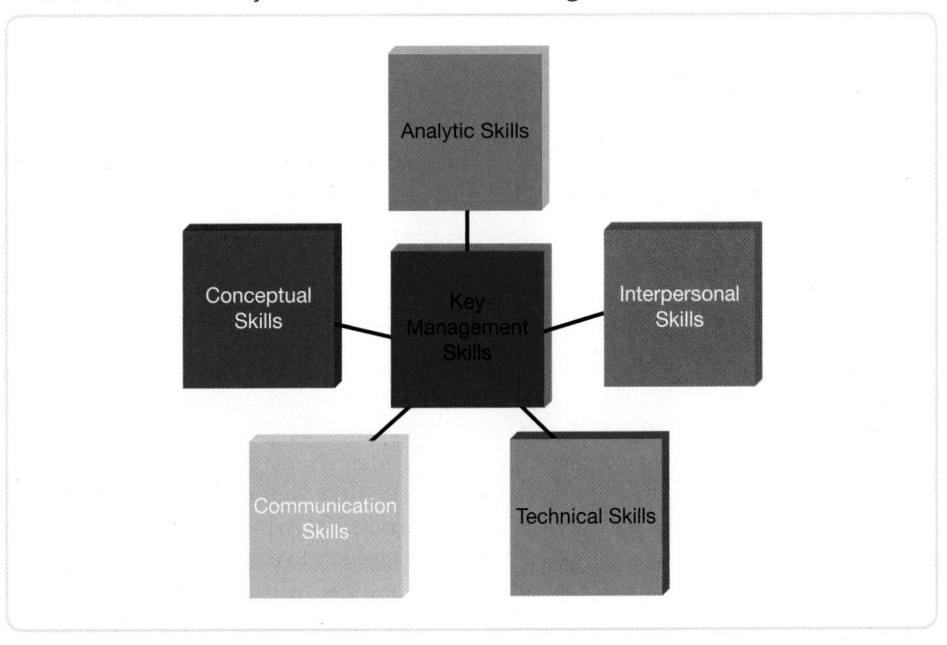

Concept Check

✓ Describe the three levels of management.

✓ Identify the various areas of management specialization, and describe the responsibilities of each.

Learning Objective

6-4 Identify the key management skills of successful managers.

marketing manager a manager who is responsible for facilitating the exchange of products between an organization and its customers or clients

human resources manager a person charged with managing an organization's human resources programs

administrative manager a manager who is not associated with any specific functional area but who provides overall administrative guidance and leadership

Career Success

Collaborate Your Way to Success

Do you know how to collaborate? According to recent research, managers at all levels value the ability to collaborate with others, not just give orders. By working together to devise innovative solutions to problems, they benefit individually from the added knowledge and experience—and their teamwork supports the organization's creativity and performance. Moreover, collaboration is a necessity in situations where you and other managers are expected to achieve shared goals by pooling your efforts.

You'll be in a better position to collaborate if you sharpen your communication skills—particularly if you're using e-mail or phone conversations that can't convey unspoken cues or nuances of body language. Listen carefully, keep an open mind, and ask questions to clarify your understanding of what your collaborator says. Simply being a better communicator can save precious time on the job, whether you're working with one person or a group, collaborating across time zones, or joining forces with colleagues across the continent.

Also be aware that effective collaboration depends on your ability to work with people of different backgrounds. Cisco Systems sees this as such an important issue that it has appointed a Chief Inclusion and Collaboration Officer to encourage diversity and collaboration within the company's workforce. The best managers are respectful of differences, ready to learn from anybody who has a great idea, and willing to share their know-how with others to get the job done.

Sources: Based on information in Michal Lev-Ram, "Cisco Opens Up About Its Struggle to Diversify Its Workforce," *Fortune*, November 19, 2014, www.fortune.com; Jack Zenger and Joseph Folkman, "Most Managers Think of Themselves as Coaches," *Harvard Business Review*, July 25, 2014, http://hbr.org; "Businesses Losing 20 Days of Work a Year Thanks to Outdated Communications," *Growth Business*, November 18, 2014, http://www.growthbusiness.co.uk.

6-4a Conceptual Skills

Conceptual skills involve the ability to think in abstract terms. Conceptual skills allow a manager to see the "big picture" and understand how the various parts of an organization or idea can fit together. Consider Engineer Jonathan Downey, who founded Airware after recognizing that the proliferation of hobby unmanned aerial vehicles (UAVs), better known as drones, represented a huge opportunity for commercial applications such as photography, agriculture, police work, and public utilities. Airware develops hardware, software, and other services for UAVs that allow them to perform a wide variety of activities. The firm has already provided services for overseas UAV makers and hopes to provide the dominant operating system platform for U.S. makers' drones as soon as the Federal Aviation Administration allows their commercial use.[9] Conceptual skills are useful in a wide range of situations, including the optimization of goals described earlier.

6-4b Analytic Skills

Employers expect managers to use **analytic skills** to identify problems correctly, generate reasonable alternatives, and select the "best" alternatives to solve problems. Top-level managers especially need these skills because they must discern the important issues from the less important ones, as well as recognize the underlying reasons for different situations. When Lee Bird became the CEO of At Home Group (formerly known as Garden Ridge), he quickly identified a number of issues that were contributing to stagnating sales of Garden Ridge home décor stores. These issues included disorganized stores, incoherent product offerings, outdated employee policies, and even unused warehouse space—which he converted into new corporate headquarters offices. Within a short time, Bird and his team identified alternatives and solutions to these issues and then set about updating the stores—which are now

conceptual skills the ability to think in abstract terms

analytic skills the ability to identify problems correctly, generate reasonable alternatives, and select the "best" alternatives to solve problems

called At Home—and employee policies, as well as reorganizing stores and refocusing the products offered.[10] Managers who use these skills not only address a situation but also correct the initial event or problem that caused it to occur. Thus, these skills are vital to running a business efficiently and logically.

6-4c Interpersonal Skills

Interpersonal skills involve the ability to deal effectively with other people, both inside and outside an organization. Examples of interpersonal skills are the ability to relate to people, understand their needs and motives, and show genuine compassion.

6-4d Technical Skills

Technical skills involve specific skills needed to accomplish a specialized activity. For example, engineers and machinists need technical skills to do their jobs. First-line managers (and, to a lesser extent, middle managers) need to understand the technical skills relevant to the activities they manage in order to train subordinates, answer questions, and provide guidance, even though the managers may not perform the technical tasks themselves. In general, top managers do not rely on technical skills as heavily as managers at other levels. Still, understanding the technical side of a business is an aid to effective management at every level.

6-4e Communication Skills

Communication skills, both oral and written, involve the ability to speak, listen, and write effectively. Managers need both oral and written communication skills. Because a large part of a manager's day is spent conversing with others, the ability to speak *and* listen is critical. Oral communication skills are used when a manager makes sales presentations, conducts interviews, and holds press conferences. Written communication skills are important because a manager's ability to prepare letters, e-mails, memos, sales reports, and other written documents may spell the difference between success and failure. Computers, smartphones, and other high-tech devices make communication in today's businesses easier and faster. To manage an organization effectively and to stay informed, it is very important that managers understand how to use and maximize the potential of digital communication devices.

How good are your managerial skills? To be successful, managers must master and simultaneously utilize a number of skills. These include technical skills that aid with specialized work, conceptual skills that foster abstract thinking, and interpersonal skills to help manage and motivate their employees. Which of these skills will you need to work on as you build your career?

Concept Check

✓ What are the key skills that successful managers should have?

✓ For each skill, provide two reasons why a successful manager should have that skill.

6-5 LEADERSHIP

Leadership has been defined broadly as the ability to influence others. Leadership is different from management in that a leader strives for voluntary cooperation, whereas a manager may have to depend on coercion to change employee behavior.

6-5a Formal and Informal Leadership

Some experts make distinctions between formal leadership and informal leadership. Formal leaders have legitimate power of position. They have *authority* within an organization to influence others to work toward the organization's objectives. Informal leaders usually have no such authority and may or may not exert their influence in support of the organization. Both formal and informal leaders make use of several kinds of power, including the ability to grant rewards or impose punishments, the possession of expert knowledge, and personal attraction or charisma. Informal leaders who identify with the organization's goals are a valuable

Learning Objective

6-5 Explain the different types of leadership.

interpersonal skills the ability to deal effectively with other people

technical skills specific skills needed to accomplish a specialized activity

communication skills the ability to speak, listen, and write effectively

leadership the ability to influence others

Entrepreneurial Success

Elon Musk's Far-Out Ideas Are Crazy like a Fox

South African-born Elon Musk has been a high-tech entrepreneur since the age of 12, when he developed and sold a videogame for several hundred dollars. He scored his first multimillion-dollar payday in 1999, from the sale of Web-based city guides for newspapers. His next multimillion-dollar payday came from creating an electronic payment system that ultimately merged with PayPal and was purchased by eBay in 2002.

Elon Musk exemplifies entrepreneurial leadership at its best, transforming bold ideas into viable businesses by inspiring employees, investors, and others to work toward his vision of the future. He used some of his fortune to launch SpaceX, now a leading rocket technology company, with an eye toward a new era of space exploration. Next, he invested in Tesla Motors, a fast-growing company developing clean, emission-free electric vehicles. Within a few years, he

took over as CEO and shifted the world of electric vehicles into high gear by giving away Tesla's patents to rivals in the automotive industry.

Even though he spends just two days a week at Tesla and three days at SpaceX, the CEO's unflagging enthusiasm, determination, and sense of purpose motivate his employees every day and add to the forward momentum of both enterprises. Under Musk's entrepreneurial leadership, his businesses are turning the seemingly impossible into reality one day at a time, day after day after day.

Sources: Based on information in Dana Hull, "Timeline: Elon Musk's Accomplishments," *San Jose Mercury News*, April 11, 2014, www.mercurynews.com; Simon Mainwaring, "21st Century Leadership: 3 Master Strokes by Elon Musk," *Forbes*, June 24, 2014, www.forbes.com; Scott Pelley, "Tesla and SpaceX: Elon Musk's Industrial Empire," *CBS News*, March 30, 2014, http://www.cbsnews.com/news/tesla-and-spacex-elon-musks-industrial-empire (accessed July 11, 2015).

asset to any organization. However, a business can be greatly hampered by informal leaders who turn work groups against management.

6-5b Styles of Leadership

For many years, finding a consensus on the most important leadership traits was difficult. Leadership was viewed as a combination of personality traits, such as self-confidence, concern for people, intelligence, and dependability. In recent years, the emphasis has been on styles of leadership. Several styles have emerged, including *autocratic*, *participative*, and *entrepreneurial*.

Autocratic leadership is very task-oriented. Decisions are made unilaterally, with little concern for employee opinions. Employees are told exactly what is expected from them and given specific guidelines, rules, and regulations on how to achieve their tasks.

Participative leadership is common in today's business organizations. Participative leaders consult workers before making decisions. This helps workers understand which goals are important and fosters a sense of ownership and commitment to reach them. Participative leaders can be classified into three groups: consultative, consensus, and democratic. *Consultative leaders* discuss issues with workers but retain the final authority for decision making. *Consensus leaders* seek input from almost all workers and make final decisions based on their support. *Democratic leaders* give final authority to the group. They collect opinions and base their decisions on the vote of the group. New Belgium Brewing frequently appears on lists of best places to work in part because of the company's "high involvement, ownership culture" and participative leader, CEO Kim Jordan. She encourages employees to own stock and make important business decisions.[11] Communication is open up and down the hierarchy. Coaching, collaborating, and negotiating are important skills for participative leaders.

autocratic leadership task-oriented leadership style in which workers are told what to do and how to accomplish it without having a say in the decision-making process

participative leadership leadership style in which all members of a team are involved in identifying essential goals and developing strategies to reach those goals

Entrepreneurial leadership is personality dependent. Although each entrepreneur is different, this leadership style is generally task-oriented, driven, charismatic, and enthusiastic.[12] The entrepreneurial personality tends to take initiative, be visionary, and be forward-looking. Their enthusiasm energizes and inspires employees. Entrepreneurial leaders tend to be very invested in their businesses, working long hours to ensure success. They may not understand why their employees do not have the same level of passion for their work. Dr. David Hung, President and CEO of drug maker Medivation, was recognized by Ernst & Young as a top entrepreneur. He beat out thousands of others for this distinction through his passion to make a difference, resilience in learning from his company's failures, and persistence in looking for the key to developing life-saving products.[13]

NANCY KASZERMAN/ZUMA PRESS, INC./ALAMY

A CEO who motivates and inspires. Howard Schultz, CEO of Starbucks, has a highly participative leadership style. He gives more power to employees and allows, encourages, and seeks feedback and advice from them. Schultz states that, "when you're surrounded by people who share a passionate commitment around a common purpose, anything is possible."

6-5c Which Leadership Style Is the Best?

Today, most management experts agree that no "best" managerial leadership style exists. Each of the styles described—autocratic, participative, and entrepreneurial—has advantages and disadvantages. For example, participative leadership can motivate employees to work effectively because they have a sense of ownership in decision making. However, the decision-making process in participative leadership takes time that subordinates could be devoting to the work itself.

Although hundreds of research studies have been conducted to prove which leadership style is best, there are no definite conclusions. Each of the leadership styles can be highly effective in the right situation. The *most* effective style depends on the right balance between interaction among employees, characteristics of the work situation, and the manager's personality.

> ## Concept Check
> ✓ Describe the major leadership styles.
>
> ✓ Which one is best?

6-6 MANAGERIAL DECISION MAKING

Decision making is the act of choosing one alternative from a set of alternatives.[14] In ordinary situations, decisions are made casually and informally. We encounter a problem, mull it over, settle on a solution, and go on. Managers, however, require a more systematic method for solving complex problems. As shown in Figure 6-9, the managerial decision-making process involves four steps: (1) identifying the

Learning Objective

6-6 Discuss the steps in the managerial decision-making process.

FIGURE 6-9 Major Steps in the Managerial Decision-Making Process

Managers require a systematic method for solving problems in a variety of situations.

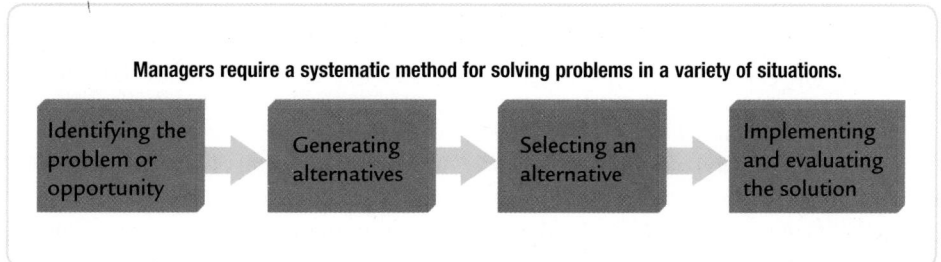

Identifying the problem or opportunity → Generating alternatives → Selecting an alternative → Implementing and evaluating the solution

entrepreneurial leadership personality-based leadership style in which the manager seeks to inspire workers with a vision of what can be accomplished to benefit all stakeholders

decision making the act of choosing one alternative from a set of alternatives

problem or opportunity, (2) generating alternatives, (3) selecting an alternative, and (4) implementing and evaluating the solution.

6-6a Identifying the Problem or Opportunity

A **problem** is the discrepancy between an actual condition and a desired condition—the difference between what is occurring and what one wishes would occur. For example, a marketing manager at Campbell's Soup Company has a problem if sales revenues for its Pepperidge Farm Goldfish crackers are declining (the actual condition). To solve this problem, the marketing manager must take steps to increase sales revenues (desired condition). Most people consider a problem to be "negative," but a problem also can be "positive." Some problems can be viewed as "opportunities."

Although accurate identification of a problem is essential before it can be solved or turned into an opportunity, this stage of decision making creates many difficulties for managers. Sometimes managers' preconceptions of the problem prevent them from seeing the actual situation. They produce an answer before the proper question has been asked, leading them to focus on insignificant issues. Also, managers may mistakenly analyze problems in terms of symptoms rather than underlying causes.

Effective managers learn to look ahead so that they are prepared when decisions must be made. They clarify situations and examine the causes of problems, asking whether the presence or absence of certain variables alters a situation. Finally, they consider how individual behaviors and values affect the way problems or opportunities are defined.

6-6b Generating Alternatives

After a problem has been defined, the next task is to generate alternatives. The more important the decision, the more attention must be devoted to this stage. Managers should be open to fresh, innovative ideas as well as obvious answers.

Certain techniques can aid in the generation of creative alternatives. Brainstorming, commonly used in group discussions, encourages participants to produce many new ideas. During brainstorming, other group members are not permitted to criticize or ridicule. Another approach, developed by the U.S. Navy, is called "Blast! Then Refine." Group members tackle a recurring problem by erasing all previous solutions and procedures. The group then re-evaluates its original objectives, modifies them if necessary, and devises new solutions. Other techniques—including trial and error—are also useful in this stage of decision making.

6-6c Selecting an Alternative

Final decisions are influenced by a number of considerations, including financial constraints, human and informational resources, time limits, legal obstacles, and political factors. Managers must select the alternative that will be most effective and practical. When publishing giant Meredith Corporation (*Family Circle and Every Day with Rachel Ray*) acquired *Eating Well* magazine, managers had to decide what focus it would have. For example, it could emphasize comfort food or health food. After analyzing the alternatives and the competition, managers decided to focus on healthy meals on a shoestring, a choice that has paid off.[15]

problem the discrepancy between an actual condition and a desired condition

CVS Backs Words with Actions

Should a drug store carry tobacco products? In 2014, CVS's top management decided that the answer was "no." CVS rings up nearly $130 billion in annual sales and operates 7,700 U.S. drug stores, many with in-store pharmacy departments. For years, CVS (like many other drug, grocery, and convenience stores) sold cigarettes at the checkout counter. Early in 2014, however, the CEO unexpectedly announced that CVS would halt all tobacco sales before the end of the year: "Cigarettes and tobacco products have no place in a setting where health care is delivered. This is the right thing to do."

One month after CVS's announcement, more than two dozen attorneys general from U.S. states and territories wrote competing drug retailers to ask them to follow suit. CVS increased the pressure by dumping tobacco products well in advance of its self-appointed deadline, but at that point, no other major drug retailer had yet agreed to drop cigarettes. Not only did CVS drop tobacco products—potentially losing up to $2 billion in yearly revenue—it also changed its name to CVS Health, to reflect the mission of "helping people on their path to better health."

Should drug stores take a stand against tobacco? Walgreens and Rite Aid, which compete with CVS, both offer various plans and products to help people stop smoking. But should retailers that sell products to protect or restore health continue to sell products that are known to be unhealthy?

Sources: Based on information in Sarah Kliff, "CVS to Stop Selling Cigarettes by Oct. 1," *Washington Post*, February 5, 2014, www.washingtonpost.com; Kelly Gilblom and Michelle Fay Cortez, "CVS's Competitors Can't Afford to Quit Tobacco," *Bloomberg News*, November 5, 2014, www.bloomberg.com; Jason Millman, "After Cutting Tobacco Sales, CVS Is Now Pressuring Other Pharmacies to Do the Same," *Washington Post*, October 20, 2014, www.washingtonpost.com; www.cvs.com.

At times, two or more alternatives or some combination of alternatives will be equally appropriate. Managers may choose solutions to problems on several levels. The word *satisfice* describes solutions that are only adequate and not ideal. When lacking time or information, managers often make decisions that "satisfice." Whenever possible, managers should try to investigate alternatives carefully and select the ideal solution.

6-6d Implementing and Evaluating the Solution

Implementation of a decision requires time, planning, preparation of personnel, and evaluation of results. Managers usually deal with unforeseen consequences even when they have carefully considered the alternatives.

The final step in managerial decision making entails evaluating a decision's effectiveness. If the alternative that was chosen removes the difference between the actual condition and the desired condition, the decision is considered effective. If the problem still exists, managers may select one of the following choices:

- Decide to give the chosen alternative more time to work.
- Adopt a different alternative.
- Start the problem identification process all over again.

Managers should be aware that failure to evaluate decisions adequately may have negative consequences.

> ## Concept Check
>
> ✓ Describe the major steps in the managerial decision-making process.
>
> ✓ Why does a manager need to evaluate the solution and look for problems after a solution has been implemented?

6-7 MANAGING TOTAL QUALITY

The management of quality is a high priority in many organizations today. Major reasons for a greater focus on quality include foreign competition, more demanding customers who have the ability to comparison shop online, and poor

> **Learning Objective**
>
> 6-7 Describe how organizations benefit from total quality management.

Total Quality Management. Prior to the 1970s, products "Made in Japan" were often considered shoddy. Not anymore. Toyota Motor Company, the maker of Lexus, worked hard to change that image by pioneering the use of total quality management practices. As a part of its total quality management practices, Toyota meticulously inspects its products and continuously strives to improve them.

financial performance resulting from reduced market shares and higher costs. Over the last few years, several U.S. firms have lost the dominant competitive positions they had held for decades.

Total quality management is a much broader concept than just controlling the quality of the product itself (which is discussed in Chapter 8). **Total quality management (TQM)** is the coordination of efforts directed at improving customer satisfaction, increasing employee participation, strengthening supplier partnerships, and facilitating an organizational atmosphere of continuous quality improvement. For TQM programs to be effective, management must address each of the following components:

- *Customer satisfaction.* Ways to improve include producing higher-quality products, providing better customer service, and showing customers that the company cares.
- *Employee participation.* This can be increased by allowing employees to contribute to decisions, develop self-managed work teams, and assume responsibility for improving the quality of their work.
- *Strengthening supplier partnerships.* Developing good working relationships with suppliers can ensure that the right supplies and materials will be delivered on time at lower costs.
- *Continuous quality improvement.* A program based on continuous improvement has proven to be the most effective long-term approach.

One tool that is used for TQM is called benchmarking. **Benchmarking** is the process of evaluating the products, processes, or management practices of another organization for the purpose of improving quality. The benchmark should be superior in safety, customer service, productivity, innovation, or in some other way.

For example, competitors' products might be disassembled and evaluated, or wage and benefit plans might be surveyed to measure compensation packages against the labor market. The four basic steps of benchmarking are identifying objectives, forming a benchmarking team, collecting and analyzing data, and acting on the results. Best practices may be discovered in any industry or organization.

Although many factors influence the effectiveness of a TQM program, two issues are crucial. First, top management must make a strong commitment to a TQM program by treating quality improvement as a top priority and giving it frequent attention. Firms that establish a TQM program but then focus on other priorities will find that their quality-improvement initiatives will fail. Second, management must coordinate the specific elements of a TQM program so that they work in harmony with each other.

Although not all U.S. companies have TQM programs, they provide many benefits. Overall financial benefits include lower operating costs, higher return on sales and on investments, and an improved ability to use premium pricing rather

total quality management (TQM) the coordination of efforts directed at improving customer satisfaction, increasing employee participation, strengthening supplier partnerships, and facilitating an organizational atmosphere of continuous quality improvement

benchmarking a process used to evaluate the products, processes, or management practices of another organization that is superior in some way in order to improve quality

than competitive pricing. Firms that do not implement TQM are sometimes afraid that the costs of doing so will be prohibitive. While implementing TQM can be costly initially, the savings from preventing future problems and integrating systems usually make up for the expense. The long-term costs of not implementing TQM can involve damage to a company's reputation and lost productivity and time spent fixing mistakes after they have happened.[16]

Concept Check

✓ Why does top management need to be strongly committed to TQM programs?

✓ Describe the major components of a TQM program.

Summary

6-1 Define what management is.

Management is the process of coordinating people and other resources to achieve an organization's goals. Managers are concerned with four types of resources—material, human, financial, and informational.

6-2 Describe the four basic management functions: planning, organizing, leading and motivating, and controlling.

Managers perform four basic functions, which do not occur according to a rigid, preset timetable. At any time, managers may engage in a number of functions simultaneously. However, each function tends to lead naturally to the next. Managers engage in planning—determining where the firm should be going and how best to get there. One method of planning that can be used is SWOT analysis, which identifies and evaluates a firm's strengths, weaknesses, opportunities, and threats. Three types of plans, from the broadest to the most specific, are strategic, tactical, and operational. Managers also organize resources and activities to accomplish results in an efficient and effective manner, and they lead and motivate others to work in the best interests of the organization. In addition, managers control ongoing activities to keep the organization on course. There are three steps in the control function: setting standards, measuring actual performance, and taking corrective action.

6-3 Distinguish among the various kinds of managers in terms of both level and area of management.

Managers—or management positions—may be classified from two different perspectives. From the perspective of level within the organization, there are top managers, who control the organization as a whole, middle managers, who implement strategies and major policies, and first-line managers, who supervise the activities of operating employees. From the viewpoint of area of management, managers most often deal with the areas of finance, operations, marketing, human resources, and administration.

6-4 Identify the key management skills of successful managers.

Managers need a variety of skills in order to run a successful and efficient business. Conceptual skills are used to think in abstract terms or see the "big picture." Analytic skills are used to identify problems correctly, generate reasonable alternatives, and select the "best" alternatives to solve problems. Interpersonal skills are used to deal effectively with other people, both inside and outside an organization. Technical skills are needed to accomplish a specialized activity, whether they are used to actually do the task or to train and assist employees. Communication skills are used to speak, listen, and write effectively.

6-5 Explain the different types of leadership.

Managers' effectiveness often depends on their styles of leadership—that is, their ability to influence others, either formally or informally. Autocratic leaders are very task oriented; they tell their employees exactly what is expected from them and give them specific instructions on how to do their assigned tasks. Participative leaders consult their employees before making decisions and can be classified into three groups: consultative, consensus, and democratic. Entrepreneurial leaders are different depending on their personalities, but they are generally enthusiastic and passionate about their work and tend to take the initiative.

6-6 Discuss the steps in the managerial decision-making process.

Decision making, an integral part of a manager's work, is the process of developing a set of possible alternative solutions to a problem and choosing one alternative from among the set. Managerial decision making involves four steps: Managers must accurately identify problems, generate several possible solutions, choose the solution that will be most effective under the circumstances, and implement and evaluate the chosen course of action.

6-7 Describe how organizations benefit from total quality management.

Total quality management (TQM) is the coordination of efforts directed at improving customer satisfaction, increasing employee participation, strengthening supplier partnerships, and facilitating an organizational atmosphere of continuous quality improvement. Another tool used for TQM is benchmarking, which involves comparing and evaluating the products, processes, or management practices of another organization that is superior in some way in order to improve quality. The five basic steps in benchmarking are identifying objectives, forming a benchmarking team, collecting data, analyzing data, and acting on the results. To have an effective TQM program, top management must make a strong, sustained commitment to the effort and must be able to coordinate all the program's elements so that they work in harmony. Benefits of TQM include lower operating costs, higher return on sales and on investment, and an improved ability to use premium pricing rather than competitive pricing.

Key Terms

You should now be able to define and give an example relevant to each of the following terms:

management (165)
planning (167)
mission (167)
strategic planning process (167)
goal (167)
objective (167)
SWOT analysis (169)
core competencies (169)
plan (169)
strategic plan (169)

tactical plan (170)
operational plan (170)
contingency plan (170)
organizing (171)
leading (171)
motivating (171)
directing (171)
controlling (172)
top manager (173)
middle manager (173)
first-line manager (174)

financial manager (174)
operations manager (174)
marketing manager (175)
human resources manager (175)
administrative manager (175)
conceptual skills (176)
analytic skills (176)
interpersonal skills (177)
technical skills (177)
communication skills (177)

leadership (177)
autocratic leadership (178)
participative leadership (178)
entrepreneurial leadership (179)
decision making (179)
problem (180)
total quality management (TQM) (182)
benchmarking (182)

Discussion Questions

1. Define the word *manager* without using the word *management* in your definition.
2. Does a healthy firm (one that is doing well) have to worry about effective management? Explain.
3. What might be the mission of a neighborhood restaurant? Of the Salvation Army? What might be reasonable objectives for these organizations?
4. What are the major elements of SWOT analysis?
5. How do a strategic plan, a tactical plan, and an operational plan differ? What do they all have in common?
6. Why are leadership and motivation necessary in a business in which people are paid for their work?
7. Compare and contrast the major styles of leadership.

8. According to this chapter, the leadership style that is most effective depends on interaction among the employees, characteristics of the work situation, and the manager's personality. Do you agree or disagree? Explain your answer.
9. What are the major benefits of a total quality management program?
10. Do you think that people are really as important to an organization as this chapter seems to indicate?
11. Discuss what happens during each of the four steps of the managerial decision-making process.
12. As you learned in this chapter, managers often work long hours at a hectic pace. Would this type of career appeal to you? Explain.

Video Case
Meet Heidi Ganahl, Top Dog at Camp Bow Wow

Even the strongest leaders welcome fresh ideas when facing difficult decisions. Heidi Ganahl had already founded and failed with two businesses when she emptied her bank account to fund Camp Bow Wow. Her vision for the business was to provide a healthy, happy, and safe day-care and overnight environment for dogs. She opened her first Camp Bow Wow in 2000 inside a refurbished former Veterans of Foreign Wars hall in Denver, Colorado, followed by a second camp nearby in 2002. At camp, each dog gets a private cabin, and counselors supervise as the "campers" play together, enjoy a swim, or romp through rough terrain. Owners can watch what's happening by clicking to view live coverage on the web-based Camper Cams installed at each location.

Within three years of founding Camp Bow Wow, Ganahl realized that she needed more money to expand the business and the brand. After exploring various alternatives, she began selling franchises in the United States and Canada. When new franchisees come on board, Ganahl is careful to explain the need for consistency in delivering services the same way at every Camp Bow Wow. She also explains the measurement standards she uses to manage the performance of the business and its franchise operations. Yet within that framework, she encourages franchisees to come forward with fresh ideas, and she seeks the input of franchisees when making important decisions about maintaining Camp Bow Wow's momentum.

Taking Camp Bow Wow from a cash-guzzling startup to a thriving, profitable franchise company has required all of Ganahl's skills in leadership and decision making. One complication she faced is that she originally relied on family members to fill management roles in the business. Over time, she found that she was making some decisions with an eye toward how it would affect her family, rather than what was best for a fast-growing business. Although her family did a good job, Ganahl quickly realized she needed to focus on her business's priorities and hire professionals with the specialized expertise to support her long-term goal of opening 1,000 Camp Bow Wows worldwide.

Camp Bow Wow operates in 122 locations and rings up $71 million in total revenues, including about $4 million in franchise fees. Recently analyzing the competition and future opportunities, Ganahl knew she would need significant financial backing for Camp Bow Wow to blossom into a major force in the dog day-care market. Thus, she sold her firm to VCA, a large pet health-care company that owns hundreds of animal hospitals and diagnostic centers. Next, applying the enthusiasm and personal touch for which she's known, Ganahl picked up the phone and called every franchise owner to deliver the news and explain the implications.

As part of the deal with VCA, Ganahl has hired a president to manage Camp Bow Wow's daily operations. Taking this step frees the founder to spend more time planning for the future and making strategic decisions about innovative new products to satisfy the changing needs of dog owners and their dogs. Ganahl is aiming high as she plans to increase the company's share of the $5 billion market for pet-related goods and services by attracting many more customers and many more franchisees in the coming years.[17]

Questions

1. When Heidi Ganahl talks with franchisees about performance expectations and measurements, what part of the management process is she describing? Why is this so important in a franchising business?
2. How would you describe Heidi Ganahl's leadership style? Why is it appropriate for her role at Camp Bow Wow?
3. Managers need five key skills to succeed. Of the five, which do you think will be most valuable to Heidi Ganahl now that she's been freed from day-to-day management to spend her time focusing on the future?

Building Skills for Career Success

1. Social Media Exercise

Crowdsourcing is a set of principles, processes, and platforms to get things done that includes putting out an open call to a group and managing the responses and output. Crowdsourcing can be like outsourcing in a bigger way because instead of contracting to one known entity, you are putting a call out to a bigger group, often a global online community, to either get many to participate or to find the person you need by casting a much wider net.

There are crowdsourcing companies that perform specific types of work such as translations (Gengo, Smartling), transcription (CastingWords), keyword marketing (Trada), even design and marketing work (99Designs, CrowdSpring). Each company operates differently. In the case of transcription or translation, you give work to a company like CastingWords or Gengo, and they in turn put the job out to their "crowd" of workers from around the world. They are like the middleman to helping you get the work done, and their distributed workforce can be less costly to them so they pass on their savings to your organization.

1. Check out a few of these crowdsourcing companies. What are your thoughts? Do you think they are effective? Why or why not?
2. Which type of leadership is most likely to include the use of crowdsourcing?
3. Can you think of other areas in businesses that can benefit from the use of crowdsourcing? What are they?

2. Building Team Skills

Over the past few years, an increasing number of employees, stockholders, and customers have demanded to know more about their companies. As a result, more companies have been taking the time to analyze their operations and to prepare mission statements that focus on the purpose of the company. The mission statement is becoming a critical planning tool for successful companies. To make effective decisions, employees must understand the purpose of their company.

Assignment

1. Divide into teams and write a mission statement for one of the following types of businesses:
   Food service, restaurant
   Banking
   Airline
   Auto repair
   Cabinet manufacturing
2. Discuss your mission statement with other teams. How did the other teams interpret the purpose of your company? What is the mission statement saying about the company?
3. Write a one-page report on what you learned about developing mission statements.

3. Researching Different Careers

A successful career requires planning. Without a plan, or roadmap, you will find it very difficult, if not impossible, to reach your desired career destination. The first step in planning is to establish your career goal. You then must set objectives and develop plans for accomplishing those objectives. This kind of planning takes time, but it will pay off later.

Assignment

Complete the following statements:

1. My career objective is to

-
-
-
-

This statement should encapsulate what you want to accomplish over the long run. It may include the type of job you want and the type of business or industry you want to work in. Examples include the following:

- My career goal is to work as a top manager in the food industry.
- My career goal is to supervise aircraft mechanics.
- My career goal is to win the top achievement award in the advertising industry.

2. My career objectives are to

-
-
-
-

Objectives are benchmarks along the route to a career destination. They are more specific than a career goal. A statement about a career objective should specify what you want to accomplish, when you will complete it, and any other details that will serve as criteria against which you can measure your progress. Examples include the following:

- My objective is to enroll in a management course at Main College in the spring semester 2016.
- My objective is to earn an A in the management course at Main College in the spring semester 2016.
- My objective is to be promoted to supervisor by January 1, 2018.
- My objective is to prepare a status report by September 30 covering the last quarter's activities by asking Charlie in Quality Control to teach me the procedures.

3. Exchange your goal and objectives statements with another class member. Can your partner interpret your objectives correctly? Are the objectives concise and complete? Do they include criteria against which you can measure your progress? If not, discuss the problem and rewrite the objective.

Endnotes

1 Based on information in Brooks Barnes, "Bob Iger, on Success Streak, Gets 2nd Contract Extension at Disney," *New York Times*, October 2, 2014, www.nytimes.com; "How Bob Iger Remade the House that Walt Built," *Chief Executive*, August 7, 2014, http://chiefexecutive.net; "Disney Offers HR Lessons, Best Practices," *Benefits Pro*, June 23, 2014, www.benefitspro.com; David A. Price, "Managing Creativity: Lessons from Pixar and Disney Animation," *Harvard Business Review*, April 9, 2014, http://hbr.org; www.thewaltdisneycompany.com (accessed July 11, 2015).

2 Gregory Wallace and Chris Isidore, "HP to Split into Two Companies," *CNN Money*, October 6, 2014, http://money.cnn.com/2014/10/06/technology/hp-restructuring-split/index.html?hpt=hp_t2 (accessed June 24, 2015).

3 Starbucks website at http://www.starbucks.com/about-us/company-information/mission-statement (accessed February 10, 2015); Amazon.com website at http://phx.corporate-ir.net/phoenix.zhtml?c=176060&p=irol-factSheet (accessed February 10, 2015); Twitter website at https://about.twitter.com/company (accessed February 10, 2015).

4 The Associated Press, "Swedish Fashion Retailer H&M Plans More Store Openings," The Star, September 25, 2014, http://www.thestar.com/business/2014/09/25/swedish_fashion_retailer_hm_plans_more_store_openings.html (accessed July 11, 2015).

5 Scott Moritz and Christina Pellegrini, "Blackberry Says Growth in Sight as Turnaround Takes Hold," *Bloomberg*, June 19, 2014, http://www.bloomberg.com/news/2014-06-19/blackberry-beats-estimates-as-cost-cutting-plan-fuels-turnaround.html (accessed June 24, 2015).

6 Spencer Jakab, "Best Buy Won't Fade to Blue," *Wall Street Journal*, August 25, 2014, http://online.wsj.com/articles/best-buy-wont-fade-to-blue-ahead-of-the-tape-1408994708 (accessed June 24, 2015); Zack's Equity Research, "Will Best Buy's Turnaround Efforts Beat Sector Weakness?" *Yahoo Finance*, September 16, 2014, http://finance.yahoo.com/news/best-buys-turnaround-efforts-beat-155002603.html (accessed June 24, 2015); Ann Zimmerman and Joan E. Solsman, "Best Buy's Turnaround Plan Models Unlikely Set of Retailers," *Wall Street Journal*, November 15, 2012, http://online.wsj.com/article/SB10001424127887324556304578119321442547426.html (accessed June 24, 2015).

7 "Hawaii Electric Light's Contingency Plans as Kilauea Lava Approaches," *KHON*, October 3, 2014, http://khon2.com/2014/10/03/hawaii-electric-lights-contingency-plans-as-kilauea-lava-approaches/ (accessed June 24, 2015).

8 Don Schwabel, "Kip Tendell: How He Created an Employee-First Culture at the Container Store," *Forbes*, October 7, 2014, http://www.forbes.com/sites/danschawbel/2014/10/07/kip-tindell-how-he-created-an-employee-first-culture-at-the-container-store/ (accessed June 24, 2015); Aaron Taube, "Why the Container Store Pays Its Employees $50,000 a Year," *Business Insider*, October 16, 2014, http://www.businessinsider.com/the-container-store-pays-employees-50000-a-year-2014-10 (accessed June 24, 2015).

9 Heather Kelly, "The CNN10 Startups: Airware," *CNN Money*, http://www.cnn.com/interactive/2014/10/tech/cnn10-startups/index.html?hpt=hp_bn5 (accessed February 10, 2015).

10 Maria Halkias, "Garden Ridge Is Evolving into At Home," *Dallas News*, June 16, 2014, http://www.dallasnews.com/business/retail/20140616-garden-ridge-is-evolving-into-at-home.ece (accessed June 24, 2015).

11 Dinah Eng, "New Belgium's Kim Jordan Is Tasting Success in Craft Brewing," *Fortune*, June 30, 2014, http://fortune.com/2014/06/12/new-belgium-kim-jordan/ (accessed June 24, 2015); Bryan Simpson, "New Belgium Brewing: How Intangibles Keep Employees Coming Back for More," *Sustainable Brands*, July 2012, http://www.sustainablebrands.com/news_and_views/jul2012/new-belgium-brewing-how-intangibles-keep-employees-coming-back-more (accessed June 24, 2015).

12 Andrew J. Dubrin, *Leadership: Research Findings, Practice and Skills*, 8th ed. (Mason, OH: South-Western/Cengage Learning, 2016).

13 "EY Entrepreneur of the Year Winner Talks Passion, Persistence, and Resilience," *Forbes*, November 16, 2014, http://www.forbes.com/sites/ey/2014/11/16/ey-entrepreneur-of-the-year-winner-talks-passion-persistence-resilience/ (accessed June 24, 2015).

14 Ricky Griffin, *Fundamentals of Management*, 8th ed. (Mason, OH: South-Western Cengage, 2016), 6.

15 Christine Haughney, "A Sale Gives a Magazine on Healthy Eating a New Lease on Life," *New York Times*, October 21, 2012, http://www.nytimes.com/2012/10/22/business/media/eating-well-magazines-new-lease-on-life.html (accessed June 24, 2015).

16 Martin Murray, "Total Quality Management (TQM)," http://logistics.about.com/od/qualityinthesupplychain/a/TQM.htm (accessed February 10, 2015).

17 Based on information in Heidi Ganahl, "My Turn: Changes to Franchise Rules Would Do Much Harm to Small-Business Owners," *Concord (NH) Monitor*, February 6, 2015, www.concordmonitor.com (accessed July 7, 2015); Caroline McMillan Portillo, "How Did She Turn a Plane Crash and Two Flops into a $71M Company? Dogs," *BizWomen*, August 12, 2014, www.bizjournals.com; Ryan Dezember, "VCA to Acquire Camp Bow Wow Chain," *Wall Street Journal*, August 4, 2014, www.wsj.com; Cengage Learning, *Camp Bow Wow* video.

CHAPTER 7

Creating a Flexible Organization

Why Should You Care?

To operate a successful business, those in charge must create an organization that operates efficiently and is able to attract employees.

Learning Objectives

Once you complete this chapter, you will be able to:

7-1 Understand what an organization is and identify its characteristics.

7-2 Explain why job specialization is important.

7-3 Identify the various bases for departmentalization.

7-4 Explain how decentralization follows from delegation.

7-5 Understand how the span of management describes an organization.

7-6 Describe the four basic forms of organizational structure.

7-7 Describe the effects of corporate culture.

7-8 Understand how committees and task forces are used.

7-9 Explain the functions of the informal organization and the grapevine in a business.

Can Structural Changes Re-Ignite McDonald's Growth?

Although McDonald's leads the world in fast-food restaurant revenues, competitors are nibbling away at its U.S. market share and profits. Some rivals are attracting customers with fancier burgers or healthier fare, while others are inviting customers to pick and choose sandwich toppings. Now, facing stagnant U.S. sales after decades of steady growth, McDonald's is getting closer to its customers by changing its organizational structure as well as its menu.

In the past, McDonald's organized its U.S. operations into three regional divisions (East, Central, and West). Managers in those regions provided ideas and input for decisions made at corporate headquarters. However, decision making was a slow process because information, analyses, and communications had to move through multiple layers of managers up and down the organization.

To speed things up, and stay in tune with local customers, the fast-food company is eliminating some management layers and switching to a four-zone structure (Northeast, South, Central, and West). States are grouped into zones not just for efficiency but also to reflect regional taste preferences. In this new structure, each zone's president has the authority to make decisions about products and promotions based on the needs and buying patterns of local customers. By expediting decision making, McDonald's hopes to respond more quickly to changes in customer buying behavior and—just as important—to more effectively fend off competitive challenges.

McDonald's has also put its menu on a diet. Too many choices was complicating ordering and adding precious seconds to preparation time—which, in turn, slowed service in the drive-through lanes and inside the restaurants. Instead, McDonald's is paring the number of menu items, adding a few healthier food choices, and allowing each zone to promote special items that prove popular with local customers. Some zones are testing "create your taste" customized ordering so customers can select the specific sandwich toppings they like. Others are testing service guarantees. Will these organizational changes enable McDonald's to reignite growth in revenues and profits?[1]

Did You Know?

With global annual revenues topping $28 billion, McDonald's serves 70 million customers each day through more than 35,000 restaurants in 100 nations.

To survive and to grow, companies such as McDonald's must constantly look for ways to improve their methods of doing business. Managers at McDonald's, like those at many organizations, maintain an organizational structure that best achieves company goals and creates products that foster long-term customer relationships.

When firms are organized, or reorganized, the focus is sometimes on achieving low operating costs. Other firms, such as Nike, emphasize providing high-quality products to ensure customer satisfaction. The issue of a firm's organizational structure is important because it can influence performance.

We begin this chapter by examining the business organization—what it is and how it functions in today's business environment. Next, we focus one by one on five characteristics that shape an organization's structure. We discuss job specialization within a company, the grouping of jobs into manageable units or departments, the delegation of power from management to workers, the span of management, and establishment of a chain of command. Then we step back for an overall view of organizational structure, describe the effects of corporate culture, and focus in on how committees and task forces are used. Finally, we look at the network of social interactions—the informal organization—that operates within the formal business structure.

7-1 WHAT IS AN ORGANIZATION?

We used the term *organization* throughout Chapter 6 without really defining it, mainly because its everyday meaning is close to its business meaning. Here, however, let us agree that an **organization** is a group of two or more people working together

organization a group of two or more people working together to achieve a common set of goals

Learning Objective

7-1 Understand what an organization is and identify its characteristics.

to achieve a common set of goals. A neighborhood dry cleaner owned and operated by a husband-and-wife team is an organization. IBM and Home Depot, which employ thousands of workers worldwide, are also organizations. Although each corporation's organizational structure is more complex than the dry-cleaning establishment, all must be organized to achieve their goals.

An inventor who goes into business to produce and market a new invention hires people, decides what each will do, determines who will report to whom, and so on. These activities are the essence of organizing, or creating, the organization. An organization chart helps to illustrate the shape of an organization.

7-1a Developing Organization Charts

An **organization chart** is a diagram that represents the positions and relationships within an organization. An example of an organization chart is shown in Figure 7-1. Each rectangle represents a particular position or person in the organization. At the top is the president, next are the vice presidents, and so on. The solid vertical lines connecting each level of the hierarchy indicate who is in the chain of command. The **chain of command** is the line of authority that extends from the highest to the lowest levels of the organization. You can see that each vice president reports directly to the president. Similarly, the plant managers, regional sales managers, and accounting department manager report to the vice presidents. An organization's chain

organization chart a diagram that represents the positions and relationships within an organization

chain of command the line of authority that extends from the highest to the lowest levels of an organization

FIGURE 7-1 A Typical Corporate Organization Chart

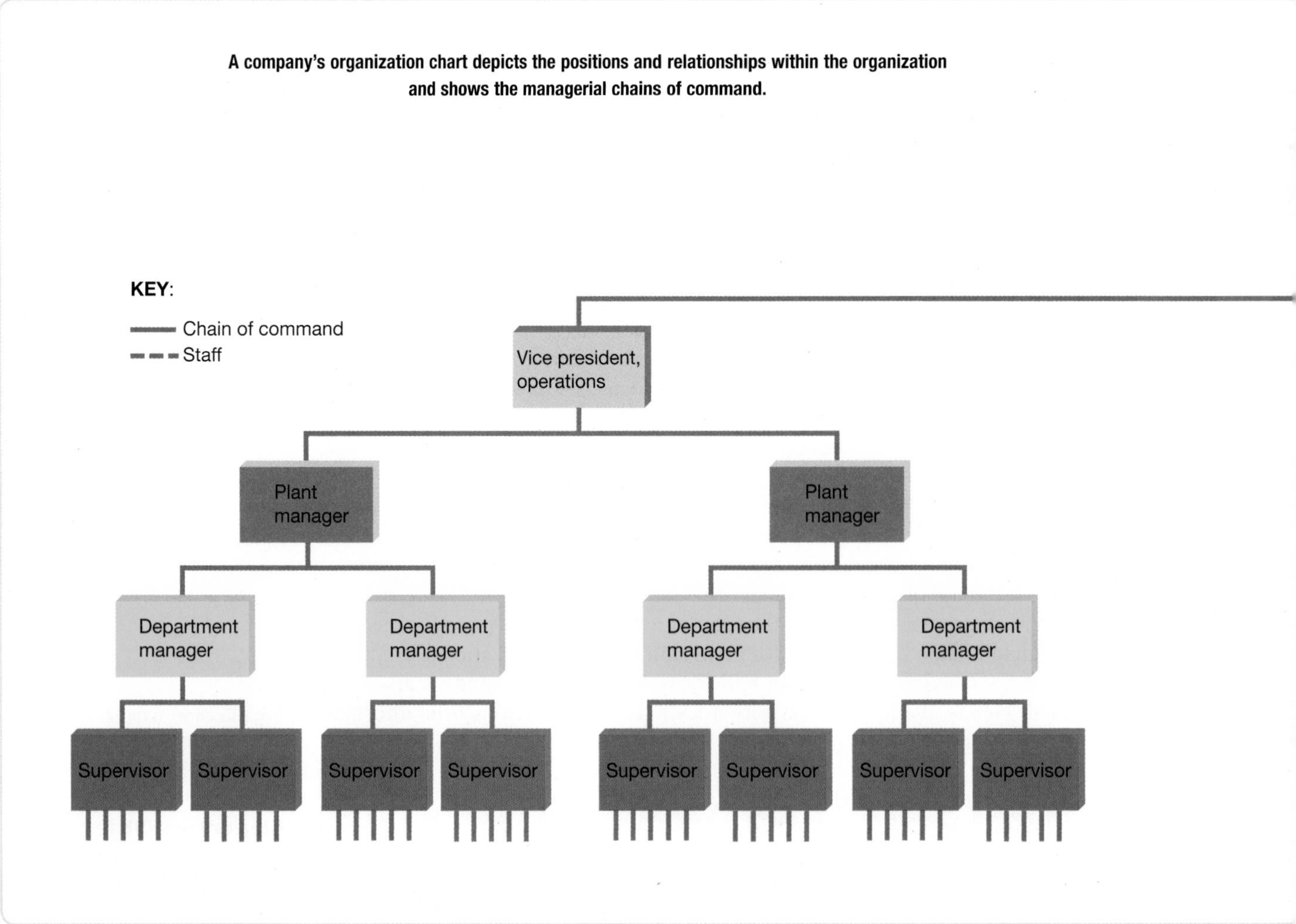

A company's organization chart depicts the positions and relationships within the organization and shows the managerial chains of command.

KEY:
— Chain of command
--- Staff

Vice president, operations

Plant manager

Plant manager

Department manager

Department manager

Department manager

Department manager

Supervisor Supervisor Supervisor Supervisor Supervisor Supervisor Supervisor Supervisor

of command can be short or long. A small local restaurant may have a very short chain of command consisting of the owner at the top and employees below. Large multinational corporations, on the other hand, may have very long chains of command. No matter what the length of the chain of command, organizations must ensure that communication along the chain is clear. Not everyone who works for an organization is part of the direct chain of command. In the chart these positions are represented by broken lines, as you can see with the directors of legal services, public affairs, and human resources. Instead, they hold *advisory*, or *staff*, positions. This difference will be examined later in the chapter when we discuss line-and-staff positions.

Most smaller organizations find organization charts useful. They clarify positions and relationships for everyone in the organization, and they help managers to track growth and change in the organizational structure. However, many large organizations, such as ExxonMobil, Kellogg's, and Procter & Gamble, do not maintain complete, detailed charts. There are two reasons for this. First, it is difficult to chart even a few dozen positions accurately, much less the thousands that characterize larger firms. Second, larger organizations are almost always changing parts of their structure. An organization chart would be outdated before it was completed. Increasingly, technology can help even large and complicated organizations implement up-to-date organization charts.

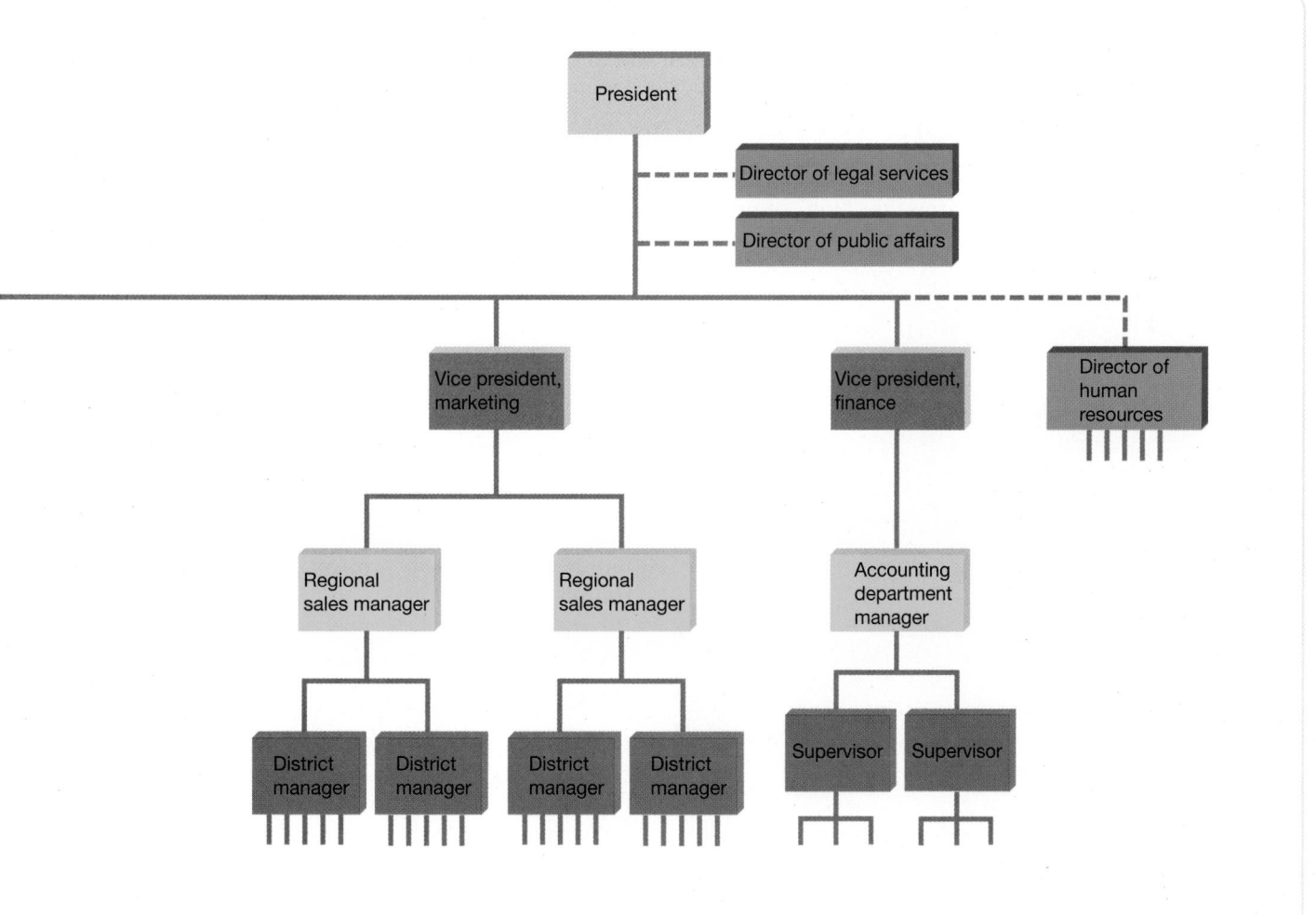

job specialization the separation of all organizational activities into distinct tasks and the assignment of different tasks to different people

7-1b Major Considerations for Organizing a Business

When a firm is started, management must decide how to organize the firm. These decisions focus on job design, departmentalization, delegation, span of management, and chain of command. In the next several sections, we discuss major issues associated with these dimensions.

7-2 JOB DESIGN

In Chapter 1, we defined *specialization* as the separation of a manufacturing process into distinct tasks and the assignment of different tasks to different people. Here we are extending that concept to *all* the activities performed within an organization.

7-2a Job Specialization

Job specialization is the separation of all organizational activities into distinct tasks and the assignment of different tasks to different people. Adam Smith, the 18th century economist whose theories gave rise to capitalism, was the first to emphasize the power of specialization in his book, *The Wealth of Nations*. According to Smith, the various tasks in a particular pin factory were arranged so that one worker drew the wire for the pins, another straightened the wire, a third cut it, a fourth ground the point, and a fifth attached the head. Smith claimed that 10 men were able to produce 48,000 pins per day. Before specialization, they could produce only 200 pins per day because each worker had to perform all five tasks!

7-2b The Rationale for Specialization

For a number of reasons, some job specialization is necessary in every organization because the "job" of most organizations is too large for one person to handle. In a firm such as Ford Motor Company, thousands of people are needed to manufacture automobiles. Others are needed to sell the cars, control the firm's finances, and so on.

Second, when a worker has to learn one specific, highly specialized task, that individual can learn it quickly and perform it efficiently. Third, a worker repeating the same job does not lose time changing operations, as the pin workers did when producing complete pins. Fourth, the more specialized the job, the easier it is to design specialized equipment. And finally, the more specialized the job, the easier the job training.

7-2c Alternatives to Job Specialization

Unfortunately, specialization can have negative consequences. The most significant drawback is the boredom and dissatisfaction employees may feel when repeating the same job. Bored employees may be absent from work frequently, not put much effort into their work, and even sabotage the company's efforts to produce quality products.

Specialization has its drawbacks. This employee has a specialized job that includes stitching a component of leather shoes. Specialization is efficient for the firm, but it can leave employees bored and dissatisfied. What do you think a firm can do to offset these problems?

To combat these problems, managers often turn to job rotation. **Job rotation** is the systematic shifting of employees from one job to another. For example, a worker may be assigned a different job every week for a four-week period and then return to the first job in the fifth week. Job rotation provides a variety of tasks so that workers are less likely to become bored and dissatisfied. Intel, for instance, encourages job rotation as a means of sharing ideas, perspectives, and best practices across the company. Job rotation helps workers stay interested in their jobs, develop new skills, and identify new roles where they may want to focus their energies in the future. According to the Society for Human Resource Management, around 38 percent of employers offer some kind of cross-training for their workers.[2]

Two other approaches—job enlargement and job enrichment—also can provide solutions to the problems caused by job specialization. These topics, along with other methods used to motivate employees, are discussed in Chapter 10.

job rotation the systematic shifting of employees from one job to another

Concept Check

✓ What are the positive and negative effects of specialization?

✓ What are three ways to reduce the negative effects of specialization?

7-3 DEPARTMENTALIZATION

After jobs are designed, they must be grouped together into "working units," or departments. This process is called **departmentalization**, which is the process of grouping jobs into manageable units. Today, the most common bases for organizing a business into effective departments are by function, by product, by location, and by customer.

Learning Objective

7-3 Identify the various bases for departmentalization.

7-3a By Function

Departmentalization by function groups jobs that relate to the same organizational activity. Under this scheme, all marketing personnel are grouped together in the marketing department, all production personnel in the production department, and so on.

departmentalization the process of grouping jobs into manageable units

departmentalization by function grouping jobs that relate to the same organizational activity

Most smaller and newer organizations departmentalize by function. Supervision is simplified because everyone is involved in the same activities and coordination is easy. The disadvantages of this method of grouping jobs are that it can lead to slow decision making and it tends to emphasize the department over the organization as a whole.

7-3b By Product

Departmentalization by product groups activities related to a particular good or service. This approach is used often by older and larger firms that produce and sell a variety of products. Each department handles its own marketing, production, financial management, and human resources activities.

Departmentalization by product makes decision making easier and provides for the integration of all activities associated with each product. However, it causes some duplication of specialized activities—such as finance—between departments. Moreover, the emphasis is placed on the product rather than on the whole organization.

7-3c By Location

Departmentalization by location groups activities according to the defined geographic area in which they are performed. Departmental areas may range from whole countries (for international firms) to regions within countries (for national firms) to areas of several city blocks (for police departments organized into precincts). For example, Ford has divisions for the Americas, Europe, Asia Pacific and Africa, and China. Departmentalization by location allows the organization to respond readily to the unique demands or requirements of different locations. Nevertheless, a large administrative staff and an elaborate control system may be needed to coordinate operations across many locations.

7-3d By Customer

Departmentalization by customer groups activities according to the needs of various customer populations. The advantage of this approach is that it allows the firm to deal efficiently with unique customers or customer groups. The biggest drawback is that a larger-than-usual administrative staff is needed.

7-3e Combinations of Bases

Many organizations use a combination of departmentalization bases. PepsiCo, for instance, is divided by product and location. It has product divisions such as Americas Beverages and Americas Foods, as well as divisions based on location such as Asia, Europe, the Middle East, and Africa.[3]

Take a moment to examine Figure 7-2. Notice that departmentalization by customer is used to organize New-Wave Fashions, Inc., into three major divisions: Men's, Women's, and Children's clothing. Then functional departmentalization is used to distinguish the firm's production and marketing activities. Finally, location is used to organize the firm's marketing efforts.

How is your school organized? These call center employees are organized by their function. Some organizations are structured in other ways. For example, if your university has more than one campus, they are organized by location but also by function such as by their business, social sciences, and math departments. Your school also might be organized by customer such as by undergraduate, graduate, and continuing education students.

departmentalization by product grouping activities related to a particular product or service

departmentalization by location grouping activities according to the defined geographic area in which they are performed

departmentalization by customer grouping activities according to the needs of various customer populations

Concept Check

✓ What are the four most common bases for departmentalization?

✓ Give an example of each.

FIGURE 7-2 Multibase Departmentalization for New-Wave Fashions, Inc.

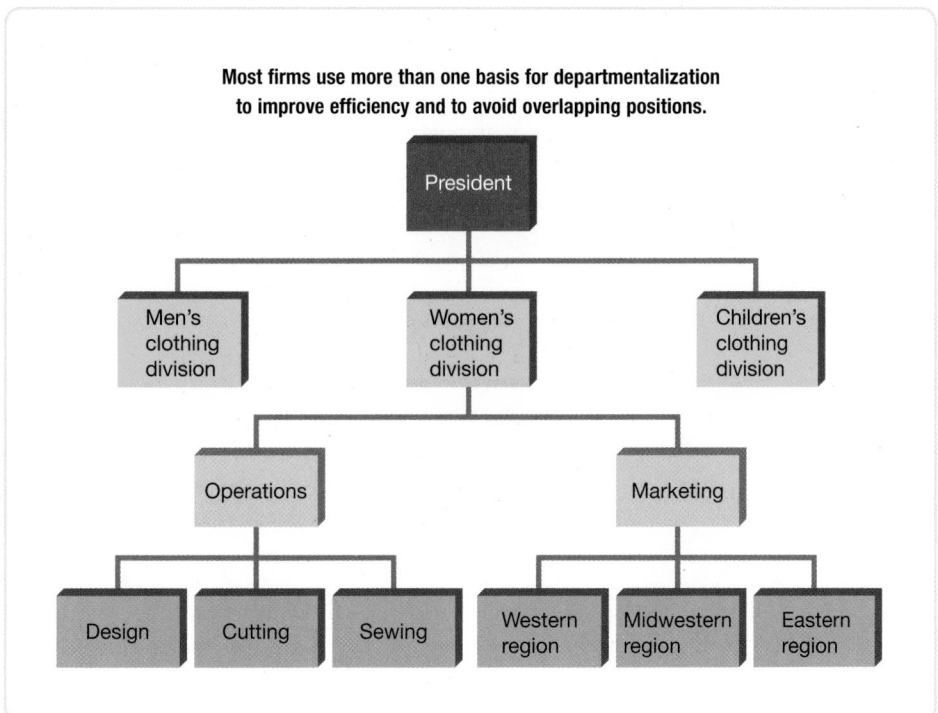

Most firms use more than one basis for departmentalization to improve efficiency and to avoid overlapping positions.

7-4 DELEGATION, DECENTRALIZATION, AND CENTRALIZATION

The third major step in the organizing process is to distribute power in the organization. **Delegation** assigns work and power to other workers. The degree of centralization or decentralization of authority is determined by the overall pattern of delegation within the organization.

Learning Objective

7-4 Explain how decentralization follows from delegation.

7-4a Delegation of Authority

Because no manager can do everything, delegation is vital to completion of a manager's work. Delegation is also important in developing the skills and abilities of subordinates. It allows those who are being groomed for higher-level positions to play increasingly important roles in decision making.

STEPS IN DELEGATION The delegation process generally involves three steps (see Figure 7-3). First, the manager must *assign responsibility*. **Responsibility** is the duty to do a job or perform a task. In most job settings, a manager simply gives the worker a job to do. Typical job assignments might range from preparing a report on the status of a new quality control program to being put in charge of a task force. Second, the manager must *grant authority*. **Authority** is the power, within the organization, to accomplish an assigned job or task. This might include the power to obtain specific information, order supplies, authorize relevant expenditures, or make certain decisions. Finally, the manager must *create accountability*. **Accountability** is the obligation of a worker to accomplish an assigned job or task.

Note that accountability is created but it cannot be delegated. Suppose that you are an operations manager for Target and are responsible for performing a specific task. You, in turn, delegate this task to someone else. You nonetheless remain accountable to your immediate supervisor for getting the task done properly. If the

delegation assigning part of a manager's work and power to other workers

responsibility the duty to do a job or perform a task

authority the power, within an organization, to accomplish an assigned job or task

accountability the obligation of a worker to accomplish an assigned job or task

FIGURE 7-3 Steps in the Delegation Process

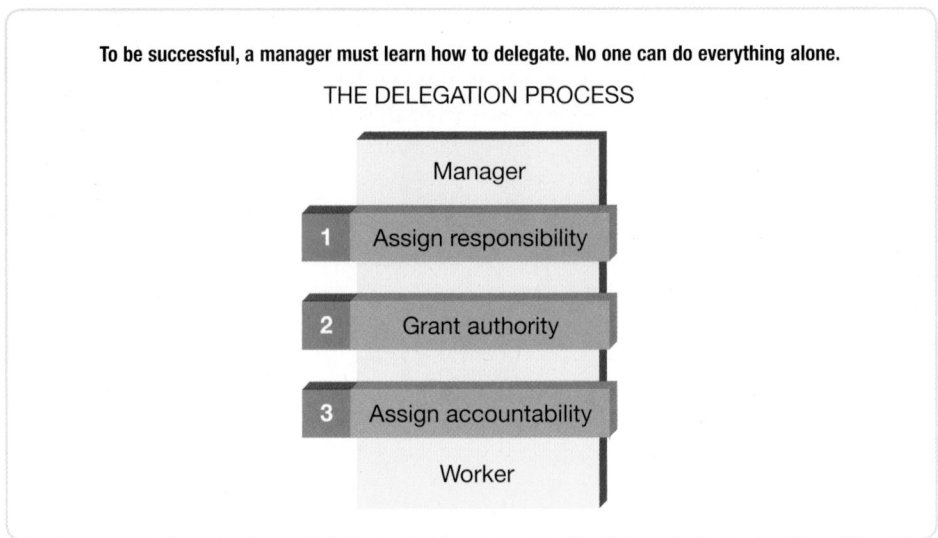

To be successful, a manager must learn how to delegate. No one can do everything alone.

THE DELEGATION PROCESS

Manager

1 Assign responsibility

2 Grant authority

3 Assign accountability

Worker

decentralized organization an organization in which management consciously attempts to spread authority widely in the lower levels of the organization

centralized organization an organization that systematically works to concentrate authority at the upper levels of the organization

other person fails to complete the assignment, you—not the person to whom you delegated the task—will be held accountable.

BARRIERS TO DELEGATION For several reasons, managers may be unwilling to delegate work. This may be because the manager does not trust the employee to complete the task, or because the manager fears the employee will perform exceptionally and attract the notice of higher level managers. Finally, some managers do not delegate because they are disorganized and they are not able to plan and assign work effectively.

7-4b Decentralization of Authority

The pattern of delegation throughout an organization determines the extent to which that organization is decentralized or centralized. In a **decentralized organization**, management consciously attempts to spread authority widely across various organization levels. A **centralized organization**, on the other hand, systematically works to concentrate authority at the upper levels. For example, shipping companies like UPS tend to be centralized, with shipping dispatches coordinated by upper management. After merging with OfficeMax, Office Depot restructured its European operations to reduce costs by centralizing and standardizing processes across all European countries.[4] Large organizations may have characteristics of both decentralized and centralized organizations.

A number of factors can influence the extent to which a firm is decentralized. One is the external environment in which the firm operates. The more complex and unpredictable this environment, the more likely it is that top management will let lower-level managers make important decisions because lower-level managers are closer to the problems. Another factor is the nature of the decision itself.

ISTOCKPHOTO.COM/STURTI

Delegate, delegate, delegate. The industrialist Andrew Carnegie once said, "No person will make a great business who wants to do it all himself or get all the credit." Delegating gives employees different tasks to do, which can enrich and enlarge their jobs. It also enables both employees and their superiors to learn new skills required for higher-level positions.

The riskier or more important the decisions that have to be made, the greater the tendency to centralize decision making. A third factor is the abilities of lower-level managers. If these managers do not have strong decision-making skills, top managers will be reluctant to decentralize. Finally, a firm that has practiced centralization or decentralization is likely to maintain that same posture in the future.

In principle, neither decentralization nor centralization is right. What works for one organization may or may not work for another. Every organization must assess its own situation and choose the level of centralization or decentralization that will work best.

Concept Check

✓ Identify and describe the three steps in the delegation process.

✓ Differentiate decentralized organization and centralized organization.

7-5 THE SPAN OF MANAGEMENT

Learning Objective

7-5 Understand how the span of management describes an organization.

The fourth major step in organizing a business is establishing the **span of management** (or **span of control**), which is the number of workers who report directly to one manager. Hundreds of years of research has shown that there is no perfect ratio of subordinates to managers. More recently, theorists have focused on the width of the span of management. This issue is complicated because the span of management may change by department within the same organization. A highly mechanized factory where all operations are standardized may allow for a wide span of management. An advertising agency, where new problems and opportunities arise every day and where teamwork is a constant necessity, will have a much narrower span of management.

7-5a Wide and Narrow Spans of Management

A *wide* span of management exists when a manager has a larger number of subordinates. A *narrow* span exists when the manager has only a few subordinates. Several factors determine the span that is best for a particular manager (see Figure 7-4). Generally, the span of management may be wide when (1) the manager and the subordinates are very competent, (2) the organization has a well-established set of standard operating procedures, and (3) few new problems are expected to arise. The span should be narrow when (1) workers are physically located far from one another,

FIGURE 7-4 The Span of Management

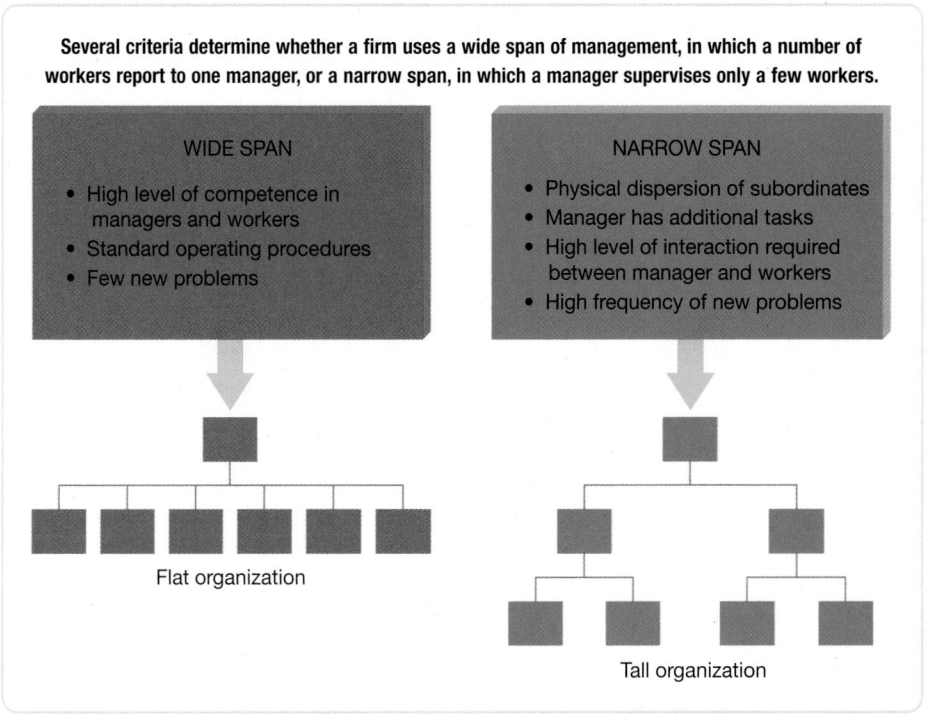

Several criteria determine whether a firm uses a wide span of management, in which a number of workers report to one manager, or a narrow span, in which a manager supervises only a few workers.

WIDE SPAN
- High level of competence in managers and workers
- Standard operating procedures
- Few new problems

NARROW SPAN
- Physical dispersion of subordinates
- Manager has additional tasks
- High level of interaction required between manager and workers
- High frequency of new problems

Flat organization

Tall organization

span of management (or span of control) the number of workers who report directly to one manager

CATHERINE YEULET/ISTOCK/THINKSTOCK

Narrow versus wide spans of management: Which is better? The manager in the middle of the photo supervises only a handful of employees. Consequently, she has a narrow span of management. Companies are constantly searching for the ideal number of employees their supervisors should manage.

Concept Check

✓ Describe the two spans of management.

✓ What are problems associated with each one?

organizational height the number of layers, or levels, of management in a firm

line structure an organizational structure in which the chain of command goes directly from person to person throughout the organization

line managers a position in which a person makes decisions and gives orders to subordinates to achieve the organization's goals

(2) the manager has much work to do in addition to supervising workers, (3) a great deal of interaction is required between supervisor and workers, and (4) new problems arise frequently.

7-5b Organizational Height

The span of management has an obvious impact on relations between managers and workers. It has a more subtle, but equally important, impact on the height of the organization. **Organizational height** is the number of layers, or levels, of management in a firm. The span of management plays a direct role in determining the height of the organization (see Figure 7-4). If the span of management is wide, fewer levels are needed, and the organization is *flat*. If the span of management is narrow, more levels are needed, and the resulting organization is *tall*.

In a tall organization, administrative costs are higher because more managers are needed. Communication may become distorted because information has to pass up and down through more levels. When companies are cutting costs, one option is to decrease organizational height in order to reduce related administrative expenses. For example, in the wake of fallout from the 2008 financial crisis and stricter rules on risky forms of investing, major Swiss bank UBS laid off 10,000 employees (15 percent of staff) and scrapped its risky fixed income business. These steps were meant to simplify the company's structure and help it return to its roots as a private banker.[5] Although flat organizations avoid these problems, their managers may perform more administrative duties simply because there are fewer managers. Wide spans of management also may require managers to spend considerably more time supervising and working with subordinates.

7-6 FORMS OF ORGANIZATIONAL STRUCTURE

Up to this point, we have focused our attention on the major characteristics of organizational structure. In many ways, this is like discussing the parts of a jigsaw puzzle one by one. It is now time to put the puzzle together. We will next discuss four basic forms of organizational structure: line, line-and-staff, matrix, and network.

7-6a The Line Structure

The simplest and oldest form of organizational structure is the **line structure**, in which the chain of command goes directly from person to person throughout the organization. Thus, a straight line could be drawn down through the levels of management, from the chief executive down to the lowest level in the organization. In a small retail store, for example, an hourly employee might report to an assistant manager, who reports to a store manager, who reports to the owner.

Managers within a line structure, called **line managers**, make decisions and give orders to subordinates to achieve the organization's goals. A line structure's simplicity and clear chain of command allow line managers to make decisions quickly with direct accountability because the decision maker only has one supervisor to whom he or she reports.

The downside of a line structure is that line managers are responsible for many activities, and therefore must have a wide range of knowledge about all of them. While this may not be a problem for small organizations with a lower volume of activities, in a larger organization, activities are more numerous and complex, thus making it more difficult for line managers to fully understand what they are in charge of. Therefore, line managers in a larger organization would have a hard time making an educated decision without expert advice from outside sources. As a result, line structures are not very effective in medium- or large-sized organizations, but are very popular in small organizations.

7-6b The Line-and-Staff Structure

A **line-and-staff structure** not only utilizes the chain of command from a line structure but also provides line managers with specialists, called staff managers. Therefore, this structure works much better for medium- and large-sized organizations than line management alone. **Staff managers** provide support, advice, and expertise to line managers, thus eliminating the major drawback of line structures. Staff managers are not part of the chain of command like line managers are, but they do have authority over their assistants (see Figure 7-5).

Personal App

Do you have a mentor?

If you're looking to move up, try to get some advice from co-workers in both line and staff positions. Not only will this broaden your understanding of the organization, it will also help you bridge the gaps between line and staff and connect with both groups.

FIGURE 7-5 Line and Staff Managers

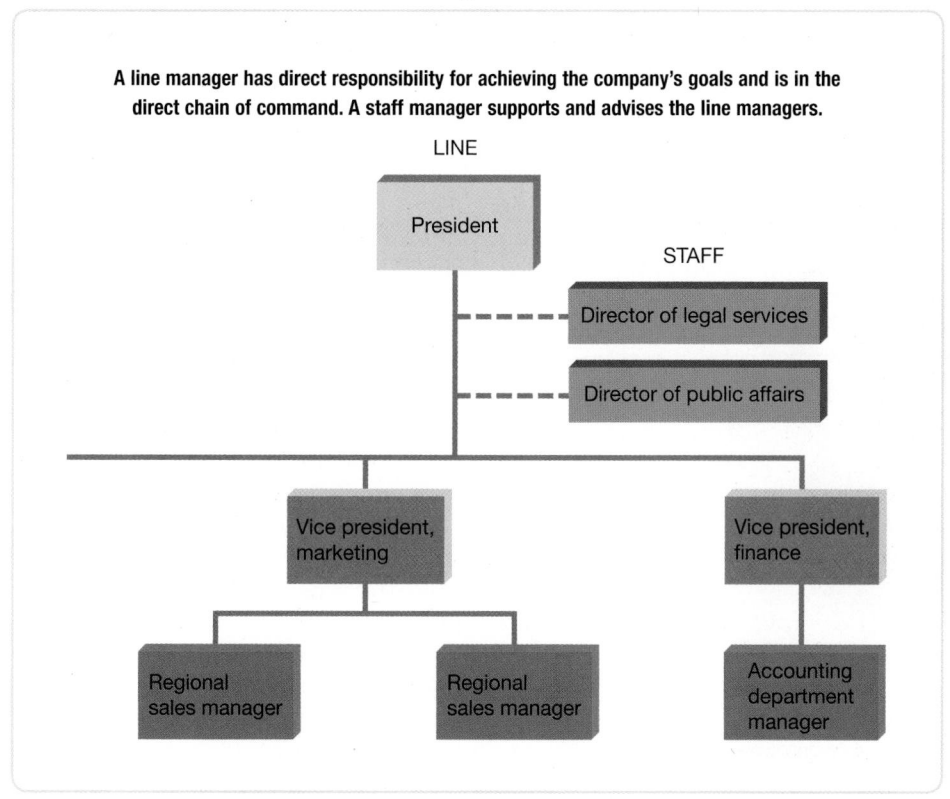

A line manager has direct responsibility for achieving the company's goals and is in the direct chain of command. A staff manager supports and advises the line managers.

line-and-staff structure an organizational structure that utilizes the chain of command from a line structure in combination with the assistance of staff managers

staff managers a position created to provide support, advice, and expertise within an organization

Ethical Success or Failure

If We Get Ethics Right, Will Compliance Follow?

During the past two decades, hundreds of corporations, as well as many educational institutions, nonprofit groups, and government agencies, have established the chief ethics officer as a staff position. This senior management-level position serves as the central point of organizational contact for formulating ethics guidelines, communicating ethical values, and dealing with reports of potential ethics violations. Often, the chief ethics officer works with the staff executive who is responsible for ensuring compliance with the various local, state, national, and international laws and regulations governing the organization's products, operations, and facilities.

At L'Oreal, which has been named one of the world's most ethical companies, the chief ethics officer makes a distinction between enforcing compliance and instilling ethical behavior. "If we get ethics right, compliance will follow," he says. The company's core ethics values are respect, integrity, courage, and transparency. Every year, L'Oreal invites all employees to participate in a global ethics day event, during which they can discuss ethical issues with the chief executive officer. The goal is to encourage the work force to ask questions and to speak up about what's happening in any division or unit.

Even organizations with a chief ethics officer may discover potentially unethical behavior at some point. Walmart, for example, is investigating allegations of bribery and corruption in Mexico, China, and other countries. The retailer has developed a detailed, multinational compliance plan and is investing $100 million in compliance technology. Both its chief ethics officer and chief compliance officer report to a committee of the board of directors to allow for top-level discussions about possible problems.

Sources: Based on information in Sue Reisinger, "Wal-Mart Compliance Chief Looking Beyond the Scandals," *Corporate Council*, October 21, 2014, www.corpcounsel.com; Elizabeth A. Harris, "After Bribery Scandal, High-Level Departures at Walmart," *New York Times*, June 4, 2014, www.nytimes.com; Rachel Louise Ensign, "Q&A: Emmanuel Lulin, L'Oreal's Chief Ethics Officer," *Wall Street Journal*, November 12, 2013, www.wsj.com; http://corporate.walmart.com (accessed January 15, 2015).

Both line and staff managers are needed for effective management, but the two positions differ in important ways. Most importantly, line managers have *line authority*, which means that they can make decisions and issue directives relating to the organization's goals. Staff managers seldom have this kind of authority. Instead, they usually have either advisory authority or functional authority. *Advisory authority* is the expectation that line managers will consult the appropriate staff manager when making decisions. *Functional authority* is a stronger form. It is the authority of staff managers to make decisions and issue directives about their areas of expertise. For example, a legal adviser for Nike can decide whether to retain a particular clause in a contract but not product pricing.

Staff managers in a line-and-staff structure tend to have more access to information than line managers. This means that line managers must rely on the staff managers for information. This is usually not an issue, unless the staff manager makes a wrong decision and there is no one else to catch his or her mistake.[6] For a variety of reasons, conflict between line managers and staff managers is fairly common in business. Staff managers often have more formal education and sometimes are younger (and perhaps more ambitious) than line managers. Line managers may perceive staff managers as a threat to their own authority and thus may resent them. For their part, staff managers may become annoyed or angry if their expert recommendations are not adopted by line management.

HANNELORE FOERSTER/GETTY IMAGES

Line-and-staff organization structure. Ronald McDonald occupies a staff position and does not have direct authority over other employees at McDonald's. Steve Easterbrook, McDonald's CEO, does have direct authority over other McDonald's employees and thus occupies a line position.

Fortunately, there are several ways to minimize the likelihood of such conflict. One way is to integrate line and staff managers into one team. Another is to ensure that the areas of responsibility of line and staff managers are clearly defined. Finally, line and staff managers both can be held accountable for the results of their activities.

7-6c The Matrix Structure

The **matrix structure** combines vertical and horizontal lines of authority, forming a matrix shape in the organization chart. The matrix structure occurs when product departmentalization is superimposed on a functionally departmentalized organization. In a matrix organization, authority flows both down and across and individuals report to more than one superior at the same time.

To understand the structure of a matrix organization, consider the usual functional arrangement, with people working in departments such as engineering, finance, and marketing. Now suppose that we assign people from these departments to a special group that is working on a new project as a team—a cross-functional team. A **cross-functional team** consists of individuals with varying specialties, expertise, and skills that are brought together to achieve a common task. Frequently, cross-functional teams are charged with the responsibility of developing new products. The manager in charge of a team is usually called a *project manager*. Any individual who is working with the team reports to *both* the project manager and the individual's superior in the functional department (see Figure 7-6).

Cross-functional team projects may be temporary, in which case the team is disbanded once the mission is accomplished, or they may be permanent. As the world becomes more connected, many companies require managers to have had cross-functional team experience. Major corporations such as GE, Whirlpool,

FIGURE 7-6 A Matrix Structure

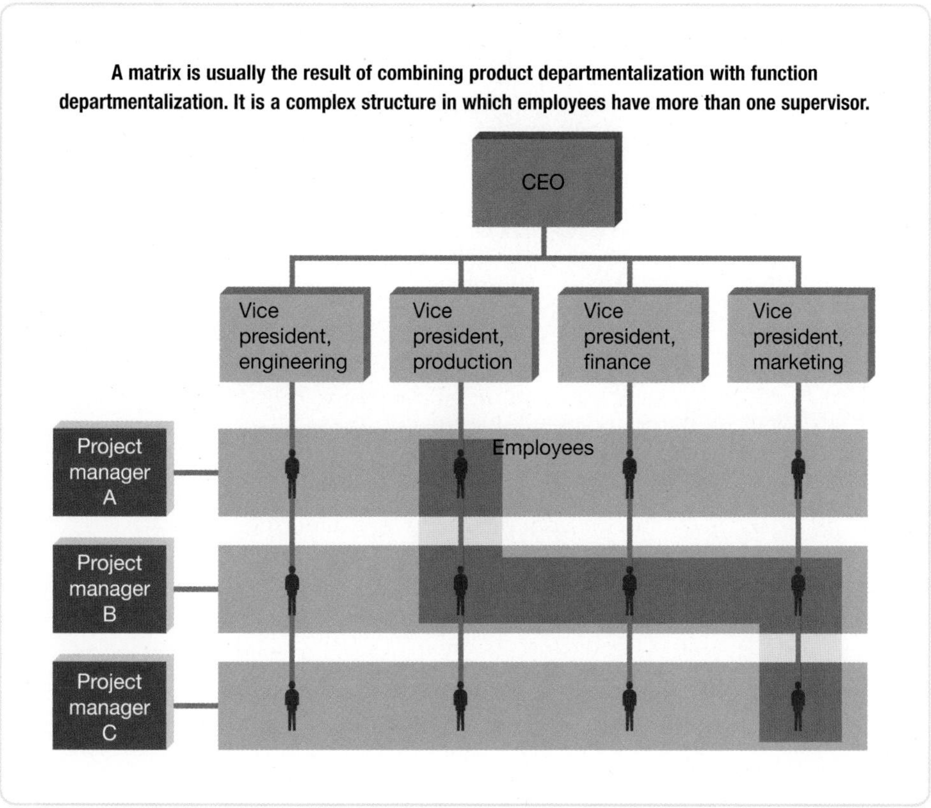

A matrix is usually the result of combining product departmentalization with function departmentalization. It is a complex structure in which employees have more than one supervisor.

CEO

Vice president, engineering | Vice president, production | Vice president, finance | Vice president, marketing

Project manager A | Project manager B | Project manager C

Employees

matrix structure an organizational structure that combines vertical and horizontal lines of authority, usually by superimposing product departmentalization on a functionally departmentalized organization

cross-functional team a team of individuals with varying specialties, expertise, and skills that are brought together to achieve a common task

Source: Ricky W. Griffin, *Fundamentals of Management*, 8th ed. Copyright © 2016, p. 180 by South-Western/Cengage Learning, Mason, OH. Adapted with permission.

and Procter & Gamble all utilize the diverse viewpoints that come out of cross-functional teams.

These teams often are empowered to make major decisions. When a cross-functional team is employed, prospective team members may receive special training because effective teamwork can require different skills. For cross-functional teams to be successful, team members must be given specific information on the job each performs. The team must also develop a sense of cohesiveness and maintain good communications among its members.

Matrix structures offer advantages over other organizational forms, added flexibility probably being the most obvious one. The matrix structure also can increase productivity, raise morale, and nurture creativity and innovation. In addition, employees experience personal development through doing a variety of jobs.

The matrix structure also has disadvantages. Having employees report to more than one supervisor can cause confusion about who is in charge. Like committees, teams may take longer to resolve problems and issues than individuals working alone. Other difficulties include personality clashes, poor communication, undefined individual roles, unclear responsibilities, and difficulties in finding ways to reward individual and team performance simultaneously. Because more managers and support staff may be needed, a matrix structure may be more expensive to maintain.

7-6d The Network Structure

In a **network structure** (sometimes called a *virtual organization*), administration is the primary function performed, and other functions such as engineering, production, marketing, and finance are contracted out to other organizations. Frequently, a network organization does not manufacture the products it sells. This type of organization has a few permanent employees consisting of top management and hourly clerical workers. Leased facilities and equipment, as well as temporary

network structure an organizational structure in which administration is the primary function, and most other functions are contracted out to other firms

Entrepreneurial Success

Entrepreneurs Set the Tone of Corporate Culture

Even the smallest business can build a strong and vibrant corporate culture—starting with the entrepreneur's vision and values. By demonstrating, communicating, celebrating, and reinforcing what's important, you can, as an entrepreneur, cultivate a strong culture to support long-term growth and success. Here are three tips from entrepreneurs and experts:

- *Hire employees who share your values and who believe in the business and its mission.* Employees whose values aren't aligned with yours are likely to be less committed and less productive. A shared belief in specific values and vision "keeps the team focused and moving forward with purpose, against all odds," explains Elena Bajic, the founder of Ivy Exec, an executive search firm.
- *Involve employees in activities that perpetuate the culture.* From awards ceremonies to after-work parties, every small business needs rituals built around the entrepreneur's values. At Stylerunner, a small business

in Sydney, Australia, employees gather for twice-weekly "gratitude sessions" where they talk about the things and people they're thankful for. This ritual reflects the co-founders' emphasis on positive thinking and on how people make a difference.

- *Live the values by applying them in every business decision and action.* Employees will take their cue from what the entrepreneur does, day in and day out, not just what he or she says. "You can delegate everything else, but you must always hold the culture in your hands," says consultant Sharon Hadary.

Sources: Based on information in Sharon Hadary, "Five Ways Entrepreneurs Can Keep a Great Corporate Culture," *Wall Street Journal*, June 12, 2014, www.wsj.com; Eric Thome, "Three Ways to Maintain Your Small-Business Culture," *Wall Street Journal*, June 12, 2014, www. wsj.com; Sarah Kimmorley, "How the Twin Sisters Behind Stylerunner Put a Quirky Company Culture at the Heart of Their Strategy," *Business Insider (Australia)*, December 19, 2014, www. businessinsider.com.au; Elena Bajic, "Corporate Culture: Creating and Cultivating Company 'Charisma,'" *Forbes.com*, May 7, 2013.

workers, are increased or decreased as the organization's needs change. Thus, there is limited formal structure associated with a network organization.

An obvious strength of a network structure is flexibility that allows the organization to adjust quickly to changes. Network structures consist of a lot of teams working together, rather than relying on one centralized leader. One noteworthy benefit is that firms with a network structure are more likely to survive the loss of an important member. Some of the challenges faced by managers in network-structured organizations include controlling the quality of work performed by other organizations, low morale and high turnover among hourly workers, and a lack of a clear hierarchy.

7-7 CORPORATE CULTURE

Most managers function within a corporate culture. A **corporate culture** is generally defined as the inner rites, rituals, heroes, and values of a firm. An organization's culture has a powerful influence on how employees think and act. It also can determine public perception of the organization.

Corporate culture generally is thought to have a very strong influence on a firm's performance over time. Hence, it is useful to be able to assess a firm's corporate culture. Common indicators include the physical setting (building or office layouts), what the company says about its corporate culture (in advertising or news releases), how the company greets guests (formal or informal reception areas), and how employees spend their time (working alone in an office or working with others).

Researchers Rob Goffee and Gareth Jones identified four distinct types of corporate cultures (see Figure 7-7). One is called the *networked culture*, characterized by a base of trust and friendship among employees, a strong commitment to the organization, and an informal environment. A small nonprofit organization may seek to build a networked culture where employees look out for each other and believe strongly in the organizational mission. Building a networked culture in such an organization is important because employees may have to work long hours for relatively little pay, and a strong sense of community and commitment helps to keep productivity high and turnover low.

Learning Objective

7-7 Describe the effects of corporate culture.

corporate culture the inner rites, rituals, heroes, and values of a firm

FIGURE 7-7 Types of Corporate Cultures

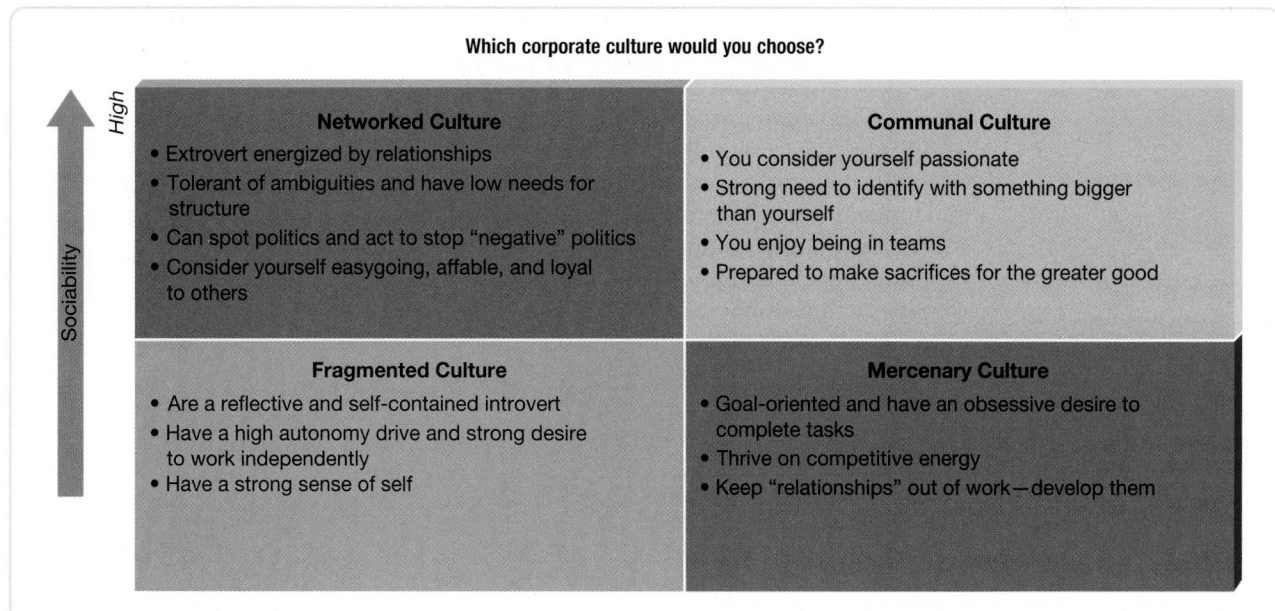

Source: "Types of Corporate Culture," in Rob Goffee and Gareth Jones, *The Character of a Corporation* (New York: HarperCollins, 1998). Copyright © 1998 by Rob Goffee and Gareth Jones. Permission granted by Rob Goffee and Gareth Jones.

Corporate Culture. Corporate culture can influence an employee's attitudes toward fitness and health. Some organizations have gyms and complimentary healthy snacks such as fruit.

ad hoc committee a committee created for a specific short-term purpose

standing committee a relatively permanent committee charged with performing some recurring task

task force a committee established to investigate a major problem or pending decision

Concept Check

✓ What is corporate culture?

✓ Explain the four types of corporate cultures.

Learning Objective

7-8 Understand how committees and task forces are used.

The phrase *mercenary culture* may have a negative connotation, but it also involves a high degree of passion, energy, sense of purpose, and excitement for one's work. Large banks and investment firms often have mercenary cultures because the environment is fast-paced, the stakes are high, and winning is important. This kind of culture can be very stressful for an employee with an incompatible personality. The term *mercenary* does not imply that employees are motivated to work only for the money, although financial gain does play a role. In this culture, employees are very intense, focused, and determined to win. For example, years after the 2008 economic crisis, Barclays, a major financial company, is still being criticized by U.S. and British regulators for its mercenary culture. Accusations include an excessive risk-taking culture and encouraging employees to win by any means. Although new CEO Antony Jenkins has vowed to restore Barclay's culture, similar allegations of conduct continue to dog the British firm.[7]

In the *fragmented culture*, employees do not become friends, and they work "at" the organization, not "for" it. Employees have a high degree of autonomy, flexibility, and equality.

The *communal culture* combines the positive traits of the networked culture and the mercenary culture—those of friendship, commitment, high focus on performance, and high energy. People's lives revolve around the product in this culture, and success by anyone in the organization is celebrated by all.[8]

Some experts believe that cultural change is needed when a company's environment changes, such as when the industry becomes more competitive, the company's performance is mediocre, or when the company is growing. It is not uncommon that companies feel they must adjust their culture in order to attract top talent. For example, many companies have formally come out in favor of same-sex marriage, including General Mills, Alcoa, and Aetna. Having a nondiscriminatory culture is seen as important for maintaining a strong workforce for many corporations.[9]

Organizations in the future will look quite different, as technology allows more to be done in small, flexible work groups that are coordinated by computers and held together by strong corporate cultures. Businesses operating in fast-changing industries will require leadership that supports trust and risk taking. Creating a culture of trust in an organization can lead to increases in growth, profit, productivity, and job satisfaction. A culture of trust can help an organization to retain the best people, inspire customer loyalty, develop new markets, and increase creativity.

Another area where corporate culture plays a vital role is the integration of two or more companies. Business leaders often cite the role of corporate cultures in the integration process as one of the primary factors affecting the success of a merger or acquisition. Experts note that corporate culture is a way of conducting business both within the company and externally. If two merging companies do not address differences in corporate culture, they are setting themselves up for missed opportunities and possibly failure.

7-8 COMMITTEES AND TASK FORCES

Today, business firms use several types of committees that affect organizational structure. An **ad hoc committee** is created for a specific short-term purpose, such as reviewing the firm's employee benefits plan. Once its work is finished, the ad hoc committee disbands. A **standing committee** is a relatively permanent committee charged with performing a recurring task. A firm might establish a budget review committee, for example, to review departmental budget requests on an ongoing basis. Finally, a **task force** is a committee established to investigate a major problem or pending decision. A firm contemplating a merger with another company might form a task force to assess the pros and cons of the merger.

Committees offer some advantages over individual action. Their several members are able to bring information and knowledge to the task at hand. Furthermore, committees tend to make more accurate decisions and to transmit their results through the organization more effectively. However, committee deliberations take longer than individual actions. In addition, unnecessary compromise may take place within the committee, or the opposite may occur, as one person dominates (and thus negates) the committee process.

Concept Check

✓ What is the difference between a committee and a task force?

✓ What are the advantages and disadvantages of using committees?

7-9 THE INFORMAL ORGANIZATION AND THE GRAPEVINE

Learning Objective

7-9 Explain the functions of the informal organization and the grapevine in a business.

So far, we have discussed the organization as a formal structure consisting of interrelated positions. This is the organization that is shown on an organization chart. There is another kind of organization, however, that does not appear on any chart. We define this **informal organization** as the pattern of behavior and interaction that stems from personal rather than official relationships. Embedded within every informal organization are informal groups and the notorious grapevine.

An **informal group** is created by the group members themselves to accomplish goals that may or may not be relevant to the organization. Workers may create an informal group to go bowling, form a union, get a particular manager fired or transferred, or meet for lunch. The group may last for several years or a few hours.

Informal groups can be powerful forces in organizations. They can restrict output, or they can help managers through tight spots. They can cause disagreement and conflict, or they can help to boost morale and job satisfaction. They have the power to improve or worsen employee performance and productivity. Clearly, managers should be aware of informal groups and determine how to utilize them.

There is power in numbers. It's common for employees to befriend one another and form informal groups within an organization. The groups provide their members with camaraderie and information, but can create both challenges and benefits for the organization.

The **grapevine** is the informal communications network within an organization. It is completely separate from—and sometimes much faster than—the organization's formal channels of communication. Formal communications usually follow a path that parallels the organizational chain of command. Information can be transmitted through the grapevine in any direction—up, down, diagonally, or horizontally across the organizational structure. Subordinates may pass information to their bosses, an executive may relay something to a maintenance worker, or there may be an exchange of information between people who work in totally unrelated departments. Information gleaned from the grapevine can run the gamut from the latest management decisions to gossip.

How should managers treat the grapevine? Certainly, it would be a mistake to try to eliminate it. People working together, day in and day out, are bound to communicate. A more rational approach is to recognize its existence. For example, managers should respond promptly and aggressively to inaccurate grapevine information to minimize the damage that such misinformation might do. Moreover, the grapevine can come in handy when managers are on the receiving end of important communications from the informal organization.

In the next chapter, we apply these and other management concepts to an extremely important business function: the production of goods and services.

informal organization the pattern of behavior and interaction that stems from personal rather than official relationships

informal group a group created by the members themselves to accomplish goals that may or may not be relevant to an organization

grapevine the informal communications network within an organization

Concept Check

✓ In what ways can informal groups affect a business?

✓ How is the grapevine used in a business organization?

Summary

7-1 Understand what an organization is and identify its characteristics.

An organization is a group of two or more people working together to achieve a common set of goals. The relationships among positions within an organization can be illustrated by means of an organization chart. Five elements—job design, departmentalization, delegation, span of management, and chain of command—help to determine what an organization chart and the organization itself look like.

7-2 Explain why job specialization is important.

Job specialization is the separation of all the activities within an organization into smaller components and the assignment of those different components to different people. Several factors combine to make specialization a useful technique for designing jobs, but high levels of specialization may cause employee dissatisfaction and boredom. One technique for overcoming these problems is job rotation.

7-3 Identify the various bases for departmentalization.

Departmentalization is the grouping of jobs into manageable units. Typical bases for departmentalization are by function, product, location, or customer. Because each of these bases provides particular advantages, most firms—especially larger ones—use a combination of different bases to address different organizational situations.

7-4 Explain how decentralization follows from delegation.

Delegation is giving part of a manager's work to other workers. It involves the following three steps: (1) assigning responsibility, (2) granting authority, and (3) creating accountability. A decentralized firm is one that delegates as much power as possible to people in the lower management levels. In a centralized firm, on the other hand, power is retained at the upper levels.

7-5 Understand how the span of management describes an organization.

The span of management is the number of workers who report directly to a manager. Spans generally are characterized as wide (many workers per manager) or narrow (few workers per manager). Wide spans generally result in flat organizations (few layers of management); narrow spans generally result in tall organizations (many layers of management).

7-6 Describe the four basic forms of organizational structure.

There are four basic forms of organizational structure. The line structure is the oldest and simplest structure, in which the chain of command moves in a straight line from person to person down through the levels of management. The line-and-staff structure is similar to the line structure, but adds specialists called staff managers to assist the line managers in decision making. The line structure works most efficiently for smaller organizations, whereas the line-and-staff structure is used by medium- and large-sized organizations. The matrix structure may be depicted as product departmentalization superimposed on functional departmentalization. With the matrix structure, an employee on a cross-functional team reports to both the project manager and the individual's supervisor in a functional department. In an organization with a network structure, the primary function performed internally is administration, and other functions are contracted out to other firms.

7-7 Describe the effects of corporate culture.

Corporate culture has both internal and external effects on an organization. An organization's culture can influence the way employees think and act, and it can also determine the public's perception of the organization. Corporate culture can affect a firm's performance over time, either negatively or positively. Creating a culture of trust, for example, can lead to increased growth, profits, productivity, and job satisfaction, while retaining the best employees, inspiring customer loyalty, developing new markets, and increasing creativity. In addition, when two or more companies undergo the integration process, their different or similar corporate cultures can affect the success of a merger or acquisition.

7-8 Understand how committees and task forces are used.

Committees and task forces are used to develop organizational structure within an organization. An ad hoc committee is created for a specific short-term purpose, whereas a standing committee is relatively permanent. A task force is created to investigate a major problem or pending decision.

7-9 Explain the functions of the informal organization and the grapevine in a business.

Informal groups are created by group members to accomplish goals that may or may not be relevant to the organization, and they can be very powerful forces. The grapevine—the informal communications network within an organization—can be used to transmit information (important or gossip) through an organization much faster than through the formal communication network. Information transmitted through the grapevine can go in any direction across the organizational structure, skipping up or down levels of management and even across departments.

Key Terms

You should now be able to define and give an example relevant to each of the following terms:

organization (189)
organization chart (190)
chain of command (190)
job specialization (192)
job rotation (193)
departmentalization (193)
departmentalization by function (193)
departmentalization by product (194)

departmentalization by location (194)
departmentalization by customer (194)
delegation (195)
responsibility (195)
authority (195)
accountability (195)
decentralized organization (196)

centralized organization (196)
span of management (or span of control) (197)
organizational height (198)
line structure (198)
line manager (198)
line-and-staff structure (199)
staff manager (199)
matrix structure (201)
cross-functional team (201)

network structure (202)
corporate culture (203)
ad hoc committee (204)
standing committee (204)
task force (204)
informal organization (205)
informal group (205)
grapevine (205)

Discussion Questions

1. In what way do organization charts create a picture of an organization?
2. What determines the degree of specialization within an organization?
3. Describe how job rotation can be used to combat the problems caused by job specialization.
4. Why do most firms employ a combination of departmentalization bases?
5. What three steps are involved in delegation? Explain each.
6. How does a firm's top management influence its degree of centralization?

7. How is organization height related to the span of management?
8. Contrast line-and-staff and matrix forms of organizational structure.
9. How does the corporate culture of a local Best Buy store compare to that of a local McDonald's?
10. Which kinds of firms probably would operate most effectively as centralized firms? As decentralized firms?
11. How do decisions concerning span of management and the use of committees affect organizational structure?

Video Case
Zappos Wants to Make Customers (and Employees) Happy

Zappos (www.zappos.com) doesn't want to simply satisfy its customers—it wants to make them happy, a major reason for its success as an Internet retailer. Founded in 1999 to sell shoes online, the business soon earned a reputation for delivering personalized, responsive customer service. Top executives didn't pressure call-center employees (known internally as members of the Customer Loyalty Team) to follow a script or end conversations quickly. In fact, they encouraged employees to stay on the phone as long as needed to answer customers' questions, discuss merchandise, add a little chit-chat, and provide a "wow" shopping experience. Delighted customers would tell their friends and click or call back for more "wow" the next time they're in the market for new shoes.

By 2009, when it was purchased by the pioneering web giant Amazon, Las Vegas-based Zappos was beginning to branch out into clothing, handbags, and other merchandise. Today, with annual sales surpassing $2 billion, the website features outerwear, beauty products, sporting goods, and many other items, as well as shoes and clothing for the whole family. In addition, the company has established an Insights division to help other companies understand and adapt the unique corporate culture that has given Zappos a vital competitive edge in the dynamic world of e-commerce.

Zappos is so famous for its upbeat, can-do culture—not to mention the many opportunities for advancement available in a fast-growing firm—that it attracts 55,000 job applications every year. During interviews, managers ask offbeat questions such as, "On a scale of one to ten, how weird are you?" The purpose is to determine whether an applicant has the personality and temperament to fit into a corporate culture where fun, change, teamwork, creativity, transparency, and personal growth are highly valued. All newly hired employees have to sign a statement confirming that they understand these core values and are committed to applying them on the job.

Delivering superior service with a virtual smile requires careful behind-the-scenes coordination. Every Zappos employee is responsible for performing specific tasks, supported by regular training plus optional courses to build new skills. Because so many orders come in by phone, the entire workforce (including the CEO) receives a month of call-center training, along with a week of training in the warehouse, to get a first-hand taste of the challenges of customer contact and order fulfillment.

In line with the corporate culture, Zappos provides the tools and the opportunities for employees to become the best they can be. For example, employees are invited to meet with an on-site life coach for assistance in setting and meeting both personal and professional goals. They can sign up to shadow a manager or employee elsewhere in the organization as a way to explore new career possibilities. Work hard, play hard is the rule at Zappos, where holiday parties, picnics, parades, and other special events bring employees together for a bit of fun. These are only some

of the ways that Zappos makes the workplace a "wow" experience for its workforce.

To keep the organization running smoothly, Zappos holds an "all hands" meeting every three months. Videotaped and available online for repeat viewing, these meetings update everyone on the latest departmental and company news, serve as team-building events, and keep employees excited and inspired about working at Zappos. In addition, the firm monitors key performance statistics and posts them at headquarters to inform employees about what's happening to the business, day by day.

Now Zappos is taking on a leadership role in Las Vegas, using its new headquarters in the former city hall as the corporate linchpin in an ambitious plan to revitalize the downtown area. Will Zappos succeed in making its community as happy as its employees and customers?[10]

Questions

1. Do you think Zappos is a decentralized or centralized organization? Do you think it should change? Explain your answer.
2. Of the four types of corporate culture, which most closely describes the culture of Zappos? What are the implications for the organization and for managers and employees?
3. What effect are quarterly meetings and daily postings of performance statistics likely to have on the grapevine inside Zappos?

Building Skills for Career Success

1. Social Media Exercise

Zappos has a reputation for being customer-centered, meaning it embraces the notion that customers come first. One of the ways that it allows employees to communicate with customers is through its blog www.zapposinsights.com/blog.

1. Take a look at this blog. What can you tell about the corporate culture of Zappos?
2. How do they approach customer service? Do you think it works? Why or why not?

2. Building Team Skills

An organization chart is a diagram showing how employees and tasks are grouped and how the lines of communication and authority flow within an organization. These charts can look very different depending on a number of factors, including the nature and size of the business, the way it is departmentalized, its patterns of delegating authority, and its span of management.

Assignment

1. Working in a team, use the following information to draw an organization chart: The KDS Design Center works

closely with two home-construction companies, ACME Homebuilders and Highmass. KDS's role is to help customers select materials for their new homes and to ensure that their selections are communicated accurately to the builders. The company is also a retailer of wallpaper, blinds, and drapery. The retail department, the ACME Homebuilders accounts, and the Highmass accounts make up KDS's three departments. The company has the following positions: president, executive vice president, managers, two appointment coordinators, two ACME Homebuilders coordinators, two Highmass coordinators, two consultants/designers for the Amex and Highmass accounts, 15 retail positions, and four payroll and billing personnel.

2. After your team has drawn the organization chart, discuss the following:
   a. What type of organizational structure does your chart depict? Is it a bureaucratic, matrix, cluster, or network structure? Why?
   b. How does KDS use departmentalization?
   c. To what extent is authority in the company centralized or decentralized?

d. What is the span of management within KDS?

e. Which positions are line positions and which are staff? Why?

3. Prepare a three-page report summarizing what the chart revealed about relationships and tasks at the KDS Design Center and what your team learned about the value of organization charts. Include your chart in your report.

3. Researching Different Careers

In the past, company loyalty and the ability to assume increasing job responsibility usually ensured advancement within an organization. While the reasons for seeking advancement (the desire for a better-paying position, more prestige, and job satisfaction) have not changed, the qualifications for career advancement have. In today's business environment, climbing the corporate ladder requires packaging and marketing yourself. To be promoted within your company or to be considered for employment with another company, it is wise to improve your skills continually. By taking workshops and seminars or enrolling in community college courses, you can keep up with the changing technology in your industry. Networking with people in your business or community can help you to find a new job. Most jobs are filled through personal contacts, proving that who you know can be important.

A list of your accomplishments on the job can reveal your strengths and weaknesses. Setting goals for improvement helps to increase your self-confidence.

Be sure to recognize the signs of job dissatisfaction. If you are feeling unhappy in your job, it may be time to move to another position or company.

Assignment
Are you prepared to climb the corporate ladder? Do a self-assessment by analyzing the following areas and summarize the results in a two-page report.

1. Skills
   - What are your most valuable skills?
   - What skills do you lack?
   - Describe your plan for acquiring new skills and improving your existing skills.

2. Networking
   - How effective are you at using a mentor?
   - Are you a member of a professional organization?
   - In which community, civic, or church groups are you participating?
   - Whom have you added to your contact list in the last six weeks?

3. Accomplishments
   - What achievements have you reached in your job?
   - What would you like to accomplish? What will it take for you to reach your goal?

4. Promotion or new job
   - What is your likelihood for getting a promotion?
   - Are you ready for a change? What are you doing or willing to do to find another job?

Endnotes

1 Based on information in Tom Huddleston, Jr., "McDonald's Latest Recipe to Reverse Declining Sales: More 'Lovin,'" *Fortune*, January 2, 2015, www.fortune.com; Julie Jargon, "McDonald's Plans to Change U.S. Structure," *Wall Street Journal*, October 30, 2014, www.wsj.com; Lisa Jennings and Jonathan Maze, "McDonald's Reorganizes US into Four Regional Divisions," *Nation's Restaurant News*, October 31, 2014, http://nrn.com (accessed June 26, 2015); Julie Jargon, "McDonald's to Pare Menu, Review Ingredients," *Wall Street Journal*, December 10, 2014, www.wsj.com; www.aboutmcdonalds.com (accessed January 15, 2015).

2 Jennifer Alsever, "Job Swaps: Are They for You?" *Fortune*, October 29, 2012, http://management.fortune.cnn.com/2012/10/24/job-swaps/ (accessed June 26, 2015).

3 PepsiCo Corporate Profile website at http://www.pepsico.com/Company/Global-Business-Units/ (accessed October 14, 2014).

4 Nick Turner, "Office Depot to Eliminate 1,100 Jobs in European Division," *Bloomberg*, October 16, 2014, http://www.bloomberg.com/news/2014-10-16/office-depot-to-eliminate-about-1-100-jobs-in-european-division.html (accessed June 26, 2015).

5 "Francesco Guerrera, "UBS Tells Why it Cut off a Limb," *Wall Street Journal*, November 12, 2012, http://online.wsj.com/article/SB1000142412788732389470457811486381797600.2.html (accessed June 26, 2015).

6 Dana Griffin, "Disadvantages of a Line & Staff Organization Structure," *Small Business*, http://smallbusiness.chron.com/disadvantages-line-staff-organization-structure-2762.html (accessed January 15, 2015).

7 Chris Dolmetsch and Keri Geiger, "Barclays Hid Traders' Role After Questions: Schneiderman," *Bloomberg*, September 17, 2014, http://www.bloomberg.com/news/2014-09-16/barclays-hid-traders-role-after-questions-schneiderman.html (accessed June 26, 2015); Matthew Heller, "SEC Fines Barclays $15M for Compliance Omissions," *CFO*, September 24, 2014, http://ww2.cfo.com/regulation/2014/09/sec-fines-barclays-15m-compliance-omissions/ (accessed June 26, 2015); Peter J. Henning, "A Triple Whammy for Barclays," *New York Times*,

November 5, 2012, http://dealbook.nytimes.com/2012/11/05/a-triple-whammy-for-barclays/ (accessed June 26, 2015).

8 Rob Goffee and Gareth Jones, "The Character of a Corporation: How Your Company's Culture Can Make or Break Your Business," *Jones Harper Business*, December 2003, 182.

9 Leslie Kwoh, "To Snag Top Talent, Companies Come out For Gay Rights," *New York Times*, November 13, 2012, http://blogs.wsj.com/atwork/2012/11/13/to-snag-top-talent-companies-come-out-for-gay-rights/ (accessed June 26, 2015); Jenna McGregor, "Corporate America's Gay-Rights Revolution," *The Washington Post*, February 27, 2014, http://www.washingtonpost.com/blogs/on-leadership/wp/2014/02/27/corporate-americas-gay-rights-evolution/ (accessed June 26, 2015).

10 Based on information in "Inside Zappos," https://jobs.zappos.com/ (accessed January 12, 2015); Ryan Mac, "Revenge of the Ripoff: How Zalando Became a $5 Billion Retailing Sensation," *Forbes*, August 18, 2014, http://www.forbes.com/sites/ryanmac/2014/07/30/zalando-europe-zappos-fashion/ (accessed June 26, 2015); "How Zappos' CEO Turned Las Vegas into a Startup Fantasyland," *Wired*, January 21, 2014, http://www.wired.com/2014/01/zappos-tony-hsieh-las-vegas/ (accessed June 26, 2015); Rhymer Rigby, "The Benefits of Workplace Levity," *Financial Times*, December 19, 2012, http://www.ft.com/cms/s/0/3983a83e-492a-11e2-9225-00144feab49a.html#axzz3fcVR33yA (accessed July 11, 2015); Carmine Gallo, "America's Happiest Employee," *Forbes*, December 26, 2012, http://www.forbes.com/sites/carminegallo/2012/12/26/americas-happiest-employee/ (accessed July 11, 2015); Mig Pascual, "Zappos: 5 Out-of-the-Box Ideas for Keeping Employees Engaged," *U.S. News & World Report*, October 30, 2012, http://money.usnews.com (accessed June 26, 2015); Lisa V. Gillespie, "Workplace Culture: Targeting Soft Skills Yields Hard Returns for Employers," *Employee Benefit News*, April 15, 2012, p. 18; Priya de Langen, "The Right Fit at Zappos," *HRM Asia*, January 5, 2012, www.hrmasia.com (accessed June 26, 2015); Cengage "Zappos" video; www.zappos.com (accessed July 11, 2015).

CHAPTER

8

Producing Quality Goods and Services

Why Should You Care?

Think for a moment about the products and services you bought in the past week. Those products and services could not be produced if it weren't for the production activities described in this chapter and that means consumers like you would not be able to purchase the products and services they need or want.

Learning Objectives

Once you complete this chapter, you will be able to:

8-1 Explain the nature of production.

8-2 Outline how the conversion process transforms raw materials, labor, and other resources into finished goods or services.

8-3 Understand the importance of service businesses to consumers, other business firms, and the nation's economy.

8-4 Describe how research and development leads to new products and services.

8-5 Discuss the components involved in planning the production process.

8-6 Explain how purchasing, inventory control, scheduling, and quality control affect production.

8-7 Summarize how technology can make American firms more productive and competitive in the global marketplace.

How Detroit Bikes Makes Bikes in Detroit

Musician and entrepreneur Zak Pashak got the idea for his bicycle manufacturing firm during a taxi ride through downtown Detroit. The cab was weaving around cyclists in the bicycle lanes, which caught Pashak's attention. He realized that more people would try commuting by bicycle if they could ride a sturdy, basic, reasonably-priced bike designed for city streets. Since 99 percent of the bikes sold in the United States are made abroad, he also saw an opportunity to build on Detroit's manufacturing heritage by mass-producing "Made in America" bicycles.

Pashak quickly recruited a handful of employees with manufacturing expertise and purchased a production facility on Detroit's west side with sufficient space to build 40,000 bikes a year. He invested hundreds of thousands of dollars to equip the factory, develop designs, and build prototypes. However, the entrepreneur soon discovered that the high cost of manufacturing every component in Detroit would force him to set too high a price for his bicycles. To keep costs down and prices reasonable, Pashak decided to import many parts but make the bicycle frames and chain guards in his factory, where all bicycles would be assembled.

The company's first product was the A-Type, a name reminiscent of Ford's "Model A" cars made in Detroit a century ago. Although Pashak initially set the ambitious goal of selling 10,000 A-Types during the first year, only 1,000 were actually sold. When he launched his second product, the B-Type, he set a more realistic first-year sales goal of 1,000, and concentrated on expanding distribution.

These days, Detroit Bikes has a workforce of 31 turning out about a dozen bicycles every business day, with new models on the way. It also faces local competition from Shinola and the Detroit Bicycle Company. All this entrepreneurial activity means Detroit is gaining new fame as a center of bicycle manufacturing—a plus for a small business named Detroit Bikes.[1]

Did you know?

Detroit Bikes' mission is "to encourage cycling by making an accessible, enjoyable bicycle while continuing Detroit's legacy of quality manufacturing and design."

Because more and more people are living in metropolitan areas and either walk or ride a bike to work, Zak Pashak, the founder of Detroit Bikes, felt there was a need for a different kind of bike that was sturdy, easy to understand, and easy to ride. Unfortunately, many of the bikes available today are geared toward performance rather than for a daily commute in a large city. A successful musician, music promoter, and entrepreneur, Pashak started Detroit Bikes with a $2 million investment. In addition to investing money, Pashak recruited a talented group of employees—many with a background in Detroit's automotive industry—to design and build bikes that are practical, functional, and reliable. In contrast to other bike manufacturers, the products produced by Detroit Bikes are low maintenance because they have three gears and a coaster brake. High performance bikes have as many as 36 gears or more and hand brakes—both components that often require high maintenance over time. And compared to the cost of a Detroit Bike, high performance bikes cost more. Although the business was slow to start, it is now recognized for quality and craftsmanship, and its bikes are now sold around the globe. According to Pashak, the near-term goal is to sell 50,000 bikes per year to shops from Detroit to Japan. With increased global interest and sales steadily climbing, he is well on his way to achieving his dream.

We begin this chapter with an overview of operations management—the activities required to produce goods and services that meet the needs of customers. In this section, we also discuss the role of manufacturing in the U.S. economy, competition in the global marketplace, and careers in operations management. Next, we describe the conversion process that makes production possible and also note the growing role of services in our economy. Then we examine more closely three important aspects of operations management: developing ideas for new products, planning for production, and effectively controlling operations after production has begun. We close the chapter with a look at the productivity trends and the ways that manufacturing can be improved through the use of technology.

8-1 WHAT IS PRODUCTION?

Have you ever wondered where a new pair of Levi's jeans comes from? Or an Apple iPhone, or a Uniroyal tire for your car? Even factory service on a Maytag clothes dryer would be impossible if it weren't for the activities described in this chapter. In fact, these products and services and millions of others like them would not exist if it weren't for production activities.

Let's begin this chapter by reviewing what an operating manager does. In Chapter 6, we described an *operations manager* as a person who manages the systems that convert resources into goods and services. This area of management is usually referred to as **operations management**, which consists of all the activities required to produce goods and services.

To produce a product or service successfully, a business must perform a number of specific activities. For example, suppose that Ford Motor Company has an idea for a new version of its popular F-150 truck that includes an aluminum body and costs between $30,000 and $50,000. The driving force behind the idea is that a truck with an aluminum body will be 700 pounds lighter than previous models. And a lighter truck equals better gas mileage and saves fuel. Marketing research must determine not only if customers are willing to pay the price for this product but also what additional features they want, and how Ford's new truck compares with the competition. Once marketing research is completed, Ford's operations managers must turn the idea into reality.

operations management all the activities required to produce goods and services

Ford's managers cannot just push the "start button" and immediately begin producing the new truck. As you will see, planning takes place both *before* anything is produced and *during* the production process.

Managers also must concern themselves with the control of operations to ensure that the organization's goals are achieved. For a product such as the Ford F-150 truck, control of operations involves a number of important issues, including product quality, performance standards, the amount of inventory of both raw materials and finished products, and production costs.

We discuss each of the major activities of operations management later in this chapter. First, however, let's take a closer look at American manufacturers and how they compete in the global marketplace.

8-1a How American Manufacturers Compete in the Global Marketplace

After World War II, the United States became the most productive country in the world. For almost 30 years, until the late 1970s, its leadership was never threatened. By then, however, manufacturers in Japan, Germany, Korea, Singapore, Sweden, and other industrialized nations were offering U.S. firms increasing competition. Now the Chinese are manufacturing everything from

Know what this Hasbro employee is holding? Not sure. Ask a young boy. The product—the KRE-O—is the latest line of transformers. While kids love the product, so does Hasbro because it is one of its most profitable product lines. The KRE-O transformers also allow Hasbro to compete with the very popular Lego transformers in both the U.S. and the global marketplace.

© LEV RADIN/SHUTTERSTOCK.COM

sophisticated electronic equipment and automobiles to less expensive everyday items. And yet, in the face of increasing competition, there is both good and bad news for U.S. manufacturers. First the bad news.

THE BAD NEWS FOR MANUFACTURERS The number of Americans employed in the manufacturing sector has decreased. Currently, just over 12 million U.S. workers are employed in manufacturing jobs—down from just over 19 million back in 1979.[2] While there are many additional factors, three major factors explain why employment in this economic sector has declined.

- Many of the U.S. manufacturing jobs that were lost were outsourced to low-wage workers in nations where there are few labor, safety, and environmental regulations.
- It costs about 20 percent more to manufacture goods in the United States than it does anywhere else in the world.[3]
- The number of unemployed factory workers increased during the economic crisis that began in 2008 because of decreased consumer demand for manufactured goods. Although the number of jobs in manufacturing has increased during the economic recovery, manufacturing employment is close to all-time lows.

As a result, manufacturing accounts for only about 9 percent of the current U.S. workforce.[4] Since 1979, 7 million jobs have been lost, and many of those jobs aren't coming back. Experts also predict that U.S. employment in the manufacturing sector will continue to decline to about 11 million jobs between now and the year 2022.[5]

THE GOOD NEWS FOR MANUFACTURERS The United States remains one of the largest manufacturing countries in the world. While some people would argue that "Made in America" doesn't mean what it used to mean, consider the following:

- U.S. manufacturers produce approximately 18 percent of total global manufacturing output.[6]
- Every year, manufacturing contributes about 12 percent of the gross domestic product and almost $2 trillion to the U.S. economy.[7]
- Manufacturing exports are nearly 60 percent of all U.S. exports.[8]
- Compared to other economic activities, manufacturing has a huge multiplier effect. For every $1 spent in manufacturing, an additional $1.35 is generated in the nation's economy because of purchases from suppliers and businesses that support manufacturers.[9]

As a result, the manufacturing sector is still a very important part of the U.S. economy. Although the number of manufacturing jobs has declined, productivity has increased. At least two very important factors account for increases in productivity: First, innovation—finding a better way to produce products—is the key factor that has enabled American manufacturers to compete in the global marketplace. Second, today's workers in the manufacturing sector are highly skilled in order to operate sophisticated equipment. Simply put, Americans are making more goods, but with fewer employees.

Social Media:

Inside Boeing's Factories

Every year, hundreds of jumbo jets roll out of Boeing's factories in Washington state and South Carolina. Now you can take a peek inside these cavernous facilities and see how Boeing aircrafts are designed, assembled, tested, and delivered. You'll find dozens of videos on the company's YouTube Channel (https://www.youtube.com/user/Boeing).

More than 130,000 people subscribe to receive notices of Boeing's new videos as they're posted. If you're interested in high-tech production techniques, you can watch robots painting the wings for a Boeing 777 aircraft. Or take a look at what happens in the interior of a jet as it's being assembled. Or watch employees talking about their area of manufacturing expertise, such as production planning. These videos are the next best thing to a guided tour through a Boeing plant.

Even more good news is that many American manufacturers that outsourced work to factories in foreign nations are once again beginning to manufacture goods in the United States. For our purposes, the term **reshoring** (sometimes referred to as onshoring or insourcing) describes a situation where U.S. manufacturers bring manufacturing jobs back to the United States. For example, General Electric, Ford, Apple, Caterpillar, Honda, Lenovo, Whirlpool, and many other U.S. firms are involved in reshoring. The primary reasons why U.S. firms are "coming back home" include increasing labor costs in foreign nations, higher shipping costs, significant quality and safety issues, faster product development when goods are produced in the United States, and federal and state subsidies to encourage manufactures to produce products in the United States.

Although there are many challenges facing U.S. manufacturers, experts predict that there could be a significant resurgence for manufacturers that can meet current and future challenges. The bottom line: The global marketplace has never been more competitive and successful U.S. firms will focus on the following:

1. Meeting the needs of customers and improving product quality.
2. Motivating employees to cooperate with management and improve productivity.
3. Reducing costs by selecting suppliers that offer higher quality raw materials and components at reasonable prices.
4. Using computer-aided and flexible manufacturing systems that allow a higher degree of customization.
5. Improving control procedures to help ensure lower manufacturing costs.
6. Using green manufacturing to conserve natural resources and sustain the planet.

For most firms, competing in the global marketplace is not only profitable but also an essential activity that requires the cooperation of everyone within the organization.

8-1b Careers in Operations Management

Although it is hard to provide information about specific career opportunities in operations management, some generalizations do apply to this management area. A basic understanding of mass production and the difference between an analytical process and a synthetic process is essential. **Mass production** is a manufacturing process that lowers the cost required to produce a large number of identical or similar products over a long period of time. An **analytical process** breaks raw materials into different component parts. For example, a barrel of crude oil refined by Marathon Oil Corporation—a Texas-based oil and energy exploration company—can be broken down into gasoline, oil, lubricants, and many other petroleum by-products. A **synthetic process** is just the opposite of the analytical one; it combines raw materials or components to create a finished product. Black & Decker uses a synthetic process when it combines plastic, steel, rechargeable batteries, and other components to produce a cordless drill.

Once you understand that operations managers are responsible for producing tangible goods or services that customers want, you must determine how you fit into the production process. Today's successful operations managers must:

1. Be able to motivate and lead people.
2. Understand how technology can make a manufacturer more productive.
3. Appreciate the cost-control processes that help lower production costs and improve product quality.

Margin glossary

reshoring a situation in which U.S. manufacturers bring manufacturing jobs back to the United States

mass production a manufacturing process that lowers the cost required to produce a large number of identical or similar products over a long period of time

analytical process a process in operations management in which raw materials are broken into different component parts

synthetic process a process in operations management in which raw materials or components are combined to create a finished product

Concept Check

✓ List the major activities in operations management.

✓ What steps have U.S. firms taken to regain a competitive edge in the global marketplace?

✓ What is the difference between an analytical and a synthetic manufacturing process? Give an example of each type of process.

CRYSTALEYESTUDIO/DREAMSTIME.COM

4. Understand the relationship between the customer, the marketing of a product, and the production of a product.

If operations management seems like an area you might be interested in, why not do more career exploration?

8-2 THE CONVERSION PROCESS

The purpose of manufacturing or a service business is to provide utility to customers. **Utility** is the ability of a good or service to satisfy a human need. Although there are four types of utilities—form, place, time, and possession—operations management focuses primarily on form utility. **Form utility** is created by people converting raw materials, finances, and information into finished products. The other types of utility—place, time, and possession—are discussed in Chapter 11.

But how does the conversion take place? How does Kellogg's convert corn, sugar, salt, and other ingredients; money from previous sales and stockholders' investments; production workers and managers; and economic and marketing forecasts into Frosted Flakes cereal products? How does H&R Block employ more than 80,000 tax preparers and convert retail locations, computers and software, and advertising and promotion into tax services for its clients. They do so through the use of a conversion process like the one illustrated in Figure 8-1. As indicated by our H&R Block example, the conversion process can be used to produce services.

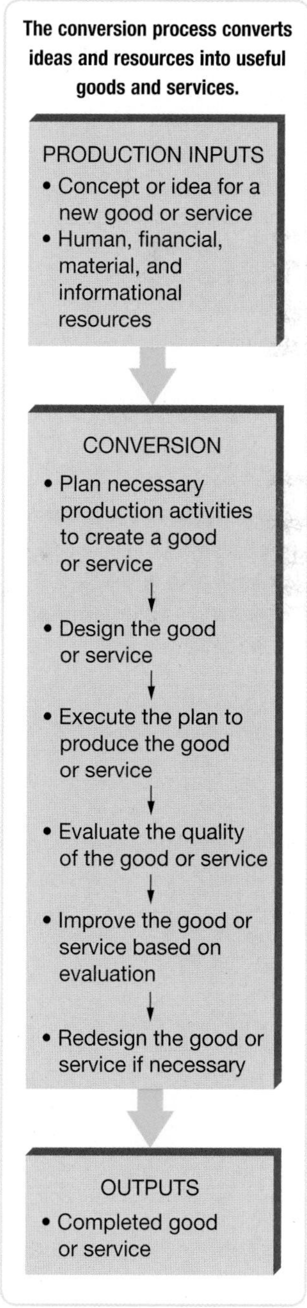

8-2a Manufacturing Using a Conversion Process

The conversion of resources into products and services can be described in several ways. We limit our discussion here to three: the focus or major resource used in the conversion process, its magnitude of change, and the number of production processes employed.

FOCUS By the *focus* of a conversion process, we mean the resource or resources that make up the major or most important *input*. The resources are financial, material, information, and people—the same resources discussed in Chapters 1 and 6. For a bank such as Citibank, financial resources are the major resource. A chemical and energy company such as Chevron concentrates on material resources. Your college or university is concerned primarily with information. And temporary employment services, such as Manpower, focus on the use of human resources.

MAGNITUDE OF CHANGE The *magnitude* of a conversion process is the degree to which the resources are physically changed. At one extreme lie such processes as the one by which the Glad Products Company produces Glad® ClingWrap. Various chemicals in liquid or powder form are combined to produce long, thin sheets of plastic Glad ClingWrap. Here, the original resources are totally unrecognizable in the finished product. At the other extreme, Southwest Airlines produces no physical change in its original resources. The airline simply provides a service and transports people from one location to another.

NUMBER OF PRODUCTION PROCESSES A single firm may employ one production process or many. In general, larger firms that make a variety of products use multiple production processes. For example, GE manufactures some of its own products, buys other merchandise from suppliers, and operates multiple divisions including a finance division, a lighting division, an appliance division, a healthcare division, and other divisions responsible for the products and services that customers

utility the ability of a good or service to satisfy a human need

form utility utility created by people converting raw materials, finances, and information into finished products

Learning Objective

8-2 Outline how the conversion process transforms raw materials, labor, and other resources into finished goods or services.

FIGURE 8-1 The Conversion Process

The conversion process converts ideas and resources into useful goods and services.

PRODUCTION INPUTS
- Concept or idea for a new good or service
- Human, financial, material, and informational resources

CONVERSION
- Plan necessary production activities to create a good or service
- Design the good or service
- Execute the plan to produce the good or service
- Evaluate the quality of the good or service
- Improve the good or service based on evaluation
- Redesign the good or service if necessary

OUTPUTS
- Completed good or service

Towering skyscraper or medieval castle? While we may not be able to answer that question, this future engineer can. Often the conversion process begins with an idea. Then the idea becomes reality when someone takes the next step and begins to focus on the resources needed to develop an idea into a good or service that meets customer needs.

Concept Check

✔ Explain how utility is related to form utility.

✔ In terms of focus, magnitude of change, and number, characterize the production processes used by a local pizza parlor, a dry-cleaning establishment, and an automobile repair shop.

associate with the GE name. Smaller firms, by contrast, may use one production process. For example, Texas-based Advanced Cast Stone, Inc., manufactures one basic product: building materials made from concrete.

8-3 THE INCREASING IMPORTANCE OF SERVICES

Learning Objective

8-3 Understand the importance of service businesses to consumers, other business firms, and the nation's economy.

The application of the basic principles of operations management to the production of services has coincided with a dramatic growth in the number and diversity of service businesses. In 1900, only 28 percent of American workers were employed in service firms. By 1950, this figure had grown to 40 percent, and by the beginning of 2015, it had risen to 86 percent.[10] In fact, the American economy is now characterized as a service economy (see Figure 8-2). A **service economy** is one in which more effort is devoted to the production of services than to the production of goods.

8-3a Planning Quality Services

Today, the managers of restaurants, laundries, real estate agencies, banks, movie theaters, airlines, travel bureaus, and other service firms have realized that they can benefit from the experience of manufacturers. And while service firms are different from manufacturing firms, both types of businesses must complete many of the same activities in order to be successful. For example, as illustrated in the middle section of Figure 8-1, service businesses must plan, design, execute, evaluate, improve, and redesign their services in order to provide the services that their customers want.

For a service firm, planning often begins with determining who the customer is and what needs the customer has. After customer needs are identified, the next step for successful service firms is to develop a plan that will enable the firm to deliver the services that their customers want or need. For example, a swimming pool repair business must develop a business plan that includes a process for hiring and training qualified employees, obtaining necessary parts and supplies, marketing the firm's

service economy an economy in which more effort is devoted to the production of services than to the production of goods

FIGURE 8-2 Service Industries

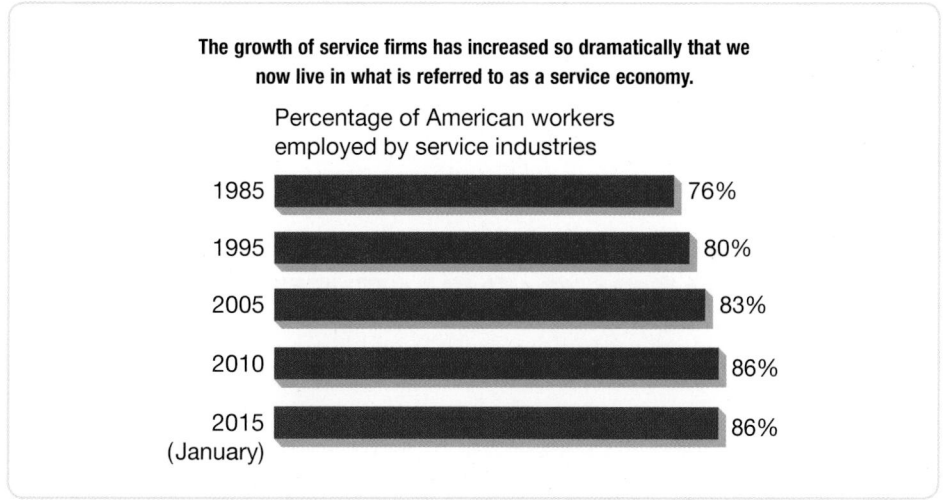

The growth of service firms has increased so dramatically that we now live in what is referred to as a service economy.

Percentage of American workers employed by service industries

Year	Percentage
1985	76%
1995	80%
2005	83%
2010	86%
2015 (January)	86%

Source: U.S. Bureau of Labor Statistics website, www.bls.gov (accessed January 20, 2015).

services, and creating management and accounting systems to control the firm's activities. Once the firm provides a service to a customer, successful firms evaluate the way they operate and measure customer satisfaction. And if necessary, redesign their services to improve the customer's experience.

8-3b Evaluating the Quality of a Firm's Services

The production of services is very different from the production of manufactured goods in the following five ways:

1. When compared to manufactured goods, customers are much more involved in obtaining the service they want or need.
2. Services are consumed immediately and, unlike manufactured goods, cannot be stored. For example, a hair stylist cannot store completed haircuts.
3. Services are provided when and where the customer desires the service. In many cases, customers will not travel as far to obtain a service.
4. Services are usually labor-intensive because the human resource is often the most important resource used in the production of services.
5. Services are intangible, and it is therefore more difficult to evaluate customer satisfaction.[11]

Compared with manufacturers, service firms often listen more carefully to customers and respond more quickly to the market's changing needs. For example, Maggiano's Little Italy restaurant is a chain of eating establishments owned by Brinker International. In order to continuously improve customer service, the restaurant encourages diners to complete online surveys that prompt diners to evaluate the food, atmosphere, service, and other variables. The information from the surveys is then used to fine-tune the way Maggiano's meets its customers' needs. Often, as a reward for completing the survey, diners are given free food the next time they visit a Maggiano's restaurant.

In addition, many service firms are now using social media to build relationships with their customers. Coldwell Banker, one of the largest real estate companies in the United States sponsors an Internet blog—for both residential and commercial clients—that can be used not only to provide information about the current real

Learning Objective

8-4 Describe how research and development leads to new products and services.

estate market, but also as a method to encourage comments and questions from customers.

Now that we understand something about the production process that is used to transform resources into goods *and* services, we can consider three major activities involved in operations management: research and development, planning for production, and operations control.

8-4 WHERE DO NEW PRODUCTS AND SERVICES COME FROM?

Imagine an automobile that can drive itself! Sound like a crazy idea. Think again. At the 2015 Consumer Electronics Show in Las Vegas, Mercedes Benz introduced a concept car that can do just that—drive for you. What's even more astonishing is that Mercedes is not the only company using research and development to create driverless cars. Toyota, Audi, Ford, General Motors, and even Google are attempting to turn a "big" idea into a marketable product. New products—like a driverless car—start with an idea. In fact, no firm can produce a product or service until it has an idea. Then assuming the idea has potential, a company's research and development activities turn the idea into a reality.

8-4a Research and Development

How did we get the Apple iPhone or the MakerBot 3D printer? We got them as a result of people working with new ideas that developed into useful products. These activities generally are referred to as research and development. For our purposes, **research and development (R&D)** involves a set of activities intended to identify new ideas that have the potential to result in new goods and services.

Today, business firms use three general types of R&D activities. *Basic research* consists of activities aimed at uncovering new knowledge. The goal of basic research is scientific advancement, without regard for its potential use in the development of goods and services. *Applied research*, in contrast, consists of activities geared toward discovering new knowledge with some potential use. *Development and implementation* involves research activities undertaken specifically to put new or existing knowledge to use in producing goods and services. For many companies, R&D is a very important part of their business operations. According to Marc Levinson, a researcher for the Congressional Research Service, "U.S. manufacturers spend far more on research and development (R&D) than those in any other country, but manufacturers' R&D spending is rising more rapidly in China, Korea, and Taiwan. Much of the R&D in the United States takes place in high technology industries."[12] The 3M company, for example, has always been known for its development and implementation research activities. Currently, 3M employs 8,400 researchers worldwide and has invested almost $8 billion over the last five years to develop new products designed to make people's lives easier and safer.[13]

8-4b Product Extension and Refinement

If a firm sells only one product or service, when customers quit buying the product or service, the firm will die. To stay in business, the firm must, at the very least, find ways to refine or extend the want-satisfying capability of its product or service. Consider television sets. Since they were introduced in the late 1930s, television sets have been constantly *refined* so that they now provide clearer, sharper pictures with less dial adjusting. During the same time, television sets also were *extended*. There are basic flat-screen televisions without added features, and many others that include

research and development (R&D) a set of activities intended to identify new ideas that have the potential to result in new goods and services

Entrepreneurial Success

Have a New Product Idea? Think Quirky

Quirky is a rather strange name for a successful business that develops and markets dozens of crowdsourced new products every year. Founded by CEO Ben Kaufman, the New York-based company invites consumers to submit ideas for products to help solve a problem or fill a need. Quirky receives as many as 4,000 ideas every week, but turns away ideas that are too complex, too similar to existing products, or too narrowly focused. After screening, the surviving ideas are posted online and the Quirky community votes on each.

Ideas that do well in the vote count are evaluated by industry experts who examine the market, legal and regulatory concerns, and competitive issues. High-potential ideas then move to Quirky's weekly evaluation meeting, which is streamed online while staff members, experts, and hundreds of participating viewers decide which merit further research and development. Next, Quirky creates prototypes to polish the design, finalize the features, and get ready for introduction.

Quirky works quickly. It has created as many as five working prototypes in a day, using 3D printers and other high-tech tools. One product, the Pluck egg yolk extractor, was available in stores within a month of being approved. Quirky rings up $100 million in annual revenues from products sold in 35,000 stores worldwide—sharing the profits with those who originate the ideas and community members who help tweak a product and suggest a name. Already, one entrepreneurial inventor has earned more than $1 million from his winning idea for a pivoting power strip.

Sources: Based on information in J. J. McCorvey, "What Happens When Crowdsourcing Stops Being Polite and Starts Getting Real," *Fast Company Design*, September 9, 2014, www. fastcodesign.com; Serena Altschul, "Today's Quirky Idea May Be Tomorrow's Must-Have Consumer Item," *CBS Sunday Morning*, March 23, 2014, www.cbsnews.com; Steve Lohr, "Quirky to Create a Smart-Home Products Company," *New York Times*, June 22, 2014, www. nytimes.com; Chris Raymond, "How Quirky Turns Ideas into Inventions," *Popular Mechanics*, January 7, 2014, www.popularmechanics.com.

DVD or Blu-Ray players and Apps that can be used to access the Internet. The latest development—high-definition television—has already become the standard. Already Samsung, LG, Sony, and other television manufacturers are taking the next step—4K Ultra High-Definition TV. Ultra high definition displays movies, sports, and other shows at four times the resolution of HD and provides incredible detail on your TV screen.

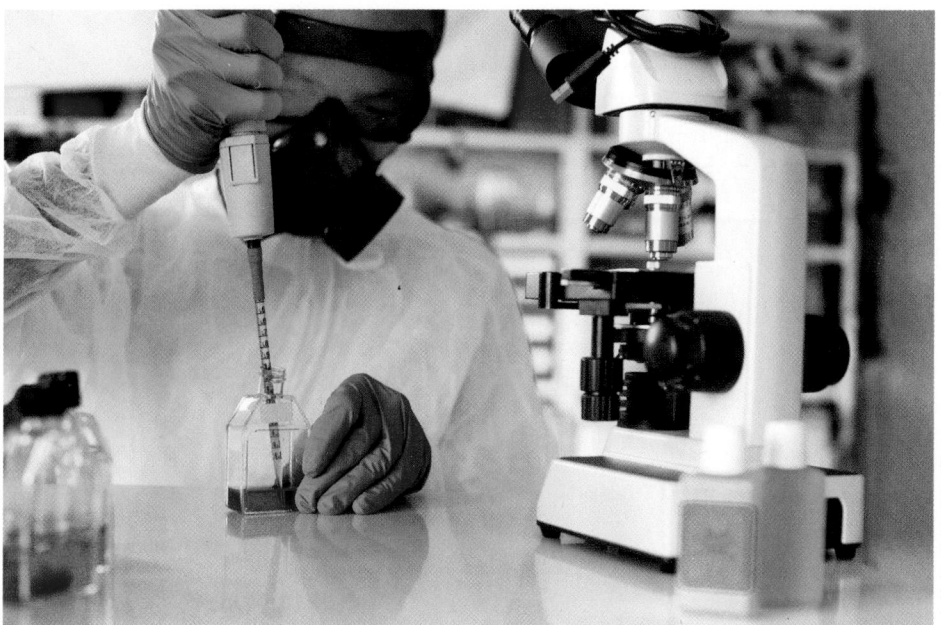

A cure for Ebola! While the world waits, scientists, researchers, and lab technicians are desperately working to find a cure for a disease that kills more than half of the people who contract the disease. Unfortunately, the search for a cure for Ebola and many other diseases is not a perfect science and it takes time, effort, research and development, and money to eventually find a cure for some very serious diseases.

Concept Check

✓ Describe how research and development leads to new products.

✓ What is the difference between basic research, applied research, and development and implementation?

✓ Explain why product extension and refinement are important.

For most firms, extension and refinement are expected results of their research, development, and implementation activities. Each refinement or extension results in an essentially "new" product whose sales make up for the declining sales of a product that was introduced earlier. When consumers were introduced to the original five varieties of Campbell's Soup, they discovered that these soups were of the highest quality, as well as inexpensive, and the soups were an instant success. Although one of the most successful companies at the beginning of the 1900s, Campbell's had to continue to innovate, refine, and extend its product line. For example, many consumers in the United States live in what is called an on-the-go society. To meet this need, Campbell's Soup has developed ready-to-serve products that can be popped into a microwave at work or school. It also continues to develop new soup flavors including Fiesta Chicken Lime Tortilla Soup, Avengers™ Fun Shaped Pasta Soup, and organic products to meet the needs of its customers.

8-5 HOW DO MANAGERS PLAN PRODUCTION?

Learning Objective

8-5 Discuss the components involved in planning the production process.

Only a few of the many ideas for new products ever reach the production stage. For those ideas that do, however, the next step is planning for production. Once a new idea for a product or service has been identified, planning for production involves three different phases: design planning, facilities planning, and operational planning (see Figure 8-3).

8-5a Design Planning

When the R&D staff at Samsung recommended to top management that the firm manufacture and market a "Smart Fridge" with a touch screen, Wi-Fi connectivity, and apps that allow consumers to update their calendars, leave notes to family members, or even provide recipe suggestions, the company could not simply swing into production the next day. Instead, a great deal of time and energy had to be invested in determining what the new refrigerator would look like, where and how

FIGURE 8-3 Planning for Production

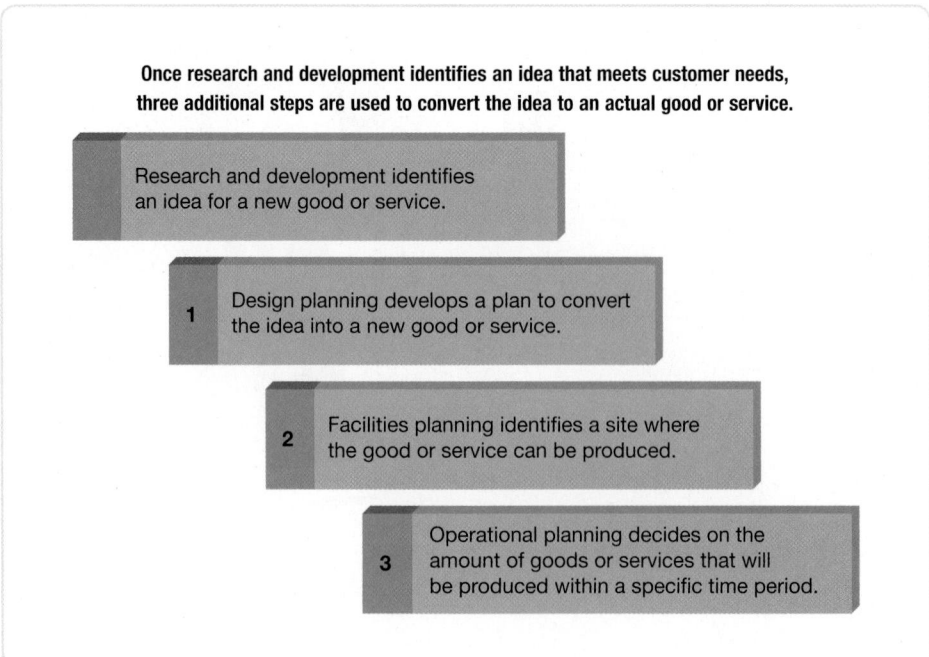

Once research and development identifies an idea that meets customer needs, three additional steps are used to convert the idea to an actual good or service.

Research and development identifies an idea for a new good or service.

1 Design planning develops a plan to convert the idea into a new good or service.

2 Facilities planning identifies a site where the good or service can be produced.

3 Operational planning decides on the amount of goods or services that will be produced within a specific time period.

it would be produced, and what options would be included. These decisions are a part of design planning. **Design planning** is the development of a plan for converting an idea into an actual product or service. The major decisions involved in design planning deal with product line, required capacity, and use of technology.

PRODUCT LINE A **product line** is a group of similar products that differ only in relatively minor characteristics. During the design-planning stage, a manufacturer like Samsung must determine how many different models to produce and what major options to offer. Likewise, a restaurant chain such as Pizza Hut must decide how many menu items to offer.

An important issue in deciding on the product line is to balance customer preferences and production requirements. Typically, marketing personnel want a "long" product line that offers customers many options. Because a long product line with more options gives customers greater choice, it is easier to sell products that meet the needs of individual customers. On the other hand, operations managers and production personnel generally want a "short" product line with fewer options because products are easier to produce.

Once the product line has been determined, each distinct product within the product line must be designed. **Product design** is the process of creating a set of specifications from which a product can be produced. For example, product engineers for Samsung must make sure that their new "Smart Fridge" keeps food frozen in the freezer compartment. At the same time, they must make sure that lettuce and tomatoes do not freeze in the crisper section of the refrigerator. The need for a complete product design is fairly obvious; products that work cannot be manufactured without it. But services should be designed carefully as well—and *for the same reason.*

REQUIRED PRODUCTION CAPACITY Capacity is the amount of products or services that an organization can produce in a given period of time. Remember Detroit Bikes—the company profiled in the Inside Business feature for this chapter. The company's capacity is up to 40,000 bikes per year in its present facilities. The capacity of a Panasonic assembly plant might be 1.3 million high-definition televisions per year. Operations managers—again working with the firm's marketing managers—must determine the required capacity. This, in turn, determines the

design planning the development of a plan for converting an idea into an actual product or service

product line a group of similar products that differ only in relatively minor characteristics

product design the process of creating a set of specifications from which a product can be produced

capacity the amount of products or services that an organization can produce in a given time

Who needs a driver? This Mercedes Benz can drive you where you want to go. In addition to Mercedes, Toyota, Audi, Ford, General Motors, and even Google are all developing driverless cars. Of course, one of the most important factors required to turn any idea—like a driverless car—into reality is design planning—the development of a plan for converting an idea into an actual product or service.

© KOBBY DAGAN/SHUTTERSTOCK.COM

amount of goods and services that will be produced and the size of the production facility. If the facility is built with too much capacity, valuable resources (plant, equipment, and money) will lie idle. If the facility offers insufficient capacity, additional capacity may have to be added later when it is much more expensive than in the initial building stage.

Capacity means about the same thing to service businesses. For example, the capacity of a restaurant such as the Hard Rock Cafe in Nashville, Tennessee, is the number of customers it can serve at one time.

USE OF TECHNOLOGY During the design-planning stage, management must determine the degree to which *automation* and *technology* will be used to produce a product or service. Here, there is a trade-off between high initial costs and low operating costs (for automation) and low initial costs and high operating costs (for human labor). Ultimately, management must choose between a labor-intensive technology and a capital-intensive technology. A **labor-intensive technology** is a process in which people must do most of the work. Housecleaning services and the New York Yankees baseball team, for example, are labor-intensive. A **capital-intensive technology** is a process in which machines and equipment do most of the work. A Sony automated assembly plant is capital intensive because there are fewer workers that operate automated machinery. In many situations, people and technology are combined to create the most efficient and most cost effective method to produce goods or services.

8-5b Site Selection and Facilities Planning

Generally, a business will choose to produce a new product in an existing factory as long as (1) the existing factory has enough capacity to handle customer demand for both the new product and established products and (2) the cost of refurbishing an existing factory is less than the cost of building a new one.

After exploring the capacity of existing factories, management may decide to build a new production facility. In determining where to locate production facilities, management must consider a number of variables, including the following:

- Locations of major customers and suppliers.
- Availability and cost of skilled and unskilled labor.
- Quality of life for employees and management in the proposed location.
- The cost of land and building costs.
- Local and state taxes, environmental regulations, and zoning laws.
- The amount of financial support and subsidies, if any, offered by local and state governments.
- Special requirements, such as great amounts of energy or water used in the production process.

Before making a final decision about where a proposed plant will be located and how it will be organized, two other factors—human resources and plant layout—should be examined.

HUMAN RESOURCES Several issues involved in site selection and facilities planning fall within the province of human resources managers. When Nestlé built its new 900,000-square-foot production facility to make liquid Nesquik® and Coffee-Mate® products in Anderson, Indiana, human resources managers were involved to make sure the necessary employees needed to staff and operate the plant were available. And when a company decides to build a new facility in a foreign country, again human resources managers are involved. For example, suppose that a U.S. firm like General Motors wants to lower labor costs by importing component parts from China. It has two choices. It can build its own manufacturing facility in a foreign country or it can outsource production to local firms. In either case, human resources

labor-intensive technology a process in which people must do most of the work

capital-intensive technology a process in which machines and equipment do most of the work

become involved in the decision. If the decision is made to build its own plant, human resources managers will have to recruit employees with the appropriate skills who are willing to relocate to a foreign country, develop training programs for local Chinese workers, or both. On the other hand, if the decision is made to outsource production to local suppliers, human resources managers must make sure that local suppliers are complying with the U.S. company's human rights policies and with all applicable national and local wage and hour laws. For General Motors, selecting suppliers in foreign countries is an important consideration when determining where to buy component parts. At a recent awards ceremony, General Motors recognized 76 companies representing 16 different countries with its Supplier of the Year award.

PLANT LAYOUT Plant layout is the arrangement of machinery, equipment, and personnel within a production facility. Three general types of plant layout are used (see Figure 8-4).

The *process layout* is used when different operations are required for creating small batches of different products or working on different parts of a product. The plant is arranged so that each operation is performed in its own particular area.

plant layout the arrangement of machinery, equipment, and personnel within a production facility

FIGURE 8-4 Facilities Planning

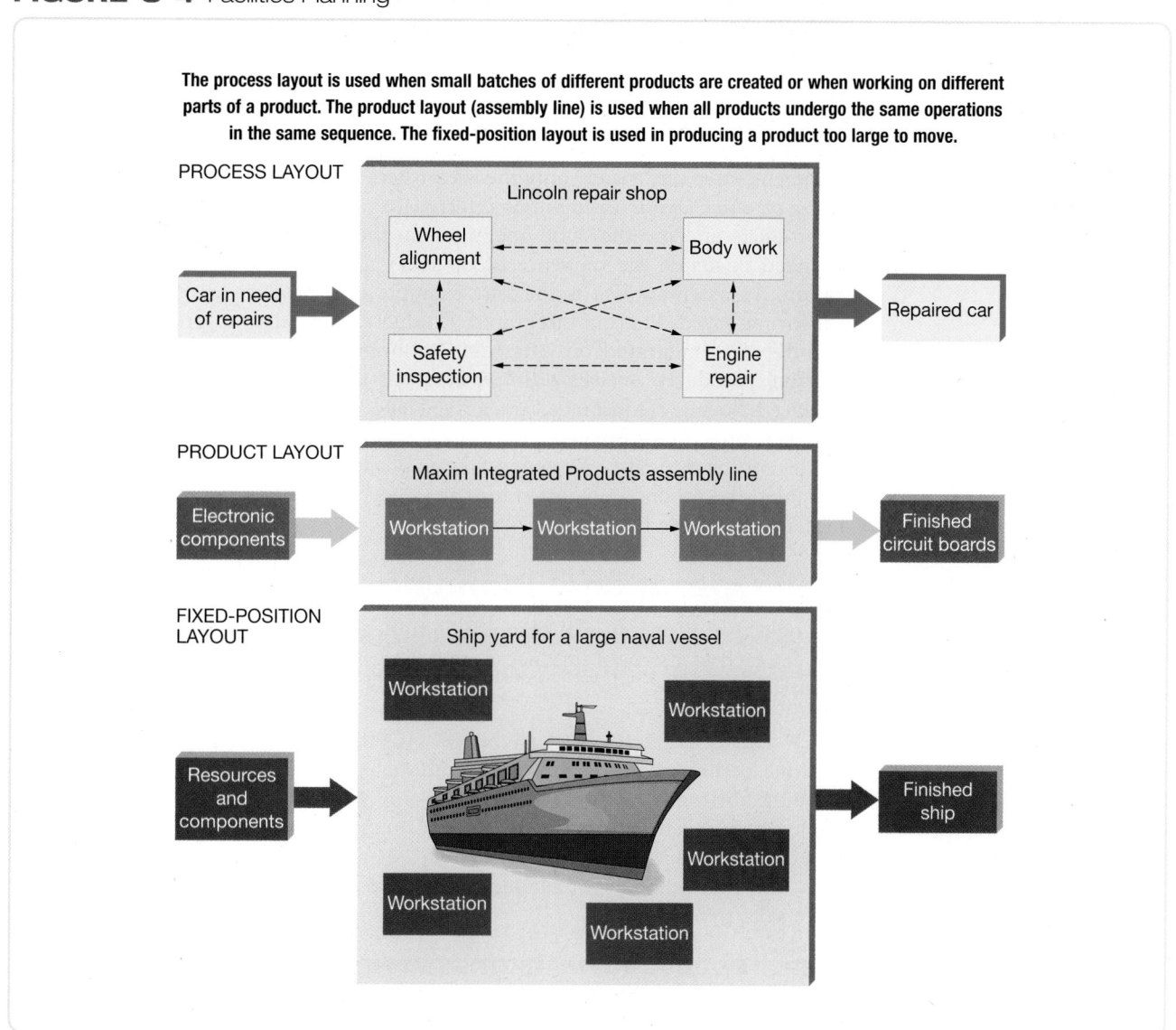

The process layout is used when small batches of different products are created or when working on different parts of a product. The product layout (assembly line) is used when all products undergo the same operations in the same sequence. The fixed-position layout is used in producing a product too large to move.

A "BIG" parking jam. At this Boeing assembly plant, space is at a premium because the finished product—a 757 jetliner—is so big. To see how large each airliner is, compare its size with the people in the photo. When a product is this large, it is easier to move people, machinery, and parts to where they are needed instead of moving the plane.

MATTHEW MCVAY/PHOTOS.COM

An auto repair facility at a local automobile dealership provides an example of a process layout. The various operations may be engine repair, bodywork, wheel alignment, and safety inspection. If you take your Lincoln Navigator for a wheel alignment, your car "visits" only the area where alignments are performed.

A *product layout* (sometimes referred to as an *assembly line*) is used when all products undergo the same operations in the same sequence. Workstations are arranged to match the sequence of operations, and work flows from station to station. An assembly line is the best example of a product layout. For example, California-based Maxim Integrated Products, Inc., uses a product layout to manufacture integrated circuits and components for consumer and business electronic products. A *fixed-position layout* is used when a very large product is produced. Boeing, for instance, uses a fixed layout plant arrangement because of the size of its products—commercial airliners. Shipbuilders also use this type of layout because of the difficulty of moving a large product such as an ocean liner. In both examples, the product remains stationary, and people and machines are moved as needed to assemble the product.

8-5c Operational Planning

The objective of operational planning is to decide on the amount of products or services each facility will produce during a specific period of time. Four steps are required.

STEP 1: SELECTING A PLANNING HORIZON A **planning horizon** is simply the time period during which an operational plan will be in effect. A common planning horizon for production plans is one year. Then, before each year is up, management must plan for the next. A planning horizon of one year generally is long enough to average out seasonal increases and decreases in sales. At the same time, it is short enough for planners to adjust production to accommodate long-range sales trends.

STEP 2: ESTIMATING MARKET DEMAND The *market demand* for a product is the quantity that customers will purchase at the going price. This quantity must be estimated for the time period covered by the planning horizon. Sales projections

planning horizon the period during which an operational plan will be in effect developed by marketing managers are the basis for market-demand estimates.

STEP 3: COMPARING MARKET DEMAND WITH CAPACITY The third step in operational planning is to compare the estimated market demand with the facility's capacity to satisfy that demand. (Remember that capacity is the amount of products or services that an organization can produce in a given time period.) One of three outcomes may result: Demand may exceed capacity, capacity may exceed demand, or capacity and demand may be equal. If they are equal, the facility should be operated at full capacity. However, if market demand and capacity are not equal, adjustments may be necessary.

STEP 4: ADJUSTING PRODUCTS OR SERVICES TO MEET DEMAND The biggest reason for changes to a firm's production schedule is changes in the amount of products or services that a company sells to its customers. For example, Indiana-based Berry Plastics produces all kinds of plastic products. One particularly successful product line for Berry Plastics is drink cups that can be

A Marie Callender pie that tastes as good as it looks. For just a moment, assume you are the production manager responsible for making thousands of pies like this one. What would your factory look like? How could plant layout improve productivity? How would you manage human resources, purchasing, and quality control? All good questions that should be answered before a single pie is produced.

Career Success

How Would You Plan for Peak Holiday Deliveries?

Imagine you work for an express package delivery service. You must prepare to deliver more than 20 million packages in a single December day, regardless of the weather. You don't know how many packages you'll handle on any given day, nor do you know where these packages are headed. You do know that if even a small fraction of these deliveries are late, a lot of recipients will be disappointed—and the shippers will be unhappy, as well.

These are challenges that FedEx and UPS face every year in planning capacity to meet peak demand for on-time deliveries during the holidays—creating career opportunities in many fields. Consider FedEx's Memphis hub, which unloads cargo from 160 jets every evening. Before sunrise, 1.8 million packages will ride 42 miles of conveyor belts to be loaded on outbound jets for delivery. That means jobs inside the sorting facility, transportation and maintenance jobs on the ground and in the air, plus engineers to plan the physical plant and data analysts to identify efficiencies.

Both UPS and FedEx employ meteorologists, so they can be ready to reroute planes and trucks around storms. They have logistics experts to devise creative ways of increasing temporary capacity—such as mobile sorting centers that can be shifted from place to place as demand fluctuates. And they have human resources planning experts to project how many extra employees will be needed for the peak season. During one recent holiday season, UPS hired 95,000 seasonal employees for its sorting and delivery operations, based on what its experts projected.

Sources: Based on information in Hiroko Tabuchi, "Crunch Time for FedEx and UPS as Last-Minute Shipping Ramps Up," *New York Times*, December 21, 2014, www.nytimes.com; Nick Carey, "UPS, FedEx Seek Ways to Manage Massive Peak Season Package Bulge," *Reuters.com*, October 23, 2014; Mae Anderson, "Retailers and Package Deliverers Take on Peak Shipping Volume Days Before Christmas," *Minneapolis Star-Tribune*, December 22, 2014, www.startribune.com; Aamer Madhani, "UPS Hopes for a Merrier Christmas in 2014," *USA Today*, December 14, 2014, www.usatoday.com.

screen-printed to promote a company or its products or services.[14] If Berry Plastics obtains a large contract to provide promotional cups to a large fast-food chain such as Sonic, Whataburger, or McDonald's, the company may need to work three shifts a day, seven days a week, until the contract is fulfilled. Unfortunately, the reverse is also true. If the company's sales force does not generate new sales, there may be only enough work for the employees on one shift.

When market demand exceeds capacity, several options are available to a firm. Production of products or services may be increased by operating the facility overtime with existing personnel or by starting a second or third work shift. For manufacturers, another response is to subcontract or outsource a portion of the work to other manufacturers. If the excess demand is likely to be permanent, the firm may expand the current facility or build another facility.

What happens when capacity exceeds market demand? Again, there are several options. To reduce output temporarily, workers may be laid off or the facility may be operated on a shorter-than-normal workweek. To adjust to a permanently decreased demand, management may shift the excess capacity of a manufacturing facility to the production of other goods or services. The most radical adjustment is to eliminate the excess capacity by selling unused manufacturing facilities.

Concept Check

✓ What are the major elements of design planning?

✓ Define capacity. Why is it important for a manufacturing business or a service business?

✓ What factors should be considered when selecting a site for a new manufacturing facility?

✓ What is the objective of operational planning? What four steps are used to accomplish this objective?

Learning Objective

8-6 Explain how purchasing, inventory control, scheduling, and quality control affect production.

8-6 OPERATIONS CONTROL

We have discussed the development of an idea for a product or service and the planning that translates that idea into the reality. Now we are ready to begin the production process. In this section, we examine four important areas of operations control: purchasing, inventory control, scheduling, and quality control (see Figure 8-5).

8-6a Purchasing

Purchasing consists of all the activities involved in obtaining required materials, supplies, components (or subassemblies), and parts from other firms. Levi Strauss, for example, must purchase denim cloth, thread, and zippers before it can produce a single pair of jeans.

The objective of purchasing is to ensure that required materials are available when they are needed, in the proper amounts, and at minimum cost. Generally, the company with purchasing needs and suppliers must develop a working relationship built on trust. In addition, many companies believe that purchasing is one area where they can promote diversity. For example, AT&T developed a Supplier Diversity Program in 1968. Today, goals for the AT&T program include purchasing a total of 21.5 percent of all products and services from minorities, women, and disabled

purchasing all the activities involved in obtaining required materials, supplies, components, and parts from other firms

FIGURE 8-5 Four Aspects of Operations Control

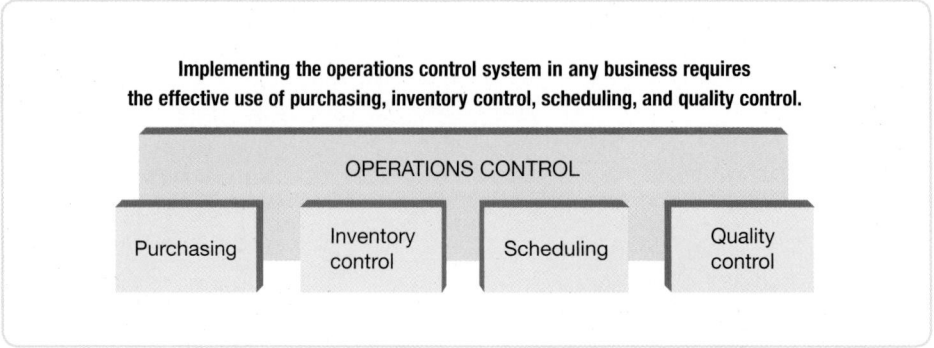

Implementing the operations control system in any business requires the effective use of purchasing, inventory control, scheduling, and quality control.

OPERATIONS CONTROL

| Purchasing | Inventory control | Scheduling | Quality control |

veteran business enterprises. In recent years, it has exceeded the goal of 21.5 percent and purchases more than $15 billion in merchandise and supplies from diverse businesses that obtain AT&T supplier certification. In recognition of its efforts to promote diverse and minority businesses, AT&T has received awards from the Women's Business Enterprise National Council, Diversity, Inc., DiversityBusiness. com and other national organizations.[15]

Purchasing personnel should constantly be on the lookout for new or backup suppliers, even when their needs are being met by their present suppliers, because problems such as strikes and equipment breakdowns can cut off the flow of purchased materials from a primary supplier at any time.

The choice of suppliers should result from careful analysis of a number of factors. The following are especially critical:

- *Price*. Comparing prices offered by different suppliers is always an essential part of selecting a supplier.
- *Quality*. Purchasing specialists always try to buy materials at a level of quality in keeping with the type of product being manufactured. The lowest acceptable quality is usually specified by product designers.
- *Reliability*. An agreement to purchase high-quality materials at a low price is the purchaser's dream. However, the dream becomes a nightmare if the supplier does not deliver.
- *Credit terms*. Purchasing specialists should determine if the supplier demands immediate payment or will extend credit.
- *Shipping costs*. The question of who pays the shipping costs should be answered before any supplier is chosen.

8-6b Inventory Control

Can you imagine what would happen if a Coca-Cola manufacturing plant ran out of the company's familiar red-and-white aluminum cans? It would be impossible to complete the manufacturing process and ship soft drinks to retailers. Management would be forced to shut the assembly line down until the next shipment of cans arrived from a supplier. The simple fact is that shutdowns are expensive because costs such as wages, rent, utilities, insurance, and other expenses still must be paid.

Operations managers are concerned with three types of inventories. A *raw-materials inventory* consists of materials that will become part of the product during the production process. The *work-in-process inventory* consists of partially completed products. The *finished-goods inventory* consists of completed goods. Each type of inventory also has a *holding cost*, or storage cost, and a *stock-out cost*, the cost of running out of inventory. **Inventory control** is the process of managing inventories in such a way as to minimize inventory costs, including both holding costs and potential stock-out costs.

Today, computer systems are being used to track inventory levels and alert managers to impending stock-outs. One of the most sophisticated methods of inventory control used today is materials requirements planning. **Materials requirements planning (MRP)** is a computerized system that integrates production planning and inventory control. One of the great advantages of an MRP system is its ability to juggle delivery schedules and lead times effectively. For a complex product such as an automobile with 4,000 or more individual parts, it is virtually impossible for individual managers to oversee the hundreds of parts that go into the finished product. However, a manager using an MRP system can arrange both order and delivery schedules so that materials, parts, and supplies arrive when they are needed.

Because large firms can incur huge inventory costs, much attention has been devoted to inventory control. The just-in-time system being used by some businesses

inventory control the process of managing inventories in such a way as to minimize inventory costs, including both holding costs and potential stock-out costs

materials requirements planning (MRP) a computerized system that integrates production planning and inventory control

Consider what happens when a firm doesn't have any inventory. In a manufacturing plant, everything shuts down until the raw materials, component parts, or subassemblies are delivered. Inventory is also a problem for retailers that sell finished goods because many customers won't wait, but simply purchase alternate goods from another business. That's why these two employees are pouring over inventory levels and making important decisions that determine when it's time to reorder inventory.

is one result of all this attention. A **just-in-time inventory (JIT) system** is designed to ensure that materials or supplies arrive at a facility just when they are needed so that storage and holding costs are minimized. For example, managers using a just-in-time inventory system at a Harley Davidson assembly plant determine the number of motorcycles that will be assembled in a specified time period. Then Harley Davidson purchasing personnel order just the parts needed to produce those motorcycles. In turn, suppliers deliver the parts in time or when they are needed on the assembly line. The benefits for Harley Davidson are enormous and include decreased inventory levels and a much more efficient manufacturing process that reduces costs and increases profits. While stories of large firms like Harley Davidson, Dell, and Toyota are common, smaller firms can also use JIT to reduce costs and improve profitability. For example, fast-food restaurants, florists, and print-on-demand publishing can all use the same JIT principles that larger firms use—and for the same reasons.

Without proper inventory control, it is impossible for operations managers to schedule the work required to produce goods and services that can be sold to customers.

8-6c Scheduling

Scheduling is the process of ensuring that materials and other resources are at the right place at the right time. As our definition implies, both place and time are important to scheduling. The *routing* of materials is the sequence of workstations that the materials will follow. Assume that Hickory White—a furniture company based in North Carolina—is scheduling production of an oval coffee table made from cherry wood. Operations managers route the needed materials (wood, screws, packaging materials, etc.) through a series of individual workstations along an assembly line. At each workstation, a specific task is performed, and then the partially finished coffee table moves to the next workstation. When routing materials, operations managers are especially concerned with the sequence of each step of the production process. For the coffee table, the top and legs must be cut before the wood is finished. (If the wood were finished before being cut, the finish would be ruined, and the coffee table would have to be stained again.)

When scheduling production, managers also are concerned with timing. The *timing* function specifies when the materials will arrive at each station and how long they will remain there. For the cherry coffee table, it may take workers 30 minutes to cut the table top and legs and another 30 minutes to drill the holes and assemble the table. Before packaging the coffee table for shipment, it must be finished with cherry stain and allowed to dry. This last step may take as long as three days depending on weather conditions and humidity.

Regardless of whether the finished product requires a simple or complex production process, operations managers are responsible for monitoring schedules—called *follow-up*—to ensure that the work flows according to the schedule.

8-6d Quality Control

Over the years, more and more managers have realized that quality is an essential "ingredient" of the good or service being produced. This view of quality provides several benefits. The number of defects decreases, which causes profits to increase.

just-in-time inventory (JIT) system a system designed to ensure that materials or supplies arrive at a facility just when they are needed so that storage and holding costs are minimized

scheduling the process of ensuring that materials and other resources are at the right place at the right time

Furthermore, making products or completing services right the first time reduces many of the rejects and much of the rework.

As mentioned earlier in this chapter, American business firms that compete in the very competitive global marketplace have taken another look at the importance of improving quality. Today, there is even a national quality award. The **Malcolm Baldrige National Quality Award** is given by the President of the United States to organizations judged to be outstanding in specific managerial tasks that lead to improved quality for both products and services. Past winners include PricewaterhouseCoopers, Nestlé Purina Petcare, Boeing Aerospace, and Ritz-Carlton Hotels, among many others. All Baldrige winners have one factor in common: They use quality control to improve their firm's products or services.

Quality control is the process of ensuring that goods and services are produced in accordance with design specifications. The major objective of quality control is to see that the organization lives up to the standards it has set for itself on quality. Some firms, such as Mercedes-Benz, have built their reputations on quality. Other firms adopt a strategy of emphasizing lower prices along with reasonable (but not particularly high) quality. Today, many firms use the techniques described in Table 8-1 to gather information and statistics that can be used to improve the quality of a firm's products or services.

Although the techniques described in Table 8-1 can provide information and statistics, it is people who must act on the information and make changes to improve the production process. And the firm's employees are often the most important component needed to improve quality.

IMPROVING QUALITY THROUGH EMPLOYEE PARTICIPATION One of the first steps needed to improve quality is employee participation. Simply put:

Personal App

Nobody likes complaints!

PATHDOC/FOTOLIA

You don't want to buy a shoddy product, and a company doesn't want to gain a reputation for poor quality. In addition to just complaining about your problem, you can actually help by providing feedback to companies to pinpoint problems and identify areas where quality improvement is needed.

Malcolm Baldrige National Quality Award an award given by the President of the United States to organizations judged to be outstanding in specific managerial tasks that lead to improved quality for both products and services

quality control the process of ensuring that goods and services are produced in accordance with design specifications

TABLE 8-1 Four Widely Used Techniques to Improve the Quality of a Firm's Products.

Technique	Description
Benchmarking	A process of comparing the way a firm produces products or services to the methods used by organizations known to be leaders in an industry in order to determine the "best practices" that can be used to improve quality.
Continuous Improvement	Continuous improvement is a never-ending effort to eliminate problems and improve quality. Often this method involves many small changes or steps designed to improve the production process on an ongoing basis.
Statistical Process Control (SPC)	Sampling to obtain data that are plotted on control charts and graphs to see if the production process is operating as it should and to pinpoint problem areas.
Statistical Quality Control (SQC)	A detailed set of specific statistical techniques used to monitor all aspects of the production process to ensure that both work-in-process and finished products meet the firm's quality standards.

Successful firms encourage employees to accept full responsibility for the quality of their work. When Toyota, once the role model for world-class manufacturing, faced a quality crisis, the company announced a quality-improvement plan based on its famous "Toyota Way." One tenet of the Toyota Way is the need to solve problems at their source, which allows factory workers to stop the production line if necessary to address a problem. Another tenet that enabled Toyota to resolve quality problems was the use of quality circles designated to deal with difficulties as they arise. A **quality circle** is a team of employees who meet on company time to solve problems of product quality. Quality circles have also been used successfully in companies such as IBM, Northrop Grumman Corporation, Lockheed Martin, and GE.

Increased effort is also being devoted to **inspection**, which is the examination of the quality of work-in-process. Employees perform inspections at various times during production. Purchased materials may be inspected when they arrive at the production facility. Component parts may be inspected before they become part of a finished product. In addition, finished goods may be inspected before they are shipped to customers. Items that are within design specifications continue on their way. Those that are not within design specifications are removed from production.

Total quality management (TQM) can also be used to improve quality of a firm's products or services. As noted in Chapter 6, a TQM program coordinates the efforts directed at improving customer satisfaction, increasing employee participation, strengthening supplier partnerships, and facilitating an organizational atmosphere of continuous quality improvement. Firms such as American Express, AT&T, Motorola, and Hewlett-Packard all have used TQM to improve product quality and, ultimately, customer satisfaction.

Another technique that businesses may use to improve not only quality but also overall performance is Six Sigma. **Six Sigma** is a disciplined approach that relies on statistical data and improved methods to eliminate defects for a firm's products and services. Although many experts agree that Six Sigma is similar to TQM, Six Sigma often has more top-level support, much more teamwork, and a new corporate attitude or culture.[16] The companies that developed, refined, and have the most experience with Six Sigma are Motorola, GE, Ford, and Honeywell. Although each of these companies is a corporate giant, the underlying principles of Six Sigma can be used by any firm, regardless of size.

quality circle a team of employees who meet on company time to solve problems of product quality

inspection the examination of the quality of work-in-process

Six Sigma a disciplined approach that relies on statistical data and improved methods to eliminate defects for a firm's products and services

International Organization for Standardization (ISO) a network of national standards institutes and similar organizations from over 160 different countries that is charged with developing standards for quality products and services that are traded throughout the globe

WORLD QUALITY STANDARDS: ISO 9000 AND ISO 14000 Without a common standard of quality, customers may be at the mercy of manufacturers and vendors. As the number of companies competing in the global marketplace has increased, so has the seriousness of this problem. To deal with the problem of standardization, the International Organization for Standardization, a nongovernmental organization with headquarters in Geneva, Switzerland, was created. The **International Organization for Standardization (ISO)** is a network of national standards institutes and similar organizations from over 160 different countries that is charged with developing standards for quality products and services that are traded throughout the globe.[17] Standardization is achieved through consensus agreements between national delegations representing all the economic stakeholders—suppliers, customers, and often governments. The member organization for the United States is the American National Standards Institute located in Washington, D.C.

Although certification is not a legal requirement to conduct business globally, ISO standards are so prevalent around the globe that many customers refuse to do business with noncertified companies. As an added bonus, companies completing the certification process often discover new, cost-efficient ways to improve their existing quality-control programs.

In 1987, the panel published ISO 9000 (*iso* is Greek for "equal"), which sets the guidelines for quality management procedures that manufacturers and service providers must use to receive certification. Certification by independent auditors and laboratory testing services serves as evidence that a company meets the standards for quality control procedures in design, production processes, and product testing.

As a continuation of this standardization process, the ISO has developed many different standards for businesses that provide goods and services to customers around the globe. For example, the ISO 14000 is a family of international standards for incorporating environmental concerns into operations and product standards. ISO standards are also updated periodically.

8-6e Production Planning: A Summary

In this chapter, the activities that firms use to produce products and services have been described. Now, toward the end of the chapter, it may help to look at a table to see how all of the "pieces of the puzzle" fit together. At the top of Table 8-2, planning for production begins with research and development, design planning, site selection and facilities planning, and operational planning—all topics described in this chapter. In the middle of Table 8-2, activities that were described in the Operations Control section (purchasing, inventory control, scheduling, and quality control) are summarized. The goal of all the planning activities in the top section and operations control activities in the middle section is to create and produce a successful product or service. Of course, the steps for planning production and operations control should always be evaluated to determine if the firm's activities can be improved.

Concept Check

✓ Why is selecting a supplier important? What factors should be considered when selecting a supplier?

✓ What costs must be balanced and minimized through inventory control?

✓ Explain in what sense scheduling is a control function of operations managers.

✓ How can a business firm improve the quality of its products or services?

TABLE 8-2 Production Planning: A Summary

Both planning for production and operations control are necessary if a firm is to produce a successful product or service.

The Process Begins with Planning for Production
1. *Research and Development* identifies ideas for a product or service.
2. *Design Planning* develops a plan for producing a product or service.
3. *Site Selection and Facilities Planning* identifies a production site, a plant layout, and if human resources are available.
4. *Operational Planning* decides on the amount of products or services that will be produced.

Then Four Operations Control Steps Are Used to Produce a Product or Service
1. *Purchasing* obtains required materials, supplies, and parts from other firms.
2. *Inventory Control* ensures that materials, supplies, and parts are available when needed.
3. *Scheduling* ensures that materials and other resources are at the right place and at the right time in the production process.
4. *Quality Control* determines if the firm has lived up to the standards it has set for itself on the quality of its products or services.

The End Result: A Successful Product or Service

8-7 IMPROVING PRODUCTIVITY WITH TECHNOLOGY

Learning Objective

8-7 Summarize how technology can make American firms more productive and competitive in the global marketplace.

No coverage of operations management would be complete without a discussion of productivity and technology. Productivity concerns all managers, but it is especially important to operations managers, the people who must oversee the creation of a firm's goods or services. In Chapter 1, *productivity* was defined as the average level of output per worker per hour. Hence, if each worker at plant A produces 75 units per day and each worker at plant B produces only 70 units per day, the workers at plant A are more productive. If one fast-food employee serves 25 customers per hour and another serves 28 per hour, the second employee is more productive.

8-7a Productivity Trends

For U.S. businesses, overall manufacturing productivity growth for output per hour averaged 2.1 percent for the period 2004–2014.[18] More specifically, the U.S. productivity growth rate for the first three quarters of 2014 was 3.2 percent.[19] (*Note:* At the time of publication, 2014 was the last year that actual statistics were available.) While the 3.2 percent increase in productivity for 2014 was slightly higher when compared with average productivity growth over the 2004–2014 period, economists, business leaders, and government officials point to the need for even larger increases in the future. In reality, there are many factors that account for increases or decreases in productivity growth rates for any country. For example, as illustrated in Figure 8-6, U.S. productivity growth was zero in 2008—the beginning of a global economic crisis. To make matters worse, it actually declined to a *negative* 0.3 percent in 2009.[20] Fortunately, as the economy began to improve, so did U.S. productivity growth rates. Many other nations in the world experienced the same pattern of growth and decline in productivity during this same time period. And for some nations including Finland, the United Kingdom, Singapore, and Australia low

FIGURE 8-6 U.S. Productivity Growth Rates

This chart describes manufacturing productivity growth rates for U.S. businesses for the period 2004 to 2014—the latest statistics available prior to publication.

(First 3 Quarters) 2014	3.2
2013	2.0
2012	1.0
2011	0.8
2010	6.2
2009	−0.3
2008	
2007	3.4
2006	0.4
2005	4.2
2004	2.4

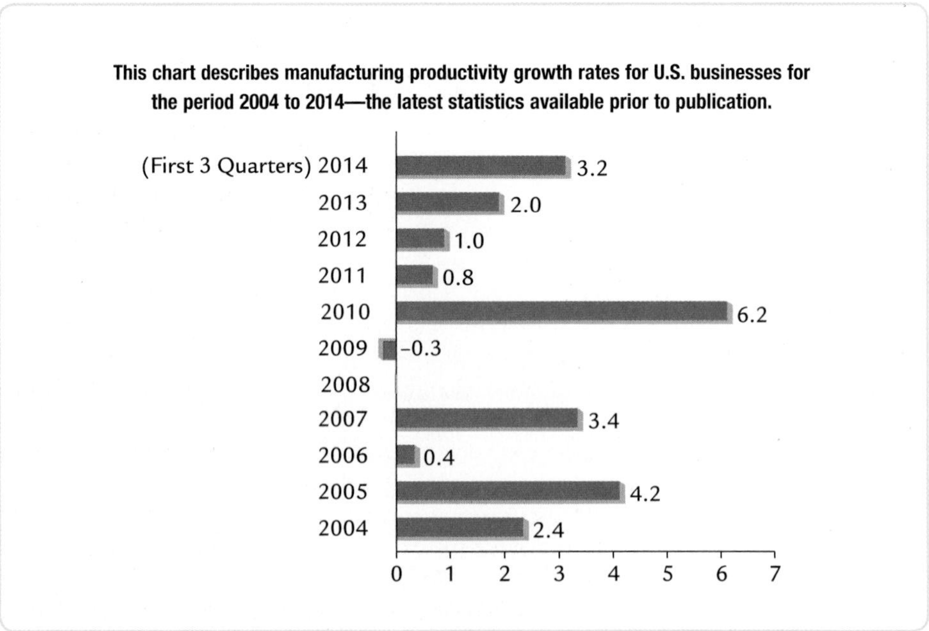

Source: Based on information in "Productivity Growth and Costs—Manufacturing 2014," The Bureau of Labor Statistics website at www.bls.gov (accessed January 22, 2015).

productivity growth or negative growth rates continued even as other nations were in economic recovery.[21]

8-7b Improving Productivity Growth

Many U.S. firms are using a number of techniques to improve productivity. For example, a large number of business firms are adopting lean manufacturing to improve productivity. **Lean manufacturing** is a concept built on the idea of eliminating waste from all of the activities required to produce a good or service. Benefits of lean manufacturing include a reduction in the amount of resources required to produce a product or service, more efficient use of employee time, improved quality, and increased profits. In addition to lean manufacturing, several other factors must be considered if U.S. firms are going to increase productivity *and* their ability to compete in the global marketplace. For example:

- The United States must stabilize its economy so that firms will invest more money in new facilities, equipment, technology, and employee training.
- Managers and executives must cooperate with employees to increase employee motivation and participation in the workplace.
- All government policies must be examined to ensure that unreasonable regulations that may be hindering productivity growth are eliminated.
- Successful techniques that have been used in manufacturing firms must be used to increase productivity in the service industry.
- Increased use of automation, robotics, and computer manufacturing systems must be used to lower production costs.
- There must be more emphasis on satisfying the customer's needs with quality goods and services.

Finally, innovation and research and development efforts to create new products and services must be increased in order for U.S. firms to compete in the global marketplace. As pointed out earlier in this chapter, U.S. manufacturers spend more on innovation and research and development than firms in other nations, but foreign firms are beginning to innovate and realize the importance of research and development.

8-7c The Impact of Automation, Robotics, and Computers on Productivity

Automation is the total or near-total use of machines to do work. The rapid increase in automated procedures has been made possible by computer technology—the same technology that led to the production of desktop computers for businesses, homes, and schools. In factories, computer technology is used in robotics and in sophisticated manufacturing systems.

ROBOTICS **Robotics** is the use of programmable machines to perform a variety of tasks by manipulating materials and tools. Robots work quickly, accurately, and steadily. For example, the iRobot Ava 500, distributed by Cisco Systems, is a robot that takes teleconferencing to the next level and allows workers to meet with other employees in an office setting or tour remote facilities that would be impossible without traveling to the physical site. The AVA 500 robot can also be used to inspect manufacturing facilities, laboratories, customer experience centers, and other remote facilities. And when the robot's work is finished, it will return to its docking station for charging.[22]

Robots are especially effective in tedious, repetitive assembly-line jobs, as well as in handling hazardous materials. Lincoln Electric, for example, provides robotic arc welders that eliminate the hot, dirty job of welding, which is key to many

lean manufacturing a concept built on the idea of eliminating waste from all of the activities required to produce a product or service

automation the total or near-total use of machines to do work

robotics the use of programmable machines to perform a variety of tasks by manipulating materials and tools

The factory of the future is already here! Thanks to automation, robotics, and computer manufacturing, manufacturing is much more efficient and employees are more productive. Because of increased efficiency and improved productivity, U.S. firms are able to compete with manufacturers both at home and in the global marketplace.

manufacturing tasks. As an added bonus, robotic arc welders are often quicker and are more precise than old-fashioned welding machines.

Robots are also useful as artificial "eyes" that can check the quality of products as they are being processed on assembly lines. To date, the automotive industry has made the most extensive use of robotics, but robots also have been used to mine coal, inspect the inner surfaces of pipes, assemble computer components, provide certain kinds of patient care in hospitals, and clean and guard buildings at night.

COMPUTER MANUFACTURING SYSTEMS People are quick to point out how computers have changed their everyday lives, but most people do not realize the impact computers have had on manufacturing. In simple terms, the factory of the future has already arrived. For most manufacturers, the changeover began with the use of computer-aided design and computer-aided manufacturing. **Computer-aided design (CAD)** is the use of computers to aid in the development of products. Ford speeds up car design, Canon designs new photocopiers, and American Greetings creates new birthday cards by using CAD.

Computer-aided manufacturing (CAM) is the use of computers to plan and control manufacturing processes. A well-designed CAM system allows manufacturers to become much more productive. Not only are a greater number of products produced, but speed and quality also increase. Using CAM systems, Toyota produces automobiles, Hasbro manufactures toys, and Apple Computer creates electronic products.

If you are thinking that the next logical step is to combine the CAD and CAM computer systems, you are right. Today, the most successful manufacturers use CAD and CAM together to form a computer-integrated manufacturing system. Specifically, **computer-integrated manufacturing (CIM)** is a computer system that not only helps to design products but also controls the machinery needed to produce the finished product. For example, manufacturers for Juicy Couture use CIM to design clothing, to establish patterns for new fashions, and then to cut the cloth needed to produce finished products that are sold in Juicy Couture Stores and select department stores in North America, Europe, Asia, Latin America, Africa, and the Middle East.[23] Other advantages of using CIM include improved flexibility, more efficient scheduling, and higher product quality—all factors that make a production facility more competitive in today's global economy.

computer-aided design (CAD) the use of computers to aid in the development of products

computer-aided manufacturing (CAM) the use of computers to plan and control manufacturing processes

computer-integrated manufacturing (CIM) a computer system that not only helps to design products but also controls the machinery needed to produce the finished product

FLEXIBLE MANUFACTURING SYSTEMS Manufacturers have known for a number of years that the mass-production and traditional assembly lines used to manufacture products present a number of problems. For example, although traditional assembly lines at General Motors, Ford, Nissan, and other automobile manufacturers turn out extremely large numbers of products economically, the system requires expensive, time-consuming retooling of equipment whenever a new product is to be manufactured. This type of manufacturing is often referred to as a continuous process. **Continuous process** is a manufacturing process in which a firm produces the same product(s) over a long period of time. Now it is possible to use flexible manufacturing systems to solve such problems. A **flexible manufacturing system (FMS)** combines electronic machines and CIM in a single production system. Instead of having to spend large amounts of time and effort to retool the traditional mechanical equipment on an assembly line for each new product, an FMS is rearranged simply by reprogramming electronic machines. Because FMSs require less time and expense to reprogram than traditional systems, manufacturers can produce smaller batches of a variety of products without raising the production cost. Flexible manufacturing is sometimes referred to as an intermittent process. An **intermittent process** is a manufacturing process in which a firm's manufacturing machines and equipment are changed to produce different products.

For most manufacturers, the driving force behind FMSs is the customer. In fact, the term *customer-driven production* is often used to describe a manufacturing system that is driven by customer needs and what customers want to buy. For example, advanced software and a flexible manufacturing system have enabled Dell Computer to change to a more customer-driven manufacturing process. Although the costs of designing and installing an FMS such as this are high, the electronic equipment is used more frequently and efficiently than the machinery on a traditional assembly line.

8-7d Sustainability and Technological Displacement

In Chapter 1, *sustainability* was defined as creating and maintaining the conditions under which humans and nature can exist in productive harmony that permit fulfilling the social, economic, and other requirements of present and future generations. While sustainability affects all aspects of a nation, its people, and the economy, the concept is especially important for manufacturers and service providers. Because of the amount of resources required to produce goods and services, these businesses must conserve resources whenever possible. As an added bonus, efforts to reduce waste and sustain the planet can often improve a firm's bottom-line profit amount.

Today, many countries around the globe produce goods and services and compete with U.S. manufacturers. And yet, U.S. producers are known for quality and innovation—especially for products that are more expensive or more complicated to manufacture. As a result, most experts agree that, because U.S. manufacturers will continue to innovate, workers who have manufacturing jobs will be highly skilled and will be able to work with automated and computer-aided manufacturing systems. Those that don't possess high-tech skills will be unemployed. Many workers will be faced with the choice of retraining for new jobs or seeking jobs in other sectors of the economy. Government, business, and education will have to cooperate to prepare workers for new roles in an automated workplace.

The next chapter discusses many of the issues caused by technological displacement. In addition, a number of major components of human resources management are described, and we see how managers use various reward systems to boost motivation, productivity, and morale.

continuous process a manufacturing process in which a firm produces the same product(s) over a long period of time

flexible manufacturing system (FMS) a single production system that combines electronic machines and CIM

intermittent process a manufacturing process in which a firm's manufacturing machines and equipment are changed to produce different products

Concept Check

✓ How might productivity be measured in a dry cleaners? In a department store? In a public school system?

✓ How can robotics, computer manufacturing systems, and flexible manufacturing systems help a manufacturer to produce products?

Summary

8-1 Explain the nature of production.

Operations management consists of all the activities that managers engage in to create goods and services. Today, U.S. companies are forced to compete in an ever-smaller world to meet the needs of more-demanding customers. As a result, U.S. manufacturers have used innovation to improve productivity. Because of innovation, fewer workers are needed, but those workers who are needed possess the skills to use automation and technology. In an attempt to regain a competitive edge, manufacturers have taken another look at the importance of improving quality and meeting the needs of their customers. They also have used new techniques to motivate employees, reduced costs, used computer-aided and flexible manufacturing systems, improved control procedures, and used green manufacturing. Competing in the global economy is not only profitable but also an essential activity that requires the cooperation of everyone within an organization. A number of career options are available for employees in operations management.

8-2 Outline how the conversion process transforms raw materials, labor, and other resources into finished goods or services.

A business transforms resources into goods and services in order to provide utility to customers. Utility is the ability of a good or service to satisfy a human need. Form utility is created by people converting raw materials, finances, and information into finished products. Conversion processes vary in terms of the major resources used to produce goods and services (focus), the degree to which resources are changed (magnitude of change), and the number of production processes that a business uses.

8-3 Understand the importance of service businesses to consumers, other business firms, and the nation's economy.

The application of the basic principles of operations management to the production of services has coincided with the growth and importance of service businesses in the United States. Today 86 percent of American workers are employed in the service industry. In fact, the American economy is now characterized as a service economy. For a service firm, planning often begins with determining who the customer is and what needs the customer has. After customer needs are identified the next step is to develop a plan that will enable the firm to deliver the services that their customers want or need.

Although it is often more difficult to measure customer satisfaction, today's successful service firms work hard at providing the services customers want. For example, compared with manufacturers, service firms often listen more carefully to customers and respond more quickly to the market's changing needs.

8-4 Describe how research and development leads to new products and services.

Operations management often begins with product research and development and often referred to as R&D. The results of R&D may be entirely new products or services or extensions and refinements of existing products or services. R&D activities are classified as basic research (aimed at uncovering new knowledge), applied research (discovering new knowledge with some potential use), and development and implementation (using new or existing knowledge to produce goods and services). If a firm sells only one product or provides only one service, when customers quit buying the product or service, the firm will die. To stay in business, the firm must, at the very least, find ways to refine or extend the want-satisfying capability of its product or service.

8-5 Discuss the components involved in planning the production process.

Planning for production involves three major phases: design planning, site selection and facilities planning, and operational planning. First, design planning is undertaken to address questions related to the product line, required production capacity, and the use of technology. Then production facilities, human resources, and plant layout must be considered. Operational planning focuses on the use of production facilities and resources. The steps for operational planning include (1) selecting a planning horizon, (2) estimating market demand, (3) comparing market demand with capacity, and (4) adjusting production of products or services to meet demand.

8-6 Explain how purchasing, inventory control, scheduling, and quality control affect production.

The major areas of operations control are purchasing, inventory control, scheduling, and quality control. Purchasing involves selecting suppliers. The choice of suppliers should result from careful analysis of a number of factors, including price, quality, reliability, credit terms, and shipping costs. Inventory control is the management of stocks of raw materials, work-in-process, and finished goods to minimize the total inventory cost. Scheduling ensures that materials and other resources are at the right place at the right time. Quality control guarantees that products and services are produced in accordance with design specifications. The major objective of quality control is to see that the organization lives up to the standards it has set for itself on quality. A number of different activities including quality circles, inspection, total quality management, and six sigma can be used to encourage employee participation and to improve quality.

8-7 Summarize how technology can make American firms more productive and competitive in the global marketplace.

Productivity is the average level of output per worker per hour. From 2004 to 2014, U.S. productivity growth averaged a 2.1 percent increase. More specifically, productivity for the first three quarters of 2014 increased 3.2 percent. Although a 3.2 percent increase was higher when compared to our average productivity growth over the 2004 to 2014 time period, economists, business leaders, and government officials point to the need for even larger increases in the future. Several factors must be considered if U.S. firms are going to increase productivity and their ability to compete in the global marketplace.

Automation, the total or near-total use of machines to do work, has for some years been changing the way work is done in factories. A growing number of industries are using programmable machines called robots. Computer-aided design, computer-aided manufacturing, and computer-integrated manufacturing use computers to help design and manufacture products. A flexible manufacturing system (FMS) combines electronic machines and CIM to produce smaller batches of products more efficiently than on the traditional assembly line. Instead of having to spend vast amounts of time and effort to retool the traditional mechanical equipment on an assembly line for each new product, an FMS is rearranged simply by reprogramming electronic machines. An FMS is sometimes referred to as an intermittent process.

Key Terms

You should now be able to define and give an example relevant to each of the following terms:

operations management (212)	product design (221)	just-in-time inventory (JIT) system (228)	automation (233)
reshoring (214)	capacity (221)	scheduling (228)	robotics (233)
mass production (214)	labor-intensive technology (222)	Malcolm Baldrige National Quality Award (229)	computer-aided design (CAD) (234)
analytical process (214)	capital-intensive technology (222)	quality control (229)	computer-aided manufacturing (CAM) (234)
synthetic process (214)	plant layout (223)	quality circle (230)	computer-integrated manufacturing (CIM) (234)
utility (215)	planning horizon (224)	inspection (230)	continuous process (235)
form utility (215)	purchasing (226)	Six Sigma (230)	flexible manufacturing system (FMS) (235)
service economy (216)	inventory control (227)	International Organization for Standardization (ISO) (230)	intermittent process (235)
research and development (R&D) (218)	materials requirements planning (MRP) (227)	lean manufacturing (233)	
design planning (221)			
product line (221)			

Discussion Questions

1. Why would Rubbermaid—a successful U.S. company—need to expand and sell its products to customers in foreign countries?
2. What steps have U.S. firms taken to regain a competitive edge in the global marketplace?
3. Do certain kinds of firms need to stress particular areas of operations management? Explain.
4. Is it really necessary for service firms to engage in research and development? In planning for production and operations control?
5. How are the four areas of operations control interrelated?
6. Is operations management relevant to nonbusiness organizations such as colleges and hospitals? Why or why not?

Video Case
Chobani Gives the World a Taste for Greek Yogurt

Entrepreneur Hamdi Ulukaya, founder and CEO of fast-growing Chobani, needed less than ten years to transform a defunct yogurt factory in rural South Edmeston, New York into the U.S. capitol of Greek yogurt production. He came up with the idea of making Greek yogurt in the United States in 2005, when he bought the factory with the help of a Small Business Administration loan from its former owner, Kraft Foods. Ulukaya spent the next 18 months experimenting with recipes while upgrading the factory, arranging a steady supply of milk and other fresh ingredients, and working out the details of what the yogurt cup would look like.

By 2007, Ulukaya had perfected his recipe and was churning out the first cases of Chobani yogurt for an ever-larger list of supermarket customers. His Greek yogurt, thicker and tangier than traditional yogurts, took the industry by storm. Ulukaya originally projected that Chobani would break even if it produced 20,000 cases of yogurt every week. By 2009, the company was getting weekly orders for 200,000 cases—ten times the founder's estimate.

Suddenly, Chobani's Greek yogurt wasn't a tiny, niche product that multinational competitors like Dannon and Yoplait could ignore. Although Ulukaya considered enlarging the factory to accommodate weekly production capacity of 400,000 cases, he decided on the much more ambitious strategy of planning for weekly production capacity of 1 million cases. This huge expansion required new equipment and an around-the-clock production schedule. At the newly enlarged plant, employees would operate machines for 10 hours, followed by a cleaning period of 4 hours to ensure product purity.

By 2012, Chobani was ringing up $1 billion in annual sales throughout North America, and the South Edmeston factory was operating at near capacity every day. According to Ulukaya, "milk is a gift from nature" and along with the freshest fruits available is what makes Chobani different from its competitors. However, Chobani was having difficulty obtaining sufficient quantities of fresh milk to further boost production in the New York plant. Whereas one cup of regular yogurt is made from one cup of milk, one cup of Greek yogurt requires three cups of milk. Ulukaya's $450 million solution to the challenge of milk availability: Build a cavernous new production facility in Twin Falls, Idaho, where Chobani can draw on an abundant local supply of milk. This plant opened in December, 2012, with a weekly production capacity of more than 2 million cases of yogurt. It serves Western states, while the original New York plant ships to Eastern states.

Even as Chobani gears up for higher production and higher market share in North America, it's also getting ready for growth halfway around the world. Ulukaya purchased a dairy near Melbourne, Australia, and invested millions of dollars to upgrade and expand yogurt production at the site. From this facility, Chobani will serve Australia and export its popular Greek yogurt to new markets in Asia. In addition, it maintains a sales office in Europe to support expansion on the continent.

Today, Chobani—a company that was started with an SBA loan in 2005—dominates the U.S. market for Greek yogurt and is the number one Greek yogurt brand in the U.S. It has expanded its product line to include Greek yogurt for children and various sizes and flavors of Greek yogurt for adults. Not long ago, Ulukaya opened a specialty yogurt shop in a trendy part of New York City. New flavor combinations that prove especially popular there may soon be transferred to the production lines in New York, Idaho, and beyond.

While a product recall in 2013 caused Chobani's market share to take a one percent drop and a corresponding drop in revenues, the company moved quickly to correct the problems that led to the recall. Today, the company is constantly looking for new ways to improve its manufacturing efficiency and increase sales revenues and profits while staying true to its mission. According to Ulukaya, "If we can't do it better, we don't do it at all."[24]

Questions

1. Do you agree with Ulukaya's decision to open a production facility in Idaho instead of buying milk and trucking it to Chobani's New York plant? In addition to the cost of transporting the milk, are there other factors that might have influenced Ulukaya's decision to build a second plant?
2. What can Chobani do to gauge market demand for Greek yogurt and for particular flavors and products in its own product line? Identify at least three specific ideas.
3. Chobani's equipment runs for 10 hours and must be idle for four hours while being cleaned. Its plants operate day and night, all week long. What are the implications for the company's purchasing, inventory control, scheduling, and quality control functions?

Building Skills for Career Success

1. Social Media Exercise

Starbucks has taken an innovative approach to improving their products and the customer experience in their stores. Their entire purpose is to create a "third place" beyond home and work where people can congregate and socialize (while having a nice cup of coffee). To engage customers, they created a website called My Starbucks Idea (http://mystarbucksidea.com) that allows customers to post their ideas and then allows customers to also vote on them.

1. Visit the http://mystarbucksidea.com site. Do you have an idea for Starbucks? If so, post it. Do you have an opinion about one of the current ideas? If so, then vote for it.
2. Do you think this is an effective way to gain customer ideas for new products? Why or why not?
3. Can you think of other ways that corporate executives at Starbucks can gauge customer interest in their products and in-store experience using social media?

2. Building Team Skills

Suppose that you are planning to build a house in the country. It will be a brick, one-story structure of approximately 2,000 square feet, centrally heated and cooled. It will have three bedrooms, two bathrooms, a family room, a dining room, a kitchen with a breakfast nook, a study, a utility room, an entry foyer, a two-car garage, a covered patio, and a fireplace. Appliances will operate on electricity and propane fuel. You have received approval and can be connected to the cooperative water system at any time. Public sewerage services are not available; therefore, you must rely on a septic system. You want to know how long it will take to build the house.

Assignment

1. In a group, identify the major activities involved in the project and sequence them in the proper order.
2. Estimate the time required for each activity.
3. Present your list of activities to the class and ask for comments and suggestions.

3. Researching Different Careers

Because service businesses are now such a dominant part of our economy, job seekers sometimes overlook the employment opportunities available in production. Two positions often found in manufacturing and production are quality-control inspector and purchasing agent.

Assignment

1. Using the *Occupational Outlook Handbook* at your local library or on the Internet (http://www.bls.gov/ooh), find the following information for the jobs of quality-control inspector and purchasing agent:
   a. Nature of work, including main activities and responsibilities
   b. Job outlook
   c. Earnings
   d. Training, qualifications, and advancement.
2. Look for other production jobs that may interest you and compile the same sort of information about them.
3. Summarize in a two-page report the key things you learned about jobs in production.

Running a Business
Part 3

Graeter's Grows Through Good Management, Organization, and Quality

Graeter's began as a tiny Cincinnati business and now enjoys a national reputation for the quality of its premium ice cream. Even though the $30 million company recently opened a new factory to support its expansion plans, it still clings fiercely to its original small-batch production method for making creamy ice cream from fresh ingredients. CEO Richard Graeter emphasizes that profits are important, but "staying true to who you are and investing in your business is what makes sure that your business is going to be here tomorrow." That's why Graeter's still makes all of its ice cream by hand, ensuring that the texture and taste meet its high standards batch after batch, year after year.

More than a Family Affair

Graeter's top-management team includes the CEO and his two cousins, Bob and Chip Graeter. As vice president of operations, Bob is responsible for manufacturing, as well as for developing new products and finding suppliers to provide ingredients such as fresh fruits, cream, eggs, and chocolates. His brother Chip oversees all of the company's ice cream shops. Rounding out the management team is a vice president of manufacturing, a controller, a vice president of sales and marketing, and a candy production manager.

"Every major decision, we make on a consensus basis," Richard says, describing the equal partnership among the three family members. "That doesn't mean we don't have a different point of view from time to time, but . . . we learn to see each other's view and discuss, debate, and get down to a decision that all of us support. The other thing that we have learned to do, something that is a little different than our parents' generation [did], is bring in outside people into the . . . executive level of the management team. . . . We now work with a couple of consultants to help us plan our strategy to look for a new vision, to develop training programs . . . all those systems that big companies have." Managers stay in close contact with employees at all levels and don't hesitate to ask for their input when solving problems and making decisions.

Inside the Org Chart

Graeter's formalized its organization structure over the years as it opened more stores and expanded beyond Cincinnati. Today, the store managers report to a group manager, who in turn reports to the vice president of retail operations. At the company's recently opened 28,000 square foot production facility, employees in each of three shifts are supervised by a shift manager, who reports to the vice president of operations. The first and third shifts are responsible for ice cream production, while the second shift is in charge of cleaning and sanitizing the facility.

Because so many Graeter's stores are located miles from headquarters, two managers "shop" each store every month, checking on quality and service. These management visits are supplemented by two monthly visits from "mystery shoppers" who buy ice cream and other products on different days, observing what employees are doing and taking note of what else is happening in the store. Their written reports give Graeter's top managers another view of the business, this time from the customer's perspective.

What's the Plan?

Change has come quickly to Graeter's, not all of it anticipated. The company was constructing its second factory to support the drive for nationwide distribution when an unexpected opportunity arose: to buy out the last franchise company operating Graeter's retail stores and take over its factory as well. The management team jumped at the chance. "A few months ago our strategy was just operate one plant," says Richard. "Now our strategy is, adapt to the opportunity that came along . . . we are operating three plants. The goal is to keep all of your assets deployed productively, so if we have these three plants, what is the most we can do out of those plants to be generating product and profit? One example would be supplying restaurants in other cities, which we really weren't considering originally because our new plant was really geared for pints, but if we have this excess capacity, the smart thing to do is figure out what we can do with that."

The newest Graeter's facility, on Regina Graeter Way in Cincinnati, was built with the capacity to produce as much as 1 million gallons of ice cream per year, although the current annual output is about 625,000 gallons. Many steps, such as putting lids on packages and moving them into refrigerated storage, are handled by automated equipment. Yet all of the ice cream is still made in small batches and by hand. Experienced technicians wield a paddle to gradually mix in ingredients such as molten chocolate, which have been pasteurized on the premises to comply with government regulations. Once the ice cream reaches the right temperature and texture, another employee hand-packs it into individual packages, which are then automatically capped, stamped with a date code, sealed, and whisked away to be kept cold until being loaded onto trucks for delivery to supermarket customers. Ice cream samples from every shift's output are tested to ensure purity and quality.

Graeter's sets weekly and monthly sales goals for its stores, based on each unit's location and other factors that affect demand. If a store doesn't meet its goals, the group manager acts quickly to find out why and help the store get back on track. As the company explores the possibility of opening Graeter's stores as far away as Los Angeles and New York, the management team is planning carefully and assessing the potential challenges and advantages of coast-to-coast operations.[25]

Questions

1. Based on this case and the two previous Graeter's cases, what are the company's most important strengths? Can you identify any weaknesses that might affect its ability to grow?

2. How would you describe the departmentalization and the organizational structure at Graeter's? Do you think Graeter's is centralized or decentralized, and what are the implications for its plans for growth?

3. The newest Graeter's plant can produce far more ice cream than is needed today. The company also makes ice cream cakes, pies, toppings, and other products at its original plant and at the plant formerly owned by a franchisee. What are the implications for Graeter's strategy and for its operational planning?

Building a Business Plan: Part 3

Now you should be ready to provide evidence that you have a management team with the necessary skills and experience to execute your business plan successfully. Only a competent management team can transform your vision into a successful business. You also should be able to describe your manufacturing and operations plans. The three chapters in Part 3 of your textbook, "Understanding the Management Process," "Creating a Flexible Organization," and "Producing Quality Goods and Services," should help you in answering some of the questions in this part of the business plan.

The Management Team Component

The management team component should include the answers to at least the following questions:

3.1. How is your team balanced in technical, conceptual, interpersonal, and other special skills needed in your business?

3.2. What will be your style of leadership?

3.3. How will your company be structured? Include a statement of the philosophy of management and company culture.

3.4. What are the key management positions, compensation, and key policies?

3.5. Include a job description for each management position and specify who will fill that position. *Note:* Prepare an organization chart and provide the résumé of each key manager for the appendix.

3.6. What other professionals, such as a lawyer, an insurance agent, a banker, and a certified public accountant, will you need for assistance?

The Manufacturing and Operations Plan Component

If you are in a manufacturing business, now is a good time to describe your manufacturing and operations plans, space requirements, equipment, labor force, inventory control, and purchasing requirements. Even if you are in a service-oriented business, many of these questions still may apply.

The manufacturing and operations plan component should include the answers to at least the following questions:

3.7. What are the advantages and disadvantages of your planned location in terms of

- Wage rates
- Unionization
- Labor pool
- Proximity to customers and suppliers
- Types of transportation available
- Tax rates
- Utility costs
- Zoning requirements

3.8. What facilities does your business require? Will you rent, lease, or purchase the facilities? Prepare a floor plan for the appendix.

3.9. Will you make or buy component parts to be assembled into the finished product? Make sure to justify your "make-or-buy" decision.

3.10. Who are your potential subcontractors and suppliers?

3.11. How will you control quality, inventory, and production? How will you measure your progress?

3.12. Is there a sufficient quantity of adequately skilled people in the local labor force to meet your needs?

Review of Business Plan Activities

Be sure to go over the information you have gathered. Check for any weaknesses and resolve them before beginning Part 4. Also, review all the answers to the questions in Parts 1, 2, and 3 to be certain that they are consistent throughout the entire business plan. Finally, write a brief statement that summarizes all the information for this part of the business plan.

Endnotes

1   Sources: Based on information in Gary Anglebrandt, "Detroit Bikes Rolls Out Second Model, Sets Sales Goal of 1,000 by Year's End," *Crain's Detroit Business*, August 24, 2014, www.crainsdetroit.com; Jen Weiczner, "Motor-less City? Bankrupt Detroit's Booming Bike Industry," *Fortune*, October 9, 2014, www.fortune.com; Jason McBride, "Cycling in Motor City," *Canadian Business*, February 19, 2014, www.canadianbusiness.com; http://detroitbikes.com.

2   The Bureau of Labor Statistics website at www.bls.gov (accessed January 20, 2015).

3   Tom Raum, "Obama Call for Manufacturing Revival a Tough Goal," the Yahoo! Finance website at http://finance.yahoo.com (accessed February 10, 2012).

4   The Bureau of Labor Statistics website at www.bls.gov (accessed January 20, 2015).

5   "Industry Employment and Output Projections to 2022," The Bureau of Labor Statistics website at www.bls.gov (accessed January 20, 2015).

6   Marc Levinson, "U.S. Manufacturing in International Perspective," Congressional Research Service website at http://fas.org/sgp/crs/misc/R42135.pdf (accessed February 20, 2014).

7   "U.S. Manufacturing in Context," The Advanced Manufacturing Portal website at www.manufacturing.gov (accessed January 20, 2015).

8   Ibid.

9   Ibid.

10 The Bureau of Labor Statistics website at www.bls.gov (accessed January 21, 2015).

11 Robert Kreitner and Carlene Cassidy, *Management*, 12th ed. (Mason, OH: Cengage Learning, 2013).

12 Marc Levinson, "U.S. Manufacturing in International Perspective," Congressional Research Service website at http://fas.org/sgp/crs/misc/R42135.pdf (accessed February 20, 2014).

13 The 3M Corporation website at www.3m.com (accessed January 21, 2015).

14 The Berry Plastics Corporation website at www.berryplastics.com (accessed January 22, 2015).

15 The AT&T Supplier website at www.attsuppliers.com (accessed January 22, 2015).

16 "What Makes Six Sigma Work," The iSixSigma website at www.isixsigma.com (accessed January 22, 2015).

17 The International Organization of Standardization (ISO) website at www.iso.org (accessed February 15, 2013).

18 The Bureau of Labor Statistics website at www.bls.gov (accessed January 22, 2015).

19 Ibid.

20 Ibid.

21 "International Labor Comparisons," The Conference Board website at www.conference-board.org (accessed January 20, 2015).

22 The KBZ Communications website at www.kbz.com (accessed January 23, 2015).

23 The Juicy Couture website at www.juicycouture.com (accessed January 23, 2015).

24 Sources: Based on information from the Chobani website at www.chobani.com (accessed January 27, 2015); Eric Goodell, "Chobani Defends Company, Twin Falls Plant Operations," the MagicValley.com website at www.magicvalley.com (accessed January 8, 2015); Bryan Gruley, "How a Turkish Immigrant Made a Billion Dollars in Eight Years Selling ... Yogurt," *Bloomberg Businessweek*, February 4, 2013, pp. 60–64; Andrew Grossman, "Yogurt Boom Leaves Dairy Farmers Behind," *Wall Street Journal*, June 26, 2012, www.wsj.com; Bill Roberts, "Twin Falls Welcomes New Chobani Yogurt Plant," *Idaho Statesman*, December 17, 2012, www.idahostatesman.com; Mark Astley, "What to Expect in 2013," *Dairy Reporter*, January 9, 2013, www.dairyreporter.com; Meghan Walsh, "Chobani Takes Gold in the Yogurt Aisle," *Bloomberg Businessweek*, July 31, 2012, www.businessweek.com.

25 Sources: Based on information from the Graeter's website at www.graeters.com (accessed January 26, 2015); Kimberly L. Jackson, "Graeter's Premium Chocolate Chip Ice Cream Lands at Stop & Shop," *Newark Star-Ledger (NJ)*, April 4, 2012, www.nj.com; "Graeter's Ice Cream Debuts in Bay Area," *Tampa Bay Times (St. Petersburg, FL)*, January 10, 2012, p. 4B; "Graeter's to Make All Ice Cream at new Cincinnati Plant," the Cincinnati Business Courier website at http://www.bizjournals.com/cincinnati/news/2011/08/12/graeters-to-make-all-ice-cream-at-new.html (accessed August 12, 2011); Jim Carper, "Graeter's Runs a Hands-on Ice Cream Plant," *Dairy Foods*, August 2011, pp. 36+; Jim Carper, "The Greater Good," *Dairy Foods*, August 2011, pp. 95+; "Graeter's Unveils New 'Mystery Flavor,'" *Dayton Daily News*, March 29, 2012, www.daytondailynews.com; Bob Driehaus, "A Cincinnati Ice Cream Maker Aims Big," *New York Times*, September 11, 2010, www.nytimes.com; Lucy May, "Graeter's Northern Kentucky Franchisee Puts Stores on the Block," *Business Courier*, August 6, 2010, http://cincinnati.bizjournals.com; interviews with company staff and Cengage videos about Graeter's.

Part 4

CHAPTER 9
Attracting and Retaining the Best Employees

Why Should You Care?

Being able to understand how to attract and keep the right people is crucial. Also, you can better understand about your own interactions with your co-workers.

Learning Objectives

Once you complete this chapter, you will be able to:

9-1 Describe the major components of human resources management.

9-2 Identify the steps in human resources planning.

9-3 Describe cultural diversity and understand some of the challenges and opportunities associated with it.

9-4 Explain the objectives and uses of job analysis.

9-5 Describe the processes of recruiting, employee selection, and orientation.

9-6 Discuss the primary elements of employee compensation and benefits.

9-7 Explain the purposes and techniques of employee training and development.

9-8 Discuss performance appraisal techniques and performance feedback.

9-9 Outline the major legislation affecting human resources management.

Netflix Stands Ready to Change

Founded in 1997 to rent DVDs by mail, Netflix was a fledgling business challenging the competitive dominance of mighty Blockbuster, which operated an extensive network of video and DVD rental stores. These days, the video format is obsolete and Blockbuster is bankrupt, but Netflix is thriving worldwide because it was smart enough and nimble enough to shift focus from renting DVDs to streaming entertainment as the technology evolved. The California-based company now streams two billion hours of movies and television every month to 53 million subscribers in 50 countries.

Credit Netflix's culture of excellence for the company's success. It hires the best managers and employees, and gives them the freedom and responsibility to do whatever it takes to move the company forward. In fact, co-founder and CEO Reed Hastings prides himself on making as few decisions as possible. He rejects the idea of rigidly controlling the workforce because "if you dummy-proof the process, you only get dummies to work there."

Instead, Netflix seeks out highly skilled, high-performance individuals and trusts them to do what's best for the company. For example, instead of having to comply with a lengthy, detailed policy for business travel and expenses, employees are told only to: "Act in Netflix's best interests." The firm's vacation policy for salaried employees is similarly informal, depending on common sense and the rhythm of the business to set the tone. Salaried employees can arrange time off as needed, as long as they consult with their managers and colleagues, and ensure proper staffing levels during busy periods.

Rather than requiring the kind of formal yearly performance reviews that are typical at other organizations, managers and employees at Netflix have spontaneous performance-appraisal conversations as occasions arise, day by day. And to keep work teams running smoothly, the company asks employees to provide feedback about what their managers and colleagues should stop doing, start doing, or keep doing.[1]

Did You Know?

Netflix, which began as a DVD-rental-by-mail business, currently rings up more than $4.4 billion in annual revenues and serves 53 million customers in 50 countries.

Netflix recruits some of the most skilled people in the tech industry and retains and keeps them satisfied by offering good compensation and trusting them to do right by the company. We begin our study of human resources management (HRM) with an overview of how businesses acquire, maintain, and develop human resources. After listing the steps by which firms match their human resources needs with the supply available, we explore several dimensions of cultural diversity. Then we examine the concept of job analysis. Next, we focus on how a firm's recruiting, selection, and orientation procedures impact a firm's success in acquiring employees. We describe forms of employee compensation, which can impact employee loyalty and productivity. Then we discuss methods of employee training, management development, and performance appraisal. Finally, we consider legislation that affects HRM practices.

9-1 HUMAN RESOURCES MANAGEMENT: AN OVERVIEW

Human resources, the people who work within an organization, are the most important and valuable resource for a business. Without them, a firm would cease to function. Organizations will expend a great deal of effort to acquire and utilize human resources fully. This effort is known as *human resources management*, or *staffing* and *personnel management*.

Human resources management (HRM) consists of all the activities involved in acquiring, maintaining, and developing an organization's human resources. HRM begins with acquisition—getting people to work for the organization. The acquisition

Learning Objective

9-1 Describe the major components of human resources management.

human resources management (HRM) all the activities involved in acquiring, maintaining, and developing an organization's human resources

Personal App

How many skills do you have?

The more skills you develop, the more valuable you are to any employer. Do your own personal skills inventory before you write a résumé or interview for a job. Then you'll be prepared to explain the special skills you can bring to an employer.

The power of people. Many firms believe their employees are their most important assets. However, unlike other assets such as machinery, capital, and products, employees can choose to leave an organization. Carefully designing compensation and reward packages can help a firm attract and retain valuable employees.

process can be very competitive, particularly for skilled employees and in fields where demand for workers exceed supply. Next, steps must be taken to retain these valuable resources. (After all, they are the only business resources that can voluntarily leave an organization.) Finally, human resources should be developed to their full capacity.

9-1a HRM Activities

Each of the three phases of HRM—acquiring, maintaining, and developing human resources—consists of related actions. Acquisition, for example, includes planning, and the various activities that lead to hiring new personnel. Altogether this phase of HRM includes five separate activities:

- *Human resources planning*—determining the firm's future human resources needs
- *Job analysis*—determining the exact nature of the positions
- *Recruiting*—attracting people to apply for positions
- *Selection*—choosing and hiring the most qualified applicants
- *Orientation*—acquainting new employees with the firm

Maintaining human resources consists primarily of encouraging employees to remain with the firm and to work effectively by using a variety of HRM programs, including the following:

- *Employee relations*—increasing employee job satisfaction through satisfaction surveys, employee communication programs, exit interviews, and fair treatment
- *Compensation*—rewarding employee effort through monetary payments
- *Benefits*—providing rewards to ensure employee well-being

The development phase of HRM is concerned with improving employees' skills and expanding their capabilities. The two important activities of this phase are:

- *Training and development*—teaching employees new skills and new jobs, and more effective ways of performing their present jobs
- *Performance appraisal*—assessing employees' current and potential performance levels

We will discuss each of these activities in more detail later in the chapter.

9-1b Responsibility for HRM

In general, HRM is a shared responsibility of line managers and staff HRM specialists. In very small organizations, the owner handles all or most HRM activities. As a firm grows in size, an owner may employ an outside party to handle some HRM functions, such as payroll and taxes, or hire a human resources manager to take over some staff responsibilities. In very large firms such as Disney, HRM activities tend to be highly specialized, with separate groups for compensation, benefits, training and development, and other staff activities. GE, for example, has divisions and offices all over the world. Because of the size and complexity of the organization, GE has hundreds of HR managers to cover different geographic areas and departments within the firm.

Specific HRM activities are assigned to those in the best position to perform them. Human resources planning and job analysis are usually carried out by staff specialists with input from line managers. Similarly, staff experts handle recruiting and selection, although line managers are involved in hiring decisions. Staff specialists devise orientation programs that are carried out by both staff specialists and line managers. Compensation systems (including benefits) most often are developed and administered by the HRM staff. However, line managers recommend pay increases and promotions. Training and development activities are the joint responsibility of staff and line managers. Performance appraisal is the job of the line manager, although HRM personnel design the firm's appraisal system in many organizations.

Concept Check

✓ What are the three phases of human resources management?

✓ Identify the activities associated with each phase.

✓ How does the responsibility of HRM change with the size of a firm?

9-2 HUMAN RESOURCES PLANNING

Human resources planning is the development of strategies to meet a firm's future human resources needs. The organization's overall strategic plan is the starting point of the process. From this, human resource planners can forecast future demand for human resources. Next, the planners must determine whether the needed human resources will be available. Finally, they have to take steps to match supply with demand.

Learning Objective

9-2 Identify the steps in human resources planning.

9-2a Forecasting Human Resources Demand

Planners should base human resource demand forecasts on all relevant information available. The firm's overall strategic plan will provide information about future business ventures, new products, and projected expansions or contractions of specific product lines. Information on past staffing levels, evolving technologies, industry staffing practices, and projected economic trends also can be helpful. Technological advances are creating new opportunities in forecasting and planning for human resources demand. Increasingly, companies are using specialized software to analyze data about their employees' demographics, performance, training, and internal movements in order to make better HR decisions. Insights gained from such technology can help managers develop more cost-effective recruiting and selection strategies, as well as recognize threats and opportunities. For example, at Black Hills, Corp., computer modeling exposed the fact that an anticipated loss of 24 percent of employees over the next five years, due to retirement, would actually result in the loss of 34 percent of the firm's total employee experience—a significant loss. Recognizing that threat, executives looked for ways to capture those employees' knowledge and experience before they retired.[2]

HRM managers use forecasting information to determine both the number of employees required and their qualifications. Planners use a wide range of methods

human resources planning the development of strategies to meet a firm's future human resources needs

Entrepreneurial Success

Hiring Your First Employee: Key Questions to Consider

Put yourself in the shoes of an entrepreneur whose startup is gaining momentum. When is the right time to hire your first employee? Here are some key questions to ask before you recruit.

- *Do you have enough work for two people (or more)?* If so, what part of the business needs the most help? Think about what skills are required to complement your own skills. Also think about how to spread the workload so that you, as the owner, will have more time to work on strategic challenges and future planning.
- *Do you have enough money?* Your budget will have to cover not only compensation and benefits, but also payroll taxes and other mandatory payments. Remember to budget for a desk and a computer or other equipment for the new employee, not to mention the cost of complying with the laws and regulations that apply to employers. Yet cost is only part of the equation:

Consider whether hiring someone will help the business increase revenue, attract larger clients, or prepare for imminent expansion.

- *Can you find qualified candidates who are accustomed to life in a startup?* Not everyone is suited to the fast pace and pressure of a small business—and to working closely with an entrepreneurial boss. Although you'll have to invest time to train and supervise your first employee, this investment will pay off if the employee understands how to function in an entrepreneurial situation.

Sources: Based on information in Eric Siu, "5 Things You Need to Know Before Hiring Your First Employee," *Entrepreneur.com* (accessed July 10, 2015), November 4, 2014; Jeffrey Hayzlett, "6 Tips to Keep in Mind When Hiring Your First Employees," *Entrepreneur.com*, September 16, 2014; Jessica Stillman, "3 Signs You're Ready to Hire Your First Employee," *Inc.*, August 27, 2014, www.inc.com (accessed July 10, 2015); Nellie Akalp, "4 Questions to Ask Before Hiring Your First Employee," Mashable, October 30, 2014, http://mashable.com/2014/10/30/questions-before-hiring/ (accessed July 27, 2015).

to predict specific personnel needs. For example, a simple method projects personnel requirements to increase or decrease in the same proportion as sales revenue. Thus, a 30 percent increase in projected sales volume over the next two years results in a forecasted personnel increase of 30 percent for the same period. (This method can be applied to specific positions and to the workforce in general. It is not, however, a very precise forecasting method.) At the other end of the spectrum are complex computer programs that perform HRM activities, such as forecasting future human resources requirements, using algorithms and demographic data.

9-2b Forecasting Human Resources Supply

A forecast of human resources supply must take into account both the present workforce and any changes that may occur within it. For example, suppose that planners project that in five years a firm that currently employs 100 engineers will need to employ 200 engineers. Forecasting is not as simple as planning to hire 100 additional engineers. Some of the firm's current engineers will leave, move to other jobs within the firm, or be promoted. Thus, planners may project the supply of current engineers in five years at 87, which means that the firm will have to hire a total of 113 new engineers. When forecasting supply, planners should also account for the organization's existing employees to determine who can be retrained to perform required tasks.

Two useful techniques for forecasting human resources supply are the replacement chart and the skills inventory. A **replacement chart** is a list of key personnel and their possible replacements within a firm. It is important to maintain this chart to ensure that top-management positions can be filled quickly in the event of an unexpected death, resignation, or retirement. Some firms provide additional training for employees who might eventually replace top managers.

A **skills inventory** is a searchable database containing information on the skills and experience of all present employees, which can be mined to find

replacement chart a list of key personnel and their possible replacements within a firm

skills inventory a computerized data bank containing information on the skills and experience of all present employees

candidates to fill available positions. For a special project, a manager may be seeking a current employee with specific information technology skills, at least six years of experience, and fluency in French. The skills inventory can quickly identify qualified employees. Skill-assessment tests, which provide the information in a skills inventory, can be administered internally or by outside vendors. Some companies, such as Halogen Software, offer customizable skills assessment and training software that allows firms to examine skills more expertly without contracting with an outside provider.

9-2c Matching Supply with Demand

Once they have forecasted the supply and demand for personnel, HR planners can devise a course of action for matching one with the other. When demand is predicted to be greater than supply, they must make

The demand for labor versus its supply: A balancing act. The supply and demand for employees with different skills is constantly shifting. In some industries, qualified workers are plentiful. In others, they are hard to find, even when the nation's unemployment rate is high.

plans to recruit new employees. The timing of recruitment efforts depends on the types of positions to be filled. Suppose that we expect to open another plant in five years that will need a plant manager and 25 maintenance workers, along with additional support staff. We can wait to recruit maintenance personnel. However, because the job of a plant manager is so critical, we may begin the process to fill that position immediately.

When the supply of employees is predicted to be greater than demand, the firm must take steps to reduce the size of its workforce. When the oversupply is expected to be temporary, companies may implement a hiring freeze, cut back employees' hours and/or benefits, or *lay off* some employees—dismiss them from the workforce until they are needed again. In the case of layoffs, it is the positions that are eliminated rather than the employees holding those positions.

Perhaps the most humane method for making personnel cutbacks is through attrition. *Attrition* is the normal reduction in the workforce that occurs when employees leave a firm due to retirement or finding a new job.

Early retirement is another option for reducing workforce size. Under early retirement, people who are within a few years of retirement are permitted to retire ahead of schedule with full benefits. To streamline operations, Microsoft used a combination of attrition, layoffs, early retirements, and firings to reduce the size of its workforce by 18,000 people, most of them from recently acquired Nokia.[3]

Buyouts are similar to early retirement in that employees are offered a severance package in order to leave their jobs. Buyouts typically offer a number of weeks of pay for every year an employee has worked plus a specified period of extension of benefits after the employee leaves.

As a last resort, unnecessary employees are sometimes simply *fired* if cause can be found, such as failure to measure up to a specified performance standard. In such cases, companies must take care to document employees' performance and should give them warning that their performance is subpar long before a pink slip is handed out. However, because of its negative impact, this method generally is used only when absolutely necessary.

Concept Check

✓ How do firms forecast the demand for human resources?

✓ What are the techniques used to forecast human resources supply?

✓ To match human resources supply and demand, how is attrition used?

9-3 CULTURAL DIVERSITY IN HUMAN RESOURCES

Today's workforce is highly diverse, with employees bringing a wide variety of beliefs, expectations, and behavioral norms to the workplace. Managers must be sensitive to and aware of these differences. For instance, European businesspeople may offer a kiss on the cheek as a greeting. Latin Americans tend to stand closer to people with whom they are talking than North Americans prefer. Without cultural sensitivity, a job applicant who will not make eye contact during an interview may be rejected for being unapproachable, when, according to his or her culture, he or she was just being polite.

A large number of women, minorities, and immigrants have entered the U.S. workforce in recent decades. It is estimated that women make up about 47 percent of the U.S. workforce; African Americans and Hispanics each make up about 12 and 16 percent of U.S. workers, respectively.[4] Women now account for the majority of workers in the financial, education, and health services industries. They make up 52 percent of management positions in the United States.[5]

Cultural (or workplace) diversity refers to the differences among people in a workforce owing to race, ethnicity, and gender. Increasing cultural diversity is forcing managers to learn to supervise and motivate people who have a broad range of value systems. In addition to cultural diversity, other changes have taken place as well. The high proportion of women in the workforce, combined with a new emphasis on participative parenting by men, has brought many family-related issues to the workplace. Today's more educated employees also want greater independence and flexibility, leading to improved quality of life.

Although cultural diversity presents a challenge, managers should view it as an opportunity rather than a limitation. When managed properly, cultural diversity can result in a stronger organization. Table 9-1 shows several benefits that creative management of cultural diversity can offer, such as cost and human resource advantages. A culturally diverse organization may gain a marketing edge because it understands different cultures and languages. Proper guidance and management of diversity in an organization also can improve creativity. People who embrace cultural diversity frequently are more flexible in the types of positions they will accept and are more comfortable working with diverse co-workers.

cultural (or workplace) diversity differences among people in a workforce owing to race, ethnicity, and gender

Because cultural diversity creates challenges along with advantages, it is important for an organization's employees to understand it. To accomplish this goal, numerous U.S. firms have trained their managers to respect and manage diversity. Diversity training programs may include recruiting minorities, training minorities to be managers, training managers to view diversity positively, teaching English as a second language, and facilitating support groups for immigrants. Many companies recognize the importance of in-depth diversity training programs. International companies are continuously expanding their business and therefore need to meld a cohesive workforce from a labor pool with ever more diverse demographics.

A diversity program will be successful only if it is systematic, is ongoing, and has a

Why hiring a diverse group of employees can benefit your business.
Organizations that hire diverse types of employees benefit from their different skills and life experiences. The different points of view of these workers can help a firm find new opportunities and ways of doing things. In addition, diverse employees often have a greater understanding of diverse customers and the goods and services they prefer.

TABLE 9-1 Advantages of Cultural Diversity

Economic Measure	Description
Cost	The cost of poorly integrating workers increases with diversity. However, companies that handle diversity well can create cost advantages over those that do a poor job. Companies can also reduce costs by hiring culturally sensitive and trained workers.
Resource acquisition	Companies develop reputations as being favorable or unfavorable employers for women and ethnic minorities. Those with the best reputations will attract and retain the best personnel.
Marketing edge	For multinational organizations, the insight and cultural sensitivity that comes from an international perspective should improve marketing efforts. The same rationale applies to marketing subpopulations domestically.
Flexibility	Culturally diverse employees often are open to a wider array of positions within a company and are more likely to move up the corporate ladder rapidly.
Creativity	Diversity of perspectives and less emphasis on conformity to norms of the past should improve the level of creativity.
Problem solving	Differences within decision making and problem-solving groups potentially produce better decisions through a wider range of perspectives and more thorough critical analysis of issues.
Bilingual skills	Cultural diversity in the workplace is valuable in the global marketplace. Employees with knowledge about another country who can communicate in that language can prevent embarrassing mistakes due to a lack of cultural sophistication. Thus, many companies seek job applicants with a background in cultures in which the company does business.

Sources: Adapted from Taylor H. Cox and Stacy Blake, "Managing Cultural Diversity: Implications for Organizational Competitiveness," *Academy of Management Executive* 5(3):46, 1991; Ricky Griffin, *Fundamentals of Management*, 8th ed. (Mason, OH: South-Western/Cengage Learning, 2016), 244–245; and Richard L. Daft and Dororthy Marcic, *Understanding Management*, 9th ed. (Mason, OH: South-Western/Cengage Learning, 2015), 388–389.

strong, sustained commitment from top leadership. Diversity training can improve workplace attitudes and behaviors, especially when it focuses on the group most resistant to diversity training, which is white male managers. Even though there may be resistance in certain situations, cultural diversity is here to stay. Its impact on organizations is widespread and will continue to grow. Management must learn to overcome the obstacles and capitalize on the advantages associated with culturally diverse human resources.

> **Concept Check**
>
> ✓ What is cultural diversity in an organization?
>
> ✓ What are some of the benefits and challenges of cultural diversity in an organization?

9-4 JOB ANALYSIS

A manager needs to understand the nature of a job before he or she can find the right person to do it. It would make no sense to hire new people without knowing why. **Job analysis** is a systematic procedure for studying positions to determine their various elements and requirements. Consider a clerk—in a large corporation, there may be 50 kinds of clerk positions, which may all differ in terms of activities performed, the level of proficiency required for each activity, and the set of qualifications demanded. These distinctions are the focus of job analysis.

The job analysis for a particular position typically consists of two parts—a job description and a job specification. A **job description** is a list of the elements that make up a particular job. It includes the duties to be performed, the working conditions, the responsibilities, and the tools and equipment that must be used on the job (see Figure 9-1).

A **job specification** is a list of the qualifications required to perform a particular job, such as certain skills, abilities, education, and experience. In addition to

Learning Objective

9-4 Explain the objectives and uses of job analysis.

job analysis a systematic procedure for studying jobs to determine their various elements and requirements

job description a list of the elements that make up a particular job

job specification a list of the qualifications required to perform a particular job

FIGURE 9-1 Job Description and Job Specification

This job description explains the job of sales coordinator and lists the responsibilities of the position.
The job specification is contained in the last paragraph.

SOUTH-WESTERN
JOB DESCRIPTION

TITLE:	Georgia Sales Coordinator		**DATE:**	3/26/15
DEPARTMENT:	College, Sales		**GRADE:**	12
REPORTS TO:	Regional Manager		**EXEMPT/NONEXEMPT:**	Exempt

BRIEF SUMMARY:

Supervise one other Georgia-based sales representative to gain supervisory experience. Captain the four members of the outside sales rep team that are assigned to territories consisting of colleges and universities in Georgia. Oversee, coordinate, advise, and make decisions regarding Georgia sales activities. Based upon broad contact with customers across the state and communication with administrators of schools, the person will make recommendations regarding issues specific to the needs of higher education in the state of Georgia such as distance learning, conversion to the semester system, potential statewide adoptions, and faculty training.

PRINCIPAL ACCOUNTABILITIES:

1. Supervises/manages/trains one other Atlanta-based sales rep.
2. Advises two other sales reps regarding the Georgia schools in their territories.
3. Increases overall sales in Georgia as well as his or her individual sales territory.
4. Assists regional manager in planning and coordinating regional meetings and Atlanta conferences.
5. Initiates a dialogue with campus administrators, particularly in the areas of the semester conversion, distance learning, and faculty development.

DIMENSIONS:

This position will have one direct report in addition to the leadership role played within the region. Revenue most directly impacted will be within the individually assigned territory, the supervised territory, and the overall sales for the state of Georgia.

KNOWLEDGE AND SKILLS:

Must have displayed a history of consistently outstanding sales in personal territory. Must demonstrate clear teamwork and leadership skills and be willing to extend beyond the individual territory goals. Should have a clear understanding of the company's systems and product offerings in order to train and lead other sales representatives. Must have the communication skills and presence to communicate articulately with higher education administrators and to serve as a bridge between the company and higher education in the state.

Concept Check

✓ What is job analysis?

✓ What is job specification?

✓ How can it be used to hire the right person for the job?

Learning Objective

9-5 Describe the processes of recruiting, employee selection, and orientation.

recruiting the process of attracting qualified job applicants

requiring certain experience, some companies also list personality characteristics in job specifications.

The job analysis is not only the basis for recruiting and selecting new employees, it is also used in other areas of HRM, including evaluation and the determination of equitable compensation levels.

9-5 RECRUITING, SELECTION, AND ORIENTATION

In an organization with jobs waiting to be filled, HRM personnel need to (1) find candidates and (2) match the right candidate with each position. Three activities are involved: recruiting, selection, and new employee orientation.

9-5a Recruiting

Recruiting is the process of attracting qualified job applicants. Because it is a vital link in a costly process (the cost of hiring an employee can be several thousand dollars), recruiting needs to be systematic. One goal of recruiters is to attract the "right number" of applicants, which is enough to allow a good match between applicants and open positions but not so many that matching requires a lot of time and effort.

For example, if there are five open positions and five applicants, the firm has no choice. It must hire all five applicants (qualified or not). At the other extreme, if several hundred job seekers apply for the five positions, HRM personnel will spend weeks processing applications.

Recruiters may seek applicants outside the firm, within the firm, or both. The source used depends on the nature of the position, the situation within the firm, and sometimes the firm's established or traditional recruitment policies.

EXTERNAL RECRUITING External recruiting is the attempt to attract job applicants from outside an organization. External recruiting may include activities on college campuses and open houses, soliciting recommendations from present employees, posting in newspapers, employment agencies, and online. The Internet is a popular medium for searching and recruiting for positions. Social networking sites like LinkedIn and even Twitter match employers with potential employees. Online job sites such as Monster.com, Indeed.com, and SimplyHired.com help potential employees search for positions by criteria such as location, industry, or pay.

Clearly, it is best to match the recruiting means with the kind of applicant being sought. Technology is helping organizations with this matching process. A survey by the Society for Human Resource Management found that 77 percent of employers look at social media sites—most notably LinkedIn, Facebook, Twitter, and Google+—for recruiting purposes. The survey also found that 69 percent of companies employ social networking tools to identify and recruit applicants with specific skills, and 67 percent use social networking to raise their brand recognition.[6]

Social Media:
Recruiting Via Social Media

Social media is a vital tool in recruiting today, used by 93 percent of recruiting professionals polled in a recent survey. Companies don't just look for talented people with particular skills—they also want to check the fit with their corporate culture by seeing what potential employees value and how they spend their time. In addition, using social media can help firms attract the attention of managers and employees who aren't actively looking for a change, but who might be interested if they see a tweet or a Facebook post about an open position. A growing number of firms have their own mobile apps or use recruiting apps, from LinkedIn and other networking sites, to reach prospective candidates on the go.

Beyond LinkedIn, one of the most popular networking sites for recruiters and applicants, many businesses are using Twitter to announce job fairs and open positions, including temporary and seasonal employment. Crate & Barrel tweets about job fairs for seasonal employees every Fall. The Container Store posts notices of open positions on its Facebook page, reasoning that its customers might want to apply or know someone who might be looking for a new job.

Maersk Drilling, based in Denmark, has been successful in recruiting employees from around the world through its Facebook page. In addition to posting photos of everyday working conditions on an oil rig, the firm asks current employees to comment about what they do, adding a personal touch to the recruiting process.

Sources: Based on information in Sharon Florentine, "3 Ways to Use Social Media to Recruit Better Tech Talent," *CIO.com*, December 4, 2014, http://www.cio.com/article/2855173/careers-staffing/3-ways-to-use-social-media-to-recruit-better-tech-talent.html (accessed July 27, 2015); Clare Bettelley, "Executives Aren't Always Right: Why Social Media Recruiting Has a Place in Every Industry," *Forbes.com*, October 6, 2014 http://www.forbes.com/sites/clarebettelley/2014/10/06/executives-arent-always-right-why-social-media-recruiting-has-a-place-in-every-industry/ (accessed July 27, 2015); Sharon Florentine, "The Next 'Sea Change' in Recruiting: Mobile," *CIO.com*, December 5, 2014; Eric Morath, "To Fill Holiday Jobs, Retailers Reach Out Through Social Media," *Wall Street Journal*, October 26, 2014, www.wsj.com (accessed July 27, 2015).

External recruiting has advantages and disadvantages. A primary advantage is that it brings people into a firm who have new perspectives and varied business backgrounds. Some firms prefer to hire recruits directly out of college because they believe that these candidates will be easier to train to fit with the corporate culture and the needs of the company. An additional benefit of hiring younger talent is that they tend to be more technologically savvy than their older counterparts, a characteristic that is highly desirable in today's workplace. A disadvantage of external recruiting is that it is often expensive, especially if private employment agencies must be used. External recruiting also may provoke resentment among present employees who wish to advance within the company.

INTERNAL RECRUITING Internal recruiting involves considering current employees as applicants for available positions. Generally, current employees are considered for *promotion* to higher-level positions. However, employees may be considered for *transfer* from one position to another at the same level.

external recruiting the attempt to attract job applicants from outside an organization

internal recruiting considering present employees as applicants for available positions

EDWARD J BOCK 111/DREAMSTIME.COM

Don't just search the classified ads to find a job. Potential employees are recruited in a variety of ways. Companies often keep statistics on their recruiting sources so they can determine which methods are the most effective for finding good employees.

selection the process of gathering information about applicants for a position and then using that information to choose the most appropriate applicant

Promoting from within provides strong motivation for current employees and helps the firm to retain quality personnel, along with their experience. The practice of *job posting*, or informing current employees of upcoming openings, is practiced by many different firms. It may be a company policy or required by union contract. The primary disadvantage of internal recruiting is that promoting a current employee leaves another position open. Not only does the firm still incur recruiting and selection costs, but it also must train two employees instead of one.

In many situations it may be impossible to recruit internally. For example, no current employee may be qualified to fill a new position, or the firm may be growing so rapidly that there is no time to reassign positions that open as a result of promotion or transfer.

9-5b Selection

Selection is the process of gathering information about applicants for a position and using that information to choose the most appropriate applicant. Note the use of the word *appropriate*. In selection, the idea is not to hire the person with the *most* qualifications but rather the applicant who is *most appropriate*. Line managers responsible for the position select applicants. However, HRM personnel usually help by developing a pool of applicants and by expediting their assessment. Common means of obtaining information about applicants' qualifications are employment applications, interviews, references, assessment centers, and online on social networking sites like LinkedIn and Facebook.

EMPLOYMENT APPLICATIONS An employment application is useful for collecting factual information on a candidate's education, work experience, and personal history (see Figure 9-2). The data from applications are used for two purposes: to identify applicants who are worthy of further scrutiny and to familiarize interviewers with applicant backgrounds. Online applications are common, which help to streamline the process and improve data gathering capabilities for the firm. In fact, paper applications are becoming rare.

Many job candidates submit résumés, and some firms require them. A *résumé* is a one- or two-page summary of the candidate's background and qualifications. It may include a description of the type of job the applicant is seeking. A résumé may be sent to a firm to request consideration for available jobs, or it may be submitted along with an employment application.

To improve the usefulness of information, HRM specialists ask current employees about experiences and characteristics that relate to their current jobs. These factors are included on the applications and may be weighted more heavily when evaluating new applicants' qualifications.

PHASINPHOTO/DREAMSTIME.COM

EMPLOYMENT TESTS Tests administered to job candidates usually focus on aptitudes, skills, abilities, or knowledge relevant to the job. Such tests (basic computer skills tests, for example) help an employer gauge how well the applicant will perform the job. Companies may use general intelligence or personality tests, but these are seldom helpful in predicting performance. Many organizations of all sizes use predictive behavior tests, which have become more affordable with improved technology.

FIGURE 9-2 Typical Employment Application

Employers use applications to collect factual information on a candidate's education, work experience, and personal history.

3M Employment Application
Form 14650 - D

3M Staffing Resource Center
3M Center, Building 224-1W-02
P.O. Box 33224
St. Paul, MN 55133-3224

Personal Data *(Print or Type)* **No.** 109060

Name (Print or Type) Last First M.I.

Name — Last | First | MI | Social Security Number

Present Address — Street Address | Home Telephone (Include Area Code) ( )
City, State and Zip | Work Telephone (Include Area Code) ( )
Internet e-mail Address

Permanent Address — *Leave blank if same as above* — Street Address | Perm. Address Telephone (Include Area Code) ( )
City, State and Zip | Date of Application

Job Interest — Position applied for | Salary desired | Date available for work
Type of position applied for: ☐ Regular ☐ Part-time ☐ Temporary ☐ Summer ☐

Authorization to Work — It is unlawful for 3M to hire individuals that are not authorized to work in the United States. Accordingly, 3M hires only citizens or aliens that are authorized to work in the United States. If you receive an offer from 3M and you accept the offer, before you will be placed on the payroll, you will be required to document that you are a U.S. Citizen or an alien that is authorized to work in the United States.
Are you a United States citizen or a lawful permanent resident? ☐ Yes ☐ No
If your answer is No, what type of Visa and employment authorization do you have?

Education History

Schools Attended (Last School First)	Attendance Dates Mo./Yr. From - To	Grad. Date	Degree Type	Major/Minor	Accum. Grade Point
Name of School (City, State)	-				.
	-				.
	-				.
	-				.
High School or GED					.

Additional Education Information (If additional space is needed, attach separate page)
Faculty person who knows you best (name, telephone)
Memberships in professional or honorary societies and any other extracurricular activities
Post graduate research, title and description
Publications/Patents Issued

Please Open Folder and Complete Additional Information

Printed with soy inks on Torchglow Opaque (made of 50% recycled fiber, including 10% post-consumer waste).

General Information and Job Requirements
Are you willing to ➔ Work Shifts ☐ Yes ☐ No | Work overtime ☐ Yes ☐ No | Work a schedule other than M/F ☐ Yes ☐ No | Work a rotation work schedule ☐ Yes ☐ No
Travel ☐ Yes ____% ☐ No | List any restrictions regarding relocation | Are you willing to relocate? ☐ Yes ☐ No
If you wish to indicate that you were referred to 3M by any of the following, please check appropriate box and specify
☐ Employment advertisement (Name of publication) ☐ Employment agency (Name of agency) ☐ 3M Employee (Name) ☐ Other
Are you under 18? ☐ Yes ☐ No | Have you ever ☐ been employed by 3M or any 3M Subsidiary ☐ previously applied to 3M or any 3M Subsidiary | If so, please check appropriate box and specify location, date, employee number - (include last two 3M performance reviews if appropriate and available.) | Date/Employee Number

Employment Record

List most current or recent employer first, include periods of unemployment, include U.S. Military Service (show rank/rate at discharge, but not type of discharge). Include previous 3M experience (summer/part time jobs and Cooperative Education assignments and any volunteer experience which relates to the position you are applying for).

Employer (company name) | Immediate supervisor's name | Your job title
Street Address | Employment dates (mo. and yr.) From To | Salary Begin End
City, State, Zip Code | Reason for leaving or why do you want to leave?
Company's Product or Service | Summarize your job duties

Employer (company name) | Immediate supervisor's name | Your job title
Street Address | Employment dates (mo. and yr.) From To | Salary Begin End
City, State, Zip Code | Reason for leaving
Company's Product or Service | Summarize your job duties

Employer (company name) | Immediate supervisor's name | Your job title
Street Address | Employment dates (mo. and yr.) From To | Salary Begin End
City, State, Zip Code | Reason for leaving
Company's Product or Service | Summarize your job duties

Employer (company name) | Immediate supervisor's name | Your job title
Street Address | Employment dates (mo. and yr.) From To | Salary Begin End
City, State, Zip Code | Reason for leaving
Company's Product or Service | Summarize your job duties

Additional Information — *(Please include any additional information you think might be helpful to use in considering you for employment, such as additional work experience, activities, accomplishments, etc.)*

Source: Courtesy of 3M.

INTERVIEWS The interview is perhaps the most widely used selection technique because it provides an opportunity for applicants and the firm to learn more about one another. Job candidates are interviewed by at least one member of the HRM staff and by the person for whom they will be working. Candidates for higher-level jobs may meet with a department head or vice president over several interviews.

Interviewers may pose problems to test the candidate's abilities, probe employment history, and learn something about the candidate's attitudes and motivation. The candidate has a chance to find out more about the job and potential co-workers. They also provide an opportunity to test the personality fit of a candidate with the organizational culture. Many organizations now conduct interviews remotely using services such as Skype or gotomeeting.com, only flying in the most promising candidates for face-to-face meetings.

Unfortunately, interviewing may be the stage at which discrimination begins. For example, suppose that a female applicant mentions that she is the mother of small children. Her interviewer may assume that she will be resistant to job-related travel. In addition, interviewers may be unduly influenced by such factors as appearance. They may also ask different questions of different applicants so that it becomes impossible to compare candidates' qualifications objectively. Some of these problems can be solved through better interviewer training and using structured interviews. In a *structured interview*, the interviewer asks only a prepared set of job-related questions. The firm also may consider using several different interviewers for each applicant, but this can be costly.

A job interview is similar to a first date. Like a date, interviews can occur in a variety of locations and through several formats. The purpose is to give the candidate and the company the opportunity to find out about each other. Can you think of any other selection methods that benefit *both* parties in the recruiting process?

REFERENCES A job candidate generally is asked to furnish the names of references—people who can verify background information and provide personal evaluations. Naturally, applicants tend to list only references who are likely to say good things. Thus, personal evaluations obtained from references may not be of much value. However, references are often contacted to verify such information as previous job responsibilities and the reason an applicant left a former job. In many cases, social networking has changed the order in which employers receive information. Employers can peruse LinkedIn accounts, for example, to see reviews and recommendations before even interviewing a candidate.

ASSESSMENT CENTERS An assessment center is used primarily to select current employees for promotion to higher-level positions. Typically, a group of employees is sent to the center for a few days. While there, they participate in activities designed to simulate the management environment and to predict managerial effectiveness. Trained observers make recommendations regarding promotion possibilities. The expense of this technique limits its use.

9-5c Orientation

Once all information about job candidates has been collected and analyzed, the company extends a job offer. If it is accepted, the candidate becomes an employee. Soon after a candidate joins a firm, he or she goes through the firm's orientation program. **Orientation** is the process of acquainting new employees with an organization. Orientation topics range from the location of the company cafeteria to career paths within the firm. The orientation itself may range widely from a half-hour informal presentation to an elaborate program involving dozens of people and lasting several days or weeks.

9-6 COMPENSATION AND BENEFITS

An effective employee reward system must (1) enable employees to satisfy basic needs, (2) provide rewards comparable with those offered by other firms, (3) be distributed fairly within the organization, and (4) recognize that different people have different needs. A firm's compensation system can be structured to meet the first three of these requirements. The fourth is more difficult because it must account for many variables. Most firms offer a number of benefits that, taken together, generally help to provide for employees' varying needs.

9-6a Compensation Decisions

Compensation is the payment employees receive in return for their labor. Its importance to employees is obvious. Because compensation can account for a significant percentage of a firm's operating costs, it is also an important consideration

Concept Check

✓ What are the differences between internal and external recruiting?

✓ Under what conditions are each one of them used?

✓ Identify and briefly describe the types of practices and tools that are used in the selection process.

Learning Objective

9-6 Discuss the primary elements of employee compensation and benefits.

orientation the process of acquainting new employees with an organization

compensation the payment employees receive in return for their labor

for management. Therefore, the firm's **compensation system**, the policies and strategies that determine employee compensation, must be designed carefully to provide for employees' needs while keeping labor costs within reasonable limits. For most firms, designing an effective compensation system requires three separate management decisions—wage level, wage structure, and individual wages.

WAGE LEVEL Management first must position the firm's general pay level relative to pay levels of comparable firms. Most firms choose a level near the industry average. However, a firm that is not in good financial shape may pay less than average, and large, prosperous organizations may pay more than average. To determine the average pay for a job, the firm may use wage surveys. A **wage survey** is a collection of data on prevailing wage rates within an industry or a geographic area. Such surveys are compiled by industry associations, local governments, personnel associations, and (occasionally) individual firms.

WAGE STRUCTURE Next, management must decide on relative pay levels for all the positions within the firm. The result of this set of decisions is called the firm's *wage structure*. The wage structure almost always is developed on the basis of a job evaluation. **Job evaluation** is the process of determining the relative worth of the various jobs within a firm. Most observers probably would agree that a secretary/administrative assistant should make more money than a custodian, but how much more?

A number of techniques may be used to evaluate jobs. The simplest is to rank all the jobs within the firm according to value. A more frequently used method is based on the job analysis. Points are allocated to each element and job requirement. For example, "college degree required" might be worth 50 points, whereas a job requiring only a high school diploma would only receive 25 points. The more points allocated, the more important the job is presumed to be (and the higher its level in the firm's wage structure).

INDIVIDUAL WAGES Finally, the company must determine the specific payments individual employees will receive. Consider the case of two secretaries. Job evaluation was used to determine the level of secretarial pay, but suppose that one secretary has 15 years of experience, can type 80 words per minute accurately, and can work in several computer programs, while the other has two years of experience, can type only 55 words per minute, and knows only one computer program. In most firms, a wage range would be established (maybe $10.00 to $15.00 per hour) to reflect the range of experience and abilities, with the more qualified secretary receiving the higher wage.

Two wage decisions come into play here. First, the employee's initial rate must be established. It is based on experience, other qualifications, and expected performance. Later, the employee may be given pay increases based on seniority and performance.

9-6b Comparable Worth

It is an established fact that women in the workforce are paid less than men, in spite of measures and legislation to counter this phenomenon. **Comparable worth** is a concept that seeks equal compensation for jobs that require equivalent levels of education, training, and skill. In recent decades, many states have taken steps to ensure that all workers have equal pay for comparable worth, but the issue is contentious. Critics argue that inflating salaries artificially for female-dominated occupations encourages women to keep these jobs rather than seek out higher-paying jobs. Addressing pay inequality is complicated. Studies have shown that, even after controlling for educational attainment and profession, wage gaps persist between men and women. Research suggests that factors behind the continuing wage disparity may include the

compensation system the policies and strategies that determine employee compensation

wage survey a collection of data on prevailing wage rates within an industry or a geographic area

job evaluation the process of determining the relative worth of the various jobs within a firm

comparable worth a concept that seeks equal compensation for jobs requiring about the same level of education, training, and skills

idea that women are less inclined to ask for raises and that working mothers are less likely to work long hours or at specific times. Some companies have revealed that closing the gap is proving more challenging than expected, even with strong support. Companies, such as Raytheon and Kimberly-Clark, are applying more formal approaches to addressing the issue, such as implementing special teams dedicated to pay equity analyses that identify areas with pay disparities, as well as where women are experiencing a "glass ceiling" that keeps them from moving up within a firm. A side effect of such efforts is more women and minorities moving into management positions.[7]

9-6c Types of Compensation

Compensation can take a variety of forms. Most forms fall into the following categories: hourly wage, weekly or monthly salary, commissions, incentive payments, lump-sum salary increases, and profit sharing.

HOURLY WAGE An **hourly wage** is a specific amount of money paid for each hour worked. People who earn wages are paid their hourly wage for the first 40 hours worked in any week. Anything in excess of 40 hours is overtime, for which they are paid one-and-one-half times their hourly wage. Workers in retail and fast-food chains, on assembly lines, and in clerical positions usually are paid an hourly wage.

WEEKLY OR MONTHLY SALARY A **salary** is a specific amount of money paid for an employee's work during a set calendar period, regardless of the actual number of hours worked. Salaried employees receive no overtime pay, but they do not lose pay when they work less than 40 hours per week. Most professional and managerial positions are salaried.

COMMISSIONS A **commission** is a payment that is a percentage of sales revenue. Sales representatives and sales managers often are paid entirely through commissions or a combination of commissions and salary.

INCENTIVE PAYMENTS An **incentive payment** is in addition to wages, salary, or commissions. Incentive payments are rewards for outstanding job performance. They may be distributed to all or only select employees. Some firms distribute incentive payments to all employees annually. The size of the payment depends on the firm's earnings and, at times, on the particular employee's length of service with the firm. Firms sometimes offer incentives to employees who exceed specific sales or production goals, a practice called *gainsharing*. For example, 12 New Jersey hospitals used a pilot gainsharing program to award financial incentives to physicians for achieving quality and efficiency goals. The three-year program, which paid out nearly $19 million to doctors, reduced costs per admission by 8.5 percent, saving the hospitals $113 million.[8] Some organizations reward outstanding workers individually through *merit pay*. This pay-for-performance approach allows management to control labor costs while encouraging employees to work more efficiently.

LUMP-SUM SALARY INCREASES In traditional reward systems, an annual pay increase is spread evenly across each paycheck that year. However, some companies offer a **lump-sum salary increase**. This gives the employee the option of taking the

hourly wage a specific amount of money paid for each hour of work

salary a specific amount of money paid for an employee's work during a set calendar period, regardless of the actual number of hours worked

incentive payment a payment in addition to wages, salary, or commissions

commission a payment that is a percentage of sales revenue

lump-sum salary increase an entire pay raise taken in one lump sum

entire pay raise in one lump sum. The employee then draws his or her "regular" pay for the rest of the year. The lump-sum payment typically is treated as an interest-free loan that must be repaid if the employee leaves the firm during the year.

PROFIT-SHARING Profit-sharing is the distribution of a percentage of a firm's profit among its employees. The idea is to motivate employees to work effectively by giving them a stake in the company's financial success. For example, every year since 1938 Hormel Foods Corporation has distributed its profits to employees in the form of dividends at the beginning of the winter holiday season. The higher the profits, the higher the dividends employees earn.[9]

9-6d Employee Benefits

An **employee benefit** is a reward in addition to regular compensation that is provided indirectly to employees. Employee benefits consist mainly of services (such as health and life insurance) that are paid for partially or totally by employers, and employee expenses (such as college tuition) that employers reimburse. Currently, the average cost of these benefits is 30 percent of an employee's total compensation.[10] Thus, a person who receives a salary of $35,000 really receives total compensation of $50,000, once $15,000 in benefits (30 percent of $50,000) is factored in.

TYPES OF BENEFITS Employee benefits take a variety of forms. *Pay for time not worked* covers such absences as vacation, holidays, and sick leave. *Insurance packages* may include health, life, and dental insurance for employees and their families. Some firms pay the entire cost of the insurance package, and others share the cost with the employee. The costs of *pension and retirement programs* also may be borne entirely by the firm or shared with the employee.

Some benefits are required by law. For example, employers must maintain *workers' compensation insurance*, which pays medical bills for injuries that occur on the job and provides income for employees who are disabled by job-related injuries. Employers must also pay for *unemployment insurance* and contribute to each employee's federal *Social Security* account.

Other benefits employers may provide include tuition-reimbursement plans; credit unions, child-care services, company cafeterias, exercise rooms, and broad employee stock-option plans. Some companies offer special benefits to U.S. military reservists who are called up for active duty.

profit-sharing the distribution of a percentage of a firm's profit among its employees

employee benefit a reward in addition to regular compensation that is provided indirectly to employees

What job benefits are crucial to you? The benefits companies provide vary widely. Large companies are often able to offer employees more benefits than small ones. However, in small firms, employees are more likely to do a broader range of tasks and advance to higher positions more quickly.

© TUPUNGATO/SHUTTERSTOCK.COM

Career Success

What Are the Job Perks at Apple?

Apple—famed for its iconic "i" products, including the iPhone, the iPad, and iTunes—employs 98,000 people worldwide in all kinds of positions. Thanks to its ongoing growth and success, the company often has openings for talented employees in functions such as product design and development, engineering, information technology, sales, customer service, finance, human resources, retailing, and administrative support.

Denise Young Smith, the head of human resources, is casting a wide recruiting net and offering a wide range of benefits to encourage diversity in Apple's workforce. For example, the company will now reimburse employees for the cost of educational courses, help them refinance student loans at subsidized rates, and offer extended new-parent leave. It also matches employees' charitable donations and donates money to non-profit groups based on the number of volunteer hours put in by Apple employees at each organization. On-site fitness and wellness centers help

employees get into shape and stay healthy. Smith explains that "for the first time, we've probably got four generations in the workplace at the same time, and we need a plethora of programs" to attract and retain the best employees.

Apple employees have the option of taking courses at Apple University, either online or in person. Some courses analyze key decisions in the company's history, illuminating Apple's corporate culture and business priorities by exploring the background, potential solutions, and actual results. Others focus on the inspirations for product design and on effective communications. Attendance is voluntary—but new hires, in particular, find the courses valuable at the start of their Apple careers.

Sources: Based on information in Michal Lev-Ram, "Apple Unveils New Perks to Attract Talent," *Fortune*, October 2, 2014, www.fortune.com (accessed July 27, 2015); Brian X. Chen, "Simplifying the Bull: How Picasso Helps to Teach Apple's Style," *New York Times*, August 10, 2014, www.nytimes.com (accessed July 27, 2015); Michal Lev-Ram, "Apple's New Voice," *Fortune*, October 6, 2014, pp. 134–5.

Increasingly, companies offer more varied benefits to attract and retain the best employees. In the high-tech industry, competition for talented employees is so intense that many firms have adopted more unusual perks, such as on-site bowling alleys, arcades, bike-repair services, and barber services, as well as free food, nap pods, free exercise classes, and concierge services that run errands for employees so they can stay at work and focus on their jobs.[11]

flexible benefit plan
compensation plan whereby an employee receives a predetermined amount of benefit dollars to spend on a package of benefits he or she has selected to meet individual needs

FLEXIBLE BENEFIT PLANS Through a **flexible benefit plan**, an employee receives a predetermined amount of benefit dollars and may allocate those dollars to various categories of benefits in the way that best fits his or her needs. Some flexible benefit plans offer a broad array of benefit options, including health care, dental care, life insurance, accidental death and dismemberment coverage for the worker and dependents, long-term disability coverage, vacation benefits, retirement savings, and dependent-care benefits. Other firms offer limited options, primarily in health and life insurance and retirement plans.

Although the cost of administering flexible plans is high, a number of organizations, including Phillips Corporation and Coca-Cola, have implemented this option. Because employees' needs are so diverse, flexible plans help firms to offer benefit packages that more specifically meet their employees' needs. Flexible plans can, in the long run, help a company to contain costs because a specified amount is allocated to cover the benefits of each employee. Furthermore, organizations that offer flexible plans with many choices may be perceived as being employee-friendly. Thus, they are in a better position to attract and retain qualified employees.

Concept Check

✓ Identify the major compensation decisions that HRM managers make.

✓ What are the different forms of compensation?

✓ What are the major types of employee benefits?

✓ How do flexible benefit plans work?

Learning Objective

9-7 Explain the purposes and techniques of employee training and development.

9-7 TRAINING AND DEVELOPMENT

Training and development are extremely important at Verizon, as evidenced by its recent induction into *Training* magazine's "Hall of Fame" list. Verizon has made

Training's "Top 125" list for 12 consecutive years, distinguishing itself through its effectiveness and efficiency, number of training hours logged by employees, and survey results. Employees log nearly 8 million training hours annually, using a range of technologies, including mobile and online learning. The company offers over 11,000 courses to employees to ensure that they continue their professional development.[12] Many top managers believe that the financial and human resources invested in training and development are well worth it. Employees at all levels of a company need training and/or development about its products, specific computer programs and protocols, customer needs, company policies and codes of conduct, applicable regulations, competitors' products, and more.

Both training and development are aimed at improving employees' skills and abilities. However, the two are usually differentiated as employee training or management development. **Employee training** is the process of teaching operations and technical employees how to do their present jobs more effectively and efficiently. **Management development** is the process of preparing managers and other professionals to assume increased responsibility in both present and future positions. Thus, training and development differ in who is being taught and the purpose of the teaching. However, both are necessary for personal and organizational growth. Companies that hope to stay competitive typically make huge commitments to employee training and development. Indeed, training accounts for about $70 billion of business spending in the U.S. and $130 billion worldwide.[13] Developing an effective training program involves analyzing needs, determining the best methods, and developing an evaluation system to gauge effectiveness. Some employers require workers to attain certifications targeted to their field to help them gain and maintain the specific skills they need. There are many different employee training methods, including Internet-based training. Internet training is growing in popularity as it can result in significant cost, travel, and time savings.

employee training the process of teaching operations and technical employees how to do their present jobs more effectively and efficiently

management development the process of preparing managers and other professionals to assume increased responsibility in both present and future positions

9-7a Analysis of Training Needs

When thinking about developing a training program, managers first must determine if training is actually needed and, if so, what types of training needs exist. Training needs can vary considerably. For example, some employees may need to improve their technical skills, while others need training on organizational procedures. Training also may focus on business ethics, product information, or customer service. Because training is expensive, it is critical that the correct training needs be identified. Employers may find that sometimes employees need motivation more than they need training.

9-7b Training and Development Methods

A number of methods are available for employee training and management development. Most of these methods can be applied to both training and management development.

- *On-the-job methods.* The trainee learns by doing the work under the supervision of an experienced employee.
- *Simulations.* The work situation is simulated in a separate area so that learning takes place away from the day-to-day pressures of work.

AUREMAR/DREAMSTIME.COM

What job training methods have you experienced, and how effective were they? Organizations train employees using a variety of methods and locations. Depending on the type of business, the training may take just a few hours or more than a year.

- *Classroom teaching and lectures.* Instructors present concepts and illustrations through a variety of techniques.
- *Conferences and seminars.* Experts and learners come together to discuss problems and exchange ideas.
- *Role-playing.* Participants act out others' roles in order to better understand them (primarily a management development tool).
- *e-Learning.* Participants train by watching videos of lectures or how-to guides, playing "games" that simulate work situations, or taking online quizzes to demonstrate their proficiency in a topic.

9-7c Evaluation of Training and Development

Training and development are expensive because the training itself can be costly and employees are not working at full productivity while they are receiving training, costing the firm further revenue. To ensure that training and development are as cost-effective as possible, the managers responsible should evaluate the company's efforts periodically.

In order to set benchmarks and gauge program effectiveness, managers should develop measurable objectives before the training starts. For example, a measurable object would be that, after receiving training, a new employee will be able to produce a report using a specified format and be able to correctly identify 20 critical terms related to the field. The results of training evaluations should be made known to all those involved in the program—including trainees and upper management. For trainees, the results of evaluations can enhance motivation and learning. For upper management, the results may be the basis for making decisions about the training program itself.

9-8 PERFORMANCE APPRAISAL

Performance appraisal is the evaluation of employees' current and potential levels of performance to allow managers to make unbiased human resources decisions. The process has three main objectives. First, managers use performance appraisals to let workers know how well they are doing and how they can improve in the future. Second, a performance appraisal provides an effective basis for distributing rewards, such as pay raises and promotions. Third, performance appraisal helps the organization monitor its employee selection, training, and development activities. If large numbers of employees continually perform below expectations, the firm may need to revise its selection process or strengthen its training and development activities. Most performance appraisal processes include a written document. An example appears in Figure 9-3.

9-8a Common Evaluation Techniques

The techniques and methods for appraising employee performance are either objective or judgmental in nature.

OBJECTIVE METHODS Objective appraisal methods use some measurable quantity as the basis for assessing performance. Units of output, dollar volume of sales, number of defective products, and number of insurance claims processed are all objective, measurable quantities. Thus, an employee who processes an average of 26 insurance claims per week is given a higher evaluation than one whose average is 19 claims per week.

Such objective measures may require adjustment depending on the work environment. Suppose that the first of our insurance claims processors works in New York City and the second works in rural Iowa. Both must visit each client because they are processing homeowners' insurance claims. The difference in their

Learning Objective

9-8 Discuss performance appraisal techniques and performance feedback.

performance appraisal the evaluation of employees' current and potential levels of performance to allow managers to make objective human resources decisions

FIGURE 9-3 Performance Appraisal

3M **Contribution and Development Summary**
FORM 37450 - B

Employee Name	Employee Number	Job Title
Department		Location
Coach/Supervisor(s) Name(s)		Review Period
		From : To :

Major Job Responsibilities

| Goals/Expectations | Contributions/Results |

Contribution (To be completed by coach/supervisor)

☐ Good Level of Contribution for this year ☐ Exceptional Level of Contribution for this year

☐ Unsatisfactory Level of Contribution for this year

page 3

Development Summary

| Areas of Strength | Development Priorities |

Career Interests

| Next job | Longer Range |

Current Mobility

☐ 0 - Currently Unable to Relocate ☐ 3 - Position Within O.U.S. Area (ex: Europe, Asia)

☐ 1 - Position In Home Country Only (Use if Home Country is Outside U.S.) ☐ 4 - Position In U.S.

☐ 2 - Position Within O.U.S. Region (e: Nordic, SEA...) ☐ 5 - Position Anywhere In The World

Development

☐ W - Well placed. Development plans achievable in current role for at least the next year ☐ X - Not well placed. Action required to resolve placement issues.

☐ C - Ready now for a move to a different job for career broadening experience **Comments on Development**

☐ I - Ready now for a move to a different job involving increased responsibility

Employee Comments

Coach/Supervisor Comments **Other Supervisor (if applicable) and/or Reviewer**

Signatures

| Coach/Supervisor | Date | Other Coach/Supervisor or Reviewer | Date |
| Employee | | | Date |

page 4

Source: Courtesy of 3M.

average weekly output may be entirely because of the long distances the Iowan must travel to visit clients. In this case, the two workers may very well be equally competent and motivated. Thus, a manager must take into account circumstances that may be hidden by a purely statistical measurement.

JUDGMENTAL METHODS Judgmental appraisal methods are used much more frequently than objective methods. They require that the manager judge or estimate the employee's performance level. These methods are based on employee ranking or rating scales. When ranking is used, the manager ranks subordinates from best to worst. This approach has drawbacks, including the lack of an absolute standard. Use of rating scales is the most popular judgmental appraisal technique. A *rating scale* consists of a number of statements, on which each employee is rated based on the degree to which the statement applies. For example, one statement might be, "This employee always does high-quality work." The supervisor would give the employee a rating, from 5 down to 1, corresponding to gradations ranging from "strongly agree" to "strongly disagree." The ratings on all the statements are added to obtain the employee's total evaluation.

AVOIDING APPRAISAL ERRORS Managers must be cautious if they are to avoid making mistakes when appraising employees. It is common to overuse one portion of an evaluation instrument, thus risking overemphasizing or underemphasizing issues. A manager must guard against allowing an employee's poor performance on one activity to influence his or her judgment of that subordinate's work

Performance feedback can help employees progress within an organization. A business usually evaluates its employees on an annual basis, but sometimes it does so quarterly and even monthly, especially when they are newly hired. Performance reviews that gather feedback about an employee from his or her peers, subordinates, and supervisors can help the person get a realistic view of his or her strengths and weaknesses.

FRIZZANTINE/DREAMSTIME.COM

on other activities. Similarly, putting too much weight on recent performance can distort an employee's evaluation. For example, if the employee is being rated on performance over the last year, a manager should not permit last month's disappointing performance to overshadow the quality of the work done in the first 11 months of the year. Finally, a manager must guard against discrimination on the basis of race, age, gender, religion, national origin, or sexual orientation.

9-8b Performance Feedback

No matter which appraisal technique is used, managers should discuss the results with the employee soon after completion. The manager should explain the basis for present rewards and should let the employee know what he or she can do to improve. The information provided to an employee in such discussions is called *performance feedback*, and the process is known as a *performance feedback interview*.

There are three major approaches to performance feedback interviews: tell-and-sell, tell-and-listen, and problem solving. In a *tell-and-sell* feedback interview, the superior tells the employee how good or bad the employee's performance has been and attempts to persuade the employee to accept the evaluation. Because the employee has no input into the evaluation, the tell-and-sell interview can lead to defensiveness, resentment, and frustration on the part of the subordinate.

With the *tell-and-listen* approach, the supervisor tells the employee what the employee has done right and wrong and then gives him or her a chance to respond. The subordinate may simply be given an opportunity to react to the supervisor's statements or may be permitted to offer a full self-appraisal.

In the *problem-solving* approach, employees evaluate their own performance and set their own goals for future performance. The supervisor is more a colleague than a judge and offers comments and advice in a noncritical manner while mutually agreeing with the employee on goals for improvement. This is the method most likely to result in employee commitment to the established goals.

To avoid some of the problems associated with the tell-and-sell interview, supervisors sometimes use a mixed approach. The mixed interview uses the tell-and-sell approach to communicate administrative decisions and the problem-solving approach to discuss employee-development issues and future performance goals.

Another approach that has become popular is called a *360-degree evaluation*. A 360-degree evaluation collects anonymous reviews about an employee from his or her peers, subordinates, and supervisors and compiles them into a feedback report for the employee. Companies that invest significant resources in employee-development efforts are especially likely to use 360-degree evaluations. An employee should not be given a feedback report without first having a one-on-one meeting with his or her supervisor. To ensure effective implementation, upper-level management should adopt this approach first and coach managers on how to use the feedback to achieve positive performance and behavioral outcomes.

Many managers find it difficult to discuss negative appraisals, leading them to ignore performance feedback. However, it is important for employees to be informed of how they can improve. Employers should emphasize employee strengths when delivering a negative appraisal. Without feedback, an employee may be unaware of his or her weaknesses and they will never be addressed. Only through tactful, honest communication can the results of an appraisal be fully used.

Concept Check

✓ What are the main objectives of performance appraisal?

✓ What methods are used?

✓ Describe the three approaches to performance feedback interviews.

9-9 THE LEGAL ENVIRONMENT OF HRM

Legislation regarding HRM practices has been passed mainly to protect the rights of employees, to promote job safety, and to eliminate discrimination in the workplace. The major federal laws affecting HRM are summarized in Table 9-2.

Learning Objective

9-9 Outline the major legislation affecting human resources management.

9-9a National Labor Relations Act and Labor–Management Relations Act

These laws are concerned with dealings between business firms and labor unions. This general area is, in concept, a part of HRM. However, because of its importance, it is often treated as a separate set of activities.

9-9b Fair Labor Standards Act

This act, passed in 1938 and amended many times since, applies primarily to wages. It established minimum wages and overtime pay rates. Many managers and other professionals, however, are exempt from this law. Salaried employees seldom get overtime when they work more than 40 hours a week.

TABLE 9-2 Federal Legislation Affecting Human Resources Management

Law	Purpose
National Labor Relations Act (1935)	Established a collective-bargaining process in labor–management relations and the National Labor Relations Board (NLRB).
Fair Labor Standards Act (1938)	Established a minimum wage and an overtime pay rate for employees working more than 40 hours per week.
Labor–Management Relations Act (1947)	Provides a balance between union power and management power, also known as the Taft–Hartley Act.
Equal Pay Act (1963)	Specifies that men and women who do equal jobs must be paid the same wage.
Title VII of the Civil Rights Act (1964)	Prohibits discrimination in employment practices based on sex, race, color, religion, or national origin.
Age Discrimination in Employment Act (1967–1986)	Prohibits personnel practices that discriminate against people aged 40 years and older. The 1986 amendment eliminated a mandatory retirement age.
Occupational Safety and Health Act (1970)	Regulates the degree to which employees can be exposed to hazardous substances and specifies the safety equipment that the employer must provide.
Employment Retirement Income Security Act (1974)	Regulates company retirement programs and provides a federal insurance program for retirement plans that go bankrupt.
Worker Adjustment and Retraining Notification (WARN) Act (1988)	Requires employers to give employees 60 days notice regarding plant closure or layoff of 50 or more employees.
Americans with Disabilities Act (1990)	Prohibits discrimination against qualified individuals with disabilities in all employment practices, including job-application procedures, hiring, firing, advancement, compensation, training, and other terms, conditions, and privileges of employment.
Civil Rights Act (1991)	Empowers employees to sue employers for sexual discrimination and collect punitive damages.
Family and Medical Leave Act (1993)	Requires an organization with 50 or more employees to provide up to 12 weeks of leave without pay on the birth (or adoption) of an employee's child or if an employee or his or her spouse, child, or parent is seriously ill.
Affordable Care Act (2010)	Requires an organization with 50 or more employees to make health insurance available to employees or pay an assessment and gives employees the right to buy health insurance from another provider if an organization's health insurance is too expensive.

9-9c Equal Pay Act

Passed in 1963, this law overlaps somewhat with Title VII of the Civil Rights Act (see next section). The Equal Pay Act specifies that men and women who are doing equal jobs must be paid the same wage. Equal jobs are ones that demand equivalent effort, skill, and responsibility and are performed under the same conditions. Discrepancies in pay are legal if they can be attributed to differences in seniority, qualifications, or performance. In spite of having this law on the books for more than half a century, women and men are not treated equally in the workplace. For example, there are only 24 female CEOs of *Fortune 500* companies—less than 5 percent—and women still earn 18 percent less than men.[14]

9-9d Civil Rights Acts

Title VII of the Civil Rights Act of 1964 forbids organizations with 15 or more employees to discriminate in employee selection and retention on the basis of sex, race, color, religion, or national origin. The purpose of Title VII is to ensure that employers make personnel decisions on the basis of employee qualifications only. As a result of this act, discrimination in employment (especially against African Americans) has been reduced in this country.

A person who believes that he or she has been discriminated against can file a complaint with the Equal Employment Opportunity Commission (EEOC), which oversees federal laws and regulations regarding discrimination in employment. If it finds that the person has, in fact, been the victim of discrimination, the commission can take legal action on his or her behalf.

The Civil Rights Act of 1991 facilitates an employee's suing and collecting punitive damages for sexual discrimination. Discriminatory promotion and termination decisions as well as on-the-job issues, such as sexual harassment, are covered by this act.

9-9e Age Discrimination in Employment Act

The general purpose of this act, which was passed in 1967 and amended in 1986, is the same as that of Title VII—to eliminate discrimination. However, as the name implies, the Age Discrimination in Employment Act is concerned with discrimination based on age. It outlaws personnel practices that discriminate against people aged 40 years or older in companies with 20 or more employees. Also outlawed are company policies that specify a mandatory retirement age. Employers must base employment decisions on ability, not on a number. For example, Dallas-based HiLine Electric Co. settled EEOC charges over the use of age-based criterion in its recruiting and hiring process. The agency identified eight job seekers, who failed to gain employment because of the company's discrimination against potential employees over the age of 50. HiLine agreed not to engage in such practices in the future and to pay $210,000 in penalties.[15]

9-9f Occupational Safety and Health Act

Passed in 1970, this act is concerned with issues of employee health and safety. For example, the act regulates the degree to which employees can be exposed to hazardous substances. It also specifies the safety equipment that the employer must provide. The Occupational Safety and Health Administration (OSHA) was created to enforce this act. Inspectors from OSHA investigate employee complaints regarding unsafe working conditions. They also make spot checks on companies operating in particularly hazardous industries, such as chemicals and mining, to ensure compliance with the law. A firm found to be in violation of federal standards can be heavily fined or shut down. Nonetheless, many people feel that issuing OSHA violations is not enough to protect workers from harm.

9-9g Employee Retirement Income Security Act

This act was passed in 1974 to protect the retirement benefits of employees. It does not require that firms provide a retirement plan. However, it does specify that if a retirement plan is provided, it must be managed in such a way that the interests of employees are protected. It also provides federal insurance for retirement plans that go bankrupt.

9-9h Affirmative Action

Affirmative action is not one act, but a series of executive orders issued by the President of the United States. It applies to all employers with 50 or more employees holding federal contracts in excess of $50,000. It prescribes that such employers (1) actively encourage job applications from members of minority groups and (2) hire qualified employees from minority groups who are not fully represented in their organizations. Many firms that do not hold government contracts voluntarily take part in affirmative action.

KATARZYNA BIALASIEWICZ/DREAMSTIME.COM

Focus on what employees and job candidates can do—not what they can't. The American Disabilities Act (ADA) requires businesses to make reasonable accommodations for applicants and employees with disabilities. The law is not the only reason why firms should hire and retain the disabled. Studies have shown that firms that do so experience positive business outcomes. Many manual and electronic devices are available today that can help the disabled work safely and productively. Something as small as slightly redesigning workstations can make it possible for people of all abilities to work in many jobs.

9-9i Americans with Disabilities Act

The Americans with Disabilities Act (ADA) prohibits discrimination against qualified individuals with disabilities in all employment practices—including job-application procedures, hiring, firing, advancement, compensation, training, and other terms and conditions of employment. All private employers and government agencies with 15 or more employees are covered by the ADA. Defining who is a qualified individual with a disability is, of course, difficult. Depending on how *qualified individual with a disability* is interpreted, more than 57 million Americans can be included under this law.[16] Although pregnancy is not a disability, the ADA also requires employers to provide reasonable accommodation to pregnant employees. It also mandates that all businesses that serve the public must make their facilities accessible to people with disabilities.

The ADA not only protects individuals with obvious physical disabilities, but also safeguards those with less visible conditions such as heart disease, diabetes, epilepsy, cancer, AIDS, and mental illnesses. Because of this law, many organizations no longer require job applicants to pass physical examinations as a condition of employment.

Employers are required to provide disabled employees with reasonable accommodation. *Reasonable accommodation* is any modification or adjustment to a job or work environment that will enable a qualified employee with a disability to perform a central job function, such as making existing facilities accessible to and usable by wheelchair-bound individuals. Reasonable accommodation also might mean restructuring a job, modifying work schedules, acquiring or modifying equipment, providing qualified readers or interpreters, or changing training programs.

Concept Check

✓ How is the National Labor Relations Act different from the Fair Labor Standards Act?

✓ How does the Civil Rights Act influence the selection and promotion of employees?

✓ What is the Occupational Safety and Health Act?

✓ What is the purpose of the Americans with Disabilities Act?

Summary

9-1 Describe the major components of human resources management.

Human resources management (HRM) is the set of activities involved in acquiring, maintaining, and developing an organization's human resources. Responsibility for HRM is shared by specialized staff and line managers. HRM activities include human resources planning, job analysis, recruitment, selection, orientation, compensation, benefits, training and development, and performance appraisal.

9-2 Identify the steps in human resources planning.

Human resources planning consists of forecasting the human resources that a firm will need and planning a course of action to match supply with demand. Layoffs, attrition, early retirement, and (as a last resort) firing are ways to reduce the size of the workforce when needed. Supply is increased through hiring.

9-3 Describe cultural diversity and understand some of the challenges and opportunities associated with it.

Cultural diversity refers to the differences among people in a workforce owing to race, ethnicity, and gender. With an increasing number of women, minorities, and immigrants in the U.S. workforce, management is faced with challenges and competitive advantages. Some organizations have implemented diversity-related training programs to make the most of cultural diversity. With proper guidance and management, a culturally diverse organization can prove beneficial to all involved.

9-4 Explain the objectives and uses of job analysis.

Job analysis provides a job description and a job specification for each position within a firm. A job description is a list of the elements that make up a particular job. A job specification is a list of qualifications required to perform a job. Job analysis is used in evaluation and in the determination of compensation levels and serves as the basis for recruiting and selecting new employees.

9-5 Describe the processes of recruiting, employee selection, and orientation.

Recruiting is the process of attracting qualified job applicants. Candidates for open positions may be recruited from within or outside a firm. In the selection process, information about candidates is obtained from applications, résumés, tests, interviews, references, assessment centers, even online social networking sites. This information is used to select the most appropriate candidate for the job. Newly hired employees will then go through an orientation program to learn about the firm and the specifics of the job.

9-6 Discuss the primary elements of employee compensation and benefits.

Compensation is the payment employees receive in return for their labor. In developing a system for paying employees, management must decide on the firm's general wage level (relative to other firms), the wage structure within the firm, and individual wages. Wage surveys and job analyses are useful in making these decisions. Employees may be paid hourly wages, salaries, or commissions. They also may receive incentive payments, lump-sum salary increases, and profit-sharing payments. Employee benefits, which are nonmonetary rewards to employees, add about 30 percent to the cost of compensation.

9-7 Explain the purposes and techniques of employee training and development.

Employee-training and management-development programs enhance the ability of employees to contribute to a firm. When developing a training program, the company should analyze training needs and then select training methods. Because training is expensive, an organization should periodically evaluate the effectiveness of its training programs.

9-8 Discuss performance appraisal techniques and performance feedback.

Performance appraisal, or evaluation, is used to provide employees with performance feedback, to serve as a basis for distributing rewards, and to monitor selection and training activities. Both objective and judgmental appraisal techniques are used. Their results are communicated to employees through three performance feedback approaches: tell-and-sell, tell-and-listen, and problem solving.

9-9 Outline the major legislation affecting human resources management.

A number of laws have been passed that affect HRM practices and that protect the rights and safety of employees.

Some of these are the National Labor Relations Act of 1935, the Labor–Management Relations Act of 1947, the Fair Labor Standards Act of 1938, the Equal Pay Act of 1963, Title VII of the Civil Rights Act of 1964, the Age Discrimination in Employment Acts of 1967 and 1986, the Occupational Safety and Health Act of 1970, the Employment Retirement Income Security Act of 1974, the Worker Adjustment and Retraining Notification Act of 1988, the Americans with Disabilities Act of 1990, the Civil Rights Act of 1991, and the Family and Medical Leave Act of 1993.

Key Terms

You should now be able to define and give an example relevant to each of the following terms:

human resources
    management (HRM) (245)
human resources planning
    (247)
replacement chart (248)
skills inventory (248)
cultural (or workplace)
    diversity (250)
job analysis (251)

job description (251)
job specification (251)
recruiting (252)
external recruiting (253)
internal recruiting (253)
selection (254)
orientation (256)
compensation (256)
compensation system (257)

wage survey (257)
job evaluation (257)
comparable worth (257)
hourly wage (258)
salary (258)
commission (258)
incentive payment (258)
lump-sum salary increase
    (258)

profit-sharing (259)
employee benefit (259)
flexible benefit plan (260)
employee training (261)
management development
    (261)
performance appraisal (262)

Discussion Questions

1. In general, on what basis is responsibility for HRM divided between line and staff managers?
2. How is a forecast of human resources demand related to a firm's organizational planning?
3. How do human resources managers go about matching a firm's supply of workers with demand?
4. What are the major challenges and benefits associated with a culturally diverse workforce?
5. What are the advantages and disadvantages of external recruiting? Of internal recruiting?
6. How is a job analysis used in the process of job evaluation?
7. Suppose that you have just opened a new Ford sales showroom and repair shop. Which of your employees would be paid wages, which would receive salaries, and which would receive commissions?
8. Why is it so important to provide feedback after a performance appraisal?
9. How accurately can managers plan for future human resources needs?
10. Are employee benefits really necessary? Why?
11. As a manager, what actions would you take if an operations employee with six years of experience on the job refused ongoing training and ignored performance feedback?
12. Why are there so many laws relating to HRM practices?
13. Of the laws discussed in the text, which are the most important, in your opinion?

Video Case
The Container Store Hires Great Employees to Sell Empty Boxes

Empty boxes are big business for the Container Store (www. containerstore.com), headquartered just outside Dallas in Coppell, Texas. Founded in 1978, the company has grown to 67 stores nationwide and $800 million in annual revenue by specializing in storage products for home and office. From stacking bins and spice racks to trash cans and toy caddies, the Container Store sells a variety of functional, stylish storage solutions for every situation.

Kip Tindell, co-founder and CEO, attributes the company's decades-long success to the high caliber of its employees. "When you're selling empty boxes, you'd better have great people," he explains. Tindell's philosophy that "one great person equals three good people" has become the cornerstone of the Container Store's approach to recruiting, hiring, training, and retaining employees. To attract and keep enthusiastic people who enjoy working with customers, the company pays above-average wages—the average Container Store retail salesperson brings in $50,000—nearly twice that of the typical retailer. It also offers numerous benefits, including medical coverage, generous discounts on store merchandise, paid vacation time, and even pet insurance.

Not surprisingly, hundreds of people apply for every job opening. The Container Store requires as many as nine interviews before managers make a decision about which "great" candidate to select. Only 3 percent of the people who apply to work for the company end up being hired. Once they're hired, new employees enter a training program to gain the skills they need for on-the-job success. All full-time employees receive more than 260 hours of intensive training during their first 12 months. Part-time workers receive 150 hours of training during the first year. The purpose is to improve employees' product knowledge, teach them how to assess customers' storage needs, and provide the techniques and tools they need to suggest creative solutions for each individual's needs. The training also covers professional development topics to prepare employees for future career advancement.

Although retailers usually experience high turnover, the Container Store's turnover is exceptionally low, because it is so selective in hiring, rewards its employees well for performance, and provides a satisfying work environment. During the recent recession, when many employers were forced to cut costs through layoffs, the CEO reassured his employees that they didn't have to worry about being laid off. Rather than reduce its workforce, the company cut back slightly on some benefits and found other ways to lower expenses during the financial crunch. When the economy turned around and profits began to rise, the Container Store restored employee benefits to their former levels. It also embarked on its most aggressive expansion ever, opening six new stores in a single year and hiring hundreds of employees to fill the newly created sales positions.

The Container Store's no-layoff policy is only one way it proves how much it values its employees. Following the principle "communication is leadership," the retailer practices transparency, allowing employees access to most types of information except specific details about what individuals are paid. Not only do employees have the information they need to do their jobs, they can get a big picture overview of the company and its challenges and accomplishments. Thanks to its reputation for putting employees first, the Container Store has been named many times to *Fortune* magazine's annual list of 100 best companies to work for in America.[17]

Questions

1. What effect does low turnover have on the Container Store's ability to forecast human resources supply and match supply with demand?
2. Do you agree with the Container Store's decision to allow employees access to all kinds of company information except individual compensation? Explain your answer.
3. If you were interviewing applicants for a sales position at the Container Store, what questions would you ask, and why?

Building Skills for Career Success

1. Social Media Exercise

LinkedIn (www.linkedin.com) is the largest and best-known social network for professionals. Many of you are probably already familiar with it.

1. Do you have a profile? If not, you might want to consider developing one because many companies recruit from LinkedIn and it can be a great tool for professional networking.
2. If you already have a profile, think about how you might improve it. Do you participate in discussion groups? Have you reached out and connected to people in industries where you want to work?

2. Building Team Skills

The New Therapy Company is soliciting a contract to provide five nursing homes with physical, occupational, speech, and respiratory therapists. The therapists will rotate among the five nursing homes. The therapists have not yet been hired, but the nursing homes expect them to be fully trained and ready to go to work in three months. The previous therapy company lost its contract because of high staff turnover owing to employee "burnout" (a common problem in this field), high costs, and low-quality care. The nursing homes want a plan specifying how the New Therapy Company will meet staffing needs, keep costs low, and provide high-quality care.

Assignment

1. Working in a group, discuss how the New Therapy Company can meet the deadline and still ensure a high quality of care. Also discuss the following:
   a. How many of each type of therapist will the company need?
   b. How will it prevent therapists from burning out?
   c. How can it retain experienced staff and still limit costs?
   d. Are promotions available for staff? What does the career ladder look like?

e. How will the company manage therapists at five different locations? How will it keep in touch with them (computer, voice mail, or monthly meetings)? Would it make more sense to have therapists work permanently at each location rather than rotate among them?

f. How will the company justify the travel costs? What other expenses might it expect?

2. Prepare a plan for the New Therapy Company to present to the nursing homes.

3. Researching Different Careers

A résumé provides a summary of your skills, abilities, and achievements. It also may include a description of the type of job you want. An effective résumé clearly communicates your career objectives, your experience and qualifications, and shows that you have given serious thought to your career.

Assignment

1. Prepare a résumé for a job that you want using the information in Appendix A (see text website).

   a. Determine your skills and decide which are important for this particular job.

   b. Decide which format—chronological or functional—will be most effective in presenting your skills and experience.

   c. Keep the résumé to one page, if possible (no more than two pages). Note that portfolio items may be attached for certain jobs, such as artwork.

2. Have several people review the résumé for accuracy.

3. Ask your instructor to comment on your résumé.

Endnotes

1 Based on information in Patty McCord, "How Netflix Reinvented HR," *Harvard Business Review*, January–February 2014, pp. 70–76; Drake Baer, "Netflix's Major HR Innovation: Treating Humans Like People," *Fast Company*, March 13, 2014, www.fastcompany.com (accessed July 1, 2015); Bill Snyder, "Netflix Founder Reed Hastings: Make as Few Decisions as Possible," *Insights by Stanford (Stanford Graduate School of Business)*, November 3, 2014, www.gsb.stanford.edu/insights (accessed July 1, 2015); www.netflix.com (accessed January 15, 2015).

2 Dave Zielinski, "Get Analytical," *HRMagazine*, November 2014, pp. 61–62.

3 Ellen Meyers, "Microsoft Will Cut 18,000 Jobs by June 2015," *Christian Science Monitor*, July 17, 2014, http://www.csmonitor.com/Business/2014/0717/Microsoft-will-cut-18-000-jobs-by-June-2015 (accessed July 1, 2015).

4 *Labor Force Characteristics by Race and Ethnicity, 2013*, U.S. Department of Labor, Bureau of Labor Statistics, May 2014, http://www.bls.gov/cps/wlf-databook-2013.pdf (accessed July 1, 2015), p. 2; *Women in the Labor Force: A Data Book*, U.S. Department of Labor, Bureau of Labor Statistics, May 2014, http://www.bls.gov/cps/wlf-databook-2013.pdf (accessed July 1, 2015), p. 2.

5 *Women in the Labor Force: A Data Book*, p. 2.

6 Miriam Salpeter, "How to Use Social Media to Land a Job," *U.S. News & World Report*, April 16, 2014, http://money.usnews.com/money/blogs/outside-voices-careers/2014/04/16/how-to-use-social-media-to-land-a-job (accessed July 1, 2015).

7 Tara Siegel Bernard, "Vigilant Eye on Gender Pay Gap," *New York Times*, November 15, 2014, p. B1.

8 Beth Fitzgerald, "Hospitals Saved $113M in Gainsharing Pilot; Second Program Underway," *NJBiz*, July 24, 2014, http://www.njbiz.com/article/20140724/NJBIZ01/140729835/Hospitals-saved-$113M-in-gainsharing-pilot;-second-program-underway (accessed July 1, 2015).

9 Hormel Foods, "Hormel Foods Distributes Annual Profit-Sharing," Press Release, November 26, 2014, http://www.hormelfoods.com/Newsroom/Press-Releases/2014/11/20141126 (accessed July 1, 2015).

10 "Employment Cost Index," U.S. Department of Labor, Bureau of Labor Statistics, Press Release, October 31, 2014, http://www.bls.gov/news.release/eci.toc.htm (accessed July 1, 2015).

11 Victor Luckerson, "10 Most Lavish Job Perks in Silicon Valley," *Time*, October 14, 2014, http://time.com/3506815/10-best-job-perks/ (accessed July 1, 2015).

12 "Training Top 10 Hall of Fame: Farmers Insurance and Verizon Inducted into Top 10 Hall of Fame," *Training*, http://www.trainingmag.com/trgmag-article/farmers-insurance-and-verizon-inducted-top-10-hall-fame (accessed January 15, 2015).

13 Josh Bersin, "Spending on Corporate Training Soars: Employee Capabilities Now a Priority," *Forbes*, February 4, 2014, http://www.forbes.com/sites/joshbersin/2014/02/04/the-recovery-arrives-corporate-training-spend-skyrockets/ (accessed July 1, 2015).

14 Caroline Fairchild, "Number of Fortune 500 Women CEOs Reaches Historic High," *Fortune*, June 3, 2014, http://fortune.com/2014/06/03/number-of-fortune-500-women-ceos-reaches-historic-high/ (accessed July 1, 2015); Lawrence H. Leith, "Why Do Women Still Earn Less than Men?" *Monthly Labor Review*, Bureau of Labor Statistics, June 2014, http://www.bls.gov/opub/mlr/2014/beyond-bls/why-do-women-still-earn-less-than-men.htm (accessed July 1, 2015).

15 Equal Employment Opportunity Commission, "HiLine Electric to Pay $210,000 to Settle EEOC Age Discrimination Suit," Press Release, October 6, 2014, http://www.eeoc.gov/eeoc/newsroom/release/10-6-14c.cfm (accessed July 1, 2015).

16 U.S. Department of Commerce, "Census Bureau Releases Disability Facts and Figures in Recognition of ADA Anniversary," July 22, 2014, http://www.commerce.gov/blog/2014/07/22/census-bureau-releases-disability-facts-and-figures-recognition-ada-anniversary (accessed July 1, 2015).

17 Based on information in Aaron Taube, "Why The Container Store Pays Its Retail Employees $50,000 a Year," *Business Insider*, October 16, 2014, http://www.businessinsider.com/the-container-store-pays-employees-50000-a-year-2014-10 (accessed July 1, 2015); Jason Heid, "Breakfast with Kip Tindell of The Container Store," *D Magazine*, November 2012, http://www.dmagazine.com/publications/d-ceo/2012/november/breakfast-with-kip-tindell-of-the-container-store (accessed July 8, 2015); Steven R. Thompson, "Container Store Uses Personal Approach in New Strategy," *Dallas Business Journal*, April 27, 2012, http://www.bizjournals.com/dallas/print-edition/2012/04/27/container-store-uses-personal-approach.html (accessed July 8, 2015); Brooke Baker, "No. 1, Small Companies: The Container Store," *Indianapolis Star*, April 7, 2012, www.indystar.com; Caitlin Keating, "No Layoffs—Ever!" *Fortune*, January 20, 2012, http://archive.fortune.com/galleries/2012/pf/jobs/1201/gallery.best-companies-no-layoffs.fortune/2.html (accessed July 8, 2015); Cengage "Container Store" video; www.containerstore.com (accessed July 8, 2015).

CHAPTER

10

Motivating and Satisfying Employees and Teams

Why Should You Care?

As you move up into management positions or operate your own business, you will need to understand what motivates others in an organization.

Learning Objectives

Once you complete this chapter, you will be able to:

10-1 Explain what motivation is.

10-2 Understand some major historical perspectives on motivation.

10-3 Describe three contemporary views of motivation: equity theory, expectancy theory, and goal-setting theory.

10-4 Explain several techniques for increasing employee motivation.

10-5 Understand the types, development, and uses of teams.

What Makes a "Best Company to Work For"?

Salesforce.com has appeared six times on *Fortune* magazine's annual list of "Best Companies to Work For." The San Francisco-based firm markets technology to help businesses maintain strong customer relationships. As an employer, Salesforce.com is in the spotlight because it invests heavily in recognizing and rewarding employee performance. For instance, its top salespeople enjoy lavish vacations in addition to companywide honors—and they take pride in their hard-earned professional achievements.

Salesforce.com recruits talented employees who have a drive to succeed and pays close attention to the basics employees need for their well-being. For example, employees have access to health insurance, dental and vision coverage, and fitness programs. Company offices are well stocked with free snacks and beverages. To make life easier for those who are out on medical leave or parental leave, Salesforce.com offers an allowance for take-out meals. Beyond the basics, employees are invited to bring their dogs to work, mingle at company-sponsored concerts and outings, and play friendly games of ping-pong to break up the office routine.

With an eye toward helping employees achieve their professional goals, Salesforce.com provides extensive training to build skills, plus mentoring and career coaching. Both managers and employees can attend internal job fairs, and switch to other projects or teams, to round out their skills and take on new challenges. Employees can also earn virtual merit badges for completing key work tasks or assisting co-workers. Visible in online trophy cases, these badges are particularly effective for motivating Millennials who are accustomed to the immediate rewards of winning points or advancing levels in digital games.

Salesforce.com encourages community involvement by giving employees six paid days each year for volunteer work. It matches charitable donations made by employees (up to $5,000 per year) and uses its philanthropic contributions to support not-for-profit groups in which employees are actively involved. Employees feel good when they have the opportunity to do good for others, and they appreciate the backing of Salesforce.com at work and in the community.[1]

Did You Know?

Founded in 1999, Salesforce.com now employs 15,000 people worldwide and rings up nearly $5 billion in annual sales of technology for customer relationship management.

To achieve its goals, any organization—be it Salesforce.com, Google, or a local convenience store—must be sure that its employees have more than the right raw materials, adequate facilities, and equipment that works. The organization also must ensure that its employees are *motivated*. A high level of employee motivation derives from effective management practices.

In this chapter, after first explaining what motivation is, we present several studies and views of motivation that have influenced management practices over the years: Taylor's ideas of scientific management, Mayo's Hawthorne Studies, Maslow's hierarchy of needs, Herzberg's motivation–hygiene theory, McGregor's Theory X and Theory Y, Ouchi's Theory Z, and reinforcement theory. Then, turning our attention to contemporary theory, we examine equity, expectancy, and goal-setting theories. Finally, we discuss specific techniques managers can use to foster employee motivation and satisfaction.

motivation the individual internal process that energizes, directs, and sustains behavior; the personal "force" that causes you or me to behave in a particular way

10-1 WHAT IS MOTIVATION?

A *motive* is something that causes a person to act. A successful athlete is said to be "highly motivated." A student who avoids work is said to be "unmotivated." We define **motivation** as the individual internal process that energizes, directs, and sustains behavior. It is the personal "force" that causes you or me to act in a particular way. For example, although job rotation may increase your job satisfaction and

Learning Objective

10-1 Explain what motivation is.

your enthusiasm for your work so that you devote more energy to it, it may not have the same impact on someone else.

Morale is an employee's attitude or feelings about the job, about superiors, and about the firm itself. To achieve organizational goals effectively, employees need more than the right raw materials, adequate facilities, and efficient equipment. High morale results mainly from the satisfaction of needs on the job or as a result of doing the job. One need that might be satisfied on the job is the need *to be recognized* as an important contributor to the organization. A need satisfied as a result of the job is the need for *financial security*. High morale leads to dedication, loyalty, and a desire to do the job well. Low morale, however, can lead to shoddy work, absenteeism, and high turnover rates as employees leave to seek more satisfying jobs with other firms. Turnover can be very costly. To minimize it, companies may try to create work environments that increase employee satisfaction. One obvious indicator of satisfaction at a specific organization is whether employees report that they like working there and whether other people want to work there. In a recent list of *Fortune* magazine's "Top 100 Companies to Work For," the top ten best companies to work for were Google, SAS, the Boston Consulting Group, Edward Jones, Quicken Loans, Genentech, Salesforce.com, Intuit, Robert W. Baird & Co., and DPR Construction.[2] Motivation, morale, and the satisfaction of employees' needs are highly intertwined considerations. Their relationships to business success and productivity have been the subject of much study since the end of the 19th century. We continue our discussion of motivation by outlining some landmarks of the early research.

10-2 HISTORICAL PERSPECTIVES ON MOTIVATION

Researchers often begin a study with a fairly narrow goal in mind, usually to test a specific hypothesis. After they develop an understanding of their subject, however, they realize that their research has broader applications. This is exactly what happened when early research into productivity grew into the study of employee motivation.

10-2a Scientific Management

Toward the end of the 19th century, Frederick W. Taylor, an American mechanical engineer, became interested in improving the efficiency of individual workers. This interest, which stemmed from his own experiences in manufacturing plants, eventually led to the development of **scientific management**, the application of scientific principles to management of work and workers.

One of Taylor's first jobs was with the Midvale Steel Company in Philadelphia, where he developed a strong distaste for waste and inefficiency. While there, he observed a practice he dubbed "soldiering." Workers "soldiered," or worked slowly, because they feared that if they worked faster, they would run out of work and lose their jobs. Taylor realized that workers could get away with this because managers had no idea what productivity levels *should* be.

After Midvale, Taylor spent several years at Bethlehem Steel. While there, he made his most significant contribution to the field of motivation. He suggested that each job be broken down into separate tasks. Then management should determine (1) the best way to perform each task and (2) the job output to expect when employees performed the tasks properly. Next, management should choose the best person for each job and train that person in doing the job properly. Finally, management should monitor workers to ensure that jobs were performed as planned.

Taylor also developed the idea that most people work only to earn money. He therefore reasoned that pay should be tied directly to output. The more a person produces, the more he or she should be paid. This gave rise to the **piece-rate system,**

FIGURE 10-1 Taylor's Piece-Rate System

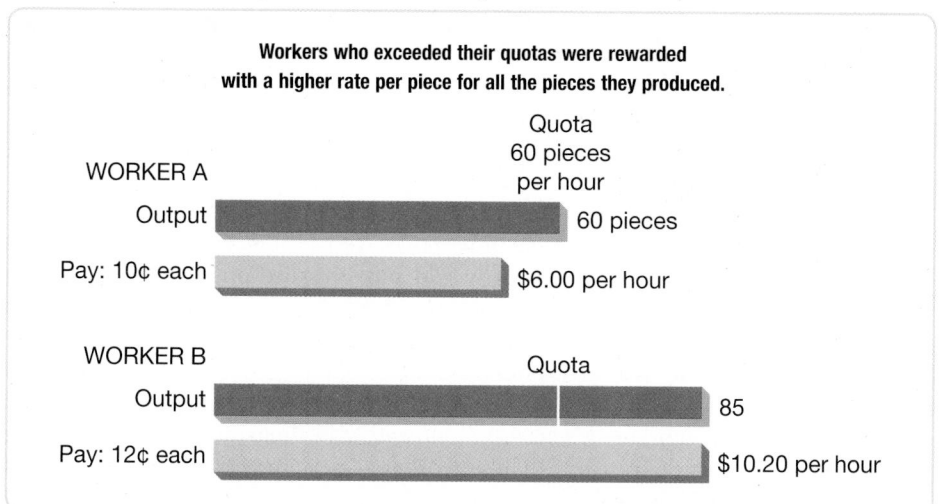

Workers who exceeded their quotas were rewarded with a higher rate per piece for all the pieces they produced.

WORKER A
Quota
60 pieces
per hour

Output — 60 pieces

Pay: 10¢ each — $6.00 per hour

WORKER B
Quota

Output — 85

Pay: 12¢ each — $10.20 per hour

under which employees are paid a certain amount for each unit of output they produce. Under Taylor's piece-rate system, each employee is assigned an output quota. If they exceed the quota, they receive a higher per unit rate for all work produced (see Figure 10-1).

When Taylor's system was put into practice at Bethlehem Steel, the results were dramatic. Average earnings per day for steel handlers rose from $1.15 to $1.88. (Do not let the low wages obscure the fact that this was an increase of more than 61 percent!) The average amount of steel handled per day increased from 16 to 57 tons. Today, the piece-rate system is still used by some manufacturers and by farmers who grow crops that are harvested by farm laborers.

Taylor's revolutionary ideas had a profound impact on management practice. However, his view of motivation was soon recognized as overly simplistic and narrow. It is true that most people expect to be paid for their work, but it is also true that people work for a variety of reasons other than pay. Therefore, simply increasing a person's pay may not increase that person's motivation or productivity.

10-2b **The Hawthorne Studies**

Between 1927 and 1932, Elton Mayo, an Australian sociologist and organizational theorist, conducted two experiments at the Hawthorne plant of the Western Electric Company in Chicago. The original objective of these studies, now referred to as

Is anyone happy? A century ago, most businesses in the United States weren't overly concerned about employee satisfaction. This is not the case today. Why do you think attitudes about employee motivation and satisfaction have changed?

ARCHIVE PHOTOS/GETTY IMAGES

the *Hawthorne Studies*, was to determine the effects of the work environment on employee productivity.

The first set of experiments tested the effect of lighting levels on productivity. One group of workers was subjected to varying lighting, while a second was not. To the amazement of the researchers, productivity increased for both groups. For the group whose lighting was varied, productivity remained high until the light was reduced to the level of moonlight!

The second set of experiments focused on the effectiveness of the piece-rate system in increasing the output of groups of workers. Researchers expected that output would increase because faster workers would put pressure on slower workers to produce more. Again, the results were not as expected. Output remained constant irrespective of the "standard" rates management set.

When faced with unexpected outcomes, the researchers concluded that *human factors* were responsible for the results. In the lighting experiments, researchers had given both groups of workers a *sense of involvement* in their jobs merely by asking them to participate in the research. These workers—perhaps for the first time—felt as though they were an important part of the organization. The level of light did not matter. In the piece-rate experiments, each group of workers informally set the acceptable rate of output for the group. To gain or retain the *social acceptance* of the group, each worker felt pressure to produce at the same rate as the group pace.

The Hawthorne Studies showed that such human factors are at least as important to motivation as pay rates. From these and other studies, the *human relations movement* in management was born. Its premise was simple: Employees who are happy and satisfied with their work are motivated to perform better. Hence, management is best served by providing a work environment that maximizes employee satisfaction.

10-2c Maslow's Hierarchy of Needs

Abraham Maslow, an American psychologist whose best-known works were published in the 1960s and 1970s, developed a theory of motivation based on a hierarchy of needs. A **need** is a personal requirement. Maslow assumed that humans are "wanting" beings who seek to fulfill a variety of needs, which he argued can be arranged from most basic to most complex in a sequence now known as **Maslow's hierarchy of needs** (see Figure 10-2).

At the bottom of the pyramid are **physiological needs**, the things we require to survive. They include food and water, clothing, shelter, and sleep. In the employment context, these needs usually are satisfied through adequate wages.

need a personal requirement

Maslow's hierarchy of needs a sequence of human needs in the order of their importance

physiological needs the things we require for survival

FIGURE 10-2 Maslow's Hierarchy of Needs

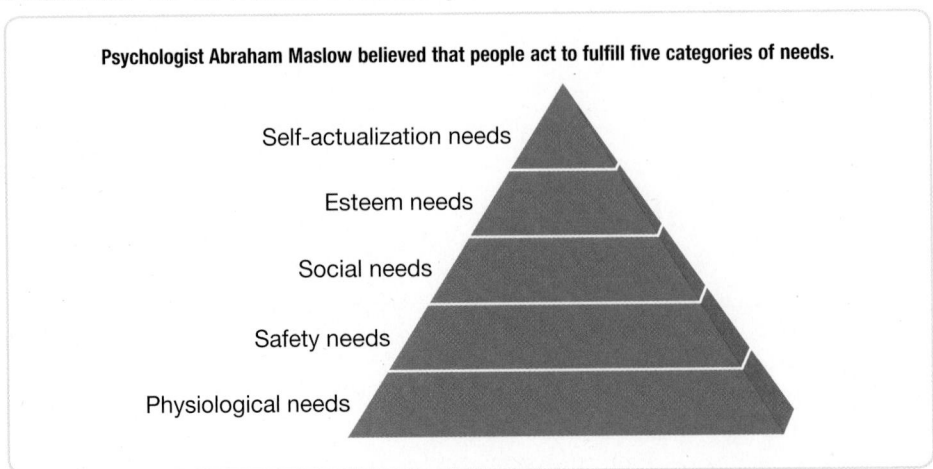

Psychologist Abraham Maslow believed that people act to fulfill five categories of needs.

- Self-actualization needs
- Esteem needs
- Social needs
- Safety needs
- Physiological needs

At the next level are **safety needs**, the things we require for physical and emotional security. Safety needs may be satisfied through job stability, health insurance, pension plans, and safe working conditions. The escalating costs of health care in today's work environment threaten some workers' sense of safety. Many firms are switching to more part-time workers for low-wage positions in order to avoid health insurance costs and fees. Under new law, large employers must provide health insurance to those who work more than 30 hours per week, or risk paying a fine.[3] The move might backfire as employees seek to satisfy their safety needs at more secure jobs.

Next are the **social needs**, the human requirements for love and affection and a sense of belonging. These needs are fulfilled in the workplace through the work environment and the informal organization and outside of the workplace by family and friends. Employers are increasingly offering their workers flexible scheduling options in order to improve their quality of lives, which includes time for family and friends. Employees who have flexible work schedules are more likely to be able to attend family events or care for children or ailing relatives. Employers can help workers satisfy social needs by providing useful feedback and fostering workplace cooperation and communication through a variety of media.

At the level of **esteem needs**, we require respect and recognition from others and a sense of our own accomplishment and worth (self-esteem). These needs may be satisfied through personal accomplishment, promotion to positions with greater responsibility, various honors and awards, and other forms of recognition.

At the top of the hierarchy are the **self-actualization needs**, which are the needs to grow, develop, and become all that we are capable of being. These are the most difficult needs to satisfy, and the means of satisfying them tend to vary with the individual. For some people, learning a new skill, starting a new career after retirement, or trying to become the best at some endeavor may be the way to realize self-actualization. Some companies reimburse employees for continuing education expenses—even another college degree—knowing they get the benefit of employees with more knowledge, as well as more satisfied employees who feel supported in their efforts to improve themselves.

Maslow suggested that people work up the hierarchy, satisfying their physiological needs before safety needs, for example. However, needs at one level do not have to be satisfied completely before needs at the next higher level come into play. People can also move up and down the hierarchy. For example, if a person loses a good job, he may find himself trying to satisfy safety needs when he only recently had focused on social needs.

Maslow's hierarchy of needs provides a guide for management and a useful way of viewing employee motivation. By and large, American business has been able to satisfy workers' basic needs, but the higher-order needs present more of a challenge. The means of satisfying these needs varies from one employee to another.

safety needs the things we require for physical and emotional security

social needs the human requirements for love and affection and a sense of belonging

esteem needs our need for respect, recognition, and a sense of our own accomplishment and worth

self-actualization needs the need to grow and develop and to become all that we are capable of being

10-2d Herzberg's Motivation–Hygiene Theory

Frederick Herzberg, an American psychologist, interviewed approximately 200 accountants and engineers in Pittsburgh in the 1950s to develop his theory of motivation. He asked them to think of a time when they had felt especially good about their jobs and

© COZYTA/SHUTTERSTOCK.COM

What satisfies employees? Companies sometimes use travel awards as incentives for better employee performance. According to the motivation–hygiene theory, when an incentive for higher performance is not provided, is that a dissatisfier?

FIGURE 10-3 Herzberg's Motivation–Hygiene Theory

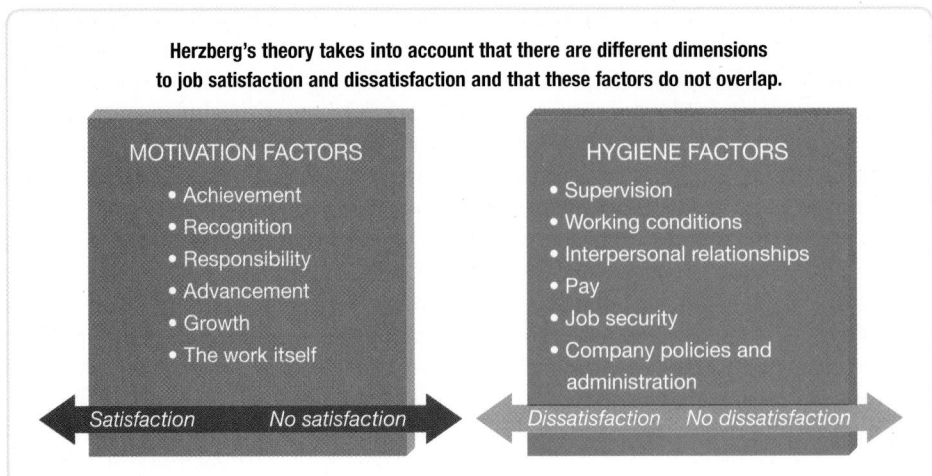

Herzberg's theory takes into account that there are different dimensions to job satisfaction and dissatisfaction and that these factors do not overlap.

MOTIVATION FACTORS
- Achievement
- Recognition
- Responsibility
- Advancement
- Growth
- The work itself

Satisfaction   No satisfaction

HYGIENE FACTORS
- Supervision
- Working conditions
- Interpersonal relationships
- Pay
- Job security
- Company policies and administration

Dissatisfaction   No dissatisfaction

their work and to describe the factor or factors that had caused them to feel that way. Next, he asked them about a time when they had felt especially bad about their work. He was surprised to find that feeling good and feeling bad resulted from entirely different factors. That is, low pay may make a particular person feel bad, but high pay does not necessarily make that same person feel good.

motivation–hygiene theory the idea that satisfaction and dissatisfaction are separate and distinct dimensions

motivation factors job factors that increase motivation, although their absence does not necessarily result in dissatisfaction

hygiene factors job factors that reduce dissatisfaction when present to an acceptable degree but that do not necessarily result in high levels of motivation

SATISFACTION AND DISSATISFACTION Before Herzberg's interviews, the general assumption was that employee satisfaction and dissatisfaction lay at opposite ends of the same scale. However, Herzberg's interviews convinced him that satisfaction and dissatisfaction are different dimensions altogether. In other words, the opposite of satisfaction is not dissatisfaction. The idea that satisfaction and dissatisfaction are separate and distinct dimensions is referred to as the **motivation–hygiene theory** (see Figure 10-3).

The job factors that Herzberg found most frequently associated with satisfaction were achievement, recognition, responsibility, advancement, growth, and the work itself. These factors generally are referred to as **motivation factors** because their presence increases motivation. However, their absence does not necessarily result in dissatisfaction. When motivation factors are present, they act as *satisfiers*.

Dissatisfaction, on the other hand, is caused by job factors such as supervision, working conditions, interpersonal relationships, pay, job security, company policies, and administration. These factors, called **hygiene factors**, reduce dissatisfaction when they are present to an acceptable degree. However, they do not necessarily result in high levels of motivation. When hygiene factors are absent, they act as *dissatisfiers*.

USING HERZBERG'S MOTIVATION–HYGIENE THEORY Herzberg provides explicit guidelines for using the motivation–hygiene theory of employee motivation. He suggests that the hygiene factors must be present to ensure that a worker can function comfortably. He warns, however, that a state of *no dissatisfaction* cannot exist. In any situation, people always will be dissatisfied with something.

According to Herzberg, managers should utilize hygiene factors to make the work environment as positive as possible, but should expect only short-term improvements in motivation. Managers must focus instead on providing those satisfiers that will enhance motivation and long-term effort.

We should note that employee pay has proven to have more effect than Herzberg's theory indicates. He suggests that pay provides only short-term, not true, motivation. Yet, in many organizations, pay is a form of recognition and reward for achievement—and recognition and achievement are both motivation factors. The effect of pay may depend on how it is distributed. If a pay increase does not depend on performance (as in across-the-board or cost-of-living raises), it may not motivate people. However, if pay is increased as a form of recognition (as in bonuses or incentives), it can play a role in motivating employees to higher performance.

10-2e Theory X and Theory Y

The concepts of Theory X and Theory Y were advanced by Douglas McGregor, an American business professor, in his book, *The Human Side of Enterprise*, in 1967. They represent opposing sets of assumptions that underlie management's attitudes and beliefs regarding workers' behavior.

Theory X is a concept of employee motivation generally consistent with Taylor's ideas about scientific management. Theory X is based on the following assumptions:

1. People dislike work and try to avoid it.
2. Because people dislike work, managers must coerce, control, and frequently threaten employees to achieve organizational goals.
3. People generally must be led because they have little ambition and will not seek responsibility; they are concerned mainly about security.

The logical outcome of such assumptions will be a highly controlled, autocratic work environment—one in which managers make all the decisions and employees take all the orders.

On the other hand, **Theory Y** is a concept of employee motivation generally consistent with the ideas of the human relations movement. Theory Y is based on the following assumptions:

1. People do not naturally dislike work. In fact, work is an important part of all of our lives.
2. People will work toward goals to which they are committed.
3. People become committed to goals when it is clear that accomplishing the goals will bring personal rewards.
4. People often seek out and willingly accept responsibility.
5. Employees have the potential to help accomplish organizational goals.
6. Organizations generally do not make full use of their human resources.

Obviously, Theory Y is much more positive than Theory X. McGregor argued that most managers behave in accordance with Theory X, but he maintained that Theory Y is more appropriate and effective as a guide for managerial action (see Table 10-1).

Theory X a concept of employee motivation generally consistent with Taylor's scientific management; assumes that employees dislike work and will function only in a highly controlled work environment

Theory Y a concept of employee motivation generally consistent with the ideas of the human relations movement; assumes responsibility and work toward organizational goals, and by doing so they also achieve personal rewards

TABLE 10-1 Theory X and Theory Y Contrasted

Area	Theory X	Theory Y
Attitude toward work	Dislike	Involvement
Control systems	External	Internal
Supervision	Direct	Indirect
Level of commitment	Low	High
Employee potential	Ignored	Identified
Use of human resources	Limited	Not limited

The human relations movement and Theories X and Y increased managers' awareness of the importance of social factors in the workplace during the second half of the 20th century. However, human motivation is a complex and dynamic process to which there is no simple key. It is clear from decades of research that neither money nor social factors alone can provide the answer.

10-2f Theory Z

William Ouchi, currently a management professor at UCLA, studied business practices in American and Japanese firms as discussed in his book, *Theory Z: How American Management Can Meet the Japanese Challenge*. He concluded that different types of management systems dominate in these two countries. In Japan, Ouchi found what he calls *type J* firms. They are characterized by lifetime employment, collective (or group) decision making, collective responsibility for the outcomes of decisions, slow evaluation and promotion, implied control mechanisms, nonspecialized career paths, and a holistic concern for employees as people.

American industry is dominated by what Ouchi calls *type A* firms, which follow a different pattern. They emphasize short-term employment, individual decision making, individual responsibility for the outcomes of decisions, rapid evaluation and promotion, explicit control mechanisms, specialized career paths, and a segmented concern for employees only as employees.

A few very successful American firms represent a blend of the type J and type A patterns. These firms, called *type Z* organizations, emphasize long-term employment, collective decision making, individual responsibility for the outcomes of decisions, slow evaluation and promotion, informal control along with some formalized measures, moderately specialized career paths, and a holistic concern for employees.

Theory Z the belief that some middle ground between type A and type J practices is best for American business

Ouchi's **Theory Z** posits that some middle ground between his type A and type J practices is best for American business (see Figure 10-4). A major part of Theory Z emphasizes participative decision making. The focus is on "we" rather than on "us versus them." Theory Z employees and managers view the organization as a family. This participative spirit fosters cooperation and encourages the dissemination of information and organizational values.

FIGURE 10-4 The Features of Theory Z

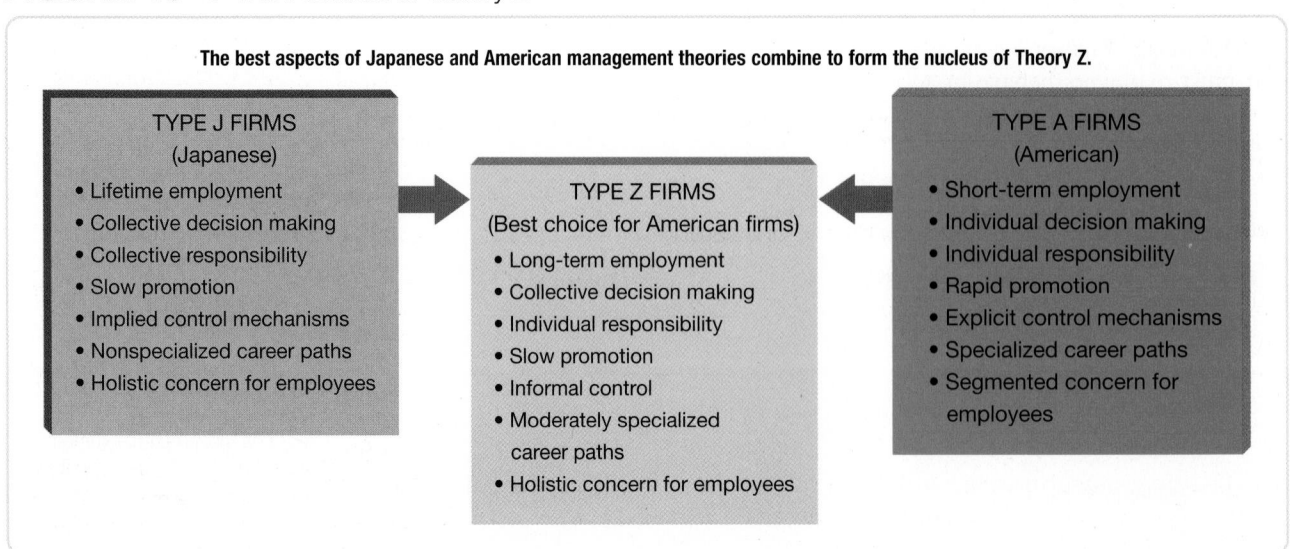

The best aspects of Japanese and American management theories combine to form the nucleus of Theory Z.

TYPE J FIRMS
(Japanese)
- Lifetime employment
- Collective decision making
- Collective responsibility
- Slow promotion
- Implied control mechanisms
- Nonspecialized career paths
- Holistic concern for employees

TYPE Z FIRMS
(Best choice for American firms)
- Long-term employment
- Collective decision making
- Individual responsibility
- Slow promotion
- Informal control
- Moderately specialized career paths
- Holistic concern for employees

TYPE A FIRMS
(American)
- Short-term employment
- Individual decision making
- Individual responsibility
- Rapid promotion
- Explicit control mechanisms
- Specialized career paths
- Segmented concern for employees

10-2g Reinforcement Theory

Reinforcement theory is based on the premise that people will repeat behavior that is rewarded and will cease behavior that is punished. A *reinforcement* is an action that follows directly from a particular behavior. It may be a pay raise after a particularly large sale to a new customer or a reprimand for coming late to work.

Reinforcements can take a variety of forms and can be used in a number of ways. A *positive reinforcement* is one that strengthens desired behavior by providing a reward, such as praise or recognition from supervisors for a job done well. A reward increases (strengthens) their willingness to perform well in the future. A *negative reinforcement* strengthens desired behavior by eliminating an undesirable task or situation. Suppose that a machine shop must be cleaned thoroughly every month—a dirty, miserable task. During a month when the workers do a less-than-satisfactory job, the boss requires them to clean the factory themselves, rather than bringing in the usual private maintenance service. The employees will be motivated to work harder the next month to avoid the unpleasant cleanup duty.

Punishment is a consequence of undesirable behavior. Common forms of punishment used in organizations include reprimands, reduced pay, disciplinary layoffs, and termination (firing). Punishment often does more harm than good by creating a negative work environment, fostering worker hostility, and encouraging employees to engage in undesirable behaviors behind the backs of supervisors.

Managers who rely on *extinction* hope to eliminate undesirable behavior by not responding to it with the hope that the behavior will eventually go "extinct." Suppose, for example, that an employee writes memo after memo to his or her manager about insignificant events. If the manager does not respond to any of these memos, the employee probably will stop writing them, and the behavior will stop.

The effectiveness of reinforcement depends on which type is used and how it is timed. Some situations lend themselves to the use of more than one approach. Generally, positive reinforcement is considered the most effective with most employees, and it is recommended when the manager has a choice.

Continual reinforcement can become tedious for both managers and employees, especially when the same behavior is being reinforced over and over again in the same way. At the start, it may be necessary to reinforce a desired behavior every time it occurs. Generally, once a desirable behavior has been more or less established, only occasional reinforcement will be needed.

Concept Check

✓ What are the major elements of Taylor's "scientific management"?

✓ What were Elton Mayo's conclusions from the Hawthorne Studies?

✓ What are the different levels in Maslow's hierarchy of needs?

✓ What are the major elements of Herzberg's motivation–hygiene theory?

✓ What are the underlying assumptions of Theory X and Theory Y?

10-3 CONTEMPORARY VIEWS ON MOTIVATION

Maslow's hierarchy of needs and Herzberg's motivation–hygiene theory are popular and widely known theories of motivation. Each takes a broader view than the narrow focus of scientific management and Theories X and Y. However, they do have a weakness: each attempts to specify *what* motivates people, but neither explains *why* or *how* motivation develops or is sustained over time. More recently, managers have explored three other models that take a more dynamic view of motivation. These are equity theory, expectancy theory, and goal-setting theory.

10-3a Equity Theory

The **equity theory** of motivation is based on the premise that people are motivated to obtain and preserve equitable treatment for themselves. As used here, *equity* is the distribution of rewards in direct proportion to each employee's contribution to the organization. Everyone need not receive the same rewards, but the rewards should be in accordance with individual contributions.

Learning Objective

10-3 Describe three contemporary views of motivation: equity theory, expectancy theory, and goal-setting theory.

reinforcement theory a theory of motivation based on the premise that rewarded behavior is likely to be repeated, whereas punished behavior is less likely to recur

equity theory a theory of motivation based on the premise that people are motivated to obtain and preserve equitable treatment for themselves

Employees want to be treated fairly. Employees compare the amount of effort they put into their jobs and the outcomes they get to that of their co-workers. This is the idea behind equity theory. At sweatshops such as this one, though, all employees are treated unfairly. Does equity theory come into play in this instance?

According to this theory, we conceive of equity in the following way. First, we develop our own input-to-outcome ratio. *Inputs* are the time, effort, skills, education, experience, and so on that we contribute to the organization. *Outcomes* are the rewards we get from the organization, such as pay, benefits, recognition, and promotions. Next, we compare this ratio to what we perceive as the input-to-outcome ratio for some other person. It might be a co-worker, a friend who works for another firm, or even an average of all the people in our organization. This person is called the *comparison other*. Note that the important consideration is that we believe our perception to be correct, whether or not it is.

If the two ratios are roughly the same, we feel that the organization is treating us equitably. In this case, we are motivated to leave things as they are. However, if our ratio is the higher of the two, we feel under-rewarded and are motivated to make changes. We may (1) decrease our own inputs by not working as hard, (2) try to increase our outcome by asking for a raise in pay, (3) try to get the comparison other to increase some inputs or receive decreased outcomes, (4) leave the work situation, or (5) conduct a new comparison with a different comparison other.

Equity theory is most relevant to pay as an outcome. Because pay is a very real measure of a person's worth to an organization, comparisons involving pay are a natural part of organizational life. Managers can try to avoid problems arising from inequity by making sure that rewards are distributed on the basis of performance and that everyone clearly understands the basis for his or her own pay.

10-3b Expectancy Theory

Expectancy theory, developed by Victor Vroom, a Canadian business professor, is a very complex model of motivation based on a simple assumption. According to expectancy theory, motivation depends on how much we want something and on how likely we think we are to get it (see Figure 10-5). Consider, for example, the case of three sales representatives who are candidates for promotion to one sales manager's job. Bill has had a very good sales year and always gets positive performance evaluations. However, he is not sure that he wants the job because it involves

expectancy theory a model of motivation based on the assumption that motivation depends on how much we want something and on how likely we think we are to get it

FIGURE 10-5 Expectancy Theory

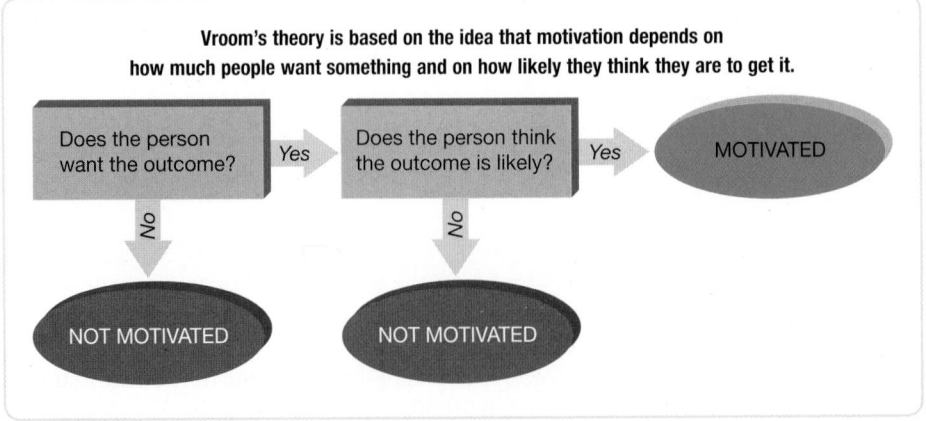

What do employees want?
That's what their managers need to determine. Different employees are motivated by different rewards. Figuring out which rewards motivate each employee is a key step in goal setting.

travel, long working hours, and stress and pressure. Paul wants the job badly, but does not think he has much chance of getting it. He has had a terrible sales year and gets only mediocre performance evaluations from his present boss. Susan wants the job as much as Paul, and she thinks that she has a pretty good shot. Her sales have improved this past year, and her evaluations are the best in the company.

Expectancy theory would predict that Bill and Paul are not very motivated to seek the promotion. Bill does not really want it, and Paul does not think that he has much of a chance of getting it. Susan, however, is very motivated to seek the promotion because she wants it and thinks that she can get it.

Expectancy theory is complex because each action we take is likely to lead to several outcomes, some of which we want and others we do not. For example, a person who works hard and puts in many extra hours may get a pay raise, be promoted, and gain valuable new job skills. However, that person also may be forced to spend less time with his or her family and to cut back on social activities.

For one person, the promotion may be paramount, the pay raise and new skills fairly important, and the loss of family and social life of negligible importance. For someone else, the family and social life may be most important, the pay raise of moderate importance, the new skills unimportant, and the promotion undesirable because of the additional hours it would require. The first person would be motivated to work hard and put in the extra hours, whereas the second person would not be motivated at all to do so. In other words, it is the bundle of outcomes combined with the individual's perception of each outcome's importance that determines motivation.

Expectancy theory is difficult to apply, but it does provide several useful guidelines for managers. It suggests that managers must recognize that (1) employees work for a variety of reasons, (2) these reasons, or expected outcomes, may change over time, and (3) it is necessary to show employees how they can attain the outcomes they desire.

10-3c Goal-Setting Theory

Goal-setting theory states that employees are motivated to achieve goals that they and their managers establish together. The goal should be very specific, moderately difficult, and one that the employee will be committed to achieve.[4] Rewards should be tied directly to goal achievement. Using goal-setting theory, a manager can design

goal-setting theory a theory of motivation suggesting that employees are motivated to achieve goals that they and their managers establish together

Concept Check

✓ What is equity theory?

✓ How do managers use it in order to decide the pay structure of employees?

✓ What is expectancy theory and how is it different from goal-setting theory?

rewards that fit employee needs, clarify expectations, maintain equity, and provide reinforcement. For example, a manager might discover that one of her employees is very motivated by the occasional day off. Therefore, the manager and the employee may work out a plan that involves a free day as a reward after he completes a project satisfactorily and ahead of schedule, as long as he is up-to-date in his other work. This theory takes into account the goal the employee has to achieve and the rewards that will accrue if the goal is accomplished.

10-4 KEY MOTIVATION TECHNIQUES

Learning Objective

10-4 Explain several techniques for increasing employee motivation.

Today, it takes more than a generous salary to motivate employees. Increasingly, companies are trying to provide motivation by satisfying employees' less-tangible needs. Businesses may use simple, low- or no-cost, or complex and expensive approaches to motivation. In this section, we discuss several specific techniques that help managers to boost employee motivation and job satisfaction.

10-4a Management by Objectives

Management by objectives (MBO) is a motivation technique in which managers and employees collaborate in setting goals. The primary purpose of MBO is to clarify the roles employees are expected to play in reaching the organization's goals.

MBO increases employee motivation by empowering them with an active role in goal-setting and performance evaluation. Most MBO programs consist of a series of five steps. The first step in setting up an MBO program is to secure the acceptance of top management. It is essential that top managers endorse and participate in the program if others in the firm are to accept it. This also provides a natural starting point for educating employees about the purposes and mechanics of MBO.

In the second step, top management and other parties must establish preliminary goals that reflect a firm's mission and strategy. The intent of an MBO program is to have these goals filter down through the organization.

The third step is the heart of MBO. It consists of three smaller steps:

1. The manager explains to each employee that he or she has accepted certain goals for the organization, or a group within the organization, and asks the individual to think about how he or she can help to achieve these goals.

2. The manager later meets with each employee individually. Together they establish individual goals for the employee. Whenever possible, the goals should be measurable and should specify the time frame for completion (usually one year).

3. The manager and the employee decide what resources the employee will need to accomplish his or her goals.

As the fourth step, the manager and employees meet periodically to review each employee's progress. They may agree to modify certain goals during these meetings if circumstances have changed. For example, a sales representative accepted a goal of increasing sales by 20 percent. However, an aggressive competitor has since entered the marketplace, making this goal unattainable. In light of this circumstance, the goal is revised down to 10 or 15 percent.

The fifth step in the MBO process is evaluation. At the end of the designated time period, the manager and each employee meet again to determine which of the individual's goals were met and which were not, and why. The employee's reward (in the form of a pay raise, praise, or promotion) is based primarily on the degree of goal attainment.

As with every other management method, MBO has advantages and disadvantages. MBO can motivate employees by involving them actively in the life of the firm. The collaboration on goal setting and performance appraisal improves communication

management by objectives (MBO) a motivation technique in which managers and employees collaborate in setting goals

and makes employees feel that they are an important part of the organization. Periodic progress reviews also enhance quality control within an organization. Shortcomings of MBO are that it must have the support of top management, it can result in a lot of paperwork, and managers may not like to work out goals with subordinates.

10-4b Job Enrichment

Job enrichment is a method of motivating employees by providing them with variety in their tasks while giving them some responsibility for, and control over, their jobs. At the same time, employees gain new skills and acquire a broader perspective about how their individual work contributes to the goals of the organization. Earlier in this chapter, we noted that Herzberg's motivation–hygiene theory is one rationale for the use of job enrichment. That is, the added responsibility and control that job enrichment confers on employees increases their satisfaction and motivation. For example, some employees at 3M and Google get to spend a fraction of their time at work on projects of their choosing.[5] This type of enrichment can motivate employees and result in benefits for the company. At times, **job enlargement**, expanding a worker's assignments to include additional but similar tasks, can lead to job enrichment. Job enlargement might mean that a worker on an assembly line who used to connect three wires to components moving down the line now connects five wires. Unfortunately, the added tasks often are just as routine as those the worker performed before the change and may not be an effective motivator over the long term.

Whereas job enlargement does not really change the routine and monotonous nature of jobs, job enrichment does. Job enrichment results in an increased sense of employee responsibility, increased control over how the job is performed, and new tasks. Job enrichment gives workers more authority and assigns tasks in complete, natural units (rather than breaking it down into the smallest possible task). Employees frequently are given fresh and challenging job assignments. By blending more planning and decision making into jobs, enrichment gives work more depth and complexity.

Job redesign is a type of job enrichment in which work is restructured in ways that cultivate the worker–job match. Job redesign can be achieved by combining tasks, forming work groups, or establishing closer customer relationships. Employees often are more motivated when jobs are combined because the increased variety of tasks presents a more rewarding challenge. Depending on the form it takes, job redesign can give employees a stronger sense of belonging to a team, a clearer image of how their work contributes to the organization as a whole, and a more personal investment in the satisfaction of clients. Furthermore, a job redesign that carefully matches worker to job can prevent stress-related injuries. Employees may play an active role in redesigning their jobs to their liking. If an employee recognizes an opportunity at work to rework his or her job in such a way as to improve efficiency or productivity, he or she may want to approach a superior with the idea.

Job enrichment works best with employees who want more challenging work. Employees must desire personal growth and have the skills and knowledge to perform more complex tasks. Lack of self-confidence, fear of failure, and distrust of management's intentions are likely to lead to ineffective performance on enriched jobs. Some workers prefer routine jobs because they find them satisfying. Job enrichment would not be appealing for these individuals. Companies that use job

TUDOR VINTILOIU/DREAMSTIME.COM

Job enlargement versus job enrichment. It's no secret. Doing the same task over and over at your job is boring. Being able to do a variety of tasks helps. Having more responsibility over how you do your job is even better.

job enrichment a motivation technique that provides employees with more variety and responsibility in their jobs

job enlargement expanding a worker's assignments to include additional but similar tasks

job redesign a type of job enrichment in which work is restructured to cultivate the worker–job match

enrichment as an alternative to specialization also face extra expenses, such as the cost of retraining.

10-4c Behavior Modification

Behavior modification is a systematic program of reinforcement to encourage desirable behavior. Behavior modification involves both rewards to encourage desirable actions and punishments to discourage undesirable actions. Rewards, such as compliments and expressions of appreciation, tend to be much more effective behavior modifiers than punishments, such as reprimands and scorn.

When applied to management, behavior modification strives to encourage desirable organizational behavior. This technique begins with identifying and measuring a *target behavior*—the behavior that is to be changed (e.g., low production levels or a high rate of absenteeism). Next, managers provide positive reinforcement in the form of a reward when employees exhibit the *desired behavior* (e.g., increased production or less absenteeism). The reward might be praise or a more tangible form of recognition, such as a gift, meal, or trip. For example, Apple offers Corporate Gifts and Rewards Program to give companies the ability to reward their staff or very loyal customers with iPods, iPhones, iPads, Mac computers, or iTunes gift cards. Finally, the levels of the target behavior are measured again to determine whether the desired changes have been achieved. If the target behavior has not changed significantly in the desired direction, the reward system must be changed to one that is likely to be more effective. The key is to devise effective rewards that will not only modify employees' behavior in desired ways, but also motivate them. To this end, experts suggest that management should reward quality, loyalty, and productivity.

10-4d Flextime

The needs and lifestyles of today's workforce are changing. Dual-income families make up a much larger share of the workforce than ever before, and women are one of its fastest-growing sectors. In addition to child-rearing duties, a growing number of employees are responsible for the care of elderly relatives. A study by Pew Research found that 40 million Americans are assisting at least one elderly parent with the daily living activities, and that 70 percent of these caretakers must come in late, leave early, or make other adjustments to do so.[6] Recognizing that these changes increase the demand for flexibility during the normal work day, many employers are offering flexible work schedules to help employees to manage their time better and increase employee motivation and job satisfaction.

Flextime is a system in which employees set their own work hours within certain limits determined by employers. Typically, the firm establishes two bands of time: the *core time*, when all employees must be at work, and the *flexible time*, when employees may choose whether to be at work. The only condition is that every employee must work a total of eight hours each day. For example, the hours between 9 and 11 a.m. and 1 and 3 p.m. might be core times, and the hours between 6 and 9 a.m., 11 a.m. and 1 p.m., and 3 and 6 p.m. might be flexible times. This would give employees the option of coming in early and getting off early, coming in later and leaving later, or taking a long lunch break. But flextime also ensures that everyone is present at certain times, when conferences with supervisors and department meetings can be scheduled. Another type of flextime allows employees to work a 40-hour work week in four days instead of five.

A study by National Work/Life Measurement Project found that 70 percent of managers and 87 percent of employees said that flexible work measures have a positive or very positive effect on productivity and significantly enhanced the quality of work.[7] However, two common problems associated with using flextime are (1) supervisors sometimes find their jobs complicated by having employees who come and go at different times and (2) employees without flextime sometimes resent co-workers who have it.

behavior modification a systematic program of reinforcement to encourage desirable behavior

flextime a system in which employees set their own work hours within employer-determined limits

Career Success

Is Flextime for You?

Would you enjoy a flextime schedule, with the leeway to start work late or leave early and make up the time on other days? Or would you prefer the predictability of a fixed schedule? When it comes to work schedules, one size doesn't fit all as people seek to balance their personal and professional obligations. And that's why a growing number of companies, nonprofit organizations, and government agencies are offering flextime.

Parents of young children and employees who care for sick relatives especially appreciate the flexibility. Although more women use flextime than men, the proportion of men who choose flextime has increased to 77 percent. What's more, 86 percent of men using flextime report higher job satisfaction—and 82 percent say it makes them more loyal to the employer.

However, some managers resist flextime, in part because it's a challenge to manage workflow when employees are on a variety of schedules. For their part, employees sometimes fear they'll be seen as less dedicated or experience a backlash if they request flextime. Now state agencies in almost a dozen states are required to allow flextime, and Vermont has laws preventing private employers from retaliating against those who request flextime or fixed schedules. Flextime is also in schools: One Idaho high school allows a flexible 15 minutes in each school day for underperforming students to work with teachers (while other students have free time).

Sources: Based on information in Kelly Wallace, "Report: Majority of Men Using Flex Time and Loving It," *CNN.com* (accessed July 11, 2015), December 12, 2014; Jennifer Ludden, "If You Want Flextime But Are Afraid to Ask, Consider Moving," *National Public Radio*, April 29, 2014, www.npr.org (accessed July 11, 2015); Teresa Wiltz, "Flextime Grows, Helping Working Families," *Detroit News*, October 19, 2014, www.detroitnews.com (accessed July 11, 2015); Kristen Johnson, "Idaho High School Uses Flex Time to Help Students," *Associated Press*, November 22, 2014, www.washingtontimes.com (accessed July 11, 2015); Susan Adams, "Workers Have More Flextime, Less Real Flexibility, Study Shows," *Forbes.com* (accessed July 11, 2015), May 2, 2014.

While most people still work standard 40-hour weeks, flexible schedules are becoming much more common and easier to manage as improvements in technology allow people to stay connected, no matter where they are or what time it is. Medical and health, education and training, administrative jobs, and accounting are all likely to offer flexible schedule options. For example, the accounting firm Ernst & Young offers flextime as a reward for working in an intense industry that requires long hours during busy times. In order to offset the 60- or 70-hour workweeks during tax season, it allows their employees to work three-day weeks or take extended breaks during the summer. Its flexible work policies have landed Ernst & Young on *Working Mother* magazine's "100 Best Companies" list for 18 years in a row.[8] Flex policies like this help to reduce employee burnout and keep turnover low in what can be a stressful industry.

part-time work permanent employment in which individuals work less than a standard work week

10-4e Part-Time Work and Job Sharing

Part-time work is permanent employment in which individuals work less than a standard work week. The specific number of hours worked varies, but part-time jobs are structured so that all responsibilities can be completed in the number of hours an employee works. Part-time work is of special interest to parents who need more time with their children. While some firms are famous for offering part-time workers benefits, such as Starbucks, REI, and Barnes & Noble, most do

ISTOCKPHOTO.COM/OLLO

Part-time pay, full-time benefits. Many employees want to work part-time but can't afford not to have benefits such as health insurance. Companies known for hiring part-time employees with full benefits include Starbucks, REI, Land's End, UPS, and Barnes & Noble.

Personal App

Can you work from home?

Depending on your career and your employer, telecommuting may be in your future. Would you like to have the option of working from home, occasionally or regularly? Do you think you'll be able to complete your work projects on schedule if you telecommute? Or would you prefer to work in an office or other workplace, where you have access to central records and can consult with colleagues and supervisors?

not offer this perk. In fact, more companies are switching to part-time workers in order to cut back on the rising cost of offering benefits, especially the health insurance benefits now required of all companies with more than 50 full-time employees. Some companies even use high-tech "workforce optimization" software that models demand so that employers can predict exactly how many workers are needed at any given time, further reducing the length of shifts and numbers of workers needed. Such "just-in-time scheduling" can yield significant cost savings for businesses; however, it can result in unpredictable schedules for employees, which may create dissatisfaction and thus higher turnover.[9]

Job sharing (sometimes referred to as *work sharing*) is an arrangement whereby two people share one full-time position. One job sharer may work from 8 a.m. to noon, and the other from 1 to 5 p.m., or they may alternate workdays. Job sharing is different than part-time work because two people share one single position, which is generally more skilled than a part-time position would be. Job sharing can be difficult to orchestrate at the beginning, but may contribute to greater job satisfaction and ease in creating work–life balance. Job sharing can actually lead people to be more productive, as they know that their time at work is limited and that someone else is directly depending on the quality of their work. Job sharing combines the security of a full-time position with the flexibility of a part-time one, which may be especially valuable for working parents. For firms, job sharing provides a unique opportunity to attract highly skilled employees who are not available on a full-time basis. In addition, companies can save on benefits expenses and avoid the disruptions of employee turnover. For employees, opting for the flexibility of job sharing may mean giving up some of the benefits, such as health insurance, received for full-time work. Job sharing is difficult if tasks are not easily divisible or if two people do not work or communicate well with one another.

10-4f Telecommuting

A growing number of companies allow **telecommuting**, working at home all the time or for a portion of the work week. Technology such as e-mail, cloud computing, smart phones, laptops, tablets, video conferencing, and overnight couriers all make working at home easier and more convenient than ever before. Working at home means that individuals can set their own hours and have more time with their families. Telecommuting has boomed 79 percent since 2005, and now comprises 2.6 percent of the U.S. workforce, excluding the self-employed. Telecommuting can be especially beneficial to the disabled, working parents, and employees taking care of elderly or disabled family members, though in fact, telecommuters include all demographic groups.[10]

A growing body of research indicates that telecommuters are actually more effective than their in-office counterparts. This is because remote workers feel pressured to counter any perception that they do not work as hard. Remote workers try harder to connect, use technology more effectively, use time more efficiently, and

job sharing an arrangement whereby two people share one full-time position

telecommuting working at home all the time or for a portion of the work week

generally experience fewer distractions than those working in a conventional office.[11]

In addition to increased productivity, companies that allow occasional telecommuting have lower real estate and travel expenses, improved morale, and the flexibility to access larger labor pools. Telecommuting also reduces fossil fuel emissions from putting fewer cars on the road. When Chinese travel website Ctrip allowed half of its employees to telecommute, the company saved $1,900 per employee in furniture and space costs over nine months. Moreover, the telecommuting employees were so efficient that they effectively netted the company an extra day of work per week. The telecommuters used fewer sick days, quit at a much lower rate, and reported much higher job satisfaction.[12]

Among the disadvantages of telecommuting are feelings of isolation, putting in long hours, and being distracted by family or household responsibilities. The stigma also remains, in spite of evidence to the contrary, that telecommuters are less productive than office-based staff. In addition, some supervisors have difficulty monitoring productivity of remote workers.

Office space—at home. Many companies are finding it cost-effective to allow employees to work at home. Working at home means that parents can spend more time with their children. Telecommuting arrangements such as this can be a win-win situation for both employees and their firms.

10-4g Employee Empowerment

Many companies are increasing employee motivation and satisfaction through the use of empowerment. **Empowerment** means making employees more involved in their jobs and in the operations of the organization by increasing their participation in decision making. With empowerment, control no longer flows exclusively from the top level of the organization downward. Empowered employees have a voice in what they do and how and when they do it. In some organizations, employees' input is restricted to individual choices, such as when to take breaks. In other companies, their responsibilities may encompass more far-reaching issues. Successful companies treat their employees like assets, empowering them to fully utilize their talents and shift responsibilities with the firm's needs. Technology clearly plays a role in empowering employees, but so does creating an open and safe workplace where employees feel like they can speak up and are heard. Allowing employees access to information, such as reports, performance data, and communications, can empower them and make them feel more satisfied with their jobs.

For empowerment to work effectively, management must be involved. Managers should set expectations, communicate standards, institute periodic evaluations, and guarantee follow-up. If effectively implemented, empowerment can lead to increased job satisfaction, improved job performance, higher self-esteem, and increased organizational commitment. Obstacles to empowerment include resistance on the part of management, distrust of management on the part of workers, inadequate training of employees, and poor communication between levels of the organization.

10-4h Employee Ownership

Some organizations have discovered that an effective technique for motivating employees is **employee ownership**—that is, employees own the company they work for by virtue of being stockholders. Employee-owned businesses directly reward employees for success. When the company enjoys increased sales or lower costs,

empowerment making employees more involved in their jobs by increasing their participation in decision making

employee ownership a situation in which employees own the company they work for by virtue of being stockholders

Entrepreneurial Success

A Time to Micromanage

Entrepreneurs are accustomed to being in charge and doing what it takes to help their businesses prosper. Yet even the most competent entrepreneurs may be tempted to cross the line from managing to micromanaging—by dictating exactly what their employees should do, when they should do it, and how to do it, for example. Unfortunately, micromanaged employees can easily become demoralized, which in turn may lead to lower performance, the opposite of what owners intended by exerting such tight control.

Does micromanaging ever make sense? According to experts, a hands-on approach can be helpful when the business is implementing a new but critical process for the first time. Entrepreneurs are aware of the big picture, so they're in an ideal position to clarify details, offer suggestions, and make decisions on the spot, if problems or questions arise. Just as important, entrepreneurs can encourage

employees as work progresses and congratulate them on successfully tackling a difficult challenge.

In general, empowered employees feel more motivated than micromanaged employees. Therefore, entrepreneurs should establish clear goals, responsibilities, and deadlines; describe how performance will be measured; and hold employees accountable for results. Finally, take the time to explain the context of complicated work assignments, says entrepreneur-turned-author Kevin Daum, and provide opportunities for employees to experience what works and what doesn't work.

Sources: Based on information in Muriel Maignan Wilkins, "Signs That You're a Micromanager," *Harvard Business Review*, November 11, 2014, http://hbr.org (accessed July 11, 2015); Doug and Polly White, "The 3-Step Cure for Micromanagement," *Entrepreneur*, June 19, 2014, www.entrepreneur.com (accessed July 11, 2015); Lindsay Broder, "When It's Appropriate to Micromanage," *Entrepreneur*, March 20, 2014, www.entrepreneur.com; Kevin Daum, "8 Tips for Empowering Employees," Inc., September 30, 2013, http://www.inc.com/kevin-daum/8-tips-for-empowering-employees.html (accessed July 27, 2015).

Concept Check

✓ What are the five steps of most MBO programs?

✓ How can companies use job enrichment as a method for motivating employees?

✓ What is behavior modification and how is it used in organizations?

✓ What benefits does a company receive when using flextime, job sharing, and telecommuting?

✓ How do employee ownership and employee empowerment help in increasing employee motivation and satisfaction?

employees benefit directly. The National Center for Employee Ownership, an organization that studies employee-owned American businesses, reports that employee stock ownership plans (ESOPs) provide considerable employee incentive and increase employee involvement and commitment. In the United States today, an estimated 14.7 million employees participate in 8,926 ESOPs and stock bonus plans.[13] Employees in an ESOP may own all or part of a company's stock. In the United States, employee-owned companies include Publix Super Markets, New Belgium Brewing Company, Harpoon Brewery, and Davey Tree Expert Company. ESOPs have also become more popular in Europe.

As a means to motivate executives and managers to feel invested in the company as they work long days, some firms provide stock options as part of the employee compensation package. An option is simply the right to buy shares of the firm within a prescribed time at a set price. If the firm does well and its stock price rises past the set price (presumably because of all the work being done by the employee), the employee can exercise the option and sell the stock to cash in on the company's success. However, not all companies choose to engage in ESOPs because they can be complex and expensive for the firm. This is particularly true of smaller organizations that may not have the means to manage such a program.

10-5 TEAMS AND TEAMWORK

Learning Objective

10-5 Understand the types, development, and uses of teams.

The concepts of teams and teamwork may be most commonly associated with sports, but they are also integral parts of business organizations. This organizational structure is popular because it encourages employees to participate more fully in business decisions. The growing number of companies organizing their workforces into teams reflects an effort to increase employee productivity and creativity because team members are working on specific goals and are given greater autonomy. This leads to greater job satisfaction as employees feel more involved in the management process.[14]

10-5a What Is a Team?

In a business organization, a **team** is two or more workers operating as a coordinated unit to accomplish a specific task or goal.[15] A team may be assigned any number of tasks or goals, from development of a new product to selling that product. A team can also be created to identify or solve a problem that an organization is experiencing. Teamwork may seem like a simple concept, but teams are a microcosm of the organization and any complications in the work environment will affect the team. It is important to take into account the different work and communication styles and personalities of team members in order to create a productive team.[16]

10-5b Types of Teams

Businesses may have several types of teams to achieve different purposes, including problem-solving teams, self-managed teams, cross-functional teams, and virtual teams.

PROBLEM-SOLVING TEAMS The most common type of team in business organizations is the **problem-solving team**. It is generally used temporarily in order to bring knowledgeable employees together to tackle a specific problem. Once the problem is solved, the team typically is disbanded.

SELF-MANAGED WORK TEAMS **Self-managed teams** are groups of employees with the authority and skills to manage themselves. Experts suggest that workers on self-managed teams are more motivated and satisfied because they have greater task variety and job control. On many work teams, members are cross-trained to perform everyone else's jobs and rotate through all the jobs for which the team is responsible. In a traditional business structure, management is responsible for hiring and firing employees, establishing budgets, purchasing supplies, conducting performance reviews, and taking corrective action. When self-managed teams are in place, they take over some or all of these management functions. The major advantages and disadvantages of self-managed teams are mentioned in Figure 10-6.

CROSS-FUNCTIONAL TEAMS Traditionally, businesses have organized employees into departments based on a common function or specialty. However, increasingly, business organizations are faced with projects that require a diversity of skills from multiple departments. A **cross-functional team** consists of individuals with varying specialties, expertise, and skills that are brought together to achieve a common task. For example, a purchasing agent might create a cross-functional team to gain insight into useful purchases for the company. This structure avoids departmental separation and allows greater efficiency when there is a single goal. Although cross-functional teams are not necessarily self-managed,

© GRAFVISION/SHUTTERSTOCK.COM

Using technology to close time and space and get more done. Skype, e-mail, and other electronic methods are allowing employees, continents away from one another, to work together effectively. Being able to hire the best employees from all around the globe to work virtually with one another can give a firm a competitive advantage. Virtual teams located in different time zones and on different continents can also enable a company to work on important projects 24/7.

team two or more workers operating as a coordinated unit to accomplish a specific task or goal

problem-solving team a team of knowledgeable employees brought together to tackle a specific problem

self-managed teams groups of employees with the authority and skills to manage themselves

cross-functional team a team of individuals with varying specialties, expertise, and skills that are brought together to achieve a common task

FIGURE 10-6 Advantages and Disadvantages of Self-Managed Teams

While self-managed teams provide advantages, managers must recognize their disadvantages.

ADVANTAGES	DISADVANTAGES
• Boosts employee morale	• Additional training costs
• Increases productivity	• Teams may be disorganized
• Aids innovation	• Conflicts may arise
• Reduces employee boredom	• Leadership role may be unclear

FIGURE 10-7
Stages of Team
Development

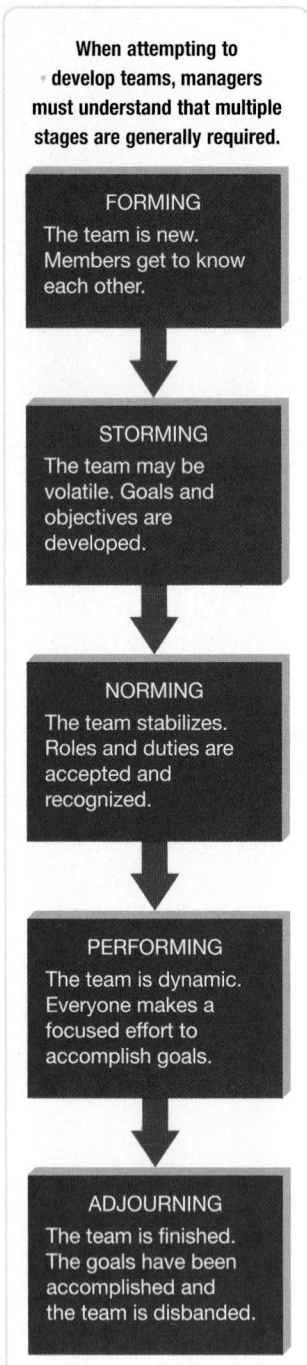

When attempting to develop teams, managers must understand that multiple stages are generally required.

FORMING
The team is new. Members get to know each other.

STORMING
The team may be volatile. Goals and objectives are developed.

NORMING
The team stabilizes. Roles and duties are accepted and recognized.

PERFORMING
The team is dynamic. Everyone makes a focused effort to accomplish goals.

ADJOURNING
The team is finished. The goals have been accomplished and the team is disbanded.

most self-managed teams are cross-functional. Cross-functional teams can also be cross-divisional. Ideally, a cross-functional team consists of a group of people with complementary skill sets and perspectives to enable the group to solve problems effectively and efficiently. The Internet and digital tools have helped strengthen the communication abilities of cross-functional teams. Increasingly, the ability to work in cross-functional teams is an important skill as the world becomes more interconnected and businesses must adapt quickly to change.

VIRTUAL TEAMS Teams do not even have to be geographically close, thanks to sophisticated communications technology. A **virtual team** consists of members who are geographically dispersed but communicate electronically. In fact, team members may never meet in person but rely solely on e-mail, video conferences, voice mail, and other technological interactions. In the global business environment, virtual or remote teams connect employees located anywhere in the world on a common task. However, distance and the lack of face-to-face interactions can make working on virtual teams difficult. Clear communication is very important, especially among team members who have never met in person. E-mail communications, for example, are easily misinterpreted. Team members must be respectful and tolerant of cultural and language differences and quirks, and focus instead on the process.[17]

10-5c Developing and Using Effective Teams

It takes time for team members to establish individual roles, relationships, and duties in order to become an effective team. As a team matures, it passes through five stages of development, as shown in Figure 10-7.

FORMING In the first stage, *forming*, team members are introduced to one another and begin to develop a social dynamic. The members of the team are unsure about how to relate to one another, what behaviors are acceptable, and what the ground rules are for the team. Through group member interaction over time, team members become more comfortable and a group dynamic emerges.

STORMING During the storming stage, the interaction may be volatile and the team may lack unity. This is the stage at which goals and objectives begin to develop. Team members will brainstorm to develop ideas and plans and establish a broad-ranging agenda. It is important for team members to grow comfortable with each other so that they can contribute openly. It is unlikely that a team leader has come forth by this stage, although an informal leader may emerge. The success or failure of the ideas in the storming stage determines how long the team will take to reach the next stage.

NORMING After storming and the first burst of activity, the team begins to stabilize during the *norming* stage. Each person's role within the group begins to solidify, and members recognize the roles of others. A sense of unity grows during this stage. If it has not occurred already, an identified leader will emerge. The group may remain somewhat in flux during norming, and may even regress back to the storming stage if any conflict, especially over the leadership role, occurs.

PERFORMING The fourth stage, *performing*, is when the team achieves its full potential, finally focusing on the assigned task. This stage may take a long time to develop, as team development issues can be complicated. The members of the team finally work in harmony under the established roles to accomplish the necessary goals.

ADJOURNING In the final stage, *adjourning*, the team is disbanded because the project is complete. Team members may be reassigned to other teams or tasks. This stage will not occur if the team is placed together for a task with no specific date of completion. For example, a marketing team may continue to develop promotional efforts for a store even after a specific promotional task has been accomplished.

virtual team a team consisting of members who are geographically dispersed but communicate electronically

When Teamwork Doesn't Work

Have you ever seen one team member take credit for a suggestion that actually came from another member? Or been part of a team with a member who dodged his or her responsibilities? What about a team that made a poor decision because members were reluctant to state opposing views? These are grey areas in teamwork, which can give rise to resentment and dysfunction rather than satisfaction and productivity.

Janine Popick, who runs a marketing services firm, says leaders should speak up when a team member tries to take credit for someone else's idea. Otherwise, employees may hold back—and some promising new product or program will never happen.

In the case of "social loafing," a member "loafs" while others carry the workload. To prevent such situations—and to highlight individual accomplishments—firms can require periodic progress reports from each team member. Team members at Skype and eBay, for example, submit a weekly Progress, Plans, and Problems report. Managers can then see what individuals have achieved, what they expect to achieve, and what challenges they face.

"Groupthink" occurs when a group makes a decision without encouraging diverse viewpoints and alternatives. Because members feel pressure to conform and avoid dissension, decisions are made without the benefit of constructive debate. Google Ventures avoids Groupthink by having team members note their ideas individually and share the best one or two with everyone. Members then vote on ideas from this pool of the best ideas and, after some group discussion, the team leader makes the final decision.

Sources: Based on information in, "Benjamin Voyer on the Psychology of Teamwork," *Economist*, January 2, 2015, www.economist.com (accessed July 11, 2015); Jake Knapp, "Note and Vote: How Google Ventures Avoids Groupthink in Meetings," *Fast Company Design*, August 26, 2014, www.fastcodesign.com (accessed July 11, 2015); Janine Popick, "Someone Is Taking Credit for Your Idea! Now What?" *Inc.com*, January 25, 2013; Kulli Koort, "5 Techniques to Make Teamwork More Manageable," *Fast Company*, October 27, 2014, www.fastcompany.com (accessed July 11, 2015).

10-5d Roles Within a Team

Within any team, each member has a role to play in helping the team attain its objectives. Each of these roles adds important dimensions to team member interactions. The group member who pushes the team toward achieving goals and objectives plays the *task-specialist role* by concentrating fully on the assigned task. In a cross-functional team, this might be the person with the most expertise relating to the current task. The *socioemotional* role is played by the individual who supports and encourages the emotional needs of the other members, placing the team members' personal needs above the task at hand. Although this may sound like an unimportant role, the socioemotional member's dedication to team cohesiveness leads to greater unity and higher productivity. Some team members play a *dual role*, which is a combination of the socioemotional and task-specialist roles. The team leader might not always play this dual role, but the team is likely to be most successful when he or she does. Sometimes an individual assumes the *nonparticipant role*. This role behavior is characterized by a person who does not contribute to accomplishing the task and does not provide favorable input with respect to team members' socioemotional needs. He or she is obviously not a desirable team member to have.

10-5e Team Cohesiveness

Developing a unit from a diverse group of personalities, specialties, backgrounds, and work styles can be challenging and complicated. In a cohesive team, the members get along and are able to accomplish their tasks effectively. Team cohesiveness is affected by different factors, internal and external to the team. To assure cohesiveness, the ideal team size is generally five to 12. Anything larger and relationship development becomes too complicated. Anything smaller and the group may be excessively burdened and tasks may not get completed. Jeff Bezos, CEO of Amazon,

Go team, go! More companies today are using team-building exercises to help their employees figure out how to work better with one another. Sprint uses team-building exercises, such as whitewater rafting, for this purpose as well as to raise money for charities.

© VILEV/SHUTTERSTOCK.COM

famously believes that a team is too large if it takes more than two small pizzas to feed everyone on it.[18] One of the most reliable ways to build cohesiveness within a team is through competition with other teams. When two teams are competing for a single prize or recognition, they are forced to become more goal-oriented and to put aside conflict. A favorable appraisal from an outsider may strengthen team cohesiveness. Because the team is being praised as a group, team members recognize their contribution as a unit. Teams are also more successful when goals have been agreed upon beforehand. A team that is clear about its objective will be able to focus on accomplishing it. Frequent interaction also builds team cohesiveness through increasing familiarity.

10-5f Team Conflict and How to Resolve It

Conflict occurs when a disagreement arises between two or more team members. Conflict traditionally has been viewed as negative, but it is unavoidable. If handled properly conflict can improve a team. For example, if two team members disagree about a proposition, both will spend extra time analyzing the situation closely to determine the best decision. As long as conflict is handled in a respectful and professional manner, it can improve the quality of work produced. However, if conflict turns hostile and affects the work environment, then steps must be taken to arrive at a compromise. Compromises can be difficult because neither party ends up getting everything he or she wants. The best solution is a middle-ground alternative in which each party is satisfied to some degree. Conflict must be acknowledged before it can be dealt with or used in a constructive manner. Ignoring conflict may cause it to simmer or grow, disrupting team progress.

10-5g Benefits and Limitations of Teams

Teamwork can be key to reducing turnover and costs and increasing productivity, customer service, and product quality. There is also evidence that working in teams leads to higher levels of job satisfaction among employees and a harmonious work environment. Thus, an increasingly large number of companies use teams as a valuable element of their organizational structures. However, the process of organizing teams can be stressful and time consuming, and there is no guarantee that the team will develop effectively. If a team lacks cohesiveness and is unable to resolve conflict, the company may experience lower productivity.

Concept Check

✓ What are the major types of teams?

✓ Highlight some differences between cross-functional teams and virtual teams.

✓ Identify and describe the stages of team development.

✓ How can team conflict be reduced?

✓ What are some of the benefits and limitations of a team?

Summary

10-1 Explain what motivation is.

Motivation is the individual internal process that energizes, directs, and sustains behavior. Motivation is affected by employee morale—that is, the employee's feelings about the job, superiors, and the firm itself. Motivation, morale, and job satisfaction are closely related.

10-2 Understand some major historical perspectives on motivation.

One of the first approaches to employee motivation was Frederick Taylor's scientific management, the application of scientific principles to the management of work and workers. Taylor believed that employees work only for money and that they must be closely supervised. This thinking led to the piece-rate system, under which employees are paid a certain amount for each unit they produce.

The Hawthorne Studies attempted to determine the effects of the work environment on productivity. Results of these studies indicated that human factors affect productivity more than physical aspects of the workplace do.

Maslow's hierarchy of needs suggests that people are motivated by five sets of needs. In ascending order of complexity, these motivators are physiological, safety, social, esteem, and self-actualization needs. People are motivated by the most basic set of needs that remains unfulfilled. As needs at one level are satisfied, people try to satisfy needs at the next level.

Frederick Herzberg found that job satisfaction and dissatisfaction are influenced by two distinct sets of factors. Motivation factors, including recognition and responsibility, affect an employee's degree of satisfaction, but their absence does not necessarily cause dissatisfaction. Hygiene factors, including pay and working conditions, affect an employee's degree of dissatisfaction but do not affect satisfaction.

Theory X is a concept of motivation that assumes that employees dislike work and will function effectively only in a highly controlled environment. Thus, to achieve an organization's goals, managers must coerce, control, and threaten employees. This theory generally is consistent with Taylor's ideas of scientific management. Theory Y is more in keeping with the results of the Hawthorne Studies and the human relations movement. It suggests that employees can be motivated to behave as responsible members of the organization.

Theory Z emphasizes long-term employment, collective decision making, and individual responsibility for the outcomes of decisions, informal control, and a holistic concern for employees.

Reinforcement theory is based on the idea that people will repeat behavior that is rewarded and will avoid behavior that is punished.

10-3 Describe three contemporary views of motivation: equity theory, expectancy theory, and goal-setting theory.

Equity theory maintains that people are motivated to obtain and preserve equitable treatment for themselves. Expectancy theory suggests that our motivation depends on how much we want something and how likely we think we are to get it. Goal-setting theory suggests that employees are motivated to achieve a goal that they and their managers establish together.

10-4 Explain several techniques for increasing employee motivation.

Management by objectives (MBO) is a motivation technique in which managers and employees collaborate in setting goals. MBO motivates employees by involving them directly in their jobs and in the organization as a whole. Job enrichment seeks to motivate employees by varying their tasks and giving them more responsibility for and control over their jobs. Job enlargement, expanding a worker's assignments to include additional tasks, is one aspect of job enrichment. Job redesign is a type of job enrichment in which work is restructured to improve the worker–job match.

Behavior modification uses reinforcement to encourage desirable behavior. Rewards for productivity, quality, and loyalty change employees' behavior in desirable ways and increase motivation.

Allowing employees to work flexible hours is another way to build motivation and job satisfaction. Flextime is a system of work scheduling that allows workers to set their own schedules, as long as they fall within the limits established by employers. Part-time work is permanent employment in which individuals work less than a standard work week. Job sharing is an arrangement whereby two people share one full-time position. Telecommuting allows employees to work at home for all or part of the work week. All of these work arrangements give employees more time outside the workplace to deal with family responsibilities or to enjoy free time.

Employee empowerment, self-managed work teams, and employee ownership are also techniques that boost employee motivation. Empowerment increases employees' involvement in their jobs by increasing their decision-making authority. Self-managed work teams are groups of employees with the authority and skills to manage themselves. When employees participate in ownership programs, such as employee stock ownership plans (ESOPs), they have more incentive to make the company succeed and therefore work more effectively.

10-5 Understand the types, development, and uses of teams.

A large number of companies use teams to increase their employees' productivity. In a business organization, a team is a group of workers functioning together as a unit to complete a common goal or purpose.

There are several types of teams that function in specific ways to achieve different purposes. A problem-solving team is a team of knowledgeable employees brought together to tackle a specific problem. Self-managed work teams involve groups of employees with the authority and skills to manage themselves. A cross-functional team is a team of individuals with varying specialties, expertise, and skills. A virtual team is a team consisting of members who are geographically dispersed and communicate electronically.

The five stages of team development are forming, storming, norming, performing, and adjourning. As a team develops, it becomes more productive and unified in order to achieve its assigned objective and goals. The four roles within teams are task specialist, socioemotional, dual, and nonparticipative. Each of these roles plays a specific part in the team's interaction. For a team to be successful, members must learn how to resolve and manage conflict so that the team can work cohesively to accomplish goals.

Key Terms

You should now be able to define and give an example relevant to each of the following terms:

motivation (273)	esteem needs (277)	equity theory (281)	part-time work (287)
morale (274)	self-actualization needs (277)	expectancy theory (282)	job sharing (288)
scientific management (274)	motivation–hygiene theory (278)	goal-setting theory (283)	telecommuting (288)
piece-rate system (274)	motivation factors (278)	management by objectives (MBO) (284)	empowerment (289)
need (276)	hygiene factors (278)	job enrichment (285)	employee ownership (289)
Maslow's hierarchy of needs (276)	Theory X (279)	job enlargement (285)	team (291)
physiological needs (276)	Theory Y (279)	job redesign (285)	problem-solving team (291)
safety needs (277)	Theory Z (280)	behavior modification (286)	self-managed teams (291)
social needs (277)	reinforcement theory (281)	flextime (286)	cross-functional team (291)
			virtual team (292)

Discussion Questions

1. How did the results of the Hawthorne Studies influence researchers' thinking about employee motivation?
2. What are the five levels of needs in Maslow's hierarchy? How are a person's needs related to motivation?
3. What are the two dimensions in Herzberg's theory? What kinds of elements affect each dimension?
4. According to equity theory, how does an employee determine whether he or she is being treated equitably?
5. According to expectancy theory, what two variables determine motivation?
6. Describe the steps involved in the MBO process.
7. What are the objectives of the MBO? What do you think might be its disadvantage?
8. How does employee participation increase motivation?
9. Identify and describe the major types of teams.
10. What are the major benefits and limitations associated with the use of self-managed teams?
11. Explain the major stages of team development.
12. What combination of motivational techniques do you think would result in the best overall motivation and reward system?
13. In what ways are team cohesiveness and team conflict related?

Video Case
Putting the Focus on People at the Fruit Guys

People are as important as profits to Chris Mittelstaedt, founder and CEO of the Fruit Guys (http://fruitguys.com). Remembering the downside of some earlier on-the-job experiences, such as not being asked to help solve problems, Mittelstaedt resolved to make employee empowerment and collaborative teamwork top priorities when he started his own business. Today, his Fruit Guys business rings up $20 million in annual sales and employs dozens of people in the San Francisco area and beyond.

Mittelstaedt's path to entrepreneurial success grew out of a need to make a change in his professional life when his wife was expecting their first child. He was unhappy at a temporary job and thinking about possible ideas for a new business of his own. In speaking with friends and family, Mittelstaedt realized that many office workers who snack on junk food might prefer something healthier if it was conveniently at hand. This led to the concept of selling weekly deliveries of fresh, ripe fruit to companies so their employees would have healthy snacks at work. Mittelstaedt named his new company the Fruit Guys and began making the rounds of corporate headquarters to sign up customers. He also connected with local growers who could provide a steady supply of apples, oranges, and other fruits in season.

As the business grew, Mittelstaedt had to hire employees to sort, package, and deliver fruits to his expanding customer base, as well as hiring employees to handle billing, human resources, and other functions. This is where his background working for other firms came into play: As the head of a small business, he wanted to motivate his employees the way he wished his managers had motivated him, by treating them fairly, showing respect for their capabilities as individuals and team members, and inviting their input as valued members of the organization. "People like to be part of something bigger than themselves,"

he says. The same is true for suppliers, which is why he pays growers fair prices and offers support to help them profit from what they produce.

Although the company has had its ups and downs over the years, Mittelstaedt has remained true to his principles of building positive relationships with customers, employees, and suppliers. Rather than setting one employee against each other in a race for advancement, the entrepreneur looks for win-win ways to develop the talents of everyone on the team. He emphasizes each employee's vital role in the company's overall success, expecting them to reach out to colleagues for coordination purposes as well as to take responsibility for completing their assigned tasks. Recognizing that employees have their own goals and dreams, Mittelstaedt encourages everyone to make the most of opportunities for participation, learning, communication, and expanded responsibilities at the Fruit Guys.

These days, Mittelstaedt's company has a healthy roster of regular customers that includes high-tech firms, law firms, accounting firms, manufacturers, and even public schools. But no matter how big the Fruit Guys gets, the founder is determined to maintain the healthy corporate culture that shows respect for the individual, fosters involvement, and fuels committed teamwork.[19]

Questions
1. When Chris Mittelstaedt says, "People like to be part of something bigger than themselves," what are the implications for employee motivation?
2. Why would an accounting firm spend money week after week for deliveries of fresh fruit for its employees? Explain your answer in terms of the motivation concepts in this chapter.
3. What other techniques would you suggest Mittelstaedt use to motivate his employees, and why?

Building Skills for Career Success

1. Social Media Exercise

Infosys is a successful software company with nearly 150,000 employees. Social media is integral to its strategy and communications approach. The company uses social media to engage younger employees in these processes and to empower them. In order to do this, the company created STRAP Surround as a social platform to engage employees and allow executives to teach. It contains blogs, discussion

forums, an in-house version of YouTube for video sharing, and a range of physical activities and games. The system has provided a mountain of data on its workforce for executives to process.

Here is one example. Employees participated in a series of live events related to a strategy execution topic. These events resulted in tens of thousands of ideas shared via social media. Through these events, management discovered some new things about the effectiveness of different communications media. For example, social media was most effective for structured questions, such as those asking about technologies for future growth, digital consumer behavior, and health care. Moderators made sure to thank participants, and the information gathered was passed along to managers. Some employees who provided particularly useful answers were chosen to become team members.[20]

1. Do you think social media is an effective way to engage employees who are in large organizations? Why or why not?
2. Do you think social media would work well in smaller companies? Why or why not?
3. Do you think that using social media changes the corporate culture and the way in which teams communicate for the better or worse? Explain your answer.

2. Building Team Skills

Empowerment makes workers feel more involved in their jobs and the operations of the organization by involving them in decision making. However, empowerment is a tool that is used inconsistently in different workplaces. If you worked in a position that did not empower you, would you want it? How do you envision empowerment looking in the workplace?

Assignment

Form small groups of three or four. Each member of the group should think about the last time you had a complaint that you brought to a company's attention. Perhaps you purchased an item that quickly malfunctioned, you wanted to exchange a pair of pants for a larger size, or you were not happy with the service you received at an auto body shop.

1. Who helped you address the problem? Was the salesperson empowered to give you a refund or an exchange? Or did the employee have to call in a manager?
2. Every group member should share their experiences with one another.

3. Discuss the following among your group:
   a. From the perspective of upper management, what are the pros and cons of empowering workers to take care of problems?
   b. What about from the perspective of the employees?
   c. How did your experiences as customers change, depending on how empowered the workers were? Did you prefer dealing with the employee or the manager?

3. Researching Different Careers

Because a manager's job varies from department to department within firms, as well as among firms, it is virtually impossible to write a generic description of a manager's job. If you are contemplating becoming a manager, you may find it helpful to shadow several managers to learn firsthand what they do.

Assignment

1. Make an appointment with managers in three firms, preferably firms of different sizes. When you make the appointments, request a tour of the facilities.
2. Ask the managers the following questions:
   a. What do you do in your job?
   b. What do you like most and least about your job? Why?
   c. What skills do you need in your job?
   d. How much education does your job require?
   e. What advice do you have for someone thinking about pursuing a career in management?
3. Summarize your findings in a two-page report. Include answers to these questions:
   a. Is management a realistic field of study for you? Why?
   b. What might be a better career choice? Why?

Running a Business

At Graeter's, Tenure Is "a Proud Number"

Although you might think working for an ice-cream company would be motivating under almost any circumstances, Graeter's doesn't take its employees' commitment for granted. Including full-time and part-time seasonal workers, the company employs about 800 people in three production facilities and dozens of ice-cream shops. Teenagers who take a summer job at a Graeter's shop often return to help out during the winter holidays and then come back to work the following summer, and the summer after that. Production employees tend to remain with the company for long periods as well, and Graeter's is relying on their experience and expertise as it expands its national distribution and opens new stores far from the Cincinnati base.

Professional Procedures with Personal Touches

Over the last few years, Graeter's has benefitted from tightening up some of its long-standing human resources management (HRM) procedures, including those for hiring and evaluating employees. David Blink, the company's controller, explains: "We hire based on potential. . . . We are looking for people who are conscientious about their work, who do a good job, who show up every day. We are a fun place to work. . . . We have turnover based on seasonal work only because we hire a lot of college kids [and] high school kids" to work during the summer months. Managers begin recruiting during the spring so that each store is fully staffed in advance of the peak ice-cream buying season. The company also accepts job applications through its website.

When filling job openings at its three factories, Graeter's looks for people with baking industry skills. On the job, employees and managers alike wear name badges that show the number of years they have worked for the firm, "and that is a proud number," says Blink. Graeter's adds a personal touch by celebrating employees' birthdays and milestones such as 25 years of service with the firm.

According to a consultant who works with top management, goals and measurement systems weren't strongly emphasized in the company's early days. "If [employees] came in and they made ice cream, if they made enough for the week, for the day, that was enough," he says.

These days, however, Graeter's sets specific production and store goals so that all employees know what is expected of them. It also has measurement systems in place to track progress toward those goals. "We have defined the behaviors that are acceptable and not acceptable within the company," the consultant continues, "We communicate that. We teach and educate people." At the retail level, Graeter's training focuses on how employees can make the in-store experience engaging, fun, and memorable for customers.

In the factory, higher production goals have given newly empowered employees achievements to boast about on the slogan T-shirts they wear. The workforce is eager to submit suggestions for improvement, and morale is high. The company also offers advancement opportunities for employees who are ready to take on more responsibility. Graeter's low rate of turnover indicates that employees feel involved with the firm and the work they do. In fact, some employees spend their entire working careers with Graeter's and eventually retire from the firm.

Benefits That Pay

The benefits package for managers and full-time employees is competitive. Graeter's offers profit sharing, and it has made a profit year after year. It also has a 401(k) retirement plan that matches employees' contributions, plus a rolling allowance for paid time-off that is separate from paid vacations and holidays, and is based on the employee's tenure with the firm. Other benefits include medical, life, and disability insurance. Store employees wear uniforms (paid for by the company) and receive a 25 percent discount when they buy Graeter's products. All managers and employees receive the training they need to be effective in their positions and to develop their professional skills.

"You Can't Do It Alone"

The management team has grown as the company moves forward with its aggressive nationwide expansion plans. CEO Richard Graeter, a great-grandson of the company's founders, believes in recruiting outstanding people, compensating them well, and giving them the autonomy they need to get things done. "In the last few months," he notes, "I have hired a vice president of sales and marketing . . . [and] we hired a vice president of finance, basically a CFO [chief financial officer] because we are big enough to support

© ISTOCKPHOTO.COM/LIVIO

that . . . Identifying the gaps in your executive team and your talent pool, and going out and finding people to fill those gaps, is probably one of my most critical functions in addition to looking out to define the strategic direction of the company. I've got some wonderful people on the team now, and they are really helping us make the jump from a small business to a medium-sized business . . . People at that level, you've got to pay them well. It's worth it, though . . . They can command the kind of salary they do because they bring the talent you need to navigate the waters."

"You can't do it alone," Richard concludes. "That is the other thing that I think my cousins and I all have come to realize; we can't do it alone. Our fathers and aunt and the folks that came before them . . . they did it all, from figuring out where to build the next store to hanging up the laundry at the end of the day." Now, to achieve the fast-growing company's ambitious goals, he's found that "you need to rely on talent that is beyond just you."[21]

Questions

1. Imagine that you're a human resources manager for Graeter's. If you were writing the job specification for an entry-level, part-time employee who will serve customers in one of the scoop shops, what qualifications would you include, and why?

2. Food production facilities like the three Graeter's factories must comply with strict regulations to ensure purity and safety. What kinds of teams might Graeter's use in these facilities, and for what specific purposes?

3. Graeter's is currently a non-union company. How might the experience of working there change if a union were to be introduced?

Building a Business Plan: Part 4

In this section of your business plan, you will expand on the type and quantity of employees that will be required to operate the business. Your human resources requirements are determined by the type of business and by the size and scale of your operation. From the preceding section, you should have a good idea of how many people you will need. Part 4 of your textbook, "Human Resources," especially Chapters 9 and 10, should help you in answering some of the questions in this part of the business plan.

The Human Resources Component

To ensure successful performance by employees, you must inform workers of their specific job requirements. Employees must know what is expected of the job, and they are entitled to expect regular feedback on their work. It is vital to have a formal job description and job specification for every position in your business. Also, you should establish procedures for evaluating performance.

The labor force component should include the answers to at least the following questions:

4.1. How many employees will you require, and what qualifications should they have—including skills, experience, and knowledge? How many jobs will be full-time? Part-time?

4.2. Will you have written job descriptions for each position?

4.3. Have you prepared a job application form? Do you know what can legally be included in it?

4.4. What criteria will you use in selecting employees?

4.5. Have you made plans for the orientation process?

4.6. Who will do the training?

4.7. What can you afford to pay in wages and salaries? Is this in line with the going rate in your region and industry?

4.8. Who will evaluate your employees?

4.9. Will you delegate any authority to employees?

4.10. Have you developed a set of disciplinary rules?

4.11. Do you plan to interview employees when they resign?

Review of Business Plan Activities

Remember that your employees are the company's most valuable and important resource. Therefore, make sure that you expend a great deal of effort to acquire and make full use of this resource. Check and resolve any issues in this component of your business plan before beginning Part 5. Again, make sure that your answers to the questions in each part are consistent with the entire business plan. Finally, write a brief statement that summarizes all the information for this part of the business plan.

Endnotes

1   Based on information in Patrick Hoge, "Newsmaker 2014: Salesforce CEO Marc Benioff Becomes a Bigger S.F. Powerhouse," *San Francisco Business Times*, December 24, 2014, www.bizjournals.com/sanfrancisco (accessed July 1, 2015); Kathleen Pender, "Rewarding Workers with Virtual Merit Badges," *San Francisco Chronicle*, September 25, 2014, www.sfgate.com (accessed July 1, 2015); Milton Moskowitz and Robert Levering, "Best Companies to Work For 2014: #7, Salesforce.com (accessed July 1, 2015)," *Fortune*, February 3, 2014, p. 110; Alex Konrad, "Salesforce Innovation Secrets: How Marc Benioff's Team Stays on Top," *Forbes*, August 20, 2014, www.forbes.com; www.salesforce.com.

2   "2014 Top 100 Best Companies to Work For," *Fortune*, http://fortune.com/best-companies/ (accessed January 26, 2015).

3   Sandhya Somashekhar, "As Health-Care Law's Mandate Nears, Firms Cut Worker Hours, Struggle with Logistics," *Washington Post*, June 23, 2014, http://www.washingtonpost.com/national/health-science/as-health-care-laws-employer-mandate-nears-firms-cut-worker-hours-struggle-with-logistics/2014/06/23/720e197c-f249-11e3-914c-1fbd0614e2d4_story.html (accessed July 1, 2015).

4   Ricky W. Griffin, *Fundamentals of Management*, 8th ed. (Mason, OH: South-Western/Cengage Learning, 2016), 302–304.

5   Michael Schein, "Why You Should Let Your Employees Do Whatever They Want," *Inc.*, February 18, 2014, http://www.inc.com/michael-schein-let-employees-do-whatever-they-want.html (accessed July 1, 2015).

6   Anne Fisher, "Can You Care for an Elderly Parent and Still Succeed at Work," *Fortune*, July 24, 2014, http://fortune.com/2014/07/24/elderly-parents-work-life-balance/ (accessed July 1, 2015).

7   Sara Sutton Fell, "5 Ways Telecommuting and Flex Time Help You Recruit the Best Workers," *Entrepreneur*, October 1, 2014, http://www.entrepreneur.com/article/237960 (accessed July 1, 2015).

8   "2014 100 Best Companies," *Working Mother*, http://www.workingmother.com/best-company-list/156592 (accessed January 26, 2015); Ernst & Young, "Ernst & Young, LLP, Marks Ninth Year Among the Top 10 on Working Mothers Best Companies List," Press Release, September 16, 2014, http://www.ey.com/US/en/Newsroom/News-releases/news-ey-marks-ninth-straight-year-among-top-10-on-working-mother-best-companies-list (accessed July 1, 2015).

9   Seth Freed Wessler, "Shift Change: 'Just-in-Time' Scheduling Creates Chaos for Workers," *NBC News*, May 2, 2014, http://www.nbcnews.com/feature/in-plain-sight/shift-change-just-time-scheduling-creates-chaos-workers-n95881 (accessed July 1, 2015).

10 Alina Tugend, "It's Clear Undefined, but Telecommuting Is Fast on the Rise," *New York Times*, March 7, 2014, http://www.nytimes.com/2014/03/08/your-money/when-working-in-your-pajamas-is-more-productive.html?_r=0 (accessed July 1, 2015).

11 Nicholas Bloom, "To Raise Productivity, Let More Employees Work at Home," *Harvard Business Review*, 92 (January–February 2014), pp. 28–29; Scott Edinger, "Why Remote Workers Are More (Yes, More) Engaged," *Harvard Business Review Blog*, August 24, 2012, http://blogs.hbr.org/cs/2012/08/are_you_taking_your_people_for.html?awid=6449339475255159080-3271 (accessed July 1, 2015).

12 Bloom, "To Raise Productivity, Let More Employees Work at Home."

13 National Center for Employee Ownership, "A Brief Overview of Employee Ownership," http://www.nceo.org/articles/employee-ownership-esop-united-states (accessed January 26, 2015).

14 Ricky W. Griffin, *Fundamentals of Management*, 8th ed. (Mason, OH: South-Western/Cengage Learning, 2016), 397.

15 Richard L. Daft and Dorothy Marcic, *Understanding Management*, 9th ed. (Mason, OH: South-Western/Cengage Learning, 2015), 588.

16 Chana R. Shoenberger, "How to Get People to Work Together," *Wall Street Journal*, September 7, 2012, http://blogs.wsj.com/atwork/2012/09/07/how-to-get-people-to-work-together (accessed July 1, 2015).

17 Paul Berry, "Communication Tips for Global Virtual Teams," *Harvard Business Review*, October 30, 2014, https://hbr.org/2014/10/communication-tips-for-global-virtual-teams/ (accessed July 1, 2015).

18 Drake Baer, "5 Brilliant Strategies Jeff Bezos Used to Build the Amazon Empire," *Business Insider*, March 17, 2014, http://www.businessinsider.com/the-strategies-jeff-bezos-used-to-build-the-amazon-empire-2014-3 (accessed July 1, 2015).

19 Based on information in Teresa Novellino, "How the Fruit Guys Made It Through the Dot-Com Bust," *Upstart Business Journal*, August 4, 2014, http://upstart.bizjournals.com/entrepreneurs/hot-shots/2014/08/04/how-the-fruitguys-made-it-through-dot-com-bust.html?page=all

(accessed July 1, 2015); Chris Mittelstaedt, "5 Employee Morale Killers," *Inc.*, March 16, 2012, www.inc.com; Chris Mittelstaedt, "Is This Your Employees' Idea of Service?" *Inc.*, June 19, 2012, www.inc.com (accessed July 1, 2015); Stacy Finz, "Fruit Guys Thrives on Adaptability, Realistic Goals," *San Francisco Chronicle*, February 12, 2012, www.sfgate.com (accessed July 1, 2015); Cengage "Fruit Guys" video; http://fruitguys.com (accessed January 26, 2015).

20 Vanessa DiMauro and Adam Zawel, "Social Media for Strategy-Focused Organizations," *Leader Networks*, June 19, 2014, http://www.leadernetworks.com/2014/06/social-media-for-strategy-focused-organizations.html (accessed July 1, 2015).

21 Based on information from Alexander Coolidge, "Graeter's Pitches Its Products Nationwide," *Cincinnati Enquirer*, June 20, 2014, http://www.cincinnati.com/story/money/2014/06/18/graeters-pitches-product-nationwide/10820875/ (accessed July 1, 2015); Kimberly L. Jackson, "Graeter's Premium Chocolate Chip Ice Cream Lands at Stop & Shop," *Newark Star-Ledger (NJ)*, April 4, 2012, www.nj.com (accessed July 1, 2015); "Graeter's Ice Cream Debuts in Bay Area," *Tampa Bay Times (St. Petersburg, FL)*, January 10, 2012, p. 4B; Jim Carper, "Graeter's Runs a Hands-on Ice Cream Plant," *Dairy Foods*, August 2011, pp. 36+; Jim Carper, "The Greater Good," *Dairy Foods*, August 2011, pp. 95+; "Graeter's Unveils New 'Mystery Flavor,'" *Dayton Daily News*, March 29, 2012, www.daytondailynews.com (accessed July 1, 2015); Bob Driehaus, "A Cincinnati Ice Cream Maker Aims Big," *New York Times*, September 11, 2010, www.nytimes.com (accessed July 27, 2015); Lucy May, "Graeter's Northern Kentucky Franchisee Puts Stores on the Block," *Business Courier*, August 6, 2010, http://cincinnati.bizjournals.com (accessed July 1, 2015); www.graeters.com (accessed January 26, 2015); interviews with company staff and Cengage videos about Graeter's.

CHAPTER 11

Building Customer Relationships Through Effective Marketing

Why Should You Care?

Marketers are concerned about building long-term customer relationships. To develop competitive product offerings, business people must identify acceptable target customer groups and understand their behaviors.

Learning Objectives

Once you complete this chapter, you will be able to:

11-1 Understand the meaning of *marketing* and the importance of managing customer relationships.

11-2 Explain how marketing adds value by creating several forms of utility.

11-3 Trace the development of the marketing concept and understand how it is implemented.

11-4 Understand what markets are and how they are classified.

11-5 Understand the two major components of a marketing strategy—target market and marketing mix.

11-6 Explain how the marketing environment affects strategic market planning.

11-7 Understand the major components of a marketing plan.

11-8 Describe how market measurement and sales forecasting are used.

11-9 Distinguish between a marketing information system and marketing research.

11-10 Identify the major steps in the consumer buying decision process and the sets of factors that may influence this process.

Starbucks: What's Not to Love

Starbucks doesn't just sell lattes and espressos—it markets a coffee-culture experience, one fresh-brewed cup at a time. Whether customers sit and sip at one of the company's 22,000 shops worldwide or use the Starbucks app to order and pay for coffee picked up at a drive-thru location, the strategy is to provide high-quality food and beverage products with convenient service in comfortable surroundings.

With the acquisition of Tazo teas and the addition of sandwiches and bakery items, Starbucks can offer variety to satisfy repeat customers while attracting new customers for breakfast, lunch, and early evening. The company also reinforces its premium positioning by introducing new specialty beverages and opening new "reserve" stores where enthusiasts can taste and buy high-end coffees. In the coming months, it will open hundreds of small express stores for city-dwellers who get coffee to go. It is also increasing the number of drive-thrus to accommodate time-pressured suburban commuters. To reach students and faculty members on college campuses, Starbucks is testing mobile trucks that park in different locations and remain open when dining halls are closed.

Starbucks has a growing presence in grocery stores, with bagged coffees, instant coffee packets, single-serve coffee pods, and ready-to-drink products like bottled Frappuccino. Its single-serve coffee maker, the Verismo, targets coffee-lovers who want to quickly brew high-quality coffee and tea at home or at work. Beyond coffee and related products, the company builds on its brand cachet and market coverage to promote gift cards for all occasions and budgets. During one recent Christmas season, more than 45 million Americans received a Starbucks gift card.

Research shows that many Starbucks customers are tech-savvy. As a result, the company engages these customers online, via mobile marketing, and through social media, where it has more than 35 million Facebook likes and 7 million Twitter followers. These customers are among the first to learn about new products, new locations, and new promotions—and they can post comments to let Starbucks know what they think.[1]

Did You Know?

Starbucks rings up $16 billion in annual revenues through 12,000 U.S. locations and 10,000 locations in 65 other countries.

Numerous organizations, like Starbucks, use marketing efforts to inform customers about their range of products that seek to satisfy customer demand and create value. Understanding customers' needs and wants are crucial to providing the products that satisfy them. Although marketing encompasses a diverse set of decisions and activities, it always begins and ends with the customer. The American Marketing Association defines **marketing** as "[t]he activity, set of institutions, and processes for creating, communicating, delivering, and exchanging offerings that have value for customers, clients, partners, and society at large."[2] The marketing process involves eight major functions and numerous related activities, all of which are essential to the marketing process (see Table 11-1).

In this chapter, we examine how marketing activities add value to products. We trace the evolution of the marketing concept and describe how organizations practice it. Next, our focus shifts to market classifications and marketing strategy. We analyze the four elements of a marketing mix and discuss uncontrollable factors in the marketing environment. Then we examine the major components of a marketing plan. We consider tools for strategic market planning, including market measurement, sales forecasts, marketing information systems, and marketing research. Finally, we look at the forces that influence consumer and organizational buying behavior.

11-1 MANAGING CUSTOMER RELATIONSHIPS

Without marketing relationships with customers, businesses would not be successful. Therefore, maintaining positive relationships with customers is an important goal for marketers. The term **relationship marketing** refers to marketing decisions

marketing the activity, set of institutions, and processes for creating, communicating, delivering, and exchanging offerings that have value for customers, clients, partners, and society at large

relationship marketing establishing long-term, mutually satisfying buyer–seller relationships

Learning Objective

11-1 Understand the meaning of *marketing* and the importance of managing customer relationships.

TABLE 11-1 Eight Major Marketing Functions

Exchange functions: All companies—manufacturers, wholesalers, and retailers—buy and sell to market their merchandise.
1. **Buying** includes obtaining raw materials to make products, knowing how much merchandise to keep on hand, and selecting suppliers.
2. **Selling** creates possession utility by transferring the title of a product from seller to customer.
Physical distribution functions: These functions involve the flow of goods from producers to customers.
3. **Transporting** involves selecting a mode of transport that provides an acceptable delivery schedule at an acceptable price.
4. **Storing** goods is often necessary to sell them at the best selling time.
Facilitating functions: These functions help the other functions to take place.
5. **Financing** helps at all stages of marketing. To buy raw materials, manufacturers often borrow from banks or receive credit from suppliers. Wholesalers may be financed by manufacturers, and retailers may receive financing from the wholesaler or manufacturer. Finally, retailers often provide financing to customers.
6. **Standardization** sets uniform specifications for products or services. Grading classifies products by size and quality, usually through a sorting process. Together, standardization and grading facilitate production, transportation, storage, and selling.
7. **Risk taking**—even though competent management and insurance can minimize risks—is a constant reality of marketing because of such losses as bad-debt expense, obsolescence of products, theft by employees, and product-liability lawsuits.
8. **Gathering** market information is necessary for making all marketing decisions.

and activities focused on achieving long-term, satisfying relationships with customers. Relationship marketing deepens and reinforces the buyer's trust in the company, which, as the customer's loyalty grows, increases a company's understanding of the customer's needs and desires. Successful marketers respond to customers' needs and strive to increase value to buyers continually over time. Eventually, this interaction becomes a solid relationship that fosters cooperation and mutual trust. The Internet has expanded and improved relationship marketing options for many firms by making targeted communication faster, cheaper, and easier. Digital technologies allow firms to connect to consumers and have a dialogue with them in real time. This not only improves the speed at which firms can innovate, but consumers are satisfied because they feel the firm is listening to them.

customer relationship management (CRM) using information about customers to create marketing strategies that develop and sustain desirable customer relationships

To build long-term customer relationships, marketers are increasingly turning to marketing research and information technology. **Customer relationship management (CRM)** focuses on using information about customers to create marketing strategies that develop and sustain desirable customer relationships. By increasing customer value over time, organizations try to retain and increase long-term profitability through customer loyalty. Kroger, for example, tracks the purchases of its 55 million loyalty-card holders and documents what customers buy at its 2,600 stores. After analyzing the data, the supermarket firm sells information about the trends it identifies to vendors like Procter & Gamble and Nestlé, who are willing to pay for the insights because it helps them more precisely target their products and messages to customer desires.[3] Because CRM is such an important part of creating and building customer loyalty, many companies offer high-tech products aimed at helping firms to identify good customers and to manage relations with them over the long-term. The accessibility of technology has contributed to a more even playing field for firms of all sizes.

RAWPIXEL/FOTOLIA LLC

Developing long-term customer relationships. Many companies spend a considerable amount of money on marketing programs to develop and maintain long-term relationships with their customers—especially the valuable ones. Often it's more profitable to retain these customers by offering them big rewards than attracting new customers who may never develop the same loyalty.

Managing customer relationships requires identifying patterns of buying behavior and using this information to focus on the most promising and profitable customers. Companies must be sensitive to customers' requirements and desires and establish communication to build customers' trust and loyalty. In some instances, it may be more profitable for a company to focus on satisfying a valuable existing customer than to attempt to attract a new one who may never develop the same level of loyalty. This involves determining how much the customer will spend over his or her lifetime. The **customer lifetime value (CLV)** is a measure of a customer's worth (sales minus costs) to a business during one's lifetime.[4] CLV also includes the intangible benefits of retaining lifetime-value customers, such as their ability to provide feedback to a company and refer new customers of similar value, but these are important considerations as well. The amount of money a company is willing to spend to retain such customers is also a factor. In general, when marketers focus on customers chosen for their lifetime value, they earn higher profits in future periods than when they focus on customers selected for other reasons.[5] Thanks to technological innovations and improved research, it is a fairly straightforward task to calculate CLV. In fact, businesses can utilize reliable free online tools to calculate CLV, including one created by the Harvard Business School.[6] Because the loss of a potential lifetime customer can result in lower profits, managing customer relationships has become a major focus of marketers.

Concept Check

✓ How can technology help to build long-term customer relationships?

✓ What are the benefits of retaining customers?

11-2 UTILITY: THE VALUE ADDED BY MARKETING

Utility is the ability of a good or service to satisfy a human need. The latest iPad, Nike Zoom running shoes, or Mercedes Benz luxury car all satisfy human needs. Thus, each possesses utility. There are four kinds of utility (see Figure 11-1).

Form utility is created by converting production inputs into finished products. Marketing efforts may influence form utility indirectly because the data gathered as part of marketing research are frequently used to determine the size, shape, and features of a product.

The three kinds of utility that are created directly by marketing are place, time, and possession utility. **Place utility** is created by making a product available at a

Learning Objective

11-2 Explain how marketing adds value by creating several forms of utility.

FIGURE 11-1 Types of Utility

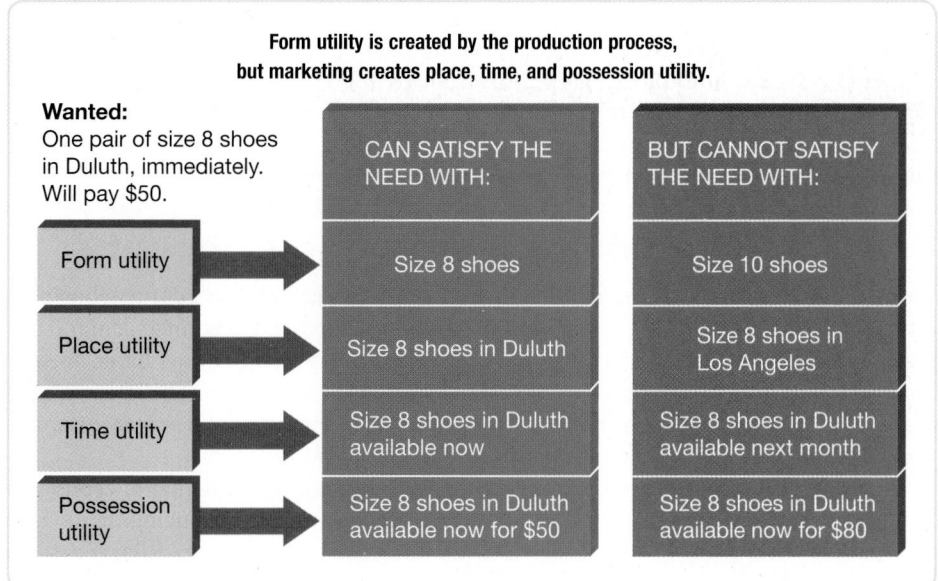

customer lifetime value (CLV) a measure of a customer's worth (sales minus costs) to a business over one's lifetime

utility the ability of a good or service to satisfy a human need

form utility utility created by converting production inputs into finished products

place utility utility created by making a product available at a location where customers wish to purchase it

Putting products at the customer's fingertips. Firms try to provide customers with products whenever and wherever they need them.

location where customers wish to purchase it. A pair of shoes is given place utility when it is shipped from a factory to a department store.

Time utility is created by making a product available when customers wish to purchase it. For example, Halloween costumes may be manufactured in April but not displayed until September, when consumers start buying them. By storing the costumes until there is a demand, the manufacturer or retailer provides time utility.

Possession utility is created by transferring title (or ownership) of a product to a buyer. For a product as simple as a pair of shoes, ownership usually is transferred by means of a sales slip or receipt. For such products as automobiles and homes, the transfer of title is a more complex process. Along with the title to products, the seller transfers the right to use that product.

Place, time, and possession utility have real value in terms of both money and convenience. This value is created and added to goods and services through a wide variety of marketing activities—from research indicating what customers want to product warranties ensuring that customers get what they pay for. Overall, these marketing activities account for about half of every dollar spent by consumers. When they are part of an integrated marketing program that delivers maximum utility to the customer, many would agree that they are worth the cost.

Place, time, and possession utility are only the most fundamental applications of marketing activities. In recent years, marketing activities have been influenced by a broad business philosophy known as the *marketing concept*.

11-3 THE MARKETING CONCEPT

The **marketing concept** is a business philosophy that a firm should provide goods and services that satisfy customers' needs through a coordinated set of activities that allow the firm to achieve its objectives. Initially, the firm communicates with potential customers to assess their product needs. Then, the firm develops a good or service to satisfy those needs. Finally, the firm continues to seek ways to provide customer satisfaction. This process is an application of the marketing concept or marketing orientation. For example, in order to satisfy the demands of an increasingly young and tech-savvy target market, T-Mobile, the fourth largest wireless carrier, has upgraded and expanded its infrastructure at significant expense, eliminated contracts, dropped international roaming charges, offered unlimited data plans that cover music streaming, and even offered to pay rivals' customers to switch to T-Mobile wireless service. Calling itself the "Un-carrier," T-Mobile has sought to attract market share away from rivals by focusing on what customers really want. The company's efforts have unsettled the wireless industry and gained it millions of new subscribers.[7]

11-3a Evolution of the Marketing Concept

From the start of the Industrial Revolution until the early 20th century, business effort was directed mainly toward the production of goods. Consumer demand for manufactured products was so great that manufacturers could almost bank on selling everything they produced. Business had a strong *production orientation*, which placed a strong emphasis on increased output and production efficiency. Marketing was limited to taking orders and distributing finished goods.

In the 1920s, production caught up with and began to exceed demand. Producers had to direct their efforts toward selling goods rather than just producing them. This new *sales orientation* was characterized by increased advertising, enlarged sales forces, and, occasionally, high-pressure selling techniques. Manufacturers produced

Concept Check

✔ Explain the four kinds of utility.

✔ Provide an example of each.

Learning Objective

11-3 Trace the development of the marketing concept and understand how it is implemented.

time utility utility created by making a product available when customers wish to purchase it

possession utility utility created by transferring title (or ownership) of a product to a buyer

marketing concept a business philosophy that a firm should provide goods and services that satisfy customers' needs through a coordinated set of activities that allow the firm to achieve its objectives

TABLE 11-2 Evolution of Customer Orientation

Business managers recognized that they were not primarily producers or sellers, but were in the business of satisfying customers' wants.

Production Orientation	Sales Orientation	Customer Orientation
Take orders	Increase advertising	Determine customer needs
Distribute goods	Enlarge sales force	Develop products to fill these needs
	Intensify sales techniques	Achieve the organization's goals

the goods they expected consumers to want, and marketing consisted primarily of promoting products through personal selling and advertising, taking orders, and delivering goods.

During the 1950s, however, businesspeople started to realize that even enormous advertising expenditures and proven sales techniques were not sufficient to gain a competitive edge. It was then that business managers recognized that they were not primarily producers or sellers, but were in the business of satisfying customers' needs. Marketers realized that the best approach was to adopt a customer orientation—in other words, the organization had to first determine what customers need and then develop goods and services to fill those particular needs (see Table 11-2).

All functional areas—research and development, production, finance, human resources, and, of course, marketing—play a role in providing customer satisfaction.

11-3b Implementing the Marketing Concept

To implement the marketing concept, a firm first must obtain information about its present and potential customers. The firm must determine not only what customers' needs are, but also how well these needs are satisfied by products currently in the market—both its own products and those of competitors. It must ascertain how its products might be improved and what opinions customers have about the firm and its marketing efforts.

The firm then must use this information to pinpoint the specific needs and potential customers toward which it will direct its marketing activities and resources. Next, the firm must mobilize its marketing resources to (1) provide a product that will satisfy its customers, (2) price the product at a level that is acceptable to buyers and will yield a profit, (3) promote the product so that potential customers will be aware of its existence and its ability to satisfy their needs, and (4) ensure that the product is distributed so that it is available to customers where and when it is needed.

Finally, the firm must again obtain marketing information—this time regarding the effectiveness of its efforts. Can the product be improved? Is it being promoted effectively? Is it being distributed efficiently? Is the price too high or too low? The firm must be ready to modify any or all of its marketing activities based on information about its customers and competitors. For example, West Elm modified its marketing activities at one new furniture store in Durham, North Carolina, after analyzing both in-store and online sales data from customers living in the area.

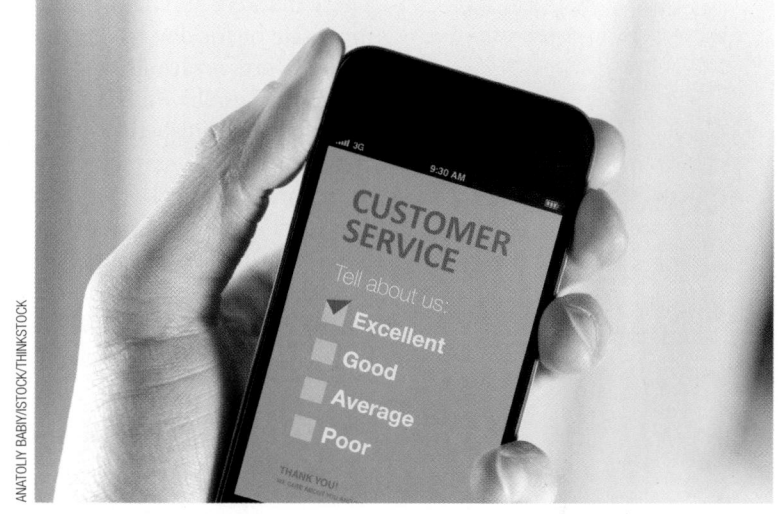

ANATOLIY BABIY/ISTOCK/THINKSTOCK

Tell us what you _really_ think. Customer satisfaction is a major element of the marketing concept. Many businesses attempt to measure customer satisfaction through surveys. Surveys can be conducted in a variety of ways: in-person, by mail or fax, or online. Online surveys have made it very inexpensive for firms to gather customer feedback.

Concept Check

✓ Identify the major components of the marketing concept.

✓ How did the customer orientation evolve?

✓ What steps are involved when implementing the marketing concept?

Although the retailer had expected younger shoppers looking for a contemporary look and stocked the store accordingly, Durham shoppers buying from the firm's website were actually buying more traditional furniture. Sales at the Durham store rallied quickly, after the store manager adjusted the store's products to better match what local shoppers were actually buying.[8]

11-4 MARKETS AND THEIR CLASSIFICATION

Learning Objective

11-4 Understand what markets are and how they are classified.

A **market** is a group of individuals or organizations, or both, that need products in a given category and that have the ability, willingness, and authority to purchase them. Markets are broadly classified as consumer or business-to-business, and marketing efforts vary depending on the intended market. Marketers should understand the general characteristics of these two groups.

Consumer markets consist of purchasers and/or household members who intend to consume or benefit from the purchased products and who do not buy products to make profits. *Business-to-business markets*, also called *industrial markets*, are grouped broadly into producer, reseller, governmental, and institutional categories. These markets purchase specific kinds of products for use in making other products for resale or for day-to-day operations. *Producer markets* consist of individuals and business organizations that buy certain products to use in the manufacture of other products. *Reseller markets* consist of intermediaries, such as wholesalers and retailers, who buy finished products and sell them for a profit. *Governmental markets* consist of federal, state, county, and local governments. They buy goods and services to maintain internal operations and to provide citizens with such products as highways, education, water, energy, and national defense. Governmental purchases total billions of dollars each year. *Institutional markets* include churches, not-for-profit private schools and hospitals, civic clubs, fraternities and sororities, charitable organizations, and foundations. Their goals are different from the typical business goals of profit, market share, or return on investment.

market a group of individuals or organizations, or both, that need products in a given category and that have the ability, willingness, and authority to purchase them

Concept Check

✓ What is a market?

✓ Identify and describe the major types of markets.

11-5 DEVELOPING MARKETING STRATEGIES

Learning Objective

11-5 Understand the two major components of a marketing strategy—target market and marketing mix.

A **marketing strategy** is a plan that will enable an organization to make the best use of its resources and advantages to meet its objectives. A marketing strategy consists of (1) the selection and analysis of a target market and (2) the creation and maintenance of an appropriate **marketing mix**, a combination of product, price, distribution, and promotion developed to satisfy a particular target market.

11-5a Target Market Selection and Evaluation

A **target market** is a group of individuals or organizations, or both, for which a firm develops and maintains a marketing mix suitable for the specific needs and preferences of that group. In selecting a target market, marketing managers examine potential markets for their possible effects on the firm's sales, costs, and profits. The managers attempt to determine whether the organization has the resources to produce a marketing mix that meets the needs of a particular target market and whether satisfying these needs is consistent with the firm's overall objectives. They also analyze the strengths and number of competitors already marketing to the target market. A target market can range in size from millions of people to only a few, depending on the product and the marketer's objectives. Zipcar is a car-sharing company that targets people who either live in cities and do not want to own a car, or those who cannot afford a car or only need one occasionally. Its target

marketing strategy a plan that will enable an organization to make the best use of its resources and advantages to meet its objectives

marketing mix a combination of product, price, distribution, and promotion developed to satisfy a particular target market

target market a group of individuals or organizations, or both, for which a firm develops and maintains a marketing mix suitable for the specific needs and preferences of that group

market treats cars as something that are needed to get around, not as a status symbol.[9] On the other hand, Rolls-Royce targets its automobiles toward a small, very exclusive market: wealthy people who want the ultimate in prestige in an automobile. Some companies target multiple markets with different products, prices, distribution systems, and promotion for each one. For example, some high-end clothing designers target multiple markets through developing affordable lines distributed at mass market retail outlets, such as Target, Kmart, and Walmart. This strategy allows designers to reach customers with varying needs and levels of disposable income. For example, Target has partnered with such high-end designers as Jason Wu, Missoni, and Joseph Altuzarra, and website NET-A-PORTER.COM to offer affordable versions of high-end products.[10] The strategy has introduced the normally elite brands to a much larger market, enhancing Target's stylish image.

Reaching the right market segments. The market for fragrances is segmented based on gender. Some fragrances are aimed at men, while others, such as the perfume featured in this photo, are aimed at women.

UNDIFFERENTIATED APPROACH A company that designs a single marketing mix and directs it at the entire market for a particular product is using an **undifferentiated approach** (see Figure 11-2). This approach assumes that individual customers in the target market for a specific kind of product have similar needs and that the organization can satisfy most customers with a single marketing mix, which consists of one type of product with little or no variation, one price, one promotional program aimed at everyone, and one distribution system to reach all customers in the total market. Products that can be marketed successfully with the undifferentiated approach include staple food items, such as sugar and salt, and some produce. An undifferentiated approach is useful in only a limited number of situations because buyers have varying needs for most product categories, which requires the market segmentation approach.

MARKET SEGMENTATION APPROACH Market segmentation is required because different consumers have different needs. A firm that markets 40-foot yachts would not direct its marketing effort toward every person in the total boat market, for instance, because not all boat buyers have the same needs. Marketing efforts directed at the wrong target market are wasted.

Instead, the firm should direct its attention toward a particular portion, or segment, of the total market for boats. A **market segment** is a group of individuals or organizations within a market that shares one or more common characteristics. The process of dividing a market into segments is called **market segmentation**. As shown in Figure 11-2, there are two market segmentation approaches: concentrated and differentiated. When an organization uses *concentrated* market segmentation, a single marketing mix is directed at a single market segment. If *differentiated* market segmentation is used, multiple marketing mixes are focused on multiple market segments.

In our boat example, one common characteristic, or *basis*, for segmentation might be end use of a boat. The firm would be interested primarily in the market segment whose uses for a boat could lead to the purchase of a 40-foot yacht. Other bases for segmentation might be income or geographic location. Variables can affect the type of boat an individual might purchase. When choosing a basis for segmentation, it is important to select a characteristic that relates to differences in customers' needs for a product. The yacht producer, for example, would not use religion to segment the boat market because people's needs for boats do not vary based on religion.

undifferentiated approach directing a single marketing mix at the entire market for a particular product

market segment a group of individuals or organizations within a market that share one or more common characteristics

market segmentation the process of dividing a market into segments and directing a marketing mix at a particular segment or segments rather than at the total market

FIGURE 11-2 General Approaches for Selecting Target Markets

The undifferentiated approach assumes that individual customers have similar needs and that most customers can be satisfied with a single marketing mix. When customers' needs vary, the market segmentation approach—either concentrated or differentiated—should be used.

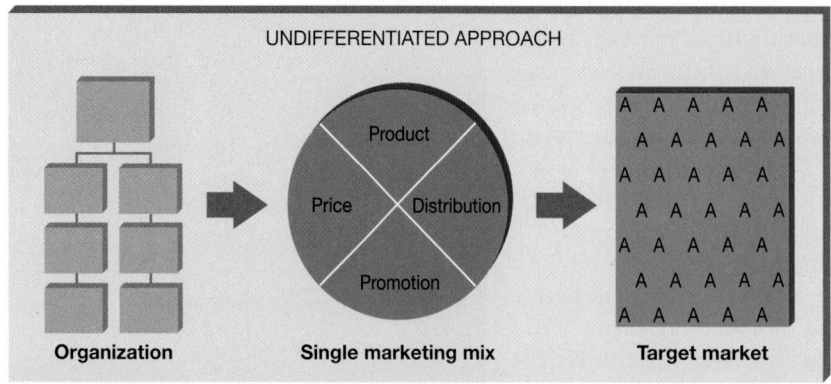

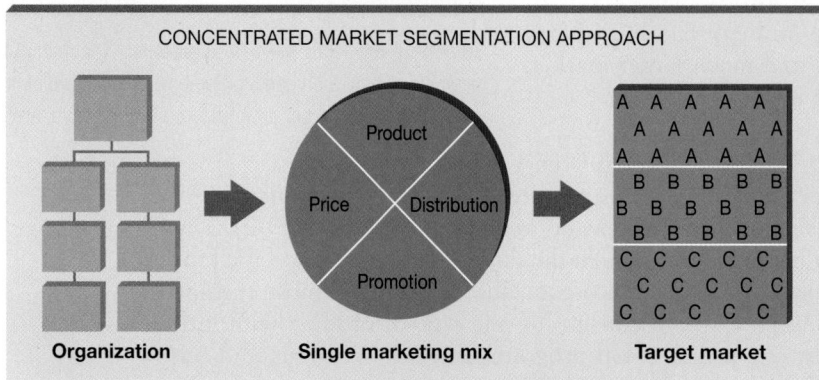

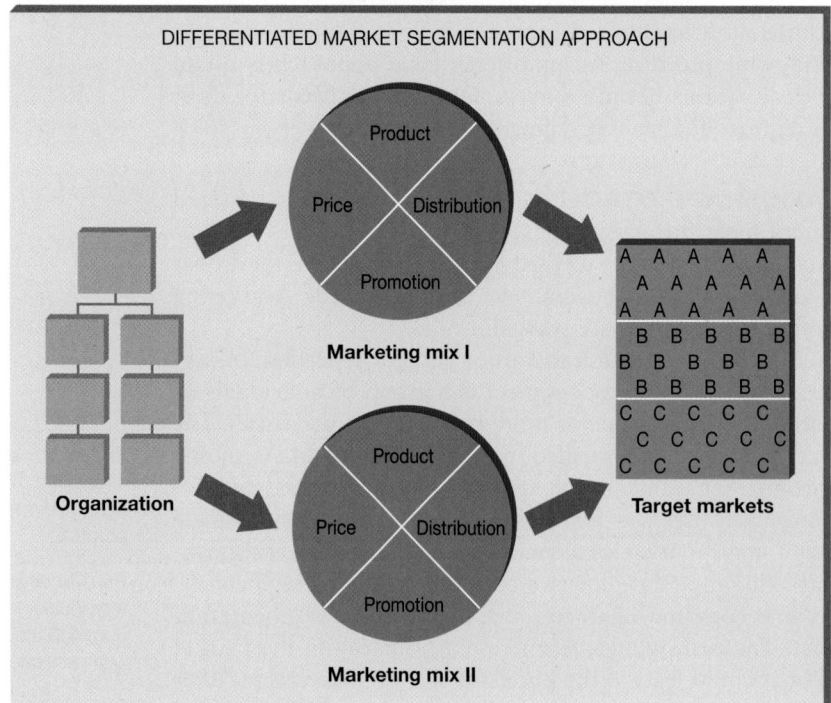

NOTE: The letters in each target market represent potential customers. Customers that have the same letters have similar characteristics and similar product needs.

Source: William M. Pride and O. C. Ferrell, *Marketing*, 18th ed. (Mason, OH: South-Western/Cengage Learning, 2016). Adapted with permission.

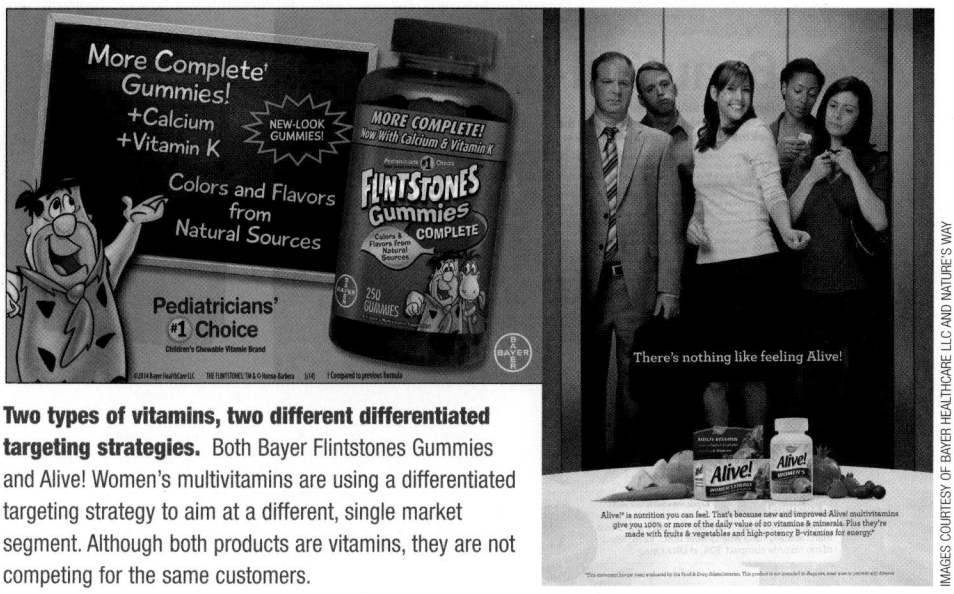

Two types of vitamins, two different differentiated targeting strategies. Both Bayer Flintstones Gummies and Alive! Women's multivitamins are using a differentiated targeting strategy to aim at a different, single market segment. Although both products are vitamins, they are not competing for the same customers.

Marketers use a wide variety of segmentation bases. Those most commonly applied to consumer markets are shown in Table 11-3. Each may be used as a single basis for market segmentation or in combination with other bases. Top-Toy, a Toys "R" Us licensee in Sweden, has turned traditional toy market segmentation on its head by choosing to segment toys by age only. It releases gender-neutral catalogs that market dolls and toy cars, for example, to girls and boys equally in Finland, Norway, Germany, Denmark, and France. Marketers are responding to the cultural trend toward total gender equality in Sweden.[11]

11-5b Creating a Marketing Mix

A business firm controls four important elements of marketing that it combines in a way that reaches the firm's target market. These are the *product* itself, the

TABLE 11-3 Common Bases of Market Segmentation

Demographic	Psychographic	Geographic	Behavioristic
Age	Personality attributes	Region	Volume usage
Gender	Motives	Urban, suburban, rural	End use
Race	Lifestyles	Market density	Benefit expectations
Ethnicity		Climate	Brand loyalty
Income		Terrain	Price sensitivity
Education		City size	
Occupation		County size	
Family size		State size	
Family life cycle			
Religion			
Social class			

Source: William M. Pride and O. C. Ferrell, *Marketing*, 18th ed. (Mason, OH: South-Western/Cengage Learning, 2016). Adapted with permission.

FIGURE 11-3 The Marketing Mix and the Marketing Environment

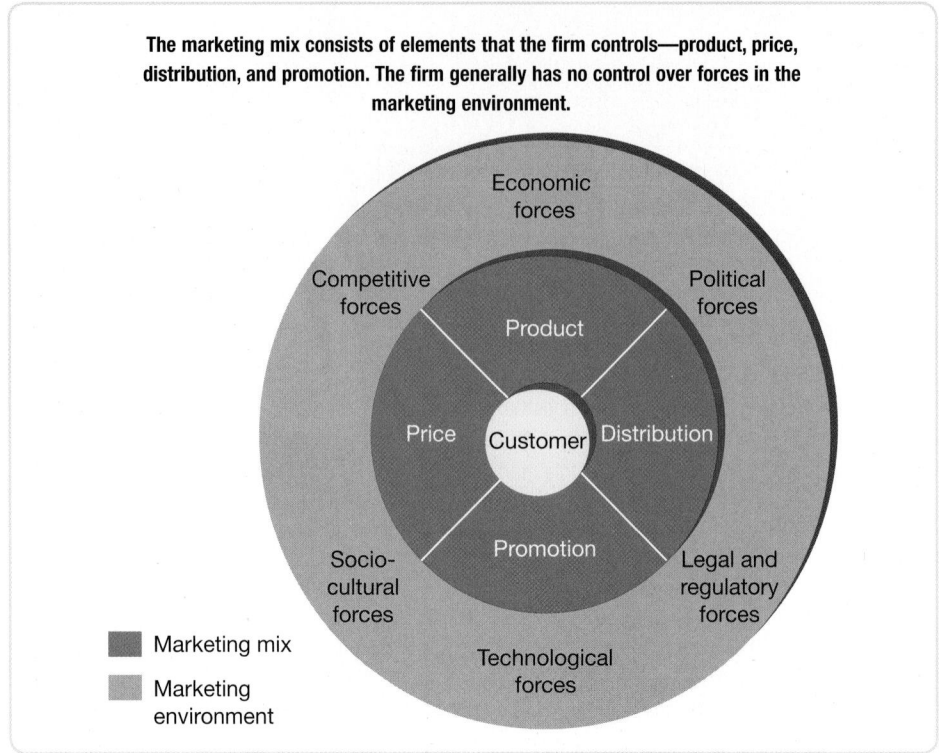

The marketing mix consists of elements that the firm controls—product, price, distribution, and promotion. The firm generally has no control over forces in the marketing environment.

Source: William M. Pride and O. C. Ferrell, *Marketing*, 18th ed. (Mason, OH: South-Western/Cengage Learning, 2016). Adapted with permission.

price of the product, the means chosen for its *distribution*, and the *promotion* of the product. When combined, these four elements form a marketing mix (see Figure 11-3).

A firm can vary its marketing mix by changing any one or more of the ingredients. Thus, a firm may use one marketing mix to reach one target market and another marketing mix to reach a different target market. For example, most automakers produce several different types and models of vehicles and aim them at different market segments based on the potential customers' age, income, and other factors.

Developing the right marketing mix. Firms have little control over the marketing environment. However, they *can* control the marketing mixes for their products—that is, the nature of the products themselves and how they are priced, distributed, and promoted. Marketers at Coca-Cola have developed a specific marketing mix for Coca-Cola Classic.

Entrepreneurial Success

Small Businesses Create Big Buzz

Unusual marketing can help small businesses with big goals but tiny budgets make a big impression. For example, the San Francisco-based Headsets.com, which sells high-quality telephone headsets to business customers, promotes certain products with "pay what you want" pricing. The company limits this offer to customers that have made a previous purchase, and allows one such purchase per customer. Although most customers choose to pay close to full price, three have opted to pay just $1. Still, Headsets.com has attracted dozens of new customers since implementing this pricing policy, and the founder is pleased with the financial return on this marketing investment.

Rock Candy Media, a marketing agency in Austin, Texas, showcased its services by shooting an inexpensive, tongue-in-cheek video about searching for additional office space in fast-growing Austin. Called "Workin' at Ikea," the video shows the founder and several employees testing out desk space at a local Ikea and taking lunch breaks in the store's restaurant. In reality, the firm was eventually able to expand into an office hub for startup businesses. By posting this and other videos on YouTube, Rock Candy demonstrated its creativity and its knowledge of digital media to prospective customers.

The CEO of Silicon Valley startup Zapier promotes his firm's software expertise by writing articles for well-known publications and websites. The idea is to communicate with decision makers who seek software for improving business processes. Not only does this catch the eye of potential customers, it also adds credibility because the publications and websites are known for authoritative content.

Sources: Based on information in John Hall, "Brands Lost Big with Content Marketing in 2014—Here's How to Recover This Year," *Forbes*, January 11, 2015, www.forbes.com (accessed July 18, 2015); Chris Gay, "Four Marketing Strategies That Paid Off for Small Companies," *Wall Street Journal*, November 3, 2014, www.wsj.com (accessed July 1, 2015); Chad Swiatecki, "Want to Office Out of Ikea? Austin Agency Gives It a Try with Guerrilla Video," *Austin Business Journal*, October 20, 2014, www.bizjournals.com/austin (accessed July 1, 2015).

The *product* ingredient of the marketing mix includes decisions about the product's design, brand name, packaging, and warranties. When McDonald's decides on brand names, package designs, sizes of orders, flavors of sauces, and recipes, these choices are all part of the product ingredient.

The *pricing* ingredient is concerned with both base prices and discounts. Pricing decisions are intended to achieve particular goals, such as to maximize profit or to make room for new models. The rebates offered by automobile manufacturers are a pricing strategy developed to boost low auto sales.

The *distribution* ingredient involves not only transportation and storage, but also selecting intermediaries. How many levels of intermediaries is ideal in the distribution of a product? Should the product be distributed as widely as possible or should distribution be restricted to specialized outlets? Companies will likely have to alter the distribution ingredient over time. For example, as customers' consumption habits shift, retailers must adapt their distribution to include online sales—but they must do so carefully or risk cannibalizing sales at their brick-and-mortar stores. At West Elm, the furniture retailer, online sales have grown to 51 percent of its revenues. The company helps its retail store managers embrace its retail website by including online sales that come from households within their zip

TASHATUVANGO/FOTOLIA LLC

codes as part of their stores' performance measures.[12] CVS Health has seen traffic at its CVS.com site and through its mobile app grow by 250 percent, and more than 1 million customers a month visit CVS.com through a mobile device. The company has enhanced its online marketing by including tools such as a "Drug Interaction Checker" and a "Family Vitamin Center" that can offer personalized recommendations for vitamins and supplements.[13]

The *promotion* ingredient focuses on providing information to target markets. The major forms of promotion are advertising, personal selling, sales promotion, and public relations. Careful planning and implementation of promotional tools is crucial to ensure their effectiveness. Distribution and promotion are discussed in more detail in Chapter 13.

These ingredients of the marketing mix are controllable elements. A firm can vary each of them to suit its organizational and marketing goals and target market needs. As we extend our discussion of marketing strategy, we will see that the marketing environment includes a number of *uncontrollable* elements as well.

Concept Check

✓ What are the major components of a marketing strategy?

✓ Describe the major approaches used in target market selection.

✓ Identify the four elements of the marketing mix.

11-6 MARKETING STRATEGY AND THE MARKETING ENVIRONMENT

Learning Objective

11-6 Explain how the marketing environment affects strategic market planning.

The marketing mix consists of elements that a firm controls and uses to reach its target market. The firm also has control of organizational resources, such as finances and data, which can be utilized to accomplish marketing goals and refine the marketing mix. All of a firm's marketing activities can be affected by external forces, which are generally uncontrollable. As Figure 11-3 illustrates, the following forces make up the external *marketing environment*:

- *Economic forces*—the effects of economic conditions on customers' ability and willingness to buy

- *Sociocultural forces*—influences in a society and its culture that result in changes in attitudes, beliefs, norms, customs, and lifestyles
- *Political forces*—influences that arise through the actions of political figures
- *Competitive forces*—the actions of competitors, who are in the process of implementing their own marketing plans
- *Legal and regulatory forces*—laws that protect consumers and competition and government regulations that affect marketing
- *Technological forces*—technological changes that can create new marketing opportunities or cause products to become obsolete rapidly

These forces influence decisions about marketing mix ingredients. Changes in the environment can affect existing marketing strategies. For example, Starbucks, recognizing that consumers are spending more time shopping online and less in conventional shopping areas where its coffee shops are found, tweaked its marketing strategy to keep customers coming in by adding beer, wine, and evening snacks to broaden its product line, as well mobile ordering to reduce time waiting in line.[14] In addition, changes in environmental forces may lead to abrupt shifts in customers'

Social Media:

Warby Parker: Social Media Star

Warby Parker markets fashionable prescription eyeglasses online at prices that undercut traditional eyewear outlets. Its social media strategy focuses on style, value, and social responsibility. For instance, its blog (http://blog.warbyparker.com) chronicles the company's donations of eyeglasses to people in need and offers sneak peeks of new products and new retail connections.

With 408,000 likes, the firm's Facebook page (http://www.facebook.com/warbyparker) is filled with posts about fashion frames, special events, and company updates. Some of this content is also featured on Warby Parker's Twitter account (http://twitter.com/warbyparker) and its Tumblr account (http://warbyparker.tumblr.com). Warby Parker's popular Instagram account (http://instagram.com/warbyparker) has attracted more than 173,000 followers who enjoy browsing photos of eyeglass frames and behind-the-scenes photos of employees at work. Finally, fans are invited to pin photos of themselves in Warby Parker glasses on the firm's Pinterest board (http://www.pinterest.com/warbyparker).

needs or wants. Consider the effect technological forces have had on printed newspapers. Years ago, very few people would have predicted that consumers would one day read their news on a computer or their phone. Yet many people now do exactly that.

11-7 DEVELOPING A MARKETING PLAN

A **marketing plan** is a written document that specifies an organization's resources, objectives, marketing strategy, and implementation and control efforts to be used in marketing a specific product or product group. The marketing plan describes the firm's current position or situation, establishes marketing objectives for the product, and specifies how the organization will attempt to achieve these objectives. Marketing plans vary with respect to the time period involved. Short-range plans are for one year or less, medium-range plans cover from over one year to five years, and long-range plans cover periods of more than five years.

Although time-consuming, developing a clear, well-written marketing plan is important. The plan helps establish a unified vision for an organization and is used for communication among the firm's employees. It covers responsibilities, tasks, and schedules for implementation, specifies how resources are to be allocated to achieve marketing objectives, and helps marketing managers monitor and evaluate the performance of the marketing strategy. Because the forces of the marketing environment are subject to change, marketing plans have to be updated frequently. Kellogg, for example, has experienced a 10 percent decline in breakfast cereal sales as consumers turn to other foods such as Greek yogurt or fast-food meals to start their day. The company, which banks on cereal for 30 percent of its sales, responded by adjusting its marketing messages to highlight the protein and other nutritional benefits of its Special K, Mini-Wheats, and Kashi brands of breakfast cereal. The company is also considering introducing healthy cereal snacks.[15]

The major components of a marketing plan are shown in Table 11-4.

Concept Check

✓ Describe the environmental forces that affect a firm's marketing decision and activities.

✓ How are marketing decisions affected by environmental forces?

Learning Objective

11-7 Understand the major components of a marketing plan.

marketing plan a written document that specifies an organization's resources, objectives, strategy, and implementation and control efforts to be used in marketing a specific product or product group

Concept Check

✓ What are the major components of a marketing plan?

✓ Why is developing a well-written marketing plan important?

TABLE 11-4 Components of the Marketing Plan

Plan Component	Component Summary	Highlights
Executive summary	One- to two-page synopsis of the entire marketing plan	
Environmental analysis	Information about the company's current situation with respect to the marketing environment	1. Assessment of marketing environment factors 2. Assessment of target market(s) 3. Assessment of current marketing objectives and performance
SWOT analysis	Assessment of the organization's strengths, weaknesses, opportunities, and threats	1. Strengths 2. Weaknesses 3. Opportunities 4. Threats
Marketing objectives	Specification of the firm's marketing objectives	Qualitative measures of what is to be accomplished
Marketing strategies	Outline of how the firm will achieve its objectives	1. Target market(s) 2. Marketing mix
Marketing implementation	Outline of how the firm will implement its marketing strategies	1. Marketing organization 2. Activities and responsibilities 3. Implementation timetable
Evaluation and control	Explanation of how the firm will measure and evaluate the results of the implemented plan	1. Performance standards 2. Financial controls 3. Monitoring procedures (audits)

Source: William M. Pride and O. C. Ferrell, *Marketing*, 18th ed. (Mason, OH: South-Western/Cengage Learning, 2016). Reprinted with permission.

Personal App

Do you have a personal marketing plan?

© RAWPIXEL/SHUTTERSTOCK.COM

Whether you're looking for a new job, aiming for a promotion, or seeking election to a school or community group, you can use the principles of a marketing plan to market yourself. Start by looking at your current situation, including your competition. Then set objectives for what you want to accomplish. What deadlines should you establish, what resources can you count on, and what steps will get you to your objective? How and when will you evaluate your performance to stay on track?

Learning Objective

11-8 Describe how market measurement and sales forecasting are used.

Concept Check

✓ Why is sales forecasting important?

✓ What methods do businesses use to forecast sales?

Learning Objective

11-9 Distinguish between a marketing information system and marketing research.

sales forecast an estimate of the amount of a product that an organization expects to sell during a certain period of time based on a specified level of marketing effort

11-8 MARKET MEASUREMENT AND SALES FORECASTING

Measuring the sales potential of specific market segments can help an organization make important decisions. An accurate measure of a market segment can help a firm to determine the feasibility of entering new segments and how best to allocate marketing resources and activities among market segments in which it is already active. All such estimates should identify the relevant time frame. As with marketing plans, these plans may be short-range for periods of less than one year, medium-range for one to five years, or long-range for more than five years. The estimates should also define the geographic boundaries of the forecast, such as a city, county, state, or group of nations. Finally, analysts should indicate whether their estimates are for a specific product item, a product line, or an entire product category.

A **sales forecast** is an estimate of the amount of a product that an organization expects to sell during a certain period of time based on a specified level of marketing effort. Managers may rely on sales forecasts when they purchase raw materials, schedule production, secure financial resources, consider plant or equipment purchases, hire personnel, and plan inventory levels. Because the accuracy of a sales forecast is so important, organizations often use several forecasting methods, including executive judgments, surveys of buyers or sales personnel, time-series analyses, correlation analyses, and market tests. The specific methods used depend on the costs involved, type of product, characteristics of the market, time span of the forecast, purposes for which the forecast is used, stability of historical sales data, availability of the required information, and expertise and experience of forecasters. To assist with complicated predictions, many companies utilize sales forecasting software.

11-9 MARKETING INFORMATION

The availability and proper utilization of accurate and timely information are critical to making effective marketing decisions. Thanks to the proliferation of information-gathering technology, marketers have access to a wealth of data. It is accessible through two major channels: a marketing information system or marketing research.

11-9a Marketing Information Systems

A **marketing information system** is a system for managing marketing information that is gathered continually from internal and external sources. Most of these systems are computer based because of the large quantities of data the system must accept, store, sort, and retrieve. *Continual* data collection is essential to ensure the most up-to-date information.

In concept, the operation of a marketing information system is simple. Data from a variety of sources are fed into the system. Data from *internal* sources include sales figures, product and marketing costs, inventory levels, and activities of the sales force. The savviest marketers also collect data from following every move consumers make on their websites and social media interactions. Data from *external* sources relate to the organization's suppliers, intermediaries, and customers. It can also come from competitors' marketing activities and economic conditions. All these data are stored and processed by the marketing information system. Marketers then choose the output format most useful for making marketing decisions, such as daily sales reports by territory and product, forecasts of sales or buying trends, and reports on changes in market share for the major brands in a specific industry. Both the information outputs and their form depend on the requirements of the personnel in the organization. It is imperative that marketers have access to and understand how to use the latest technologies in order to maximize the efficiency and effectiveness of marketing information systems. Increasingly, businesses are using "big data analytics" to mine useful information from all the data collected to build customer profiles that allow them to target just the right messages and products. Kohl's, for example, could use such information to present a personalized coupon on a shopper's smartphone when she lingers in the shoe department—based on shoes she had looked at on Kohls.com.[16]

11-9b Marketing Research

Marketing research is the process of systematically gathering, recording, and analyzing data concerning a particular marketing problem. Marketing research is an important step of the marketing process because it involves collecting and analyzing data on what consumers want and need, their consumption habits, trends, and changes in the marketing environment. The Internet has made marketing research easier and cheaper than ever. Social media sites, such as Facebook and Twitter, can help small firms gauge potential market demand and try out product ideas for little or no cost. The Internet also offers numerous databases and other sources of valuable information on competitors, target markets, and the marketing environment. When conducting marketing research, businesses commonly use external marketing research companies to do one or more of the steps in Table 11-5.

Table 11-5 outlines a six-step procedure for conducting marketing research. It is particularly well suited to test new products, determine various characteristics of consumer markets, and evaluate promotional activities.

11-9c Using Technology to Gather and Analyze Marketing Information

Marketers have more access to reliable data and programs for analyzing them than ever before. Technology has allowed even small firms an unprecedented level of access to high-quality data.

A *database* is a collection of information arranged for easy access and retrieval. Using databases, marketers tap into sources such as internal sales reports, newspaper

Can you hear me now? Would you be interested in having a pre-recruited group of your customers ready and willing to participate in data collection surveys at a moment's notice? If so, you might want to sign up for online software such as PortalPanel, produced by the marketing research company Toluna. Data gathered from good marketing research can be invaluable. Poor quality data can be disastrous and may lead marketers to make the wrong decisions.

marketing information system a system for managing marketing information that is gathered continually from internal and external sources

marketing research the process of systematically gathering, recording, and analyzing data concerning a particular marketing problem

TABLE 11-5 The Six Steps of Marketing Research

1. Define the problem	The problem is stated clearly and accurately, as it will determine the research issues and approaches, the right questions to ask, and the types of solutions that are acceptable. This is a crucial step that should not be rushed.
2. Make a preliminary investigation	The preliminary investigation aims to develop a sharper definition of the problem and a set of tentative answers, which are developed by examining internal information and published data and by talking with persons who have experience with the problem. These answers will be tested by further research.
3. Plan the research	At this stage, researchers know what facts are needed to resolve the identified problem and what facts are available. They make plans on how to gather needed but missing data.
4. Gather factual information	Once a plan is in place, researchers can collect primary information by mail, interviews, observation, and get secondary information from commercial or government data sources. The choice depends on the plan and the available sources of information.
5. Interpret the information	Facts by themselves do not always provide a sound solution to a marketing problem. They must be interpreted and analyzed to determine the choices available to management.
6. Reach a conclusion	Once the data have been evaluated, researchers seek to draw conclusions and make recommendations. These may be obvious or not, depending on intangible factors and whether data used were complete. When there are gaps in the data, it is important for researchers to state this.

articles, company news releases, government economic reports, and bibliographies. Many marketers use commercial databases, such as LEXIS-NEXIS, to obtain information for marketing decisions. A great deal of information that used to be obtainable only for a high price from companies specializing in producing commercial databases is now available via the Internet. Firms occasionally need to access the broad and in-depth information contained in large commercial databases, such as Dun & Bradsteet's Global Commercial database, with 225 million business records.[17]

Information provided by a single firm on household demographics, purchases, television viewing behavior, and responses to promotions such as coupons and free samples is called *single-source data*. Consumers often use multiple devices to view shows and movies, including televisions, smartphones, and computers, making it difficult for companies to track media consumption habits and needs. To solve this problem, Facebook and Nielsen formed a partnership to compile accurate single-source data about how people are watching shows and when. The partnership represents a step forward in helping marketers track consumer media consumption over multiple devices.[18]

Online information services offer subscribers access to e-mail, websites, downloadable files, news, databases, and research materials. By subscribing to mailing lists, marketers can receive electronic newsletters and participate in online discussions with other network users. This ability to communicate online with customers, suppliers, and employees improves the capability of a firm's marketing information system and helps the company track its customers' changing desires and buying habits.

The *Internet* is a powerful communication medium, linking customers and companies around the world and providing affordable information to companies and customers. *Advertising Age* and Nielsen, for example, both have websites that are highly useful when conducting marketing research. While most Web pages are open to all Internet users, some companies, such as U.S. West and Turner Broadcasting System, also maintain internal Web pages, called *intranets*, which allow employees to access internal data and facilitate communication among departments.

Table 11-6 lists a variety of useful resources for secondary information, which is existing information that has been gathered by other organizations. As can be seen in Table 11-6, secondary information can come from a variety of sources, including governments, trade associations, general publications and news outlets, and corporate information.

Concept Check

✓ Data from a marketing information system is collected from which internal and external sources?

✓ What are the major reasons for conducting marketing research?

✓ Identify and describe the six steps of the marketing research process.

✓ How does technology facilitate collecting and analyzing marketing information?

TABLE 11-6 Sources of Secondary Information

Government sources	
Economic census	www.census.gov/
Export.gov—country and industry market research	www.export.gov/mrktresearch/index.asp
National Technical Information Services	www.ntis.gov/
Strategis—Canadian trade	http://strategis.ic.gc.ca/
Trade associations and shows	
American Society of Association Executives	www.asaecenter.org/
Directory of Associations	http://www.marketingsource.com/directories
Trade Show News Network	www.tsnn.com/
Magazines, newspapers, video, and audio news programming	
Google Video Search	http://www.google.com/videohp?hl=en
Media Jumpstation	www.directcontactpr.com/jumpstation/
Google News Directory	https://news.google.com/
Yahoo! Video Search	http://video.search.yahoo.com/
Corporate information	
The Public Register Online	www.annualreportservice.com/
Bitpipe	www.bitpipe.com/
Business Wire—press releases	www.businesswire.com/
Hoover's Online	www.hoovers.com/
Open Directory Project	http://dmoz.org/
PR Newswire—press releases	www.prnewswire.com/

Source: Adapted from "Data Collection: Low-Cost Secondary Research," KnowThis.com, www.knowthis.com/principles-of-marketing-tutorials/data-collection-low-cost-secondary-research/ (accessed December 5, 2014).

Many companies also use social media outlets to solicit feedback from customers on their existing or upcoming products. While there is always a risk that customers will give a company or its products bad reviews online, most firms deem the risk worthwhile to conduct the low-cost research they need to be successful. If handled correctly, consumer complaints can be an important source of data on how to improve goods and services.

11-10 TYPES OF BUYING BEHAVIOR

Buying behavior may be defined as the decisions and actions of people involved in buying and using products.[19] **Consumer buying behavior** refers to the purchasing of products for personal or household use, not for business purposes. **Business buying behavior** is the purchasing of products by producers, resellers, governmental units, and institutions. Because a firm's success depends in large part on buyers' reactions to a marketing strategy, it is important to understand buying behavior. Marketing managers are better able to predict customer responses to marketing strategies and to develop a satisfying marketing mix if they are aware of the factors that affect buying behavior.

11-10a Consumer Buying Behavior

Consumers' buying behaviors differ for different types of products. For frequently purchased low-cost items, a consumer uses routine response behavior,

Learning Objective

11-10 Identify the major steps in the consumer buying decision process and the sets of factors that may influence this process.

buying behavior the decisions and actions of people involved in buying and using products

consumer buying behavior the purchasing of products for personal or household use, not for business purposes

business buying behavior the purchasing of products by producers, resellers, governmental units, and institutions

Ethical Success or Failure

Should E-Cigarettes Be Marketed to Young People?

The U.S. market for electronic cigarettes is approaching $2 billion yearly as brands like Blu eCigs and NJoy spend millions of dollars to promote their products. E-cigarette marketers are differentiating their products with various colors and flavors like bubble gum and chocolate. Although television advertising for traditional cigarettes has been banned since 1971, e-cigarette brands can advertise on television and, in fact, are expanding into multiple media. But should e-cigarette marketing be limited to avoid influencing consumers under the age of 21?

A study by RTI International points to a significant increase in the number of e-cigarette commercials being seen by children and young adults. Surveys indicate that more U.S. teenagers have tried e-cigarettes than have tried traditional cigarettes. Health advocates worry about the increase in e-cigarette use among middle school students and high school students because nicotine affects brain development. However, despite the nicotine content, many teens do not perceive "vaping"—using e-cigarettes—to be harmful.

Now the U.S. Food and Drug Administration is considering whether and how to regulate e-cigarettes. It may soon outlaw sales to under-age consumers and require health warnings on e-cigarette packaging. The United Kingdom bans e-cigarette commercials that glamorize or encourage smoking, but the United States has no such rules for e-cigarette advertising. Still, individual companies like Blu eCigs are trying to minimize the amount of advertising seen by under-age audiences. Should more be done to restrict e-cigarette marketing?

Sources: Based on information in Sally Satel, "Will the F.D.A. Kill Off E-Cigs?" *New York Times*, January 18, 2015, www.nytimes.com (accessed July 18, 2015); Tripp Mickle, "Survey: U.S. Teens' E-Cigarette Use Tops Traditional Cigarettes," *Wall Street Journal*, December 16, 2014, www.wsj.com (accessed July 18, 2015); Emma Hall, "Ads for Vodka and E-Cigarettes Flout U.K. Rules," *Advertising Age*, December 24, 2014, www.adage.com (accessed July 18, 2015); Michael Sebastian, "FDA's E-Cigs Rules Leave the Way Clear for Unfettered Advertising," *Advertising Age*, April 25, 2014, www.adage.com (accessed July 18, 2015); Hope T. Jackson, "E-Cigarette TV Ads Target Kids, Study Finds," *ABC News*, June 2, 2014, http://abcnews.go.com (accessed July 18, 2015).

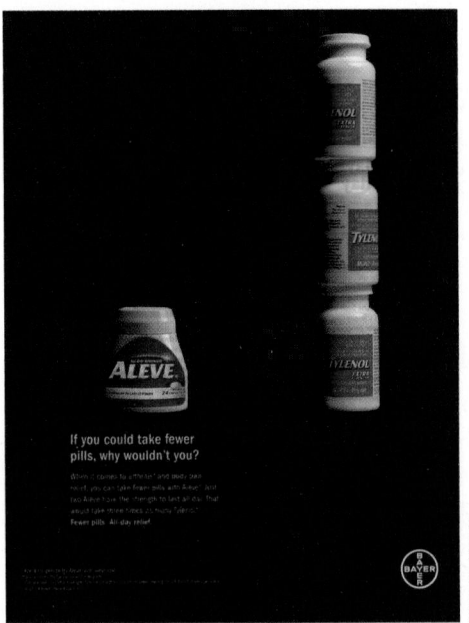

COURTESY OF AARP

Problem recognition. Problem recognition is the first stage of the consumer buying-decision process. This advertisement is attempting to stimulate problem recognition regarding the amount of Tylenol pills consumers have to take to get results compared to Aleve.

which involves very little search or decision–making effort. The buyer uses limited decision making for purchases made occasionally, or when more information is needed about an unknown product in a well-known product category. When buying an unfamiliar or expensive item, or one that is seldom purchased, the consumer engages in extended decision making. Consumers have become empowered by information found on the Internet that allows them to compare prices and features and read reviews about goods and services without stepping into a store. In situations where they would have relied on salespeople in the past, consumers now feel informed enough by online research to make purchasing decisions themselves. In this environment, marketing and customer service are increasingly important.[20]

A person deciding on a purchase goes through some or all of the steps shown in Figure 11-4. First, the consumer acknowledges that a problem exists that might be solved by a good or service. Then, the buyer looks for information, which may include brand names, product characteristics, warranties, and other features, as well as product reviews. Next, the buyer weighs the various alternatives, makes a choice, and acquires the item. In the after-purchase stage, the consumer evaluates the suitability of the product, which will affect future purchases. As Figure 11-4 shows, the buying process is influenced by situational factors (physical surroundings, social surroundings, time, purchase reason, and buyer's mood and condition), psychological factors (perception, motives, learning, attitudes, personality, and lifestyle), and social factors (family, roles, reference groups, online social networks, social class, culture, and subculture).

FIGURE 11-4 Consumer Buying Decision Process and Possible Influences on the Process

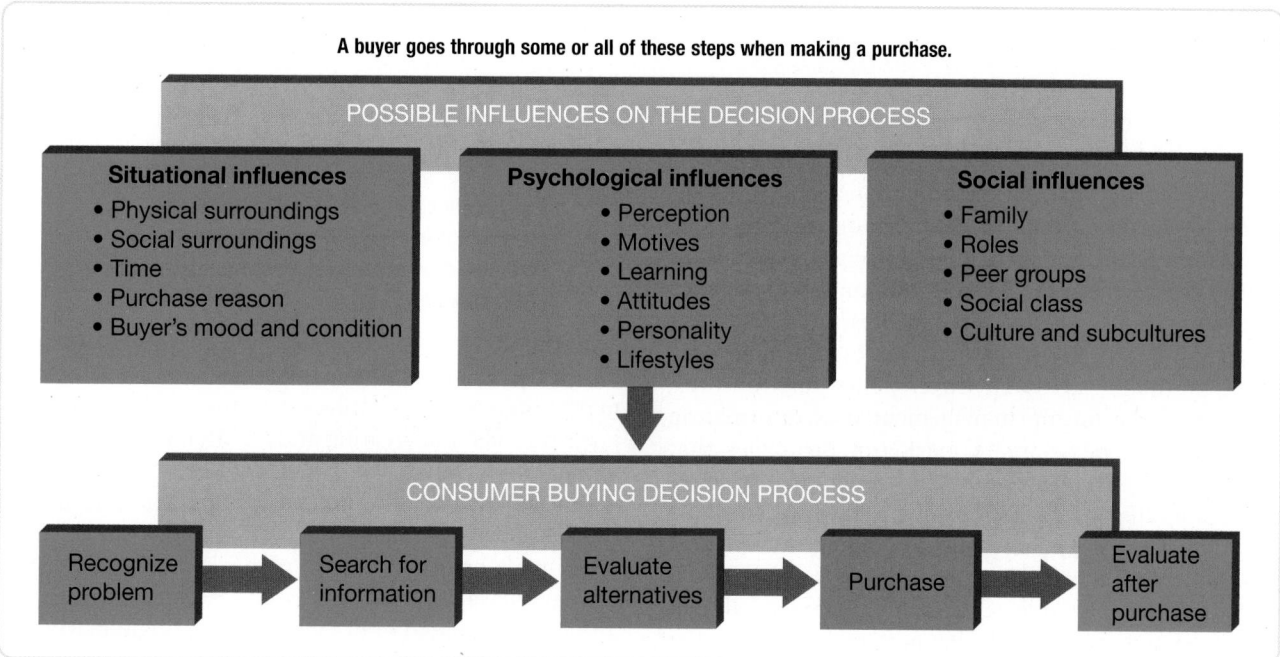

Source: William M. Pride and O. C. Ferrell, *Marketing*, 18th ed. (Mason, OH: South-Western/Cengage Learning, 2016). Adapted with permission.

Consumer buying behavior is also affected by the ability to buy, called one's *buying power*, which is largely determined by income. As every taxpayer knows, not all income is available for spending. For this reason, marketers consider income in three different ways. **Personal income** is the income an individual receives from all sources *less* the Social Security taxes the individual must pay. **Disposable income** is personal income *less* all additional personal taxes. These taxes include income, estate, gift, and property taxes levied by local, state, and federal governments. **Discretionary income** is disposable income *less* savings and expenditures on food, clothing, and housing. Discretionary income is of particular interest to marketers because consumers have the most choice in spending it. Consumers use their discretionary income to purchase a wide variety of items ranging from automobiles and vacations to movies and pet food. Although many marketers prefer to target 18-to-49-year-olds, more companies are recognizing that the U.S.'s 76 million Baby Boomers—those born between 1946 and 1964—remain a highly desirable market because they have the most discretionary income relative to other groups.[21]

11-10b Business Buying Behavior

Business buyers are generally better informed than consumers and consider a product's quality, its price, and the service provided by suppliers. Business purchases can be large, and a committee or a group of people, rather than just one person, often decides on purchases. Committee members must consider the organization's objectives, purchasing policies, resources, and personnel. The process of business buying is different than consumer buying. It occurs through description, inspection, sampling, or negotiation. Because business transactions can be more complicated and orders tend to be larger, obtaining complete and correct information on buyers and sellers is important.

personal income the income an individual receives from all sources *less* the Social Security taxes the individual must pay

disposable income personal income *less* all additional personal taxes

discretionary income disposable income *less* savings and expenditures on food, clothing, and housing

Concept Check

✓ Why is it important to understand buying behavior?

✓ How does a customer's decision-making time vary with the type of product?

✓ What are the five stages of the consumer buying decision process?

✓ What are the possible influences on this process?

✓ What is the difference between disposable income and discretionary income?

Summary

11-1 Understand the meaning of *marketing* and the importance of managing customer relationships.

Marketing is an organizational function and a set of processes for creating, communicating, and delivering value to customers and for managing customer relationships in ways that benefit the organization and its stakeholders. Maintaining positive relationships with customers is crucial. Relationship marketing is establishing long-term, mutually satisfying buyer–seller relationships. Customer relationship management uses information about customers to create marketing strategies that develop and sustain desirable customer relationships. Managing customer relationships requires identifying patterns of buying behavior and focusing on the most profitable customers. Customer lifetime value (CLV) is a combination of purchase frequency, average value of purchases, and brand-switching patterns over the entire span of a customer's relationship with the company.

11-2 Explain how marketing adds value by creating several forms of utility.

Marketing adds value in the form of utility, or the power of a good or service to satisfy a need. It creates place utility by making products available where customers want them, time utility by making products available when customers want them, and possession utility by transferring the ownership of products to buyers.

11-3 Trace the development of the marketing concept and understand how it is implemented.

From the Industrial Revolution until the early 20th century, businesspeople focused on the production of goods. From the 1920s to the 1950s, the emphasis moved to the selling of goods. During the 1950s, businesspeople recognized that their enterprises involved not only producing and selling products, but also satisfying customers' needs. They began to implement the marketing concept, a business philosophy that involves the entire organization in the dual processes of meeting the customers' needs and achieving the organization's goals.

Implementation of the marketing concept begins and ends with customers—first to determine what customers' needs are and then to evaluate how well the firm is meeting these needs.

11-4 Understand what markets are and how they are classified.

A market consists of people with a need, the ability to buy, and the desire and authority to purchase. Markets are classified as consumer and business-to-business or industrial, which includes producer, reseller, governmental, and institutional markets.

11-5 Understand the two major components of a marketing strategy—target market and marketing mix.

A marketing strategy is a plan for the best use of an organization's resources to meet its objectives. Developing a marketing strategy involves selecting and analyzing a target market and creating and maintaining a marketing mix that will satisfy the target market. A target market is chosen through the undifferentiated or the market segmentation approach. A market segment is a group of individuals or organizations within a market that have similar characteristics and needs. Businesses that use an undifferentiated approach design a single marketing mix and direct it at the entire market for a particular product. The market segmentation approach directs a marketing mix at a segment of a market.

The four elements of a firm's marketing mix are product, price, distribution, and promotion. The product ingredient includes decisions about the product's design, brand name, packaging, and warranties. The pricing ingredient is concerned with base prices and various types of discounts. Distribution involves not only transportation and storage but also the selection of intermediaries. Promotion focuses on providing information to target markets. The elements of the marketing mix can be varied to suit broad organizational goals, marketing objectives, and target markets.

11-6 Explain how the marketing environment affects strategic market planning.

To achieve a firm's marketing objectives, marketing-mix strategies must begin with an assessment of the marketing environment, which, in turn, influences decisions about marketing-mix ingredients. Marketing activities are affected by the external forces that make up the marketing environment. These forces include economic, sociocultural, political, competitive, legal and regulatory, and technological forces. Economic forces affect customers' ability and willingness to buy. Sociocultural forces are social and cultural factors, such as attitudes, beliefs, and lifestyles that affect customers' buying choices. Political forces and legal and regulatory forces influence marketing planning through laws that protect consumers and regulate competition. Competitive forces involve the actions of competitors. Technological forces can create new marketing opportunities or cause a product to become obsolete.

11-7 Understand the major components of a marketing plan.

A marketing plan is a written document that specifies an organization's resources, objectives, strategy, and implementation and control efforts to be used in marketing a specific product or product group. The marketing plan describes a firm's current position, establishes marketing objectives, and specifies the methods the organization will use to achieve these objectives. Marketing plans can be short-range for one year or less, medium-range for two to five years, or long-range for periods of more than five years.

11-8 Describe how market measurement and sales forecasting are used.

Market measurement and sales forecasting are used to estimate sales potential and predict product sales in specific market segments.

11-9 Distinguish between a marketing information system and marketing research.

Strategies are monitored and evaluated through marketing research and marketing information systems, which store and process internal and external data and produce reports in a form that aids marketing decision making. A marketing information system manages marketing information that is gathered continually from internal and external sources. Marketing research is the process of systematically gathering, recording, and analyzing data concerning a particular marketing problem. Technology is making information for marketing decisions more accessible. Electronic communication tools can be very useful for accumulating accurate and affordable information. Information technologies that are changing the way marketers obtain and use information are databases, online information services, and the Internet. Many companies are using social media to obtain research data and feedback from customers.

11-10 Identify the major steps in the consumer buying decision process and the sets of factors that may influence this process.

Buying behavior consists of the decisions and actions of people involved in buying and using products. Consumer buying behavior refers to the purchase of products for personal or household use. Organizational buying behavior is the purchase of products by producers, resellers, governments, and institutions. Understanding buying behavior helps marketers predict how buyers will respond to marketing strategies. The consumer buying decision process consists of five steps: recognizing the problem, searching for information, evaluating alternatives, purchasing, and post-purchase evaluation. Factors affecting the consumer buying decision process fall into three categories: situational influences, psychological influences, and social influences.

Key Terms

You should now be able to define and give an example relevant to each of the following terms:

marketing (305)
relationship marketing (305)
customer relationship management (CRM) (306)
customer lifetime value (CLV) (307)
utility (307)
form utility (307)
place utility (307)

time utility (308)
possession utility (308)
marketing concept (308)
market (310)
marketing strategy (310)
marketing mix (310)
target market (310)
undifferentiated approach (311)

market segment (311)
market segmentation (311)
marketing plan (317)
sales forecast (318)
marketing information system (319)
marketing research (319)
buying behavior (321)

consumer buying behavior (321)
business buying behavior (321)
personal income (323)
disposable income (323)
discretionary income (323)

Discussion Questions

1. What is relationship marketing?
2. How is a marketing-oriented firm different from a production-oriented firm or a sales-oriented firm?

3. What are the major requirements for a group of individuals and organizations to be a market? How does a consumer market differ from a business-to-business market?

4. What are the major components of a marketing strategy?
5. What is the purpose of market segmentation? What is the relationship between market segmentation and the selection of target markets?
6. Describe the forces in the marketing environment that affect an organization's marketing decisions.
7. What is a marketing plan, and what are its major components?
8. What new information technologies are changing the ways that marketers keep track of business trends and customers?
9. Why do marketers need to understand buying behavior?
10. Is it a good strategy to focus most marketing efforts on the most profitable customers?
11. How might adoption of the marketing concept benefit a firm? How might it benefit the firm's customers?
12. Is marketing information as important to small firms as it is to larger firms? Explain.
13. How does the marketing environment affect a firm's marketing strategy?

Video Case
Raleigh Wheels Out Steel Bicycle Marketing

From its 19th century roots as a British bicycle company, Raleigh has developed a worldwide reputation for marketing sturdy, comfortable, steel-frame bicycles. The firm, named for the street in Nottingham, England, where it was originally located, was a trendsetter in designing and manufacturing bicycles. When Raleigh introduced steel-frame bicycles equipped with three-speed gear hubs in 1903, it revolutionized the industry and set off a never-ending race to improve the product's technology. In the pre-auto era, its bicycles became a two-wheeled status symbol for British consumers, and the brand maintained its cachet for decades. Although Raleigh's chopper-style bicycles were hugely popular in the 1970s, international competition and changing consumer tastes have taken a toll during the past few decades.

Now Raleigh markets a wide variety of bicycles to consumers in Europe, Canada, and the United States. Its U.S. division, based in Kent, Washington, has been researching new bicycles for contemporary consumers and developing models that are lighter, faster, and better. Inspired by the European lifestyle and tradition of getting around on bicycles, and its long history in the business, Raleigh is looking to reinvigorate sales and capture a larger share of the nearly $6 billion U.S. bicycle market.

Raleigh's U.S. marketers have been observing the "messenger market," customers who ride bicycles through downtown streets to deliver documents and small packages to businesses and individuals. They have also noted that many everyday bicycle riders dress casually, in T-shirts and jeans, rather than in special racing outfits designed for speed. Targeting consumers who enjoy riding bicycles as a lifestyle, Raleigh's marketers are focusing on this segment's specific needs and preferences as they develop, price, promote, and distribute new models.

In recent years, Raleigh's marketers have stepped up the practice of bringing demonstration fleets to public places where potential buyers can hop on one of the company's bicycles and pedal for a few minutes. The idea is to allow consumers who enjoy bicycling to actually experience the fun feeling of riding a Raleigh. The marketers are also fanning out to visit bicycle races and meet bicyclists in cities and towns across America, encouraging discussions about Raleigh and about bicycling in general and seeking feedback about particular Raleigh products.

Listening to consumers, Raleigh's marketers recognized that many had misperceptions about the weight of steel-frame bicycles. Although steel can be quite heavy, Raleigh's bicycles are solid yet light, nimble, and easy to steer. Those who have been on bicycles with steel frames praise the quality of the ride, saying that steel "has a soul," according to market research.

To stay in touch with its target market, Raleigh is increasingly active in social media. It has several thousand fans who visit its Facebook page to see the latest product concepts and post their own photos and comments about Raleigh bicycles. It also uses Twitter to keep customers informed and answer questions about its bicycles and upcoming demonstration events. The company's main blog communicates the latest news about everything from frame design and new bike colors under consideration to product awards and racing activities. It has a separate blog about both the fun and the challenges of commuting by bicycle, a topic in which its customers are intensely interested because so many do exactly that. By listening to customers and showing that it understands the daily life of its target market, Raleigh is wheeling toward higher sales in a highly competitive marketplace.[22]

Questions
1. Is Raleigh using the marketing concept? Explain.
2. What type of approach does Raleigh use to select target markets?
3. Of the four categories of segmentation variables, which is most important to Raleigh's segmentation strategy, and why?

Building Skills for Career Success

1. Social Media Exercise

Comcast, the cable and communications provider, was one of the first companies to use Twitter for customer service. Developed by Frank Eliason, the company's first Director of Digital Care, Bill Gerth currently manages the ComcastCares feed on Twitter. Gerth and the Comcast team scan Twitter for complaints about service and contact the customers to see how Comcast can remedy the situation. This has altered the culture of the organization and prompted other companies to utilize Twitter for customer service. Visit the site at @comcastcares on Twitter.

1. After exploring @comcastcares on Twitter, do you think that this helps with customer service? Why or why not?
2. Do you see other applications for Twitter for a communications giant like Comcast?

2. Building Team Skills

Review the text definitions of *market* and *target market*. Markets can be classified as consumer or industrial. Buyer behavior consists of the decisions and actions of those involved in buying and using goods or services. By examining aspects of a company's products, you can determine the company's target market and the characteristics important to members of that target market.

Assignment

1. Working in teams of three to five, identify a company and a few of its most popular products.
2. List and discuss characteristics that customers may find important, including price, quality, brand name, variety of services, salespeople, customer service, special offers, promotional campaign, packaging, convenience of use, convenience of purchase, location, guarantees, store/office decor, and payment terms.
3. Write a description of the company's primary customer (target market).

3. Researching Different Careers

Before interviewing for a job, you should learn all you can about the company to help prepare you to ask meaningful questions during the interview. To find out more about a company, you can conduct market research before you interview.

Assignment

1. Choose at least two local companies for which you might like to work.
2. Contact your local Chamber of Commerce. (The Chamber of Commerce collects information about local businesses and most of its services are free.) Ask for the information you desire.
3. Call the Better Business Bureau in your community (or check online) to determine if there are any complaints against the companies you are researching.
4. Prepare a report summarizing your findings.

Endnotes

1 Based on information in Venessa Wong, "Coffee, Mate," *Bloomberg Businessweek*, January 19, 2015, p. 78; John Kell, "Nearly 46 Million Americans Received Starbucks Gift Cards This Holiday," *Fortune*, January 5, 2015, www.fortune.com (accessed July 27, 2015); Ciara Linnane, "Starbucks' New Plan to Win Over Coffee Snobs, Commuters," *MarketWatch*, September 5, 2014 www.marketwatch.com (accessed July 1, 2015); Christine Champagne and Teressa Iezzi, "Coffee Week: Dunkin' Donuts and Starbucks: A Tale of Two Coffee Marketing Giants," *Fast Company Create*, August 21, 2014, www.fastcocreate.com (accessed July 1, 2015); Lisa Jennings, "Starbucks to Add Delivery in 2015," *Nation's Restaurant News*, October 31, 2014, www.nrn.com (accessed July 1, 2015); www.starbucks.com (accessed July 27, 2015).

2 "Definition of Marketing," American Marketing Association, https://www.ama.org/AboutAMA/Pages/Definition-of-Marketing.aspx (accessed January 27, 2015).

3 Vipal Monga, "The Big Mystery: What's Big Data Really Worth," *Wall Street Journal*, October 12, 2014, http://online.wsj.com/articles/whats-all-that-data-worth-1413157156 (accessed July 1, 2015).

4 V. Kumar, *Customer Lifetime Value* (Hanover, MA: now Publishers, 2008), p. 5.

5 Rajkumar Venkatesan and V. Kumar, "A Customer Lifetime Value Framework for Customer Selection and Resource Selection and Resource Allocation Strategy," *Journal of Marketing 68*, (October 2004), 106–125.

6 Dennis Price, "How Much Is a Customer REALLY Worth?" *Insider Retail*, March 18, 2012, https://www.insideretail.com.au/blog/2012/03/18/how-much-is-a-customer-really-worth/ (accessed July 18, 2015); Customer Lifetime Value Calculator, http://hbsp.harvard.edu/multimedia/flashtools/cltv/index.html (accessed January 27, 2015).

7 Mark Bergen, "Pretty in Pink: How the CMO and un-CEO Roused T-Mobile," *Advertising Age*, August 11, 2014, http://adage.com/article/digital/cmo-ceo-roused-t-mobile/294513/ (accessed July 1, 2015); James O'Toole, "T-Mobile Is at a Crossroads, so Is the U.S. Wireless Industry," *CNN*, June 8, 2014, http://money.cnn.com/2014/06/08/technology/mobile/tmobile-sprint/ (accessed July 1, 2015).

8 Beth Kowitt, "At West Elm There's No Place Like Home," *Fortune*, December 22, 2014, http://fortune.com/2014/12/04/west-elm-retail-online-sales/ (accessed July 1, 2015).

9 "Is Zipcar for Me?," *Zipcar*, http://www.zipcar.com/is-it (accessed January 27, 2015).

10 Tamara Walsh, "Target Turns Heads in a Big Way at New York Fashion Week," *The Motley Fool*, September 14, 2014, http://www.fool.com/investing/general/2014/09/14/target-turns-heads-in-a-big-way-at-new-york-fashio.aspx (accessed July 1, 2015); "Luxury Fashion Brand Altuzarra Brings Limited-Edition Collection to Target this Fall," *Target*, Press Release, May 22, 2014, https://corporate.target.com/discover/article/luxury-fashion-brand-Altuzarra-brings-limited-edit (accessed July 1, 2015).

11 David Crouch, "Toys R Us's Stockholm Superstore Goes Gender Neutral," *The Guardian*, December 23, 2013, http://www.theguardian.com/world/2013/dec/23/toys-r-us-stockholm-gender-neutral (accessed

July 1, 2015); Anna Molin, "In Sweden, Playtime Goes Gender-Neutral for the Holidays," *Wall Street Journal*, November 28, 2012, http://online.wsj.com/article/SB10001424127887324205404578147373422297406.html (accessed July 1, 2015).

12 Kowitt, "At West Elm There's No Place Like Home."

13 Antoinette Alexander, "CVS's Digital Strategy Pays Off," *Retailing Today*, January 22, 2014, http://www.retailingtoday.com/article/cvs%E2%80%99s-digital-strategy-pays (accessed July 1, 2015).

14 CNBC, "Booze Plays Key Role in Starbucks' Revenue Plan," MSN Quotes, December 4, 2014, http://www.mnsquotes.com/booze-plays-key-role-in-starbucks-revenue-plan/ (accessed July 8, 2015).

15 Sara Eisen, "How Brands Are Responding to New Breakfast Habits," *CNBC*, June 28, 2014, http://www.cnbc.com/id/101789253 (accessed July 1, 2015).

16 Barbara Thau, "How Big Data Helps Stores Like Macy's and Kohl's Track You Like Never Before," *Forbes*, January 24, 2014, http://www.forbes.com/sites/barbarathau/2014/01/24/why-the-smart-use-of-big-data-will-transform-the-retail-industry/ (accessed July 1, 2015).

17 Dun & Bradstreet, http://www.dnb.com/company.html (accessed January 27, 2015).

18 "Facebook, Nielsen Partner to Track Mobile TV Viewing," *CBS News*, July 16, 2014, http://www.cbsnews.com/news/facebook-nielsen-partner-to-track-mobile-tv-viewing/ (accessed July 1, 2015).

19 William M. Pride and O. C. Ferrell, *Marketing*, 18th ed. (Mason, OH: South-Western/Cengage Learning, 2016), 192.

20 Christine Crandell, "The New Corporate Power Couple," *Forbes*, February 25, 2012, http://www.forbes.com/sites/christinecrandell/2012/02/25/the-new-corporate-power-couple/ (accessed December 24, 2012).

21 Stewart Elliott, "Go Where the Money Is, AARP Tells Marketers," *New York Times*, July 13, 2014, http://www.nytimes.com/2014/07/14/business/media/go-where-the-money-is-aarp-tells-marketers.html?_r=0 (accessed July 1, 2015).

22 "BRAINy Awards Honor Individuals," *Bicycle Retailer and Industry News*, April 15, 2010, www.bicycleretailer.com/news/newsDetail/3961.html (accessed July 1, 2015); Francis Lawell, "Raleigh: Cycling to Success?" *Business Review (UK)*, (February 2009), pp. 16ff; "Industry Overview 2013," *National Bicycle Dealers Association*, http://nbda.com/articles/industry-overview-2013-pg34.htm (accessed January 13, 2015); www.raleigh.co.uk/ (accessed July 1, 2015); www.raleighusa.com (accessed July 1, 2015).

FUNSTOCK/ISTOCK/THINKSTOCK

Creating and Pricing Products That Satisfy Customers

Learning Objectives

Once you complete this chapter, you will be able to:

12-1 Explain what a product is and how products are classified.

12-2 Discuss the product life-cycle and how it leads to new-product development.

12-3 Define *product line* and *product mix* and distinguish between the two.

12-4 Identify the methods available for changing a product mix.

12-5 Explain the uses and importance of branding, packaging, and labeling.

12-6 Describe the economic basis of pricing and the means by which sellers can control prices and buyers' perceptions of prices.

12-7 Identify the major pricing objectives used by businesses.

12-8 Examine the three major pricing methods that firms employ.

12-9 Explain the different strategies available to companies for setting prices.

12-10 Describe three major types of pricing associated with business products.

Why Should You Care?

To be successful, a business person must understand how to develop and manage a mix of appropriately priced products and to change the mix of products as customers' needs change.

GoldieBlox Gets the Gold for Capitalizing on Free Marketing Opportunities

Debbie Sterling, engineer turned entrepreneur, started GoldieBlox with an idea for a new construction toy that would inspire pre-teen girls to experience the excitement and possibilities of engineering. She came up with a golden-haired character named Goldie and selected the brand name GoldieBlox as a play on words, combining the character's name with the concept of building blocks. After writing a story about Goldie building a spinning machine for her dog, Sterling designed a toy construction set, complete with blocks, wheels, and other parts, setting a price that was competitive with other toy block sets.

The next step was to prepare for introduction by financing the initial production run. Sterling turned to the Kickstarter website and within days, she had raised $285,000 from consumers, promising each a branded item in exchange for their financial support. She also sought out media attention to build brand awareness, which drew thousands of buyers to pre-order the set at the company's e-commerce site. Once Toys "R" Us agreed to stock the set, the product had a national retail launchpad. It quickly zoomed to the top of Amazon.com's list of most popular holiday toys. The product won several awards, including "Educational Toy of the Year," and Sterling soon expanded the product line with new construction sets.

Next, Sterling entered a contest to have her toys featured for free in a nationally-aired commercial during the 2014 Super Bowl. When she won the contest, the combination of the publicity and the commercial seen by 111 million viewers gave GoldieBlox a huge boost in brand recognition. Barely two years after the first product debuted, GoldieBlox was featured as a float during the Macy's Thanksgiving Day Parade, adding to the buzz surrounding the brand and its ever-expanding product line. Building on this success, Sterling released a new Goldie action figure and a brief animated video starring Goldie, as well as a free mobile app that teaches children the basics of animation. What's next for GoldieBlox? [1]

Did You Know?

GoldieBlox was the first small business ever to advertise its product nationally during the Super Bowl.

A **product** like GoldieBlox has everything one receives in an exchange, including all tangible and intangible attributes and expected benefits. In addition to a sweet and satisfying taste, Oreo cookies come in a familiar package marked with an iconic label. The brand also has the intangible benefit of being an American classic, a favorite snack for more than a century. A car includes tangible benefits, such as a warranty and a GPS navigation system, and intangible attributes, such as status and the memories generated from road trips. Developing and managing products effectively, including these tangible and intangible benefits, are crucial to an organization's ability to maintain successful marketing mixes.

A product can be a good, a service, or an idea. A *good* is a real, physical thing that we can touch, such as an Oreo cookie. A *service* is the result of applying human or mechanical effort to a person or thing. A service is a change we pay others to make for us. A real estate agent's services result in a change in the ownership of real property. A barber's services result in a change in your hairstyle. An *idea* may take the form of philosophies, lessons, concepts, or advice. Often ideas are bundled with a good or service. Thus, we might buy a book (a good) that provides ideas on how to lose weight. Alternatively, we might join Weight Watchers for ideas on how to lose weight and for help (service) in doing so.

In this chapter, we first look at the different aspects of products. We examine product classifications and describe the four stages, or life-cycles, through which every product progresses. Next, we illustrate how firms manage products by modifying or deleting existing ones and developing new products. We also discuss branding,

product everything one receives in an exchange, including all tangible and intangible attributes and expected benefits; it may be a good, a service, or an idea

packaging, and labeling. Then our focus shifts to pricing. We explain competitive factors that influence sellers' pricing decisions and explore buyers' perceptions of prices. After considering organizational objectives that can be accomplished through pricing, we outline several methods for setting prices. Finally, we describe pricing strategies by which sellers can reach target markets successfully.

12-1 CLASSIFICATION OF PRODUCTS

Different classes of products are directed at different target markets according to their varying needs and wants. A product's classification largely determines what kinds of distribution, promotion, and pricing are appropriate in marketing it.

Products can be grouped into two general categories: consumer and business (also called *business-to-business* or *industrial products*). A product purchased to satisfy personal and family needs is a **consumer product**. A product bought by a business for resale, for making other products, or for use in a firm's operations is a **business product**. The same item can be both a consumer and a business product, depending on the buyer's end use. Light bulbs are a consumer product when you use them in your home, but are a business product if you purchase them for use in an office.

12-1a Consumer Product Classifications

The traditional and most widely accepted system of classifying consumer products consists of three categories: convenience, shopping, and specialty products. These groupings are based primarily on characteristics of buyers' purchasing behavior.

A **convenience product** is a relatively inexpensive, frequently purchased item for which buyers want to exert only minimal effort to procure. Examples include bread, gasoline, newspapers, soft drinks, and chewing gum. The buyer spends little time in planning the purchase of a convenience item or in comparing available brands or sellers.

A **shopping product** is an item for which buyers are willing to expend considerably more effort on planning and purchasing. Shopping products cost

Consumer products can be classified into convenience, shopping, and specialty. Goldfish, a convenience product, is an item you are likely to grab off the shelf without much thought as you walk through the snack aisle of a grocery store. By contrast, people may spend a considerable amount of time and effort engaged in comparison shopping behavior when buying a product, like a handbag.

Concept Check

✓ Identify the general categories of products.

✓ Describe the classifications of consumer products.

✓ Based on their characteristics, business products can be classified into what categories?

Learning Objective

12-2 Discuss the product life-cycle and how it leads to new-product development.

more than convenience products and buyers allocate ample time for comparing prices, product features, qualities, services, and warranties between different stores and brands. Appliances, upholstered furniture, men's suits, bicycles, and mobile phones are examples of shopping products. These products are expected to last for a fairly long time and thus are purchased less frequently than convenience items.

A **specialty product** possesses one or more unique characteristics for which a group of buyers is willing to expend considerable purchasing effort. Buyers know exactly what they want and will not accept a substitute. When seeking out specialty products, purchasers do not compare alternatives. Examples include unique sports cars, a rare imported beer, or original artwork.

12-1b Business Product Classifications

Based on their characteristics and intended uses, business products can be classified into the following categories: raw materials, major equipment, accessory equipment, component parts, process materials, supplies, and services.

A **raw material** is a basic material that becomes part of a physical product. It usually comes from mines, forests, oceans, or recycled solid wastes. Raw materials are generally bought and sold according to grades and specifications.

Major equipment includes large tools and machines used for production purposes. Examples of major equipment are lathes, cranes, and stamping machines. Some major equipment is custom-made for a particular organization, but other items are standardized products that perform one or several tasks for many types of organizations.

Accessory equipment is standardized equipment used in a firm's production or office activities. Examples include hand tools, photocopiers, fractional horsepower motors, and calculators. Compared with major equipment, accessory items are usually less expensive and are purchased routinely with less negotiation.

A **component part** becomes part of a physical product and is either a finished item ready for assembly or a product that needs little processing prior to assembly. Although it becomes an element of a larger product, a component part can often be identified easily. Clocks, tires, computer chips, and switches are examples of component parts.

A **process material** is used directly in the production of another product. Unlike a component part, a process material is not readily identifiable in the finished product. Like raw materials, process materials are purchased according to industry standards or to the specifications of the individual purchaser. Examples include industrial glue and food preservatives.

A **supply** facilitates production and operations but does not become part of a finished product. Paper, pencils, oils, and cleaning agents are examples.

A **business service** is an intangible product that an organization uses in its operations. Examples include financial, legal, online, janitorial, and marketing research services. Purchasers must decide whether to provide their own services internally or to hire a contractor from outside the organization.

12-2 THE PRODUCT LIFE-CYCLE

In a way, products are like people. They are born, they live, and they die. Every product progresses through a **product life-cycle**, a series of stages in which a product's sales revenue and profit increase, reach a peak, and then decline. A firm must be able to launch, modify, and delete products from its offering in response to changes in product life-cycles. Otherwise, the firm's profits will disappear, and the firm will fail. Depending on the product, life-cycle stages vary in length. In this section, we discuss the stages of the life-cycle and how marketers can use this information.

FIGURE 12-1 Product Life-Cycle

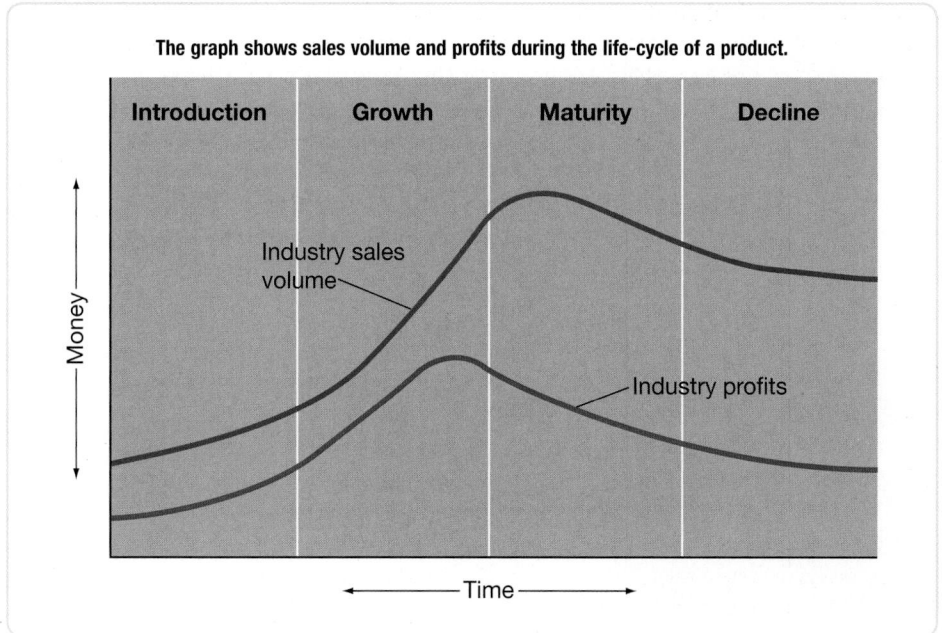

The graph shows sales volume and profits during the life-cycle of a product.

Source: William M. Pride and O. C. Ferrell, *Marketing*, 18th ed. (Mason, OH: South-Western/Cengage Learning, 2016). Adapted with permission.

12-2a Stages of the Product Life-Cycle

Generally, the product life-cycle is composed of four stages—introduction, growth, maturity, and decline—as shown in Figure 12-1. Some products progress through these stages rapidly, in a few weeks or months, while others can take years. The Koosh Ball, popular in the late 1980s, had a short life-cycle. In contrast, Parker Brothers' Monopoly game, which was introduced nearly a century ago, is still going strong.

INTRODUCTION In the *introduction stage*, customer awareness and acceptance of the new product are low. Sales rise gradually as a result of promotion and distribution activities. There are no competitors at this stage. High development and marketing costs result in low profit, or even in a loss, initially. The price can be high as the firm recoups research and development expenses and ramps up production. Customers are primarily people who want to be at the forefront of owning the new product. The marketing challenge at this stage is to make potential customers aware of the product's existence and its features, benefits, and uses.

A new product is seldom an immediate success. Marketers must monitor early buying patterns and be prepared to modify the product promptly if necessary. The firm should attempt to price the product to attract the market segment that has the greatest desire and ability to purchase it. Plans for distribution and promotion should suit the targeted market segment. All ingredients of the marketing mix may need to be adjusted quickly to maintain sales growth during the introduction stage.

GROWTH In the *growth stage*, sales increase rapidly as consumers gain awareness of the product. Other firms have begun to market competing products. The competition and decreased unit costs (owing to mass production) result in a lower price, which reduces the profit per unit. Industry profits reach a peak and begin to decline during this stage. To meet the needs of the growing market, the originating firm offers modified versions of the product and expands distribution.

Do you have one of these?

Think back to toys that were wildly popular when you were younger. How many do you still see in stores? This shows how quickly some products can pass through the stages of the product life-cycle.

Saying "goodbye" to the pay telephone. The pay telephone is in the decline stage of the product life-cycle. Do you recall seeing one? If so, when and where? You might have a hard time remembering.

Management's goal in the growth stage is to stabilize and strengthen the product's position by encouraging brand loyalty. To beat the competition, the company may further improve the product or expand the product line to appeal to additional market segments. For example, to compete with the Apple iPhone, Samsung, LG, and others have introduced their own touchscreen smartphones with features aimed at capturing different market segments and gaining market share in the growing industry.

Management also may compete by lowering prices if increased production efficiency has resulted in sufficient savings. As the product becomes more widely accepted, marketers may be able to broaden the network of distributors. Marketers can also emphasize customer service and prompt credit for defective products. During this period, promotional efforts attempt to build brand loyalty among customers.

MATURITY Sales are still increasing at the beginning of the *maturity stage*, but the rate of increase has slowed. Later on, the sales curve peaks and begins to decline, as do industry profits. Product lines are simplified, markets are segmented more carefully, and price competition increases, which forces weaker competitors to leave the industry. Marketers continue to introduce refinements and extensions of the original product to the market.

During a product's maturity stage, its market share may be strengthened by redesigned packaging or style changes. For example, Weiman's redesigned its floor-cleaning product bottles and propelled the product to new levels of growth. The company changed its old lime-green bottles to a more ergonomic-shaped white custom container with cheerful images to help the cleaners stand out among brightly colored rival cleaning products. The redesigned package also gained more functionality with sprayer tops. These changes helped the products triple their sales.[2] Redesigned packaging may convince consumers to use the product more often or in new ways.

Pricing strategies are flexible during the maturity stage. Markdowns and price incentives are not uncommon, although price increases may work to offset production and distribution costs. Marketers may offer incentives and assistance of various kinds to dealers to encourage them to support mature products, especially in the face of competition from private-label brands. New promotional efforts and aggressive personal selling may be necessary during this period of intense competition.

DECLINE During the *decline stage*, sales volume decreases sharply and profits continue to fall. The number of competing firms declines, and the only survivors in the marketplace are firms that specialize in marketing the product. Production and marketing costs become the most important determinant of profit.

When a product adds to the success of the overall product line, the company may retain it. Otherwise, management must determine when to eliminate it. A product usually declines because of technological advances or environmental factors, or because consumers have switched to competing brands. Therefore, few changes are made in the product itself during this stage. Instead, management may raise the price to cover costs, reprice to maintain market share, or lower the price to reduce inventory. Management will narrow distribution to the most profitable existing markets. During this period, the company probably will not spend heavily on promotion, although it may use some advertising and sales incentives to slow the product's decline. The company may choose to eliminate less-profitable versions of the product from the product line or may decide to drop the product entirely. For example, to regain ground after significant declines in a very competitive electronics market, HP is aggressively cutting items from unprofitable product lines, including half of its 2,100 laser printers. Having so many products largely similar to one another can be a risk, as they compete for the same consumers.[3]

12-2b Using the Product Life-Cycle

When making marketing strategy decisions, managers must be aware of the life-cycle stage of each product for which they are responsible and to estimate how long the product is expected to remain in that stage. For example, if a product is expected to remain in the maturity stage for a long time, there is no rush to develop a replacement product. A firm risks speeding the decline of an existing product by releasing a replacement before the earlier product has reached the decline stage. Even so, a firm will be willing to take that risk in some cases. In other situations, a company will attempt to extend a product's life-cycle. Extending its life can be an important tool in maintaining a product's profitability. A condiment staple since its introduction more than 140 years ago, Heinz Ketchup has extended its life through packaging innovations, such as squeeze bottles and single-serving containers, releasing different flavors, like balsamic and jalapeño, and even experimenting with purple and green-colored ketchup.

Concept Check

✓ Explain the four stages of the product life-cycle.

✓ How does knowledge of the product life-cycle relate to the introduction of new products?

12-3 PRODUCT LINE AND PRODUCT MIX

A **product line** is a group of similar products that differ only in relatively minor characteristics. Generally, the products within a product line are related to each other in the way they are produced, marketed, or used. Procter & Gamble, for example, manufactures and markets several shampoos, including Pantene, Head & Shoulders, and Ivory.

While organizations may start a new product line, many opt to introduce new products within existing product lines. It is less costly than starting a new product line and permits them to apply the experience and knowledge they have acquired to the production and marketing of new products.

An organization's **product mix** consists of all the products the firm offers for sale. For example, Procter & Gamble has over 80 brands—some of which are well-known, such as Gillette and Febreze, and others that are less familiar in the United States, such as Lenor and Ariel–that fall into several product lines.[4] Two "dimensions" are often applied to a firm's product mix. The *width* of the mix is the number of product lines it contains. The *depth* of the mix is the average number of individual products within each line. These measures are general—no exact numbers correspond to these categories. Some organizations offer a broad product mix as a means of trying to be competitive in many different categories.

Learning Objective

12-3 Define *product line* and *product mix* and distinguish between the two.

product line a group of similar products that differ only in relatively minor characteristics

product mix all the products a firm offers for sale

Concept Check

✓ How does a product line differ from a product mix?

✓ Can a product line be a product mix?

Part of a Product Line. These products are part of Gatorade's product line. Gatorade has over 40 flavors in its sports drink product line.

ISTOCKPHOTO.COM/LOVLEAH

12-4 MANAGING THE PRODUCT MIX

Learning Objective

12-4 Identify the methods available for changing a product mix.

To provide products that satisfy people in a firm's target market or markets and that also achieve the organization's objectives, a marketer must develop, adjust, and maintain an effective product mix. The same product mix is rarely effective for long. As customers' product preferences and attitudes change, their desire for a product may diminish or grow. A firm may also need to alter its product mix to adapt to changes in the competition. For example, a marketer may have to introduce a new product, modify an existing one, or eliminate a product from the mix because one or more competitors have grown more dominant in the market segment. A marketer may also expand the firm's product mix to take advantage of excess marketing and production capacity. For example, Campbell Soup Company has a wide product mix consisting of many different brands. It frequently expands its product mix by adding new offerings to its different product lines, such as soups and juices. The company plans to introduce 200 new products this year in order to keep up with changing consumer tastes and needs.[5] A firm must be careful when altering the product mix that the changes made bring about improvements in the mix. There are three major ways to improve a product mix: change an existing product, delete a product, or develop a new product.

12-4a Managing Existing Products

A product mix can be changed by deriving additional products from existing ones. This can be accomplished through product modifications and by line extensions.

PRODUCT MODIFICATIONS Product modification refers to changing one or more of a product's characteristics. For this approach to be effective, several conditions must be met. First, the product must be modifiable. Second, existing customers must be able to perceive that a modification has been made, assuming that the modified item is still directed at the same target market. Third, the modification should make the product more consistent with customers' desires so that it provides greater satisfaction. For example, General Mills adjusted the recipe for its long-selling Cheerios breakfast cereal to avoid using genetically modified ingredients in order to address health and environmental concerns some consumers have about genetically modified organisms.[6]

Existing products can be altered in three primary ways: in quality, function, and aesthetics. *Quality modifications* are changes that relate to a product's dependability and durability and are usually achieved by alterations in the materials or production process. *Functional modifications* affect a product's versatility, effectiveness, convenience, or safety. They usually require redesign of the product. Typical product

product modification the process of changing one or more of a product's characteristics

categories that have undergone extensive functional modifications include home appliances, office and farm equipment, and consumer electronics. *Aesthetic modifications* change the sensory appeal of a product by altering its taste, texture, sound, smell, or visual characteristics. Because a buyer's purchasing decision is affected by sensory stimuli, an aesthetic modification may impact purchases. Through aesthetic modifications, a firm can differentiate its product from competing brands and gain market share if customers find the modified product more appealing.

LINE EXTENSIONS A **line extension** is the development of a product closely related to one or more products in the existing product line but designed specifically to meet somewhat different customer needs. For example, Campbell Soup Company launched V8-branded protein shakes and protein bars that include familiar V8 vegetables along with plant-based proteins like quinoa and brown rice to gain a place in the rapidly growing market for adult on-the-go snacks and meals.[7]

Many of the so-called new products introduced each year are in fact line extensions. Line extensions are more common than new products because they are a less-expensive, lower-risk alternative for increasing sales. A line extension may focus on a different market segment or be an attempt to increase sales within the same market segment by more precisely satisfying that segment's needs, hopefully taking away market share from competitors.

12-4b Deleting Products

To maintain an effective product mix, an organization often has to eliminate some products. This is called **product deletion**. A weak and unprofitable product costs a company time, money, and resources that could be used to modify other products or develop new ones. A weak product's unfavorable image can negatively impact the customer perception and sales of other products sold by the firm.

Most organizations find it difficult to delete a product because of the costs associated with bringing the product to market or for more emotional reasons. Some firms drop weak products only after they have become severe financial burdens. A better approach is to conduct a systematic review of the product's impact on the overall effectiveness of a firm's product mix. Such a review should analyze a product's contribution to a company's sales for a given period and should include estimates of future sales, costs, and profits. This review should help a firm to determine whether changes in the marketing strategy might improve the product's performance.

A product-deletion program can improve a firm's performance. *Encyclopaedia Britannica*, once a prestige product in many homes, stopped issuing print editions for the first time in its 244 years. Now, Internet users can access about half of its content online via an advertising-supported free website or all of it via online subscription for $70 per year. This model allows the firm to update content more frequently and is cheaper for the company to maintain.[8]

© VALESTOCK/SHUTTERSTOCK.COM

Line extensions help companies like Frito Lay to be more competitive and to maintain or increase their market shares. Frito Lay's first line extension, after its initial introduction of original, was the barbecue flavor. It has since expanded its product mix through its use of product line extensions including such flavors as Sour Cream & Onion, Dill Pickle, and Pico de Gallo.

line extension development of a new product that is closely related to one or more products in the existing product line but designed specifically to meet somewhat different customer needs

product deletion the elimination of one or more products from a product line

© GIUSEPPE COSTANTINO/SHUTTERSTOCK.COM

New Product? Not Yet! Google Glass, a new product recently developed by Google, allows users to view e-mails, apps, and shoot videos in a hands-free format through voice commands. Google had to withdraw the product from the market due to technical issues.

FIGURE 12-2
Phases of New-Product
Development

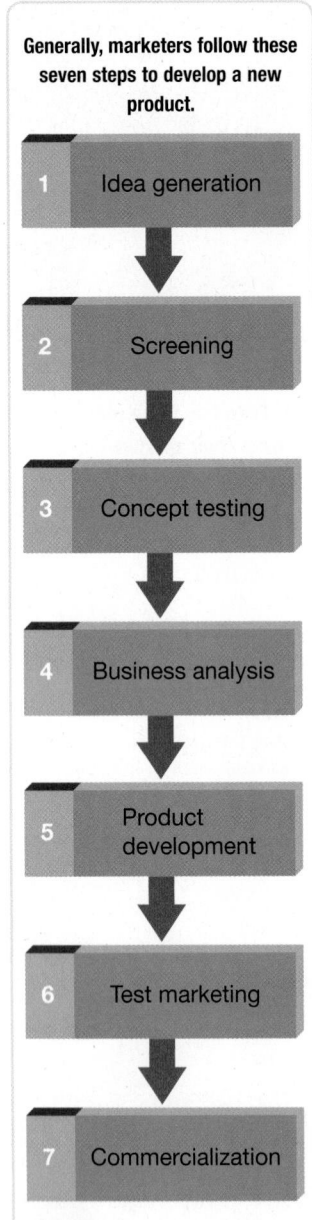

Generally, marketers follow these seven steps to develop a new product.

1. Idea generation
2. Screening
3. Concept testing
4. Business analysis
5. Product development
6. Test marketing
7. Commercialization

Source: William M. Pride and O. C. Ferrell, *Marketing*, 18th ed. (Mason, OH: South-Western/Cengage Learning, 2016). Adapted with permission.

12-4c Developing New Products

Developing and introducing new products is frequently time consuming, expensive, and risky. Aerion Corporation, for example, has spent more than ten years and $100 million developing a new supersonic business jet that will be able to fly from San Francisco to Tokyo in 6.5 hours.[9] Thousands of new products are introduced annually. For most firms, more than half of new products will fail. Although developing new products is risky, failing to introduce new products can be just as hazardous. Successful new products can produce benefits for an organization, including survival, profits, a sustainable competitive advantage, and a favorable public image.

New products are generally grouped into three categories on the basis of their degree of similarity to existing products. *Imitations* are products designed to compete with existing products of other firms. The success of Apple's iPad, for instance, spawned many tablet computer competitors. *Adaptations* are variations of existing products that are intended for an established market. Product refinements and extensions are the adaptations considered most often, although imitative products may also include some refinement and extension. *Innovations* are entirely new products. They may give rise to a new industry or revolutionize an existing one. Innovative products take considerable time, effort, and money to develop. They are by far the riskiest new product to develop and launch and are therefore less common than adaptations and imitations. While other companies market exercise watches and monitors, Lark uses sensors in an iPhone to monitor exercise, diet, sleep, and other factors and offers coaching on how to maximize health and happiness via an app.[10] As shown in Figure 12-2, the process of developing a new product consists of seven phases.

IDEA GENERATION Idea generation involves looking for product ideas that will help a firm to achieve its objectives. Although some organizations get their ideas almost by chance, firms trying to maximize product-mix effectiveness develop systematic approaches for generating new-product ideas. Ideas may come from virtually any stakeholder associated with the firm, including managers, researchers, engineers, competitors, advertising agencies, management consultants, private research organizations, customers, salespersons, or top executives. Sometimes, large firms with superior experience and resources may mentor small firms and help them generate ideas to help their businesses grow. Business incubators exist all over the country that pair new businesses with established ones so that the new business can learn about marketing and branding from experts. Goldman Sachs, Walmart, Chase Bank, and Staples have all hosted events and programs to counsel start-ups. Jim Koch of Boston Beer Company, maker of Sam Adams, partners with the small business lender, Accion, for the Brewing the American Dream program, which offers speed coaching sessions and loans to small businesses.[11]

SCREENING During screening, ideas that do not match organizational resources and objectives are rejected. In this phase, a firm's managers consider whether the organization has personnel with the correct expertise to develop and market the proposed product. Management may reject a good idea because the company lacks the necessary skills and abilities to make the product a success. The largest number of product ideas is rejected during the screening phase.

CONCEPT TESTING Concept testing is a phase in which a product idea is presented to a sample of potential buyers through a written or oral description (and perhaps drawings) to determine their attitudes and initial buying intentions. An organization may test one or several concepts when developing a product idea. Concept testing is a low-cost means for an organization to determine consumers' initial reactions to an idea before investing considerable resources in product research and development (R&D). Product development personnel use the results of concept testing to make product attributes and benefits reflect the characteristics and features

BucketFeet: A Gift of Hand-Decorated Sneakers Creates a $1 Million Business

Raaja Nemani and Aaron Firestein never expected to start a shoe company. Firestein was traveling through Argentina when he met Nemani and gave his new friend a one-of-a-kind pair of hand-decorated sneakers to wear as he backpacked his way from continent to continent. Nemani was struck by the positive reactions to the artistic sneakers he wore as he trekked through 25 countries.

The two entrepreneurs soon teamed up to launch Chicago-based BucketFeet, marketing athletic shoes and flip-flops featuring designs from artists around the world, priced competitively with well-known sneaker brands. Their idea was to give artists a new outlet and a way to reach consumers who like to express themselves through the originality of artistic footwear. Choosing from among thousands of original designs available on BucketFeet's website or in selected stores, consumers can suit their own tastes and express their individuality through what they wear on their feet.

Early on, BucketFeet experienced some marketing stumbles as Nemani and Firestein learned to plan for the ups and downs of demand, gained experience with suppliers, and experimented with different styles and different ways of involving artists and consumers. Now the company has surpassed $1 million in annual sales and established nationwide distribution through national retailers, such as Nordstrom, as well as dozens of independent boutiques. To stay close to their customers, Nemani and Firestein invite visitors to view and buy the latest shoe styles at BucketFeet's Chicago and New York studios.

Sources: Based on information in Alexia Elejalde-Ruiz, "Bucketfeet Doubles Down on Fulton Market," *Chicago Tribune*, October 17, 2014, www.chicagotribune.com (accessed July 29, 2015); Courtney Subramanian, "Fancy Footwork: Bucketfeet Gives Artists a New Kind of Canvas," *Fortune*, May 16, 2014, www.fortune.com (accessed July 29, 2015); Lizette Chapman, "How I Built It: Art-Inspired Shoes Take Bucketfeet to Next Level," *Wall Street Journal*, August 13, 2014, www.wsj.com (accessed July 29, 2015); Caroline Howard, "30 Under 30 Who Are Changing the World 2014," *Forbes*, January 20, 2014, www.forbes.com (accessed July 29, 2015).

most important to potential customers. The questions asked vary considerably depending on the type of product idea being tested. The following are typical:

- Which benefits of the proposed product are especially attractive to you?
- Which features are of little or no interest to you?
- What are the primary advantages of the proposed product over the one you currently use?
- If this product were available at an appropriate price, how often would you buy it?
- How could this proposed product be improved?

BUSINESS ANALYSIS Business analysis generates tentative ideas about a potential product's financial performance, including profitability. During this stage, the firm considers how the new product, if it were introduced, would affect the firm's overall sales, costs, and profits. Marketing personnel usually work up preliminary sales and cost projections at this point, with the help of R&D and production managers.

PRODUCT DEVELOPMENT In the product development phase, the company must find out if it is technically feasible to produce the product and if the product can be made at a low enough cost for the company to generate a profit. If a product idea makes it to this point, it is transformed into a working model, or prototype. Often, this step is time consuming and expensive for the organization. If a product moves through this step successfully, then it is ready for test marketing.

TEST MARKETING Test marketing is the limited introduction of a product in several towns or cities that are representative of the intended target market. Its aim

TABLE 12-1 Examples of Product Failures

Company	Product
Microsoft	Zune (2006)
Apple	Newton (1993)
Barbie	Earring Magic Ken (1993)
Coca-Cola	New Coke (1985)
Colgate	Kitchen Entrees (1982)
Ford	Edsel (1957)
Barnes & Noble	the Nook (2009)

Source: Adapted from: "25 Biggest Product Flops of All Time," *Daily Finance*, http://www.dailyfinance.com/photos/top-25-biggest-product-flops-of-all-time/ (accessed February 5, 2015); Jillian Berman, "22 of the Most Epic Product Fails in History," Business Insider, July 31, 2014, http://www.businessinsider.com/biggest-product-failures-in-business-history-2014-7 (accessed July 6, 2015).

is to determine buyers' probable reactions. Marketers experiment with advertising, pricing, and packaging in different test markets and measure the extent of brand awareness, brand switching, and repeat purchases that result from alterations in the marketing mix. Whole Foods, for example, test marketed reduced prices on produce and other grocery products in Austin, Texas, where the company faces intense competition for consumers of organic and natural foods.[12]

COMMERCIALIZATION During commercialization, the organization completes plans for full-scale manufacturing and marketing and prepares project budgets. In the early part of the commercialization phase, marketing management analyzes the results of test marketing to determine necessary changes in the marketing mix. Test marketing may reveal, for example, that marketers must change the product's physical attributes, modify the distribution plan, alter promotional efforts, or change the price. Most new products are marketed in stages, beginning in selected geographic areas and expanding into adjacent areas over a period of time.

12-4d Why Do Products Fail?

Despite this rigorous process for developing product ideas, most new products end up as failures. In fact, many well-known companies have produced market failures (see Table 12-1).

Why does a new product fail? Mainly because the product and its marketing program are not planned and tested as thoroughly as they should be. For example, Amazon's Fire cell phone failed largely because it didn't have any features that stood out in a competitive field of innovative mobile phones, and the phone was priced at the upper end of the market. The company will likely introduce a new version of the phone in the future that addresses these marketing stumbles.[13] To save on development costs, a firm may market-test a product before the kinks are worked out, or may not test its entire marketing mix. Or, when problems show up in the testing stage, a firm may try to recover its product development costs by pushing ahead with full-scale marketing anyway. Finally, some firms try to market new products with inadequate financing.

12-5 BRANDING, PACKAGING, AND LABELING

Three important features of a product (particularly a consumer product) are its brand, package, and label. These features may be used to associate a product with a successful product line or to distinguish it from existing products. They may be

Concept Check

✓ What are the ways to improve a product mix? Describe two approaches to use existing products to strengthen a product mix.

✓ Why is it important to delete certain products? The largest number of product ideas is rejected during which stage?

✓ What is the aim of test marketing?

✓ Describe the seven phases of new-product development.

Learning Objective

12-5 Explain the uses and importance of branding, packaging, and labeling.

designed to attract customers at the point of sale or to provide information to potential buyers. Because the brand, package, and label are integral elements of the product, they deserve careful attention during product planning.

12-5a What Is a Brand?

A **brand** is a name, term, symbol, design, or any combination that identifies a seller's products and distinguishes it from other sellers' products. A **brand name** is the part of a brand that can be spoken. It may include letters, words, numbers, or pronounceable symbols, such as the ampersand in *Procter & Gamble*. A **brand mark**, on the other hand, is the part of a brand that is a symbol or distinctive design, such as the Nike "swoosh." A **trademark** is a brand name or brand mark that is registered with the U.S. Patent and Trademark Office and thus is legally protected from use by anyone except its owner. A **trade name** is the complete and legal name of an organization, such as Pizza Hut or Cengage Learning (the publisher of this text).

12-5b Types of Brands

Brands are often classified according to who owns them: manufacturers or stores. A **manufacturer (or producer) brand**, as the name implies, is a brand that is owned by the manufacturer. Many foods (Kellogg's Frosted Flakes), major appliances (Whirlpool), gasolines (Exxon Mobil), automobiles (Honda), and clothing (Levi's) are sold as manufacturers' brands. Some consumers prefer manufacturer brands because they are usually nationally known, offer consistent quality, and are widely available.

A **store (or private) brand** is a brand that is owned by an individual wholesaler or retailer. Among the better-known store brands are Kenmore and Craftsman, both owned by Sears. Owners of store brands claim that they can offer lower prices, earn greater profits, and improve customer loyalty by offering their own brands. Some companies that manufacture private brands also produce their own manufacturer brands. They often find such operations profitable because they can use excess capacity and avoid most marketing costs. Many private-branded grocery products are produced by companies that specialize in making private-label products. Most supermarkets rely heavily on their store brands. According to the Private Label Manufacturer's Association, the popularity and quality of store brands is on the rise, particularly among consumers who seek out good value without sacrificing quality.[14]

Consumer confidence is the most important element in the success of a branded product, whether the brand is owned by a producer or by a retailer. Because branding identifies each product, customers can easily repurchase products that provide satisfaction, performance, and quality. Moreover, they can just as easily avoid or ignore unsatisfactory products. In supermarkets, the products most likely to keep their shelf space are the brands with large market shares and strong customer loyalty.

A **generic product (or generic brand)** is a product with no brand at all. Its plain package carries only the name of the product—applesauce, peanut butter, or potato chips. Generic products, available in supermarkets since 1977, are sometimes made by the major producers that manufacture name brands.

12-5c Benefits of Branding

Both buyers and sellers benefit from branding. Because brands are easily recognizable, they reduce the amount

brand a name, term, symbol, design, or any combination of these that identifies a seller's products as distinct from those of other sellers

brand name the part of a brand that can be spoken

brand mark the part of a brand that is a symbol or distinctive design

trademark a brand name or brand mark that is registered with the U.S. Patent and Trademark Office and thus is legally protected from use by anyone except its owner

trade name the complete and legal name of an organization

manufacturer (or producer) brand a brand that is owned by a manufacturer

store (or private) brand a brand that is owned by an individual wholesaler or retailer

generic product (or generic brand) a product with no brand at all

You can easily recognize a manufacturer's brand because it is not sold by just one retailer. This brand was initiated by the manufacturer and is owned and supported by the manufacturer. Gillette razors are sold in many retail stores.

Social Media:

Going Boldly Where No Cookie Has Gone Before

The Oreo brand may be more than 100 years old, but its social media marketing is as youthful as a brand born yesterday. Owned by Mondelēz, Oreo has been moving full speed ahead on social media since 2012, its centenary year. Today, the black-and-white sandwich cookie's fun ritual of "twist, lick, and dunk" is recognized worldwide, thanks to the company's social media attention, supported by other marketing efforts.

To engage cookie-lovers of all ages, Oreo uses Facebook, Twitter, YouTube, Instagram, and Vine. During its 100th birthday celebration, the brand posted new Facebook content every day, using creative visuals of the cookie adapted to current events and pop culture. At the start of Gay Pride Week, the brand posted a rainbow-colored Oreo cookie on its Facebook page, generating a huge amount of publicity and public attention. On the day of the Mars Rover Curiosity landing, the brand's Facebook page featured an open-faced Oreo cookie with red crème bisected by tire tracks.

Oreo's marketers recognize that social media content must be timely to grab attention. During the 2013 Super Bowl, when a blackout plunged the stadium into darkness, Oreo quickly posted a tweet that was retweeted more than 10,000 times: "Power out? No problem," including a link to a photo of an Oreo with the caption: "You can still dunk in the dark." More recently, Oreo's marketers created a popular series of social-media videos showing Oreos as ingredients in meals and beverages, accompanied by the hashtag #OreoSnackHack.

Sources: Based on information in Danielle Sacks, "Oreo Tags Pop Culture," *Fast Company*, October 21, 2014, www.fastcompany.com (accessed July 29, 2015); Michelle Castillo, "Oreo Turns Snack Hacks into Web Series," *Adweek*, April 11, 2014, www.adweek.com (accessed July 29, 2015); Christopher Heine, "Thanks to Oreo, More Marketers Will Be Huddled Up in Super Bowl War Rooms," *Adweek*, January 31, 2014, www.adweek.com (accessed July 29, 2015).

brand loyalty extent to which a customer is favorable toward buying a specific brand

brand equity marketing and financial value associated with a brand's strength in a market

of time buyers spend on shopping, as they can quickly identify the brands they prefer. Choosing particular brands, such as Chanel, Polo, Patagonia, or Nike, can be a way of expressing oneself and identifying with certain lifestyle characteristics and values. Brands also help to reduce the perceived risk of purchase. Finally, customers may receive a psychological reward from owning a brand that symbolizes status. The Lexus brand is an example.

Branding helps a firm to introduce a new product that carries a familiar brand name because buyers already know the brand. Branding aids sellers in their promotional efforts because promotion of each branded product indirectly promotes other products of the same brand. H.J. Heinz, for example, markets many products with the Heinz brand name, such as ketchup, vinegar, gravies, barbecue sauce, and steak sauce.

One chief benefit of branding is the creation of **brand loyalty**, the extent to which a customer is favorable toward buying a specific brand. The stronger the brand loyalty, the greater is the likelihood that buyers will consistently choose the brand. There are three levels of brand loyalty: recognition, preference, and insistence. *Brand recognition* is the level of loyalty at which customers are aware that the brand exists and will purchase it if their preferred or familiar brands are unavailable. This is the weakest form of brand loyalty. *Brand preference* is the level of brand loyalty at which a customer prefers one brand over competing brands. However, if the preferred brand is unavailable, the customer is willing to substitute another brand. *Brand insistence* is the strongest and least common level of brand loyalty. Brand-insistent customers will not buy substitutes. Apple is a brand known for having brand-insistent customers. Every time Apple releases a new product, customers will stand in line for hours, even days, just to be among the first to purchase it. Brand loyalty in general seems to be declining, partly due to marketers' increased dependence on discounted prices, coupons, and other short-term promotions, and partly because of the enormous array of new products with similar characteristics. It is also easier than ever to comparison shop for products that meet customer, needs at the lowest possible price.

Brand equity is the marketing and financial value associated with a brand's strength in a market. Although difficult to measure, brand equity represents the value of a brand to an organization. The top ten most valuable brands in the world are shown in Table 12-2. The four major factors that contribute to brand equity are brand awareness, brand associations, perceived brand quality, and brand loyalty. Brand awareness leads to brand familiarity—buyers are more likely to select a familiar brand. The symbolic associations of a brand connect it to a personality type or lifestyle. For example, customers associate Michelin tires with protecting family members, Nike products with pushing yourself athletically ("Just Do It"), and Dr Pepper with a unique taste. When consumers are unable to judge for themselves

TABLE 12-2 Top Ten Most Valuable Brands in the World

Brand	Brand Value (million $)	Brand	Brand Value (million $)
1. Apple	118,863	6. GE	45,480
2. Google	107,439	7. Samsung	45,462
3. Coca-Cola	81,563	8. Toyota	42,392
4. IBM	72,244	9. McDonald's	42,254
5. Microsoft	61,154	10. Mercedes-Benz	34,338

Source: "Best Global Brands 2014," *Interbrand*, http://www.bestglobalbrands.com/2014/ranking/ (accessed February 5, 2015).

the quality of a product, they may rely on a brand's perceived level of quality. Finally, brand loyalty is a valued element of brand equity because it reduces both a brand's vulnerability to competitors and the need to spend tremendous resources to attract new customers. Loyalty also increases brand visibility and encourages retailers to carry the brand. Sometimes, large firms opt to purchase a well-known brand rather than to compete with it. Facebook, for instance, acquired the popular photo-sharing platform, Instagram, with the intention of minimizing competition and making money off of the service.[15]

12-5d Choosing and Protecting a Brand

A number of issues should be considered when selecting a brand name. The name should be easy for customers to say, spell, and recall. Short, one-syllable names such as *Tide* often satisfy this requirement. Words, numbers, and letters can be combined to yield brand names such as Nokia's Lumia 830 phone or BMW's Z4 Roadster. The brand name should suggest, in a positive way, the product's uses, special characteristics, and major benefits, and should be distinctive enough to set it apart from competing brands.

It is important that a firm select a brand that can be protected through registration, reserving it for exclusive use by that firm. Some brands, because of their designs, are infringed on more easily than others. Registration protects trademarks domestically for ten years and can be renewed indefinitely. To protect its exclusive right to the brand, the company must ensure that the selected brand will not be considered an infringement on any existing brand already registered with the U.S. Patent and Trademark Office. This task may be complicated by the fact that courts determine infringement and base their decisions on whether a brand causes consumers to be confused, mistaken, or deceived about the source of the product. McDonald's is one company that is known for aggressively protecting its trademarks against infringement. It has brought charges against a number of companies with *Mc* names because of concerns that the use of the prefix might give consumers the impression that these companies are associated with or owned by McDonald's.

A firm does not want a brand name to become a generic term that refers to a general product category. Generic terms cannot be legally protected as exclusive brand names. For example, names such as *yo-yo*, *aspirin*, *escalator*, and *thermos*—all exclusively brand names at one time—eventually were declared generic terms that refer to product categories. As such, they can no longer be protected. To ensure that a brand name does not become a generic term, the firm should spell the name with a capital letter and use it as an adjective to modify the name of the general product class, as in Jell-O Brand Gelatin. An organization can deal directly with this problem by advertising that its brand is a trademark and should not be used generically. Firms also can use the registered trademark symbol ® to indicate that the brand is trademarked.

12-5e Branding Strategies

The basic branding decision for any firm is how to brand its products. A producer may market its products under its own brands, private brands, or both. A retail store may carry only producer brands, its own brands, or both. Once either type of firm decides to brand, it chooses one of two branding strategies: individual branding or family branding.

Individual branding is the strategy in which a firm uses a different brand for each of its products. For example, Procter & Gamble uses individual branding for its line of bar soaps, which includes Ivory, Safeguard, and Olay. Individual branding offers two major advantages: a problem with one product will not affect the good name of the firm's other products and the different brands can be directed toward different market segments.

Family branding is the strategy in which a firm uses the same brand for all or most of its products. Sony, Dell, IBM, and Xerox use family branding for their product mixes. A major advantage of family branding is that successful promotion for any one item that carries the family brand can help all other products with the same brand name. In addition, a new product has a head-start when its brand name is already known and accepted by customers.

12-5f Brand Extensions

A **brand extension** occurs when an organization uses one of its existing brands to brand a new product in a different product category. Iams, a popular maker of dog food, partnered with VPI Pet Insurance to extend its brand into pet insurance.[16] A brand extension should not be confused with a line extension. A *line extension* refers to using an existing brand on a new product in the same product category, such as a new flavor or new sizes. Pringles engages in line extension when releasing a new flavor, such as its holiday flavors Cinnamon & Sugar or White Chocolate Peppermint. Marketers must be careful not to extend a brand too many times or extend too far outside the original product category. Either action may weaken the brand.

12-5g Packaging

Packaging consists of all the activities involved in developing and providing a container with graphics for a product. The package is a vital part of the product. It can make the product more versatile, safer, or easier to use. Through its shape, size, appearance, and printed message, a package can influence purchasing decisions.

PACKAGING FUNCTIONS Effective packaging is a combination of function and aesthetics. The basic function of packaging materials is to protect the product and maintain its functional form. Fluids such as milk, orange juice, and hair spray need packages that preserve and protect the product inside. Packaging should prevent damage that would affect the product's usefulness and increase costs. Because product tampering has become a problem for marketers of many types of goods, packaging techniques have been developed to counter this danger. Some packages are also designed to foil shoplifting.

Another function of packaging is to offer consumer convenience. For example, individual-serving boxes or plastic bags that contain liquids and do not require refrigeration appeal strongly to parents of small children and to young adults with

individual branding the strategy in which a firm uses a different brand for each of its products

family branding the strategy in which a firm uses the same brand for all or most of its products

brand extension using an existing brand to brand a new product in a different product category

packaging all the activities involved in developing and providing a container with graphics for a product

active lifestyles. The size or shape of a package may relate to the product's storage, convenience of use, or replacement rate. Small, single-serving cans of vegetables, for instance, may prevent waste and make storage easier.

A third function of packaging is to promote a product by communicating its features, uses, benefits, and image. Sometimes a firm develops a reusable package to make its product more desirable. For example, CleanPath multi-surface cleaners employ Replenish technology which allows them to be sold as cleaner concentrate in pods that screw onto the bottom of a spray bottle. Consumers purchase the bottle once, add water, and the pod releases the correct amount of cleaner concentrate. The system saves on plastic and water waste and is cheaper than many competitors' products.[17]

PACKAGE DESIGN CONSIDERATIONS Many factors must be weighed when developing packages. Obviously, one major consideration is cost. Expensive packaging can affect the final cost of a product.

Marketers also must decide whether to package the product in single or multiple units. Multiple-unit packaging can increase demand by increasing the amount of the product available at the point of consumption (in the home, for example). However, multiple-unit packaging does not work for infrequently used products because buyers generally prefer not to have an excess supply or to store products for a long time. However, multiple-unit packaging can make storage and handling easier (as in the case of twelve-packs used for soft drinks). It can also facilitate special price offers, such as two-for-one sales. Multiple-unit packaging may encourage customers to try a product several times, but it may also backfire and deter them from trying the product if they cannot purchase just one.

Marketers should consider how much consistency is desirable among an organization's package designs. To promote an overall company image, a firm may decide that all packages must be similar or include a distinct design element. This approach, called *family packaging*, is often used only for lines of products, as with Campbell's soups, Weight Watchers foods, and Planters nuts. The best policy is sometimes no consistency, especially if a firm's various products are unrelated or aimed at different target markets.

Packages also play an important promotional role. Through verbal and nonverbal symbols, the package informs potential buyers about the product's content, uses, features, advantages, and hazards. Firms can create desirable images and associations by choosing particular colors, designs, shapes, and textures. Many cosmetics manufacturers, for example, design their packages to create impressions of richness, luxury, and exclusivity. The package performs another promotional function when it is designed to be safer or more convenient to use than competitors'.

Packaging also must meet the needs of intermediaries. Wholesalers and retailers consider whether a package is easy to transport, handle, and store. Resellers may refuse to carry certain products if their packages are too cumbersome.

Finally, firms must consider the issue of environmental responsibility when developing packages. Companies must balance consumers' desires for convenience against the need to preserve the environment. Reducing packaging will help with global waste problems because about one-half of all garbage consists of plastic packaging. When deciding on the best packaging for its organic yogurt products, Stonyfield Farm chose lightweight plastic because it costs less to ship and is durable. It partners with Preserve, a company that makes recycled toothbrushes and home goods out of yogurt containers, to reduce packaging waste. Stonyfield Farm encourages recycling at Whole Foods drop-offs.[18]

Heinz turns the ketchup bottle on its head. The original design of the ketchup bottle made it difficult for customers to get the ketchup out. To solve this problem, Heinz put the cap on the bottom of the bottle and made the opening larger. In addition, Heinz made the bottle squeezable.

12-5h Labeling

Labeling is the presentation of information on a product or its package. The *label* is the part of a package that contains information, including the brand name and mark, the registered trademark symbol ®, the package size and contents, product claims, directions for use and safety precautions, ingredients, the name and address of the manufacturer, and the Universal Product Code (UPC) symbol, which is used for automated checkout and inventory control.

A number of federal regulations specify information that *must* be included in the labeling for certain products:

- Garments must be labeled with the name of the manufacturer, country of manufacture, fabric content, and cleaning instructions.
- Food labels must contain the most common term for ingredients.
- Any food product for which a nutritional claim is made must have nutrition labeling that follows a standard format.
- Food product labels must state the number of servings per container, the serving size, the number of calories per serving, the number of calories derived from fat, and the amounts of specific nutrients.
- Non-edible items such as shampoos and detergents must carry safety precautions and instructions for use.

Such regulations are aimed at protecting customers from misleading product claims and the improper (and thus unsafe) use of products. Food manufacturers are not allowed to make misleading health claims about their products.

Labels also may carry the details of written, or express, warranties. An **express warranty** is a written explanation of the producer's responsibilities in the event that a product is found to be defective or otherwise unsatisfactory.

12-6 PRICING PRODUCTS

A product is a set of attributes and benefits that has been designed to satisfy its market while earning a profit for its seller. Pricing is an integral part of this equation. Each product has a price at which consumers' desires and expectations are balanced with a firm's need to make a profit. We will now look more closely at how businesses go about determining a product's price.

12-6a The Meaning and Use of Price

The **price** of a product is the amount of money a seller is willing to accept in exchange for the product at a given time and under given circumstances. At times, the price results from negotiations between buyer and seller. In many business situations, however, the price is fixed by the seller. Suppose that a seller sets a price of $10 for a product. The seller is saying, "Anyone who wants this product can have it here and now in exchange for $10."

Each interested buyer then makes a personal judgment regarding the product's utility, often in terms of a dollar value. A particular person who feels that he or she will get at least $10 worth of want satisfaction (or value) from the product is likely to buy it. If that person can get more want satisfaction by spending $10 in some other way, he or she will not buy the product.

Price thus serves the function of *allocator*. First, it allocates goods and services among those who are willing and able to buy them. (As we noted in Chapter 1, the answer to the economic question "For whom to produce?" depends primarily on prices.) Second, price allocates financial resources (sales revenue) among producers according to how well they satisfy customers' needs. Third, price helps customers to allocate their own financial resources among various want-satisfying products.

Learning Objective

12-6 Describe the economic basis of pricing and the means by which sellers can control prices and buyers' perceptions of prices.

labeling the presentation of information on a product or its package

express warranty a written explanation of the producer's responsibilities in the event that a product is found to be defective or otherwise unsatisfactory

price the amount of money a seller is willing to accept in exchange for a product at a given time and under given circumstances

12-6b Price and Non-Price Competition

Before a product's price can be set, an organization must determine whether it will compete based on price alone, or on a combination of factors. The choice influences pricing decisions as well as other marketing-mix variables.

Price competition occurs when a seller emphasizes a product's low price and sets a price that equals or beats competitors' prices. To use this approach most effectively, a seller must have the flexibility to change prices often, rapidly, and aggressively in response to competitors' price changes. Price competition allows a marketer to set prices based on product demand or in response to changes in the firm's finances. Competitors can do likewise, however, which is a major drawback of price competition. If circumstances force a seller to raise prices, competing firms may be able to maintain their lower prices. Some retailers, such as Staples,

How low can you go? Price competition is fierce among fast food restaurants. McDonald's launched the first dollar menu in its industry in 2002. It was not long before many of its competitors followed suit with their own value menus.

have taken price competition to a whole new level. They use sophisticated algorithms to instantly alter prices on products offered through their websites based on geography, customer proximity to competitors, buying habits, and other information stored about the customer.[19] The Internet has made it more difficult than ever for sellers to compete on the basis of price, as consumers can quickly and easily conduct comparison-shopping online.

Non-price competition is competition based on factors other than price. It is used most effectively when a seller can make its product stand out through distinctive product quality, customer service, promotion, packaging, or other features. Buyers must be able to perceive these characteristics and consider them desirable. Once customers have chosen a brand for non-price reasons, they may not be as attracted to competing firms and brands. In this way, a seller can build customer loyalty to its brand. A method of non-price competition, **product differentiation**, is the process of developing and promoting differences between one's product and all similar products. Vibram Five Fingers shoes, for example, are sufficiently differentiated from the competition that marketers do not compete on price. The shoes have highly distinct styling and are unlike any other shoe on the market. Modeled on the shape of a foot, including individual toes, they appeal to runners and other athletes who want to protect their feet while having a barefoot experience.[20]

12-6c Buyers' Perceptions of Price

In setting prices, managers should consider the price sensitivity of the target market. Members of one market segment may be more influenced by price than members of another. Consumer price sensitivity can also vary between products. For example, buyers may be more sensitive to price when purchasing gasoline than when purchasing running shoes.

Buyers will tolerate a narrow range of prices for certain items and a wider range for others. Consider the varying prices of soft drinks—from 15 cents per ounce at the movies down to 1.5 cents per ounce on sale at the grocery store. Management should be aware of consumers' price limits and the products to which they apply. The firm also should take note of buyers' perceptions of a given product in relation to competing products. A premium price may be appropriate if a product

price competition an emphasis on setting a price equal to or lower than competitors' prices to gain sales or market share

non-price competition competition based on factors other than price

product differentiation the process of developing and promoting differences between one's product and all similar products

Concept Check

✓ What factors must be considered when pricing products?

✓ How does a change in price affect the demand and supply of a product?

✓ Differentiate price competition and non-price competition.

✓ Why is it important to consider the buyer's sensitivity to price when pricing products?

What is the Real Price...?

Should customers have to check the fine print to figure out the real price of an airline ticket or a hotel room? In some cases, customers don't know the final price until they follow the asterisk in an ad or read the details in a tiny type size at the bottom of the screen or printed page. Because many travel services are subject to taxes and fees that are not always prominently disclosed, customers may be surprised when a bargain turns out to be nowhere near as good as it appeared at first glance.

Airlines and travel websites often promote low prices to grab attention and boost sales. After customers complained about "hidden" fees and taxes added at the end of a purchase, U.S. regulators began requiring airlines to disclose the full price at the start. Some airlines are pushing for change, saying fees and taxes should be disclosed separately because they are government-imposed and not under the airline's pricing control.

A growing number of resorts and hotels are adding all-in-one fees to cover parking, fitness facilities, and other services. The companies explain that bundled pricing is more convenient for guests. However, not all guests use these services—and some guests are complaining about the final price, especially when they weren't aware of the added fees at the time of booking. Should fees and other extras be in the fine print or in the price?

Sources: Based on information in Kate Rice, "Except for Southwest, Airlines Oppose Regulation of Fee Disclosure," *Travel Weekly*, October 1, 2014, www.travelweekly.com (accessed July 29, 2015); Caroline Mayer, "8 Ways To Combat Outrageous Hidden Travel Fees," *Forbes*, May 27, 2014, www.forbes.com (accessed July 29, 2015); Christopher Elliott, "Bill Aims to Scuttle New Airfare Pricing Rule," *Chicago Tribune*, February 7, 2012, www.chicagotribune.com (accessed July 29, 2015).

is considered superior to others in its category, or if the product has inspired strong brand loyalty. On the other hand, a lower price may be necessary if buyers have even a slightly negative product perception.

Sometimes buyers equate price and quality. Managers involved in pricing decisions should determine whether this outlook is widespread in the target market. If it is, a higher price may improve a product's image, making it more desirable.

12-7 PRICING OBJECTIVES

Learning Objective

12-7 Identify the major pricing objectives used by businesses.

Before setting prices for a firm's products, management must determine pricing objectives that are in line with organizational and marketing objectives. Of course, one objective of pricing is to make a profit, but this may not be a firm's primary objective. One or more of the following factors may be just as important.

12-7a Survival

A firm may have to price its products to survive—either as an organization or as a player in a particular market. This usually means that the firm will cut its price to attract customers, even if it must operate at a loss for a while. Obviously, such a goal cannot be pursued on a long-term basis, for consistent losses would cause the business to fail.

12-7b Profit Maximization

Concept Check

✓ Explain the various types of pricing objectives.

✓ Which ones usually will result in a firm having lower prices?

Many firms may state that their goal is to maximize profit, but this goal is impossible to define (and thus impossible to achieve). What, exactly, is the *maximum* profit? How does a firm know when it has been reached? Firms that wish to set profit goals should express them as either specific dollar amounts, or percentage increases, over previous profits.

12-7c Target Return on Investment

The *return on investment* (ROI) is the amount earned as a result of a financial investment. Some firms set an annual percentage ROI as a quantifiable means to gauge the success of their pricing goal.

12-7d Market-Share Goals

A firm's *market share* is its proportion of total industry sales. Some firms attempt, through pricing, to maintain or increase their market shares. Both U.S. cola giants, Coke and Pepsi, continually try to gain market share through aggressive pricing and other marketing efforts.

12-7e Status-Quo Pricing

In pricing their products, some firms are guided by a desire to maintain the status quo. This is especially true in industries that depend on price stability. If such a firm can maintain its profit or market share simply by matching the competition—charging about the same price as competitors for similar products—then it will do so.

12-8 PRICING METHODS

Once a firm has developed its pricing objectives, it must select a pricing method to reach that goal. Two factors are important to every firm engaged in setting prices. The first is recognition that the market, and not the firm's costs, ultimately determines the price at which a product will sell. The second is awareness that costs and expected sales can be used only to establish a *price floor*, the minimum price at which the firm can sell its product without incurring a loss. In this section, we look at three kinds of pricing methods: cost-based, demand-based, and competition-based pricing.

What does a product's price communicate to you?
How buyers perceive a product is often determined by its price. High prices communicate quality and status—which is why the makers of luxury goods such as Rolex watches are often reluctant to sell them at a discount. The producers of these goods don't want to "cheapen" their brands for a quick sales boost because it could hurt the image of these brands.

12-8a Cost-Based Pricing

Using the simplest method of pricing, *cost-based pricing*, the seller first determines the total cost of producing (or purchasing) one unit of the product. The seller then adds an amount to cover additional costs (such as insurance or interest) and profit. The amount that is added is called the **markup**. The total of the cost plus the markup is the product's selling price.

A firm's management can calculate markup as a percentage of total costs. Suppose, for example, that the total cost of manufacturing and marketing 1,000 DVD players is $100,000, or $100 per unit. If the manufacturer wants a markup that is 20 percent above costs, the selling price will be $100 plus 20 percent of $100, or $120 per unit.

Markup pricing is easy to apply and is used by many businesses (mostly retailers and wholesalers). However, it has two major flaws. The first is the difficulty of determining the best markup percentage. If the percentage is too high, the product may be overpriced for its market and too few units will be sold to cover the cost of producing and marketing it. If the markup percentage is too low, the seller forgoes profit it could have earned by assigning a higher price.

Learning Objective

12-8 Examine the three major pricing methods that firms employ.

markup the amount a seller adds to the cost of a product to determine its basic selling price

The second problem with markup pricing is that it separates pricing from other business functions. The product is priced *after* production quantities are determined, *after* costs are incurred, and almost without regard for the market or the marketing mix. To be most effective, the cost of various business functions should be integrated. *Each* should have an impact on all marketing decisions.

Cost-based pricing can also be calculated through breakeven analysis. For any product, the **breakeven quantity** is the number of units that must be sold for the total revenue (from all units sold) to equal the total cost (of all units sold). **Total revenue** is the total amount received from the sales of a product. We estimate projected total revenue as the selling price multiplied by the number of units sold.

The costs involved in operating a business can be broadly classified as either fixed or variable. A **fixed cost** is a cost incurred no matter how many units of a product are produced or sold. Rent, for example, is a fixed cost because it remains the same whether 1 or 1,000 units are produced. A **variable cost** is a cost that depends on the number of units produced. The cost of fabricating parts for a stereo receiver is a variable cost. The more units produced, the more efficient production will be and the per-unit cost of the parts will go down. The **total cost** of producing a certain number of units is the sum of the fixed costs and the variable costs attributed to those units.

If we assume a particular selling price, we can find the breakeven quantity either graphically or by using a formula. Figure 12-3 graphs the total revenue earned and the total cost incurred by the sale of various quantities of a hypothetical product. With fixed costs of $40,000, variable costs of $60 per unit, and a selling price of $120, the breakeven quantity is 667 units (represented in Figure 12-3 as the intersection of the total revenue and total cost curves). To find the breakeven quantity, first deduct the variable cost from the selling price to determine how much money the sale of one unit contributes toward offsetting fixed costs. Divide that contribution into the total fixed costs to arrive at the breakeven quantity. If the firm sells more than 667 units at $120 each, it will earn a profit. If it sells fewer units, it will suffer a loss.

FIGURE 12-3 Breakeven Analysis

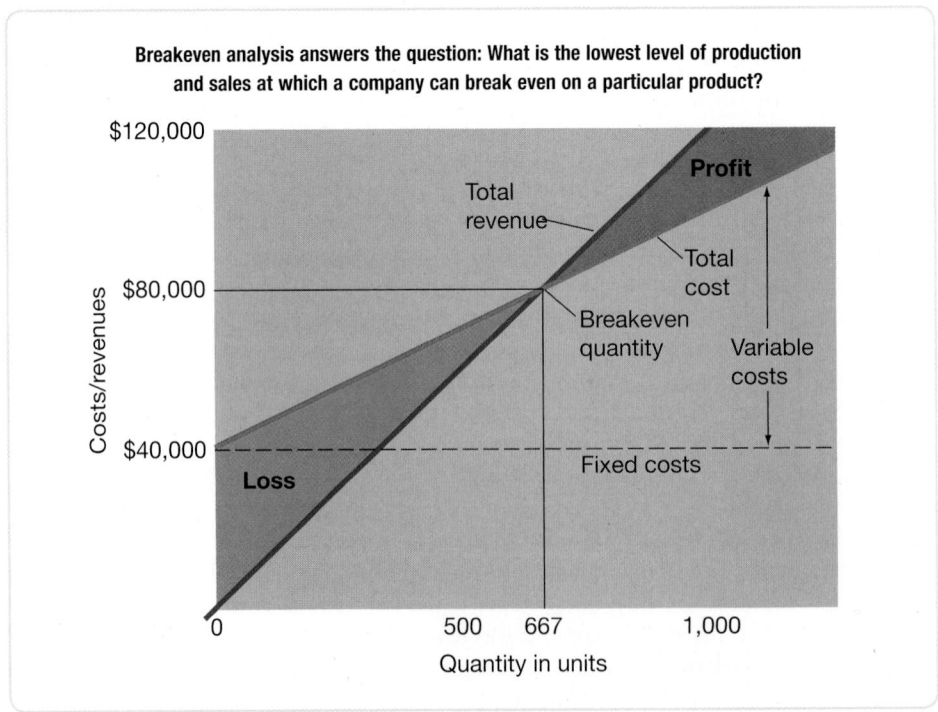

breakeven quantity the number of units that must be sold for the total revenue (from all units sold) to equal the total cost (of all units sold)

total revenue the total amount received from the sales of a product

fixed cost a cost incurred no matter how many units of a product are produced or sold

variable cost a cost that depends on the number of units produced

total cost the sum of the fixed costs and the variable costs attributed to a product

12-8b Demand-Based Pricing

Rather than basing the price of a product on its cost, companies sometimes use a pricing method based on the level of demand for the product: *demand-based pricing*. This method results in a higher price when product demand is strong and a lower price when demand is weak. To use this method, a marketer estimates the amount of a product that customers will demand at different prices and then chooses the price that should generate the highest total revenue. Obviously, the effectiveness of this method depends on the firm's ability to estimate demand accurately.

A firm may favor a demand-based pricing method called *price differentiation* if it wants to use more than one price in the marketing of a specific product. Price differentiation can be based on such considerations as time of the purchase, type of customer, or type of distribution channel. The use of so-called *dynamic pricing*—which raises prices during periods of high demand—is growing, especially for nontraditional car ride-sharing services like Uber and Lyft, as well as restaurants looking for a more even flow of customers throughout the day. Restaurants can utilize an app or online booking service such as Savored (now owned by Groupon) to offer customers a discount for dining at 5 pm on a Wednesday, when demand is low, rather than at 8 pm on a Friday, when demand is high.[21] For price differentiation to work, the company must be able to segment a market on the basis of different strengths of demand. The company must then be able to keep the segments separate enough so that those who buy at lower prices cannot sell to buyers in segments that are charged a higher price. This isolation can be accomplished, for example, by selling to geographically separated segments. However, the Internet has made price differentiation for products more difficult.

Compared with cost-based pricing, demand-based pricing places a firm in a better position to attain higher profit levels, assuming that buyers value the product at levels sufficiently above the product's cost. To use demand-based pricing, however, management must be able to estimate demand at different price levels, which may be difficult to assess accurately.

Why you might have paid twice as much for your plane ticket as the person sitting next to you. Airlines use demand-based pricing because the number of passengers that can be put on a specific flight is limited. The sophisticated software the companies use constantly re-prices seats based on the number of tickets customers are purchasing at any given time as well as historical data.

12-8c Competition-Based Pricing

In using *competition-based pricing*, an organization considers costs and revenue secondary to competitors' prices. The importance of this method increases if competing products are similar and the organization is serving markets in which price is the crucial variable of the marketing strategy. A firm that uses competition-based pricing may choose to sell below competitors' prices, slightly above competitors' prices, or at the same level. The price that your bookstore paid to the publishing company of this text was determined using competition-based pricing. Competition-based pricing can help to attain a pricing objective to increase sales or market share. Competition-based pricing may also be combined with other cost approaches to arrive at a profitable level.

> ### Concept Check
> ✓ List and explain the three kinds of pricing methods.
> ✓ Give an advantage and a disadvantage for each method.

12-9 PRICING STRATEGIES

A *pricing strategy* is a course of action designed to achieve pricing objectives. The extent to which a business uses any of the following strategies depends on its pricing and marketing objectives, the markets for its products, the degree of product differentiation, the product's life-cycle stage, and other factors. Figure 12-4 is a list

Learning Objective

12-9 Explain the different strategies available to companies for setting prices.

FIGURE 12-4 Types of Pricing Strategies

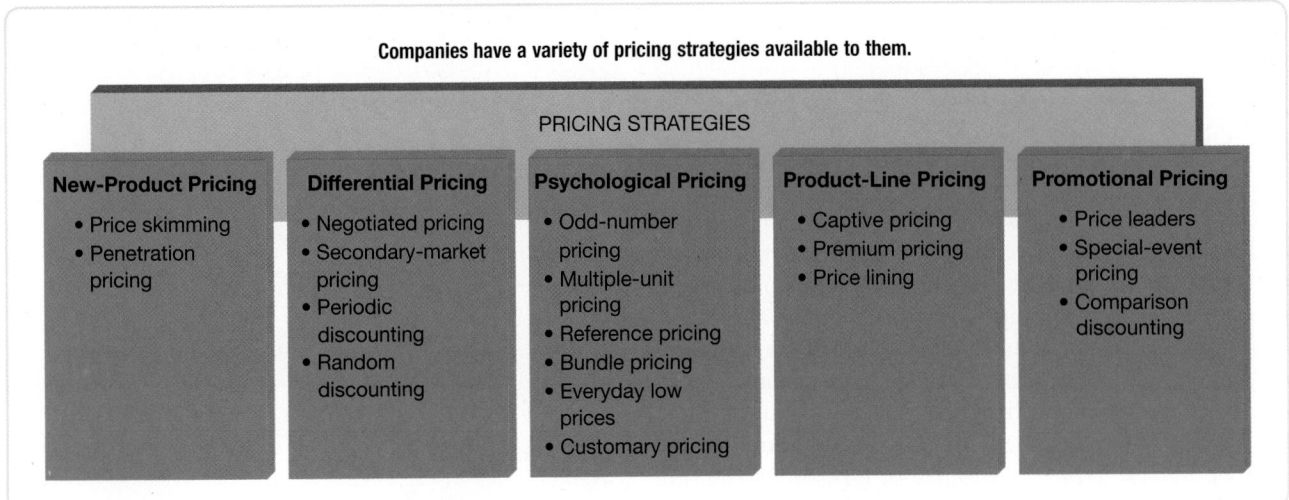

Companies have a variety of pricing strategies available to them.

PRICING STRATEGIES

New-Product Pricing	**Differential Pricing**	**Psychological Pricing**	**Product-Line Pricing**	**Promotional Pricing**
• Price skimming • Penetration pricing	• Negotiated pricing • Secondary-market pricing • Periodic discounting • Random discounting	• Odd-number pricing • Multiple-unit pricing • Reference pricing • Bundle pricing • Everyday low prices • Customary pricing	• Captive pricing • Premium pricing • Price lining	• Price leaders • Special-event pricing • Comparison discounting

of the major types of pricing strategies. We discuss these strategies in the remainder of this section.

12-9a New-Product Pricing

The two primary types of new-product pricing strategies are price skimming and penetration pricing. An organization can use either one, or even both, over a period of time.

PRICE SKIMMING Some consumers are willing to pay a high price for an innovative product, either because of its novelty or because of the prestige or status that ownership confers. **Price skimming** is the strategy of charging the highest possible price for a product during the introduction stage of its life-cycle. This strategy helps to recover the high costs of R&D quickly. In addition, a skimming policy may hold down demand for the product, which is helpful if the firm's production capacity is limited during the introduction stage. A danger is that a price-skimming strategy may make the product appear more lucrative than it actually is to potential competitors, encouraging more competitors to enter the market.

PENETRATION PRICING At the opposite extreme, **penetration pricing** is the strategy of setting a low price for a new product to build market share quickly. The seller hopes that building a large market share will discourage competitors from entering the market. If the low price stimulates sales, the firm also may be able to order longer production runs, which usually results in lower production costs per unit. A disadvantage of penetration pricing is that it places a firm in a less flexible position on pricing. It is more difficult to raise prices significantly than it is to lower them.

12-9b Differential Pricing

An important issue in pricing decisions is whether to use a single price or different prices for the same product. *Differential pricing* means charging different prices to different buyers for the same quality and quantity of product. For differential pricing to be effective, the market must consist of multiple segments with different price sensitivities. When this method is employed, caution should be used to avoid confusing or antagonizing customers. Differential pricing can take several forms, including negotiated pricing, secondary-market pricing, periodic discounting, and random discounting.

price skimming the strategy of charging the highest possible price for a product during the introduction stage of its life-cycle

penetration pricing the strategy of setting a low price for a new product

NEGOTIATED PRICING Negotiated pricing occurs when the final price is established through bargaining between the seller and the customer. Negotiated pricing occurs at all levels of distribution and is common in a variety of industries. Even when there is a predetermined stated price or a price list, manufacturers, wholesalers, and retailers may negotiate to establish the final sales price. Consumers commonly negotiate prices for houses, cars, and used equipment.

SECONDARY-MARKET PRICING Secondary-market pricing means setting one price for the primary target market and a different price for another market. The price charged in the secondary market is often, but not always, lower. Examples of secondary markets include a geographically isolated domestic market, a market in a foreign country, and a segment willing to purchase a product during off-peak times (such as "early bird" diners at restaurants and off-peak users of mobile phones).

PERIODIC DISCOUNTING Periodic discounting is the temporary reduction of prices on a patterned or systematic basis. For example, many retailers have annual holiday sales, and apparel stores have seasonal sales. From the marketer's point of view, a problem with periodic discounting is that customers can predict when the reductions will occur and may delay their purchases until they can take advantage of the lower prices.

RANDOM DISCOUNTING To alleviate the problem of customers holding off on purchases until a discount period, some organizations employ **random discounting**. That is, they reduce their prices temporarily on a nonsystematic basis. When price reductions of a product occur randomly, current users of that brand are not able to predict when reductions will occur. They therefore will not delay their purchases in anticipation of purchasing the product at a lower price. Marketers also use random discounting to attract new customers.

12-9c Psychological Pricing

Psychological pricing strategies encourage purchases based on emotional responses rather than on economically rational ones. These strategies are used primarily for consumer products rather than business products.

ODD-NUMBER PRICING Many retailers believe that consumers respond more positively to odd-number prices such as $4.99 than to whole-dollar prices such as $5. **Odd-number pricing** is the strategy of setting prices using odd numbers that are slightly below whole-dollar amounts. Nine and five are the most popular ending figures for odd-number prices.

MULTIPLE-UNIT PRICING Many retailers (supermarkets in particular) practice **multiple-unit pricing**, setting a single price for two or more units, such as two cans for 99 cents, rather than 50 cents per can. Especially for frequently purchased products, this strategy can increase the amount of an item that is sold. Customers who see the single price and who expect eventually to use more than one unit of the product will purchase multiple units to save money.

REFERENCE PRICING Reference pricing means pricing a product at a moderate level and positioning it next to a more expensive model or brand in the hope that the customer will use the higher price as a reference price (i.e., a comparison price). Because of the comparison, the customer is expected to view the moderate price favorably.

BUNDLE PRICING Bundle pricing is the packaging together of two or more products, usually of a complementary nature, to be sold for a single price. To be attractive to customers, the single price usually is considerably less than the sum of the prices of the individual products. Because the products are complementary, such as shampoo and conditioner, the customer will also find convenience value from purchasing them

negotiated pricing establishing a final price through bargaining

secondary-market pricing setting one price for the primary target market and a different price for another market

periodic discounting temporary reduction of prices on a patterned or systematic basis

random discounting temporary reduction of prices on an unsystematic basis

odd-number pricing the strategy of setting prices using odd numbers that are slightly below whole-dollar amounts

multiple-unit pricing the strategy of setting a single price for two or more units

reference pricing pricing a product at a moderate level and positioning it next to a more expensive model or brand

bundle pricing packaging together two or more complementary products and selling them for a single price

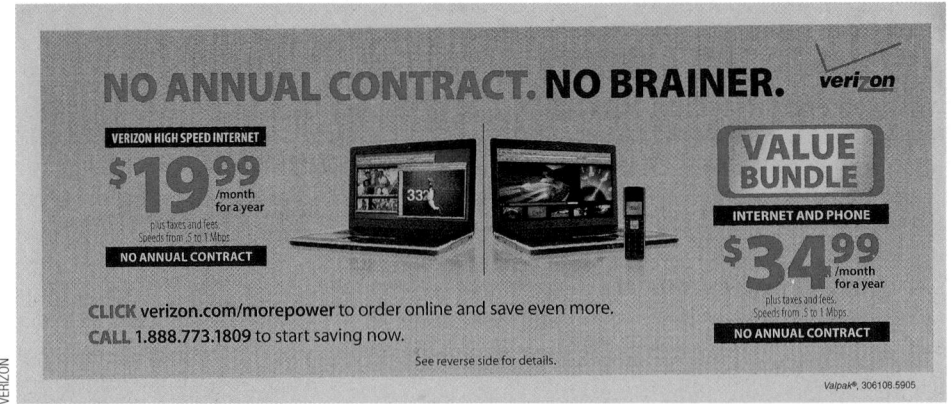

VERIZON

together. The firm may find bundling to be a valuable strategy because, by bundling slow-moving products with more popular ones, an organization can stimulate sales and increase revenues. Selling products as a package rather than individually also may result in cost savings for the organization. It is common for telecommunications providers to sell service bundles of cable, Internet, and phone service for one price.

EVERYDAY LOW PRICES (EDLPS) To reduce or eliminate frequent short-term price reductions, some organizations use an approach referred to as **everyday low prices (EDLPs)**. When EDLPs are used, a marketer sets a low price for its products on a consistent basis, rather than setting high prices and frequently discounting them. EDLPs, though not deeply discounted, are set far enough below competitors' prices to make customers feel confident that they are receiving a good deal. EDLPs are employed by retailers such as Walmart and by manufacturers such as Procter & Gamble. A company that uses EDLPs benefits from reduced promotional costs, reduced losses from frequent markdowns, and more stability in sales. However, customers may not trust the EDLP and assume the deal is merely a marketing gimmick.

CUSTOMARY PRICING In **customary pricing**, certain goods are priced primarily on the basis of tradition. It is not as common as it once was, but examples of customary, or traditional, prices are those set for candy bars and chewing gum.

12-9d Product-Line Pricing

Rather than considering products on an item-by-item basis when determining pricing strategies, some marketers employ product-line pricing. *Product-line pricing* means establishing and adjusting the prices of multiple products within a product line. Product-line pricing can provide marketers with flexibility in price setting. For example, marketers can set prices high so that one product is highly profitable, whereas another has a low price to increase market share.

When marketers employ product-line pricing, they have several strategies from which to choose. These include captive pricing, premium pricing, and price lining.

CAPTIVE PRICING When **captive pricing** is used, the basic product in a product line is priced low, but the price on the items required to operate or enhance it are higher. Two common examples of captive pricing are razor blades and printer ink. The razor handle and the printer are generally priced quite low, but the razor blades and the printer ink replacement cartridges are usually very expensive.

PREMIUM PRICING **Premium pricing** occurs when the highest-quality product or the most-versatile version of similar products in a product line is assigned the highest price. Other products in the line are priced to appeal to more price-sensitive shoppers, or to those seeking product-specific features. Marketers that employ

everyday low prices (EDLPs) setting a low price for products on a consistent basis

customary pricing pricing on the basis of tradition

captive pricing pricing the basic product in a product line low, but pricing related items at a higher level

premium pricing pricing the highest-quality or most-versatile products higher than other models in the product line

premium pricing often realize a significant portion of profits from the premium-priced products. Examples of product categories in which premium pricing is common are small kitchen appliances, beer, ice cream, and television cable service.

PRICE LINING Price lining is the strategy of selling goods only at certain predetermined prices that reflect definite price breaks. For example, a shop may sell men's ties only at $22 and $37. This strategy is used in clothing and accessory stores. It eliminates minor price differences from the buying decision—both for customers and for managers who buy merchandise to sell in these stores.

12-9e Promotional Pricing

Price, as an ingredient in the marketing mix, often is coordinated with promotions. The two variables sometimes are so interrelated that the pricing policy is promotion-oriented. Examples of promotional pricing include price leaders, special-event pricing, and comparison discounting.

PRICE LEADERS Sometimes a firm prices a few products below the usual markup, near cost, or below cost, which results in **price leaders**. This type of pricing is used most often in supermarkets and restaurants to attract customers by giving them especially low prices on a few items. Management hopes that customers will purchase regularly priced items as well, which will offset the reduced revenues from the price leaders.

SPECIAL-EVENT PRICING To increase sales volume, many organizations coordinate price with advertising or sales promotions for seasonal or special occasions. **Special-event pricing** involves advertised sales or price cutting linked to a holiday, season, or event. If the pricing objective is survival, then special sales events may be designed to generate the necessary operating capital.

COMPARISON DISCOUNTING Comparison discounting sets the price of a product at a specific level and compares it with a higher price. The higher price may be the product's previous price, the price of a competing brand, the product's price at another retail outlet, or a manufacturer's suggested retail price. Comparison discounting can significantly impact customers' decisions. Because this pricing strategy can lead to deceptive pricing practices, the Federal Trade Commission has established guidelines for comparison discounting. If the higher price against which the comparison is made is the price formerly charged for the product, sellers must have made the previous price available to customers for a reasonable period of time. If sellers present the higher price as the one charged by other retailers in the same trade area, they must be able to demonstrate the veracity of the claim. When they present the higher price as the manufacturer's suggested retail price, then the higher price must be similar to the price at which a reasonable proportion of the product was sold.

price lining the strategy of selling goods only at certain predetermined prices that reflect definite price breaks

price leaders products priced below the usual markup, near cost, or below cost

special-event pricing advertised sales or price cutting linked to a holiday, season, or event

comparison discounting setting a price at a specific level and comparing it with a higher price

Concept Check

✓ Identify the five categories of pricing strategies.

✓ Describe two specific pricing strategies in each category.

12-10 PRICING BUSINESS PRODUCTS

Many of the pricing issues discussed thus far in this chapter deal with pricing in general. However, setting prices for business products is different from setting prices for consumer products because of factors such as the size of purchases, transportation considerations, and geographic issues. We examine three types of pricing associated with business products: geographic pricing, transfer pricing, and discounting.

12-10a Geographic Pricing

Geographic pricing strategies deal with delivery costs. The pricing strategy that requires the buyer to pay the delivery costs is called *FOB origin pricing*. It stands for

Learning Objective

12-10 Describe three major types of pricing associated with business products.

"free on board at the point of origin," which means that the price does not include freight charges. Thus the buyer must pay the transportation costs from the seller's warehouse to the buyer's place of business. *FOB destination* indicates that the price does include freight charges, and thus the seller pays these charges.

12-10b Transfer Pricing

When one unit in an organization sells a product to another unit, **transfer pricing** occurs. The price is determined by calculating the cost of the product. A transfer price can vary depending on the types of costs included in the calculations. The choice of the costs to include depends on the company's management strategy and the nature of the units' interactions. An organization also must ensure that transfer pricing is fair to all units involved in the purchases.

12-10c Discounting

A **discount** is a deduction from an item's price. Producers and sellers offer a wide variety of discounts to their customers, including trade, quantity, cash, and seasonal discounts and allowances. *Trade discounts* are taken off the list prices that are offered to marketing intermediaries, or middlemen. *Quantity discounts* are discounts given to customers who buy in large quantities, which makes sellers' per-unit selling cost lower for larger purchases. *Cash discounts* are offered for prompt payment. A seller may offer a discount of "2/10, net 30," meaning that the buyer receives a 2 percent discount if the first payment occurs within ten days and is paid in full within 30 days. A *seasonal discount* is a price reduction to buyers who purchase out of season. This discount encourages off-season sales and ensures steady production throughout the year. An *allowance* is a reduction in price to achieve a desired goal. Trade-in allowances, for example, are price reductions granted for turning in used equipment when purchasing new equipment. Table 12-3 describes some of the reasons for using these discounting techniques and some examples.

Concept Check

✓ Describe the three types of pricing associated with business products.

✓ Differentiate between FOB origin and FOB destination pricing.

✓ Explain the five types of discounts for business products.

TABLE 12-3 Discounts Used for Business Markets

Type	Reasons for Use	Examples
Trade (functional)	To attract and maintain effective resellers by compensating them for performing certain functions, such as transportation, warehousing, selling, and providing credit.	A college bookstore pays about one-third less for a new textbook than the retail price.
Quantity	To encourage customers to buy large quantities when making purchases and, in the case of cumulative discounts, to encourage customer loyalty.	Companies that serve business markets offer a 2 percent discount if an account is paid within ten days.
Seasonal	To allow a marketer to use resources more efficiently by stimulating sales during off-peak periods.	Hotels offer companies deeply discounted accommodations for holding large meetings or conventions there during off-peak months.
Allowance	In the case of a trade-in allowance, to assist the buyer in making the purchase and potentially earn a profit on the resale of used equipment. In the case of a promotional allowance, to ensure that dealers participate in advertising and sales support programs.	A farm equipment dealer takes a farmer's used tractor as a trade-in on a new one. Nabisco pays a promotional allowance to a supermarket for setting up and maintaining a large end-of-aisle display for a two-week period.

Source: Adapted from William M. Pride and O. C. Ferrell, *Foundations of Marketing* (Mason, OH: South-Western/Cengage Learning, 2015), 351.

transfer pricing prices charged in sales between an organization's units

discount a deduction from the price of an item

Summary

12-1 Explain what a product is and how products are classified.

A product is everything one receives in an exchange, including all attributes and expected benefits. The product may be a manufactured item, a service, an idea, or a combination.

Products are classified according to their ultimate use. Classification affects a product's distribution, promotion, and pricing. Consumer goods, which include convenience, shopping, and specialty products, are purchased to satisfy personal and family needs. Business products are purchased for resale, in making other products, or for use in a firm's operations. Business products can be classified as raw materials, major equipment, accessory equipment, component parts, process materials, supplies, and services.

12-2 Discuss the product life-cycle and how it leads to new-product development.

Every product moves through a series of four stages—introduction, growth, maturity, and decline—which together form the product life-cycle. As the product progresses through these stages, its sales and profitability increase, peak, and decline. Marketers keep track of the life-cycle stage of products in order to estimate when a new product should be introduced to replace a declining one.

12-3 Define product line and product mix and distinguish between the two.

A product line is a group of similar products marketed by a firm. They are related to each other in the way they are produced, marketed, and consumed. The firm's product mix includes all the products it offers for sale. The width of a mix is the number of product lines it contains. The depth of the mix is the average number of individual products within each line.

12-4 Identify the methods available for changing a product mix.

Customer satisfaction and organizational objectives require marketers to develop, adjust, and maintain an effective product mix. Marketers may improve a product mix by changing existing products, deleting products, and developing new products.

New products are developed through a series of seven steps. The first step, idea generation, involves developing a pool of product ideas. Screening, the second step, removes from consideration those product ideas that do not match organizational goals or resources. Concept testing, the third step, is a phase in which a sample of potential buyers is exposed to a proposed product through a written or oral description in order to determine their initial reactions and buying intentions. The fourth step, business analysis, generates information about potential sales, costs, and profits. During the development step, the product idea is transformed into mock-ups and prototypes to determine if product production is technically feasible and can be produced at reasonable costs. Test marketing is an actual launch of the product in selected cities chosen for their representativeness of target markets. Finally, during commercialization, plans for full-scale production and marketing are refined and implemented. Most product failures result from inadequate product planning and development.

12-5 Explain the uses and importance of branding, packaging, and labeling.

A brand is a name, term, symbol, design, or any combination of these that identifies a seller's products as distinct from those of other sellers. Brands can be classified as manufacturer brands, store brands, or generic brands. A firm can choose between two branding strategies—individual or family branding, which are used to associate (or *not* associate) particular products with existing products, producers, or intermediaries. Packaging protects goods, increases consumer convenience, and enhances marketing efforts by communicating product features, uses, benefits, and image. Labeling provides customers with product information, some of which is required by law.

12-6 Describe the economic basis of pricing and the means by which sellers can control prices and buyers' perceptions of prices.

A product is a set of attributes and benefits that has been designed to satisfy its market while earning a profit for its seller. Each product has a price at which it balances consumers' desires and expectations with a firm's need to make a profit. The price of a product is the amount of money a seller is willing to accept in exchange for the product at a given time and under given circumstances. Price thus serves the function of *allocator*. It allocates goods and services among those who are willing and able to buy them. It allocates financial resources among producers according to how well they satisfy customers' needs. Price also helps customers to allocate their own financial resources among products.

Price competition occurs when a seller emphasizes a product's low price and sets a price that equals or beats competitors' prices. To use this approach most effectively, a seller must have the flexibility to change prices often. Price competition allows a marketer to set prices based on demand. The Internet has made it more difficult than ever for sellers to compete on price. Non-price competition is based on factors other than price. It is used most effectively when a seller can make its product stand out from the competition by differentiating product quality, customer service, promotion, packaging, or other features. Buyers must be able to perceive these distinguishing characteristics and consider them desirable. Buyers' perceptions of prices are affected by the importance of the product to them, the range of prices they consider acceptable, their perceptions of competing products, and their association of quality with price.

12-7 Identify the major pricing objectives used by businesses.

Objectives of pricing include survival, profit maximization, target return on investment, achieving market goals, and maintaining the status quo. Firms sometimes have to price products to survive, which usually requires cutting prices to attract customers. The return on investment (ROI) is the amount earned as a result of the investment in developing and marketing the product. Some firms set an annual percentage ROI as the pricing goal. Other firms use pricing to maintain or increase their market share. In industries in which price stability is important, firms often price their products by charging about the same as competitors.

12-8 Examine the three major pricing methods that firms employ.

The three major pricing methods are cost-based pricing, demand-based pricing, and competition-based pricing. When cost-based pricing is employed, a proportion of the cost is added to the total cost to determine the selling price. When demand-based pricing is used, the price will be higher when demand is higher, and the price will be lower when demand is lower. A firm that uses competition-based pricing may choose to price below competitors' prices, at the same level as competitors' prices, or slightly above competitors' prices.

12-9 Explain the different strategies available to companies for setting prices.

Pricing strategies fall into five categories: new-product pricing, differential pricing, psychological pricing, product-line pricing, and promotional pricing. Price skimming and penetration pricing are two strategies used for pricing new products. Differential pricing can be accomplished through negotiated pricing, secondary-market pricing, periodic discounting, and random discounting. Types of psychological pricing strategies are odd-number pricing, multiple-unit pricing, reference pricing, bundle pricing, everyday low prices, and customary pricing. Product-line pricing can be achieved through captive pricing, premium pricing, and price lining. The major types of promotional pricing are price-leader pricing, special-event pricing, and comparison discounting.

12-10 Describe three major types of pricing associated with business products.

Setting prices for business products is different from setting prices for consumer products because of several factors, including the size of purchases, transportation considerations, and geographic issues. The three types of pricing associated with business products are geographic pricing, transfer pricing, and discounting.

Key Terms

You should now be able to define and give an example relevant to each of the following terms:

product (330)	business service (332)	manufacturer (or producer) brand (341)	express warranty (346)
consumer product (331)	product life-cycle (332)	store (or private) brand (341)	price (346)
business product (331)	product line (335)	generic product (or generic brand) (341)	price competition (347)
convenience product (331)	product mix (335)	brand loyalty (342)	non-price competition (347)
shopping product (331)	product modification (336)	brand equity (342)	product differentiation (347)
specialty product (332)	line extension (337)	individual branding (344)	markup (349)
raw material (332)	product deletion (337)	family branding (344)	breakeven quantity (350)
major equipment (332)	brand (341)	brand extension (344)	total revenue (350)
accessory equipment (332)	brand name (341)	packaging (344)	fixed cost (350)
component part (332)	brand mark (341)	labeling (346)	variable cost (350)
process material (332)	trademark (341)		total cost (350)
supply (332)	trade name (341)		price skimming (352)

penetration pricing (352)

negotiated pricing (353)

secondary-market pricing (353)

periodic discounting (353)

random discounting (353)

odd-number pricing (353)

multiple-unit pricing (353)

reference pricing (353)

bundle pricing (353)

everyday low prices (EDLPs) (354)

customary pricing (354)

captive pricing (354)

premium pricing (354)

price lining (355)

price leaders (355)

special-event pricing (355)

comparison discounting (355)

transfer pricing (356)

discount (356)

Discussion Questions

1. What does the purchaser of a product obtain besides the good, service, or idea itself?
2. What major factor determines whether a product is a consumer or a business product?
3. What are the four stages of the product life-cycle? How can a firm determine which stage a particular product is in?
4. Under what conditions does product modification work best?
5. Why do products have to be deleted from a product mix?
6. Why must firms introduce new products?
7. What is the difference between manufacturer brands and store brands? Between family branding and individual branding?
8. What is the difference between a line extension and a brand extension?
9. For what purposes is labeling used?
10. Compare and contrast the characteristics of price and non-price competition.
11. How might buyers' perceptions of price influence pricing decisions?
12. What are the five major categories of pricing strategies? Give at least two examples of specific strategies that fall into each category.
13. Identify and describe the main types of discounts that are used in the pricing of business products.
14. Some firms do not delete products until they become financially threatening. What problems may result from this practice?
15. Under what conditions would a firm be most likely to use non-price competition?
16. Under what conditions would a business most likely decide to employ one of the differential pricing strategies?
17. For what types of products are psychological pricing strategies most likely to be used?

Video Case
Mi Ola Strives for a Marketing Splash

Helena Fogarty got the idea for her startup bikini manufacturing firm, Mi Ola ("My Wave"), when she learned to surf while on vacation from her fast-paced New York City fashion career. As much as she enjoyed the fun of riding a wave, she was frustrated with the fit and durability of her swimwear. Based on her experience, Fogarty identified a profitable opportunity to make a business splash with colorful bikini tops and bottoms designed to look good and to stay in place, in and out of the surf.

The target market is the segment of women who are active in water sports and seek the benefits of stylish swimwear that fits properly, wears well wash after wash, and protects the skin. Fogarty manufactures her bikinis domestically so she can be closer to her U.S. customers, monitor product quality, and have easy access to the newest fabrics. For added appeal and differentiation, she markets her products as "Made in America."

Being the head designer, not just the founder, Fogarty puts her own personal taste into every product she creates. She plans for new products by researching what female surfers want and need, analyzing their comments and complaints about competing products, and coming up with ideas for solving customer problems. Once she develops new designs, she asks female surfers to test the tops and bottoms and then provide in-depth feedback about how the bikini pieces look, how they fit, how they feel, and how they can be improved. If a new item receives mixed reactions, she probes for more information. But if she hears mostly negative comments, she'll take that product back to the drawing board for a redesign. Because she's in the fashion business, Fogarty moves quickly to catch the newest trends while building in innovative features for functionality valued by women surfers.

Mi Ola is a new and unknown brand, so Fogarty is using a combination of social media and public relations to build awareness and attract the attention of retailers and customers alike. She appreciates the ability to post product photos on Facebook and, within a short time, read comments and count "likes" to gauge customer reactions. In addition, she posts product updates on Twitter and harnesses the visual qualities of Instagram, Pinterest, and YouTube to convey her brand's unique image of fashion and function.

Fogarty's background includes working with top style brands, such as Chanel, which means she understands that the fashion world revolves around the introduction of seasonal clothing collections. To be competitive, she must have her products ready during the periods when store buyers typically review new collections and place orders. As Mi Ola grows, she has had to make difficult decisions about how many pieces of each design, each color, and each size she will pay to manufacture. Here, the objective is to invest in sufficient inventory to meet projected demand without having an ocean of unsold bikinis left at the end of the season.

The entrepreneur is realistic about the need to make marketing decisions without complete information and within the framework of a young company's limited resources. Fogarty believes in careful analysis, and she consults her expert advisory board for advice—but she is also determined to proceed aggressively toward higher market share month after month.[22]

Questions

1. How would you classify Mi Ola's consumer products? Explain your answer.
2. In which stage of the product life-cycle would you place Mi Ola's products? In this stage, would you expect Helena Fogarty to put more emphasis on developing new products, deleting existing products, or modifying existing products? Why?
3. What is Helena Fogarty doing to build brand equity for Mi Ola?

Building Skills for Career Success

1. Social Media Exercise

Creating and pricing products that satisfy customers

As a division of PepsiCo that manufacturers, markets, and sells thousands of snack food products, Frito-Lay has been a front-runner in social media marketing for the past few years. The company started its Lay's "Do Us a Flavor" campaign in 2012 to boost consumer interaction and create a larger presence on social media. The company encouraged consumers to submit a new flavor of Lay's chips that they would like to try. Various flavors were then submitted such as Chicken and Waffles, Spicy Taco, and even Cappuccino. The company chose four finalists and had their internal culinary experts create the finalists' flavors to be sold in stores and voted on by consumers. Consumers could vote by visiting the company's website or using the hashtag of their favorite flavor on various social media sites such as Twitter, Facebook, and Instagram. After the voting period, the winning flavor was announced and each finalist was rewarded with a prize. Based on the success of this first campaign, Frito-Lay has held the competition numerous times in many countries around the world and will likely continue this trend.

1. Visit the https://www.dousaflavor.com website. What do you think are the most important elements of this promotional program?
2. What can other companies learn from Frito-Lay's utilization of crowdsourcing for promotion purposes?

2. Building Team Skills

In his book, *The Post-Industrial Society*, Peter Drucker wrote:

Society, community, and family are all conserving institutions. They try to maintain stability and to prevent, or at least slow down, change. But the organization of the post-capitalist society of organizations is a destabilizer. Because its function is to put knowledge to work—on tools, processes, and products; on work; on knowledge itself—it must be organized for constant change. It must be organized for innovation.

New product development is important in this process of systematically abandoning the past and building a future. Current customers can be sources of ideas for new goods and services and ways of improving existing ones.

Assignment

1. Working in teams of five to seven, brainstorm ideas for new products for your college.
2. Construct questions to ask currently enrolled students (your customers). Sample questions might include:
   a. Why did you choose this college?
   b. How can this college be improved?
   c. What products do you wish were available?
3. Conduct the survey and review the results.
4. Prepare a list of improvements and/or new products for your college.

3. Researching Different Careers

Standard & Poor's Industry Surveys, designed for investors, provide insight into various industries and the companies that compete within those industries. The "Basic Analysis" section gives overviews of industry trends and issues. The other sections define some basic industry terms, report the latest revenues and earnings of more than 1,000 companies, and occasionally list major reference books and trade associations.

Assignment

1. Identify an industry in which you might like to work.
2. Find the industry in *Standard & Poor's*. (*Note: Standard & Poor's* uses broad categories of industry. For example, an apparel or home-furnishings store would be included under "Retail" or "Textiles.")
3. Identify the following:
   a. Trends and issues in the industry
   b. Opportunities and/or problems that might arise in the industry in the next five years
   c. Major competitors within the industry. (These companies are your potential employers.)
4. Prepare a report of your findings.

Endnotes

1. Based on information in Jennifer Reingold, "Watch Out Disney: This Toy Startup's Coming for You," *Fortune*, November 26, 2014, http://fortune.com/2014/11/26/goldieblox-toy-startup/ (accessed July 7, 2015); "R.I. Woman's GoldieBlox Now Has Free Mobile App," *Providence Journal*, November 17, 2014, www.providencejournal.com; Ariel Schwartz, "How GoldieBlox Went from a Scrappy Kickstarter to Making Important Toys for Girls," *Fast Company*, September 15, 2014, http://www.fastcoexist.com/3035356/how-goldieblox-went-from-a-scrappy-kickstarter-to-making-important-toys-for-girls (accessed July 7, 2015); Bourree Lam, "Do Toy Companies Need More Women at the Top?" *The Atlantic*, September 19, 2014, http://www.theatlantic.com/business/archive/2014/09/do-toy-companies-need-more-women-at-the-top/380295/ (accessed July 12, 2015); Adam Vaccaro, "The Girls-Only Toy Maker That's Exploding Stereotypes," *Inc.*, April 23, 2014, http://www.inc.com/audacious-companies/adam-vaccaro/goldieblox.html (accessed July 12, 2015).

2. Anne Marie Mohan, "New Floor Cleaning Bottle Triples Weiman's Sales," *Packaging World*, February 2, 2015, http://www.packworld.com/package-design/redesign/new-floor-cleaning-bottle-triples-weimans-sales (accessed June 29, 2015).

3. Ben Worthen, "What's Gone Wrong with H-P?" *Wall Street Journal*, November 6, 2012, http://online.wsj.com/article/SB10001424052972070204755404578101943429107284.html (accessed July 12, 2015); Jon Swartz, "HP to Eliminate Another 11,000 to 16,000 Jobs," *USA Today*, May 23, 2014, http://www.usatoday.com/story/tech/2014/05/22/hewlett-packard-ceo-meg-whitman-quarterly-results/9443279/ (accessed June 29, 2015).

4. Procter & Gamble, http://www.pg.com/en_US/brands/all_brands.shtml (accessed February 5, 2015).

5. Campbell Soup Company, "Campbell to Launch More than 200 New Products in Fiscal 2015 to Meet Evolving Consumer Preferences," Press Release, July 21, 2014, http://www.campbellsoupcompany.com/newsroom/press-releases/2014/072114-campbell-to-launch-more-than-200-new-products-in-fiscal-2015 (accessed June 29, 2015).

6. Bruce Horovitz, "Cheerios Drops Genetically Modified Ingredients," *USA Today*, February 2, 2014, http://www.usatoday.com/story/money/business/2014/01/02/cheerios-gmos-cereals/4295739/ (accessed July 7, 2015).

7. Campbell Soup Company, "Campbell to Launch More than 200 New Products in Fiscal 2015 to Meet Evolving Consumer Preferences."

8. Robert Channick, "Encyclopaedia Britannica Sees Digital Growth, Aims to Draw New Users," *Chicago Tribune*, September 10, 2014, http://www.chicagotribune.com/business/ct-britannica-digital-0911-biz-20140910-story.html#page=1 (accessed July 7, 2015).

9. Thomas Black, "The Slow Takeoff of Robert Bass's Supersonic Business Jet," *Business Week*, November 13, 2014, http://www.businessweek.com/articles/2014-11-13/aerion-as2-supersonic-business-jet-could-fly-by-2019#r=most popular? (accessed July 7, 2015).

10. Leah Yamshon, "HealthKit App Lark Talks to You to Help You Stay Active," *MacWorld*, October 2, 2014, http://www.macworld.com/article/2690816/healthkit-app-lark-talks-to-you-to-help-you-stay-active.html (accessed July 7, 2015); Larklife, Lark Technologies, http://lark.com/ (accessed February 5, 2015).

11. Boston Beer Company, "Samuel Adams Expands Brewing the American Dream Program," Press Release, April 3, 2014, via Brewbound, http://www.brewbound.com/news/samuel-adams-expands-brewing-the-american-dream-program (accessed June 29, 2015).

12. "Whole Foods to Try Price Cuts at Some Stores," *Richmond Times-Dispatch*, October 2, 2014, http://www.timesdispatch.com/business/retail/whole-foods-to-try-price-cuts-at-some-stores/article_a991ba28-4a34-11e4-a74e-001a4bcf6878.html (accessed June 29, 2015).

13. JP Mangalindan, "Why Amazon's Fire Phone Failed," *Fortune*, September 29, 2014, http://fortune.com/2014/09/29/why-amazons-fire-phone-failed/ (accessed June 29, 2015).

14. "Store Brands Facts," Private Label Manufacturers Association (PLMA), http://plma.com/storeBrands/facts14a.html (accessed February 3, 2015); Bonnie S. Benwick, "Store Brands, the (Now) Welcome Option," *Washington Post*, February 25, 2014, http://www.washingtonpost.com/lifestyle/food/store-brands-the-now-welcome-option/2014/02/24/be4808c6-99b0-11e3-80ac-63a8ba7f7942_story.html (accessed July 7, 2015).

15. Timothy Stenovec, "Facebook Didn't Ruin Instagram, Actually Made It 10 Times as Big," *Huffington Post*, December 10, 2014, http://www.huffingtonpost.com/2014/12/10/facebook-instagram_n_6304884.html (accessed July 7, 2015).

16. "Pet Insurance," Iams, http://www.iams.com/pet-health/dog-article/save-on-health-insurance-for-pets (accessed February 3, 2015).

17. Replenish, http://myreplenish.com/ (accessed December 15, 2014); CleanPath, http://mycleanpath.com/ (accessed December 15, 2014).

18. "5 Questions About #5 Plastic Cups," Stonyfield Farm, http://www.stonyfield.com/blog/5-cups/ (accessed December 15, 2014).

19. Jennifer Valentino-Devries, Jeremy Singer-Vine, and Ashkan Soltani, "Websites Vary Prices, Deals Based on User Information," *Wall Street Journal*, December 23, 2012, http://online.wsj.com/article/SB10001424127887323777204578189391813881534.html (accessed July 7, 2015); Lindsay Wise, "Online Prices Can Change by the Hour, and by the Shopper," *Kansas City Star*, December 1, 2012, http://www.kansascity.com/2012/12/01/3944160/online-prices-can-change-by-the.html (accessed June 29, 2015).

20. Vibram Five Fingers, www.vibramfivefingers.com/index.htm (accessed February 6, 2015).

21. Donna Fenn, "Some Business Go Creative on Prices, Applying Technology," *New York Times*, January 22, 2014, http://www.nytimes.com/2014/01/23/business/smallbusiness/with-new-thinking-and-technology-some-businesses-get-creative-with-pricing.html?_r=0 (accessed July 7, 2015).

22. Based on information in Michella Ore, "Polished Role Models: Helena Fogarty," *Polish Magazine*, July 1, 2014, http://www.polishmagazine.com/2014/07/mi-ola/ (accessed July 12, 2015); Bernadette Tansey, "Turning a Business into a One-Way Ticket to Paradise," *CNBC.com*, July 2, 2012, http://www.cnbc.com/id/48018693 (accessed July 12, 2015); Mi Ola website at http://mi-ola.com (accessed July 7, 2015); Cengage Learning, *Mi Ola Swimwear* video.

CHAPTER 13

Distributing and Promoting Products

Why Should You Care?

Not only is it important to create and maintain a mix of products that satisfies customers but also to make these products available at the *right place* and *time* and to communicate with customers effectively.

Learning Objectives

Once you complete this chapter, you will be able to:

13-1 Identify the various distribution channels and explain the concept of market coverage.

13-2 Understand how supply-chain management facilitates partnering among channel members.

13-3 Discuss the need for wholesalers, describe the services they provide, and identify the major types of wholesalers.

13-4 Distinguish among the major types of retailers and shopping centers.

13-5 Explain the five most important physical distribution activities.

13-6 Explain how integrated marketing communications works to have the maximum impact on the customer.

13-7 Understand the basic elements of the promotion mix.

13-8 Explain the three types of advertising and describe the major steps of developing an advertising campaign.

13-9 Recognize the kinds of salespersons, the steps in the personal-selling process, and the major sales management tasks.

13-10 Describe sales promotion objectives and methods.

13-11 Understand the types and uses of public relations.

INSIDE BUSINESS

Under Armour Gaining in the Race against Nike

Aiming to become the world's largest sports brand, Under Armour has a multipronged distribution and promotion strategy to reach more customers in more markets. The fast-growing Baltimore-based company is celebrating its 20th anniversary and is fast approaching its goal of generating $4 billion in annual revenue. Led by founder and CEO Kevin Plank, Under Armour's mission is "[t]o make all athletes better through passion, design, and the relentless pursuit of innovation."

Under Armour puts the brand at the heart of its marketing, targeting performance-oriented consumers and professional athletes with an ever-widening range of apparel, footwear, and sports accessory products. The firm's two largest retail partners, Dick's Sporting Goods and Sports Authority, feature Under Armour products in special in-store branded departments. These store areas emphasize the width and breadth of the product mix, and focus attention on the brand's associations with performance and innovation.

In addition to distributing products through sporting-goods stores, Under Armour operates its own Brand House stores to showcase a full range of products in a carefully-controlled retail atmosphere. For example, the 10,000-square-foot Brand House in New York City is located in a trendy area and features interactive digital displays, a huge media wall, and a private area where VIPs can receive personalized attention. Under Armour also maintains online stores to sell directly to consumers in many nations.

To support its aggressive growth strategy, Under Armour will soon open a third U.S. distribution center in Tennessee, supplementing the current distribution centers in Maryland and California. The new million-square-foot facility will house logistical and transportation functions and can be doubled in size if needed, as Under Armour continues its race to overtake industry-leader Nike. Although the company's advertising budget is less than one-third that of Nike's budget, Under Armour's innovation image and memorable multimedia and digital campaigns—such as "I Will What I Want" for its women's products—help it stand out in this intensely competitive marketplace.[1]

Did You Know?

Founded in 1996, Under Armour currently rings up $3 billion in annual sales in the Americas, Europe, Australia, and Asia.

Successful companies, like Under Armour, use a particular approach to distribution and marketing channels that gives them a sustainable competitive advantage. More than two million firms in the United States help to move products from producers to consumers. Store chains such as Dollar General, Starbucks, Old Navy, and Walmart operate retail outlets where consumers make purchases. Some retailers, such as Avon Products and Amway, send their salespeople to the homes of customers. Other retailers, such as Lands' End and REI, sell in stores, online, through catalogs, or a combination of the three. Still others, such as Amazon, sell exclusively online.

In this chapter, we first examine the various distribution channels through which products move as they progress from producer to ultimate user, as well as supply-chain management. Then we discuss marketing intermediaries, wholesalers and retailers, and examine major types of shopping centers. Next, we focus on retailers, including the types of retailing stores, nonstore retailing, and shopping centers. We then explore the physical distribution function and the major modes of transportation that are used to move goods. Then we discuss integrated marketing communication and the elements of the promotion mix: advertising, personal selling, sales promotion, and public relations.

13-1 DISTRIBUTION CHANNELS AND MARKET COVERAGE

Learning Objective

13-1 Identify the various distribution channels and explain the concept of market coverage.

distribution channel (or marketing channel) a sequence of marketing organizations that directs a product from the producer to the ultimate user

middleman (or marketing intermediary) a marketing organization that links a producer and user within a marketing channel

merchant middleman a middleman that actually takes title to products by buying them

functional middleman a middleman that helps in the transfer of ownership of products but does not take title to the products

retailer a middleman that buys from producers or other middlemen and sells to consumers

A **distribution channel (or marketing channel)** is a sequence of marketing organizations that directs a product from the producer to the ultimate user. Every marketing channel begins with the producer and ends with either the consumer or the business user.

A marketing organization that links a producer and user within a marketing channel is called a **middleman (or marketing intermediary)**. For the most part, middlemen are concerned with the transfer of *ownership* of products. A **merchant middleman** (or, more simply, a *merchant*) is an intermediary that actually takes title to products by buying them. A **functional middleman**, on the other hand, helps in the transfer of ownership of products but does not take title to the products.

13-1a Commonly Used Distribution Channels

Different channels of distribution generally are used to move consumer and business products. Figure 13-1 illustrates the most common distribution channels for consumer and business products.

PRODUCER TO CONSUMER This channel, often called the *direct channel*, includes no marketing intermediaries. Practically all services and a few consumer goods are distributed through a direct channel. Examples of marketers that sell goods directly to consumers include Mary Kay Cosmetics and Avon Products.

Producers sell directly to consumers for several reasons. They can better control the quality and price of their products. They do not have to pay (through discounts) for the services of intermediaries. Also, they can maintain closer relationships with customers.

PRODUCER TO RETAILER TO CONSUMER A **retailer** is a middleman that buys from producers or other middlemen and sells to consumers. Producers sell directly to retailers when the retailers are large enough to buy in large quantities.

FIGURE 13-1 Distribution Channels

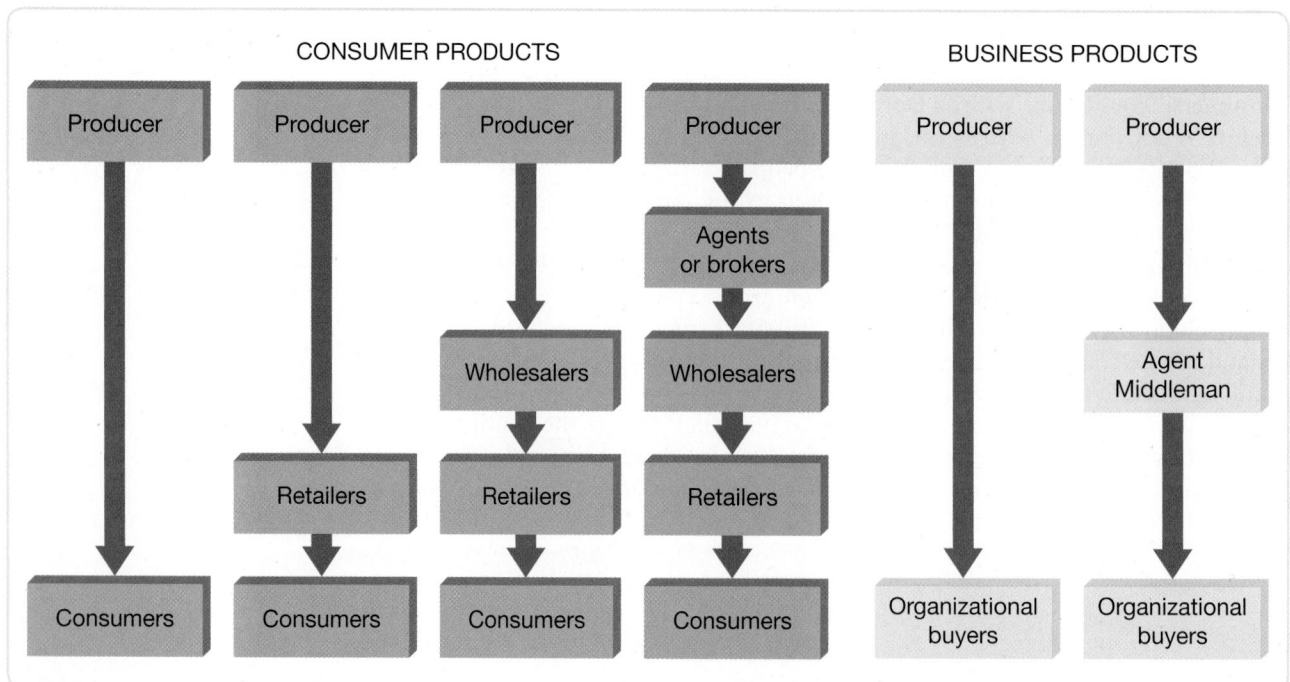

This channel is used most often for products that are bulky, such as furniture and automobiles, for which additional handling would increase selling costs. It is also the usual channel for perishable products, such as fruits and vegetables, and for high-fashion products that must reach the consumer in the shortest possible time.

PRODUCER TO WHOLESALER TO RETAILER TO CONSUMER This channel is known as the *traditional channel* because many consumer goods (especially convenience goods) pass through wholesalers to retailers. A **wholesaler** is a middleman that sells products to other firms. These firms may be retailers, industrial users, or other wholesalers. A producer uses wholesalers when its products are carried by so many retailers that the producer cannot manage and distribute all of them. For example, chewing gum or soft drink manufacturers may use this type of channel.

PRODUCER TO AGENT TO WHOLESALER TO RETAILER TO CONSUMER Producers can use agents to reach wholesalers. Agents are functional middlemen that do not take title to products and that are compensated by commissions paid by producers. Often the products with which agents deal are inexpensive, frequently purchased items. For example, to reach a large number of potential customers, a small manufacturer of gas-powered lawn edgers might choose to use agents to market them to wholesalers. The wholesalers then sell the product to a large network of retailers. This channel is also used for seasonal products (such as Christmas decorations) and by producers that do not have in-house sales forces.

PRODUCER TO ORGANIZATIONAL BUYER In this direct channel, the manufacturer's own sales force sells directly to organizational buyers, or business users. Heavy machinery, airplanes, and major equipment usually are distributed in this way. The very short channel allows the producer to provide customers with expert and timely services, such as delivery, machinery installation, and repairs.

PRODUCER TO AGENT MIDDLEMAN TO ORGANIZATIONAL BUYER Manufacturers use this channel to distribute such items as operating supplies, accessory equipment, small tools, and standardized parts. The agent is an independent intermediary between the producer and the user. Agents generally represent sellers.

wholesaler a middleman that sells products to other firms

USING MULTIPLE CHANNELS
Often a manufacturer uses different distribution channels to reach different market segments. For example, candy bars may be sold through channels containing wholesalers and retailers, as well as channels in which the producer sells them directly through large retailers. Multiple channels are also used to increase sales or to capture a larger share of the market with the goal of selling as much merchandise as possible.

13-1b Level of Market Coverage

As with other marketing decisions, producers must analyze all relevant factors when deciding which distribution channels and intermediaries to use. Marketers should weigh the firm's production capabilities and marketing resources, the target

ISTOCKPHOTO.COM/MEDIAPHOTOS

Using multiple marketing channels. Sometimes, companies use multiple marketing channels rather than just one. College textbook publishers often sell their products through multiple marketing channels. This textbook can be purchased directly from the publisher. It can also be purchased at a campus bookstore, or through Amazon.

market and buying patterns of potential customers, and the product itself. After evaluating these factors, the producer chooses the correct level of *intensity of market coverage*. Then the producer selects channels and intermediaries to implement that coverage.

Intensive distribution is the use of all available outlets for a product. It gives a product the widest possible exposure in the marketplace. The manufacturer saturates the market by selling to any intermediary of good financial standing that is willing to stock and sell the product. For the consumer, intensive distribution means being able to shop at a convenience store and spend minimum time selecting and buying the product. Many convenience goods, including candy, gum, and soft drinks, are distributed intensively.

Selective distribution is the use of only a portion of the available outlets for a product in each geographic area. Manufacturers of goods such as furniture, major home appliances, and clothing typically prefer selective distribution. For instance, you may prefer Hanes brand socks, which are distributed through retailers such as Target and Sears.

Exclusive distribution is the use of only a single retail outlet for a product in a large geographic area. Exclusive distribution usually is limited to prestigious products. It is appropriate, for instance, for specialty goods such as grand pianos, fine china, and expensive jewelry. The producer usually places many requirements (such as inventory levels, sales training, service quality, and warranty procedures) on exclusive dealers. For example, Patek Philippe watches, which may sell for $500,000 or more, are available in only a few select locations.

13-2 PARTNERING THROUGH SUPPLY-CHAIN MANAGEMENT

Supply-chain management is a long-term partnership among channel members working together to create a distribution system that reduces inefficiencies, costs, and redundancies while creating a competitive advantage and satisfying customers. Supply-chain management requires cooperation throughout the entire marketing channel, including manufacturing, research, sales, advertising, and shipping. Supply chains focus not only on producers, wholesalers, retailers, and customers, but also on component-parts suppliers, shipping companies, communication companies, and other organizations that participate in product distribution. Suppliers strongly influence what items retail stores carry. This phenomenon, called *category management*, is a common practice for mass merchandisers, supermarkets, and convenience stores. Through category management, the retailer asks a supplier in a particular category how to stock the shelves. Many retailers and suppliers believe this process enhances efficiency.

Traditionally, buyers and sellers have had an adversarial relationship when negotiating purchases. Supply-chain management, however, encourages cooperation in reducing the costs of inventory, transportation, administration, and handling. It also speeds order-cycle times, and increases profits for all channel members. When buyers, sellers, marketing intermediaries, and facilitating agencies work together, customers' needs regarding delivery, scheduling, packaging, and other requirements are better met. Meeting customer needs through a highly innovative, fast, and efficient distribution system helped clothing company Zara grow to be the world's largest fashion retailer. Trendy items are produced close to the market so they can be on the shelves quickly, and thus command the highest prices, while less trendy items are made where they can be produced most cheaply.[2]

Technology has enhanced the implementation of supply-chain management significantly. Through computerized integrated information sharing, channel members reduce costs and improve customer service. Firms can take advantage of hundreds of

Concept Check

✓ How do the different types of middlemen link a producer to a user within a marketing channel?

✓ Describe the six distribution channels. Give an example of each.

✓ Explain the three intensities of market coverage. Which types of products are generally associated with each of the different intensity levels (convenience, shopping, or specialty)?

Learning Objective

13-2 Understand how supply-chain management facilitates partnering among channel members.

intensive distribution the use of all available outlets for a product

selective distribution the use of only a portion of the available outlets for a product in each geographic area

exclusive distribution the use of only a single retail outlet for a product in a large geographic area

supply-chain management long-term partnership among channel members working together to create a distribution system that reduces inefficiencies, costs, and redundancies while creating a competitive advantage and satisfying customers

electronic trading communities comprised of businesses selling to other businesses, including auctions, exchanges, e-procurement hubs, and multisupplier online catalogs. As many major industries transform their processes, the end result is increased productivity by reducing inventory, shortening cycle time, and reducing wasted human effort.

Concept Check

✓ How does supply-chain management encourage cooperation between buyers and sellers?

✓ How has technology enhanced the implementation of supply-chain management?

13-3 MARKETING INTERMEDIARIES: WHOLESALERS

Wholesalers are possibly the most misunderstood of marketing intermediaries. Producers sometimes try to cut out wholesalers in favor of dealing directly with retailers or consumers. However, wholesalers increase distribution efficiency. The marketing activities performed by wholesalers *must* be performed by other channel members if wholesalers are eliminated, which means that cutting out wholesalers may not reduce distribution costs.

13-3a Wholesalers Provide Services to Retailers and Manufacturers

Wholesalers help retailers by

- Buying in large quantities and selling to retailers in smaller quantities and delivering goods to retailers.
- Stocking in one place the variety of goods that retailers otherwise would have to buy from many producers.
- Providing assistance in other vital areas, including promotion, market information, and financial aid.

Wholesalers help manufacturers by

- Performing functions similar to those provided to retailers.
- Providing a sales force, reducing inventory costs, assuming credit risks, and furnishing market information.

13-3b Types of Wholesalers

Wholesalers generally fall into two categories: merchant wholesalers, and agents and brokers. Of these, merchant wholesalers constitute the largest portion. They account for about four-fifths of all wholesale establishments and employees.

MERCHANT WHOLESALERS A **merchant wholesaler** is a middleman that purchases goods in large quantities and sells them to other wholesalers or retailers and to institutional, farm, government, professional, or industrial users.

Merchant wholesalers have the following characteristics:

- They usually operate one or more warehouses at which they receive, take title to, and store goods. These wholesalers are sometimes called *distributors* or *jobbers*.

Learning Objective

13-3 Discuss the need for wholesalers, describe the services they provide, and identify the major types of wholesalers.

merchant wholesaler a middleman that purchases goods in large quantities and sells them to other wholesalers or retailers and to institutional, farm, government, professional, or industrial users

ISTOCKPHOTO.COM/STURTI

Wholesalers facilitate trade by connecting manufacturers with retailers. A general-merchandise wholesaler buys many types of products from a broad range of manufacturers, warehouses the products, and then sells them to retailers. So, instead of having to contact hundreds of different manufacturers to stock their shelves, retailers need to contact only a small number of wholesalers.

- Most merchant wholesalers are businesses composed of salespeople, order takers, receiving and shipping clerks, inventory managers, and office personnel.
- The successful merchant wholesaler must analyze available products and market needs. It must be able to adapt the type, variety, and quality of its products to changing market conditions.
- Merchant wholesalers may be classified as full-service or limited-service wholesalers depending on the number of services they provide. A **full-service wholesaler** performs the entire range of wholesaler functions. These functions include delivering goods, supplying warehousing, arranging for credit, supporting promotional activities, and providing general customer assistance.

A full-service wholesaler can be of three different types:

- A **general-merchandise wholesaler** deals in a wide variety of products, such as drugs, hardware, nonperishable foods, cosmetics, detergents, and tobacco.
- A **limited-line wholesaler** stocks only a few product lines but carries numerous product items within each line.
- A **specialty-line wholesaler** carries a select group of products within a single line. Food delicacies, such as shellfish, represent a product handled by this type of wholesaler.

AGENTS AND BROKERS Agents and brokers are functional middlemen. Functional middlemen do not take title to products. They perform a small number of marketing activities and are paid a commission that is a percentage of the sales price.

An **agent** is a middleman that expedites exchanges, represents a buyer or a seller, and often is hired permanently on a commission basis. When agents represent producers, they are known as *sales agents* or *manufacturer's agents*. As long as the products represented do not compete, a sales agent may represent one or several manufacturers on a commission basis. The agent solicits orders for the manufacturers within a specific territory. As a rule, the manufacturers ship the merchandise and bill the customers directly. The manufacturers also set the prices and other conditions of the sales. The sales agent provides immediate entry into a territory, regular calls on customers, selling experience, and a known, predetermined selling expense (a commission that is a percentage of sales revenue).

A **broker** is a middleman that specializes in a particular commodity, represents either a buyer or a seller, and is likely to be hired on a temporary basis. Food brokers which sell grocery products to resellers are the exception to this rule. They generally have long-term relationships with clients. Brokers may perform only the selling function or both buying and selling using their established contacts and specialized knowledge of their fields.

13-4 MARKETING INTERMEDIARIES: RETAILERS

Retailers are the final link between producers and consumers. Retailers may buy from either wholesalers or producers. They can sell goods, services (such as auto repairs or haircuts), or both. Sears, Roebuck & Co. sells consumer goods, financial services, and repair services for home appliances purchased at Sears.

The U.S. Census estimates that the United States has nearly 1.1 million retail establishments ringing up total sales of more than $4 trillion.[3] Most retailers are small, with annual revenues well under $1 million. However, some retailers are very large. Table 13-1 lists the ten largest retail organizations in the U.S., their sales revenues, and number of stores.

---

full-service wholesaler a middleman that performs the entire range of wholesaler functions

general-merchandise wholesaler a middleman that deals in a wide variety of products

limited-line wholesaler a middleman that stocks only a few product lines but carries numerous product items within each line

specialty-line wholesaler a middleman that carries a select group of products within a single line

agent a middleman that expedites exchanges, represents a buyer or a seller, and often is hired permanently on a commission basis

broker a middleman that specializes in a particular commodity, represents either a buyer or a seller, and is likely to be hired on a temporary basis

Concept Check

✓ What services do wholesalers provide to producers and to retailers?

✓ Identify and describe the various types of wholesalers.

Learning Objective

13-4 Distinguish among the major types of retailers and shopping centers.

TABLE 13-1 The Ten Largest U.S. Retailers

Rank	Company	Sales (in millions)	# of Stores
1	Walmart	$334,302	4,779
2	Kroger	$93,598	3,519
3	Costco	$74,740	447
4	Target	$71,279	1,793
5	The Home Depot	$69,951	1,965
6	Walgreens	$68,068	7,998
7	CVS Caremark	$65,618	7,621
8	Lowe's	$52,210	1,717
9	Amazon.com	$43,962	N/A
10	Safeway	$37,534	1,335

Source: National Retail Federation, "Top 100 Retailers Chart 2014," https://nrf.com/2014/top100-table (accessed January 5, 2015).

13-4a Types of Retail Stores

One way to classify retailers is by the number of stores owned and operated by the firm.

1. An **independent retailer** is a firm that operates only one retail outlet. Most retailers are independent, one-store operators that generally provide personal service and a convenient location.

2. A **chain retailer** is a company that operates more than one retail outlet. By adding outlets, chain retailers reach new geographic markets. As sales increase, chains usually buy merchandise in larger quantities and thus take advantage of quantity discounts. They also wield more power in their dealings with suppliers. There are fewer chain retailers than independent retailers.

Another way to classify retail stores is by store size and the kind and number of products carried. We will now take a closer look at store types based on these dimensions.

DEPARTMENT STORES These large retail establishments consist of several sections, or departments, that sell a wide assortment of products. According to the U.S. Census, a **department store** is a retail store that (1) employs 25 or more persons and (2) sells at least home furnishings, appliances, family apparel, and household linens and dry goods, each in a different part of the store. Macy's, Harrods, and Printemps are examples of large international department stores. Sears, Roebuck & Co. and JCPenney are also department stores. Traditionally, department stores have been service-oriented. Along with the goods they sell, these retailers provide credit, delivery, personal assistance, liberal return policies, and pleasant shopping atmospheres.

DISCOUNT STORES A **discount store** is a self-service general-merchandise outlet that sells products at lower-than-usual prices. These stores operate on smaller markups and higher merchandise turnover than other retailers and offer minimal customer services. Popular discount stores include Kmart, Walmart, and Target.

independent retailer a firm that operates only one retail outlet

chain retailer a company that operates more than one retail outlet

department store a retail store that (1) employs 25 or more persons and (2) sells at least home furnishings, appliances, family apparel, and household linens and dry goods, each in a different part of the store

discount store a self-service general-merchandise outlet that sells products at lower-than-usual prices

© NORTHFOTO/SHUTTERSTOCK.COM

Accessing customers through different types of retailers. When people are asked to name a retailer, they often think of brick-and-mortar establishments like the ones shown in this photo. However, retailing goes on in all kinds of places, including in people's homes and workplaces, online, over the phone and on TV, and even on the streets.

Entrepreneurial Success

Mobile Goes Retro: Food Trucks and More

A growing number of entrepreneurial retailers are going mobile—selling products from a van or truck parked near busy shopping or commercial streets. The idea is to make snacks, clothing, jewelry, and other products available where consumers work, live, or commute. Being able to move between locations is a definite advantage for entrepreneurs who want to reach buyers at different times and places. It also allows entrepreneurs to adapt to the needs and buying patterns of consumers in each location, so they can build a loyal customer base over time.

Compared with the cost of a traditional store or restaurant location, mobile boutiques and food trucks are much less costly to equip and operate. In fact, thanks to lower overhead and limited inventory investment, some mobile businesses may show profits within two years. For example, Jeanine Romo and Stacey Steffe, who own Le Fashion Truck in Los Angeles, spent less than $20,000 to start their mobile boutique selling locally-made apparel and accessories. They estimate that the average monthly cost to operate a mobile retail business is $2,000 to $3,000, including fuel and insurance.

Food trucks, initially popularized by entrepreneurs like Roy Choi of Kogi BBQ, cruise the streets in many areas. No wonder the U.S. market for food-truck meals will soon reach $2.7 billion per year. Food trucks are a good way to break into the restaurant business, test new product ideas, or test new locations—as long as customers can find out, via Twitter or other social media, where and when the next stop will be.

Sources: Based on information in Tafi Mukunyadzi, "Food Truck Trend Lets Boston Restaurateurs Test-Drive New Ideas," *Daily Free Press (Boston University)*, December 4, 2014, http://dailyfreepress.com (accessed August 6, 2015); Tamara Best, "Shops on Wheels, but the Goods Aren't Sold from the Trunk," *New York Times*, November 26, 2014, www.nytimes.com (accessed August 6, 2015); Alison Damast, "Food Trucks and College Business Majors: A Most Delicious Match," *Fortune*, September 10, 2014, www.fortune.com (accessed August 6, 2015).

WAREHOUSE SHOWROOMS A **warehouse showroom** is a retail facility with five basic characteristics: (1) a large, low-cost building, (2) warehouse materials-handling technology, (3) vertical merchandise displays, (4) a large, on-premises inventory, and (5) minimal service. Some of the best-known showrooms are operated by big furniture retailers, including IKEA. These operations employ few personnel and offer few services. Most customers carry away purchases in the manufacturer's carton, although some warehouse showrooms will deliver for a fee.

CONVENIENCE STORES A **convenience store** is a small food store that sells a limited variety of products but remains open well beyond normal business hours. Because convenience stores are common, most patrons of a particular store live within a mile of it. White Hen Pantry, 7-Eleven, Circle K, and Open Door Pantry stores, for example, are convenience stores found either regionally or nationally in the U.S. Limited product mixes and higher prices keep convenience stores from threatening the business of other grocery retailers. There are more than 152,000 convenience stores in the United States.[4]

SUPERMARKETS A **supermarket** is a large self-service store that sells primarily food and household products. It stocks canned, fresh, frozen, and processed foods, paper products, and cleaning supplies. Supermarkets also may sell such items as housewares, toiletries, toys and games, drugs, stationery, books and magazines, plants and flowers, and a few clothing items. Supermarkets like Kroger, Publix, and H-E-B are large-scale operations that emphasize low prices and one-stop shopping for household needs.

SUPERSTORES A **superstore** is a large retail store that carries not only food and nonfood products ordinarily found in supermarkets but also additional product lines such as housewares, hardware, small appliances, clothing, personal-care

warehouse showroom a retail facility in a large, low-cost building with a large on-premises inventory and minimal service

convenience store a small food store that sells a limited variety of products but remains open well beyond normal business hours

supermarket a large self-service store that sells primarily food and household products

superstore a large retail store that carries not only food and nonfood products ordinarily found in supermarkets but also additional product lines

products, garden products, and automotive merchandise. Superstores also provide services, including automotive repair, snack bars and restaurants, photo printing, and banking. Target, Walmart, and H-E-B operate some superstores.

WAREHOUSE CLUBS The **warehouse club** is a large-scale members-only establishment that combines features of cash-and-carry wholesaling with discount retailing. For an annual fee, small retailers or individuals may become members and purchase products at wholesale prices for business use, resale, or personal use.

Because their product lines are shallow and sales volumes are high, warehouse clubs like Sam's Club and Costco can offer a broad range of merchandise, including perishable and nonperishable foods, beverages, books, appliances, housewares, automotive parts, hardware, and furniture.

TRADITIONAL SPECIALTY STORES A **traditional specialty store** carries a narrow product mix with deep product lines. Traditional specialty stores are sometimes called *limited-line retailers*. If they have depth in one product category, such as baked goods or jewelry, they may be called *single-line retailers*. Specialty stores usually offer deeper product mixes than department stores. They attract customers by emphasizing service, atmosphere, and location. Consumers who are dissatisfied with the impersonal atmosphere of large retailers often find the attention offered by specialty stores appealing. Specialty stores include chains such as the Gap, Bath and Body Works, and Foot Locker, as well as many independent stores.

OFF-PRICE RETAILERS An **off-price retailer** is a store that buys manufacturers' seconds, overruns, returns, and off-season merchandise at below-wholesale prices and sells them to consumers at deep discounts. Off-price retailers sell limited lines of national-brand and designer merchandise, usually clothing, shoes, or housewares. Off-price retailers include T.J. Maxx, Burlington Coat Factory, and Nordstrom Rack. Off-price stores charge up to 50 percent less than department stores for comparable merchandise, but offer few customer services. They often include community dressing rooms and central checkout counters. Some off-price retailers have a no-returns, no-exchanges policy.

CATEGORY KILLERS A **category killer** is a very large specialty store that concentrates on a single product line and competes by offering low prices and an enormous number of products. These stores are called *category killers* because they take business away from smaller, higher-cost retail stores. Category killers, such as Best Buy and Toys "R" Us, are seeing increased competition from Internet retailing. The cost of maintaining such large stores can drain a company of its profits.

13-4b Types of Nonstore Selling

Nonstore retailing is selling that does not take place in conventional store facilities. Consumers may purchase products without ever visiting a store. This form of retailing accounts for an increasing percentage of total retail sales. Nonstore retailers use direct selling, direct marketing, and vending machines.

DIRECT SELLING **Direct selling** is the marketing of products to customers through face-to-face sales

Killing the competition? Or not? Home Depot is an example of a category killer. Category killers aren't likely to annihilate all of the competition though. Small retailers with less product variety and higher prices have found it difficult to compete against category killers. However, small retailers that carry a smaller inventory of products that are different from those stocked by category killers and compete on the basis of service, rather than price, can survive.

presentations at home or in the workplace. Traditionally called *door-to-door selling*, direct selling in the United States began with peddlers more than a century ago and is now a major industry with $31.63 billion in U.S. sales annually.[5] Instead of the door-to-door approach, many companies today—such as Mary Kay, Amway, and Avon—use other approaches. They can identify customers by mail, telephone, or the Internet and then set up appointments. Direct selling sometimes involves the "party plan," which can occur in the customer's home or workplace. Direct selling through the party plan requires effective salespeople who identify potential hosts and provide encouragement and incentives for them to organize a gathering. Companies that commonly use the party plan are Tupperware, Stanley Home Products, and Pampered Chef.

DIRECT MARKETING **Direct marketing** is the use of the telephone, Internet, and nonpersonal media to communicate product and organizational information to customers, who then can purchase products via mail, telephone, or the Internet. Direct marketing is a type of nonstore retailing and can occur through catalog marketing, direct-response marketing, telemarketing, television home shopping, and online.

In **catalog marketing**, an organization provides a catalog from which customers make selections and place orders by mail, telephone, or the Internet. Catalog marketing began in 1872 when Montgomery Ward issued its first catalog to rural families. There are thousands of catalog marketing companies in the U.S., many of which publish online. Some catalog marketers sell products spread over multiple product lines, while others are more specialized. Catalog companies, such as Burpee and Newport News, offer considerable depth in only one major product line. The advantages of catalog marketing include efficiency and convenience for customers because they do not have to visit a store. The retailer benefits by being able to locate in remote, low-cost areas, save on expensive store fixtures, and reduce both personal selling and store operating expenses. Disadvantages are that catalog marketing is inflexible, provides limited service, and is most effective for only a selected set of products.

Direct-response marketing occurs when a retailer advertises a product and makes it available through mail, telephone, or online orders. This marketing method has resulted in some products gaining widespread popularity. You may have heard of the Shake Weight, Snuggie, and Magic Bullet—all of which became popular through direct response television marketing campaigns. Direct-response marketing can also be conducted by sending letters, samples, brochures, or booklets to prospects on a mailing list.

Telemarketing is the performance of marketing-related activities by telephone. Some organizations use a prescreened list of prospective clients. Telemarketing has many advantages, such as generating sales leads, improving customer service, speeding up payments on past-due accounts, raising funds for nonprofit organizations, and gathering market data.

However, increasingly restrictive telemarketing laws have made it a less appealing marketing method. In 2003, U.S. Congress implemented a national do-not-call registry, which has more than 223 million numbers on it. The Federal Trade Commission (FTC) enforces violations and companies are subject to fines of up to $16,000 for each call made to numbers on the list. The Federal Communications Commission (FCC) ruled that companies are no longer allowed to call customers using prerecorded marketing calls—"robocalls"—and requires an "opt-out" mechanism for consumers who do not wish to receive calls. Companies that make telemarketing phone calls must pay for access to the do-not-call registry and must obtain updated numbers from the registry at least every three days. However, new technologies and less expensive calling rates mean that some unscrupulous firms are ignoring the National Do Not Call Registry and using robocalls for telemarketing purposes. The FTC fined VMS $3.4 million for repeatedly making telemarketing calls to registered phone numbers.[6]

direct marketing the use of the telephone, Internet, and nonpersonal media to introduce products to customers, who then can purchase them via mail, telephone, or the Internet

catalog marketing a type of marketing in which an organization provides a catalog from which customers make selections and place orders by mail, telephone, or the Internet

direct-response marketing a type of marketing in which a retailer advertises a product and makes it available through mail, telephone, or online orders

telemarketing the performance of marketing-related activities by telephone

Television home shopping presents products to television viewers, encouraging them to order through toll-free numbers and pay with credit cards. Home Shopping Network (HSN) originated and popularized this format. Most homes in the U.S. receive at least one home shopping channel.

Online retailing makes products available to buyers through computer connections. Most bricks-and-mortar retailers have websites to sell products, provide information about their company, or distribute coupons. Online retailing is a rapidly growing segment that most retailers view as vital to business. Retailers frequently offer exclusive online sales, or may reward customers who visit their websites with special in-store coupons and other promotions and discounts. Although online retailing represents a major retailing venue, security remains an issue. Some Internet users retain concerns about identity theft and credit-card number theft when shopping online.

Automatic vending is the use of machines to dispense products. It accounts for less than 2 percent of all retail sales. Automatic vending is one of the most impersonal forms of retailing. Small, standardized, routinely purchased products can be sold in machines because they do not readily spoil and consumers appreciate the convenience. Customers can now find a wide variety of products dispensed via vending machine, even high-end items such as gold bars (Dubai) and caviar (Beverly Hills), as well as shoes and food. Box Brands, for example, developed the Burritobox to dispense warm custom burritos and plans to expand the concept to college campuses. The company is also developing Pizzaboxes to dispense hot pizza. Jamba Juice has installed JambaGo machines with healthy drink options in hundreds of schools as well as stores.[7]

Utilizing multiple retail approaches. Many retailers use multiple marketing strategies to reach potential customers. IKEA operates more than 350 retail stores in 43 countries. It also engages in direct marketing through catalog and online retailing.

13-4c Types of Shopping Centers

The *planned shopping center* is a self-contained retail facility constructed by independent owners and consisting of various stores. Shopping centers are designed and promoted to serve diverse groups of customers with widely differing needs. The management of a shopping center strives for a coordinated mix of stores, a comfortable atmosphere, adequate parking, pleasant landscaping, and special events to attract customers. The convenience of shopping for most family and household needs in a single location is an important element of shopping-center appeal. A planned shopping center is one of four types: lifestyle, neighborhood, community, or regional.

LIFESTYLE SHOPPING CENTERS A **lifestyle shopping center** is a shopping center that has an open-air configuration and is occupied by upscale national chain specialty stores. The lifestyle shopping center model is popular because it combines shopping with the feel of strolling along Main Street. Some lifestyle shopping centers, like The Domain in Austin, Texas, include residences above the stores, as well as activities and culture in their design in order to attract a wide variety of people.

NEIGHBORHOOD SHOPPING CENTERS A **neighborhood shopping center** typically consists of several small convenience and specialty stores. Businesses in neighborhood shopping centers might include small grocery stores, drugstores, gas stations, and fast-food restaurants. These retailers serve consumers who live less than ten minutes away, usually within a two to three-mile radius. Unlike in a lifestyle shopping center, most purchases in the neighborhood shopping center are based on convenience or personal contact. These retailers generally make only limited efforts to coordinate their promotional activities.

television home shopping a form of selling in which products are presented to television viewers, who can buy them by calling a toll-free number and paying with a credit card

online retailing retailing that makes products available to buyers through computer connections

automatic vending the use of machines to dispense products

lifestyle shopping center an open-air-environment shopping center with upscale chain specialty stores

neighborhood shopping center a planned shopping center consisting of several small convenience and specialty stores

Lifestyle Shopping Center. Lifestyle shopping centers include specialty retailers, restaurants, and areas for cultural activities in an open-air setting.

STEVE ROSSET/SHUTTERSTOCK.COM

community shopping center a planned shopping center that includes one or two department stores and some specialty stores, along with convenience stores

regional shopping center a planned shopping center containing large department stores, numerous specialty stores, restaurants, movie theaters, and sometimes even hotels

Concept Check

✓ Describe the major types of retail stores. Give an example of each.

✓ How does nonstore retailing occur?

✓ What are the four most common types of shopping centers, and what type of store does each typically contain?

Learning Objective

13-5 Explain the five most important physical distribution activities.

physical distribution all those activities concerned with the efficient movement of products from the producer to the ultimate user

inventory management the process of managing inventories in such a way as to minimize inventory costs, including both holding costs and potential stock-out costs

COMMUNITY SHOPPING CENTERS A **community shopping center** includes one or two department stores and some specialty stores, along with convenience stores. It attracts consumers from a wider geographic area who will drive longer distances to find products and specialty items unavailable in neighborhood shopping centers. Community shopping centers, which are carefully planned and coordinated, generate traffic with special events such as art exhibits, automobile shows, and sidewalk sales. The management of a community shopping center maintains a mix of tenants so that the center offers wide product mixes and deep product lines.

REGIONAL SHOPPING CENTERS A **regional shopping center** usually has large department stores, numerous specialty stores, restaurants, movie theaters, and sometimes even hotels. It carries a similar mix of merchandise to that available in a downtown shopping district.

Regional shopping centers carefully coordinate management and marketing activities to reach the 150,000 or more customers in their target market. These large centers usually advertise, hold special events, and may even provide transportation for customers. National chain stores can gain leases in regional shopping centers more easily than small independent stores because they are better able to meet the centers' financial requirements.

13-5 PHYSICAL DISTRIBUTION

Physical distribution is all those activities concerned with the efficient movement of products from the producer to the ultimate user. Physical distribution, therefore, is the movement of the products themselves—both goods and services—through their channels of distribution. It combines several interrelated business functions, the most important of which are inventory management, order processing, warehousing, materials handling, and transportation. Because these functions and their costs are highly interrelated, marketers view physical distribution as an integrated effort that supports other marketing activities. The overall goal of distribution is to get the right product to the right place at the right time and at minimal total cost.

13-5a Inventory Management

We define **inventory management** as the process of managing inventories in such a way as to minimize inventory costs, including both holding costs and potential stock-out costs.

Holding costs are the expenses of storing products until they are purchased or shipped to customers. *Stock-out costs* are sales lost when items are not in inventory. Marketers seek to balance these two costs so that the company always has sufficient inventory to satisfy customer demand, but with little surplus because storing unsold products can be very expensive.

Holding costs include the money invested in inventory, the cost of storage space, insurance costs, and inventory taxes. Often even a relatively small reduction in inventory can generate a large increase in available working capital. Sometimes firms discover that risking some stockout costs can be cheaper than having too much inventory. Generally speaking, inventory management software helps companies maintain the correct levels of inventory and knows when to place orders.

13-5b Order Processing

Order processing consists of activities involved in receiving and filling customers' purchase orders. It may include not only the means by which customers order products but also procedures for billing and granting credit.

Fast, efficient order processing can provide a dramatic competitive edge. Those in charge of purchasing goods for intermediaries are especially concerned with their suppliers' promptness and reliability in order processing. To them, promptness and reliability mean minimal inventory costs as well as the ability to order goods when they are needed rather than weeks in advance. The Internet is providing new opportunities for improving services associated with order processing.

13-5c Warehousing

Warehousing is the set of activities involved in receiving and storing goods and preparing them for reshipment. Goods are stored to create time utility, meaning they are held until they are needed for use or sale. Warehousing includes the following activities:

- *Receiving goods.* The warehouse accepts delivered goods and assumes responsibility for them.
- *Identifying goods.* Records are made of the quantity of each item received. Items may be marked, coded, or tagged for identification.
- *Sorting goods.* Delivered goods may have to be sorted before being stored.
- *Dispatching goods to storage.* Items must be moved to storage areas, where they can be found later.
- *Holding goods.* The goods are protected in storage until needed.
- *Recalling, picking, and assembling goods.* Items that are to leave the warehouse must be selected from storage and assembled efficiently.
- *Dispatching shipments.* Each shipment is packaged and directed to the proper transport vehicle. Shipping and accounting documents are prepared.

A firm may use its own private warehouses or rent space in public warehouses. A *private warehouse*, owned and operated by a particular firm, can be designed to serve the firm's specific needs. However, the organization must take on the task of financing the facility and determining the best location for it. Generally, only companies that deal in large quantities of goods, such as UPS or Walmart, can justify the expense of private warehouses.

Public warehouses are open to all individuals and firms. Most are located on the outskirts of cities, where rail and truck transportation is easily available. They provide storage facilities, areas for sorting and assembling shipments, and office and display spaces for wholesalers and retailers. Public warehouses also will hold—and issue receipts for—goods used as collateral for borrowed funds.

order processing activities involved in receiving and filling customers' purchase orders

warehousing the set of activities involved in receiving and storing goods and preparing them for reshipment

13-5d Materials Handling

Materials handling is the actual physical handling of goods—in warehouses as well as during transportation. Proper materials-handling procedures and techniques can increase the efficiency and capacity of a firm's warehouse and transportation system, as well as reduce product breakage and spoilage.

Materials handling attempts to reduce the number of times a product is handled. One method is called *unit loading*. Several smaller cartons, barrels, or boxes are combined into a single standard-size load that can be moved efficiently by forklift, conveyer, or truck.

13-5e Transportation

As a part of physical distribution, **transportation** is simply the shipment of products to customers. The greater the distance between seller and purchaser, the more important is the choice of the means of transportation and the particular carrier.

A firm that offers transportation services is called a **carrier**. A *common carrier* is a transportation firm whose services are available to all shippers. Railroads, airlines, and most long-distance trucking firms are common carriers. A *contract carrier* is available for hire by one or several shippers. Contract carriers do not serve the general public, and the number of firms they can handle at a time is limited by law. A *private carrier* is owned and operated by the shipper.

A shipper can hire agents called *freight forwarders* to handle transportation. Freight forwarders pick up shipments, ensure that the goods are loaded onto carriers, and assume responsibility for their safe delivery. Freight forwarders have the capacity to group multiple small shipments into one large load, thereby saving smaller firms money by charging them a lower rate.

The six major criteria used for selecting transportation modes are compared in Table 13-2. These six criteria are cost, speed, dependability, load flexibility, accessibility, and frequency.

Obviously, the *cost* of a transportation mode is an important consideration. However, it is not the only one. Higher-cost modes of transportation can convey important benefits. *Speed* is measured by the total time that a carrier possesses the

materials handling the actual physical handling of goods, in warehouses as well as during transportation

transportation the shipment of products to customers

carrier a firm that offers transportation services

TABLE 13-2 Characteristics of Transportation Modes

Selection Criteria	Railroads	Trucks	Pipelines	Waterways	Airplanes
Cost	Moderate	High	Low	Very low	Very high
Speed	Average	Fast	Slow	Very slow	Very fast
Dependability	Average	High	High	Average	High
Load flexibility	High	Average	Very low	Very high	Low
Accessibility	High	Very high	Very limited	Limited	Average
Frequency	Low	High	Very high	Very low	Average
Percent of use*	26.4%	40.2%	17.5%	7.5%	0.2%
Products carried	Coal, grain, lumber, heavy equipment, paper and pulp products, chemicals	Clothing, computers, books, groceries and produce, livestock	Oil, processed coal, natural gas, wood chips	Chemicals, bauxite, grain, motor vehicles, agricultural implements	Flowers, food (highly perishable), technical instruments, emergency parts and equipment, overnight mail

*Note: Percent of use values do not add up to 100%. 8.4% of freight shipments were categorized as Multimodal, and 1.6% were categorized as Other/Unknown.

Source: "3-1 Freight Shipments Within the U.S. by Mode," U.S. Bureau of Transportation Statistics, *Pocket Guide to Transportation 2014,* http://www.rita.dot.gov/bts/sites/rita.dot.gov.bts/files/publications/pocket_guide_to_transportation/2014/3_Moving_Goods/table3_1 (accessed January 5, 2015).

products, including time required for pickup and delivery, handling, and movement between point of origin and destination. Usually there is a direct relationship between cost and speed, meaning faster modes of transportation are more expensive. A transportation mode's *dependability* is determined by its consistency of service. *Load flexibility* is the degree to which a transportation mode can be adapted for moving different kinds of products with varying requirements, such as controlled temperatures or humidity levels. *Accessibility* refers to a transportation mode's ability to move goods over a specific route or network. *Frequency* refers to how frequently a marketer can ship products by a specific transportation mode. Whereas pipelines provide continuous shipments, railroads and waterways follow specific schedules for moving products from one location to another. In Table 13-2, each transportation mode is compared according to these six selection criteria and the percentage of use (ton-miles) for each mode.

RAILROADS Although usage has declined over the years, the railroad remains one of the most important modes of transportation in the United States. Rail is also the least expensive mode for many products. Almost all railroads are common carriers, although a few coal-mining companies operate their own lines. Many commodities carried by railroads could not be transported easily by any other means.

TRUCKS The trucking industry consists of common, contract, and private carriers. Trucks are a very popular transportation mode because they have the advantage of being able to move goods to areas not served by railroads. They can handle freight quickly and economically, and they can carry a wide range of shipments. Many shippers favor this mode because it offers door-to-door service, less stringent packaging requirements than ships and airplanes, and flexible delivery schedules. Railroad and truck carriers sometimes team up to provide a form of transportation called *piggyback*, wherein truck trailers are loaded onto railroad flatcars for much of the distance and then pulled by trucks to the final destination.

AIRPLANES Air transport is the fastest, but most expensive, means of transportation. All certified airlines are common carriers. Supplemental or charter lines are contract carriers. Because of the high cost, uneven geographic distribution of airports, and reliance on weather conditions, airlines carry only a tiny fraction of intercity freight. Only high-value, perishable items or goods that are needed immediately usually are shipped by air.

WATERWAYS Cargo ships and barges offer the least expensive, but slowest, form of transportation. They are used mainly for bulky, nonperishable goods such as iron ore, bulk wheat, motor vehicles, and agricultural implements. Of course, shipment by water is limited to cities located on navigable waterways. Many international distributors will combine this mode with a land mode to transport products to their destination.

PIPELINES Pipelines are a highly specialized mode of transportation. They are used primarily to carry petroleum and natural gas. Such products as semiliquid coal and wood chips also can be shipped through pipelines, although their use can be controversial when they cut across animal migratory pathways or spring a leak in remote areas.

integrated marketing communications coordination of promotion efforts to ensure maximal informational and persuasive impact on customers

Concept Check

✓ How is inventory management a balancing act between stock-out costs and holding costs?

✓ Explain the seven major warehousing activities.

✓ What is the goal of materials handling?

✓ Describe the major characteristics of the primary transportation modes.

13-6 WHAT IS INTEGRATED MARKETING COMMUNICATIONS?

Integrated marketing communications is the coordination of promotion efforts to ensure maximum informational and persuasive impact on customers. A major goal of integrated marketing communications is to send a consistent message to customers.

Learning Objective

13-6 Explain how integrated marketing communications works to have the maximum impact on the customer.

Integrated marketing communications helps organizations coordinate and manage promotions in order to create a consistent message. This approach fosters long-term customer relationships and the efficient use of promotional resources. The concept of integrated marketing communications has been increasingly accepted for several reasons. Mass-media advertising, a very popular promotional method in the past, is used less today because of its high costs and variable audience sizes. Marketers now take advantage of highly targeted promotional tools, such as cable TV, direct mail, DVDs, the Internet, special-interest magazines, and podcasts. Database marketing allows marketers to be more precise in targeting individual customers.

Because the overall costs of marketing communications are significant, management demands systematic evaluations of communication efforts to ensure that promotional resources are used efficiently. Although the fundamental role of promotion has not changed, the specific communication vehicles employed and the precision with which they are used are evolving.

13-7 THE PROMOTION MIX: AN OVERVIEW

Learning Objective

13-7 Understand the basic elements of the promotion mix.

Promotion is communication about an organization and its products that is intended to inform, persuade, or remind target-market members. Promotion is not limited to business. Charities use promotion to inform us about their cause or issue, to persuade us to donate, and to remind us to do so.

Even the Internal Revenue Service uses promotion (in the form of publicity) to remind us of the April 15 deadline for filing tax returns. The promotion with which we are most familiar—advertising—attempts to inform, persuade, or remind us to buy particular products. But advertising is only one aspect of promotion.

A **promotion mix** (sometimes called a *marketing-communications mix*) is the particular combination of promotion methods a firm uses to reach a target market. The makeup of a mix depends on many factors, including the firm's promotional resources and objectives, the nature of the target market, the product characteristics, and the feasibility of the various promotional methods. The four elements of the promotion mix are advertising, personal selling, sales promotion, and public relations, as illustrated in Figure 13-2.

FIGURE 13-2 Possible Elements of a Promotion Mix

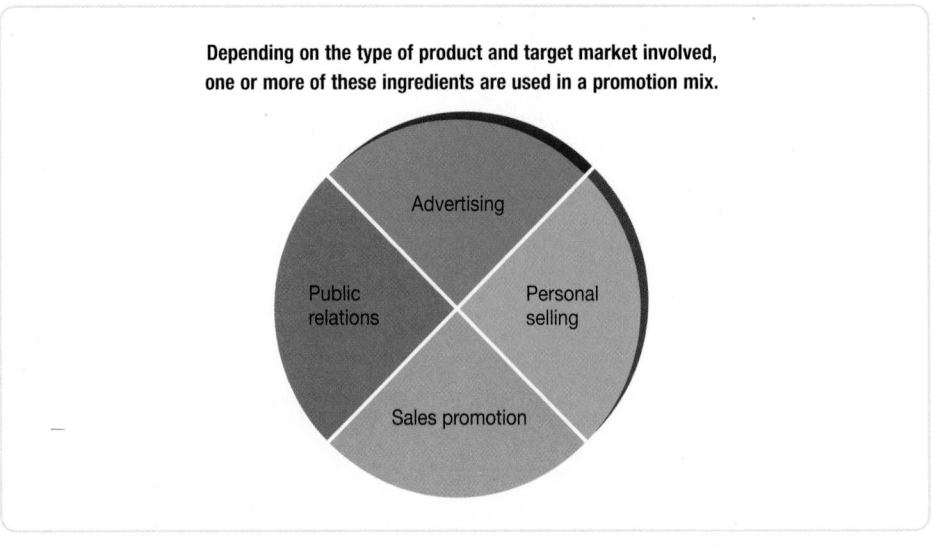

Depending on the type of product and target market involved, one or more of these ingredients are used in a promotion mix.

- Advertising
- Personal selling
- Sales promotion
- Public relations

Source: William M. Pride and O. C. Ferrell, *Marketing: Concepts and Strategies*, 18th ed. (Mason, OH: South-Western/Cengage Learning, 2016). Adapted with permission.

Concept Check

✓ What is the major goal of integrated marketing communications?

✓ Why is integrated marketing communications being increasingly accepted?

promotion communication about an organization and its products that is intended to inform, persuade, or remind target-market members

promotion mix the particular combination of promotion methods a firm uses to reach a target market

Advertising is a paid nonpersonal message communicated to a select audience through a mass medium. Advertising is flexible and can reach a very large or a small, carefully chosen target group. **Personal selling** is personal communication aimed at informing customers and persuading them to buy a firm's products. It is more expensive to reach a consumer through personal selling than through advertising, but this method provides immediate feedback and often is more persuasive than advertising. **Sales promotion** is the use of activities or materials as direct inducements to customers or salespersons, which can add value to the product and increase the customer's incentive to make a purchase. **Public relations** is a broad set of communication activities used to create and maintain favorable relationships between an organization and various public groups, both internal and external. Public-relations activities are numerous and varied and can be a very effective form of promotion.

While it is possible for a marketer to only use one ingredient of the promotion mix, it is more likely that two, three, or four of these ingredients will be used, depending on the type of product and target market involved.

Concept Check

✓ What are the major elements of a promotion mix?

✓ How can each element help a firm reach a target market?

13-8 ADVERTISING

Advertising is a very important element of the promotion mix. Organizations currently spend around $140 billion annually on advertising in the U.S.[8] In this section, we discuss the types of advertising and how to develop an advertising campaign.

13-8a Types of Advertising by Purpose

Depending on its purpose and message, advertising may be classified into one of three groups: primary demand, selective demand, or institutional.

PRIMARY-DEMAND ADVERTISING Primary-demand advertising is advertising aimed at increasing the demand for all brands of a product within a specific industry. Trade and industry associations, such as The National Pork Producers Council and The California Milk Processor Board, use primary-demand advertising. To reach out to a new generation of potential home buyers, the National Association of Realtors launched a multimedia campaign to highlight the value of local realtors' insights and the accurate data available through realtor.com to those seeking to buy a home.[9]

SELECTIVE-DEMAND ADVERTISING Selective-demand (or brand) advertising is advertising that is used to sell a particular brand of product. It is by far the most common type of advertising, and it accounts for the majority of advertising expenditures.

Selective-demand advertising that aims at persuading consumers to make purchases within a short time is called *immediate-response advertising*. Most local advertising is of this type.

Often local advertisers promote products with immediate appeal. Selective advertising aimed at keeping the public aware of a firm's name or product is called *reminder advertising*.

Comparative advertising compares the sponsored brand with one or more identified competing brands. The association shows the sponsored brand to be as good as or better than the other identified competing brands. Marketers must be careful when using this technique to present information truthfully and not to obscure or distort facts.

INSTITUTIONAL ADVERTISING Institutional advertising is advertising designed to enhance a firm's image or reputation. Some large firms allocate a portion of advertising dollars to build goodwill, rather than to stimulate sales directly. For

Learning Objective

13-8 Explain the three types of advertising and describe the major steps of developing an advertising campaign.

advertising a paid nonpersonal message communicated to a select audience through a mass medium

personal selling personal communication aimed at informing customers and persuading them to buy a firm's products

sales promotion the use of activities or materials as direct inducements to customers or salespersons

public relations communication activities used to create and maintain favorable relationships between an organization and various public groups, both internal and external

primary-demand advertising advertising whose purpose is to increase the demand for *all* brands of a product within a specific industry

selective-demand (or brand) advertising advertising that is used to sell a particular brand of product

institutional advertising advertising designed to enhance a firm's image or reputation

Harnessing the power of social media—or not? Social media allows a business to reach out to customers in a context that is familiar and comfortable to them. Firms attempt to measure the effectiveness of their social media efforts by gathering statistics on the number of followers and fans they have, traffic to their websites, and mentions of their products on social networking sites.

example, Whole Foods launched its first national campaign to highlight its values regarding sustainable business practices and its high standards for food quality. The "Values Matter" campaign seeks to distinguish the company from conventional grocers that are increasingly offering organic and natural products desired by consumers.[10] A positive public image helps an organization to attract customers, employees, and investors.

13-8b Major Steps in Developing an Advertising Campaign

An advertising campaign is developed in several stages, which can vary in the order in which they are implemented. Factors affecting a campaign include the company's resources, products, and target audiences. The development of a campaign in any organization includes the following steps in some form:

1. IDENTIFY AND ANALYZE THE TARGET AUDIENCE The target audience is the group toward which a firm's advertisements are directed. To pinpoint the organization's target audience and develop an effective campaign, marketers analyze various factors, such as the geographic distribution of potential customers, their age, sex, race, income, and education, and their attitudes toward the product, the nature of the competition, and the product's features. It is crucial to correctly identify the target market because all subsequent efforts will fail if not directed at the right audience.

2. DEFINE THE ADVERTISING OBJECTIVES The goals of an advertising campaign should be stated precisely and in quantifiable terms. Objectives should give specific details about the actual and desired position of the company and how it will arrive there, including a timetable for achieving goals. For example, advertising objectives that focus on sales will stress increasing sales by a certain percentage or dollar amount, or expanding the firm's market share by a specific amount.

3. CREATE THE ADVERTISING PLATFORM An advertising platform includes the important selling points, or features, that an advertiser will incorporate into the advertising campaign. These should be features that are lacking in competitors' products and that are important to customers. Although research into what consumers view as important issues is expensive, it is the most productive way to determine what to include in an advertising platform.

4. DETERMINE THE ADVERTISING APPROPRIATION The advertising appropriation is the total amount of money designated for advertising in a given time period. Developing an acceptable advertising appropriation is critical—too little and promotional efforts will not meet demand, too much will waste resources and reduce the funds available for other activities. Advertising appropriations may be based on historical or forecasted sales, what competitors spend on advertising, or executive judgment. Companies that spend the most on advertising in the U.S. include Procter & Gamble, AT&T, General Motors, Comcast, and Ford Motor Company.[11]

5. DEVELOP THE MEDIA PLAN A media plan outlines a timetable for advertisements and which media will be used. Although cost-effectiveness is not easy to measure, the primary concern of the media planner is to reach the largest proportion of the target audience possible for each dollar spent. Media planners must also consider the location and demographics of the target market, the content of the message, and the characteristics of the audiences reached by various media. The media planner begins with general media decisions, selects subclasses within each medium, and chooses specific media vehicles for the campaign. The advantages and disadvantages of the major media classes are shown in Table 13-3.

6. CREATE THE ADVERTISING MESSAGE The content and form of a message are influenced by the product's features, the characteristics of the target audience, the objectives of the campaign, and the choice of media. An advertiser must consider these factors to choose words and illustrations that will be meaningful and appealing to the target audience. The copy, or words, of an advertisement will vary depending on the media choice, but attempt to engage the audience and move them through attention, interest, desire, and action. Artwork and visuals should complement copy by being visually attractive and communicating an idea quickly.

7. EXECUTE THE CAMPAIGN Execution of an advertising campaign requires extensive planning, scheduling, and coordinating because the tasks are carried out

TABLE 13-3 Advantages and Disadvantages of Major Media Classes

	Advantages	Disadvantages
Television	Reaches large audiences, high frequency available, dual impact of audio and video, highly visible, high prestige, geographic and demographic selectivity, difficult to ignore	Very expensive, highly perishable message, size of audience not guaranteed, amount of prime time limited, lack of selectivity in target market
Direct mail	Little wasted circulation, highly selective, circulation controlled by advertiser, few distractions, personal, stimulates actions, easy to measure performance, hidden from competitors	Very expensive, lacks editorial content to attract readers, often thrown away unread as junk mail, criticized as invasion of privacy, consumers must choose to read the ad
Newspapers	Reaches large audience, purchased to be read, geographic flexibility, short lead time, frequent publication, favorable for cooperative advertising	Not selective for socioeconomic groups or target market, short life, limited reproduction capabilities, large advertising volume limits exposure
Radio	Reaches a large proportion of consumers, mobile and flexible, low relative costs, ad can be changed quickly, high level of geographic and demographic selectivity, encourages use of imagination	Lacks visual imagery, short life of message, listeners' attention limited, market fragmentation, difficult buying procedures, limited media and audience research
Yellow Pages	Wide availability, action and product category oriented, low relative costs, ad frequency and longevity, nonintrusive	Market fragmentation, extremely localized, slow updating, lack of creativity, long lead times, requires large space to be noticed
Magazines	Demographic selectivity, good reproduction, long life, prestige, geographic selectivity when regional issues available	High costs, 30- to 90-day average lead time, high level of competition, limited reach, communicates less frequently
Internet	Immediate response, potential to reach a precisely targeted audience, ability to track customers and build databases, highly interactive medium	Costs of precise targeting can be high, inappropriate ad placement, effects difficult to measure, concerns about security and privacy
Outdoor	Allows for frequent repetition, low cost, message can be placed close to point of sale, geographic selectivity, operable 24 hours a day, high creativity	Message must be short and simple, no demographic selectivity, seldom attracts readers' full attention, criticized as traffic hazard and blight on landscape, much wasted coverage, limited capabilities
Social Media	Target, interact, and connect more personally with customers, receive real-time feedback, direct messages to specific individuals, effectively reach target market/followers	Restricted number of contacts per message because of highly targeted nature, new mediums—unsure of best applications and how to calculate ROI, large time commitment to monitor

Sources: Adapted from William F. Arens, Michael Weigold, and Christian Arens, *Contemporary Advertising & Integrated Communications*, 14th ed. (Burr Ridge, IL: Irwin/McGraw-Hill, 2013); George E. Belch and Michael Belch, *Advertising and Promotion: An Integrated Marketing Communications Perspective*, 9th ed. (Burr Ridge, IL: Irwin/McGraw-Hill, 2012).

TABLE 13-4 Most Effective Advertisers

Ranking	Advertiser
1	Unilever
2	Coca-Cola
3	Procter & Gamble
4	PepsiCo
5	Nestlé

Source: Effie Worldwide, "2014 Effie Effectiveness Index: Overview," July 2014, http://www.effieindex.com/rankings/ (accessed July 15, 2015).

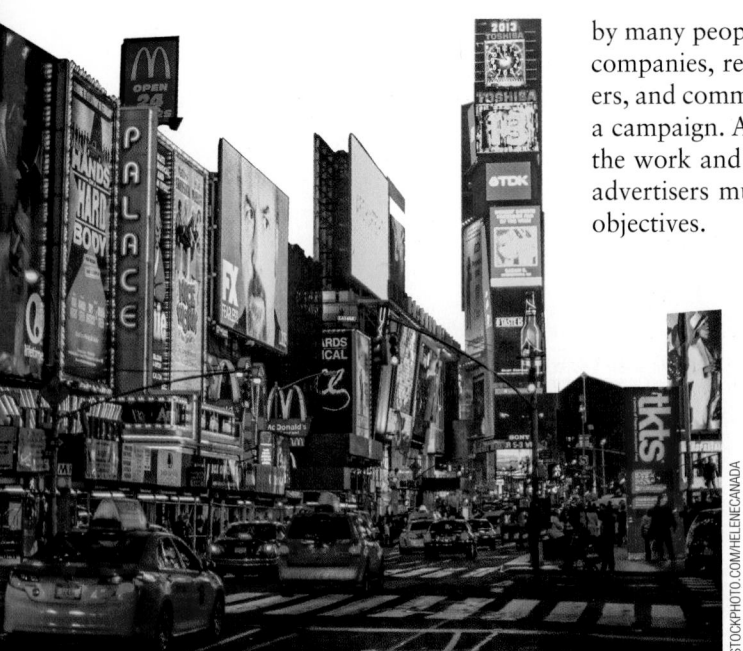

by many people and groups and must be completed on time. Production companies, research organizations, media firms, printers, photoengravers, and commercial artists are just a few of the potential contributors to a campaign. Advertising managers must constantly assess the quality of the work and take corrective action when necessary. In some instances, advertisers must make changes in the middle of the campaign to meet objectives.

8. EVALUATE ADVERTISING EFFECTIVENESS A campaign's success should be compared against original objectives at regular intervals before, during, and after campaign launch. An advertiser should be able to track the impact of the campaign on sales and market share, as well as changes in customer attitudes and brand awareness. Data from past and current sales and responses to coupon offers and customer surveys administered by research organizations are some of the ways in which advertising effectiveness can be evaluated. Table 13-4 shows the five advertisers with the most effective campaigns according to the Effie Effectiveness Index, a global ranking system for advertising effectiveness. This ranking takes into account factors such as ROI, sales growth, and brand awareness in relation to money spent on promotional activities.

13-8c Advertising Agencies

Advertisers can plan and produce their own advertising with help from in-house media personnel, or they can hire advertising agencies. An **advertising agency** is an independent firm that plans, produces, and places advertising for clients. Many large ad agencies also help with sales promotion and public relations. The cost to a firm can be moderate, especially for large campaigns. It is usually around 15 percent commission. Some firms opt to use a combination of in-house advertising talent and outside specialists.

13-8d Social and Legal Considerations in Advertising

Critics of U.S. advertising have two main complaints—that it is wasteful and that it can be deceptive. Although advertising (like any other activity) can be performed inefficiently, evidence shows that it is not wasteful.

- Advertising is the most effective and least expensive means of communicating product information to a large number of individuals and organizations.

advertising agency an independent firm that plans, produces, and places advertising for its clients

- Advertising encourages competition. It thus leads to the development of new and improved products, wider product choices, and lower prices.
- Advertising revenues support mass-communication media—newspapers, magazines, radio, and television, effectively paying for news coverage and entertainment programming.
- Advertising provides job opportunities in fields ranging from sales to film production.

A number of government and private agencies scrutinize advertising for false or misleading claims or offers that might harm consumers. At the national level, the Federal Trade Commission (FTC), the Food and Drug Administration (FDA), and the Federal Communications Commission (FCC) oversee advertising practices. Advertising also may be monitored by state and local agencies, better business bureaus, and industry associations.

Concept Check

✓ Describe the major types of advertising by purpose.

✓ Explain the eight major steps in developing an advertising campaign.

13-9 PERSONAL SELLING

Learning Objective

13-9 Recognize the kinds of salespersons, the steps in the personal-selling process, and the major sales management tasks.

Personal selling is the most adaptable of all promotional methods because the person presenting the message can modify it to suit the individual buyer. However, it is also the most expensive method because it involves salespeople communicating with customers one at a time or in small groups. Many selling situations demand the face-to-face contact and adaptability of personal selling. This is especially true of industrial sales, in which a single purchase may amount to millions of dollars. Obviously, sales of that size must be based on carefully planned presentations, personal contact with customers, and thorough negotiations.

13-9a Kinds of Salespersons

Because most businesses employ different salespersons to perform different functions, marketing managers must select the kinds of sales personnel that will be most effective in selling the firm's products. Salespersons may be identified as order getters, order takers, and support personnel. A single individual can, and often does, perform all three functions.

order getter a salesperson who is responsible for selling a firm's products to new customers and increasing sales to present customers

creative selling selling products to new customers and increasing sales to present customers

order taker a salesperson who handles repeat sales in ways that maintain positive relationships with customers

sales support personnel employees who aid in selling but are more involved in locating prospects, educating customers, building goodwill for the firm, and providing follow-up service

ORDER GETTERS An **order getter** is responsible for what is sometimes called **creative selling**—selling a firm's products to new customers and increasing sales to current customers. An order getter must be able to perceive buyers' needs, supply customers with information about the product, and persuade them to buy it.

ORDER TAKERS An **order taker** handles repeat sales and customer demands to maintain positive relationships. *Inside order takers* receive incoming mail, online, and telephone orders for businesses. Salespersons in retail stores are also inside order takers. *Outside* (or *field*) *order takers* travel to customers. Often the buyer and the field salesperson develop a mutually beneficial relationship of placing, receiving, and delivering orders. Both inside and outside order takers are active salespersons and produce a large proportion of their companies' sales.

SUPPORT PERSONNEL Sales support personnel aid in selling but are more involved in

MICHAELJUNG/ISTOCK/THINKSTOCK

The pros and cons of personal selling. Personal selling is more effective than advertising. It's easy to ignore an advertisement. Saying "no" to a salesperson is much harder. The main drawback of personal selling is that it's expensive, which is why it's generally used to sell high-dollar goods and services.

missionary salesperson a salesperson—generally employed by a manufacturer—who visits retailers to persuade them to buy the manufacturer's products

trade salesperson a salesperson—generally employed by a food producer or processor—who assists customers in promoting products, especially in retail stores

technical salesperson a salesperson who assists a company's current customers in technical matters

FIGURE 13-3 The Six Steps of the Personal-Selling Process

Personal selling is not only the most adaptable of all promotional methods but also the most expensive.

1. Prospecting
2. Approaching the prospect
3. Making the presentation
4. Answering objections
5. Closing the sale
6. Following up

Source: William M. Pride and O. C. Ferrell, *Marketing: Concepts and Strategies*, 18th ed. (Mason, OH: South-Western/Cengage Learning, 2016). Adapted with permission.

locating prospects (likely first-time customers), educating customers, building goodwill for the firm, and providing follow-up service. The most common categories of support personnel are missionary, trade, and technical salespersons.

A **missionary salesperson**, who usually works for a manufacturer, visits retailers to persuade them to buy the manufacturer's products. If the retailers agree, they buy the products from wholesalers, who are the manufacturer's actual customers.

A **trade salesperson**, who generally works for a food producer or processor, assists customers in promoting products, especially in retail stores. A trade salesperson may obtain additional shelf space for the products, restock shelves, set up displays, and distribute samples. Because trade salespersons usually are order takers as well, they are not strictly support personnel.

A **technical salesperson** assists a company's current customers in technical matters. He or she may explain how to use a product, how it is made, how to install it, or how a system is designed. A technical salesperson should be formally educated in science or engineering.

Firms usually need to employ sales personnel from several of these categories. Factors that affect which marketing personnel are hired include the number of customers and their characteristics, the product's attributes, complexity, price, the distribution channels used by the company, and the company's approach to advertising.

13-9b The Personal-Selling Process

No two selling situations are exactly alike, and no two salespeople perform their jobs in exactly the same way. Most salespeople, however, follow the six-step procedure illustrated in Figure 13-3.

PROSPECTING The first step in personal selling is to research potential buyers and choose the most likely customers, or prospects. Business associates and customers, public records, telephone and trade-association directories, and company files can all be good sources of new prospects. The salesperson concentrates on those prospects who have the financial resources, willingness, and authority to buy the product.

APPROACHING THE PROSPECT First impressions are often lasting. Therefore, a salesperson's first contact with a prospect is crucial to successful selling. A salesperson should be friendly and knowledgeable about the product, the prospect's needs, and how the product can meet those needs. Those salespeople who demonstrate an understanding of and sensitivity to a customer's situation are more likely to make a good first impression, and make a sale.

MAKING THE PRESENTATION The next step is actual delivery of the sales presentation, which often includes a product demonstration. The salesperson points out the product's features, its benefits, and how it is superior to competitors' merchandise. The salesperson may list other clients (if given permission) during the presentation.

During a demonstration, the salesperson may suggest that the prospect try out the product personally. The demonstration and product trial should underscore specific points made during the presentation.

ANSWERING OBJECTIONS The prospect may raise objections or ask questions at any time during the process. This is the salesperson's chance to eliminate objections that could prevent a sale, to point out additional features, or to mention special services the company offers.

CLOSING THE SALE To close the sale, the salesperson asks the prospect to buy the product. This is the critical point in the selling process. Many experienced salespeople utilize a *trial closing*, in which they ask questions before the actual close in a tone that assumes a successful sale. Typical questions are: "When would you want delivery?" and "Do you want the standard model or the one with the special options package?" They allow the salesperson to gauge the likelihood and imminence of a sale.

FOLLOWING UP The salesperson's job does not end with a sale. He or she must follow up to ensure that the product is delivered on time, in the right quantity, and in proper operating condition. During follow-up, the salesperson also makes it clear that he or she is available in case problems develop. Follow-up is essential to the selling process because it leaves a good impression and helps to increase the likelihood of future sales.

13-9c Major Sales Management Tasks

A firm's success often hinges on the competent management of its sales force. Although some companies operate efficiently without one, most firms rely on a strong sales force—and the revenue it brings in—for their success.

Sales managers must:

- Set sales objectives in concrete, quantifiable terms and specify a specific period of time and geographic area.
- Adjust the size of the sales force to meet changes in the firm's marketing plan and the marketing environment.
- Attract and hire effective salespersons.
- Develop a training program and decide where, when, how, and for whom to conduct the training.
- Formulate a fair and adequate compensation plan to retain qualified employees.
- Motivate salespersons to keep their productivity high.
- Define sales territories and determine scheduling and routing of the sales force.
- Evaluate the operation holistically, through sales reports, communications with customers, and invoices.

Concept Check

✓ What are the advantages and disadvantages of using personal selling?

✓ Identify the three types of salespersons.

✓ Describe the six steps of the personal-selling process.

13-10 SALES PROMOTION

Sales promotion consists of activities or materials that are direct inducements to customers or salespersons. Receiving a free sample at the supermarket or being invited to join a frequent-flyer program are examples of sales promotions. Sales promotion techniques can significantly affect sales and are often used to enhance and supplement other promotional methods. Firms have dramatically increased spending on sales promotions as they increase in importance as part of the promotion mix.

Learning Objective

13-10 Describe sales promotion objectives and methods.

13-10a Sales Promotion Objectives

Sales promotion activities may be used singly or in combination to achieve one goal or a set of goals. Marketers use sales promotion activities and materials for a number of purposes, including

1. To attract new customers
2. To encourage trial of a new product
3. To invigorate the sales of a mature brand
4. To boost sales to current customers
5. To reinforce advertising
6. To increase traffic in retail stores

Personal App

Do sales promotion tools affect your buying decision?

You're the target market for many products, and different marketers use different sales promotion methods to encourage you to try and buy. Do you use coupons? Do you enjoy trying free samples? Do you ever notice the displays in stores where you shop? Are you enrolled in any frequent-user programs? All of these are sales promotion methods designed to attract you to a product or business and influence your buying decision.

7. To smooth out customer demand
8. To build up reseller inventories
9. To neutralize the competition's promotional efforts
10. To increase the attractiveness of shelf placement and displays

Sales promotion objectives should be consistent with the organization's general goals and with its marketing and promotional objectives.

13-10b Sales Promotion Methods

Most sales promotion methods can be classified as promotional techniques for either consumer sales or trade sales.

A **consumer sales promotion method** attracts consumers to particular retail stores and motivates them to purchase certain new or established products. A **trade sales promotion method** encourages wholesalers and retailers to stock and actively promote a manufacturer's product. Incentives such as money, merchandise, marketing assistance, and gifts may provide incentives to resellers to purchase products or support a firm in other ways. Of the combined dollars spent on sales promotion and advertising, about one-half is spent on trade promotions, one-fourth on consumer promotions, and one-fourth on advertising.

13-10c Selection of Sales Promotion Methods

Several factors affect a marketer's choice of sales promotion methods, including

1. The objectives of the promotional effort
2. Product characteristics—size, weight, cost, durability, uses, features, and hazards
3. Target-market profiles—age, gender, income, location, density, usage rate, and buying patterns
4. Distribution channels and availability of appropriate resellers
5. The competitive and regulatory forces in the environment

REBATES A **rebate** is a return of part of the purchase price of a product. Usually the rebate is offered by the producer to consumers who submit a coupon and a specific proof of purchase. Rebating is a relatively low-cost promotional method, but consumers may not be attracted by it because they view it to be too complicated or time consuming.

COUPONS A **coupon** reduces the retail price of a particular item by a stated amount at the time of purchase. Coupons may be worth anywhere from a few cents to a few dollars. Customers can find coupons in newspapers, magazines, direct mail, and shelf dispensers in stores. Some coupons are precisely targeted at customers. After declining throughout the 1990s, the popularity of coupons has rebounded,

consumer sales promotion method a sales promotion method designed to attract consumers to particular retail stores and to motivate them to purchase certain new or established products

trade sales promotion method a sales promotion method designed to encourage wholesalers and retailers to stock and actively promote a manufacturer's product

rebate a return of part of the purchase price of a product

coupon reduces the retail price of a particular item by a stated amount at the time of purchase

largely because consumers can visit coupon websites, and companies send coupons via email or smartphone to loyal customers. Target, for instance, offers customers customized coupons via its Cartwheel app.[12] RetailMeNot gives consumers access to digital coupon offers and promo codes from 50,000 stores and restaurants via a website or smartphone app.[13]

SAMPLES A **sample** is a free product given to customers to encourage trial and purchase. Marketers utilize samples to increase awareness of a product, which can increase sales volume in the early stages of a product's life cycle and improve distribution. Samples may be offered via online coupons, direct mail, or in stores. It is the most expensive sales promotion technique. Established brands, such as cosmetics companies, may use free samples to attract customers and renew interest in a brand. Interactions, a company that operates sampling tables for many national retailers including Costco, reported that its beer sampling at many retailers boosted sales by an average of 71 percent and its frozen pizza samples by 600 percent.[14] Organizations must consider such factors as seasonal demand for the product, market characteristics, and prior advertising when designing a free sample campaign.

PREMIUMS A **premium** is a gift that a producer offers a customer in return for buying its product. It is used to attract competitors' customers, introduce different sizes of established products, add variety to other promotional efforts, and stimulate consumer loyalty. Creativity is essential when using premiums. To stand out and achieve a significant number of redemptions, the premium must suit the target audience and the brand's image. The premium must also be recognizable and desirable to customers. Premiums are placed on or inside packages and can be distributed through retailers or the mail.

FREQUENT-USER INCENTIVES A **frequent-user incentive** is a program developed to reward customers who engage in repeat (frequent) purchases. Such programs are used commonly by service businesses such as airlines, hotels, and auto rental agencies. Frequent-user incentives foster customer loyalty because the customer is given an additional reason to continue patronizing the company or group of companies.

sample a free product given to customers to encourage trial and purchase

premium a gift that a producer offers a customer in return for buying its product

frequent-user incentive a program developed to reward customers who engage in repeat (frequent) purchases

Do you use coupons?
Companies give away coupons to increase the sales of their products and encourage consumers who are unfamiliar with their products to give them a try.

© CREATISTA/SHUTTERSTOCK.COM

Ethical Success or Failure

On-Campus Branding: What's Your Experience?

Microsoft has student representatives demonstrating its software on more than 300 college campuses. Target promotes dorm merchandise via Twitter and YouTube, sponsors freshmen events, and buses incoming students to nearby stores for midnight shopping trips. Red Bull underwrites lectures, races, and other events at hundreds of colleges to boost its energy drink brand. American Eagle gives free T-shirts to student reps who help freshmen during move-in days. Amethyst Jeans parks its colorful brand van on college campuses and gives away free jeans to thousands of female students.

Some colleges and universities welcome brand-supported activities and giveaways that benefit students, and most students who represent brands enjoy the experience. "We are the people who understand what kinds of things the students will be open to," explains one student rep. "It's marketing for the students, by the students."

However, students sometimes feel pressured. One told a reporter: "Although you may want to support your friends, you may not always be interested in supporting the company." An enthusiastic student rep says, "My friends threaten to block me because I am constantly posting" brand-related messages on Facebook and Twitter. For their part, some school administrators are uneasy about the ongoing onslaught of on-campus marketing. Do you think brands should be doing so much sales promotion on campus?

Sources: Based on information in Diego Vasquez, "Smart Ways to Target Back-to-College Kids," *Media Life*, August 7, 2014, http://www.medialifemagazine.com (accessed August 6, 2015); Sandra O'Loughlin, "How Target Became the Big Brand on Campus," *Event Marketer*, May 7, 2014, www.eventmarketer.com (accessed August 6, 2015); "Marketers Hitting Campus Harder than Ever," *Advertising Age*, October 16, 2011, www.adage.com (accessed August 6, 2015); Natasha Singer, "On Campus, It's One Big Commercial," *New York Times*, September 11, 2011, pp. Bu1–Bu4; Karl Greenberg, "Chick-fil-A, MillerCoors, UPS Go to College," *MediaPost*, December 7, 2011, www.mediapost.com (accessed August 6, 2015).

---

point-of-purchase display promotional material placed within a retail store

trade show an industry-wide exhibit at which many sellers display their products

buying allowance a temporary price reduction to resellers for purchasing specified quantities of a product

cooperative advertising an arrangement whereby a manufacturer agrees to pay a certain amount of a retailer's media cost for advertising the manufacturer's products

Concept Check

✓ Why do marketers use sales promotion?

✓ What are the two classifications of sales promotion methods?

✓ What factors affect the choice of sales promotion used?

POINT-OF-PURCHASE DISPLAYS A **point-of-purchase display** is promotional material placed within a retail store. The display is usually located near the product being promoted. It may hold merchandise or information and encouragements to buy the product. Most point-of-purchase displays are prepared and set up by manufacturers and wholesalers.

TRADE SHOWS A **trade show** is an industry-wide exhibit at which many sellers display their products. Some trade shows are organized exclusively for dealers—to permit manufacturers and wholesalers to show their latest lines to retailers. Others are promotions designed to stimulate consumer awareness and interest, such as annual home shows or boat shows.

BUYING ALLOWANCES A **buying allowance** is a temporary price reduction to resellers for purchasing specified quantities of a product. A laundry detergent manufacturer might give retailers $1 for each case of detergent purchased. A buying allowance is an incentive to resellers to handle new products and may stimulate purchase of items in large quantities. A shortcoming of buying allowances is that competitors can counter quickly with their own buying allowances.

COOPERATIVE ADVERTISING **Cooperative advertising** is an arrangement whereby a manufacturer agrees to pay a certain amount of a retailer's media cost for advertising the manufacturer's products. To be reimbursed, a retailer must show proof that the advertisements did appear. Not all retailers take advantage of available cooperative advertising offers, either because they cannot afford to advertise or choose not to.

13-11 PUBLIC RELATIONS

As noted earlier, public relations is a broad set of communication activities used to create and maintain favorable relationships between an organization and various public groups, both internal and external. These groups may include customers, employees, stockholders, suppliers, educators, the media, government officials, and society in general.

Learning Objective

13-11 Understand the types and uses of public relations.

13-11a Types of Public-Relations Tools

Organizations use a variety of public-relations tools to convey messages and to create images. Public-relations professionals prepare written materials such as brochures, newsletters, company magazines, annual reports, and news releases. They also create corporate-identity materials such as logos, business cards, signs, and stationery. Speeches, YouTube videos, and social media accounts on at Twitter, Instagram, and Facebook are additional public-relations tools through which companies can communicate information and ideas or respond to negative information about the firm.

Another public-relations tool is event sponsorship, in which a company pays for all or part of a special event such as a concert, sports competition, festival, or play. Sponsoring special events is an effective way for organizations to increase brand recognition and receive media coverage, sometimes with relatively little investment. The energy drink brand Red Bull, for example, underscores its reputation for giving consumers energy through sponsoring athletes and teams, acts of daring, and rock concerts. Perhaps most notably, Red Bull sponsored Felix Baumgartner in his mission to be the first man to break the speed of sound during a free fall. Baumgartner caught the attention of the world when he successfully jumped from 128,000 feet, the edge of space—giving Red Bull a lot of attention.[15]

Publicity is an important part of public relations, as it increases public awareness of a firm or brand through mass media communications at no cost to the business. **Publicity** is communication in news-story form about an organization, its products, or both. Organizations use publicity to provide information about products, to announce new product launches, expansions, or research, and to strengthen the company's image. Public-relations personnel sometimes organize events, such as grand openings with prizes and celebrities, to generate news coverage of a company.

publicity communication in news-story form about an organization, its products, or both

Social Media:
UPS and FedEx Are Social Media Savvy

Although UPS and FedEx began package delivery in the 20th century, both transportation firms are savvy in the ways of 21st century social media. On Facebook, for example, UPS has collected 1.5 million "likes" for its steady stream of messages and videos. Visitors to the UPS Facebook page (www.facebook.com/ups) can see what happens in busy UPS sorting hubs, find out how the company supports charities, and even learn how to wrap a package securely.

UPS maintains two Twitter accounts, one for general information (http://twitter.com/ups) and one for customer service assistance (http://twitter.com/upshelp). Given the huge number of temporary employees it hires for the busy year-end holiday season, UPS also uses social media to recruit job candidates across the country. It began uploading videos to a company YouTube channel (www.youtube.com/user/ups) years ago, and some of its videos have logged more than 2.5 million views.

Rival FedEx has attracted 1 million "likes" on its Facebook page (www.facebook.com/FedEx), where it posts announcements and videos about delivery services, corporate changes, social responsibility initiatives, and promotions. The firm's YouTube channel (www.youtube.com/user/fedex/custom) features FedEx commercials, as well as videos about preparing and tracking shipments, sporting events sponsored by the company, and behind-the-scenes technology. The FedEx blog (http://blog.van.fedex.com/) presents insights by managers and employees about logistical issues, sports sponsorships, and more.

The FedEx Twitter account (http://twitter.com/fedex), with more than 200,000 followers, features delivery success stories, ideas to help customers improve shipping practices, and causes supported by the company. A separate Twitter account (http://twitter.com/FedExHelp) is designated for customer service questions and concerns. And, like UPS, FedEx uses social media to communicate with job-seekers.

Sources: Based on information in Rita Pyrillis, "How Mobile Delivers Talent for UPS," *Talent Management*, July 28, 2014, www.talentmgt.com; Laura Stevens, "UPS Plans to Use Social Media to Deliver the Needed Holiday Workers," *Wall Street Journal*, September 16, 2014, www.wsj.com; Ekaterina Walter, "The Big Brand Theory: How FedEx Achieves Social Customer Service Success," *Social Media Today*, May 27, 2013, www.socialmediatoday.com.

Event sponsorships are intended to promote a positive image of a firm. Event sponsorships are a public-relations tool. They are often used in conjunction with advertising, personal selling, and sales promotions.

PCN PHOTOGRAPHY/ALAMY LIMITED

news release a typed page of about 300 words provided by an organization to the media as a form of publicity

feature article a piece (of up to 3,000 words) prepared by an organization for inclusion in a particular publication

captioned photograph a picture accompanied by a brief explanation

press conference a meeting at which invited media personnel hear important news announcements and receive supplementary textual materials and photographs

Concept Check

✓ What are the common tools of public relations?

✓ What is publicity, and why do organizations use it?

✓ What are the four common types of publicity?

The most widely used tool of publicity is the **news release**. It is generally one typed page of about 300 words provided by an organization to the media as a form of publicity. The release includes the firm's name, address, phone number, and contact person. A **feature article**, which may run as long as 3,000 words, is usually written for inclusion in a particular publication. For example, a software firm might send an article about its new product to a computer magazine. A **captioned photograph**, a picture accompanied by a brief explanation, is an effective way to illustrate a new or improved product. A **press conference** allows invited media personnel to hear important news announcements and to receive supplementary materials and photographs. Finally, letters to the editor, special newspaper or magazine editorials, and videos may be prepared and distributed to appropriate media for possible use in news stories.

13-11b Uses of Public Relations

Public relations can be used to promote many things, including people, places, activities, and ideas. Public relations focuses on enhancing the reputation of the total organization by increasing public awareness of a company's products, brands, or activities and by fostering desirable company images, such as that of innovativeness, dependability, or social responsibility. By getting the media to report on a firm's accomplishments, public relations helps a company to maintain public visibility. Effective management of public-relations efforts also can reduce the amount of unfavorable coverage surrounding negative events. For example, after McDonald's received criticism about the ingredients in some of its products, the company countered with a series of YouTube videos starring former MythBusters co-host Grant Imahara exploring how McDonald's makes its iconic burgers, as well as the quality of its ingredients and suppliers.[16]

Summary

13-1 Identify the various distribution channels and explain the concept of market coverage.

A marketing channel is a sequence of marketing organizations that directs a product from producer to ultimate user. The marketing channel for a particular product is concerned with the transfer of ownership of that product. Merchant middlemen (merchants) actually take title to products, whereas functional middlemen simply aid in the transfer of title.

The channels used for consumer products include the direct channel from producer to consumer, the channel from producer to retailer to consumer, the channel from producer to wholesaler to retailer to consumer, and the channel from producer to agent to wholesaler to retailer to consumer. There are two major channels of industrial products: producer to user and producer to agent middleman to user.

Channels and intermediaries are chosen to implement a given level of market coverage. Intensive distribution is the use of all available outlets for a product, providing the widest market coverage. Selective distribution uses a portion of the available outlets in an area. Exclusive distribution uses only a single retail outlet for a product in a large geographic area.

13-2 Understand how supply-chain management facilitates partnering among channel members.

Supply-chain management is a long-term partnership among channel members working together to create a distribution system that reduces inefficiencies, costs, and redundancies, while creating a competitive advantage and satisfying customers. Cooperation is required among all channel members, including manufacturing, research, sales, advertising, and shipping. When all channel partners work together, delivery, scheduling, packaging, and other customer requirements are better met. Technology makes supply-chain management easier to implement.

13-3 Discuss the need for wholesalers, describe the services they provide, and identify the major types of wholesalers.

Wholesalers are intermediaries that purchase from producers or other intermediaries and sell to industrial users, retailers, or other wholesalers. Wholesalers perform many functions in a distribution channel. If they are eliminated, other channel members—such as the producer or retailers—must perform these functions. Wholesalers provide retailers with assistance in promoting products, collecting information and financing. They provide manufacturers with sales assistance, reduce their inventory costs, furnish market information, and extend credit to retailers.

Merchant wholesalers buy and then sell products. Commission merchants and brokers are essentially agents and do not take title to the goods they distribute. Sales branches and offices are owned by the manufacturers and resemble merchant wholesalers and agents, respectively.

13-4 Distinguish among the major types of retailers and shopping centers.

Retailers are intermediaries that buy from producers or wholesalers and sell to consumers. In-store retailers include department stores, discount stores, warehouse showrooms, convenience stores, supermarkets, superstores, warehouse clubs, traditional specialty stores, off-price retailers, and category killers. Nonstore retailers use direct selling, direct marketing, and automatic vending, instead of conventional stores. Types of direct marketing include catalog marketing, direct-response marketing, telemarketing, television home shopping, and online retailing.

There are four major types of shopping centers: lifestyle, neighborhood, community, and regional. Each of these centers has a varying mix of stores and serves geographic areas of different sizes.

13-5 Explain the five most important physical distribution activities.

Physical distribution consists of activities designed to move products from producers to ultimate users. Its five major functions are inventory management, order processing, warehousing, materials handling, and transportation. These interrelated functions are integrated into marketing efforts.

13-6 Explain how integrated marketing communications works to have the maximum impact on the customer.

Integrated marketing communications is the coordination of promotion efforts to achieve maximum informational and persuasive impact on customers.

13-7 Understand the basic elements of the promotion mix.

Promotion is communication about an organization and its products that is intended to inform, persuade, or remind target market members. The major ingredients of a promotion mix are advertising, personal selling, sales promotion, and public relations. The role of promotion is to facilitate exchanges directly or indirectly and to help an organization maintain favorable relationship with groups in the marketing environment.

13-8 Explain the three types of advertising and describe the major steps of developing an advertising campaign.

Advertising is a paid nonpersonal message communicated to a specific audience through a mass medium. Primary-demand advertising promotes the products of an entire industry rather than just a single brand. Selective-demand advertising promotes a particular brand of product. Institutional advertising is image-building advertising for a firm.

An advertising campaign is developed in several stages. A firm first identifies and analyzes its advertising target. The goals of the campaign must be clearly defined. Then the firm develops the advertising platform and determines the size of the advertising budget. The next steps are to develop a media plan, to create the advertising message, and to execute the campaign. Finally, promotion managers must evaluate the effectiveness of the advertising efforts before, during, and/or after the campaign.

13-9 Recognize the kinds of salespersons, the steps in the personal-selling process, and the major sales management tasks.

Personal selling is personal communication aimed at informing customers and persuading them to buy a firm's products. It is the most adaptable promotional method because the salesperson can modify the message to fit individual buyers. The major types are order getters, order takers, and support personnel. The six steps in the personal-selling process are prospecting, approaching the prospect, making the presentation, answering objections, closing the sale, and following up. Sales managers are involved directly in setting sales force objectives, recruiting, selecting, and training salespersons, compensating and motivating sales personnel, creating sales territories, and evaluating sales performance.

13-10 Describe sales promotion objectives and methods.

Sales promotion is the use of activities and materials as direct inducements to customers and salespersons. Sales promotions enhance and supplement other promotional methods. Methods of sales promotion include rebates, coupons, samples, premiums, frequent-user incentives, point-of-purchase displays, trade shows, buying allowances, and cooperative advertising.

13-11 Understand the types and uses of public relations.

Public relations is a broad set of communication activities used to create and maintain favorable relationships between an organization and various public groups, both internal and external. Organizations use a variety of public relations tools to convey messages and create images. Brochures, newsletters, company magazines, and annual reports are written public-relations tools. Speeches, event sponsorship, and publicity are other public-relations tools. Publicity is communication in news-story form about an organization, its products, or both. Types of publicity include news releases, feature articles, captioned photographs, and press conferences. Public relations can also be used to promote people, places, activities, and ideas. It can be used to enhance the reputation of an organization and reduce the unfavorable effects of negative events.

Key Terms

You should now be able to define and give an example relevant to each of the following terms:

distribution channel (or marketing channel) (364)
middleman (or marketing intermediary) (364)
merchant middleman (364)
functional middleman (364)
retailer (364)
wholesaler (365)
intensive distribution (366)
selective distribution (366)
exclusive distribution (366)
supply-chain management (366)

merchant wholesaler (367)
full-service wholesaler (368)
general-merchandise wholesaler (368)
limited-line wholesaler (368)
specialty-line wholesaler (368)
agent (368)
broker (368)
independent retailer (369)
chain retailer (369)
department store (369)
discount store (369)

warehouse showroom (370)
convenience store (370)
supermarket (370)
superstore (370)
warehouse club (371)
traditional specialty store (371)
off-price retailer (371)
category killer (371)
nonstore retailing (371)
direct selling (371)
direct marketing (372)
catalog marketing (372)

direct-response marketing (372)
telemarketing (372)
television home shopping (373)
online retailing (373)
automatic vending (373)
lifestyle shopping center (373)
neighborhood shopping center (373)
community shopping center (374)

regional shopping center (374)

physical distribution (374)

inventory management (374)

order processing (375)

warehousing (375)

materials handling (376)

transportation (376)

carrier (376)

integrated marketing communications (377)

promotion (378)

promotion mix (378)

advertising (379)

personal selling (379)

sales promotion (379)

public relations (379)

primary-demand advertising (379)

selective-demand (or brand) advertising (379)

institutional advertising (379)

advertising agency (382)

order getter (383)

creative selling (383)

order taker (383)

sales support personnel (383)

missionary salesperson (384)

trade salesperson (384)

technical salesperson (384)

consumer sales promotion method (386)

trade sales promotion method (386)

rebate (386)

coupon (386)

sample (387)

premium (387)

frequent-user incentive (387)

point-of-purchase display (388)

trade show (388)

buying allowance (388)

cooperative advertising (388)

publicity (389)

news release (390)

feature article (390)

captioned photograph (390)

press conference (390)

Discussion Questions

1. What are the most common marketing channels for consumer products? For industrial products?
2. What are the three levels of market coverage? What types of products is each used for?
3. List the services performed by wholesalers. For whom is each service performed?
4. Identify three kinds of full-service wholesalers. What factors are used to classify wholesalers into one of these categories?
5. What can nonstore retailers offer their customers that in-store retailers cannot?
6. What is physical distribution? Which major functions does it include?
7. Many producers sell to consumers both directly and through middlemen. How can such a producer justify competing with its own middlemen?
8. In what situations might a producer use agents or commission merchants rather than its own sales offices or branches?
9. If a middleman is eliminated from a marketing channel, under what conditions will costs decrease? Under what conditions will costs increase? Will the middleman's functions be eliminated? Explain.
10. What is integrated marketing communications, and why is it becoming increasingly accepted?
11. Identify and describe the major ingredients of a promotion mix.
12. Identify and give examples of the three major types of salespersons.
13. What are the major tasks involved in managing a sales force?
14. What are the major differences between consumer and trade sales promotion methods? Give examples of each.
15. What is the difference between publicity and public relations? What is the purpose of each?
16. Why do firms use event sponsorship?

Video Case
Honest Tea Plus Coca-Cola Equals National Distribution

When Seth Goldman and Barry Nalebuff co-founded Honest Tea in 1998, their idea was to "democratize organics." The two met when Nalebuff was Goldman's professor at Yale University's School of Management. A few years later, Goldman recognized an opportunity to market a distinctly different, healthy, bottled beverage made with organic ingredients, and he teamed up with Nalebuff to form Maryland-based Honest Tea. The entrepreneurs decided on tea because it has widespread appeal, and Nalebuff suggested the company's name, a play on words that reflects natural rather than synthetic ingredients.

Despite the challenges facing traditional products in the soft-drink industry, Honest Tea made inroads because its beverages taste good, have fewer calories than many competing beverages, and cater to the growing market for organic foods. However, the company had difficulty obtaining distribution at first. Retailers were unsure about stocking beverages that were far less sweet than so many already on store shelves. Finally, they found a positive reception at a natural-foods grocery chain, which agreed to buy 15,000 bottles. That order helped establish Honest Tea as a serious competitor and laid the foundation for approaching other multi-store regional retailers.

Eight years after it began operations, Honest Tea had increased annual sales to $13.5 million and was shipping 1.5 million cases of bottled drinks every year. Yet when the mainstream supermarket giant Safeway was ready to stock Honest Tea's products in all its stores, Goldman and Nalebuff realized they lacked the ability to deliver coast to coast. To make the leap from regional to national brand, Honest Tea needed a partner with a dependable distribution network to serve the entire U.S. market.

Enter Coca-Cola, which in 2008 invested enough to buy 40 percent of the Honest Tea company. Coca-Cola saw this investment as a way to enhance its own line of soft-drinks. Honest Tea gained a partner with huge buying and marketing power, as well as distribution to every corner of the country. Once Coca-Cola was involved in the distribution process, Honest Tea was able to supply Safeway and a host of other large retailers. In 2011, Coca-Cola purchased the rest of Honest Tea and left the founding management in charge to continue the company's success.

Within a few years, Honest Tea had leveraged the Coca-Cola network to expand market coverage from 15,000 stores to more than 100,000 stores throughout the United States. Its annual revenues have skyrocketed to more than $130 million as it introduces new products and enters new channels. For example, Honest Tea has begun marketing a line of bottled lemonades exclusively in Whole Foods Markets. It has also created a lightly-sweetened herbal

tea, called Heavenly Lemon Tulsi, which is now being sold through restaurants and stores. In addition, Honest Tea markets K-Cup pods for people who want to use single-serve coffee makers to make organic tea at home. On the other hand, the company dropped its CocoaNova line of brewed cacao herbal beverages after it found that stores were confused about whether to stock these products with chocolate drinks or coffee drinks.

The new products and expanded distribution have led to double-digit growth for Honest Tea, which has now sold more than 1 billion units and is racing toward its second billion. Just as important, the company has been able to expand its purchasing of sustainably-sourced sugar and other ingredients, and reinvest in the communities where its ingredients are produced.[17]

Questions

1. How would you describe Honest Tea's ideal level of market coverage? Why would this intensity of market coverage be appropriate for such beverages?
2. Should Honest Tea use the same distribution channels for its K-Cup pods as it uses for its bottled and canned tea beverages? Explain your answer.
3. What aspects of physical distribution are particularly important for Honest Tea's products that are packaged in glass bottles?

Building Skills for Career Success

1. Social Media Exercise

Distributing and Promoting Products

Recently, Coca-Cola's "Share a Coke" campaign helped the company boost U.S. sales of its carbonated beverage by more than 2 percent. Beginning with a campaign to re-engage Australian consumers with the brand, "Share a Coke" allowed people to buy bottles of Coca-Cola with their name on them and share these personalized bottles, either digitally or physically, with their friends and the rest of the world. In our current social media-dominated environment, personalization is paramount, offering consumers a way to talk, connect, and share their experiences with others. "Share a Coke" encouraged consumers to post their personalized bottles on social media platforms like Facebook, Instagram, Tumblr, and Twitter, and inspired viral videos, including a famous "Share a Coke" marriage proposal. Coca-Cola's "Summer of Sharing" generated a level of consumer-driven buzz that effectively reversed the decline in sales that the company had suffered for the past few years. Visit http://www.coca-cola.co.uk/share-a-coke and take a look at the United Kingdom's "Share a Coke" story.

1. Do you think that social media buzz is an effective way to promote a product? Why or why not?
2. Have you ever participated in a social media campaign like "Share a Coke"? If so, how did your participation in the campaign impact your purchase decision?

2. Building Team Skills

Surveys are a common tool in marketing research. The information they provide can reduce business risk and facilitate decision making. Retail outlets often survey their customers' wants and needs by distributing comment cards or questionnaires.

The following is an example of a customer survey that a local photography shop might distribute to its customers.

Assignment

1. Working in teams of three to five, choose a local retailer.
2. Classify the retailer according to the major types.

3. Design a survey to help the retailer to improve customer service. (You may find it beneficial to work with the retailer and actually administer the survey to customers. Prepare a report of the survey results.)
4. Present your findings to the class.

3. Researching Different Careers

When you are looking for a job, the people closest to you can be a great resource. Family members and friends may be able to answer your questions directly or put you in touch with someone else who can. This type of "networking" can lead to an "informational interview," in which you meet with someone who will answer your questions about a career or a company and who can provide inside information on related fields and other helpful hints.

Assignment

1. Choose a retailer or wholesaler and a position within the company that interests you.
2. Call the company and ask to speak to the person in that particular position. Explain that you are a college student interested in the position and ask to set up an informational interview.
3. Prepare a list of questions to ask in the interview. The questions should focus on:
   a. The training and experience recommended for the position
   b. How the person entered the position and advanced within the organization
   c. What he or she likes and dislikes about the work
   d. Present your findings to the class

Customer Survey

To help us to serve you better, please take a few minutes to answer the following questions. Your opinions are important to us.

1. Do you live/work in the area? (Circle one or both if they apply.)
2. Why did you choose us? (Circle all that apply.)

   Close to home   Quality
   Close to work   Full-service photography shop
   Convenience   Other
   Good service

3. How did you learn about us? (Circle one.)

   Newspaper
   Flyer/coupon
   Passing by
   Recommended by someone
   Other

4. How frequently do you have photos printed? (Please estimate.)
   ___ Times per month
   ___ Times per year
5. Which aspects of our photography shop do you think need improvement?
6. Our operating hours are from 8:00 a.m. to 7:00 p.m. weekdays and from 9:30 a.m. to 6:00 p.m. Saturdays. We are closed on Sundays and legal holidays. If changes in our operating hours would serve you better, please specify your preferences.
7. Age (Circle one.)

   Under 25
   26–39
   40–59
   Over 60

   Comments:

Running a Business
Part 5

Graeter's Is "Synonymous with Ice Cream"

When a 140-year-old company finally redesigns its logo and launches its first national ad campaign, that's big news. Graeter's, the beloved Cincinnati-based maker of premium, hand-packed ice cream, is still managed by direct descendants of its founders. Its new logo is just one part of a major rebranding effort to support the company's first big planned expansion. "If we don't continue to improve and innovate, somebody will come and do it better than us," says Chip Graeter, the company's vice president of retail stores. "And we don't want that to happen."

Quality Builds the Brand

Graeter's considers as its competitors not only Häagen-Dazs and Ben & Jerry's, national premium ice-cream brands that have much bigger marketing budgets, but also all kinds of premium-quality desserts and edible treats. Taking that wide-angle view means its competition is both broad and fierce. One thing the company is firm about, however, is maintaining the quality of its dense, creamy product (it's so dense that one pint of Graeter's ice cream weighs about a pound). Graeter's quality standards call for adhering to its simple, original family recipe—which now includes more all-natural ingredients, like beet juice instead of food dye and dairy products from hormone-free cows—and an original, artisanal production process that yields only about two gallons per machine every 20 minutes. "We were always all-natural," says CEO Richard Graeter II, "but now we're being militant about it."

That hard-earned premium quality is what built the Graeter's brand from its earliest days when refrigeration was unknown and ice cream was a true novelty. Today, "Graeter's in Cincinnati is synonymous with ice cream," says a company executive. "People will say, 'Let's go get a Graeter's.' They don't say, 'Let's go get an ice cream.'" Quality is also what the current management team hopes will propel Graeter's beyond its current market, which consists of a few dozen company-owned retail stores in Ohio, Missouri, Kentucky, and nearby states, and the freezer cases of about 6,000 supermarkets and grocery stores, particularly the Kroger chain. Graeter's is also on the menu in some fine restaurants and country clubs. The company operates an online store and will ship ice cream overnight via UPS to any of the 48 continental states (California is its biggest shipping market). Graeter's also sells a limited line of candies, cakes, and other bakery goods, and its ice-cream line includes smoothies and sorbets.

Expanding to New Markets

Graeter's ambitious expansion plans are backed by a recent increase in production capacity from one factory to three (one of the new factories was built, and the other purchased). The plans call for distributing Graeter's delectable, seasonal flavors to even more supermarkets and grocery stores, and for gradually opening new retail stores, perhaps as far away as Los Angeles and New York. The Kroger chain is Graeter's biggest distribution partner. Of the tens of thousands of brands Kroger carries, says the chain, pricey Graeter's commands the strongest brand loyalty. It was through Kroger, in fact, that Graeter's managers hit upon the idea of conducting a trial expansion to Denver, a new market for the brand.

Kroger owns the King Soopers chain of grocery stores in Denver, and research showed that more Denver ice-cream buyers choose premium brands than cheaper choices, suggesting that Graeter's might do well there. So Graeter's chose 12 flavors to send to 30 King Soopers stores in Denver as a test market, with the goal of selling two or three gallons a week. The test was an unqualified success. Within a few weeks, the company was selling an average of five gallons a week per store.

"I'd like to be coast to coast," admits Graeter's CEO. In fact, the management team would like to explore selling Graeter's in Canada, perhaps within the next five years. "The challenge, of course, is to preserve the integrity of the product as we grow. But we have done that for more than 100 years, and I'd argue that it's better now than ever."

Promoting the Brand

Graeter's had already gotten a big free boost from a positive mention on the *Oprah Winfrey Show* in 2002, when the influential talk-show host called it the best ice cream she had ever tasted. "We were shipping about 40 orders a day," says CEO Richard Graeter II. "After her show, the next day we probably shipped 400." National attention continues with occasional exposure on the Food Network, the Fine Living

© ISTOCKPHOTO.COM/LUMO

Channel, the Travel Channel, and even the History Channel. "How does that happen?" asks one of the firm's executives. "It happens because we have a product and a process and a growth that is exciting."

Still, says George Denman, the company's vice president of sales and marketing, Graeter's faces the same challenge in new markets as any "small, regional niche player" and one with a limited marketing budget: "establishing a relationship with the consumer, building brand awareness [through] trial and repeat. . . . So obviously when we roll into a marketplace one of the first things we do is we demo the product. We get it out in front of the consumer and get them to taste it, because the product sells itself." The company has also been reducing its price to distributors, who pass the savings along to stores that can then advertise that Graeter's pints are on sale. "If a consumer has maybe been buying Ben & Jerry's and never considered ours, because maybe that dollar price point difference was too high, this gives her the opportunity to try us. And once she tries us, we know we've brand-switched that consumer right then," says Denman.

Marketing Communications

Through its Cincinnati-based ad agency, Graeter's does some local advertising, including attractive point-of-sale displays in supermarkets and grocery stores and some radio ads, occasional print ads, and billboards. The company launches small-scale promotions for the introduction of a new flavor or to celebrate National Ice Cream Month or other occasions. To support the brand's nationwide presence in grocery stores, the company began airing commercials nationally for the first time in 2014. However, brand loyalty for this family business has grown mostly through word of mouth that endures across generations. "We are the beneficiary of that loyalty that our customers have built up over so many years, multiple generations," says one of the company's executives. "Our customers have told us they were introduced to the product through their grandmother, or a special time. . . .

They don't come to our stores because they have to; they come because they want to."

"We use the traditional [marketing] methods," says Denman. "We are also doing nontraditional methods. We are looking at electronic couponing, where consumers will be able to go to our website as a new consumer . . . and secure a dollar-off coupon to try Graeter's, just for coming to our website or joining up on Facebook. We've done loyalty programs with Kroger where they have actually direct-mailed loyal consumers and offered . . . discounts as well. . . . So far it's worked well for us. We've had to go back and look at the return on investment on each of these programs and cut some things out and improve on some other things, but in the end we have been very pleased with the results."

"Quality . . . We Never Changed"

"We ship our product, and that was something that for the first hundred years you never thought about. I mean, who would think about shipping ice cream from Cincinnati to California? But it is our number-one market for shipping, so all those things you can change," says Richard Graeter, the CEO. "The most important thing, the quality of the product and how we make it, that we never changed."[18]

Questions

1. What are the elements of Graeter's marketing mix? Which are most likely to be affected by external forces in the marketing environment?
2. Graeter's ice-cream line includes smoothies and sorbets. Do you think it should consider other brand extensions such as yogurt, low-fat ice cream, coffee drinks, or other related products? Why or why not?
3. How might Graeter's capitalize on its valuable capacity for word-of-mouth promotion in expanding to new markets where, despite some national publicity like the *Oprah Winfrey Show*, its name is still not widely known?

Building a Business Plan: Part 5

This part is one of the most important components of your business plan. In this part, you will present the facts that you have gathered on the size and nature of your market(s). State market size in dollars and units. How many units and what is the dollar value of the products you expect to sell in a given time period? Indicate your primary and secondary sources of data and the methods you used to estimate total market size and your market share. Part 5 of your textbook covers all marketing-related topics. These chapters should help you to answer the questions in this part of the business plan.

The Marketing Plan Component

The marketing plan component is and should be unique to your business. Many assumptions or projections used in the analysis may turn out differently; therefore, this component should be flexible enough to be adjusted as needed. The marketing plan should include answers to at least the following questions:

5.1 What are your target markets, and what common identifiable need(s) can you satisfy?

5.2 What are the competitive, legal, political, economic, technological, and sociocultural factors affecting your marketing efforts?

5.3 What are the current needs of each target market? Describe the target market in terms of demographic, geographic, psychographic, and product-usage characteristics. What changes in the target market are anticipated?

5.4 What advantages and disadvantages do you have in meeting the target market's needs?

5.5 How will your product, distribution, promotion, and price satisfy customer needs?

5.6 How effectively will your products meet these needs?

5.7 What are the relevant aspects of consumer behavior and product use?

5.8 What are your company's projected sales volume, market share, and profitability?

5.9 What are your marketing objectives? Include the following in your marketing objectives:

- Product introduction, improvement, or innovation
- Sales or market share
- Profitability
- Pricing
- Distribution
- Advertising (Prepare advertising samples for the appendix.)

Make sure that your marketing objectives are clearly written, measurable, and consistent with your overall marketing strategy.

5.10 How will the results of your marketing plan be measured and evaluated?

Review of Business Plan Activities

Remember that even though it will be time-consuming, developing a clear, well-written marketing plan is important. Therefore, make sure that you have checked the plan for any weaknesses or problems before proceeding to Part 6. Also, make certain that all your answers to the questions in this and other parts are consistent throughout the business plan. Finally, write a brief statement that summarizes all the information for this part of the business plan.

The information contained in this section will also assist you in completing the online *Interactive Business Plan*.

Endnotes

1 Based on information in E. J. Schultz, "Ad Age's 2014 Marketer of the Year: Under Armour," *Advertising Age*, December 8, 2014, http://adage.com/article/news/marketer-year-armour/296088/ (accessed July 7, 2015); Scott Harrison, "Under Armour Confirms Plans to Invest $100m in Mt. Juliet, Create 1,500 Jobs," *Nashville Business Journal*, October 2, 2014, http://www.bizjournals.com/nashville/blog/2014/10/under-armour-confirms-plans-to-invest-100m-in-mt.html?page=all (accessed July 7, 2015); Lorraine Mirabella, "Under Armour Surpasses Adidas to Become No. 2 Sports Brand," *Baltimore Sun*, September 8, 2014, http://articles.baltimoresun.com/2014-09-08/business/bs-bz-under-armour-beats-adidas-20140908_1_armour-ceo-kevin-plank-market-leader-nike (accessed July 7, 2015); Kim Adams, "Fast-Growing Under Armour Gaining Speed in Global Market," *Medill Reports*, March 11, 2014, http://news.medill.

northwestern.edu/chicago/news.aspx?id=228798 (accessed July 7, 2015); Lorraine Mirabella, "Under Armour's Brand House in SoHo Opens," *Baltimore Sun*, April 24, 2014, http://articles.baltimoresun.com/2014-04-24/business/bal-consuming-under-armour-soho-store-opening-20140423_1_harbor-east-store-brand-house-armourwill (accessed July 7, 2015).

2 Suzy Hansen, "How Zara Grew into the World's Largest Fashion Retailer," *New York Times*, November 11, 2012, http://www.nytimes.com/2012/11/11/magazine/how-zara-grew-into-the-worlds-largest-fashion-retailer.html (accessed July 7, 2015); "Learnings from International Retail: Zara," *The Free Press Journal*, December 11, 2014, http://freepressjournal.in/learnings-from-international-retail-zaras/ (accessed July 7, 2015).

3 U.S. Census Bureau, "Economic Census: Industry Snapshots: Retail Trade," http://thedataweb.rm.census.gov/TheDataWeb_HotReport2/

econsnapshot/2012/snapshot.hrml?NAICS=44-45 (accessed January 5, 2015).

4 "Fact Sheets," National Association of Convenience Stores, http://www.nacsonline.com/Research/FactSheets/pages/default.aspx (accessed January 5, 2015).

5 "Fast Facts," Direct Selling 411, http://www.directselling411.com/about-direct-selling/ (accessed January 5, 2015).

6 *Do Not Call*, http://www.donotcall.gov (accessed January 5, 2015); Jeff Rossen and Avni Patel, "Telemarketer Agrees to $3.4 Million FTC Penalty over Unwanted Calls," *Today*, May 27, 2014, http://www.today.com/news/telemarketer-agrees-3-4-million-ftc-penalty-over-unwanted-calls-2D79710375 (accessed July 7, 2015).

7 Ulrike Lemmin-Woolfrey, "8 Vending Machines You Didn't Know You Needed," *CNN*, June 23, 2014; "Vending Machines Go Gourmet for Upscale Consumers," *Dallas Morning News*, July 8, 2014, http://www.dallasnews.com/business/retail/20140708-vending-machines-go-gourmet-for-upscale-customers.ece (accessed July 7, 2015).

8 "U.S. Ad Spending Totals by Medium," *Advertising Age*, December 29, 2014, p. 14.

9 National Association of Realtors, "National Association of Realtors Announces Major National Advertising Campaign," Press Release, July 14, 2014, http://www.realtor.org/news-releases/2014/07/national-association-of-realtors-announces-major-national-advertising-campaign (accessed July 7, 2015).

10 Matt MacVey, "Whole Foods Rolls out First National Advertising Campaign," *Advertising Age*, November 18, 2014, http://adage.com/article/cmo-strategy/foods-rolls-national-advertising-campaign/295901/ (accessed July 7, 2015).

11 "25 Largest U.S. Advertisers," *Advertising Age*, December 29, 2014, p. 8.

12 Target, http://cartwheel.target.com/ (accessed January 6, 2015).

13 Jane L. Levere, "A Campaign to Pique the Interest of Those Who Revel in a Deal," *New York Times*, August 11, 2014, http://www.nytimes.com/2014/08/12/business/media/a-campaign-to-pique-the-interest-of-those-who-revel-in-a-deal.html?_r=0 (accessed July 7, 2015).

14 Joe Pinsker, "The Psychology behind Costco's Free Samples," *The Atlantic*, October 1, 2014, http://www.theatlantic.com/business/archive/2014/10/the-psychology-behind-costcos-free-samples/380969/ (accessed July 7, 2015).

15 Red Bull Stratos, http://www.redbullstratos.com/ (accessed January 6, 2015).

16 Katie Little, "McDonald's Shuts Down Pink Slime Question ... Again," *CNBC*, October 13, 2014, http://www.cnbc.com/id/102082873 (accessed July 7, 2015).

17 Based on information in Fran Tarkenton, "Small Business Advice: How to Strike and Sustain a Successful Business Partnership," *Washington Post*, February 3, 2015, http://www.washingtonpost.com/business/on-small-business/small-business-advice-how-to-strike-and-sustain-a-successful-business-partnership/2015/02/03/c72cafb0-abd8-11e4-9c91-e9d2f9fde644_story.html (accessed July 15, 2015); Thomas Heath, "Even After Sale to Coca-Cola, Bethesda-Based Honest Tea 'Work in Progress,'" *Washington Post*, June 29, 2014, www.washingtonpost.com (accessed July 7, 2015); Monica Watrous, "Q&A: Honest Tea Steeped in Success," *Food Business News*, December 8, 2014, www.foodbusinessnews.net (accessed July 7, 2015); Cengage Learning, *Honest Tea* video.

18 Based on information from Alexander Coolidge, "Graeter's Pitches Its Products Nationwide," *Cincinnati Enquirer*, June 20, 2014, http://www.cincinnati.com/story/money/2014/06/18/graeters-pitches-product-nationwide/10820875/ (accessed July 7, 2015); Kimberly L. Jackson, "Graeter's Premium Chocolate Chip Ice cream Lands at Stop & Shop," *Newark Star-Ledger (NJ)*, April 4, 2012, www.nj.com; "Graeter's Ice cream Debuts in Bay Area," *Tampa Bay Times (St. Petersburg, FL)*, January 10, 2012, p. 4B; Jim Carper, "Graeter's Runs a Hands-on Ice cream Plant," *Dairy Foods*, August 2011, pp. 36+; Jim Carper, "The Greater Good," *Dairy Foods*, August 2011, pp. 95+; "Graeter's Unveils New 'Mystery Flavor,'" *Dayton Daily News*, March 29, 2012, http://m.daytondailynews.com/news/news/local/graeters-unveils-new-mystery-flavor-1/nMzb9/ (accessed August 6, 2015); Bob Driehaus, "A Cincinnati Ice Cream Maker Aims Big," *New York Times*, September 11, 2010, http://www.nytimes.com/2010/09/12/us/12icecream.html?_r=0 (accessed July 15, 2015); Lucy May, "Graeter's Northern Kentucky Franchisee Puts Stores on the Block," *Business Courier*, August 6, 2010, http://cincinnati.bizjournals.com (accessed July 7, 2015); www.graeters.com (accessed July 7, 2015); interviews with company staff and Cengage videos about Graeter's.

CHAPTER

14

Exploring Social Media and e-Business

Why Should You Care?

Question: How important is social media and e-business for a business today? Answer: Today, more and more businesses are using social media and e-business to reach new customers and increase sales and profits.

Learning Objectives

Once you complete this chapter, you will be able to:

14-1 Examine why it is important for a business to use social media.

14-2 Discuss how businesses use social media tools.

14-3 Explain the business objectives for using social media.

14-4 Describe how businesses develop a social media plan.

14-5 Explain the meaning of e-business.

14-6 Understand the fundamental models of e-business.

14-7 Identify the factors that will affect the future of the Internet, social media, and e-business.

Taco Bell's Recipe for Social Media Success

Taco Bell's recipe for social media success includes a bold tactic that few businesses would dare to try. For one day, it temporarily wiped all messages off its Facebook and Twitter accounts and displayed a single post, labeled with the hashtag #OnlyInTheApp. The hashtag referred to Taco Bell's new app (application) for ordering customized menu items, paying for them, and arranging pick-up in the store or at the drive-through window. This unusual social media tactic caught the attention of customers as well as reporters for conventional media outlets, increasing the audience for Taco Bell's new app introduction. Within 24 hours, three-quarters of Taco Bell's 6,000 U.S. stores had received at least one customer order via the new app. Within two months, the app—available for Apple and Android systems—had been downloaded nearly 2 million times.

Smart phones and other mobile devices are popular among Millennials—people born after 1980, and for Taco Bell, Millennials are a key customer group. That's why the restaurant chain has an active social media presence integrated with traditional advertising. To support the app introduction, for example, Taco Bell aired a television commercial about the speed and convenience of mobile ordering and uploaded the commercial to YouTube, where it has been viewed more than 800,000 times. A few months after the social media blackout, Taco Bell used the hashtag #OnlyInTheApp on Facebook and Twitter to promote its giveaway of one free Doritos Locos Taco with every purchase made with the app. That promotion resulted in a surge of mobile orders.

Taco Bell also uses social media to obtain customer feedback and generate interest in new menu items it develops. When the company developed the Quesalupa, which is a combination of a quesadilla and a chalupa, the restaurant chain selected Toledo, Ohio as the only test market. It ran a local ad campaign promoting the product and invited customers to post comments on social media, using the hashtag #Quesalupa. Taco Bell then analyzed the number and content of comments to understand what customers liked and disliked before deciding whether to launch the product nationally.[1]

Did You Know?

Taco Bell has 6,000 U.S. restaurants, 9.9 million Facebook likes, 1.5 million Twitter followers, and 550,000 Instagram followers.

For Taco Bell, the company profiled in the Inside Business feature for this chapter, tacos, enchiladas, burritos, and other food items are big business. And with 6,000 stores in 21 countries, this company sells a lot of food. In order to increase brand awareness, the company uses social media, e-business, and its new #OnlyInTheApp mobile app to build revenues and profits. In fact, Taco Bell is an excellent example of how social media, e-business, and mobile apps are changing the way companies do business in today's competitive business environment.

Take a moment to think about how social media and e-business affect your own life. In just a few short years, it has changed the way we communicate with each other, it has changed the way we meet people, and it has changed the way we shop. In this chapter, we explore how these trends affect both individuals and businesses.

We begin this chapter by examining why social media is important for both individuals and business firms. Next, we discuss how companies can use social media to build relationships with customers, the goals for social media, the steps to build a social media plan, and ways to measure the effectiveness of a firm's social media activities. In the last part of this chapter, we take a close look at how firms use technology to conduct business on the Internet and what growth opportunities and challenges affect both social media and e-businesses.

14-1 WHY IS SOCIAL MEDIA IMPORTANT?

Learning Objective

14-1 Examine why it is important for a business to use social media.

If you are a "digital native" (typically defined as anyone born after 1980), you know exactly what social media is because you have grown up with computers and technology and are very comfortable sharing information about yourself. If you are anyone else, social media seems like a strange (but exciting) phenomenon where millions of people freely share, create, vote, and connect with other people effortlessly using Internet-based technologies.

14-1a What Is Social Media and How Popular Is It?

Today, there are many definitions of social media because it is still developing and continually changing. For our purposes, **social media** represents the online interactions that allow people and businesses to communicate and share ideas, personal information, and information about products and services. Simply put, social media is about people. It is about a culture of participation, meaning that people can now discuss, vote, create, connect, and advocate much easier than ever before. For example, you can post your plans for a weekend trip on Facebook. Then you can share a travel itinerary and chronicle your trip through videos, photos, and ratings on Facebook. People can also use Twitter to raise awareness about bone-marrow donations in order to help a friend find a match. While it's hard to imagine, many popular social media sites like Facebook and Twitter were just created in the past 10 to 15 years (see Figure 14-1).

So how popular are social media sites? A recent Pew Internet Research study found that 71 percent of U.S. adults who use the Internet are active on Facebook, 28 percent are on LinkedIn, 28 percent are on Pinterest, 26 percent are on Instagram, and 23 percent are on Twitter.[2] And more than half of these adults are active on two or more social media sites. Among the most popular worldwide are Facebook, which has more than 1.2 billion users; YouTube, which has more than 1 billion users; and LinkedIn, the professional networking site with 300 million users. These numbers increase daily as consumers log onto social media from home, from work, and from smartphones to stay in touch with family and friends, reconnect with old friends or classmates, share photos and videos, and post messages about what's happening in their lives.

social media the online interactions that allow people and businesses to communicate and share ideas, personal information, and information about products and services

ANDREBLAIS/DREAMSTIME.COM

A new kind of surfing! Surfing the Internet doesn't require water or waves, but is one of the most popular activities for people around the globe. Social media and technology have changed the way people communicate and share ideas, personal information, and information about products and services. Simply put: It's the new way more and more people obtain the information they need to live their lives.

14-1b Why Businesses Use Social Media

Social media has completely changed the business environment. Early on, companies saw potential in the sheer number of people using social media and that made using social media a top priority for many business firms. By using social media, companies could share information about their products and services and improve customer service. Now many companies, large and small, are using social media to learn about customers' likes and dislikes, seek public input about products and marketing, create a community feeling, polish brand image, and promote particular products. Macy's, for example, is active on Facebook, YouTube, Pinterest, Twitter, and a blog designed to be read on mobile screens. The company

FIGURE 14-1 Timeline for the Development of Social Media

Like computer technology, developments in social media have been not
only rapid, they have also changed the way people connect.

	SOCIAL MEDIA BREAKTHROUGH
1991	• AOL
1995	• Classmates.com; Yahoo
1996	• AOL instant messenger
1998	• MoveOn.org, Google
1999	• Napster, Blogger, Epinions, LiveJournal
2001	• Wikipedia, StumbleUpon
2002	• Friendster, Technorati
2003	• LinkedIn, Wordpress, MySpace, Hi5, Photobucket, Delicious
2004	• Gmail, Flickr, Facebook, Yelp, Digg
2005	• YouTube, Mashable, Reddit, Bebo
2006	• Twitter
2007	• Tumblr
2008	• Apple's App Store
2009	• Foursquare
2010	• Pinterest, Instagram
2011	• Google +, Snapchat
2012	• Facebook sells stock to the public
2013	• Twitter sells stock to the public
2014	• Smart electronics and crowdfunding became popular
The Future	• Who knows what the next generation of social media will mean for both individuals and business?

uses its Facebook site to provide fashion tips and news about new products and
to communicate with its 14 million-plus Facebook fans. Macy's also maintains
multiple Twitter accounts to highlight special in-store events, announce discounts
and clearance sales, and recruit college students and graduates for internships
and job opportunities. Often it uses a **hashtag**, either a word or a short phrase
preceded by the pound sign (#), to identify different topics, such as #GoRed for
tweets showing how Macy's supports the American Heart Association's healthy-
heart campaign.[3] On Pinterest, Macy's virtual bulletin boards hold thousands of
"pinned" images representing the latest in beauty products, fashions, bridal registry
items, and home décor. Its YouTube channel includes Macy's commercials, coverage
of the annual Thanksgiving Day Parade, behind-the-scenes designer interviews, and
videos about fashion trends.

hashtag a word or a short phrase
preceded by the pound sign (#), to
identify different topics

Ethical Success or Failure

Should Social Media Disclose Experiments to Users?

Should social media users be involved in experiments without their knowledge or permission? Facebook is one of many networks with an entire team of researchers who analyze what users post and how they interact. Facebook made headlines not long ago when news broke out that it had manipulated the news feeds of nearly 700,000 users. The researchers wanted to determine whether positive posts trigger positive feelings and sharing of such feelings, as well as whether negative posts trigger negative feelings and sharing of those feelings. They learned that the answer to both questions is yes—and their experiment also triggered an ethical controversy.

Some academic researchers and privacy advocates argued that users should have been notified in advance that they would be part of an experiment and should have been given a choice about participating. Privacy advocates also expressed concern about how much user information Facebook and other social media networks collect and how they use the data for marketing research. For its part, Facebook noted that users give their consent to research and analyses when they register and agree to the site's terms of service, a document that covers several screens of online text. Since this issue came to light, Facebook and other sites have been looking more carefully at their research processes and asking internal review boards to examine proposed studies. Do you think social media sites should disclose experiments and allow users to opt out if they choose?

Sources: Based on information in, "Social Media Ethics," *PBS Religion & Ethics Newsweekly*, January 9, 2015, www.pbs.org/wnet/religionandethics; Sharon Jayson, "Social Media Research Raises Privacy and Ethics Issues," *USA Today*, March 12, 2014, www.usatoday.com; Reed Albergotti and Elizabeth Dwoskin, "Facebook Study Sparks Soul-Searching and Ethical Questions," *Wall Street Journal*, June 30, 2014, www.wsj.com.

Concept Check

✓ According to material in this section, what are the reasons why people use social media?

✓ How has social media changed the environment for business firms?

Of course, companies want to encourage *viral* sharing of product or brand messages and images, meaning that a large number of people mention the brand or share the content repeatedly on social media sites. For instance, Samsung provided Oscars host Ellen DeGeneres with one of its smartphones before a recent Academy Awards show. Not only did she show it on stage, she used it to snap a selfie with other celebrities and immediately tweeted the photo. It was retweeted more than 3 million times, giving Samsung tens of millions of dollars worth of social media exposure within hours.[4]

The fact that so many people are actively sharing information about themselves and their likes and dislikes online for all to see was a driving force behind many companies' attempts to develop a social media presence. Unlike social media, traditional marketing messages were top down—meaning that companies used television, newspapers, and magazine ads to promote their product to a large audience without any opportunity for feedback. With social media, this is no longer the case. If people have bad experiences with a product or service, they tend to let the world know by writing about it on a blog, mentioning it on Facebook, or tweeting about it. Not long ago, one customer tweeted her annoyance after waiting to talk with a Citibank service representative. To her surprise, a Citibank representative quickly tweeted back to ask for the customer's phone number so the bank could solve the problem. As a result of Citibank's attention to social media, it receives tweeted compliments in addition to tweeted complaints. Other banks using social media to stay in touch with customers' concerns and comments include Bank of America, Capital One, JP Morgan Chase, TD Bank, and Wells Fargo. The bottom line: While companies no longer have much control over what is said about their products or services, they still often respond to negative comments about the company and its products or services made by their customers. Even if the company's response doesn't completely resolve the issue, customers appreciate the company's effort to improve customer service. For more information about why businesses use social media (and the benefits for a business), see Figure 14-2.

FIGURE 14-2 The Six Most Important Benefits for a Business That Uses Social Media

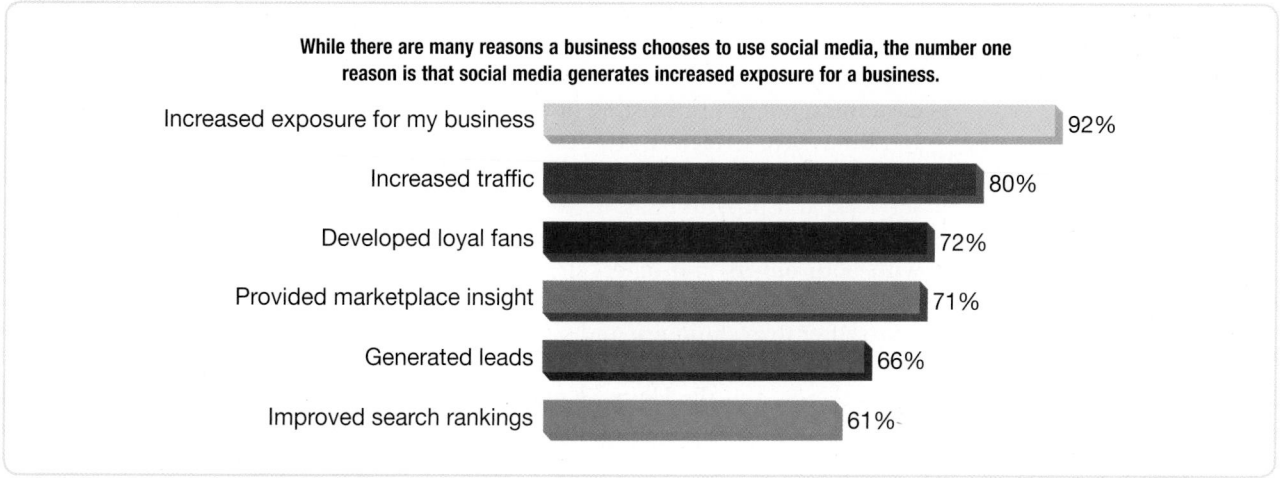

While there are many reasons a business chooses to use social media, the number one reason is that social media generates increased exposure for a business.

- Increased exposure for my business — 92%
- Increased traffic — 80%
- Developed loyal fans — 72%
- Provided marketplace insight — 71%
- Generated leads — 66%
- Improved search rankings — 61%

Source: Michael A. Stelzner, "2014 Social Media Marketing Industry Report," The SocialMediaExaminer.com website at www.socialmediaexaminer.com (accessed February 27, 2015).

14-2 SOCIAL MEDIA TOOLS FOR BUSINESS USE

For a business, part of what makes social media so challenging is the sheer number of ways to interact with other businesses and both existing and potential customers. Companies are using social media because it allows the company to

- connect with customers;
- listen to its main stakeholders (including but not limited to customers);
- provide another means of customer service;
- develop content that is valuable to customers; and
- engage customers in product development and formulation.

For example, **social content sites** allow companies to create and share information about their products and services via blogs, videos, photos, and podcasts. Commercials, for example, can go viral on social media, especially when linked to major sporting events like the Super Bowl or the World Cup. To build buzz for their Super Bowl commercials, some companies post them on social media content sites before the big game. Budweiser regularly does this, allowing its ads to rack up 20 million views or more before kickoff time. It also publicizes hashtags like #BestBuds keyed to the commercials as a way of encouraging ad-related comments on social media.[5] For businesses selling to other businesses, social content sites can also include webinars and online promotional materials. For an overview of how businesses can use social media tools, take another look at Figure 14-2.

14-2a Business Use of Blogs

For businesses, blogs have become one of the most widely used tools for the effective use of social media.

Learning Objective

14-2 Discuss how businesses use social media tools.

social content sites allow companies to create and share information about their products and services

© FUZZBONES/SHUTTERSTOCK.COM

Companies use social media to ... While you can fill in the blank, companies use social media to connect with customers. Other more specific reasons for the increased use of social media include listening to customers, improving customer service, providing information about products and services, and generating new ideas for products and services.

A **blog** is a website that allows a company to share information in order to increase customers' knowledge about its products and services, as well as to build trust. Once a story or information is posted, customers can provide feedback through comments, which is one of the most important ways of creating a conversation with customers, not as just existing or potential customers, but as people.

Blogs are effective at developing better relationships with customers, attracting new customers, telling stories about the company's products or services, and providing an active forum for testing new ideas. For example, the Brooklyn-based online crafts marketplace Etsy uses its blogs to communicate with both buyers and sellers. Its blog posts, some written by artisans and some by Etsy personnel, profile online shops, highlight new fashion trends, teach do-it-yourself craft techniques, and showcase unusual and unique items for sale. Etsy also maintains blogs for its marketplaces in Australia, France, Germany, the Netherlands, and the United Kingdom, as well as a blog only for Etsy news and a "Seller Handbook" blog to help sellers succeed on Etsy.[6] Etsy invites comments on all these blogs and pays close attention to the feedback so it can better serve the needs of sellers and buyers. By including information about webinars and promotional materials, blogs are also effective for businesses that are selling to other businesses.

blog a website that allows a company to share information in order to not only increase the customer's knowledge about its products and services, but also to build trust

media sharing sites allow users to upload photos, videos, and podcasts

podcasts digital audio or video files that people listen to or watch online on tablets, computers, MP3 players, or smartphones

14-2b Photos, Videos, and Podcasts

In addition to blogs, another tool for social content is **media sharing sites**, which allow users to upload photos, videos, and podcasts. Today, photo sharing provides a method for a company to tell a compelling story about its products or services through postings on either the company's website or a social media site. Before participating in media sharing, managers and employees should consider the following three factors:

- Who will create the photos, videos, and podcasts that will be used?
- How will the content be distributed to interested businesses and consumers?
- How much will it cost to create and distribute the material?

Videos have also gained popularity because of their ability to tell stories. Entertainment companies, for example, now traditionally use YouTube as a way to showcase movie trailers. And Home Depot and Lowes have also posted great do-it-yourself videos on their YouTube channels. Companies know that YouTube and others sites are useful because they are already recognized by other businesses and consumers as a source of both entertainment and information.

Podcasts are digital audio or video files that people listen to or watch online on tablets, computers, MP3 players, or smartphones. Think of podcasts as radio shows that are distributed through various means (like iTunes) and not linked to a scheduled time period. The great thing about podcasts is that they are available for download at any time. Bill Marriott, former CEO of Marriott Hotels, has always used an audio recorder to "write" his blog entries. The company posts those podcasts for download on the Marriott on the Move blog, alongside the transcribed version that's posted on the blog itself.

14-2c Social Media Ratings

Social media enables shoppers to access opinions, recommendations, and referrals from others who have

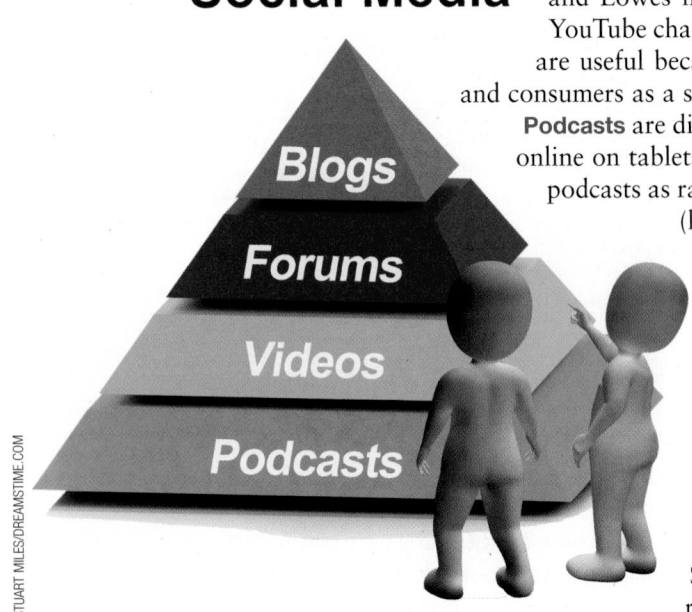

Social Media

Blogs

Forums

Videos

Podcasts

STUART MILES/DREAMSTIME.COM

bought a product or service. This type of information is available via a social media site and can include reviews and ratings, as well as information on sales promotions programs like Groupon and LivingSocial. Both of these sites provide information about companies that offer deep discounts to customers that redeem an offer.

Sites for ratings and reviews are based on the idea that consumers trust the opinions of others when it comes to purchasing products and services. According to Bazaarvoice, adding just one review results in a 10 percent increase in orders. That increase jumps to 25 percent when a product goes from zero to 30 reviews.[7] Based on the early work of Amazon and eBay, new sites have sprung up allowing consumers to rate local businesses or compare products and services. One of the most popular, Yelp, combines customer ratings with social networking and is now one of the largest local review directories on the Web. Consumer reviews are especially influential in certain purchase situations. Travel services and restaurants, for example, are an area where ratings make a difference in buying decisions. Knowing this, Wyndham Hotel Group puts the ratings of consumers who use TripAdvisor directly on its websites so travelers can see what others say about the hotels. By examining the reviews on other sites, plus any social media comments posted elsewhere, Wyndham can get a good sense of its online reputation and identify specific areas for improvement.[8]

14-2d Social Games

Social games are another area of growth in social media. A **social game** is "a multiplayer, competitive, goal-oriented activity with defined rules of engagement and online connectivity among a community of players."[9] One of the most important aspects of social media is entertainment and games like Angry Birds and FarmVille serve that purpose. Indeed, research shows that the "gamification" of social media is a huge trend because people like the competition, social status, and rewards that they can earn through social gaming.[10] For businesses that create games, it can be very profitable. Rovio Entertainment's Angry Birds games have been downloaded more than 2 billion times, creating huge demand for game-related goods and services. Still, Rovio and its rivals, including King Digital Entertainment, are feeling intense competitive pressure as players set aside old favorites to try new games and access different games via mobile apps. In fact, some companies are creating their own mobile game apps with social media links. For instance, the sandwich chain Schlotzsky's increased brand engagement with a mobile game app in which players "stack" sandwich ingredients and share their results on social media.[11]

While some businesses elect to create their own games, others promote particular brands or products within another firm's game. For example, Honda sponsored a promotion in which players of the Zynga social game, Words with Friends, earned extra points and special tips when they played and uncovered words that describe the new Honda Accord, words such as "tech" and "luxury."[12]

social game a multiplayer, competitive, goal-oriented activity with defined rules of engagement and online connectivity among a community of players

Concept Check

✓ What is a blog? How can a business use blogs to develop relationships with customers?

✓ What types of content can be used on a media sharing site? What factors should be considered when developing content for a media sharing site?

✓ Describe two ways that businesses can use "gamification" to generate sales revenue.

14-3 ACHIEVING BUSINESS OBJECTIVES THROUGH SOCIAL MEDIA

Although the popularity of social media is a recent phenomenon, many businesses are already using it to achieve important objectives. Some of these goals are long-term—such as building brand awareness and brand reputation—while others are more short-term—such as increasing website traffic or generating sales leads. Regardless of how social media is used, there are a lot of business opportunities. In this section, we explore a few ways that companies have used social media effectively to achieve business objectives.

Learning Objective

14-3 Explain the business objectives for using social media.

14-3a Social Media Communities

For a business, social media can be used to build a community. **Social media communities** are social networks based on the relationships among people.[13] These electronic communities encourage two-way communication, allow for people to develop profiles, and identify other people to connect with by using technology and the Internet. People in each community can be called friends, fans, followers, or connections. Popular social networking sites include Facebook (the largest), LinkedIn (for professionals), Twitter, Google+, YouTube, Pinterest, and many others. Visual content is particularly valuable because it encourages more people to share with other people in social media communities. Three Brothers Bakery in Houston has found that mouth-watering photos of wedding cakes and other bakery goods, posted on Pinterest, encourage photo sharing and bring potential customers to its website for more information.[14] To see how many businesses use the top seven social media community sites, see Figure 14-3.

There are social communities for every interest, ethnic group, and lifestyle. Different types of social communities include forums and wikis. A **forum** is an interactive version of a community bulletin board that focuses on threaded discussions. These are particularly popular with people who share a common interest such as video games. Another community based on social media is a wiki. A **wiki** is a collaborative online working space that enables members to contribute content that can be shared with other people. With wikis, members of the community are the editors and gatekeepers ensuring that the content is correct and updated. Wikipedia—the free online encyclopedia—is the best example of a wiki.

Today, many companies and nonprofit organizations are using social media to build communities in order to achieve important objectives. Using social media to promote its lending programs, the nonprofit organization, Kiva, has helped build communities around the globe by matching lenders and struggling would-be entrepreneurs. Using Kiva to identify potential borrowers, anyone who can lend at least $25 can loan money to people who need a bit of cash to go into business or keep a business running. To date, there are 1.3 million Kiva lenders that have funded loans of more than $675 million to people in 86 different countries.[15]

social media communities social networks based on the relationships among people

forum an interactive version of a community bulletin board that focuses on threaded discussions

wiki a collaborative online working space that enables members to contribute content that can be shared with other people

FIGURE 14-3 The Top Seven Social Media Networking Sites Used by Businesses

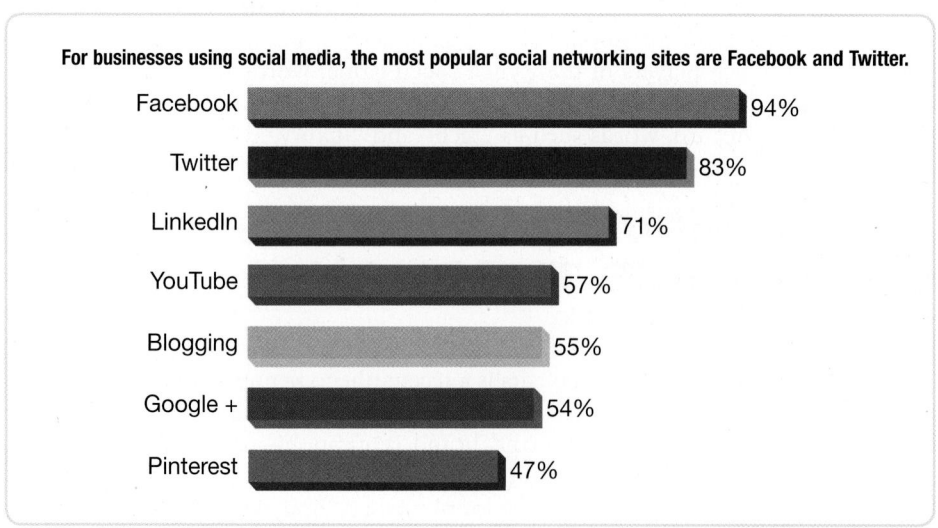

For businesses using social media, the most popular social networking sites are Facebook and Twitter.

- Facebook 94%
- Twitter 83%
- LinkedIn 71%
- YouTube 57%
- Blogging 55%
- Google + 54%
- Pinterest 47%

Source: Michael A. Stelzner, "2014 Social Media Marketing Industry Report," The SocialMediaExaminer.com website at www. socialmediaexaminer.com (accessed February 27, 2015).

14-3b Crisis and Reputation Management

One of the most important reasons for listening to stakeholders is to determine whether there is a crisis brewing. A majority of companies believe that their company is less than a year away from some potential crisis moment and monitor social media for conversations that may predict a crisis.[16] During a crisis, companies can use social media to answer questions, reassure the public, and present positive information to help rebuild their reputations. General Motors recently faced a crisis when it had to recall more than a million cars to fix faulty ignition switches. As the recall proceeded, some car owners posted negative comments and asked specific questions on GM's Facebook page and Twitter account. The company had 20 employees ready to monitor electronic communities and respond. By responding quickly with private messages tailored to individual situations and providing updates about the recall, GM demonstrated its commitment to serving its customers.[17] To preserve a favorable reputation, experts advise businesses to train employees in social media etiquette, avoid misunderstandings by carefully wording posts, and remember that social media conversations go on all day, every day, all around the world.[18]

14-3c Listening to Stakeholders

Listening to people, whether they are customers or not, is always an important aspect of a company's social media plan. Indeed, listening is often the first step when developing a social media strategy. Listening to the conversations unfolding on Facebook or Twitter, for example, can be important to understanding just what people think about a company's products and services. By monitoring Facebook, Twitter, and other social media sites, Domino's Pizza found out that people were

Career Success

Do You Have a Future in Social Media?

Social media is opening new career opportunities every day. A study conducted for Facebook found that its global growth has led to new jobs in marketing, engineering, software, and even computer design and manufacturing. If you want a career specifically in social media, you can follow a variety of paths to future success.

As an example, both businesses and nonprofit organizations hire *social media managers* to plan and implement communication campaigns, monitor company or brand mentions, coordinate the work of technical and non-technical personnel, and report on results and trends. This position generally pays about $47,000 per year, depending on the employer's size and location. Another example is the *online community manager*, someone who oversees a company's brand or community on Facebook and other social-media sites. This manager, who is paid about $48,000 per year, plans targeted promotions to attract and engage participants, establishes and enforces participant guidelines,

and supervises technical maintenance and upgrades.

A *digital strategist* must have the education and background to research emerging digital trends and their potential effect on the company, prepare long-range plans to engage customers and other stakeholders, and coordinate internal and external resources to support the company's plans. This job pays, on average, about $64,000. At the very top of the career ladder is the *chief social media officer* or *chief digital officer*, a senior-level position with a six-figure salary. This executive formulates organization-wide strategies for a consistent, compelling presence across social media platforms and at the same time maintains a good reputation for the business.

Sources: Based on information in David Goldman, "Facebook Claims It Created 4.5 Million Jobs," *CNN Money*, January 20, 2015, http://money.cnn.com; Sharon Florentine, "Should You Hire a Chief Social Media Officer?" *CIO.com*, January 7, 2015; Neha Sampat, "Every Company Needs a Chief Digital Officer," *Techcrunch.com*, November 22, 2014; Matt Kapko, "10 Top Jobs By Salary for Social Media Pros," *CIO.com*, July 17, 2014.

not very happy with its product quality. Customers described the sauce as "tasting like ketchup" and the crust as "tasting like cardboard." Unfortunately, there were enough comments of a similar nature for the company to use traditional marketing research to verify this information. They found the sentiment to be true and the company then developed a plan to reinvent every aspect of the company—and its pizza products. Did the plan work? Same store sales increased more than 14 percent.[19]

14-3d Targeting Customers

Many companies are using social media to increase awareness and build their brand among customers. It is especially valuable in targeting the Millennials. **Millennials** are tech-savvy digital natives born after 1980. When the U.K. fashion firm Burberry began researching the market for luxury apparel, it found that 60 percent of the world's population is under 30 years old. It also realized that this demographic group is increasingly affluent in developing nations. Therefore, the company decided to target Millennials worldwide as the key to revitalizing sales and building a loyal customer base for future success. Burberry's designers created new collections of styles that appeal to Millennials' fashion tastes while building on the company's 160-year heritage.

Despite high brand awareness, Burberry still faced a challenge in communicating its move toward hipper styles for today's Millennial lifestyle. To accomplish this, it engaged its tech-savvy target market through social media marketing. Burberry started live-streaming its fashion shows online and for viewing on mobile devices, allowing customers to place orders with a few clicks even before the end of a show. Burberry also encourages consumers to purchase anything they see via Twitter's "Buy" button. In fact, with every new fashion season, Burberry has added to its digital marketing. One recent collection was introduced via Facebook, Twitter, YouTube, Instagram, Pinterest, and Google+, as well as several social media sites in China. Thanks to its aggressive social media outreach, Burberry has attracted 17 million Facebook likes, 4 million Twitter followers, 21 million YouTube video views, 130,000 Pinterest followers, and 3.6 million Instagram followers. At the same time, the firm has increased sales and profits.[20]

Millennials tech-savvy digital natives born after 1980

social media marketing the utilization of social media technologies, channels, and software to create, communicate, deliver, and exchange offerings that have value for an organization

14-3e Social Media Marketing

Social media marketing is the "utilization of social media technologies, channels, and software to create, communicate, deliver and exchange offerings that have value for an organization."[21] As companies become more comfortable with social media, we can expect even more companies to use social media to market products and services to their customers. Already, research indicates that companies are shifting their advertising money from traditional marketing (like television and magazines) to digital marketing (like Internet search engines and social media). Experts now predict that social media will account for 26 percent of all online spending by 2016.[22] The primary reason is simple: People are spending more time on social media sites. Often the first step for a business that wants to use social media is to go to LinkedIn, Facebook, Twitter, or some other popular social media site. As you can tell from the information in Figure 14-4, companies like Facebook make using their technology as easy as possible to connect with potential or existing customers.

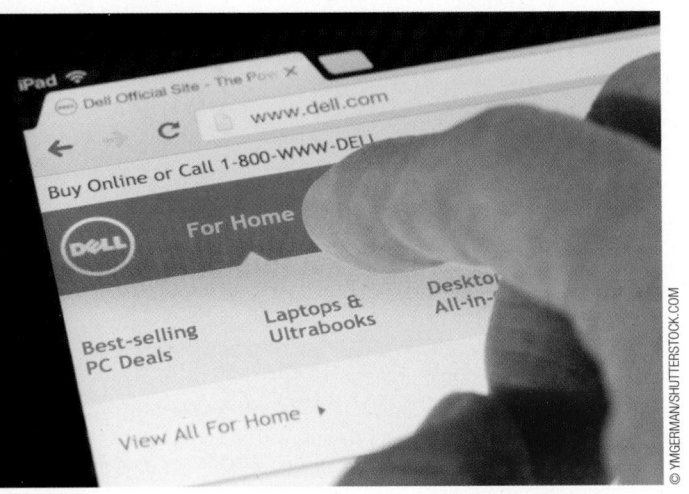

© YMGERMAN/SHUTTERSTOCK.COM

Listen. Learn. Deliver. That's what Dell is about. At the age of 19, Michael Dell invested $1,000 and started a company that would be a game changer in the highly competitive technology industry. Today, Dell is not only successful, but also one of the most admired companies in the U.S. The reason is simple: At Dell, meeting the needs of the customer—both businesses and individuals—is the most important factor in Dell's business plan.

FIGURE 14-4 Facebook's Marketing Solutions for Other Businesses

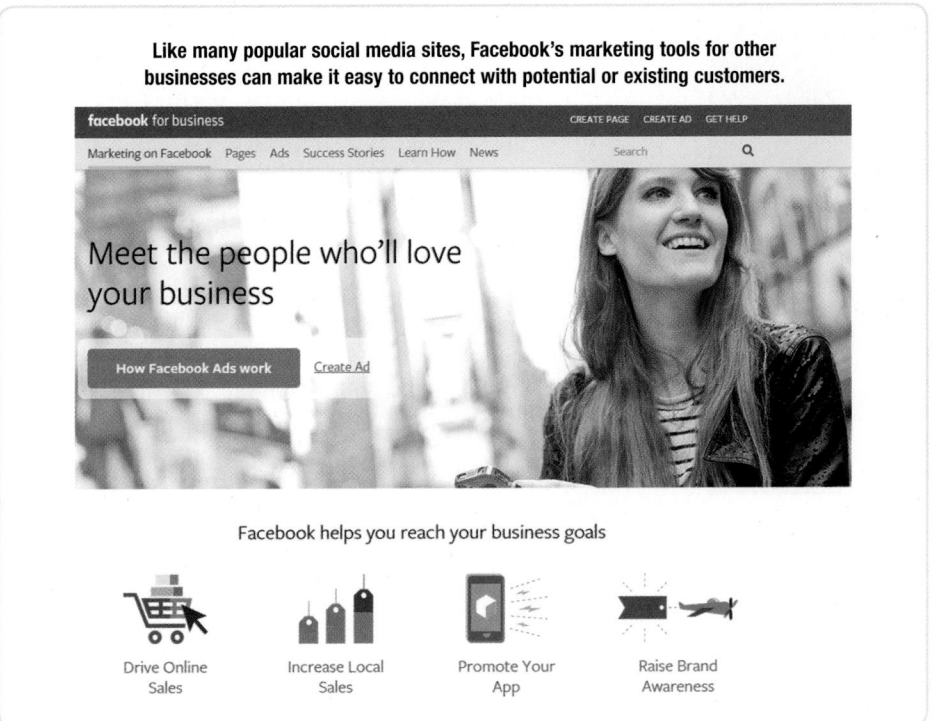

Like many popular social media sites, Facebook's marketing tools for other businesses can make it easy to connect with potential or existing customers.

Courtesy of Facebook

Today, many companies have been quite successful using social media marketing not only to develop customer awareness, but also to obtain sales leads and increase actual sales. HubSpot, for example, is a software company that helps small and medium-sized companies develop inbound marketing programs. **Inbound marketing** is a marketing term that describes new ways of gaining attention, and ultimately, customers by creating content on a website that pulls customers in. Tools used for inbound marketing programs include search engine optimization, blogging, videos, and social media. In order to market its software products, HubSpot shunned traditional advertising and began to practice what it preached. First, the company developed its own inbound marketing program by creating valuable content and marketing information that was then distributed through social media and search engine websites. Companies interested in HubSpot's software were required to enter contact information (name, phone number, and e-mail address) in order to view the information. People provided contact information because they believed the company's software could help them improve their marketing activities. As a result of HubSpot's inbound marketing program, the cost of generating new sales leads was reduced, the number of customers increased, and sales increased.

Companies also use social media to sell goods and services, invite customer feedback, and reinforce a positive brand image. General Electric, for example, is a social media innovator with award-winning Vine video campaigns, striking Instagram and Pinterest photos of its industrial products, more than 338,000 followers on Twitter, 1.3 million Facebook followers, a popular YouTube channel, a Google+ community, and a Tumblr blog. GE's social media presence creates a cutting-edge image, connects the company with inventors worldwide, and sets the stage for global sales of locomotives, turbines, jet engines, and medical devices, among other products. Through GE's LinkedIn account, the

inbound marketing a marketing term that describes new ways of gaining attention and ultimately customers by creating content on a website that pulls customers in

Where do ideas for new products or services come from? Although most companies still use research to develop new ideas for products and services, a growing number of companies are using social media to tap into customer-driven ideas. Each year, Starbucks, for example, receives thousands of ideas for new products and suggestions for improving the customer's in store experience on its website www.mystarbucksidea.com.

company's salespeople can find decision-makers in customer organizations and facilitate sales research and sales calls.[23]

As important as social media marketing is, it is only one aspect of digital marketing. Indeed, digital marketing or online marketing is comprised of several areas, including

- *online public relations*—developing social media press kits;
- *search engine optimization*—using keywords in a company's website in order to rank higher in search engine results;
- *search engine marketing*—buying ads like Google's AdWords to increase traffic to a company's website;
- *display advertising*—buying banner ads;
- *e-mail marketing*—targeting customers through opt-in e-mail campaigns; and
- *content marketing*—developing photos, videos, podcasts, blog posts, and other tools to increase the value to the customer.

From an ethical perspective, every company and every employee should identify itself during digital interactions and be transparent about its role in social media. Intel, which makes computer chips, is one of many businesses that require disclosure of ties to the company when employees participate in social media conversations. From a legal perspective, businesses in highly-regulated industries like pharmaceuticals must comply with government guidelines when planning social-media messages about their products.[24]

crowdsourcing outsourcing tasks to a group of people in order to tap into the ideas of the crowd

14-3f **Generating New Product Ideas**

Companies can use social media to conduct much of their consumer-based research. Using insight gained from Facebook or Twitter, for example, allows a company to modify existing products and services and develop new ones. **Crowdsourcing** involves outsourcing tasks to a group of people in order to tap into the ideas of the crowd. In some cases valuable information can be obtained by crowd voting. Frito Lay, for example, has used crowd voting for the last few years when they allowed people to create and then vote for their favorite television spots for its popular Doritos brand. The winners are then featured during the Super Bowl. Their effort "Crash the Super Bowl" has been wildly successful.[25]

Companies can even build communities for specific brands in order to obtain information and new ideas from consumers. The Danish toymaker LEGO has created an online site called LEGO Ideas (http://ideas.lego.com) where brand enthusiasts can post and vote on new product ideas. Ideas that attract at least 10,000 votes are presented to the company's review board, which checks for fit with current products and the target market. Then LEGO makes a final selection of which ideas to put into production. Out of this process has come new products like LEGO's Doctor Who set and its WALL-E set, among others. LEGO benefits from its customers' creativity and the goodwill generated by seeking the community's input. Just as important, the creators receive credit for their ideas plus a small royalty from product sales.[26]

Concept Check

✓ In your own words, describe how social media can help businesses to connect with other businesses and consumers.

✓ For a business, why are crisis and reputation management, listening to stakeholders, and targeting specific types of customers important activities?

✓ How can social media be used to market and advertise a firm's products or services?

✓ How can social media help a firm generate new product ideas and recruit employees?

14-3g Recruiting Employees

For years, companies have used current employees to recruit new employees based on the theory that "birds of a feather flock together." The concept is simple: Current employees' friends and family may prove to be good job candidates. Social media takes that concept to a whole new level. LinkedIn, the largest social network for professionals, has been used quite effectively by large corporations, small businesses, nonprofit organizations, and government agencies that want to recruit new employees. Because LinkedIn hosts more than 300 million professional profiles, employers using the site can save time, reduce their recruiting costs, and see more information about individual candidates. Companies like Accenture, Ford, General Electric, Home Depot, IBM, and Oracle have all had recruiting success with LinkedIn.[27]

14-4 DEVELOPING A SOCIAL MEDIA PLAN

Before developing a plan to use social media, it is important to determine how social media can improve the organization's overall performance and how it "fits" with a company's objectives and other promotional activities. For example, if a social media plan attempts to improve customer service, it needs to link to the company's other efforts to improve customer service.

14-4a Steps to Build a Social Media Plan

Once it is determined how social media links to the company's other activities, there are several steps that should be considered.

STEP 1: LISTEN TO DETERMINE OPPORTUNITIES As pointed out earlier in this chapter, social media is often used to "listen" to what customers like and don't like about a company's products or services. For example, reading comments on social media sites can yield some insight into how consumers are reacting to a price increase for an existing product or service. Monitoring social media sites also allows managers and employees to enter the conversation and tell the company's side of the story. In addition, companies can monitor social media sites to gather information about competitors as well as what is being said about the industry.

After the listening phase, it is important to analyze the information to identify the company's strengths and weaknesses before taking the next step—setting objectives.

STEP 2: ESTABLISH SOCIAL MEDIA OBJECTIVES After listening to and analyzing the information obtained from social media sites, it is important to use that information to develop specific objectives. For social media, an objective is a

Personal App

Make a Good Impression Using Social Media

When you use social media to promote yourself to potential employers, what you post and how often you post can affect your ability to make a good impression. Above all, keep two factors in mind. First, photos, career goals, work experience, and personal information, should showcase your professional side. Second, don't post inappropriate material that would detract from the professional career-oriented image you are trying to project to prospective employers.

Learning Objective

14-4 Describe how businesses develop a social media plan.

statement about what a social media plan should accomplish. Each objective should be specific, measurable, achievable, realistic, and oriented toward the future.

For most companies, the most popular objectives are increasing brand awareness, acquiring new customers, introducing new products, retaining current customers, and gaining customer insight.[28] Other objectives that are often important include improving search engine ranking, showcasing public relations activities, increasing website traffic, and generating sales leads.[29] All objectives need to be linked to specific actions that can be used to accomplish each objective.

STEP 3: SEGMENT AND TARGET THE SOCIAL CUSTOMER Ideally, a company will have developed a customer profile that describes a typical customer in terms of age, income, gender, ethnicity, etc. When segmenting or targeting customers, it also helps to know how they think, how they spend their time, how much they buy, and how often they buy. More information about potential customers will help you develop a social media plan to achieve a company's objectives. Lack of information about customers can lead to wasted time and money and the inability to successfully achieve the firm's social media objectives. For example, most companies feel that they must use Facebook and Twitter. But if their core customer does not use these social media sites, then it does not make sense to use them. Additionally, it is important to really understand how customers use social media.

- Do they create content like photos, videos, blog posts, etc.?
- Do they use social media for ratings and reviews?
- Do they post product reviews and ratings on Facebook accounts?
- Do they spend a lot of time using social media?

In fact, a business should consider all available and relevant information about potential and existing customers when creating a social media plan. Some of the information that can help you target just the "right" social media customer is illustrated in Figure 14-5.

STEP 4: SELECT SOCIAL MEDIA TOOLS The search for the right social media tool(s) usually begins with the company's social media objectives, outlined in Step 2. It also helps to review the target customer or segment of the market the company is trying to reach (Step 3). With this information, the next step is to choose the right social media tools to reach the right customers. A company can use social media communities, blogs, photos, videos, podcasts, or games to reach potential or existing customers. For example, if the goal is to recruit college students for college entry-level jobs, LinkedIn may be a good choice. Remember, it is not necessary (or even advisable) to use all of the above tools. It is also possible for a business to build a social media community—especially when the objective is to fund local community projects or nonprofit organizations. Often money for worthwhile projects is obtained through crowdfunding. **Crowdfunding** is a method of raising money from a large group of people who donate small amounts of money using the Internet and social media.

STEP 5: IMPLEMENT AND INTEGRATE THE PLAN Once social media tools have been identified, a company can implement and integrate the social media plan. Because a social media plan doesn't necessarily have a start and stop date, it is different from traditional advertising campaigns. Some social media activities continue and have a life of their own. For example, Zappos, a very successful and well-respected online retailer, is a company who is always "on" in terms of its social media. Indeed, they do very little traditional advertising and instead rely on social media to promote products, monitor customer service, and

crowdfunding a method of raising money from a large group of people who donate small amounts of money using the Internet and social media

FIGURE 14-5 Types of Information That Can Help Target Different Social Media Customers

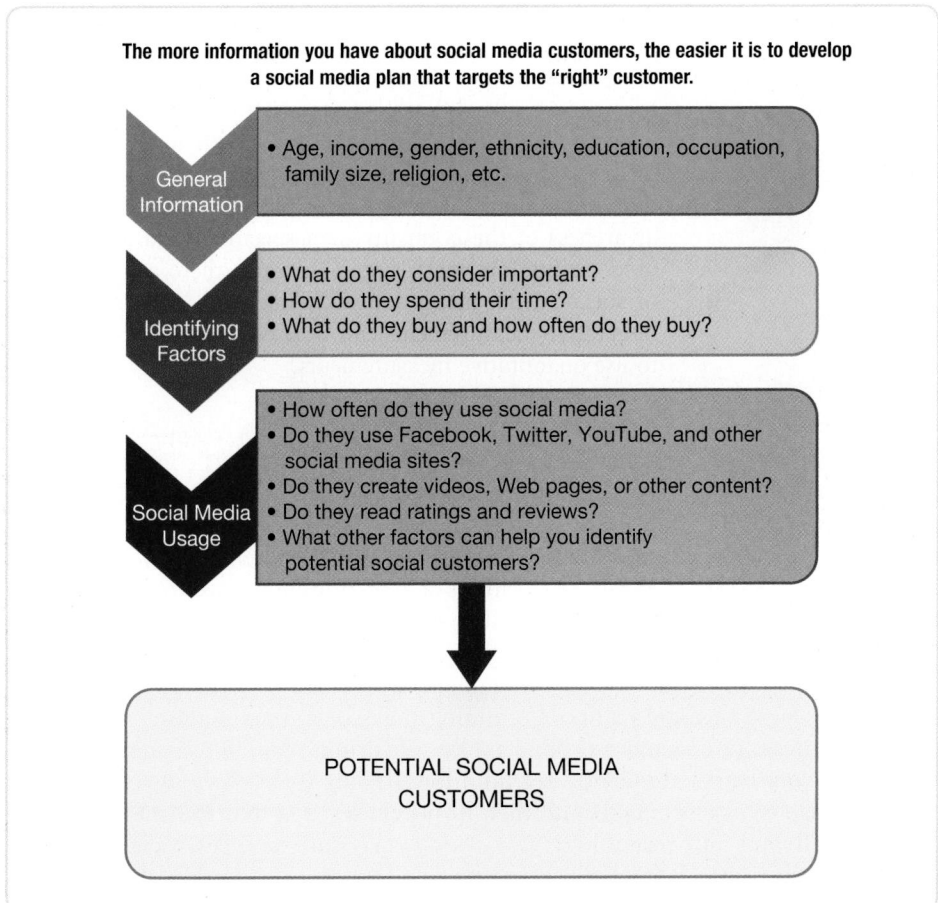

The more information you have about social media customers, the easier it is to develop a social media plan that targets the "right" customer.

General Information
- Age, income, gender, ethnicity, education, occupation, family size, religion, etc.

Identifying Factors
- What do they consider important?
- How do they spend their time?
- What do they buy and how often do they buy?

Social Media Usage
- How often do they use social media?
- Do they use Facebook, Twitter, YouTube, and other social media sites?
- Do they create videos, Web pages, or other content?
- Do they read ratings and reviews?
- What other factors can help you identify potential social customers?

POTENTIAL SOCIAL MEDIA CUSTOMERS

enhance the company's reputation. Some companies, on the other hand, feel that it is important to have a mix of short- and long-term social media promotion. In this case, it's important to key the content and presentation to each social media site, and to coordinate the timing of promotions. For example, Coca-Cola is constantly adding new features to its Facebook page, which has more than 91 million likes. One day, the company might post its latest TV commercial. The next day, it might invite visitors to send branded greetings to friends from its Facebook page. On Twitter, where Coca-Cola has nearly 3 million followers, it posts messages about new products and initiates conversations about other promotional activities. Knowing that customers post thousands of social-media messages about its brand every day, Coca-Cola monitors these sites very carefully, responds quickly to questions and comments, and provides specific guidelines for posting by employees, agencies, and spokespeople. Finally, like a growing number of companies, Coca-Cola integrates its social media and traditional marketing efforts for maximum impact, using hashtags and sharing images and taglines to tie each campaign together.[30] For example, it is not unusual to see the Twitter icon at the end of a television commercial. This signals to consumers that more information about the product or service is provided on Twitter. Indeed, as companies increase the amount of money spent on digital marketing and social media, they will attempt to tie online and offline promotions together in order to get "more bang for the buck."

Social media—success or failure. Because social media cost both time and money, it is important to evaluate a firm's social media plan and make adjustments if necessary. For most firms, social media measurements are *quantitative* and include number of visitors, number of comments, and other numerical measurements. A firm can also use *qualitative* measurements to detect the mood, attitudes, or emotions of people who visit a firm's social media sites.

14-4b Measuring and Adapting a Social Media Plan

Because social media is a relatively new method of reaching customers, many companies struggle when attempting to measure social media. Often companies use the same measurements that have been used with long-established media channels like television, newspapers, and radio to determine the effect of social media on the customer's awareness of the company or a specific brand and if sales (and profits) are increasing. Generally, there are two types of social media measurement. While both quantitative and qualitative measurements can be used, most companies tend to use quantitative measurements.

QUANTITATIVE SOCIAL MEDIA MEASUREMENT
Quantitative social media measurement consists of using numerical measurements, such as counting the number of website visitors, number of fans and followers, number of leads generated, and the number of new customers. Table 14-1 shows a few popular quantitative ways to measure social media. Coca-Cola counts not only the number of social media likes and followers but also the number of times its brands are mentioned each day. Although such measures help the company gauge brand awareness and sentiment, determining how social media interactions affect actual purchases of consumer products, like soft drinks, can be difficult. Business-to-business marketers frequently set additional goals to track how social media activities lead to sales contacts and then to purchases. SAP North America, which markets software and technology services to corporations, uses social media to generate leads and facilitate the sales process. It created a series of blog posts about data analysis, and tweeted about the posts. Each tweet included a unique identifier so SAP could track people who clicked to read the blog post. When blog visitors registered to obtain free information, SAP captured those details for future sales calls. In addition, SAP used unique identifiers to determine when a current customer or a customer in the sales pipeline accessed its social media content. By

TABLE 14-1 Quantitative Measurements for Selected Social Media Websites

Type of Social Media	Typical Measurements
Blogs	• Unique visitors • Number of views • Ratio of visitors to posted comments
Twitter	• Number of followers • Number of tweets and retweets • Click through rate (CTR) of tweeted links • Visits to website from tweeted links
Facebook	• Number of likes • Number of comments • Growth of wall response • Visits to websites from Facebook links
YouTube	• Number of videos • Number of visitors • Ratio of comments to the number of videos • Number of embedded links

quantitative social media measurement using numerical measurements, such as counting the number of website visitors, number of fans and followers, number of leads generated, and the number of new customers

© D.R.3D/SHUTTERSTOCK.COM

tracking such contacts, SAP learned that its social media content helped generate sales revenues valued at more than $10 million.[31]

A number of companies are using key performance indicators to measure their social media activities. **Key performance indicators (KPIs)** are measurements that define and measure the progress of an organization toward achieving its objectives. Generally, KPIs are *quantitative* (based on numbers like the number of Twitter followers).

If measuring the success or failure of social media activities with KPIs, the first step is to connect KPIs with objectives. The second step is to set a benchmark—a number that shows what success should look like. For example, Ford said that if 144,000 people visited the Ford Fiesta website within a specified time, it would indicate that the company's social media plan to introduce the new subcompact car to Millennials was successful. When measured, more than 300,000 people had visited the website. In fact, the plan worked so well that Ford decided to revamp the plan to introduce the 2014 Ford Fiesta.[32]

QUALITATIVE SOCIAL MEDIA MEASUREMENT Qualitative social media measurement is the process of accessing the opinions and beliefs about a brand. This process primarily uses sentiment analysis to categorize what is being said about a company. **Sentiment analysis** is a measurement that uses technology to detect the mood, attitudes, or emotions of people who experience a social media activity. Other measurements for determining customer sentiment include:

- *Customer satisfaction score*—defined as the relative satisfaction of customers.
- *Issue resolution rate*—the percentage of customer service inquiries resolved satisfactorily using social media.
- *Resolution time*—defined as the amount of time taken to resolve customer service issues.

When compared to quantitative measurement, it should be noted that many of these qualitative social media measurements are more subjective in nature.

14-4c The Cost of Maintaining a Social Media Plan

Basic Assumption: Social media is not free and can be quite expensive. Because social media costs both time and money, it is important to measure the success of a social media plan and make adjustments and changes if needed. Based on quantitative and qualitative measurements, the company may also try to determine if it is getting a positive return on its investment in social media.

After reviewing results for social media activities against pre-established benchmarks, it may be necessary to make changes and update the plan to increase the effectiveness of the social media plan. A social media plan, for example, must provide current and up-to-date information in order to keep customers coming back to see what's new. Without updates, customers lose interest and the number of returning customers can drop dramatically. After all, one of the major objectives of social media activities is to provide customers and stakeholders with current and useful information about the company and its products or services. Once it is determined that updates and changes are needed, many of the same steps described in this section may be used to improve a firm's social media plan. It is also important to create future social media plans based on what worked and what didn't work in previous plans.

Social media is particularly important to businesses that use e-business to sell their products and services online. In the next section, we take a close look at how e-business firms are organized, satisfy needs online, and earn profits.

key performance indicators (KPIs) measurements that define and measure the progress of an organization toward achieving its objectives

qualitative social media measurement the process of accessing the opinions and beliefs about a brand and primarily uses sentiment analysis to categorize what is being said about a company

sentiment analysis a measurement that uses technology to detect the mood, attitudes, or emotions of people who experience a social media activity

Concept Check

✓ What are the steps required to develop a social media plan?

✓ What is the difference between quantitative and qualitative measurements? Which type of measurement do you think is the most reliable when measuring the effectiveness of a company's social media plan?

14-5 DEFINING E-BUSINESS

Learning Objective

14-5 Explain the meaning of e-business.

In Chapter 1, we defined *business* as the organized effort of individuals to produce and sell, for a profit, the goods and services that satisfy society's needs. Working from this original definition, then, **e-business (or electronic business)**, can be defined as the organized effort of individuals to produce and sell, for a profit, the goods and services that satisfy society's needs *through the facilities available on the Internet*. Sometimes people use the term *e-commerce* instead of *e-business*. In a strict sense, e-business is used when you're talking about all business activities and practices conducted on the Internet by an individual firm or industry. On the other hand, e-commerce is a part of e-business and usually refers only to buying and selling activities conducted online. E-commerce already accounts for more than $3 trillion in yearly purchases from U.S. manufacturers, which means e-business is an even more significant factor in the U.S. economy.[33] In this chapter, we generally use the term *e-business* because of its broader definition and scope.

With the popularity of smartphones and tablet computers capable of functions such as Internet access and e-mail, many companies are using **mobile marketing**, communicating with and selling to customers through mobile devices. Mobile marketing covers a range of activities, such as optimizing websites for viewing on smartphones and tablets to delivering promotional messages and discounts via mobile devices. Because 28 percent of retail purchasing is currently completed via mobile devices, many stores are investing more heavily in mobile marketing.[34] A growing number of companies have *apps* to make mobile transactions faster and more convenient for customers. For example, Starbucks offers an easy-to-use app for customers to pay for their lattes or espressos directly from a smartphone or tablet. Every week, customers initiate more than 7 million mobile payments to Starbucks using this app.[35]

14-5a Organizing e-Business Resources

As noted in Chapter 1, to be organized, a business must combine *human*, *material*, *informational*, and *financial resources*. This is true of e-business, too (see Figure 14-6),

FIGURE 14-6 Combining e-Business Resources

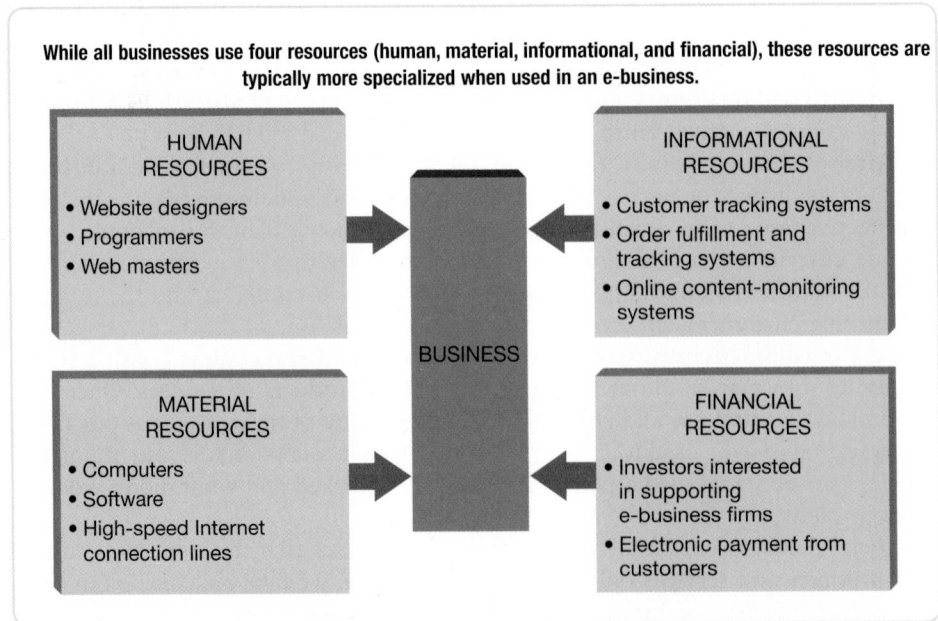

While all businesses use four resources (human, material, informational, and financial), these resources are typically more specialized when used in an e-business.

HUMAN RESOURCES
- Website designers
- Programmers
- Web masters

INFORMATIONAL RESOURCES
- Customer tracking systems
- Order fulfillment and tracking systems
- Online content-monitoring systems

BUSINESS

MATERIAL RESOURCES
- Computers
- Software
- High-speed Internet connection lines

FINANCIAL RESOURCES
- Investors interested in supporting e-business firms
- Electronic payment from customers

e-business (or electronic business) the organized effort of individuals to produce and sell, for a profit, the goods and services that satisfy society's needs *through the facilities available on the Internet*

mobile marketing communicating with and selling to customers through mobile devices

Entrepreneurial Success

Advice from Teenage App Entrepreneurs

Thinking about starting an e-business? Consider the advice of these teenage entrepreneurs, who entered the world of e-business by creating smartphone apps and related goods or services:

1. *Never stop networking.* Ryan Orbuch and Michael Hansen of Boulder, Colorado, were in high school when they developed a popular iPhone app called "Finish," which helps people stop procrastinating and start planning more effectively. These app entrepreneurs are constantly networking at local events and national conferences to learn from the ideas and experiences of other people who have started successful e-businesses and developed apps.

2. *Follow your passion.* When Michael Sayman was a high school junior in Miami, he created a popular game app called "4 Snaps." Not only did he earn money, he was invited to be an intern at Facebook after graduation.

Sayman believes that aspiring app entrepreneurs should follow their passion and embrace the excitement of ever-changing advances in technology.

3. *Experiment, experiment, experiment.* Australian high school student Jake Coppinger invented an app linked to a "smart" glove that allows users to control Internet-connected devices with basic hand gestures. Coppinger tapped online resources to follow up on materials and technologies as he developed prototypes of the app and glove, winning prestigious awards for his innovations. He says entrepreneurs should keep experimenting and tinkering as they pursue their e-business goals.

Sources: Based on information in "Teen's App Helps Pay Family's Bills," *National Public Radio*, May 5, 2014, www.npr.org; "An Intelligent Glove, a Smartphone App and a Teen's Perspective on What's Missing in School," *Knowledge @Wharton High School*, August 15, 2014, http://kwhs.wharton.upenn.edu; Matt Richtel, "The Youngest Technorati," *New York Times*, March 8, 2014, www.nytimes.com.

but in this case, the resources may be more specialized than in a typical business. For example, people who can design, create, and maintain websites are only a fraction of the specialized human resources required by e-businesses. Material resources must include specialized computers, sophisticated equipment and software, and high-speed Internet connections. Computer programs that track the number of customers who view a firm's website are generally among the specialized informational resources required. Financial resources, the money required to start and maintain the firm and allow it to grow, usually reflect greater participation by individual entrepreneurs, venture capitalists, and investors willing to invest in a high-tech firm instead of conventional financial sources such as banks.

In an effort to reduce the cost of specialized resources that are used in e-business, many firms have turned to outsourcing. **Outsourcing** is the process of finding outside vendors and suppliers that provide professional help, parts, or materials at a lower cost. For example, a firm that needs computer programmers and specialized software to complete a project may turn to an outside firm located in another part of the United States, India, or an Eastern European country.

14-5b Satisfying Needs Online

Today more and more people are using computers, the Internet, and social media as a way to connect with people. The Internet can also be used to purchase products or services. Let's start with two basic assumptions.

- The Internet has created some new customer needs that did not exist before the creation of the Internet.
- e-Businesses can satisfy those needs, as well as more traditional ones.

Restoration Hardware (www.restorationhardware.com), for instance, gives customers anywhere in the world access to the same virtual store of hardware and

outsourcing the process of finding outside vendors and suppliers that provide professional help, parts, or materials at a lower cost

eBay: A very popular e-Business website! eBay empowers consumers to buy and sell anything, anytime, anywhere. For a company that was started in 1995, eBay is a very successful company. Today, over 149 million people from around the globe use eBay to buy and sell more than 700 million items listed on its website.

decorative items. In addition to purchasing products, the Internet can be used by both individuals and business firms to obtain information. For example:

- Internet users can access newspapers, magazines, and radio and television programming at a time and place convenient to them.
- The Internet provides the opportunity for two-way interaction between an Internet firm and the viewer. For example, the CNN news site (www.cnn.com) and other news-content sites encourage dialogue among users.
- Customers can respond to information on the Internet by requesting more information or posing specific questions, which may lead to purchasing a product or service.
- Finally, the Internet allows customers to choose the content they are offered. Knowing the interests of a customer allows an Internet firm to direct appropriate, smart advertising to a specific customer. For the advertiser, knowing that its advertisements are being directed to the most likely customers represents a better way to spend advertising dollars.

14-5c Creating e-Business Profit

Business firms can increase profits either by increasing sales revenue or by reducing expenses through a variety of e-business activities.

INCREASING SALES REVENUE Each source of sales revenue flowing into a firm is referred to as a **revenue stream**. One way to increase revenues is to sell merchandise on the Internet. Because the opportunity to shop on the Internet is virtually unrestricted, traditional retailers like Macy's (www.macys.com) and Walmart (www.walmart.com) can obtain additional revenue by selling to a global customer base 24 hours a day, seven days a week. However, shifting revenues earned from customers inside a real store to revenues earned from these same customers online does not create any real new revenue for a firm. The goal is to find *new customers* and generate *new sales* so that *total revenues are increased.*

Intelligent information systems also can help to generate sales revenue for Internet firms such as Amazon.com (www.amazon.com). Such systems store information about each customer's purchases, along with a variety of other information about the buyer's preferences. Using this information, the system can assist the customer the next time he or she visits the website. For example, if the customer has bought a Carrie Underwood CD in the past, the system might suggest CDs by similar artists who have either appeared on *American Idol* or won Country Music Awards.

Although some customers may not make a purchase online, the existence of the firm's website and the services and information it provides may lead to increased sales in the firm's physical stores. For example, Honda's website (www.honda.com) can provide basic comparative information for shoppers so that they are better prepared for their visit to an automobile showroom.

In addition to selling products or services online, e-business revenue streams are created by advertising placed on Web pages and by subscription fees charged for access to online services and content. For example, Hoover's (www.hoovers.com),

revenue stream a source of revenue flowing into a firm

a comprehensive source for company and industry information, makes some of its online content free for anyone who visits the site, but more detailed information is available only by paid subscription.

Many Internet firms that distribute news, magazine and newspaper articles, and similar content generate revenue from commissions earned from sellers of products linked to the site. Online shopping malls, for example, now provide groups of related vendors of electronic equipment and computer hardware and software with a new method of selling their products and services. In many cases, the vendors share online sales revenues with the site owners.

REDUCING EXPENSES Reducing expenses is the second major way in which e-business can help to increase profitability. Providing online access to information that customers want can reduce the cost of dealing with customers. Sprint (www. sprint.com), for instance, is just one company that maintains an extensive website where potential customers can learn more about products and services, and where current customers can access personal account information, send questions to customer service, and purchase additional products or services. With such extensive online services, Sprint does not have to maintain as many physical store locations as it would without these online services. We examine more examples of how e-business contributes to profitability throughout this chapter, especially as we focus on some of the business models for activity on the Internet.

business model represents a group of common characteristics and methods of doing business to generate sales revenues and reduce expenses

business-to-business (or B2B) model a model used by firms that conduct business with other businesses

Concept Check

✓ What are the four major factors contained in the definition of e-business?

✓ How do e-businesses generate revenue streams, reduce expenses, and earn a profit?

14-6 FUNDAMENTAL MODELS OF E-BUSINESS

A **business model** represents a group of common characteristics and methods of doing business to generate sales revenues and reduce expenses. Each of the models discussed in the following text represents a primary e-business model. Regardless of the type of business model, planning often depends on if the e-business is a new firm or an existing firm adding an online presence—see Figure 14-7. It also helps to keep in mind that in order to generate sales revenues and earn profits, a business—especially an e-business—must meet the needs of its customers.

Learning Objective

14-6 Understand the fundamental models of e-business.

14-6a Business-to-Business (B2B) Model

Some firms use the Internet mainly to conduct business with other businesses. These firms are generally referred to as having a **business-to-business (or B2B) model**.

When examining B2B firms, two clear types emerge. In the first type, the focus is simply on facilitating sales transactions between businesses. For example, Dell manufactures computers to specifications that customers enter on the Dell website (www.dell.com). A large portion of Dell's online orders are from corporate clients who are well informed about the products they need and are looking for fairly priced, high-quality computer products that will be delivered quickly. By dealing directly with Dell, customers eliminate costs associated with wholesalers and retailers, thereby helping to reduce the price they pay for equipment.

A second, more complex type of B2B model involves a company and its suppliers. Today, suppliers use the Internet to bid on products and services they wish to sell to a business customer and learn about the customer's rules and procedures

STUART MILES/DREAMSTIME.COM

FIGURE 14-7 Planning for a New Internet Business or Building an Online Presence for an Existing Business

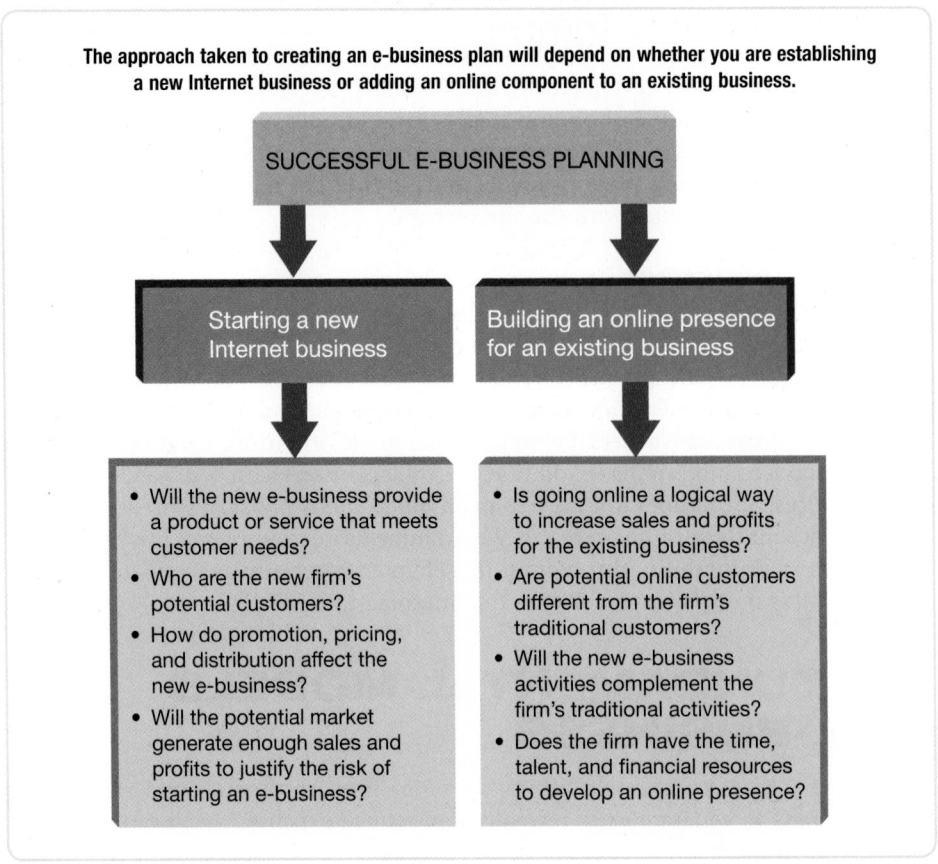

The approach taken to creating an e-business plan will depend on whether you are establishing a new Internet business or adding an online component to an existing business.

SUCCESSFUL E-BUSINESS PLANNING

Starting a new Internet business

- Will the new e-business provide a product or service that meets customer needs?
- Who are the new firm's potential customers?
- How do promotion, pricing, and distribution affect the new e-business?
- Will the potential market generate enough sales and profits to justify the risk of starting an e-business?

Building an online presence for an existing business

- Is going online a logical way to increase sales and profits for the existing business?
- Are potential online customers different from the firm's traditional customers?
- Will the new e-business activities complement the firm's traditional activities?
- Does the firm have the time, talent, and financial resources to develop an online presence?

that must be followed. For example, Ford, General Motors, and Chrysler have developed a B2B model to link thousands of suppliers that sell the automobile makers parts, supplies, and raw materials worth millions of dollars each year. Although the B2B site is expensive to start and maintain, there are significant savings for all three automakers. Given the potential savings, it is no wonder that many other manufacturers and their suppliers are beginning to use the same kind of B2B systems that are used by the automakers.

14-6b Business-to-Consumer (B2C) Model

In contrast with the B2B model, firms such as Walmart (www.walmart.com) and Warby Parker (www.warbyparker.com) clearly are focused on individual consumers. These companies are referred to as having a **business-to-consumer (or B2C) model**. In a B2C situation, understanding how consumers behave online is critical to a firm's success. Typically, a business firm that uses a B2C model must answer the following questions:

- Will consumers use websites merely to simplify and speed up comparison shopping?
- Will consumers purchase services and products online or end up buying at a traditional retail store?
- What sorts of products and services are best suited for online consumer shopping?
- Are consumers willing to wait for purchases to be delivered, will they pay for next-day delivery, or will they collect online purchases from a convenient pickup site?

business-to-consumer (or B2C) model a model used by firms that focus on conducting business with individual consumers

Concept Check

✓ What are the two fundamental e-business models?

✓ Assume that you are the owner of a small company that produces outdoor living furniture. Describe how you could use the B2C business model to sell your products to consumers.

In addition to providing round-the-clock global access to all kinds of products and services, B2C firms often attempt to build long-term relationships with their customers. Often, firms will make a special effort to make sure that the customer is satisfied and that problems, if any, are solved quickly. Specialized software also can help build good customer relationships. Tracking the decisions and buying preferences as customers navigate a website, for instance, helps management to make well-informed decisions about how best to serve online customers. In essence, this is Orbitz's (www.orbitz.com) online selling approach. By tracking and analyzing customer data, the online travel company can provide individualized service to its customers. Although a "little special attention" may increase the cost of doing business for a B2C firm, the customer's repeated purchases will repay the investment many times over.

Today, B2B and B2C models are the most popular business models for e-business. And yet, there are other business models that perform specialized e-business activities to generate revenues. Most of the business models described in Table 14-2 are modified versions of the B2B and B2C models.

14-7 THE FUTURE OF THE INTERNET, SOCIAL MEDIA, AND E-BUSINESS

Since the beginning of commercial activity on the Internet, developments in computer technology, social media, and e-business have been rapid with spectacular successes such as Facebook, Amazon, Google, eBay, and Pinterest. However, success is not guaranteed just because it is a "technology" firm. Even firms with a promising idea must develop a business plan to turn the idea into a reality—and a successful business. Today, most firms involved in the Internet, social media, and e-business use a very intelligent approach to the initial start-up phase and expansion and development. The long-term view held by the vast majority of analysts is that the Internet, social media, and e-business will continue to expand to meet the needs of businesses and consumers.

14-7a Internet Growth Potential

To date, only a small percentage of the global population uses the Internet. In June 2014, estimates suggest that about 3 billion of the 7 billion people in the world (about 40 percent) use the Web.[36] Clearly, there is much more growth opportunity.

© VDOVICHENKO DENIS/SHUTTERSTOCK.COM

Want to shop 24 hours a day, 7 days a week. Then go to Walmart.com. While everyone recognizes Walmart as the world's largest retailer known for everyday low prices, another corporate goal is to provide consumers with the best Internet shopping experience available. To achieve this goal, Walmart now offers more than 1,000,000 products and services online, and its website and e-commerce software makes it easy for consumers to place an order with a computer, tablet, or mobile device.

Learning Objective

14-7 Identify the factors that will affect the future of the Internet, social media, and e-business.

TABLE 14-2 Other Business Models That Perform Specialized e-Business Activities

Although modified versions of B2B or B2C, these business models perform specialized e-business activities to generate revenues.	
Advertising e-business model	Advertisements that are displayed on a firm's website in return for a fee. Examples include pop-up and banner advertisements on search engines and other popular Internet and social media sites.
Brokerage e-business model	Online marketplaces where buyers and sellers are brought together to facilitate an exchange of goods and services. One example is eBay (www.ebay.com), which provides a site for buying and selling virtually anything.
Consumer-to-consumer model	Peer-to-peer software that allows individuals to share information over the Internet. Examples include BitTorrent (www.bittorrent.com), which allows users to exchange digital media files.
Subscription and pay-per-view e-business models	Content that is available only to users who pay a fee to gain access to a website. Examples include investment information provided by Standard & Poor's (www.netadvantage.standardandpoors.com) and business research provided by Forrester Research, Inc. (www.forrester.com).

Internet users in the United States comprise of approximately 10 percent of all Internet users.[37] Of the almost 323 million people making up the U.S. population, 279 million use the Internet. With approximately 86 percent of the U.S. population already using the Internet, potential growth in the United States is limited.[38] On the other hand, the number of Internet users in the world's developing countries is expected to increase dramatically.

Although the number of global Internet users is expected to increase, that's only part of the story. Perhaps the more important question is why people are using the Internet. Primary reasons for using the Internet include the ability to connect with other people, to obtain information, or to purchase a firm's products or services. Of particular interest to business firms is the growth of social media. For example, Facebook now has more than 1.2 billion users worldwide. And because only 17 percent of the world population currently uses Facebook, the number of Facebook users is expected to continue to increase for years to come. In fact, the number of users for other social media sites like LinkedIn, Google+, Twitter, YouTube, and Pinterest, is also expected to increase.

Experts also predict that the number of companies using e-business to increase sales and reduce expenses will continue to increase. Firms that adapt existing business models to an online environment will continue to dominate development. For example, books, CDs, clothing, hotel accommodations, car rentals, and travel reservations are products and services well suited to online buying and selling. These products or services will continue to be sold in the traditional way, as well as in a more cost-effective and efficient fashion over the Internet.

14-7b Ethical and Legal Concerns

The social and legal concerns for the Internet, social media, and e-business extend beyond those shared by all businesses. Essentially, the Internet is a new "frontier" without borders and with little control by governments or other organizations.

ETHICS AND SOCIAL RESPONSIBILITY Socially responsible and ethical behavior by individuals and businesses on the Internet are major concerns. For example, an ethically questionable practice in cyberspace is the unauthorized access and use of information discovered through computerized tracking of users once they are connected to the Internet. Essentially, a user may visit a website and unknowingly receive a small piece of software code called a **cookie**. This cookie can track where the user goes on the Internet and measure how long the user stays at any particular website. Although this type of software may produce valuable customer information, it also can be viewed as an invasion of privacy, especially since users may not even be aware that their movements are being monitored. AT&T and Verizon Wireless also use cookies to track web browsing on mobile devices for advertising purposes, which raises privacy concerns because customers are automatically tracked unless they specifically opt out.[39] Shoppers with smartphones may be tracked when they enter stores equipped to follow *electronic beacons* sent by the store's mobile apps. Kohl's, Macy's, and other retailers, for example, offer free downloadable apps that send e-mails with discounts and product information based on an individual shopper's movement within a store. Unlike the situation with cookies, however, shoppers must download the app to be tracked—but in exchange, they benefit by receiving personalized discounts.[40]

Some firms also practice data mining. **Data mining** refers to the practice of searching through data records looking for useful information. Customer registration forms typically require a variety of information before a user is given access to a site. Based on an individual's information, data mining analysis can then provide what might be considered private and confidential information about individuals. For

cookie a small piece of software sent by a website that tracks an individual's Internet use

data mining the practice of searching through data records looking for useful information

instance, assume an individual frequents a website that provides information about a life-threatening disease. If this information is sent to an insurance company, the company might refuse to insure this individual, thinking that there is a higher risk associated with someone who wants more information about this disease.

Besides the unauthorized use of cookies to track online behavior, there are several other threats to users' privacy and confidentiality. Monitoring an employee's computer usage may be intended to help employers police unauthorized Internet use on company time. However, the same records can also give a firm the opportunity to observe what otherwise might be considered private and confidential information. Today, legal experts suggest that, at the very least, employers need to disclose the level of surveillance to their employees and consider the corporate motivation for monitoring employees' behavior.

INTERNET CRIME Because the Internet is often regarded as an unregulated frontier, both individuals and business users must be particularly aware of online risks and dangers. For example, a general term that describes software designed to infiltrate a computer system without the user's consent is **malware**. Malware is often based on the creator's criminal or malicious intent and can include computer viruses, spyware, deceptive adware, and other software capable of criminal activities. A more specific term used to describe disruptive software is computer virus. The potentially devastating effects of both malware and computer viruses have given rise to a software security industry.

In addition to the risk of computer viruses, identity theft is one of the most common computer crimes that impacts both individuals and business users. A recent study conducted by Javelin Strategy and Research determined that over 13 million Americans were victims of identity theft in just one year. This represents an increase of more than 500,000 victims compared to the previous year's research study.[41] In recent years, major firms such as Anthem, J.P. Morgan Chase, and Home Depot have been hacked by thieves who stole sensitive data about tens of millions of customers.[42]

Most consumers are also concerned about fraud. Because the Internet allows easy creation of websites, access from anywhere in the world, and anonymity for the creator, it is almost impossible to know with certainty that the website, organization, or individuals that you believe you are interacting with are what they seem. As always, caveat emptor ("let the buyer beware") is a good suggestion to follow whether on the Internet or not.

malware a general term that describes software designed to infiltrate a computer system without the user's consent

cloud computing a type of computer usage in which services stored on the Internet is provided to users on a temporary basis

14-7c Future Challenges for Computer Technology, Social Media, and e-Business

Today, more information is available than ever before. Although individuals and business users may think we are at the point of information overload, the amount of information will only increase in the future. In order to obtain more information in the future, both business users and individuals must consider the cost of obtaining information and computer technology. In an effort to reduce expenses and improve accessibility, some companies and individuals are now using cloud computing. **Cloud computing** is a type of computer usage in which services stored on the Internet is provided to users on a temporary basis. When cloud computing is used, a third party makes processing power, software applications, databases, and storage available for on-demand use from anywhere. Instead of running software and storing data on their employer's computer network or

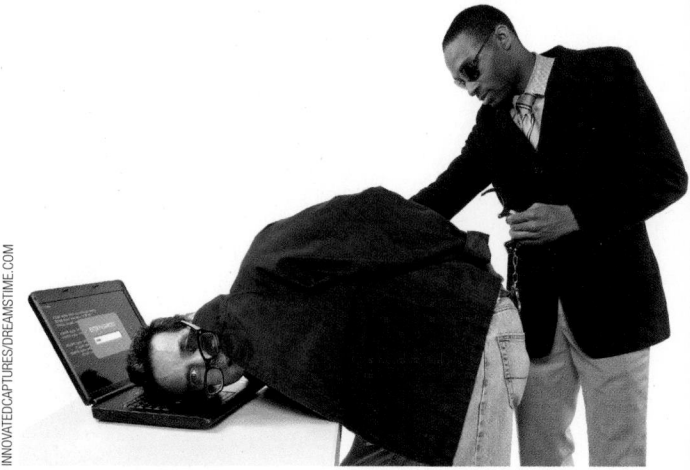

INNOVATEDCAPTURES/DREAMSTIME.COM

Busted! A recent study by Javelin Strategy and Research indicates that 13 million Americans were victims of identity theft in one year. What's worse is that the number increased when compared to the previous year. While it would be nice if computer hackers and identity thieves were always caught and punished, the reality is that everyone has to be careful and take steps to protect their identity.

their individual computers, employees log onto the third party's system and use (and pay for) only the applications and data storage they actually need. In addition to just cost, there are a number of external and internal factors that a business must consider.

Although the environmental forces at work are complex, it is useful to think of them as either *internal* or *external* forces that affect how a business uses computer technology. Internal environmental forces are those that are closely associated with the actions and decisions taking place within a firm. As shown in Figure 14-8, typical internal forces include a firm's planning activities, organizational structure, human resources, management decisions, information database, and available financing. A shortage of skilled employees needed for a specialized project, for instance, can undermine a firm's ability to sell its services to clients. Unlike the external environmental forces affecting the firm, internal forces such as this one are more likely to be under the direct control of management. In this case, management can either hire the needed staff or choose to pass over a prospective project. In addition to the obvious internal factors that affect how a company operates, a growing number of firms are concerned about how their use of technology affects the environment. The term **green IT** is now used to describe all of a firm's activities to support a healthy environment and sustain the planet. Many offices, for example, are reducing the amount of paper they use by storing data and information on computers.

In contrast, external environmental forces affect a company's use of technology and originate outside the organization. These forces are unlikely to be controllable by a company. Instead, managers and employees of a company generally will react to these forces, attempting to shield the organization from any negative effects and finding ways to take advantage of opportunities in an ever-changing technology environment. The primary external environmental forces affecting a company's use

FIGURE 14-8 Internal and External Forces That Affect an e-Business

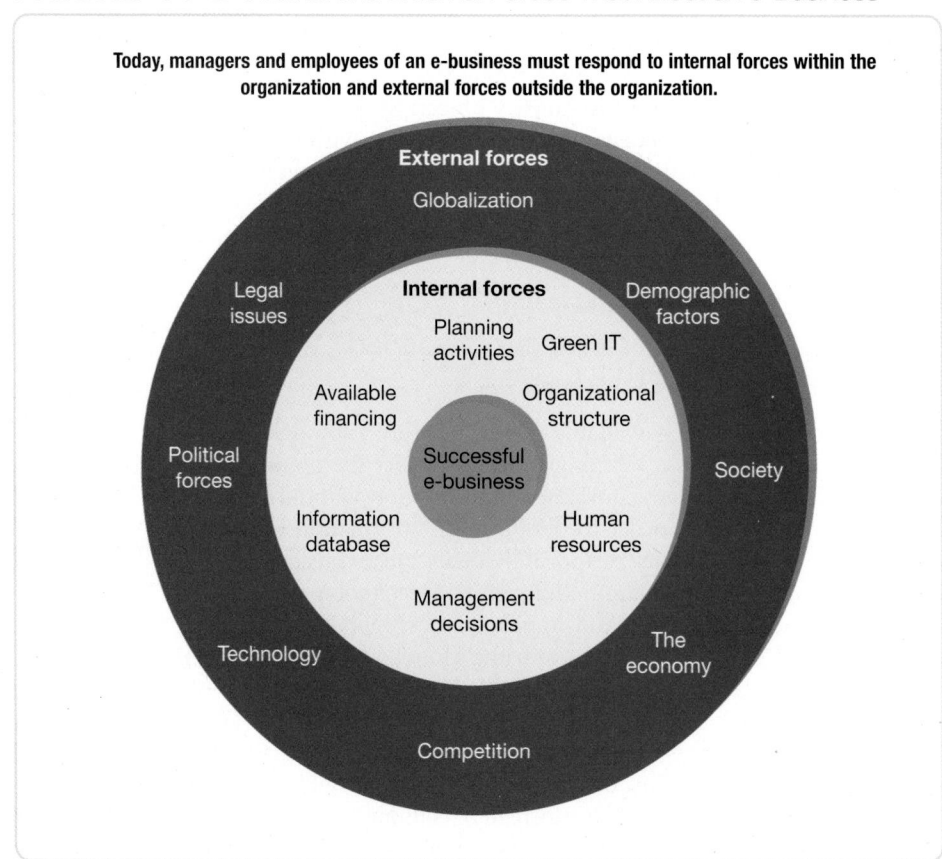

Today, managers and employees of an e-business must respond to internal forces within the organization and external forces outside the organization.

External forces
Globalization
Legal issues
Demographic factors

Internal forces
Planning activities
Green IT
Available financing
Organizational structure

Political forces
Successful e-business
Society

Information database
Human resources

Management decisions

Technology
The economy

Competition

green IT a term used to describe all of a firm's activities to support a healthy environment and sustain the planet

of technology include globalization, demographic, societal, economic, competitive, technological, and political and legal forces.

In this chapter, we have explored how both individuals and businesses use social media. We also examined how e-business is changing the way that firms do business. In Chapter 15, we examine a business firm's need for information and why accounting is a major source of information for business.

Summary

14-1 Examine why it is important for a business to use social media.

Millions of people of all ages use social media to interact with people and share ideas, personal information, and information about products and services. Today, about 71 percent of U.S. adults use the Internet or some sort of social media platform like Facebook, LinkedIn, Google+, Twitter, or Pinterest according to a recent Pew Internet Research Study. The primary reason for using social media is to stay in touch with family and friends. Other reasons include reconnecting with friends and posting messages about what's going on in their lives. Early on, companies saw the potential in the sheer numbers of people using social media. Even though companies have used social media to share information about their products and services and improve customer service, many are still uncomfortable with this new method of communicating with customers because they do not have much control over what is said about their products or services.

14-2 Discuss how businesses use social media tools.

Companies use social media to connect with customers, listen to stakeholders, provide customer service, provide information to customers, and engage customers in product development. To share social content (information about products and services), companies can use blogs, photos, videos, and podcasts. In addition, social media also enables shoppers to access opinions, recommendations, and referrals from others within and outside their own social circle. Rating and review sites are based on the idea that people trust the opinions of others when it comes to purchasing products and services. Social games are another area of growth in social media. A social game (like Angry Birds or FarmVille) is a multiplayer, competitive, goal-oriented activity with defined rules of engagement and online connectivity among a community of players. While some businesses elect to create their own game, others choose to place advertising into a game.

14-3 Explain the business objectives for using social media.

Although its popularity is a recent phenomenon, many businesses are already using social media to achieve important goals and objectives. In fact, there are many ways for businesses to use social media to take advantage of business opportunities to build connections with other businesses and consumers. For example, businesses can use social media to build a community. Social media communities are social networks based on the relationships among people. Today, there are social communities for every interest, ethnic group, and lifestyle. Different types of communities include both forums and wikis. Other reasons for using social media include crisis and reputation management, listening to stakeholders, targeting customers, social media marketing, generating new product ideas, and recruiting employees. For a business, social media marketing is especially important because it can not only develop customer awareness, but also obtain sales leads and increase actual sales.

14-4 Describe how businesses develop a social media plan.

Before developing a plan to use social media, it is important to determine how social media can improve the organization's overall performance and how it "fits" with a company's objectives and other promotional activities. Once it is determined how social media links to the company's other activities, the first step is to listen to what customers like and don't like about a company's products or services. Typically, the second step is to establish social media objectives that are specific, measurable, achievable, realistic, and oriented toward the future. After listening and establishing objectives, the third step is to identify the customer or market segment a business is trying to reach with a social media promotion. The fourth step is to select the social media tool that will be used to reach customers. While it is not necessary (or even advisable) to use all of the available tools, a company can use social media communities, blogs, photos, videos, podcasts, or games to reach potential or existing customers. Once social media tools have been identified, a company can implement and integrate the social media plan.

Both quantitative and qualitative measurements can be used to determine the effectiveness of a social media plan. Quantitative social media measurement consists of using numerical measurements. Key performance indicators (KPIs), for example, are quantitative measurements. Qualitative measurement is the process of accessing the opinions and beliefs about a brand and primarily uses sentiment analysis to categorize what is being said about a company. Because social media costs both time and money, it is important to maintain, update, and measure the success of a social media plan and make adjustments and changes if needed.

14-5 Explain the meaning of e-business.

e-Business, or electronic business, can be defined as the organized effort of individuals to produce and sell, for a profit, the goods and services that satisfy society's needs *through the facilities available on the Internet*. The human, material, information, and financial resources that any business requires are highly specialized for e-business. In an effort to reduce the cost of e-business resources, many firms have turned to outsourcing. It is also possible to use mobile marketing to increase sales and profits.

Using e-business activities, it is possible to satisfy new customer needs created by the Internet as well as traditional ones in unique ways. Meeting customer needs is especially important when an e-business is trying to earn profits by increasing sales and reducing expenses. Each source of revenue flowing into the firm is referred to as a revenue stream.

14-6 Understand the fundamental models of e-business.

e-Business models focus attention on the identity of a firm's customers. Firms that use the Internet mainly to conduct business with other businesses generally are referred to as having a business-to-business, or B2B, model. When examining B2B firms, two clear types emerge. In the first type of B2B, the focus is simply on facilitating sales transactions between businesses. A second, more complex type of the B2B model involves a company and its suppliers. In contrast to the focus of the B2B model, firms such as Amazon or Warby Parker are focused on individual buyers and are thus referred to as having a business-to-consumer, or B2C, model. In a B2C situation, understanding how consumers behave online is critical to the firm's success. Successful B2C firms often make a special effort to build long-term relationships with their customers. While B2B and B2C models are the most popular e-business models, there are other models that perform specialized e-business activities to generate revenues (see Table 14-2).

14-7 Identify the factors that will affect the future of the Internet, social media, and e-business.

Since the beginning of commercial activity on the Internet, developments in computer technology, social media, and e-business have been rapid. However, success is not guaranteed just because it is a "technology" firm. Even firms with a promising idea must develop a business plan to turn an idea into a reality—and a successful business. Today, most firms involved in computer technology, social media, and e-business use a more intelligent approach to development and realize the need to satisfy customer needs. The long-term view held by the vast majority of analysts is that use of the Internet will continue to expand along with related technologies. Because approximately 86 percent of Americans now have access to the Internet, potential growth is limited in the United States. On the other hand, only 3 billion of the 7 billion people in the world use the Web. Clearly, the number of Internet users in the world's developing countries is expected to increase dramatically.

The future of computer technology and the Internet will be influenced by advances in technology, the increasing popularity of social media, and the increasing use of e-business. Other factors including ethics, social responsibility, and Internet crime will all impact the way that businesses and consumers use computer technology and the Internet. Although the environmental forces at work are complex, it is useful to think of them as either internal or external forces that affect how businesses use computer technology. Internal environmental forces are those that are closely associated with the actions and decisions taking place within a firm. In contrast, external environmental forces are those factors affecting an e-business originating outside an organization.

Key Terms

You should now be able to define and give an example relevant to each of the following terms:

social media (402)	podcasts (406)	wiki (408)	crowdfunding (414)
hashtag (403)	social game (407)	Millennials (410)	quantitative social media
social content sites (405)	social media communities	social media marketing (410)	measurement (416)
blog (406)	(408)	inbound marketing (411)	key performance indicators
media sharing sites (406)	forum (408)	crowdsourcing (412)	(KPIs) (417)

qualitative social media measurement (417)

sentiment analysis (417)

e-business (or electronic business) (418)

mobile marketing (418)

outsourcing (419)

revenue stream (420)

business model (421)

business-to-business (or B2B) model (421)

business-to-consumer (or B2C) model (422)

cookie (424)

data mining (424)

malware (425)

cloud computing (425)

green IT (426)

Discussion Questions

1. Given the fast pace of everyday life, most people often feel there is not enough time to do everything that needs to be done. Yet, people do find time to post personal information, photos, etc., on Facebook, Twitter, blogs, and other social media sites. Why do you think people are so fascinated with social media?

2. How can a small cosmetics wholesaler located in Jacksonville, Florida use e-business and social media to increase its customer base, increase revenues, and reduce expenses?

3. Is outsourcing good for an e-business firm? The firm's employees? Explain your answer.

4. What distinguishes a B2B from a B2C e-business model?

5. Experts predict that the Internet, social media, and e-business will continue to expand along with related computer technologies. What effect will this expansion have on how businesses connect with customers in the future?

Video Case

Luke's Lobster: Entrepreneurs Use Social Networking to Claw Their Way Up the Food Chain

When Luke Holden decided to open up a restaurant in 2009, using social media to promote it seemed like a no-brainer. "Word-of-mouth from friends is stronger than any other form of advertising in my opinion," says the 27-year-old.

Holden didn't start out in the restaurant business, though. After graduating from Georgetown University, he went to work on Wall Street as a financial analyst. A couple of years later, the banking crisis hit. When many of his coworkers started getting laid off, he began thinking about a backup plan for himself.

One thing Holden had noticed about New York City was that there were no restaurants serving good lobster rolls for a decent price: "They were all selling for $24, but you got only a little lobster, a lot of mayo, and more filler," he says. The Maine native sensed an opportunity. Plus, he knew where to find a good lobster supplier: his dad, Jeff Holden, who owns a seafood processing company in Portland, Maine. Luke had worked for his father when he was younger. If he purchased seafood directly from his father, rather than through a wholesaler, he figured he could offer a big lobster roll for a small price.

Because the restaurant business in New York City is very competitive, Holden figured he better not quit his day job right away. Instead, he posted an ad on Craigslist to find a partner who could help him get the business up and running. That's how he came across Ben Conniff. Conniff was fresh out of Yale and looking to get into the restaurant business, too. After coming up with a business plan and raising some money,

he and Holden hired some employees and opened Luke's Lobster, a tiny eatery in New York City's East Village. Conniff worked the day shift. Holden worked nights and weekends.

Fortunately, Luke's Lobster quickly found a following. Better yet, customers got online to rave about the restaurant's generously portioned rolls as well as their $15 price. Health- and environmentally conscious diners who want to know where their food is coming from were also attracted to the eatery. "We know the exact source of all our food," Holden says. "We can trace it from the bottom of the ocean to the East Village."

To further spread the word out about the restaurant, Holden and Conniff signed up with the social networking site Foursquare. Foursquare has a GPS-enabled, mobile-phone app that recommends businesses in the area where you're located based on what you and your friends in your network have said they like. People with the app can automatically "check in" with a business on Foursquare. They can let their friends know where they are and comment on their experience. When customers accumulate enough check-ins, they qualify for discounts and freebies. "Forget about loyalty cards and coupons. This makes it so it's more digital and virtual," Holden says about Foursquare. "It's a digital wallet that you can carry around, and it's constantly rewarding you."

In addition to using Foursquare to get customers in the door, Holden and Conniff use it to help manage Luke's. The data they get from Foursquare allows them to categorize their customers by gender, age, and arrival time. Analyzing the arrival times of customers helps the restaurant ramp up for busy periods and offer specials when business is slow.

The entrepreneurs didn't limit their social networking to Foursquare, however. They use a combination of Facebook, Twitter, Tumblr, Pinterest, and Vimeo to post photos and videos about Luke's, make announcements about specials and contests, and provide links to the restaurant's website and blog. The crew at Luke's also "listens" to what people on the Web are saying about the restaurant and replies to them. "Responding to folks who mention us is our way of bringing them into the family and incorporating their feedback into our business," Holden says.

Six months after setting up shop in the East Village, business was so good that Holden and Conniff were able to open up a second location. At that point, Holden felt comfortable enough to leave the banking business. Since then, the men have opened up more Luke's Lobster restaurants in New York City, and in Washington, D.C. In 2011, the Luke's chain rolled out a food truck in the New York area. The employees who work the truck use Twitter to update customers on its whereabouts.

Thanks to a good product and social networking strategy, New York City has been awash with information about Luke's Lobster. HauteLiving.com even named it the city's best lobster restaurant. What's interesting is that without doing any traditional advertising whatsoever, Holden and Conniff have achieved so much success—including landing a spot on the *Today Show* with Kathie Lee Gifford. With a little more angling, it's looking like they could net some cookbook or reality TV offers.[43]

Questions

1. What factors have contributed to the success of Luke's Lobster?
2. Why have Holden and Conniff shunned traditional advertising? Is that a good idea? Why or why not?
3. Pick another type of business and describe how it could use social media networking to promote its products or services?

Building Skills for Career Success

1. Social Media Exercise

The purpose of the first part of this chapter is to introduce you to social media and its importance to business. After reading the chapter, choose a business that you either know something about, want to start, or is the company you already work for.

Assignment

1. Develop a social media plan for that business using what you learned in this chapter.
2. What are the objectives of your social media plan?
3. What social media tools would you choose and why? How would you measure success?
4. Prepare a report that describes how this exercise has helped you understand the material in this chapter.

2. Building Team Skills

After graduating from college with a degree in marketing, your first job was working in the marketing department for a fast-food chain located in the southwestern part of the United States. After three years, you were promoted and became director of the chain's social media program. While monitoring posts about the company on Facebook and Twitter, you notice the following post from one of the firm's former employees.

"Got fired today, but I was tired of serving low-quality food with expired expiration dates. Don't eat there or any of the chain's restaurants unless you want to get deathly ill."

To make matters worse, a couple of other employees who had recently been fired chimed in and made posts of a similar nature.

Assignment

1. Working in small teams, create a response that can be used to convince consumers that your company is committed to food freshness and quality and that these posts were made by employees who had been terminated.
2. Choose a spokesperson that will read your response to the rest of the class.
3. As a class, discuss the pros and cons of each response developed by each team.
4. Ask all members of the class to vote on the best response.
5. Finally, each team should prepare a report for the company's management that describes what happened and the response that was made to tell the company's side of this issue and restore consumer confidence in the firm's food products.

3. Researching Different Careers

Today, there are a wide assortment of career opportunities in companies that are involved in technology, social media, and e-business. In addition to existing businesses, there are new technology companies springing up every day. In many cases, these firms want people with a fresh outlook on how technology, social media, and e-business companies can differentiate their products or services from those of other companies in the same industry. They often prefer individuals without preconceived notions about how to proceed. Website managers, designers, creative artists, and content specialists are just a few of the positions available. Many large online job sites, such as Monster.com, can help you to find out about employment opportunities and the special skills required for various jobs.

Assignment

1. Identify a website that provides information about careers in technology, social media, or e-business.
2. Summarize at least three positions that appear to be in high demand.
3. What are some of the special skills required to fill these jobs?
4. What salaries and benefits typically are associated with these positions?
5. Which job seems most appealing to you personally? Why?

Endnotes

1 Based on information in Jon Chavez, "Toledo to Determine Fate of Taco Bell Item," *Toledo Blade*, February 3, 2015, www.toledoblade.com; Ron Ruggless, "Taco Bell Offers Free Doritos Locos Tacos to App Users," *Nation's Restaurant News*, January 5, 2015, www.nrn.com; Amy Gesenhues, "A CMO's View: Taco Bell's Chris Brandt Makes Mobile a Priority & It Has Paid Off with Nearly 2M App Downloads," *Marketing Land.com*, January 21, 2015; Lauren Johnson, "Why Did Taco Bell Just Wipe Out Its Social Media Accounts?" *Adweek*, October 28, 2014, www.adweek.com; Lauren Johnson, "Taco Bell Explains Its Social Media Blackout and How It Lit Up Mobile Orders within Minutes," *Adweek*, October 30, 2014, www.adweek.com.

2 Maeve Duggan, Nicole B. Ellison, Cliff Lampe, Amanda Lenhart, and Mary Madden, "Social Media Update 2014," *Pew Research Center*, January 9, 2015, www.pewinternet.org.

3 Rosemary Feitelberg, "Macy's to Sponsor Go Red for Women Red Dress Collection," *WWD*, January 14, 2015, www.wwd.com.

4 Mark Bergen, "Forget the Selfie: Samsung Is Out-Innovating Apple in Marketing," *Advertising Age*, April 11, 2014, www.adage.com.

5 Maura Judkis, "Budweiser 'Puppy Love' Commercial for Super Bowl Wins America's Heart," *Washington Post*, January 31, 2014, www.washingtonpost.com; Tim Nudd, "The 20 Most Viral Ads of 2014," *Adweek*, November 20, 2014, www.adweek.com.

6 Nicole Fallon, "Etsy Shares 5 Secrets to Seller Success," *Business News Daily.com*, February 3, 2015, www.businessnewsdaily.com.

7 Stefany Zaroban, "Product Reviews Boost Revenue per Online Visit 62 %," Internet Retailer, January 22, 2015, www.internetretailer.com.

8 The Wyndam Hotel website, February 24, 2015, www.wyndam.com.

9 Tracy L. Tuten and Michael R. Solomon, *Social Media Marketing* (Upper Saddle River, NJ: Pearson Publishing, 2013), p. 147.

10 Dave Chaffey, "2011 Marketing Trends," *the Smart Insights*, March 1, 2012, www.smartinsights.com/digital-p.marketing-strategy/online-marketing-mix/2011-digital-marketing-trends/.

11 Michael Barris, "Schlotzsky's Engages Customers with Mobile Games on App," *Mobile Marketer*, October 7, 2014, www.mobilemarketer.com.

12 Shara Tibken, "Zynga Revs Up Mobile Ads with Honda Campaign," *CNet*, October 16, 2012, http://news.cnet.com.

13 Tracy L. Tuten and Michael R. Solomon, *Social Media Marketing* (Upper Saddle River, NJ: Pearson Publishing, 2013), p. 5.

14 Janice Jucker, "Popular Houston Bakery Shares Top 3 Reasons to Use Pinterest," *Houston Business Journal*, December 17, 2014, www.bizjournals.com/houston.

15 The Kiva website, February 24, 2015, www.kiva.org.

16 Stephanie Rosendahl, "Top 5 Tips for Reputation Management through Social Media," *the Articlebase*, July 7, 2011, http://articlebase.com/internet-marketingarticles/top-5-tips-for-reputation-managmenet-through-social-media-4997832.html.

17 David Welch, "GM Executives Help Scour Social Media to Spot Vehicle Flaws," *Automotive News*, November 24, 2014, www.autonews.com; Vindu Goel, "G.M. Uses Social Media to Manage Customers and Its Reputation," *New York Times*, March 23, 2014, www.nytimes.com.

18 David Gerzof-Richard, "Don't Make These Social-Media Blunders That Businesses Keep Repeating," *Entrepreneur.com*, June 10, 2014, www.entrepreneur.com.

19 Emily Bryson York, "Domino's Reports 14 Percent Same-Store Sales Hike for First Quarter," *The Advertising Age*, April 1, 2012, www.advertisingage.com.

20 "Fashion Designers Strutting Their Stuff," *The Economist*, website at www3.economist.com, February 14, 2015; Gemma Taylor, "Burberry Total Sales Rise 9% in Q3," *Retail Gazette*, January 15, 2013, www.retailgazette.co.uk; Nina Easton, "Angela Ahrendts: The Secrets Behind Burberry's Growth," *Fortune*, June 19, 2012, http://management.fortune.cnn.com; Maureen Morrison, "A Focus on Digital Makes Burberry Relevant to a New Generation," *Advertising Age*, December 10, 2012, www.adage.com; Caryn Rousseau, "Classic Fashion Brand Burberry Goes Digital," *Bloomberg*, December 26, 2012, www.bloomberg.com; Di Gallo, "Luxury Brand Burberry Moves Beyond the Tartan," *Social Media Week*, August 14, 2012, http://socialmediaweek.org; Emily Cronin, "Burberry: Entrenched in the Digisphere," *Telegraph (London)*, November 24, 2012, http://fashion.telegraph.co.uk.

21 Tracy L. Tuten and Michael R. Solomon, *Social Media Marketing* (Upper Saddle River, NJ: Pearson Publishing, 2013), p. 5.

22 Shar VanBoskirk with Christine Spivey Overby, "US Interactive Marketing Forecast 2011 to 2016," *Forrester Research*, August 24, 2011, www.forrester.com August 24, 2011.

23 Ted Mann, "GE Touts Its New-Media Cred," *Wall Street Journal*, December 1, 2014, www.wsj.com; John Dix, "How GE Uses Social Tools to Support Its Digital Strategies," *Network World*, May 21, 2014, www.networkworld.com; Wendy Frink, "How 122-Year-Old General Electric Is Killing It on Social Media," *Entrepreneur.com*, April 8, 2014.

24 Joanna Belbey, "FDA Readies Social Media Rules for Big Pharma," *Forbes*, August 6, 2014, www.forbes.com.

25 "Doritos Wants You to Pick Its Super Bowl Ad," *Great Ideas*, January 26, 2015, www.greatideas.com.

26 Lego to Immortalize Doctor Who," *Independent (Ireland)*, February 4, 2015, www.independent.ie; Sarah Whitten, "Allons-y! Lego Is About to Get a Little More Sonic," *CNBC*, February 6, 2015, http://www.cnbc.com; https://ideas.lego.com.

27 LinkedIn, February 25, 2015, www.linkedin.com.

28 Melissa Barker, Donald Barker, Nicholas Bormann, and Krista E. Neher, *Social Media Marketing: A Strategic Approach* (Mason, OH: Cengage Publishing, 2013), p. 31.

29 Ibid.

30 Jeff Fromm, "How Coke's Super Bowl Ad Will #MakeItHappy And Sell More Soda To Millennials," *Forbes.com*, February 1, 2015; Coca-Cola Social Media Principles, www.coca-colacompany.com/stories/online-social-media-principles.

31 Louis Julig, "Four Ways to Measure the Impact of Social Media: A Case Study," *Social Media Examiner.com*, September 24, 2014.

32 Stephen Edelstein, "Ford Relaunches Fiesta Movement Social Media Campaign," Digital Trends website at www.digitaltrends.com (accessed February 20, 2013).

33 "2012 E-Stats," *E-Stats*, U.S. Department of Commerce, May 22, 2014, http://www.census.gov/econ/estats.

34 Tom Kaneshige, "What Retailers Think of Mobile Marketing," *CIO*, February 10, 2015, http://www.cio.com.

35 Marcus Wohlsen, "Forget Apple Pay. The Master of Mobile Payments Is Starbucks," *Wired*, November 3, 2014, www.wired.com.

36 The Internet World Stats, February 26, 2015, www.internetworldstats.com.

37 The Internet Live Stats, February 26, 2015, www.internetlivestats.com.

38 Ibid.

39 Brian X. Chen and Natasha Singer, "Verizon Wireless to Allow Complete Opt Out of Mobile 'Supercookies,'" *New York Times*, January 30, 2015, www.nytimes.com; Elizabeth Weise, "AT&T: Customers Can Opt Out of Tracking in Advance," *USA Today*, November 15, 2014, www.usatoday.com.

40 Chris Fleisher, "Beacons Track Shoppers' Smartphones Amid Retailers' Aisles," *Pittsburgh Tribune-Review*, December 18, 2014, http://triblive.com; Rick Romell, "Kohl's to Launch Personalized Marketing Effort," *Milwaukee Journal Sentinel*, November 2, 2014, www.vnews.com.

41 The Javelin Strategy and Research, February 5, 2014, www.idsafety.net.

42 Anna Wilde Mathews and Danny Yadron, "Health Insurer Anthem Hit by Hackers," *Wall Street Journal*, February 4, 2015, www.wsj.com.

43 Based on information from Luke's Lobster, February 26, 2015, www.lukeslobster.com; "Foursquare: Social Media for Small Businesses," *CBSNews*, June 13, 2011, www.cbsnews.com; Katy Finneran, "Food Trucks' Tasty Tweets," *FOXBusiness*, May 13, 2011, http://foxbusiness.com; Dana Schuster, "On a Roll!" *New York Post*, May 11, 2011, www.nypost.com; Alexandra Wolfe, "Luke Holden's Luke's Lobster," *Businessweek*, October 14, 2010, www.businessweek.com; Benjamin Wallace, "On a Roll," *New York Magazine*, June 20, 2010, http://nymag.com.

Using Management and Accounting Information

Learning Objectives

Once you complete this chapter, you will be able to:

15-1 Examine how information can reduce risk when making a decision.

15-2 Discuss management's information requirements.

15-3 Outline the five functions of an information system.

15-4 Explain why accurate accounting information and audited financial statements are important.

15-5 Read and interpret a balance sheet.

15-6 Read and interpret an income statement.

15-7 Describe business activities that affect a firm's cash flow.

15-8 Summarize how managers evaluate the financial health of a business.

Why Should You Care?

Question: How important is management and accounting information for a successful business? Answer: It would be extremely difficult to manage even a small business without management and accounting information.

ISTOCKPHOTO.COM/ALEXSL

Amazon Web Services Delivers in the Cloud

Amazon Web Services (AWS), founded in 2006 by e-commerce giant Amazon.com, has become the runaway leader in cloud computing services. It now serves more than a million businesses, including established corporations like Unilever, Dole Food Company, and Siemens, as well as up-and-coming firms like Netflix, Spotify, and Pinterest. AWS also serves U.S. government agencies such as the Centers for Disease Control and Prevention (CDC) and the Food and Drug Administration (FDA), and nonprofit organizations like the Public Broadcasting Service (PBS).

Rather than have to invest heavily in servers and other hardware plus specialized software to store and process data, AWS's customers have convenient "pay-as-you-go" access to some of the world's fastest, cutting-edge network technology. Customers can use AWS to power their websites, host their databases, run business applications, supplement in-house information systems, deliver digital content, and more.

AWS maintains a global network of data centers, packed with more than 3.5 million servers, to manage cloud computing for customers in 190 countries. Because customers rely on AWS to have all systems available all day, every day, AWS has worked hard to minimize any outages. During one recent year, AWS experienced only 2.4 hours of downtime. In fact, its technology is designed to withstand unexpected spikes in usage and sustained periods of heavy demand. For example, when Netflix uploads a new season of popular programs like *House of Cards*, AWS's data centers are ready to accommodate the tens of thousands of subscribers who will click to view it over the course of the first week. On the other hand, if a small business needs access to cloud-based data storage for just a few minutes every hour, it pays only for that level of usage.

Every year, AWS improves its technology offerings, often coupled with a cut in price. Since 2006, the company has lowered its prices 46 times. Not surprisingly, this has put pricing pressure on competitors like Microsoft and Google, which are both seeking to increase their market share in cloud computing services. AWS is now expanding into areas that have traditionally been strengths of Microsoft and Google, such as providing e-mail and electronic calendar services for corporations. What will AWS introduce next? [1]

Did You Know?

Amazon Web Services (AWS) runs more than 3.5 million servers as part of its cloud computing services for Netflix, Pinterest, and thousands of other organizations worldwide.

Information—that's what this chapter is all about! We begin this chapter with information about Amazon Web Services (AWS)—the company profiled in the Inside Business feature. While many people think of Amazon as a large online retailer, this Internet-based firm is branching out into many other areas of technology to meet the needs of its customers. For example, AWS is the runaway leader in cloud computing and has technology firms like Microsoft and Google playing catch-up. By providing access to its cloud, AWS is increasing both its sales and profits and at the same time meeting the information needs of over a million customers. Customers like Netflix, the U.S. Food and Drug Administration, and the Public Broadcasting Service can use AWS's state-of-the-art technology that is not only reliable, but more cost effective than what they could purchase on their own to obtain the information they need to make decisions and improve productivity.

In this chapter, we begin by describing why employees need information. The first three major sections in this chapter answer the following questions:

- How can information reduce risk when making a decision?
- What is a management information system?
- How do employees use a management information system?

Next, we look at why accounting information is important, attempts to improve financial reporting, and careers in the accounting industry. Then we examine the basic accounting equation and the three most important financial statements: the balance sheet, the income statement, and the statement of cash flows. Finally, we take a look at how managers evaluate the firm's financial health.

15-1 HOW CAN INFORMATION REDUCE RISK WHEN MAKING A DECISION?

As we noted in Chapter 1, information is one of the four major resources (along with material, human, and financial resources) managers must have to operate a business. Although a successful business uses all four resources efficiently, it is information that helps managers reduce risk when making a decision.

Learning Objective

15-1 Examine how information can reduce risk when making a decision.

15-1a Information and Risk

To improve the decision-making process and reduce risk, the information used by individuals and business firms must be relevant or useful to meet a specific need. Using relevant information results in better decisions.

Relevant information → Better intelligence and knowledge → Better decisions

For businesses, better intelligence and knowledge that lead to better decisions are especially important because they can provide a *competitive edge* over competitors and improve a firm's *profits*.

Theoretically, with accurate and complete information, there is no risk whatsoever. On the other hand, a decision made without any information is a gamble. These two extreme situations are rare in business. For the most part, business decision makers see themselves located someplace between the extremes. As illustrated in Figure 15-1, when the amount of available information is high, there is less risk; when the amount of available information is low, there is more risk.

Remember back in Chapter 8 (Producing Quality Goods and Services), we discussed Ford Motor Company's plans to produce a new Ford truck that is 700 pounds lighter than the current model. To help make a very important decision that affected the future of the number one selling truck in the U.S., executives at Ford relied on information. Without any information, Ford executives might as well have made the decision by flipping a coin—heads we make a lighter truck or tails we don't. For a decision this important that could impact both sales and profits for the entire company, executives began by gathering information from customers. Simply put: Did customers think a lighter truck was a good idea if it could improve gas mileage. Customers provided Ford with additional information about the price that they were willing to pay for the truck and also about features and options they

FIGURE 15-1 The Relationship Between Information and Risk

When the amount of available information is high, managers tend to make better decisions. On the other hand, when the amount of information is low, there is a high risk of making a poor decision.

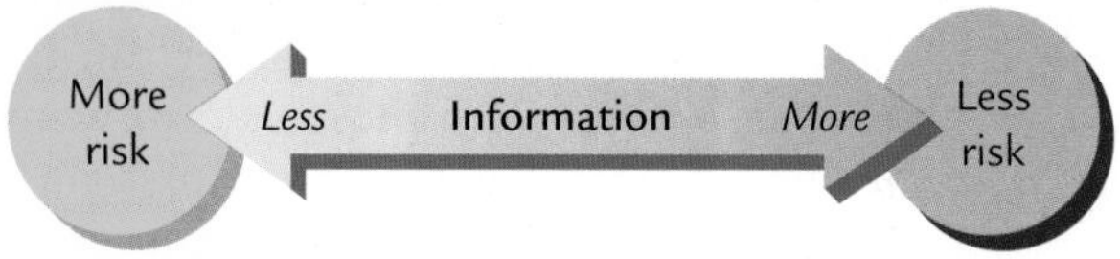

More risk ← *Less* Information *More* → Less risk

would like on a new truck. Information was also obtained from Ford's own product engineers, production employees, marketing employees, and key executives. Only after all of the information was obtained and analyzed, did Ford make the decision to produce and market the new truck. Thus, information, when understood properly, produces knowledge and empowers managers and employees to make better decisions.

15-1b Information Rules

Marketing research continues to show that discounts influence almost all car and truck buyers. Simply put, if dealers lower their prices, they will sell more cars and trucks. This relationship between buyer behavior and price can be thought of as an information rule that usually will guide the marketing manager correctly. An information rule emerges when research confirms the same results each time that it studies the same or a similar set of circumstances.

Because of the volume of information they receive each day and their need to make decisions on a daily basis, businesspeople try to accumulate information rules to shorten the time they spend analyzing choices. Information rules are the "great simplifiers" for all decision makers. Business research is continuously looking for new rules that can be put to good use and looking to discredit old ones that are no longer valid. This ongoing process is necessary because business conditions rarely stay the same for very long.

15-1c The Difference Between Data and Information

data numerical or verbal descriptions that usually result from some sort of measurement

information data presented in a form that is useful for a specific purpose

Many people use the terms *data* and *information* interchangeably, but the two differ in important ways. **Data** are numerical or verbal descriptions that usually result from some sort of measurement. Your current wage level, the amount of last year's sales revenues and after-tax profit for Google, and the current retail prices of Dell computers are all data. Most people think of data as being numerical only, but they can be nonnumerical as well. A description of an individual as a "tall, athletic person with short, dark hair" certainly would qualify as data.

Information is data presented in a form that is useful for a specific purpose. For example, the Container Store has earned a reputation as one of the best employers in the nation. It also has a history of paying female and male employees the same amount when they perform the same duties in the workplace. To verify that employees receive the same pay for the same job, a human resources manager must compare the wages paid to male and female employees. The manager might begin with a stack of computer printouts listing every sales associate employed by the firm, along with each associate's current wages. The manager would be hard pressed to make any sense of all the names and numbers. Such printouts consist of data rather than information.

Now suppose that the manager uses a computer to graph the average wages paid to men and to women. The result is information because the manager can use it to compare wages paid to men with those paid to women over the last year. For a manager, information presented in a practical, useful form, such as a graph, simplifies the decision-making process.

© ARINDAMBANERJEE/SHUTTERSTOCK.COM

Two *Big* Names in Technology! Although they were small start-ups when computers were just beginning to change the way businesses obtain and use information, today both companies are large, successful corporations. Even now, both Intel and Hewlett-Packard invest heavily in research and development to produce state-of-the-art products to meet the ever changing information needs of businesses and individuals.

15-1d Knowledge Management

The average company maintains a great deal of data that can be transformed into information. Typical data include records pertaining to personnel, inventory, sales, expenses, and accounting. Often each type of data is stored in individual departments within an organization. However, the data can be used more effectively when they are organized into a database. A **database** is a single collection of data and information stored in one place that can be used by people throughout an organization to make decisions. Although databases are important, the way the data and information are used is even more important—and more valuable to the firm. As a result, management information experts now use the term **knowledge management (KM)** to describe a firm's procedures for generating, using, and sharing the data and information.

MAKING SMART DECISIONS How do managers and employees sort out relevant and useful information from the spam, junk mail, and useless data? Today, three different software applications can actually help to improve and speed the decision-making process for people at different levels within an organization. First, a **decision-support system (DSS)** is a type of software program that provides relevant data and information to help a firm's employees make decisions. It also can be used to determine the effect of changing different variables and answer "what if" type questions. For example, a manager at Georgia-based Pulte Homes may use a DSS to determine prices for new homes built in an upscale, luxury subdivision. By entering the number of homes that will be built along with different costs associated with land, labor, materials, building permits, promotional costs, and all other costs, a DSS can help to determine a base price for each new home. It is also possible to increase or decrease the building costs and determine new home prices for each set of assumptions with a DSS. Although similar to a DSS, an **executive information system (EIS)** is a computer-based system that facilitates and supports the decision-making needs of top managers and senior executives by providing easy access to both internal and external information.

An **expert system** is a type of computer program that uses artificial intelligence to imitate a human's ability to think. An expert system uses a set of rules that analyze information supplied by the user about a particular activity or problem. Based on the information supplied, the expert system then provides recommendations or suggests specific actions in order to help make decisions. Expert systems, for example, have been used to schedule manufacturing tasks, diagnose illnesses, determine credit limits for credit card customers, evaluate loan applications, and develop electronic games.

BUSINESS APPLICATION SOFTWARE In addition to decision support, executive information, and expert systems, a number of business software applications can improve both decision making and productivity. Early business application software typically performed a single function. Today, however, *integrated*

database a single collection of data and information stored in one place that can be used by people throughout an organization to make decisions

knowledge management (KM) a firm's procedures for generating, using, and sharing the data and information

decision-support system (DSS) a type of software program that provides relevant data and information to help a firm's employees make decisions

executive information system (EIS) a computer-based system that facilitates and supports the decision-making needs of top managers and senior executives by providing easy access to both internal and external information

expert system a type of computer program that uses artificial intelligence to imitate a human's ability to think

Social Media:
The Small Business Administration Is Big on Social Media

The U.S. Small Business Administration (SBA) knows that small businesses are active on social media, so it has joined the conversation with a presence on Twitter, Facebook, and YouTube. Its national Twitter account (http://twitter.com/sbagov) has more than 166,000 followers who read tweets and watch videos about applying for a loan, complying with accounting and tax rules, preparing to import or export, and other topics of interest to small businesses. For more information about these and other topics, business owners can go to the SBA's YouTube channel (www.youtube.com/user/sba), which has over 9,000 subscribers. The SBA's Facebook page (www.facebook.com/SBAgov) has posts with links to articles, videos, and resources for startups and established businesses alike.

Knowing that tweets and Facebook posts are necessarily brief, the SBA also maintains a series of blogs (www.sba.gov/blogs) where experts provide detailed information and analyze current issues of interest to small businesses. For example, entrepreneurs can read blog entries about how to start a new business, how to qualify for a loan, and how to sell goods and services to the U.S. government.

TABLE 15-1 Current Business Application Software Used to Improve Productivity

Word processing	Users can prepare and edit written documents and store them in the computer or on a memory device.
Desktop publishing	Users can combine text and graphics in professional reports, newsletters, and pamphlets.
Accounting	Users can record routine financial transactions and prepare financial reports at the end of the accounting period.
Database management	Users can electronically store large amounts of data and transform the data into information.
Graphics	Users can display and print pictures, drawings, charts, and diagrams.
Spreadsheets	Users can organize numerical data into a grid of rows and columns.

Learning Objective

15-2 Discuss management's information requirements.

management information system (MIS) a system that provides managers and employees with the information they need to perform their jobs as effectively as possible

software combines many functions in a single package. Integrated packages allow for the easy linking of text, numerical data, graphs, photographs, and even audio-visual clips. A business report prepared using the Microsoft Office package, for instance, can include all these components.

Integration offers at least two other benefits. Once data have been entered into an application in an integrated package, the data can be used in another application without having to reenter the data. In addition, once a user learns one application, it is much easier to learn another application in an integrated package. From a career standpoint, you should realize that employers will assume that you possess, or will possess after training, a high degree of working comfort with several of the software applications described in Table 15-1.

Typically, data, information, databases, knowledge management, and computer software all become important parts of a firm's management information system.

15-2 WHAT IS A MANAGEMENT INFORMATION SYSTEM?

A **management information system (MIS)** is a system that provides managers and employees with the information they need to perform their jobs as effectively as possible. The purpose of an MIS (sometimes referred to as an information technology system or simply IT system) is to distribute timely and useful information from both internal and external sources to the managers and employees who need it.

15-2a A Firm's Information Requirements

Employees and managers have to plan for the future, implement their plans in the present, and evaluate results against what has been accomplished in the past. Of course, the specific types of information they need depend on their work area and on their level within the firm.

Today, many firms are organized into five areas of management: *finance*, *operations*, *marketing*, *human resources*, and *administration*. Managers in each of these areas need specific information in order to make decisions (see Figure 15-2).

- *Financial managers* are obviously most concerned with a firm's finances. They must ensure that the firm's managers and employees, lenders and suppliers, stockholders and potential investors, and government agencies have the information they need to measure the financial health of the firm.

FIGURE 15-2 Management Information System (MIS)

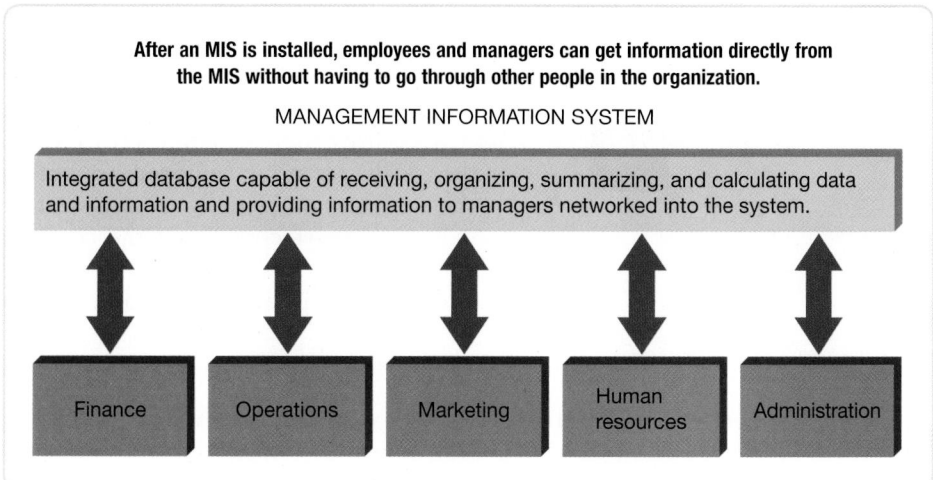

After an MIS is installed, employees and managers can get information directly from the MIS without having to go through other people in the organization.

MANAGEMENT INFORMATION SYSTEM

Integrated database capable of receiving, organizing, summarizing, and calculating data and information and providing information to managers networked into the system.

Finance | Operations | Marketing | Human resources | Administration

Source: Adapted from Ricky W. Griffin, *Management* (Mason, OH: Cengage Learning, 2013). Reprinted with permission.

- *Operations managers* are concerned with present and future sales levels, current inventory levels of work in process and finished goods, and the availability and cost of the resources required to produce products and services.

- *Marketing managers* need to have detailed information about a firm's products and services and those offered by competitors. Such information includes pricing strategies, new promotional campaigns, and products that competitors are test marketing. Information concerning the firm's customers, current and projected market share, and new and pending product legislation is also important to marketing managers.

- *Human resources managers* must be aware of anything that pertains to a firm's employees. Key examples include current wage levels and benefits packages both within the firm and in firms that compete for valuable employees, current legislation and court decisions that affect employment practices, and the firm's plans for growth, expansion, or mergers.

- *Administrative managers* are responsible for the overall management of the organization. Thus, they are concerned with the coordination of information—just as they are concerned with the coordination of material, human, and financial resources.

Administrative managers must ensure that the information is used in a consistent manner throughout the firm. Suppose, for example, that General Electric (GE) is designing a new plant in China to manufacture energy-efficient light bulbs that will open in five years. GE's management will want answers to many questions: Is the capacity of the plant consistent with marketing plans based on sales projections? Will human resources managers be able to recruit U.S. employees with the appropriate skills who are willing to relocate to a foreign country and hire and train Chinese workers to staff the plant?

© MASTER_ART/SHUTTERSTOCK.COM

Why a management information system? Assume you are a marketing manager and must develop a brochure about a new product. In this situation, you may need information from many different people within the organization. If your firm has a management information system you can use it to obtain the needed information. As an added bonus, the system not only provides the information you need, but the information other employees need to perform their jobs.

And do sales projections indicate enough income to cover the expected cost of the plant? Next, administrative managers must make sure that all managers and employees are able to use the information technology that is available. Certainly, this requires that all employees receive the skills training required to access the information. Finally, administrative managers must commit to the costs of updating the firm's MIS and providing additional training when necessary.

15-2b Costs and Limits of the System

Can employees, managers, and executives have too much information? The answer is yes. The truth is that each group needs relevant information that helps them make better decisions. And yet, too much information that must be analyzed can lead to information overload. Another problem related to information overload is the amount of worthless information, junk e-mails, and advertising that contribute to information overload. Just for a moment, think about the time employees spend reading e-mails that have been sent to everyone in a firm instead of the one or two people who really need to receive the e-mail. Unfortunately, there are other misuses of information technology that do nothing but rob employees of time that could be devoted to more productive activities. In addition to lower employee productivity, the cost of computers, software, and related equipment can be staggering. Although it would be nice for all employees to have new computers and the latest software applications, in reality, even the largest and most profitable business firms cannot afford to waste money on unnecessary computer hardware and software. One of the main goals of a firm's information technology officer is to make sure that a firm has the equipment necessary to provide information the employees need to make effective decisions—*at a reasonable cost*. As mentioned in the Inside Business feature, many firms are now using cloud computing to lower the cost of technology. When cloud computing is used, a third party makes processing power, software applications, databases, and storage available for on demand use at a lower total cost than owning the same technology.

In reality, an MIS must be tailored to the needs of the organization it serves. In some firms, a tendency to save on initial costs may result in a system that is too small or overly simple. Such a system generally ends up serving only one or two management levels or a single department. Managers in other departments "give up" on the system as soon as they find that it cannot process their data.

Almost as bad is an MIS that is too large or too complex for the organization. Unused capacity and complexity do nothing but increase the cost of owning and operating the system. In addition, a system that is difficult to use probably will not be used at all.

Concept Check

✔ How do the information requirements of managers differ by management area?

✔ What happens if a business has a management information system that is too large?

✔ What happens if a business has a management information system that is too small?

15-3 HOW DO EMPLOYEES USE A MANAGEMENT INFORMATION SYSTEM?

Learning Objective

15-3 Outline the five functions of an information system.

To provide information, an MIS must perform five specific functions. It must (1) collect data, (2) store the data, (3) update the data, (4) process the data into information, and (5) present the information to users (see Figure 15-3).

FIGURE 15-3 Five Management Information System Functions

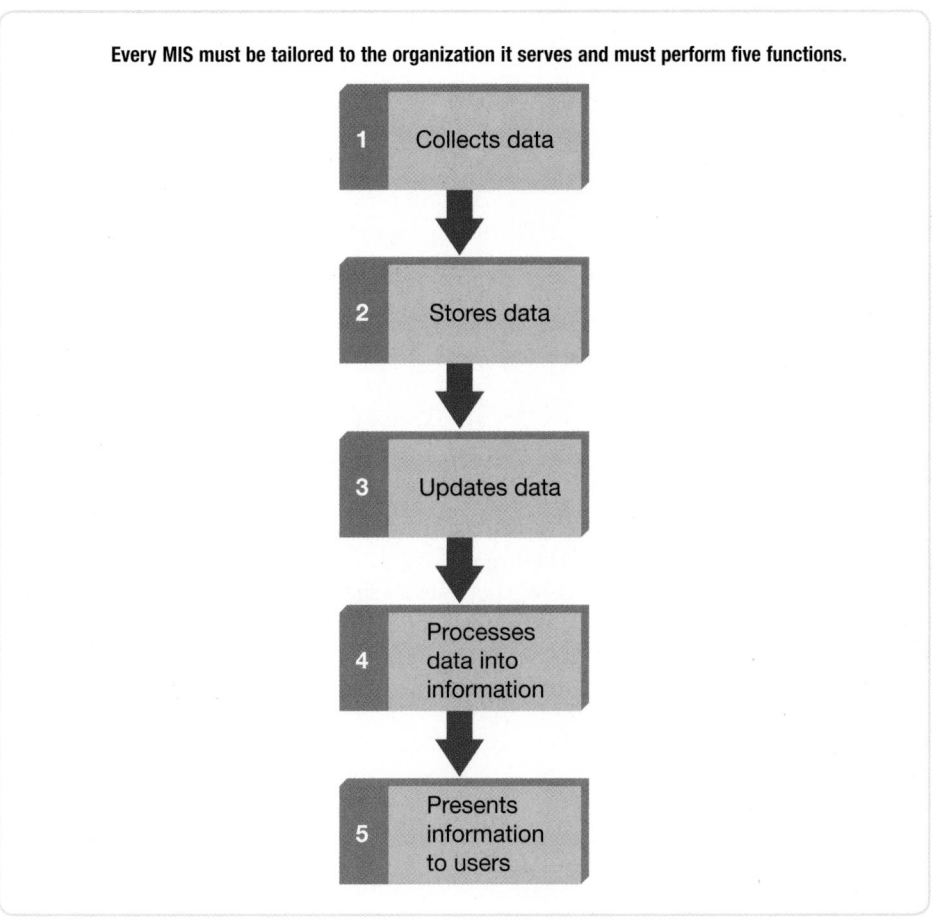

Every MIS must be tailored to the organization it serves and must perform five functions.

1. Collects data
2. Stores data
3. Updates data
4. Processes data into information
5. Presents information to users

15-3a Step 1: Collecting Data

A firm's employees, with the help of an MIS system, must gather the data and information needed to establish the firm's *database*. The database should include all past and current data that may be useful in managing the firm. Clearly, the data entered into the system must be *relevant* to the needs of the firm's employees. And perhaps most important, the data must be *accurate*. Irrelevant data are simply useless; inaccurate data can be disastrous. There are two data sources: *internal* and *external*.

Typically, most of the data gathered for an MIS come from internal sources. The most common internal sources of information are managers and employees, company records and reports, accounting data, and minutes of meetings.

External sources of data include customers, suppliers, financial institutions and banks, trade and business publications, industry conferences, online computer services, lawyers, government sources, and firms that specialize in gathering marketing research for organizations.

SCOTT PROKOP/DREAMSTIME.COM

Many businesses turn to IBM when they need to process data into information. One name that has always been known for cutting-edge technology is IBM. In fact, some of the most important technological advances that enable managers, employees, and individuals to process data into useful information are the result of IBM's research and development activities.

Personal App

Better Knowledge = Better Decisions

When gathering external data for important professional or personal decisions, ask yourself: Are you using reliable, timely, and objective sources? Can the data be double-checked? Are more up-to-date data and information available? What additional data do you need to make a more informed decision?

Whether the source of the data is internal or external, always remember the following two cautions:

1. The cost of obtaining data from some external sources, such as marketing research firms, can be quite high.

2. Although computers generally do not make mistakes, the people who use them can make or cause errors. When data (or information) and your judgment disagree, always check the data.

15-3b Step 2: Storing Data

An MIS must be capable of storing data until they are needed. Typically, the method chosen to store data depends on the size and needs of the organization. Small businesses may enter data and then store them directly on an employee's computer. Generally, medium-sized to large businesses store data in a larger computer system and provide access to employees through a computer network.

15-3c Step 3: Updating Data

Today, an MIS must be able to update stored data regularly to ensure that the information presented to managers and employees is accurate, complete, and up-to-date. The frequency with which the data are updated depends on how fast they change and how often they are used. When it is vital to have current data, updating may occur as soon as the new data are available. For example, Macy's, a national retailer that sells a wide range of merchandise including apparel and accessories for men, women, and children, cosmetics, home furnishing, and other consumer goods, has cash registers that automatically transmit data on each item sold in each store to a central computer. The computer adjusts the store's inventory records accordingly. In addition to maintaining accurate inventory records, sales representatives can tell customers where they can obtain merchandise if the store where they are shopping is out of the merchandise they want. Data and information may also be entered into a firm's data bank at certain intervals—every 24 hours, weekly, or monthly.

15-3d Step 4: Processing Data

Some data are used in the form in which they are stored, whereas other data require processing to extract, highlight, or summarize the information they contain. **Data processing** is the transformation of data into a form that is useful for a specific purpose.

For verbal data, this processing consists mainly of extracting the pertinent material from storage and combining it into a report. Most business data, however, are in

data processing the transformation of data into a form that is useful for a specific purpose

the form of numbers—large groups of numbers, such as daily sales totals or production costs for a specific product. Fortunately, computer software can process large volumes of numbers quickly, and their contents can be summarized through the use of statistics. A **statistic** is a measure that summarizes a particular characteristic of an entire group of numbers.

15-3e Step 5: Presenting Information

An MIS must be capable of presenting information in a usable form. That is, the method of presentation—reports, tables, graphs, or charts, for example—must be appropriate for the information itself and for the uses to which it will be put.

BUSINESS REPORTS Verbal information may be presented in list or paragraph form. Employees often are asked to prepare formal business reports. A typical business report includes

- An introduction
- The body of the report
- The conclusions
- The recommendations

The *introduction*, which sets the stage for the remainder of the report, describes the problem to be studied in the report, identifies the research techniques that were used, and previews the material that will be presented in the report. The *body* of the report should objectively describe the facts that were discovered in the process of completing the report. The *conclusions* are statements of fact that describe the findings contained in the report. The *recommendations* section presents suggestions on how the problem might be solved. Like the conclusions, the recommendations should be specific, practical, and based on the evidence contained in the report.

VISUAL DISPLAYS AND TABLES A visual display can also be used to present information and may be a diagram that represents several items of information in a manner that makes comparison easier. Figure 15-4 illustrates examples of visual displays including graphs, bar charts, and pie charts generated by a computer.

A tabular display is used to present verbal or numerical information in columns and rows. It is most useful in presenting information about two or more related variables. A table, for example, can be used to illustrate the number of salespeople in each region of the country, sales for different types of products, and total sales for all products (see Table 15-2). Information that is to be manipulated—for example, to calculate loan payments—is usually displayed in tabular form.

Tabular displays generally have less impact than visual displays. However, displaying the information that could be contained in a multicolumn table such as the one shown in Table 15-2 would require several bar or pie charts.

Sometimes a graph is worth a 1,000 words. Graphs, bar charts, and tables are often used when reporting information about sales, profits, expenses, and many other factors that measure not only past performance, but also help plan for the future. Fortunately, computer software can produce both visual displays and tables with a click of a mouse—once you have the data and information you want to include in your presentation.

© ANDRESR/SHUTTERSTOCK.COM

statistic a measure that summarizes a particular characteristic of an entire group of numbers

Concept Check

✓ List the five functions of an MIS.

✓ What are the components of a typical business report?

✓ What types of information could be illustrated in a visual display? In a tabular display?

FIGURE 15-4 Typical Visual Displays Used in Business Presentations

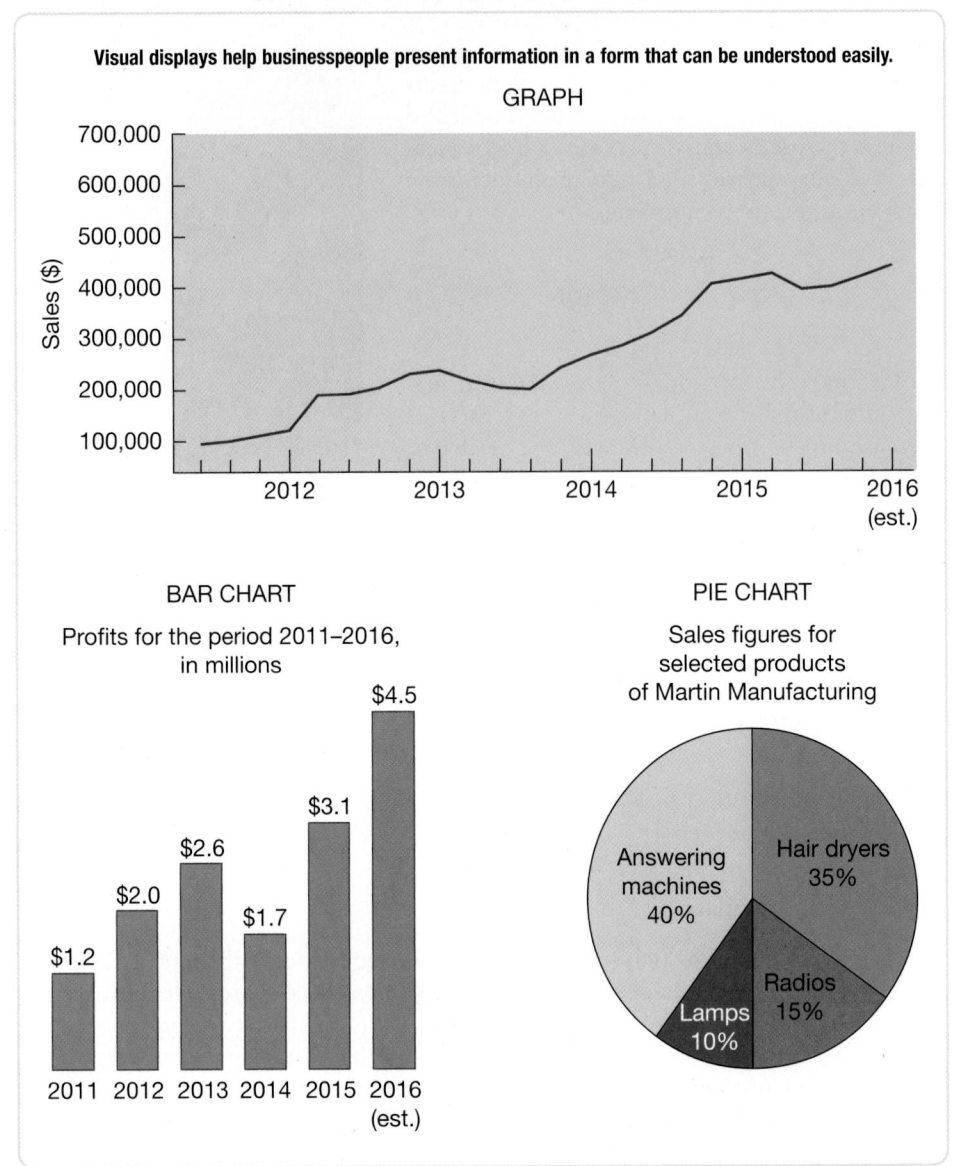

Visual displays help businesspeople present information in a form that can be understood easily.

GRAPH

BAR CHART

Profits for the period 2011–2016, in millions

PIE CHART

Sales figures for selected products of Martin Manufacturing

TABLE 15-2 Typical Three-Column Table Used in Business Presentations

Tables are most useful for displaying information about two or more variables.
All-Star Technology Projected Sales

Section of the Country	Number of Salespeople	Consumer Products ($)	Industrial Products ($)
Eastern territory	15	1,500,000	3,500,000
Midwestern territory	20	2,000,000	5,000,000
Western territory	10	1,000,000	4,000,000
TOTAL	45	4,500,000	12,500,000

15-4 WHY ACCOUNTING INFORMATION IS IMPORTANT

In today's competitive business environment, all successful firms use information to make decisions. In order to obtain needed information, firms use an MIS like the one described in the first part of this chapter. Executives, managers, and employees also rely on the firm's accounting system to provide needed financial information. **Accounting** is the process of systematically collecting, analyzing, and reporting financial information. Just for a moment, think about the following three questions:

1. Did Coca Cola's sales revenue increase last year?
2. How much federal income tax did Walmart pay last year?
3. How much cash does Google have that can be used to acquire other business firms and pay its debts?

In each case, the firm's accountants and its accounting system provide the answers to these questions and many others. Although accounting information can be used to answer questions about what has happened in the past, it can also be used to help make decisions about the future.

Because the information provided by a firm's accountants and its accounting system is so important, managers and employees, stockholders, financial analysts, bankers, lenders, suppliers, government agencies, and other interested groups must be able to "trust the numbers." To improve the accuracy of a firm's accounting information and its financial statements, businesses rely on audits conducted by accountants employed by public accounting firms.

Learning Objective

15-4 Explain why accurate accounting information and audited financial statements are important.

accounting the process of systematically collecting, analyzing, and reporting financial information

---

Entrepreneurial Success

Avoid These Top Three Accounting Mistakes

Most entrepreneurs have to watch every penny during the startup phase—and the last thing they need is an accounting problem. Here are the three most common accounting mistakes made by entrepreneurs, and how to avoid them.

1. *Mixing business and personal finances.* Sole proprietors, in particular, might think it's easier to write business checks and make business deposits using a personal checking account, or using a personal credit card to buy office supplies. This is a mistake because it blurs the line between personal and business finances, making it difficult to tell what is a company expense and what is not. Commingling business and personal finances can also complicate tax returns. Bottom line: Set up separate business and personal accounts.

2. *Misunderstanding or misinterpreting regulations.* Every business must comply with basic legislative and regulatory requirements that affect accounting—such

as filing tax returns and meeting tax payment deadlines. As a business grows, it faces other issues such as how to handle accounting for employee benefits like health insurance. The rules are complex and ever-changing, with penalties for noncompliance. Bottom line: Be aware of the local, state, and federal laws and regulations that affect accounting.

3. *Skimping on professional accounting advice.* As tempting as it may be to save money when starting a business, mistakes like missing a tax deadline or commingling business and personal finances can be costly. Bottom line: Consult an accountant who has experience working with small businesses.

Sources: Based on information in Dana Brownlee, "Entrepreneurship: It Takes a Village," *Entrepreneur.com*, January 28, 2015; Tim Devaney and Tom Stein, "Avoid These Five Common Small Business Accounting Mistakes," *Forbes.com*, April 28, 2014; Mike Trabold, "Top 3 Regulatory Issues Accountants Should Monitor This Year for Small Business Clients," *Accounting Today.com*, January 20, 2014.

15-4a Why Audited Financial Statements Are Important?

An **audit** is an examination of a company's financial statements and the accounting practices that produced them. The purpose of an audit is to make sure that a firm's financial statements have been prepared in accordance with **generally accepted accounting principles (GAAPs)**. GAAPs have been developed to provide an accepted set of guidelines and practices for U.S. companies reporting financial information and the accounting profession. At the time of publication, the Financial Accounting Standards Board (FASB), which establishes and improves accounting standards for U.S. companies, is working toward establishing a new set of standards that combines GAAPs with the International Financial Reporting Standards (IFRS) to create one set of accounting standards that can be used by both U.S. and multinational firms. IFRS are now used in more than 110 different countries around the world.[2] For multinational firms like Johnson & Johnson, Royal Dutch Shell, ExxonMobil, Walmart, and Toyota, the benefits of global accounting standards are huge because preparing financial statements and accounting records that meet global standards saves both time and money.

Although the Securities and Exchange Commission (SEC) must approve changes to the way U.S. firms report financial information, the SEC has expressed its support for high-quality globally accepted accounting standards that would benefit U.S. investors and other interested parties. Yet, at the time of publication, no official date has been announced for a conversion of GAAPs and IFRS. The final decision regarding whether to incorporate IFRS into the financial reporting system for U.S. issuers now rests with the SEC Commissioners.[3]

If an accountant determines that a firm's financial statements present financial information fairly and conform to GAAPs, then he or she will issue the following statement:

In our opinion, the financial statements ... present fairly, in all material respects the financial position of the company ... in conformity with generally accepted accounting principles.

Although an audit and the resulting report do not *guarantee* that a company has not "cooked" the books, it does imply that, on the whole, the company has followed GAAPs. Also, it should be noted that without the audit function and GAAPs, there would be very little oversight or supervision. The validity of a firm's financial statements and its accounting records would drop quickly, and firms would find it difficult to obtain debt financing, acquire goods and services from suppliers, find investor financing, or prepare documents requested by government agencies.

15-4b Accounting Fraud, Ethical Behavior, and Reform

Which of the following firms has been convicted or accused of accounting fraud?

a. Diamond Foods (U.S. Snack Food Company)
b. Mahindra Satyam (Indian Information Technology Company)
c. Bernie Madoff Investment Securities (Wall Street Investment Firm)
d. Autonomy Software (British Software Development Firm)
e. All of the above

Unfortunately, the answer to the question is e—all of the above. Each company is a business that has been plagued by accounting problems. In one case, accounting problems led to imprisonment for Bernie Madoff, the founder of Madoff Investment Securities. In other cases, the value of the corporation's stock plummeted because the firm had inflated sales or underreported expenses. And as you can tell from the options to the above question, the companies can operate in any industry and be located any place on the globe. The bottom line: The accounting

audit an examination of a company's financial statements and the accounting practices that produced them

generally accepted accounting principles (GAAPs) an accepted set of guidelines and practices for U.S. companies reporting financial information and for the accounting profession

problems at these companies—and similar problems at even more companies—have forced many investors, lenders and suppliers, and government regulators to question the motives behind fraudulent and unethical accounting practices.

Today, much of the pressure on corporate executives to "cook" the books is driven by the desire to look good to Wall Street analysts and investors. For a company like California-based Diamond Foods, executives involved falsified costs in order to boost earnings and meet estimates by stock analysts.[4] If a company reports sales and profit figures that are higher than expected, the company's stock value can increase dramatically. Greed—especially when executive salaries and bonuses are tied to a company's stock value—is another factor that can lead some corporate executives to use unethical accounting methods to inflate a firm's sales revenues and profit amount. Former Diamond Foods CEO, Michael Mendes, agreed to pay $125,000 to settle a separate charge of negligence and give back $4 million he received in bonuses to the company.[5]

Four heads are better than one! When managers and employees plan for the future, one important question always surfaces in a meeting like the one in this photo: How much is it going to cost? In almost every situation, managers and employees use accurate and reliable accounting information to answer that important question.

Unfortunately, the ones hurt when companies (and their accountants) report inaccurate or misleading accounting information often are not the high-paid corporate executives. In many cases, it's the employees who lose their jobs if the company files for bankruptcy, as well as the money they invested in the company's retirement program. In addition, investors, lenders, and suppliers who relied on fraudulent accounting information in order to make a decision to invest in or lend money to the company also usually experience a loss.

To help ensure that corporate financial information is accurate and to prevent the type of accounting scandals that have occurred in the past, Congress enacted the Sarbanes–Oxley Act in 2002. Key components include the following:[6]

- The Securities and Exchange Commission (SEC) is required to establish a full-time five-member public company accounting oversight board.
- Executive and financial officers are required to certify periodic financial reports and are liable for intentional violations of securities reporting requirements.
- Accounting firms are prohibited from providing many types of non-audit and consulting services to the companies they audit.
- Auditors must maintain financial documents and audit work papers for five years.
- Auditors, accountants, and employees can be imprisoned for up to 20 years and subject to fines for destroying financial documents and willful violations of the securities laws.
- A public corporation must change its lead auditing firm every five years.
- There is added protection for whistle-blowers who report violations of the Sarbanes–Oxley Act.

Although most people welcome the Sarbanes–Oxley Act, complex rules make compliance more expensive and time-consuming for corporate management and more difficult for accounting firms. Yet, most people agree that the cost of compliance is justified.

15-4c Different Types of Accounting

Although many people think that all accountants do the same tasks, there are special areas of expertise within the accounting industry. In fact, accounting is usually broken down into two broad categories: managerial and financial.

Managerial accounting provides managers and employees within the organization with the information needed to make decisions about a firm's financing, investing, marketing, and operating activities. By using managerial accounting information, both managers and employees can evaluate how well they have done in the past and what they can expect in the future.

Financial accounting, on the other hand, generates financial statements and reports for interested people outside of an organization. Typically, stockholders, financial analysts, bankers, lenders, suppliers, government agencies, and other interested groups use the information provided by financial accounting to determine how well a business firm has achieved its goals. In addition to managerial and financial accounting, additional special areas of accounting include the following:

- *Cost accounting*—determining the cost of producing specific products or services;
- *Tax accounting*—planning tax strategy and preparing tax returns for firms or individuals;
- *Government accounting*—providing basic accounting services to ensure that tax revenues are collected and used to meet the goals of state, local, and federal agencies; and
- *Not-for-profit accounting*—helping not-for-profit organizations to account for all donations and expenditures.

15-4d Careers in Accounting

What is the typical day like for accountants? While each day may be different than the next and depending on if they are self-employed, work for a business firm, or work for an accounting firm, accountants typically do the following:

- Ensure the business is using generally accepted accounting procedures.
- Examine financial statements to be sure that they are accurate.
- Calculate the amount of taxes owed, prepare tax returns, and ensure that taxes are paid properly and on time.
- Organize and maintain financial records.
- Assist employees, managers, and owners to improve financial decisions.
- Suggest ways to reduce costs, increase revenues, and improve profits.

According to the *Occupational Outlook Handbook*, published by the Department of Labor, job opportunities for accountants, as well as auditors in the accounting area, are expected to experience a 13 percent increase or average employment growth between now and the year 2022.[7] And more good news: Salaries for employees in the accounting industry are often higher than the salaries for other industries.

Accounting can be an exciting and rewarding career. To be successful in the accounting industry, employees must

- be responsible, honest, and ethical;
- have a strong background in financial management;
- know how to use a computer and software to process data into accounting information; and
- be able to communicate with people who need accounting information.

Today, accountants generally are classified as either private accountants or public accountants. A *private accountant* is employed by a specific organization. On the other hand, a *public accountant* works on a fee basis for clients and may be self-employed or be the employee of an accounting firm. Accounting

---

managerial accounting provides managers and employees with the information needed to make decisions about a firm's financing, investing, marketing, and operating activities

financial accounting generates financial statements and reports for interested people outside an organization

Concept Check

✓ What purpose do audits and GAAPs serve in today's business world?

✓ How do the major provisions of the Sarbanes–Oxley Act affect a public company's audit procedures?

✓ Based on the information in this section, would you choose accounting as a career?

firms range in size from one-person operations to huge international firms with hundreds of accounting partners and thousands of employees. Today, the largest accounting firms, sometimes referred to as the "Big Four," are Pricewaterhouse-Coopers (PwC), Ernst & Young, KPMG, and Deloitte Touche Tohmatsu.

Typically, public accounting firms include on their staffs at least one **certified public accountant (CPA)**, an individual who has met state requirements for accounting education and experience and has passed a rigorous accounting examination. More information about general requirements and the CPA profession can be obtained by contacting the American Institute of CPAs (AICPA) at www.aicpa.org. State requirements usually include a college degree or a specified number of hours of college course work and generally at least one year of on-the-job experience. Details regarding specific state requirements for practice as a CPA can be obtained by contacting the state's board of accountancy. For even more information about a career in accounting visit The Big 4 Accounting Firms website at www.big4account-ingfirms.org and click on the tab "How to become an Accountant."

15-5 THE ACCOUNTING EQUATION AND THE BALANCE SHEET

At the beginning of this chapter, *information* was defined as data presented in a form that is useful for a specific purpose. Now, we examine how financial *data* is transformed into financial *information* and reported on three very important financial statements—the balance sheet, income statement, and statement of cash flows. We begin by describing why the fundamental accounting equation is the basis for a firm's balance sheet.

15-5a The Accounting Equation

The accounting equation is a simple statement that forms the basis for the accounting process. This equation shows the relationship between a firm's assets, liabilities, and owners' equity.

- **Assets** are the resources a business owns—cash, inventory, equipment, and real estate.
- **Liabilities** are the firm's debts—borrowed money it owes to others that must be repaid.
- **Owners' equity** is the difference between total assets and total liabilities—what would be left for the owners if the firm's assets were sold and the money used to pay off its liabilities.

The relationship between assets, liabilities, and owners' equity is shown by the following **accounting equation**:

$$\text{Assets} = \text{Liabilities} + \text{Owners' equity}$$

Whether a business is a small corner grocery store or a global giant like Procter & Gamble, the total dollar amount for assets must equal the sum of its liabilities and owners' equity. To use this equation, a firm's accountants must record raw data—that is, the firm's day-to-day financial transactions—using the double-entry system of bookkeeping. The **double-entry bookkeeping system** is a system in which each financial transaction is recorded as two separate accounting entries to maintain the balance shown in the accounting equation. At the end of a specific accounting period, all of the financial transactions

certified public accountant (CPA) an individual who has met state requirements for accounting education and experience and has passed a rigorous accounting examination

assets the resources that a business owns

liabilities a firm's debts and obligations

owners' equity the difference between a firm's assets and its liabilities

accounting equation the basis for the accounting process: *Assets = Liabilities + Owners' equity*

double-entry bookkeeping system a system in which each financial transaction is recorded as two separate accounting entries to maintain the balance shown in the accounting equation

Learning Objective

15-5 Read and interpret a balance sheet.

© ALEXMILLOS/SHUTTERSTOCK.COM

What's missing in this photo? Answer: *Owners' equity.* The accounting equation is Assets = Liabilities + ***Owners' equity***. Whether a business is an independent retailer in a shopping mall, a small service business, or a corporate giant like Apple, General Motors, or Walmart, the total for each side of the accounting equation must be equal at the end of an accounting period.

can now be summarized in the firm's financial statements. This information is presented in a standardized format to make the statements as accessible as possible to managers, employees, lenders, suppliers, stockholders, potential investors, and government agencies. In fact, the form of the financial statements is pretty much the same for all businesses, from a neighborhood video store or small dry cleaner to giant corporations such as Home Depot, Boeing, and Bank of America. A firm's financial statements are prepared at least once a year and included in the firm's annual report. An **annual report** is a report distributed to stockholders and other interested parties that describes a firm's operating activities and its financial condition. Most firms also have financial statements prepared semiannually, quarterly, or monthly.

15-5b The Balance Sheet

Question: *Where could you find the total amount of assets, liabilities, and owners' equity for The Hershey Company?*

Answer: The firm's balance sheet.

A **balance sheet** (sometimes referred to as a **statement of financial position**) is a summary of the dollar amounts of a firm's assets, liabilities, and owners' equity accounts at the end of a specific accounting period. The balance sheet must demonstrate that assets are equal to liabilities plus owners' equity, and the accounting equation is still in balance. Most people think of a balance sheet as a statement that reports the financial condition of a business firm such as The Hershey Company, but balance sheets apply to individuals, too. For example, Marty Campbell graduated from college three years ago and obtained a position as a sales representative for an office supply firm. After going to work, he established a checking and savings account and purchased an automobile, stereo, television, and furniture for his apartment. Marty paid cash for some purchases, but he had to borrow money to pay for the larger ones. Figure 15-5 shows Marty's current personal balance sheet.

Marty Campbell's assets total $26,500, and his liabilities amount to $10,000. Although the difference between total assets and total liabilities is referred to as *owners' equity* or *stockholders' equity* for a business, it is normally called *net worth* for an individual. As reported on Marty's personal balance sheet, net worth is

annual report a report distributed to stockholders and other interested parties that describes the firm's operating activities and its financial condition

balance sheet (or **statement of financial position**) a summary of the dollar amounts of a firm's assets, liabilities, and owners' equity accounts at the end of a specific accounting period

FIGURE 15-5 Personal Balance Sheet

Often, individuals determine their net worth by subtracting the value of their liabilities from the value of their assets.

Marty Campbell
Personal Balance Sheet
December 31, 20XX

ASSETS			LIABILITIES		
Cash	$ 2,500		Automobile loan	$ 9,500	
Savings account	5,000		Credit card balance	500	
Automobile	15,000		TOTAL LIABILITIES		$10,000
Stereo	1,000				
Television	500				
Furniture	2,500		NET WORTH (Owners' Equity)		16,500
TOTAL ASSETS		$26,500	TOTAL LIABILITIES AND NET WORTH		$26,500

FIGURE 15-6 Business Balance Sheet

A balance sheet (sometimes referred to as a statement of financial position) summarizes a firm's assets, liabilities, and owners' equity. Note that assets ($340,000) equal liabilities plus owners' equity ($340,000) and the accounting equation is still in balance.

NORTHEAST ART SUPPLY, INC.

Balance Sheet
December 31, 20XX

ASSETS

Current assets

Cash		$ 59,000
Marketable securities		10,000
Accounts receivable	$ 40,000	
Less allowance for doubtful accounts	2,000	38,000
Notes receivable		32,000
Merchandise inventory		41,000
Prepaid expenses		2,000
Total current assets		$182,000

Fixed assets

Delivery equipment	$110,000	
Less accumulated depreciation	20,000	$ 90,000
Furniture and store equipment	$62,000	
Less accumulated depreciation	15,000	47,000
Total fixed assets		137,000

Intangible assets

Patents		$ 21,000
Total intangible assets		21,000
TOTAL ASSETS		$340,000

LIABILITIES AND STOCKHOLDERS' EQUITY

Current liabilities

Accounts payable	$ 35,000	
Notes payable	25,675	
Salaries payable	4,000	
Taxes payable	5,325	
Total current liabilities		$ 70,000

Long-term liabilities

Mortgage payable on store equipment	$ 40,000	
Total long-term liabilities		$ 40,000
TOTAL LIABILITIES		$110,000

Stockholders' equity

Common stock (25,000×$6)	$ 150,000	
Retained earnings	80,000	
TOTAL OWNERS' EQUITY		230,000
TOTAL LIABILITIES AND OWNERS' EQUITY		$340,000

$16,500. The total assets ($26,500) and the total liabilities *plus* net worth ($26,500) are equal. Thus, the accounting equation (Assets = Liabilities + Owners' equity) is still in balance.

Figure 15-6 shows the balance sheet for Northeast Art Supply, a small whole-sale business that sells picture frames, paints, canvases, and other artists' supplies to retailers in New England. Note that assets are reported on the left side of the statement, and liabilities and stockholders' equity are reported on the right side. Let's work through the different accounts in Figure 15-6.

15-5c Assets

On a balance sheet, assets are listed in order from the *most liquid* to the *least liquid*. The **liquidity** of an asset is the ease with which it can be converted into cash.

CURRENT ASSETS Current assets are assets that can be converted quickly into cash or that will be used in one year or less. Because cash is the most liquid asset, it is listed first. Next are *marketable securities*—stocks, bonds, and other investments—that can be converted into cash in a matter of days.

Next are the firm's receivables. Its *accounts receivable*, which result from allowing customers to make credit purchases, generally are paid within 30 to 60 days. However, the firm expects that some of these debts will not be collected. Thus, it has reduced its accounts receivables by a 5 percent *allowance for doubtful accounts*. The firm's *notes receivable* are receivables for which customers have signed promissory notes. They generally are repaid over a longer period of time than the firm's accounts receivable.

liquidity the ease with which an asset can be converted into cash

current assets assets that can be converted quickly into cash or that will be used in one year or less

Not your typical asset. For this jewelry store, Rolex watches are assets that are both valuable and beautiful. Proper accounting records will monitor the number of watches in the store's inventory and the value of the inventory. These same accounting records will help employees know when it is time to purchase more watches to make sure customers can buy the watches they want when they want to make a purchase.

fixed assets assets that will be held or used for a period longer than one year

depreciation the process of apportioning the cost of a fixed asset over the period during which it will be used

intangible assets assets that do not exist physically but that have a value based on the rights or privileges they confer on a firm

current liabilities debts that will be repaid in one year or less

Northeast's *merchandise inventory* represents the value of goods on hand for sale to customers. Since Northeast Art Supply is a wholesale business, the inventory listed in Figure 15-6 represents finished goods ready for sale to retailers. For a manufacturing firm, inventory also may represent raw materials that will become part of a finished product or work that has been partially completed but requires further processing.

Northeast Art's last current asset is *prepaid expenses*, which are assets that have been paid for in advance but have not yet been used. An example is insurance premiums. They are usually paid at the beginning of the policy year. The unused portion (say, for the last four months of the time period covered by the policy) is a prepaid expense. For Northeast Art, all current assets total $182,000.

FIXED ASSETS **Fixed assets** are assets that will be held or used for a period longer than one year. They generally include land, buildings, and equipment used in the continuing operation of the business. Although Northeast Art owns no land or buildings, it does own delivery equipment that originally cost $110,000. It also owns furniture and store equipment that originally cost $62,000.

Note that the values of both fixed assets are decreased by their *accumulated depreciation*. **Depreciation** is the process of apportioning the cost of a fixed asset over the period during which it will be used. The depreciation amount allotted to each year is an expense for that year, and the value of the asset must be reduced by the amount of depreciation expense. In the case of Northeast's delivery equipment, $20,000 of its value has been depreciated since it was purchased. Its value at this time is $110,000 less $20,000, or $90,000. In a similar fashion, the original value of furniture and store equipment ($62,000) has been reduced by depreciation totaling $15,000. Furniture and store equipment now has a reported value of $47,000. For Northeast Art, all fixed assets total $137,000.

INTANGIBLE ASSETS **Intangible assets** are assets that do not exist physically but that have a value based on the rights or privileges they confer on a firm. They include patents, copyrights, trademarks and brands, and goodwill. By their nature, intangible assets are long-term assets—they are of value to the firm for a number of years.

Northeast Art Supply lists a *patent* for a special oil paint that the company purchased from the inventor. The firm's accountants estimate that the patent has a current market value of $21,000. The firm's intangible assets total $21,000. Now it is possible to total all three types of assets for Northeast Art. As calculated in Figure 15-6, total assets are $340,000.

15-5d Liabilities and Owners' Equity

The liabilities and the owners' equity accounts complete the balance sheet. The firm's liabilities are separated into two categories—current and long-term liabilities.

CURRENT LIABILITIES A firm's **current liabilities** are debts that will be repaid in one year or less. Northeast Art Supply purchased merchandise from its suppliers on credit. Thus, its balance sheet includes an entry for accounts payable. *Accounts payable* are short-term obligations that arise as a result of a firm making credit purchases.

Notes payable are obligations that have been secured with promissory notes. They are usually short-term obligations, but they may extend beyond one year. Only those that must be paid within the year are listed under current liabilities.

Northeast Art also lists *salaries payable* and *taxes payable* as current liabilities. These are both expenses that have been incurred during the current accounting period but will be paid in the next accounting period. For Northeast Art, current liabilities total $70,000.

LONG-TERM LIABILITIES Long-term liabilities are debts that need not be repaid for at least one year. Northeast Art lists only one long-term liability—a $40,000 *mortgage payable* for store equipment. As you can see in Figure 15-6, Northeast Art's current and long-term liabilities total $110,000.

OWNERS' OR STOCKHOLDERS' EQUITY For a sole proprietorship or partnership, the owners' equity is shown as the difference between assets and liabilities. In a partnership, each partner's share of the ownership is reported separately in each owner's name. For a corporation, the owners' equity usually is referred to as *stockholders' equity*. The dollar amount reported on the balance sheet is the total value of stock plus retained earnings that have accumulated to date. **Retained earnings** are the portion of a business's profits not distributed to stockholders.

The original investment by the owners of Northeast Art Supply was $150,000 and was obtained by selling 25,000 shares at $6 per share. In addition, $80,000 of Northeast Art's earnings have been reinvested in the business since it was founded. Thus, owners' equity totals $230,000.

As the two grand totals in Figure 15-6 show, Northeast Art's assets and the sum of its liabilities and owners' equity are equal—at $340,000. The accounting equation (Assets = Liabilities + Owners' equity) is still in balance.

> ## Concept Check
>
> ✓ How are current assets distinguished from fixed assets?
>
> ✓ Why are fixed assets depreciated on a firm's balance sheet?
>
> ✓ How do you determine the dollar amount of owners' equity for a sole proprietorship, or a partnership, or a corporation?
>
> ✓ If a business firm has assets worth $170,000 and liabilities that total $40,000, what is the value of the owners' equity?

15-6 THE INCOME STATEMENT

Question: *Where can you find the profit amount for Apple, Inc.?*
Answer: The firm's income statement.

An **income statement** is a summary of a firm's revenues and expenses during a specified accounting period—one month, three months, six months, or a year. The income statement is sometimes called the *earnings statement* or *the statement of income and expenses*. Let's begin our discussion by constructing a personal income statement for Marty Campbell. Having worked as a sales representative for an office supply firm for the past three years, Marty now earns $33,600 a year, or $2,800 a month. After deductions, his take-home pay is $1,900 a month. As illustrated in Figure 15-7, Marty's typical monthly expenses include payments for an automobile loan, credit card payments, apartment rent, utilities, food, clothing, and recreation and entertainment.

Although the difference between income and expenses is referred to as *profit* or *loss* for a business, it is normally referred to as a *cash surplus* or *cash deficit* for an individual. Fortunately for Marty, he has a surplus of $250 at the end of each month. He can use this surplus for savings, investing, or paying off debts. It is also possible to use the information from a personal income statement to construct a personal budget. A *personal budget* is a specific plan for spending your income—over the next month or a specified time period.

Figure 15-8 shows the income statement for Northeast Art Supply. For a business,

Revenues *less* **Cost of goods sold** *less* **Operating expenses equals Net income**

Learning Objective

15-6 Read and interpret an income statement.

long-term liabilities debts that need not be repaid for at least one year

retained earnings the portion of a business's profits not distributed to stockholders

income statement a summary of a firm's revenues and expenses during a specified accounting period

FIGURE 15-7 Personal Income Statement

By subtracting expenses from income, anyone can construct a personal income
statement and determine if he or she has a surplus or deficit at the end of each month.

Marty Campbell
Personal Income Statement
For the month ended December 31, 20XX

INCOME (Take-home pay)		$1,900
LESS MONTHLY EXPENSES		
Automobile loan	$ 250	
Credit card payment	100	
Apartment rent	500	
Utilities	200	
Food	250	
Clothing	100	
Recreation & entertainment	250	
TOTAL MONTHLY EXPENSES		1,650
CASH SURPLUS (or profit)		$ 250

15-6a Revenues

Revenues are the dollar amounts earned by a firm from selling goods, providing services, or performing business activities. Like most businesses, Northeast Art Supply obtains its revenues solely from the sale of its products or services. The revenues section of its income statement begins with gross sales. **Gross sales** are the total dollar amount of all goods and services sold during the accounting period. Deductions made from this amount are

- *sales returns*—merchandise returned to the firm by its customers;
- *sales allowances*—price reductions offered to customers who accept slightly damaged or soiled merchandise; and
- *sales discounts*—price reductions offered to customers who pay their bills promptly.

The remainder is the firm's net sales. **Net sales** are the actual dollar amounts received by the firm for the goods and services it has sold after adjustment for returns, allowances, and discounts. For Northeast Art, net sales are $451,000.

15-6b Cost of Goods Sold

The standard method of determining the **cost of goods sold** by a retailing or a wholesaling firm can be summarized as follows:

Cost of goods sold = Beginning inventory + Net purchases − Ending inventory

According to Figure 15-8, Northeast Art Supply began its accounting period on January 1 with a merchandise inventory that cost $40,000. During the next 12 months, the firm purchased merchandise valued at $346,000. After deducting *purchase discounts*, however, it paid only $335,000 for this merchandise. Thus, during

revenues the dollar amounts earned by a firm from selling goods, providing services, or performing business activities

gross sales the total dollar amount of all goods and services sold during the accounting period

net sales the actual dollar amounts received by a firm for the goods and services it has sold after adjustment for returns, allowances, and discounts

cost of goods sold the dollar amount equal to beginning inventory *plus* net purchases *less* ending inventory

FIGURE 15-8 Business Income Statement

An income statement summarizes a firm's revenues and expenses during a specified accounting period. For Northeast Art Supply, net income after taxes is $30,175.

NORTHEAST ART SUPPLY, INC.

Income Statement
for the Year Ended
December 31, 20XX

Revenues

Gross sales		$465,000	
Less sales returns and allowances	$ 9,500		
Less sales discounts	4,500	14,000	
Net sales			$451,000

Cost of goods sold

Beginning inventory, January 1, 20XX		$ 40,000	
Purchases	$346,000		
Less purchase discounts	11,000		
Net purchases		335,000	
Cost of goods available for sale		$375,000	
Less ending inventory December 31, 20XX		41,000	
Cost of goods sold			334,000
Gross profit			$117,000

Operating expenses

Selling expenses

Sales salaries	$ 22,000		
Advertising	4,000		
Sales promotion	2,500		
Depreciation—store equipment	3,000		
Depreciation—delivery equipment	4,000		
Miscellaneous selling expenses	1,500		
Total selling expenses		$ 37,000	

General expenses

Office salaries	$ 28,500		
Rent	8,500		
Depreciation—furniture	1,500		
Utilities expense	2,500		
Insurance expense	1,000		
Miscellaneous expense	500		
Total general expense		42,500	
Total operating expenses			79,500
Net income from operations			$ 37,500
Less interest expense			2,000
NET INCOME BEFORE TAXES			$ 35,500
Less federal income taxes			5,325
NET INCOME AFTER TAXES			$ 30,175

the year, Northeast had total *goods available for sale* valued at $40,000 plus $335,000, for a total of $375,000.

Twelve months later, at the end of the accounting period on December 31, Northeast had sold all but $41,000 worth of the available goods. The cost of goods sold by Northeast was therefore $375,000 less ending inventory of $41,000, or $334,000. It is now possible to calculate gross profit. A firm's **gross profit** is its net sales *less* the cost of goods sold. For Northeast Art Supply, gross profit was $117,000.

15-6c Operating Expenses

A firm's **operating expenses** are all business costs other than the cost of goods sold. Total operating expenses generally are divided into two categories: selling expenses or general expenses.

Selling expenses are costs related to the firm's marketing activities. For Northeast Art Supply, selling expenses total $37,000. *General expenses* are costs incurred in managing a business, in this case, a total of $42,500. Now it is possible to total both selling and general expenses. As Figure 15-8 shows, total operating expenses for the accounting period are $79,500.

gross profit a firm's net sales *less* the cost of goods sold

operating expenses all business costs other than the cost of goods sold

Ethical Success or Failure

Timing Counts in Tesco's Accounting Scandal

Tesco, the largest grocery chain in the United Kingdom, has spent months unraveling the roots of an accounting scandal that relates to when income from promotional deals with suppliers was reported in its financial statements. The issue became public in September 2014, when the retailer first announced its discovery that some rebates paid by suppliers were being booked as income too early. In addition, some costs were being booked later than they should have been. As a result of recognizing some income early and some costs late, Tesco's profits were overstated by more than $400 million.

Even before this accounting problem came to light, Tesco was locked in a profit-sapping price war as it sought to regain market share lost to supermarket rivals, discount stores, and online merchants. The company was also dealing with multi-million-dollar losses from opening and then closing many U.S. convenience stores.

Once Tesco reported the accounting irregularities, it hired an outside accounting firm and a legal team to conduct an investigation. U.K. regulators also began their own investigations, with the full cooperation of Tesco and its accounting firm. However, the final results of all these inquiries won't be known for many months, because of the vast amount of data that must be examined and the possibility that irregularities could have spanned more than one year.

Sources: Based on information in Kamal Ahmed, "Tesco: Where It Went Wrong," *BBC.com*, January 19, 2015; Ian Walker and Costas Paris, "Tesco Faces Fresh Accounting Investigation," *Wall Street Journal*, December 22, 2014, www.wsj.com; "Tesco Accounts Face Fresh Inquiry," *BBC.com*, December 22, 2014; Russell Lynch, "Tesco to Face Criminal Probe After £263 Million Hole Found in Profits," *The Independent (UK)*, October 29, 2014, www.independent.co.uk.

15-6d Net Income

When revenues exceed expenses, the difference is called **net income**. When expenses exceed revenues, the difference is called **net loss**. As Figure 15-8 shows, Northeast Art's *net income from operations* is computed as gross profit ($117,000) less total operating expenses ($79,500). For Northeast Art, net income from operations is $37,500. From this amount, *interest expense* of $2,000 is deducted to obtain a *net income before taxes* of $35,500. The interest expense is deducted in this section of the income statement because it is not an operating expense. Rather, it is an expense that results from financing the business.

Northeast Art's *federal income taxes* are $5,325. Although these taxes may or may not be payable immediately, they are definitely an expense that must be deducted from income. This leaves Northeast Art with a *net income after taxes* of $30,175. This amount may be used to pay a dividend to stockholders, it may be retained or reinvested in the firm, it may be used to reduce the firm's debts, or all three.

15-7 THE STATEMENT OF CASH FLOWS

Cash is vital to any business. Both the SEC and the FASB require all publicly traded companies to include a statement of cash flows, along with their balance sheet and income statement, in their annual report. The **statement of cash flows** illustrates how the company's operating, investing, and financing activities affect cash during an accounting period. Whereas a firm's balance sheet reports dollar values for assets, liabilities, and owners' equity and an income statement reports the firm's dollar amount of profit or loss, the statement of cash flows focuses on how much cash is on hand to pay the firm's bills. Executives and managers can also use the information on a firm's statement of cash flows to determine how much cash is available

One very important financial statement. Managers, employees, investors, and other interested groups want to know if a business is profitable. To answer that question, a firm's accountants prepare income statements—usually on a monthly, quarterly, semiannual, and annual basis. For all interested parties, "the bottom line" is all important because it tells how much profit or loss a company earned during the accounting period.

to pay dividends to stockholders. Finally, the information on the statement of cash flows can be used to evaluate decisions related to a firm's future investments and financing needs. Outside stakeholders including investors, lenders, and suppliers are also interested in a firm's statement of cash flows. Investors want to know if a firm can pay dividends. Before extending credit to a firm, lenders and suppliers often use the information on the statement of cash flows to evaluate the firm's ability to repay its debts.

A statement of cash flows for Northeast Art Supply is illustrated in Figure 15-9. It provides information concerning the company's cash receipts and cash payments and is organized around three different activities: operating, investing, and financing.

- *Cash flows from operating activities.* This is the first section of a statement of cash flows. It addresses the firm's primary revenue source—providing goods and services. Typical adjustments include adding the amount of depreciation to a firm's net income. Other adjustments for increase or decrease in amounts for accounts receivable, inventory, accounts payable, and income taxes payable are also required to reflect a true picture of cash flows from operating activities.

- *Cash flows from investing activities.* The second section of the statement is concerned with cash flow from investments. This includes the purchase and sale of land, equipment, and other assets and investments.

- *Cash flows from financing activities.* The third and final section deals with the cash flow from all financing activities. It reports changes in debt obligation and owners' equity accounts. This includes loans and repayments, the sale and repurchase of the company's own stock, and cash dividends.

The totals of all three activities are added to the beginning cash balance to determine the ending cash balance. For Northeast Art Supply, the ending cash balance is $59,000. Note that this is the same amount reported for the cash account on the firm's balance sheet. Together, the statement of cash flows, balance sheet, and income statement illustrate the results of past business decisions and reflect the firm's ability to pay debts and dividends and to finance new growth.

Concept Check

✓ What is the purpose of the statement of cash flows?

✓ In a statement of cash flows, what is included in the operating activities section? In the investing activities section? In the financial activities section?

FIGURE 15-9 Statement of Cash Flows

A statement of cash flows summarizes how a firm's operating, investing, and financing activities affect its cash during a specified accounting period. For Northeast Art Supply, the amount of cash at the end of the year reported on the statement of cash flows is $59,000—the same amount reported for the cash account on the firm's balance sheet.

NORTHEAST ART SUPPLY, INC.

Statement of Cash Flows for the Year Ended December 31, 20XX

Cash flows from operating activities		
Net Income		$30,175
Adjustments to reconcile net income to net cash flows		
Depreciation	$ 8,500	
Decrease in accounts receivable	1,000	
Increase in inventory	(5,000)	
Increase in accounts payable	6,000	
Increase in income taxes payable	3,000	13,500
Net cash provided by operating activities		$43,675
Cash flows from investing activities		
Purchase of equipment	$ (2,000)	
Purchase of investments	(10,000)	
Sale of investments	20,000	
Net cash provided by investing activities		8,000
Cash flows from financing activities		
Payments on debt	$(23,000)	
Payment of dividends	(5,000)	
Net cash provided by financing activities		(28,000)
NET INCREASE IN CASH		$23,675
Cash at beginning of year		35,325
CASH AT END OF YEAR		$59,000

15-8 EVALUATING FINANCIAL STATEMENTS

Learning Objective

15-8 Summarize how managers evaluate the financial health of a business.

All three financial statements—the balance sheet, the income statement, and the statement of cash flows—can provide answers to a variety of questions about a firm's ability to do business and stay in business, its profitability, and its value as an investment. To evaluate a firm's financial health, often the first step is to compare a firm's financial data with its own financial results over recent accounting periods and with other firms in similar industries.

15-8a Comparing Financial Data

Many firms compare their financial results with their own historical financial results, with those of competing firms, and with industry averages. Comparisons are possible as long as accountants follow GAAPs. Except for minor differences in format and terms, the balance sheet, income statement, and statement of cash flows of Procter & Gamble, for example, will be similar to those of other large corporations, such as Clorox, Colgate-Palmolive, and Unilever, in the consumer goods industry. Comparisons among firms give executives, managers, and employees a general idea of a firm's standing within the industry. Competitors' financial statements can be

FIGURE 15-10 Comparisons of Present and Past Financial Statements for Microsoft Corporation

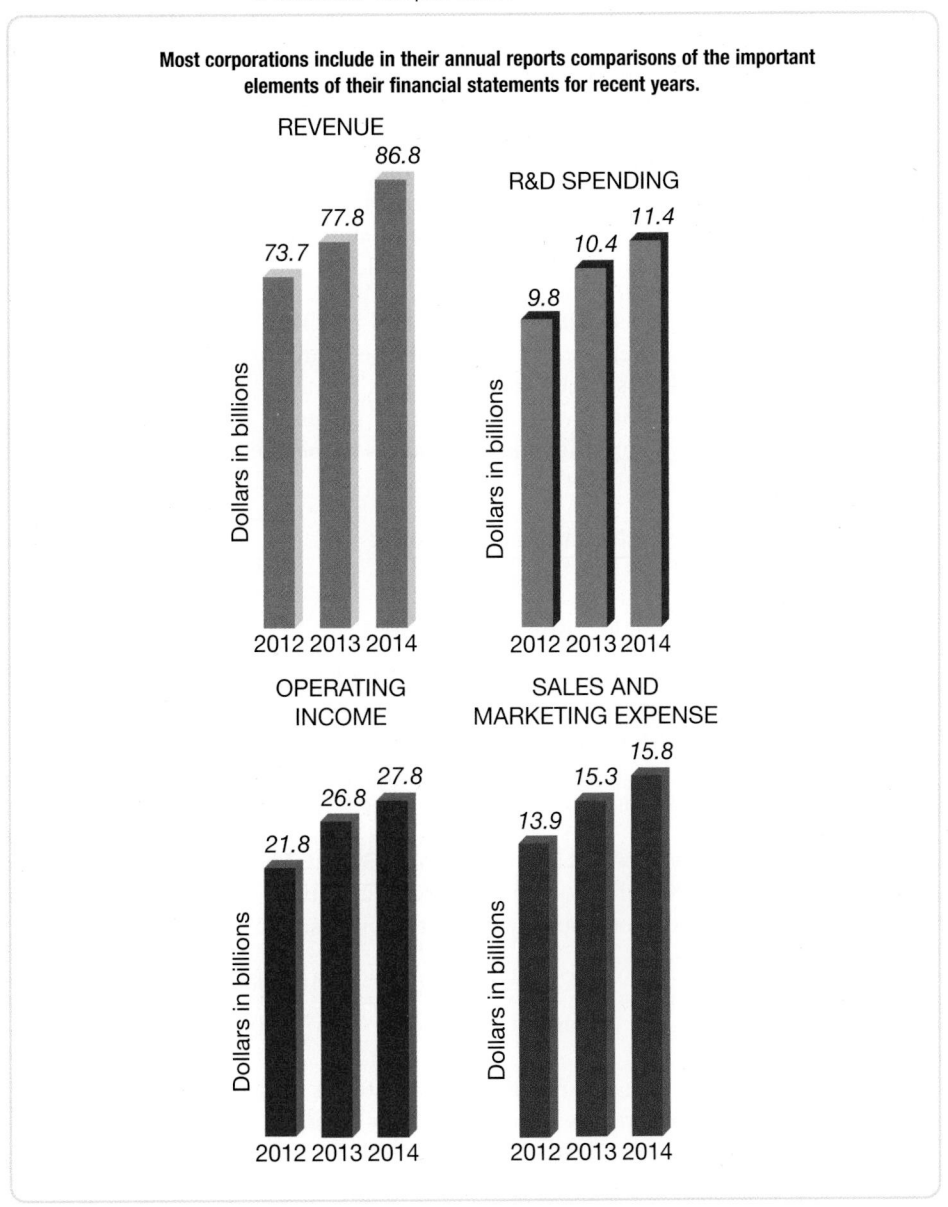

Most corporations include in their annual reports comparisons of the important elements of their financial statements for recent years.

REVENUE

R&D SPENDING

OPERATING INCOME

SALES AND MARKETING EXPENSE

Source: Adapted from the Microsoft Corporation 2014 Annual Report, www.microsoft.com (accessed February 4, 2015).

obtained from their annual reports—if they are public corporations. Industry averages are published by reporting services such as D&B (formerly Dun & Bradstreet), BizMiner, and Hoover's, Inc., as well as by some industry trade associations.

Today, most corporations include in their annual reports comparisons of the important elements of their financial statements for recent years. For example, Figure 15-10 shows comparisons—of revenue, research and development (R&D) costs, operating income, and sales and marketing expenses—for Microsoft Corporation, a world leader in the computer software industry. By examining these data, an operating manager can tell whether R&D expenditures have been increasing or decreasing over the past three years. The vice president of marketing can determine if the total amount of sales and marketing expenses is changing. Stockholders and potential investors, on the other hand, may be more concerned with increases or decreases in Microsoft's revenues and operating income over the same time period. Still another type of analysis of a firm's financial health involves computation of financial ratios.

15-8b Financial Ratios

A **financial ratio** is a number that shows the relationship between two elements of a firm's financial statements. While it is possible to calculate many different financial ratios, we'll only discuss three different ratios that are used to measure a firm's profitability, its ability to pay its debts, and how often it sells its inventory. Like the individual elements in financial statements, these ratios can be compared with those of competitors, with industry averages, and with the firm's past ratios from previous accounting periods. The information required to form these ratios is found in a firm's balance sheet, income statement, and statement of cash flows (in our examples for Northeast Art Supply, Figures 15-6, 15-8, and 15-9).

MEASURING A FIRM'S ABILITY TO EARN PROFITS A firm's net income after taxes indicates whether the firm is profitable. It does not, however, indicate how effectively the firm's resources are being used. For this latter purpose, a return on sales ratio can be computed. **Return on sales** (or **profit margin**) is a financial ratio calculated by dividing net income after taxes by net sales. For Northeast Art Supply,

$$\text{Return on sales} = \frac{\text{Net income after taxes}}{\text{Net sales}} = \frac{\$30,175}{\$451,000}$$

$$= 0.067, \text{ or } 6.7 \text{ percent}$$

The return on sales indicates how effectively the firm is transforming sales into profits. A higher return on sales is better than a low one. Today, the average return on sales for all business firms is between 4 and 5 percent. With a return on sales of 6.7 percent, Northeast Art Supply is above average. A low return on sales can be increased by reducing expenses and increasing sales.

MEASURING A FIRM'S ABILITY TO PAY ITS DEBTS A current ratio can be used to evaluate a firm's ability to pay its current liabilities. A firm's **current ratio** is computed by dividing current assets by current liabilities. For Northeast Art Supply,

$$\text{Current ratio} = \frac{\text{Current assets}}{\text{Current liabilities}} = \frac{\$182,000}{\$70,000} = 2.60$$

This means that Northeast Art Supply has $2.60 of current assets for every $1 of current liabilities. The average current ratio for all industries is 2.0, but it varies greatly from industry to industry. A high current ratio indicates that a firm can pay its current liabilities. A low current ratio can be improved by repaying current liabilities, by reducing dividend payments to stockholders to increase the firm's cash balance, or by obtaining additional cash from investors.

MEASURING HOW WELL A FIRM MANAGES ITS INVENTORY A firm's **inventory turnover** is the number of times the firm sells its merchandise inventory in one year. It is approximated by dividing the cost of goods sold in one year by the average value of the inventory.

The average value of the inventory can be found by adding the beginning inventory value and the ending inventory value (given on the income statement) and dividing the sum by 2. For Northeast Art Supply, average inventory is $40,500. Thus

$$\text{Inventory turnover} = \frac{\text{Cost of goods sold}}{\text{Average inventory}} = \frac{\$334,000}{\$40,500}$$

$$= 8.2 \text{ times per year}$$

financial ratio a number that shows the relationship between two elements of a firm's financial statements

return on sales (or **profit margin**) a financial ratio calculated by dividing net income after taxes by net sales

current ratio a financial ratio computed by dividing current assets by current liabilities

inventory turnover a financial ratio calculated by dividing the cost of goods sold in one year by the average value of the inventory

Northeast Art Supply sells its merchandise inventory 8.2 times each year, or about once every 45 days. The average inventory turnover for all firms is about 9 times per year, but turnover rates vary widely from industry to industry. For example, supermarkets may have inventory turnover rates of 20 or higher, whereas inventory turnover rates for furniture stores are generally well below the national average. The quickest way to improve inventory turnover is to order merchandise in smaller quantities at more frequent intervals.

Like the three ratios described in this section, the calculations for other financial ratios, including return on owners' equity, earnings per share, working capital, and debt-to-equity, are based on the information contained in a firm's balance sheet, income statement, and statement of cash flows. For more detailed information on ratio analysis, you may want to read more on the topic in an accounting or finance textbook or use an Internet search engine.

This chapter ends our discussion of management and accounting information. In Chapter 16, we see why firms need financing, how they obtain it, and how they ensure that funds are used effectively in keeping with the organization's goals.

Concept Check

✓ What are the benefits of comparing a firm's current financial information with information for previous accounting periods, with industry averages, and with financial information for competitors?

✓ Explain the calculation procedures for and significance of each of the following:

  a. Return on sales.

  b. The current ratio.

  c. Inventory turnover.

Summary

15-1 Examine how information can reduce risk when making a decision.

Information produces knowledge and empowers managers and employees to make better decisions. Because of the volume of information they receive each day and their need to make decisions on a daily basis, businesspeople use information rules to shorten the time spent analyzing choices. Information rules emerge when business research confirms the same results each time it studies the same or a similar set of circumstances. Although many people use the terms *data* and *information* interchangeably, there is a difference. Data are numerical or verbal descriptions that usually result from some sort of measurement. Information is data presented in a form that is useful for a specific purpose. A database is a single collection of data and information stored in one place that can be used by people throughout an organization to make decisions. Management information experts now use the term *knowledge management* (KM) to describe a firm's procedures for generating, using, and sharing the data and information. To aid the decision-making process, managers and employees can use a decision-support system (DSS), an executive information system (EIS), expert system, and business application software to make decisions and to report data and information.

15-2 Discuss management's information requirements.

A management information system (MIS) is a means of providing managers with the information they need to perform their jobs as effectively as possible. The purpose of an MIS (sometimes referred to as an information technology system or simply IT system) is to distribute timely and useful information from both internal and external sources to the decision makers who need it. The specific types of information managers need depend on their area of management and level within the firm. The size and complexity of an MIS must be tailored to the information needs of the organization it serves.

15-3 Outline the five functions of an information system.

The five functions performed by an MIS system are collecting data, storing data, updating data, processing data into information, and presenting information. Data may be collected from internal sources and external sources. An MIS must be able to store data until they are needed and to update them regularly to ensure that the information presented to managers and employees is accurate, complete, and timely. Data processing is the MIS function that transforms stored data into a form useful for a specific purpose. Finally, the processed data (which now can be called information) must be presented for use. Verbal information generally is presented in the form of a report. Numerical information most often is displayed in graphs, charts, or tables.

15-4 Explain why accurate accounting information and audited financial statements are important.

Accounting is the process of systematically collecting, analyzing, and reporting financial information. It can be used to answer questions about what has happened in the past; it also can be used to help make decisions about the future. The purpose of an audit is to make sure that a firm's financial statements have been prepared in accordance with generally accepted accounting principles (GAAPs). To help ensure that corporate financial information is accurate and in response to accounting scandals, the Sarbanes–Oxley Act was signed into law. This law contains a number of provisions designed to restore public confidence in the accounting industry. Although many people think all accountants do the same thing, typical areas of expertise include managerial, financial, cost, tax, government, and not-for-profit. A private accountant is employed by a private firm. A public accountant performs accounting work for various individuals or firms on a fee basis. Most accounting firms include on their staffs at least one CPA.

15-5 Read and interpret a balance sheet.

A balance sheet (sometimes referred to as a statement of financial position) is a summary of a firm's assets, liabilities, and owners' equity accounts at the end of an accounting period. This statement must demonstrate that the accounting equation is in balance. On the balance sheet, assets are categorized as current, fixed, or intangible. Similarly, liabilities can be divided into current liabilities and long-term liabilities. For a sole proprietorship or partnership, owners' equity is shown as the difference between assets and liabilities. For corporations, the owners' equity is the total value of stock plus retained earnings that have accumulated to date.

15-6 Read and interpret an income statement.

An income statement is a summary of a firm's revenues and expenses during the specified accounting period. On the income statement, the company's gross profit is computed by subtracting the cost of goods sold from net sales. Operating expenses and interest expense then are deducted to compute net income before taxes. Finally, income taxes are deducted to obtain the firm's net income after taxes.

15-7 Describe business activities that affect a firm's cash flow.

Both the Securities and Exchange Commission (SEC) and the Financial Accounting Standards Board (FASB) require all publicly traded companies to include a statement of cash flows in their annual reports. This statement illustrates how the company's operating, investing, and financing activities affect cash during an accounting period. The information in this statement helps employees, investors, and other interested people to evaluate the financial health of a business. Together, the cash flow statement, balance sheet, and income statement illustrate the results of past decisions and the business's ability to pay debts and dividends as well as to finance new growth.

15-8 Summarize how managers evaluate the financial health of a business.

The firm's financial statements and its accounting information become more meaningful when compared with the company's corresponding information from previous accounting periods, for competitors, and for the industry in which the firm operates. Such comparisons permit managers, employees, lenders, investors, and other interested people to pick out trends in growth, borrowing, income, and other business variables and to determine whether the firm is on the way to accomplishing its long-term goals. A number of financial ratios can be computed from the information in a firm's financial statements. These ratios provide a picture of a firm's profitability, its ability to pay its debts, and how often it sells its inventory. Like the information on the firm's financial statements, these ratios can and should be compared with corresponding information for previous years, for competitors, and for the industry in which the firm operates.

Key Terms

You should now be able to define and give an example relevant to each of the following terms:

data (436)
information (436)
database (437)
knowledge management (KM) (437)
decision-support system (DSS) (437)
executive information system (EIS) (437)
expert system (437)
management information system (MIS) (438)
data processing (442)
statistic (443)

accounting (445)
audit (446)
generally accepted accounting principles (GAAPs) (446)
managerial accounting (448)
financial accounting (448)
certified public accountant (CPA) (449)
assets (449)
liabilities (449)
owners' equity (449)
accounting equation (449)

double-entry bookkeeping system (449)
annual report (450)
balance sheet (or statement of financial position) (450)
liquidity (451)
current assets (451)
fixed assets (452)
depreciation (452)
intangible assets (452)
current liabilities (452)
long-term liabilities (453)
retained earnings (453)
income statement (453)

revenues (454)
gross sales (454)
net sales (454)
cost of goods sold (454)
gross profit (455)
operating expenses (455)
net income (456)
net loss (456)
statement of cash flows (456)
financial ratio (460)
return on sales (or profit margin) (460)
current ratio (460)
inventory turnover (460)

Discussion Questions

1. Do managers really need all the kinds of information discussed in this chapter? If not, which kinds can they do without?
2. How can confidential data and information (such as the wages of individual employees) be kept confidential and yet still be available to managers who need them?
3. Bankers usually insist that prospective borrowers submit audited financial statements along with a loan application. Why should financial statements be audited by a CPA?
4. What can be said about a firm whose owners' equity is a negative amount? How could such a situation come about?
5. Do the balance sheet, income statement, and statement of cash flows contain all the information you might want as a potential lender or investor? What other information would you like to examine?
6. Of the three financial ratios discussed in this chapter, which do you think is the most important financial ratio? Why?

Video Case
Making the Numbers or Faking the Numbers?

Will sales and profits meet the expectations of investors and Wall Street analysts? Managers at public corporations must answer this important question quarter after quarter, year after year. In an ideal world—one in which there is never an economic crisis, expenses never go up, and customers never buy competing products—the corporation's price for a share of its stock would soar, and investors would cheer as every financial report showed ever-higher sales revenues, profits, and earnings.

In the real world, however, many uncontrollable and unpredictable factors can affect a corporation's performance and its stock price. For example, when technology giant IBM announced lower-than-expected earnings in late 2014, analysts and investors were disappointed *and* the value of its stock dropped by 7 percent in just one day. Other factors include customers purchasing fewer products or services or postponing purchases, competitors lowering their prices or introducing superior products, increasing expenses, climbing interest rates, and plummeting buying power. Faced with the prospect of releasing financial results that fall short of Wall Street's expectations, managers may feel intense pressure to "make the numbers" using a variety of accounting techniques. In some cases, managers may even resort to accounting fraud to increase sales and profits and reduce expenses. A recent study by the accounting firm PricewaterhouseCoopers found that accounting fraud is on the increase when compared to a similar study conducted three years ago.

For example, executives and board members at Groupon—the premier source for consumers who want to take advantage of daily deals—found itself having to answer difficult questions about how it reported revenues and expenses. As a result of increased scrutiny by both regulators and investors, the company was forced to reexamine its accounting practices and tighten its audit procedures. Another company—Diamond Foods—was also accused by the Securities and Exchange Commission (SEC) of underreporting expenses and the cost of raw materials to boost profits and meet Wall Street and investor expectations. Eventually, Diamond Foods was forced to restate its earnings and its executives faced both SEC scrutiny and civil lawsuits filed by investors.

Under the Sarbanes–Oxley Act, the CEO and CFO now must certify the corporation's financial reports. Immediately after this legislation became effective, hundreds of companies restated their earnings, a sign that stricter accounting controls were having the intended effect. Now that stricter regulation has been in force for some time, fewer and fewer corporations are announcing restatements. The chief reason for the decline is that corporations and their accounting firms have learned to dig deeper and analyze the process used to produce the figures for financial statements, as well as checking the numbers themselves.

Because accounting rules are open to interpretation, managers sometimes find themselves facing ethical dilemmas when a corporation feels pressure to live up to Wall Street's expectations. Consider the hypothetical situation at Commodore Appliances, a fictional company that sells to Home Depot, Lowe's, and other major retail chains. Margaret, the vice president of sales, has told Rob, a district manager, that the company's sales are down 10 percent in the current quarter. She points out that sales in Rob's district are down 20 percent and states that higher-level managers want him to improve this month's figures using "book and hold," which means recording future sales transactions in the current period.

Rob hesitates, saying that he needs more time to get sales momentum going. He thinks "book and hold" is not a good business practice, even if it is legal. Margaret hints that Rob will lose his job if his sales figures don't look better and stresses that he will need the book-and-hold approach for one month only. Rob realizes that if he doesn't go along, he won't be working at Commodore for very much longer.

Meeting with Kevin, one of Commodore's auditors, Rob learns that book and hold meets GAAPs. Kevin emphasizes that customers must be willing to take title to the goods before they're delivered or billed. Any book-and-hold sales must be real, backed by documentation such as e-mails to and from buyers, and the transactions must be completed in the near future.

Rob is at a crossroads: His sales figures must be higher if Commodore is to achieve its performance targets, yet he doesn't know exactly when (or if) he actually would complete any book-and-hold sales he might report this month. He doesn't want to mislead anyone, but he also doesn't want to lose his job or put other people's jobs in jeopardy by refusing to do what he is being asked to do. Rob is confident that he can improve his district's sales over the long term. However, Commodore's executives are pressuring Rob to make the sales figures look better right now. What should he do?[8]

Questions

1. What are the ethical and legal implications of using accounting practices such as the book-and-hold technique to accelerate revenues and inflate corporate earnings?

2. Why would Commodore's auditor insist that Rob document any sales booked under the book-and-hold technique?

3. If you were in Rob's situation, would you agree to use the book-and-hold technique this month to accelerate revenues? Justify your decision.

4. Imagine that Commodore has taken out a multimillion-dollar loan that must be repaid next year. How might the lender react if it learned that Commodore was using the book-and-hold method to make revenues look higher than they really are?

Building Skills for Career Success

1. Social Media Exercise

All of the Big Four accounting firms are active on Twitter, as well as posting messages, content, and photos on Facebook, listing job openings on LinkedIn, and posting videos on YouTube. The idea is to connect with clients and potential job candidates, interact with clients and potential clients, engage employees, showcase the firm's expertise, and polish their reputations.

Assignment

1. Choose one of the Big Four accounting firms and take a look at its Twitter, Facebook, LinkedIn, or YouTube websites.

2. How does the accounting firm you chose use social media? Are they trying to reach potential job candidates, existing clients and potential clients, or employees?

3. Do you think that social media is an effective way for an accounting firm to reach the target audience?

2. Building Team Skills

This has been a bad year for Park Avenue Furniture. The firm increased sales revenues to $1,400,000, but total expenses ballooned to $1,750,000. Although management realized that some of the firm's expenses were out of control, including cost of goods sold ($700,000), salaries ($450,000), and advertising costs ($140,000), it could not contain expenses. As a result, the furniture retailer lost $350,000. To make matters worse, the retailer applied for a $350,000 loan at Fidelity National Bank and was turned down. The bank officer, Mike Nettles, said that the firm already had too much debt. At that time, liabilities totaled $420,000; owners' equity was $600,000.

Assignment

1. In groups of three or four, analyze the financial condition of Park Avenue Furniture.
2. Discuss why you think the bank officer turned down Park Avenue's loan request.
3. Prepare a detailed plan of action to improve the financial health of Park Avenue Furniture over the next 12 months.

3. Researching Different Careers

To improve productivity, employers expect employees to use computers and computer software. Typical business applications include e-mail, word processing, spreadsheets, and graphics. By improving your skills in these areas, you can increase your chances not only of being employed but also of being promoted once you are employed.

Assignment

1. Assess your computer skills by placing a check in the appropriate column in the following table:

Software	Skill Level			
	None	Low	Average	High
e-Mail				
Word processing				
Desktop publishing				
Accounting				
Database management				
Graphics				
Spreadsheet				
Internet research				

2. Describe your self-assessment in a written report. Specify the skills in which you need to become more proficient, and outline a plan for doing this.

Endnotes

1. Based on information in Shira Ovide and Greg Bensinger, "Amazon Starts Email Service for Companies," *Wall Street Journal*, January 28, 2015, www.wsj.com; John Morris, "Amazon Web Services Wants to Run Your World," *ZDNet.com*, November 19, 2014; and the AWS Amazon website at www.aws.amazon.com (accessed February 6, 2015).
2. "Ian Maackintosh Delivers Prepared Remarks at the AICPA SEC Conference," The International Financial Accounting Standards website at www.ifrs.com (accessed December 9, 2014).
3. "IFRS FAQs," the International Financial Accounting Standards website at www.ifrs.com (accessed February 2, 2015).
4. "SEC Charges Diamond Foods with Accounting Fraud," The SFGate website at www.sfgate.com (accessed January 13, 2014).
5. Ibid.
6. The Sarbanes Oxley Act Compliance Professionals Association website at www.sarbanes-oxley-association.com (accessed February 3, 2015).
7. *Occupational Outlook Handbook*, The U.S. Bureau of Labor Statistics website at www.bls.gov/oco/ocos001.htm (accessed February 4, 2015).
8. Based on information from Andrew Ross Sorkin, "The Truth Hidden by IBM's Buybacks," *The New York Times* website at www.nytimes.com (accessed October 20, 2014); Michael Cohn, "Accounting Fraud on the Rise at U.S. Companies," The Accounting Today website at www.accountingtoday.com (accessed February 19, 2014); Sarah N. Lynch, "Diamond Foods to Pay $5 million to Settle SEC Fraud Case," the Reuters website at www.reuters.com (accessed January 9, 2014); Jonathon Weil, "Groupon IPO Scandal Is the Sleaze that's Legal," the Bloomberg website at www.bloomberg.com (accessed April 4, 2012); Walter Pavlo, "Groupon Accounting Scandal, and We're Surprised," the Forbes website at www.forbes.com (accessed April 3, 2012); The Office Depot website at www.officedepot.com (accessed April 12, 2012); Matt Krantz, "Companies Are Making Fewer Accounting Mistakes," *USA Today*, March 1, 2010, www.usatoday.com; Jane Sasseen, "White-Collar Crime: Who Does Time?" *BusinessWeek*, February 6, 2006, www.businessweek.com; Stephen Labaton, "Four Years Later, Enron's Shadow Lingers as Change Comes Slowly," *New York Times*, January 5, 2006, C1; *Making the Numbers at Commodore Appliance* (Cengage video).

Why Should You Care?

The old saying goes, "Money makes the world go around." For business firms, this is true. It's hard to operate a business without money. In this chapter, we discuss how financial management is used to obtain money and ensure that it is used effectively.

Learning Objectives

Once you complete this chapter, you will be able to:

16-1 Understand why financial management is important in today's uncertain economy.

16-2 Identify a firm's short- and long-term financial needs.

16-3 Summarize the process of planning for financial management.

16-4 Identify the services provided by banks and financial institutions for their business customers.

16-5 Describe the advantages and disadvantages of different methods of short-term debt financing.

16-6 Evaluate the advantages and disadvantages of equity financing.

16-7 Evaluate the advantages and disadvantages of long-term debt financing.

Alibaba and the $25 Billion IPO

One of the world's premier e-business companies was founded in a tiny apartment in Hangzhou, China by Jack Ma, an English teacher with entrepreneurial ambitions. Ma learned about the Internet during a visit to the United States in 1995, and immediately became intrigued by the business possibilities. After starting an Internet-related business and then working for a digital advertising agency, Ma realized that Chinese manufacturers had no way to connect with customers and suppliers worldwide. In 1999, he gathered 17 friends at his apartment and explained his idea of an online marketplace to serve Chinese businesses. They chose the name Alibaba because it has global appeal and is associated with opening doors to treasure.

Early on, the U.S. investment bank Goldman Sachs led a round of investors in providing Alibaba with $5 million. The wealthy chairman of SoftBank, a leading Japanese telecommunications and Internet firm, was part of a second round of investments worth $20 million. In return, these investors received a small ownership stake in Alibaba—as did the 17 people who joined Ma in cofounding the company.

Next, Ma became interested in launching a marketplace for consumer shopping. SoftBank's chairman agreed to invest, and Taobao ("searching for treasure") began operations in 2003. Two years later, with both marketplaces booming, Alibaba received a number of offers to buy some or all of its operations. Instead, the company accepted a $1 billion investment from Yahoo, which wanted to expand in China. Now, Jack Ma and his cofounders owned only a small part of Alibaba—but that stake was growing in value as revenues skyrocketed.

In 2014, Alibaba prepared to raise billions of dollars for expansion by selling shares of stock on the New York Stock Exchange. Demand for shares in Alibaba reached a fever pitch as U.S. investors learned more about the firm's success ($8.5 billion in annual revenue, with 500 million consumers buying, and 8.5 million businesses selling in its marketplaces every year). On September 19, 2014, Alibaba's initial public offering of stock raised $25 billion—the largest IPO in history, up to that point.[1]

Did You Know?

Founded in 1999, Alibaba now serves more than 100 million online buyers every day, with the long-term goal of serving 2 billion online buyers around the world.

Question: How important is financial management for a business firm like Alibaba—the company profiled in the Inside Business feature for this chapter?

Answer: Very Important! Although Alibaba sold stock and raised $25 billion—the largest initial public stock offering in history—keep in mind that smart investors looked at the company's history, its plans for expansion, *and* the way it managed its finances. It also helps to remember that Alibaba's success didn't happen overnight. The company struggled to find the financing it needed to grow and expand during the early years. After finding investors willing to invest the initial money needed to expand operations, Alibaba was able to create an online marketplace to serve both businesses and customers. Today, the company has experienced tremendous growth and every day 100 million online buyers purchase goods and services from 8.5 million businesses. Quite a success story for a company started in 1999, when Jack Ma and 17 friends met in his apartment and began Alibaba.

The fact is that finances are necessary for the efficient operation of any business firm. Without money, creditors and lenders can't be paid, employees don't get paychecks, and the business may close its doors and cease to exist. On the other hand, when a company—like Alibaba—manages its finances it can not only pay its bills and employees, but can grow and expand in order to meet the needs of its customers and society.

In this chapter we examine why financial management is important. Then, we discuss how firms find the financing required to meet two needs of all business organizations: the need for money to start a business and keep it going, and the need to manage that money effectively. We also look at how firms develop financial plans and evaluate financial performance. Then we examine typical banking services and compare various methods of obtaining short-term and long-term financing.

16-1 WHY FINANCIAL MANAGEMENT?

Learning Objective

16-1 Understand why financial management is important in today's uncertain economy.

Financial management can make the difference between success and failure for both large and small businesses. For example, executives at Cisco Systems use aggressive financial planning to anticipate the technology firm's need for financing. Founded in 1984, to make switches and routers for computer systems, today Cisco Systems has billions of dollars on hand to fuel plans for future growth. One way Cisco maintains its market leadership is by investing more than $5 billion, year after year, to research and develop innovative products and services for Internet-based communication and collaboration. Without financial planning, Cisco Systems would not be able to fund its research and development efforts. Effective financial management also enables Cisco Systems to buy other companies that strengthen or complement its position in key areas, pay its bills on time, pay employees, pay taxes, and distribute dividends to its stockholders. Finally, financial management has helped Cisco Systems employ over 70,000 people and ring up $47 billion in annual revenue and become a leader in the very competitive technology industry.[2]

Managers and employees must find the money needed to keep a business operating and fund all the goals and objectives that a successful business wants to achieve. A business that cannot pay its bills may have to close its doors and even be forced to file for bankruptcy protection. Fortunately, the number of business firms filing for bankruptcy has decreased when compared to the large number of firms filing bankruptcy during the worst part of the recent economic crisis, as illustrated in Figure 16-1. And now that the nation's economy is improving, the number of bankruptcies should continue to decline.

16-1a The Need for Financial Management

Financial management consists of all the activities concerned with obtaining money and using it effectively. To some extent, financial management can be viewed as a two-sided problem. On one side, the uses of funds often dictate the type or types of financing needed by a business. On the other side, the activities a business can

FIGURE 16-1 Business Bankruptcies in the United States

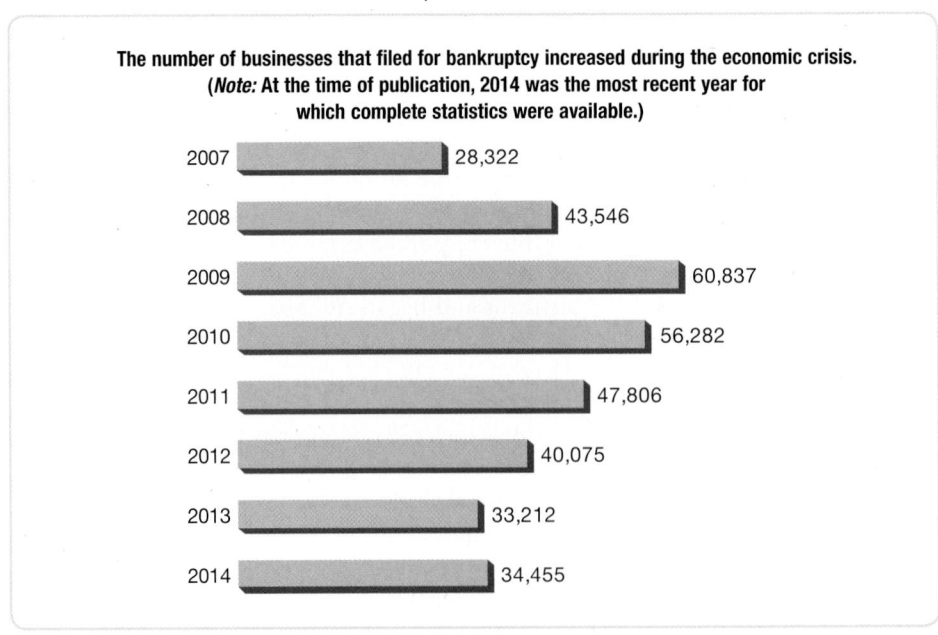

The number of businesses that filed for bankruptcy increased during the economic crisis.
(*Note:* At the time of publication, 2014 was the most recent year for which complete statistics were available.)

Year	Number
2007	28,322
2008	43,546
2009	60,837
2010	56,282
2011	47,806
2012	40,075
2013	33,212
2014	34,455

Source: Based on The American Bankruptcy Institute website at www.abiworld.org (accessed February 21, 2015).

financial management all the activities concerned with obtaining money and using it effectively

undertake are determined by the types of financing available. Financial managers must ensure that funds are available when needed, that they are obtained at the lowest possible cost, and that they are used as efficiently as possible. In addition, proper financial management must also ensure that:

- Financing priorities are established in line with organizational goals and objectives.
- Spending is planned and controlled.
- Sufficient financing is available when it is needed, both now and in the future.
- A firm's credit customers pay their bills on time, and the number of past due accounts is reduced.
- Bills are paid promptly to protect the firm's credit rating and its ability to borrow money.
- The funds required for paying the firm's taxes are available when needed to meet tax deadlines.
- Excess cash is invested in certificates of deposit (CDs), government securities, or conservative, marketable securities.

16-1b Financial Reform After the Economic Crisis

The job of financial managers became a bit easier as the nation's economy stabilized. Still, it became apparent that something needed to be done to stabilize the financial system and prevent future economic meltdowns. In the wake of the crisis that affected both business firms and individuals, a cry for more regulations and reforms became a high priority. To meet this need, President Obama signed the Dodd–Frank Wall Street Reform and Consumer Protection Act into law on July 21, 2010. This law was designed to create a sound economic foundation that would encourage job growth, protect consumers, rein in Wall Street, end financial bailouts, and prevent another financial crisis. Even with the new regulations, some experts and politicians still argue the law went too far while others argue the law did not go far enough and there is a need for additional regulations and increased government oversight. There has also been debate about limiting the amount of executive pay and bonuses, limiting the size of the largest financial firms, and curbing speculative investment techniques that were used by banks before the crisis.

The Dodd–Frank Act also provided new regulations to protect American families from unfair, abusive financial and banking practices. For business firms, the impact of new regulations could increase the time and cost of obtaining both short- and long-term financing.

16-1c Careers in Finance

A career in finance can be rewarding. As an added bonus, the Bureau of Labor Statistics projects there will be about a 9 percent increase in the number of jobs in the financial sector of the economy between now and 2022.[3]

Today, there are many different types of positions in finance. At the executive level, most large business firms have a chief financial officer for financial management.

Inventory: How do you determine the right amount? For Home Depot managers, determining the right amount of inventory for each store is a perplexing problem. If they order too much, money that could be used for other purposes is not available. If they don't order enough, the stores may run out of inventory and there are no appliances to sell. In this situation, customers could go to another retailer like Lowe's or Best Buy.

Don't let this photo give you the wrong impression! A career in finance can be rewarding and may provide above average financial rewards. Still, to be successful, you have to have a background in accounting, finance, or mathematics, computer skills, and be able to communicate with people both inside and outside the organization. Above all, you must be honest.

A **chief financial officer (CFO)** is a high-level corporate executive who manages a firm's finances and reports directly to the company's chief executive officer or president. Although some executives in finance do make $300,000 a year or more, many entry-level and lower-level positions that pay quite a bit less are available. Typical job titles in finance include bank officer, consumer credit officer, financial analyst, financial planner, loan officer, insurance analyst, and investment account executive.

People in finance must have certain traits and skills. One of the most important priorities for someone interested in a finance career is honesty. Be warned: Investors, lenders, and other corporate executives expect financial managers to be above reproach. Moreover, both federal and state government entities have enacted legislation to ensure that corporate financial statements reflect the "real" status of a firm's financial position. In addition to honesty, managers and employees in the finance area must:

1. Have a strong background in accounting or mathematics.
2. Know how to use a computer to analyze data.
3. Be an expert at both written and oral communication.

Depending on qualifications, work experience, and education, starting salaries generally begin at $30,000 to $35,000 a year, but it is not uncommon for college graduates to earn higher salaries. In addition to salary, many employees have attractive benefits and other perks that make a career in financial management attractive.

16-2 THE NEED FOR FINANCING

Learning Objective

16-2 Identify a firm's short- and long-term financial needs.

Money is needed both to start a business and to keep it going. The original investment of the owners, along with money they may have borrowed, should be enough to open the doors. After that, ideally sales revenues should be used to pay the firm's expenses and provide a profit as well.

This is exactly what happens in a successful firm—over the long run. However, income and expenses may vary from month to month or from year to year. Temporary financing may be needed when expenses are high or sales are low. Then, too, situations such as the opportunity to purchase a new facility or expand an existing plant may require more money than is currently available within a firm.

16-2a Short-Term Financing

Short-term financing is money that will be used for one year or less. As illustrated in Table 16-1, there are many short-term financing needs, but three deserve special attention. First, certain business practices may affect a firm's cash flow and create a need for short-term financing. **Cash flow** is the movement of money into and out of an organization. The goal is to have sufficient money coming into the firm in any period to cover the firm's expenses during that period. This goal, however, is

TABLE 16-1 Comparison of Short- and Long-Term Financing

Whether a business seeks short- or long-term financing depends on what the money will be used for.

Short-Term Financing Needs	Long-Term Financing Needs
Cash-flow problems	Business start-up costs
Speculative production	Mergers and acquisitions
Current inventory needs	New product development
Monthly expenses	Long-term marketing activities
Short-term promotional needs	Replacement of equipment
Unexpected emergencies	Expansion of facilities

chief financial officer (CFO) a high-level corporate executive who manages a firm's finances and reports directly to the company's chief executive officer or president

short-term financing money that will be used for one year or less

cash flow the movement of money into and out of an organization

not always achieved. For example, California-based Callaway Golf offers credit to retailers that carry the firm's golf clubs, balls, clothing, and golf accessories. Credit purchases made by Callaway's retailers generally are not paid until 30 to 60 days (or more) after the transaction. Callaway therefore may need short-term financing to pay its bills until its customers have paid theirs.

A second major need for short-term financing is speculative production. **Speculative production** refers to the time lag between the actual production of goods and when the goods are sold. Consider what happens when a firm such as Connecticut-based Stanley Black & Decker begins to manufacture power and small hand tools for sale during the Christmas season. Manufacturing begins in March, April, and May, and the firm negotiates short-term financing to buy materials and supplies, to pay wages and rent, and to cover inventory costs until its products eventually are sold to wholesalers and retailers later in the year. Take a look at Figure 16-2. Although Stanley Black & Decker manufactures and sells finished products all during the year, expenses peak during the first part of the year. During this same period, sales revenues are low. Once the firm's finished products are shipped to retailers and wholesalers and payment is received (usually within 30 to 60 days), sales revenues are used to repay short-term financing.

A third need for short-term financing is to increase inventory. Retailers that range in size from Walmart to the neighborhood drugstore need short-term financing to build up their inventories before peak selling periods. For example, Dallas-based Bruce Miller Nurseries must increase the number of shrubs, trees, and flowering plants that it makes available for sale during the spring and summer growing seasons. To obtain this merchandise inventory from growers or wholesalers, it uses short-term financing and repays the loans when the merchandise is sold.

16-2b Long-Term Financing

Long-term financing is money that will be used for longer than one year. Long-term financing obviously is needed to start a new business. As Table 16-1 shows, it is also needed for business mergers and acquisitions, new product development, long-term marketing activities, replacement of equipment that has become obsolete, and expansion of facilities.

The amounts of long-term financing needed by large firms can seem almost unreal. The 3M Company—a large multinational corporation known for research

FIGURE 16-2 Cash Flow for a Manufacturing Business

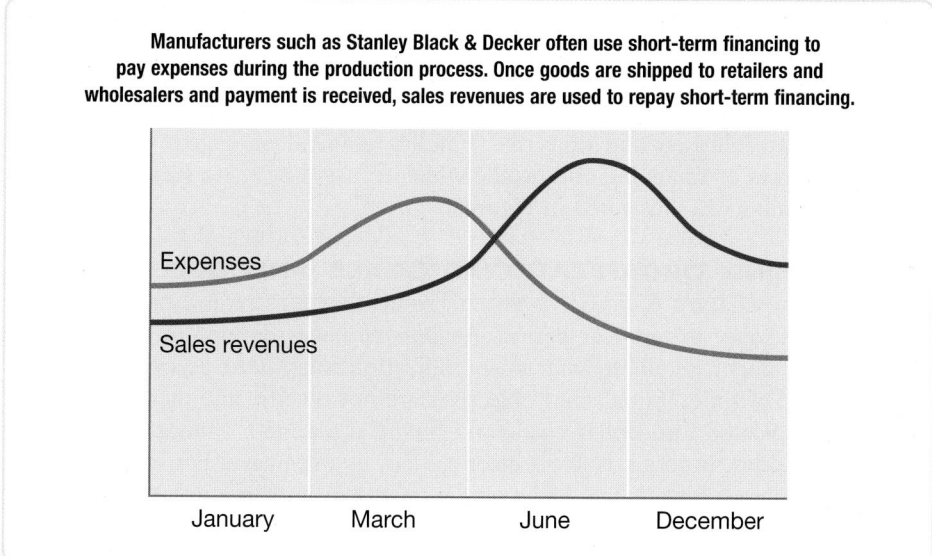

Manufacturers such as Stanley Black & Decker often use short-term financing to pay expenses during the production process. Once goods are shipped to retailers and wholesalers and payment is received, sales revenues are used to repay short-term financing.

speculative production the time lag between the actual production of goods and when the goods are sold

long-term financing money that will be used for longer than one year

Does Starbucks worry about risk and return? Starbucks' managers, like the managers of all businesses, worry about risk and return. While people are lined up to purchase coffee, food items, and other products offered in this Starbucks, what would happen if the coffee retailer chose a poor location and there weren't enough customers? In fact, a company's success is often tied to how well managers can reduce or manage the risks associated with any type of business.

---

and development—spent $1.8 billion in 2014 and has invested $8 billion over the last five years to develop new products designed to make people's lives easier and safer.[4]

16-2c The Risk–Return Ratio

According to financial experts, business firms will find it more difficult to raise both short- and long-term financing in the future for two reasons. First, financial reform and increased regulations will lengthen the process required to obtain financing. Second, both lenders and investors are more cautious about who receives financing. As a result of these two factors, financial managers must develop a strong financial plan that describes how the money will be used and how it will be repaid.

When developing a financial plan for a business, a financial manager must also consider the risk–return ratio when making decisions that affect the firm's finances. The **risk–return ratio** is based on the principle that a high-risk decision should generate higher financial returns for a business. On the other hand, more conservative decisions (with less risk) often generate lesser returns. Although financial managers want higher returns, they often must strive for a balance between risk and return. For example, Ohio-based American Electric Power may consider investing millions of dollars to fund research into new solar technology that could enable the company to use the sun to generate electrical power. Yet, financial managers (along with other managers throughout the organization) must determine the potential return before committing to such a costly research project.

16-3 PLANNING—THE BASIS OF SOUND FINANCIAL MANAGEMENT

In Chapter 6, we defined a *plan* as an outline of the actions by which an organization intends to accomplish its goals and objectives. A **financial plan**, then, is a plan for obtaining and using the money needed to implement an organization's goals and objectives.

16-3a Developing the Financial Plan

Financial planning (like all planning) begins with establishing a set of valid goals and objectives. Financial managers must then determine how much money is needed to accomplish each goal and objective. Finally, financial managers must identify available sources of financing and decide which to use. The three steps involved in financial planning are illustrated in Figure 16-3.

ESTABLISHING ORGANIZATIONAL GOALS AND OBJECTIVES As pointed out in Chapter 6, a *goal* is an end result that an organization expects to achieve over a one- to ten-year period. An *objective* was defined in Chapter 6 as a specific statement detailing what an organization intends to accomplish over a shorter period of time. If goals and objectives are not specific and measurable, they cannot be translated into dollar costs, and financial planning cannot proceed. For large corporations, both goals and objectives can be expensive. For example, have you ever wondered how much McDonald's spends on advertising? Well, to reach almost 70 million customers it serves each day in over 100 countries, the world's most famous fast-food restaurant chain spends over $800 million each year.[5]

Concept Check

✓ How does short-term financing differ from long-term financing? Give two business uses for each type of financing.

✓ What is speculative production? How is it related to a firm's cash-flow problems?

Learning Objective

16-3 Summarize the process of planning for financial management.

risk–return ratio a ratio based on the principle that a high-risk decision should generate higher financial returns for a business and more conservative decisions often generate lower returns

financial plan a plan for obtaining and using the money needed to implement an organization's goals and objectives

FIGURE 16-3 The Three Steps of Financial Planning

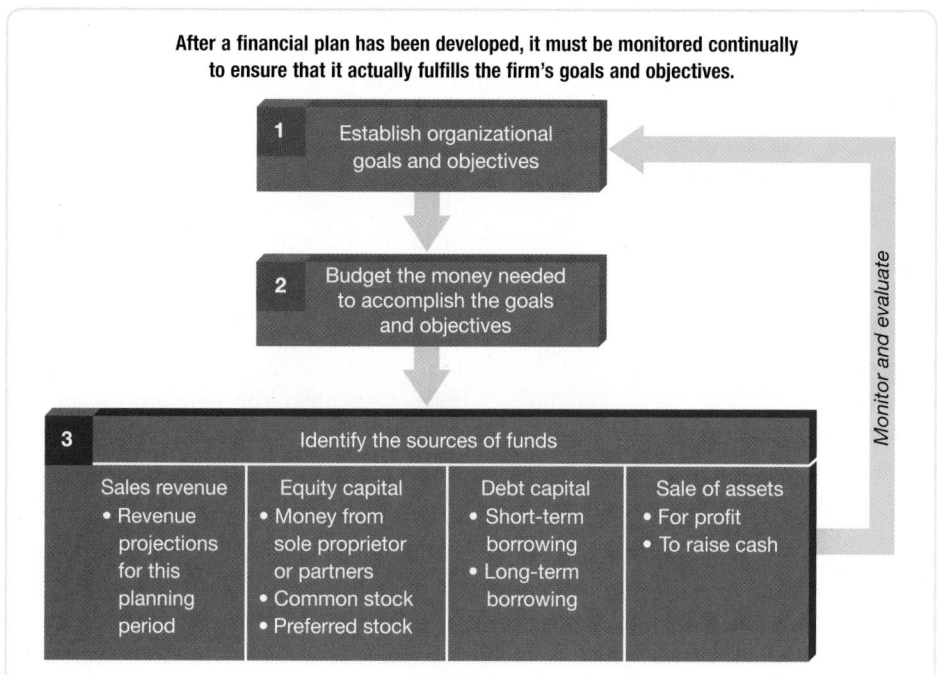

After a financial plan has been developed, it must be monitored continually to ensure that it actually fulfills the firm's goals and objectives.

1 Establish organizational goals and objectives

2 Budget the money needed to accomplish the goals and objectives

3 Identify the sources of funds

Sales revenue	Equity capital	Debt capital	Sale of assets
• Revenue projections for this planning period	• Money from sole proprietor or partners • Common stock • Preferred stock	• Short-term borrowing • Long-term borrowing	• For profit • To raise cash

Monitor and evaluate

BUDGETING FOR FINANCIAL NEEDS Once planners know what the firm's goals and objectives are for a specific period—say, the next calendar year—they can construct a budget that projects the costs the firm will incur and the sales revenues it will receive. Specifically, a **budget** is a financial statement that projects income, expenditures, or both over a specified future period.

Usually, the budgeting process begins with the construction of departmental budgets for sales and various types of expenses. Financial managers can easily combine each department's budget for sales and expenses into a company-wide cash budget. A **cash budget** estimates cash receipts and cash expenditures over a specified period. Notice in the cash budget for Stars and Stripes Clothing, shown in Figure 16-4, cash sales and collections are listed at the top for each calendar

budget a financial statement that projects income, expenditures, or both over a specified future period

cash budget a financial statement that estimates cash receipts and cash expenditures over a specified period

FIGURE 16-4 Cash Budget for Stars and Stripes Clothing

A company-wide cash budget projects sales, collections, purchases, and expenses over a specified period to anticipate cash gains and losses.

STARS AND STRIPES CLOTHING
Cash Budget   From January 1, 2015 to December 31, 2015

	First Quarter ($)	Second Quarter ($)	Third Quarter ($)	Fourth Quarter ($)	Total ($)
Cash sales and collections	150,000	160,000	150,000	185,000	645,000
Less payments					
Purchases	110,000	80,000	90,000	60,000	340,000
Wages/salaries	25,000	20,000	25,000	30,000	100,000
Rent	10,000	10,000	12,000	12,000	44,000
Other expenses	4,000	4,000	5,000	6,000	19,000
Taxes	8,000	8,000	10,000	10,000	36,000
Total payments	157,000	122,000	142,000	118,000	539,000
Cash gain or (loss)	(7,000)	38,000	8,000	67,000	106,000

NASIR1164/DREAMSTIME.COM

BUDGET

EXPENSES

quarter. Payments for purchases and routine expenses are listed in the middle section. Using this information, it is possible to calculate the anticipated cash gain or loss at the end of each quarter for this retail clothing store.

Most firms today use one of two approaches to budgeting. In the *traditional* approach, each new budget is based on the dollar amounts contained in the budget for the preceding year. These amounts are modified to reflect any revised goals, and managers are required to justify only new expenditures. The problem with this approach is that it leaves room for padding budget items to protect the (sometimes selfish) interests of the manager or his or her department. This problem is essentially eliminated through zero-base budgeting. **Zero-base budgeting** is a budgeting approach in which every expense in every budget must be justified.

To develop a plan for long-term financing needs, managers often construct a capital budget. A **capital budget** estimates a firm's expenditures for major assets, including new product development, expansion of facilities, replacement of obsolete equipment, and mergers and acquisitions. For example, Berkshire Hathaway purchased Duracell—a company known for batteries. Berkshire Hathaway, a company known for purchasing well-managed and innovative companies, constructed a capital budget to determine the best way to finance the acquisition valued at over $6 billion in late 2014.[6]

zero-base budgeting a budgeting approach in which every expense in every budget must be justified

capital budget a financial statement that estimates a firm's expenditures for major assets and its long-term financing needs

Entrepreneurial Success

Celebrity Investors Bring Cash and Star Power

Basketball star Carmelo Anthony is a high-profile investor in the ride-service company Lyft, known for its easy app access. Actor Ashton Kutcher is a high-profile investor in Popchips, a snack company. Anthony and Kutcher, plus Lady Gaga, Rapper Curtis "50 Cent" Jackson, Justin Timberlake, Lindsay Lohan, Jared Leto, Rapper Nas, Bono, Ryan Seacrest, and other celebrity investors, bring more than money to equity investments in entrepreneurial firms. They also bring their considerable star power, which helps to build brand awareness, attract customers, and attract more investors over time.

Celebrities, like other investors, are always looking for opportunities to put their money to work. Investing in startups or small, fast-growing companies with significant future revenue potential can benefit both the celebrity and the entrepreneurial firm. Kutcher, for example, has a large social-media following and is often in the spotlight, which can keep his investments in the headlines, as well. Anthony favors

tech-related investments and is articulate when interviewed about the tech firms he has a stake in. Of course, celebrities must be open about having a financial arrangement with a company they tout. Not only is this the ethical thing to do, it also ensures that the public makes the connection between the celebrity and the firm.

Not every celebrity investment turns out well, but when they do, the rewards can be worthwhile. Only a few years after Rapper 50 Cent invested in Vitaminwater, it was purchased by Coca-Cola—and its investors got a hefty return on their equity stakes.

Sources: Based on information in Katie Roof, "Not Just VCs, Celebs Look to Invest in the Next Big Thing," *Fox Business*, January 12, 2015, www.foxbusiness.com; Sarah E. Needleman, "Startup Investors Become Pitchmen, Under Loosened Securities Rules," *Wall Street Journal*, October 2, 2014, www.wsj.com; "50 Cent: Turning Notoriety into Opportunity," *CBS News*, March 24, 2013, www.cbsnews.com; Felix Gillette, "Why Celebrities Spend So Much Time Tweeting about Startups," *Bloomberg.com*, February 13, 2014.

IDENTIFYING SOURCES OF FUNDS The four primary sources of funds, listed in Figure 16-3, are sales revenue, equity capital, debt capital, and proceeds from the sale of assets. Future sales revenue generally provides the greatest part of a firm's financing. Figure 16-4 shows that for Stars and Stripes Clothing, sales for the year are expected to cover all expenses and to provide a cash gain of $106,000. However, Stars and Stripes has a problem in the first quarter, when sales are expected to fall short of expenses by $7,000. In fact, one of the primary reasons for financial planning is to provide management with adequate lead time to solve this type of cash-flow problem.

A second type of funding is **equity capital**. For a sole proprietorship or partnership, equity capital is provided by the owner or owners of the business. For a corporation, equity capital is money obtained from the sale of shares of ownership in the business. Equity capital is used almost exclusively for long-term financing.

A third type of funding is **debt capital**, which is borrowed money. Debt capital may be borrowed for either short- or long-term use—and a short-term loan seems made to order for Stars and Stripes Clothing's shortfall problem. The firm probably would borrow the needed $7,000 (or perhaps a bit more) at some point during the first quarter and repay it from second-quarter sales revenue.

Proceeds from the sale of assets are the fourth type of funding. Selling assets is a drastic step. However, it may be a reasonable last resort when sales revenues are declining and equity capital or debt capital cannot be found. Assets also may be sold to increase a firm's cash balance or when they are no longer needed or do not "fit" with the company's core business. Procter & Gamble, one of the world's leading consumer goods companies, agreed to sell its Iams pet food division to Mars for $2.9 billion. Procter & Gamble's decision will allow the corporate giant to concentrate on its core business and increase cash on hand.[7]

16-3b Monitoring and Evaluating Financial Performance

It is important to ensure that financial plans are implemented properly and to catch potential problems before they become major ones. Despite efforts to raise additional financing, reduce expenses, and increase sales to become profitable, SkyMall, the in-flight catalog found in the seat pockets on many commercial airlines, filed for bankruptcy in 2015.[8]

To prevent such problems, financial managers should establish a means of monitoring financial performance. Interim budgets (weekly, monthly, or quarterly) may be prepared for comparison purposes. These comparisons point up areas that require additional or revised planning—or at least areas calling for a more careful investigation. Budget comparisons can also be used to improve the firm's future budgets.

Personal App

Do You Have a Financial Plan?

PATHDOC/FOTOLIA LLC

Take a moment to write down your short-term and long-term financing needs. Paying for college is a long-term need, for example, as is buying a home. What kinds of short-term financing needs do you have? What can you do to meet your short- and long-term needs in the coming months and years?

equity capital money received from the owners or from the sale of shares of ownership in a business

debt capital borrowed money obtained through loans of various types

Concept Check

✓ What is the function of a cash budget? A capital budget?

✓ What is the difference between equity capital and debt capital?

✓ Describe the four sources of funds for a business.

✓ How does a financial manager monitor and evaluate a firm's financing?

16-4 FINANCIAL SERVICES PROVIDED BY BANKS AND OTHER FINANCIAL INSTITUTIONS

Learning Objective

16-4 Identify the services provided by banks and financial institutions for their business customers.

For a business owner, it helps to know your banker. Banking services can be divided into three broad categories: traditional services, electronic banking services, and international services.

16-4a Traditional Banking Services for Business Clients

Traditional services provided by banks and other financial institutions include savings and checking accounts, loans, processing credit- and debit-card transactions, and providing professional advice.

SAVINGS AND CHECKING ACCOUNTS Savings accounts provide a safe place to store money and a very conservative means of investing. The usual *passbook savings account* earns between 0.05 and 0.50 percent in banks and savings and loan associations (S&Ls) and slightly more in credit unions. A business with excess cash it is willing to leave on deposit with a bank for a set period of time can earn a higher rate of interest. To do so, the business firm buys a certificate of deposit. A **certificate of deposit (CD)** is a document stating that the bank will pay the depositor a guaranteed interest rate on money left on deposit for a specified period of time. At the time of publication, CDs were paying between 0.50 and 1.30 percent. The rate can vary depending on the financial institution and the amount of time until maturity.

Business firms (and individuals) also deposit money in checking accounts so that they can write checks to pay for purchases. A **check** is a written order for a bank or other financial institution to pay a stated dollar amount to the business or person indicated on the face of the check. For businesses, monthly charges are based on the average daily balance in the checking account and/or the number of checks written.

BUSINESS LOANS Banks, savings and loan associations, credit unions, and other financial institutions provide short- and long-term loans to businesses. *Short-term business loans* must be repaid within one year or less. To help ensure that short-term money will be available when needed, many firms establish a line of credit. A **line of credit** is a loan that is approved before the money is actually needed. Because all the necessary paperwork is already completed and the loan is preapproved, the business can obtain the money later without delay, as soon as it is required. Even with a line of credit, a firm may not be able to borrow money if the bank does not have sufficient funds available. For this reason, some firms prefer a **revolving credit agreement**, which is a guaranteed line of credit. Under this type of agreement, the bank guarantees that the money will be available when the borrower needs it. In return for the guarantee, the bank charges a commitment fee. Although commitment fees are often negotiated between the financial institution and the borrower, typical fees range from 0.25 to 1.0 percent of the *unused* portion of the revolving credit agreement. The usual interest is charged for the portion that *is* borrowed.

Long-term business loans are repaid over a period of years. The average length of a long-term business loan is generally 3 to 7 years but sometimes as long as 15 to 20 years. Most lenders require some type of collateral for long-term loans. **Collateral** is real estate or property (e.g., stocks, bonds, equipment, or any other asset of value) pledged as security for a loan.

Repayment terms and interest rates for both short- and long-term loans are arranged between the lender and the borrower. For businesses, repayment terms may include monthly, quarterly, semiannual, or annual payments.

certificate of deposit (CD) a document stating that the bank will pay the depositor a guaranteed interest rate on money left on deposit for a specified period of time

check a written order for a bank or other financial institution to pay a stated dollar amount to the business or person indicated on the face of the check

line of credit a loan that is approved before the money is actually needed

revolving credit agreement a guaranteed line of credit

collateral real estate or property pledged as security for a loan

THE BASICS OF GETTING A LOAN According to many financial experts, preparation is the key when applying for a business loan. To begin the process, you should get to know potential lenders before requesting debt financing. Although there may be many potential lenders that can provide the money you need, the logical place to borrow money is where your business does its banking. This fact underscores the importance of maintaining adequate balances in the firm's bank accounts. Before applying for a loan, you may also want to check your firm's credit rating with a national credit bureau such as D&B (formerly known as Dun & Bradstreet). Typically, business owners will be asked to fill out a loan application. In addition to the loan application, the lender will also want to see your current business plan. Be sure to explain what your business is, how much funding you require to accomplish your goals, and how the loan will be repaid. Most lenders insist that you submit current financial statements that have been prepared by an independent certified public accountant. Then compile a list of references that includes your suppliers, other lenders, or the professionals with whom you are associated. You may also be asked to discuss the loan request with a loan officer. Hopefully, your loan request will be approved. If not, try to determine why your loan request was rejected. Think back over the loan process and determine what you could do to improve your chances of getting a loan the next time you apply.

16-4b Credit and Debit Card Transactions

While consumers use credit cards to pay for everything from tickets on American Airlines to Zebco fishing gear, a recent Gallup poll indicates that Americans have fewer cards than they had a few years ago. In fact, the percentage of Americans that don't have even one credit card increased to 29 percent in 2014 up from 22 percent in 2008.[9] Still, merchants accept and even encourage customers to use credit cards to pay for their purchases. The reason is simple: Often consumers that don't have the cash to make a purchase will use a credit card to make the purchase. By depositing charge slips in a bank or other financial institution, the merchant can convert credit-card sales into cash. In return for processing the merchant's credit-card transactions, the financial institution charges a fee that generally ranges between 1.5 and 4 percent. Typically, small, independent businesses pay more than larger stores or chain stores. Let's assume that you use a Visa credit card to purchase a new, stainless steel refrigerator for $2,300 from Gold Star Appliances, a retailer in Richardson, Texas. At the end of the day, the retailer deposits your charge slip, along with other charge slips, checks, and currency collected during the day, at its bank. If the bank charges Gold Star Appliances 3 percent to process each credit-card transaction, the bank deducts a processing fee of $69 ($2,300 × 0.03 = $69) for the customer's credit-card transaction and immediately deposits the remainder ($2,231) in Gold Star Appliances' account. The number of credit-card transactions, the total dollar amount of credit sales, and how well the merchant can negotiate the fees the financial institution charges determine actual fees.

Do not confuse debit cards with credit cards. Although they may look alike, there are important differences. A **debit card** electronically subtracts the amount of a customer's purchase from her or his bank account at the moment the purchase is made. (By contrast, when you use your credit card, the credit-card company extends short-term financing, and you do not make payment until you receive your next statement.) At the time of the publication of your text, approximately 250 million Americans had at least one debit card.[10] Debit cards are used most commonly to obtain cash at automatic teller machines (ATMs) and to purchase products and services from retailers.

A bank with an open door! Although Chase Bank is the largest bank in the United States, it still wants more customers. Like many competitors, the bank offers cash rewards on credit and debit card purchases, competitive rates for savings, certificates of deposit, loans, online banking, and many other services. Check it out at www.chase.com.

debit card a card that electronically subtracts the amount of a customer's purchase from her or his bank account at the moment the purchase is made

16-4c Electronic Banking Services

An **electronic funds transfer (EFT) system** is a means of performing financial transactions through a computer terminal. The following four EFT applications are changing how banks help firms do business:

1. *Automatic teller machines (ATMs).* An ATM is an electronic bank teller—a machine that provides almost any service a human teller can provide. Once the customer is properly identified, the machine dispenses cash from the customer's checking or savings account or makes a cash advance charged to a credit card. ATMs are located in bank parking lots, supermarkets, drugstores, and even gas stations. Customers have access to them at all times of the day or night. There may be a fee for each transaction.

2. *Automated clearinghouses (ACHs).* Designed to reduce the number of paper checks, automated clearinghouses process checks, recurring bill payments, Social Security benefits, and employee salaries. For example, large companies use the ACH network to transfer wages and salaries directly into their employees' bank accounts, thus eliminating the need to make out individual paychecks.

3. *Point-of-sale (POS) terminals.* A POS terminal is a computerized cash register located in a retail store and connected to a bank's computer. Assume you want to pay for purchases at a Walmart Supercenter. You begin the process by pulling your bank credit or debit card through a magnetic card reader. A central processing center notifies a computer at your bank that you want to make a purchase. The bank's computer immediately adds the amount to your account for a credit-card transaction. In a similar process, the bank's computer deducts the amount of the purchase from your bank account if you use a debit card. Finally, the amount of your purchase is added to the store's account. The Walmart store then is notified that the transaction is complete, and the cash register prints out your receipt.

4. *Electronic check conversion (ECC).* Electronic check conversion is a process used to convert information from a paper check into an electronic payment for merchandise, services, or bills. When you give your completed check to a store cashier at a Best Buy store, the check is processed through an electronic system that captures your banking information and the dollar amount of the check. Once the check is processed, the funds to pay for your transaction are transferred into the business firm's account. Finally, you are asked to sign a receipt, and you get a voided (canceled) check back for your records. ECC also can be used for checks you mail to pay for a purchase or to pay on an account.

EFTs are fast, and they eliminate the costly processing of paper checks. However, some customers are reluctant to use online banking or EFT systems. Some simply do not like "the technology," whereas others fear that the computer will garble their accounts. Early on, in 1978, Congress responded to such fears by passing the Electronic Funds Transfer Act, which protects the customer in case the bank makes an error or the customer's credit or debit card is stolen.

16-4d International Banking Services

For international businesses, banking services are extremely important. Depending on the needs of an international firm, a bank can help by providing a letter of credit or a banker's acceptance.

A **letter of credit** is a legal document issued by a bank or other financial institution guaranteeing to pay a seller a stated amount for a specified period of time—usually thirty to sixty days. With a letter of credit, certain conditions, such as delivery of the merchandise, may be specified before payment is made.

electronic funds transfer (EFT) system a means of performing financial transactions through a computer terminal

letter of credit a legal document issued by a bank or other financial institution guaranteeing to pay a seller a stated amount for a specified period of time

A **banker's acceptance** is a written order for a bank to pay a third party a stated amount of money on a specific date. With a banker's acceptance, no conditions are specified. It is simply an order to pay without any strings attached.

Both a letter of credit and a banker's acceptance are popular methods of paying for import and export transactions. Imagine that you are a business owner in the United States who wants to purchase some leather products from a small business in Florence, Italy. You offer to pay for the merchandise with your company's check drawn on an American bank, but the Italian business owner is worried about payment. To solve the problem, your bank can issue either a letter of credit or a banker's acceptance to guarantee that payment will be made. In addition to a letter of credit and a banker's acceptance, banks also can use EFT technology to speed international banking transactions.

One other international banking service should be noted. Banks and other financial institutions provide for currency exchange. If you place an order for Japanese merchandise valued at $50,000, how do you pay for the order? Do you use U.S. dollars or Japanese yen? To solve this problem, you can use the bank's currency-exchange service. To make payment, you can use either currency, and if necessary, the bank will exchange one currency for the other to complete your transaction.

Concept Check

✓ Describe the traditional banking services provided by financial institutions.

✓ What are the major advantages of electronic banking services?

✓ How can a bank or other financial institution help American businesses to compete in the global marketplace?

16-5 SOURCES OF SHORT-TERM DEBT FINANCING

The decision to borrow money does not necessarily mean that a firm is in financial trouble. On the contrary, astute financial management often means regular, responsible borrowing of many different kinds to meet different needs. In this section, we examine the sources of *short-term debt financing* available to businesses. In the next two sections, we look at long-term financing options: equity capital and debt capital.

Learning Objective

16-5 Describe the advantages and disadvantages of different methods of short-term debt financing.

16-5a Sources of Unsecured Short-Term Financing

Short-term debt financing is usually easier to obtain than long-term debt financing for three reasons:

1. For the lender, the shorter repayment period means less risk of nonpayment.
2. The dollar amounts of short-term loans are usually smaller than those of long-term loans.
3. A close working relationship normally exists between the short-term borrower and the lender.

Most lenders do not require collateral for short-term financing. Remember in the last section that *collateral* was defined as real estate or property pledged as security for a loan. If they do require collateral, it is usually because they are concerned about the size of a particular loan, the borrowing firm's poor credit rating, or the general prospects of repayment.

Unsecured financing is financing that is not backed by collateral. A company seeking unsecured short-term financing has several options.

TRADE CREDIT Manufacturers and wholesalers often provide financial aid to retailers by allowing them 30 to 60 days (or more) in which to pay for merchandise. This delayed payment, known as **trade credit**, is a type of short-term financing extended by a seller who does not require immediate payment after delivery of merchandise. It is the most popular form of short-term financing, because most manufacturers and wholesalers do not charge interest for trade credit. In fact, from 70 to 90 percent of all transactions between businesses involve some trade credit.

banker's acceptance a written order for a bank to pay a third party a stated amount of money on a specific state

unsecured financing financing that is not backed by collateral

trade credit a type of short-term financing extended by a seller who does not require immediate payment after delivery of merchandise

Does Discount Tire use trade credit and take cash discounts? Answer: You bet! For retailers like Discount Tire, using trade credit to purchase inventory can help manage the firm's cash flow and reduce the need to borrow money. Taking advantage of cash discounts can also reduce the cost of inventory. In turn, lower costs for financing and inventory can enable Discount Tire to lower its prices compared to its competitors or increase the firm's profits, or both.

Assume that furniture manufacturer and retailer Ethan Allen receives a shipment of luxury bedding from a manufacturer. Along with the merchandise, the manufacturer sends an invoice that states the terms of payment. Ethan Allen now has two options for payment. First, it may pay the invoice promptly and take advantage of any cash discount the manufacturer offers. Cash-discount terms are specified on the invoice. For instance, "2/10, net 30" means that the customer—Ethan Allen—may take a "2" percent discount if it pays the invoice within ten days of the invoice date. If the dollar amount of the invoice is $200,000, the cash discount is $4,000 ($200,000 × 0.02 = $4,000). If the cash discount is taken, Ethan Allen only has to pay the manufacturer $196,000 ($200,000 – $4,000 = $196,000).

A second option is to wait until the end of the credit period before making payment. If payment is made between 11 and 30 days after the date of the invoice, Ethan Allen must pay the entire amount. As long as payment is made before the end of the credit period, the business maintains the ability to purchase additional merchandise using the trade-credit arrangement.

PROMISSORY NOTES ISSUED TO SUPPLIERS A **promissory note** is a written pledge by a borrower to pay a certain sum of money to a creditor at a specified future date. Suppliers uneasy about extending trade credit may be less reluctant to offer credit to customers who sign promissory notes. Unlike trade credit, however, promissory notes usually require the borrower to pay interest. Although repayment periods may extend to one year, most short-term promissory notes are repaid in 60 to 180 days.

A promissory note offers two important advantages to the firm extending the credit.

1. A promissory note is legally binding and an enforceable contract.
2. A promissory note is a negotiable instrument.

Because a promissory note is negotiable, the manufacturer, wholesaler, or company extending credit may be able to discount, or sell, the note to its own bank. If the note is discounted, the dollar amount received by the company extending credit is slightly less than the maturity value because the bank charges a fee for the service. The company extending credit recoups most of its money immediately, and the bank collects the entire amount when the note matures.

UNSECURED BANK LOANS Banks and other financial institutions offer unsecured short-term loans to businesses at interest rates that vary with each borrower's credit rating. The **prime interest rate** is the lowest rate charged by a bank for a short-term loan. Figure 16-5 traces the fluctuations in the average prime rate charged by U.S. banks from 1990 to January 2015. This lowest rate generally is reserved for large corporations with excellent credit ratings. Organizations with good to high credit ratings may pay the prime rate plus "2" percent. Firms with questionable credit ratings may have to pay the prime rate plus "4" percent. (The fact that a banker charges a higher interest rate for a higher-risk loan is a practical application of the risk–return ratio discussed earlier in this chapter.) Of course, if the banker believes that loan repayment may be a problem, the borrower's loan application may well be rejected.

When a business obtains a short-term bank loan, interest rates and repayment terms may be negotiated. As a condition of the loan, a bank may require that a *compensating balance* be kept on deposit at the bank. Compensating balances, if required, are typically 10 to 20 percent of the borrowed funds. The bank may also

promissory note a written pledge by a borrower to pay a certain sum of money to a creditor at a specified future date

prime interest rate the lowest rate charged by a bank for a short-term loan

FIGURE 16-5 Average Prime Interest Rate Paid by U.S. Businesses, 1990–January 2015

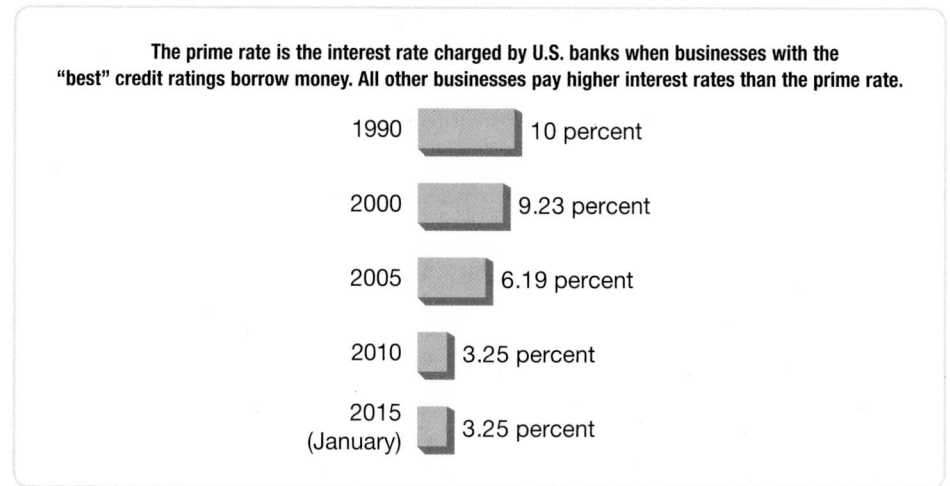

The prime rate is the interest rate charged by U.S. banks when businesses with the "best" credit ratings borrow money. All other businesses pay higher interest rates than the prime rate.

1990	10 percent
2000	9.23 percent
2005	6.19 percent
2010	3.25 percent
2015 (January)	3.25 percent

Source: Federal Reserve Bank website, www.federalreserve.gov (accessed February 21, 2015).

require that every commercial borrower *clean up* (pay off completely) its short-term loans at least once each year and not use it again for a period of 30 to 60 days.

COMMERCIAL PAPER Large firms with excellent credit reputations like Microsoft, Procter & Gamble, and Boeing can raise large sums of money quickly by issuing commercial paper. **Commercial paper** is a short-term promissory note issued by a large corporation. The maturity date for commercial paper is normally 270 days or less.

Commercial paper is secured only by the reputation of the issuing firm; no collateral is involved. The interest rate a corporation pays when it sells commercial paper is tied to its credit rating and its ability to repay the commercial paper. In most cases, corporations selling commercial paper pay interest rates below the interest rates charged by banks for short-term loans. Thus, selling commercial paper is cheaper than getting short-term financing from a bank.

Although it is possible to purchase commercial paper in smaller denominations, larger amounts—$100,000 or more—are quite common. Money obtained by selling commercial paper is most often used to purchase inventory, finance a firm's accounts receivable, pay salaries and other necessary expenses, and solve cash-flow problems.

16-5b Sources of Secured Short-Term Financing

If a business cannot obtain enough money through unsecured financing, it must put up collateral to obtain additional short-term financing. Almost any asset can serve as collateral. However, *inventories* and *accounts receivable* are the assets most commonly pledged for short-term financing. Even when it is willing to pledge collateral to back up a loan, a firm that is financially weak may have difficulty obtaining short-term financing.

LOANS SECURED BY INVENTORY Normally, manufacturers, wholesalers, and retailers have large amounts of money invested in finished goods. In addition, manufacturers carry raw materials and work-in-process inventories. All three types of inventory may be pledged as collateral for short-term loans. However, lenders prefer the much more salable finished merchandise to raw materials or work-in-process inventories.

commercial paper a short-term promissory note issued by a large corporation.

A lender may insist that inventory used as collateral be stored in a public warehouse. In this situation, the receipt issued by the warehouse is retained by the lender. Without this receipt, the public warehouse will not release the merchandise. The lender releases the warehouse receipt—and the merchandise—to the borrower when the borrowed money is repaid. In addition to paying the interest on the loan, the borrower must pay for storage in the public warehouse. As a result, this type of loan is more expensive than an unsecured short-term loan.

LOANS SECURED BY RECEIVABLES As defined in Chapter 15, *accounts receivable* are amounts owed to a firm by its customers. A firm can pledge its accounts receivable as collateral to obtain short-term financing. A lender may advance 70 to 80 percent of the dollar amount of the receivables. First, however, it conducts a thorough investigation to determine the *quality* of the receivables. (The quality of the receivables is the credit standing of the firm's customers, coupled with the customers' ability to repay their credit obligations when they are due.) If a favorable determination is made, the loan is approved. Like most business loans, the borrower and the lender negotiate interest rates and repayment terms.

factor a firm that specializes in buying other firms' accounts receivable

16-5c Factoring Accounts Receivable

Accounts receivable may be used in one other way to help raise short-term financing: They can be sold to a factoring company (or factor). A **factor** is a firm that specializes in buying other firms' accounts receivable. The factor buys the accounts receivable for less than their face value; however, it collects the full face value dollar amount when each account is due. The factor's profit is the difference between the face value of the accounts receivable and the amount the factor has paid for them. Generally, the amount of profit the factor receives is based on the risk the factor assumes. Risk, in this case, is the probability that the accounts receivable will not be repaid when they mature.

Even though the firm selling its accounts receivable gets less than face value, it does receive needed cash immediately. Moreover, it has shifted both the task of collecting and the risk of nonpayment to the factor, which now owns the accounts receivable. Generally, customers whose accounts receivable have been factored are given instructions to make their payments directly to the factor.

16-5d Cost Comparisons

Table 16-2 compares the various types of short-term financing. As you can see, trade credit is the least expensive. Factoring of accounts receivable is typically the highest-cost method shown.

Concept Check

✓ How important is trade credit as a source of short-term financing?

✓ Why would a supplier require a customer to sign a promissory note?

✓ What is the prime rate? Who gets the prime rate?

✓ Explain how factoring works. Of what benefit is factoring to a firm that sells its receivables?

TABLE 16-2 Comparison of Short-Term Financing Methods

Type of Financing	Cost	Repayment Period	Businesses That May Use It	Comments
Trade credit	Low, if any	30–60 days	All businesses with good credit	Usually no finance charge
Promissory note issued to suppliers	Moderate	One year or less	All businesses	Usually unsecured but requires legal document
Unsecured bank loan	Moderate	One year or less	All businesses	Promissory note is required and compensating balance may be required
Commercial paper	Moderate	270 days or less	Large corporations with high credit ratings	Usually available only to large firms
Secured loan	High	One year or less	Firms with questionable credit ratings	Inventory or accounts receivable often used as collateral
Factoring	High	None	Firms that have large numbers of credit customers	Accounts receivable sold to a factor

For many purposes, short-term financing suits a firm's needs perfectly. At other times, long-term financing may be more appropriate. In this case, a business may try to raise equity capital or long-term debt capital.

16-6 SOURCES OF EQUITY FINANCING

Sources of long-term financing vary with the size and type of business. As mentioned earlier, a sole proprietorship or partnership acquires equity capital (sometimes referred to as *owners' equity*) when the owner or partners invest money in the business. For corporations, equity-financing options include the sale of stock and the use of profits not distributed to owners. All three types of businesses can also obtain venture capital and use long-term debt capital (borrowed money) to meet their financial needs.

Learning Objective

16-6 Evaluate the advantages and disadvantages of equity financing.

16-6a Selling Stock

Some equity capital is used to start every business— sole proprietorship, partnership, or corporation. In the case of corporations, stockholders who buy shares in the company provide equity capital.

INITIAL PUBLIC OFFERING AND THE PRIMARY MARKET An **initial public offering (IPO)** occurs when a corporation sells common stock to the general public for the first time. Alibaba, the Chinese e-commerce site profiled in the Inside Business feature for this chapter, used an IPO to raise $25 billion, and it is the largest IPO in history. And at the time of the publication of your text, there are more companies that plan to use IPOs to raise capital as the economy continues to improve. Although a larger than usual number of companies in the healthcare and financial industry are using IPOs to raise capital at this time, corporations in other industries also use IPOs to raise money. In fact, as illustrated in Figure 16-6, the largest IPOs for companies listed on U.S. stock exchanges—Alibaba, Visa, Enel SpA, Facebook, and General Motors—involve companies from a number of different industries.

initial public offering (IPO) occurs when a corporation sells common stock to the general public for the first time

FIGURE 16-6 The All-Time Largest Initial Public Offerings for U.S. Companies

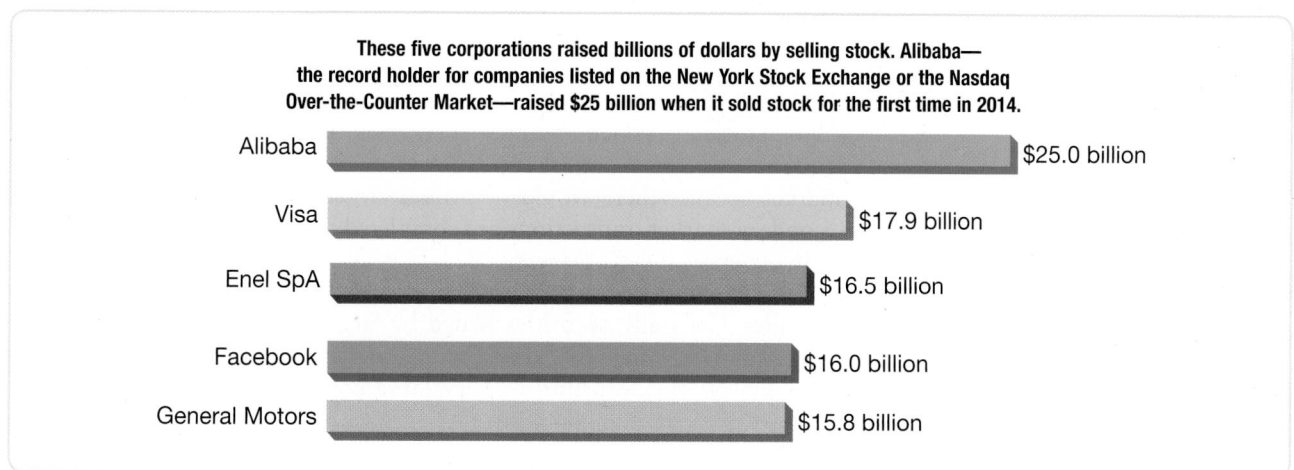

These five corporations raised billions of dollars by selling stock. Alibaba— the record holder for companies listed on the New York Stock Exchange or the Nasdaq Over-the-Counter Market—raised $25 billion when it sold stock for the first time in 2014.

Alibaba	$25.0 billion
Visa	$17.9 billion
Enel SpA	$16.5 billion
Facebook	$16.0 billion
General Motors	$15.8 billion

Source: Renaissance Capital, Greenwich, CT (www.renaissancecapital.com), (accessed February 17, 2015) and Elzio Bareto, "Alibaba IPO Ranks as World's Biggest After Additional Shares Sold," Reuters website at www.reuters.com (accessed September 22, 2014).

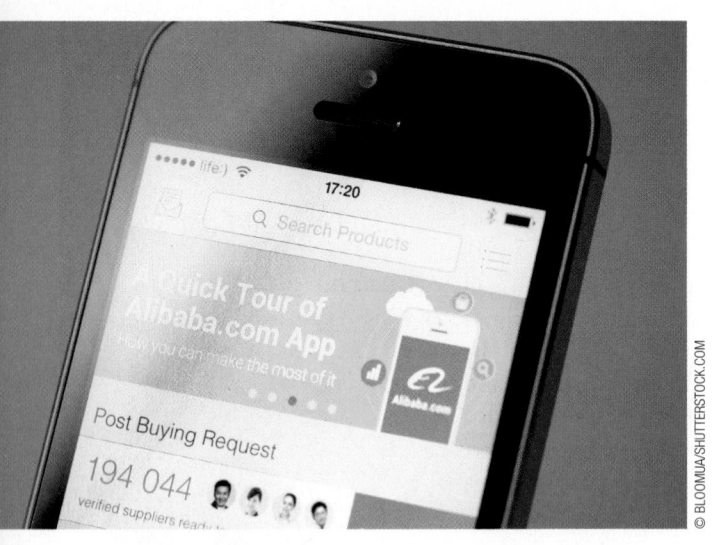

Just another app? Not really! The Alibaba app, along with its Internet website, connects 500 million buyers and 8.5 million sellers each year. And while Alibaba—the Chinese e-commerce site—has experienced tremendous success since it was founded in 1999, it has grand plans for the future and will use money from its $25 billion IPO to fund expansion.

Established companies that plan to raise capital by selling subsidiaries to the public can also use IPOs. In late 2014, eBay announced plans to spin off its PayPal business by mid-2015.[11] Monies from the IPO will be used to increase the parent company's cash balance, allow eBay to concentrate on its core business, and provide funding for growth opportunities and expansion. In addition to using an IPO to increase the cash balance for the parent company, corporations often sell shares in a subsidiary when shares can be sold at a profit or when the subsidiary no longer fits with its current business plan. Finally, some corporations will sell a subsidiary that is growing more slowly than the rest of the company's operating divisions.

When a corporation uses an IPO to raise capital, the stock is sold in the primary market. The **primary market** is a market in which an investor purchases financial securities (via an investment bank) directly from the issuer of the securities. An **investment banking firm** is an organization that assists corporations in raising funds, usually by helping to sell new issues of stocks, bonds, or other financial securities.

Although a corporation can have only one IPO, it can sell additional stock after the IPO, assuming that there is a market for the company's stock. Even though the cost of selling stock (often referred to as *flotation costs*) is high, the *ongoing* costs associated with this type of equity financing are low for two reasons. First, the corporation does not have to repay money obtained from the sale of stock because the corporation is under no legal obligation to do so. If you purchase corporate stock and later decide to sell your stock, you may sell it to another investor—not the corporation.

A second advantage of selling stock is that a corporation is under no legal obligation to pay dividends to stockholders. As noted in Chapter 4, a *dividend* is a distribution of earnings to the stockholders of a corporation. For any reason (e.g., if a company has a bad year), the board of directors can vote to omit dividend payments. Earnings then are retained for use in funding business operations. Of course, corporate management may hear from unhappy stockholders if expected dividends are omitted too frequently.

THE SECONDARY MARKET Although a share of corporate stock is only sold one time in the primary market, the stock can be sold again and again in the secondary market. The **secondary market** is a market for existing financial securities that are traded between investors. Although a corporation does not receive money each time its stock is bought or sold in the secondary market, the ability to obtain cash by selling stock investments is one reason why investors purchase corporate stock. Without the secondary market, investors would not purchase stock in the primary market because there would be no way to sell shares to other investors. Usually, secondary-market transactions are completed through a securities exchange or the over-the-counter (OTC) market.

A **securities exchange** is a marketplace where member brokers meet to buy and sell securities. Generally, securities issued by larger corporations are traded at the New York Stock Exchange (NYSE) or at regional exchanges located in different parts of the country. The securities of very large corporations may be traded at more than one of these exchanges. Securities of firms also may be listed on foreign securities exchanges—in Tokyo or London, for example.

Stocks issued by several thousand companies are traded in the OTC market. The **over-the-counter (OTC) market** is a network of dealers who buy and sell

primary market a market in which an investor purchases financial securities (via an investment bank) directly from the issuer of those securities

investment banking firm an organization that assists corporations in raising funds, usually by helping to sell new issues of stocks, bonds, or other financial securities

secondary market a market for existing financial securities that are traded between investors

securities exchange a marketplace where member brokers meet to buy and sell securities

over-the-counter (OTC) market a network of dealers who buy and sell the stocks of corporations that are not listed on a securities exchange

the stocks of corporations that are not listed on a securities exchange. The term *over-the-counter* was coined more than 100 years ago when securities actually were sold "over the counter" in stores and banks. Many stocks are traded through an *electronic* exchange called the Nasdaq (pronounced "nazzdack"). The Nasdaq is now one of the largest securities markets in the world. Today, the Nasdaq is known for its forward-looking, innovative, growth companies, including Intel, Microsoft, Cisco Systems, and Apple Computer.

There are two types of stock: common and preferred. Each type has advantages and drawbacks as a means of long-term financing.

COMMON STOCK A share of **common stock** represents the most basic form of corporate ownership. In return for the financing provided by selling common stock, management must make certain concessions to stockholders that may restrict or change corporate policies. Every corporation must hold an annual meeting, at which the holders of common stock may vote for the board of directors. Often, stockholders are also asked to approve or disapprove of major corporate actions.

Few investors will buy common stock unless they believe that their investment will increase in value. As already mentioned, stockholders may receive dividends if the corporation's board of directors approves a dividend distribution. Also, stockholders can profit from their investment if a corporate stock increases in value. Additional information on the reasons why investors purchase stocks and how to evaluate stock investments is provided in Appendix A, "Understanding Personal Finances and Investments."

PREFERRED STOCK As noted in Chapter 4, the owners of **preferred stock** must receive their dividends before holders of common stock receive theirs. Also, preferred stockholders know the dollar amount of their dividend because it is stated on the stock certificate. When compared to common stockholders, preferred stockholders also have first claim (after creditors) on assets if the corporation is dissolved or declares bankruptcy. Even so, as with common stock, the board of directors must approve dividends on preferred nazzck, and this type of financing does not represent a debt that must be legally repaid. In return for preferential treatment, preferred stockholders generally give up the right to vote at a corporation's annual meeting.

Although a corporation usually issues only one type of common stock, it may issue many types of preferred stock with varying dividends or dividend rates. For example, New York–based JPMorgan Chase has one common-stock issue but five preferred-stock issues.[12]

16-6b Retained Earnings

Most large corporations distribute only a portion of their after-tax earnings to stockholders. The portion of a corporation's profits *not* distributed to stockholders is called **retained earnings**. Because they are undistributed profits, retained earnings are considered a form of equity financing.

Social Media:
Tweet to Chuck

The financial services firm Charles Schwab is a heavy user of social media to educate, inform, and inspire people to invest for their future. The company maintains six Twitter accounts, including one where the CEO (@WaltBettinger) discusses basic financial principles, corporate leadership, and other topics of interest to consumers and businesspeople. The main Twitter account (@CharlesSchwab) has more than 55,000 followers and features posts about personal finance and sources of additional information. The firm's Twitter posts for people who actively buy and sell securities (@Schwab4Traders) covers topics such as formulating a strategy for trades and timing trades. Schwab also has separate Twitter accounts for investment advisors (@Schwab4RIAs), career opportunities (@SchwabJobs), and customer service questions (@SchwabService).

More than 133,000 people have clicked to like Schwab's Facebook page (www.facebook.com/CharlesSchwab), where they can view videos about investing and read posts related to personal finance and the economy. Dozens of videos on Schwab's YouTube channel (www.youtube.com/user/CharlesSchwab) tell the stories of people making real-life financial decisions, showcase the company's services, and analyze economic conditions. Schwab is also active on LinkedIn to connect with current customers, potential customers, and potential employees.

common stock stock whose owners may vote on corporate matters but whose claims on profits and assets are subordinate to the claims of others

preferred stock stock whose owners usually do not have voting rights but whose claims on dividends and assets are paid before those of common-stock owners

retained earnings the portion of a corporation's profits not distributed to stockholders

The amount of retained earnings in any year is determined by corporate management and approved by the board of directors. Most small and growing corporations pay no cash dividend—or a very small dividend—to their stockholders. All or most earnings are reinvested in the business for research and development, expansion, or the funding of major projects. Reinvestment tends to increase the value of the firm's stock while it provides essentially cost-free financing for the business. More mature corporations may distribute 40 to 60 percent of their after-tax profits as dividends. Utility companies and other corporations with very stable earnings often pay out as much as 80 to 90 percent of what they earn. For a large corporation, retained earnings can amount to a hefty bit of financing. For example, as reported in its last annual report, the total amount of retained earnings for General Electric was over $149 billion.[13]

16-6c Venture Capital, Angel Investors, and Private Placements

To establish a new business or expand an existing one, an entrepreneur may try to obtain venture capital. In Chapter 5, we defined *venture capital* as money invested in small (and sometimes struggling) firms that have the potential to become very successful. Most venture capital firms do not invest in the typical small business—a neighborhood convenience store or a local dry cleaner—but in firms that have the potential to become extremely profitable. Today, most venture capital firms are investing in companies that build the nation's infrastructure, develop computer software, or provide information or social media services. For example, Zynga—the company behind such popular games as FarmVille and Words With Friends—received venture capital before selling stock to the public.[14]

Generally, a venture capital firm consists of a pool of investors, a partnership established by a wealthy family, or a joint venture formed by corporations with money to invest. In return for financing, these investors generally receive an equity or ownership position in the business and share in its profits. Although venture capital firms are willing to take chances, they have also been more selective about where they invest their money after the recent economic crisis.

Another source of capital for a startup business is an angel investor. An **angel investor** is an investor who provides financial backing for small business startups or entrepreneurs. Often, an angel investor may be an entrepreneur's family member or a wealthy friend and provides the financial support needed to start a business. Unlike venture capitalists, angel investors are often focused on helping a business or an entrepreneur succeed rather than earning huge profits. And angel investors often provide more favorable financial terms when compared with venture capitalists, bankers, and other financial institutions. In return for providing needed financing, angel investors can become an owner with equity in the firm. In other cases, angel investors loan money to a small business and become a lender like a bank or other financial institution.

Another method of raising capital is through a private placement. A **private placement** occurs when stock and other corporate securities are sold directly to insurance companies, pension funds, or large institutional investors. When compared with selling stocks and other corporate securities to the public, there are often fewer government regulations and the cost is generally less when the securities are sold through a private placement. Typically, terms between the buyer and seller are negotiated when a private placement is used to raise capital.

©ANTHONY CORREIA/SHUTTERSTOCK.COM

You can buy Twitter stock on the New York Stock Exchange. While most people recognize the bird in this photo as the symbol for Twitter, did you know that you can buy Twitter's stock because it's listed on the New York Stock Exchange. The ability to obtain cash by selling stock investments in the secondary market is one reason why investors purchase corporate stock.

angel investor an investor who provides financial backing for small business startups or entrepreneurs

private placement occurs when stock and other corporate securities are sold directly to insurance companies, pension funds, or large institutional investors

Concept Check

✓ What are the advantages of financing through the sale of stock?

✓ From a corporation's point of view, how does preferred stock differ from common stock?

✓ What is venture capital? An angel investor? A private placement?

Ethical Success or Failure

Should Fans Be Able to Buy Securities Linked to Athletes?

Investors can now buy and sell shares of stock tied to the future earnings of Buffalo Bills football player E.J. Manuel. Another investment option is to trade shares tied to the future earnings of Vernon Davis of the San Francisco 49ers, Mohamed Sanu of the Cincinnati Bengals, and Michael Brockers of the St. Louis Rams, among other athletes.

Share values for each of the above athletes are based on a brand contract between the athlete and Fantex, a California-based firm that operates the exclusive online brokerage exchange for such trades. When Fantex signed an agreement with E.J. Manuel, for example, it acquired the right to 10 percent of the quarterback's future football-related earnings, including his contract with the Buffalo Bills and any endorsement fees. Then Fantex prepared an initial public offering to sell 523,700 shares that "track" Manuel's brand performance on its exchange. In return, the quarterback received nearly $5 million. If Manuel makes more money from endorsements, or signs a more lucrative football contract,

his brand performance could increase—and some of these earnings may be passed along to investors.

Although fans may be enthusiastic about a player's shares, they also must be aware of the potential risks, because these investments are, as Fantex notes, highly speculative. One risk is that a player may be injured or dropped from a team, reducing future income. Another risk is that the player could be involved in a scandal that reduces his endorsement value. Two important questions: Do you think this type of security should be available to investors? Would you want to own shares tied to the performance of a football player or other athlete?

Sources: Based on information in Brian Feldt, "Rams' Defensive Tackle Brockers Taking His Brand Public via IPO," *St. Louis Business Journal*, February 3, 2015, www.bizjournals.com; Michael Sanserino, "Sports Brokerage Fantex Adds More Players as Season Approaches," *Pittsburgh Post-Gazette*, August 22, 2014, www.post-gazette.com; Brian Korn, "Investors Buying Stock in NFL Player through First Fantex IPO," *Harvard Law School Forum on Corporate Governance and Financial Regulation*, May 10, 2014, http://blogs.law.harvard.edu; William Alden, "Fantex Signs Chicago Bears' Alshon Jeffery for an I.P.O.," *New York Times*, September 18, 2014, www.nytimes.com; William Alden, "Fantex Completes Second Football Player I.P.O., Though Demand Is Slack," *New York Times*, July 21, 2014, www.nytimes.com.

16-7 SOURCES OF LONG-TERM DEBT FINANCING

As pointed out earlier in this chapter, businesses borrow money on a short-term basis for many valid reasons other than desperation. There are equally valid reasons for long-term borrowing. In addition to using borrowed money to meet the long-term needs listed in Table 16-1, successful businesses often use the financial leverage it creates to improve their financial performance. **Financial leverage** is the use of borrowed funds to increase the return on owners' equity. The principle of financial leverage works as long as a firm's earnings are larger than the interest charged for the borrowed money.

To understand how financial leverage can increase a firm's return on owners' equity, study the information for Texas-based Cypress Springs Plastics presented in Table 16-3. Pete Johnston, the owner of the firm, is trying to decide how best to finance a $100,000 purchase of new high-tech manufacturing equipment.

- He could borrow $100,000 and pay 7 percent annual interest.
- He could invest an additional $100,000 in the firm.

Assuming that the firm earns $95,000 a year and that annual interest for this loan totals $7,000 ($100,000 × 0.07 = $7,000), the return on owners' equity for Cypress Springs Plastics would be higher if the firm borrowed the additional financing. Return on owners' equity is determined by dividing a firm's profit by the dollar amount of owners' equity. Based on the calculations illustrated in Table 16-3, Cypress Springs Plastics' return on owners' equity equals 17.6 percent if Johnston borrows the additional $100,000. The firm's return on owners' equity would decrease to 15.8 percent if Johnston invests an additional $100,000 in the business.

Learning Objective

16-7 Evaluate the advantages and disadvantages of long-term debt financing.

financial leverage the use of borrowed funds to increase the return on owners' equity

TABLE 16-3 Analysis of the Effect of Additional Capital from Debt or Equity for Cypress Springs Plastics, Inc.

Additional Debt		Additional Equity	
Owners' equity	$500,000	Owners' equity	$500,000
Additional equity	+0	Additional equity	+100,000
Total owner's equity	$500,000	Total owner's equity	$600,000
Loan (@ 7%)	+100,000	No loan	+0
Total capital	$600,000	Total capital	$600,000
Year-End Earnings			
Gross profit	$95,000	Gross profit	$95,000
Less loan interest	−7,000	No interest	−0
Profit	$88,000	Profit	$95,000
Return on owners' equity	17.6%	Return on owners' equity	15.8%
($88,000 ÷ $500,000 = 17.6%)		($95,000 ÷ $600,000 = 15.8%)	

The most obvious danger when using financial leverage is that the firm's earnings may be lower than expected. If this situation occurs, the fixed interest charge actually works to reduce or eliminate the return on owners' equity. Of course, borrowed money eventually must be repaid.

For a small business, long-term debt financing is generally limited to loans. Large corporations have the additional option of issuing corporate bonds.

16-7a Long-Term Loans

Many businesses satisfy their long-term financing needs, such as those listed in Table 16-1, with loans from commercial banks and other financial institutions. Manufacturers and suppliers of heavy machinery may also provide long-term debt financing by granting credit to their customers.

term-loan agreement a promissory note that requires a borrower to repay a loan in monthly, quarterly, semiannual, or annual installments

TERM-LOAN AGREEMENTS A **term-loan agreement** is a promissory note that requires a borrower to repay a loan in monthly, quarterly, semiannual, or annual installments. As discussed earlier in this chapter, repayment may be as long as 15 to 20 years, but long-term business loans normally are repaid in 3 to 7 years.

Assume that Pete Johnston, the owner of Cypress Springs Plastics, decides to borrow $100,000 and take advantage of the principle of financial leverage illustrated in Table 16-3. Although the firm's return on owners' equity does increase, interest must be paid each year and, eventually, the loan must be repaid. To pay off a $100,000 loan over a three-year period with annual payments, Cypress Springs Plastics must pay $33,333 on the loan balance plus $7,000 annual interest, or a total of $40,333 the first year. Although the amount of interest decreases each year because of the previous year's payment on the loan balance, annual payments of this amount are still a large commitment for a small firm such as Cypress Springs Plastics.

The interest rate and repayment terms for term loans often are based on factors such as the reasons for borrowing, the borrowing firm's credit rating, and the value of collateral. Although long-term loans occasionally may be unsecured,

A firm known for light bulbs is so much more. It's true that many people think of light bulbs when they see the GE symbol in this photo, but the firm is one of the largest corporations in the world. In fact, it has divisions for healthcare, energy management, aviation, *and* finance. Its finance division offers commercial loans, financial programs, home loans, credit cards, personal loans, and other financial services.

the lender usually requires some type of collateral. Acceptable collateral includes real estate, stocks, bonds, equipment, or any asset with value. Lenders may also require that borrowers maintain a minimum amount of working capital.

16-7b Corporate Bonds

In addition to loans, large corporations may choose to issue bonds in denominations of $1,000 to $50,000. Although the usual face value for corporate bonds is $1,000, the total face value of all the bonds in an issue usually amounts to millions of dollars. In fact, one of the reasons why corporations sell bonds is so that they can borrow a lot of money from a lot of different bondholders and raise larger amounts of money than could be borrowed from one lender. A **corporate bond** is a corporation's written pledge that it will repay a specified amount of money with interest. Interest rates for corporate bonds vary with the financial health of the company issuing the bond. Specific factors that increase or decrease the interest rate that a corporation must pay when it issues bonds include

- The corporation's ability to pay interest each year until maturity.
- The corporation's ability to repay the bond at maturity.

For bond investors, the interest rate on corporate bonds is an example of the risk–return ratio discussed earlier in this chapter. Simply put: Investors expect a higher return when they purchase high-risk, speculative bond issues—see Figure 16-7. As a result, corporations must pay higher interest if investors are concerned about continued interest payments or eventual repayment of a corporate bond.

Today, most corporate bonds are registered bonds. A **registered bond** is a bond registered in the owner's name by the issuing company. Many corporations do not issue actual bonds. Instead, the bonds are recorded electronically, and the specific details regarding the bond issue, along with the current owner's name and address, are maintained by computer. Computer entries are safer because they cannot be stolen, misplaced, or destroyed, and make it easier to transfer when a bond is sold.

The **maturity date** is the date on which the corporation is to repay the borrowed money. Until a bond's maturity, a corporation pays interest to the bond owner at the stated rate. For example, owners of Adobe Systems bonds that mature in 2020 receive 4.750 percent per year for each bond. For each $1,000 bond issued, the corporation must pay bondholders $47.50 ($1,000 × 0.04750 = $47.50) each year. Because interest for corporate bonds is usually paid semiannually, the owner of an Adobe Systems bond will receive a $23.75 payment every six months for each bond they own. On the maturity date, a registered owner will receive cash equaling the face value of the bond.

TYPES OF BONDS Corporate bonds are generally classified as debentures, mortgage bonds, or convertible bonds. Most corporate bonds are debenture bonds. A **debenture bond** is a bond backed only by the reputation of the issuing

corporate bond a corporation's written pledge that it will repay a specified amount of money with interest

registered bond a bond registered in the owner's name by the issuing company

maturity date the date on which a corporation is to repay borrowed money

debenture bond a bond backed only by the reputation of the issuing corporation

FIGURE 16-7 The Risk–Return Ratio for Corporate Bond Investors

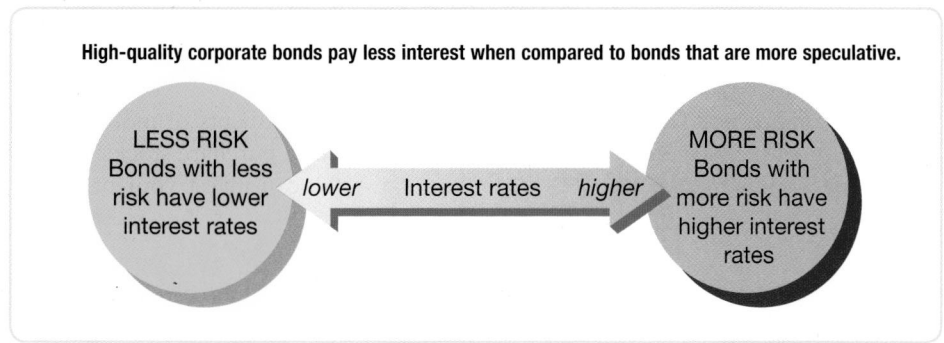

High-quality corporate bonds pay less interest when compared to bonds that are more speculative.

LESS RISK
Bonds with less risk have lower interest rates

lower   Interest rates   *higher*

MORE RISK
Bonds with more risk have higher interest rates

corporation. To make its bonds more appealing to investors, a corporation may issue mortgage bonds. A **mortgage bond** is a corporate bond secured by various assets of the issuing firm. The corporation can also issue convertible bonds. A **convertible bond** can be exchanged, at the owner's option, for a specified number of shares of the corporation's common stock. For example, Wesco—a leading wholesaler and distributor of electrical products—has issued convertible bonds that mature in 2029. Each bond can be converted to 34.6433 shares of Wesco common stock. A corporation can gain in three ways by issuing convertible bonds. First, convertibles usually carry a lower interest rate than nonconvertible bonds. Second, the conversion feature attracts investors who are interested in the speculative gain that conversion to common stock may provide. Third, if the bondholder converts to common stock, the corporation no longer has to redeem the bond at maturity.

REPAYMENT PROVISIONS FOR CORPORATE BONDS Maturity dates for bonds generally range from 10 to 30 years after the date of issue. Some bonds are callable before the maturity date; that is, a corporation can buy back, or redeem, them. For these bonds, the corporation may pay the bond owner a call premium. The amount of the call premium, if any, is specified, along with other provisions, in the bond indenture. The **bond indenture** is a legal document that details all the conditions relating to a bond issue.

A corporation may use one of three methods to ensure that it has sufficient funds available to redeem a bond issue. First, it can issue the bonds as **serial bonds**, which are bonds of a single issue that mature on different dates. For example, a company may use a 25-year $200 million bond issue to finance its expansion. None of the bonds mature during the first 15 years. Thereafter, 10 percent of the bonds mature each year until all the bonds are retired at the end of the 25th year. Second, the corporation can establish a sinking fund. A **sinking fund** is a sum of money to which deposits are made each year for the purpose of redeeming a bond issue. When Union Pacific Corporation sold a $275 million bond issue, the company agreed to contribute to a sinking fund until the bond's maturity in the year 2025. Third, a corporation can pay off an old bond issue by selling new bonds. Although this may appear to perpetuate the corporation's long-term debt, a number of utility companies and railroads use this repayment method.

A corporation that issues bonds must also appoint a **trustee**, an individual or an independent firm that acts as the bond owner's representative. A trustee's duties are handled most often by a commercial bank or other large financial institution. The corporation must report to the trustee periodically regarding its ability to make interest payments and eventually redeem the bonds. In turn, the trustee transmits this information to the bond owners, along with its own evaluation of the corporation's ability to pay.

16-7c Cost Comparisons

Table 16-4 compares some of the methods that can be used to obtain long-term equity *and* debt financing. Although the initial flotation cost of issuing stock is high, selling common stock is generally a popular option for most financial managers. Once the stock is sold and upfront costs are paid, the *ongoing* costs of using stock to finance a business are low. The type of long-term financing that generally has the highest *ongoing* costs is a long-term loan (debt).

To a great extent, firms are financed through the investments of individuals—money that people have deposited in banks or have used to purchase stocks, mutual funds, and bonds. In Appendix A, we look at how you can invest your money in business.

---

mortgage bond a corporate bond secured by various assets of the issuing firm

convertible bond a bond that can be exchanged, at the owner's option, for a specified number of shares of the corporation's common stock

bond indenture a legal document that details all the conditions relating to a bond issue

serial bonds bonds of a single issue that mature on different dates

sinking fund a sum of money to which deposits are made each year for the purpose of redeeming a bond issue

trustee an individual or an independent firm that acts as a bond owner's representative

Concept Check

✓ Describe how financial leverage can increase return on owners' equity.

✓ For a corporation, what are the advantages of corporate bonds over long-term loans?

✓ Describe the three methods used to ensure that funds are available to redeem corporate bonds at maturity.

TABLE 16-4 Comparison of Long-Term Financing Methods

Type of Financing	Repayment	Repayment Period	Cost/Dividends/Interest	Businesses That May Use It
Equity				
Common stock	No	None	High initial cost; low ongoing costs because dividends not required	All corporations that sell stock to investors
Preferred stock	No	None	Dividends not required but must be paid before common stockholders receive any dividends	Large corporations that have an established investor base of common stockholders
Debt				
Long-term loan	Yes	Usually 3–7 years	Interest rates between 3 and 12 percent depending on economic conditions, the financial stability of the company requesting the loan, and the amount of the loan	All firms that can meet the lender's repayment and collateral requirements
Corporate bond	Yes	Usually 10–30 years	Interest rates between 3.5 and 10 percent depending on the financial stability of the company issuing the bonds and economic conditions	Large corporations that are financially healthy

Summary

16-1 Understand why financial management is important in today's uncertain economy.

Financial management consists of all the activities concerned with obtaining money and using it effectively. Financial management can be viewed as a two-sided problem. On one side, the uses of funds often dictate the type or types of financing needed by a business. On the other side, the activities a business can undertake are determined by the types of financing available. Financial managers must ensure that funds are available when needed, that they are obtained at the lowest possible cost, and that they are used as efficiently as possible. In the wake of the economic crisis, the Dodd–Frank Wall Street Reform and Consumer Protection Act was signed into law. And today, there is an ongoing debate if more regulations are needed. Still, there are a number of rewarding jobs in finance for qualified job applicants.

16-2 Identify a firm's short- and long-term financial needs.

Short-term financing is money that will be used for one year or less. There are many short-term needs, but cash flow, speculative production, and inventory are three for which financing is often required. Long-term financing is money that will be used for more than one year. Such financing may be required for a business start-up, for a merger or an acquisition, for new product development, for long-term marketing activities, for replacement of equipment, or for expansion of facilities. According to financial experts, business firms will find it more difficult to raise both short- and long-term financing in the future because of increased regulations and more cautious lenders. Financial managers must also consider the risk–return ratio when making financial decisions.

16-3 Summarize the process of planning for financial management.

A financial plan begins with an organization's goals and objectives. Next, a firm's goals and objectives are "translated" into departmental budgets that detail expected income and expenses. From these budgets, which may be combined into an overall cash budget, the financial manager determines what funding will be needed. Whereas departmental and cash budgets emphasize short-term financing needs, a capital budget can be used to estimate a firm's expenditures for major assets and its long-term financing needs. The four principal sources of financing are sales revenues, equity capital, debt capital, and proceeds from the sale of assets. Once the needed funds have been obtained, the financial manager is responsible for monitoring and evaluating the firm's financial activities.

16-4 Identify the services provided by banks and financial institutions for their business customers.

Banks and other financial institutions offer today's business customers a tempting array of services. Among the most important banking services are savings accounts and certificates of deposit, checking accounts, short- and long-term loans, and credit-card and debit-card processing. Increased use of electronic funds transfer systems (automated teller machines, automated clearinghouse systems, point-of-sale terminals, and electronic check conversion) also will change the way that business firms bank and conduct typical business transactions. For firms in the global marketplace, a bank can provide letters of credit and banker's acceptances that will reduce the risk of nonpayment for sellers. Banks and financial institutions also can provide currency exchange to reduce payment problems for import or export transactions.

16-5 Describe the advantages and disadvantages of different methods of short-term debt financing.

Most short-term financing is unsecured; that is, no collateral is required. Sources of unsecured short-term financing include trade credit, promissory notes issued to suppliers, unsecured bank loans, and commercial paper. Sources of secured short-term financing include loans secured by inventory and accounts receivable. A firm may also sell its receivables to factors. Trade credit is the least-expensive source of short-term financing. The cost of financing through other sources generally depends on the source and on the credit rating of the firm that requires the financing. Factoring is generally the most expensive approach.

16-6 Evaluate the advantages and disadvantages of equity financing.

The first time a corporation sells stock to the general public is referred to as an initial public offering (IPO). With an IPO, the stock is sold in the primary market. Once sold in the primary market, investors buy and sell stock in the secondary market. Usually, secondary market transactions are completed through a securities exchange or the over-the-counter market. Common stock is voting stock; holders of common stock elect the corporation's directors and often must approve changes to the corporate charter. Holders of preferred stock must be paid dividends before holders of common stock are paid any dividends. Another source of equity funding is retained earnings, which is the portion of a business's profits *not* distributed to stockholders. Venture capital—money invested in small (and sometimes struggling) firms that have the potential to become very successful—is yet another source of equity funding. Angel investors can also provide the money needed to start or expand small businesses. Finally, a private placement can be used to sell stocks and other corporate securities.

16-7 Evaluate the advantages and disadvantages of long-term debt financing.

For a small business, debt financing is generally limited to loans. Large corporations have the additional option of issuing corporate bonds. Regardless of whether the business is small or large, it can take advantage of financial leverage. Financial leverage is the use of borrowed funds to increase the return on owners' equity. The rate of interest for long-term loans usually depends on the financial status of the borrower, the reason for borrowing, and the kind of collateral pledged to back up the loan. Long-term business loans are normally repaid in 3 to 7 years but can be as long as 15 to 20 years. Money realized from the sale of corporate bonds must be repaid when the bonds mature. In addition, the corporation must pay interest on that money from the time the bonds are issued until maturity. Maturity dates for bonds generally range from 10 to 30 years after the date of issue. Three types of bonds—debentures, mortgage bonds, and convertible bonds—are sold to raise debt capital. When comparing the cost of long-term financing, the ongoing costs of using stock (equity) to finance a business are low. The most expensive is a long-term loan (debt).

Key Terms

You should now be able to define and give an example relevant to each of the following terms:

financial management (468)
chief financial officer (CFO) (470)
short-term financing (470)
cash flow (470)
speculative production (471)
long-term financing (471)

risk–return ratio (472)
financial plan (472)
budget (473)
cash budget (473)
zero-base budgeting (474)
capital budget (474)
equity capital (475)

debt capital (475)
certificate of deposit (CD) (476)
check (476)
line of credit (476)
revolving credit agreement (476)

collateral (476)
debit card (477)
electronic funds transfer (EFT) system (478)
letter of credit (478)
banker's acceptance (479)
unsecured financing (479)

trade credit (479)

promissory note (480)

prime interest rate (480)

commercial paper (481)

factor (482)

initial public offering
    (IPO) (483)

primary market (484)

investment banking
    firm (484)

secondary market (484)

securities exchange (484)

over-the-counter (OTC)
    market (484)

common stock (485)

preferred stock (485)

retained earnings (485)

angel investor (486)

private placement (486)

financial leverage (487)

term-loan agreement (488)

corporate bond (489)

registered bond (489)

maturity date (489)

debenture bond (489)

mortgage bond (490)

convertible bond (490)

bond indenture (490)

serial bonds (490)

sinking fund (490)

trustee (490)

Discussion Questions

1. During an economic crisis, many financial managers and corporate officers are criticized for (a) poor decisions, (b) lack of ethical behavior, (c) large salaries, (d) lucrative severance packages worth millions of dollars, and (e) extravagant lifestyles. Is this criticism justified? Justify your opinion.

2. If you were the financial manager of Stars and Stripes Clothing, what would you do with the excess cash that the firm expects in the second and fourth quarters? (See Figure 16-4.)

3. Develop a *personal* cash budget for the next six months. Explain what you would do if there are budget shortfalls

or excess cash amounts at the end of any month during the six-month period.

4. Why would a lender offer unsecured short-term loans when it could demand collateral?

5. How can a small-business owner or corporate manager use financial leverage to improve the firm's profits and return on owners' equity?

6. In what circumstances might a large corporation sell stock rather than bonds to obtain long-term financing? In what circumstances would it sell bonds rather than stock?

Video Case
Moonworks Partners with Bank Rhode Island to Finance Growth

If Jim Moon's father hadn't installed gutter guards to keep out leaves and avoid clogs, Moonworks might not have become a reality. Jim Moon originally opened a kitchen remodeling business after he graduated from the University of Rhode Island in 1983. Ten years later, his life took a different turn when he returned home to visit his parents and listened to his father praise the new gutter guards he recently installed. Moon watched the company's informational video and was so impressed that he decided to sell his kitchen remodeling business and start a new company, Gutter Helmet of New England.

The company, based in Woonsocket, Rhode Island, was initially a one-man operation financed by money from family and friends. The business continued to expand at a fast pace during the home-improvement boom of the 1990s and into the early 2000s, as Moon hired salespeople and installers, rented space to store equipment, and bought trucks. Preparing for future growth, Moon wanted to purchase his own building—with plenty of room for expansion—and stop paying rent. But when he approached his bank, he learned that it didn't handle business loans smaller than $250,000. Moon immediately closed his checking account and withdrew the $40,000 he had deposited, determined to find a bank that was interested in financing his entrepreneurial activities.

He approached Bank Rhode Island, a community bank that served both consumers and businesses. Bank officials took the time to get to know Moon and his company, and dig into the financial details of his business plan. Satisfied that the company would be able to repay the debt, they approved the firm's application for a mortgage on a commercial building Moon was ready to buy.

Every quarter, Moon and his managers would update the bank about how business was going and discuss any new plans in the works. Every year, he made sure the bank received a copy of the company's annual financial statements. Even when the home-improvement market began to change and sales of gutter guards slowed, Moon stayed in touch with his bank to let them know what he was doing. During the economic downturn that hurt many businesses, Moon identified an opportunity to diversify beyond gutter guards and began installing replacement windows.

By the time Moon sat down to talk about borrowing money for expanding into new products and, later, new territories, the bank was very familiar with the company, its management, its repayment record, and its ability to repay new loans. Because of the working relationship between Moonworks and Bank Rhode Island, Moon's business was able to obtain a working capital line of credit to cover current expenses, a term loan to provide initial working capital for expansion, and a new line of credit for entering another territory. Moon also agreed to personally guarantee a company loan, demonstrating his faith in the future strength of his business.

Thanks to careful financial management during both good and bad economic times, Moon's company—renamed Moonworks in 2009—has successfully diversified into other home-improvement products and services. With annual sales topping $13 million and a workforce of nearly 100 people, plus the knowledgeable support of its banking professionals,

Moonworks is poised to continue its record of sales and success in the future.[15]

Questions

1. What steps did Jim Moon take to build a relationship between his business and Bank Rhode Island?
2. What collateral, if any, do you think Moonworks can use as security for a future loan? Explain your answer.
3. Put yourself into the shoes of the banker handling the Moonworks' account. What questions would you ask if the company asks for additional debt financing?

Building Skills for Career Success

1. Social Media Exercise

Turbo Tax is probably one of the best-known tax preparation services in the world. One of the reasons for its popularity is that it provides software that both small business firms and individuals need to make financial decisions and prepare tax returns. Another reason for its popularity is the company's use of social media through its YouTube channel. Each video on the TurboTax channel illustrates how a company can use social media to provide valuable information to customers. You can check out Turbo Tax videos at www.youtube.com/user/TurboTax.

1. Visit the YouTube channel for Turbo Tax (www.youtube.com/user/TurboTax). Do you think social media is an effective method of obtaining the tax information you might need to prepare your taxes?
2. Can you think of other companies that could use videos on a YouTube channel to share information that their customers could use?

2. Building Team Skills

Suppose that for the past three years you have been repairing lawn mowers in your garage. Your business has grown steadily, and you recently hired two part-time workers. Your garage is no longer adequate for your business; it is also in violation of the city code, and you have already been fined for noncompliance. You have decided that it is time to find another location for your shop and that it also would be a good time to expand your business. If the business continues to grow in the new location, you plan to hire a full-time employee to repair small appliances. You are concerned, however, about how you will get the money to move your shop and get it established in a new location.

Assignment

1. With all class members participating, use brainstorming to identify the following:
    a. The funds you will need to accomplish your business goals

b. The sources of short-term financing available to you
    c. Problems that might prevent you from getting a short-term loan
    d. How you will repay the money if you get a loan
2. Have a classmate write the ideas on the board.
3. Discuss how you can overcome any problems that might hamper your current chances of getting a loan and how your business can improve its chances of securing short-term loans in the future.
4. Summarize what you learned from participating in this exercise.

3. Researching Different Careers

Financial managers are responsible for determining the best way to raise funds at the lowest possible cost, for ensuring that the funds are used to accomplish their firm's goals and objectives, and for developing and implementing their firm's financial plan. Their decisions have a direct impact on the firm's level of success and if the firm is profitable or not.

Assignment

1. Investigate the job of financial manager by searching for information available in the library or on the Internet, by interviewing a financial manager, or both.
2. Find answers to the following questions:
    a. What skills do financial managers need?
    b. How much education is required?
    c. What is the starting salary? Top salary?
    d. What will the job of financial manager be like in the future?
    e. What opportunities are available?
    f. What types of firms are most likely to hire financial managers? What is the employment potential?
3. Prepare a report on your findings.

Graeter's Recipe for Growth: New Systems, Social Media, and Financing

Graeter's still makes ice cream by hand, just like the founders did in 1870. But in every other respect, it's a very different business from the mom-and-pop firm founded by the great-grandparents of Richard, Robert, and Chip Graeter. With the rise of communication technologies such as social media, Graeter's can stay in touch with customers and see what people say about its brand. Technology is also a factor in the new systems Graeter's recently installed to keep the business running smoothly as it pursues fast-paced growth. Just as important, the company has arranged financing to support its long-term plans for national expansion.

Graeter's Social Side

Even a small business can have a big presence in social media. Graeter's has designated an employee to manage all of the company's activities on Facebook, Twitter, and YouTube. With over 170,000 Facebook "likes," Graeter's engages its brand fans in conversations about new or favorite flavors, the size of its chocolate chunks, and more. It posts a new message or photo every few days, and reveals the names of mystery flavors on Facebook in advance of other publicity. As a result, fans return to its Facebook page often. In addition, Graeter's tweets frequently and periodically posts videos on its YouTube channel. Graeter's also monitors "mentions" of its brand on other social-media sites. For example, hundreds of consumers have shared images of Graeter's ice cream on the Pinterest site. As other people add their comments and click to "like," the conversation continues and the word of mouth builds buzz for Graeter's.

New Growth, New Systems

Paul Porcino, a consultant working with the Graeter family, observes that small, entrepreneurial firms often have only "a very small amount of information, and … it hasn't been pulled together in any meaningful way." The first step was to define what Graeter's executives needed to know to run the business. For example, they needed to be able to track unit sales online, in each store, and to each wholesale customer,

and to measure both costs and profitability by product and distribution channel.

Despite some technical challenges during implementation, Graeter's has already experienced some of the benefits of collecting better information. When management noticed that overall bakery sales weren't up to par, "we had to adjust," comments Porcino. The remedy was surprising: "We actually reduced the number of products we were selling in the store. . . . It wasn't very clear exactly how much we were selling, but at least [we had] the good-enough gut sense in terms of the ones that were not selling, and we . . . adjusted the total inventory line."

Counting on Accounting

Graeter's controller, David Blink, is responsible for preparing "all financial statements, all reports, payroll, [and] any ad hoc reports that any of the managers would need. I handle a lot of the reporting for the retail side as well as the manufacturing side," he says. With these reports in hand, the Graeter's team can make informed decisions about how many seasonal employees to hire, which products to keep, how much to invest in new equipment, and other issues that arise day by day. Although an outside payroll company actually prints the employees' checks, Blink's department collects and analyzes payroll data as input for management decisions.

Money Matters

With expansion on the menu, the Graeter's recognized they needed a new production facility. After scouting possible locations, Graeter's signed a 20-year deal with Cincinnati, paying a token amount for land and borrowing $10 million from the city to pay for construction of a new 28,000-square-foot factory. The loan carried low interest rates and would be repaid over 20 years. In turn, Cincinnati issued $10 million in bonds to provide Graeter's with this funding. The package of financial incentives that Graeter's received toward its new Bond Hill factory was worth $3.3 million. In exchange, Graeter's committed to "stay and grow" in Cincinnati for at least 20 years, creating dozens of new jobs when the facility opened in 2010 and additional jobs as Graeter's growth continued.

© ISTOCKPHOTO.COM/LIVIO

As opening day for the Bond Hill facility approached, Graeter's was presented with an unexpected opportunity. Its largest franchisee wanted to sell the franchise operation, complete with stores and an ice-cream factory, and Graeter's had the right to buy the franchise back. "That was not planned, not part of our strategic vision," explains Richard Graeter, "but the opportunity came up, and we had to look at it." After examining what the business had done in the past and where it was going in the future, the three great-grandsons of Graeter's founders put together the financing to buy the stores and factory from the franchisee. Now Graeter's has the right combination of ingredients for expanding from coast to coast and beyond.[16]

Assignment

1. Suppose you were writing a social media plan for Graeter's, with two objectives: to improve brand awareness in new markets and to build online orders during holiday periods. What quantitative and qualitative measurements would you use to evaluate the results of your plan?

2. Graeter's uses information to track cash, sales revenue, and expenses on a daily basis. How does this type of accounting system facilitate effective decision making?

3. What kinds of questions do you think Cincinnati officials asked Graeter's owners before agreeing to loan the company $10 million? Why would Graeter's go with this financing arrangement rather than borrowing from a bank to pay for the Bond Hill factory?

Building a Business Plan: Part 6

Now that you have a marketing plan, the next big and important step is to prepare an information and financial plan. One of the biggest mistakes an entrepreneur makes when faced with a need for financing is not being prepared. The information contained in Chapter 14 (Exploring Social Media and e-Business), Chapter 15 (Using Management and Accounting Information), and Chapter 16 (Mastering Financial Management) will help you prepare this section of the business plan and determine the amount of financing you need to start your business. With the help of information in the last three chapters of the text, the task may be easier than you think.

In this last section, you should also provide some information about your exit strategy, and discuss any potential trends, problems, or risks that you may encounter. Now is also the time to go back and prepare the executive summary, which should be placed at the beginning of the business plan.

The Information and Accounting Plan Component

Information and accounting systems are important if your business is to succeed. Your information plan should answer at least the following questions:

6.1. How will you gather information about competitors, their products, and the prices that they charge for their products and services?

6.2. Explain how you will develop a management information system to collect, store, update, process data, and present information.

6.3. Will your business have an e-business component? If so, explain how you sell your products or services online.

6.4. Are there ways that you can use social media to promote products and services and reach out to your customers?

6.5. Who will create and maintain the accounting system that you use to record routine business transactions for your business?

6.6. Will you hire an accountant to prepare financial statements for your firm?

The Financial Plan Component

Your financial plan should answer at least the following questions about the investment needed, sales and cash-flow forecasts, breakeven analysis, and sources of funding:

6.7. What is the actual amount of money you need to open your business (start-up budget) and the amount needed to keep it open (operating budget)? Prepare a realistic budget.

6.8. How much money do you have, and can you obtain additional financing, if needed, from investors or lenders?

6.9. Prepare a projected income statement by month for the first year of operation and by quarter for the second and third years.

6.10. Prepare projected balance sheets for each of the first three years of operation.

6.11. Prepare a breakeven analysis. How many units of your products or service will have to be sold to cover your costs?

6.12. Reinforce your final projections by comparing them with industry averages for your chosen industry.

The Exit Strategy Component

Your exit strategy component should at least include answers to the following questions:

6.13. How do you intend to get yourself (and your money) out of the business?

6.14. Will your children take over the business, or do you intend to sell it later?

6.15. Do you intend to grow the business to the point of an IPO?

6.16. How will investors get their money back?

The Critical Risks and Assumptions Component

Your critical risks and assumptions component should answer at least the following questions:

6.17. What will you do if your market does not develop as quickly as you predicted? What if your market develops too quickly?

6.18. What will you do if your competitors underprice or make your product obsolete?

6.19. What will you do if there is an unfavorable industry-wide trend?

6.20. What will happen if trained workers are not available as predicted?

6.21. What will you do if there is an erratic supply of products or raw materials?

The Appendix Component

Supplemental information and documents often are included in an appendix. Here are a few examples of some documents that can be included:

- Résumés of owners and principal managers
- Advertising samples and brochures
- An organization chart
- Floor plans

Review of Business Plan Activities

As you have discovered, writing a business plan involves a long series of interrelated steps. As with any project involving a number of complex steps and calculations, your business plan should be reviewed carefully and revised before you present it to potential investors.

Remember, there is one more component you need to prepare after your business plan is completed: The executive summary should be written last, but because of its importance, it appears after the introduction.

The Executive Summary Component

In the executive summary, give a one- to two-page overview of your entire business plan. This is the most important part of the business plan and is of special interest to busy bankers, investors, and other interested parties. Remember, this section is a summary; more detailed information is provided in the remainder of your business plan.

Make sure that the executive summary captures the reader's attention instantly in the first sentence by using a key selling point or benefit of the business.

Your executive summary should include answers to at least the following:

6.22. *Company information*. What product or service do you provide? What is your competitive advantage? When will the company be formed? What are your company objectives? What is the background of you and your management team?

6.23. *Market opportunity*. What is the expected size and growth rate of your market, your expected market share, and any relevant market trends?

Once again, review your answers to all the questions in the preceding parts to make sure that they are all consistent throughout the entire business plan.

Although many would-be entrepreneurs are excited about the prospects of opening their own business, remember that it takes a lot of hard work, time, and in most cases a substantial amount of money. While the business plan provides an enormous amount of information about your business, it is only the first step. Once it is completed, it is now your responsibility to implement the plan. Good luck in your business venture.

The information contained in "Building a Business Plan" will also assist you in completing the online *Interactive Business Plan*.

Endnotes

1   Based on information in Paul Mozur, "Alibaba Profit Surges, But a Revenue Gain of 40% Still Misses Forecasts," *New York Times*, January 29, 2015, www.nytimes.com; Charlie Rose, "Jack Ma," *Bloomberg Businessweek*, January 29, 2015, p. 36; David Barboza, "The Jack Ma Way," *New York Times*, September 7, 2014, BU1–BU4-5; Rana Foroohar, "The Capitalist: Jack Ma," *Time*, December 22, 2014, pp. 134–138.

2   The Cisco Systems website at www.cisco.com (accessed February 13, 2015).

3   The U.S. Bureau of Labor Statistics website at http://bls.gov (accessed February 12, 2015).

4   The 3M Corporation website at www.3m.com (accessed February 22, 2015).

5   The McDonald's Corporate website at www.aboutmcdonalds.com (accessed February 14, 2015).

6   Jonathan Stempel and Devika Krishna Kuman, "Buffet's Berkshire Hathaway Buys P&G's Duracell," The Reuters website at www.reuters.com (accessed November 13, 2014).

7   Barret Brunsman, "Procter & Gamble to Sell Pet Food Business for $2.9 Billion," The Cincinnati Business Courier website at www.bizjournals.com (accessed April 8, 2014).

8   Ben Mutzabaugh and Kevin McCoy, "Air Catalog SkyMall Seeks Bankruptcy Protection," The USA Today website at www.usatoday.com (accessed January 23, 2015).

9   The CreditCards.com website at www.creditcards.com (accessed February 15, 2015).

10   Ibid.

11   Chris Isidore, "EBay Spinning Off PayPal as Separate Company," The MoneyCNN website at www.money.cnn.com (accessed September 30, 2014).

12   The JPMorgan Chase website at www.jpmorganchase.com (accessed February 17, 2015).

13   The General Electric website at www.ge.com (accessed February 17, 2015).

14   Russ Garland, "Zynga Inc: Venture Capital Investment Up Despite Fund-Raising Constraints," The 4-Traders.com website at www.4-traders.com (accessed January 20, 2012).

15   Based on information from the company website at www.moonworkshome.com (accessed February 19, 2015); Patrick Anderson, "Building Future in Home Improvement," *Providence (RI) Business News*, May 20, 2013, p. 10; "The Story Behind Moonworks," Moonworks website at www.moonworkshome.com; and Cengage Learning, *Moonworks* video.

16   Sources: Based on information from the Graeter's company website at www.graeter.com (accessed February 20, 2015); Kimberly L. Jackson, "Graeter's Premium Chocolate Chip Ice Cream Lands at Stop & Shop," *Newark Star-Ledger (NJ)*, April 4, 2012, www.nj.com; "Graeter's Ice Cream Debuts in Bay Area," *Tampa Bay Times (St. Petersburg, FL)*, January 10, 2012, p. 4B; Jim Carper, "Graeter's Runs a Hands-on Ice Cream Plant," *Dairy Foods*, August 2011, pp. 36+; Jim Carper, "The Greater Good," *Dairy Foods*, August 2011, pp. 95+; "Graeter's Unveils New 'Mystery Flavor,'" *Dayton Daily News*, March 29, 2012, www.daytondailynews.com; Bob Driehaus, "A Cincinnati Ice Cream Maker Aims Big," *New York Times*, September 11, 2010, www.nytimes.com; Lucy May, "Graeter's Northern Kentucky Franchisee Puts Stores on the Block," *Business Courier*, August 6, 2010, http://cincinnati.bizjournals.com; www.graeters.com; interviews with company staff and Cengage videos about Graeter's.

Glossary

A

absolute advantage the ability to produce a specific product more efficiently than any other nation.

accessory equipment standardized equipment used in a firm's production or office activities.

account executive an individual, sometimes called a stockbroker or registered representative, who buys and sells securities for clients.

accountability the obligation of a worker to accomplish an assigned job or task.

accounting the process of systematically collecting, analyzing, and reporting financial information.

accounting equation the basis for the accounting process: *Assets = Liabilities + Owners' equity.*

ad hoc committee a committee created for a specific short-term purpose.

administrative law the regulations created by government agencies established by legislative bodies.

administrative manager a manager who is not associated with any specific functional area but who provides overall administrative guidance and leadership.

advertising a paid nonpersonal message communicated to a select audience through a mass medium.

advertising agency an independent firm that plans, produces, and places advertising for its clients.

affirmative action program a plan designed to increase the number of minority employees at all levels within an organization.

agency a business relationship in which one party, called the principal, appoints a second party, called the agent, to act on its behalf.

agency shop a workplace in which employees can choose not to join the union but must pay dues to the union anyway.

agent a middleman that expedites exchanges, represents a buyer or a seller, and often is hired permanently on a commission basis.

alien corporation a corporation chartered by a foreign government and conducting business in the United States.

analytic skills the ability to identify problems correctly, generate reasonable alternatives, and select the "best" alternatives to solve problems.

analytical process a process in operations management in which raw materials are broken into different component parts.

angel investor an investor who provides financial backing for small business startups or entrepreneurs.

annual report a report distributed to stockholders and other interested parties that describes the firm's operating activities and its financial condition.

appellate court a court that hears cases appealed from lower courts.

arbitration the step in a grievance procedure in which a neutral third party hears the two sides of a dispute and renders a binding decision.

asset allocation the process of spreading your money among several different types of investments to lessen risk.

assets the resources that a business owns.

audit an examination of a company's financial statements and the accounting practices that produced them.

authority the power, within an organization, to accomplish an assigned job or task.

autocratic leadership task-oriented leadership style in which workers are told what to do and how to accomplish it without having a say in the decision-making process.

automatic vending the use of machines to dispense products.

automation the total or near-total use of machines to do work.

automobile liability insurance insurance that covers financial losses resulting from injuries or damage caused by the insured vehicle.

automobile physical damage insurance insurance that covers damage to an insured vehicle.

B

balance of payments the total flow of money into a country minus the total flow of money out of that country over some period of time.

balance of trade the total value of a nation's exports minus the total value of its imports over some period of time.

balance sheet (or statement of financial position) a summary of the dollar amounts of a firm's assets, liabilities, and owners' equity accounts at the end of a specific accounting period.

banker's acceptance a written order for a bank to pay a third party a stated amount of money on a specific state.

bankruptcy a legal procedure designed both to protect an individual or business that cannot meet its financial obligations and to protect the creditors involved.

bargaining unit the specific group of employees represented by a union.

barter a system of exchange in which goods or services are traded directly for other goods or services without using money.

behavior modification a systematic program of reinforcement to encourage desirable behavior.

benchmarking a process used to evaluate the products, processes, or management practices of another organization that is superior in some way in order to improve quality.

beneficiary person or organization named in a life insurance policy as a recipient of the proceeds of that policy on the death of the insured.

bill of lading document issued by a transport carrier to an exporter to prove that merchandise has been shipped.

binding contract an agreement that requires an intermediary to purchase products from a particular supplier, not from the supplier's competitors.

blog a website that allows a company to share information in order to not only increase the customer's knowledge about its products and services, but also to build trust.

board of directors the top governing body of a corporation, the members of which are elected by the stockholders.

bond indenture a legal document that details all the conditions relating to a bond issue.

boycott a refusal to do business with a particular firm.

boycott in restraint of trade an agreement between businesses not to sell or buy from a particular entity.

brand a name, term, symbol, design, or any combination of these that identifies a seller's products as distinct from those of other sellers.

brand equity marketing and financial value associated with a brand's strength in a market.

brand extension using an existing brand to brand a new product in a different product category.

brand loyalty extent to which a customer is favorable toward buying a specific brand.

brand mark the part of a brand that is a symbol or distinctive design.

brand name the part of a brand that can be spoken.

breach of contract the failure of one party to fulfill the terms of a contract when there is no legal reason for that failure.

breakeven quantity the number of units that must be sold for the total revenue (from all units sold) to equal the total cost (of all units sold).

broker a middleman that specializes in a particular commodity, represents either a buyer or a seller, and is likely to be hired on a temporary basis.

budget a financial statement that projects income, expenditures, or both over a specified future period.

bundle pricing packaging together two or more complementary products and selling them for a single price.

business the organized effort of individuals to produce and sell, for a profit, the goods and services that satisfy society's needs.

business buying behavior the purchasing of products by producers, resellers, governmental units, and institutions.

business cycle the recurrence of periods of growth and recession in a nation's economic activity.

business ethics the application of moral standards to business situations.

business interruption insurance insurance protection for a business whose operations are interrupted because of a fire, storm, or other natural disaster.

business model represents a group of common characteristics and methods of doing business to generate sales revenues and reduce expenses.

business plan a carefully constructed guide for the person starting a business.

business product a product bought for resale, for making other products, or for use in a firm's operations.

business service an intangible product that an organization uses in its operations.

business-to-business (or B2B) model a model used by firms that conduct business with other businesses.

business-to-consumer (or B2C) model a model used by firms that focus on conducting business with individual consumers.

buying allowance a temporary price reduction to resellers for purchasing specified quantities of a product.

buying behavior the decisions and actions of people involved in buying and using products.

C

capacity the amount of products or services that an organization can produce in a given time.

capital budget a financial statement that estimates a firm's expenditures for major assets and its long-term financing needs.

capital gain the difference between a security's purchase price and its selling price.

capital-intensive technology a process in which machines and equipment do most of the work.

capitalism an economic system in which individuals own and operate the majority of businesses that provide goods and services.

captioned photograph a picture accompanied by a brief explanation.

captive pricing pricing the basic product in a product line low, but pricing related items at a higher level.

carrier a firm that offers transportation services.

cash budget a financial statement that estimates cash receipts and cash expenditures over a specified period.

cash flow the movement of money into and out of an organization.

cash surrender value the amount payable to the holder of a whole life insurance policy if the policy is canceled.

catalog marketing a type of marketing in which an organization provides a catalog from which customers make selections and place orders by mail, telephone, or the Internet.

category killer a very large specialty store that concentrates on a single product line and competes on the basis of low prices and product availability.

caveat emptor a Latin phrase meaning "let the buyer beware".

centralized organization an organization that systematically works to concentrate authority at the upper levels of the organization.

certificate of deposit (CD) a document stating that the bank will pay the depositor a guaranteed interest rate on money left on deposit for a specified period of time.

certified public accountant (CPA) an individual who has met state requirements for accounting education and experience and has passed a rigorous accounting examination.

chain of command the line of authority that extends from the highest to the lowest levels of an organization.

chain retailer a company that operates more than one retail outlet.

check a written order for a bank or other financial institution to pay a stated dollar amount to the business or person indicated on the face of the check.

chief financial officer (CFO) a high-level corporate executive who manages a firm's finances and reports directly to the company's chief executive officer or president.

closed corporation a corporation whose stock is owned by relatively few people and is not sold to the general public.

closed shop a workplace in which workers must join the union before they are hired; outlawed by the Taft–Hartley Act.

cloud computing a type of computer usage in which services stored on the Internet is provided to users on a temporary basis.

code of ethics a guide to acceptable and ethical behavior as defined by the organization.

coinsurance clause a part of a fire insurance policy that requires the policyholder to purchase coverage at least equal to a specified percentage of the replacement cost of the property to obtain full reimbursement for losses.

collateral real estate or property pledged as security for a loan.

collective bargaining the process of negotiating a labor contract with management.

command economy an economic system in which the government decides *what* goods and services will be produced, *how* they will be produced, *for whom* available goods and services will be produced, and *who* owns and controls the major factors of production.

commercial paper a short-term promissory note issued by a large corporation.

commission a payment that is a percentage of sales revenue.

common law the body of law created by court decisions rendered by judges; also known as case law or judicial law.

common stock stock owned by individuals or firms who may vote on corporate matters but whose claims on profits and assets are subordinate to the claims of others.

communication skills the ability to speak, listen, and write effectively.

community of interests a situation in which one firm buys the stock of a competing firm to reduce competition between the two.

community shopping center a planned shopping center that includes one or two department stores and some specialty stores, along with convenience stores.

comparable worth a concept that seeks equal compensation for jobs requiring about the same level of education, training, and skills.

comparative advantage the ability to produce a specific product more efficiently than any other product.

comparison discounting setting a price at a specific level and comparing it with a higher price.

compensation the payment employees receive in return for their labor.

compensation system the policies and strategies that determine employee compensation.

competition rivalry among businesses for sales to potential customers.

component part an item that becomes part of a physical product and is either a finished item ready for assembly or a product that needs little processing before assembly.

computer-aided design (CAD) the use of computers to aid in the development of products.

computer-aided manufacturing (CAM) the use of computers to plan and control manufacturing processes.

computer-integrated manufacturing (CIM) a computer system that not only helps to design products but also controls the machinery needed to produce the finished product.

conceptual skills the ability to think in abstract terms.

consideration the value or benefit that one party to a contract furnishes to the other party.

consumer buying behavior the purchasing of products for personal or household use, not for business purposes.

consumer price index (CPI) a monthly index that measures the changes in prices of a fixed basket of goods purchased by a typical consumer in an urban area.

consumer product a product purchased to satisfy personal and family needs.

consumer products goods and services purchased by individuals for personal consumption.

consumer sales promotion method a sales promotion method designed to attract consumers to particular retail stores and to motivate them to purchase certain new or established products.

consumerism all activities undertaken to protect the rights of consumers.

contingency plan a plan that outlines alternative courses of action that may be taken if an organization's other plans are disrupted or become ineffective.

continuous process a manufacturing process in which a firm produces the same product(s) over a long period of time.

contract a legally enforceable agreement between two or more competent parties who promise to do or not to do a particular thing.

controlling the process of evaluating and regulating ongoing activities to ensure that goals are achieved.

convenience product a relatively inexpensive, frequently purchased item for which buyers want to exert only minimal effort.

convenience store a small food store that sells a limited variety of products but remains open well beyond normal business hours.

convertible bond a bond that can be exchanged, at the owner's option, for a specified number of shares of the corporation's common stock.

cookie a small piece of software sent by a website that tracks an individual's Internet use.

cooperative advertising an arrangement whereby a manufacturer agrees to pay a certain amount of a retailer's media cost for advertising the manufacturer's products.

copyright the exclusive right to publish, perform, copy, or sell an original work.

core competencies approaches and processes that a company performs well that may give it an advantage over its competitors.

corporate bond a corporation's written pledge that it will repay a specified amount of money with interest.

corporate citizenship adopting a strategic approach to fulfilling economic, ethical, environmental, and social responsibilities.

corporate culture the inner rites, rituals, heroes, and values of a firm.

corporate officers the chairman of the board, president, executive vice presidents, corporate secretary, treasurer, and any other top executive appointed by the board of directors.

corporation an artificial person created by law with most of the legal rights of a real person, including the rights to start and operate a business, to buy or sell property, to borrow money, to sue or be sued, and to enter into binding contracts.

cost of goods sold the dollar amount equal to beginning inventory *plus* net purchases *less* ending inventory.

countertrade an international barter transaction.

coupon reduces the retail price of a particular item by a stated amount at the time of purchase.

court of limited jurisdiction a court that hears only specific types of cases.

court of original jurisdiction the first court to recognize and hear testimony in a legal action.

craft union an organization of skilled workers in a single craft or trade.

creative selling selling products to new customers and increasing sales to present customers.

crime a violation of a public law.

cross-functional team a team of individuals with varying specialties, expertise, and skills that are brought together to achieve a common task.

crowdfunding a method of raising money from a large group of people who donate small amounts of money using the Internet and social media.

crowdsourcing outsourcing tasks to a group of people in order to tap into the ideas of the crowd.

cultural (or workplace) diversity differences among people in a workforce owing to race, ethnicity, and gender.

currency devaluation the reduction of the value of a nation's currency relative to the currencies of other countries.

current assets assets that can be converted quickly into cash or that will be used in one year or less.

current liabilities debts that will be repaid in one year or less.

current ratio a financial ratio computed by dividing current assets by current liabilities.

customary pricing pricing on the basis of tradition.

customer lifetime value (CLV) a measure of a customer's worth (sales minus costs) to a business over one's lifetime.

customer relationship management (CRM) using information about customers to create marketing strategies that develop and sustain desirable customer relationships.

customs (or import) duty a tax on a foreign product entering a country.

D

damages a monetary settlement awarded to a party injured through a breach of contract.

data numerical or verbal descriptions that usually result from some sort of measurement.

data mining the practice of searching through data records looking for useful information.

data processing the transformation of data into a form that is useful for a specific purpose.

database a single collection of data and information stored in one place that can be used by people throughout an organization to make decisions.

debenture bond a bond backed only by the reputation of the issuing corporation.

debit card a card that electronically subtracts the amount of a customer's purchase from her or his bank account at the moment the purchase is made.

debt capital borrowed money obtained through loans of various types.

decentralized organization an organization in which management consciously attempts to spread authority widely in the lower levels of the organization.

decision making the act of choosing one alternative from a set of alternatives.

decision-support system (DSS) a type of software program that provides relevant data and information to help a firm's employees make decisions.

deed a written document by which the ownership of real property is transferred from one person or organization to another.

deflation a general decrease in the level of prices.

delegation assigning part of a manager's work and power to other workers.

demand the quantity of a product that buyers are willing to purchase at each of various prices.

department store a retail store that (1) employs 25 or more persons and (2) sells at least home furnishings, appliances, family apparel, and household linens and dry goods, each in a different part of the store.

departmentalization the process of grouping jobs into manageable units.

departmentalization by customer grouping activities according to the needs of various customer populations.

departmentalization by function grouping jobs that relate to the same organizational activity.

departmentalization by location grouping activities according to the defined geographic area in which they are performed.

departmentalization by product grouping activities related to a particular product or service.

depreciation the process of apportioning the cost of a fixed asset over the period during which it will be used.

depression a severe recession that lasts longer than a typical recession and has a larger decline in business activity when compared to a recession.

deregulation the process of removing existing government regulations, forgoing proposed regulations, or reducing the rate at which new regulations are enacted.

design planning the development of a plan for converting an idea into an actual product or service.

direct marketing the use of the telephone, Internet, and nonpersonal media to introduce products to customers, who then can purchase them via mail, telephone, or the Internet.

direct selling the marketing of products to customers through face-to-face sales presentations at home or in the workplace.

direct-response marketing a type of marketing in which a retailer advertises a product and makes it available through mail, telephone, or online orders.

directing the combined processes of leading and motivating.

discharge by mutual assent termination of a contract by mutual agreement of all parties.

discount a deduction from the price of an item.

discount store a self-service general-merchandise outlet that sells products at lower-than-usual prices.

discretionary income disposable income less savings and expenditures on food, clothing, and housing.

disposable income personal income *less* all additional personal taxes.

distribution channel (or marketing channel) a sequence of marketing organizations that directs a product from the producer to the ultimate user.

dividend a distribution of earnings to the stockholders of a corporation.

domestic corporation a corporation in the state in which it is incorporated.

domestic system a method of manufacturing in which an entrepreneur distributes raw materials to various homes, where families process them into finished goods to be offered for sale by the merchant entrepreneur.

double-entry bookkeeping system a system in which each financial transaction is recorded as two separate accounting entries to maintain the balance shown in the accounting equation.

draft issued by the exporter's bank, ordering the importer's bank to pay for the merchandise, thus guaranteeing payment once accepted by the importer's bank.

dumping exportation of large quantities of a product at a price lower than that of the same product in the home market.

E

e-business (or electronic business) the organized effort of individuals to produce and sell, for a profit, the goods and services that satisfy society's needs *through the facilities available on the Internet.*

economic community an organization of nations formed to promote the free movement of resources and products among its members and to create common economic policies.

economic model of social responsibility the view that society will benefit most when business is left alone to produce and market profitable products that society needs.

economics the study of how wealth is created and distributed.

economy the way in which people deal with the creation and distribution of wealth.

electronic funds transfer (EFT) system a means of performing financial transactions through a computer terminal.

embargo a complete halt to trading with a particular nation or in a particular product.

employee benefit a reward in addition to regular compensation that is provided indirectly to employees.

employee ownership a situation in which employees own the company they work for by virtue of being stockholders.

employee training the process of teaching operations and technical employees how to do their present jobs more effectively and efficiently.

empowerment making employees more involved in their jobs by increasing their participation in decision making.

endorsement the payee's signature on the back of a negotiable instrument.

endowment life insurance life insurance that provides protection and guarantees the payment of a stated amount to the policyholder after a specified number of years.

entrepreneur a person who risks time, effort, and money to start and operate a business.

entrepreneurial leadership personality-based leadership style in which the manager seeks to inspire workers with a vision of what can be accomplished to benefit all stakeholders.

Equal Employment Opportunity Commission (EEOC) a government agency with the power to investigate complaints of employment discrimination and the power to sue firms that practice it.

equity capital money received from the owners or from the sale of shares of ownership in a business.

equity theory a theory of motivation based on the premise that people are motivated to obtain and preserve equitable treatment for themselves.

esteem needs our need for respect, recognition, and a sense of our own accomplishment and worth.

ethics the study of right and wrong and of the morality of the choices individuals make.

everyday low prices (EDLPs) setting a low price for products on a consistent basis.

excise tax a tax on the manufacture or sale of a particular domestic product.

exclusive distribution the use of only a single retail outlet for a product in a large geographic area.

executive information system (EIS) a computer-based system that facilitates and supports the decision-making needs of top managers and senior executives by providing easy access to both internal and external information.

expectancy theory a model of motivation based on the assumption that motivation depends on how much we want something and on how likely we think we are to get it.

expense ratio all the different management fees, 12b-1 fees, and additional operating costs for a specific fund.

expert system a type of computer program that uses artificial intelligence to imitate a human's ability to think.

Export-Import Bank of the United States an independent agency of the U.S. government whose function is to assist in financing the exports of American firms.

exporting selling and shipping raw materials or products to other nations.

express warranty a written explanation of the responsibilities of the producer (or seller) in the event that a product is found to be defective or otherwise unsatisfactory.

extended coverage insurance protection against damage caused by wind, hail, explosion, vandalism, riots or civil commotion, falling aircraft, and smoke.

external recruiting the attempt to attract job applicants from outside an organization.

F

factor a firm that specializes in buying other firms' accounts receivable.

factors of production resources used to produce goods and services.

factory system a system of manufacturing in which all the materials, machinery, and workers required to manufacture a product are assembled in one place.

family branding the strategy in which a firm uses the same brand for all or most of its products.

family of funds a group of mutual funds managed by one investment company.

feature article a piece (of up to 3,000 words) prepared by an organization for inclusion in a particular publication.

federal deficit a shortfall created when the federal government spends more in a fiscal year than it receives.

Federal Trade Commission (FTC) a five-member committee charged with the responsibility of investigating illegal trade practices and enforcing antitrust laws.

fidelity bond an insurance policy that protects a business from theft, forgery, or embezzlement by its employees.

financial accounting generates financial statements and reports for interested people outside an organization.

financial leverage the use of borrowed funds to increase the return on owners' equity.

financial management all the activities concerned with obtaining money and using it effectively.

financial manager a manager who is primarily responsible for an organization's financial resources.

financial plan a plan for obtaining and using the money needed to implement an organization's goals and objectives.

financial planner an individual who has had at least two years of training in investments, insurance, taxation, retirement planning, and estate planning and has passed a rigorous examination.

financial ratio a number that shows the relationship between two elements of a firm's financial statements.

fire insurance insurance that covers losses due to fire.

first-line manager a manager who coordinates and supervises the activities of operating employees.

fiscal policy government influence on the amount of savings and expenditures; accomplished by altering the tax structure and by changing the levels of government spending.

fixed assets assets that will be held or used for a period longer than one year.

fixed cost a cost incurred no matter how many units of a product are produced or sold.

flexible benefit plan compensation plan whereby an employee receives a predetermined amount of benefit dollars to spend on a package of benefits he or she has selected to meet individual needs.

flexible manufacturing system (FMS) a single production system that combines electronic machines and CIM.

flextime a system in which employees set their own work hours within employer-determined limits.

foreign corporation a corporation in any state in which it does business except the one in which it is incorporated.

foreign-exchange control a restriction on the amount of a particular foreign currency that can be purchased or sold.

form utility utility created by people converting raw materials, finances, and information into finished products.

forum an interactive version of a community bulletin board that focuses on threaded discussions.

franchise a license to operate an individually owned business as though it were part of a chain of outlets or stores.

franchisee a person or organization purchasing a franchise.

franchising the actual granting of a franchise.

franchisor an individual or organization granting a franchise.

free enterprise the system of business in which individuals are free to decide what to produce, how to produce it, and at what price to sell it.

frequent-user incentive a program developed to reward customers who engage in repeat (frequent) purchases.

full disclosure requirement that investors should have access to all important facts about stocks, bonds, and other securities so that they can make informed decisions.

full-service wholesaler a middleman that performs the entire range of wholesaler functions.

functional middleman a middleman that helps in the transfer of ownership of products but does not take title to the products.

G

General Agreement on Tariffs and Trade (GATT) an international organization of 160 nations dedicated to reducing or eliminating tariffs and other barriers to world trade.

general partner a person who assumes full or shared responsibility for operating a business.

general-merchandise wholesaler a middleman that deals in a wide variety of products.

generally accepted accounting principles (GAAPs) an accepted set of guidelines and practices for U.S. companies reporting financial information and for the accounting profession.

generic product (or generic brand) a product with no brand at all.

goal an end result that an organization is expected to achieve over a one- to ten-year period.

goal-setting theory a theory of motivation suggesting that employees are motivated to achieve goals that they and their managers establish together.

grapevine the informal communications network within an organization.

green IT a term used to describe all of a firm's activities to support a healthy environment and sustain the planet.

green marketing the process of creating, making, delivering, and promoting products that are environmentally safe.

grievance procedure a formally established course of action for resolving employee complaints against management.

gross domestic product (GDP) the total dollar value of all goods and services produced by all people within the boundaries of a country during a one-year period.

gross profit a firm's net sales *less* the cost of goods sold.

gross sales the total dollar amount of all goods and services sold during the accounting period.

H

hard-core unemployed workers with little education or vocational training and a long history of unemployment.

hashtag a word or a short phrase preceded by the pound sign (#), to identify different topics.

health care insurance insurance that covers the cost of medical attention, including hospital care, physicians' and surgeons' fees, prescription medicines, and related services.

health maintenance organization (HMO) an insurance plan that directly employs or contracts with selected physicians and hospitals to provide health care services in exchange for a fixed, prepaid monthly premium.

high-risk investment an investment made in the uncertain hope of earning a relatively large profit in a short time.

hostile takeover a situation in which the management and board of directors of a firm targeted for acquisition disapprove of the merger.

hourly wage a specific amount of money paid for each hour of work.

human resources management (HRM) all the activities involved in acquiring, maintaining, and developing an organization's human resources.

human resources manager a person charged with managing an organization's human resources programs.

human resources planning the development of strategies to meet a firm's future human resources needs.

hygiene factors job factors that reduce dissatisfaction when present to an acceptable degree but that do not necessarily result in high levels of motivation.

I

implied warranty a guarantee imposed or required by law.

import duty (tariff) a tax levied on a particular foreign product entering a country.

import quota a limit on the amount of a particular good that may be imported into a country during a given period of time.

importing purchasing raw materials or products in other nations and bringing them into one's own country.

inbound marketing a marketing term that describes new ways of gaining attention and ultimately customers by creating content on a website that pulls customers in.

incentive payment a payment in addition to wages, salary, or commissions.

income statement a summary of a firm's revenues and expenses during a specified accounting period.

independent retailer a firm that operates only one retail outlet.

individual branding the strategy in which a firm uses a different brand for each of its products.

industrial union an organization of both skilled and unskilled workers in a single industry.

inflation a general rise in the level of prices.

informal group a group created by the members themselves to accomplish goals that may or may not be relevant to an organization.

informal organization the pattern of behavior and interaction that stems from personal rather than official relationships.

information data presented in a form that is useful for a specific purpose.

initial public offering (IPO) occurs when a corporation sells common stock to the general public for the first time.

injunction a court order requiring a person or group either to perform some act or to refrain from performing some act.

inland marine insurance insurance that protects against loss or damage to goods shipped by rail, truck, airplane, or inland barge.

insider trading the practice of board members, corporate managers, and employees buying and selling a corporation's stock.

inspection the examination of the quality of work-in-process.

institutional advertising advertising designed to enhance a firm's image or reputation.

insurable risk a risk that insurance companies will assume.

insurance the protection against loss that the purchase of an insurance policy affords.

insurance policy the contract between an insurer and the person or firm whose risk is assumed.

insurer (or insurance company) a firm that agrees, for a fee, to assume financial responsibility for losses that may result from a specific risk.

intangible assets assets that do not exist physically but that have a value based on the rights or privileges they confer on a firm.

integrated marketing communications coordination of promotion efforts to ensure maximal informational and persuasive impact on customers.

intensive distribution the use of all available outlets for a product.

interlocking directorate an arrangement in which members of the board of directors of one firm are also directors of a competing firm.

intermittent process a manufacturing process in which a firm's manufacturing machines and equipment are changed to produce different products.

internal recruiting considering present employees as applicants for available positions.

international business all business activities that involve exchanges across national boundaries.

International Monetary Fund (IMF) an international bank with 188 member nations that makes short-term loans to developing countries experiencing balance-of-payment deficits.

International Organization for Standardization (ISO) a network of national standards institutes and similar organizations from over 160 different countries that is charged with developing standards for quality products and services that are traded throughout the globe.

interpersonal skills the ability to deal effectively with other people.

inventory control the process of managing inventories in such a way as to minimize inventory costs, including both holding costs and potential stock-out costs.

inventory management the process of managing inventories in such a way as to minimize inventory costs, including both holding costs and potential stock-out costs.

inventory turnover a financial ratio calculated by dividing the cost of goods sold in one year by the average value of the inventory.

investment banking firm an organization that assists corporations in raising funds, usually by helping to sell new issues of stocks, bonds, or other financial securities.

invisible hand a term created by Adam Smith to describe how an individual's personal gain benefits others and a nation's economy.

involuntary bankruptcy a bankruptcy procedure initiated by creditors.

J

job analysis a systematic procedure for studying jobs to determine their various elements and requirements.

job description a list of the elements that make up a particular job.

job enlargement expanding a worker's assignments to include additional but similar tasks.

job enrichment a motivation technique that provides employees with more variety and responsibility in their jobs.

job evaluation the process of determining the relative worth of the various jobs within a firm.

job redesign a type of job enrichment in which work is restructured to cultivate the worker–job match.

job rotation the systematic shifting of employees from one job to another.

job security protection against the loss of employment.

job sharing an arrangement whereby two people share one full-time position.

job specialization the separation of all organizational activities into distinct tasks and the assignment of different tasks to different people.

job specification a list of the qualifications required to perform a particular job.

joint venture an agreement between two or more groups to form a business entity in order to achieve a specific goal or to operate for a specific period of time.

jurisdiction the right of a particular union to organize particular groups of workers.

just-in-time inventory (JIT) system a system designed to ensure that materials or supplies arrive at a facility just when they are needed so that storage and holding costs are minimized.

K

key performance indicators (KPIs) measurements that define and measure the progress of an organization toward achieving its objectives.

knowledge management (KM) a firm's procedures for generating, using, and sharing the data and information.

L

labeling the presentation of information on a product or its package.

labor union an organization of workers acting together to negotiate their wages and working conditions with employers.

labor-intensive technology a process in which people must do most of the work.

law a rule developed by a society to govern the conduct of and relationships among its members.

leadership the ability to influence others.

leading the process of influencing people to work toward a common goal.

lean manufacturing a concept built on the idea of eliminating waste from all of the activities required to produce a product or service.

lease an agreement by which the right to use real estate, equipment, or other assets is temporarily transferred from its owner to the user.

letter of credit a legal document issued by a bank or other financial institution guaranteeing to pay a seller a stated amount for a specified period of time.

liabilities a firm's debts and obligations.

licensing a contractual agreement in which one firm permits another to produce and market its product and use its brand name in return for a royalty or other compensation.

life insurance insurance that pays a stated amount of money on the death of the insured individual.

lifestyle shopping center an open-air-environment shopping center with upscale chain specialty stores.

limit order a request that a security be bought or sold at a price that is equal to or better than some specified price.

limited liability a feature of corporate ownership that limits each owner's financial liability to the amount of money that he or she has paid for the corporation's stock.

limited partner a person who invests money in a business but has no management responsibility or liability for losses beyond the amount he or she invested in the partnership.

limited-liability company (LLC) a form of business ownership that combines the benefits of a corporation and a partnership while avoiding some of the restrictions and disadvantages of those forms of ownership.

limited-line wholesaler a middleman that stocks only a few product lines but carries numerous product items within each line.

line extension development of a new product that is closely related to one or more products in the existing product line but designed specifically to meet somewhat different customer needs.

line managers a position in which a person makes decisions and gives orders to subordinates to achieve the organization's goals.

line of credit a loan that is approved before the money is actually needed.

line structure an organizational structure in which the chain of command goes directly from person to person throughout the organization.

line-and-staff structure an organizational structure that utilizes the chain of command from a line structure in combination with the assistance of staff managers.

liquidity the ease with which an investment can be converted into cash.

lockout a firm's refusal to allow employees to enter the workplace.

long-term financing money that will be used for longer than one year.

long-term liabilities debts that need not be repaid for at least one year.

lump-sum salary increase an entire pay raise taken in one lump sum.

M

macroeconomics the study of the national economy and the global economy.

maintenance shop a workplace in which an employee who joins the union must remain a union member as long as he or she is employed by the firm.

major equipment large tools and machines used for production purposes.

Malcolm Baldrige National Quality Award an award given by the President of the United States to organizations judged to be outstanding in specific managerial tasks that lead to improved quality for both products and services.

malware a general term that describes software designed to infiltrate a computer system without the user's consent.

management the process of coordinating people and other resources to achieve the goals of an organization.

management by objectives (MBO) a motivation technique in which managers and employees collaborate in setting goals.

management development the process of preparing managers and other professionals to assume increased responsibility in both present and future positions.

management information system (MIS) a system that provides managers and employees with the information they need to perform their jobs as effectively as possible.

managerial accounting provides managers and employees with the information needed to make decisions about a firm's financing, investing, marketing, and operating activities.

manufacturer (or producer) brand a brand that is owned by a manufacturer.

market a group of individuals or organizations, or both, that need products in a given category and that have the ability, willingness, and authority to purchase them.

market allocation an agreement to divide a market among potential competitors.

market economy an economic system in which businesses and individuals decide what to produce and buy, and the market determines quantities sold and prices.

market order a request that a security be purchased or sold at the current market price.

market price the price at which the quantity demanded is exactly equal to the quantity supplied.

market segment a group of individuals or organizations within a market that share one or more common characteristics.

market segmentation the process of dividing a market into segments and directing a marketing mix at a particular segment or segments rather than at the total market.

market value the price of one share of a stock at a particular time.

marketing the activity, set of institutions, and processes for creating, communicating, delivering, and exchanging offerings that have value for customers, clients, partners, and society at large.

marketing concept a business philosophy that a firm should provide goods and services that satisfy customers' needs through a coordinated set of activities that allow the firm to achieve its objectives.

marketing information system a system for managing marketing information that is gathered continually from internal and external sources.

marketing manager a manager who is responsible for facilitating the exchange of products between an organization and its customers or clients.

marketing mix a combination of product, price, distribution, and promotion developed to satisfy a particular target market.

marketing plan a written document that specifies an organization's resources, objectives, strategy, and implementation and control efforts to be used in marketing a specific product or product group.

marketing research the process of systematically gathering, recording, and analyzing data concerning a particular marketing problem.

marketing strategy a plan that will enable an organization to make the best use of its resources and advantages to meet its objectives.

markup the amount a seller adds to the cost of a product to determine its basic selling price.

Maslow's hierarchy of needs a sequence of human needs in the order of their importance.

mass production a manufacturing process that lowers the cost required to produce a large number of identical or similar products over a long period of time.

materials handling the actual physical handling of goods, in warehouses as well as during transportation.

materials requirements planning (MRP) a computerized system that integrates production planning and inventory control.

matrix structure an organizational structure that combines vertical and horizontal lines of authority, usually by superimposing product departmentalization on a functionally departmentalized organization.

maturity date the date on which a corporation is to repay borrowed money.

media sharing sites allow users to upload photos, videos, and podcasts.

mediation the use of a neutral third party to assist management and the union during their negotiations.

merchant middleman a middleman that actually takes title to products by buying them.

merchant wholesaler a middleman that purchases goods in large quantities and sells them to other wholesalers or retailers and to institutional, farm, government, professional, or industrial users.

merger the purchase of one corporation by another.

microeconomics the study of the decisions made by individuals and businesses.

middle manager a manager who implements the strategy and major policies developed by top management.

middleman (or marketing intermediary) a marketing organization that links a producer and user within a marketing channel.

Millennials tech-savvy digital natives born after 1980.

minority a racial, religious, political, national, or other group regarded as different from the larger group of which it is a part and that is often singled out for unfavorable treatment.

mission a statement of the basic purpose that makes an organization different from others.

missionary salesperson a salesperson—generally employed by a manufacturer—who visits retailers to persuade them to buy the manufacturer's products.

mixed economy an economy that exhibits elements of both capitalism and socialism.

mobile marketing communicating with and selling to customers through mobile devices.

monetary policies Federal Reserve's decisions that determine the size of the supply of money in the nation and the level of interest rates.

monopolistic competition a market situation in which there are many buyers along with a relatively large number of sellers who differentiate their products from the products of competitors.

monopoly a market (or industry) with only one seller, and there are barriers to keep other firms from entering the industry.

morale an employee's feelings about the job, about superiors, and about the firm itself.

mortgage bond a corporate bond secured by various assets of the issuing firm.

motivating the process of providing reasons for people to work in the best interests of an organization.

motivation the individual internal process that energizes, directs, and sustains behavior; the personal "force" that causes you or me to behave in a particular way.

motivation factors job factors that increase motivation, although their absence does not necessarily result in dissatisfaction.

motivation–hygiene theory the idea that satisfaction and dissatisfaction are separate and distinct dimensions.

multilateral development bank (MDB) an internationally supported bank that provides loans to developing countries to help them grow.

multinational enterprise a firm that operates on a worldwide scale without ties to any specific nation or region.

multiple-unit pricing the strategy of setting a single price for two or more units.

municipal bond sometimes called a muni, a debt security issued by a state or local government.

mutual fund a company that pools the money of many investors—its shareholders—to invest in a variety of different securities.

mutual insurance company an insurance company that is owned collectively by its policyholders and is thus a cooperative.

N

national debt the total of all federal deficits.

National Labor Relations Board (NLRB) the federal agency that enforces the provisions of the Wagner Act.

need a personal requirement.

negligence a failure to exercise reasonable care, resulting in injury to another.

negotiable instrument a written document that (1) is a promise to pay a stated sum of money and (2) can be transferred from one person or firm to another.

negotiated pricing establishing a final price through bargaining.

neighborhood shopping center a planned shopping center consisting of several small convenience and specialty stores.

net asset value (NAV) is equal to the current market value of a mutual fund's portfolio minus the mutual fund's liabilities divided by the number of outstanding shares.

net income occurs when revenues exceed expenses.

net loss occurs when expenses exceed revenues.

net sales the actual dollar amounts received by a firm for the goods and services it has sold after adjustment for returns, allowances, and discounts.

net worth is the difference between the value of your total assets and your total liabilities.

network structure an organizational structure in which administration is the primary function, and most other functions are contracted out to other firms.

news release a typed page of about 300 words provided by an organization to the media as a form of publicity.

no-fault auto insurance a method of paying for losses suffered in an automobile accident; enacted by state law, that requires that those suffering injury or loss be reimbursed by their own insurance companies, without regard to who was at fault in the accident.

non-price competition competition based on factors other than price.

nonstore retailing a type of retailing whereby consumers purchase products without visiting a store.

nontariff barrier a nontax measure imposed by a government to favor domestic over foreign suppliers.

not-for-profit corporation a corporation organized to provide a social, educational, religious, or other service rather than to earn a profit.

O

objective a specific statement detailing what an organization intends to accomplish over a shorter period of time.

ocean marine insurance insurance that protects the policyholder against loss or damage to a ship or its cargo on the high seas.

odd-number pricing the strategy of setting prices using odd numbers that are slightly below whole-dollar amounts.

off-price retailer a store that buys manufacturers' seconds, overruns, returns, and off-season merchandise for resale to consumers at deep discounts.

oligopoly a market (or industry) in which there are few sellers.

online retailing retailing that makes products available to buyers through computer connections.

open corporation a corporation whose stock can be bought and sold by any individual.

operating expenses all business costs other than the cost of goods sold.

operational plan a type of plan designed to implement tactical plans.

operations management all the activities required to produce goods and services.

operations manager a manager who manages the systems that convert resources into goods and services.

order getter a salesperson who is responsible for selling a firm's products to new customers and increasing sales to present customers.

order processing activities involved in receiving and filling customers' purchase orders.

order taker a salesperson who handles repeat sales in ways that maintain positive relationships with customers.

organization a group of two or more people working together to achieve a common set of goals.

organization chart a diagram that represents the positions and relationships within an organization.

organizational height the number of layers, or levels, of management in a firm.

organizing the grouping of resources and activities to accomplish some end result in an efficient and effective manner.

orientation the process of acquainting new employees with an organization.

outsourcing the process of finding outside vendors and suppliers that provide professional help, parts, or materials at a lower cost.

over-the-counter (OTC) market a network of dealers who buy and sell the stocks of corporations that are not listed on a securities exchange.

overtime time worked in excess of 40 hours in one week (under some union contracts, time worked in excess of eight hours in a single day).

owners' equity the difference between a firm's assets and its liabilities.

P

packaging all the activities involved in developing and providing a container with graphics for a product.

part-time work permanent employment in which individuals work less than a standard work week.

participative leadership leadership style in which all members of a team are involved in identifying essential goals and developing strategies to reach those goals.

partnership a voluntary association of two or more persons to act as co-owners of a business for profit.

patent the exclusive right to make, use, or sell a newly invented product or process.

penetration pricing the strategy of setting a low price for a new product.

perfect (or pure) competition the market situation in which there are many buyers and sellers of a product, and no single buyer or seller is powerful enough to affect the price of that product.

performance the fulfillment of all obligations by all parties to the contract.

performance appraisal the evaluation of employees' current and potential levels of performance to allow managers to make objective human resources decisions.

periodic discounting temporary reduction of prices on a patterned or systematic basis.

personal budget a specific plan for spending your income.

personal income the income an individual receives from all sources *less* the Social Security taxes the individual must pay.

personal property all property other than real property.

personal selling personal communication aimed at informing customers and persuading them to buy a firm's products.

physical distribution all those activities concerned with the efficient movement of products from the producer to the ultimate user.

physiological needs the things we require for survival.

picketing marching back and forth in front of a place of employment with signs informing the public that a strike is in progress.

piece-rate system a compensation system under which employees are paid a certain amount for each unit of output they produce.

place utility utility created by making a product available at a location where customers wish to purchase it.

plagiarism knowingly taking someone else's words, ideas, or other original material without acknowledging the source.

plan an outline of the actions by which an organization intends to accomplish its goals and objectives.

planning establishing organizational goals and deciding how to accomplish them.

planning horizon the period during which an operational plan will be in effect.

plant layout the arrangement of machinery, equipment, and personnel within a production facility.

podcasts digital audio or video flies that people listen to or watch online on tablets, computers, MP3 players, or smartphones.

point-of-purchase display promotional material placed within a retail store.

pollution the contamination of water, air, or land through the actions of people in an industrialized society.

possession utility utility created by transferring title (or ownership) of a product to a buyer.

power of attorney a legal document that serves as evidence that an agent has been appointed to act on behalf of a principal.

preferred provider organizations (PPOs) an insurance plan that offers the services of doctors and hospitals at discount rates or gives breaks in copayments and deductibles.

preferred stock stock owned by individuals or firms who usually do not have voting rights but whose claims on dividends are paid before those of common-stock owners.

premium a gift that a producer offers a customer in return for buying its product.

premium the fee charged by an insurance company.

premium pricing pricing the highest-quality or most-versatile products higher than other models in the product line.

press conference a meeting at which invited media personnel hear important news announcements and receive supplementary textual materials and photographs.

price the amount of money a seller is willing to accept in exchange for a product at a given time and under given circumstances.

price competition an emphasis on setting a price equal to or lower than competitors' prices to gain sales or market share.

price discrimination the practice in which producers and wholesalers charge larger firms a lower price for goods than they charge smaller firms.

price fixing an agreement between two businesses about the prices to be charged for goods.

price leaders products priced below the usual markup, near cost, or below cost.

price lining the strategy of selling goods only at certain predetermined prices that reflect definite price breaks.

price skimming the strategy of charging the highest possible price for a product during the introduction stage of its life-cycle.

primary market a market in which an investor purchases financial securities (via an investment bank) directly from the issuer of those securities.

primary-demand advertising advertising whose purpose is to increase the demand for *all* brands of a product within a specific industry.

prime interest rate the lowest rate charged by a bank for a short-term loan.

principle of indemnity in the event of a loss, an insured firm or individual cannot collect from the insurer an amount greater than the actual dollar amount of the loss.

private law the body of law that governs the relationships between two or more individuals or businesses.

private placement occurs when stock and other corporate securities are sold directly to insurance companies, pension funds, or large institutional investors.

problem the discrepancy between an actual condition and a desired condition.

problem-solving team a team of knowledgeable employees brought together to tackle a specific problem.

process material a material that is used directly in the production of another product but is not readily identifiable in the finished product.

producer price index (PPI) an index that measures prices that producers receive for their finished goods.

product everything one receives in an exchange, including all tangible and intangible attributes and expected benefits; it may be a good, a service, or an idea.

product deletion the elimination of one or more products from a product line.

product design the process of creating a set of specifications from which a product can be produced.

product differentiation the process of developing and promoting differences between one's products and all competitive products.

product liability insurance insurance that protects the policyholder from financial losses due to injuries suffered by others as a result of using the policyholder's products.

product life-cycle a series of stages in which a product's sales revenue and profit increase, reach a peak, and then decline.

product line a group of similar products that differ only in relatively minor characteristics.

product mix all the products a firm offers for sale.

product modification the process of changing one or more of a product's characteristics.

productivity the average level of output per worker per hour.

profit what remains after all business expenses have been deducted from sales revenue.

profit-sharing the distribution of a percentage of a firm's profit among its employees.

progressive tax a tax that requires the payment of an increasing proportion of income as the individual's income increases.

promissory note a written pledge by a borrower to pay a certain sum of money to a creditor at a specified future date.

promotion communication about an organization and its products that is intended to inform, persuade, or remind target-market members.

promotion mix the particular combination of promotion methods a firm uses to reach a target market.

property anything that can be owned.

proportional tax a tax whose percentage rate remains constant as the tax base increases.

prospectus a detailed, written description of a new security, the issuing corporation, and the corporation's top management.

proxy a legal form listing issues to be decided at a stockholders' meeting and enabling stockholders to transfer their voting rights to some other individual or individuals.

proxy fight a technique used to gather enough stockholder votes to control a targeted company.

public law the body of law that deals with the relationships between individuals or businesses and society.

public liability insurance insurance that protects the policyholder from financial losses due to injuries suffered by others as a result of negligence on the part of a business owner or employee.

public relations communication activities used to create and maintain favorable relationships between an organization and various public groups, both internal and external.

publicity communication in news-story form about an organization, its products, or both.

purchasing all the activities involved in obtaining required materials, supplies, components, and parts from other firms.

pure risk a risk that involves only the possibility of loss, with no potential for gain.

Q

qualitative social media measurement the process of accessing the opinions and beliefs about a brand and primarily uses sentiment analysis to categorize what is being said about a company.

quality circle a team of employees who meet on company time to solve problems of product quality.

quality control the process of ensuring that goods and services are produced in accordance with design specifications.

quantitative social media measurement using numerical measurements, such as counting the number of website visitors, number of fans and followers, number of leads generated, and the number of new customers.

R

random discounting temporary reduction of prices on an unsystematic basis.

ratification approval of a labor contract by a vote of the union membership.

raw material a basic material that actually becomes part of a physical product; usually comes from mines, forests, oceans, or recycled solid wastes.

real property land and anything permanently attached to it.

rebate a return of part of the purchase price of a product.

recession two or more consecutive three-month periods of decline in a country's GDP.

recruiting the process of attracting qualified job applicants.

recycling converting used materials into new products or components for new products in order to prevent their unnecessary disposal.

reference pricing pricing a product at a moderate level and positioning it next to a more expensive model or brand.

regional shopping center a planned shopping center containing large department stores, numerous specialty stores, restaurants, movie theaters, and sometimes even hotels.

registered bond a bond registered in the owner's name by the issuing company.

regressive tax a tax that takes a greater percentage of a lower income than of a higher income.

reinforcement theory a theory of motivation based on the premise that rewarded behavior is likely to be repeated, whereas punished behavior is less likely to recur.

relationship marketing establishing long-term, mutually satisfying buyer–seller relationships.

replacement chart a list of key personnel and their possible replacements within a firm.

research and development (R&D) a set of activities intended to identify new ideas that have the potential to result in new goods and services.

reshoring a situation in which U.S. manufacturers bring manufacturing jobs back to the United States.

responsibility the duty to do a job or perform a task.

retailer a middleman that buys from producers or other middlemen and sells to consumers.

retained earnings the portion of a business's profits not distributed to stockholders.

return on sales (or profit margin) a financial ratio calculated by dividing net income after taxes by net sales.

revenue stream a source of revenue flowing into a firm.

revenues the dollar amounts earned by a firm from selling goods, providing services, or performing business activities.

revolving credit agreement a guaranteed line of credit.

risk the possibility that a loss or injury will occur.

risk management the process of evaluating the risks faced by a firm or an individual and then minimizing the costs involved with those risks.

risk–return ratio a ratio based on the principle that a high-risk decision should generate higher financial returns for a business and more conservative decisions often generate lower returns.

robotics the use of programmable machines to perform a variety of tasks by manipulating materials and tools.

S

S corporation a corporation that is taxed as though it were a partnership.

safety needs the things we require for physical and emotional security.

salary a specific amount of money paid for an employee's work during a set calendar period, regardless of the actual number of hours worked.

sales agreement a type of contract by which ownership is transferred from a seller to a buyer.

sales forecast an estimate of the amount of a product that an organization expects to sell during a certain period of time based on a specified level of marketing effort.

sales promotion the use of activities or materials as direct inducements to customers or salespersons.

sales support personnel employees who aid in selling but are more involved in locating prospects, educating customers, building goodwill for the firm, and providing follow-up service.

sample a free product given to customers to encourage trial and purchase.

Sarbanes-Oxley Act of 2002 provides sweeping new legal protection for employees who report corporate misconduct.

scheduling the process of ensuring that materials and other resources are at the right place at the right time.

scientific management the application of scientific principles to management of work and workers.

secondary market a market for existing financial securities that are traded between investors.

secondary-market pricing setting one price for the primary target market and a different price for another market.

securities exchange a marketplace where member brokers meet to buy and sell securities.

selection the process of gathering information about applicants for a position and then using that information to choose the most appropriate applicant.

selective distribution the use of only a portion of the available outlets for a product in each geographic area.

selective-demand (or brand) advertising advertising that is used to sell a particular brand of product.

self-actualization needs the need to grow and develop and to become all that we are capable of being.

self-insurance the process of establishing a monetary fund that can be used to cover the cost of a loss.

self-managed teams groups of employees with the authority and skills to manage themselves.

seniority the length of time an employee has worked for an organization.

sentiment analysis a measurement that uses technology to detect the mood, attitudes, or emotions of people who experience a social media activity.

serial bonds bonds of a single issue that mature on different dates.

Service Corps of Retired Executives (SCORE) a group of businesspeople who volunteer their services to small businesses through the SBA.

service economy an economy in which more effort is devoted to the production of services than to the production of goods.

shop steward an employee elected by union members to serve as their representative.

shopping product an item for which buyers are willing to expend considerable effort on planning and making the purchase.

short-term financing money that will be used for one year or less.

sinking fund a sum of money to which deposits are made each year for the purpose of redeeming a bond issue.

Six Sigma a disciplined approach that relies on statistical data and improved methods to eliminate defects for a firm's products and services.

skills inventory a computerized data bank containing information on the skills and experience of all present employees.

slowdown a technique whereby workers report to their jobs but work at a slower pace than normal.

small business one that is independently owned and operated for profit and is not dominant in its field.

Small Business Administration (SBA) a governmental agency that assists, counsels, and protects the interests of small businesses in the United States.

small-business development centers (SBDCs) university-based groups that provide individual counseling and practical training to owners of small businesses.

small-business institutes (SBIs) groups of senior and graduate students in business administration who provide management counseling to small businesses.

small-business investment companies (SBICs) privately owned firms that provide venture capital to small enterprises that meet their investment standards.

social audit a comprehensive report of what an organization has done and is doing with regard to social issues that affect it.

social content sites allow companies to create and share information about their products and services.

social game a multiplayer, competitive, goal-oriented activity with defined rules of engagement and online connectivity among a community of players.

social media the online interactions that allow people and businesses to communicate and share ideas, personal information, and information about products and services.

social media communities social networks based on the relationships among people.

social media marketing the utilization of social media technologies, channels, and software to create, communicate, deliver, and exchange offerings that have value for an organization.

social needs the human requirements for love and affection and a sense of belonging.

social responsibility the recognition that business activities have an impact on society and the consideration of that impact in business decision making.

socioeconomic model of social responsibility the concept that business should emphasize not only profits but also the impact of its decisions on society.

sole proprietorship a business that is owned (and usually operated) by one person.

span of management (or span of control) the number of workers who report directly to one manager.

special-event pricing advertised sales or price cutting linked to a holiday, season, or event.

specialization the separation of a manufacturing process into distinct tasks and the assignment of the different tasks to different individuals.

specialty product an item that possesses one or more unique characteristics for which a significant group of buyers is willing to expend considerable purchasing effort.

specialty-line wholesaler a middleman that carries a select group of products within a single line.

specific performance the legal requirement that the parties to a contract fulfill their obligations according to the contract.

speculative production the time lag between the actual production of goods and when the goods are sold.

speculative risk a risk that accompanies the possibility of earning a profit.

staff managers a position created to provide support, advice, and expertise within an organization.

stakeholders all the different people or groups of people who are affected by an organization's policies, decisions, and activities.

standard of living a loose, subjective measure of how well off an individual or a society is, mainly in terms of want satisfaction through goods and services.

standing committee a relatively permanent committee charged with performing some recurring task.

statement of cash flows a statement that illustrates how the company's operating, investing, and financing activities affect cash during an accounting period.

statistic a measure that summarizes a particular characteristic of an entire group of numbers.

statute a law passed by the U.S. Congress, a state legislature, or a local government.

statutory law all the laws that have been enacted by legislative bodies.

stock the shares of ownership of a corporation.

stock dividend a dividend in the form of additional stock.

stock insurance company an insurance company owned by stockholders and operated to earn a profit.

stock split the division of each outstanding share of a corporation's stock into a greater number of shares.

stockholder a person who owns a corporation's stock.

store (or private) brand a brand that is owned by an individual wholesaler or retailer.

strategic alliance a partnership formed to create competitive advantage on a worldwide basis.

strategic plan an organization's broadest plan, developed as a guide for major policy setting and decision making.

strategic planning process the establishment of an organization's major goals and objectives and the allocation of resources to achieve them.

strike a temporary work stoppage by employees, calculated to add force to their demands.

strikebreaker a non-union employee who performs the job of a striking union member.

supermarket a large self-service store that sells primarily food and household products.

superstore a large retail store that carries not only food and nonfood products ordinarily found in supermarkets but also additional product lines.

supply an item that facilitates production and operations but does not become part of a finished product.

supply the quantity of a product that producers are willing to sell at each of various prices.

supply-chain management long-term partnership among channel members working together to create a distribution system that reduces inefficiencies, costs, and redundancies while creating a competitive advantage and satisfying customers.

sustainability creates and maintains the conditions under which humans and nature can exist in productive harmony, that permit fulfilling the social, economic, and other requirements of present and future generations.

SWOT analysis the identification and evaluation of a firm's strengths, weaknesses, opportunities, and threats.

syndicate a temporary association of individuals or firms organized to perform a specific task that requires a large amount of capital.

synthetic process a process in operations management in which raw materials or components are combined to create a finished product.

T

tactical plan a smaller scale plan developed to implement a strategy.

target market a group of individuals or organizations, or both, for which a firm develops and maintains a marketing mix suitable for the specific needs and preferences of that group.

task force a committee established to investigate a major problem or pending decision.

team two or more workers operating as a coordinated unit to accomplish a specific task or goal.

technical salesperson a salesperson who assists a company's current customers in technical matters.

technical skills specific skills needed to accomplish a specialized activity.

telecommuting working at home all the time or for a portion of the work week.

telemarketing the performance of marketing-related activities by telephone.

television home shopping a form of selling in which products are presented to television viewers, who can buy them by calling a toll-free number and paying with a credit card.

tender offer an offer to purchase the stock of a firm targeted for acquisition at a price just high enough to tempt stockholders to sell their shares.

term life insurance life insurance that provides protection to beneficiaries for a stated period of time.

term-loan agreement a promissory note that requires a borrower to repay a loan in monthly, quarterly, semiannual, or annual installments.

Theory X a concept of employee motivation generally consistent with Taylor's scientific management; assumes that employees dislike work and will function only in a highly controlled work environment.

Theory Y a concept of employee motivation generally consistent with the ideas of the human relations movement; assumes responsibility and work toward organizational goals, and by doing so they also achieve personal rewards.

Theory Z the belief that some middle ground between type A and type J practices is best for American business.

time utility utility created by making a product available when customers wish to purchase it.

top manager an upper-level executive who guides and controls the overall fortunes of an organization.

tort a violation of a private law.

total cost the sum of the fixed costs and the variable costs attributed to a product.

total quality management (TQM) the coordination of efforts directed at improving customer satisfaction, increasing employee participation, strengthening supplier partnerships, and facilitating an organizational atmosphere of continuous quality improvement.

total revenue the total amount received from the sales of a product.

trade credit a type of short-term financing extended by a seller who does not require immediate payment after delivery of merchandise.

trade deficit a negative balance of trade.

trade name the complete and legal name of an organization.

trade sales promotion method a sales promotion method designed to encourage wholesalers and retailers to stock and actively promote a manufacturer's product.

trade salesperson a salesperson—generally employed by a food producer or processor—who assists customers in promoting products, especially in retail stores.

trade show an industry-wide exhibit at which many sellers display their products.

trademark a brand name or brand mark that is registered with the U.S. Patent and Trademark Office and thus is legally protected from use by anyone except its owner.

trading company provides a link between buyers and sellers in different countries.

traditional specialty store a store that carries a narrow product mix with deep product lines.

transfer pricing prices charged in sales between an organization's units.

transportation the shipment of products to customers.

trust a business combination created when one firm obtains control of an entire industry and can set prices and manipulate trade to suit its own interest.

trustee an individual or an independent firm that acts as a bond owner's representative.

tying agreement a contract that forces an intermediary to purchase unwanted products along with the products it actually wants to buy.

U

undifferentiated approach directing a single marketing mix at the entire market for a particular product.

unemployment rate the percentage of a nation's labor force unemployed at any time.

Uniform Commercial Code (UCC) a set of laws designed to eliminate differences among state regulations affecting business and to simplify interstate commerce.

uninsurable risk a risk that insurance companies will not assume.

union security protection of the union's position as the employees' bargaining agent.

union shop a workplace in which new employees must join the union after a specified probationary period.

union–management relations (or labor relations) the dealings between labor unions and business management both in the bargaining process and beyond it.

universal life insurance life insurance that combines insurance protection with an investment plan that offers a potentially greater return than that guaranteed by a whole life insurance policy.

unlimited liability a legal concept that holds a business owner personally responsible for all the debts of the business.

unsecured financing financing that is not backed by collateral.

usury the practice of charging interest in excess of the maximum legal rate.

utility the ability of a good or service to satisfy a human need.

V

variable cost a cost that depends on the number of units produced.

venture capital money that is invested in small (and sometimes struggling) firms that have the potential to become very successful.

virtual team a team consisting of members who are geographically dispersed but communicate electronically.

voluntary agreement a contract requirement consisting of an offer by one party to enter into a contract with a second party and acceptance by the second party of all the terms and conditions of the offer.

voluntary bankruptcy a bankruptcy procedure initiated by an individual or business that can no longer meet its financial obligations.

W

wage survey a collection of data on prevailing wage rates within an industry or a geographic area.

warehouse club a large-scale members-only establishment that combines features of cash-and-carry wholesaling with discount retailing.

warehouse showroom a retail facility in a large, low-cost building with a large on-premises inventory and minimal service.

warehousing the set of activities involved in receiving and storing goods and preparing them for reshipment.

whistle-blowing informing the press or government officials about unethical practices within one's organization.

whole life insurance life insurance that provides both protection and savings.

wholesaler a middleman that sells products to other firms.

wiki a collaborative online working space that enables members to contribute content that can be shared with other people.

wildcat strike a strike not approved by the strikers' union.

workers' compensation insurance insurance that covers medical expenses and provides salary continuation for employees who are injured while at work.

World Trade Organization (WTO) powerful successor to GATT that incorporates trade in goods, services, and ideas.

Z

zero-base budgeting a budgeting approach in which every expense in every budget must be justified.

Name Index

A

AAMCO Transmissions, 150
Abercrombie & Fitch, 40
Accenture, 413
Accion, 338
Adelphia, 42
Advanced Cast Stone, Inc., 216
Advertising Age, 320
Aerion Corporation, 338
Aetna, 204
African Development Bank (AFDB), 92–93
Airware, 176
Alcoa, 204
Alibaba, 119–120, 467, 483
Altuzarra, Joseph, 311
Amazon, 167, 293, 330, 340, 363, 365, 369, 407, 420, 423, 434
Amazon Web Services (AWS), 434
America Online (AOL), 150, 403
American Airlines, 126, 477
American Eagle, 388
American Electric Power, 472
American Express, 5, 230
American Heart Association, 403
American Institute of CPAs (AICPA), 449
American Marketing Association, 305
Amethyst Jeans, 388
Amway, 363, 372
Angry Birds, 407
Annie's Homegrown, 106
Anthem, 425
Anthony, Carmelo, 474
Anytime Fitness, 151
Apple Computer, Inc., 50, 94, 115, 118, 135, 140, 150, 214, 260, 286, 334, 338, 340, 342–343, 403, 485
Archer Daniels Midland Company (ADM), 76
Ariel, 335
Armstrong, Waymon, 141
Arthur Anderson, 42
Asian Development Bank (ADB), 92
Association of Southeast Asian Nations, 89
At Home Group, 176–177

AT&T, 39–40, 226–227, 230, 380, 424
Audi, 218
Autonomy Software, 446
Avis, 151
Avon Products, 95, 363–364, 372

B

B Lab, 115
Bajic, Elena, 202
Bank of America, 404, 450
Bank Rhode Island, 493
Barclays, 204
Bark & Co., 133
Barnes & Noble, 287, 340
Baskin-Robbins, 155
Bates, Timothy, 153
Bath and Body Works, 371
Baumgartner, Felix, 389
Bayer, 313
Bazaarvoice, 407
Bebo, 403
Ben & Jerry's, 396–397
Bergeron, Melanie, 158
Berkowitz, John, 138
Berkshire Hathaway, 119, 126, 474
Bernie Madoff Investment Securities, 446
Berry Plastics, 225–226
Best Buy, 170, 371, 469, 478
Bethlehem Steel, 274–275
Bezos, Jeff, 293–294
Bird, Lee, 176–177
Birtcher, Goodman, 193
BitTorrent, 423
Black & Decker, 214
Black Hills, Corp., 247
BlackBerry, 170
Blink, David, 299, 495
Blogger, 403
Blu eCigs, 322
BlueKai, 126
BMW, 122–123, 343
Boeing Company, 62–63, 71, 78, 224, 229, 450, 481
Bono, 474
Borzacchiello, Maureen, 140
Bostic, Jim, 149
Boston Beer Company, 338
Boston Consulting Group, 274

Box, Inc., 125
Box Brands, 373
Brand House, 363
Branson, Richard, 173
Brinker International, 217
Brockers, Michael, 487
Bruce Miller Nurseries, 471
BucketFeet, 339
Budweiser, 405
Buffett, Warren, 119, 126
Burberry, 410
Burch, Sharon, 146
Bureau of Labor Statistics, 469
Burger King Corporation, 154–155
Burlington Coat Factory, 371
Burpee, 372
Bush, George W., 69–70

C

Caesars Entertainment, 62–63
California Milk Processor Board, 379
Callaway Golf, 471
Camp Bow Wow, 185
Campbell, Marty, 450–451, 453–454
Campbell Soup Company, 220, 336–337, 345
Capital One, 404
Carl's Jr., 154–155
Carnegie, Andrew, 196
Caterpillar, 214
Cengage Learning, 341
Centers for Disease Control and Prevention (CDC), 30, 434
Central American Free Trade Agreement (CAFTA), 89
Century 21, 154
Cereal Partners Worldwide, 124
Chanel, 342, 360
Charles Schwab, 485
Chase Bank, 338, 477
Chipotle Mexican Grill, 40, 61, 154
Chobani, 238
Choi, Roy, 370
Chrysler, 26, 422
Circle K, 370
Cisco Systems, 176, 233, 468, 485
Citibank, 404

Citicorp, 193
Claman, Priscilla, 138
Classmates.com, 403
CleanPath, 345
Clinton, Bill, 52
Clorox, 458
CNN, 420
Coca-Cola, 49, 53, 55, 61, 121, 151, 260, 314, 340, 343, 349, 382, 394, 415–416, 474
Coffee Club, 39
Coldwell Banker, 217
Colgate-Palmolive, 49, 77, 340, 458
Columbia Pictures Entertainment, Inc., 77
Combustion Associates of Corona, California, 69
Comcast, 380
Commodore Appliances, 464
Compaq Computer, 150
Conniff, Ben, 429–430
Consumer Product Safety Commission, 51
Container Store, 171–172, 253, 269–270, 436
Contreras-Sweet, Maria, 142, 147
Coppinger, Jake, 419
Costco, 150, 369, 371, 387
Craftsman, 341
Craigslist, 429
Crate & Barrel, 253
Creative Display Solutions, 140
Credit Suisse, 125
Ctrip, 289
Cuya, Juan Alejandro Rodriguez, 39
CVS Caremark, 55, 181, 316, 369
Cypress Springs Plastics, 487–488

D

D&B (Dun & Bradstreet), 320, 459, 477
Dairy Queen, 150
D'Aloisio, Nick, 8
Daum, Kevin, 290
Davey Tree Expert Company, 290
Davis, Vernon, 487

DeGeneres, Ellen, 404
Delicious, 403
Dell, Michael, 410
Dell Computer, 235, 344, 410, 421, 436
Deloitte Touche Tohmatsu, 449
Denman, George, 397
Denny's Inc., 151
Detroit Bikes, 211, 221–222
Diamond Foods, 446–447, 464
Dick's Sporting Goods, 363
Digg, 403
Discount Tire, 480
Dole Food Company, 434
Dollar General, 363
The Domain, 373
Domino's Pizza, 409–410
Doritos, 412
Dow Chemical Company, 78
Downey, Jonathan, 176
DPR Construction, 274
Dr. Pepper Company, 151, 342
DuBois, Kathleen, 149
Dudley, Joe, 4–5
Dunkin' Donuts, 154–155
DuPont, 30
Duracell, 126, 474

E

Easterbrook, Steve, 200
Eastman Kodak, 147
Eating Well magazine, 180
eBay, 293, 407, 420, 423, 484
Edward Jones, 274
Ellison, Larry, 125
Encyclopaedia Britannica, 337
Enel SpA, 483
Enron, 42
Entrepreneur magazine, 109
Environmental Protection
    Agency (EPA), 31, 59–60
Epinions, 403
Equal Employment Opportunity
    Commission (EEOC), 56, 266
Ernst & Young, 287, 449
Ethan Allen, 480
Etsy, 406
European Bank for
    Reconstruction and
    Development, 93
Export-Import Bank of the
    United States (Ex-Im Bank), 91–92
ExxonMobil, 191, 341, 446

F

Facebook, 5, 30, 99, 109, 126,
    130, 133, 135, 253–254,
    305, 316, 319–320, 326,
    342–343, 359, 388–389,
    397, 401–404, 408–412,
    414–415, 423–424, 430,
    437, 483, 485, 495
Fantex, 487

FarmVille, 407, 486
Febreze, 335
Federal Communications
    Commission (FCC), 372, 383
Federal Express, 150
Federal Reserve, 22
Federal Trade Commission
    (FTC), 39–41, 53, 61, 355,
    372, 383
FedEx, 225, 389
Financial Accounting Standards
    Board (FASB), 446, 456
Fine Living Channel, 396–397
Firestein, Aaron, 339
Fish Flops, 26
Flickr, 403
Fogarty, Helena, 359–360
Food and Drug Administration
    (FDA), 51, 322, 383, 434
Food Network, 396
Foot Locker, 371
Ford, Gerald, 52
Ford Motor Company, 15, 26,
    58, 76, 140, 192, 194,
    212, 214, 218, 230, 235,
    340, 380, 413, 417, 422,
    435–436
Forrester Research, Inc., 423
Fortune magazine, 266, 270,
    273–274
Foursquare, 403, 429–430
Friedman, Thomas L., 70
Friendster, 403
Frito Lay, 106, 337, 412
Fruit Guys, 297
FunBug, 105

G

Gabhawala, Rekha, 154
Gamble, James, 114
Ganahl, Heidi, 185
Gap, 371
Gatorade, 336
Genentech, 274
General Agreement on Tariffs
    and Trade (GATT), 86–87
General Electric (GE), 69, 115,
    147, 201, 214–216, 230,
    247, 343, 411–413, 439,
    486, 488
General Mills, 12, 106, 124, 204,
    336
General Motors (GM), 19, 26, 30,
    77, 142, 165, 218, 223, 235,
    380, 409, 422, 483
General Nutrition Centers (GNC),
    150
Gerber, 39–40
Gibson, Earnest III, 39
Gifford, Kathie Lee, 430
Gillette, 335, 341
Glad Products Company, 215
Gmail, 403
Goffee, Rob, 203
Gold Star Appliances, 477

GoldieBlox, 330
Goldman, Seth, 393–394
Goldman Sachs, 338, 467
Goodrich, Ben, 82
Google, 218, 274, 285, 343, 403,
    423, 434, 436
Google Glass, 337
Google+, 253, 403, 408,
    410–411, 424
Google Ventures, 293
GoPro, 105–106
gotomeeting.com, 255
Government Accountability
    Office (GAO), 82
Graeter, Chip, 98, 160, 240, 396,
    495
Graeter, Louis Charles, 98, 160
Graeter, Regina, 98, 160
Graeter, Richard II, 98, 160, 240,
    299–300, 396–397, 495–496
Graeter, Robert (Bob), 98–99,
    160, 240, 495
Graeter's Ice Cream, 9, 98–99,
    160–161, 240–241, 299–
    300, 396–397, 495–496
Great Clips, 155
Griswold, Daniel T., 72
Groupon, 351, 407, 464
Gruma SA, 76
Gucci, 311
Gutter Helmet of New England,
    493

H

H&M, 61, 168
H&R Block, 150
Häagen-Dazs, 396
Habitat for Humanity, 123
Halliburton, 42
Halogen Software, 249
Halvorsen, Elizabeth, 147
Hampton Hotels, 151
Hansen, Michael, 419
Hard Rock Cafe, 222
Hard Rock Hotel & Casino, 57
Harley Davidson, 228
Harmon, Josh, 44–45
Harpoon Brewery, 290
Harrington, Emily, 148
Harrods, 369
Harvard Business School, 307
Hastings, Reed, 245
HauteLiving.com, 430
Headsets.com, 315
H-E-B, 370–371
Heinz, 335, 342, 345
Hendricks, Brian, 139
Hershey Company, 450
Herzberg, Frederick, 277–279
Hewlett-Packard (HP), 49, 167,
    230, 335, 436
Hi5, 403
Hickory White, 228
HiLine Electric Co., 266
Hilton Hotels, 47
Hines, John, 150

Hispanic PR Wire, 119
History Channel, 397
Hochberg, Fred P., 91
Holden, Jeff, 429
Holden, Luke, 429–430
Home Depot, 24, 190, 369, 371,
    406, 413, 425, 450, 464,
    469
Home Shopping Network (HSN),
    373
Honda, 26, 214, 341, 407, 420
Honest Tea, 393–394
Honeywell, 230
Hoover's, Inc., 420–421, 459
Hormel Foods Corporation, 259
HubSpot, 411
Hufbauer, Gary, 82
The Human Side of Enterprise
    (McGregor), 279
Hung, David, 179
Hyundai, 76

I

Iams, 344
IBM, 147, 190, 230, 343–344,
    413, 441, 463
Iger, Bob, 165
IKEA, 61, 315, 370, 373
Imahara, Grant, 390
Inc. magazine, 109
Indeed.com, 253
Instagram, 42–43, 130, 133, 135,
    316, 342–343, 360, 389,
    401, 403, 410–411
Intel Corporation, 150, 436, 485
Inter-American Development
    Bank (IDB), 91–92
Internal Revenue Service, 378
International Financial Reporting
    Standards (IFRS), 446
International Franchise
    Association, 155
International Monetary Fund
    (IMF), 83–84, 93
Intuit, 274
Ivory, 344
Ivy Exec, 202
IVY Planning Group, 109–110

J

Jackson, Curtis, 474
Jamba Juice, 373
Javelin Strategy and Research,
    425
JCPenney, 106, 369
Jell-O, 343
Jenkins, Antony, 204
Jenny Craig, 150
Jerome Cheese, 60
Jobs, Steve, 118, 150
Johnson, Cameron, 137
Johnson & Johnson, 30, 446
Johnston, Pete, 487–488
Jones, Gareth, 203
Jones, Hannah, 59

Jordan, Kim, 178
Josephson, Michael, 45
JPMorgan Chase, 125, 404, 425, 485
Juicy Couture, 234

K

Kaufman, Ben, 219
Kellogg's, 191, 317, 341
Kenmore, 341
Kennedy, John F., 51, 87
Keurig Green Mountain, Inc., 39
Kickstarter, 330
Kimberly-Clark, 258
King Digital Entertainment, 407
King Soopers, 396
Kiva, 408
Klein, Marvin, 65
Klippert, Joel, 34–35
Klippert, LeeAnn, 34–35
KlipTech, 34–35
Kmart, 311, 369
Koch, Jim, 338
Koehn, Nancy F., 139
Kogi BBQ, 370
Kohl's, 319, 424
KPMG, 449
Kroc, Ray, 115
Kroger, 306, 369–370, 396–397
Krummer, Robert, Jr., 145
Kutcher, Ashton, 474

L

Lady Gaga, 474
Lamy, Pascal, 93–94
Land's End, 287, 363
Le Fashion Truck, 370
Leading Edge Aviation Services, Inc., 58–59
LEGO, 412
Lenor, 335
Lenovo, 214
Leto, Jared, 474
Levinson, Marc, 218
Levi's, 341
LEXIS-NEXIS, 320
Lexus, 342
LG, 334
Lincoln Electric, 233
LinkedIn, 5, 93, 253–254, 256, 402–403, 408, 410–414, 424, 485
LiveJournal, 403
LivingSocial, 407
L.L. Bean, Inc., 141
Lockheed Martin, 230
Lohan, Lindsay, 474
Lohr, Ross, 130
L'Oreal, 200
Lowe's, 24, 369, 406, 464, 469
Luke's Lobster, 429–430
Lyft, 351, 474

M

Ma, Jack, 467
Macy's, 11, 71, 330, 369, 402–403, 420, 424, 441
Madison, Sophie, 135
Maersk Drilling, 253
Maggiano's Little Italy, 217
Magic Bullet, 372
Mahindra Satyam, 446
Mantega, Guido, 96
Manuel, E. J., 487
Marathon Oil Corporation, 214
Marriott, Bill, 406
Marriott International, 5, 406
Mars, 61, 115
Marshall, John, 114
Marx, Karl, 18
Mary Kay Cosmetics, 364, 372
Mashable, 403
Maslow, Abraham, 276–277
Mattel, Inc., 23
Maxim Integrated Products, Inc., 224
Mayo, Elton, 275–276
Mayo Clinic, 166
Maytag, 52
McDonald's Corporation, 95, 115, 121, 140, 150–151, 154, 189, 200, 315, 343, 347, 390, 472
McGregor, Douglas, 279–280
McMillion, Denver, 149
Meeker, Matt, 133
Mendes, Michael, 447
Mercedes-Benz, 218, 229, 307, 343
Meredith Corporation, 180
MetLife, 110
Mi Ola, 359–360
Michelin, 342
Microsoft Corporation, 27, 115, 249, 340, 343, 388, 434, 459, 481, 485
Midvale Steel Company, 274
Mills, Karen, 141
Missoni, 311
Mittelstaedt, Chris, 297
Mondelēz, 342
Monster.com, 253
Montgomery Ward, 372
Moon, Jim, 493–494
Moonworks, 493–494
Moore, Ann, 121
Morgan Stanley, 125
Motorola, 230
MoveOn.org, 403
Mrs. Fields Cookies, 10
Musk, Elon, 38, 178
MySpace, 403

N

Nader, Ralph, 52
Nalebuff, Barry, 393–394
Nanigian, Daniel J., 156
Nanmac Corporation, 156

Napster, 403
Nas, 474
National Association of Realtors, 379
National Center for Employee Ownership, 290
National Pork Producers Council, 379
National Work/Life Measurement Project, 286
Nault, Hailey, 152
Nemani, Raaja, 339
Nestlé, 61, 95, 124, 222, 306, 382
Nestlé Purina Petcare, 229
NET-A-PORTER.COM, 311
Netflix, 83, 245, 434
New Belgium Brewing Company, 61, 178, 290
New United Motor Manufacturing, Inc. (NUMMI), 77
Newport News, 372
New-Wave Fashions, Inc., 194–195
Nielsen, 320
Nike, 50, 59, 307, 341–342, 363
Nissan, 26, 235
NJoy, 322
Nokia, 249, 343
Nordstrom, 339
Nordstrom Rack, 371
North American Free Trade Agreement (NAFTA), 88–89
Northeast Art Supply, 451–458, 460–461
Northrop Grumman Corporation, 230

O

Obama, Barack, 469
Obama, Michelle, 55
Occupational Outlook Handbook (Dept. of Labor), 448
Occupational Safety and Health Administration (OSHA), 266
Office Depot, 196
Olay, 344
Old Navy, 363
Olyai, Nikki, 137
Open Door Pantry, 370
Oracle Corporation, 125, 413
Orbitz, 423
Orbuch, Ryan, 419
Oreo, 342
Organization of Petroleum Exporting Countries, 90
Ouchi, William, 280
Outback Steakhouse, 150

P

P. Terry's, 47
Pampered Chef, 372
Panda Express, 154
Panera, 55

Parker Brothers, 333
Parrish, Roland G., 153
Pashak, Zak, 211
Patagonia, 342
Patek Philippe, 366
Patel, Mit, 152
PayPal, 484
Pencil Makers Association, 80
PepsiCo, 110, 151, 155, 194, 349, 382
Petty, Herman, 153
Pew Internet Research, 402
Pew Research, 286
Philip Morris, 78
Phillips Corporation, 260
Photobucket, 403
Pier 1 Imports, 69
Pinterest, 130, 133, 316, 360, 402–403, 408, 410–411, 423–424, 430, 434, 495
Pizza Hut Inc., 151, 221, 341
Plank, Kevin, 363
Planters, 345
Polaroid, 141
Polo, 342
Popchips, 474
Popick, Janine, 293
Porcino, Paul, 495
PortionPac Chemical, 65
PricewaterhouseCoopers (PwC), 229, 449, 463
Pringles, 344
Printemps, 369
Private Label Manufacturer's Association, 341
Procter, William, 114
Procter & Gamble Company (P&G), 30, 41, 46–47, 106, 114, 140, 147, 191, 202, 306, 335, 341, 344, 354, 380, 382, 449, 458, 475, 481
Project Repat, 130
Public Broadcasting Service (PBS), 434
Publix Super Markets, 290, 370
Pulte Homes, 437

Q

Questor Corporation, 74
Quicken Loans, 274
Quirky, 219
Qwest, 42

R

RadioShack, 154
Raleigh, 326
Raytheon, 258
Red Bull, 41, 388–389
Red Cross, 5
Reddit, 403
REI, 287, 363
Restoration Hardware, 419–420
RetailMeNot, 387
Rite Aid, 181

Ritz-Carlton Hotels, 229
R.J. Reynolds Tobacco Company, 51
Robare Group, Ltd., 41
Robert W. Baird & Co., 274
Robinson, Dan, 26
Robinson, Madison, 26
Rock Candy Media, 315
Roebuck, Alvah, 120
Rolex, 349, 452
Rolls-Royce, 311
Romanias, Chris, 154
Romo, Jeanine, 370
Roosevelt, Franklin D., 28, 48
Rothstein, Nathan, 130
Rousseff, Dilma, 96
Rovio Entertainment, 407
Royal Crown Companies, Inc., 151
Royal Dutch Shell, 446
RTI International, 322
Ruiz, Manny, 119

S

Safeguard, 344
Safeway, 369, 393–394
Salesforce.com, 273–274
Sam Adams, 338
Sam's Club, 371
Samsung, 220, 334, 343, 404
Sanu, Mohamed, 487
SAP North America, 416–417
SAS, 274
Save the Children Organization, 5
Savored, 351
Sayman, Michael, 419
Schlotzsky's, 407
Schultz, Howard, 179
Seacrest, Ryan, 474
Sears, Richard, 120
Sears, Roebuck & Co., 120, 142, 341, 368–369
Sears Holdings Corporation, 116
Securities and Exchange Commission (SEC), 41, 446–447, 456, 464
Selmon, Amaya, 139
Service Corps of Retired Executives (SCORE), 147–148
7-Eleven Inc., 151, 370
Shake Weight, 372
Sheets, Ellen, 158
Shell, Richard, 149
Siemens, 434
SimplyHired.com, 253
Singer Sewing Company, 152
SkyMall, 475
Skype, 255, 291, 293
Slater, Samuel, 27
Small Business Administration (SBA), 30, 91, 133, 146–147, 437
Smartfood, 106
Smith, Adam, 14–15, 192
Smith, Denise Young, 260

Smith, Gary, 109–110
Smith, Janet, 109–110
Snapchat, 403
Snuggie, 372
Social Security Administration, 110
Society for Human Resource Management, 253
SoftBank, 467
Sony Corporation, 77, 115–116, 344
Sorber, Alicia, 158
Sorber, Brig, 158
Sorber, Jon, 158
SpaceX, 178
Spalding, 74
SportClips, 155
Sports Authority, 363
Spotify, 434
Sprint, 421
Standard & Poor's, 423
Stanley Black & Decker, 471
Stanley Home Products, 372
Staples, Inc., 40, 150, 338, 347
Starbucks, 49, 55, 167, 287, 305, 316, 363, 412, 418, 472
Stars and Stripes Clothing, 473, 475
StartUpPc, 139
Stav, Julie, 8
Steffe, Stacey, 370
Steinbrecher, Susan, 138
Sterling, Debbie, 330
Stonyfield Farm, 345
Strand, Cheryl, 138
Strife, Carly, 133
The Student magazine, 173
StumbleUpon, 403
Stylerunner, 202
SUBWAY, 151, 153, 155
Summly app, 8

T

Taco Bell, 401
Taobao, 467
Target, 46, 110, 311, 369, 371, 387–388
Taylor, Frederick W., 274–275
Tazo, 305
TCBY Enterprises, Inc., 153
TD Bank, 404
Technorati, 403
Tesco, 456
Tesla Motors, 38, 178
Theory Z: How American Management Can Meet the Japanese Challenge (Ouchi), 280
Thomasville, 25
Thornton, Beth, 149
Three Brothers Bakery, 408
3M Company, 218, 285, 471–472
Timberlake, Justin, 474
Tindell, Kip, 171, 269–270
T.J. Maxx, 371

T-Mobile, 308
Toluna, 319
Top-Toy, 313
Toyota Motor Company, 19, 26, 76–77, 182, 218, 230, 343, 446
Toys "R" Us, 313, 330, 371
Training magazine, 260–261
Trammel, Angela, 152–153
Trammel, Ernest, 152–153
Trans-Pacific Partnership (TPP), 90
Travel Channel, 397
Trinity Industries, 44–45
TripAdvisor, 407
Tumblr, 316, 403, 411, 430
Tupperware, 372
Turner Broadcasting System, 320
Twitter, 5, 30, 43, 93, 99, 109, 130, 133, 135, 167, 253, 305, 316, 319, 326, 342, 359, 388–389, 401–403, 408–412, 414–415, 417, 424, 430, 437, 485–486, 495
Two Men and a Truck, 158

U

Uber, 351
Ulukaya, Hamdi, 238
Under Armour, 363
Unilever, 30, 99, 382, 434, 458
Union Carbide, 77
Union Pacific Corporation, 490
UPS, 196, 225, 287, 375, 389, 396
US Airways, 126
U.S. Census, 368–369
U.S. Department of Labor, 448
U.S. Patent and Trademark Office, 341, 343
U.S. West, 320

V

V8, 337
VB Solutions, Inc., 139
Verizon Wireless, 110, 260–261, 354, 424
Vibram Five Fingers, 347
Vimeo, 430
Vine, 342, 411
Virgin Group, 173
Visa, 3–4, 477, 483
Vitaminwater, 474
VMS, 372
Volkswagen AG, 76, 81, 95–96, 116
VPI Pet Insurance, 344
Vroom, Victor, 282–283

W

Walgreens, 181, 369
Walmart, 11, 17, 41, 50, 69,

106, 125, 311, 338, 354, 363, 369, 371, 375, 420, 422–423, 446, 471, 478
Walsh, John, 40
Walt Disney Company, 165, 247
Walton, Sam, 11, 125
Warby Parker, 316, 422
The Wealth of Nations (Smith), 14, 192
Weight Watchers, 330, 345
Weiman's, 334
Weisberg, Syd, 65
Wells Fargo, 404
Wendy's International, Inc., 154
Werdelin, Henrik, 133
Wesco, 490
West Elm, 309–310, 315–316
Western Electric Company, 275–276
Wheeler, Jaden, 139
Whirlpool, 95, 201, 214, 341
White Hen Pantry, 370
Whitman, Meg, 167
Whole Foods, 340, 345, 380, 394
Wikipedia, 403, 408
Withey, Annie, 106
Woodman, Nick, 105–106
Woodman Labs, 105
Wordpress, 403
Words with Friends, 407, 486
Workday, Inc., 175
Working Mother magazine, 287
World Bank, 91
The World Is Flat (Friedman), 70
World Trade Organization (WTO), 87–88
WorldCom, 42
Wu, Jason, 311
Wyndham Hotel Group, 407

X

Xerox, 141, 344

Y

Yahoo!, 8, 403, 467
Yelp, 403, 407
Yodle, 138
Yoplait Yogurt, 74
YouTube, 42, 93, 130, 315, 342, 360, 388–390, 401–403, 406, 408, 410–411, 424, 437, 485, 495

Z

Zapier, 315
Zappos, 11, 207–208, 414
Zara, 366
Zebco, 477
Ziehli, Joyce, 40
Zipcar, 310–311
Zynga, 407, 486

Subject Index

A

absolute advantage, 70–71
abusive behavior, programs to reduce, 57–58
accessibility, of transportation, 376, 377
accessory equipment, 332
accountability, creating, 195
accounting
  audits, 446
  in business plan, 497
  careers in, 448–449
  defined, 445
  fraud, 446–447, 463–464
  at Graeter's, 495
  software for, 438
  Tesco scandal, 456
  top mistakes, 445
  types of, 447–448
accounting equation, 449–450
accounts payable, 452
accounts receivable, 451
  as collateral, 481, 482
  factoring, 482
accumulated depreciation, 452
acquisition
  and corporate culture, 204
  growth through, 125–127
  of people, 245–246
  trend for future, 127
ad hoc committee, 204
adaptations, product, 338
adjourning stage, of team development, 292
administrative managers, 175, 439–440
advertisers, most effective, 382
advertising. See also specific types of advertising
  defined, 379
  e-business revenue streams, 420–421
  ethical questions related to, 41
  and franchising, 154
  major steps in developing campaign, 380–382
  mass-media, 378
  in promotion mix, 378
  social and legal considerations in, 382–383
  types of by purpose, 379–380

advertising agencies, 382
advertising appropriation, 380
advertising e-business model, 423
advertising platform, 380
advisory authority, 200
advisory positions, 191
aesthetic modifications, to products, 337
affirmative action, 56–57, 267
Affordable Care Act (2010), 265
Africa, economic outlook for, 84
Age Discrimination in Employment Act (1967–1986), 265, 266
agents, 365, 368
air transport, 377
alien corporation, 116
"all hands" meetings, at Zappos, 208
allocator, price as, 346
allowances
  in discounting, 356
  for doubtful accounts, 451
alternative sources of energy, 61
alternatives, in managerial decision making, 180–181
Amendments to the Equal Credit Opportunity Act (1976, 1994), 54
American Recovery and Reinvestment Act (2009), 60
Americans with Disabilities Act (ADA) of 1990, 265, 267
analytic skills, of managers, 7, 176–177
analytical process, 214
anational companies, 78
angel investor, 486
annual report, 450
antidumping duties, 80
appendix, business plan, 146, 498
applications, employment, 254, 255
applied research, 218
appraisal, performance, 246, 247
apps, 418, 419
articles of incorporation, 117
articles of partnership, 111–112
Asia, economic outlook for, 84
assembly line, 223, 224, 235
assessment centers, 256

assets, 451–452
  as collateral, 481–482
  defined, 449
  employees as, 246
  lack of in sole proprietorships, 108–109
  sale of, as source of funds, 475
Association of Southeast Asian Nations, 89
associations, brand, 342
athletes, securities linked to, 487
attrition, personnel cutbacks through, 249
audit, 446
authority
  advisory, 200
  decentralization of, 196–197
  delegation of, 195–196
  functional, 200
  granting, 195
  of leaders, 177
  line, 200
authors, e-mail addresses of, 10
autocratic leadership, 178, 179
automated clearinghouses (ACHs), 478
automatic teller machines (ATMs), 478
automatic vending, 373
automation, 222, 233
awareness, brand, 342

B

B Corp certification, 116, 130
B2B model, 421–422
B2C model, 422–423
balance of payments, 72, 81
balance of trade, 21, 71–72
balance sheet, 450–451
banker's acceptance, 479
bankruptcies, 140, 468
banks
  financing international business, 91–94
  multilateral development, 91–93
  role in exportation payments, 75–76
  services provided by, 476–479
bar charts, 444
barter, 27, 77–78

bases, for market segmentation, 311, 313
basic research, 218
behavior modification, 286
benchmarking, 182, 229, 417
benefit corporation, 116
benefits, 247, 259–260
  defined, 246
  at Graeter's, 299
  for part-time workers, 287–288
  when job sharing, 288
benefits-to-the-community component, business plan, 102, 146
bicycles
  manufacturing, 211
  marketing, 326
big data analytics, 319
bilingual skills, and cultural diversity, 251
bill of lading, 75
"Blast! Then Refine" approach, 180
blogs, 405–406, 416
board of directors, 118
body, business report, 443
Boeing Ethics Line, 63
bond indenture, 490
bonds, 489–490, 491
bootstrapping, 105
brainstorming, 180
branches, exporting firms, 76
brand advertising, 379
brand associations, 342
brand awareness, 342
brand equity, 342–343
brand extensions, 344
brand insistence, 342
brand loyalty, 334, 342, 343, 347
brand mark, 341
brand name, 341, 343
brand preference, 342
brand recognition, 342
branding
  benefits of, 341–343
  Graeter's, 396–397
  on-campus, 388
  strategies, 344
brands
  choosing and protecting, 343
  defined, 341
  most valuable, 343
  types of, 341

Brazil, economy of, 95–96
breakeven quantity, 350
bribes, 41
brokerage e-business model, 423
brokers, 368
budget
  capital, 474
  cash, 473–474
  defined, 473
  interim, 475
  personal, 453
budgeting for financial needs, 473–474
bullying, programs to reduce, 57–58
bundle pricing, 348, 353–354
bureaucratic red tape, 81
business
  achieving objectives through social media, 407–413
  activities of, 10–12
  bankruptcies, 468
  changing world of, 4–10
  considerations for organizing, 192
  defined, 10, 418
  development of, 27–29
  ethical issues in suppliers' factories, 50
  legal help, aspects requiring, 116
  in mixed economy, 16–17
  public responsibilities of, 51–55
  reasons social media is used in, 402–405
  reasons to study, 5–8
  response to environmental concerns, 60–61
  selecting type of, 100
  social media benefits for, 405
  social media tools for, 405–407
  starting your own, 7–8
  start-ups, closures, and bankruptcies in U.S. from 2000, 140
  text features for students of, 8–10
  today, in U.S., 27–32
business analysis, in product development, 338, 339
business and personal finances, mixing, 445
business application software, 437–438
business balance sheet, 451
business buying behavior, 321, 323
business communications, ethical questions related to, 41
business cycle, 21–23
business environment, current, 29–31

business ethics, defined, 39. See also ethics
business income statement, 453, 455
business loans, 149, 476–477. See also loans
business model, 421
business ownership
  corporations, 114–121
  partnerships, 109–114
  sole proprietorships, 106–109
  special types of, 121–125
business plan
  appendix, 498
  company and industry component, 146, 162
  components of, 100, 102, 145–146
  critical risks and assumptions component, 146, 497
  defined, 100, 144
  executive summary, 146, 498
  exit strategy component, 146, 497
  financial plan in, 146, 497
  human resources component, 301
  importance of, 144–145
  information and accounting plan component, 497
  introduction component, 100, 102, 146
  management team component, 146, 242
  manufacturing and operations plan component, 146, 242
  marketing plan component, 146, 398
  reviewing, 498
  for service firms, 216–218
  steps in creating, 101
business products, 331, 332. See also products
  distribution channels for, 364, 365
  pricing, 355–356
business profits, 12, 17
business reports, 443
business service, 332
business skills and knowledge, of partners, 112
business-to-business (B2B) model, 421–422
business-to-business marketing, 416
business-to-business markets, 310
business-to-business products, 331, 332
business-to-consumer (B2C) model, 422–423
buyers, perceptions of price, 347–348
buying, as function of marketing, 306

buying allowance, 388
buying behavior, 321–323, 331
buying power, 323
buyouts, 249

C

CAD, 234
CAFTA-DR, 84, 89
call premium, 490
CAM, 234
Canada, economic outlook for, 83
Canadian Free Trade Agreement, 89
capacity
  adjusting products or services to meet demand, 225–226
  comparing market demand with, 225
  defined, 222
  required production, 221–222
capital, 13
  ability of small businesses to raise, 144, 145
  availability of for partnerships, 112
  debt, 475
  ease of raising, for corporations, 119–120
  for entrepreneurs, sources of, 145
  equity, 475, 483
  lack of in sole proprietorships, 108–109
  relation to growth, 125
  and small business failure, 139–140
  venture, 149–150, 486
capital budget, 474
capital-intensive technology, 222
capitalism, 14–17
captioned photograph, 390
captive pricing, 354
careers
  in accounting, 448–449
  in business, 5
  and business cycle, 22
  choosing, 5–6
  in finance, 469–470
  in operations management, 214–215
  in social media, 409
carrier, 376
cars, driverless, 218, 221
Cartwheel app, 387
cash budget, 473–474
cash deficit, 453
cash discounts, 356
cash flows
  defined, 470
  from financing activities, 457
  from investing activities, 457
  from operating activities, 457
  statement of, 456–458

cash surplus, 453
catalog marketing, 372
category killers, 371
category management, 366
caveat emptor, 48, 425
C-corporations, 114
celebrity investors, 474
Central American Free Trade Agreement (CAFTA), 89
centralized organization, 196–197
certificate of deposit (CD), 476
certified public accountant (CPA), 449
chain of command, 190–191, 199
chain retailer, 369
change
  ability to adapt to in small business, 143
  magnitude of, 215
charts, 444
checks, 476
chief digital officer, 409
chief ethics (compliance) officer, 44, 200
chief financial officer (CFO), 470
chief social media officer, 409
chief sustainability officer (CSO), 59
Children's Online Privacy Protection Act (2000), 54
China
  economic outlook for, 84
  small businesses exporting to, 156
  tariffs, 80, 81
  trade with Brazil, 96
Cigarette Labeling Act (1965), 54
cigarettes, 55, 181
CIM, 234–235
circular flow, in mixed economy, 16
Civil Rights Act (1964), 55, 265, 266
Civil Rights Act (1991), 265, 266
classroom teaching and lectures, 262
Clayton Antitrust Act (1914), 48
Clean Air Act amendments, 60
clean environment, paying for, 61
cleaning up, short-term loans, 481
closed corporation, 115
closing sale, in personal-selling process, 384–385
closure
  of sole proprietorships, 107
  in U.S. from 2000, 140
cloud computing, 425–426, 434, 440
CLV, 307
codes of ethics, 43, 44–45
coffee makers, lock-out technology in, 39
cohesiveness, of teams, 293–294

collaboration, importance of, 176

collateral, 476, 479, 481, 489

command economies, 17–18

commercial databases, 320

commercial paper, 481, 482

commercialization, of new products, 338, 340

commercials, 405

commissions, 258

commitment fees, 476

committees, 204–205

common carrier, 376

Common Market, 88

Common Market of the Southern Cone (MERCOSUR), 90

common stock, 117, 485, 491

Commonwealth of Independent States, 90

communal culture, 203, 204

communication skills, of managers, 177

communication tool, business plan as, 144

communications
ethical questions related to, 41
informal, 205
integrated marketing, 377–378
role in collaboration, 176

communism, 18

communities, social media, 408, 414

community involvement, and corporate citizenship, 98

community shopping centers, 374

companies, role in encouraging ethics, 44–46

company and industry component, business plan, 146, 162

comparable worth, 257–258

comparative advantage, 70–71

comparative advertising, 379

comparison discounting, 355

comparison other, in equity theory, 282

compensating balances, 480

compensation, 247
comparable worth, 257–258
decisions, 256–257
defined, 246, 256
and equity theory, 282
and motivation, 279
types of, 258–259

compensation system, 257

competition
defined, 23
encouraging, 52
non-price, 347
price, 347
small businesses as providing, 142
between teams, 294
types of, 23–27

competition-based pricing, 351

competitive environment, 29–30

competitive forces, in marketing environment, 316

competitors, ethical expectations of, 39

complaints
and right to be heard, 52
as source of data, 321

compliance, relation to ethics, 200

compliance officer, 44, 200

component part, 332

compromises, 294

computer manufacturing systems, 234

computer technology, future challenges for, 425–427

computer viruses, 425

computer-aided design (CAD), 234

computer-aided manufacturing (CAM), 234

computer-integrated manufacturing (CIM), 234

concentrated market segmentation, 311, 312

concept testing, in product development, 338–339

conceptual skills, of managers, 7, 176

conclusions, business report, 443

conferences, 262

confidence, consumer, 341

confidentiality, threats to, 424–425

conflict
within corporations, 121
of interest, 40–41
in line-and-staff structure, 200–201
in teams, resolving, 294

conglomerate merger, 126, 127

consensus basis, for decisions, 240

consensus leaders, 178

constant dollars, 19

consultative leaders, 178

consumer advocates, 52

Consumer Bill of Rights, 51, 52

consumer buying behavior, 321–323

consumer confidence, 341

consumer confidence index, 21

consumer convenience, packaging offering, 344–345

Consumer Credit Reporting Reform Act (1997), 54

consumer education, 52, 53

consumer markets, 310

consumer price index (CPI), 20

Consumer Product Safety Commission Act (1972), 54

consumer products, 16, 331–332, 364–365. *See also* products

consumer reviews, 407

consumer sales promotion method, 386

consumerism, 51–53

consumers
in B2C model, 422–423
basic rights of, 51–52
becoming better informed, 8
buying behavior, 321–323
complaints from as source of data, 321
in distribution channels, 364–365
higher prices for, due to trade restrictions, 82
household members as, 16
perceptions of price, 347–348
restriction of choices, 82

consumer-to-consumer model, 423

content marketing, 412

contingency plan, 170–171

continual data collection, 318

continual reinforcement, 281

continuity
in partnerships, 113
in sole proprietorships, 108, 109

continuous improvement, 229

continuous process, 235

continuous quality improvement, in TQM, 182

contract carrier, 376

contract disputes, in franchising, 154–155

control. *See also* operations control
foreign-exchange, 80
inventory, 226, 227–228, 231
in marketing plan, 317
quality, 226, 228–231
span of, 197–198

controlling, as management function, 172

convenience, packaging offering, 344–345

convenience product, 331

convenience stores, 370

conversion process, 215–216

convertible bond, 490

cookie, 424

cooperative advertising, 388

core competencies, 169

core time, 286

corporate bonds, 489–490, 491

corporate charter, 117

corporate citizenship, 47, 62–63

corporate culture
defined, 203
entrepreneurs as setting tone for, 202
types of, 203–204
at Zappos, 207–208

Corporate Gifts and Rewards Program, at Apple, 286

corporate growth, 125–127

corporate officers, 118

corporate profits, 21

corporate raider, 126

Corporate Responsibility magazine, 47

corporate structure, 118

corporations, 130
advantages of, 119–120
as artificial persons, 114, 118, 120
compared to S corporations and LLCs, 123
conflict within, 121
defined, 114
disadvantages of, 120–121
forming, 115–118
IPOs, 483–484
organizational structure of, 118
ownership, 115
performing as good citizens, 49
relative percentages of in U.S., 106
total sales receipts of, in U.S., 107

corrective action, 51, 172

cost
advantages of cultural diversity, 251
of incorporation, 120–121
inventory, 375
involved in operating businesses, 350
of long-term financing, 490–491
of maintaining social media plan, 417
of management information systems, 440
related to inventory control, 227–228
of selling stock, 484
shipping, 227
of short-term financing, 482
of transportation, 376

cost accounting, 448

cost of goods sold, 454–455

cost-based pricing, 349–350

countertrade, 77–78

coupon, 386–387

co-workers, as factor affecting ethics, 42

CPA, 449

CPI, 20

creative selling, 383

creativity, from cultural diversity, 251

credit
availability of, for partnerships, 112
letter of, 75, 478, 479
line of, 476
revolving credit agreement, 476
terms, role in purchasing decisions, 227
trade, 479–480, 482

Credit Card Accountability, Responsibility, and Disclosure Act (2009), 54
Credit Card Liability Act (1970), 54
credit card transactions, 477
creditors, ethical expectations of, 39
crime, Internet, 425
crisis management, through social media, 409
critical risks and assumptions component, business plan, 146, 497
cross-functional teams, 201–202, 291–292
cross-training, 193
crowdfunding, 414
crowdsourcing, 412
CSO, 59
Cuba, 18
cultural barriers, 81
cultural diversity, 6, 250–251
cultural norms, as factor affecting ethics, 42
culture, 203–204
currency
    appreciation of Brazil's, 96
    devaluation, 80–81
    foreign-exchange control, 80
    in international business, 75–76
currency exchange, 479
current assets, 451–452
current liabilities, 452–453, 460
current ratio, 460
customary pricing, 354
customer lifetime value (CLV), 307
customer loyalty, 306
customer orientation, 309
customer relationship management (CRM), 306
customer satisfaction, 182, 309, 417
customer service, through social media, 404
customer-driven production, 235, 412
customers
    in B2C model, 422–423
    branding benefits for, 341–342
    departmentalization by, 194
    ethical expectations of, 39
    involvement in services, 216–218
    marketing's role in relationship with, 305–307
    personal relationships in small businesses, 143
    satisfying needs online, 419–420
    segmenting or targeting, for social media plan, 414, 415
    targeting through social media, 410

D

data
    defined, 436
    external sources of, 319, 441–442
    financial, comparing, 458–459
    versus information, 436
    internal sources of, 319, 441
    for marketing, 318–321
    for MIS, collecting, 441–442
    storing, MIS capability for, 442
    updating, in MIS, 442
data mining, 424–425
data processing, 442–443
database management software, 438
database marketing, 378
databases, 319–320, 437, 441
debenture bond, 489–490
debit card transactions, 477
debt capital, 475
debt financing, 446, 479, 487
debts, measuring firm's ability to pay, 460
decentralized organization, 196–197
decision making
    and consumer buying behavior, 322–323
    and decentralization, 196–197
    managerial, 179–181
    participative, in Theory Z, 280
    software for, 437
decision-support system (DSS), 437
decline stage, product life-cycle, 333, 334–335
deflation, 19
delegation
    of authority, 195–196
    barriers to, 196
    defined, 195
    steps in, 195–196
deletion, product, 337
demand
    adjusting products or services to meet, 225–226
    comparing with capacity, 225
    defined, 24
    and equilibrium price, 24–25
    estimating market, 224–225
    forecasting human resources, 247–248
    peak, planning for, 225
    for personnel, matching supply with, 249
    for safe products, 51
demand-based pricing, 351
democratic leaders, 178
demonstration, in personal-selling process, 384
department stores, 369
departmentalization, 193–195, 201
dependability, of transportation, 376, 377

depreciation, 452
depression, defined, 21–22
depth, product mix, 335
design
    computer-aided, 234
    job, 192–193
    packaging, 345
    product, 221
design planning, 220–222, 231
desired behavior, in behavior modification, 286
desk assignments, temporary, 193
desktop publishing software, 438
devaluation, currency, 80–81
development
    evaluation of, 262
    and implementation, 218
    management, 261
    methods, 261–262
    training and, 246, 247, 260–262
development phase, of HRM, 247
differential pricing, 351, 352–353
differentiated market segmentation, 311, 312, 313
digital marketing, 410, 412
digital native, 402
digital strategist, 409
direct channel, 364
direct investment, 77
direct mail, in advertising campaign, 381
direct marketing, 372–373
direct selling, 371–372
directing, as management function, 171–172
director, of social responsibility program, 62
direct-response marketing, 372
disabilities, protection of individuals with, 267
disaster loans, from SBA, 149
discount, defined, 356
discount store, 369
discounting, 353, 355, 356
discretionary income, 323
discrimination
    in employment, 266
    against individuals with disabilities, 267
    during interviews, 255
    reverse, 56
display advertising, 412
disposable income, 323
dissatisfaction, employee, 278
dissatisfiers, 278
distribution
    as element of marketing mix, 314, 315–316
    exclusive, 366
    intensive, 366
    level of market coverage, 365–366
    physical, 374–377
    selective, 366

distribution channels, 364–365
distribution industries, 136
distributors, 367
diversity
    cultural, 6, 250–251
    in human resources, 250–251
    promoting through purchasing, 226–227
dividends, 117, 484, 485
Do Not Call Implementation Act (2003), 54
Dodd–Frank Wall Street Reform and Consumer Protection Act (2010), 54, 469
domestic corporation, 116
domestic jobs, protecting, 82
domestic system, 27
Dominican Republic-Central America FTA (CAFTA-DR), 84, 89
do-not-call registry, 372
door-to-door selling, 372
double taxation, of corporations, 121
double-entry bookkeeping system, 449–450
draft, from bank, 75
driverless cars, 218, 221
drones, 176
"Drug Interaction Checker", CVS Health, 316
DSS, 437
dual roles, on team, 293
dual-branded franchises, 153
dumping, 80
dynamic pricing, 351

E

early retirement, 249
earnings
    relative, of male and female workers, 57
    retained, 453, 485–486
earnings statement, 453–456
Ebola, cure for, 219
e-business, 11
    defined, 418
    fundamental models of, 421–423
    future of, 423–427
    organizing resources, 418–419
    profit, creating, 420–421
    satisfying needs online, 419–420
e-cigarettes, 55, 322
e-commerce, 418
economic benefits, of higher education, 5
economic community, 88
economic crisis, financial reform after, 469
economic environment, 31
economic forces, in marketing environment, 316
economic indicators, 20–21

economic model of social responsibility, 49
economic outlook for trade, 83–86
economic performance
  measuring, 18–21
  outlook for, 83–86
economic systems
  capitalism, 14–17
  command economies, 17–18
  differences in, 13
  key issues challenging, 31–32
  types of, 12–18
economics, defined, 12
economies
  defined, 13
  economic indicators measuring, 20–21
  effect of productivity growth, 18
  service, 29, 216, 217
EDLPs, 354
education
  consumer, 52, 53
  economic benefits of higher, 52
EIS, 437
e-learning, 262
electronic beacons, 424
electronic business, 418
electronic check conversion (ECC), 478
electronic exchange, 485
Electronic Funds Transfer Act (1978), 478
electronic funds transfer (EFT) system, 478
e-mail marketing, 412
embargo, 80
emergency preparedness, 30
Emerging Leaders Program, SBA, 147
employee benefits, 246, 247, 259–260
employee empowerment, 289
employee ownership, 289–290
employee participation
  improving quality through, 229–230
  in total quality management, 182
employee relations, 246
employee stock ownership plans (ESOPs), 290
employee training, 261
employees
  as assets, 246
  being successful, 6–7
  characteristics of, 6–7
  at Container Store, 269–270
  and corporate culture, 202, 203–204
  difficulty in hiring by sole proprietors, 109
  ethical expectations of, 39
  in Herzberg's motivation-hygiene theory, 278–279

hiring first, 248
and leadership styles, 178–179
management information system use by, 440–444
personal relationships in small businesses, 143
at Zappos, 208
employment
  in manufacturing, 213
  small businesses as providing, 142
employment applications, 254, 255
employment practices, 55–58
Employment Retirement Income Security Act (1974), 265, 267
employment tests, 254
empowerment, 289
Encyclopaedia Britannica, 337
energy sources, renewable, 61
enforcement, of company policies, procedures, and ethical codes, 43
Entrepreneur magazine, 109
entrepreneurial leadership, 178, 179
entrepreneurial spirit, 137
entrepreneurs, 13
  average age of, 137
  and corporate culture, 202
  ethical decisions for, 124
  franchising as path towards success as, 152
  global, advice from, 75
  micromanaging by, 290
  motivation of, 138
  personal factors, 137
  reasons for failure of, 139–140
  sources of capital for, 145
  teenagers as, 139, 419
  tips for becoming, 138
  women as, 138–139
environmental analysis, for marketing plan, 317
environmental forces, affecting e-business, 426
environmental laws, 59–60
environmental responsibility, of packaging, 345
environments
  affecting business, 29–31
  concern for, 58–61
  influencing decentralization, 196
  marketing, 314, 316–317
Equal Credit Opportunity Act (1974), 54
Equal Pay Act (1963), 265, 266
equilibrium (market price), 24–25
equipment, as business product, 332
equity
  brand, 342–343
  defined, 281

owners', 449, 450, 453, 483, 487
  stockholders', 450, 453
equity capital, 475, 483
equity financing, 483–487, 491
equity theory, 281–282
ESOPs, 290
esteem needs, 276, 277
ethical behavior
  in accounting, 446–447
  encouraging, 43–47
  factors affecting, 41–43
ethical decisions, guidelines for making, 45–46
ethical issues, 39–41
  disclosure of experiments on social media, 404
  for entrepreneurs, 124
  marketing of e-cigarettes to young people, 322
  on-campus branding, 388
  securities linked to athletes, 487
  in teamwork, 293
ethics
  defined, 39
  for Internet, social media, and e-business, 424–425
  relation to compliance, 200
  and social media use, 412
ethics (compliance) officer, 44
euro, 88
Eurofactories, 77
European Economic Community, 88
European Union (EU), 83–84, 88
evaluation
  of advertising campaigns, 382
  of financial performance, 475
  of financial statements, 458–461
  in marketing plan, 317
  in MBO process, 284
  performance appraisal, 262–264
  of target market, 310–313
  of training and development, 262
event sponsorship, 389, 390
everyday low prices (EDLPs), 354
exchange functions, of marketing, 306
exclusive distribution, 366
executive compensation packages, 40
executive information system (EIS), 437
executive summary
  in business plan, 146, 498
  for marketing plan, 317
executives, commitment to social responsibility programs, 62
exit strategy component, business plan, 146, 497

expansion, 22
expectancy theory, 282–283
expenses
  incorporation, 120–121
  operating, 455
  prepaid, 452
  reducing in e-business, 421
experimenting, in e-business, 419
expert system, 437
export assistance, sources of, 90–91
export–import agent, 76
export–import merchant, 74
exporting, 71–73
  entering international business through, 74–76
  role in U.S. economy, 84, 85–86
express warranty, 346
extended decision making, by consumers, 322
extension, product, 218–220
external data sources
  for marketing, 319
  for MIS, 441–442
external environment
  as affecting e-business, 426–427
  influencing decentralization, 196
external recruiting, 253
extinction, in reinforcement theory, 281

F
facilitating functions, of marketing, 306
facilities planning, 220, 222–224, 231
factor, 482
factories, ethical issues in supplier, 50
factors of production, 13
factory system, of manufacturing, 27
failure
  product, 340
  of small businesses, 8, 139–140, 144
Fair Credit Billing Act (1974), 54
Fair Credit Reporting Act (1971), 54
Fair Debt Collection Practices Act (1977), 54
Fair Labor Standards Act (1938), 265
Fair Packaging and Labeling Act (1966), 54
fairness, in business, 39–40
Family and Medical Leave Act (1993), 265
family branding, 344
family packaging, 345
"Family Vitamin Center", CVS Health, 316

favorable balance of trade, 72
feature article, 390
federal deficit, 22
Federal Hazardous Substances
Labeling Act (1960), 54
federal income taxes, 456
federal regulations, for labeling,
346
Federal Trade Commission Act
(1914), 48
feedback, performance, 264
female workers, relative earnings
of, 57. *See also* women
field order takers, 383
finance, careers in, 469–470
finances, mixing business and
personal, 445
financial accounting, 448
Financial Accounting Standards
Board (FASB), 446
financial assistance, SBA,
149–150
financial benefits, of TQM
programs, 182–183
financial data, comparing,
458–459
financial institutions, 476–479
financial leverage, 487–488
financial management, 468–470
financial managers, 174, 438,
469, 472, 473
financial needs, budgeting for,
473–474
financial performance, monitoring
and evaluating, 475
financial plan, 146, 472–475, 497
financial ratios, 460–461
financial resources, 10, 166,
174, 418–419
financial security, need for, 274
financial services, 476–479
financial statements, 446, 450,
458–461
financing
cash flows from, 457
for corporations, 119–120
as function of marketing, 306
for Graeter's, 495–496
international business, 91–94
long-term, 470, 471–472,
483–491
need for, 470–472
for partnerships, 112
short-term, 470–471, 479–483
of small businesses, 144, 145
for sole proprietorships,
108–109
finished-goods inventory, 227
firing employees, 249
first-line managers, 173, 174
fiscal policy, 22
fixed assets, 452
fixed cost, 350
fixed-position layout, 223, 224
flat organizations, 197, 198
flexible benefit plans, 260

flexible manufacturing system
(FMS), 235
flexible workspaces, 193
flextime, 286–287
flotation costs, 484, 490
FOB destination, 356
FOB origin pricing, 355–356
focus, of conversion process,
215
follow-up, 228, 385
food product labels, 346
Food Quality Protection Act
(1996), 60
food trucks, 370
forecasting
human resources demand,
247–248
human resources supply,
248–249
foreign corporation, 116
foreign-exchange control, 80
form utility, 215, 307
formal communications, 205
formal leadership, 177–178
forming stage, of team
development, 292
forums, 408
fragmented culture, 203, 204
fragrances, market for, 311
franchise, defined, 150
franchise agreement, 151
franchisee, 150, 151, 154
franchising, 150–156
advantages of, 153–154
by Camp Bow Wow, 185
defined, 150
disadvantages of, 154–155
and entrepreneurial success,
152
by Graeter's, 160
growth of, 152–153
success of, 153
by Two Men and a Truck, 158
types of, 150–151
franchisor, 150, 151, 153–154
fraud
accounting, 446–447,
463–464
online, 425
free enterprise, 4
free trade, 70
free-market economy, 15, 18
freight forwarders, 376
"French pot" manufacturing
method, at Graeter's, 98
frequency, of transportation,
376, 377
frequent-user incentive, 387
full-service wholesaler, 368
function, departmentalization by,
193–194, 201
functional authority, 200
functional middleman, 364, 368
functional modifications, to
products, 336–337
funds, sources of, 475

G

gainsharing, 258
games, social, 407
gamification of social media, 407
garbage, environmental issues
related to, 58
garment labels, 346
gathering information, as
function of marketing, 306
GDP, 19–20, 84, 85
General Agreement on Tariffs
and Trade (GATT), 86–87
general expenses, 455
general managers, 175
general partners, 110, 113, 120
generally accepted accounting
principles (GAAPs), 446
general-merchandise wholesaler,
368
generic brand, 341
generic product, 341
generic terms, 343
geographic pricing strategies,
355–356
Get Your Share (Stav), 8
global entrepreneurs, advice
from, 75
global environment, 30
global marketplace, American
manufacturers in, 212–214
global perspectives, in small
business, 155–156
globalization, 83, 94, 155–156.
See also international
business
goals
defined, 167
establishing, 167–168
as factor affecting ethics, 42
for financial plan, 472
in management by objectives,
284–285
goal-setting theory, 283–284
go-between representatives, 74
going price, accepting, 24
goods, as products, 330
goods available for sale, 455
Google Glass, 337
government
export assistance programs, 90
fiscal policy, 22
increased involvement in
business, 48
regulation of corporations
by, 121
role in capitalism, 15
role in command economies,
17–18
role in encouraging ethics, 43
role in mixed economy, 16, 17
social media use by agencies
of, 30
government accounting, 448
governmental markets, 310
grapevine, 205

graphics, software for, 438
graphs, 444
Great Depression, 28, 48
Greek yogurt production, 238
green business, 31
green IT, 426
green marketing, 61
green vehicles, 38
green washing, 61
gross domestic product (GDP),
19–20, 83, 85
gross profit, 455
gross sales, 454
groups, informal, 205
Groupthink, 293
growth
from within, 125
of franchising, 152–153
Internet, potential for,
423–424
productivity, 232, 233
through mergers and
acquisitions, 125–127
growth stage, product life-cycle,
333–334

H

hard-core unemployed, training
programs for, 57
hashtag, 403
Hawthorne Studies, 275–276
health
of citizens, protecting with
trade restrictions, 82
public, businesses'
responsibility to, 53, 55
height, organizational, 198
Herzberg's motivation-hygiene
theory, 277–279
higher education, economic
benefits of, 5
hiring, 31, 109, 248
holding costs, 227, 375
honesty, in business, 39–40
Horatio Alger Award, 4
horizontal merger, 126, 127
hostile takeover, 125–126
hoteling, 193
hourly wage, 258
households, in mixed economy,
16
human factors, in Hawthorne
Studies, 276
human relations movement, 276,
279, 280
human resources, 10, 166
acquiring, 245–246
in business plan, 301
cultural diversity in, 250–251
developing, 246
in e-business, 418–419
forecasting demand, 247–248
forecasting supply, 248–249
importance of leading and
motivating to, 171–172

importance of to companies, 168

maintaining, 246

matching supply with demand, 249

in site selection and facilities planning, 222–223

human resources management (HRM)

activities, 246

defined, 245

at Graeter's, 299

legal environment of, 265–267

phases of, 245–246

responsibility for, 247

human resources managers, 175, 222–223, 247, 439

human resources planning, 246, 247–249

The Human Side of Enterprise (McGregor), 279

hygiene factors, 278

I

idea generation, in product development, 338

ideas, as products, 330

identity theft, 425

IFRS, 446

IMF, 83–84, 93

imitations, product, 338

immediate-response advertising, 379

implementation research, 218

import duty, 79–80

import quota, 80

importing, 71–73, 84, 85–86

inbound marketing, 411

Inc. magazine, 109

incentive payment, 258

income

national, 21

net, 456

types of, 323

income levels, disparity in, 55–56

income statement, 453–456, 457

income taxes, 456

incorporation

difficulty and expense of, 120–121

process of, 115–118

independence, of small-business owners, 143–144

independent retailer, 369

India, economic outlook for, 84

individual branding, 344

individual factors, affecting ethics, 42

individual wages, 257

industrial markets, 310

industrial products, 331, 332

industries

attracting small businesses, 135–136

protecting new or weak with trade restrictions, 82

inflation, 19

inflation rate, 21

inflation-adjusted dollars, 19–20

informal communications, 205

informal groups, 205

informal leadership, 177–178

informal organization, 205

information

versus data, 436

defined, 436

firm requirements regarding, 438–440

gathering, as function of marketing, 306

for marketing, 318–321

presentation of in MIS, 443–444

as resource, 10, 166, 418–419

risk and, 435–436

rules, 436

information and accounting plan component, business plan, 497

information overload, 440

information technology system, 438

infringement, on existing brands, 343

initial public offering (IPO), 120, 125, 467, 483–484

innovations, 213, 233, 235

for international business, 75

product, 338

technical, 141–142

input

for conversion process, 215

in equity theory, 282

input-to-outcome ratio, 282

inside order takers, 383

inspection, of work-in-process, 230

institutional advertising, 379–380

institutional markets, 310

insurance packages, 259

intangible assets, 452

intangible attributes, of products, 330

integrated marketing communications, 377–378

integrated software, 437–438

intelligent information systems, 420

intensity of market coverage, 366

intensive distribution, 366

interest expense, 456

interest rate

on corporate bonds, 489

prime, 21, 480, 481

interim budgets, 475

intermediary, marketing, 364

intermittent process, 235

internal data sources

for marketing, 319

for MIS, 441

internal environmental forces, affecting e-business, 426

internal recruiting, 253–254

international banking services, 478–479

international business

basis for, 70–73

defined, 70

extent of, 83–86

financing, 91–94

methods of entering, 73–78

restrictions to, 78–82

international economic organizations, working to foster trade, 88–90

International Financial Reporting Standards (IFRS), 446

International Franchise Association, 155

international markets

exporting to, 74–76

steps in entering, 79

International Monetary Fund (IMF), 83, 84, 93

International Organization for Standardization (ISO), 230–231

international resources, misallocation of, 82

international trade, 69–70

economic outlook for, 83–86

by small businesses, 155–156

international trade agreements, 86–90

International Trade Loan program, SBA, 156

Internet

in advertising campaign, 381

crime on, 425

external recruiting through, 253

as factor affecting ethics, 43

future of, 423–427

gathering and analyzing marketing information, 320

growth potential of, 423–424

marketing research on, 319

and price competition, 347

reasons for using, identifying, 424

relationship marketing and, 306

satisfying needs online, 419–420

use by small businesses, 155

Internet training, 261

interpersonal skills, of managers, 7, 177

Interstate Commerce Act (1887), 48

interviews, 255, 256

intranets, 320

introduction, business report, 443

introduction component, business plan, 100, 102, 146

introduction stage, product life-cycle, 333

inventory, 452

as collateral, 481–482

measuring how well firms manage, 460–461

short-term financing, using to increase, 471

inventory control, 226, 227–228, 231

inventory management, 374–375

inventory turnover, 460–461

investing activities, cash flows from, 457

investment banking firm, 484

investments

frozen in partnerships, 113–114

return on, 349

investors

angel, 486

becoming better informed, 8

celebrity, 474

ethical expectations of, 39, 40

invisible hand, 14

involvement, worker sense of, 276

iRobot Ava 500, 233

ISO 14000, 231

ISO 9000, 231

issue resolution rate, 417

"It Can Wait" promotion campaign, 55

IT system, 438

J

Japan, economic outlook for, 84

Japanese management theories, 280

job analysis, 246, 247, 251–252, 257

job applicants, attracting, 253

job description, 251, 252

job design, 192–193

job enlargement, 193, 285

job enrichment, 193, 285–286

job evaluation, 257

job loss, due to trade restrictions, 82

job posting, 254

job redesign, 285

job rotation, 193

job sharing, 288

job specialization, 192–193

job specification, 251–252

jobbers, 367

joint ventures, 76, 124

judgmental appraisal methods, 263

just-in-time inventory (JIT) system, 227–228

just-in-time scheduling, 288

K

Kefauver-Harris Drug Amendments (1962), 54
Kennedy Round (1964-1967), 87
key performance indicators (KPIs), 417
knowledge, as factor affecting ethics, 42
knowledge management (KM), 437–438

L

labeling, 346
labor, 13
labor force component, business plan, 146, 301
labor unions, 48
labor-intensive technology, 222
Labor–Management Relations Act (1947), 265
laissez-faire capitalism, 14–15
land and natural resources, 13
Latin America, economic outlook for, 84
lawsuits, product-liability, 51
layoffs, 249
leadership, 118, 177–179, 185
leading, as management function, 171–172
lean manufacturing, 233
lectures, 262
legal considerations
    in advertising, 382–383
    for Internet, social media, and e-business, 424–425
legal environment of HRM, 265–267
legal forces, in marketing environment, 316
legal help, business aspects that may require, 116
legal monopoly, 27
letter of credit, 75, 478, 479
liabilities, 449, 452–453, 460
licensing, 73–74
lifestyle shopping centers, 373, 374
limited liability, 119
limited monopoly, 27
limited partners, 110, 113
limited-liability company (LLC), 121, 122–123, 130
limited-liability partnership (LLP), 113
limited-line retailers, 371
limited-line wholesaler, 368
limited-service wholesalers, 368
line authority, 200
line extensions, 337, 344
line managers, 198–201, 247, 254
line of credit, 476
line structure, 198–199
line-and-staff structure, 199–201

liquidity, 451
listening to stakeholders, through social media, 409–410, 413
load flexibility, 376, 377
Loads of Hope program, 46–47
loans
    getting, 477
    long-term, 488–489, 491
    from SBA, 149
    secured short-term, 481–482
    types of, 476
    unsecured short-term, 480–481
local help, for international business, 75
location, departmentalization by, 194
lock-out technology, in coffee makers, 39
logo, Graeter's, 396
"long" product line, 221
long-term assets, 452
long-term business loans, 476
long-term financing, 471–472
    compared to short-term financing, 470
    cost comparisons, 490–491
    defined, 471
    equity capital, 483–487
    sources of, 487–491
long-term liabilities, 453
loss, 12, 453, 456
loyalty
    brand, 334, 342, 343, 347
    customer, 306
lump-sum salary increases, 258–259
luxury goods, pricing, 349

M

macroeconomics, 13
magazines, in advertising campaign, 381
magnitude, of conversion process, 215
Magnuson–Moss Warranty–Federal Trade Commission Act (1975), 54
major equipment, 332
Malcolm Baldrige National Quality Award, 229
male and female workers, relative earnings of, 57
malware, 425
management. See also specific types of management
    areas of, 438
    attitudes toward social responsibility, 49
    coordinated effort of all levels of, 173
    decision making by, 179–181
    defined, 165
    disagreements, in

partnerships, 113
    functions, 167–172
    human relations movement in, 276, 279, 280
    levels of, 173–174
    as process, 167
    and product life-cycle, 334
    resources of, 165–166
    and small business failure, 139, 140
    span of, 197–198
    specialization, areas of, 174–175
Management Assistance Program, SBA, 146–148
management by objectives (MBO), 284–285
management courses, SBA, 147
management development, 261
management functions, 7
management information system (MIS), 438–440
    costs and limits of, 440
    defined, 438
    employee use of, 440–444
    functions of, 440–441
management skills, 7, 109
management team component, business plan, 146, 242
management tool, business plan as, 144–145
management workshops, SBA, 147
managerial accounting, 448
managerial decision making, 179–181
managers
    coordinated effort of all levels of, 173
    and decentralization, 197
    kinds of, 173–175
    leadership, 177–179
    in line structure, 198–199
    in line-and-staff structure, 199
    in matrix structure, 201, 202
    in network structure, 203
    planning for production by, 220–226
    skills of, 7, 175–177, 185
manufacturer (producer) brand, 341
manufacturers
    cash flow for, 471
    wholesalers as providing services to, 367
manufacturer's agents, 368
manufacturing
    bicycle, 211
    computer systems for, 234
    flexible systems for, 235
    lean, 233
    sustainability of, 235
    in U.S., 212–214
    using conversion process, 215–216

manufacturing and operations plan component, business plan, 146, 242
manufacturing businesses, 10, 27–28
market coverage, level of, 365–366
market demand
    adjusting products or services to meet, 225–226
    comparing with capacity, 225
    estimating, 224–225
market economy, 15, 18
market price, 24–25
market segmentation, 311–313, 351
market segments, 311, 318
marketable securities, 451
marketing
    bicycles, 326
    database, 378
    defined, 305
    direct, 372–373
    of e-cigarettes to young people, 322
    by Graeter's, 397
    inbound, 411
    information for, 318–321
    integrated marketing communications, 377–378
    major functions of, 306
    managing customer relationships, 305–307
    mobile, 418
    product failure, 340
    and product life-cycle, 333–334
    relationship, 305–306
    by small businesses, 315
    social media, 410–412
    test, 338, 339–340
    top down, 404
    utility and, 307–308
marketing channels, 364–365
marketing concept, 308–310
marketing edge, from cultural diversity, 251
marketing environment, 314, 316–317
marketing implementation, in marketing plan, 317
marketing information systems, 318–319
marketing intermediaries, 10–11, 364
    retailers, 368–374
    wholesalers, 367–368
marketing managers, 175, 439
marketing mix, 310, 312, 313–316
marketing objectives, in marketing plan, 317
marketing plan, 317, 318
marketing plan component, business plan, 146, 398

marketing research, 212, 319, 320

marketing strategies
   defined, 310
   developing, 310–316
   and marketing environment, 316–317
   in marketing plan, 317

marketing-communications mix, 378–379

markets
   defined, 310
   target, 310–313
   types of, 310

market-share goals, pricing and, 349

markup, 349–350

Maslow's hierarchy of needs, 276–277

mass production, 214

mass-communication media, 382

mass-media advertising, 378

material resources, 10, 165–166, 418–419

materials
   as business product, 332
   scheduling of, 226, 228, 231

materials handling, 376

materials requirements planning (MRP), 227

matrix structure, 201–202

maturity date, bonds, 489, 490

maturity stage, product life-cycle, 333, 334

MBO, 284

MDB, 91–92

Meat Inspection Act (1906), 48

media plan, 380–381

media sharing sites, 406

mentors, 138, 199

mercenary culture, 203, 204

merchandise exporting, 72

merchandise inventory, 452

merchant middleman (merchant), 364

merchant wholesalers, 367–368

MERCOSUR, 90

mergers, 125–127, 204

merit pay, 258

message, advertising, 381

messenger market, for bicycles, 326

Mexico, economic outlook for, 84

microeconomics, 13

micromanaging, 290

middle managers, 173

middleman, 364, 365

Millennials, 401, 410

minorities, 55–56

Minority Business Development Agency, 148

minority franchisees, 152–153

minority-owned businesses, 148–149, 226–227

MIS, 438

mission statement, 114, 167, 168

missionary salesperson, 384

mixed economy, 15–16

mixed feedback interview, 264

mobile marketing, 418

mobile retailers, 370

monetary policies, 22

monitoring financial performance, 475

monopolistic competition, 23, 25

monopoly, 23, 26–27

monthly salary, 258

morale, defined, 274

mortgage bond, 490

mortgage payable, 453

most-favored-nation status (MFN), 86

motivating, as management function, 171–172

motivation
   contemporary views on, 281–284
   defined, 273–274
   high level of employee, 273
   historical perspectives on, 274–281
   key techniques, 284–290
   to start business, 138

motivation factors, 278

motivation–hygiene theory, 277–279

motive, defined, 273

Motor Vehicle Safety Act (1966), 54

MRP, 227

multibase departmentalization, 194–195

multilateral development bank (MDB), 91–93

multinational enterprises, 76, 78

multiple-unit packaging, 345

multiple-unit pricing, 353

multiplier effect, of manufacturing, 213

"mystery shoppers", for Graeter's, 240

N

NAFTA, 88–89

narrow span of management, 197–198

national debt, 22

National Do Not Call Registry, 372

National Environmental Policy Act (1970), 60

National Export Initiative (NEI), 90

National Franchise Mediation Program, 154–155

national goals, for production, 17

national income, 21

National Labor Relations Act (1935), 265

national security, protecting with trade restrictions, 82

National Small Business Week, 141

nations
   economic indicators measuring economy of, 20–21
   economic systems of, 12–18

natural monopoly, 27

natural resources, 13

needs
   analysis of training, 261
   businesses satisfying, 11
   defined, 276
   financial, budgeting for, 473–474
   Maslow's hierarchy of, 276–277
   satisfaction of, and morale, 274
   satisfying online, 419–420
   utility and, 307

negative balance of trade, 71–72

negative profit, 12

negative reinforcement, 281

negotiated pricing, 353

neighborhood shopping centers, 373

net income, 456

net loss, 456

net sales, 454

net worth, 450–451

network structure, 202–203

networked culture, 203

networking, in e-business, 419

new housing starts, 21

new-product development, 338–340

new-product pricing strategies, 352

news release, 390

newspapers, in advertising campaign, 381

Noise Control Act (1972), 60

nondiscriminatory culture, 204

nonparticipant role, on team, 293

non-price competition, 347

nonstore retailing, 371–373

norming stage, of team development, 292

North American Free Trade Agreement (NAFTA), 88–89

North Korea, 18

notes payable, 453

notes receivable, 451

not-for-profit accounting, 448

not-for-profit corporations, 123

Nutrition Labeling and Education Act (1990), 54

O

obesity, as public health issue, 53, 55

objections, answering in personal-selling process, 384

objective appraisal methods, 262–263

objectives
   for advertising campaign, 380
   business, achieving through social media, 407–413
   defined, 167
   establishing, 167–168
   for financial plan, 472
   management by, 284–285
   in marketing plan, 317
   pricing, 348–349
   sales promotion, 385–386
   social media, setting, 413–414

Occupational Outlook Handbook (Department of Labor), 448

Occupational Safety and Health Act (1970), 265, 266

odd-number pricing, 353

off-price retailers, 371

Oil Pollution Act (1990), 60

oligopoly, 23, 26

on-campus branding, 388

"100 Best Companies" list, 287

ongoing costs, of selling stock, 484, 490

online applications, 254

online community manager, 409

online information services, 320

online marketing, 410, 412

online networking, 5–6. See also social media

online presence, building for existing business, 422

online public relations, 412

online retailing, 373

online shopping malls, 421

on-the-job training methods, 261

open corporation, 115, 121

OPEN YouTube channel, 109

operating activities, cash flows from, 457

operating expenses, 455

operational plan, 170

operational planning, 220, 224–226, 231

operations control, 212, 226–231

operations management
   careers in, 214–215
   defined, 212
   operations control, 226–231
   planning for production, 220–226
   research and development, 218–220

operations managers, 174, 212, 214–215, 227, 232, 439

opportunities
   determining for social media plan, 413
   as factors affecting ethics, 42, 43
   identifying in decision making, 180
   in SWOT analysis, 169

optimization, of conflicting goals, 168
oral communication skills, 177
order getter, 383
order processing, 375
order taker, 383
organization charts, developing, 190–191
Organization of Petroleum Exporting Countries (OPEC), 90
organizational buyers, 365
organizational height, 198
organizational meeting, to form corporation, 117–118
organizational relationships, ethical issues related to, 40
organizational structure
  line structure, 198–199
  line-and-staff structure, 199–201
  matrix structure, 201–202
  network structure, 202–203
organizations
  decentralization of authority in, 196–197
  defined, 189–190
  informal, 205
organized effort of individuals, in a business, 10–11
organizing, as management function, 171
orientation, of new employees, 246, 247, 256
outcomes
  in equity theory, 282
  in expectancy theory, 282–283
outdoor advertising, 381
output per hour, productivity growth for, 232
output quota, in piece-rate system, 275
outside (field) order takers, 383
outsourcing, 222–223, 419
overseas jobs, preparing for, 87
over-the-counter (OTC) market, 484–485
owner, HRM activities by, 247
owners' equity, 449, 450, 453, 483, 487
ownership, 105–107
  of corporations, 115
  ease of transfer of, for corporations, 120
  employee, 289–290
  pride of, in partnership, 112
  of small businesses, 143–144
  sole proprietor's pride in, 107

P

packaging, 344–345
participative decision making, 280
participative leadership, 178, 179
partnership agreement, 111–112

partnerships, 109–114
  advantages of, 112–113, 120
  articles of partnership, 111–112
  defined, 109
  disadvantages of, 113–114, 120
  relative percentages of in U.S., 106
  supplier, in total quality management, 182
  total sales receipts of, in U.S., 107
  types of partners, 110
part-time work, 287–288
party plan, direct selling through, 372
passbook savings account, 476
pass-through taxation, for LLCs, 122
patents, 452
pay, employee, 10, 468
pay for time not worked, 259
"pay what you want" pricing, 315
payments
  balance of, 72, 81
  incentive, 258
  when exporting, 74, 75–76
pay-per-view e-business model, 423
peak demand, planning for, 225
peak period (prosperity), 21
penetration pricing, 352
pension and retirement programs, 259
perceived brand quality, 342–343
perfect (pure) competition, 23–25
performance
  financial, monitoring and evaluating, 475
  measuring actual, 172
performance appraisal, 246, 247, 262–264
performance feedback, 264
performance feedback interviews, 264
performing stage, of team development, 292
periodic discounting, 353
perks, for employees, 260
perpetual life, of corporations, 120
personal balance sheet, 450–451
personal budget, 453
personal finances, mixing business and, 445
personal goals, as factor affecting ethics, 42
personal income, 323
personal income statement, 453–454
personal marketing plan, 318

personal relationships, in small businesses, 143
personal selling, 378, 379, 383–385
personal values, as factor affecting ethics, 42
personnel management, 245
photo sharing sites, 406
physical distribution, 374–377
physical distribution functions, of marketing, 306
physiological needs, 276
pie charts, 444
piece-rate system, 274–275, 276
piggyback transportation, 377
pipelines, 377
place utility, 307–308
plagiarism, 40
planned shopping centers, 373–374
planning
  defined, 167
  design, 220–222, 231
  for e-business, 422
  facilities, 220, 222–224, 231
  financial, 472–475
  human resources, 246, 247–249
  as management function, 167–171
  materials requirements, 227
  operational, 220, 224–226, 231
  for production, 220–226, 231
  quality services, 216–217
  role in production, 212
  and small business failure, 140
planning horizon, selecting, 224
plans
  defined, 169
  types of, 169–171
plant layout, 223–224
podcasts, 406
point-of-purchase display, 388
point-of-sale (POS) terminals, 478
poison pills, 126
political forces, in marketing environment, 316
pollution, 58–59
porcupine provisions, 126
positive reinforcement, 281
possession utility, 307, 308
potential, limited, of small businesses, 144
preference, brand, 342
preferred stock, 117, 485, 491
premium, 387
premium pricing, 354–355
prepaid expenses, 452
presentation
  of information, in MIS, 443–444
  in personal-selling process, 384

press conference, 390
price competition, 26, 347
price differentiation, 351
price floor, 349
price leaders, 355
price lining, 355
price sensitivity, 347–348
price skimming, 352
prices
  buyers' perceptions of, 347–348
  defined, 346
  as element of marketing mix, 314, 315
  during maturity stage of product life-cycle, 334
  meaning and use of, 346
  real, 348
  role in purchasing decisions, 227
  trade restrictions as raising, 82
pricing
  bundled, 348
  business products, 355–356
  competition-based, 351
  cost-based, 349–350
  demand-based, 351
  dynamic, 351
  methods, 349–351
  objectives, 348–349
  products, 346–348
  strategies, 351–355
pride of ownership, 107, 112
primary market, 484
primary-demand advertising, 379
prime interest rate, 21, 480, 481
privacy, threats to, 424–425
private accountant, 448
private brand, 341
private carrier, 376
private placement, 486
private warehouses, 375
problem, identifying, 180
problem recognition, 322
problem solving, from cultural diversity, 251
problem-solving feedback interview, 264
problem-solving teams, 291
process layout, 223–224
process materials, 332
processing data, 442–443
producer brand, 341
producer markets, 310
producer price index (PPI), 20
producers, in distribution channels, 364–365
product deletion, 337
product design, 221
product development phase, 338, 339
product differentiation, 25, 26, 347
product layout, 223, 224

product life-cycle, 332–335
product line, 221, 335, 336
product markets, 16
product mix
    defined, 335
    managing, 336–340
product modification, 336–337
product safety, 51
product trial, in personal-selling
    process, 384
production, 212–215
    customer-driven, 235
    operations control, 226–231
    planning for, 220–226, 231
    speculative, 471
production capacity, required,
    221–222
production industries, 136
production orientation, 308
production processes, number
    of, 215–216
productivity
    defined, 18, 232
    growth rates for U.S.
        businesses, 2004 to
        2014, 232
    historical perspectives on,
        274–276
    impact of automation,
        robotics, and computers
        on, 233–235
    importance in global
        marketplace, 18–19
    improving growth of, 233
    improving with technology,
        232–235
    in manufacturing, 213
    trends in, 232–233
product-liability lawsuits, 51
product-line pricing, 352,
    354–355
products
    adjusting to meet demand,
        225–226
    branding, 340–344
    business, pricing, 355–356
    classification of, 331–332
    defined, 330
    departmentalization by, 194,
        201
    developing new, 219, 338–340
    distribution channels for,
        364–365
    as element of marketing mix,
        313–314, 315
    extension and refinement of,
        218–220
    failure of, 340
    generating ideas for through
        social media, 412
    generic, 341
    labeling, 346
    managing existing, 336–337
    market-demand estimates,
        225
    operational planning, 224–226

packaging, 344–345
planning for production,
    220–226
pricing, 346–348
research and development,
    218–220
professional accounting advice,
    445
profit, 12, 17
    corporate, 21
    creating in e-business,
        420–421
    defined, 453
    gross, 455
    measuring firm's ability to
        earn, 460
    in partnerships, 113
    and product life-cycle,
        333–334
    in sole proprietorships, 107
profit margin, 460
profit maximization, pricing for,
    348
profit-sharing, 259
project manager, 201
promissory notes, 480, 482
promotion, 253, 254, 256
    defined, 378
    as element of marketing mix,
        314, 316
    by Graeter's, 396–397
    integrated marketing
        communications,
        377–378
    sales, 378, 379, 385–388
    through packaging, 345
promotion mix, 378–379
promotional allowance, 356
promotional pricing, 352, 355
prospecting, in personal-selling
    process, 384
prosperity, 21
protective tariffs, 79–80
proxy, voting by, 117
proxy fight, 126
psychological factors,
    influencing buying process,
    322, 323
psychological pricing, 352,
    353–354
public accountant, 448
public health, businesses'
    responsibility to, 53, 55
public relations, 378, 379, 389–
    390, 412
public responsibilities of
    business, 51–55
public utilities, 27
public warehouses, 375, 482
publications, SBA, 149
publicity, 389–390
punishment, in reinforcement
    theory, 281
purchase discounts, 454
purchasing, 226–227, 231
pure competition, 23–25

Pure Food and Drug Act (1906),
    48
purpose statement, 114

Q

qualified individual, with a
    disability, 267
qualitative social media
    measurement, 416, 417
quality
    management of, 181–183
    perceived brand, 342–343
    of receivables, 481
    role in purchasing decisions,
        227
    of services, 216–218
    standards of, 230–231
    techniques to improve,
        229–230
quality circles, 230
quality control, 226, 228–231
quality modifications, to
    products, 336
quantitative social media
    measurement, 416–417
quantity discounts, 356
quotas, 56, 80, 275

R

radio, in advertising campaign,
    381
railroads, 377
random discounting, 353
rating scales, 263
ratings, social media, 406–407
ratios, financial, 460–461
raw data, 449
raw materials, 332
raw-materials inventory, 227
real (currency), in Brazil, 96
real GDP, 19–20
real price, 348
reasonable accommodation,
    under ADA, 267
rebate, 386
receivables, 451, 481, 482
recession, 21
recognition
    brand, 342
    need for, 274
    pay as form of, 279
recommendations section,
    business report, 443
record keeping, for small
    businesses, 143
recovery (expansion), 22
recruiting, 247, 248, 249
    defined, 246, 252
    external, 253
    internal, 253–254
    via social media, 253, 413
recycling, 60–61
redesigned packaging, 334
reference pricing, 353

references, 256
refinement, product, 218–220
reform
    accounting, 446–447
    financial, after economic
        crisis, 469
regional shopping centers,
    374
registered bond, 489
registered trademark symbol ®,
    343
registration, brand, 343
regular corporations, 123
regulations, misunderstanding or
    misinterpreting, 445
regulatory forces, in marketing
    environment, 316
reinforcement theory, 281
relationship marketing, 305–306
relationships
    with customer in service firms,
        217–218
    in small businesses, 143
reliability, role in purchasing
    decisions, 227
reminder advertising, 379
renewable energy sources, 61
replacement chart, for
    personnel, 248
reports
    annual, 450
    business, 443
    required for corporations, 121
reputation management, through
    social media, 409
research, marketing, 319, 320
research and development
    (R&D), 218–220, 231, 233
reseller markets, 310
reshoring, 214
resolution time, 417
resource acquisition, from
    cultural diversity, 251
Resource Conservation and
    Recovery Act (1984), 60
resource markets, 16
resource owners, 16
Resource Recovery Act (1970), 60
resources
    for conversion process, 215
    e-business, organizing,
        418–419
    kinds of, 10, 165–166
    scheduling of, 226, 228, 231
    for secondary information,
        320–321
responsibility, assigning, 195
restrictions, to international
    business, 78–82
résumés, submitting, 254
retailers, 10–11, 368–374
    defined, 364
    in distribution channels,
        364–365
    largest, 369
    mobile, 370

nonstore retailing, 371–373
shopping centers, 373–374
types of retail stores, 369–371
wholesalers as providing
services to, 367
retailing, 136
retained earnings, 453, 485–486
retirement plans, 267
retirement programs, 259
return on investment (ROI), 349
return on owners' equity, 487
return on sales (profit margin),
460
reusable packages, 345
revenue, 350, 454
revenue stream, 420
revenue tariffs, 79
reverse discrimination, 56
reviews, through social media,
407
revolving credit agreement, 476
rights
of consumers, 51–52
in franchise agreement, 151
of stockholders, 117
risk
in factoring, 482
and information, 435–436
risk taking, as function of
marketing, 306
risk–return ratio, 472, 489
robocalls, 372
robotics, impact on productivity,
233–234
ROI, 349
role-playing, 262
roles, within teams, 293
routine response behavior,
321–322
routing, of materials, 228

S
S corporations, 121–122, 123,
130, 160
safety, right to, 51
safety needs, 276, 277
salaries, 57, 258–259
salaries payable, 453
sales
of assets, as source of funds,
475
gross, 454
net, 454
personal selling, 383–385
and product life-cycle,
333–334
return on, 460
sales agents, 368
sales allowances, 454
sales discounts, 454
sales forecast, 318
sales managers, 385
sales offices, exporting firms, 76
sales orientation, of business,
308–309

sales promotion
defined, 379
methods, 386–388
objectives, 385–386
in promotion mix, 378
sales returns, 454
sales revenue
in e-business, increasing,
420–421
exchanged for additional
resources, 16
forecasting human resources
demand and, 248
relationship with profit, 12
as source of funds, 475
by type of ownership, 107
sales support personnel,
383–384
salespersons, kinds of, 383–384
sample, 387
Sarbanes–Oxley Act (2002), 43,
44, 45, 447, 464
satisfaction
customer, 182, 309, 417
employee, 274, 278
"satisfice," making decisions
that, 181
satisfiers, 278
savings, 17
savings accounts, 476
SBA, 146–150
SBDCs, 148–149
SBICs, 150
SBIs, 148
scarcity, dealing with, 13
scheduling, of materials and
resources, 226, 228, 231
scientific management, 274–275
screening, in product
development, 338
search engine marketing, 412
search engine optimization, 412
seasonal discounts, 356
seating assignments, temporary,
193
secondary information,
resources for, 320–321
secondary market, 484–485
secondary-market pricing, 353
secrecy, lack of in corporations,
121
secured short-term financing,
481–482
securities exchange, 484
securities linked to athletes,
487
segmentation, market, 311–313
segmenting customers, for
social media plan, 414
selection
of employees, 246, 247,
254–256
of target market, 310–313
selective distribution, 366
selective-demand (brand)
advertising, 379

self-actualization needs, 276,
277
self-managed teams, 291
sellers, branding benefits for,
342
selling
assets, 475
as function of marketing, 306
online, 420
personal, 378, 379, 383–385
stock, 119–120, 125, 483–
485, 490
selling expenses, 455
seminars, 262
sentiment analysis, 417
serial bonds, 490
service businesses, 10
Service Corps of Retired
Executives (SCORE),
147–148
service economy, 29, 216, 217
service industries, 136, 217
services
adjusting to meet demand,
225–226
as benefits, 259
business, 332
evaluating quality of, 217–218
increasing importance of,
216–218
market-demand estimates,
225
operational planning, 224–226
planning for production,
220–226
as products, 330
quality of, 216–218
research and development,
218–220
sustainability of, 235
sexual harassment, programs to
reduce, 57–58
shares of ownership, of
corporation, 115
shark repellents, 126
Sherman Antitrust Act (1890),
48
shipping costs, role in
purchasing decisions, 227
shopping centers, types of,
373–374
shopping product, 331–332
"short" product line, 221
short-term business loans, 476
short-term financing, 470–471
cost comparisons, 482–483
factoring accounts receivable,
482
sources of secured, 481–482
sources of unsecured,
479–481
showrooms, 370
significant others, as factor
affecting ethics, 42
simulations, 261
single-line retailers, 371

single-source data, 320
sinking fund, 490
site selection, 222–224, 231
situational factors, influencing
buying process, 322, 323
Six Sigma, 230
skill-assessment tests, 249
skills, of managers, 7, 175–177
skills inventory, 248–249
Small Business Administration
(SBA)
financial assistance, 149–150
financing international
business, 91
help for global markets from,
155–156
help for minority-owned small
businesses, 148–149
innovation among small-
business workers, 141
Management Assistance
Program, 146–148
publications from, 149
small business, definition of
by, 133
social media use by, 437
Small Business Saturday, 30,
135
small businesses, 17
advantages of, 143–144
business plan, 144–146
defined, 133
disadvantages of, 144
failure of, 8, 139–140, 144
franchising, 150–156
global perspectives in,
155–156
importance to U.S. economy,
134, 140–142
industries attracting, 135–136
marketing by, 315
minority-owned, 148–149
during recession, 142
resources on social media,
109
size standards, 133–134
solving unemployment
problems, 142
starting, 7–8
teenagers as owners of, 139
women as owners of, 138–
139
small-business development
centers (SBDCs), 148–149
small-business institutes (SBIs),
148
small-business investment
companies (SBICs),
149–150
small-business sector, 134–135
smartphones, and public health,
55
smoking, as public health issue,
55
social acceptance, 276
social audit, 62–63

social considerations in
advertising, 382–383
social content sites, 405
social factors, 42–43, 322, 323
social games, 407
social loafing, 293
social media
achieving business objectives
through, 407–413
advancing career through, 5–6
in advertising campaign, 381
benefits for businesses using,
405
Boeing's use of, 213
careers in, 409
Charles Schwab's use of, 485
consumer education through,
53
defined, 30, 402
experiments on, disclosure
of, 404
future of, 423–427
gathering and analyzing
marketing information, 321
government agency use of, 30
Graeter's use of, 495
harnessing power of, 380
importance of, 402–405
International Monetary Fund
use of, 93
making good impression
through, 413
marketing research on, 319
marketing through, 316, 326
Oreo branding on, 342
popularity of, 402
ratings, 406–407
reasons businesses use,
402–405
recruiting via, 253
service firm use of, 217–218
Small Business Administration
use of, 437
small business resources, 109
Taco Bell's recipe for success,
401
in technology environment,
30–31
timeline for development of,
403
tools, selecting, 414
tools for business use,
405–407
use by UPS and FedEx, 389
social media communities, 408,
414
social media managers, 409
social media marketing, 410–412
social media plan
cost of maintaining, 417
implementing and integrating,
414–415
measuring and adapting,
416–417
steps to build, 413–415
social needs, 276, 277

social responsibility, 38
appointment of program
director, 62
arguments for/against
increased, 49–50
benefit corporations, 116
commitment of top executives
to, 62
defined, 46
employment practices and,
55–58
environmental concerns and,
58–61
evolution of in business,
47–51
historical evolution of
business, 47–49
implementing program of,
62–63
for Internet, social media, and
e-business, 424–425
planning, 62
pros and cons of, 49–51
public responsibilities of
business, 51–55
views of, 49
Social Security, 259
socialism, 17–18
society
impact of business decisions
on, 49
small businesses as filling
needs of, 142
sociocultural forces, in
marketing environment, 316
socioeconomic model of social
responsibility, 49–50
socioemotional role, on team,
293
software, business, 437–438
solar energy, 81
soldiering, 274
sole proprietorships
accounting mistakes, 445
advantages of, 107–108, 120
defined, 106
disadvantages of, 108–109,
120
relative percentages of in
U.S., 106
total sales receipts of, in U.S.,
107
solutions, implementing and
evaluating, 181
span of management (span of
control), 197–198
special-event pricing, 355
specialization
defined, 28
job, 192–193
management, 174–175
specialized management, of
corporations, 120
specialty product, 332
specialty stores, 371
specialty-line wholesaler, 368

speculative production, 471
speed, of transportation,
376–377
sponsorship, event, 389, 390
spreadsheets, software for, 438
staff HRM specialists, 247
staff managers, 199–201
staff positions, 191
staffing, 148, 245, 247
stakeholders, 12, 39, 409–410,
413
standard of living, 27
standardization, as function of
marketing, 306
standards
of quality, 230–231
setting, 172
standing committee, 204
start-up, 107, 112, 140
statement of cash flows,
456–458
statement of financial position,
450–451
statement of income and
expenses, 453–456
states
choosing where to
incorporate, 115–116
top ten merchandise-
exporting, 72
statistical process control (SPC),
229
statistical quality control (SQC),
229
status-quo pricing, 349
steel-frame bicycles, 326
stock, 115
common, 485, 491
preferred, 485, 491
selling, 119–120, 125,
483–485, 490
stock options, 290
stockholders, 115, 117
stockholders' equity, 450, 453
stock-out costs, 227, 375
storage cost, 227
store (private) brand, 341
storing
data, MIS capability for, 442
as function of marketing, 306
storming stage, of team
development, 292
strategic alliances, 77
strategic plan, 169–170
strategic planning process, 167
strengths, in SWOT analysis,
169
structured interviews, 255
subscription e-business model,
423
success rate, for franchises, 153
Super Bowl commercials, 405
supermarkets, 370
superstores, 370–371
Supplier Diversity Program,
226–227

supplier partnerships, in TQM,
182
suppliers' factories, ethical
issues in, 50
supply
as business product, 332
defined, 24
and equilibrium price, 24–25
forecasting human resources,
248–249
of money, size of, 22
for personnel, matching with
demand, 249
supply-chain management,
366–367
support personnel, in personal
selling, 383–384
surveys, 257, 309
survival, pricing products for,
348
sustainability, 31, 235
SWOT analysis, 169, 317
syndicates, 124–125
synthetic process, 214

T
tabular display, 443, 444
tactical plan, 170
Taiwan, 81
takeovers, 125–127
tall organizations, 197, 198
tangible attributes, of products,
330
target audience, for advertising
campaign, 380
target behavior, in behavior
modification, 286
target market, selection and
evaluation of, 310–313
targeting customers
for social media plan, 414, 415
through social media, 410
tariffs, 79–80, 81, 86–87
task forces, 204–205
task-specialist role, on team,
293
tax accounting, 448
taxes, 17, 108, 113, 121–122
taxes payable, 453
team-building exercises, 294
teams
benefits and limitations of, 294
in business, 290
cohesiveness of, 293–294
competition between, 294
conflict in, resolving, 294
defined, 291
ethical issues related to, 293
roles within, 293
stages of development, 292
types of, 291–292
technical innovation, provided
by small businesses,
141–142
technical salesperson, 384

technical skills, of managers, 7, 177
technological displacement, 235
technological forces, in marketing environment, 316
technology
  capital-intensive, 222
  in customer relationship management, 306
  in design planning, 222
  development of, 28
  in external recruiting, 253
  future challenges for, 425–427
  gathering and analyzing marketing information, 319–321
  in human resources planning, 247
  improving productivity with, 232–235
  labor-intensive, 222
  and supply-chain management, 366–367
  teamwork through, 291
technology environment, 30–31
teenagers, as entrepreneurs, 139, 419
telecommuting, 288–289
telemarketing, 372
Telephone Consumer Protection Act (1991), 54
television, in advertising campaign, 381
television home shopping, 373
tell-and-listen feedback interview, 264
tell-and-sell feedback interview, 264
temporary seating assignments, 193
tender offer, 126
term-loan agreement, 488–489
test marketing, 338, 339–340
Theory X, 279–280
Theory Y, 279–280
Theory Z, 280
Theory Z: How American Management Can Meet the Japanese Challenge (Ouchi), 280
threats, in SWOT analysis, 169
three-column tables, in business presentations, 444
360-degree evaluation, 264
time differences, and international business, 75
time utility, 307, 308
timing function, in scheduling, 228
Title VII of the Civil Rights Act (1964), 265, 266
tobacco products, 55, 181
Tokyo Round (1973-1979), 87
"Top 100 Companies to Work For" list, 274
top down marketing, 404
top managers, 62, 173, 182, 284

total cost, 350
total quality management (TQM), 181–183, 230
total revenue, 350
totally owned facilities, 77
Toyota Way, 230
trade, 70, 83–86
Trade Act of 2002, 69
trade associations, role in encouraging ethics, 44
trade credit, 479–480, 482
trade deficit, 72, 73
trade discounts, 356
Trade Expansion Act (1962), 87
trade name, 341
trade restrictions, 79–82
trade sales promotion method, 386
trade salesperson, 384
trade show, 388
trade-in allowance, 356
trademark, 341, 343
trading companies, 77
traditional approach to budgeting, 474
traditional banking services, 476–477
traditional channel, 365
traditional specialty stores, 371
training
  and development, 246, 247, 260–262
  diversity, 250–251
  employee, 261
  evaluation of, 262
  for hard-core unemployed, 57
  methods, 261–262
  needs analysis, 261
Training magazine, 260–261
transfer pricing, 356
transferring, from one position to another, 253
Trans-Pacific Partnership (TPP), 90
transparency, at Container Store, 270
transportation, 376–377
transporting, as function of marketing, 306
trial closing, 385
trough phase, business cycle, 22
truck carriers, 377
trust, culture of, 204
trustee, 490
Truth in Lending Act (1968), 54
T-shirt quilts, 130
20th century economy, 28–29
21st century economy, 29
type A firms, 280
type J firms, 280
type Z organizations, 280

U

undifferentiated approach, in marketing, 311, 312

unemployment, 57, 142
unemployment insurance, 259
unemployment rate, 20
unfavorable balance of trade, 71–72
Uniform Partnership Act, 109
unit loading, 376
United States
  absolute advantage, 70
  average prime interest rate, 481
  bankruptcies in, 468
  business in, today, 27–32
  business ownership in, 106–107
  capitalism in, 15–17
  cultural diversity in workforce, 250
  economic outlook for, 83
  entrepreneurial activity in, 136
  events shaping economy, 1940 to 2000, 28–29
  export assistance programs, 90
  exports and imports, 84, 85–86
  GDP in, 19–20, 83, 85
  improving productivity growth in, 233
  management theories of, 280
  manufacturers in, 212–214
  national debt, 22
  productivity growth rate, 2004 to 2014, 232
  protection of domestic jobs in, 82
  real GDP in, 19–20
  retailers in, 368–369
  small-business sector in, 134–135
  start-ups, closures, and bankruptcies in, from 2000, 140
  trade deficit in, 72, 73
  unemployment rate, 20
Universal Product Code (UPC) symbol, 346
unlimited liability, 108, 113
unmanned aerial vehicles (UAVs), 176
unsecured financing, 479–481, 482
updating data, in MIS, 442
Uruguay Round (1986-1993), 87
U.S. Export Assistance Centers, 155–156
utility, 215, 307–308

V

value, added by marketing, 307–308
values, as factor affecting ethics, 42
"Values Matter" campaign, Whole Foods, 380
vaping, 322

variable cost, 350
venture capital, 149–150, 486
vertical merger, 126, 127
video sharing sites, 406
viral sharing, on social media, 404
virtual organization, 202–203
virtual teams, 291, 292
viruses, computer, 425
visual displays, 443–444

W

wage level, 257
wage structure, 257
wage survey, 257
wages, hourly, 258
warehouse clubs, 371
warehouse showrooms, 370
warehousing, 375
warranty, express, 346
waste, environmental issues related to, 58
Water Pollution Control Act Amendment (1972), 60
Water Quality Improvement Act (1970), 60
waterways, 377
weaknesses, in SWOT analysis, 169
wealth, defined, 12
Wealth of Nations (Smith), 14, 192
websites
  career development, 5
  text, 9
weekly salary, 258
Western Europe, economic outlook for, 83–84
Whistleblower Protection Act (1989), 45
whistle-blowing, 44–45
wholesalers, 136, 364, 365, 367–368
wide span of management, 197–198
width, product mix, 335
wikis, 408
wind-energy, 14
women
  comparable worth, 257–258
  and Equal Pay Act, 266
  as franchisees, 152–153
  relative earnings of male and female workers, 57
  SBA help for, 148
  as small-business owners, 138–139
  in U.S. workforce, 250
Women's Business Centers (WBCs), 139, 148
word processing software, 438
work sharing, 288
Worker Adjustment and Retraining Notification (WARN) Act (1988), 265

workers' compensation
insurance, 259
workforce, culturally diverse, 6
workforce optimization software,
288
"Workin' at Ikea" video, 315
working at home, 288–289
Working Mother magazine, 287

work-in-process inventory,
227
workplace diversity, 6,
250–251
workspaces, flexible, 193
The World Is Flat (Friedman), 70
world quality standards,
230–231

World Trade Organization (WTO),
87
written communication skills,
177

Y

Yellow Pages, 381

yogurt production, 238
young people, marketing of
e-cigarettes to, 322

Z

zero-base budgeting, 474